NEGIMA! OMNIBUS 9

Ken Akamatsu

TRANSLATED & ADAPTED BY
Alethea Nibley & Athena Nibley

LETTERING AND RETOUCH BY
Steve Palmer

KC
KODANSHA
COMICS

A Kodansha Comics Trade Paperback Original.

Published in the United States by Kodansha Comics, an imprint of Kodansha USA Publishing, LLC, New York.

Publication rights for this English edition arranged through Kodansha Ltd., Tokyo.

First published in Japan in 2008 by Kodansha Ltd., Tokyo, as *Maho sensei Negima!* volumes 25, 26 and 27.

ISBN 978-1-61262-273-6

Printed in the United States of America.

www.kodanshacomics.com

9 8 7 6 5 4 3 2 1

Translator & Adaptor: Alethea Nibley & Athena Nibley
Lettering: Steve Palmer

CONTENTS

A Word from the Author

Presenting *Negima!* volume 25! Finally, the Negi Party vs. Fate Party battle begins! Now is the time to show the fruits of their training.

At any rate, the enemies have very powerful pactio cards, too, so it will become almost the first artifact vs. artifact battle in the history of Negima. (*There was just a little bit of that at the school festival.) What does destiny hold for the partners!?

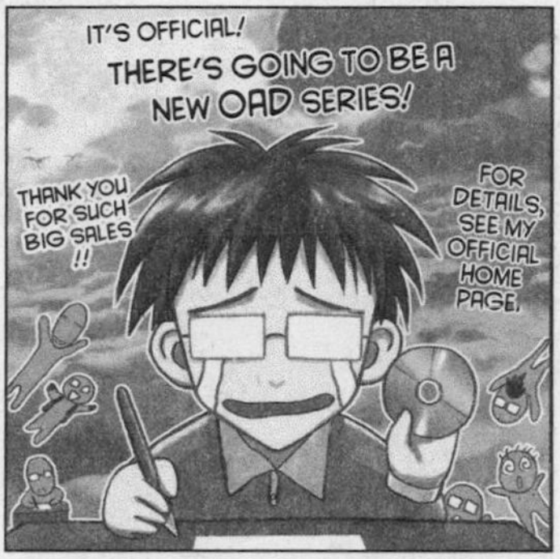
IT'S OFFICIAL!
THERE'S GOING TO BE A NEW OAD SERIES!
FOR DETAILS, SEE MY OFFICIAL HOME PAGE.
THANK YOU FOR SUCH BIG SALES !!

...And now I have a big announcement!! It was so popular that they've already decided to make a new OAD series! The next one will be a tinge different than what we've seen until now! For details, see my official home page! (^^)

Ken Akamatsu
www.ailove.net

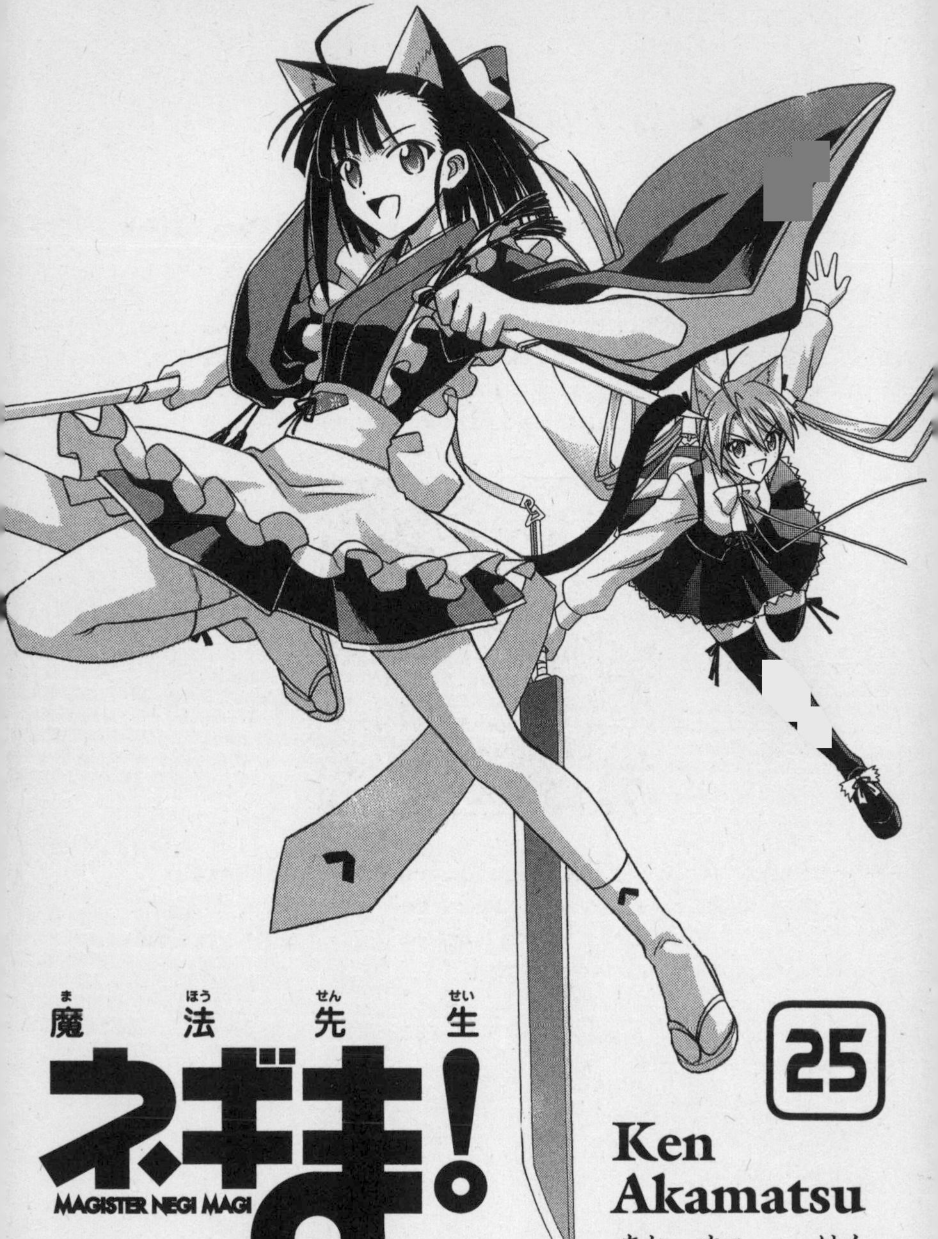

魔法先生ネギま!

MAGISTER NEGI MAGI

25

Ken Akamatsu

赤松健

CONTENTS

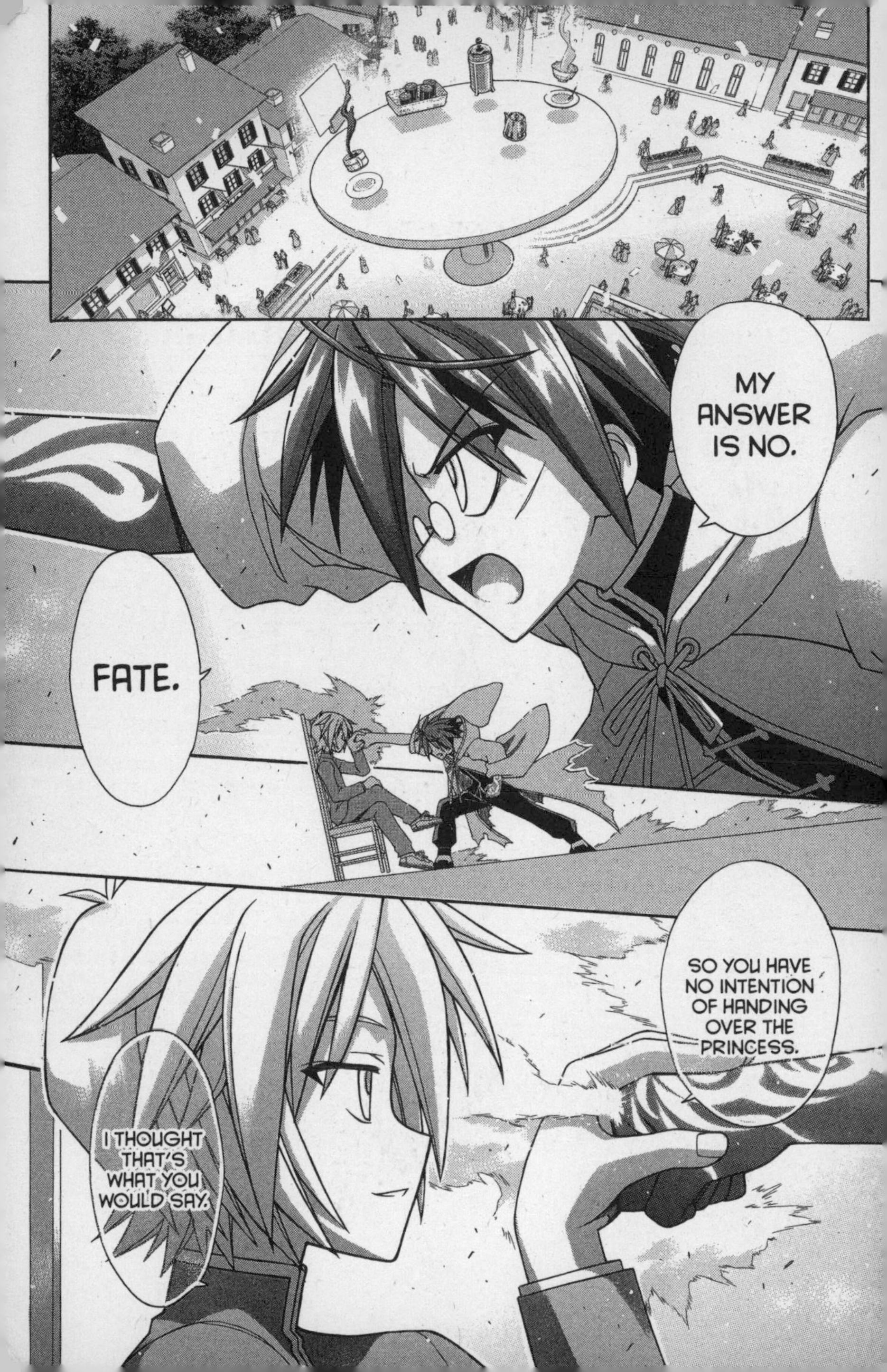
MY ANSWER IS NO.
FATE.
SO YOU HAVE NO INTENTION OF HANDING OVER THE PRINCESS.
I THOUGHT THAT'S WHAT YOU WOULD SAY.

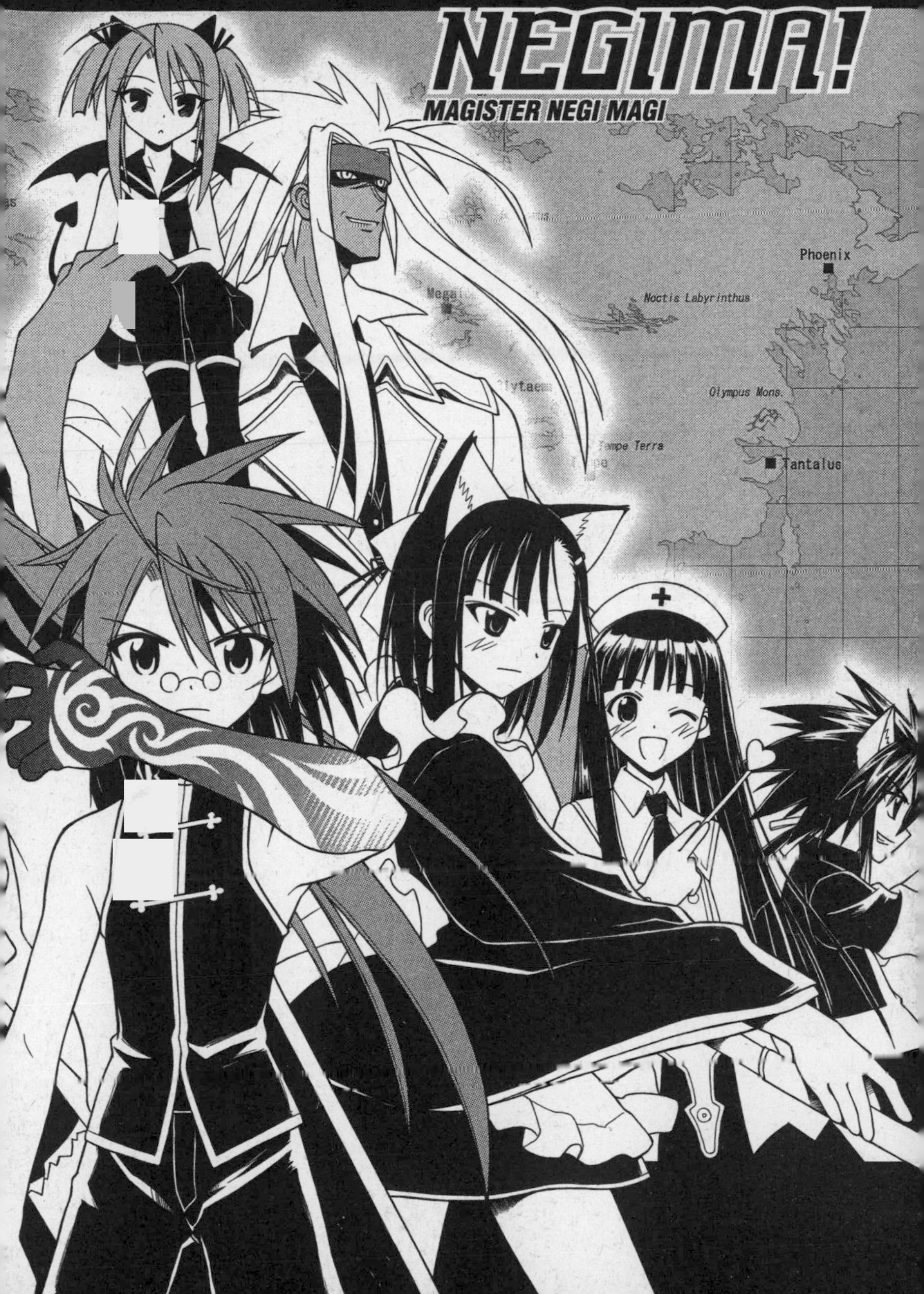
NEGIMA!
MAGISTER NEGI MAGI
Phoenix
Noctis Labyrinthus
Olympus Mons.
Tempe Terra
Tantalus

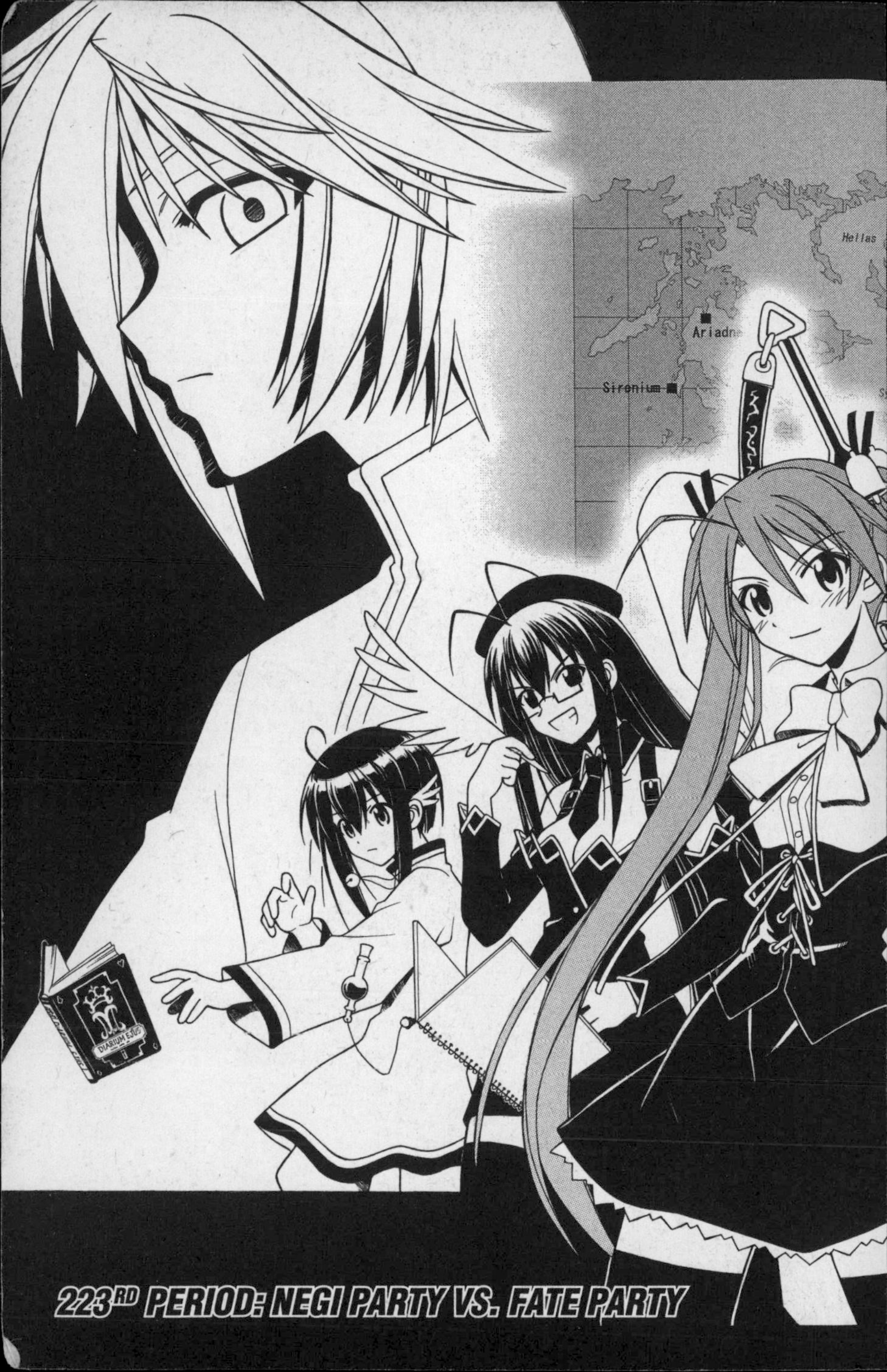
Hellas
Ariadne
Sirenium
DIARIUM EJUS

223RD PERIOD: NEGI PARTY VS. FATE PARTY

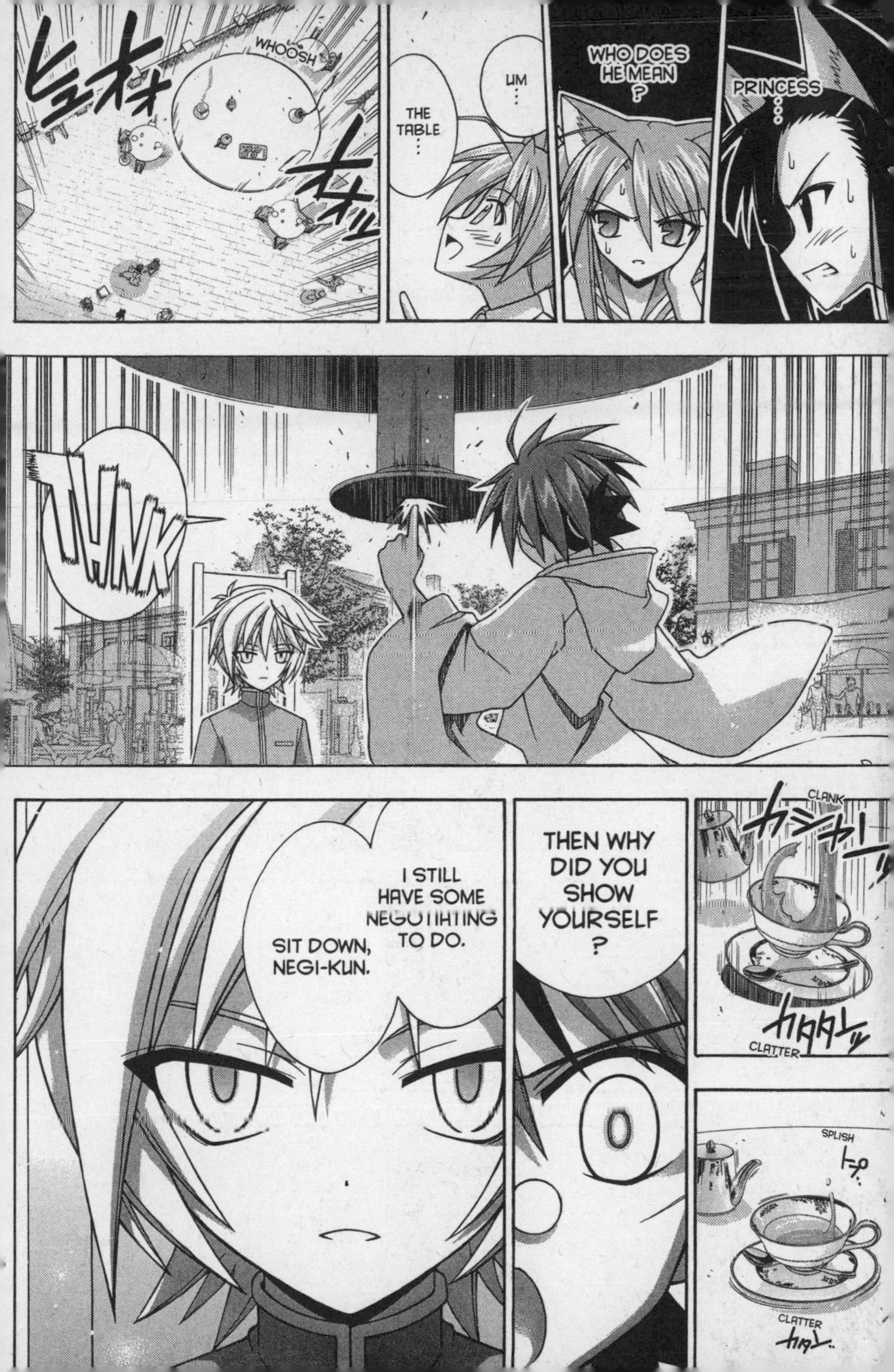
PRINCESS . . .
WHO DOES HE MEAN ?
UM . . .
THE TABLE . . .
WHOOSH
ヒュオオ
THUNK
CLANK
CLATTER
SPLISH
CLATTER
THEN WHY DID YOU SHOW YOURSELF ?
I STILL HAVE SOME NEGOTIATING TO DO.
SIT DOWN, NEGI-KUN.

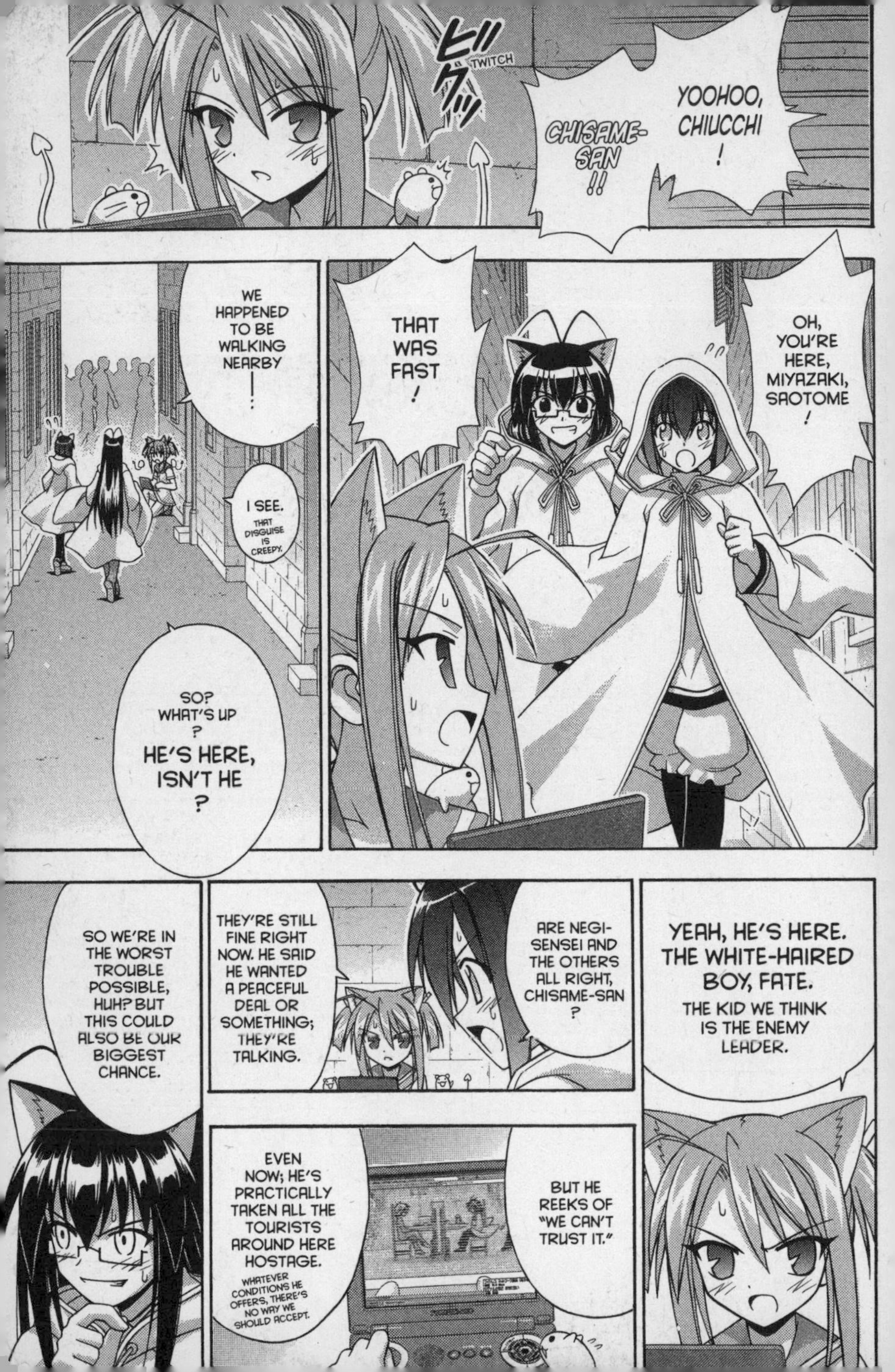

YOOHOO, CHIUCCHI!
CHISAME-SAN!!
TWITCH
OH, YOU'RE HERE, MIYAZAKI, SAOTOME!
THAT WAS FAST!
WE HAPPENED TO BE WALKING NEARBY!
I SEE. THAT DISGUISE IS CREEPY.
SO? WHAT'S UP? HE'S HERE, ISN'T HE?
YEAH, HE'S HERE. THE WHITE-HAIRED BOY, FATE. THE KID WE THINK IS THE ENEMY LEADER.
ARE NEGI-SENSEI AND THE OTHERS ALL RIGHT, CHISAME-SAN?
THEY'RE STILL FINE RIGHT NOW. HE SAID HE WANTED A PEACEFUL DEAL OR SOMETHING; THEY'RE TALKING.
BUT HE REEKS OF "WE CAN'T TRUST IT."
EVEN NOW; HE'S PRACTICALLY TAKEN ALL THE TOURISTS AROUND HERE HOSTAGE. WHATEVER CONDITIONS HE OFFERS, THERE'S NO WAY WE SHOULD ACCEPT.
SO WE'RE IN THE WORST TROUBLE POSSIBLE, HUH? BUT THIS COULD ALSO BE OUR BIGGEST CHANCE.

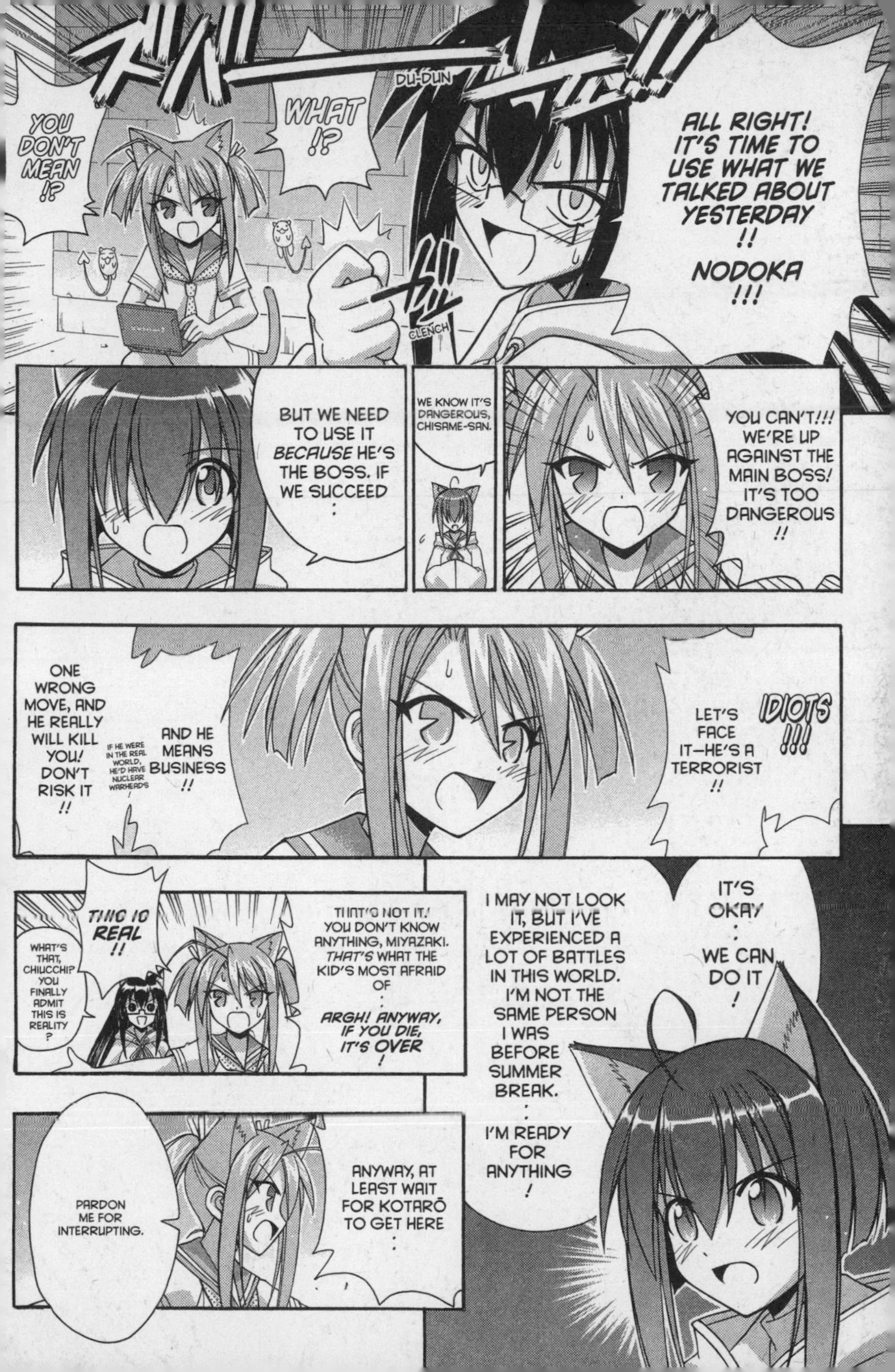
ALL RIGHT! IT'S TIME TO USE WHAT WE TALKED ABOUT YESTERDAY!! NODOKA!!!
DU-DUN
CLENCH
WHAT!?
YOU DON'T MEAN!?
YOU CAN'T!!! WE'RE UP AGAINST THE MAIN BOSS! IT'S TOO DANGEROUS!!
WE KNOW IT'S DANGEROUS, CHISAME-SAN.
BUT WE NEED TO USE IT BECAUSE HE'S THE BOSS. IF WE SUCCEED:
IDIOTS!!!
LET'S FACE IT—HE'S A TERRORIST!!
AND HE MEANS BUSINESS!!
IF HE WERE IN THE REAL WORLD, HE'D HAVE NUCLEAR WARHEADS!
ONE WRONG MOVE, AND HE REALLY WILL KILL YOU! DON'T RISK IT!!
IT'S OKAY: WE CAN DO IT!
I MAY NOT LOOK IT, BUT I'VE EXPERIENCED A LOT OF BATTLES IN THIS WORLD. I'M NOT THE SAME PERSON I WAS BEFORE SUMMER BREAK. : I'M READY FOR ANYTHING!
THAT'S NOT IT! YOU DON'T KNOW ANYTHING, MIYAZAKI. THAT'S WHAT THE KID'S MOST AFRAID OF: ARGH! ANYWAY, IF YOU DIE, IT'S OVER!
THIS IS REAL!!
WHAT'S THAT, CHIUCCHI? YOU FINALLY ADMIT THIS IS REALITY?
ANYWAY, AT LEAST WAIT FOR KOTARŌ TO GET HERE:
PARDON ME FOR INTERRUPTING.

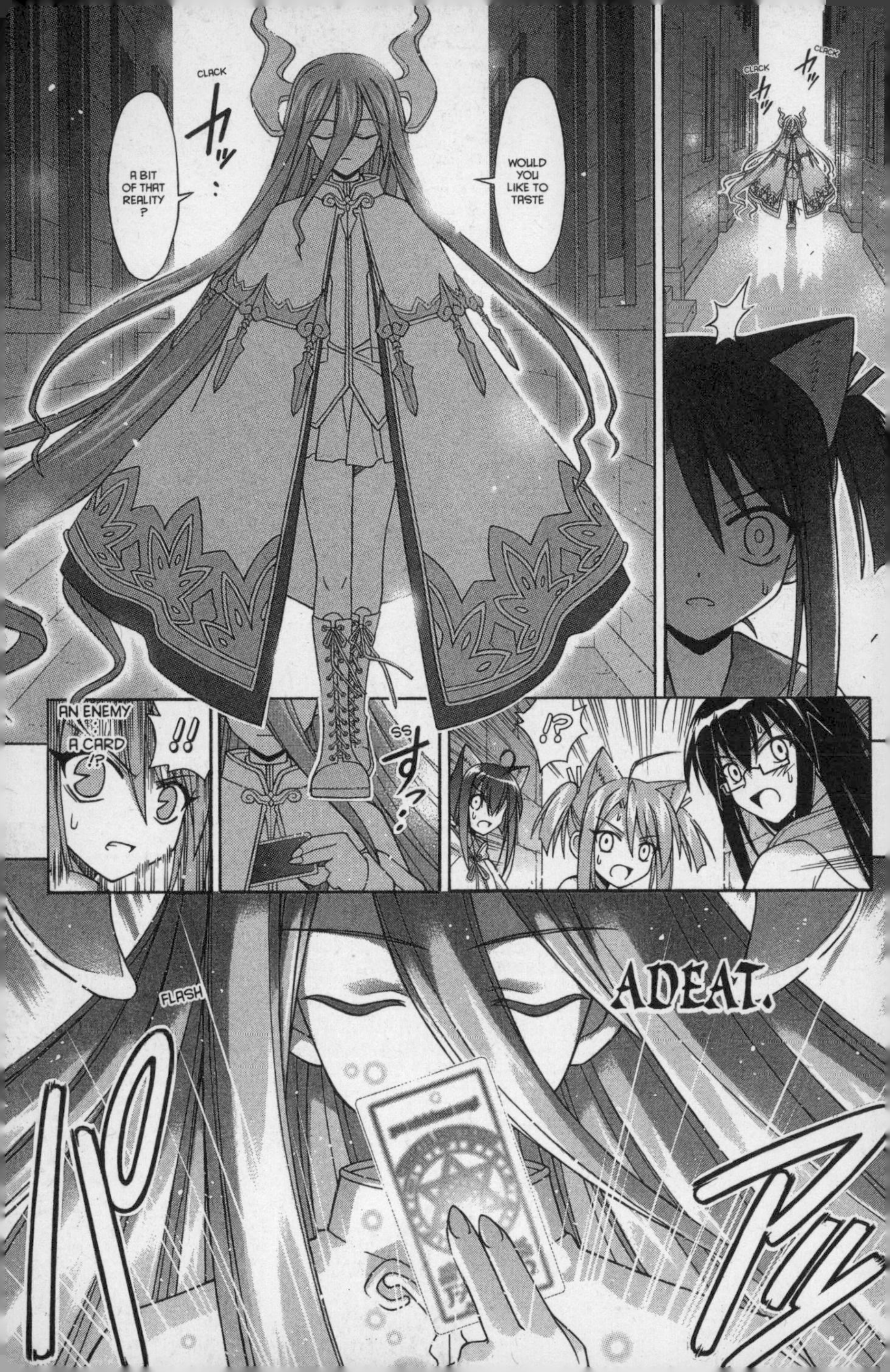
CLACK
ガッ
CLACK
ガッ
WOULD YOU LIKE TO TASTE
A BIT OF THAT REALITY?
CLACK
カッ
!?
SS
すっ
!!
AN ENEMY
A CARD
!?
ADEAT.
FLASH

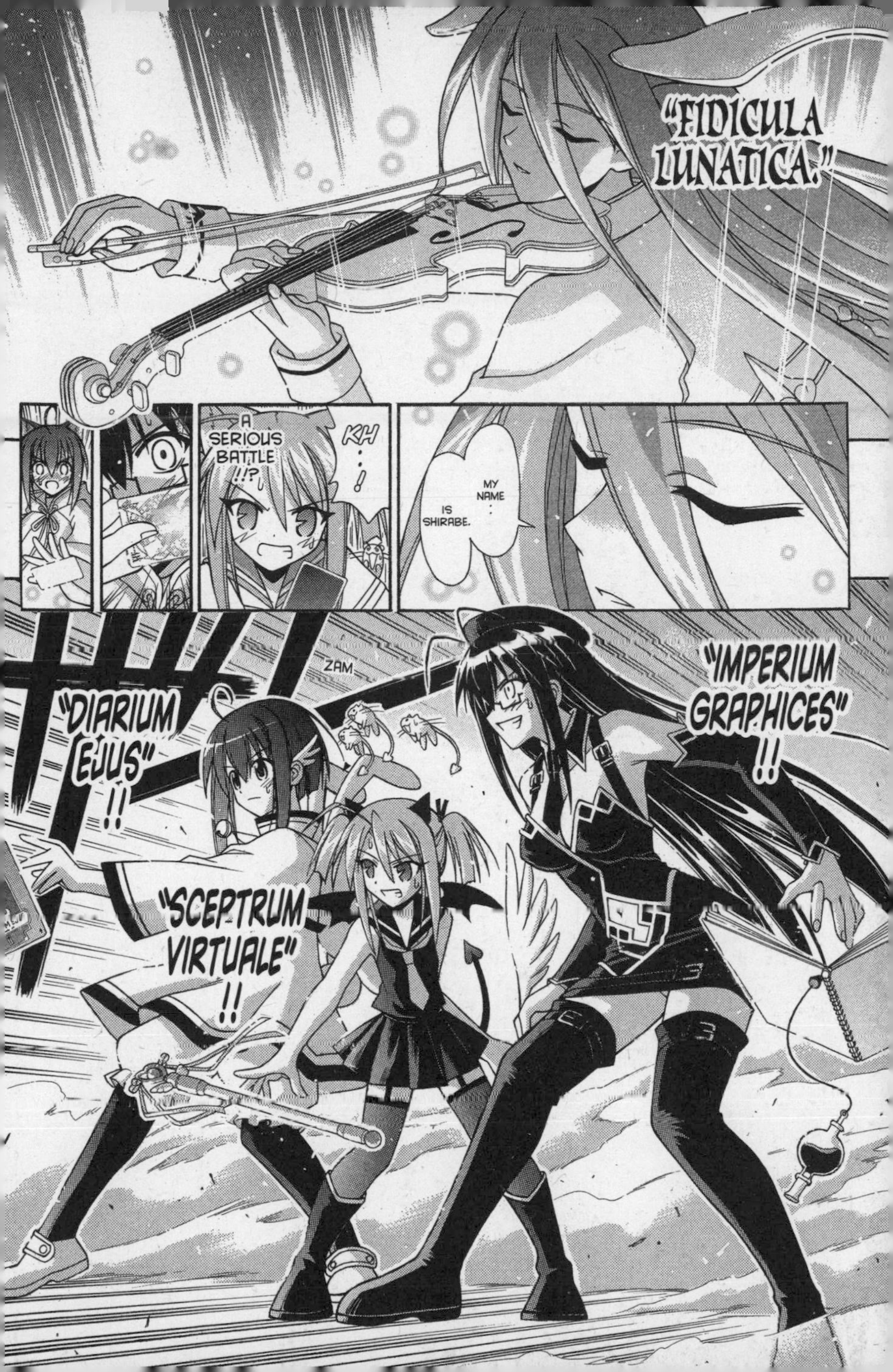
"FIDICULA LUNATICA."
MY NAME... IS SHIRABE.
KH...!
A SERIOUS BATTLE!!?
"IMPERIUM GRAPHICES"!!
ZAM
"DIARIUM EJUS"!!
"SCEPTRUM VIRTUALE"!!

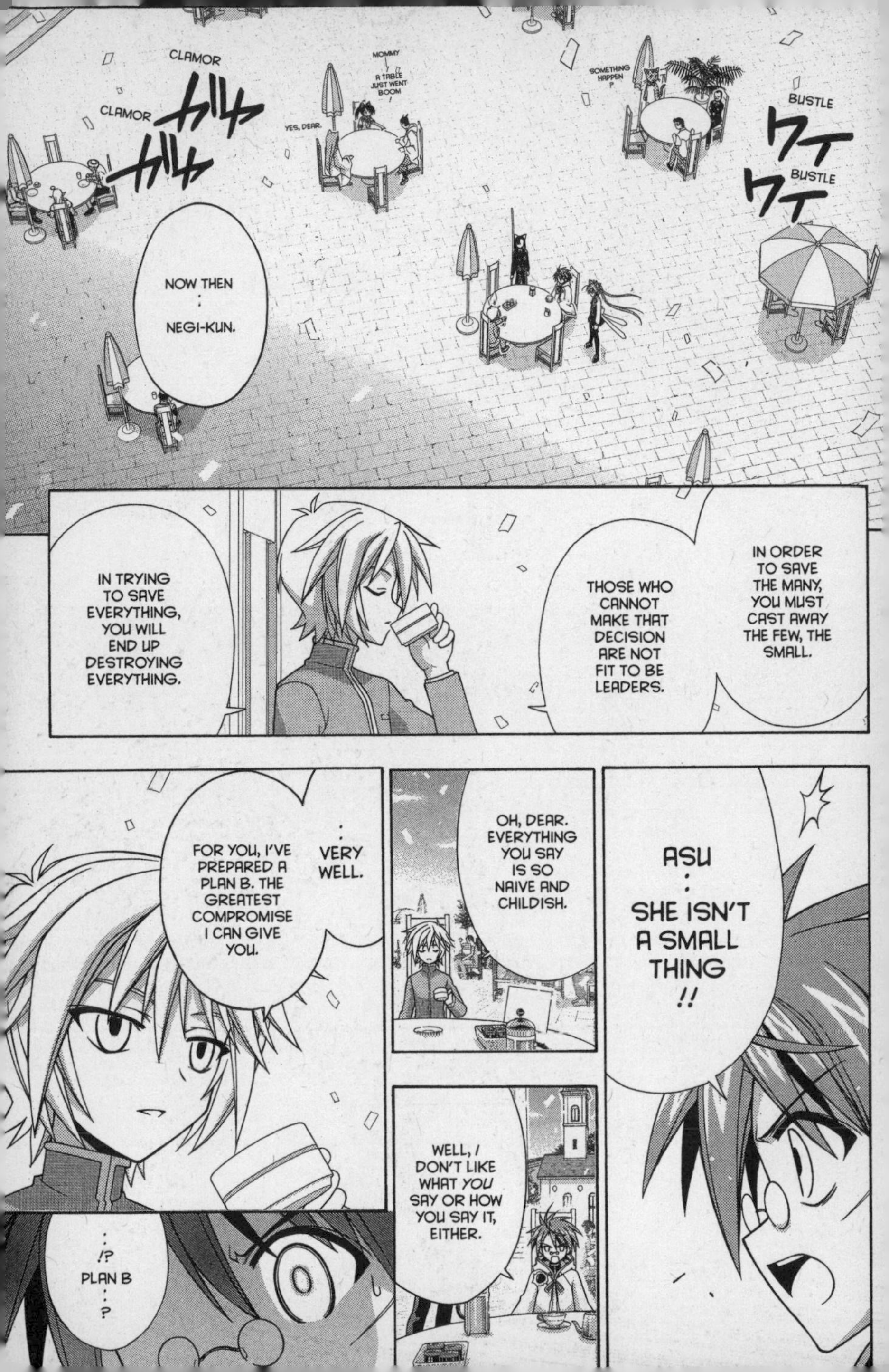
BUSTLE
ワイ
BUSTLE
ワイ
SOMETHING HAPPEN ?
MOMMY ! A TABLE JUST WENT BOOM !
YES, DEAR.
CLAMOR
ガヤ
CLAMOR
ガヤ
NOW THEN : NEGI-KUN.
IN ORDER TO SAVE THE MANY, YOU MUST CAST AWAY THE FEW, THE SMALL.
THOSE WHO CANNOT MAKE THAT DECISION ARE NOT FIT TO BE LEADERS.
IN TRYING TO SAVE EVERYTHING, YOU WILL END UP DESTROYING EVERYTHING.
ASU : SHE ISN'T A SMALL THING !!
OH, DEAR. EVERYTHING YOU SAY IS SO NAIVE AND CHILDISH.
WELL, I DON'T LIKE WHAT *YOU* SAY OR HOW YOU SAY IT, EITHER.
: VERY WELL.
FOR YOU, I'VE PREPARED A PLAN B. THE GREATEST COMPROMISE I CAN GIVE YOU.
: : !? PLAN B : : ?

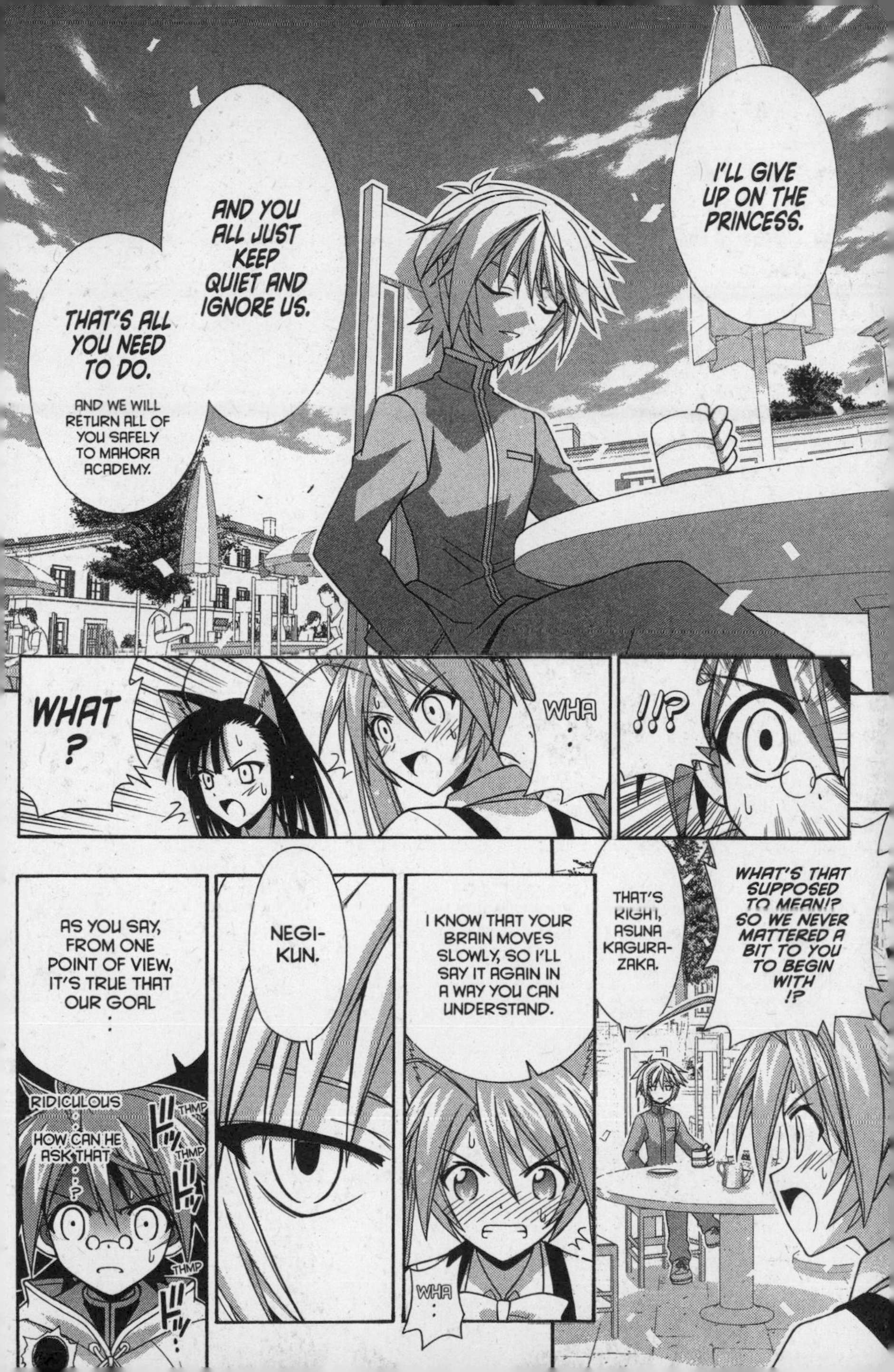

I'LL GIVE UP ON THE PRINCESS.
AND YOU ALL JUST KEEP QUIET AND IGNORE US.
THAT'S ALL YOU NEED TO DO.
AND WE WILL RETURN ALL OF YOU SAFELY TO MAHORA ACADEMY.
!!?
WHA...
WHAT?
WHAT'S THAT SUPPOSED TO MEAN!? SO WE NEVER MATTERED A BIT TO YOU TO BEGIN WITH!?
THAT'S RIGHT, ASUNA KAGURAZAKA.
I KNOW THAT YOUR BRAIN MOVES SLOWLY, SO I'LL SAY IT AGAIN IN A WAY YOU CAN UNDERSTAND.
WHA...
NEGI-KUN.
AS YOU SAY, FROM ONE POINT OF VIEW, IT'S TRUE THAT OUR GOAL...
RIDICULOUS...
HOW CAN HE ASK THAT...?
THMP
THMP
THMP

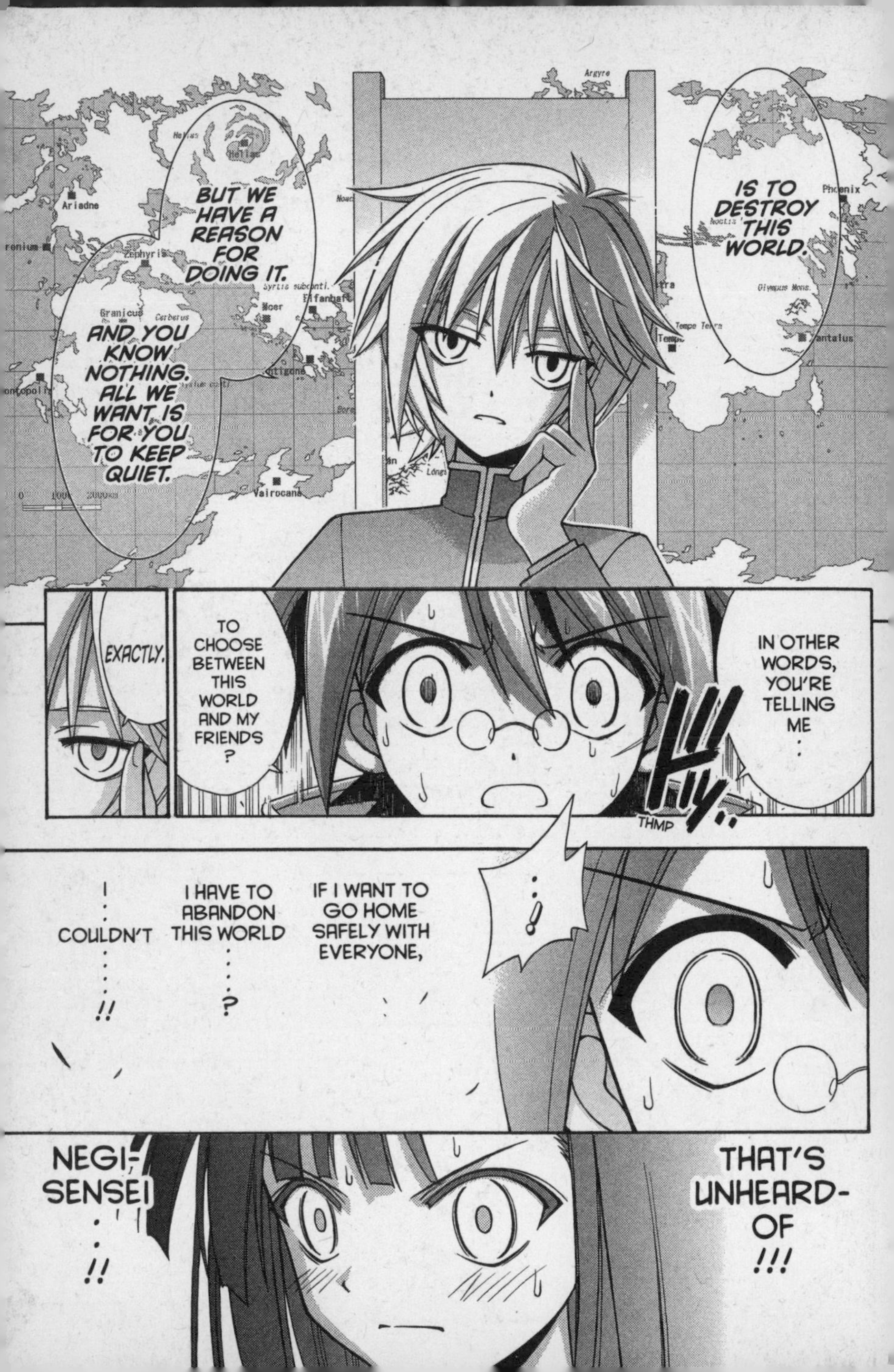

Argyre
Phoenix
Noctis
Olympus Mons
Tempe Terra
Tantalus
Helias
Ariadne
Zephyris
Granicus
Cerberus
Vairocana
IS TO DESTROY THIS WORLD.
BUT WE HAVE A REASON FOR DOING IT.
AND YOU KNOW NOTHING. ALL WE WANT IS FOR YOU TO KEEP QUIET.
IN OTHER WORDS, YOU'RE TELLING ME ...
THMP
TO CHOOSE BETWEEN THIS WORLD AND MY FRIENDS ?
EXACTLY.
...!
IF I WANT TO GO HOME SAFELY WITH EVERYONE,
I HAVE TO ABANDON THIS WORLD ....?
I ... COULDN'T .....!!
THAT'S UNHEARD-OF !!!
NEGI-SENSEI ...!!

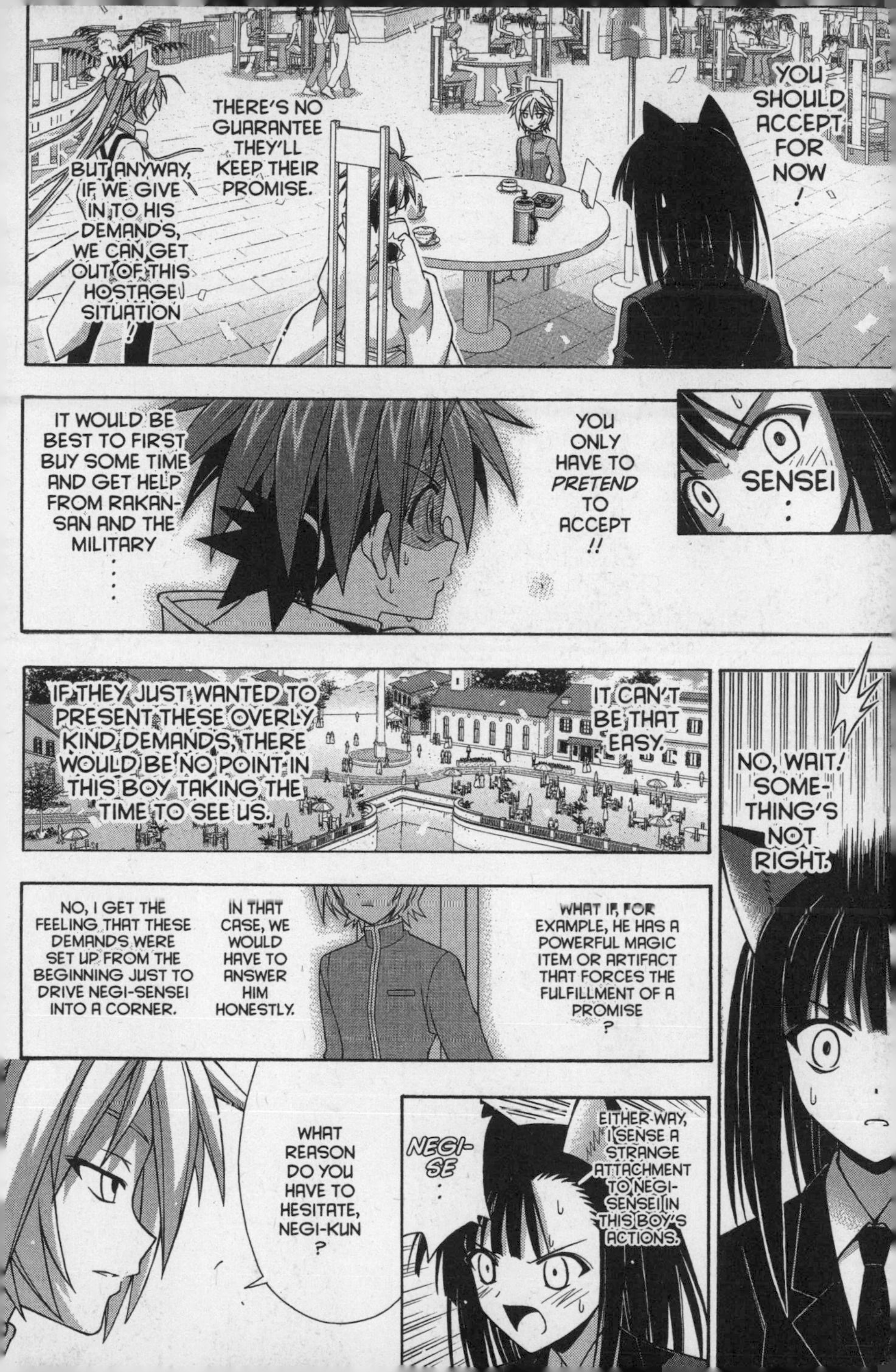

YOU SHOULD ACCEPT FOR NOW!
THERE'S NO GUARANTEE THEY'LL KEEP THEIR PROMISE.
BUT ANYWAY, IF WE GIVE IN TO HIS DEMANDS, WE CAN GET OUT OF THIS HOSTAGE SITUATION!
SENSEI...
YOU ONLY HAVE TO PRETEND TO ACCEPT!!
IT WOULD BE BEST TO FIRST BUY SOME TIME AND GET HELP FROM RAKAN-SAN AND THE MILITARY...
NO, WAIT! SOMETHING'S NOT RIGHT.
IT CAN'T BE THAT EASY.
IF THEY JUST WANTED TO PRESENT THESE OVERLY KIND DEMANDS, THERE WOULD BE NO POINT IN THIS BOY TAKING THE TIME TO SEE US.
WHAT IF, FOR EXAMPLE, HE HAS A POWERFUL MAGIC ITEM OR ARTIFACT THAT FORCES THE FULFILLMENT OF A PROMISE?
IN THAT CASE, WE WOULD HAVE TO ANSWER HIM HONESTLY.
NO, I GET THE FEELING THAT THESE DEMANDS WERE SET UP FROM THE BEGINNING JUST TO DRIVE NEGI-SENSEI INTO A CORNER.
EITHER WAY, I SENSE A STRANGE ATTACHMENT TO NEGI-SENSEI IN THIS BOY'S ACTIONS.
NEGI-SE...
WHAT REASON DO YOU HAVE TO HESITATE, NEGI-KUN?

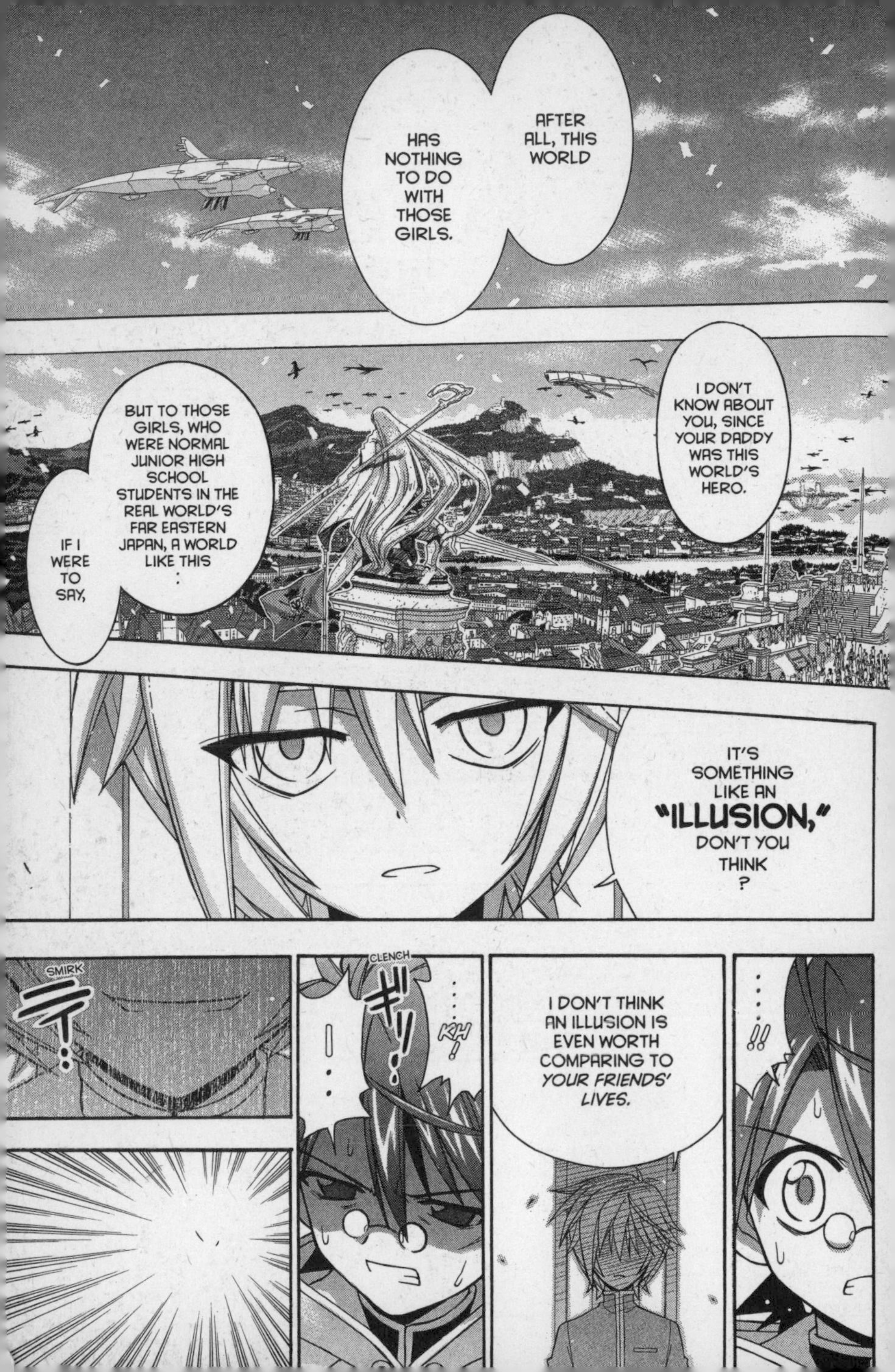

AFTER ALL, THIS WORLD
HAS NOTHING TO DO WITH THOSE GIRLS.
I DON'T KNOW ABOUT YOU, SINCE YOUR DADDY WAS THIS WORLD'S HERO.
BUT TO THOSE GIRLS, WHO WERE NORMAL JUNIOR HIGH SCHOOL STUDENTS IN THE REAL WORLD'S FAR EASTERN JAPAN, A WORLD LIKE THIS :
IF I WERE TO SAY,
IT'S SOMETHING LIKE AN "ILLUSION," DON'T YOU THINK ?
...!!
I DON'T THINK AN ILLUSION IS EVEN WORTH COMPARING TO YOUR FRIENDS' LIVES.
CLENCH
ギリッ
...KH!
...
SMIRK
ニイ

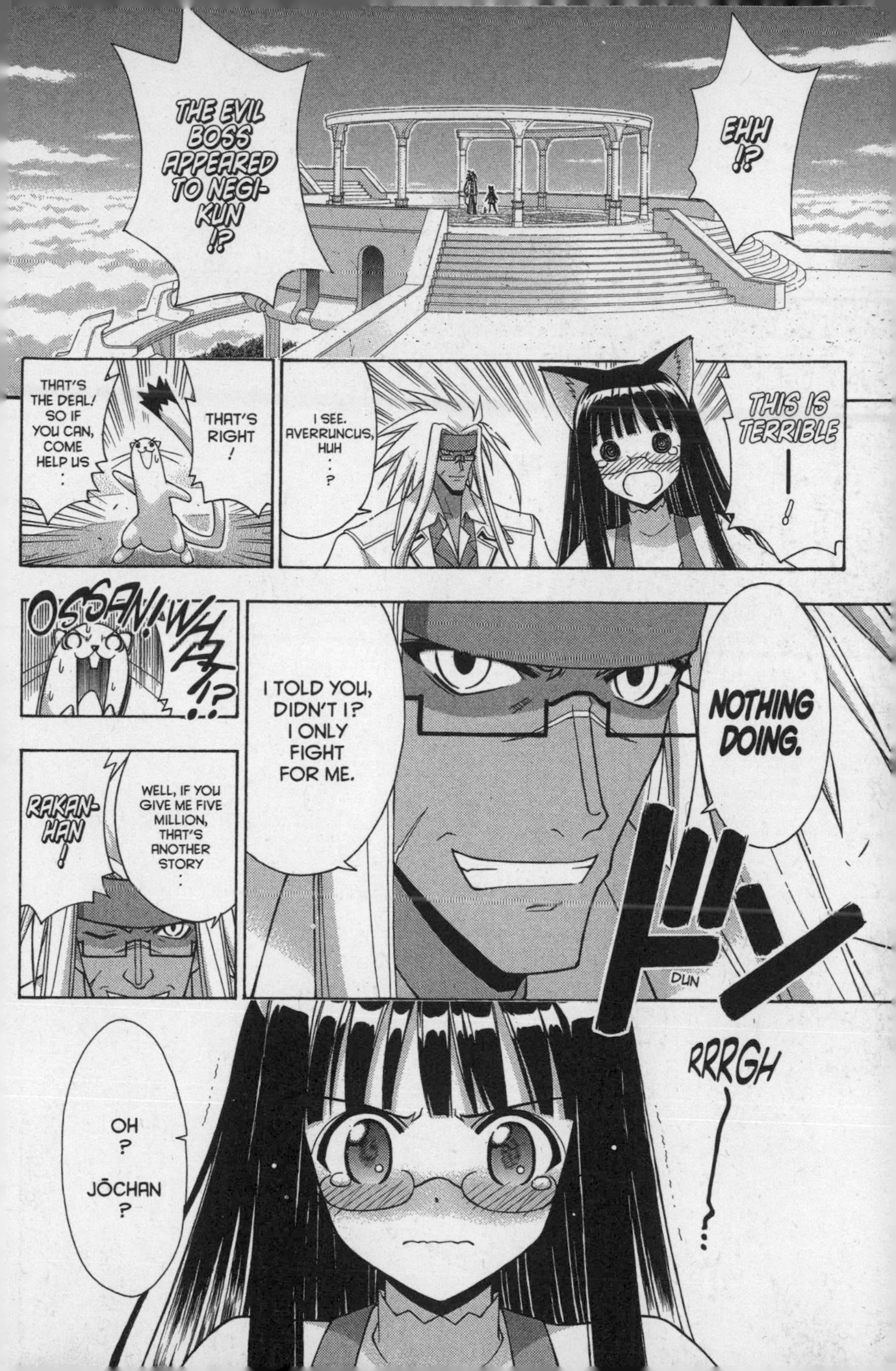
EHH !?
THE EVIL BOSS APPEARED TO NEGI-KUN !?
THIS IS TERRIBLE — !
I SEE. AVERRUNCUS, HUH . . ?
THAT'S RIGHT !
THAT'S THE DEAL! SO IF YOU CAN, COME HELP US . .
NOTHING DOING.
I TOLD YOU, DIDN'T I? I ONLY FIGHT FOR ME.
DUN
OSSAN! WHAT !? . .
WELL, IF YOU GIVE ME FIVE MILLION, THAT'S ANOTHER STORY . .
RAKAN-HAN !
RRRGH . . .
OH ? JŌCHAN ?

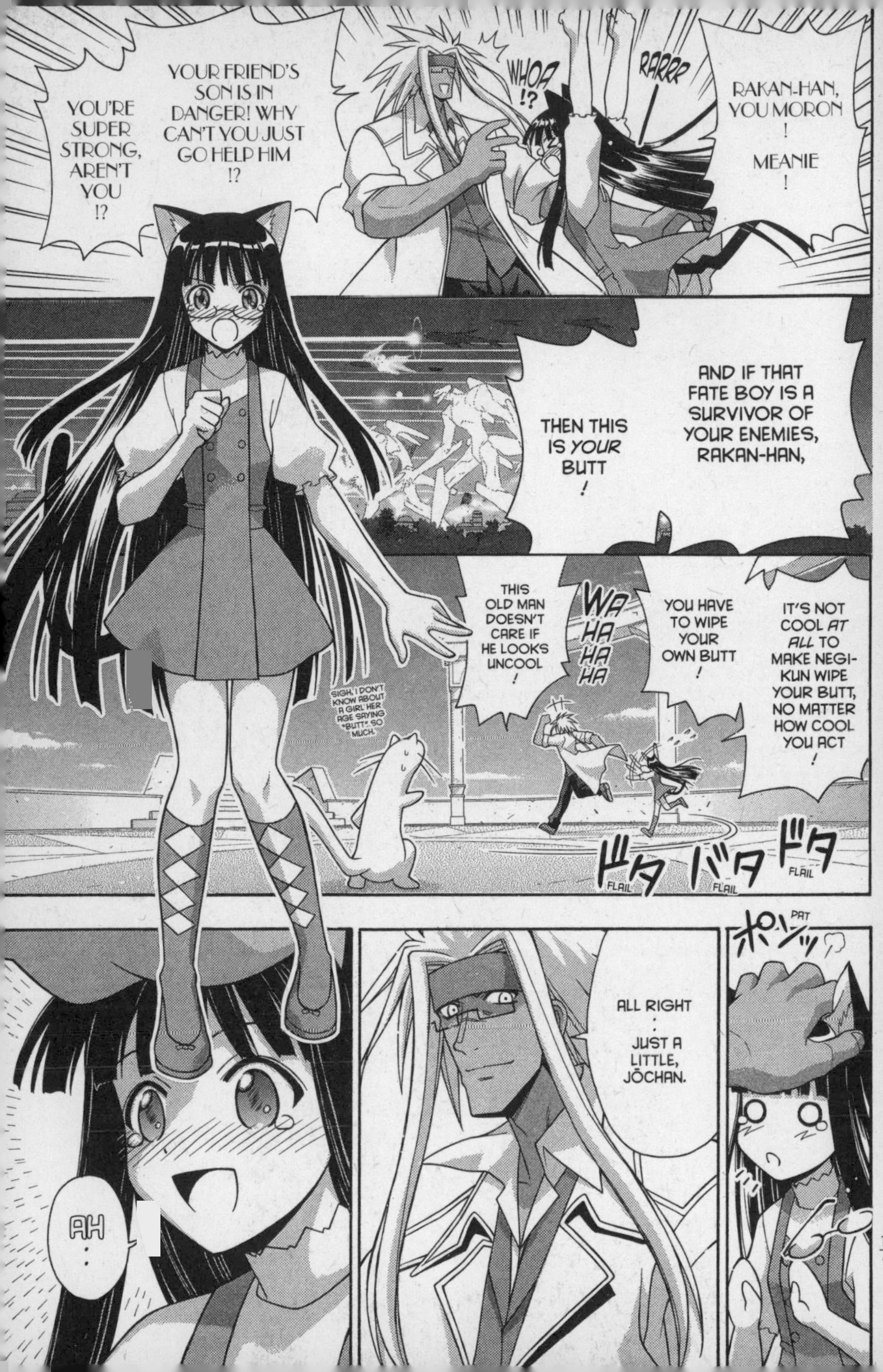
RAKAN-HAN, YOU MORON! MEANIE!
RARRR
WHOA!?
YOUR FRIEND'S SON IS IN DANGER! WHY CAN'T YOU JUST GO HELP HIM!?
YOU'RE SUPER STRONG, AREN'T YOU!?
AND IF THAT FATE BOY IS A SURVIVOR OF YOUR ENEMIES, RAKAN-HAN,
THEN THIS IS *YOUR* BUTT!
IT'S NOT COOL *AT ALL* TO MAKE NEGI-KUN WIPE YOUR BUTT, NO MATTER HOW COOL YOU ACT!
YOU HAVE TO WIPE YOUR OWN BUTT!
WAHAHAHA
THIS OLD MAN DOESN'T CARE IF HE LOOKS UNCOOL!
SIGH, I DON'T KNOW ABOUT A GIRL HER AGE SAYING "BUTT" SO MUCH.
ドタ FLAIL
バタ FLAIL
ドタ FLAIL
ポンッ PAT
ALL RIGHT... JUST A LITTLE, JŌCHAN.
AH...

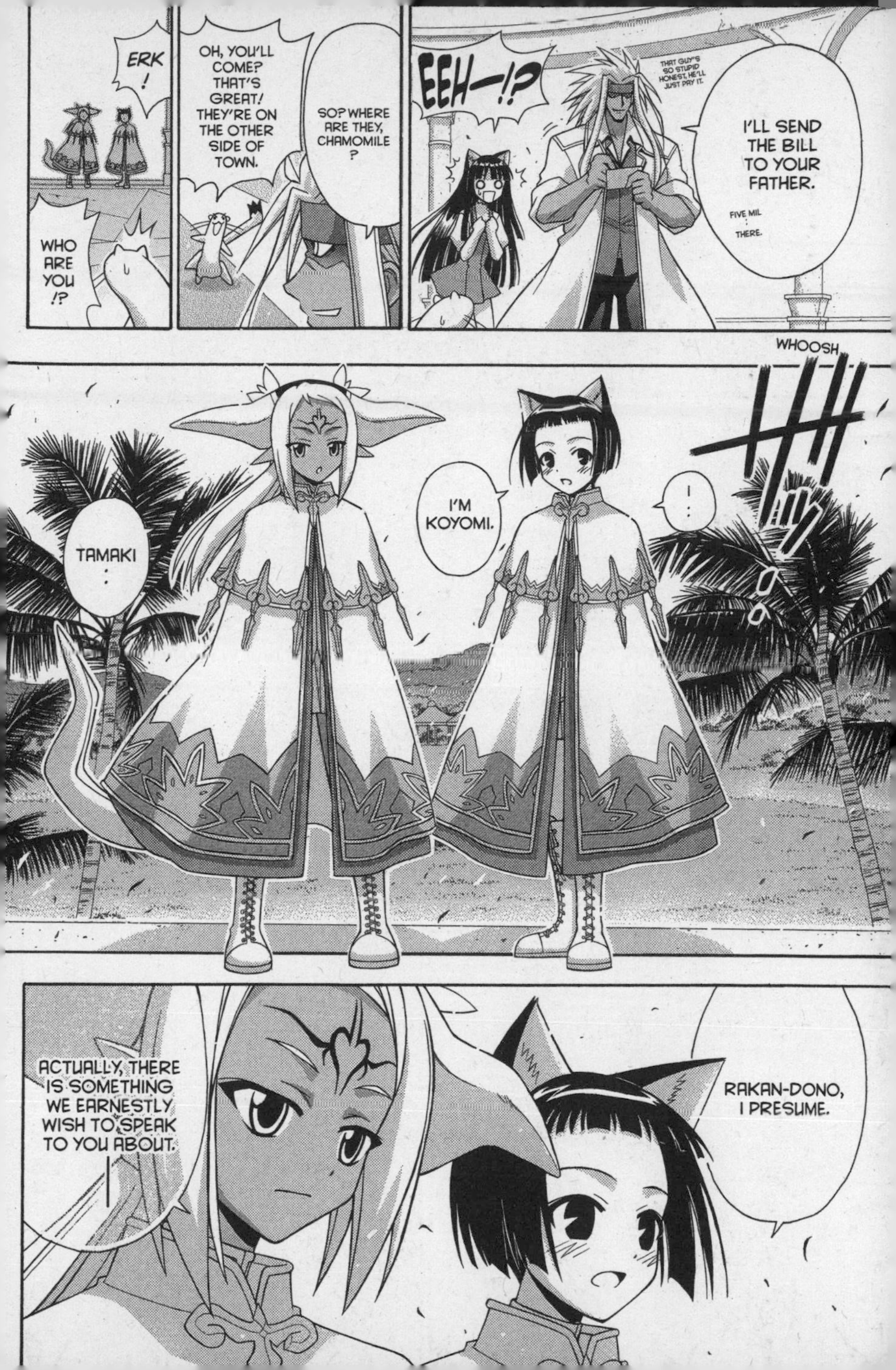
I'LL SEND THE BILL TO YOUR FATHER.
FIVE MIL : THERE.
THAT GUY'S SO STUPID HONEST, HE'LL JUST PAY IT.
EEH—!?
SO? WHERE ARE THEY, CHAMOMILE ?
OH, YOU'LL COME? THAT'S GREAT! THEY'RE ON THE OTHER SIDE OF TOWN.
ERK !
WHO ARE YOU !?
WHOOSH
! ...
I'M KOYOMI.
TAMAKI ...
RAKAN-DONO, I PRESUME.
ACTUALLY, THERE IS SOMETHING WE EARNESTLY WISH TO SPEAK TO YOU ABOUT—

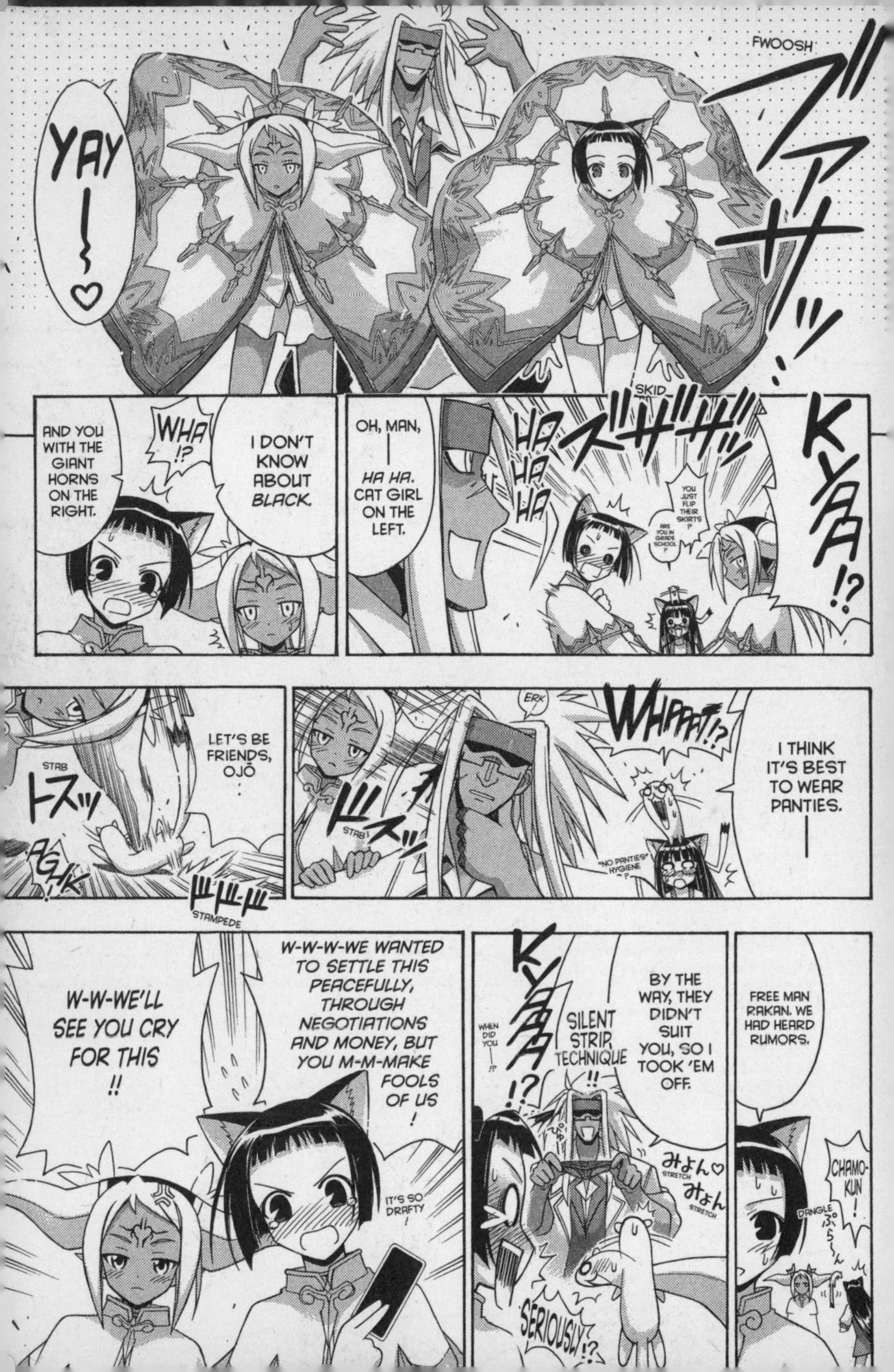
FWOOSH
ブァサッ!!
YAY!~♡
KYAA!?
SKID
ズザザッ
HA HA HA
YOU JUST FLIP THEIR SKIRTS!?
ARE YOU IN GRADE SCHOOL!?
OH, MAN, — HA HA. CAT GIRL ON THE LEFT.
I DON'T KNOW ABOUT BLACK.
WHA!?
AND YOU WITH THE GIANT HORNS ON THE RIGHT.
I THINK IT'S BEST TO WEAR PANTIES. —
WHAAAT!?
ERK!
"NO PANTIES" HYGIENE...?
STAB
ドスッ
LET'S BE FRIENDS, OJŌ
STAB
トスッ
AGHK!
STAMPEDE
FREE MAN RAKAN. WE HAD HEARD RUMORS.
CHAMO-KUN!
DANGLE
ぷら～ん
BY THE WAY, THEY DIDN'T SUIT YOU, SO I TOOK 'EM OFF.
SILENT STRIP TECHNIQUE!!
みょん♡
STRETCH
みょん
STRETCH
KYAA!?
WHEN DID YOU —!?
SERIOUSLY!?
W-W-W-WE WANTED TO SETTLE THIS PEACEFULLY, THROUGH NEGOTIATIONS AND MONEY, BUT YOU M-M-MAKE FOOLS OF US!
W-W-WE'LL SEE YOU CRY FOR THIS!!
IT'S SO DRAFTY!

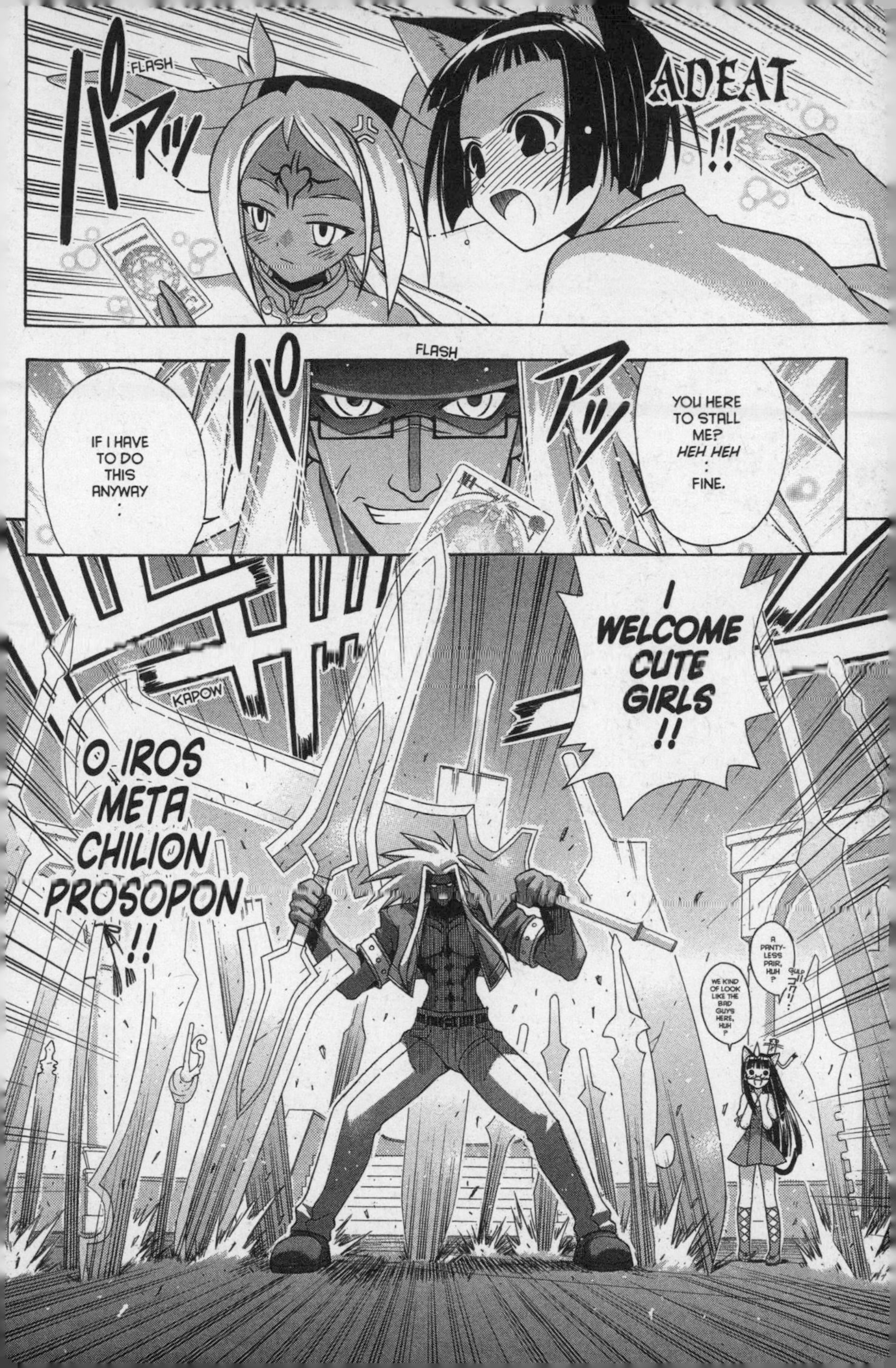
ADEAT !!
FLASH
YOU HERE TO STALL ME? HEH HEH : FINE.
FLASH
IF I HAVE TO DO THIS ANYWAY :
I WELCOME CUTE GIRLS !!
GULP
A PANTY-LESS PAIR, HUH ?
WE KIND OF LOOK LIKE THE BAD GUYS HERE, HUH ?
KAPOW
O IROS META CHILION PROSOPON !!

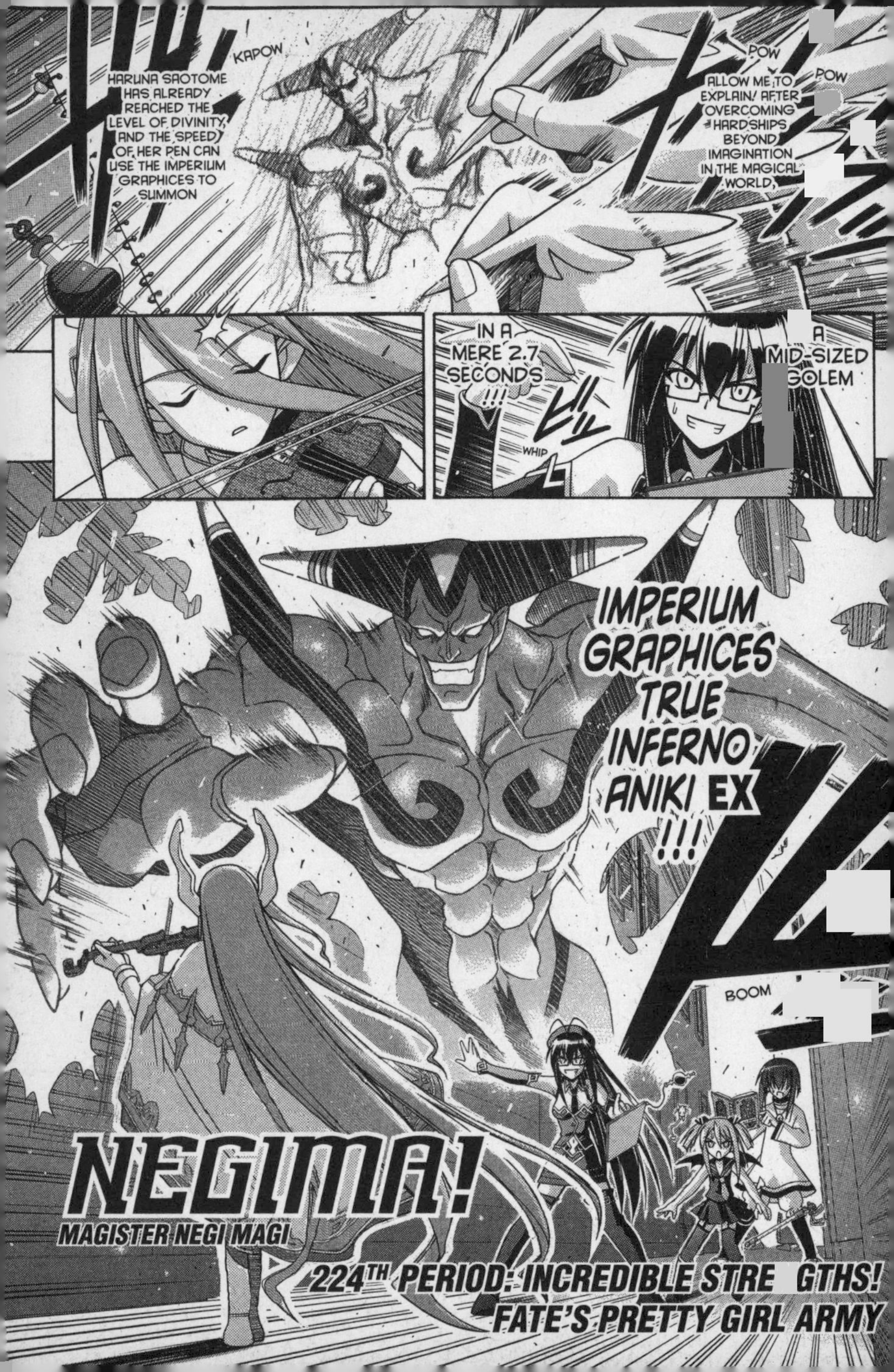

POW
POW
ALLOW ME TO EXPLAIN! AFTER OVERCOMING HARDSHIPS BEYOND IMAGINATION IN THE MAGICAL WORLD,
KAPOW
HARUNA SAOTOME HAS ALREADY REACHED THE LEVEL OF DIVINITY, AND THE SPEED OF HER PEN CAN USE THE IMPERIUM GRAPHICES TO SUMMON
A MID-SIZED GOLEM
IN A MERE 2.7 SECONDS !!!
WHIP
IMPERIUM GRAPHICES TRUE INFERNO ANIKI EX !!!
BOOM
NEGIMA!
MAGISTER NEGI MAGI
224TH PERIOD: INCREDIBLE STRE GTHS! FATE'S PRETTY GIRL ARMY

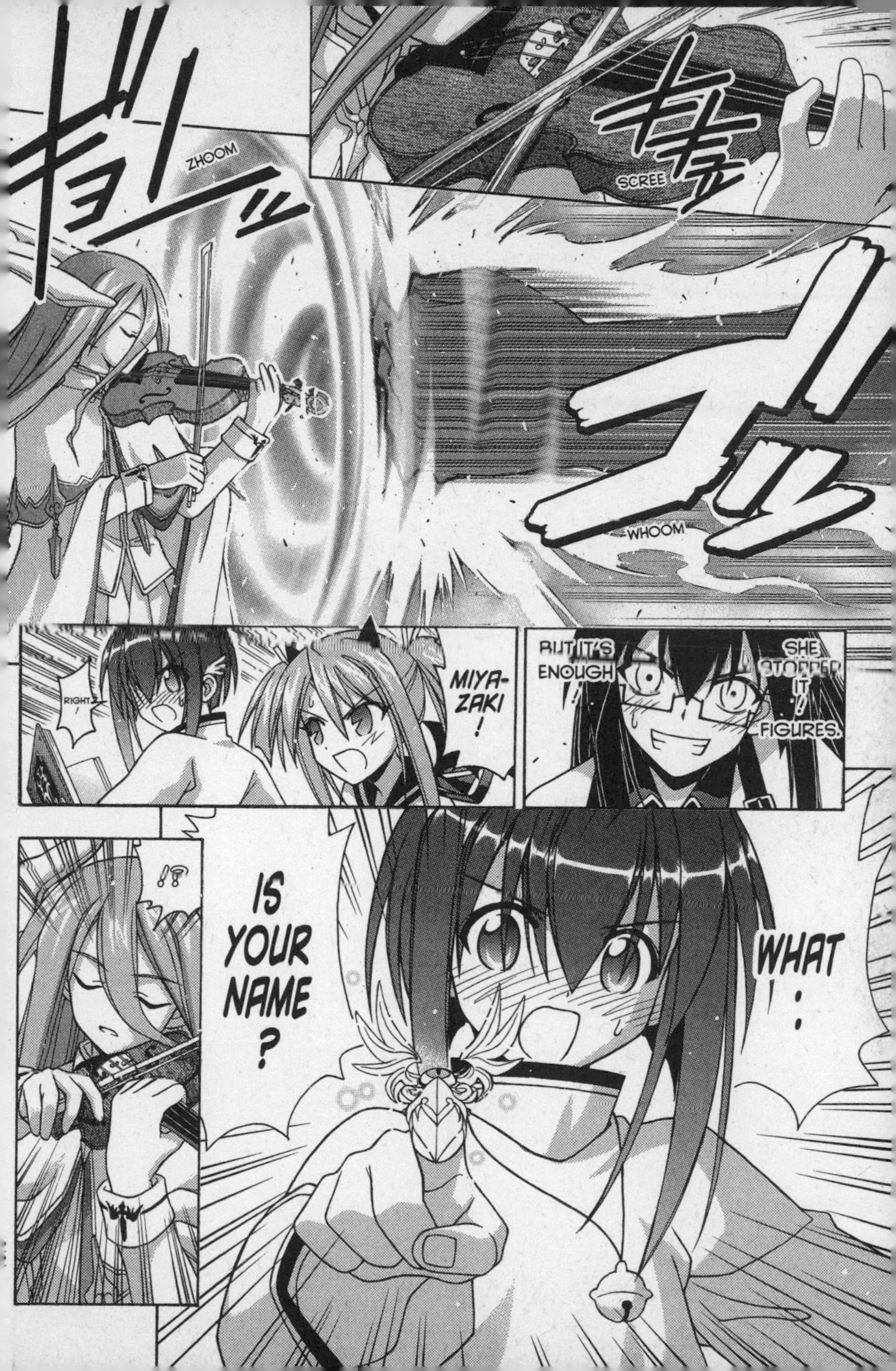
SCREE
WHOOM
ZHOOM
SHE STOPPED IT! FIGURES.
BUT IT'S ENOUGH!
MIYA-ZAKI!
RIGHT!
WHAT...
IS YOUR NAME?
!?

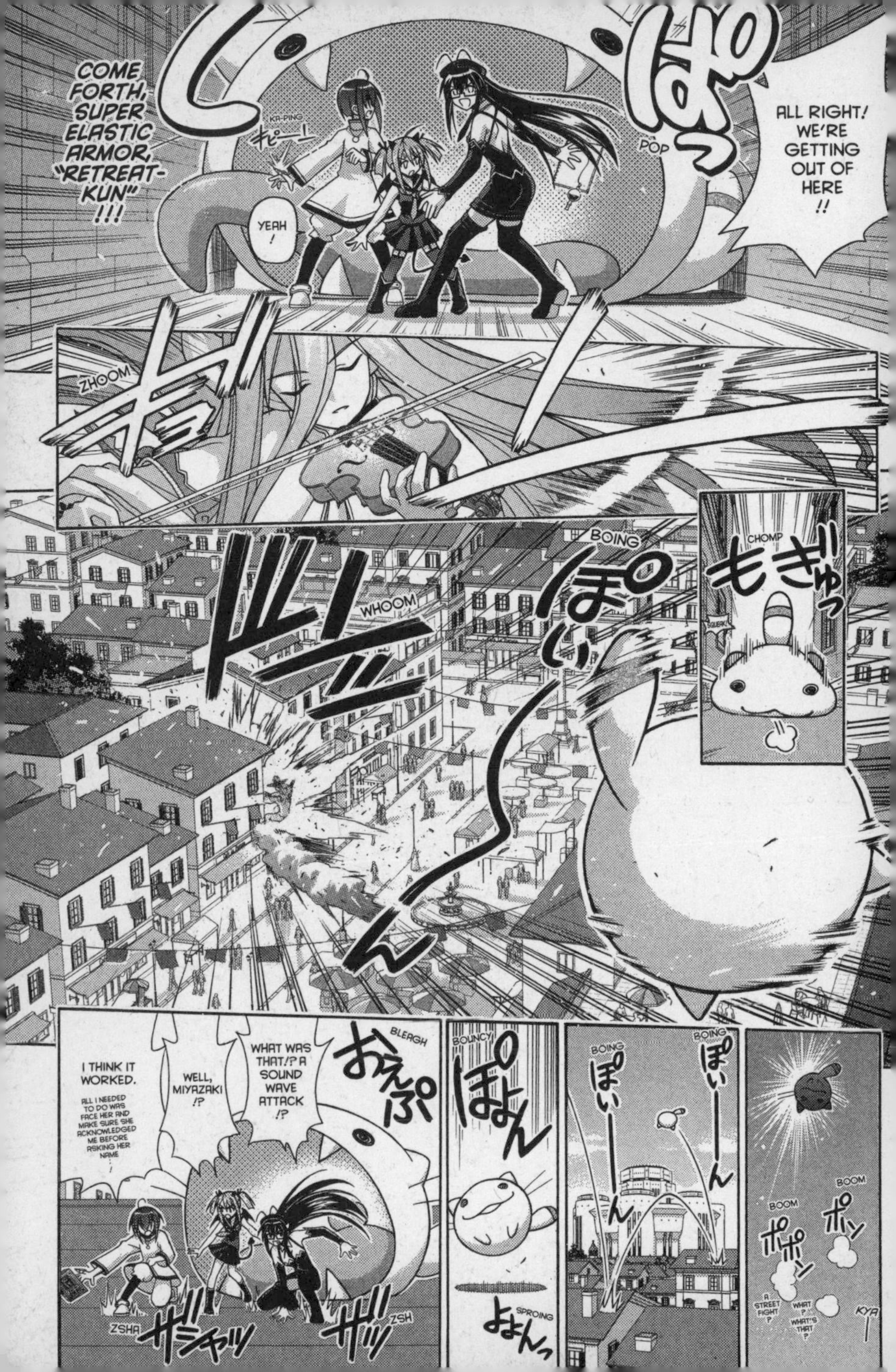
くぱっ
POP
ALL RIGHT! WE'RE GETTING OUT OF HERE!!
COME FORTH, SUPER ELASTIC ARMOR, "RETREAT-KUN"!!!
KA-PING
YEAH!
ZHOOM
CHOMP
もぎゅっ
SQUEAK
BOING
ぽいぃ〜ん
WHOOM
BOOM
ポン
BOOM
ポポン
KYA—
A STREET FIGHT?
WHAT?
WHAT'S THAT?
BOING
ぽいーん
BOING
ぽいーん
BOUNCY
ぽよん
SPROING
よよんっ
BLEAGH
おえっぷ
WHAT WAS THAT!? A SOUND WAVE ATTACK!?
WELL, MIYAZAKI!?
I THINK IT WORKED.
ALL I NEEDED TO DO WAS FACE HER AND MAKE SURE SHE ACKNOWLEDGED ME BEFORE ASKING HER NAME...!
ZSH
ZSHA

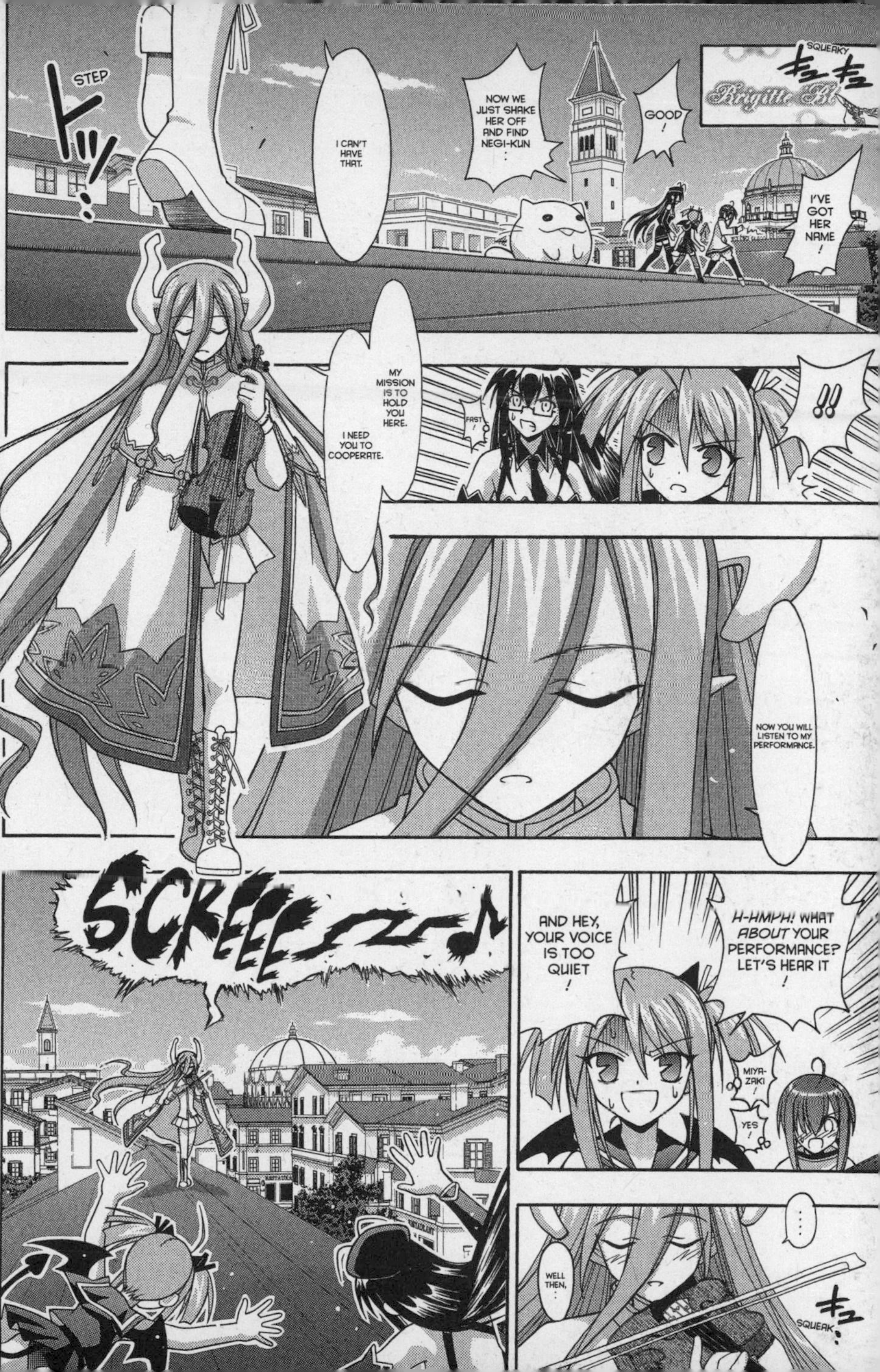
SQUEAKY
キュ キュ
Brigitte B
I'VE GOT HER NAME!
GOOD!
NOW WE JUST SHAKE HER OFF AND FIND NEGI-KUN...
I CAN'T HAVE THAT.
STEP
ドッ!
!!
FAST!
NOW YOU WILL LISTEN TO MY PERFORMANCE.
MY MISSION IS TO HOLD YOU HERE.
I NEED YOU TO COOPERATE.
H-HMPH! WHAT ABOUT YOUR PERFORMANCE? LET'S HEAR IT!
AND HEY, YOUR VOICE IS TOO QUIET!
MIYAZAKI!
YES!
....!
WELL THEN, ..
キュ
SQUEAK!
SCREEEE♪

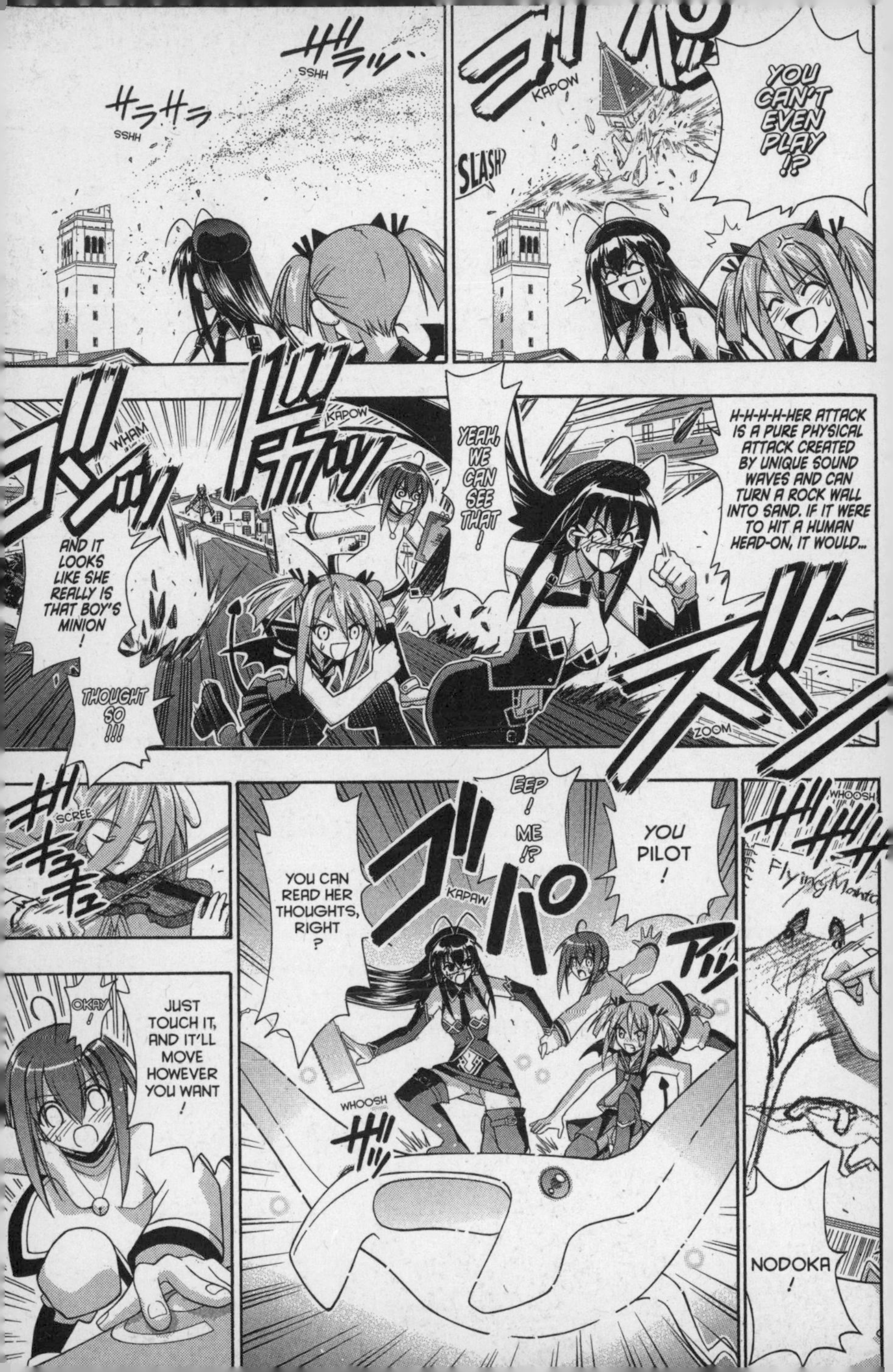
KAPOW
SLASH
YOU CAN'T EVEN PLAY !?
SSHH
SSHH
H-H-H-H-HER ATTACK IS A PURE PHYSICAL ATTACK CREATED BY UNIQUE SOUND WAVES AND CAN TURN A ROCK WALL INTO SAND. IF IT WERE TO HIT A HUMAN HEAD-ON, IT WOULD...
ZOOM
YEAH, WE CAN SEE THAT !
KAPOW
WHAM
AND IT LOOKS LIKE SHE REALLY IS THAT BOY'S MINION !
THOUGHT SO !!!
WHOOSH
NODOKA !
YOU PILOT !
EEP ! ME !?
YOU CAN READ HER THOUGHTS, RIGHT ?
KAPAW
WHOOSH
SCREE
JUST TOUCH IT, AND IT'LL MOVE HOWEVER YOU WANT !
OKAY !

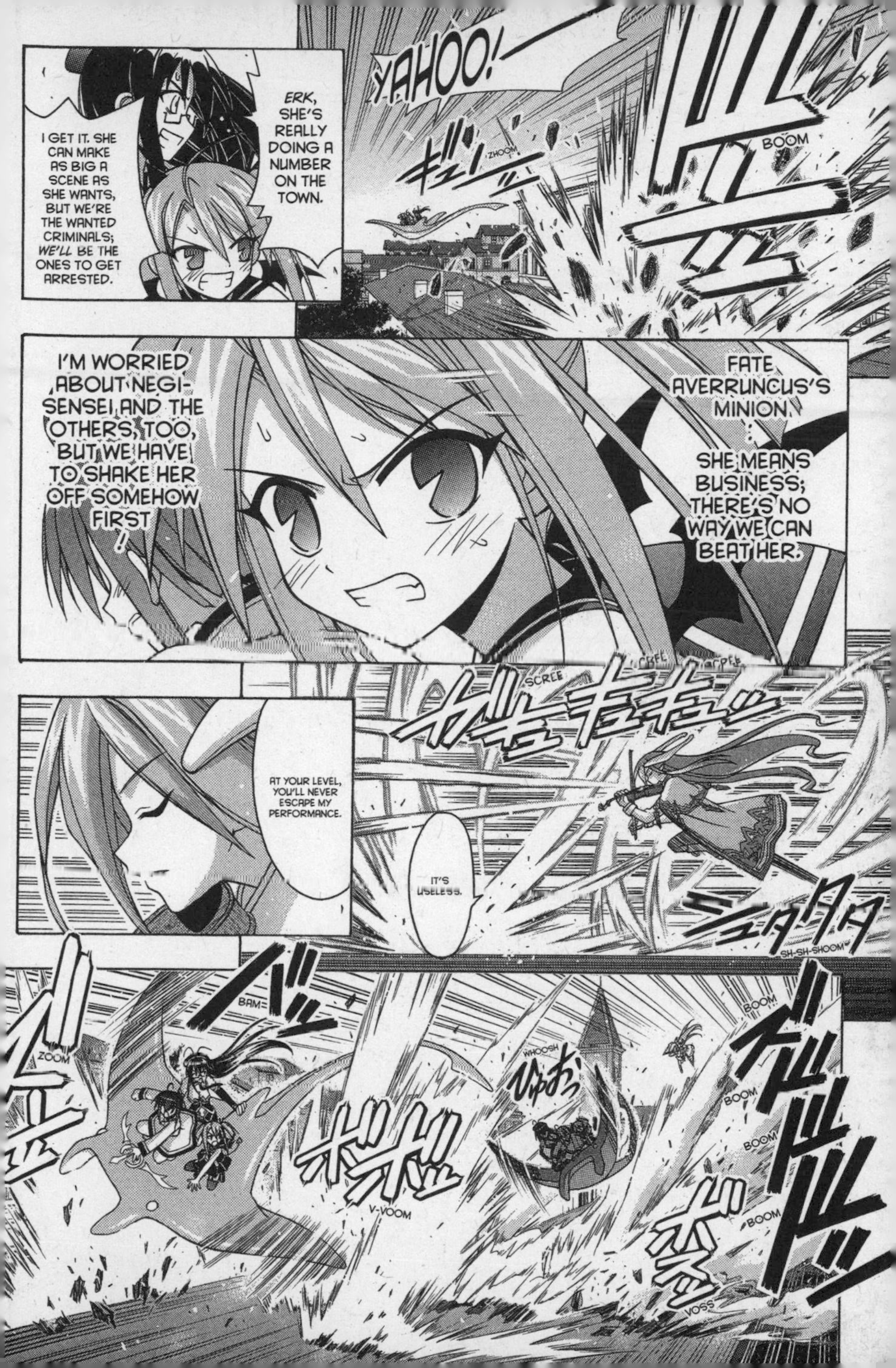
YAHOO!
ZHOOM
BOOM
ERK, SHE'S REALLY DOING A NUMBER ON THE TOWN.
I GET IT. SHE CAN MAKE AS BIG A SCENE AS SHE WANTS, BUT WE'RE THE WANTED CRIMINALS; WE'LL BE THE ONES TO GET ARRESTED.
FATE AVERRUNCUS'S MINION...
SHE MEANS BUSINESS; THERE'S NO WAY WE CAN BEAT HER.
I'M WORRIED ABOUT NEGI-SENSEI AND THE OTHERS, TOO, BUT WE HAVE TO SHAKE HER OFF SOMEHOW FIRST...!
SCREE
AT YOUR LEVEL, YOU'LL NEVER ESCAPE MY PERFORMANCE.
IT'S USELESS.
SH-SH-SHOOM
BOOM
BOOM
BOOM
BOOM
WHOOSH
VOSS
BAM
V-VOOM
ZOOM

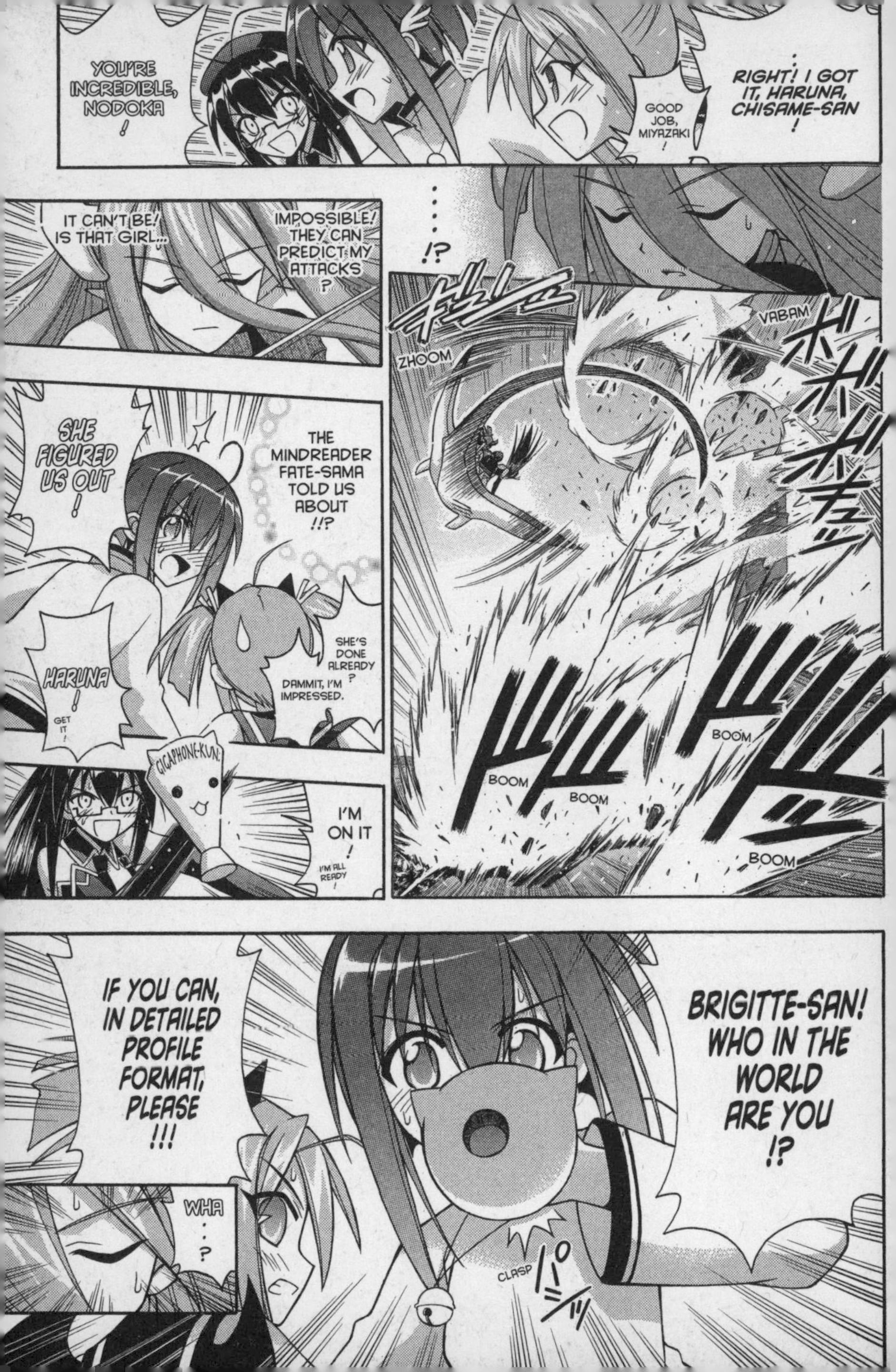
RIGHT! I GOT IT, HARUNA, CHISAME-SAN!
GOOD JOB, MIYAZAKI!
YOU'RE INCREDIBLE, NODOKA!
...!?
IMPOSSIBLE! THEY CAN PREDICT MY ATTACKS?
IT CAN'T BE! IS THAT GIRL...
VABAM
ZHOOM
BOOM
BOOM
BOOM
BOOM
THE MINDREADER FATE-SAMA TOLD US ABOUT!!?
SHE FIGURED US OUT!
SHE'S DONE ALREADY?
DAMMIT, I'M IMPRESSED.
HARUNA!
GET IT!
I'M ON IT!
I'M ALL READY
GIGAPHONE-KUN!
BRIGITTE-SAN! WHO IN THE WORLD ARE YOU!?
IF YOU CAN, IN DETAILED PROFILE FORMAT, PLEASE!!!
CLASP
WHA...?

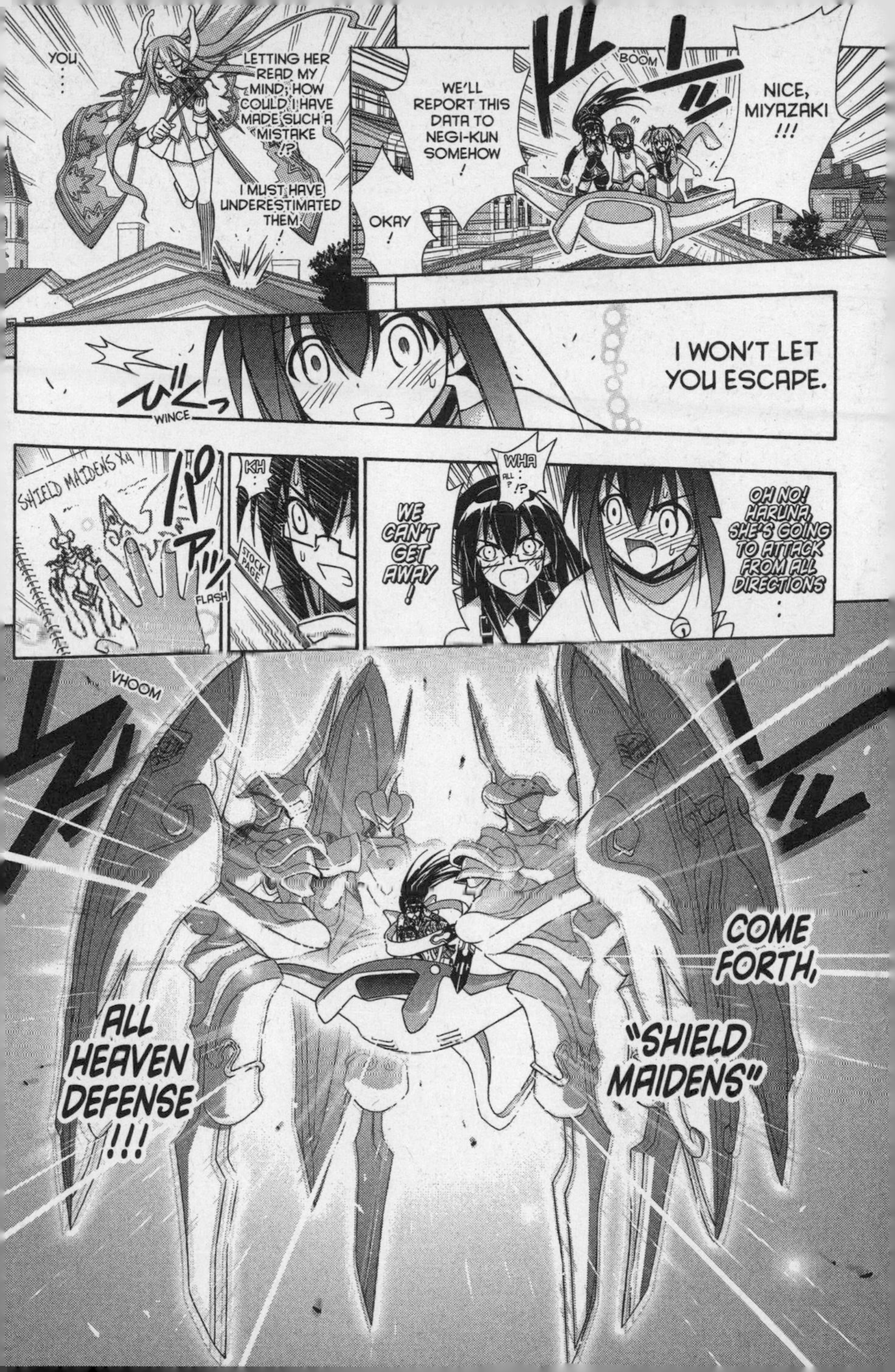
NICE, MIYAZAKI!!!
BOOM
WE'LL REPORT THIS DATA TO NEGI-KUN SOMEHOW!
OKAY!
LETTING HER READ MY MIND, HOW COULD I HAVE MADE SUCH A MISTAKE!?
YOU...
I MUST HAVE UNDERESTIMATED THEM!
I WON'T LET YOU ESCAPE.
WINCE
OH NO! HARUNA, SHE'S GOING TO ATTACK FROM ALL DIRECTIONS...
WHA... ALL?!?
WE CAN'T GET AWAY!
KH
STOCK PAGE
FLASH
SHIELD MAIDENS X4
COME FORTH, "SHIELD MAIDENS"
ALL HEAVEN DEFENSE!!!
VHOOM

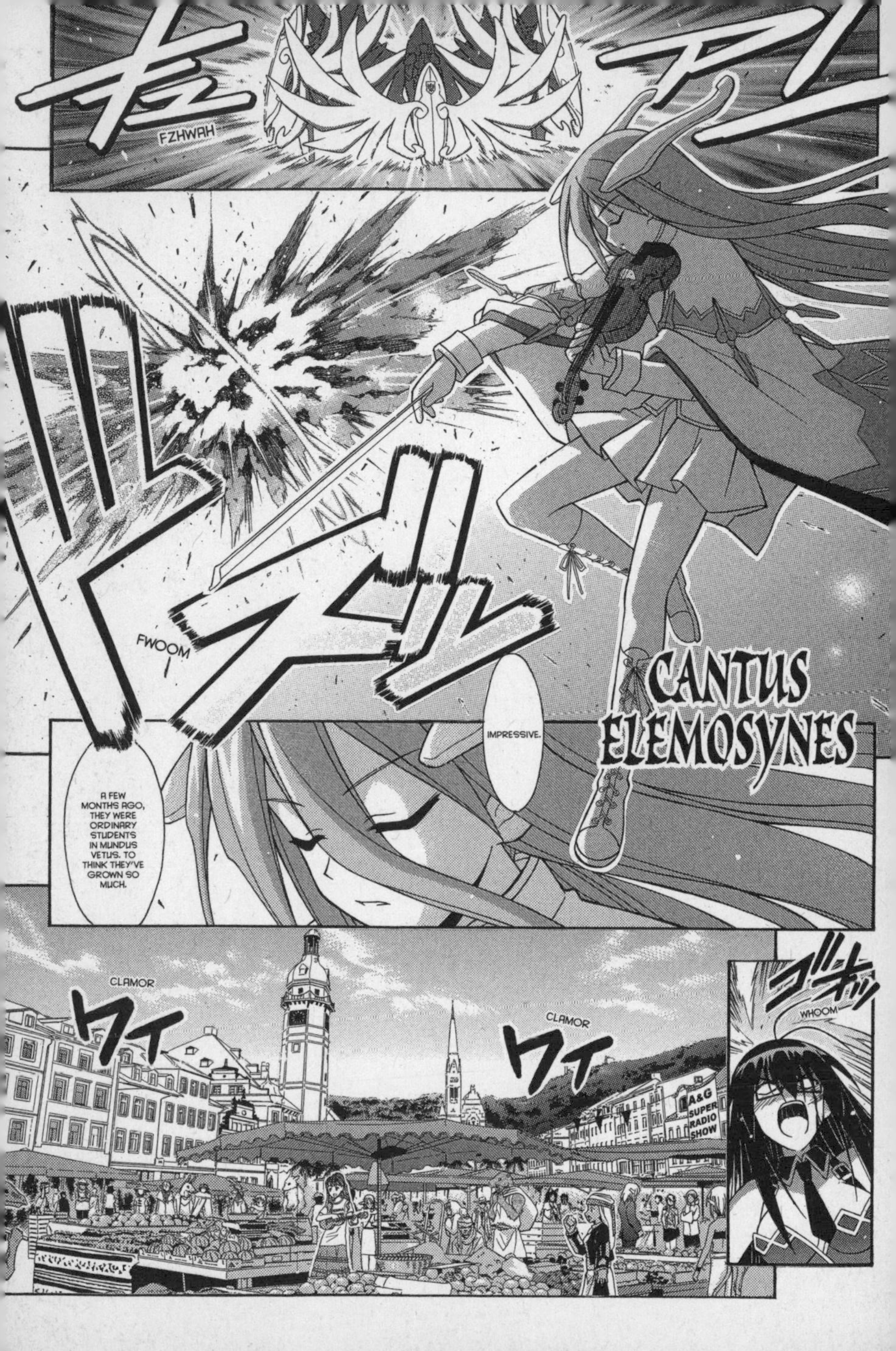
FZHWAH
FWOOM
CANTUS ELEMOSYNES
IMPRESSIVE.
A FEW MONTHS AGO, THEY WERE ORDINARY STUDENTS IN MUNDUS VETUS. TO THINK THEY'VE GROWN SO MUCH.
WHOOM
CLAMOR
CLAMOR
A&G SUPER RADIO SHOW

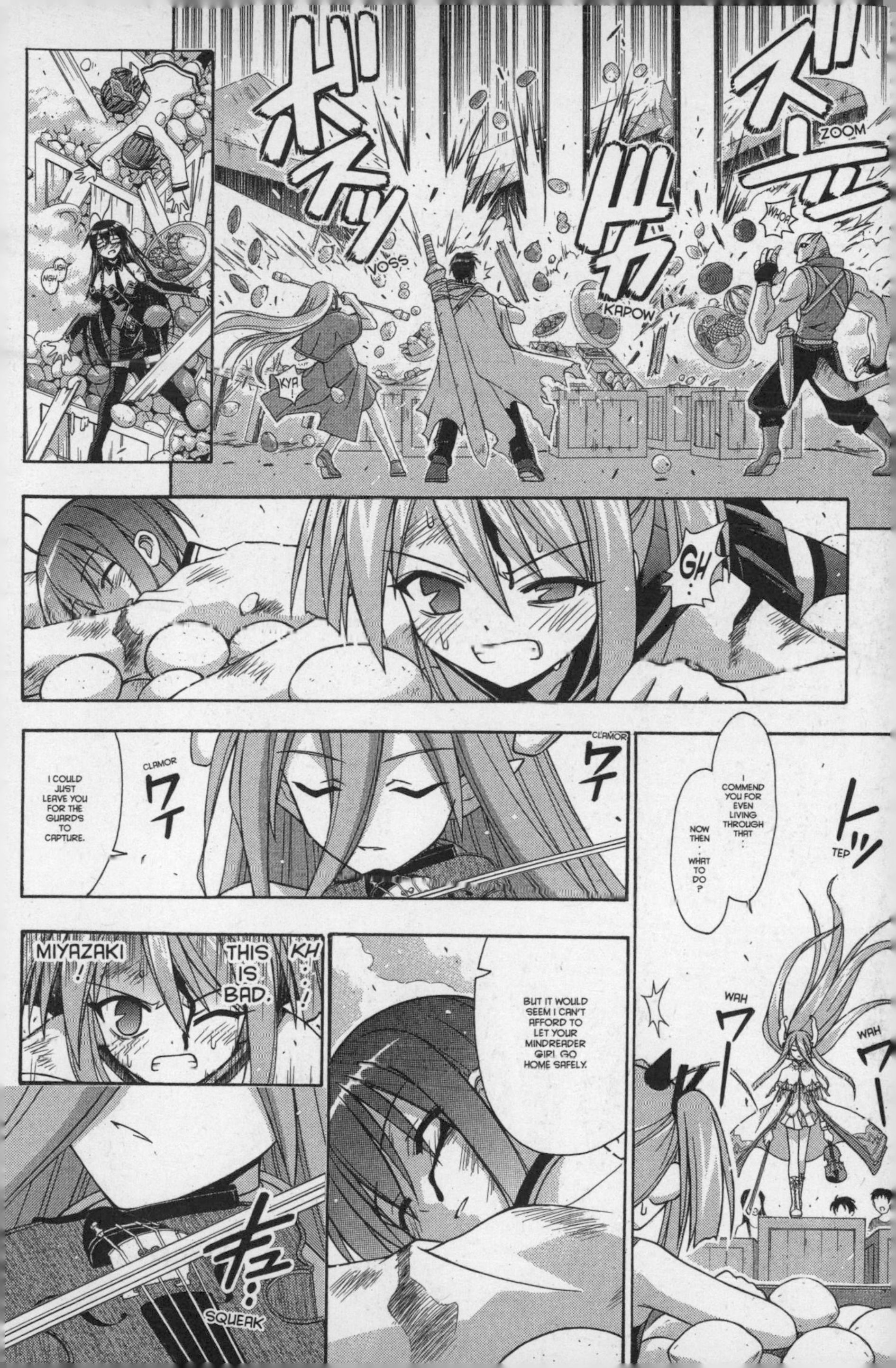
ZOOM
WHOA!
KAPOW
VOSS
KYA!
UGH
NGH
GH...!
I COMMEND YOU FOR EVEN LIVING THROUGH THAT...
NOW THEN... WHAT TO DO?
TEP
WAH
WAH
CLAMOR
CLAMOR
I COULD JUST LEAVE YOU FOR THE GUARDS TO CAPTURE.
BUT IT WOULD SEEM I CAN'T AFFORD TO LET YOUR MINDREADER GIRL GO HOME SAFELY.
KH...!
THIS IS BAD.
MIYAZAKI!
SQUEAK

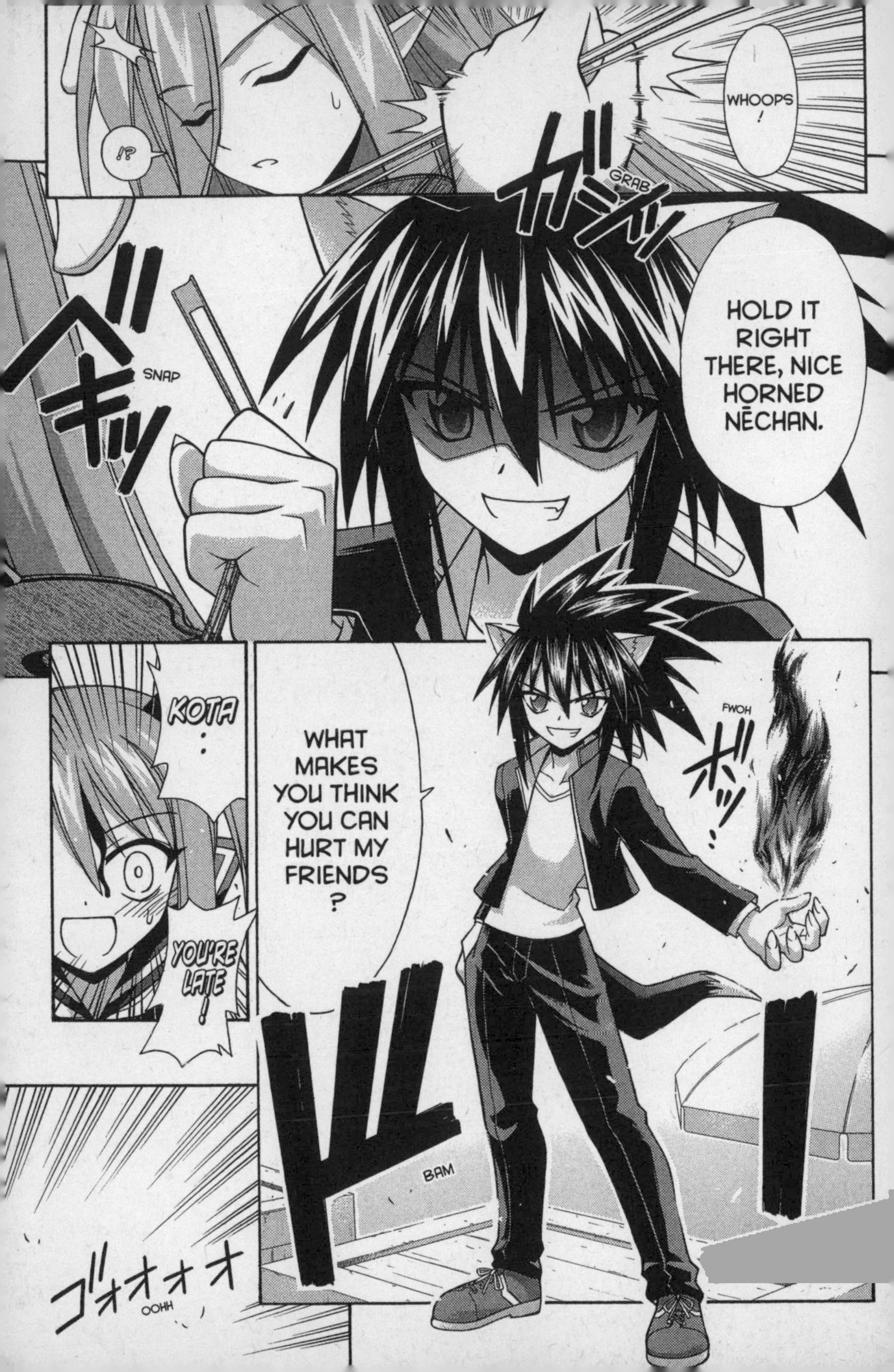
WHOOPS!
!?
GRAB
HOLD IT RIGHT THERE, NICE HORNED NĒCHAN.
SNAP
FWOH
WHAT MAKES YOU THINK YOU CAN HURT MY FRIENDS?
BAM
KOTA...
YOU'RE LATE!
OOHH

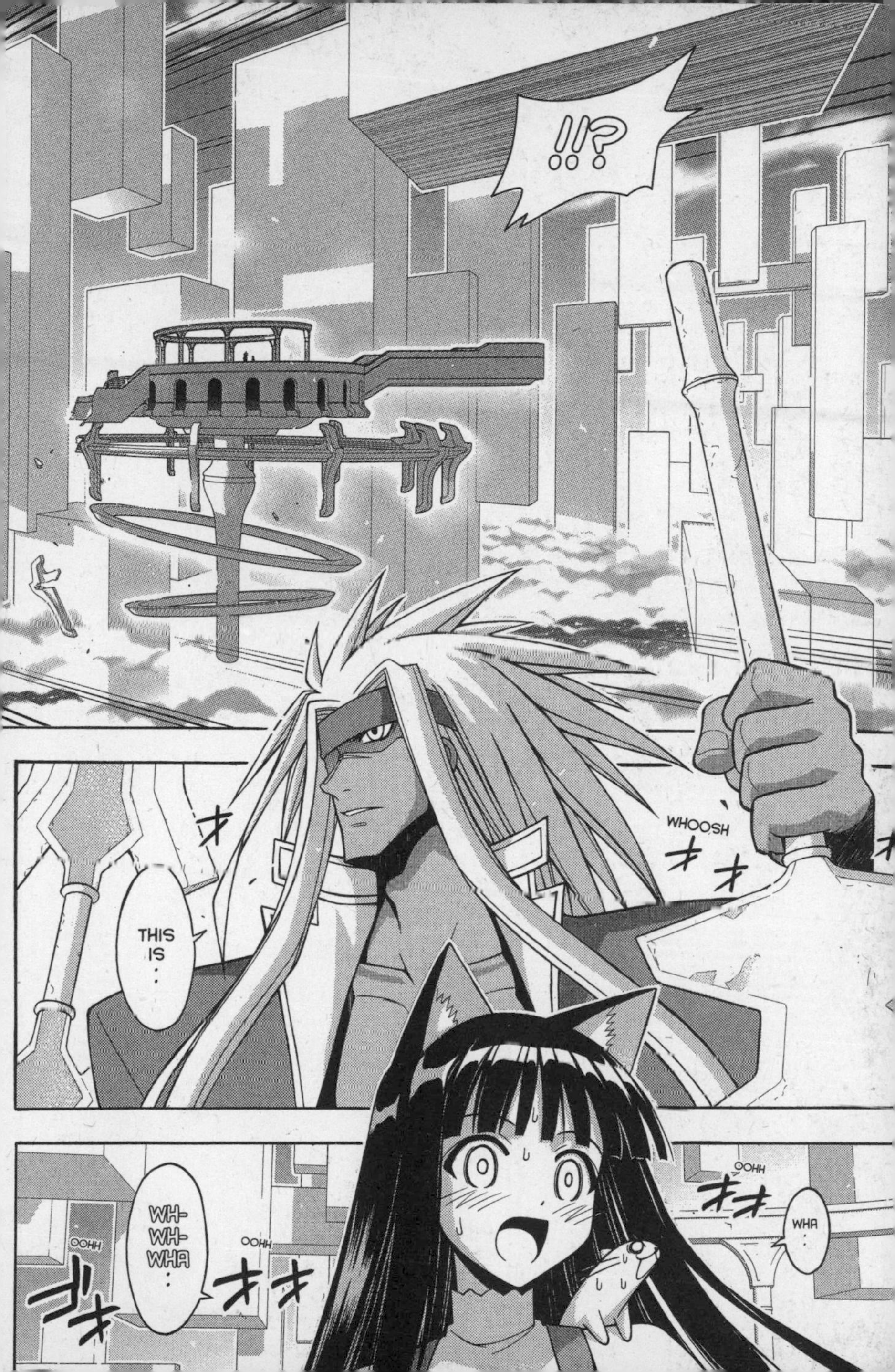
!!?
WHOOSH
THIS IS . . .
OOHH
WHA . . .
OOHH
OOHH
WH-WH-WHA . . .

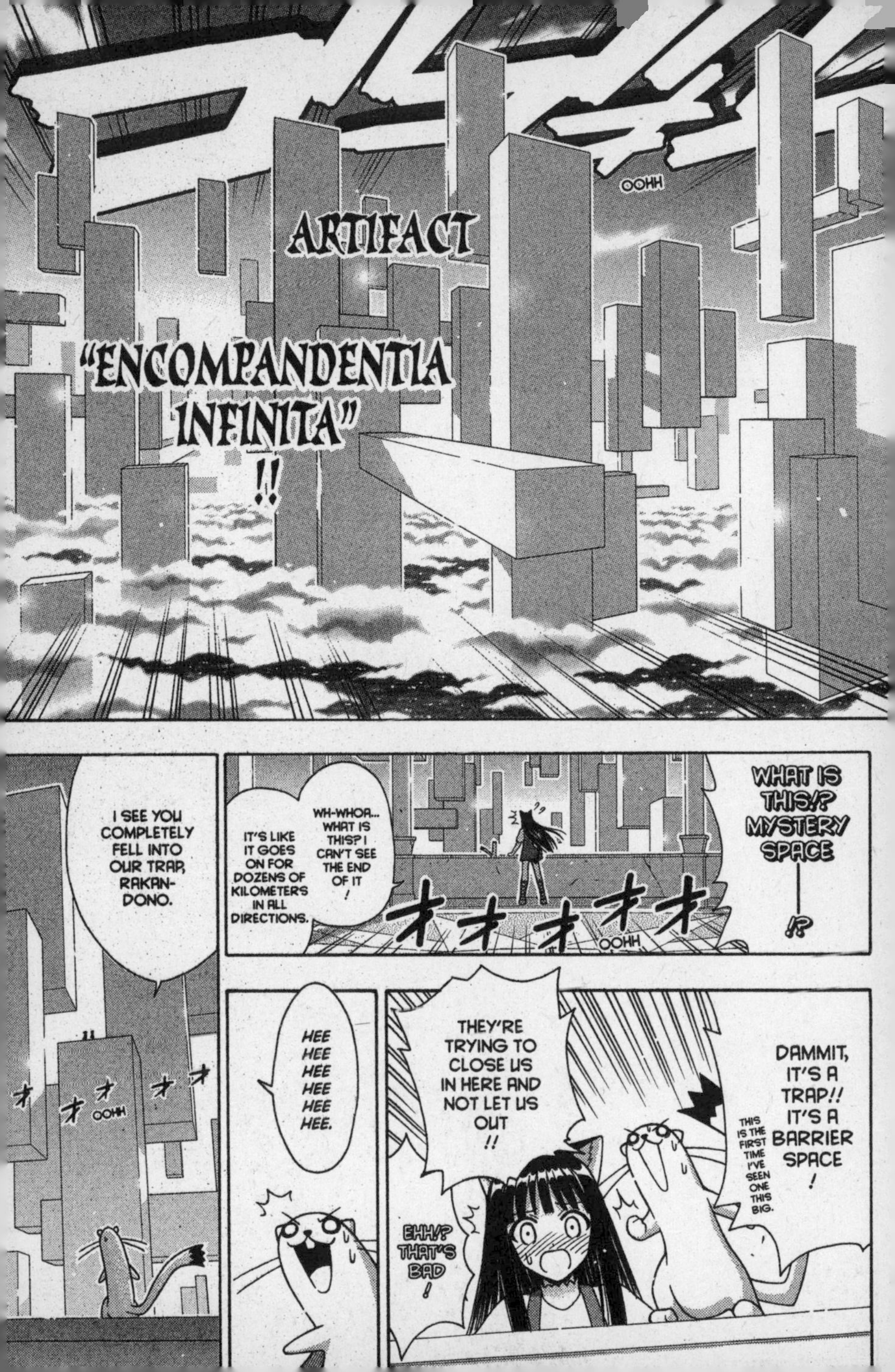

OOHH
ARTIFACT
"ENCOMPANDENTIA INFINITA" !!
WHAT IS THIS!? MYSTERY SPACE —— !?
WH-WHOA... WHAT IS THIS? I CAN'T SEE THE END OF IT!
IT'S LIKE IT GOES ON FOR DOZENS OF KILOMETERS IN ALL DIRECTIONS.
OOHH
DAMMIT, IT'S A TRAP!! IT'S A BARRIER SPACE!
THIS IS THE FIRST TIME I'VE SEEN ONE THIS BIG.
THEY'RE TRYING TO CLOSE US IN HERE AND NOT LET US OUT!!
EHH!? THAT'S BAD!
HEE HEE HEE HEE HEE HEE.
I SEE YOU COMPLETELY FELL INTO OUR TRAP, RAKAN-DONO.
OOHH

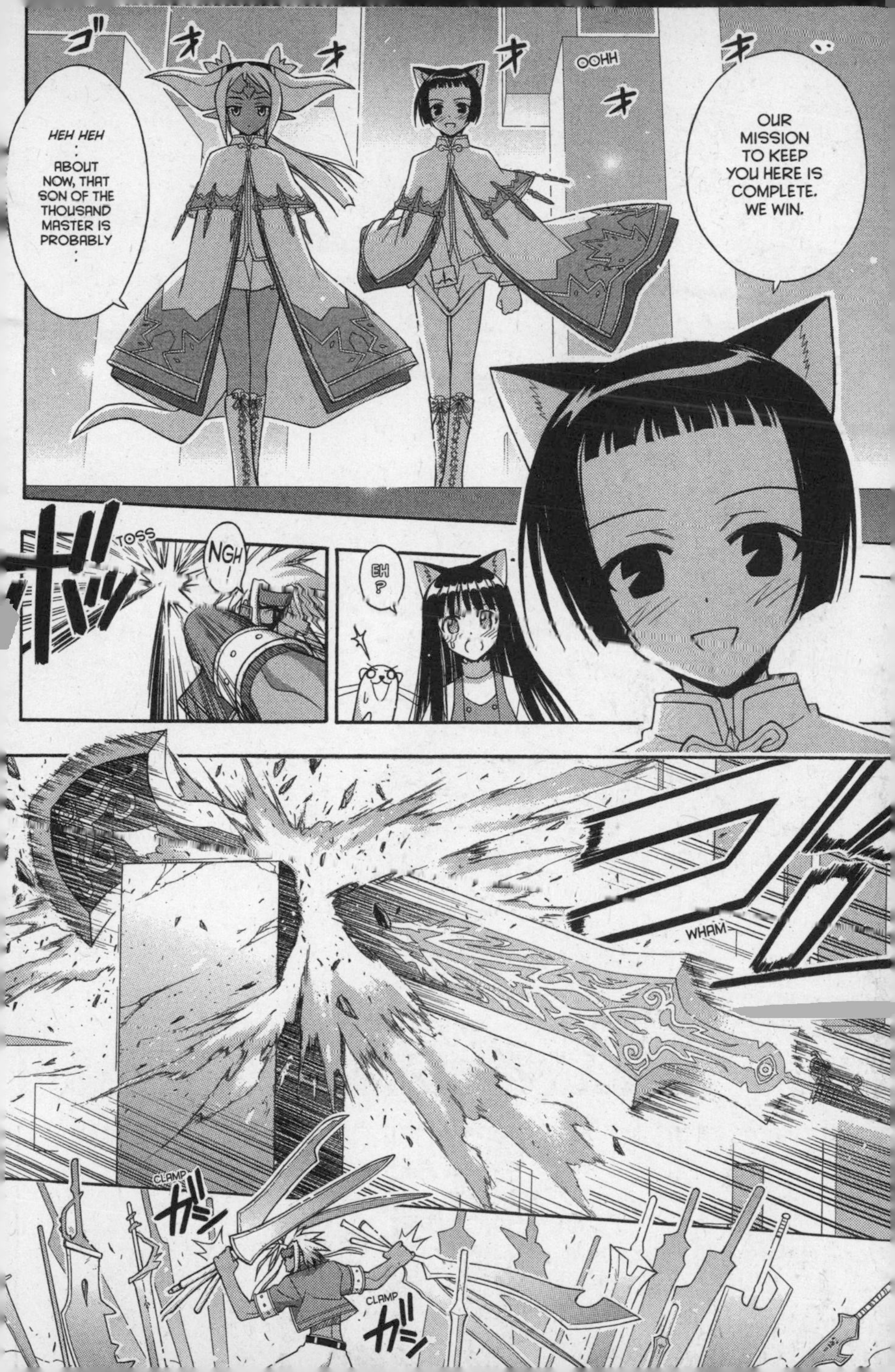
OOHH
OUR MISSION TO KEEP YOU HERE IS COMPLETE. WE WIN.
HEH HEH . . . ABOUT NOW, THAT SON OF THE THOUSAND MASTER IS PROBABLY . . .
EH?
NGH!
TOSS
WHAM
CLAMP
CLAMP

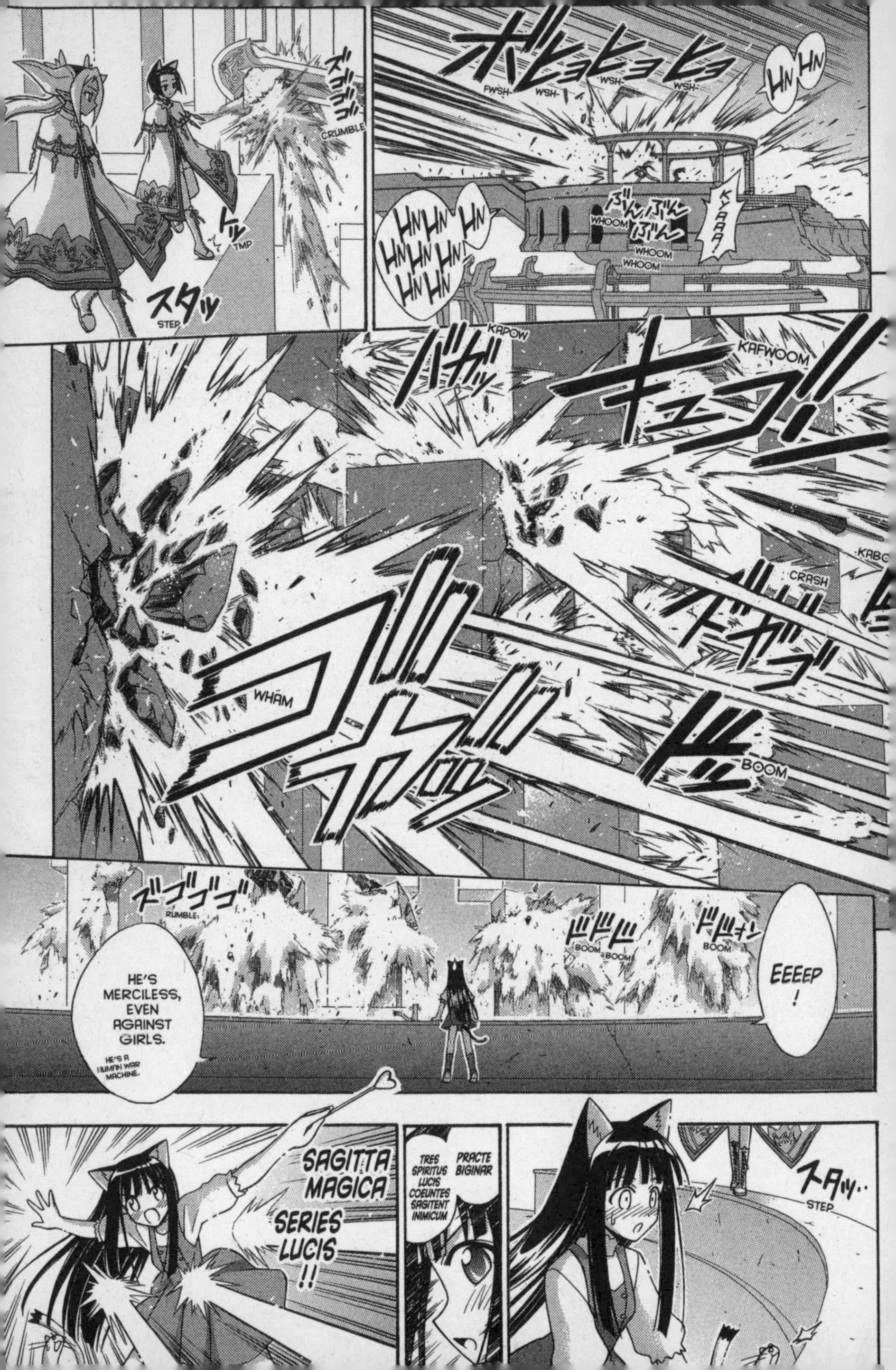

FWSH- WSH- WSH- WSH-
HN HN
HN HN HN HN HN HN HN HN HN
ぶんぶんぶん
WHOOM WHOOM WHOOM
KYAAA!
ズゴゴゴ
CRUMBLE
トッ
TMP
スタッ
STEP
KAFWOOM
KAPOW
KABO
CRASH
WHAM
BOOM
EEEEP!
BOOM
BOOM BOOM
ズゴゴゴ
RUMBLE
HE'S MERCILESS, EVEN AGAINST GIRLS.
HE'S A HUMAN WAR MACHINE.
スタッ..
STEP
PRACTE BIGINAR
TRES SPIRITUS LUCIS COEUNTES SAGITENT INIMICUM
SAGITTA MAGICA
SERIES LUCIS!!

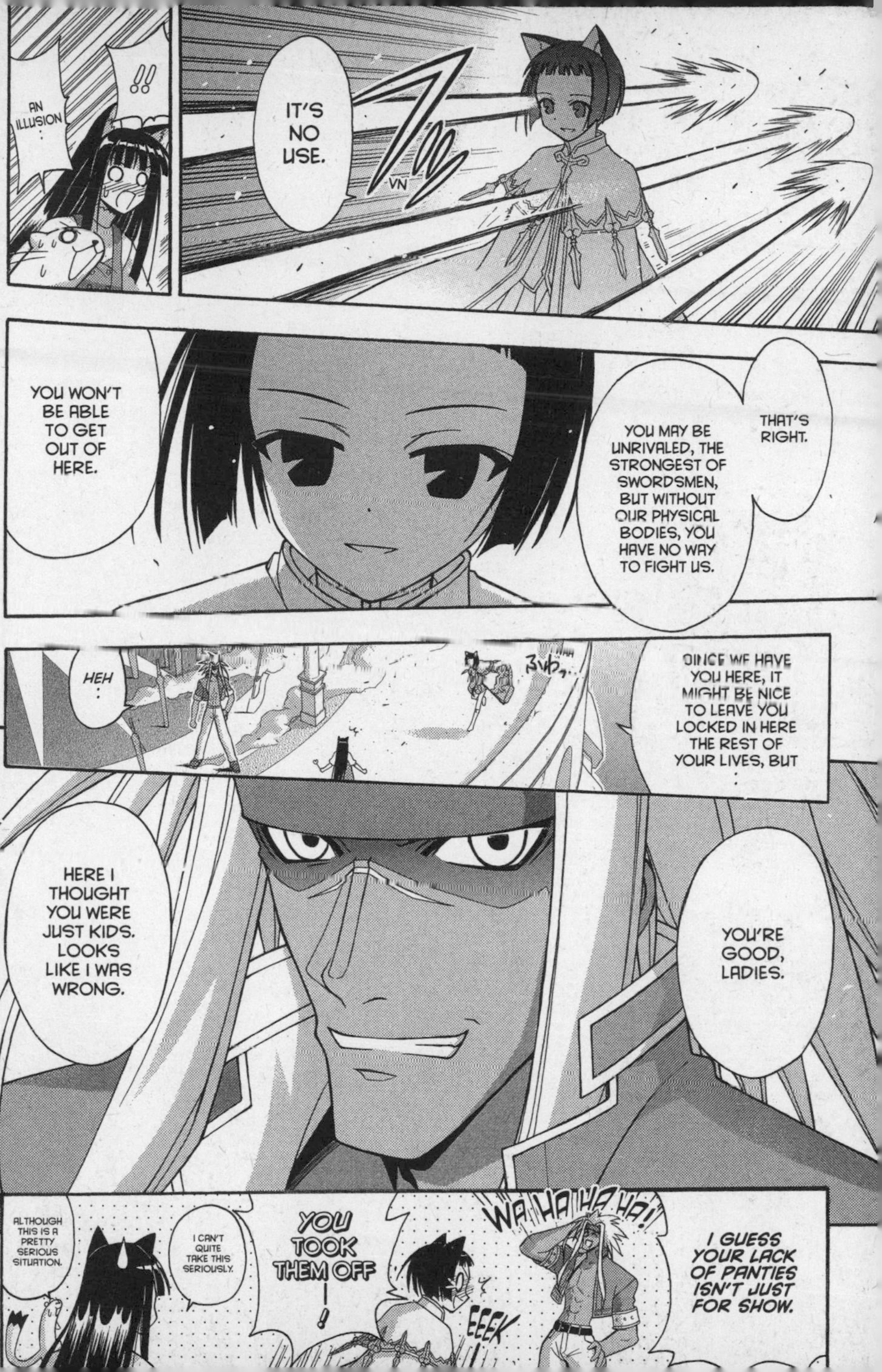
IT'S NO USE.
VN
!!
AN ILLUSION…
THAT'S RIGHT.
YOU MAY BE UNRIVALED, THE STRONGEST OF SWORDSMEN, BUT WITHOUT OUR PHYSICAL BODIES, YOU HAVE NO WAY TO FIGHT US.
YOU WON'T BE ABLE TO GET OUT OF HERE.
SINCE WE HAVE YOU HERE, IT MIGHT BE NICE TO LEAVE YOU LOCKED IN HERE THE REST OF YOUR LIVES, BUT…
HEH…
YOU'RE GOOD, LADIES.
HERE I THOUGHT YOU WERE JUST KIDS. LOOKS LIKE I WAS WRONG.
I GUESS YOUR LACK OF PANTIES ISN'T JUST FOR SHOW.
WA HA HA HA HA!
YOU TOOK THEM OFF—!
EEEK!
I CAN'T QUITE TAKE THIS SERIOUSLY.
ALTHOUGH THIS IS A PRETTY SERIOUS SITUATION.

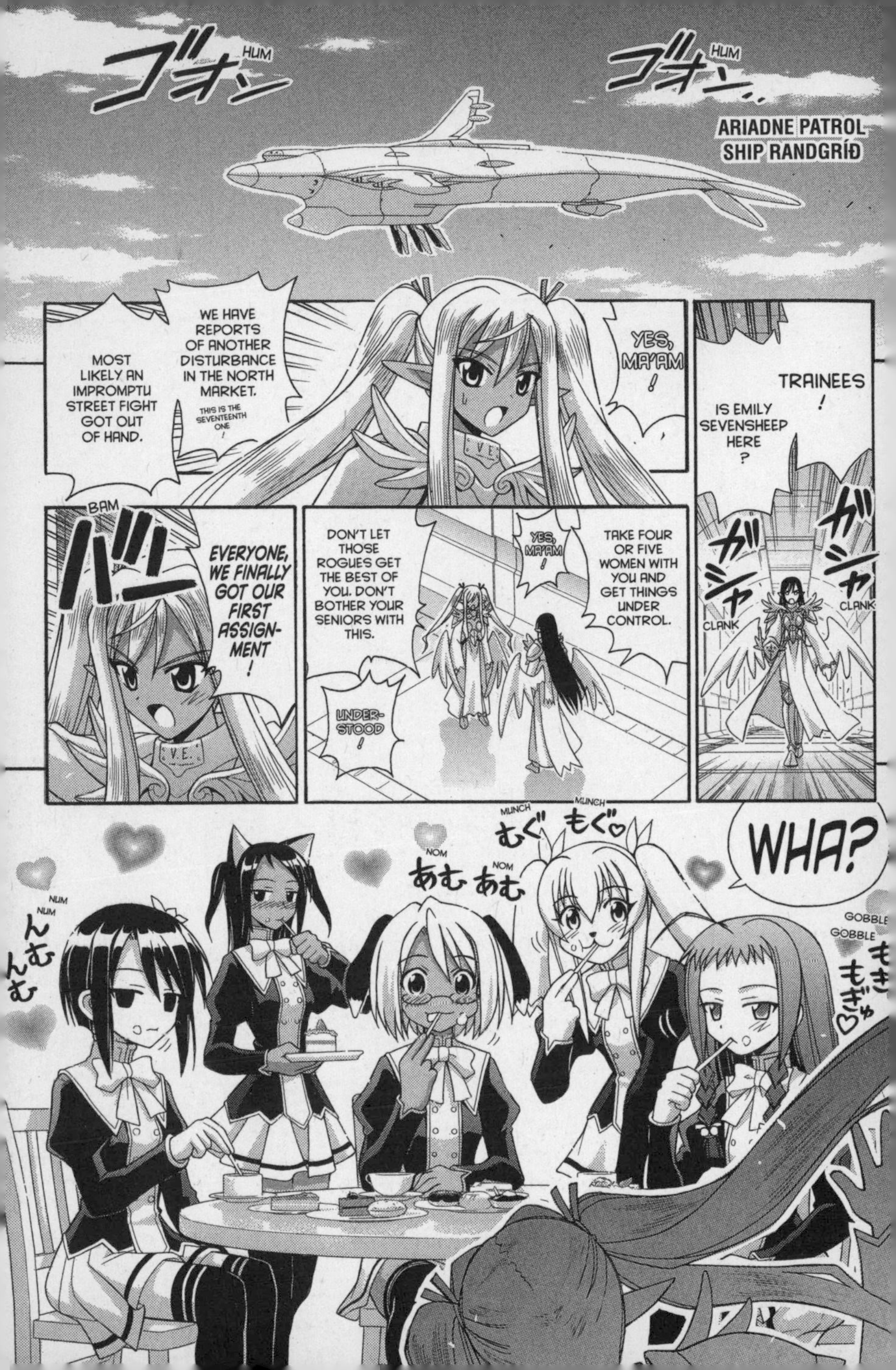

ゴオン HUM
ゴオン HUM
ARIADNE PATROL SHIP RANDGRÍÐ
TRAINEES!
IS EMILY SEVENSHEEP HERE?
ガシャ CLANK
ガシャ CLANK
YES, MA'AM!
WE HAVE REPORTS OF ANOTHER DISTURBANCE IN THE NORTH MARKET.
MOST LIKELY AN IMPROMPTU STREET FIGHT GOT OUT OF HAND.
THIS IS THE SEVENTEENTH ONE!
TAKE FOUR OR FIVE WOMEN WITH YOU AND GET THINGS UNDER CONTROL.
YES, MA'AM!
DON'T LET THOSE ROGUES GET THE BEST OF YOU. DON'T BOTHER YOUR SENIORS WITH THIS.
UNDER-STOOD!
バン BAM
EVERYONE, WE FINALLY GOT OUR FIRST ASSIGN-MENT!
WHA?
もきもぎゅ GOBBLE GOBBLE
もぐ MUNCH
むぐ MUNCH
あむ NOM
あむ NOM
んむ NUM
んむ NUM

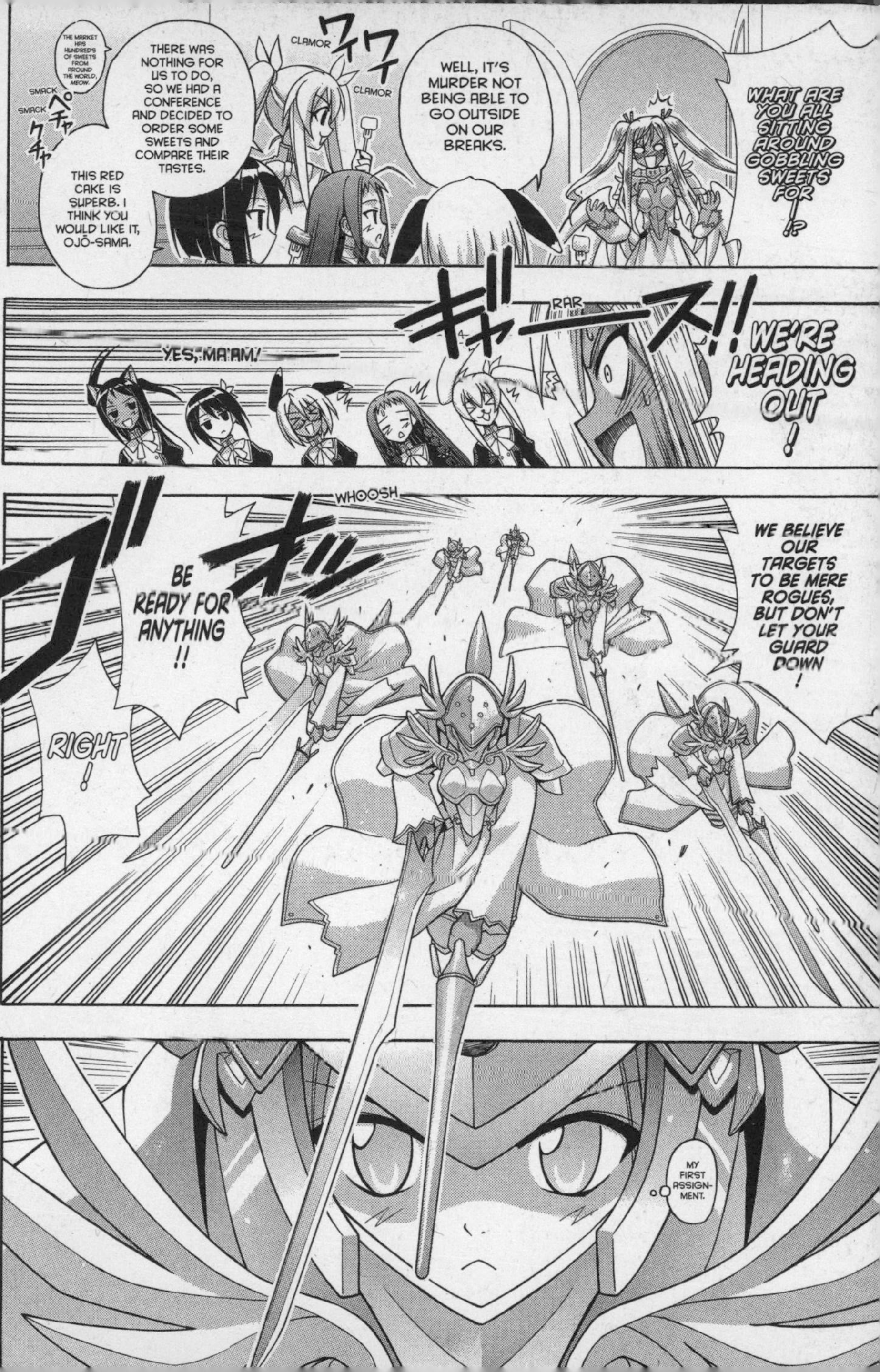
WHAT ARE YOU ALL SITTING AROUND GOBBLING SWEETS FOR !?
WELL, IT'S MURDER NOT BEING ABLE TO GO OUTSIDE ON OUR BREAKS.
CLAMOR ワイワイ CLAMOR
THERE WAS NOTHING FOR US TO DO, SO WE HAD A CONFERENCE AND DECIDED TO ORDER SOME SWEETS AND COMPARE THEIR TASTES.
THE MARKET HAS HUNDREDS OF SWEETS FROM AROUND THE WORLD, MEOW.
SMACK SMACK ペチャクチャ
THIS RED CAKE IS SUPERB. I THINK YOU WOULD LIKE IT, OJŌ-SAMA.
WE'RE HEADING OUT!
RAR ギャース!!
YES, MA'AM!
WE BELIEVE OUR TARGETS TO BE MERE ROGUES, BUT DON'T LET YOUR GUARD DOWN!
WHOOSH ゴオッ
BE READY FOR ANYTHING!!
RIGHT!
MY FIRST ASSIGNMENT.

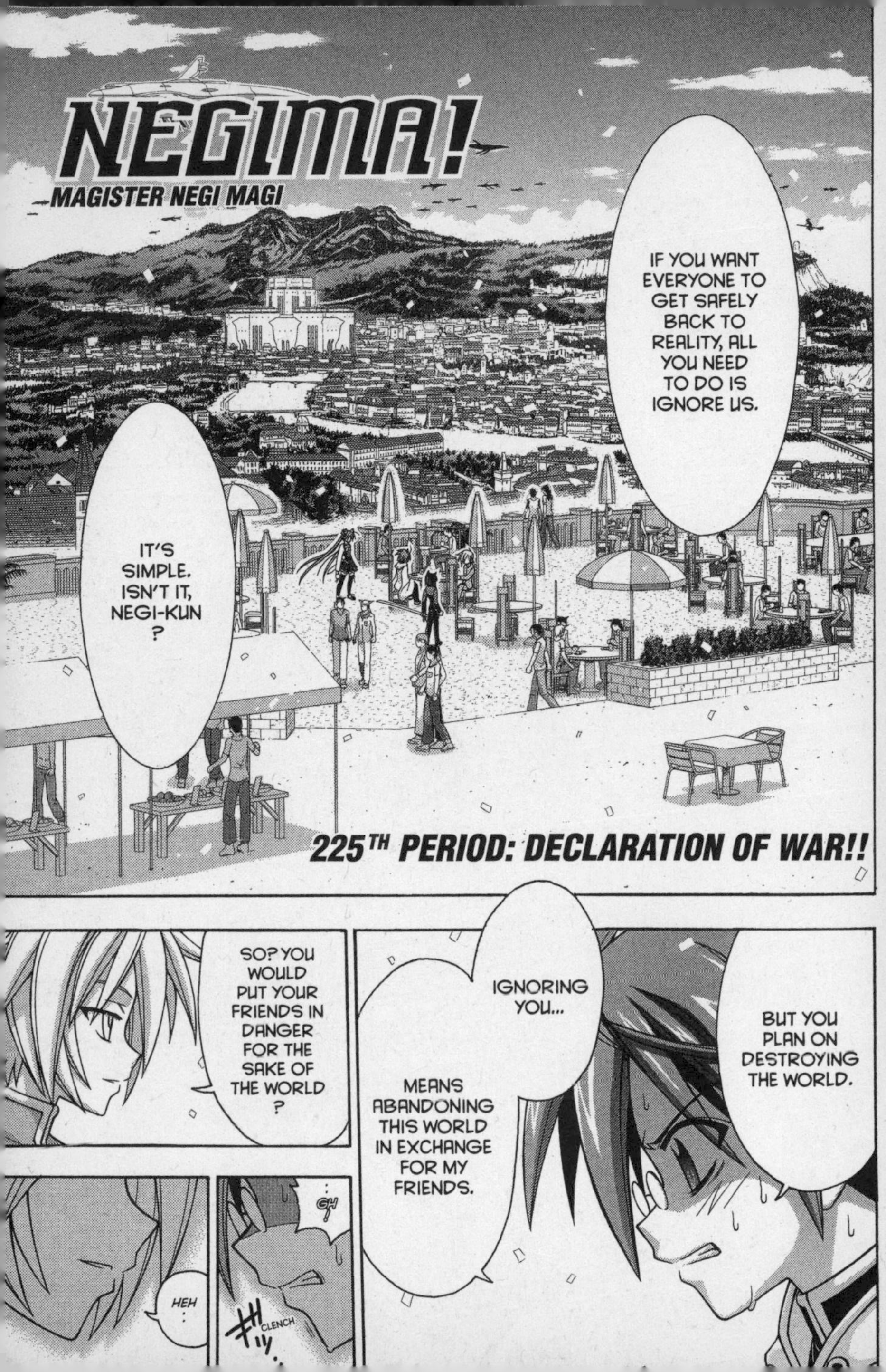
NEGIMA!
MAGISTER NEGI MAGI
IF YOU WANT EVERYONE TO GET SAFELY BACK TO REALITY, ALL YOU NEED TO DO IS IGNORE US.
IT'S SIMPLE. ISN'T IT, NEGI-KUN?
225TH PERIOD: DECLARATION OF WAR!!
BUT YOU PLAN ON DESTROYING THE WORLD.
IGNORING YOU...
MEANS ABANDONING THIS WORLD IN EXCHANGE FOR MY FRIENDS.
SO? YOU WOULD PUT YOUR FRIENDS IN DANGER FOR THE SAKE OF THE WORLD?
...GH!
CLENCH
HEH...

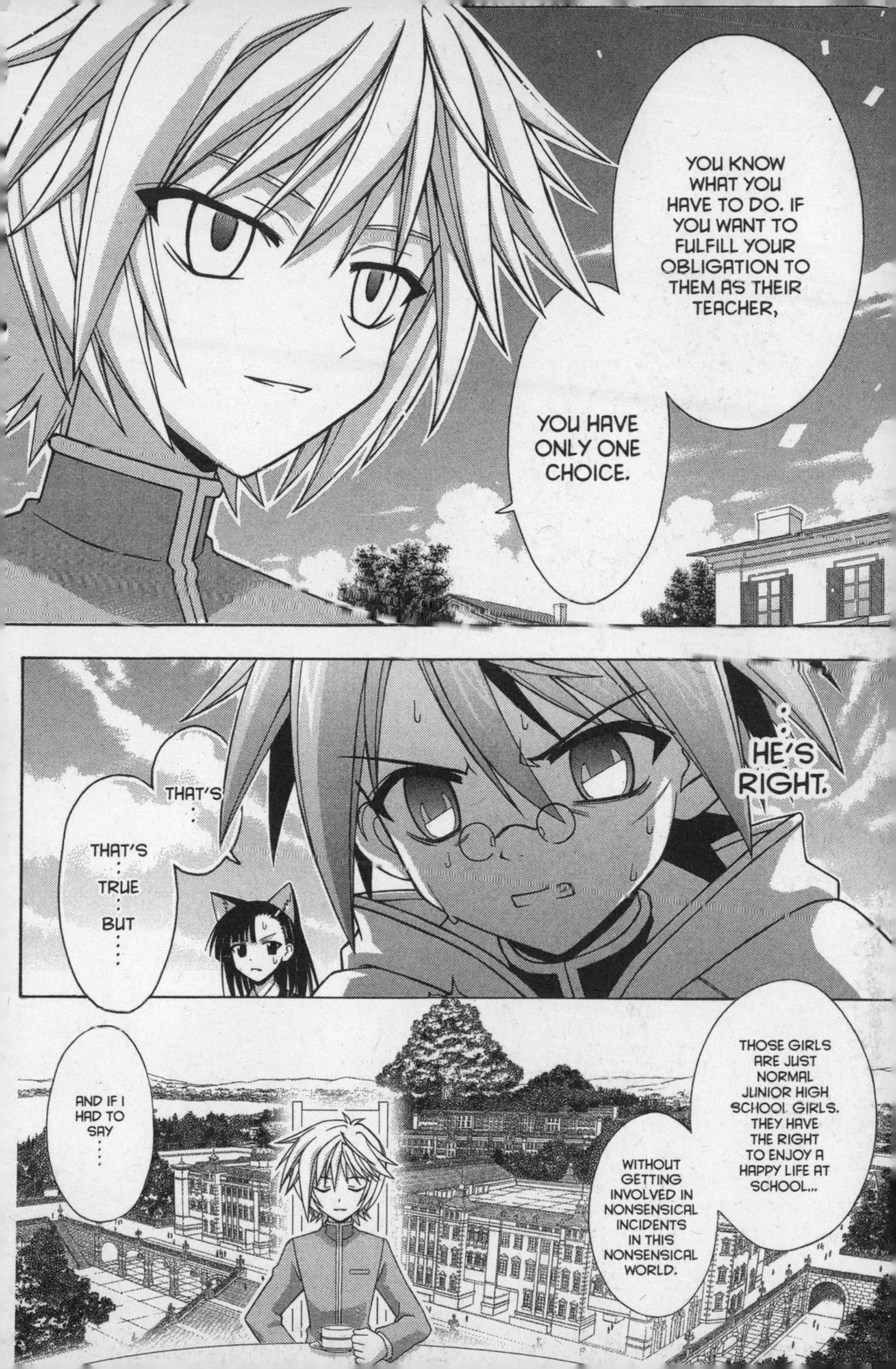
YOU KNOW WHAT YOU HAVE TO DO. IF YOU WANT TO FULFILL YOUR OBLIGATION TO THEM AS THEIR TEACHER,
YOU HAVE ONLY ONE CHOICE.
...HE'S RIGHT.
THAT'S... THAT'S... TRUE... BUT...
THOSE GIRLS ARE JUST NORMAL JUNIOR HIGH SCHOOL GIRLS. THEY HAVE THE RIGHT TO ENJOY A HAPPY LIFE AT SCHOOL...
WITHOUT GETTING INVOLVED IN NONSENSICAL INCIDENTS IN THIS NONSENSICAL WORLD.
AND IF I HAD TO SAY...

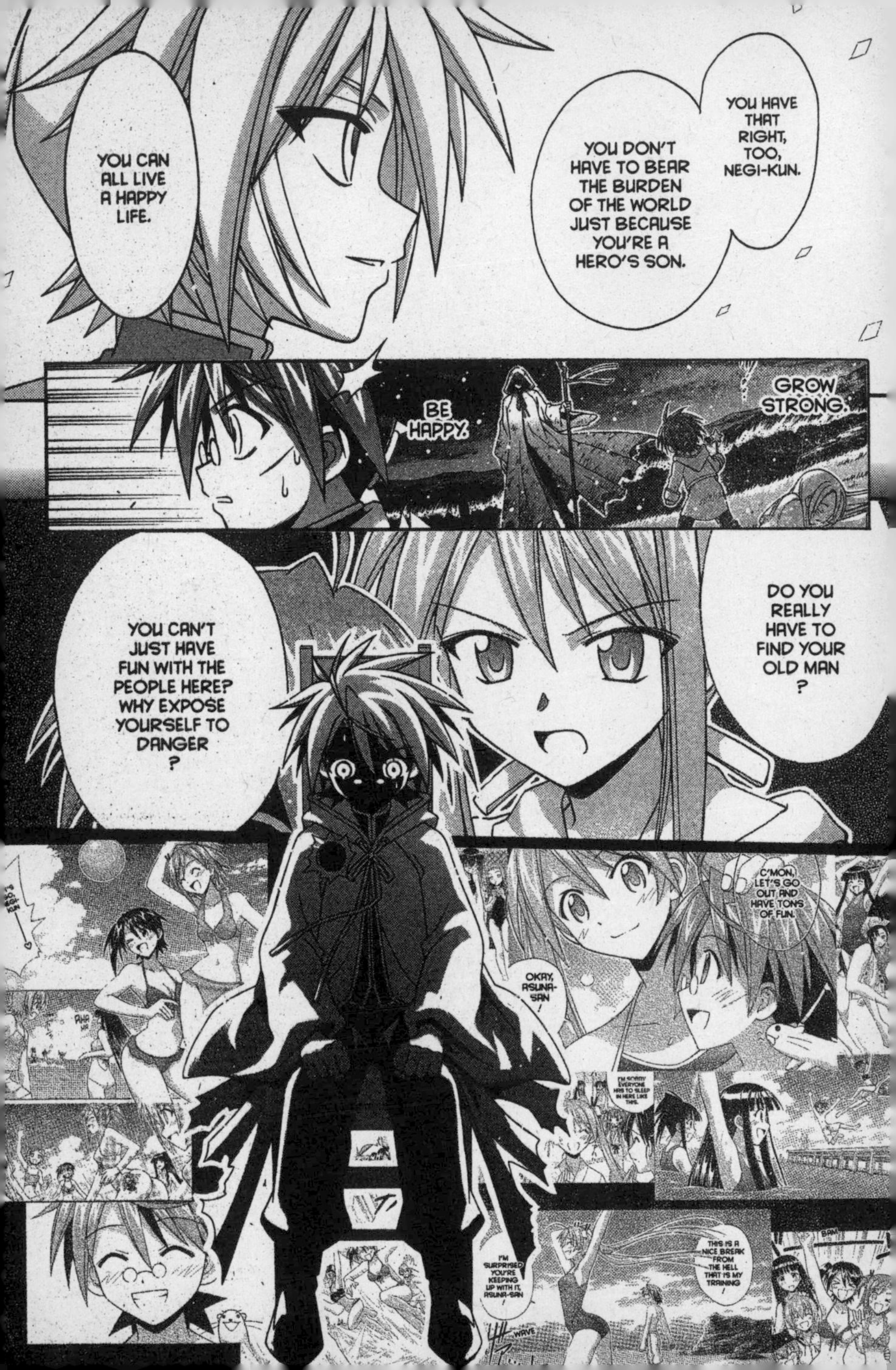
YOU HAVE THAT RIGHT, TOO, NEGI-KUN.
YOU DON'T HAVE TO BEAR THE BURDEN OF THE WORLD JUST BECAUSE YOU'RE A HERO'S SON.
YOU CAN ALL LIVE A HAPPY LIFE.
GROW STRONG.
BE HAPPY.
DO YOU REALLY HAVE TO FIND YOUR OLD MAN?
YOU CAN'T JUST HAVE FUN WITH THE PEOPLE HERE? WHY EXPOSE YOURSELF TO DANGER?
C'MON, LET'S GO OUT AND HAVE TONS OF FUN.
OKAY, ASUNA-SAN!
AHA HA
I'M SORRY EVERYONE HAS TO SLEEP IN HERE LIKE THIS.
BAM
THIS IS A NICE BREAK FROM THE HELL THAT IS MY TRAINING!
I'M SURPRISED YOU'RE KEEPING UP WITH IT, ASUNA-SAN!
WAVE

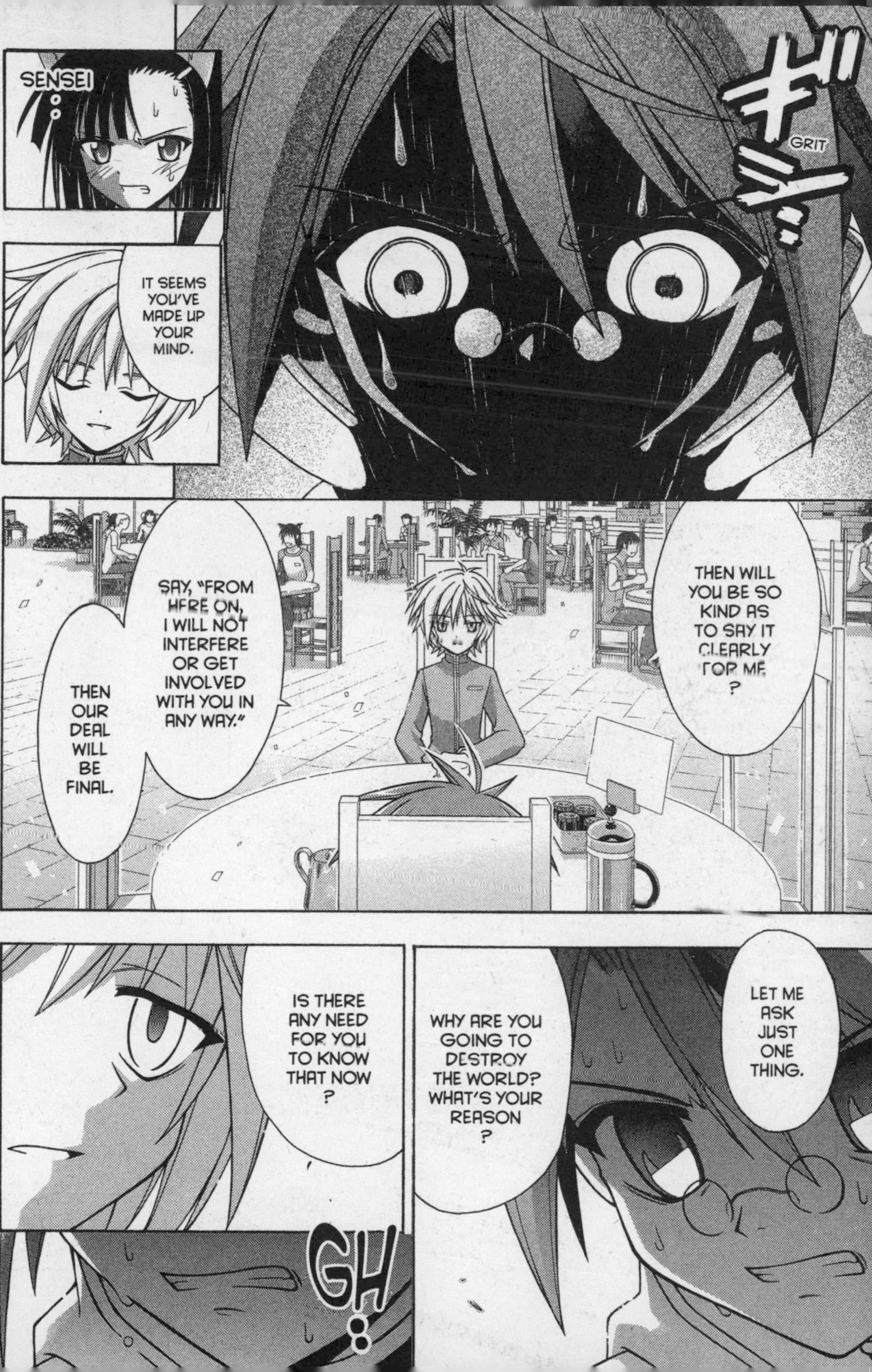
GRIT
SENSEI...
IT SEEMS YOU'VE MADE UP YOUR MIND.
THEN WILL YOU BE SO KIND AS TO SAY IT CLEARLY FOR ME?
SAY, "FROM HERE ON, I WILL NOT INTERFERE OR GET INVOLVED WITH YOU IN ANY WAY."
THEN OUR DEAL WILL BE FINAL.
LET ME ASK JUST ONE THING.
WHY ARE YOU GOING TO DESTROY THE WORLD? WHAT'S YOUR REASON?
IS THERE ANY NEED FOR YOU TO KNOW THAT NOW?
GH...

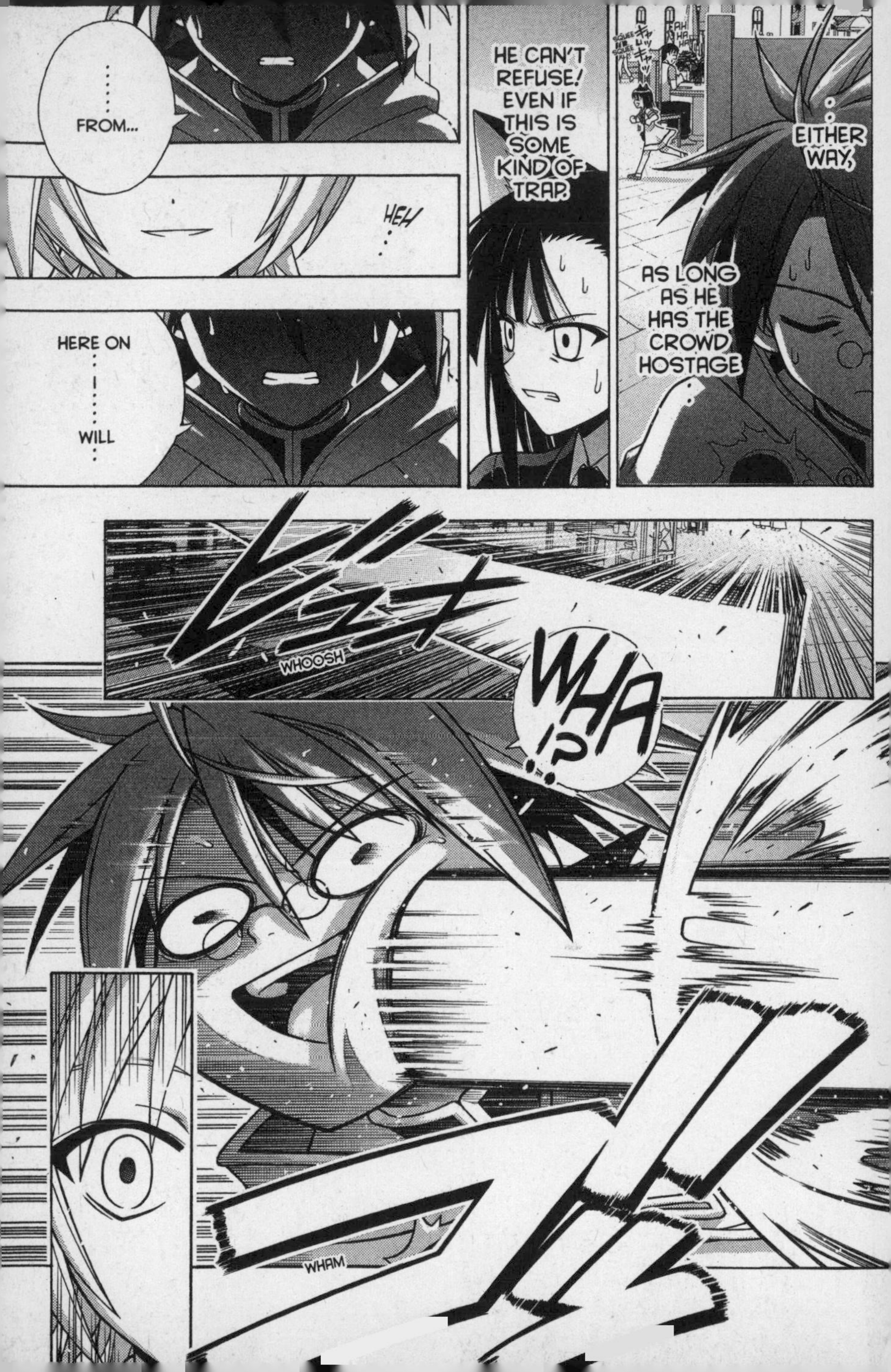

AH HA HA
SQUEE SQUEE
...EITHER WAY,
AS LONG AS HE HAS THE CROWD HOSTAGE
HE CAN'T REFUSE! EVEN IF THIS IS SOME KIND OF TRAP.
......FROM...
HEH...
HERE ON... I...... WILL...
WHOOSH
WHA!?
WHAM

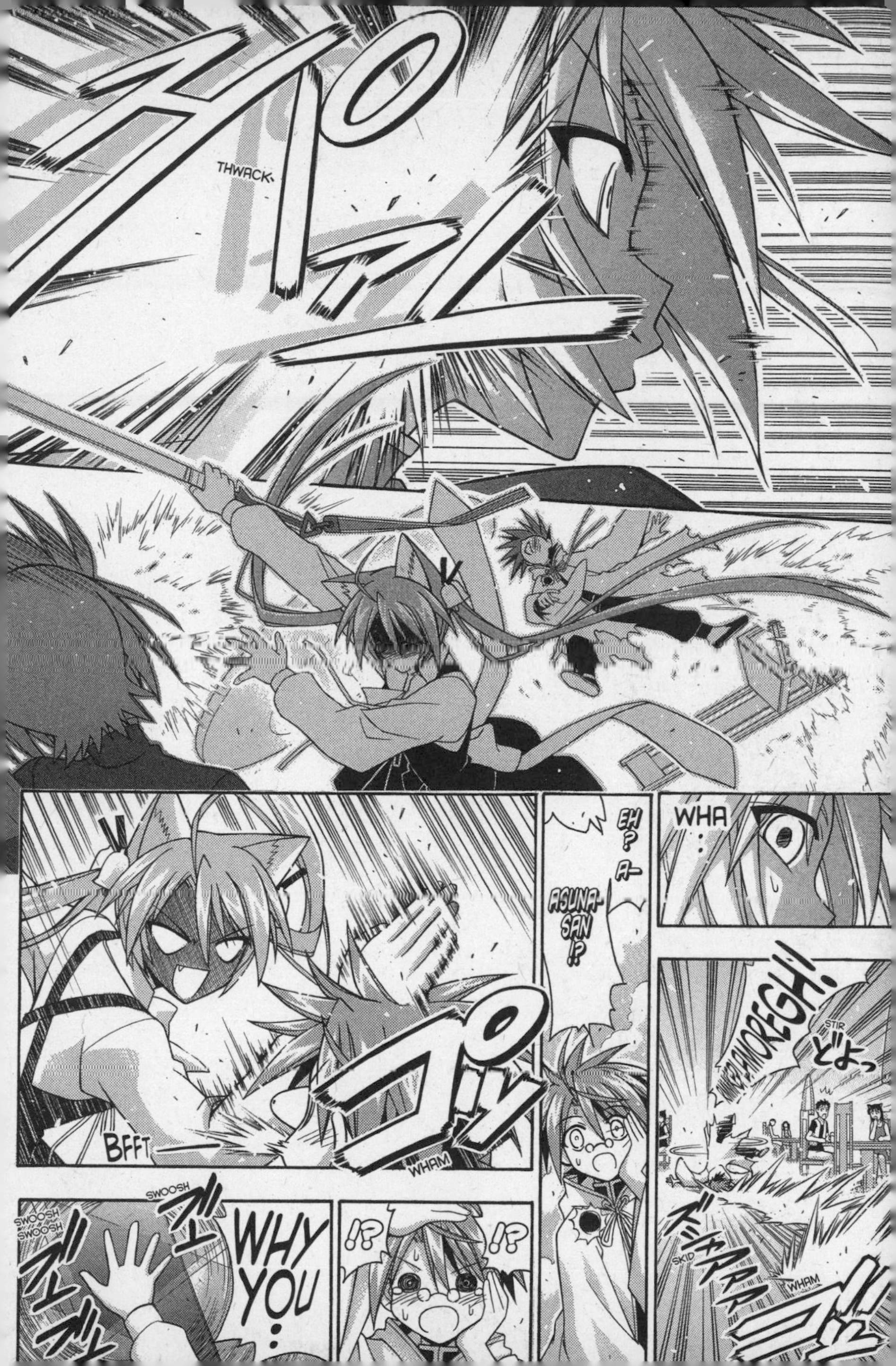
THWACK
WHA...
EH? A—
ASUNA-SAN!?
BFFT—
WHAM
STIR
どよっ
SKID
WHAM
!?
!?
SWOOSH
WHY YOU...
SWOOSH SWOOSH

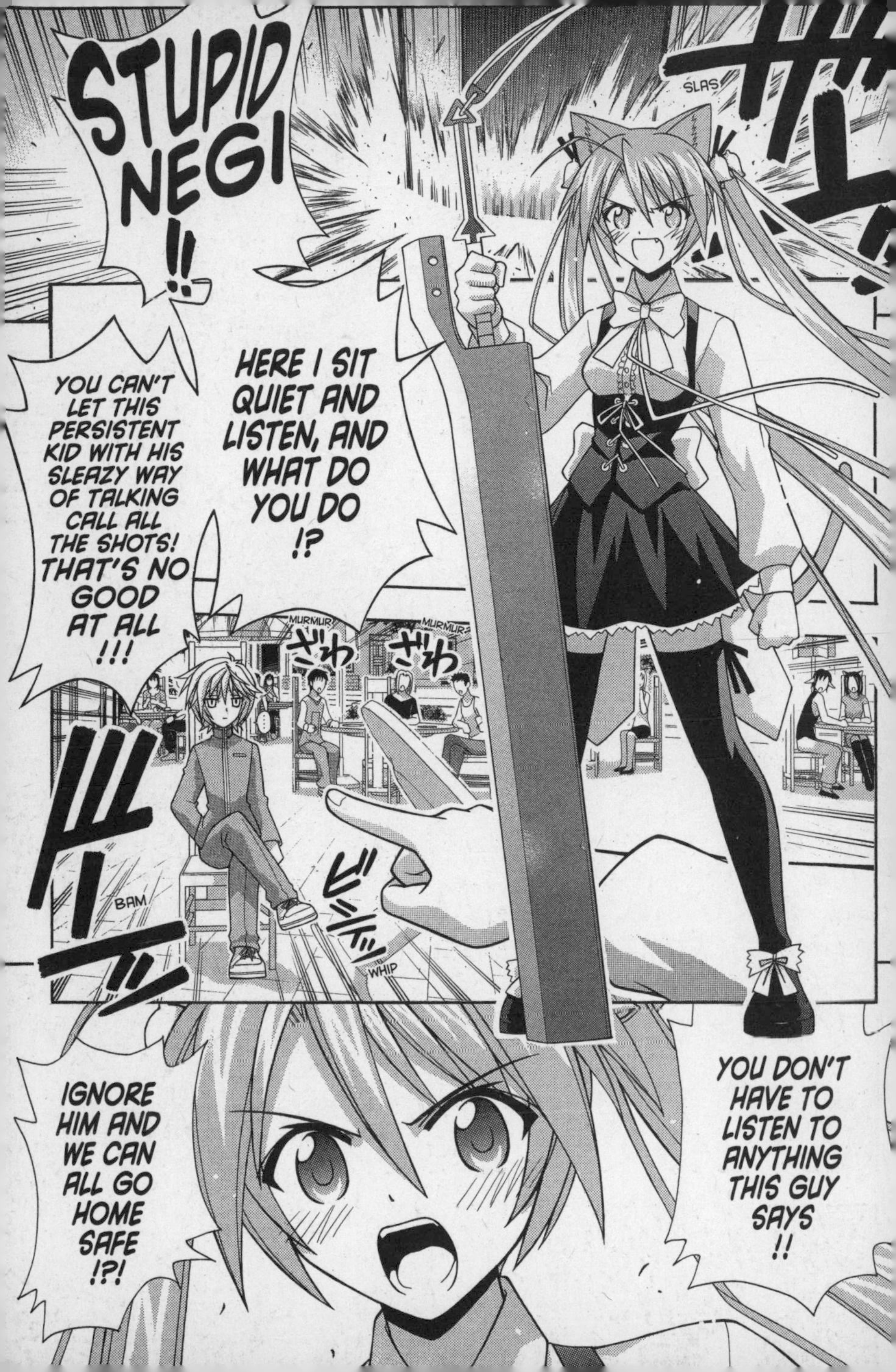
SLAS
STUPID NEGI !!
HERE I SIT QUIET AND LISTEN, AND WHAT DO YOU DO !?
YOU CAN'T LET THIS PERSISTENT KID WITH HIS SLEAZY WAY OF TALKING CALL ALL THE SHOTS! THAT'S NO GOOD AT ALL !!!
MURMUR
ざわ
MURMUR
ざわ
BAM
WHIP
YOU DON'T HAVE TO LISTEN TO ANYTHING THIS GUY SAYS !!
IGNORE HIM AND WE CAN ALL GO HOME SAFE !?!

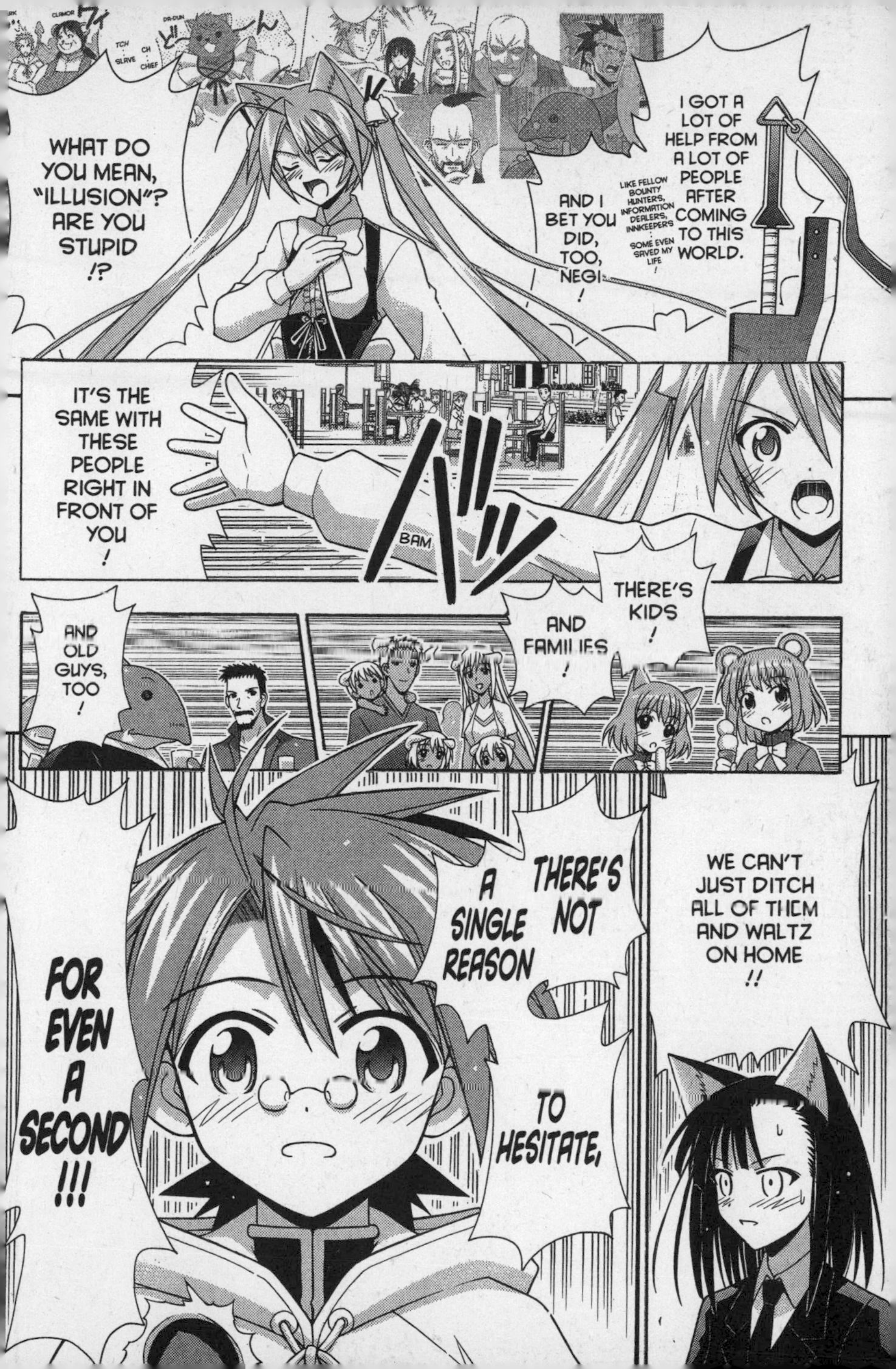

I GOT A LOT OF HELP FROM A LOT OF PEOPLE AFTER COMING TO THIS WORLD.
LIKE FELLOW BOUNTY HUNTERS, INFORMATION DEALERS, INNKEEPER'S... SOME EVEN SAVED MY LIFE!
AND I BET YOU DID, TOO, NEGI!
DA-DUN
CH... CHIEF
TCH... SLAVE
CLAMOR
WHAT DO YOU MEAN, "ILLUSION"? ARE YOU STUPID!?
IT'S THE SAME WITH THESE PEOPLE RIGHT IN FRONT OF YOU!
BAM
THERE'S KIDS!
AND FAMILIES!
AND OLD GUYS, TOO!
WE CAN'T JUST DITCH ALL OF THEM AND WALTZ ON HOME!!
THERE'S NOT A SINGLE REASON TO HESITATE, FOR EVEN A SECOND!!!

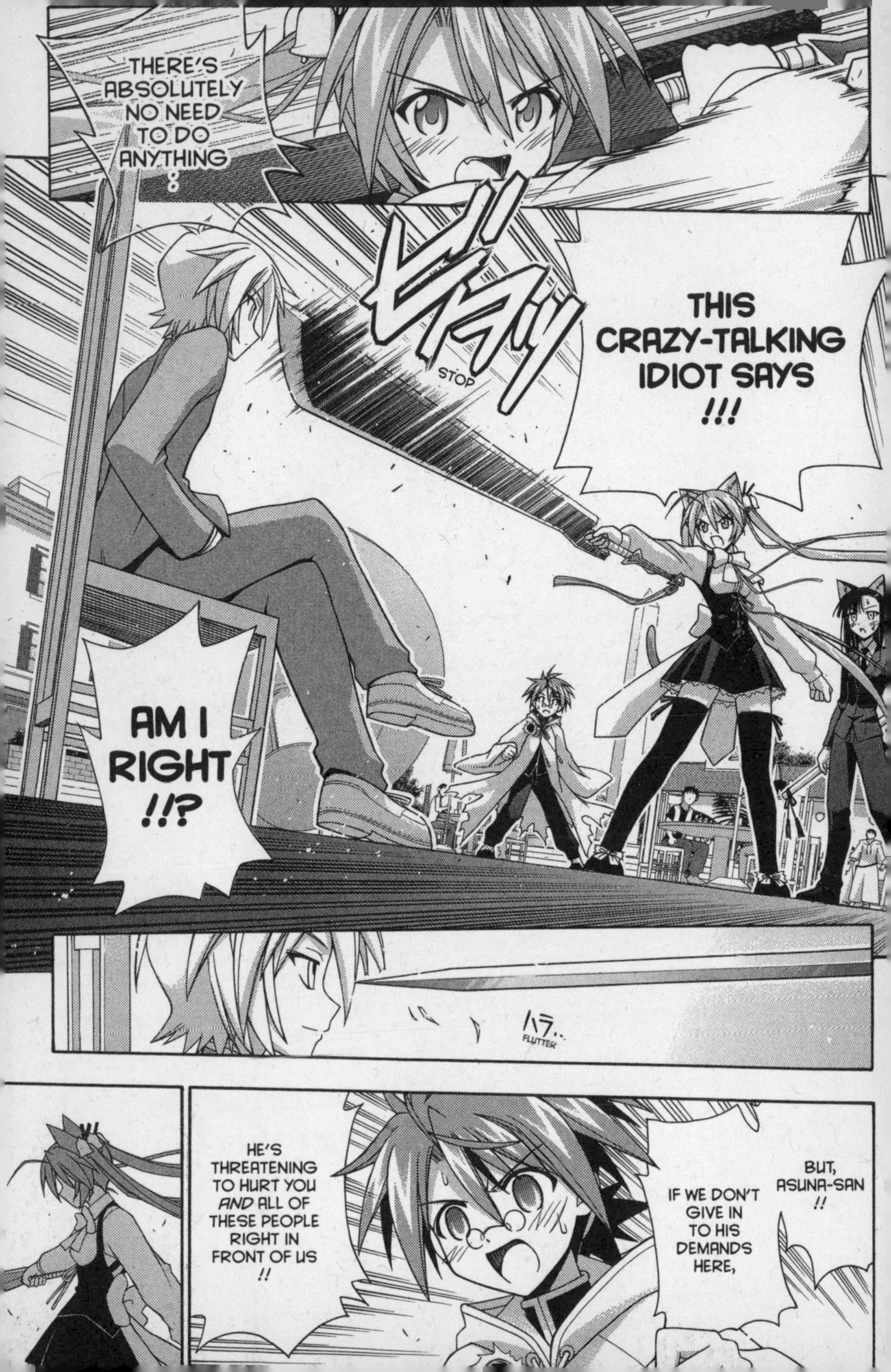
THERE'S ABSOLUTELY NO NEED TO DO ANYTHING
STOP
THIS CRAZY-TALKING IDIOT SAYS !!!
AM I RIGHT !!?
ハラ..
FLUTTER
BUT, ASUNA-SAN !!
IF WE DON'T GIVE IN TO HIS DEMANDS HERE,
HE'S THREATENING TO HURT YOU *AND* ALL OF THESE PEOPLE RIGHT IN FRONT OF US !!

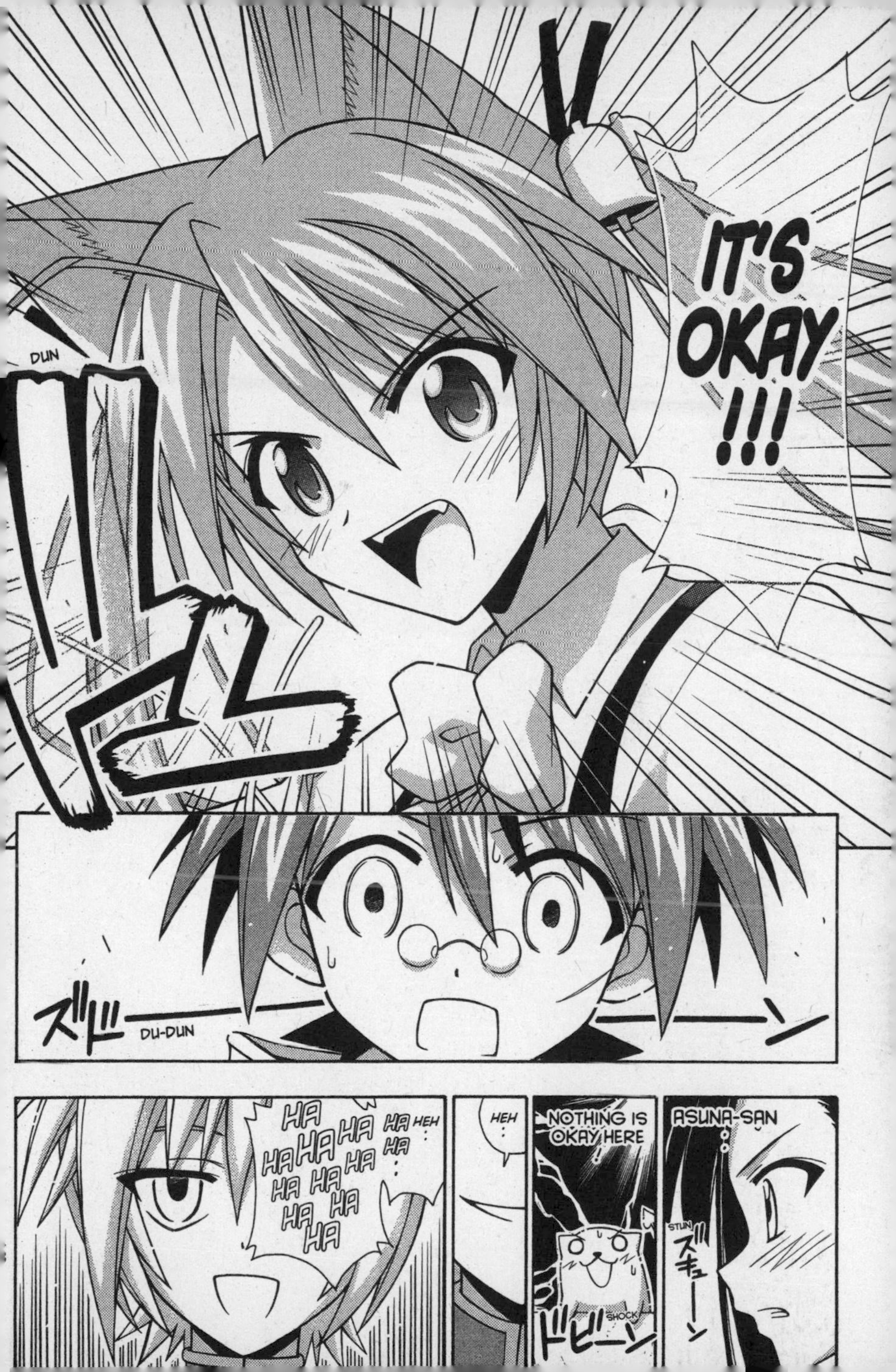
IT'S OKAY!!!
DUN
DU-DUN
ASUNA-SAN...
STUN
NOTHING IS OKAY HERE
SHOCK
HEH...
HA HA HA HA HA HA HA HA HA HA HA HA HA HA HA...
HEH...

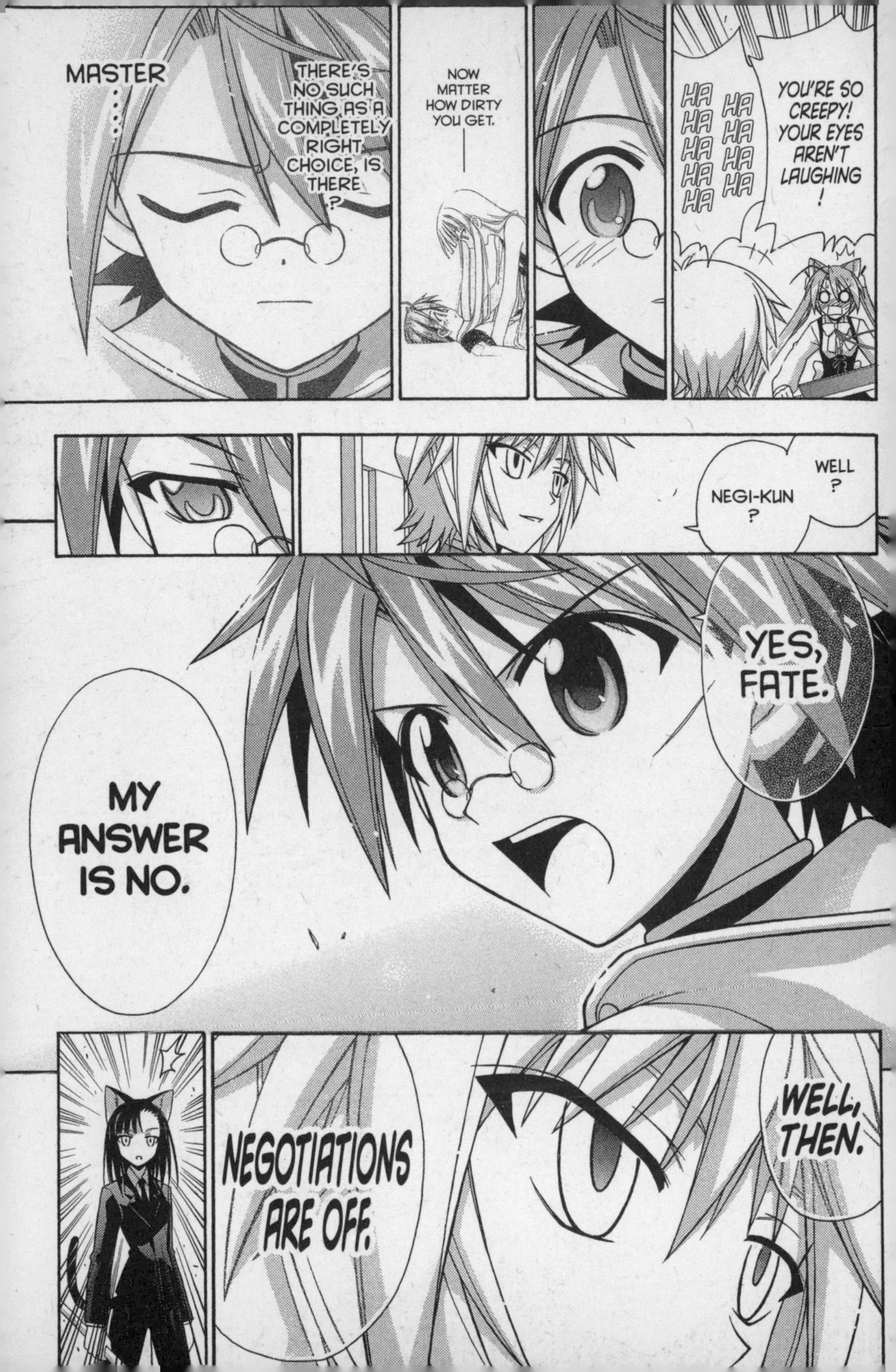
YOU'RE SO CREEPY! YOUR EYES AREN'T LAUGHING!
HA HA HA HA HA
HA HA HA HA HA HA
NOW MATTER HOW DIRTY YOU GET.
THERE'S NO SUCH THING AS A COMPLETELY RIGHT CHOICE, IS THERE?
MASTER......
WELL?
NEGI-KUN?
YES, FATE.
MY ANSWER IS NO.
WELL, THEN.
NEGOTIATIONS ARE OFF.

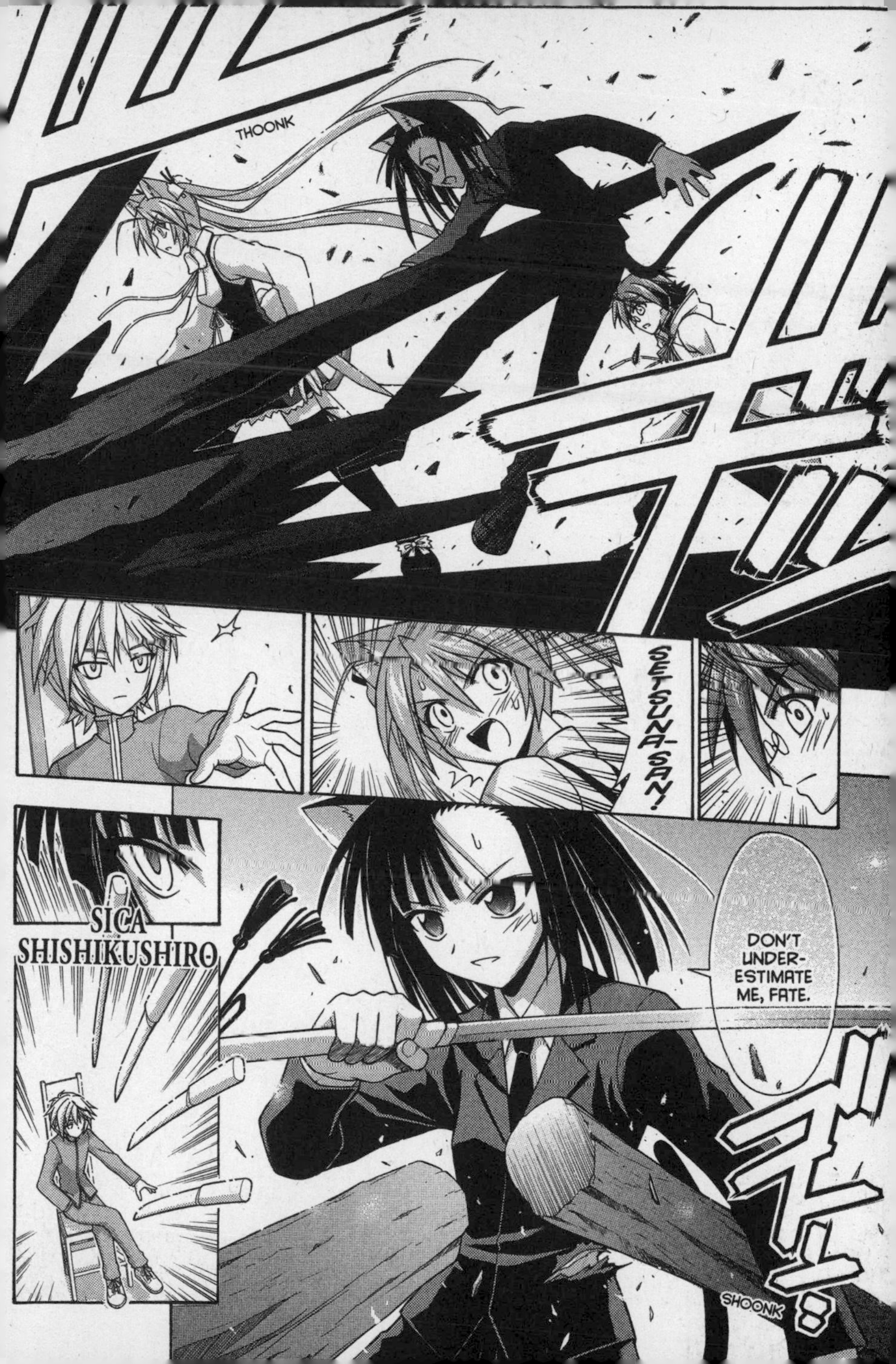
THOONK
SETSUNA-SAN!
SICA SHISHIKUSHIRO
DON'T UNDER-ESTIMATE ME, FATE.
SHOONK

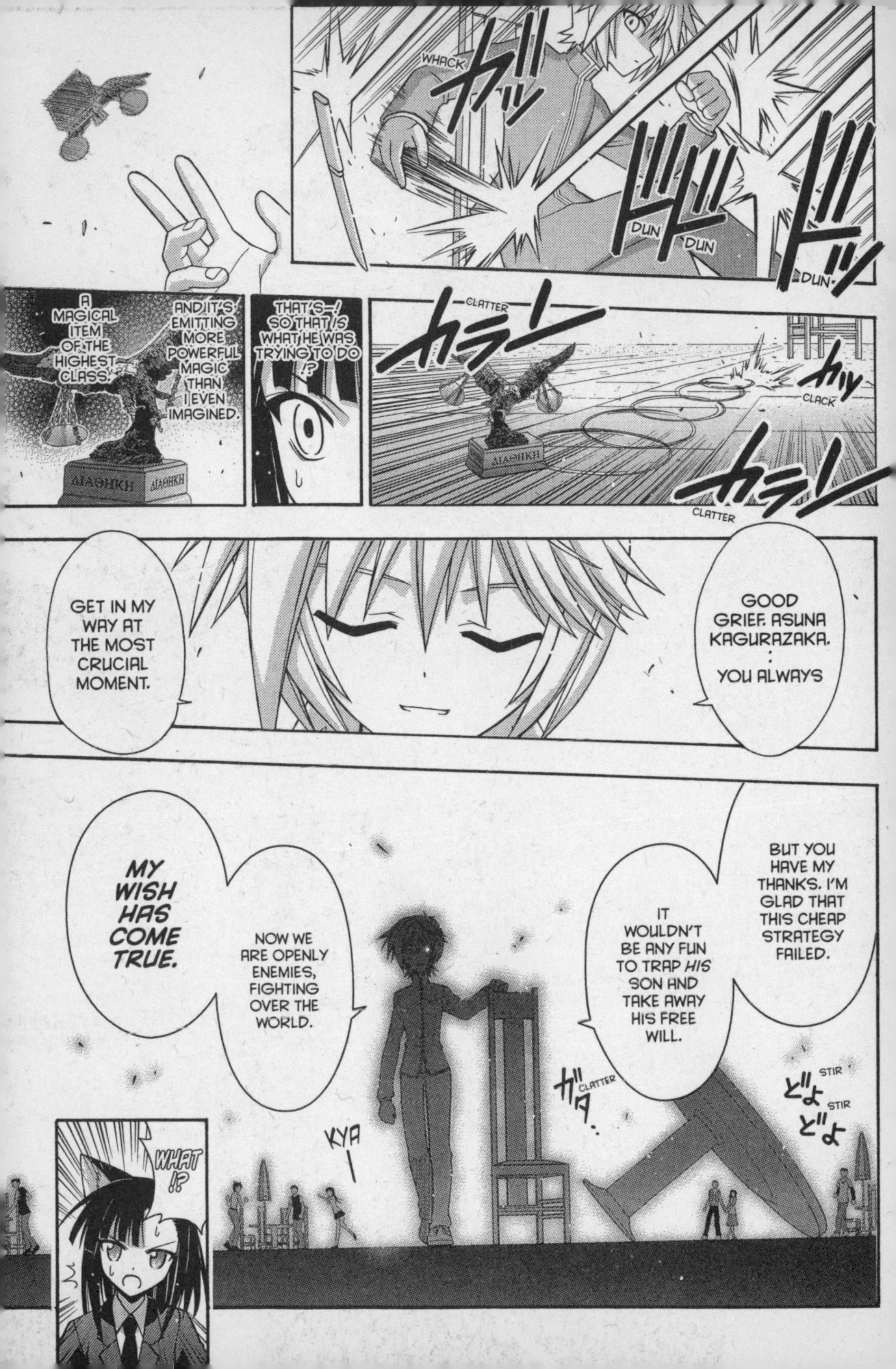
WHACK
DUN
DUN
DUN
CLATTER
CLACK
CLATTER
ΔΙΑΘΗΚΗ
THAT'S—! SO THAT *IS* WHAT HE WAS TRYING TO DO!?
AND IT'S EMITTING MORE POWERFUL MAGIC THAN I EVEN IMAGINED.
A MAGICAL ITEM OF THE HIGHEST CLASS.
ΔΙΑΘΗΚΗ
ΔΙΑΘΗΚΗ
GOOD GRIEF. ASUNA KAGURAZAKA. : YOU ALWAYS
GET IN MY WAY AT THE MOST CRUCIAL MOMENT.
BUT YOU HAVE MY THANKS. I'M GLAD THAT THIS CHEAP STRATEGY FAILED.
IT WOULDN'T BE ANY FUN TO TRAP *HIS* SON AND TAKE AWAY HIS FREE WILL.
NOW WE ARE OPENLY ENEMIES, FIGHTING OVER THE WORLD.
MY WISH HAS COME TRUE.
STIR
STIR
CLATTER
KYA
WHAT!?

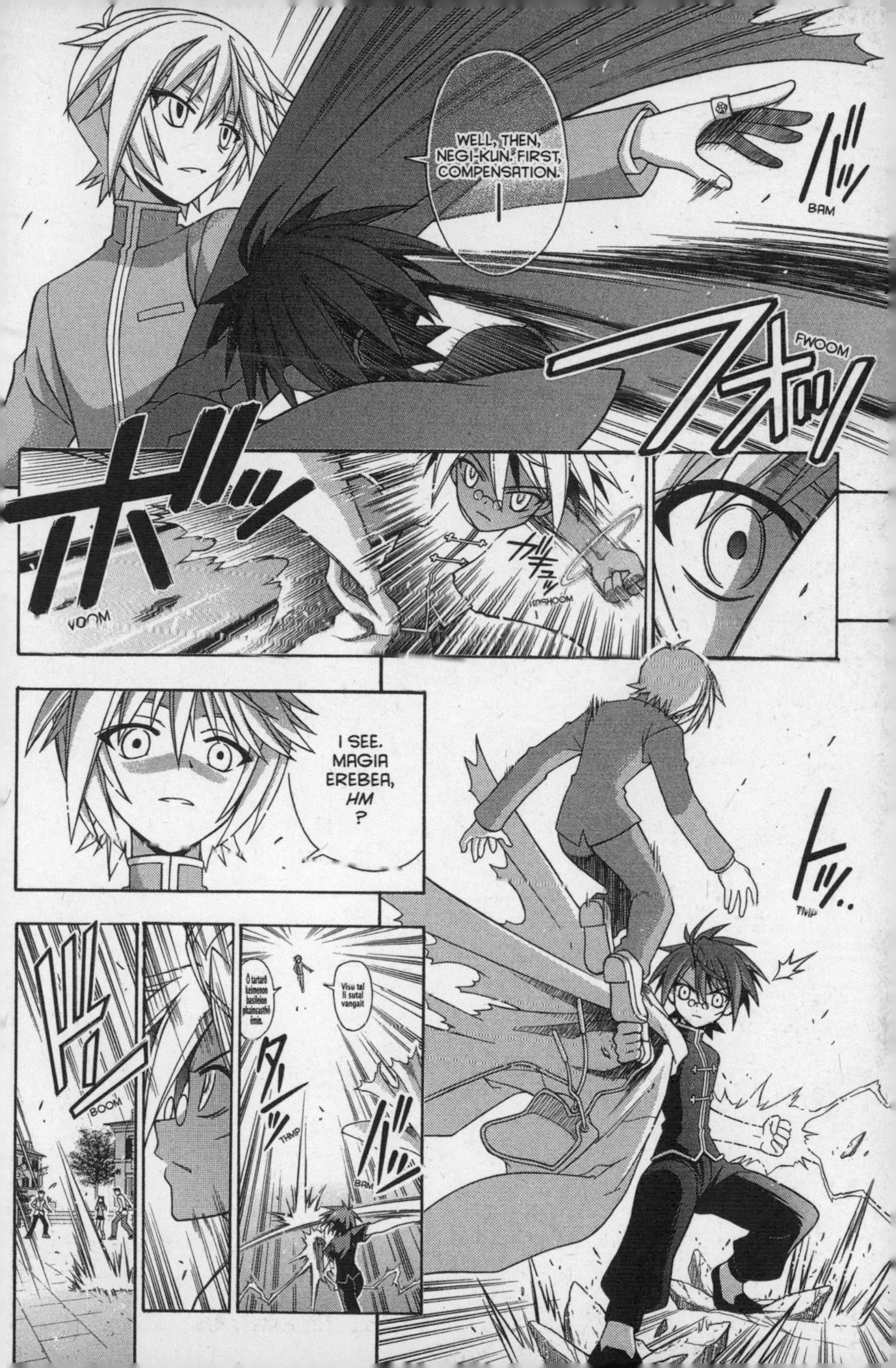
WELL, THEN, NEGI-KUN. FIRST, COMPENSATION.
BAM
FWOOM
SHOOM
VOOM
TMP..
I SEE. MAGIA EREBEA, HM?
Visu tal li sutal vangait
Ō tartarō keimenon basileion phainsasthō ēmin.
BAM
THMP
BOOM

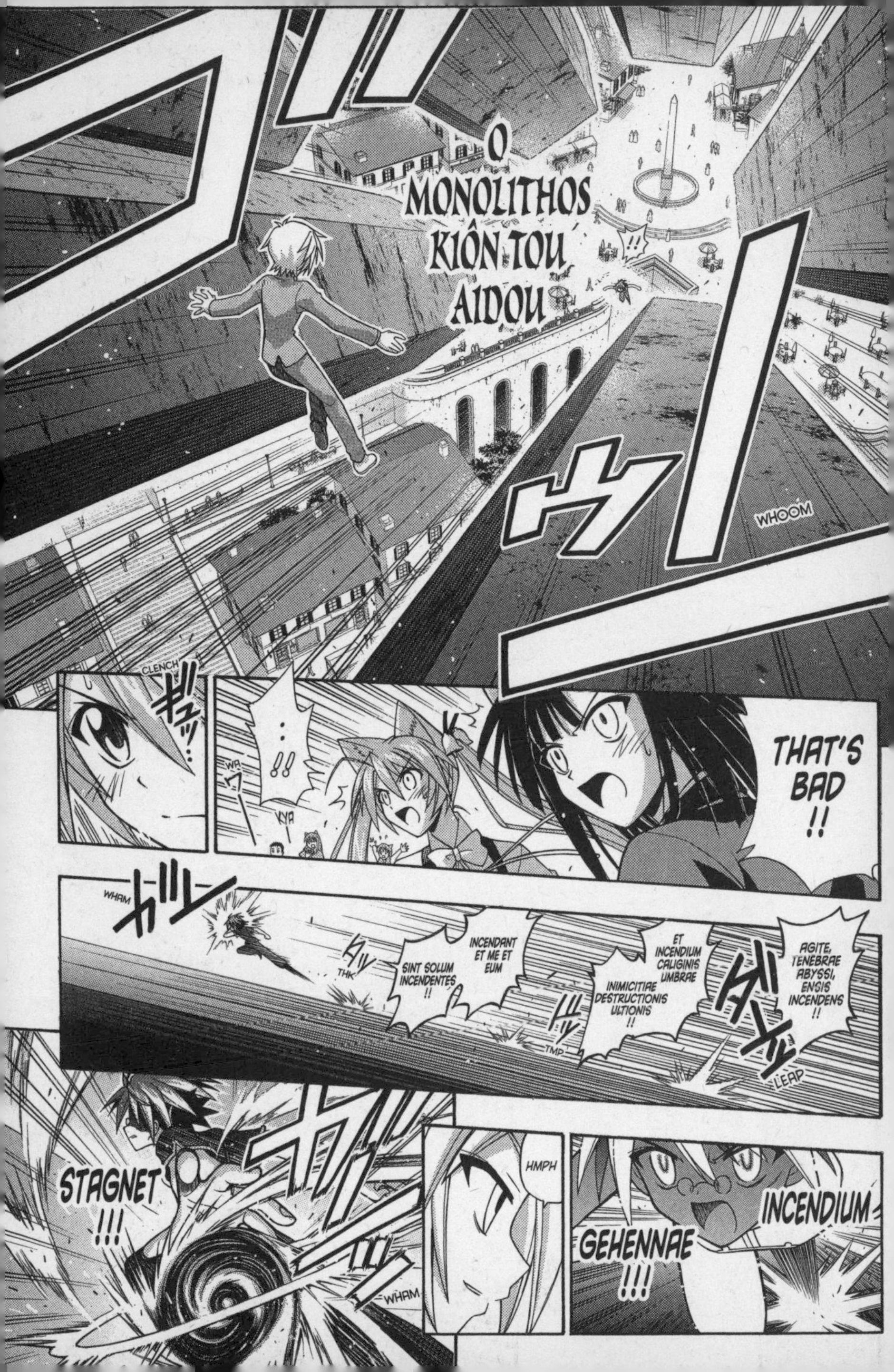
O MONOLITHOS KIÔN TOU AIDOU
!!
WHOOM
THAT'S BAD !!
!!
WA
KYA
CLENCH
AGITE, TENEBRAE ABYSSI, ENSIS INCENDENS !!
LEAP
ET INCENDIUM CALIGINIS UMBRAE
INIMICITIAE DESTRUCTIONIS ULTIONIS !!
TMP
INCENDANT ET ME ET EUM
SINT SOLUM INCENDENTES !!
THK
WHAM
INCENDIUM GEHENNAE !!!
HMPH
STAGNET !!!
WHAM

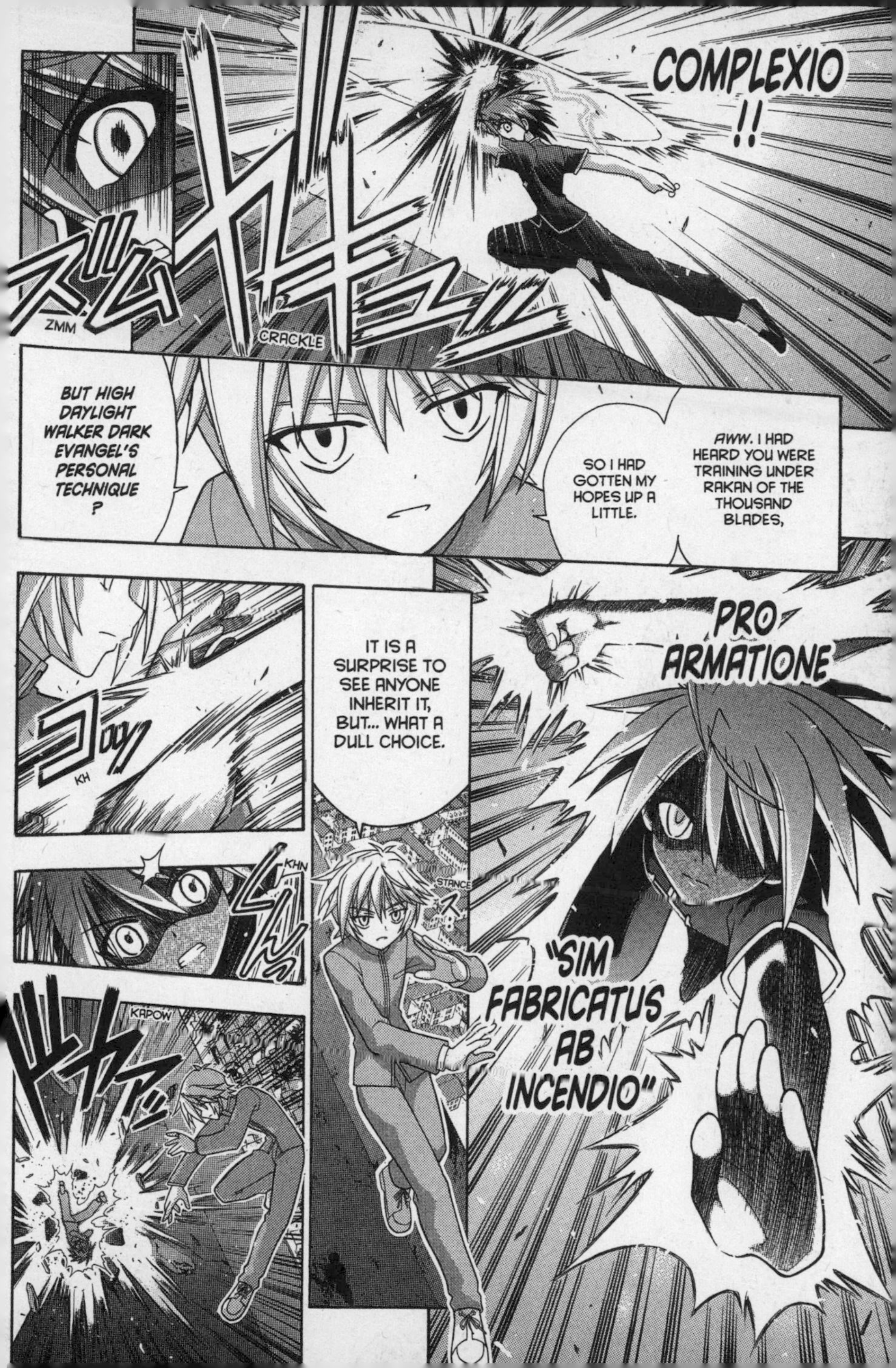
COMPLEXIO !!
CRACKLE
ZMM
AWW. I HAD HEARD YOU WERE TRAINING UNDER RAKAN OF THE THOUSAND BLADES,
SO I HAD GOTTEN MY HOPES UP A LITTLE.
BUT HIGH DAYLIGHT WALKER DARK EVANGEL'S PERSONAL TECHNIQUE ?
PRO ARMATIONE
"SIM FABRICATUS AB INCENDIO"
IT IS A SURPRISE TO SEE ANYONE INHERIT IT, BUT... WHAT A DULL CHOICE.
STANCE
KH
KHN
KAPOW

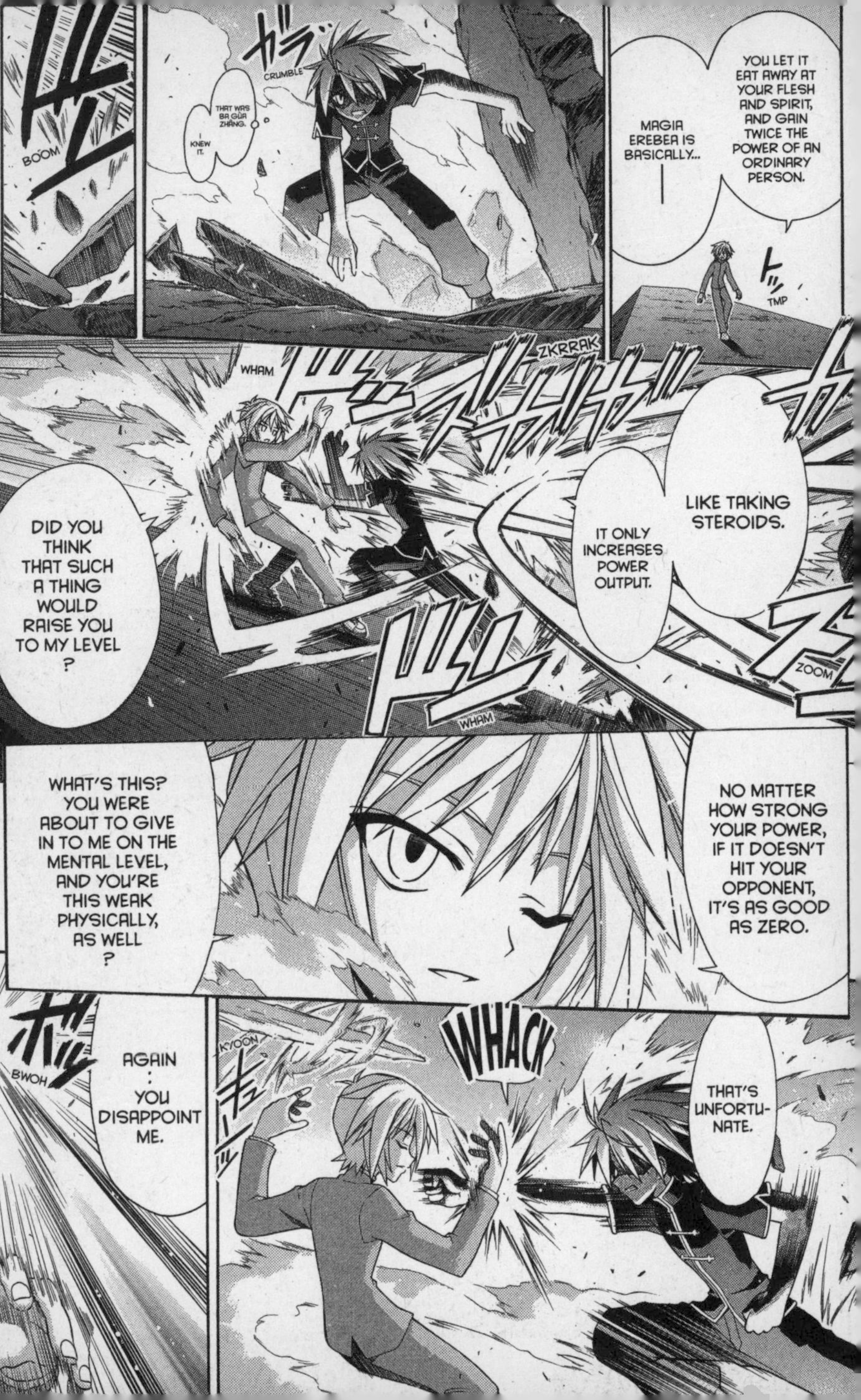
YOU LET IT EAT AWAY AT YOUR FLESH AND SPIRIT, AND GAIN TWICE THE POWER OF AN ORDINARY PERSON.
MAGIA EREBEA IS BASICALLY...
TMP
CRUMBLE
THAT WAS BA GUA ZHANG.
I KNEW IT.
BOOM
LIKE TAKING STEROIDS.
IT ONLY INCREASES POWER OUTPUT.
ZOOM
ZKRRAK
WHAM
WHAM
DID YOU THINK THAT SUCH A THING WOULD RAISE YOU TO MY LEVEL ?
NO MATTER HOW STRONG YOUR POWER, IF IT DOESN'T HIT YOUR OPPONENT, IT'S AS GOOD AS ZERO.
WHAT'S THIS? YOU WERE ABOUT TO GIVE IN TO ME ON THE MENTAL LEVEL, AND YOU'RE THIS WEAK PHYSICALLY, AS WELL ?
THAT'S UNFORTU-NATE.
WHACK
KYOON
AGAIN : YOU DISAPPOINT ME.
BWOH

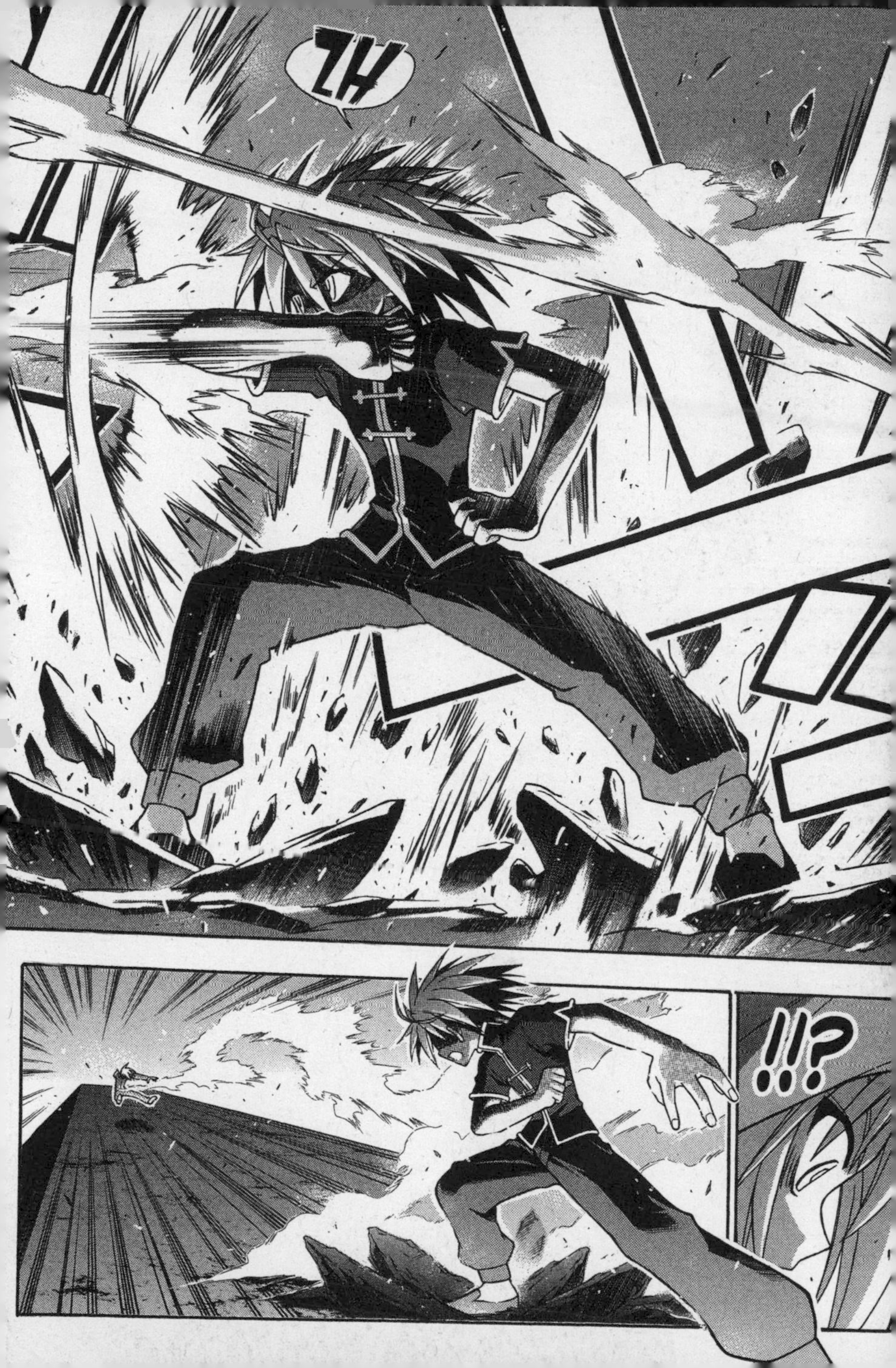
ZH
!!?

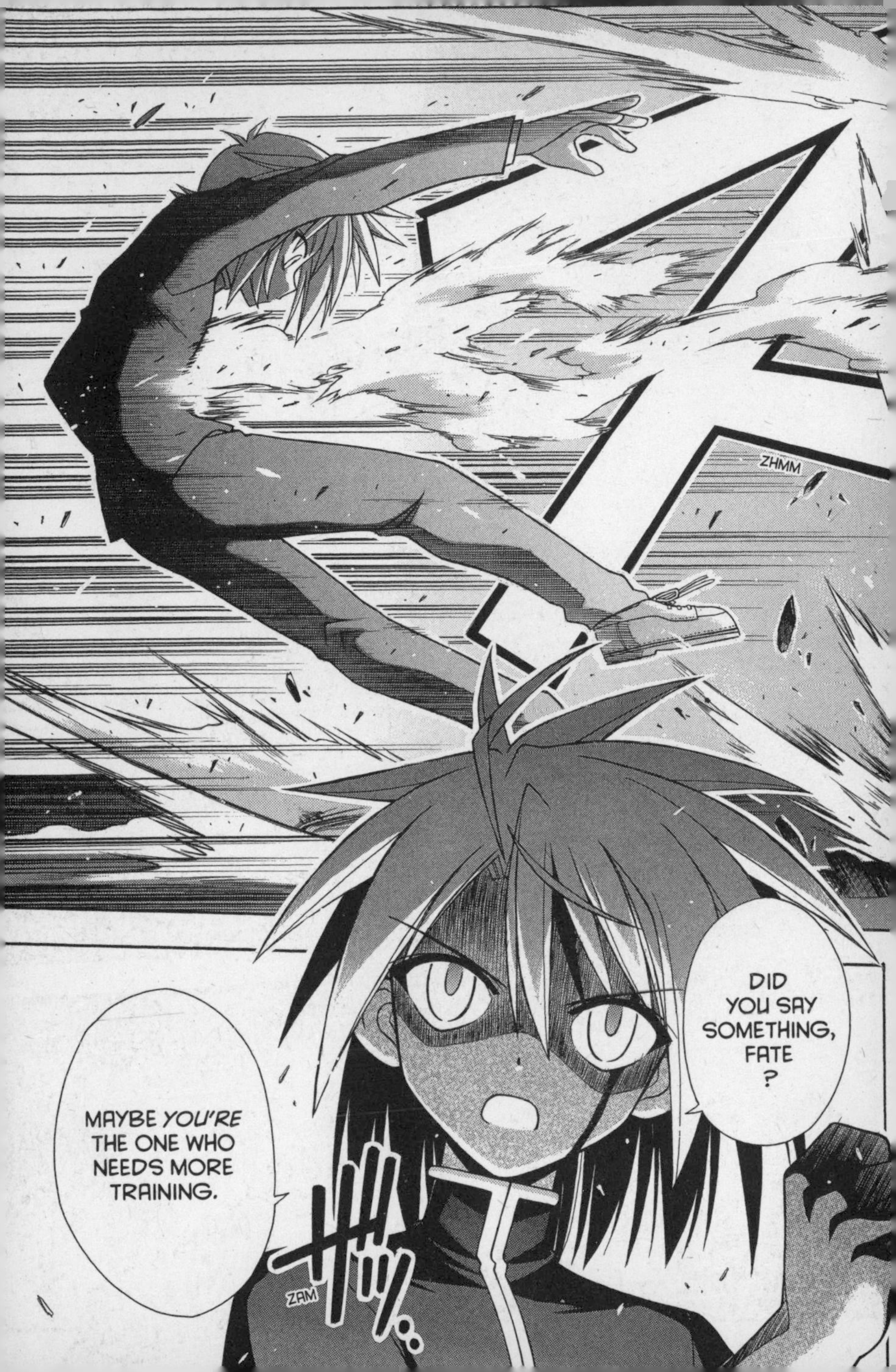
ZHMM
DID YOU SAY SOMETHING, FATE?
MAYBE *YOU'RE* THE ONE WHO NEEDS MORE TRAINING.
ZAM

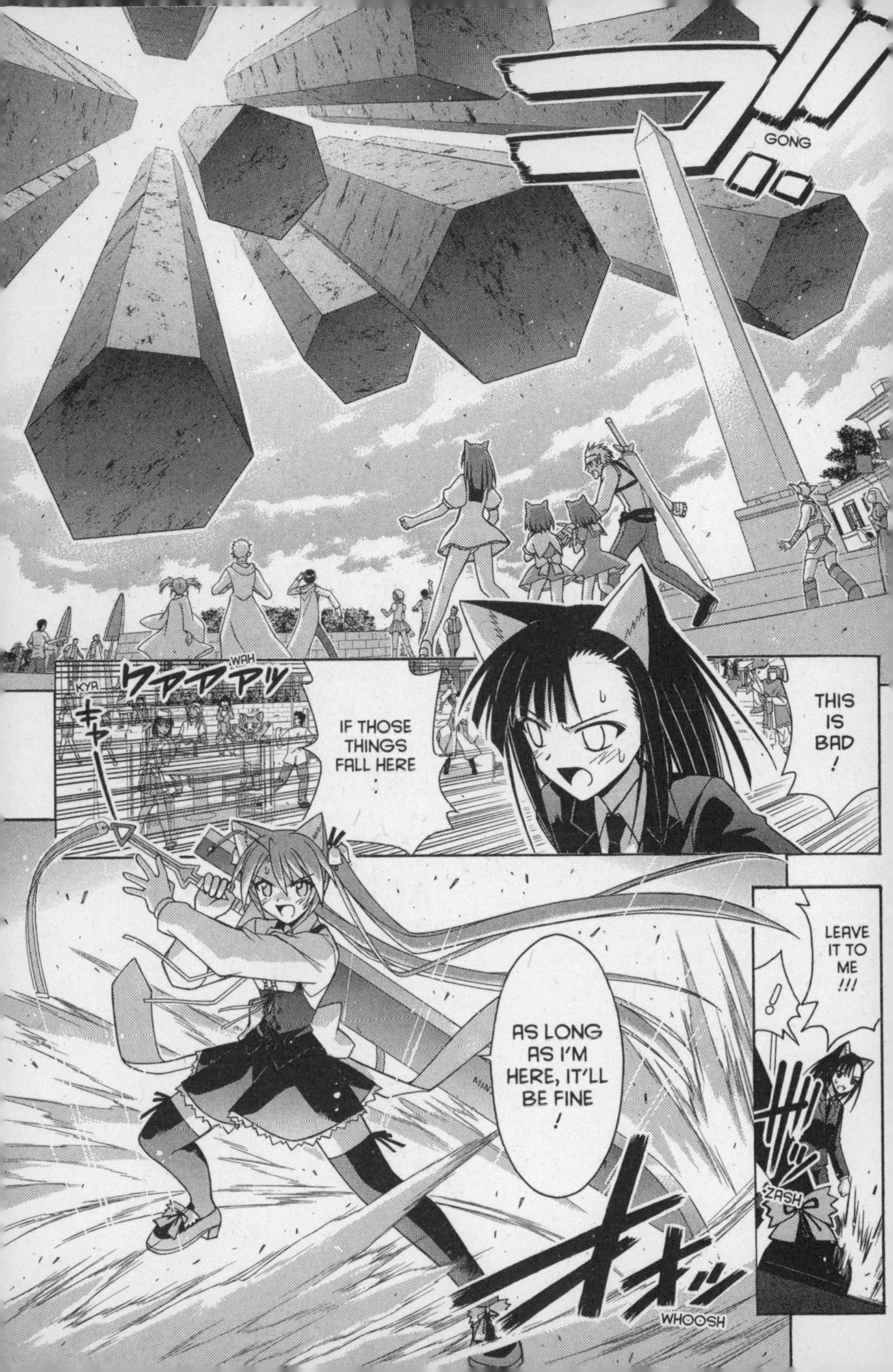
GONG
THIS IS BAD!
IF THOSE THINGS FALL HERE...
WAH
KYA
LEAVE IT TO ME!!!
!
ZASH
AS LONG AS I'M HERE, IT'LL BE FINE!
WHOOSH

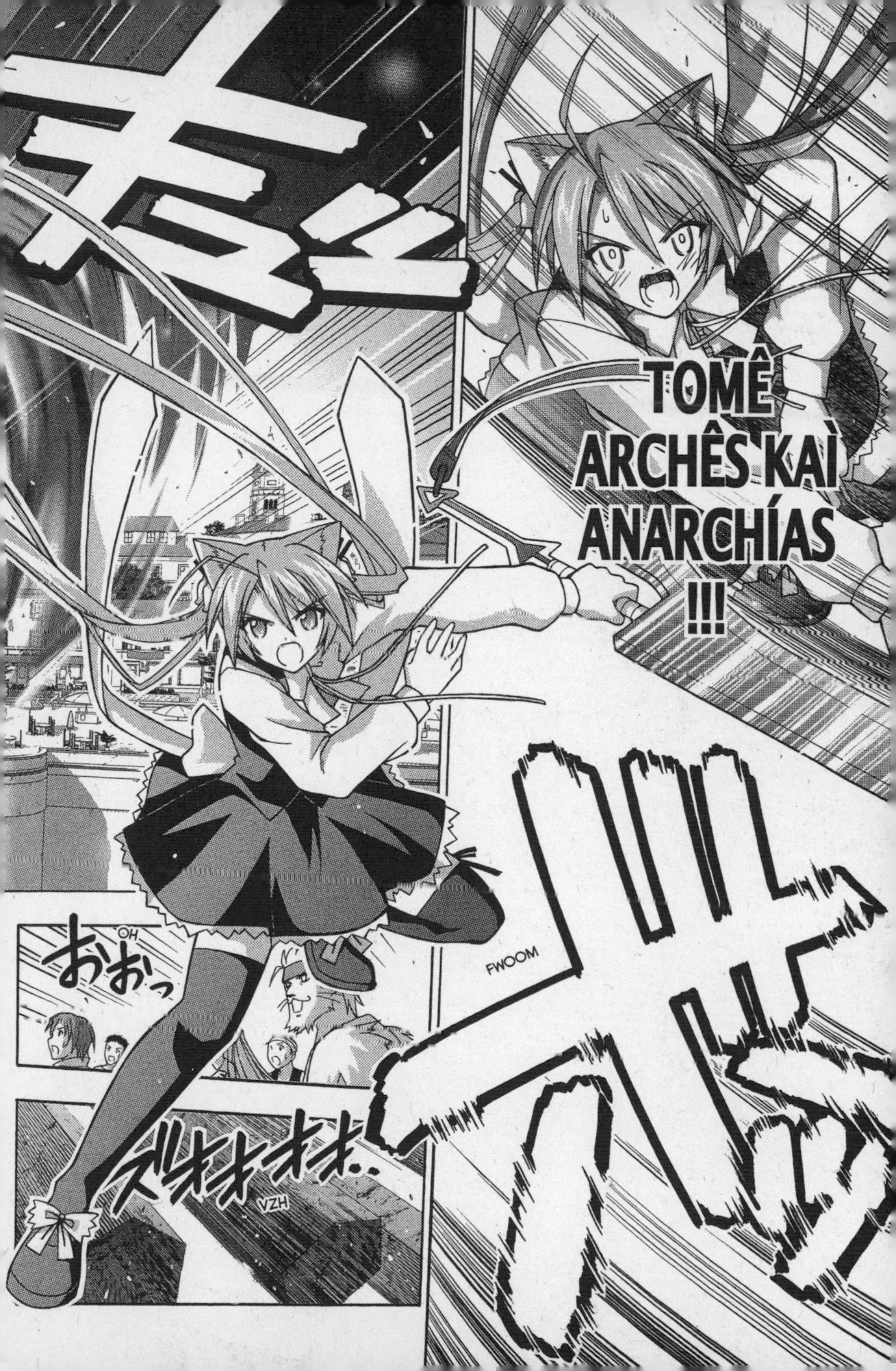
TOMÊ ARCHÊS KAÌ ANARCHÍAS !!!
FWOOM
おおっ
OH
VZH

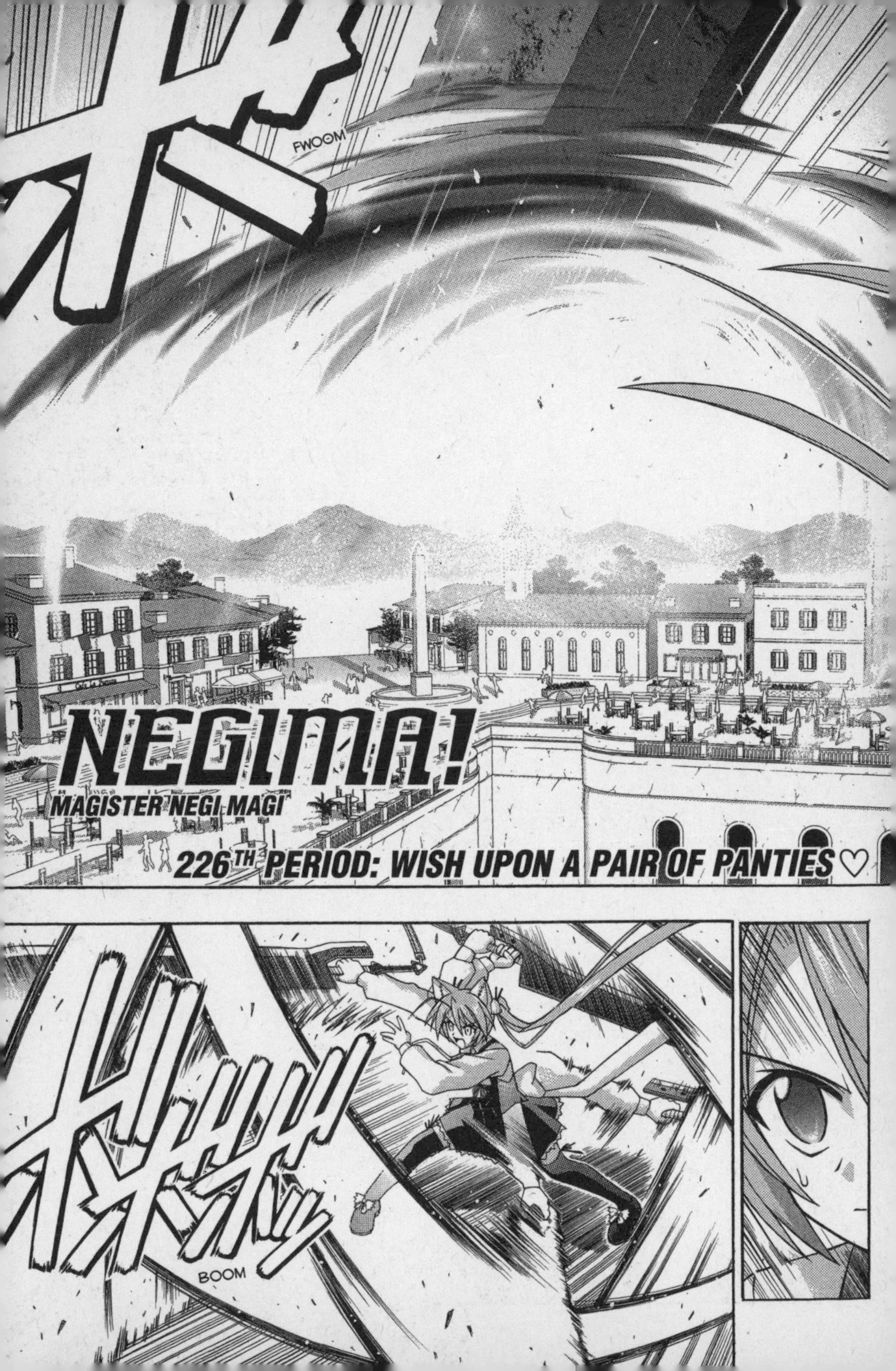
FWOOM
NEGIMA!
MAGISTER NEGI MAGI
226TH PERIOD: WISH UPON A PAIR OF PANTIES ♡
BOOM

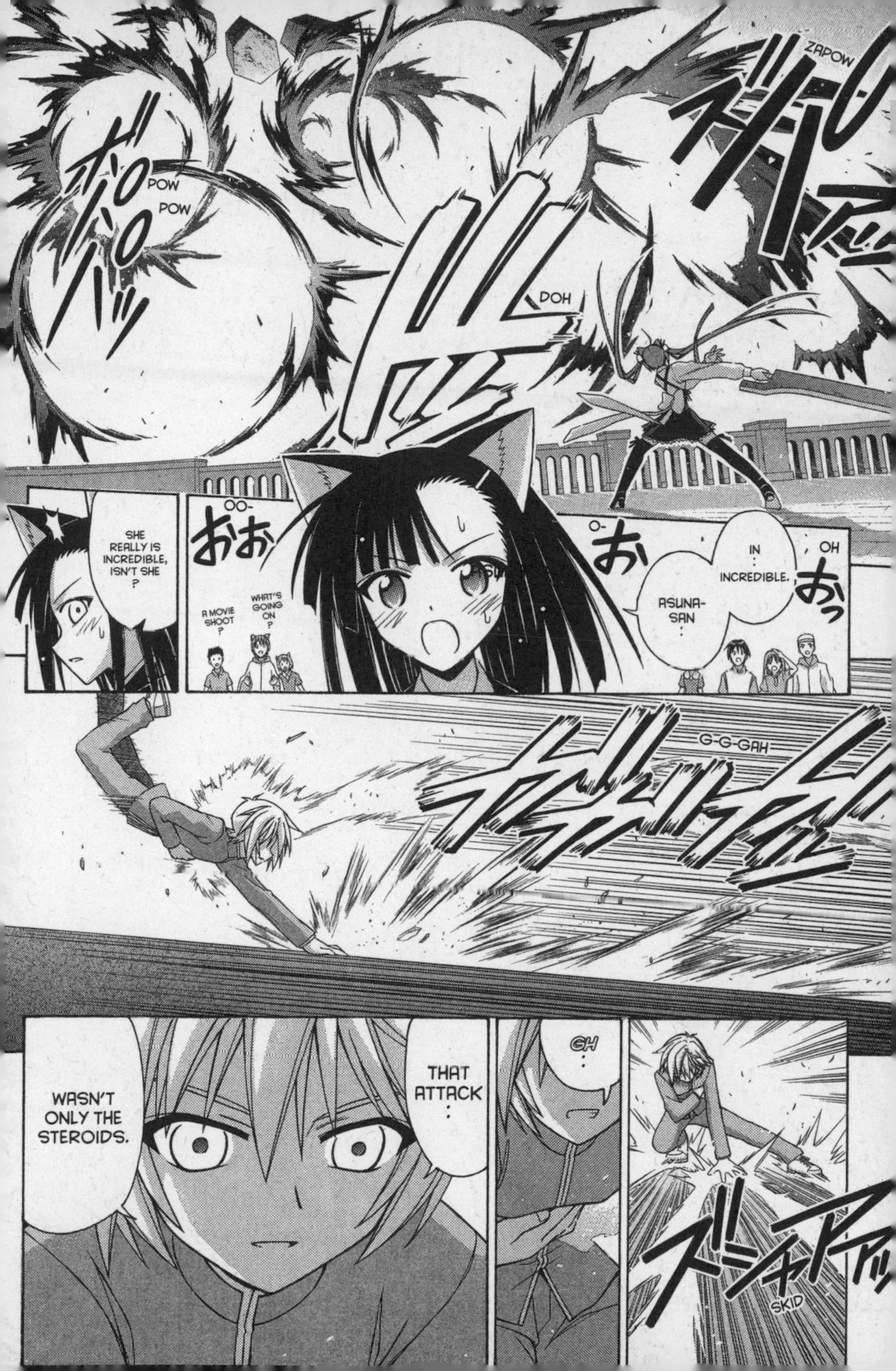
ZAPOW
DOH
POW
POW
OH
おっ
IN...
INCREDIBLE.
ASUNA-SAN...
O-
お
OO-
おお
WHAT'S GOING ON?
A MOVIE SHOOT?
SHE REALLY IS INCREDIBLE, ISN'T SHE?
G-G-GAH
SKID
GH...
THAT ATTACK...
WASN'T ONLY THE STEROIDS.

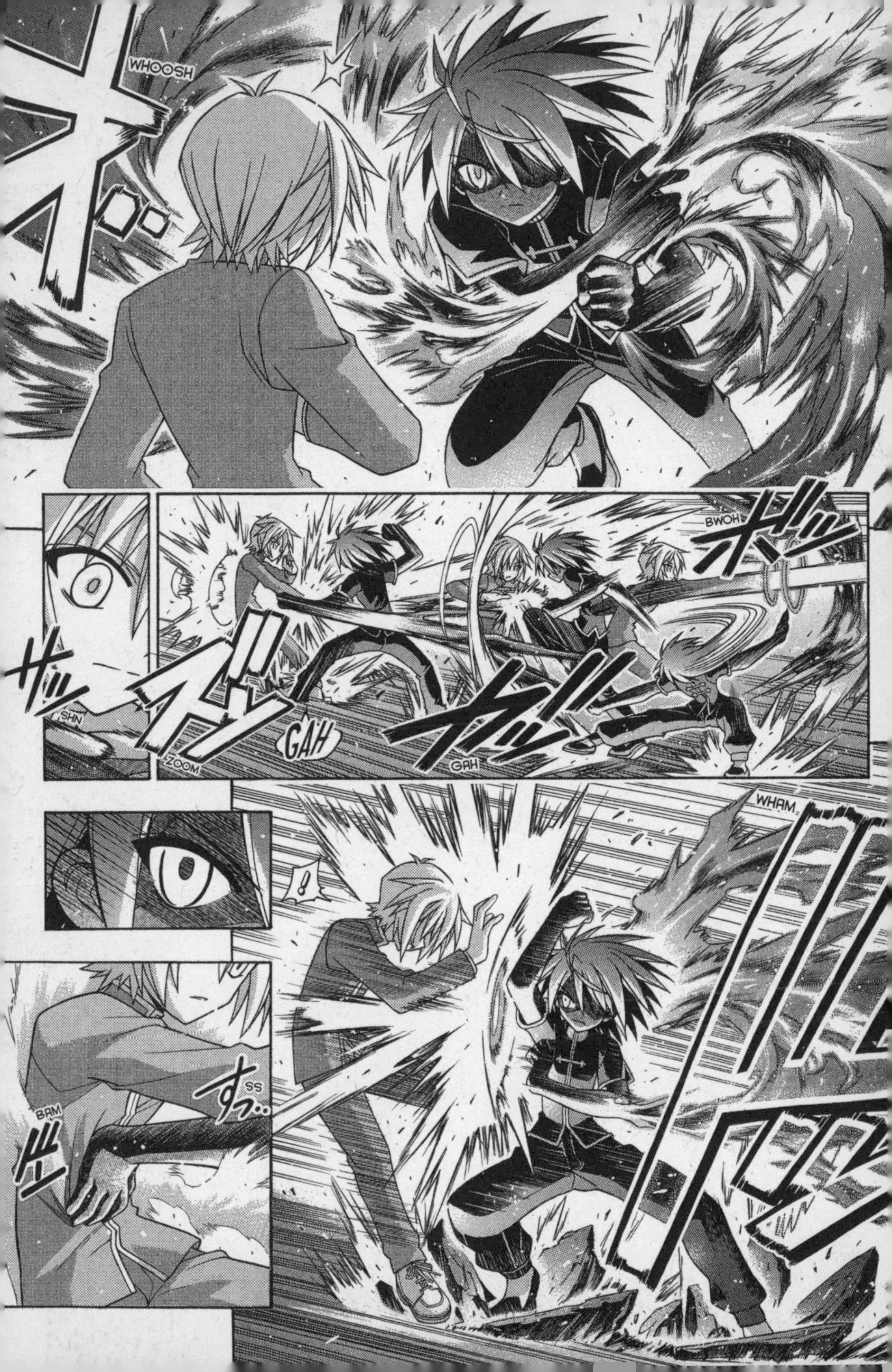

WHOOSH
BWOH
GAH
GAH
ZOOM
SHN
WHAM
!
SS
BAM

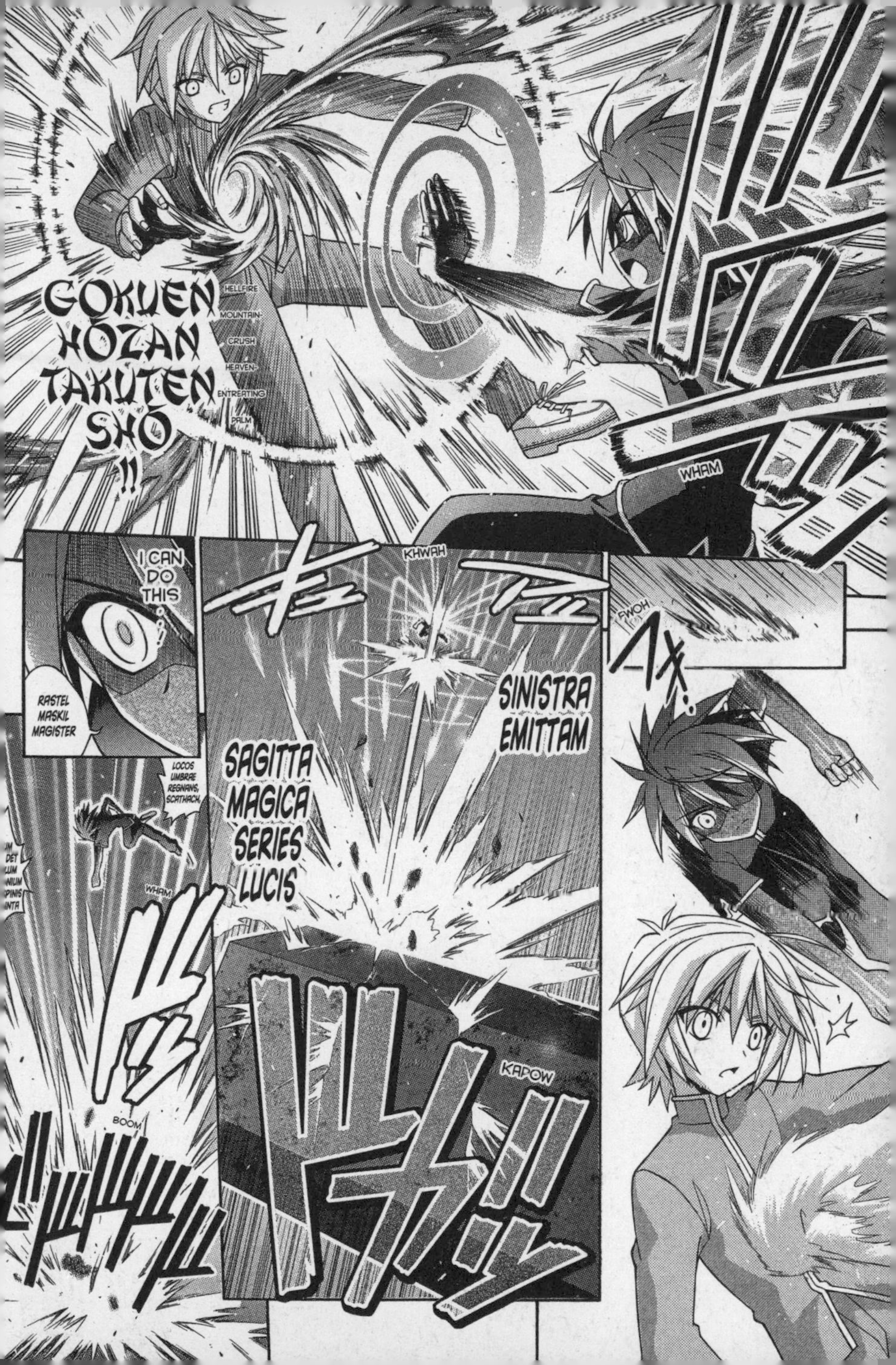

GOKUEN HŌZAN TAKUTEN SHŌ!!
HELLFIRE MOUNTAIN-CRUSH HEAVEN-ENTREATING PALM
WHAM
FWOH
KHWAH
SINISTRA EMITTAM
SAGITTA MAGICA SERIES LUCIS
KAPOW
I CAN DO THIS...!
RASTEL MASKIL MAGISTER
LOCOS UMBRAE REGNANS, SCATHACH,
WHAM
BOOM

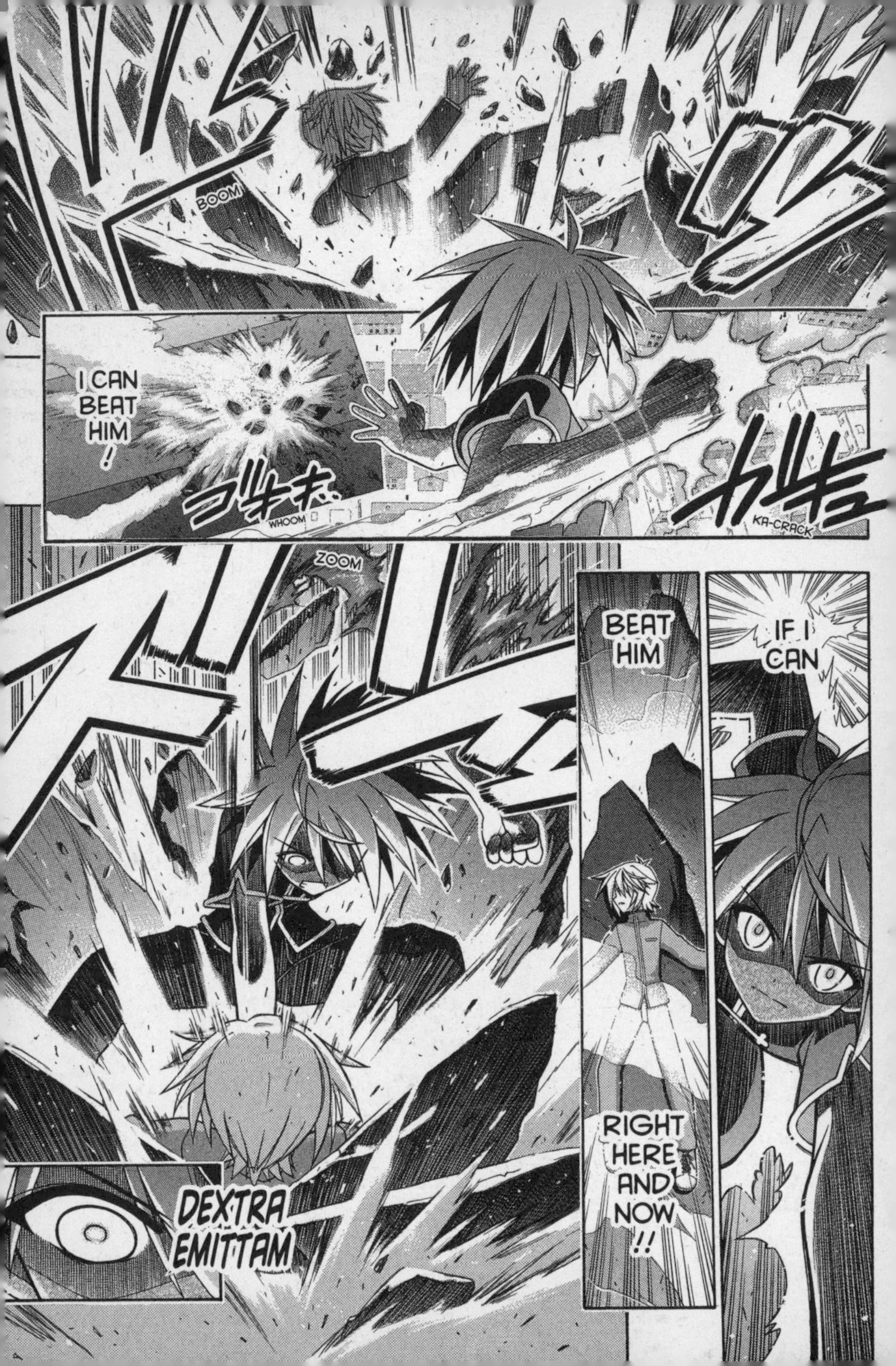
BOOM
KA-CRACK
I CAN BEAT HIM!
WHOOM
IF I CAN
BEAT HIM
RIGHT HERE AND NOW!!
ZOOM
DEXTRA EMITTAM

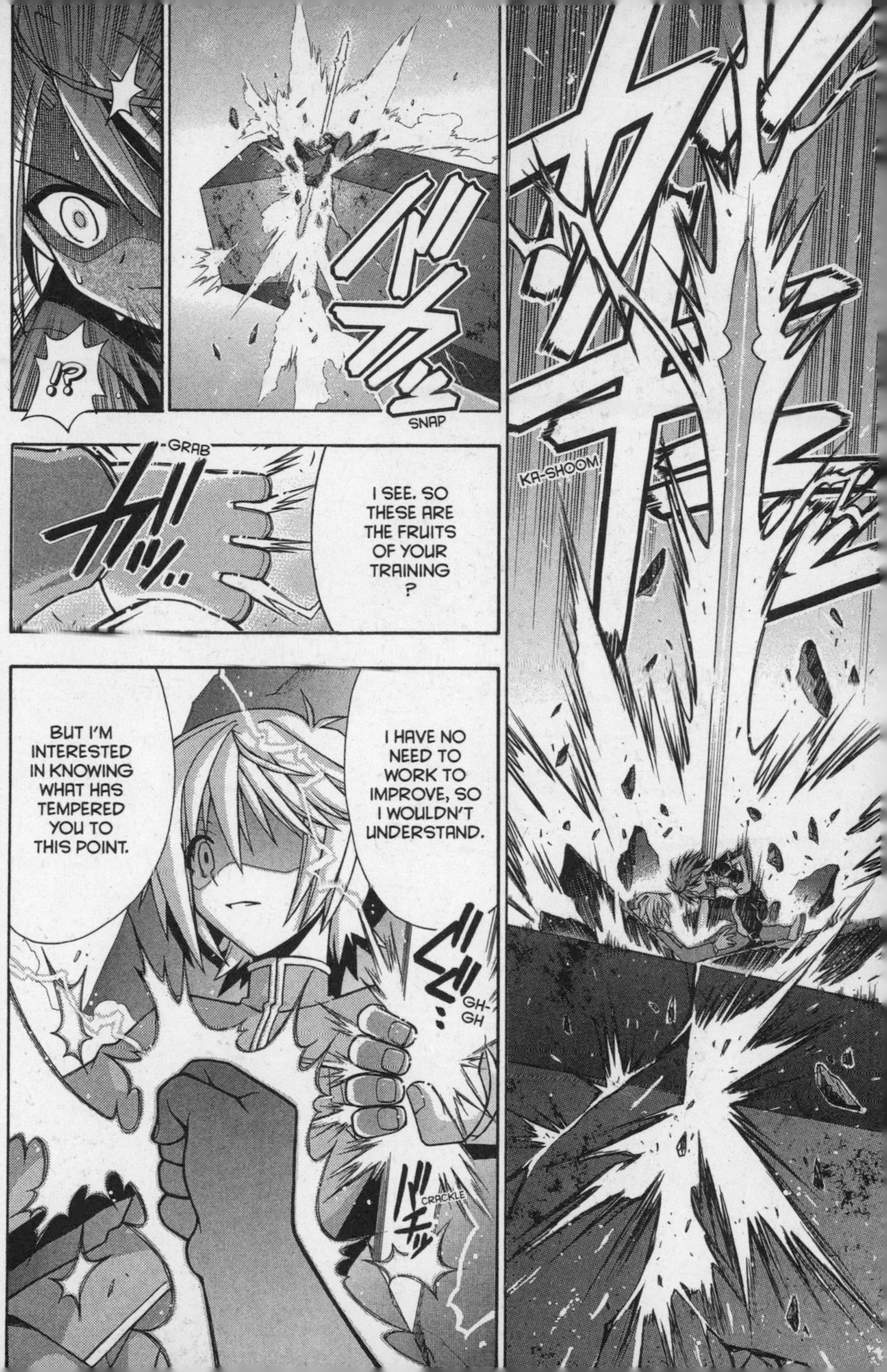
KA-SHOOM
SNAP
!?
-GRAB
I SEE. SO THESE ARE THE FRUITS OF YOUR TRAINING ?
I HAVE NO NEED TO WORK TO IMPROVE, SO I WOULDN'T UNDERSTAND.
BUT I'M INTERESTED IN KNOWING WHAT HAS TEMPERED YOU TO THIS POINT.
GH-GH
CRACKLE

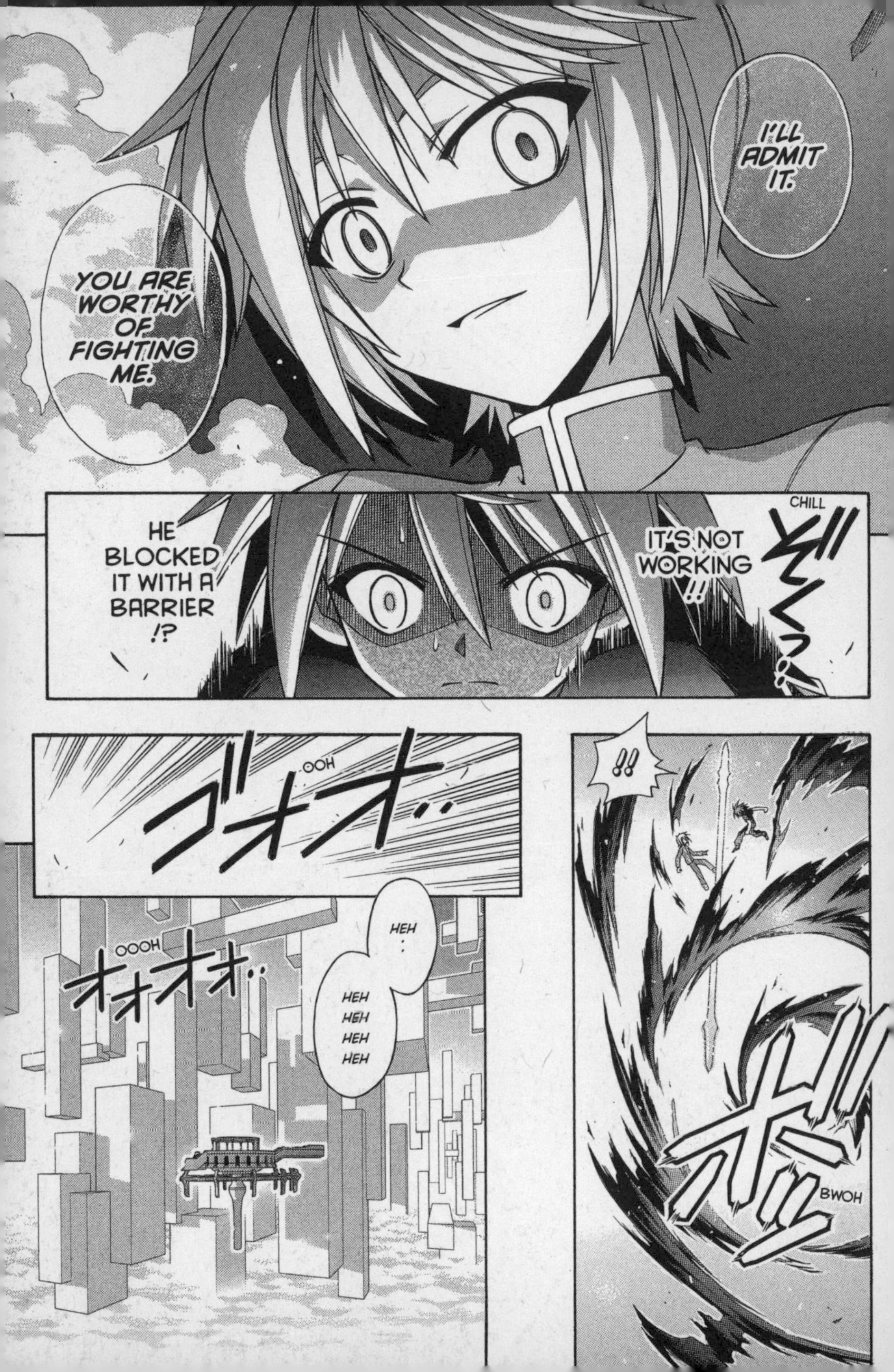

I'LL ADMIT IT.
YOU ARE WORTHY OF FIGHTING ME.
CHILL
IT'S NOT WORKING!!
HE BLOCKED IT WITH A BARRIER!?
!!
BWOH
OOH
HEH :
HEH HEH HEH HEH
OOOH

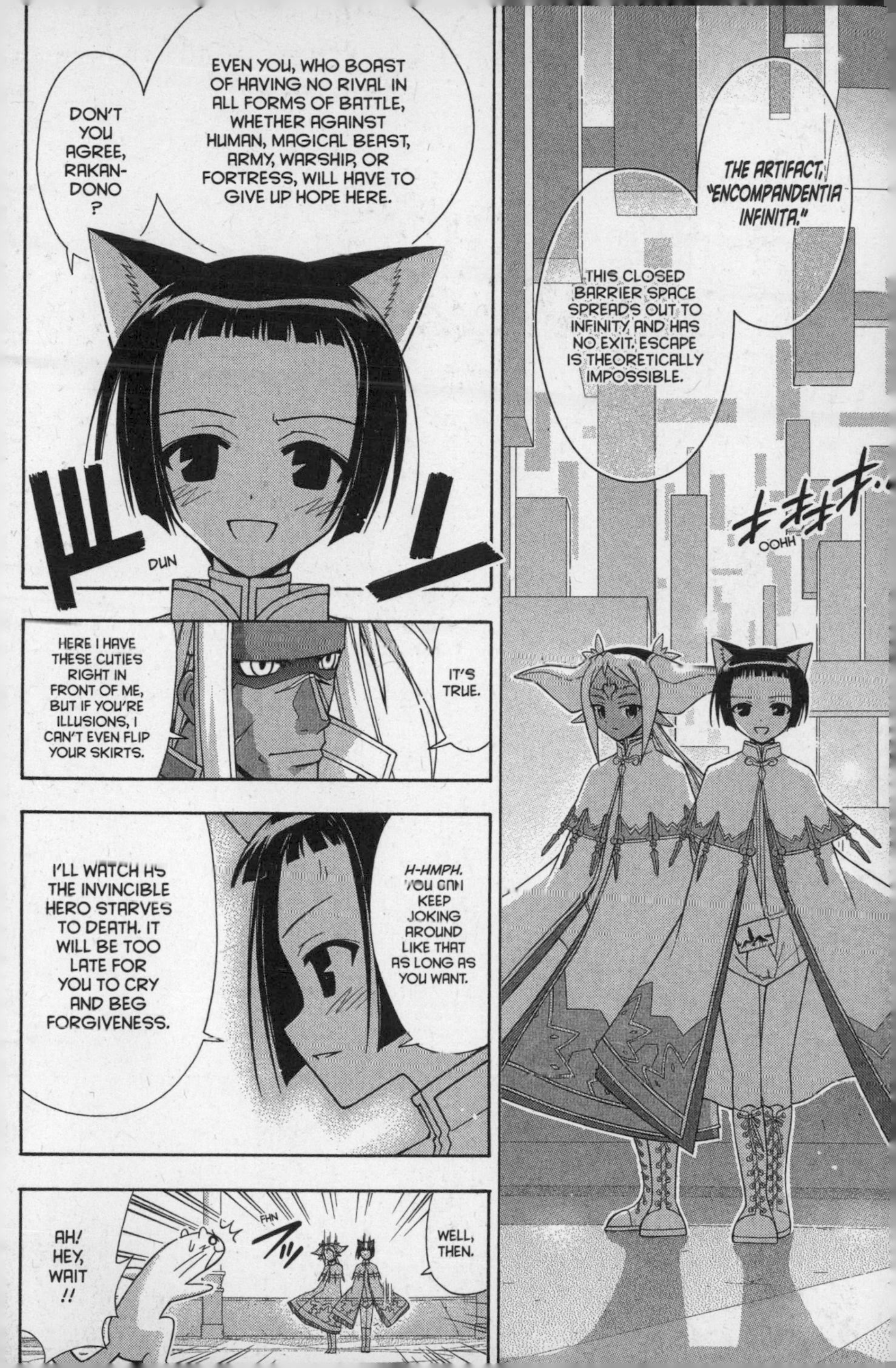
THE ARTIFACT, "ENCOMPANDENTIA INFINITA."
THIS CLOSED BARRIER SPACE SPREADS OUT TO INFINITY AND HAS NO EXIT. ESCAPE IS THEORETICALLY IMPOSSIBLE.
OOHH
EVEN YOU, WHO BOAST OF HAVING NO RIVAL IN ALL FORMS OF BATTLE, WHETHER AGAINST HUMAN, MAGICAL BEAST, ARMY, WARSHIP, OR FORTRESS, WILL HAVE TO GIVE UP HOPE HERE.
DON'T YOU AGREE, RAKAN-DONO ?
DUN
IT'S TRUE.
HERE I HAVE THESE CUTIES RIGHT IN FRONT OF ME, BUT IF YOU'RE ILLUSIONS, I CAN'T EVEN FLIP YOUR SKIRTS.
H-HMPH. YOU CAN KEEP JOKING AROUND LIKE THAT AS LONG AS YOU WANT.
I'LL WATCH AS THE INVINCIBLE HERO STARVES TO DEATH. IT WILL BE TOO LATE FOR YOU TO CRY AND BEG FORGIVENESS.
WELL, THEN.
FHN
AH! HEY, WAIT !!

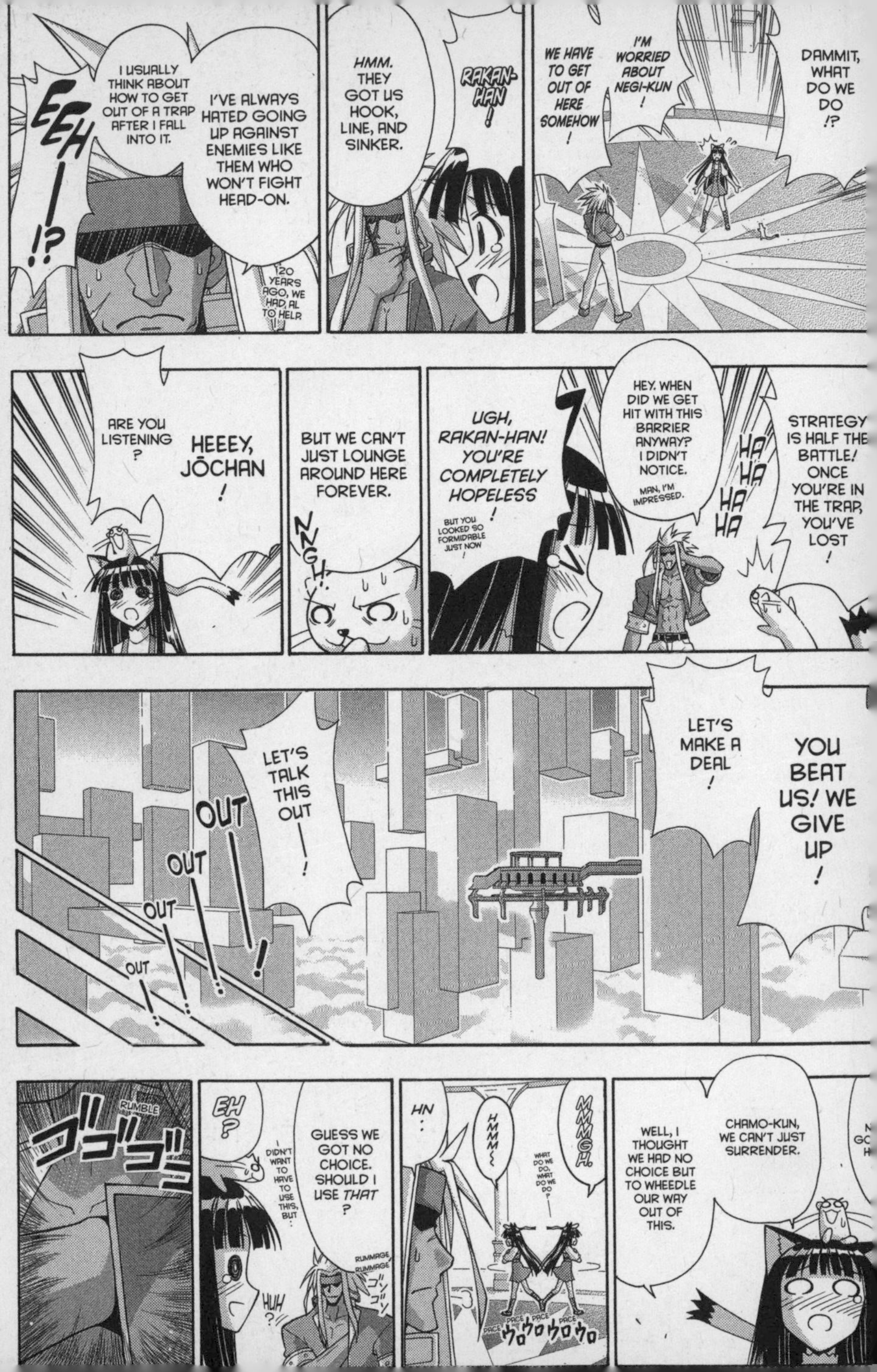
DAMMIT, WHAT DO WE DO!?
I'M WORRIED ABOUT NEGI-KUN!
WE HAVE TO GET OUT OF HERE SOMEHOW!
RAKAN-HAN!
HMM. THEY GOT US HOOK, LINE, AND SINKER.
I'VE ALWAYS HATED GOING UP AGAINST ENEMIES LIKE THEM WHO WON'T FIGHT HEAD-ON.
I USUALLY THINK ABOUT HOW TO GET OUT OF A TRAP AFTER I FALL INTO IT.
EEH--!?
120 YEARS AGO, WE HAD AL TO HELP!
STRATEGY IS HALF THE BATTLE! ONCE YOU'RE IN THE TRAP, YOU'VE LOST!
HA HA HA HA
HEY. WHEN DID WE GET HIT WITH THIS BARRIER ANYWAY? I DIDN'T NOTICE.
MAN, I'M IMPRESSED.
UGH, RAKAN-HAN! YOU'RE COMPLETELY HOPELESS!
BUT YOU LOOKED SO FORMIDABLE JUST NOW!
BUT WE CAN'T JUST LOUNGE AROUND HERE FOREVER.
NNGH!!
HEEEY, JŌCHAN!
ARE YOU LISTENING?
YOU BEAT US! WE GIVE UP!
LET'S MAKE A DEAL!
LET'S TALK THIS OUT!
OUT
OUT
OUT
OUT
CHAMO-KUN, WE CAN'T JUST SURRENDER.
WELL, I THOUGHT WE HAD NO CHOICE BUT TO WHEEDLE OUR WAY OUT OF THIS.
MMMGH.
HMMM~
WHAT DO WE DO, WHAT DO WE DO?
HN...
PACE PACE PACE PACE
ウロウロウロウロ
GUESS WE GOT NO CHOICE. SHOULD I USE THAT?
EH?
I DIDN'T WANT TO HAVE TO USE THIS, BUT...
RUMMAGE RUMMAGE
ゴソゴソ
HUH?
RUMBLE
ゴゴゴゴ

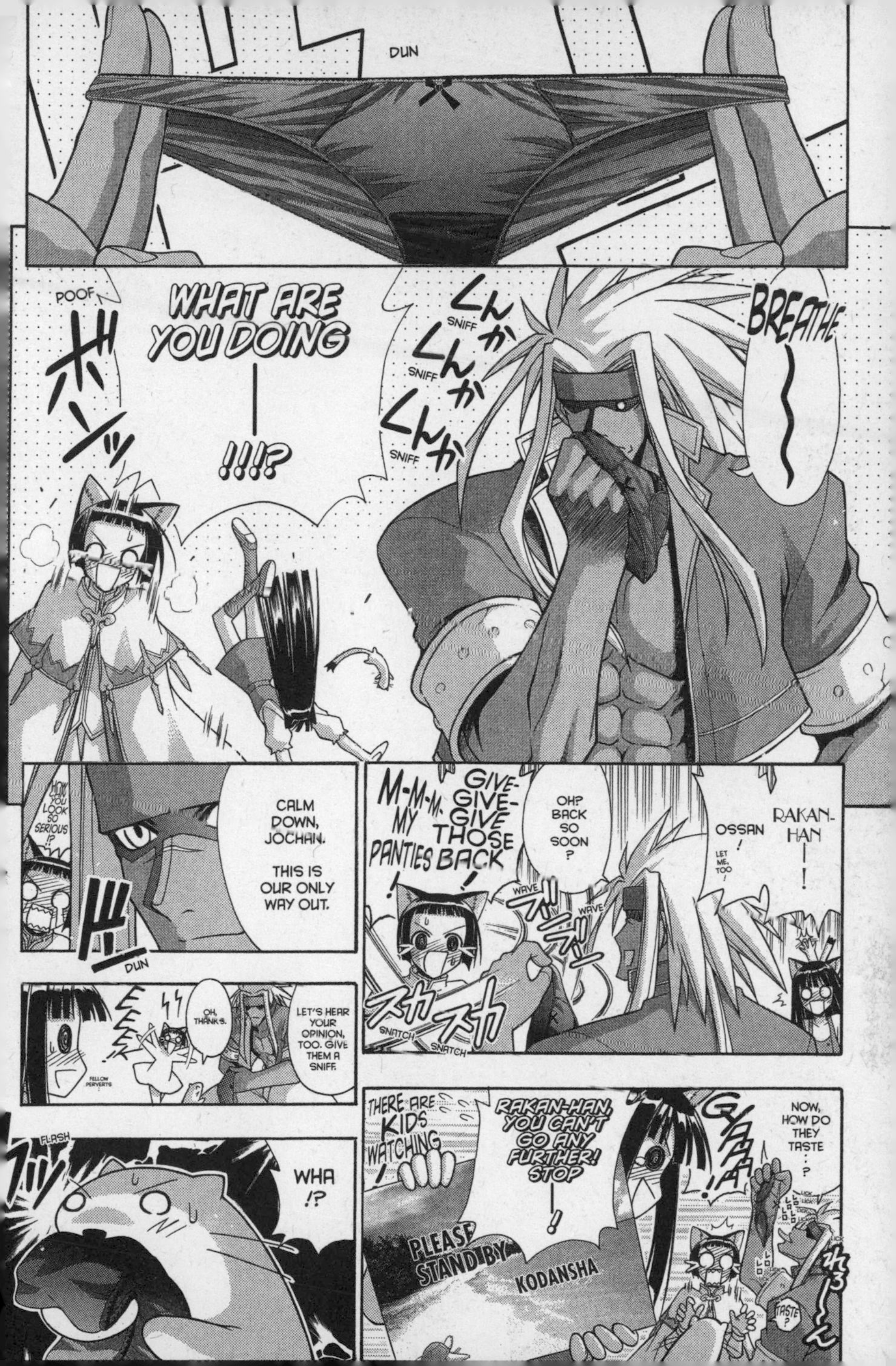

DUN
BREATHE~~
SNIFF
SNIFF
SNIFF
WHAT ARE YOU DOING—!!!!?
POOF
RAKAN-HAN—!
OSSAN! LET ME, TOO!
OH? BACK SO SOON?
GIVE-GIVE-GIVE THOSE BACK!
M-M-M-MY PANTIES!
WAVE
WAVE
SNATCH
SNATCH
CALM DOWN, JOCHAN. THIS IS OUR ONLY WAY OUT.
HOW CAN YOU LOOK SO SERIOUS!?
DUN
LET'S HEAR YOUR OPINION, TOO. GIVE THEM A SNIFF.
OH, THANKS.
FELLOW PERVERTS!
NOW, HOW DO THEY TASTE...?
TASTE?
GYAA!
RAKAN-HAN, YOU CAN'T GO ANY FURTHER! STOP—!
THERE ARE KIDS WATCHING!
PLEASE STAND BY
KODANSHA
WHA!?
FLASH

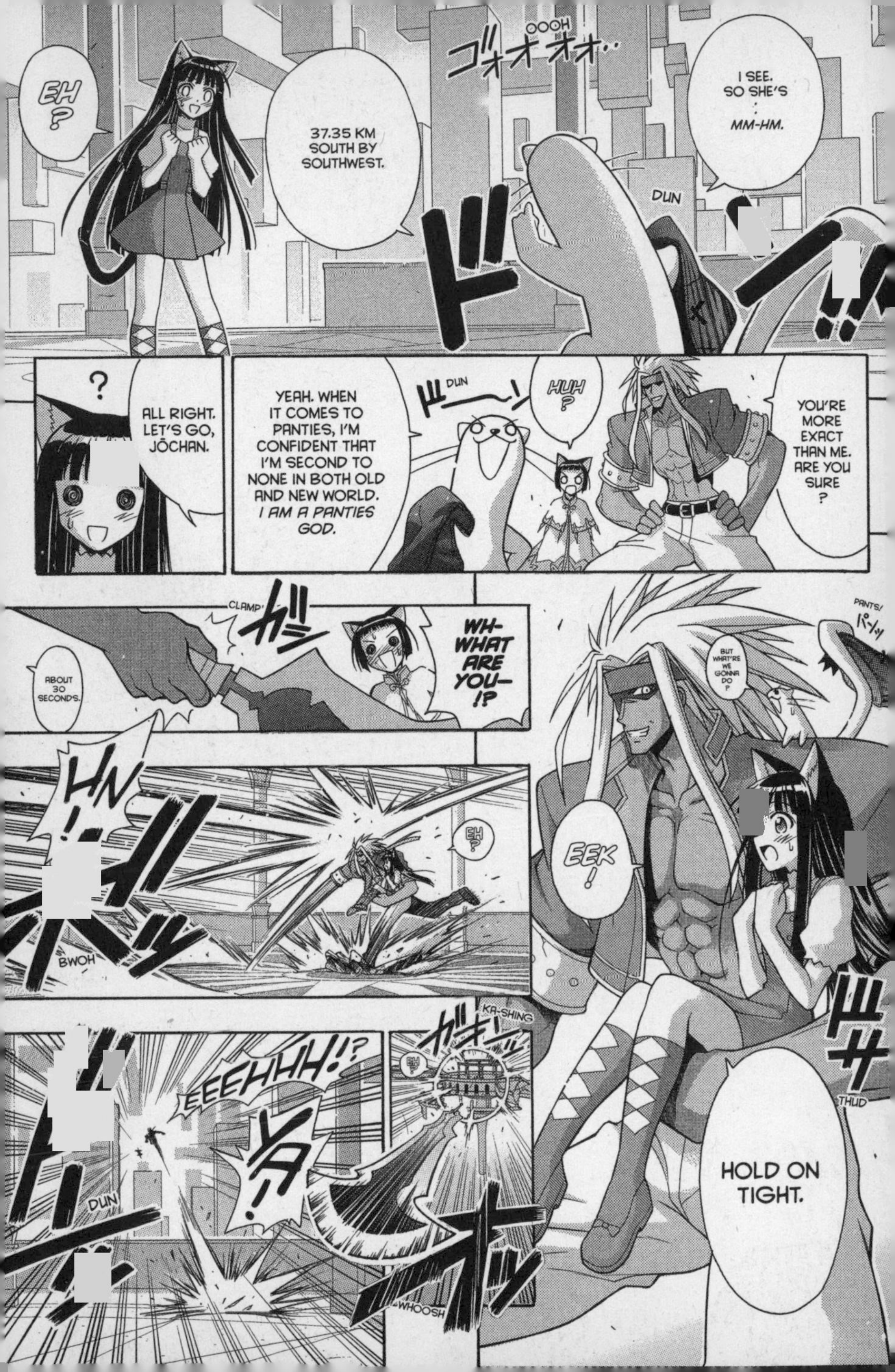
OOOH
I SEE. SO SHE'S :
MM-HM.
DUN
37.35 KM SOUTH BY SOUTHWEST.
EH ?
YOU'RE MORE EXACT THAN ME. ARE YOU SURE ?
HUH ?
DUN
YEAH. WHEN IT COMES TO PANTIES, I'M CONFIDENT THAT I'M SECOND TO NONE IN BOTH OLD AND NEW WORLD. I AM A PANTIES GOD.
?
ALL RIGHT. LET'S GO, JŌCHAN.
PANTS!
BUT WHAT'RE WE GONNA DO ?
EEK !
THUD
HOLD ON TIGHT.
CLAMP
WH- WHAT ARE YOU- !?
ABOUT 30 SECONDS.
HN !
EH ?
BWOH
KA-SHING
EH ?
EEEHHH!!?
YA!
WHOOSH
DUN

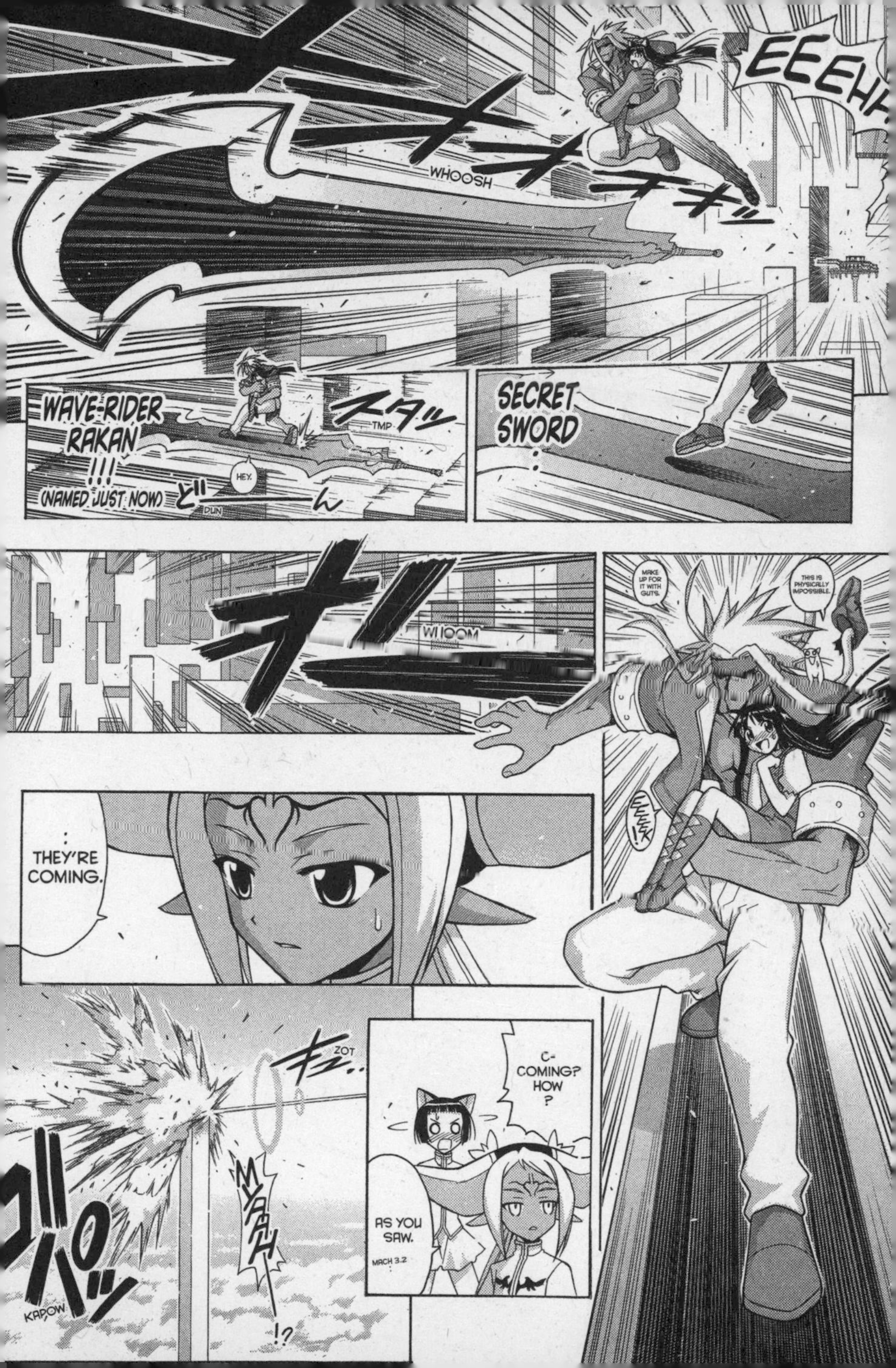
EEEHH
WHOOSH
SECRET SWORD
:
WAVE-RIDER RAKAN!!!
(NAMED JUST NOW)
TMP
HEY.
DUN
THIS IS PHYSICALLY IMPOSSIBLE.
MAKE UP FOR IT WITH GUTS.
EEEEK!
WHOOM
:
THEY'RE COMING.
C-COMING? HOW?
AS YOU SAW.
MACH 3.2
ZOT
MYAAH!?
KAPOW

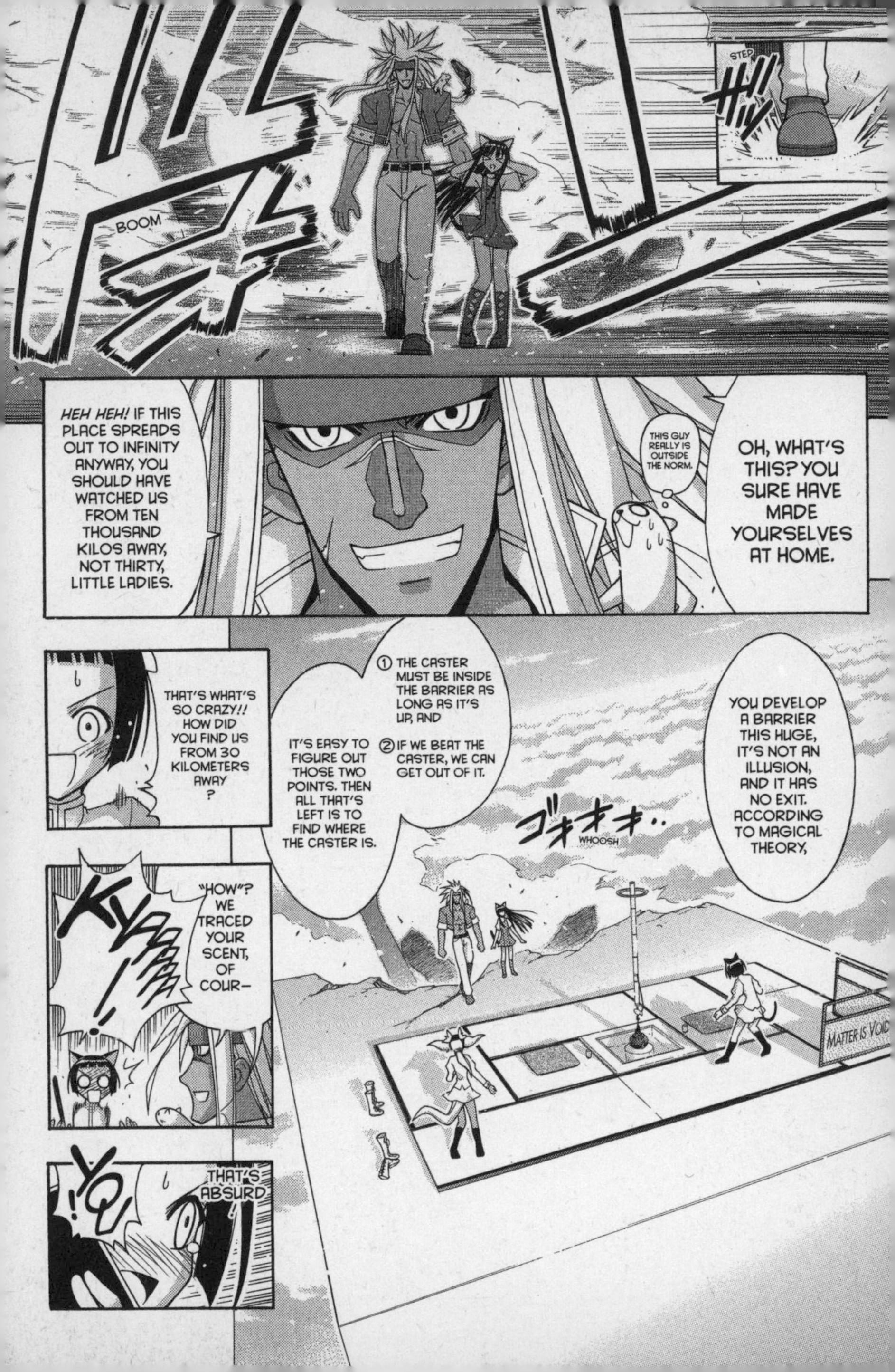
STEP
BOOM
OH, WHAT'S THIS? YOU SURE HAVE MADE YOURSELVES AT HOME.
THIS GUY REALLY IS OUTSIDE THE NORM.
HEH HEH! IF THIS PLACE SPREADS OUT TO INFINITY ANYWAY, YOU SHOULD HAVE WATCHED US FROM TEN THOUSAND KILOS AWAY, NOT THIRTY, LITTLE LADIES.
YOU DEVELOP A BARRIER THIS HUGE, IT'S NOT AN ILLUSION, AND IT HAS NO EXIT. ACCORDING TO MAGICAL THEORY,
① THE CASTER MUST BE INSIDE THE BARRIER AS LONG AS IT'S UP, AND
② IF WE BEAT THE CASTER, WE CAN GET OUT OF IT.
IT'S EASY TO FIGURE OUT THOSE TWO POINTS. THEN ALL THAT'S LEFT IS TO FIND WHERE THE CASTER IS.
ゴオオオ..
WHOOSH
MATTER IS VOID
THAT'S WHAT'S SO CRAZY!! HOW DID YOU FIND US FROM 30 KILOMETERS AWAY ?
"HOW"? WE TRACED YOUR SCENT, OF COUR–
KYAAAA!!
THAT'S ABSURD
YOU!?

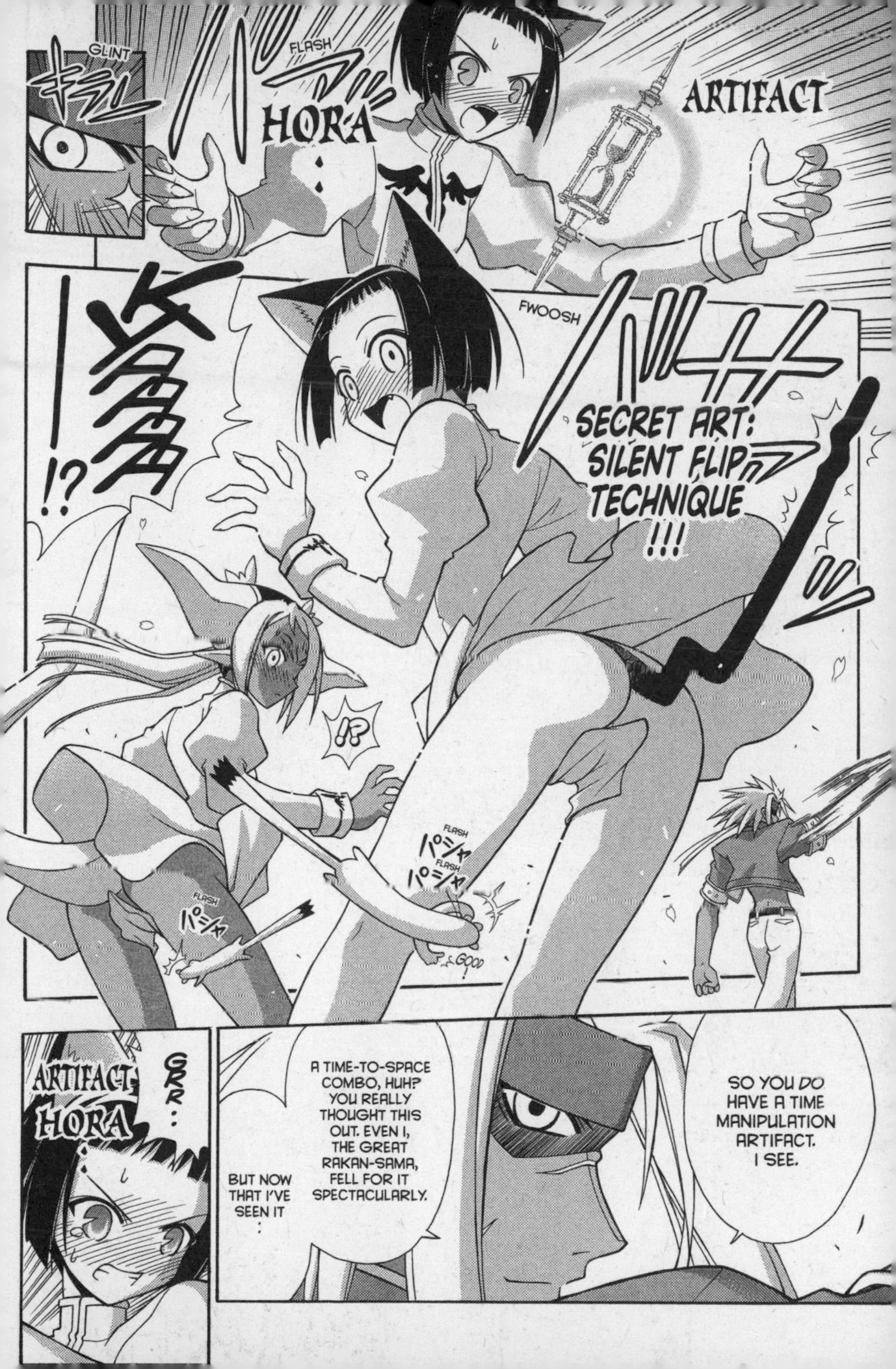

ARTIFACT
HORA
FLASH
GLINT
FWOOSH
SECRET ART: SILENT FLIP TECHNIQUE !!!
!?
!?
FLASH
FLASH
FLASH
GOOD
SO YOU DO HAVE A TIME MANIPULATION ARTIFACT. I SEE.
A TIME-TO-SPACE COMBO, HUH? YOU REALLY THOUGHT THIS OUT. EVEN I, THE GREAT RAKAN-SAMA, FELL FOR IT SPECTACULARLY.
BUT NOW THAT I'VE SEEN IT :
GRR...
ARTIFACT, HORA

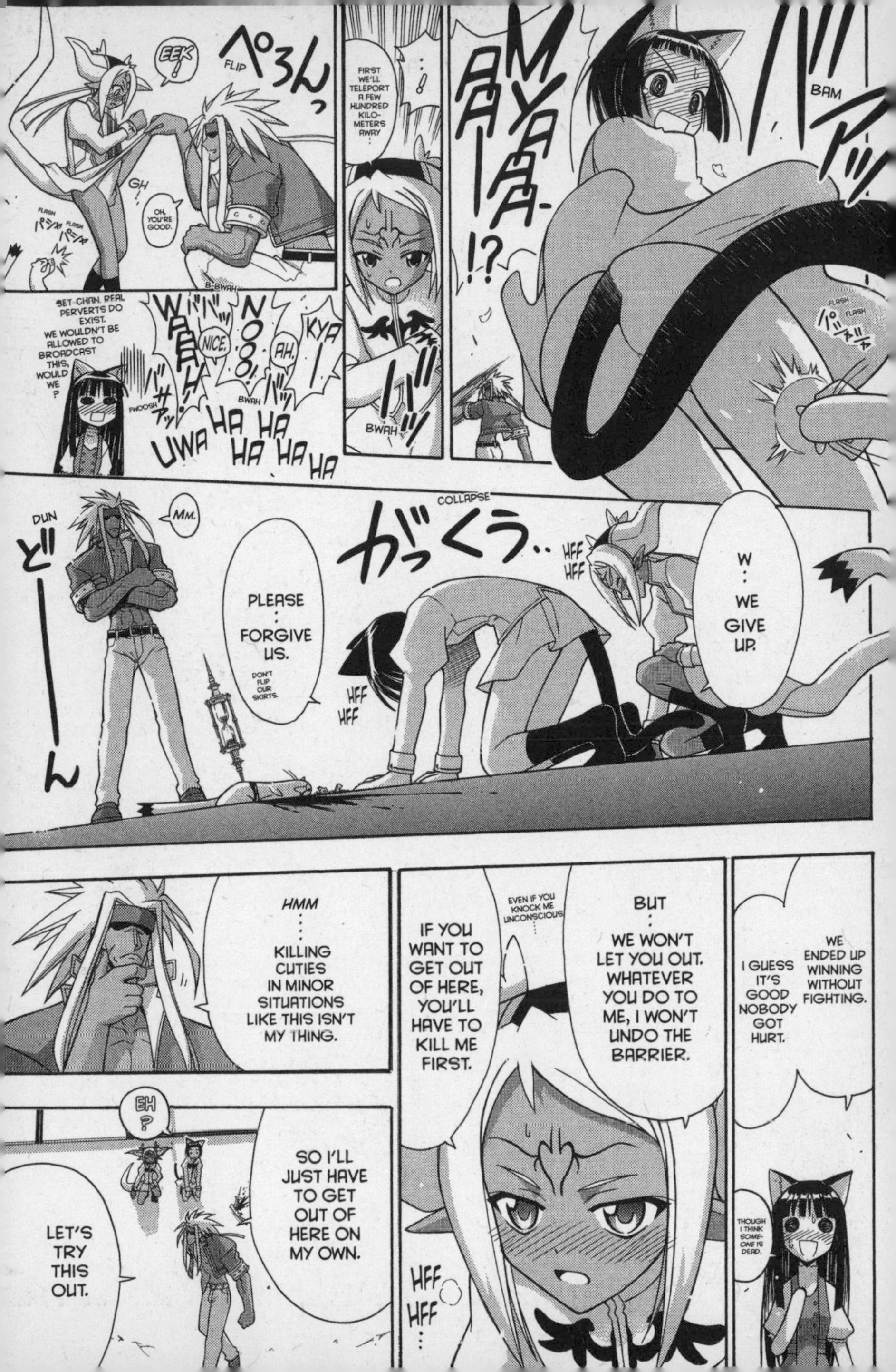

MYAAA-!?
BAM
FLASH FLASH
FIRST WE'LL TELEPORT A FEW HUNDRED KILOMETERS AWAY...
...!
BWAH
EEK!
FLIP
ぺろん
GH
OH, YOU'RE GOOD.
FLASH FLASH
B-BWAH
KYA!
AH.
NOOO!
NICE.
WAAH!
BWAH
PWOOSH
SET-CHAN, REAL PERVERTS DO EXIST. WE WOULDN'T BE ALLOWED TO BROADCAST THIS, WOULD WE?
UWA HA HA HA HA HA
W... WE GIVE UP.
HFF HFF
COLLAPSE
がっくう..
PLEASE... FORGIVE US.
DON'T FLIP OUR SKIRTS.
HFF HFF
MM.
DUN
WE ENDED UP WINNING WITHOUT FIGHTING.
I GUESS IT'S GOOD NOBODY GOT HURT.
THOUGH I THINK SOMEONE IS DEAD.
BUT... WE WON'T LET YOU OUT. WHATEVER YOU DO TO ME, I WON'T UNDO THE BARRIER.
EVEN IF YOU KNOCK ME UNCONSCIOUS...
IF YOU WANT TO GET OUT OF HERE, YOU'LL HAVE TO KILL ME FIRST.
HFF HFF...
HMM... KILLING CUTIES IN MINOR SITUATIONS LIKE THIS ISN'T MY THING.
EH?
SO I'LL JUST HAVE TO GET OUT OF HERE ON MY OWN.
LET'S TRY THIS OUT.

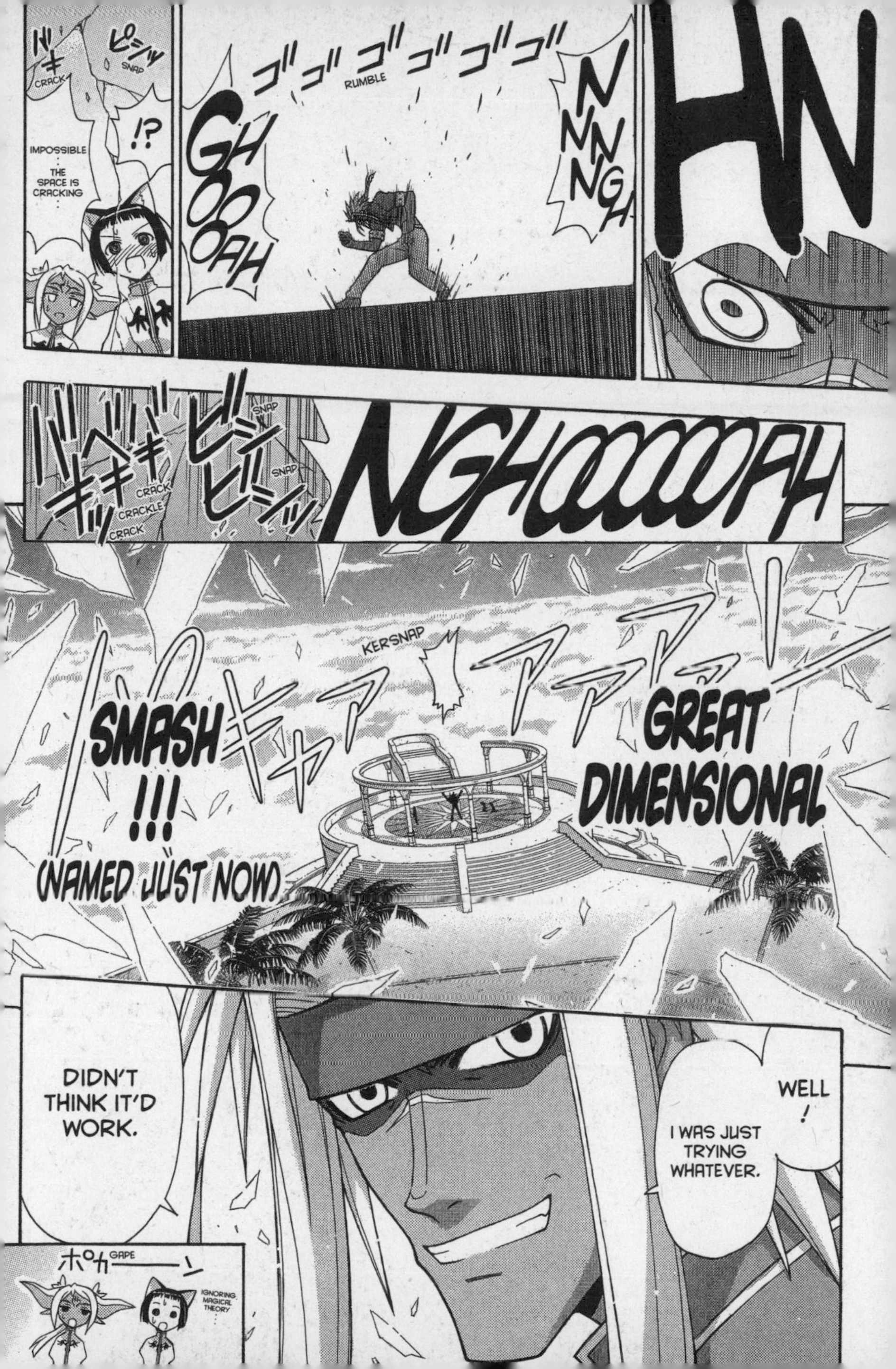
HN
NNNNGH
GHOOOAH
ゴゴゴゴゴゴ
RUMBLE
ピシッ
SNAP
バキ
CRACK
!?
IMPOSSIBLE...
THE SPACE IS CRACKING...
NGHOOOOOAH
SNAP
SNAP
CRACK
CRACKLE
CRACK
GREAT DIMENSIONAL SMASH!!!
(NAMED JUST NOW)
KERSNAP
WELL!
I WAS JUST TRYING WHATEVER.
DIDN'T THINK IT'D WORK.
ポカーン
GAPE
IGNORING MAGICAL THEORY...

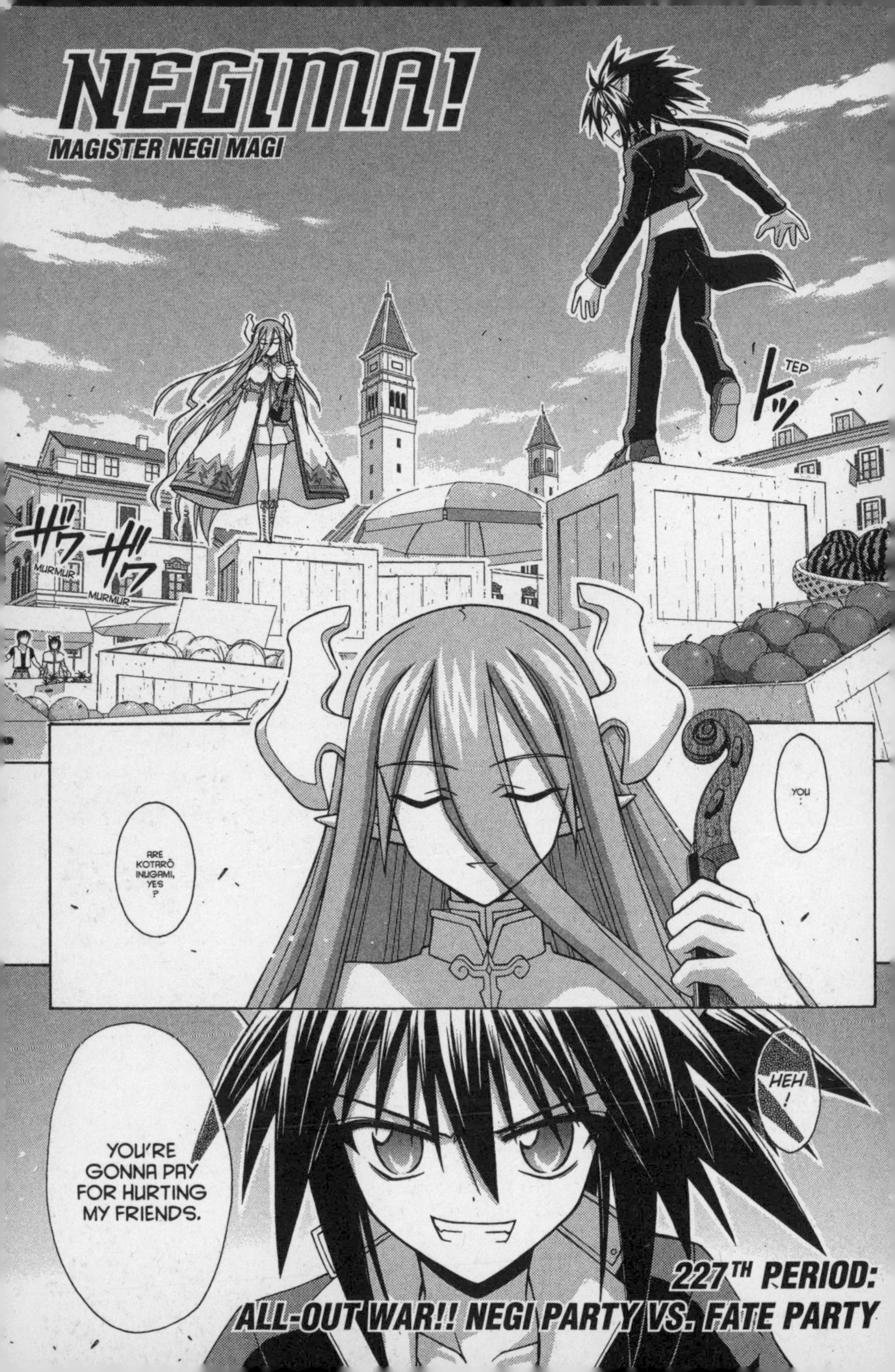
NEGIMA!
MAGISTER NEGI MAGI
TEP
MURMUR
MURMUR
YOU...
ARE KOTARŌ INUGAMI, YES?
HEH!
YOU'RE GONNA PAY FOR HURTING MY FRIENDS.
227TH PERIOD:
ALL-OUT WAR!! NEGI PARTY VS. FATE PARTY

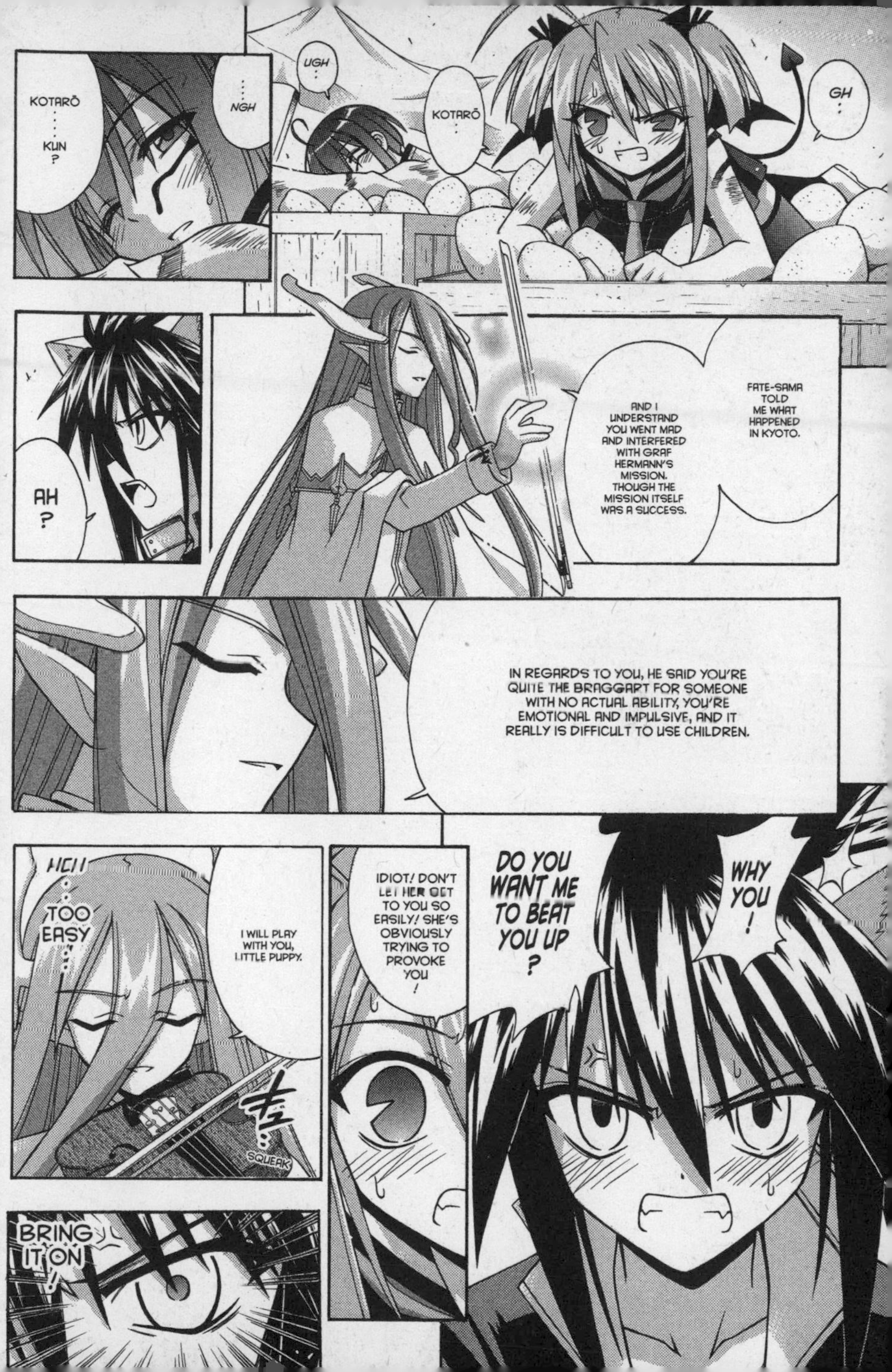

GH...
KOTARŌ...
UGH...
...NGH
KOTARŌ... KUN?
FATE-SAMA TOLD ME WHAT HAPPENED IN KYOTO.
AND I UNDERSTAND YOU WENT MAD AND INTERFERED WITH GRAF HERMANN'S MISSION. THOUGH THE MISSION ITSELF WAS A SUCCESS.
AH?
IN REGARDS TO YOU, HE SAID YOU'RE QUITE THE BRAGGART FOR SOMEONE WITH NO ACTUAL ABILITY, YOU'RE EMOTIONAL AND IMPULSIVE, AND IT REALLY IS DIFFICULT TO USE CHILDREN.
WHY YOU!
DO YOU WANT ME TO BEAT YOU UP?
IDIOT! DON'T LET HER GET TO YOU SO EASILY! SHE'S OBVIOUSLY TRYING TO PROVOKE YOU!
I WILL PLAY WITH YOU, LITTLE PUPPY.
HEH... TOO EASY...
SQUEAK
BRING IT ON!

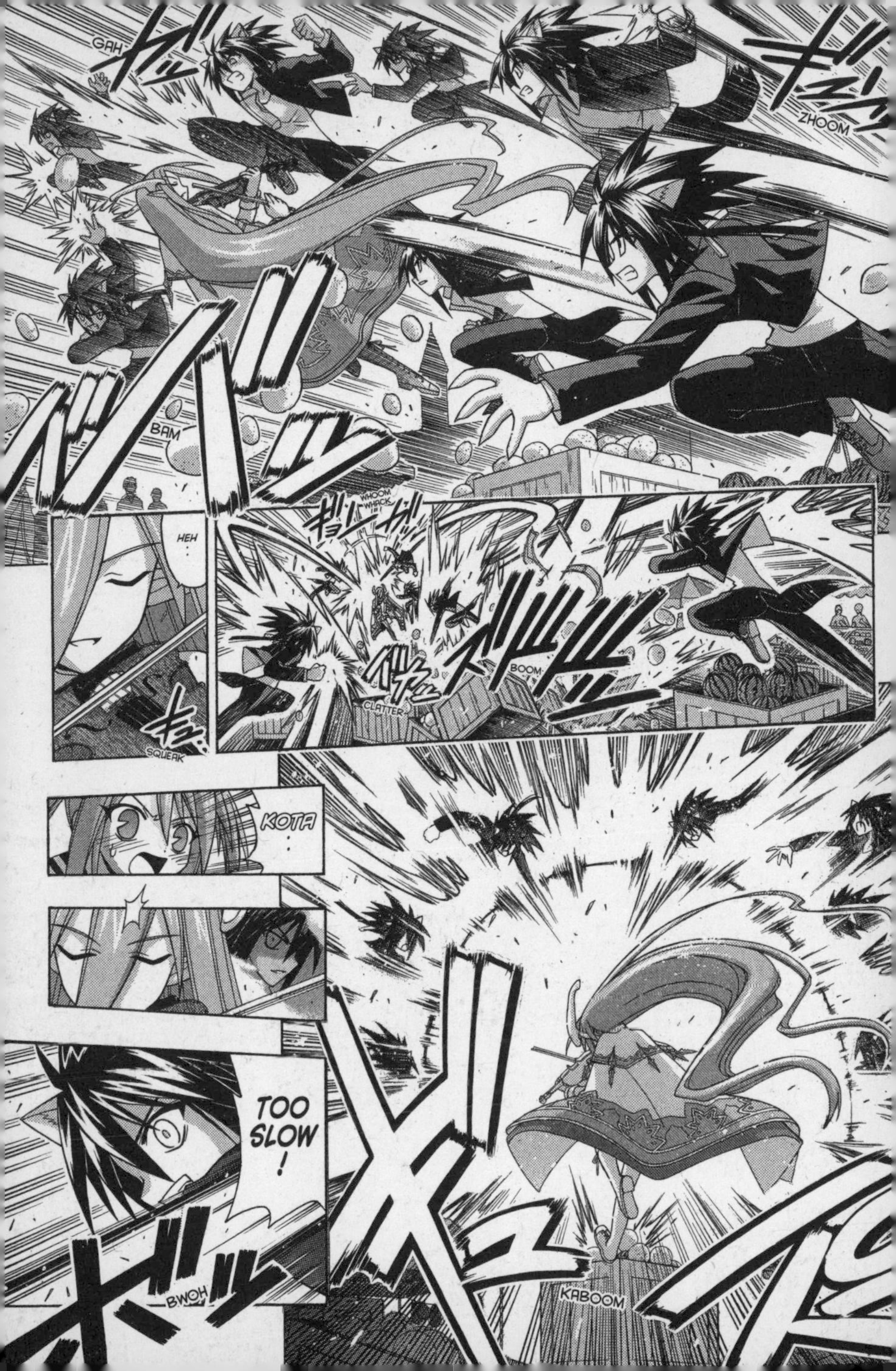
ZHOOM
GAH
BAM
WHOOM
WHACK
BOOM
CLATTER
HEH
...
SQUEAK
KABOOM
KOTA
...
TOO SLOW
!
BWOH

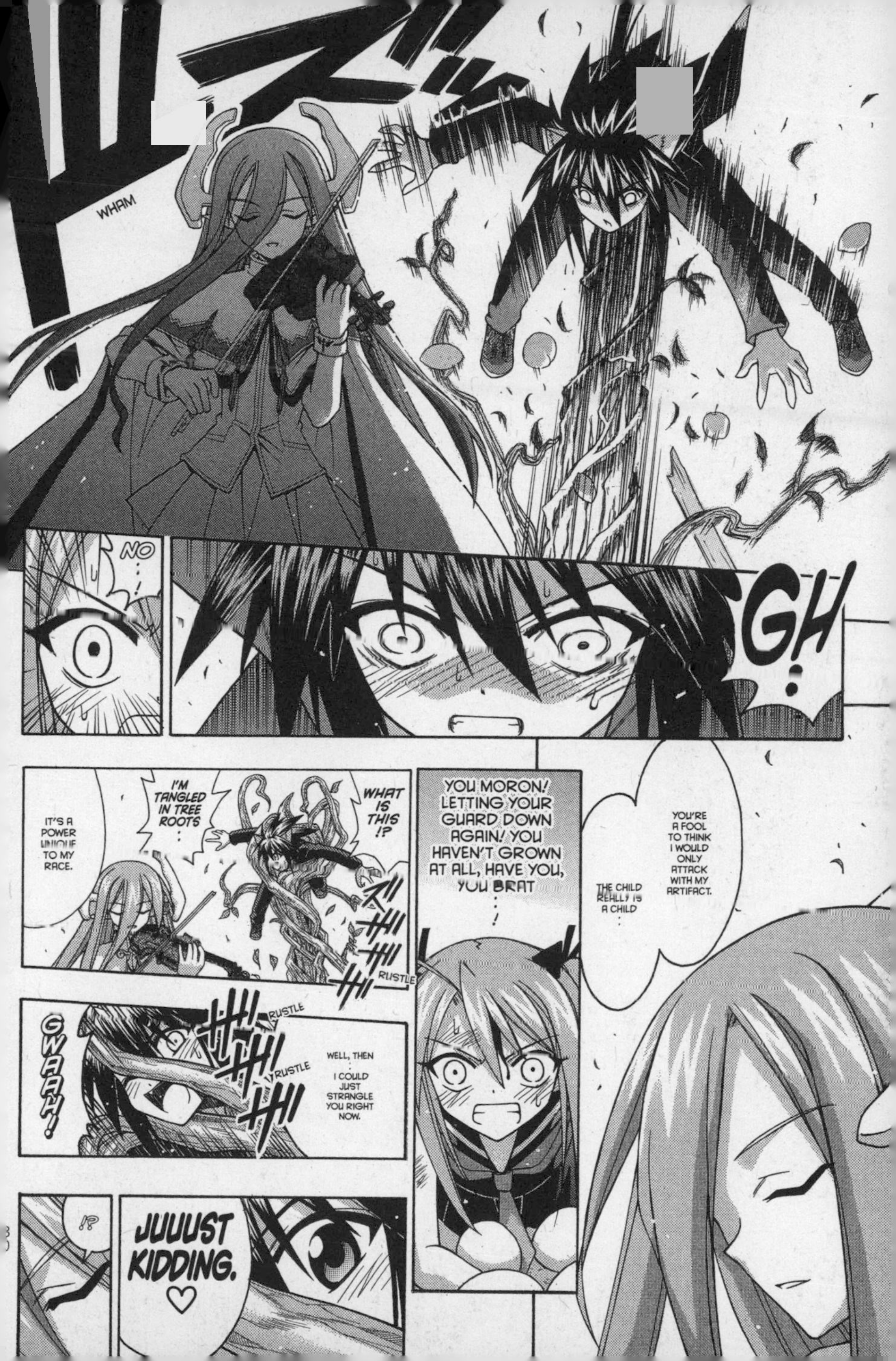
WHAM
GH!
NO...!
YOU'RE A FOOL TO THINK I WOULD ONLY ATTACK WITH MY ARTIFACT.
THE CHILD REALLY IS A CHILD...
YOU MORON! LETTING YOUR GUARD DOWN AGAIN! YOU HAVEN'T GROWN AT ALL, HAVE YOU, YOU BRAT...!
WHAT IS THIS!?
I'M TANGLED IN TREE ROOTS...
IT'S A POWER UNIQUE TO MY RACE.
RUSTLE
WELL, THEN... I COULD JUST STRANGLE YOU RIGHT NOW.
RUSTLE
RUSTLE
GWAAAH!
JUUUST KIDDING. ♥
!?

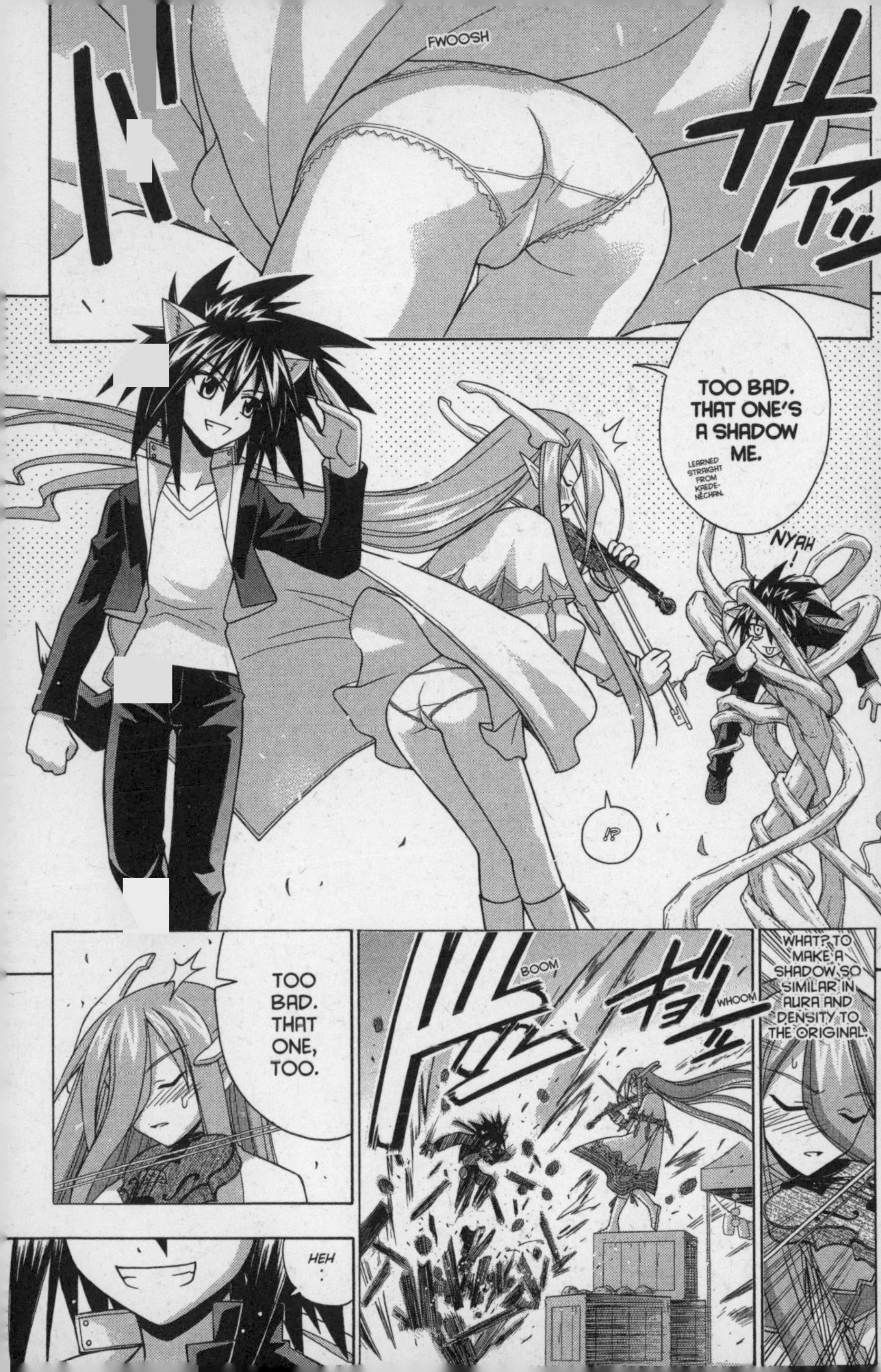
FWOOSH
TOO BAD. THAT ONE'S A SHADOW ME.
LEARNED STRAIGHT FROM KAEDE-NĒCHAN.
NYAH!
!?
WHAT? TO MAKE A SHADOW SO SIMILAR IN AURA AND DENSITY TO THE ORIGINAL.
BOOM
WHOOM
TOO BAD. THAT ONE, TOO.
HEH

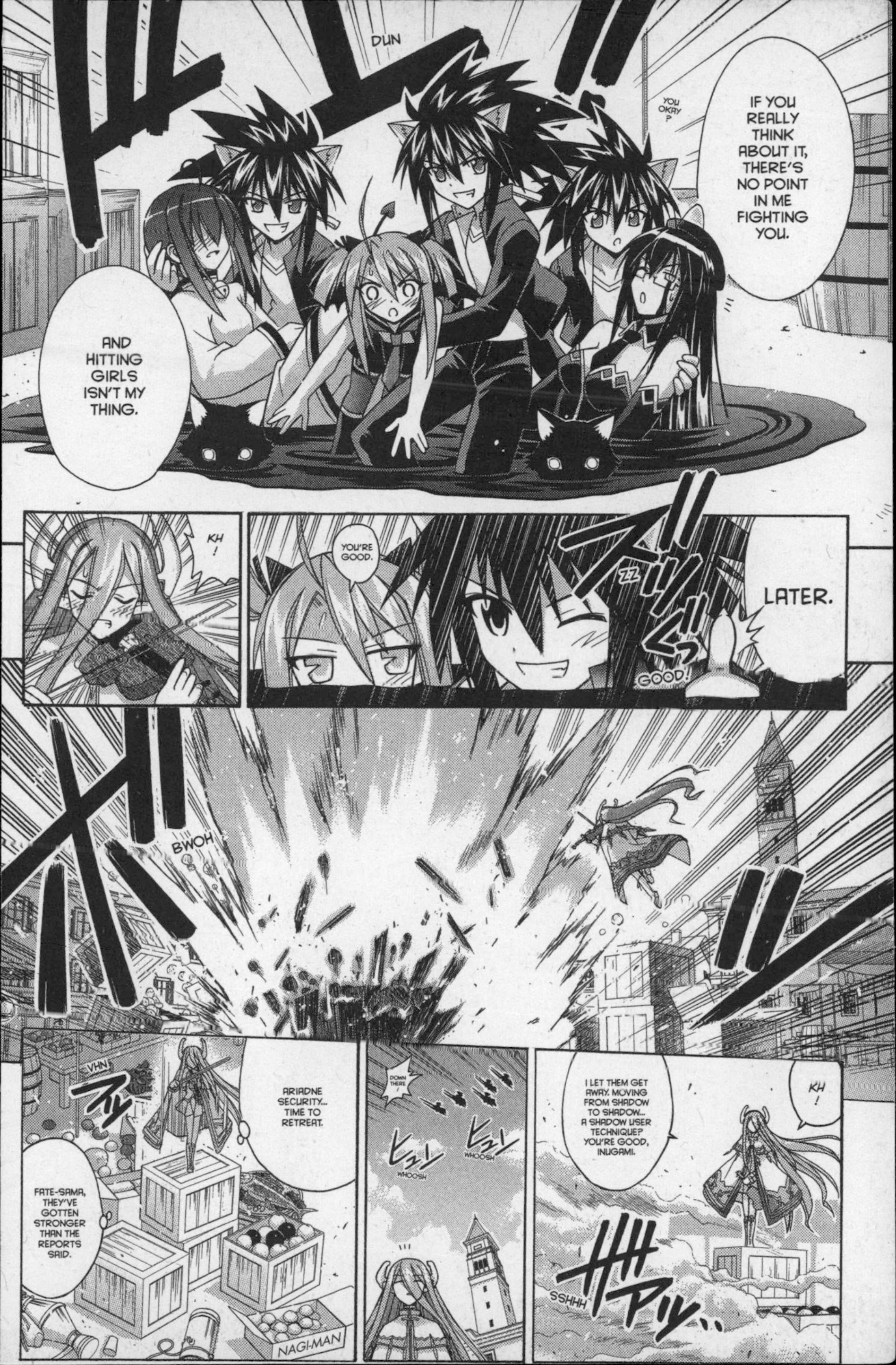
DUN
YOU OKAY?
IF YOU REALLY THINK ABOUT IT, THERE'S NO POINT IN ME FIGHTING YOU.
AND HITTING GIRLS ISN'T MY THING.
YOU'RE GOOD.
LATER.
GOOD!
KH!
BWOH
KH!
I LET THEM GET AWAY. MOVING FROM SHADOW TO SHADOW... A SHADOW USER TECHNIQUE? YOU'RE GOOD, INUGAMI.
SSHHH
DOWN THERE
WHOOSH
WHOOSH
VHN
ARIADNE SECURITY... TIME TO RETREAT.
FATE-SAMA, THEY'VE GOTTEN STRONGER THAN THE REPORTS SAID.
NAGI-MAN

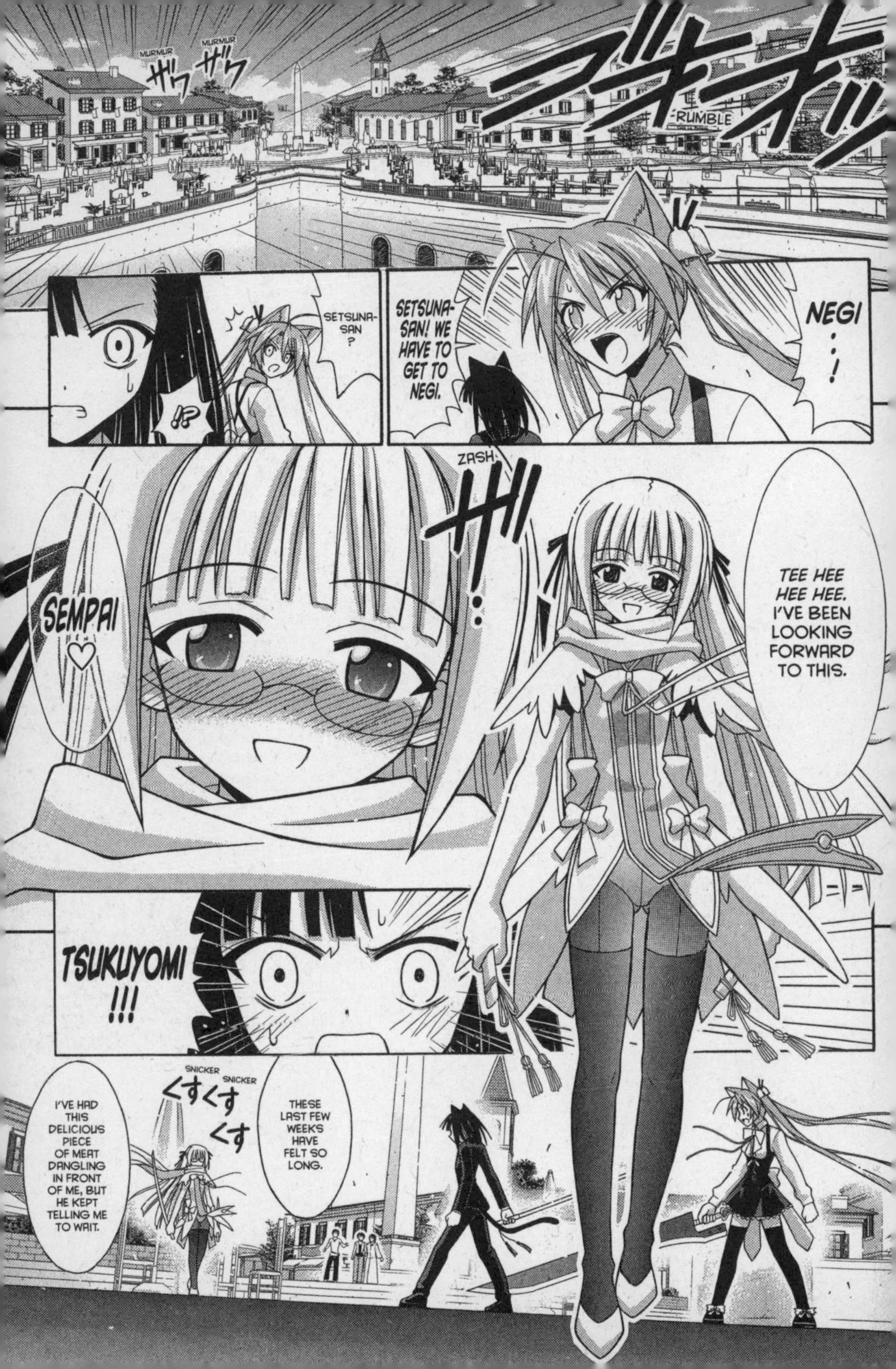

RUMBLE
MURMUR MURMUR
ザワ ザワ
NEGI...!
SETSUNA-SAN! WE HAVE TO GET TO NEGI.
SETSUNA-SAN?
!?
TEE HEE HEE HEE. I'VE BEEN LOOKING FORWARD TO THIS.
ZASH
ザッ
!..
SEMPAI ♥
TSUKUYOMI!!!
THESE LAST FEW WEEKS HAVE FELT SO LONG.
SNICKER SNICKER
くすくす くす
I'VE HAD THIS DELICIOUS PIECE OF MEAT DANGLING IN FRONT OF ME, BUT HE KEPT TELLING ME TO WAIT.

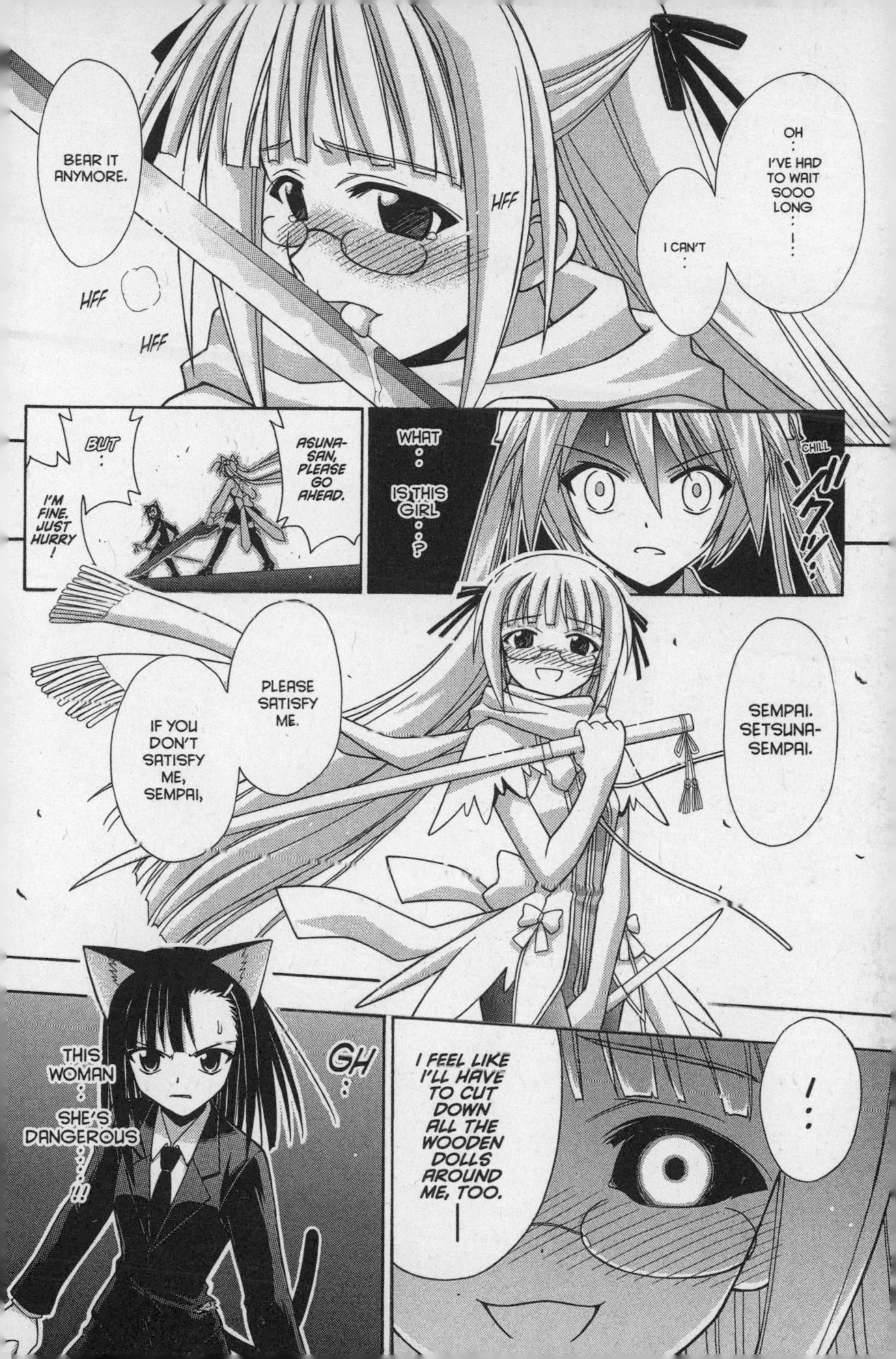

OH... I'VE HAD TO WAIT SOOO LONG......
I CAN'T...
BEAR IT ANYMORE.
HFF
HFF
HFF
CHILL
WHAT.. IS THIS GIRL...?
ASUNA-SAN, PLEASE GO AHEAD.
BUT...
I'M FINE. JUST HURRY!
SEMPAI. SETSUNA-SEMPAI.
PLEASE SATISFY ME.
IF YOU DON'T SATISFY ME, SEMPAI,
!..
I FEEL LIKE I'LL HAVE TO CUT DOWN ALL THE WOODEN DOLLS AROUND ME, TOO. —
GH..
THIS WOMAN.. SHE'S DANGEROUS...!!

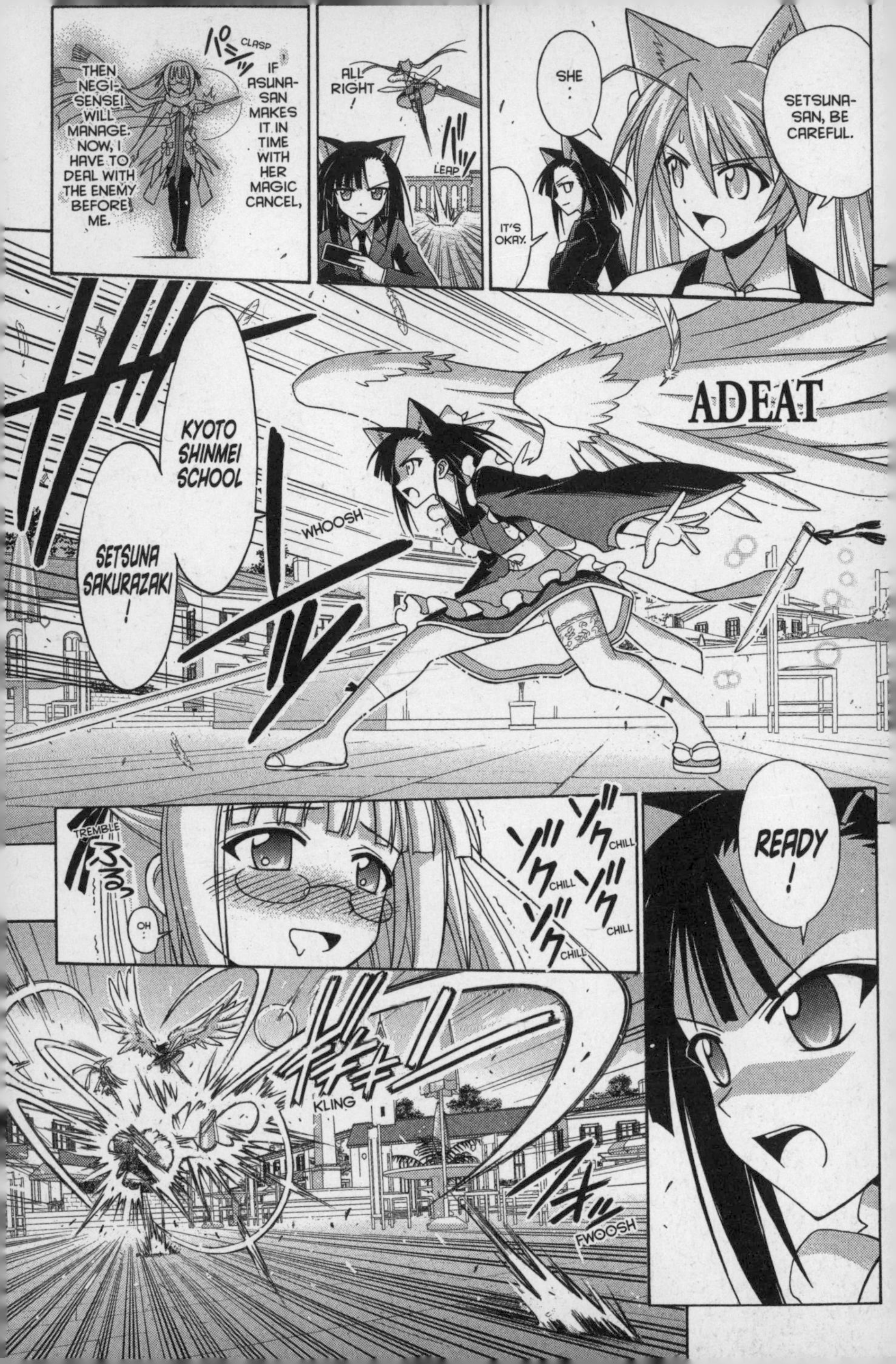
SETSUNA-SAN, BE CAREFUL.
SHE :
IT'S OKAY.
ALL RIGHT!
IF ASUNA-SAN MAKES IT IN TIME WITH HER MAGIC CANCEL,
LEAP
CLASP
THEN NEGI-SENSEI WILL MANAGE. NOW, I HAVE TO DEAL WITH THE ENEMY BEFORE ME.
ADEAT
KYOTO SHINMEI SCHOOL
SETSUNA SAKURAZAKI!
WHOOSH
READY!
CHILL
CHILL
CHILL
CHILL
TREMBLE
OH :
KLING
FWOOSH

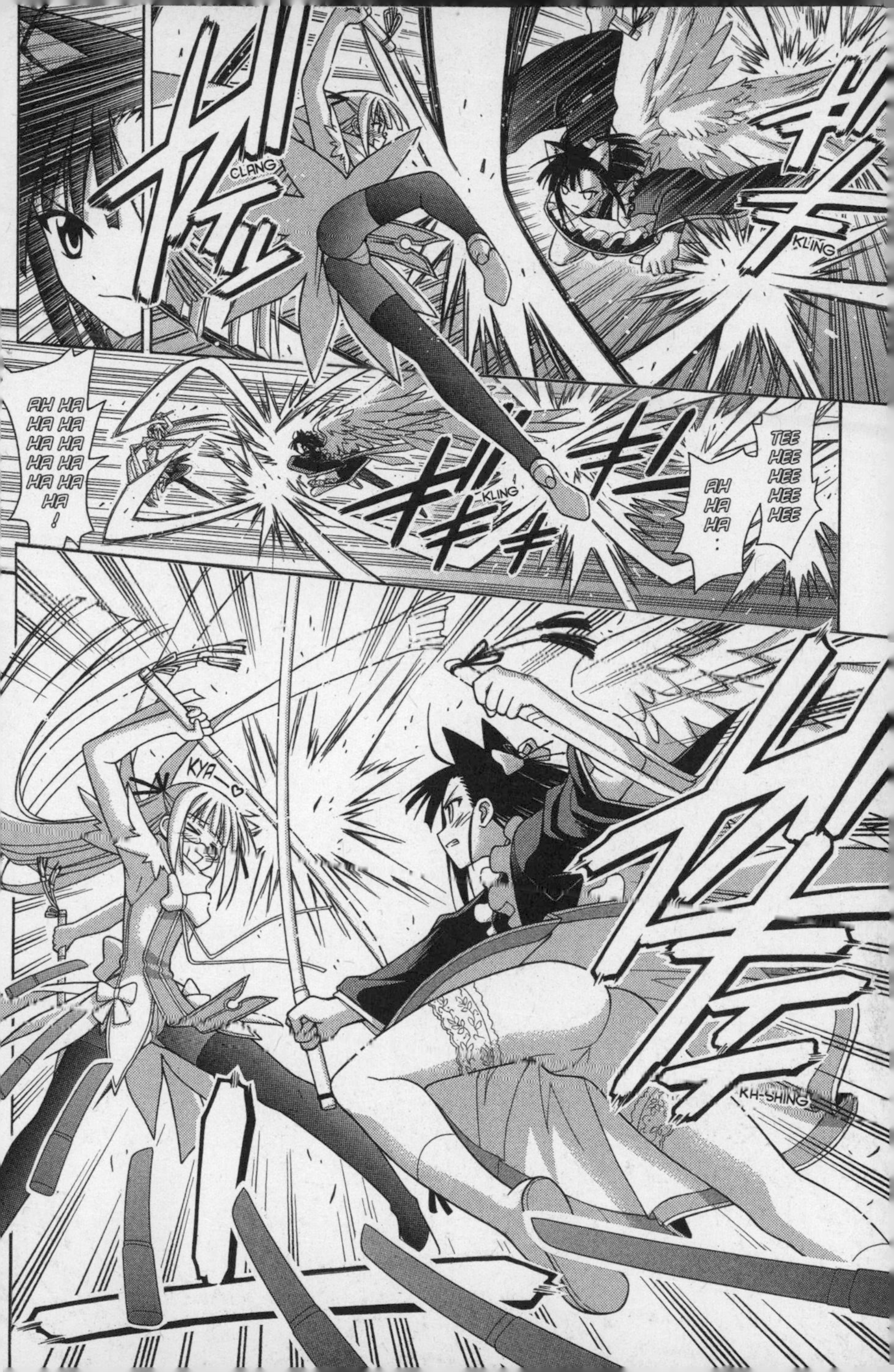
KLING
CLANG
TEE HEE HEE HEE HEE
AH HA HA...
KLING
AH HA HA HA HA HA HA HA HA HA HA!
KH-SHING
KYA—♡

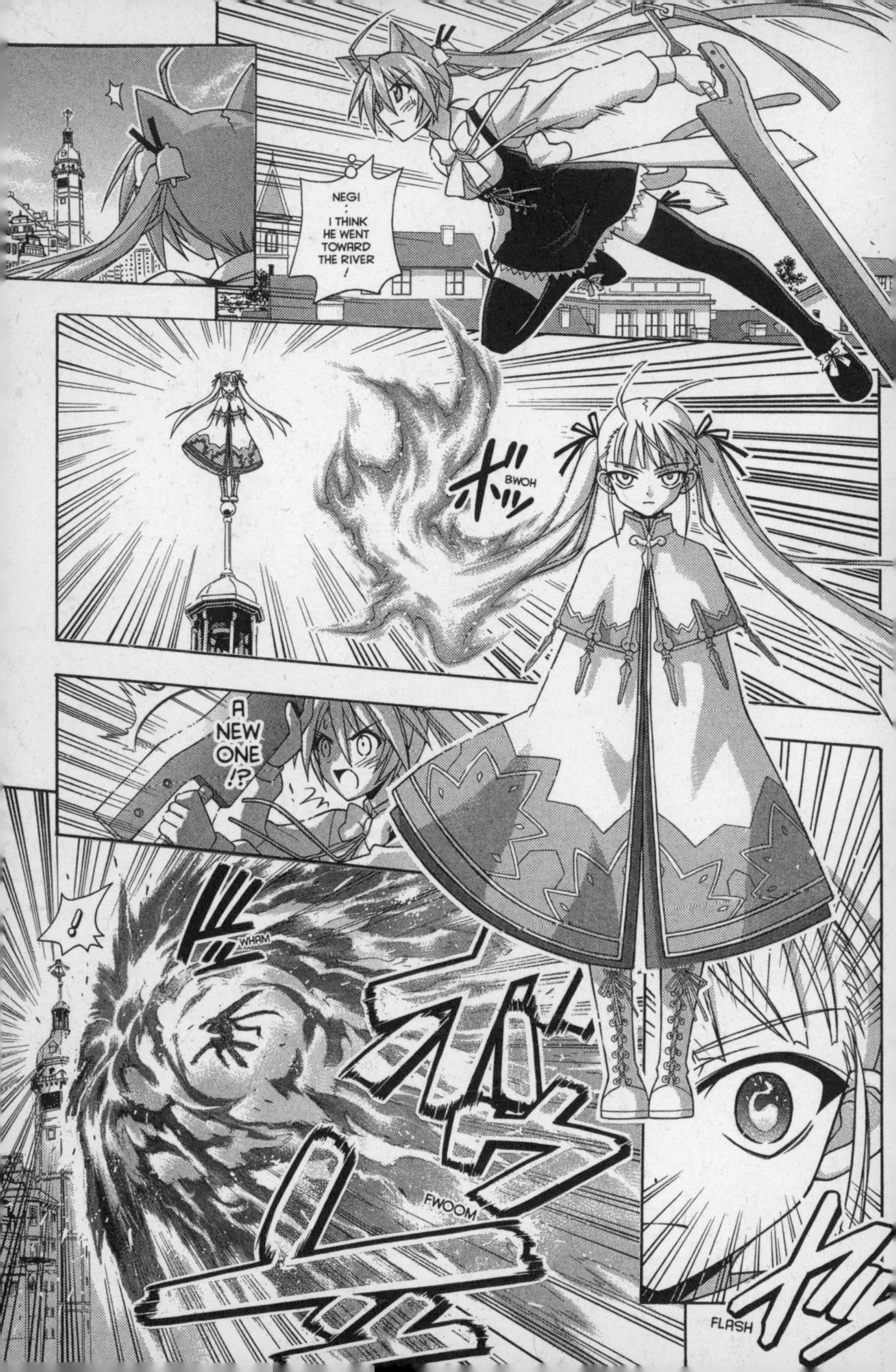
NEGI : I THINK HE WENT TOWARD THE RIVER !
ボッ
BWOH
A NEW ONE !?
FLASH
WHAM
!
FWOOM

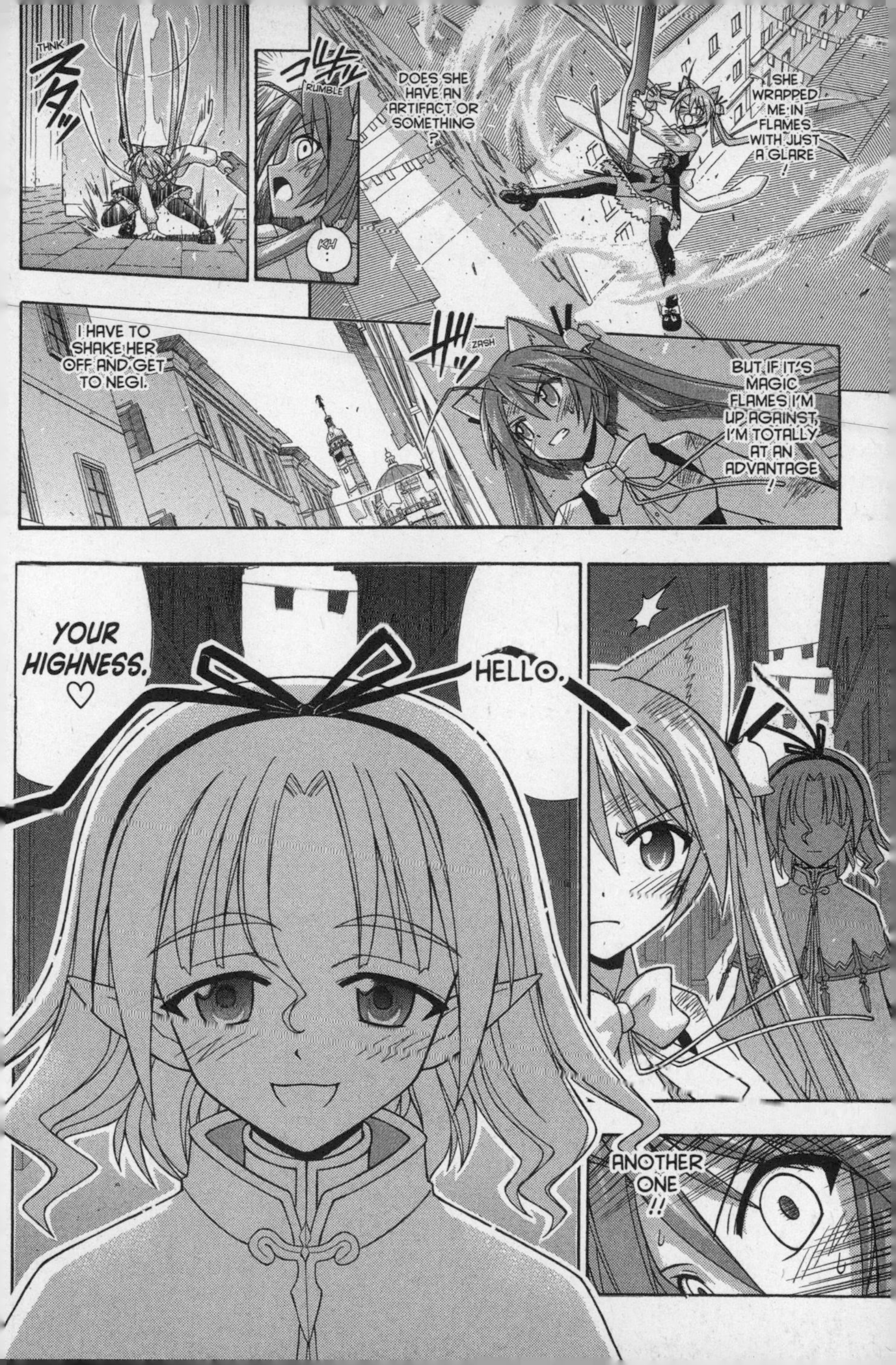

SHE WRAPPED ME IN FLAMES WITH JUST A GLARE!
DOES SHE HAVE AN ARTIFACT OR SOMETHING?
RUMBLE
KH...
THNK
BUT IF IT'S MAGIC FLAMES I'M UP AGAINST, I'M TOTALLY AT AN ADVANTAGE!
ZASH
I HAVE TO SHAKE HER OFF AND GET TO NEGI.
ANOTHER ONE!!
HELLO.
YOUR HIGHNESS. ♡

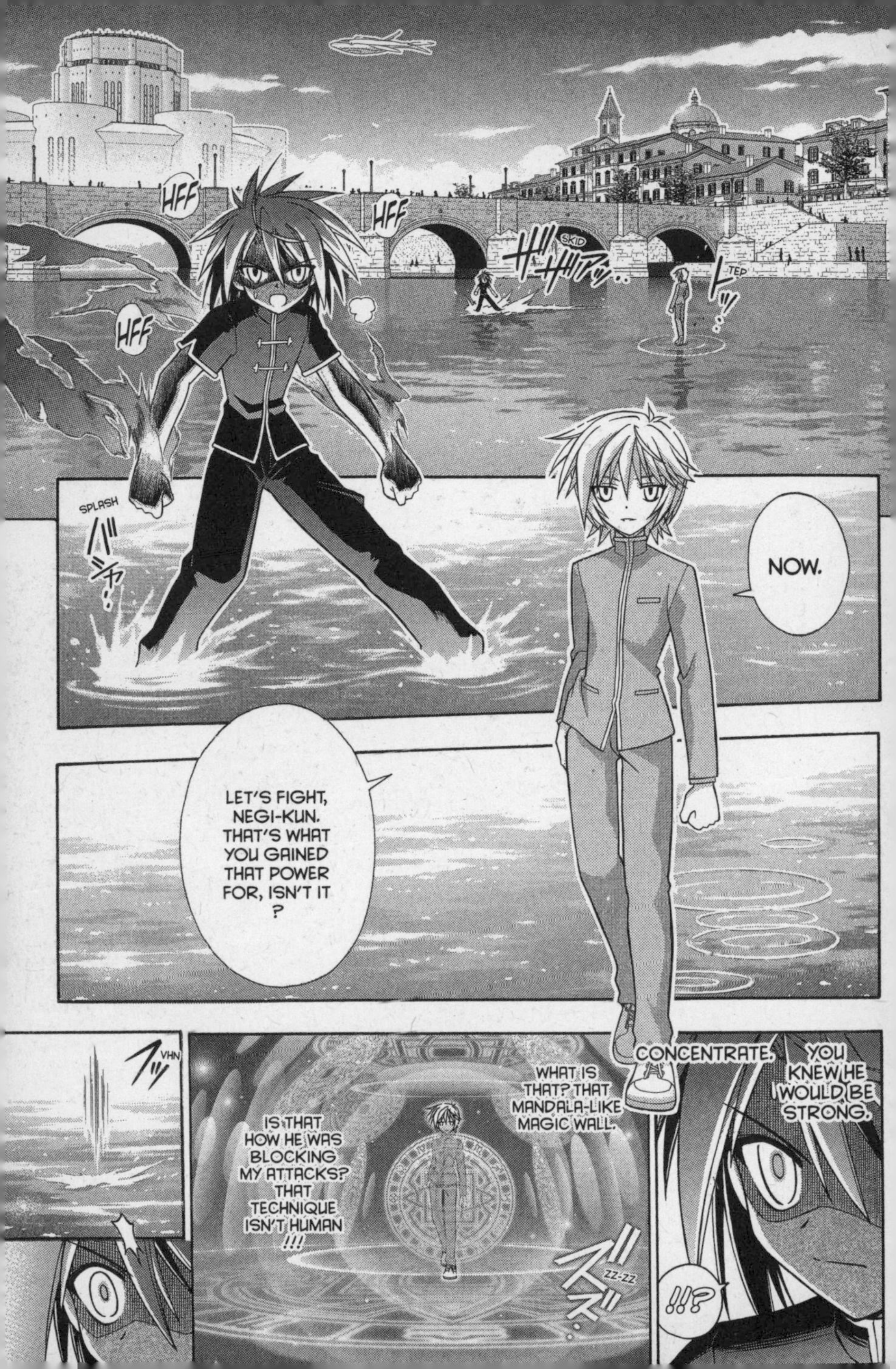
TEP
SKID
HFF
HFF
HFF
SPLASH
NOW.
LET'S FIGHT, NEGI-KUN. THAT'S WHAT YOU GAINED THAT POWER FOR, ISN'T IT?
CONCENTRATE.
YOU KNEW HE WOULD BE STRONG.
!!?
WHAT IS THAT? THAT MANDALA-LIKE MAGIC WALL.
ZZ-ZZ
IS THAT HOW HE WAS BLOCKING MY ATTACKS? THAT TECHNIQUE ISN'T HUMAN!!!
VHN

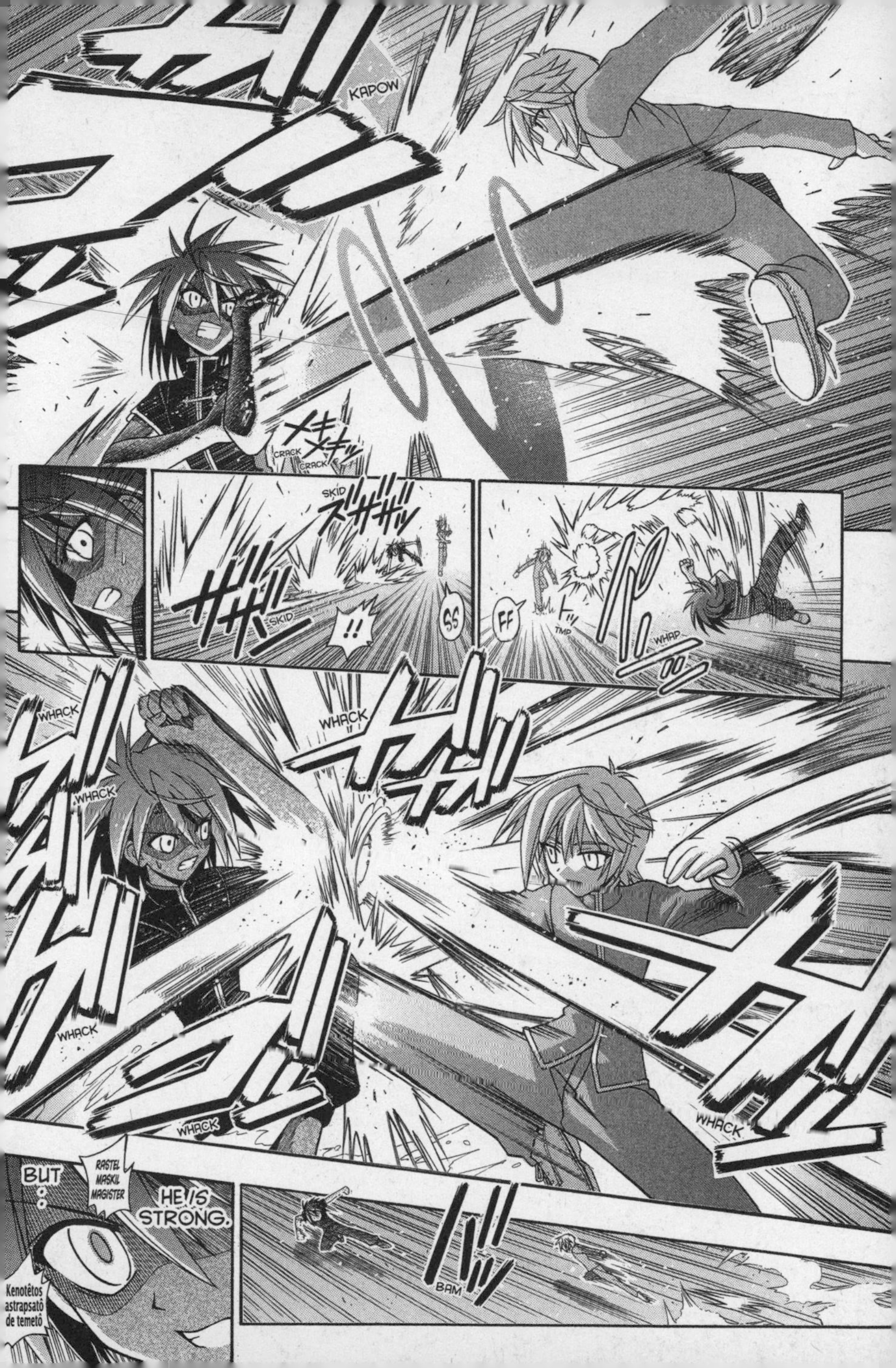
KAPOW
CRACK
CRACK
WHAP
TMP
FF
SS
SKID
!!
SKID
WHACK
WHACK
WHACK
WHACK
WHACK
WHACK
BAM
HE IS STRONG.
RASTEL MASKIL MAGISTER
BUT...
Kenotêtos astrapsatô de temetô

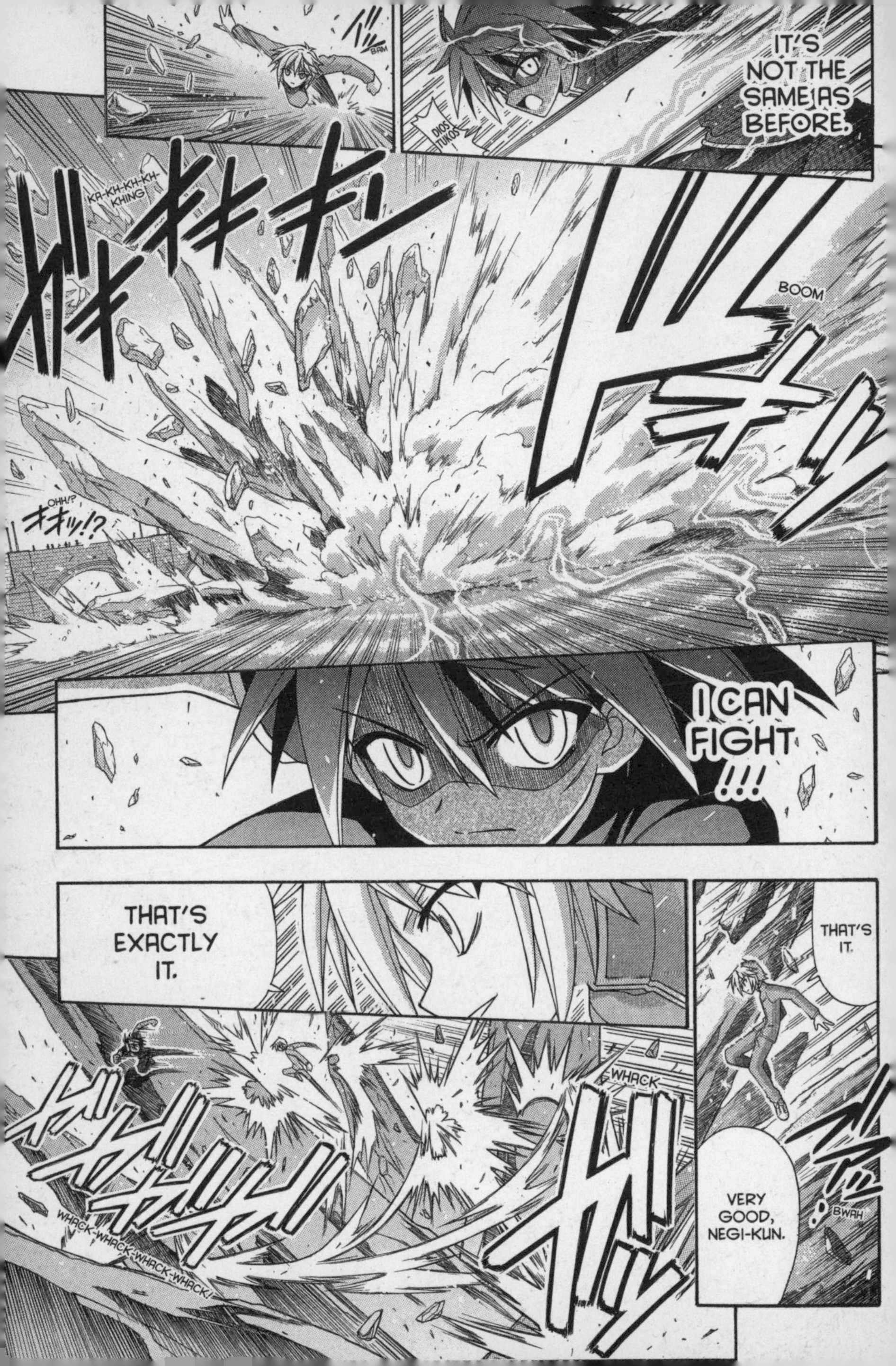

IT'S NOT THE SAME AS BEFORE.
DIOS TUKOS
BAM
BOOM
KA-KH-KH-KH-KHING
OHH!?
I CAN FIGHT !!!
THAT'S IT.
BWAH
VERY GOOD, NEGI-KUN.
THAT'S EXACTLY IT.
WHACK
WHACK-WHACK-WHACK-WHACK!

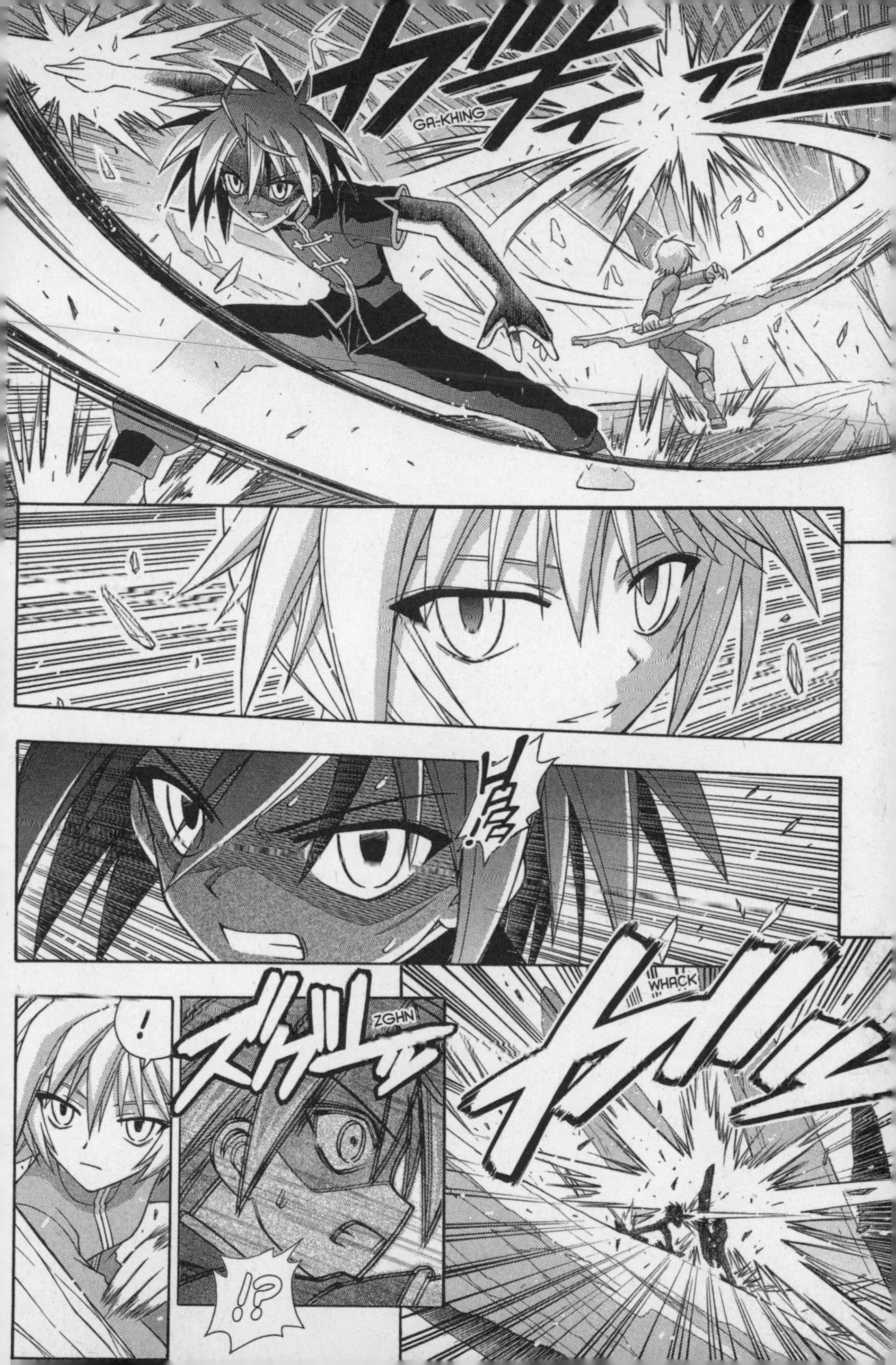
GA-KHING
WHACK
ZGHN
!?
!

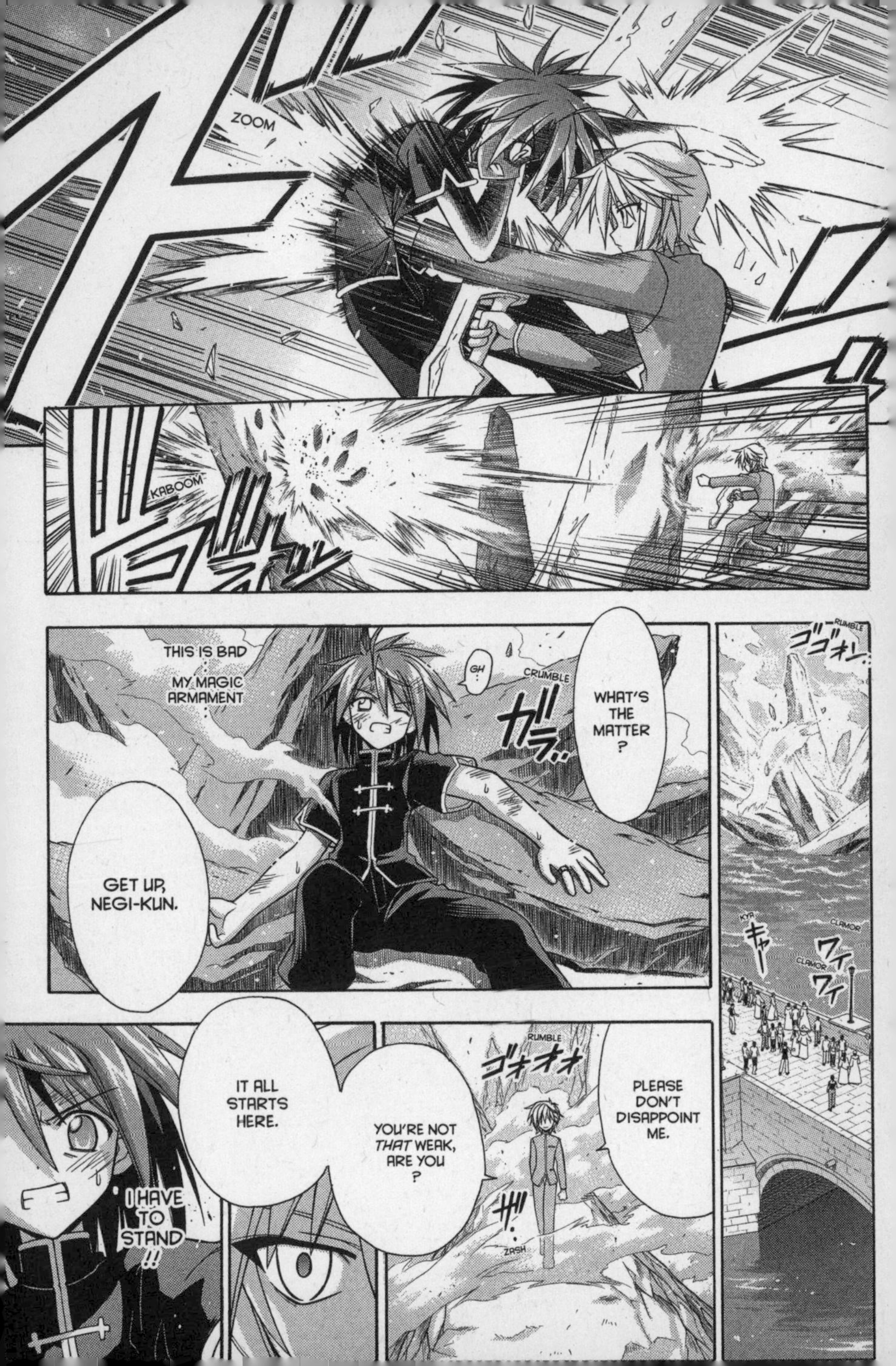
ZOOM
KABOOM
RUMBLE
KYA
CLAMOR
CLAMOR
WHAT'S THE MATTER ?
CRUMBLE
GH...
THIS IS BAD... MY MAGIC ARMAMENT...
GET UP, NEGI-KUN.
PLEASE DON'T DISAPPOINT ME.
RUMBLE
ZASH
YOU'RE NOT *THAT* WEAK, ARE YOU ?
IT ALL STARTS HERE.
I HAVE TO STAND !!

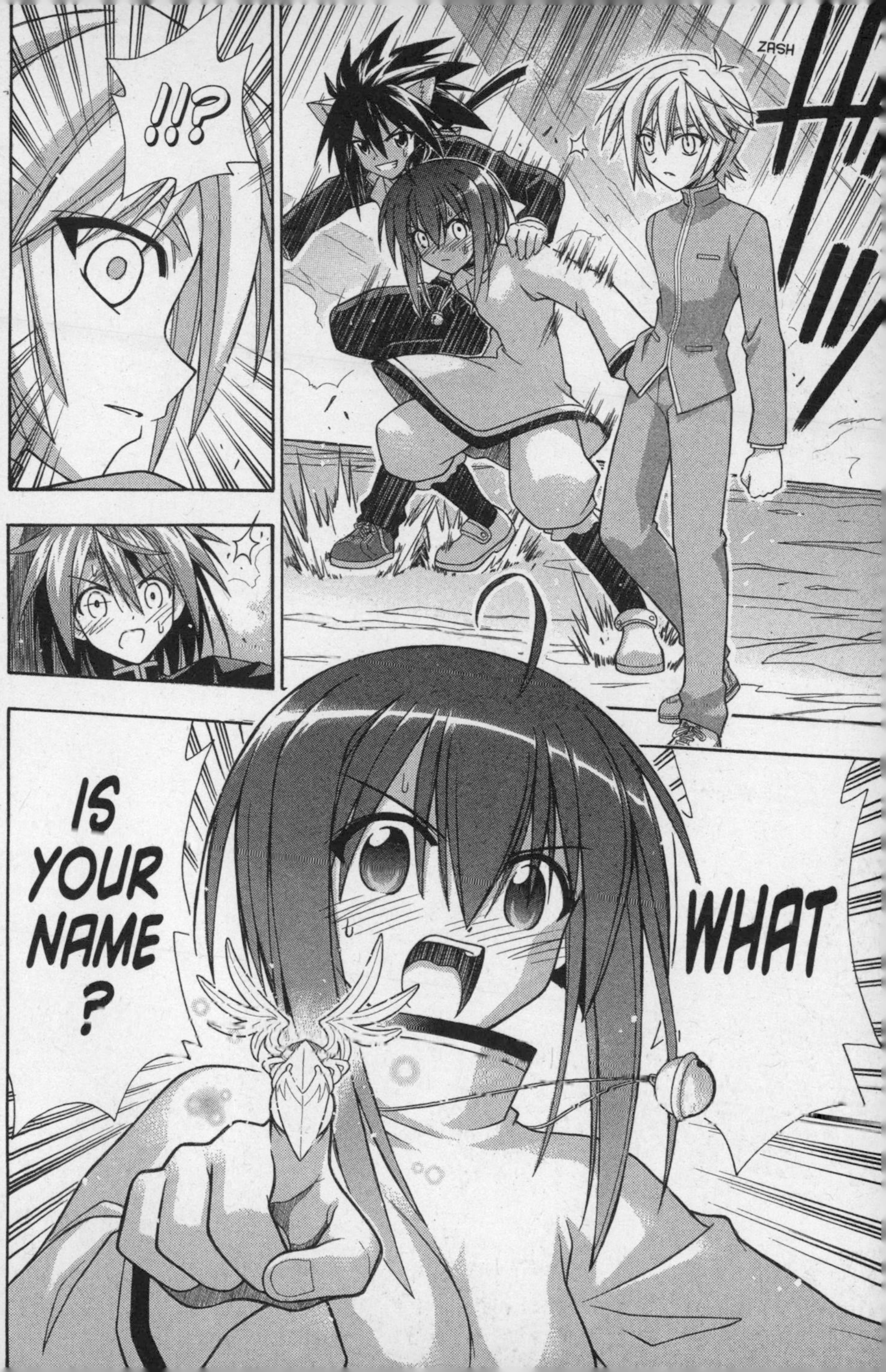
ZASH
!!?
WHAT
IS YOUR NAME ?

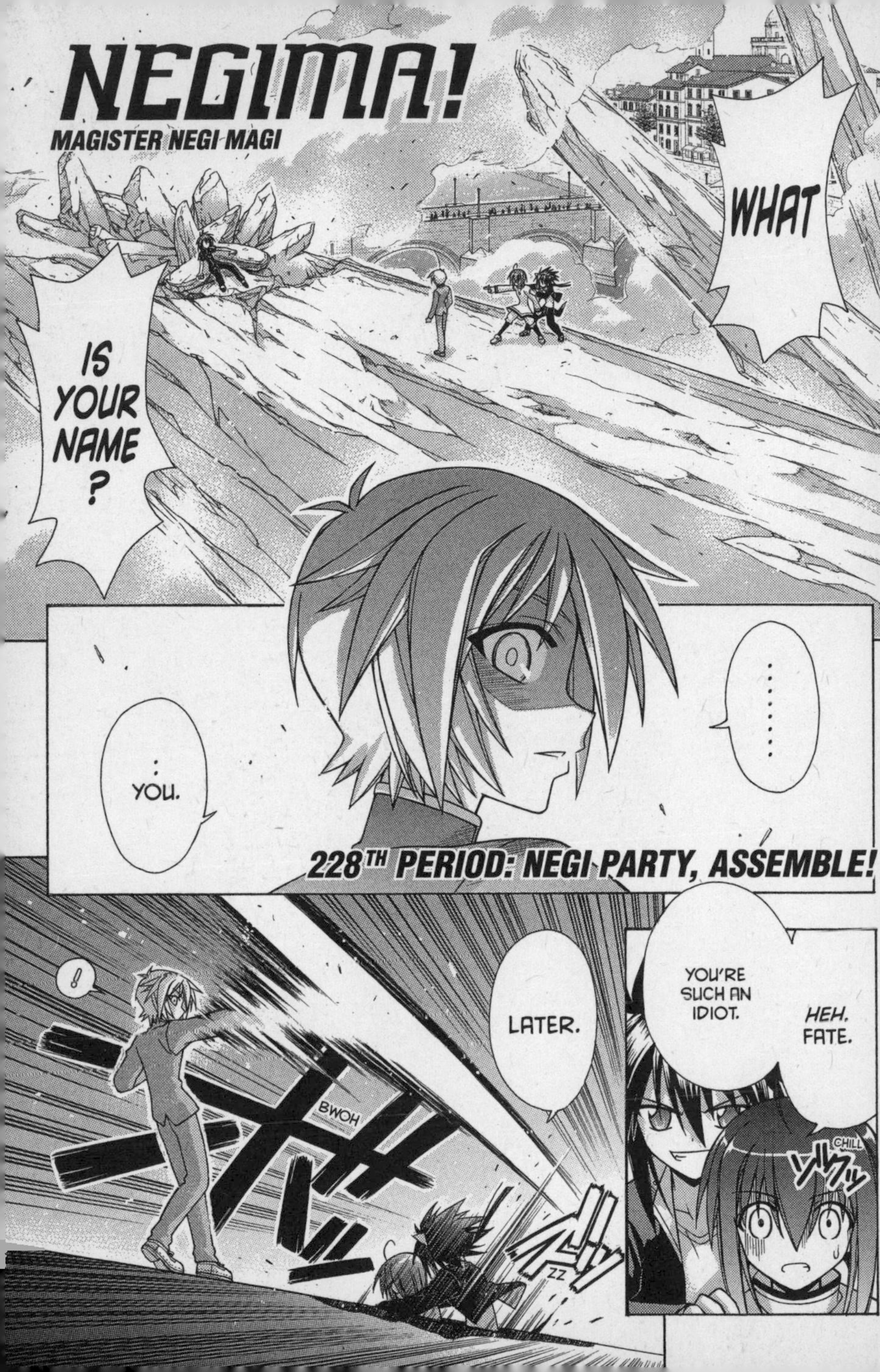
NEGIMA!
MAGISTER NEGI MAGI
WHAT
IS YOUR NAME ?
......
: YOU.
228TH PERIOD: NEGI PARTY, ASSEMBLE!
HEH. FATE.
YOU'RE SUCH AN IDIOT.
CHILL
LATER.
!
BWOH
ZZ

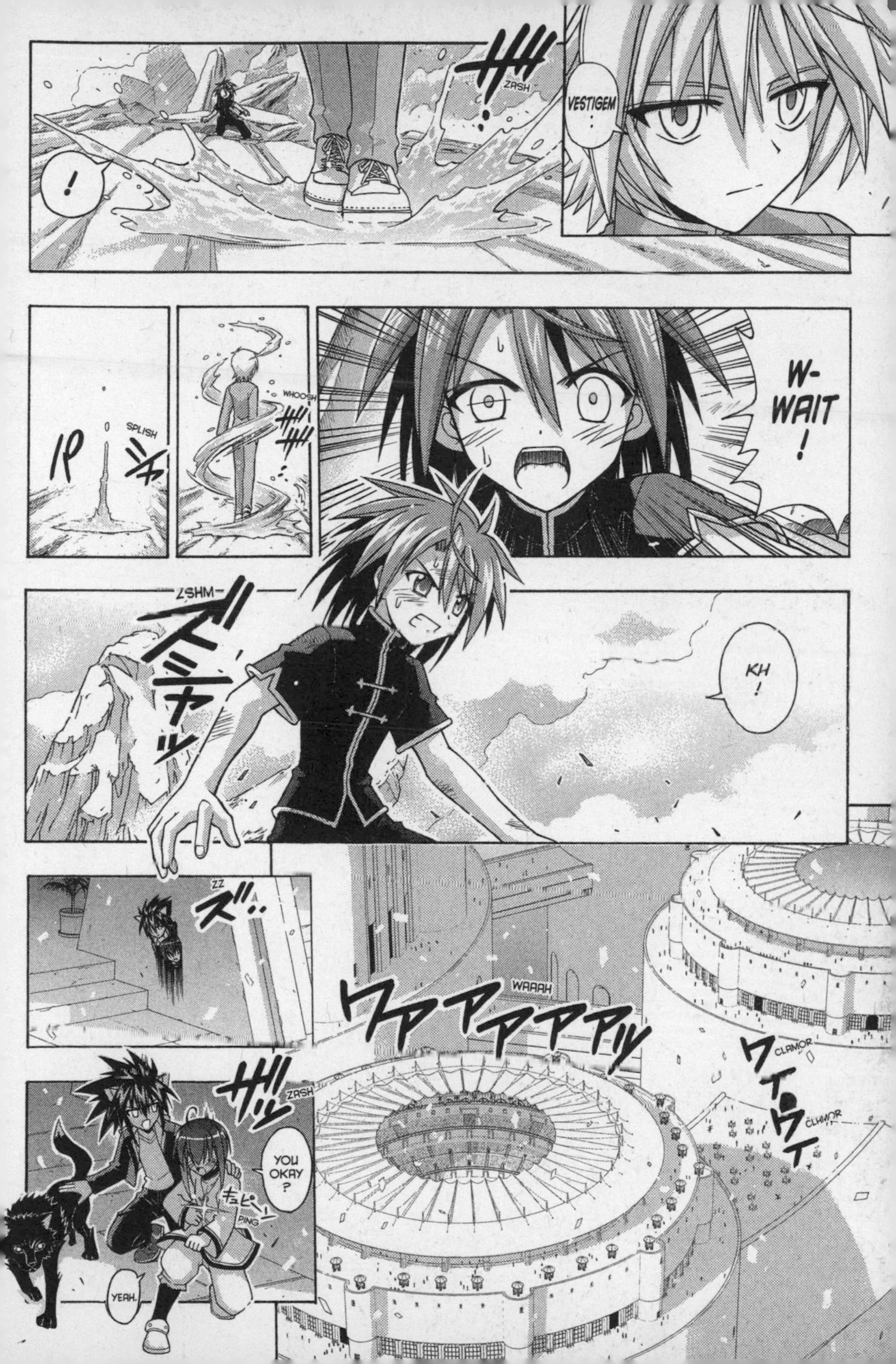

VESTIGEM...
ZASH
!
W-WAIT!
WHOOSH
SPLISH
ZSHM
KH!
WAAAH
CLAMOR
CLAMOR
ZZ
ZASH
YOU OKAY?
PING
YEAH.

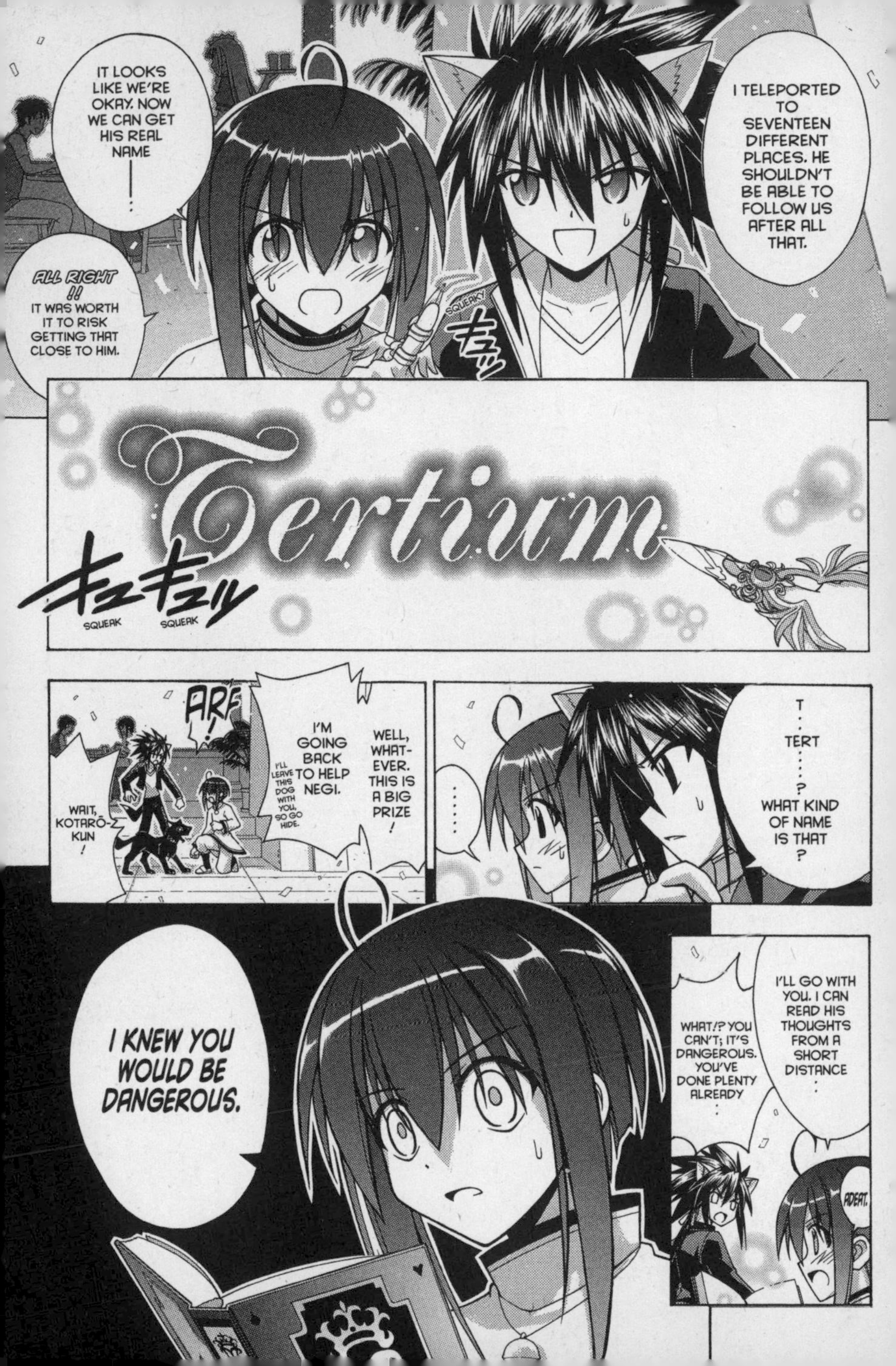
I TELEPORTED TO SEVENTEEN DIFFERENT PLACES. HE SHOULDN'T BE ABLE TO FOLLOW US AFTER ALL THAT.
IT LOOKS LIKE WE'RE OKAY. NOW WE CAN GET HIS REAL NAME
...
SQUEAKY
ALL RIGHT!! IT WAS WORTH IT TO RISK GETTING THAT CLOSE TO HIM.
Tertium
SQUEAK SQUEAK
T... TERT.....? WHAT KIND OF NAME IS THAT?
......
WELL, WHAT-EVER. THIS IS A BIG PRIZE!
I'M GOING BACK TO HELP NEGI.
I'LL LEAVE THIS DOG WITH YOU, SO GO HIDE.
ARF!
WAIT, KOTARŌ-KUN!
I'LL GO WITH YOU. I CAN READ HIS THOUGHTS FROM A SHORT DISTANCE...
WHAT!? YOU CAN'T; IT'S DANGEROUS. YOU'VE DONE PLENTY ALREADY...
ADEAT.
I KNEW YOU WOULD BE DANGEROUS.

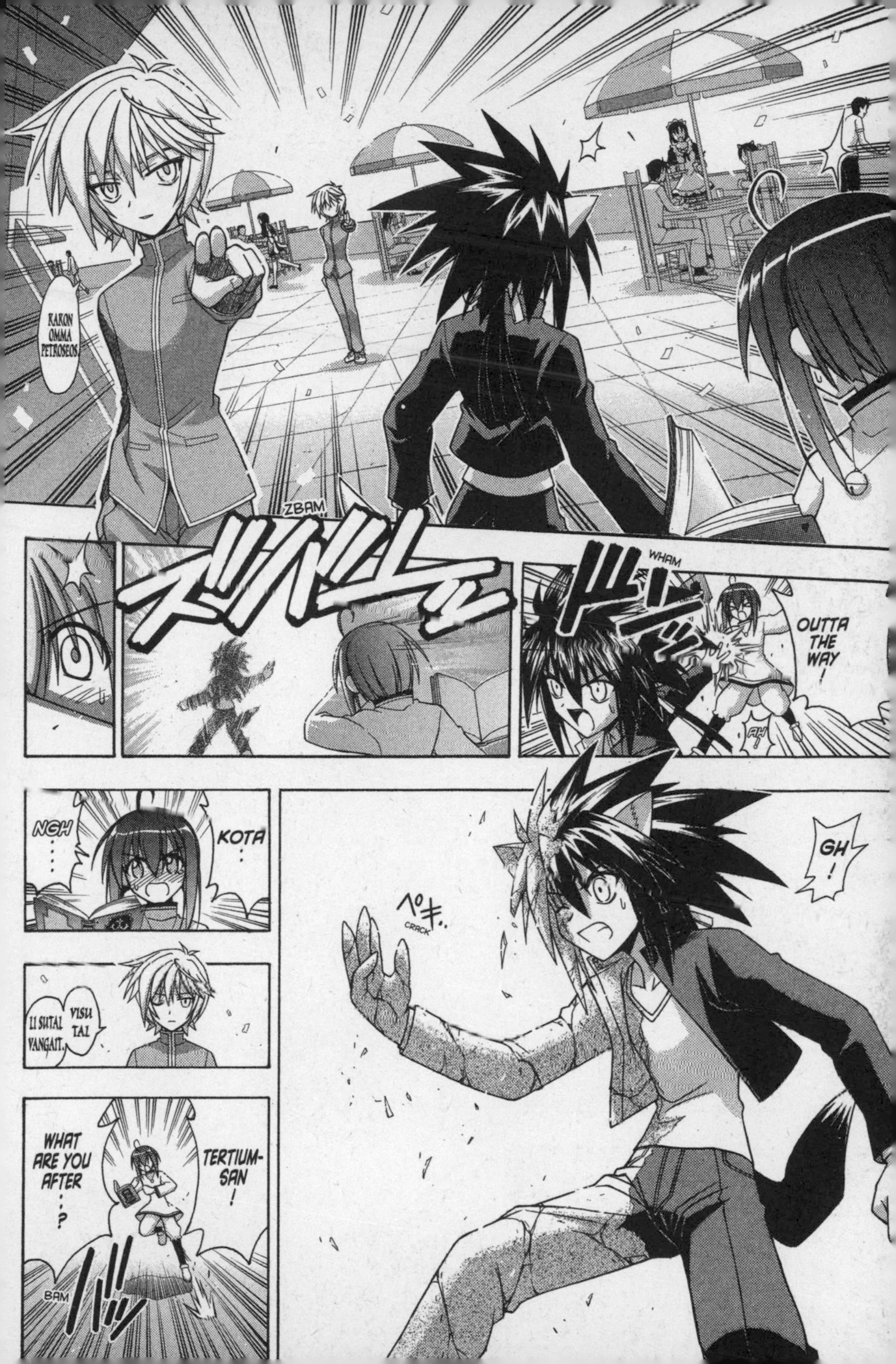
KARON OMMA PETROSEOS
WHAM
OUTTA THE WAY!
AH!
ZBAM
GH!
ペキ
CRACK
KOTA...
NGH...
VISU TAI
LI SUTAL VANGAIT.
TERTIUM-SAN!
WHAT ARE YOU AFTER...?
BAM

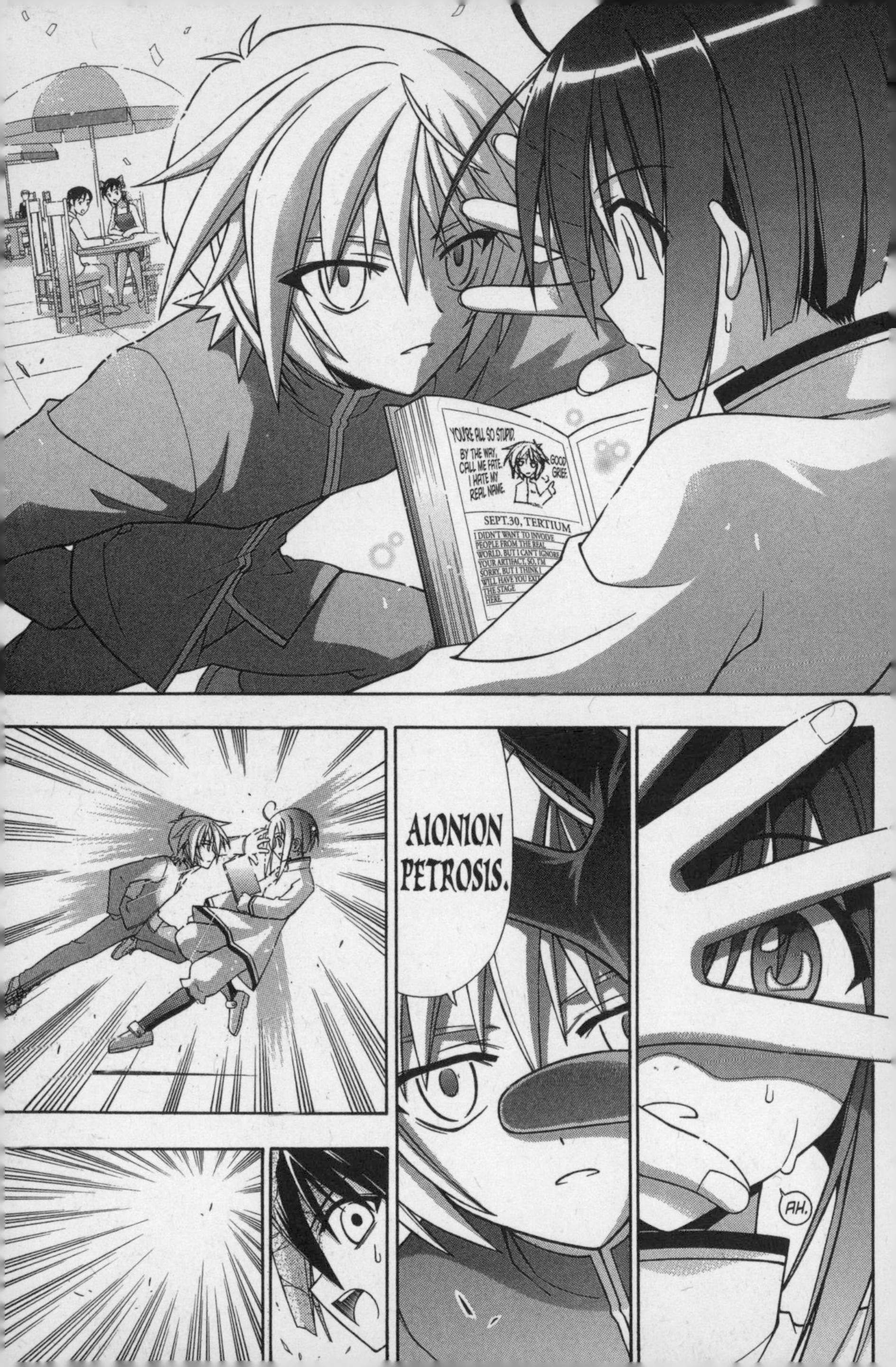
YOU'RE ALL SO STUPID.
BY THE WAY, CALL ME FATE. I HATE MY REAL NAME.
GOOD GRIEF.
SEPT.30, TERTIUM
I DIDN'T WANT TO INVOLVE PEOPLE FROM THE REAL WORLD, BUT I CAN'T IGNORE YOUR ARTIFACT, SO, I'M SORRY, BUT I THINK I WILL HAVE YOU EXI THE STAGE HERE.
AH.
AIONION PETROSIS.

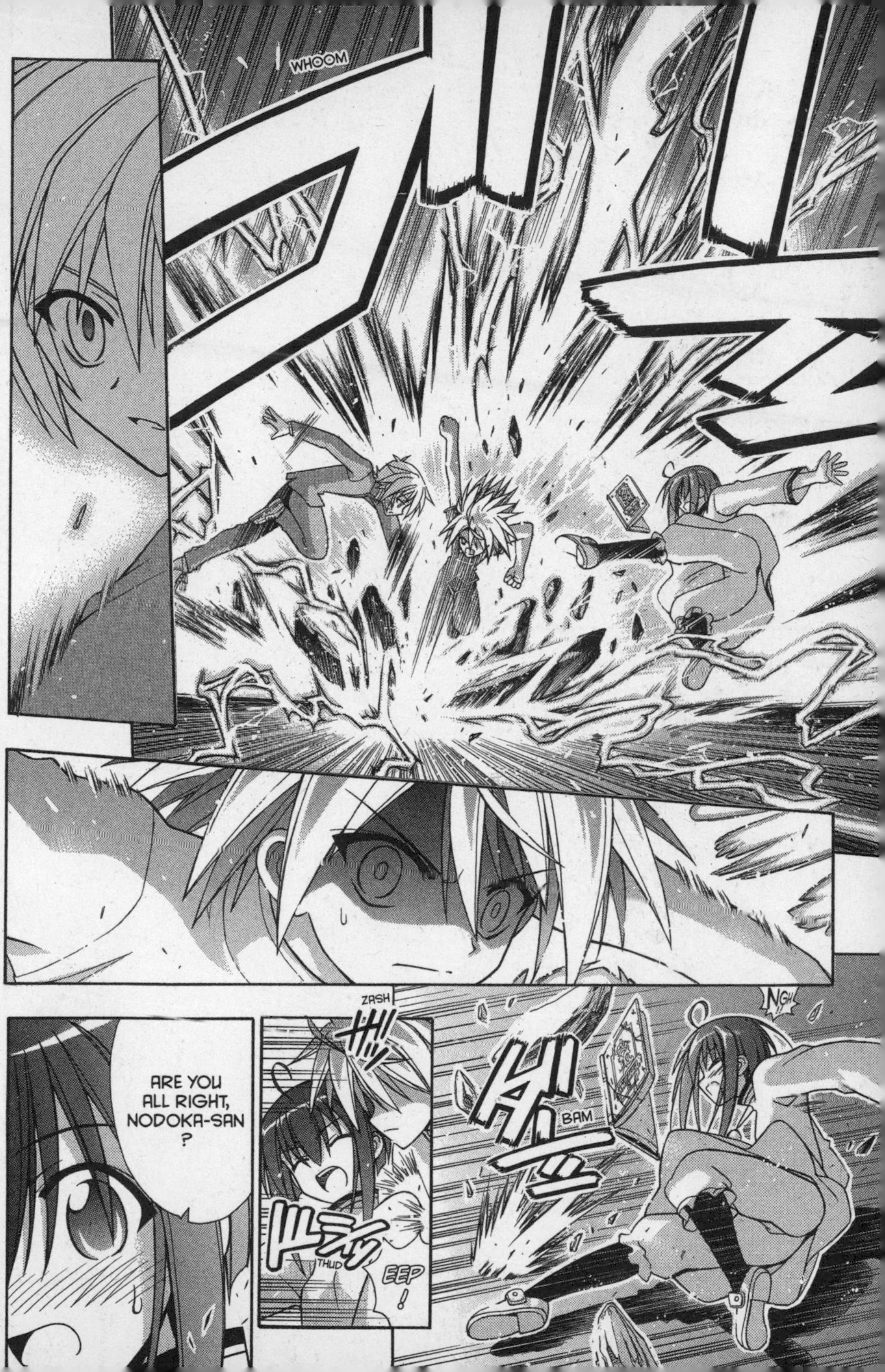
WHOOM
NGH
BAM
ZASH
ARE YOU ALL RIGHT, NODOKA-SAN ?
THUD
EEP !

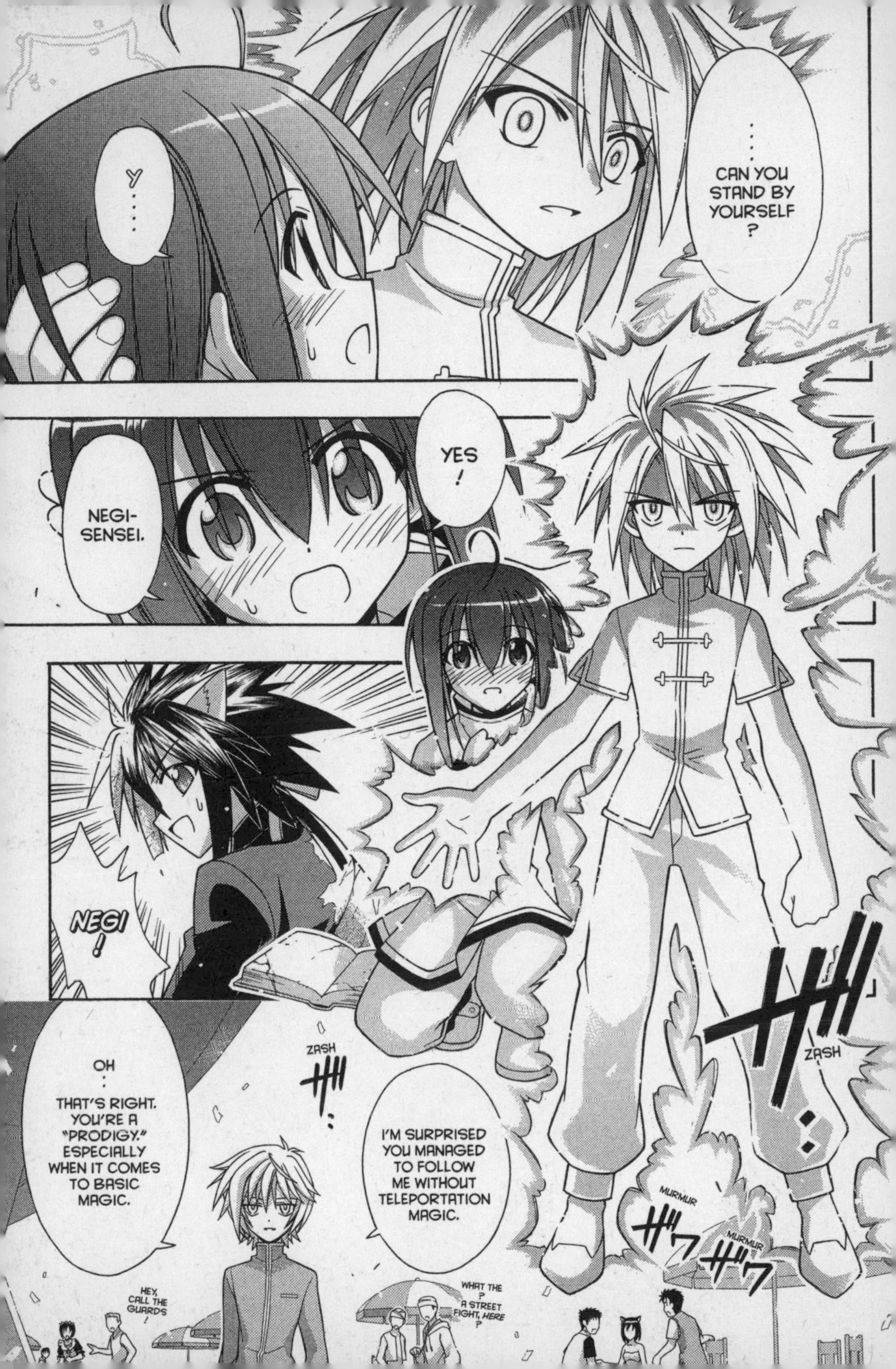

... CAN YOU STAND BY YOURSELF?
Y....
YES!
NEGI-SENSEI.
NEGI!
ZASH
I'M SURPRISED YOU MANAGED TO FOLLOW ME WITHOUT TELEPORTATION MAGIC.
ZASH
OH: THAT'S RIGHT. YOU'RE A "PRODIGY." ESPECIALLY WHEN IT COMES TO BASIC MAGIC.
MURMUR
MURMUR
WHAT THE? A STREET FIGHT, HERE?
HEY, CALL THE GUARDS!

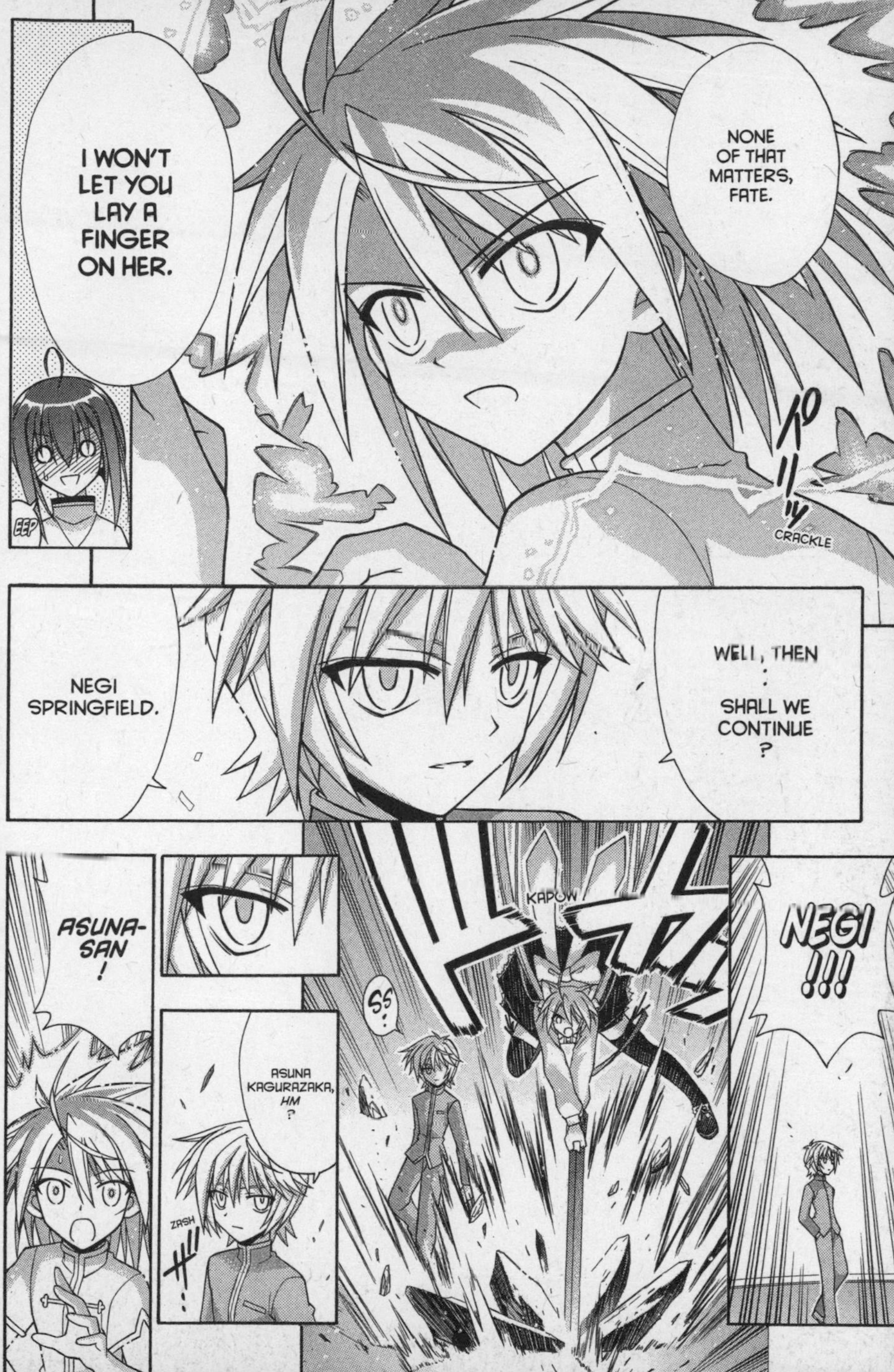
NONE OF THAT MATTERS, FATE.
CRACKLE
I WON'T LET YOU LAY A FINGER ON HER.
EEP
WELL, THEN... SHALL WE CONTINUE?
NEGI SPRINGFIELD.
NEGI!!!
KAPOW
SS
ASUNA KAGURAZAKA, HM?
ZASH
ASUNA-SAN!

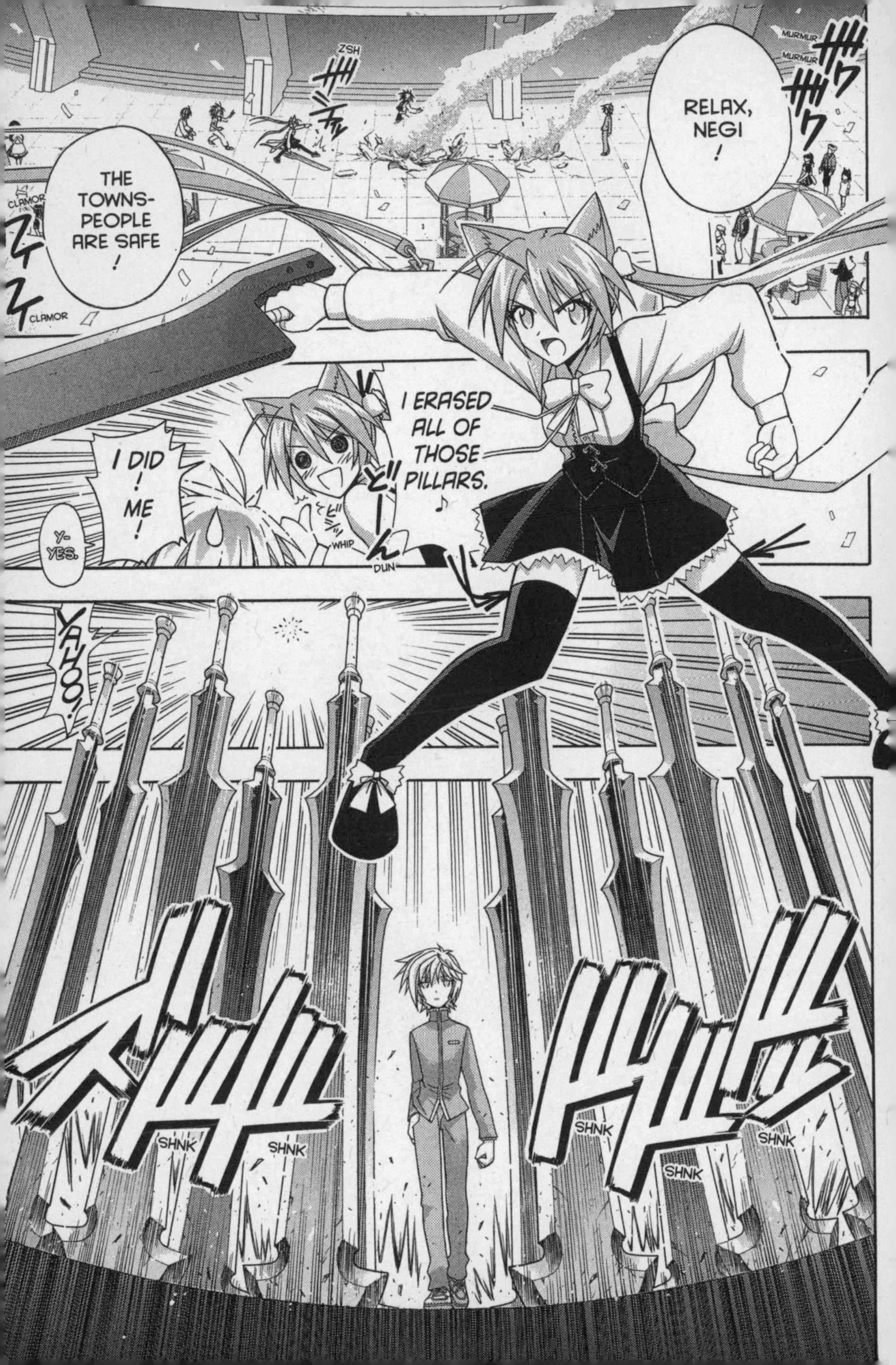
MURMUR
MURMUR
RELAX, NEGI!
ZSH
THE TOWNS-PEOPLE ARE SAFE!
CLAMOR
CLAMOR
I ERASED ALL OF THOSE PILLARS. ♪
I DID! ME!
WHIP
DUN
Y-YES.
YAHOO!
SHNK
SHNK
SHNK
SHNK
SHNK

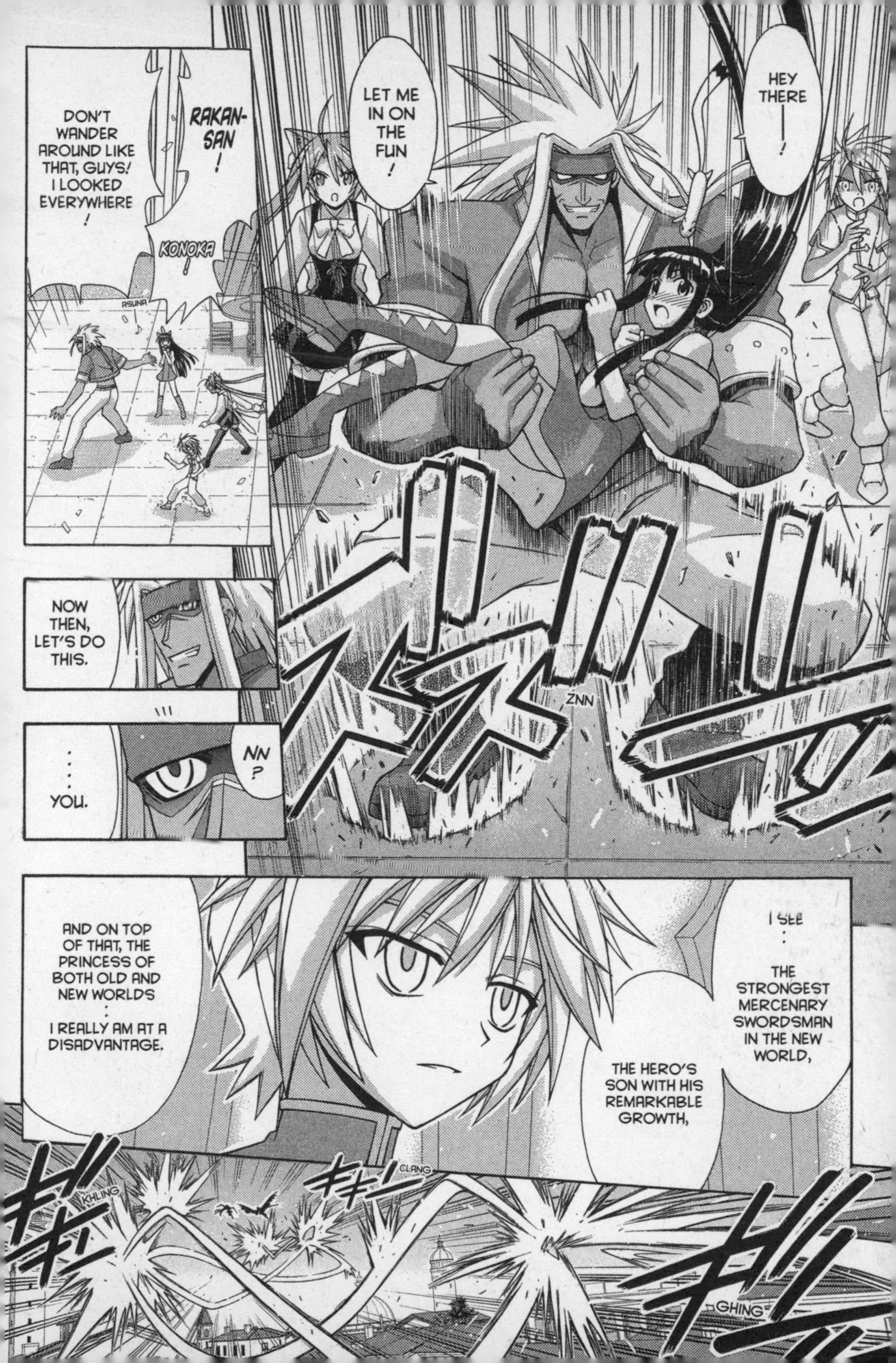

HEY THERE—!
LET ME IN ON THE FUN!
ZNN
RAKAN-SAN!
DON'T WANDER AROUND LIKE THAT, GUYS! I LOOKED EVERYWHERE!
KONOKA!
ASUNA
NOW THEN, LET'S DO THIS.
NN?
... YOU.
I SEE...
THE STRONGEST MERCENARY SWORDSMAN IN THE NEW WORLD,
THE HERO'S SON WITH HIS REMARKABLE GROWTH,
AND ON TOP OF THAT, THE PRINCESS OF BOTH OLD AND NEW WORLDS...
I REALLY AM AT A DISADVANTAGE.
CLANG
KHLING
GHING

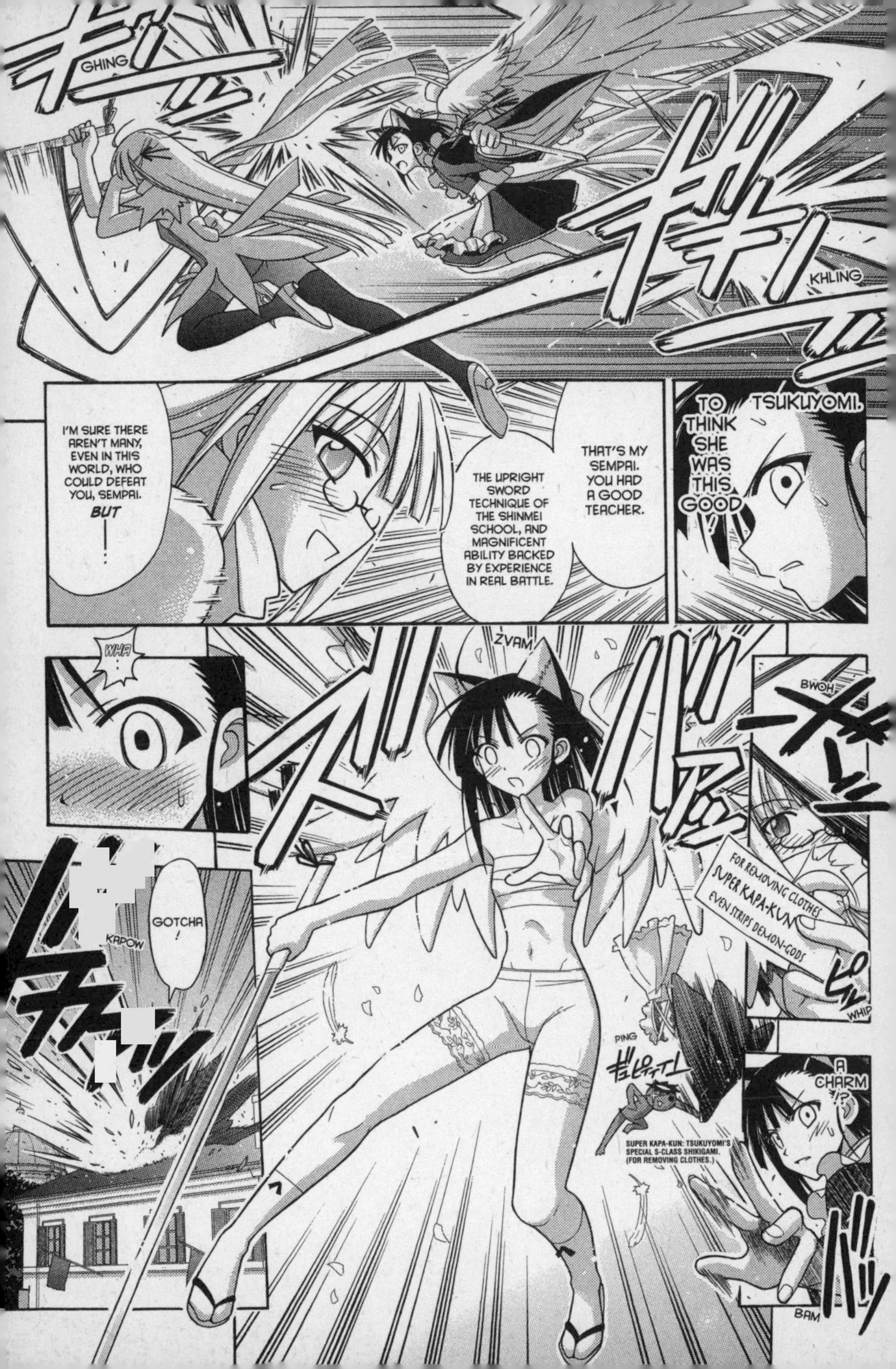
GHING
KHLING
TSUKUYOMI.
TO THINK SHE WAS THIS GOOD!
THAT'S MY SEMPAI. YOU HAD A GOOD TEACHER.
THE UPRIGHT SWORD TECHNIQUE OF THE SHINMEI SCHOOL, AND MAGNIFICENT ABILITY BACKED BY EXPERIENCE IN REAL BATTLE.
I'M SURE THERE AREN'T MANY, EVEN IN THIS WORLD, WHO COULD DEFEAT YOU, SEMPAI. BUT—!
BWOH
FOR REMOVING CLOTHES SUPER KAPA-KUN EVEN STRIPS DEMON-GODS
WHIP
ZVAM
WHA...
A CHARM!?
BAM
PING
SUPER KAPA-KUN: TSUKUYOMI'S SPECIAL S-CLASS SHIKIGAMI. (FOR REMOVING CLOTHES.)
GOTCHA!
KAPOW

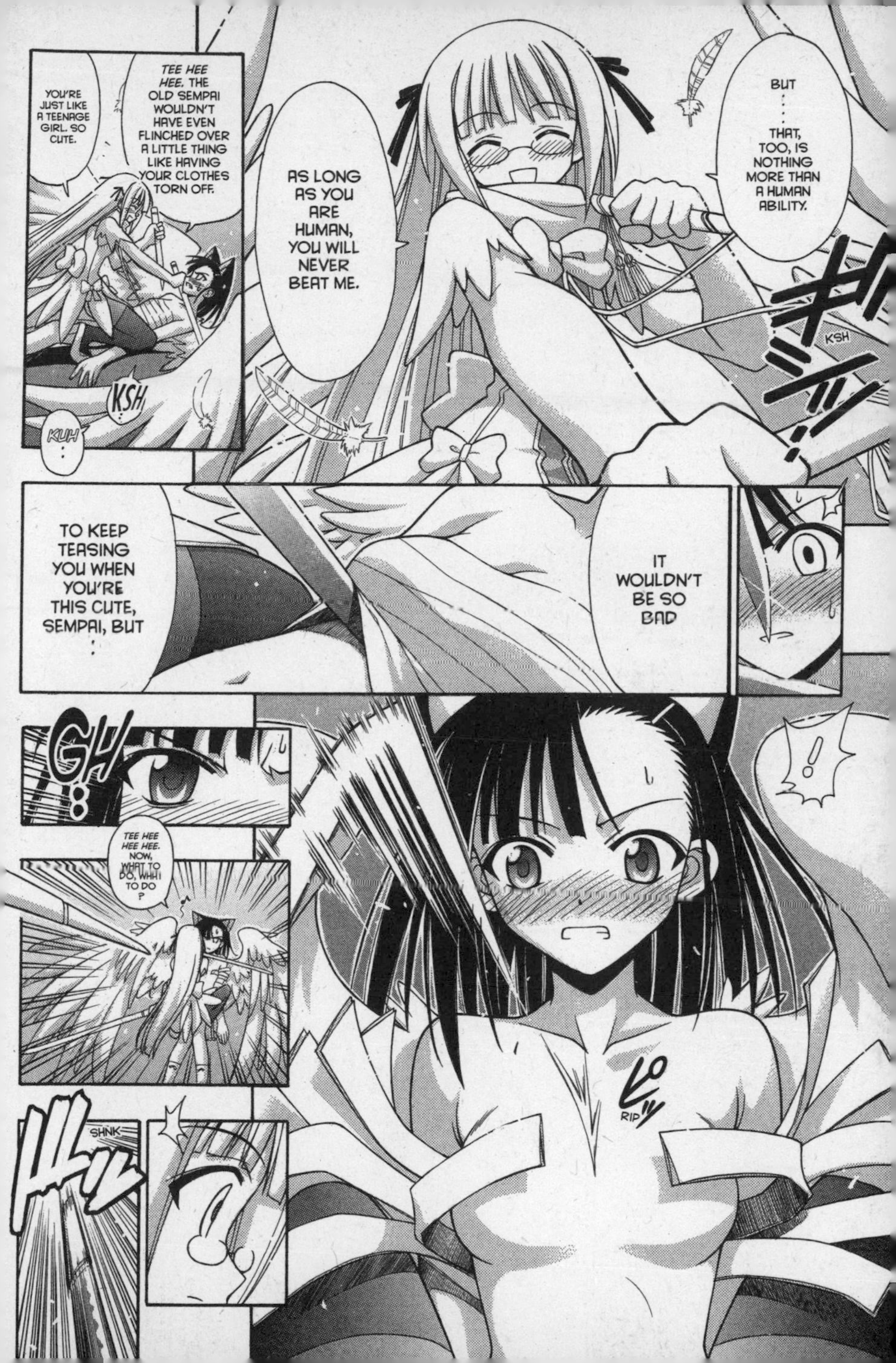
BUT ... THAT, TOO, IS NOTHING MORE THAN A HUMAN ABILITY.
AS LONG AS YOU ARE HUMAN, YOU WILL NEVER BEAT ME.
KSH
TEE HEE HEE. THE OLD SEMPAI WOULDN'T HAVE EVEN FLINCHED OVER A LITTLE THING LIKE HAVING YOUR CLOTHES TORN OFF.
YOU'RE JUST LIKE A TEENAGE GIRL. SO CUTE.
KSH
KUH ...
IT WOULDN'T BE SO BAD
TO KEEP TEASING YOU WHEN YOU'RE THIS CUTE, SEMPAI, BUT ...
!
RIP
GH
TEE HEE HEE HEE. NOW, WHAT TO DO, WHAT TO DO?
SHNK

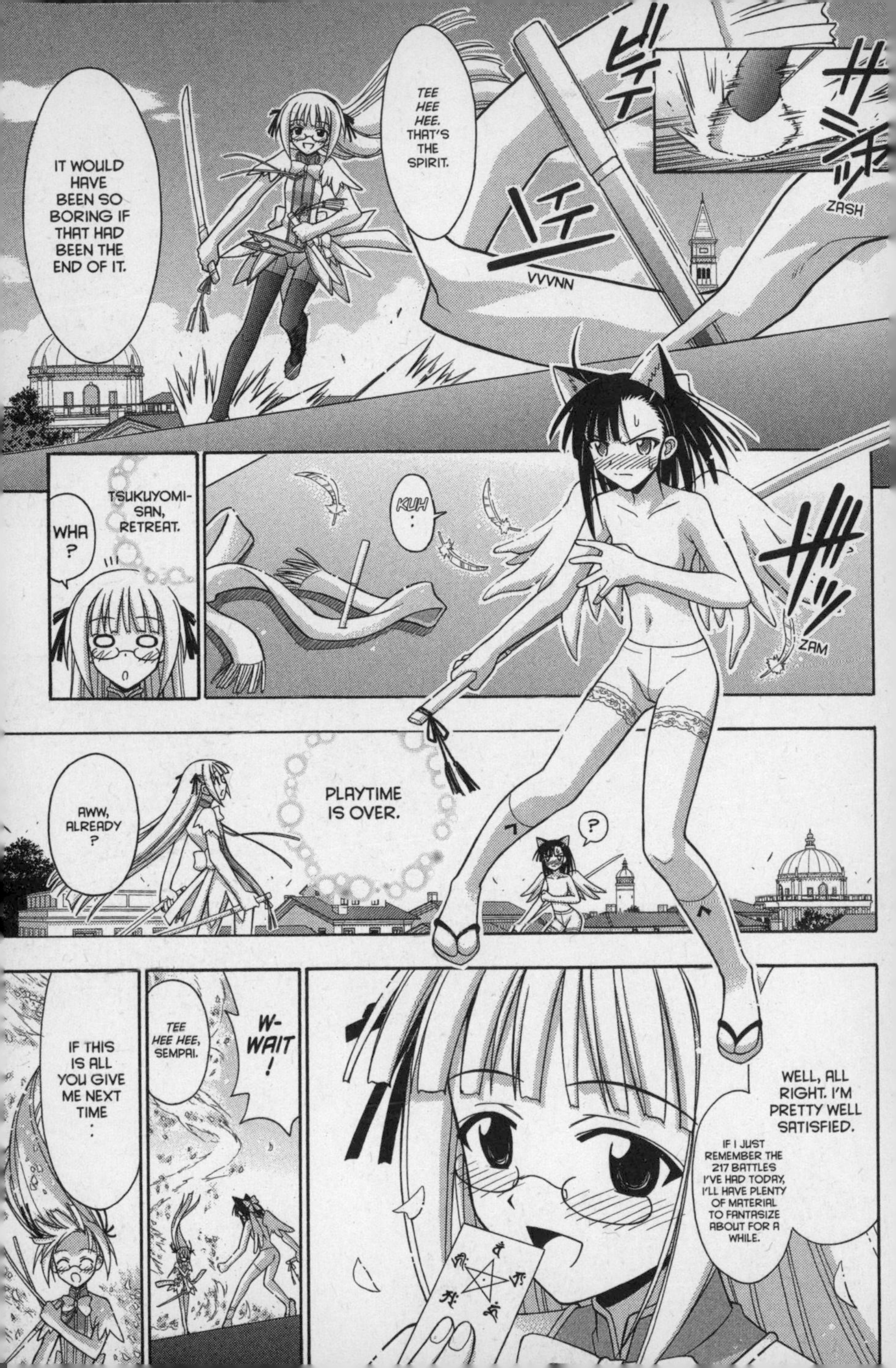
ZASH
VVVNN
TEE HEE HEE. THAT'S THE SPIRIT.
IT WOULD HAVE BEEN SO BORING IF THAT HAD BEEN THE END OF IT.
ZAM
KUH...
TSUKUYOMI-SAN, RETREAT.
WHA?
PLAYTIME IS OVER.
?
AWW, ALREADY?
WELL, ALL RIGHT. I'M PRETTY WELL SATISFIED.
IF I JUST REMEMBER THE 217 BATTLES I'VE HAD TODAY, I'LL HAVE PLENTY OF MATERIAL TO FANTASIZE ABOUT FOR A WHILE.
W-WAIT!
TEE HEE HEE, SEMPAI.
IF THIS IS ALL YOU GIVE ME NEXT TIME...

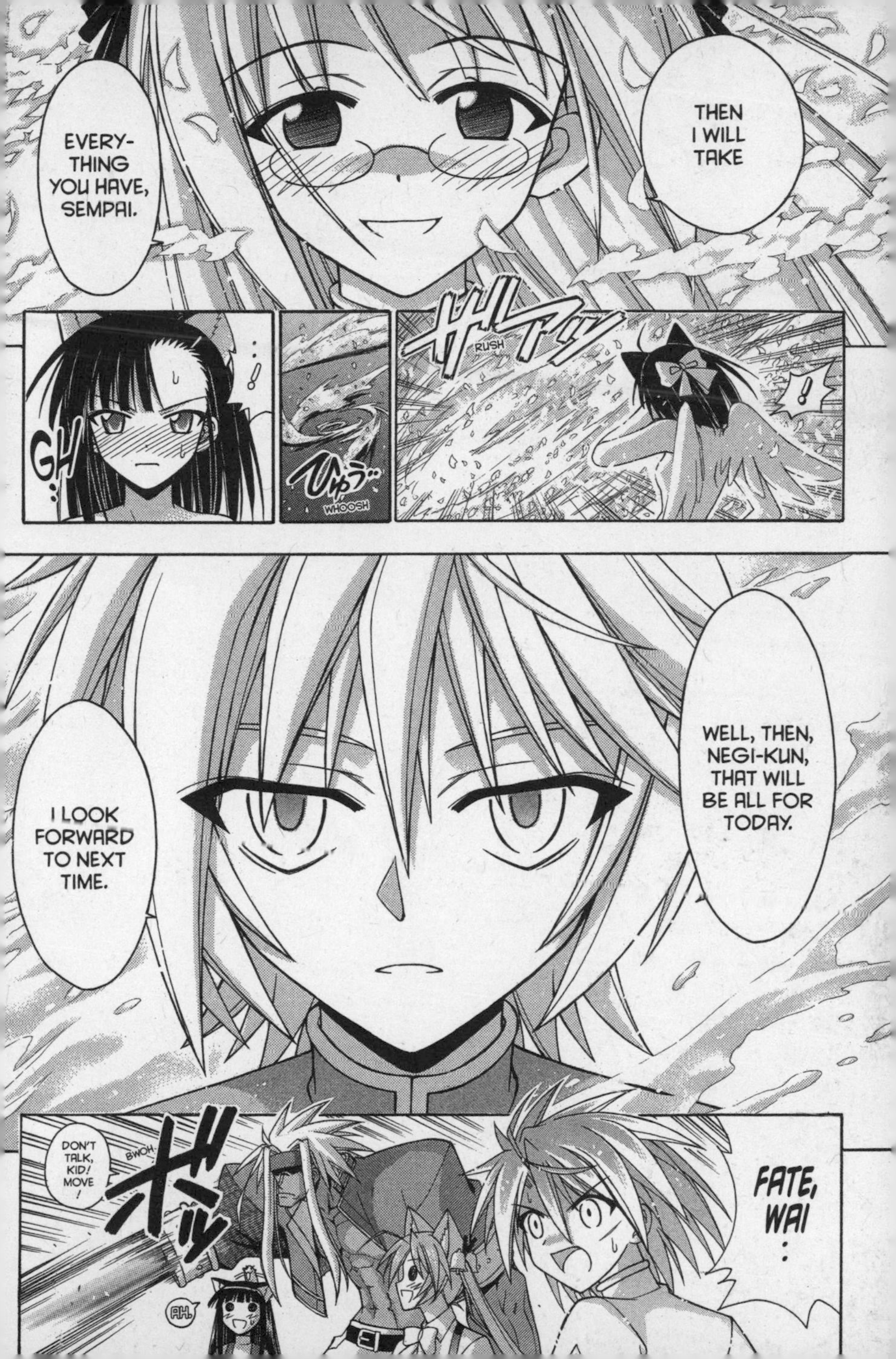
THEN I WILL TAKE
EVERY-THING YOU HAVE, SEMPAI.
RUSH
!
WHOOSH
...!
GH
WELL, THEN, NEGI-KUN, THAT WILL BE ALL FOR TODAY.
I LOOK FORWARD TO NEXT TIME.
FATE, WAI :
BWOH
DON'T TALK, KID! MOVE!
AH,

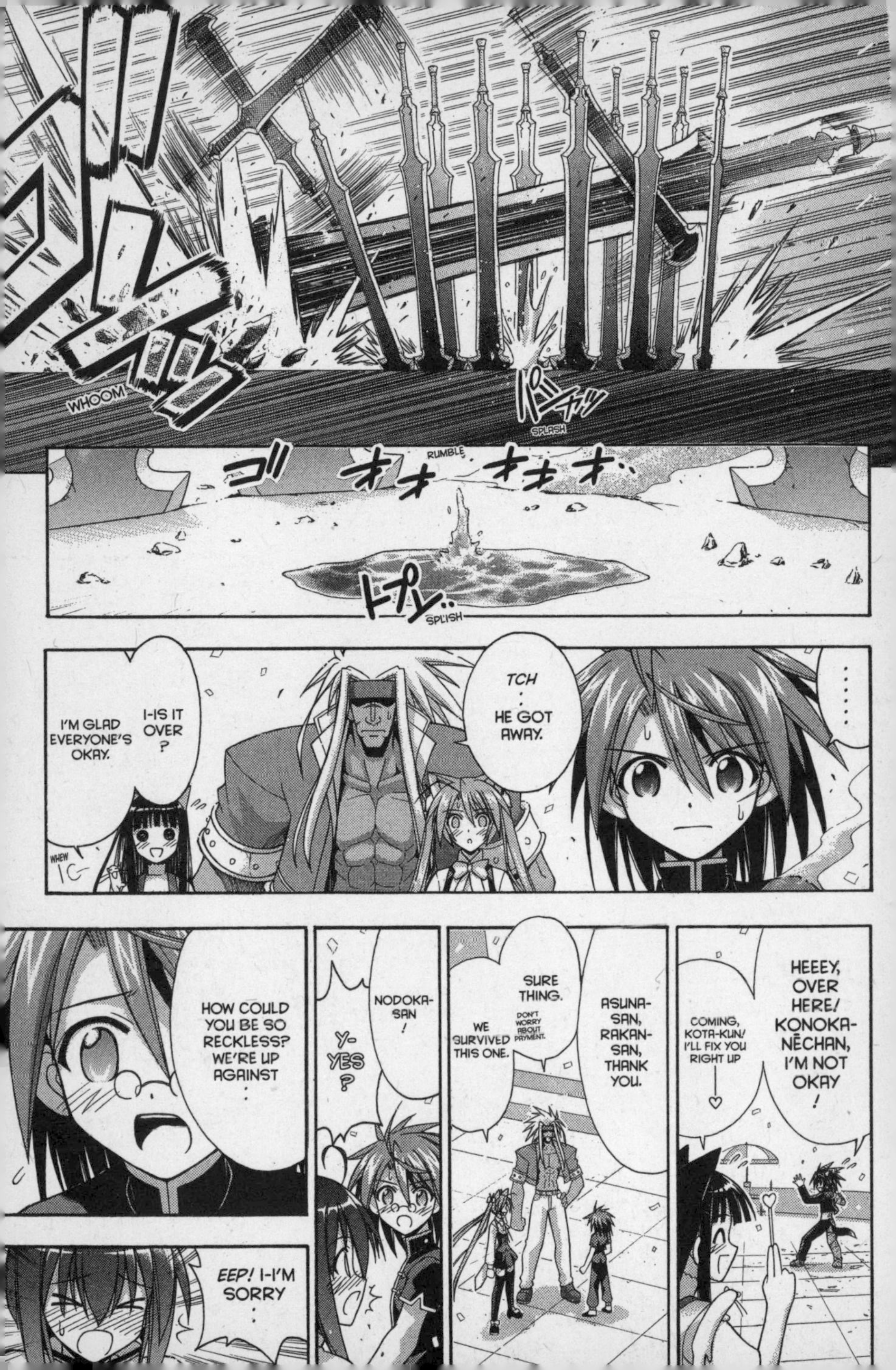
SPLASH
WHOOM
RUMBLE
SPLISH
......
TCH : HE GOT AWAY.
I-IS IT OVER ?
I'M GLAD EVERYONE'S OKAY.
WHEW
HEEEY, OVER HERE! KONOKA-NĒCHAN, I'M NOT OKAY!
COMING, KOTA-KUN! I'LL FIX YOU RIGHT UP ♡
ASUNA-SAN, RAKAN-SAN, THANK YOU.
SURE THING.
DON'T WORRY ABOUT PAYMENT.
WE SURVIVED THIS ONE.
NODOKA-SAN!
Y-YES?
HOW COULD YOU BE SO RECKLESS? WE'RE UP AGAINST :
EEP! I-I'M SORRY :

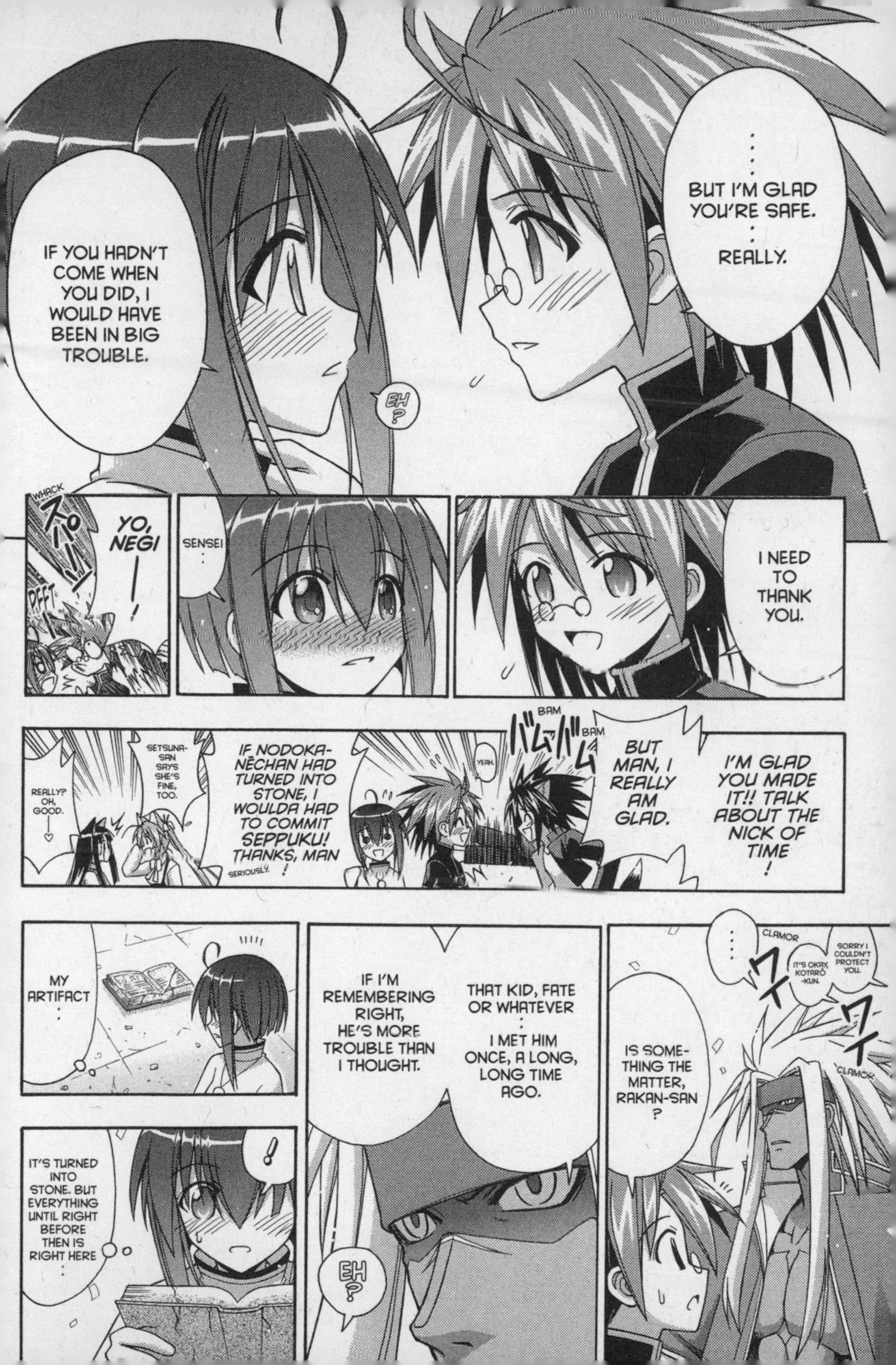

...
BUT I'M GLAD YOU'RE SAFE.
...
REALLY.
EH?
IF YOU HADN'T COME WHEN YOU DID, I WOULD HAVE BEEN IN BIG TROUBLE.
I NEED TO THANK YOU.
SENSEI
...
WHACK
YO, NEGI!
PFFT
I'M GLAD YOU MADE IT!! TALK ABOUT THE NICK OF TIME!
BAM
BAM
BUT MAN, I REALLY AM GLAD.
YEAH.
IF NODOKA-NĒCHAN HAD TURNED INTO STONE, I WOULDA HAD TO COMMIT SEPPUKU! THANKS, MAN!
SERIOUSLY.
SETSUNA-SAN SAYS SHE'S FINE, TOO.
REALLY? OH, GOOD. ♡
...
CLAMOR
SORRY I COULDN'T PROTECT YOU.
IT'S OKAY, KOTARŌ-KUN.
CLAMOR
IS SOMETHING THE MATTER, RAKAN-SAN?
THAT KID, FATE OR WHATEVER ... I MET HIM ONCE, A LONG, LONG TIME AGO.
IF I'M REMEMBERING RIGHT, HE'S MORE TROUBLE THAN I THOUGHT.
EH?
MY ARTIFACT ...
!
IT'S TURNED INTO STONE. BUT EVERYTHING UNTIL RIGHT BEFORE THEN IS RIGHT HERE

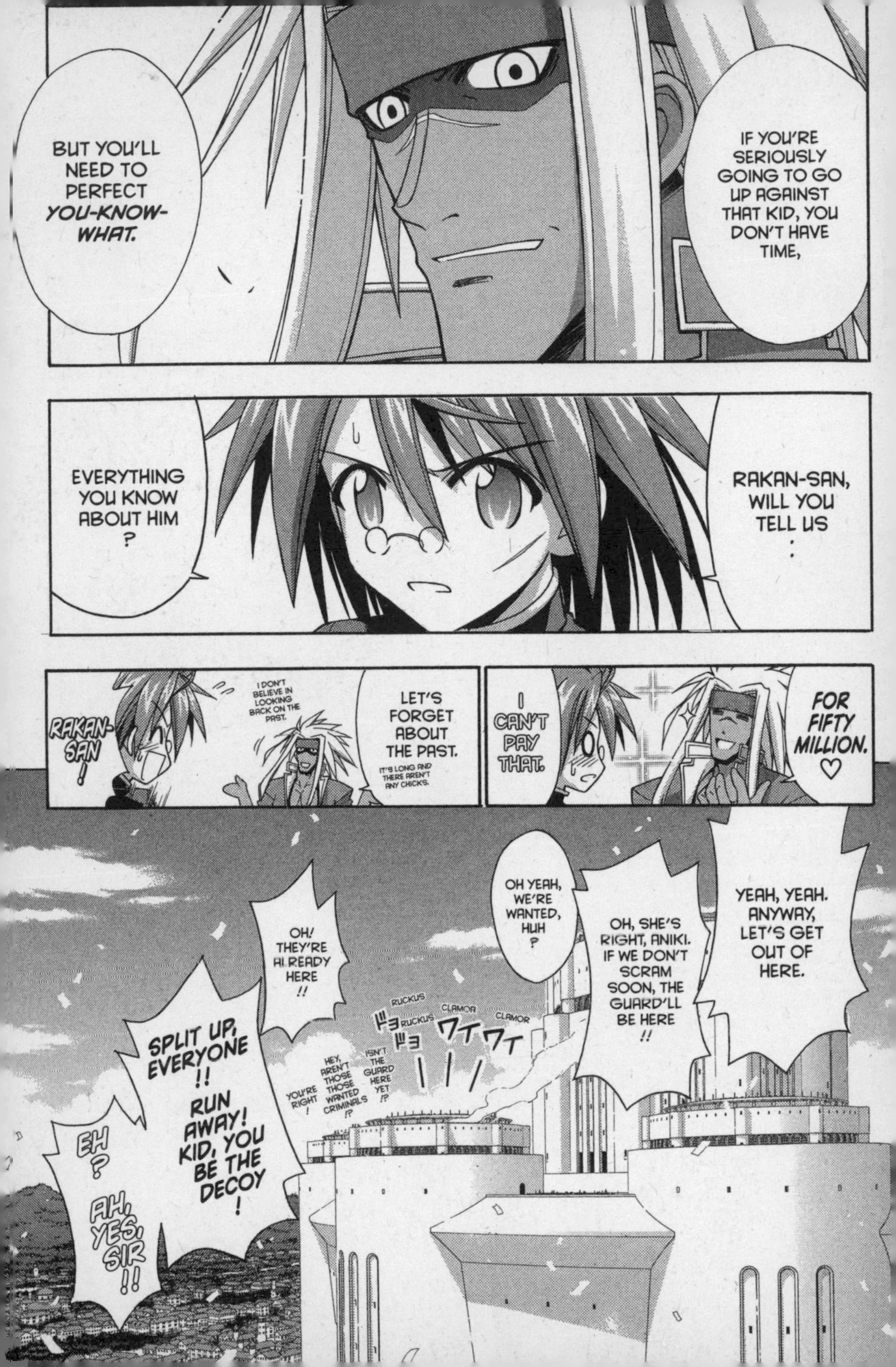
IF YOU'RE SERIOUSLY GOING TO GO UP AGAINST THAT KID, YOU DON'T HAVE TIME,
BUT YOU'LL NEED TO PERFECT *YOU-KNOW-WHAT.*
RAKAN-SAN, WILL YOU TELL US :
EVERYTHING YOU KNOW ABOUT HIM ?
FOR FIFTY MILLION. ♡
I CAN'T PAY THAT.
LET'S FORGET ABOUT THE PAST.
I DON'T BELIEVE IN LOOKING BACK ON THE PAST.
IT'S LONG AND THERE AREN'T ANY CHICKS.
RAKAN-SAN!
YEAH, YEAH. ANYWAY, LET'S GET OUT OF HERE.
OH, SHE'S RIGHT, ANIKI. IF WE DON'T SCRAM SOON, THE GUARD'LL BE HERE!!
OH YEAH, WE'RE WANTED, HUH?
OH! THEY'RE ALREADY HERE!!
ワイワイ CLAMOR CLAMOR
ドヨドヨ RUCKUS RUCKUS
ISN'T THE GUARD HERE YET!?
HEY, AREN'T THOSE THOSE WANTED CRIMINALS!?
YOU'RE RIGHT!
SPLIT UP, EVERYONE!! RUN AWAY! KID, YOU BE THE DECOY!
EH?
AH, YES, SIR!!

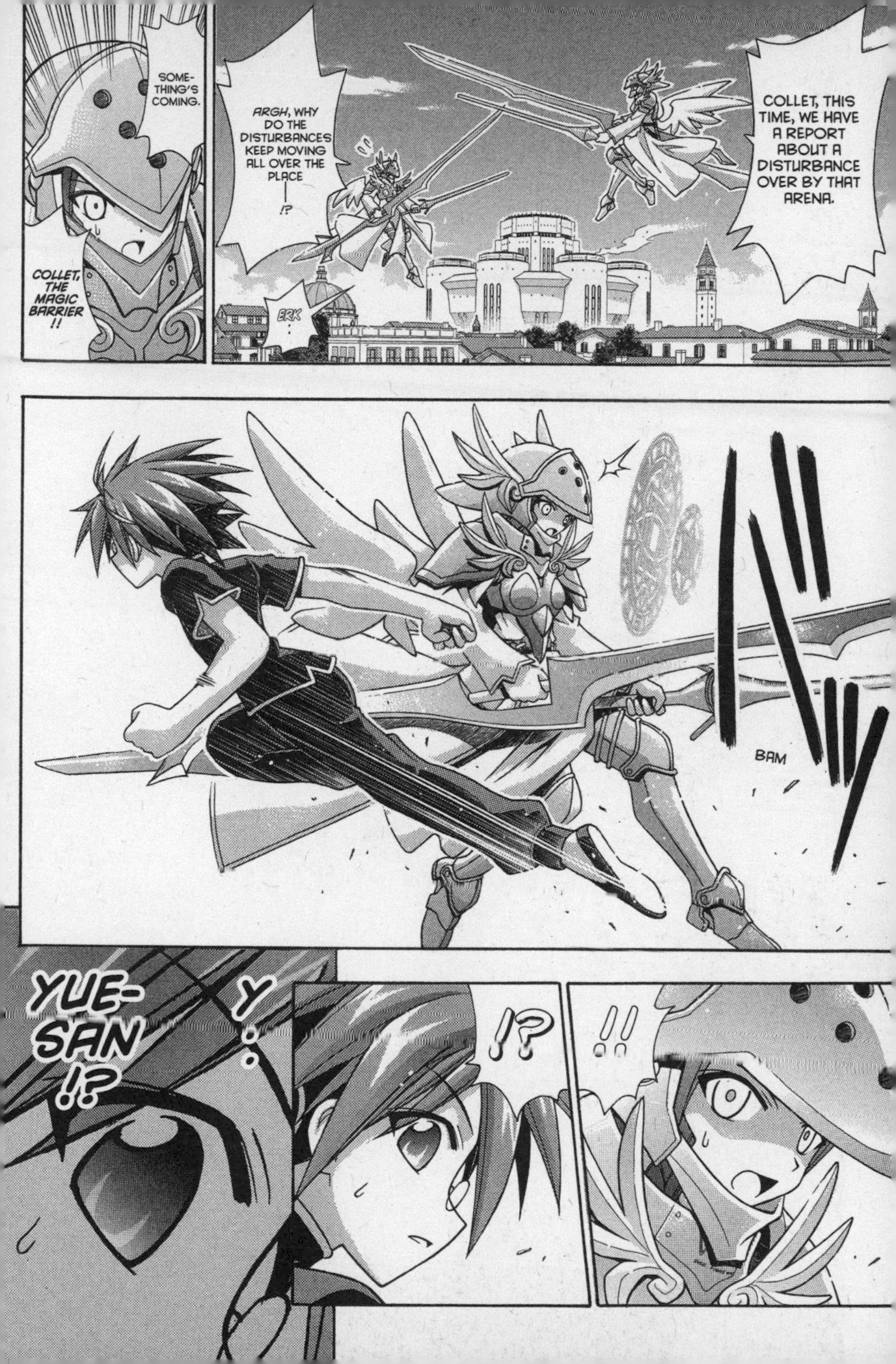
COLLET, THIS TIME, WE HAVE A REPORT ABOUT A DISTURBANCE OVER BY THAT ARENA.
ARGH, WHY DO THE DISTURBANCES KEEP MOVING ALL OVER THE PLACE—
!?
ERK
SOME-THING'S COMING.
COLLET, THE MAGIC BARRIER!!
BAM
!!
!?
Y...
YUE-SAN!?

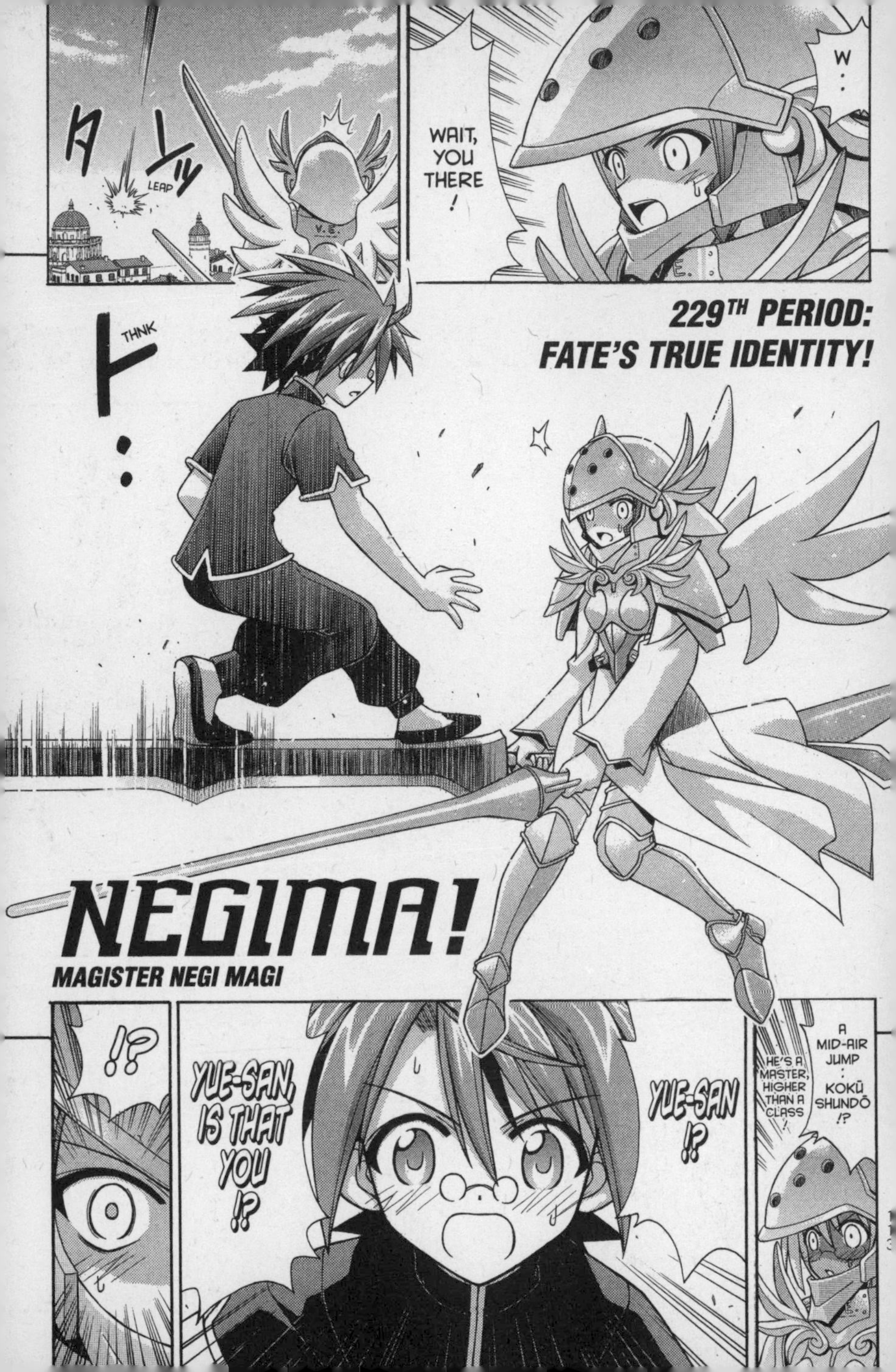
W :
WAIT, YOU THERE !
LEAP
THNK
229TH PERIOD: FATE'S TRUE IDENTITY!
NEGIMA!
MAGISTER NEGI MAGI
A MID-AIR JUMP : KOKŪ SHUNDŌ !?
HE'S A MASTER, HIGHER THAN A CLASS !
YUE-SAN !?
YUE-SAN, IS THAT YOU !?
!?

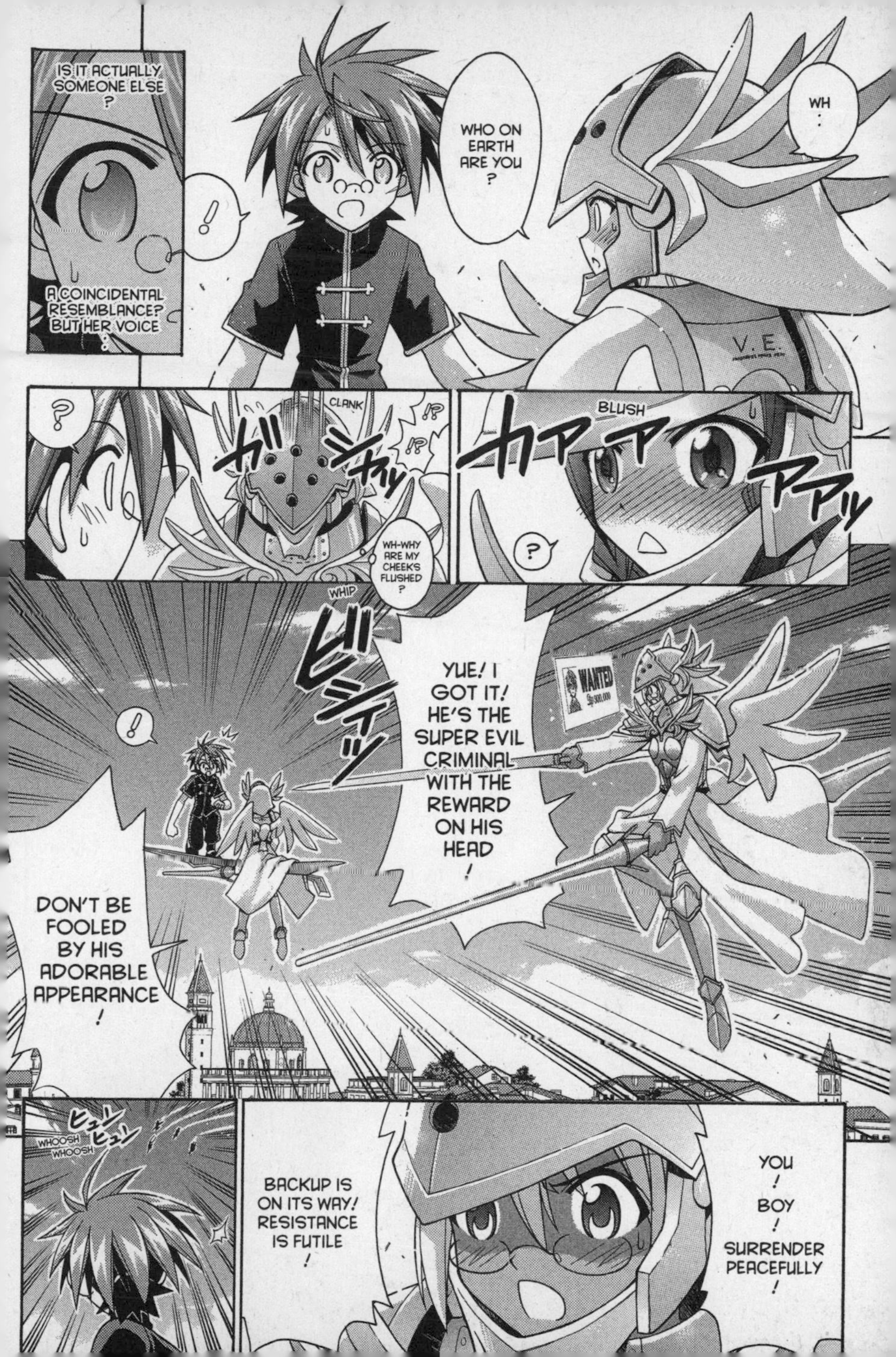
WH :
WHO ON EARTH ARE YOU ?
!
IS IT ACTUALLY SOMEONE ELSE ?
A COINCIDENTAL RESEMBLANCE? BUT HER VOICE :
BLUSH
?
CLANK
!?
!?
WH-WHY ARE MY CHEEK'S FLUSHED ?
?
WHIP
YUE! I GOT IT! HE'S THE SUPER EVIL CRIMINAL WITH THE REWARD ON HIS HEAD !
WANTED
!
DON'T BE FOOLED BY HIS ADORABLE APPEARANCE !
YOU ! BOY ! SURRENDER PEACEFULLY !
BACKUP IS ON ITS WAY! RESISTANCE IS FUTILE !
WHOOSH WHOOSH

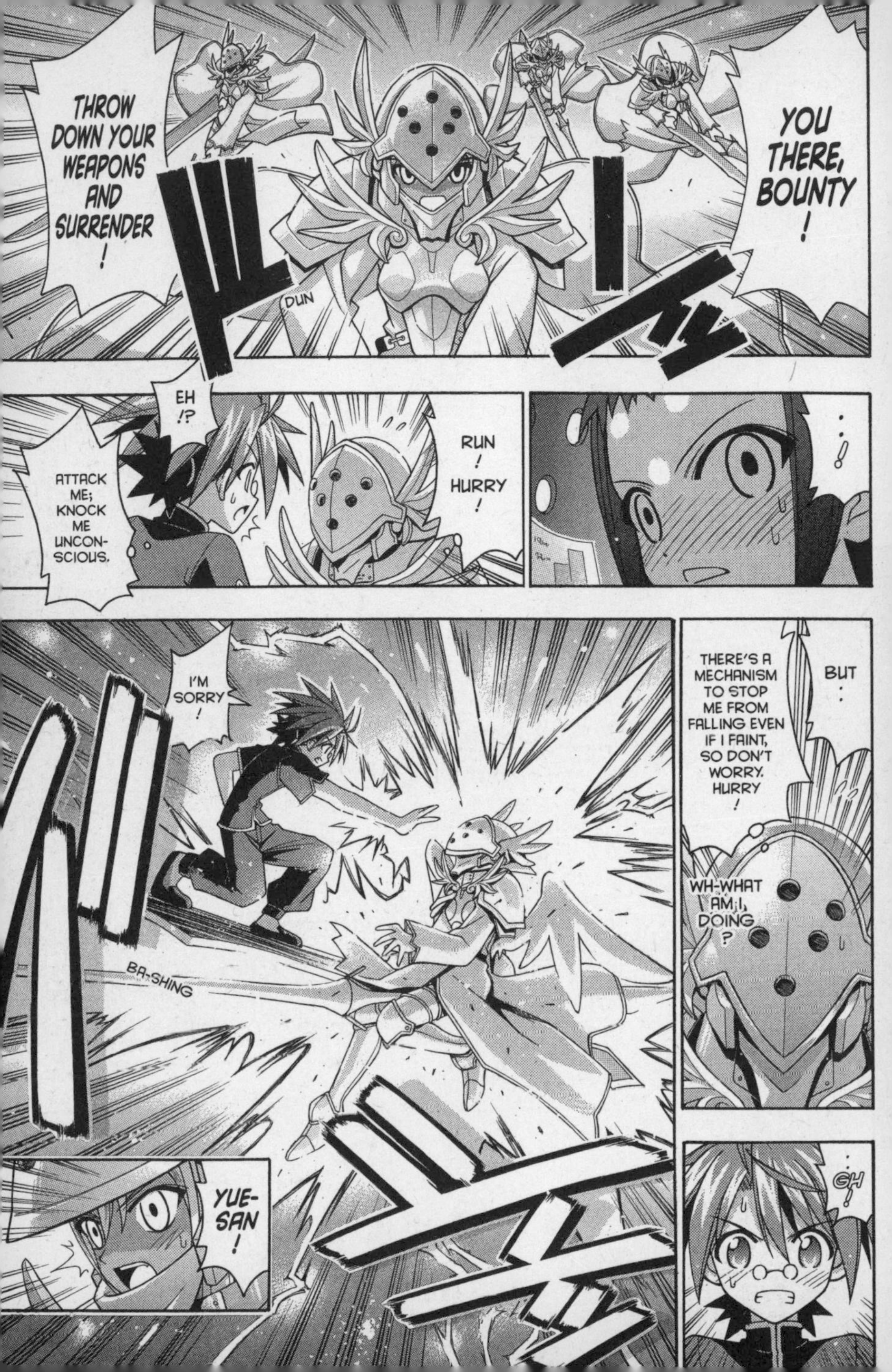
YOU THERE, BOUNTY!
THROW DOWN YOUR WEAPONS AND SURRENDER!
DUN
:.!
RUN! HURRY!
EH!?
ATTACK ME; KNOCK ME UNCONSCIOUS.
BUT...
THERE'S A MECHANISM TO STOP ME FROM FALLING EVEN IF I FAINT, SO DON'T WORRY. HURRY!
WH-WHAT AM I, DOING?
GH!
I'M SORRY!
BA-SHING
YUE-SAN!

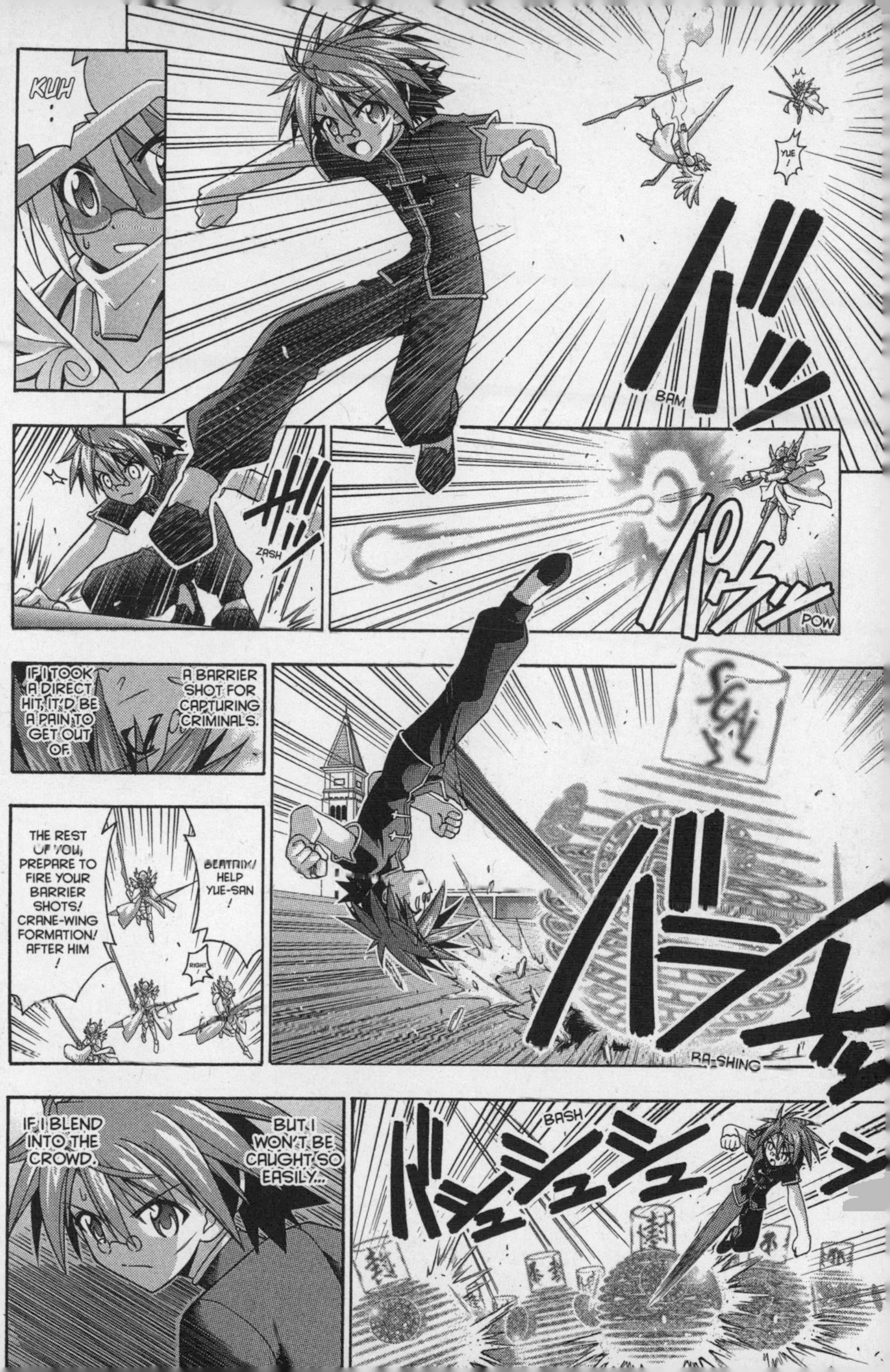

YUE!
BAM
KUH...
POW
ZASH
BA-SHING
A BARRIER SHOT FOR CAPTURING CRIMINALS.
IF I TOOK A DIRECT HIT, IT'D BE A PAIN TO GET OUT OF.
BEATRIX! HELP YUE-SAN!
THE REST OF YOU, PREPARE TO FIRE YOUR BARRIER SHOTS! CRANE-WING FORMATION! AFTER HIM!
RIGHT!
BASH
BUT I WON'T BE CAUGHT SO EASILY...
IF I BLEND INTO THE CROWD.

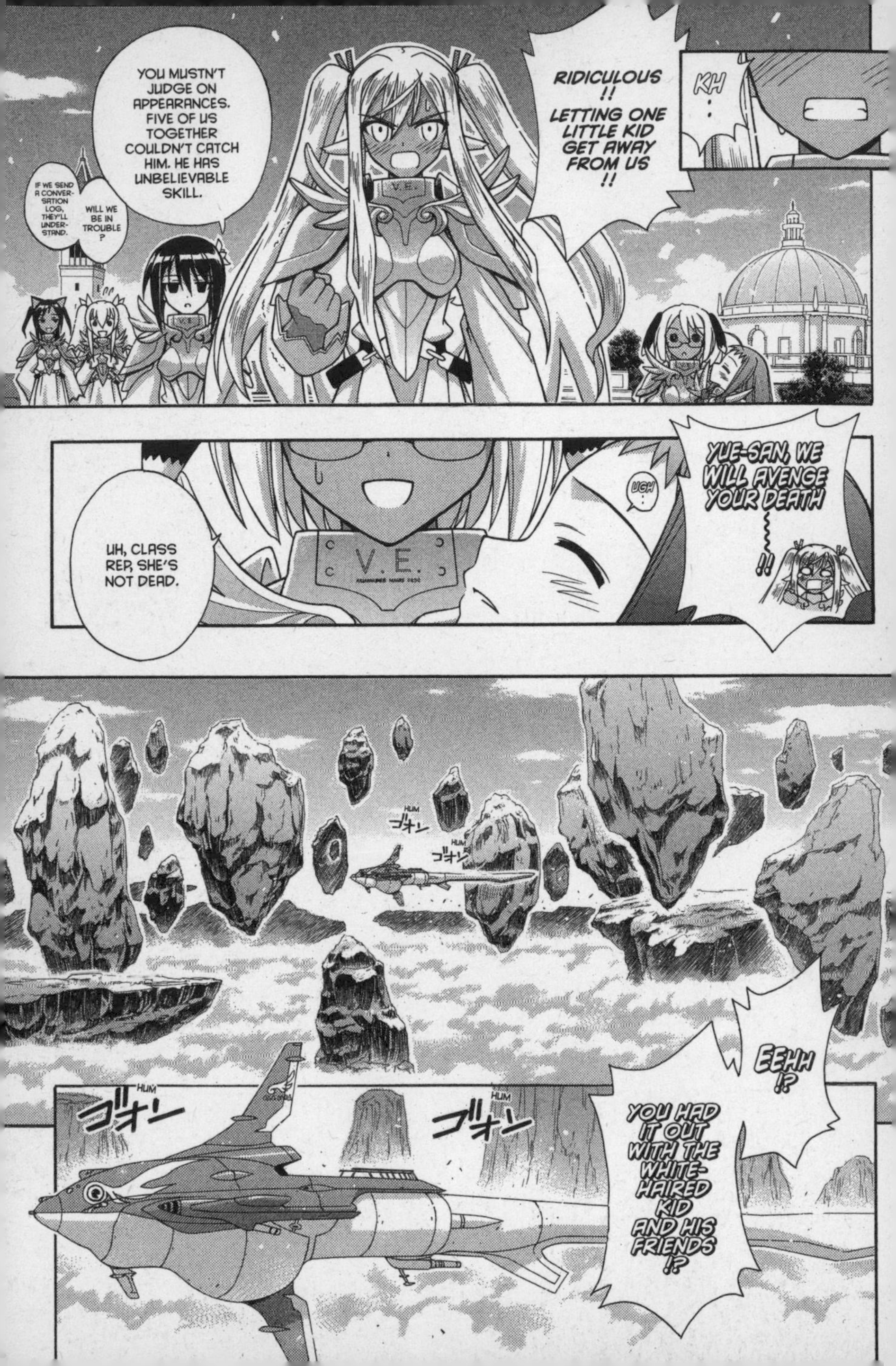
KH...
RIDICULOUS!! LETTING ONE LITTLE KID GET AWAY FROM US!!
YOU MUSTN'T JUDGE ON APPEARANCES. FIVE OF US TOGETHER COULDN'T CATCH HIM. HE HAS UNBELIEVABLE SKILL.
WILL WE BE IN TROUBLE?
IF WE SEND A CONVERSATION LOG, THEY'LL UNDERSTAND.
V.E.
YUE-SAN, WE WILL AVENGE YOUR DEATH!!
UGH
UH, CLASS REP, SHE'S NOT DEAD.
HUM ゴオン
HUM ゴオン
EEHH!?
YOU HAD IT OUT WITH THE WHITE-HAIRED KID AND HIS FRIENDS!?
HUM ゴオン
HUM ゴオン

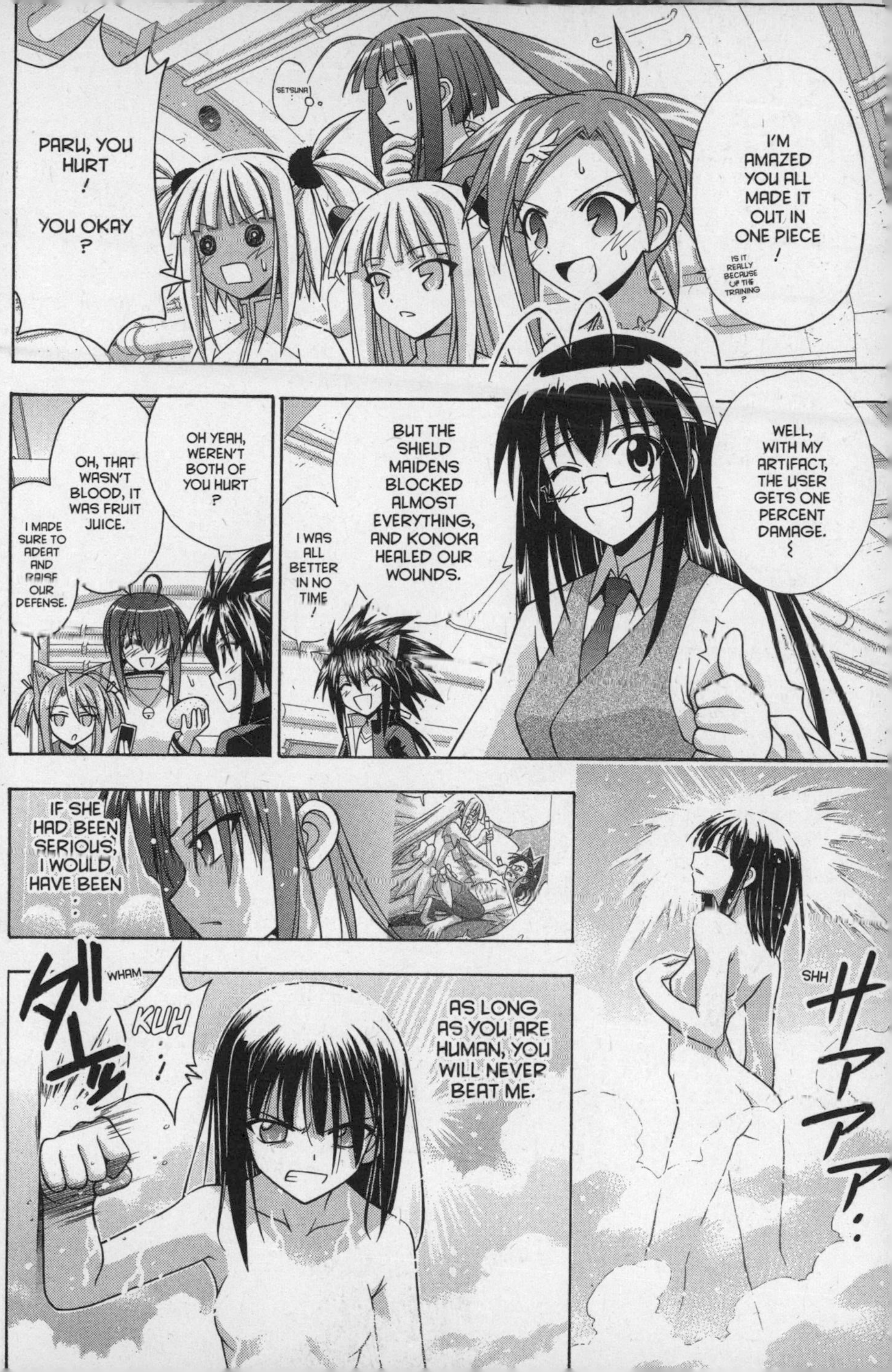
I'M AMAZED YOU ALL MADE IT OUT IN ONE PIECE!
IS IT REALLY BECAUSE OF THE TRAINING?
SETSUNA...
PARU, YOU HURT! YOU OKAY?
WELL, WITH MY ARTIFACT, THE USER GETS ONE PERCENT DAMAGE.
BUT THE SHIELD MAIDENS BLOCKED ALMOST EVERYTHING, AND KONOKA HEALED OUR WOUNDS.
I WAS ALL BETTER IN NO TIME!
OH YEAH, WEREN'T BOTH OF YOU HURT?
OH, THAT WASN'T BLOOD, IT WAS FRUIT JUICE.
I MADE SURE TO ADEAT AND RAISE OUR DEFENSE.
SHH
IF SHE HAD BEEN SERIOUS, I WOULD HAVE BEEN...
AS LONG AS YOU ARE HUMAN, YOU WILL NEVER BEAT ME.
KUH...!
WHAM

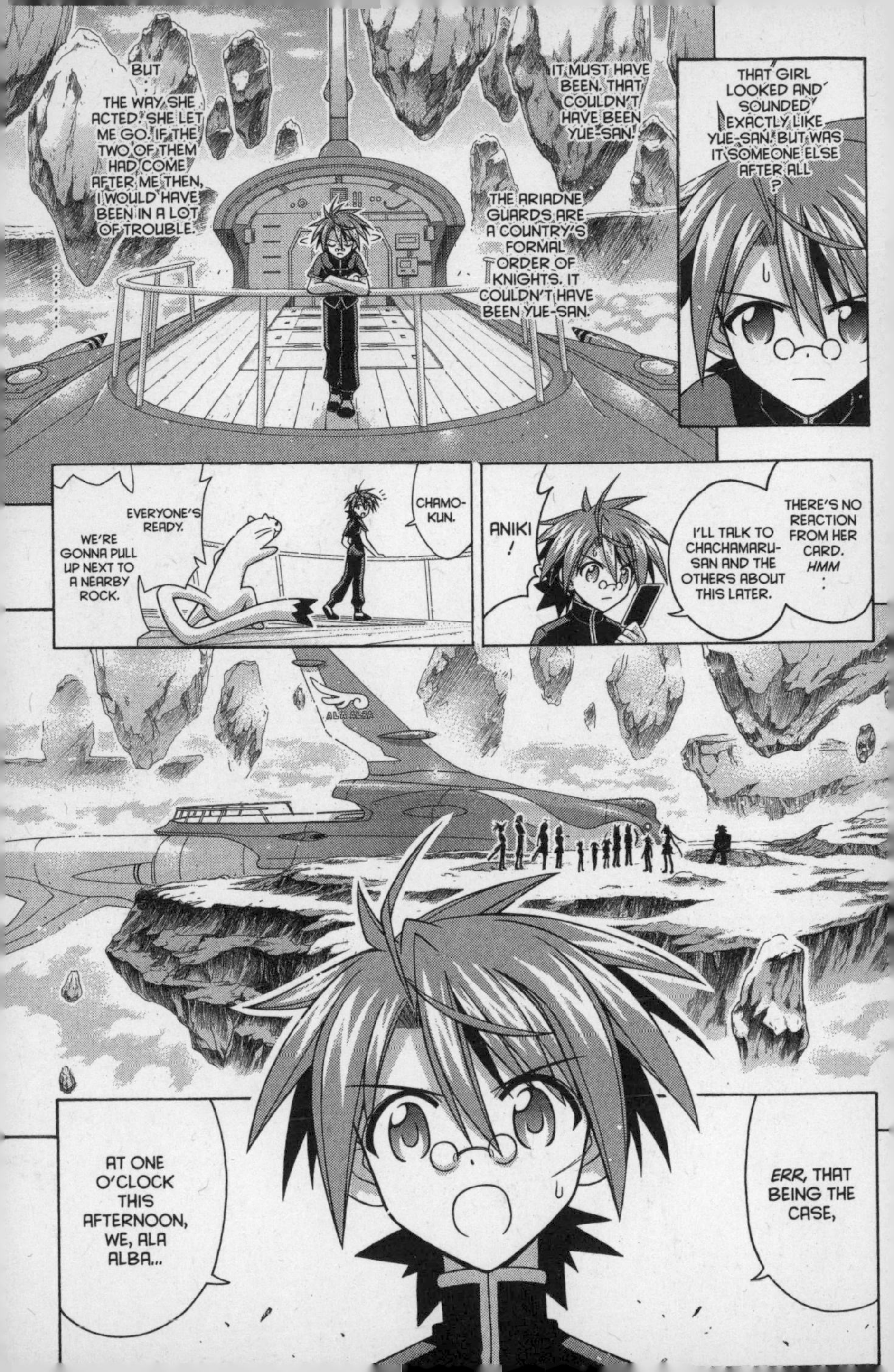
THAT GIRL LOOKED AND SOUNDED EXACTLY LIKE YUE-SAN. BUT WAS IT SOMEONE ELSE AFTER ALL?
IT MUST HAVE BEEN. THAT COULDN'T HAVE BEEN YUE-SAN.
THE ARIADNE GUARDS ARE A COUNTRY'S FORMAL ORDER OF KNIGHTS. IT COULDN'T HAVE BEEN YUE-SAN.
BUT...
THE WAY SHE ACTED. SHE LET ME GO. IF THE TWO OF THEM HAD COME AFTER ME THEN, I WOULD HAVE BEEN IN A LOT OF TROUBLE.
......
THERE'S NO REACTION FROM HER CARD. *HMM*...
I'LL TALK TO CHACHAMARU-SAN AND THE OTHERS ABOUT THIS LATER.
ANIKI!
CHAMO-KUN.
EVERYONE'S READY.
WE'RE GONNA PULL UP NEXT TO A NEARBY ROCK.
ALA ALBA
ERR, THAT BEING THE CASE,
AT ONE O'CLOCK THIS AFTERNOON, WE, ALA ALBA...

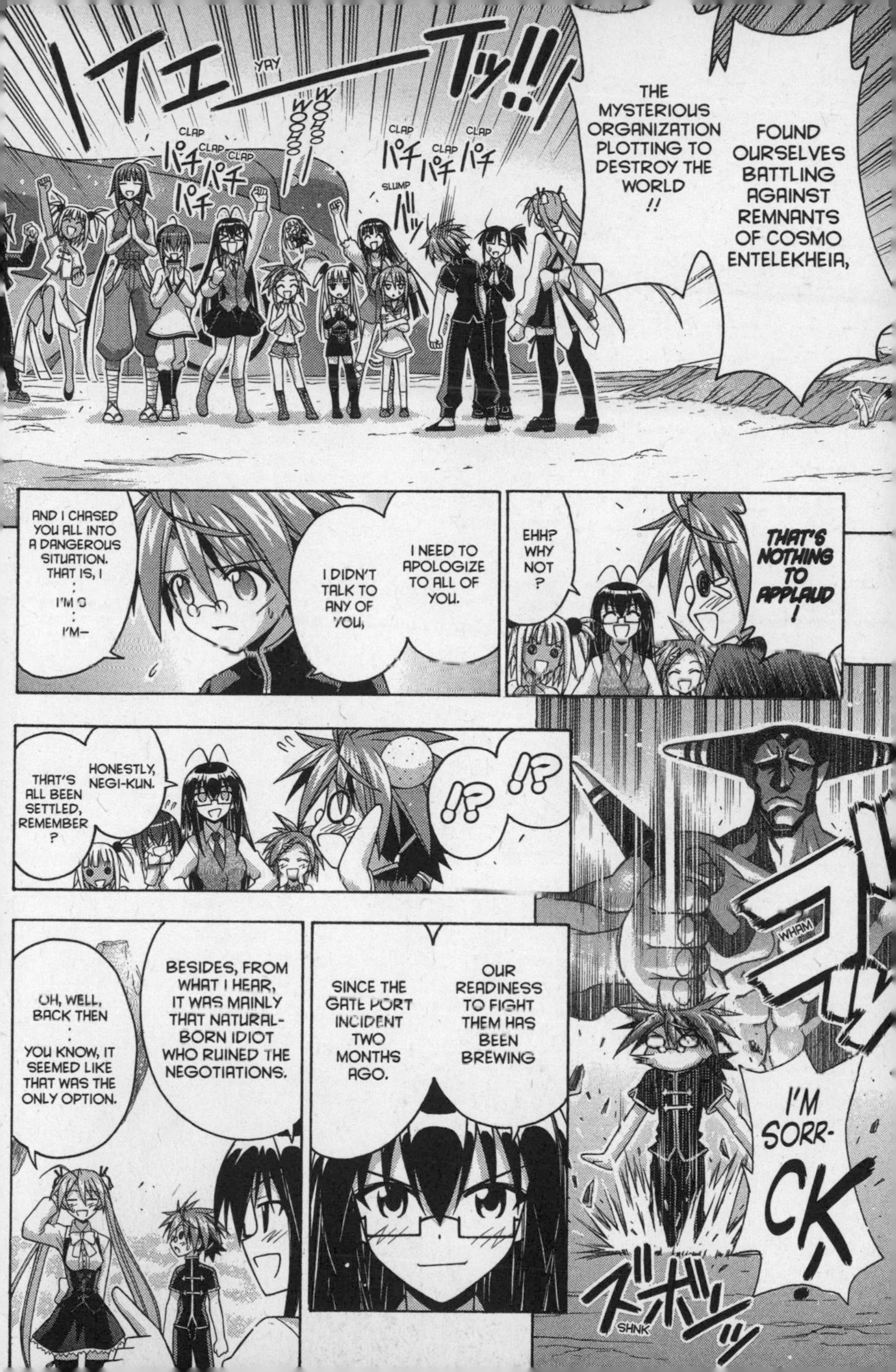

FOUND OURSELVES BATTLING AGAINST REMNANTS OF COSMO ENTELEKHEIA,
THE MYSTERIOUS ORGANIZATION PLOTTING TO DESTROY THE WORLD!!
イエーーイッ!!
YAY
WOOHOO WOOHOO
パチ CLAP パチ CLAP パチ CLAP
パチ CLAP パチ CLAP パチ CLAP
バッ
SLUMP
THAT'S NOTHING TO APPLAUD!
EHH? WHY NOT?
I NEED TO APOLOGIZE TO ALL OF YOU.
I DIDN'T TALK TO ANY OF YOU,
AND I CHASED YOU ALL INTO A DANGEROUS SITUATION. THAT IS, I... I'M... I'M—
WHAM
I'M SORR-CK!
SHNK
!? !?
HONESTLY, NEGI-KUN.
THAT'S ALL BEEN SETTLED, REMEMBER?
OUR READINESS TO FIGHT THEM HAS BEEN BREWING
SINCE THE GATE PORT INCIDENT TWO MONTHS AGO.
BESIDES, FROM WHAT I HEAR, IT WAS MAINLY THAT NATURAL-BORN IDIOT WHO RUINED THE NEGOTIATIONS.
OH, WELL, BACK THEN... YOU KNOW, IT SEEMED LIKE THAT WAS THE ONLY OPTION.

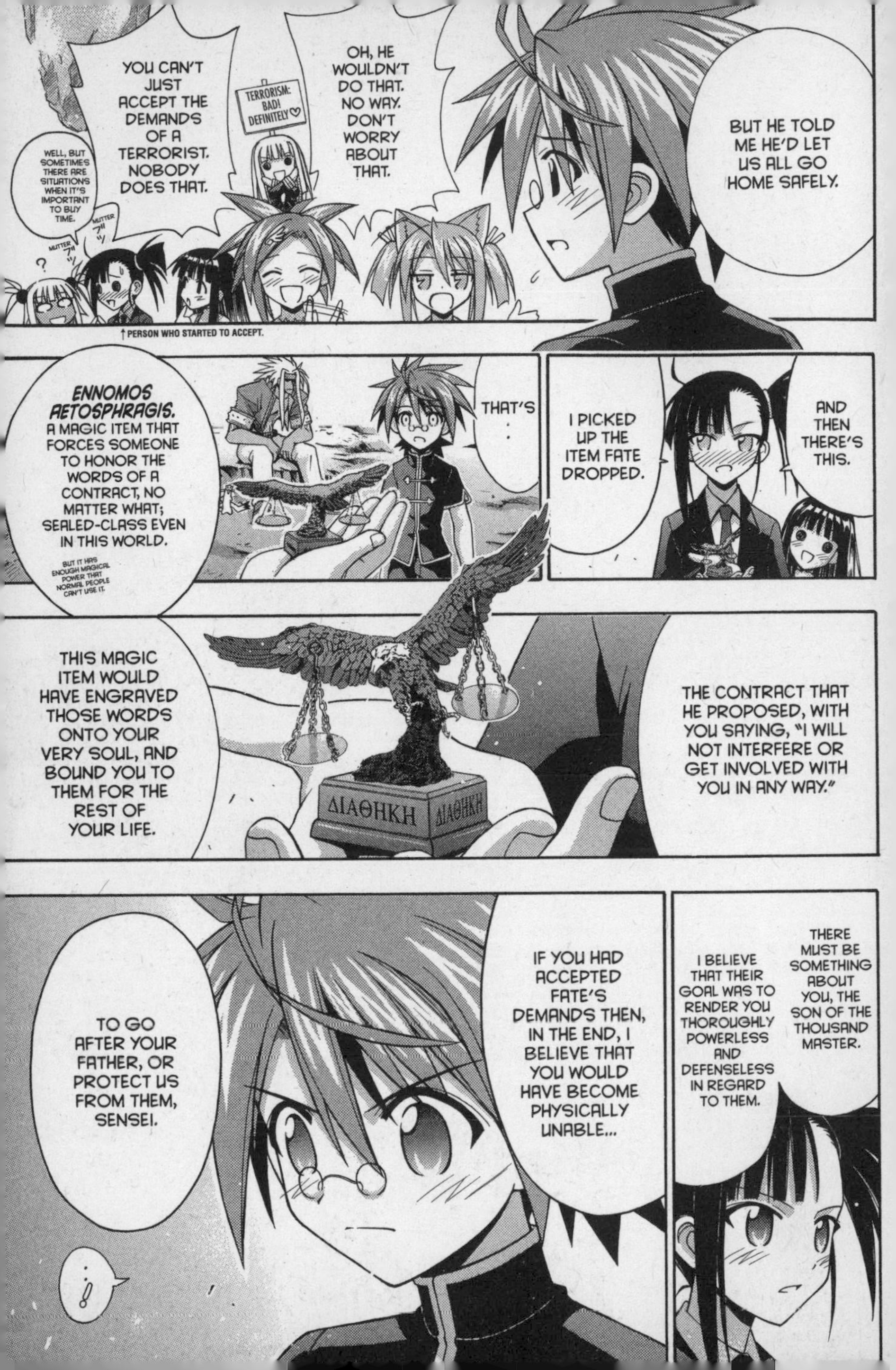
BUT HE TOLD ME HE'D LET US ALL GO HOME SAFELY.
OH, HE WOULDN'T DO THAT. NO WAY. DON'T WORRY ABOUT THAT.
TERRORISM: BAD! DEFINITELY♡
YOU CAN'T JUST ACCEPT THE DEMANDS OF A TERRORIST. NOBODY DOES THAT.
WELL, BUT SOMETIMES THERE ARE SITUATIONS WHEN IT'S IMPORTANT TO BUY TIME.
MUTTER
MUTTER
?
↑PERSON WHO STARTED TO ACCEPT.
AND THEN THERE'S THIS.
I PICKED UP THE ITEM FATE DROPPED.
THAT'S ..
ENNOMOS AETOSPHRAGIS. A MAGIC ITEM THAT FORCES SOMEONE TO HONOR THE WORDS OF A CONTRACT, NO MATTER WHAT; SEALED-CLASS EVEN IN THIS WORLD.
BUT IT HAS ENOUGH MAGICAL POWER THAT NORMAL PEOPLE CAN'T USE IT.
THE CONTRACT THAT HE PROPOSED, WITH YOU SAYING, "I WILL NOT INTERFERE OR GET INVOLVED WITH YOU IN ANY WAY."
THIS MAGIC ITEM WOULD HAVE ENGRAVED THOSE WORDS ONTO YOUR VERY SOUL, AND BOUND YOU TO THEM FOR THE REST OF YOUR LIFE.
ΔΙΑΘΗΚΗ
ΔΙΑΘΗΚΗ
THERE MUST BE SOMETHING ABOUT YOU, THE SON OF THE THOUSAND MASTER.
I BELIEVE THAT THEIR GOAL WAS TO RENDER YOU THOROUGHLY POWERLESS AND DEFENSELESS IN REGARD TO THEM.
IF YOU HAD ACCEPTED FATE'S DEMANDS THEN, IN THE END, I BELIEVE THAT YOU WOULD HAVE BECOME PHYSICALLY UNABLE...
TO GO AFTER YOUR FATHER, OR PROTECT US FROM THEM, SENSEI.
..!

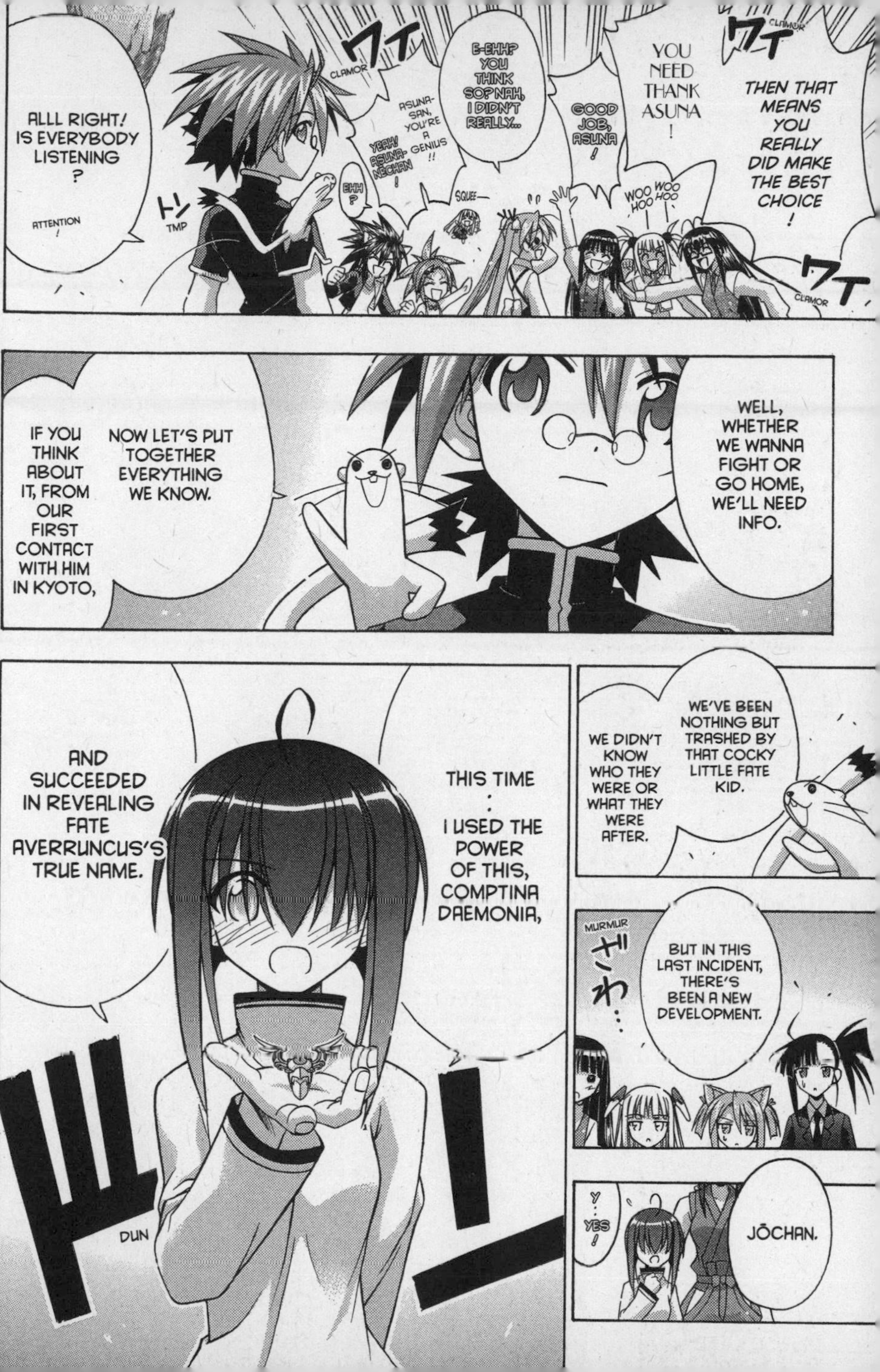
THEN THAT MEANS YOU REALLY DID MAKE THE BEST CHOICE!
CLAMOR
YOU NEED THANK ASUNA!
GOOD JOB, ASUNA!
WOO HOO WOO HOO
E-EHH? YOU THINK SO? NAH, I DIDN'T REALLY...
ASUNA-SAN, YOU'RE A GENIUS!!
YEAH! ASUNA-NECHAN!
SQUEE—
EHH?
CLAMOR
CLAMOR
ALLL RIGHT! IS EVERYBODY LISTENING?
TMP
ATTENTION!
WELL, WHETHER WE WANNA FIGHT OR GO HOME, WE'LL NEED INFO.
NOW LET'S PUT TOGETHER EVERYTHING WE KNOW.
IF YOU THINK ABOUT IT, FROM OUR FIRST CONTACT WITH HIM IN KYOTO,
WE'VE BEEN NOTHING BUT TRASHED BY THAT COCKY LITTLE FATE KID.
WE DIDN'T KNOW WHO THEY WERE OR WHAT THEY WERE AFTER.
BUT IN THIS LAST INCIDENT, THERE'S BEEN A NEW DEVELOPMENT.
MURMUR
JŌCHAN.
Y... YES!
THIS TIME: I USED THE POWER OF THIS, COMPTINA DAEMONIA,
AND SUCCEEDED IN REVEALING FATE AVERRUNCUS'S TRUE NAME.
DUN

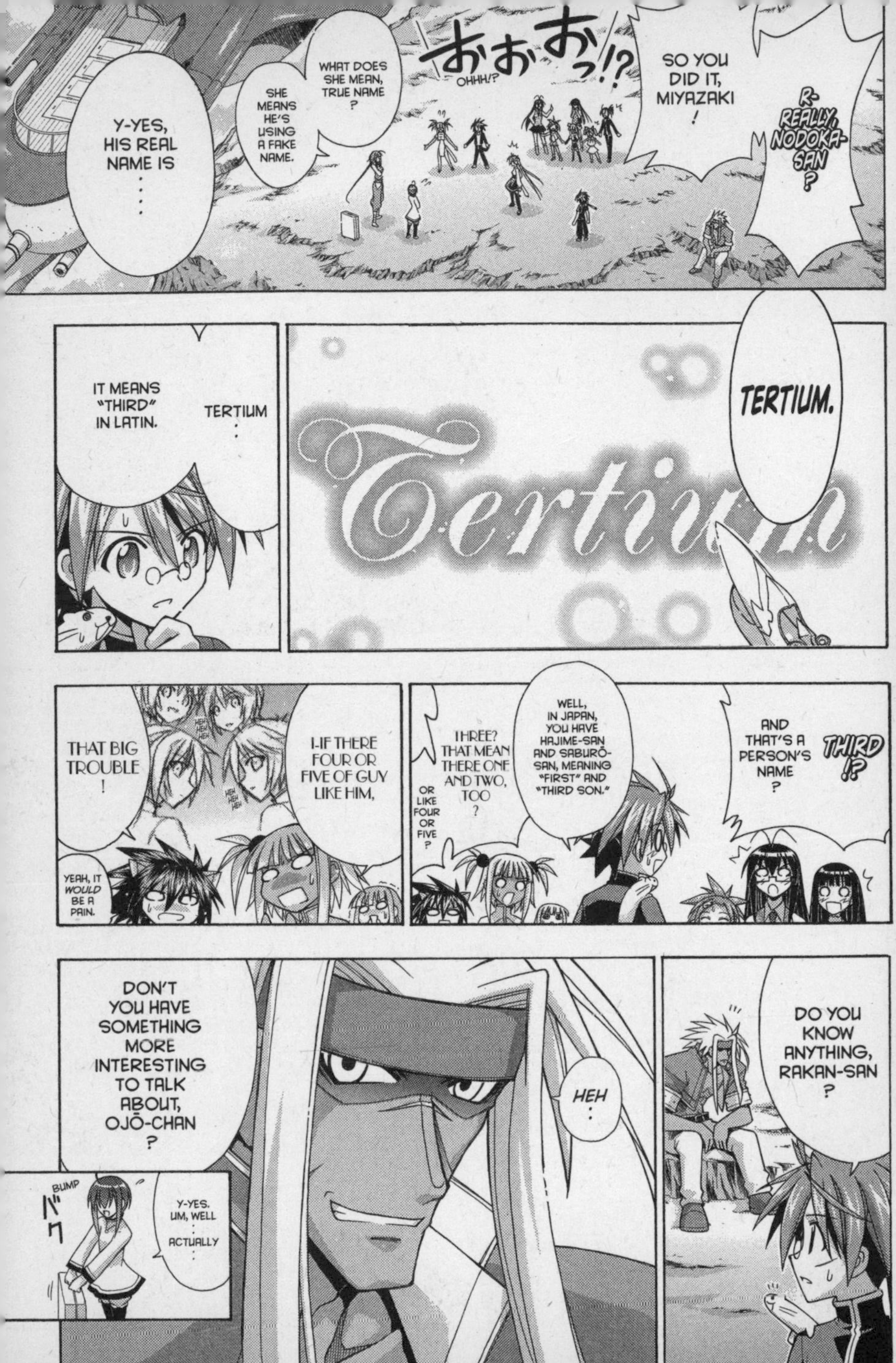
R-REALLY, NODOKA-SAN?
SO YOU DID IT, MIYAZAKI!
おぉおっ!!?
OHHH!?
WHAT DOES SHE MEAN, TRUE NAME?
SHE MEANS HE'S USING A FAKE NAME.
Y-YES, HIS REAL NAME IS ......
TERTIUM.
Tertium
TERTIUM ..
IT MEANS "THIRD" IN LATIN.
THIRD!?
AND THAT'S A PERSON'S NAME?
WELL, IN JAPAN, YOU HAVE HAJIME-SAN AND SABURŌ-SAN, MEANING "FIRST" AND "THIRD SON."
THREE? THAT MEAN THERE ONE AND TWO, TOO?
OR LIKE FOUR OR FIVE?
I-IF THERE FOUR OR FIVE OF GUY LIKE HIM,
HEH HEH HEH
HEH HEH HEH
THAT BIG TROUBLE!
YEAH, IT WOULD BE A PAIN.
DO YOU KNOW ANYTHING, RAKAN-SAN?
HEH ..
DON'T YOU HAVE SOMETHING MORE INTERESTING TO TALK ABOUT, OJŌ-CHAN?
Y-YES. UM, WELL ... ACTUALLY ...
バク
BUMP

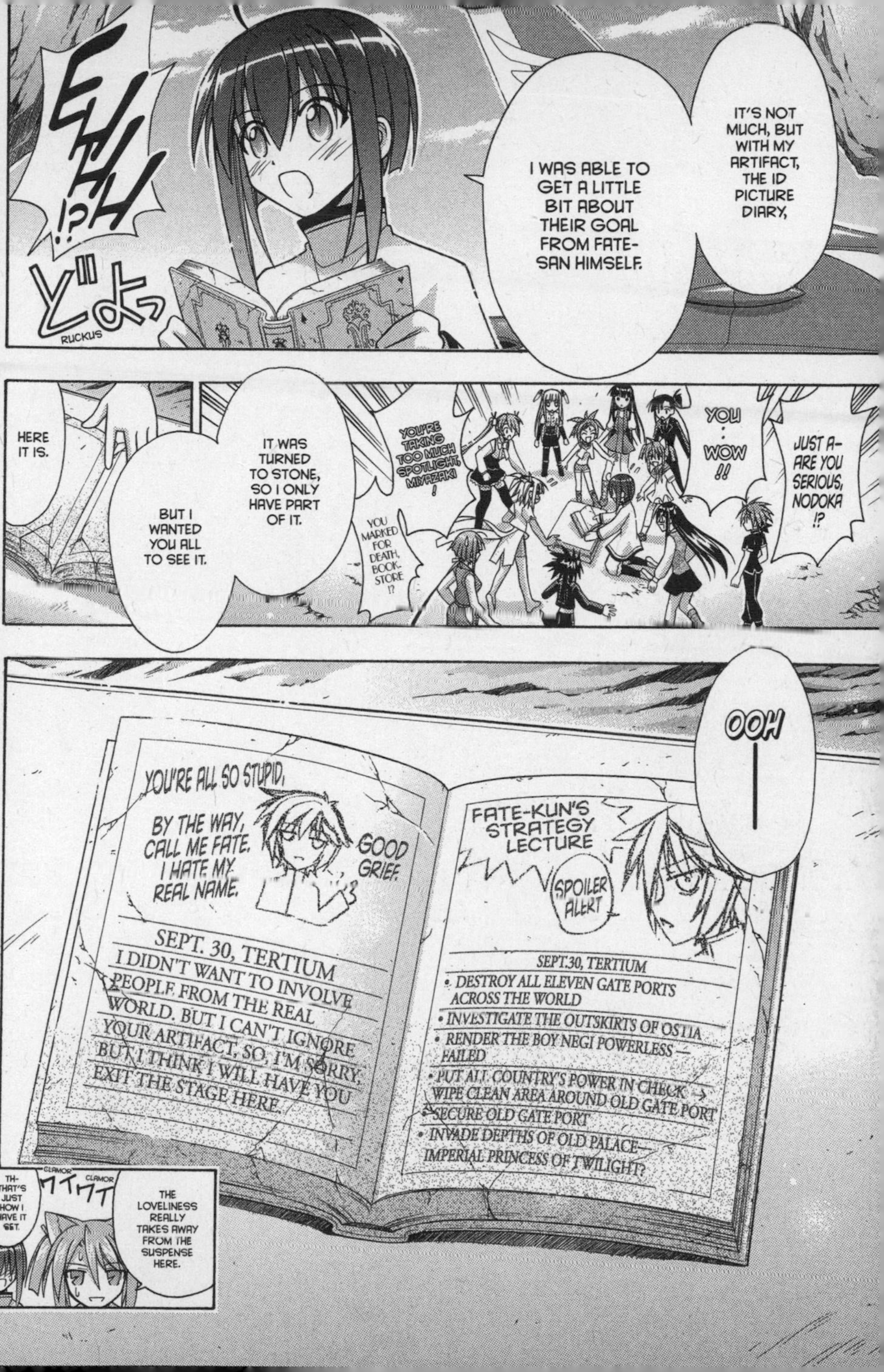
IT'S NOT MUCH, BUT WITH MY ARTIFACT, THE ID PICTURE DIARY,
I WAS ABLE TO GET A LITTLE BIT ABOUT THEIR GOAL FROM FATE-SAN HIMSELF.
EHHHH!?
どよっ
RUCKUS
JUST A— ARE YOU SERIOUS, NODOKA!?
YOU... WOW!!
YOU'RE TAKING TOO MUCH SPOTLIGHT, MIYAZAKI!
YOU MARKED FOR DEATH, BOOKSTORE!?
IT WAS TURNED TO STONE, SO I ONLY HAVE PART OF IT.
BUT I WANTED YOU ALL TO SEE IT.
HERE IT IS.
OOH—
FATE-KUN'S STRATEGY LECTURE
SPOILER ALERT
SEPT.30, TERTIUM
• DESTROY ALL ELEVEN GATE PORTS ACROSS THE WORLD
• INVESTIGATE THE OUTSKIRTS OF OSTIA
• RENDER THE BOY NEGI POWERLESS — FAILED
• PUT ALL COUNTRY'S POWER IN CHECK
WIPE CLEAN AREA AROUND OLD GATE PORT →
• SECURE OLD GATE PORT
• INVADE DEPTHS OF OLD PALACE— IMPERIAL PRINCESS OF TWILIGHT?
YOU'RE ALL SO STUPID,
BY THE WAY, CALL ME FATE. I HATE MY REAL NAME.
GOOD GRIEF.
SEPT. 30, TERTIUM
I DIDN'T WANT TO INVOLVE PEOPLE FROM THE REAL WORLD. BUT I CAN'T IGNORE YOUR ARTIFACT, SO, I'M SORRY. BUT I THINK I WILL HAVE YOU EXIT THE STAGE HERE.
THE LOVELINESS REALLY TAKES AWAY FROM THE SUSPENSE HERE.
ワイワイ
CLAMOR CLAMOR
TH-THAT'S JUST HOW I HAVE IT SET.

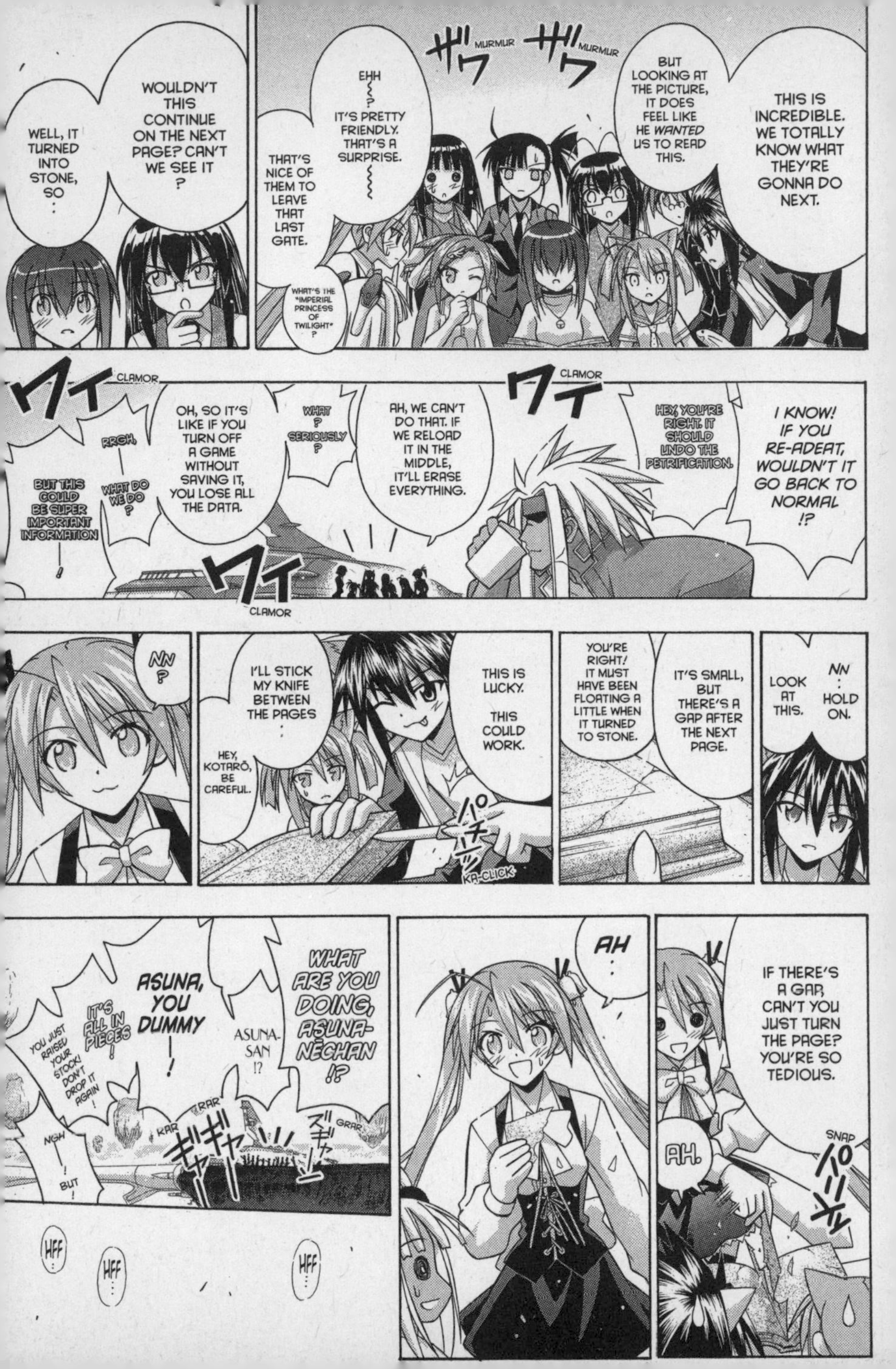
THIS IS INCREDIBLE. WE TOTALLY KNOW WHAT THEY'RE GONNA DO NEXT.
BUT LOOKING AT THE PICTURE, IT DOES FEEL LIKE HE *WANTED* US TO READ THIS.
MURMUR MURMUR
EHH~? IT'S PRETTY FRIENDLY. THAT'S A SURPRISE.
THAT'S NICE OF THEM TO LEAVE THAT LAST GATE.
WHAT'S THE "IMPERIAL PRINCESS OF TWILIGHT"?
WOULDN'T THIS CONTINUE ON THE NEXT PAGE? CAN'T WE SEE IT?
WELL, IT TURNED INTO STONE, SO...
I KNOW! IF YOU RE-ADEAT, WOULDN'T IT GO BACK TO NORMAL!?
HEY, YOU'RE RIGHT. IT SHOULD UNDO THE PETRIFICATION.
CLAMOR
AH, WE CAN'T DO THAT. IF WE RELOAD IT IN THE MIDDLE, IT'LL ERASE EVERYTHING.
WHAT? SERIOUSLY?
OH, SO IT'S LIKE IF YOU TURN OFF A GAME WITHOUT SAVING IT, YOU LOSE ALL THE DATA.
RRGH, WHAT DO WE DO?
BUT THIS COULD BE SUPER IMPORTANT INFORMATION!
CLAMOR
CLAMOR
NN: HOLD ON.
LOOK AT THIS.
IT'S SMALL, BUT THERE'S A GAP AFTER THE NEXT PAGE.
YOU'RE RIGHT! IT MUST HAVE BEEN FLOATING A LITTLE WHEN IT TURNED TO STONE.
THIS IS LUCKY. THIS COULD WORK.
I'LL STICK MY KNIFE BETWEEN THE PAGES:
HEY, KOTARŌ, BE CAREFUL.
KA-CLICK
NN?
IF THERE'S A GAP, CAN'T YOU JUST TURN THE PAGE? YOU'RE SO TEDIOUS.
SNAP
AH.
AH...
WHAT ARE YOU DOING, ASUNA-NĒCHAN!?
ASUNA-SAN!?
ASUNA, YOU DUMMY!
IT'S ALL IN PIECES!
YOU JUST RAISED YOUR STOCK! DON'T DROP IT AGAIN!
GRAR
GRAR
KAR
NGH! BUT!
HFF...
HFF...
HFF...

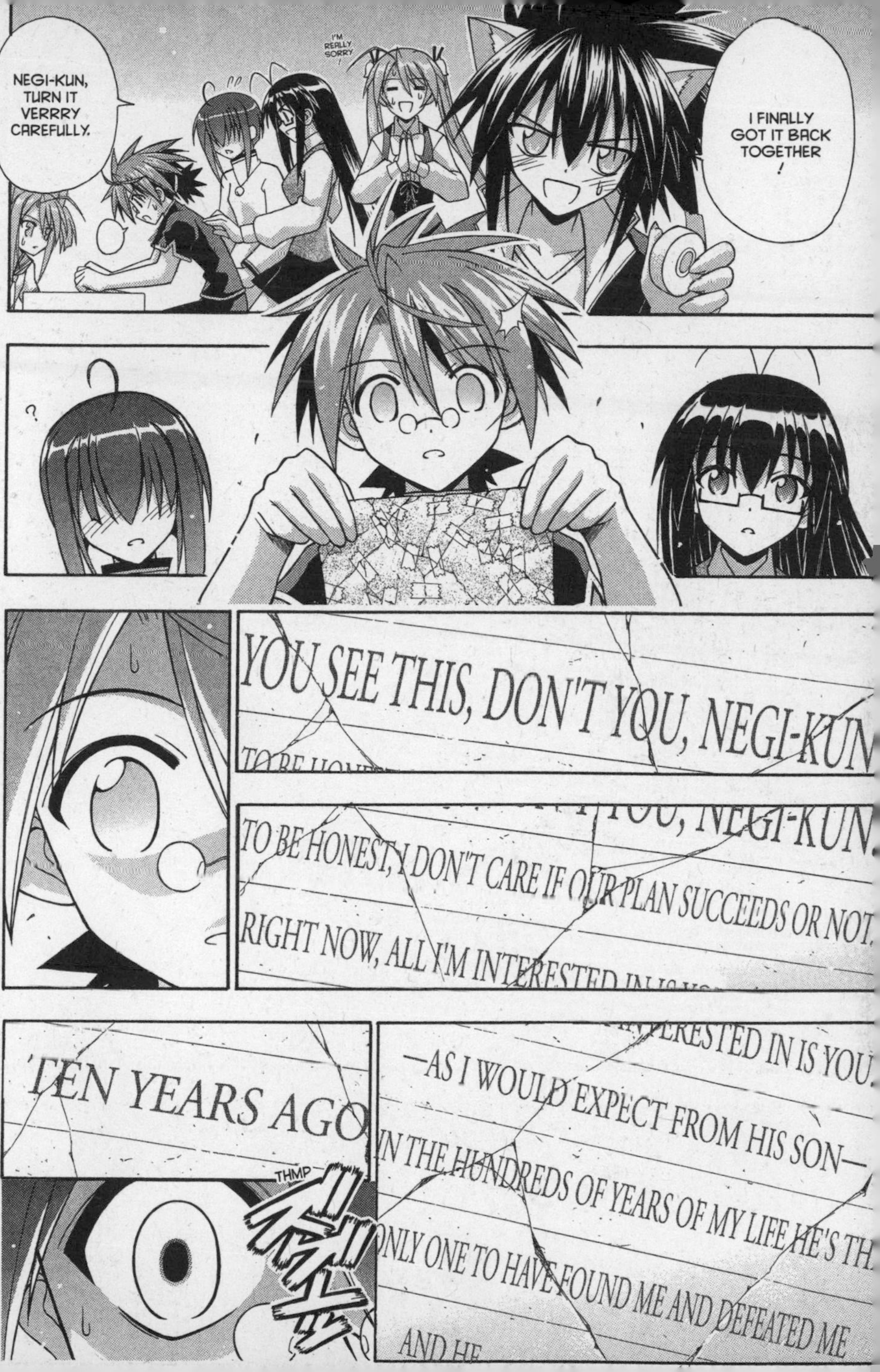
I FINALLY GOT IT BACK TOGETHER!
I'M REALLY SORRY!
NEGI-KUN, TURN IT VERRRY CAREFULLY.
?
YOU SEE THIS, DON'T YOU, NEGI-KUN
TO BE HONEST, I DON'T CARE IF OUR PLAN SUCCEEDS OR NOT.
RIGHT NOW, ALL I'M INTERESTED IN IS
INTERESTED IN IS YOU.
—AS I WOULD EXPECT FROM HIS SON—
IN THE HUNDREDS OF YEARS OF MY LIFE HE'S THE
ONLY ONE TO HAVE FOUND ME AND DEFEATED ME
AND HE
TEN YEARS AGO
THMP

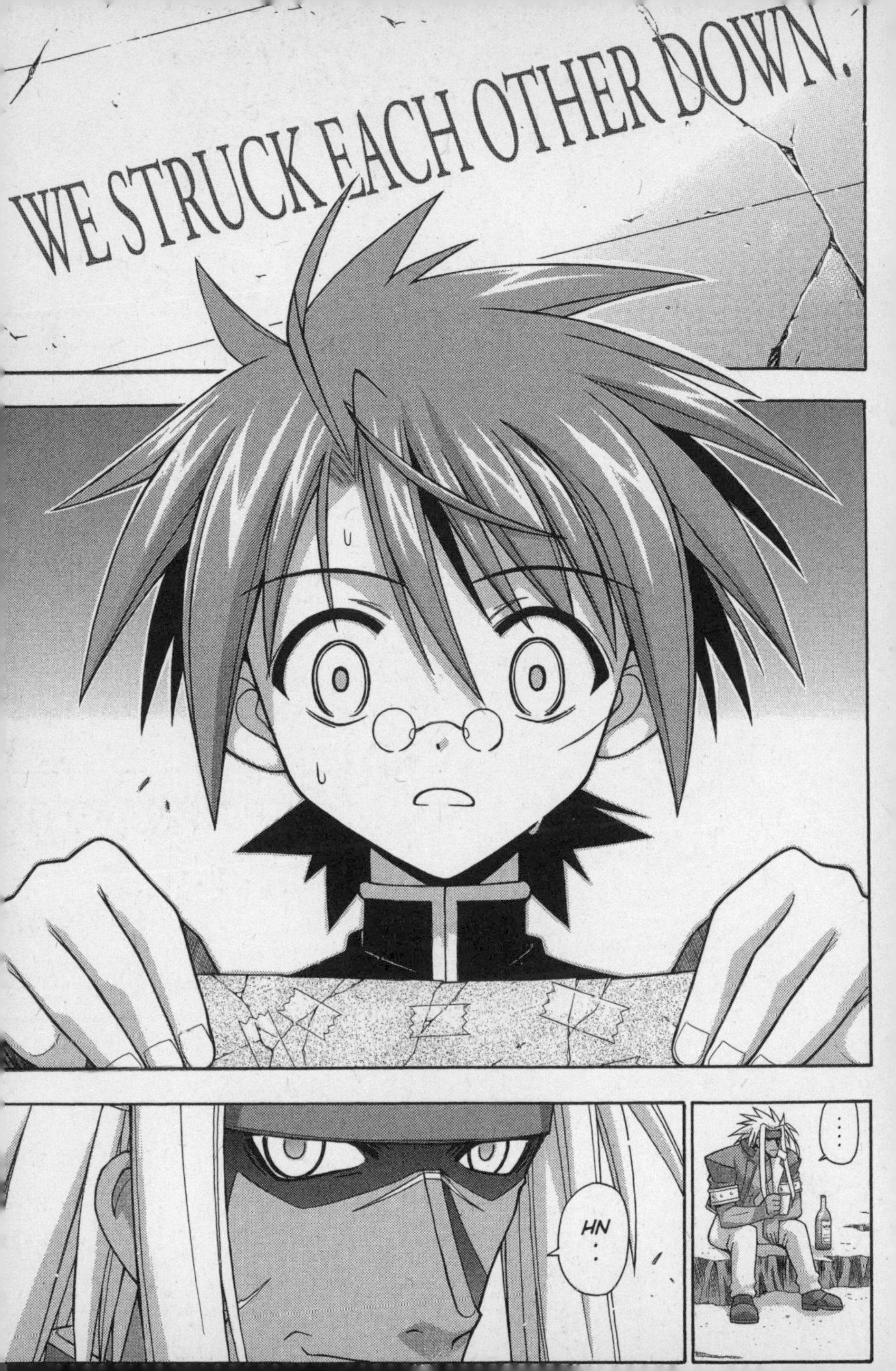
WE STRUCK EACH OTHER DOWN.
....
HN...

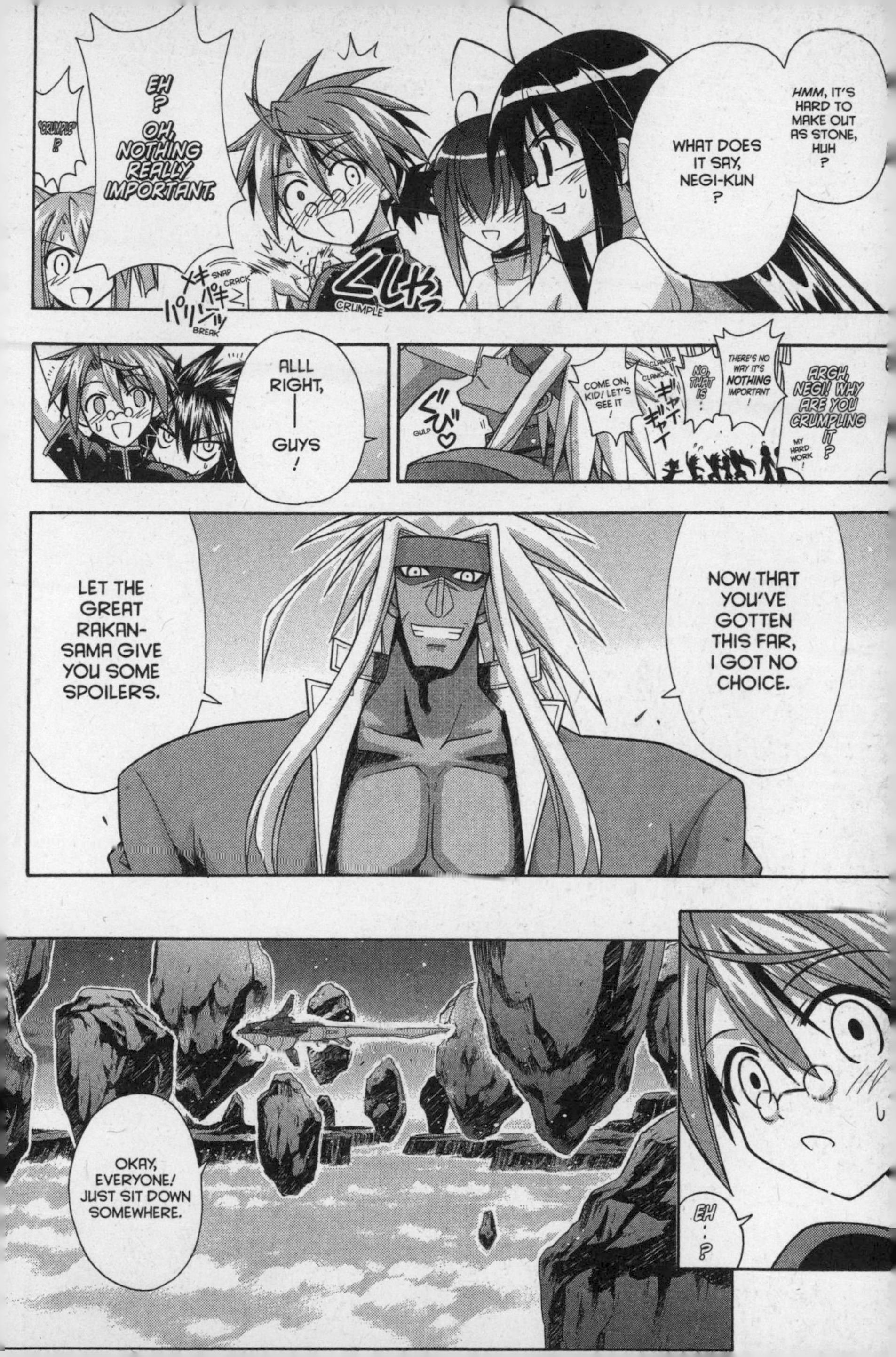
HMM, IT'S HARD TO MAKE OUT AS STONE, HUH?
WHAT DOES IT SAY, NEGI-KUN?
EH? OH, NOTHING REALLY IMPORTANT.
CRUMPLE
SNAP CRACK BREAK
"CRUMPLE"!?
ARGH, NEGI!! WHY ARE YOU CRUMPLING IT?
MY HARD WORK!
THERE'S NO WAY IT'S NOTHING IMPORTANT!
NO, THAT IS...
CLAMOR CLAMOR
COME ON, KID! LET'S SEE IT!
GULP
ALLL RIGHT, GUYS!
NOW THAT YOU'VE GOTTEN THIS FAR, I GOT NO CHOICE.
LET THE GREAT RAKAN-SAMA GIVE YOU SOME SPOILERS.
EH...?
OKAY, EVERYONE! JUST SIT DOWN SOMEWHERE.

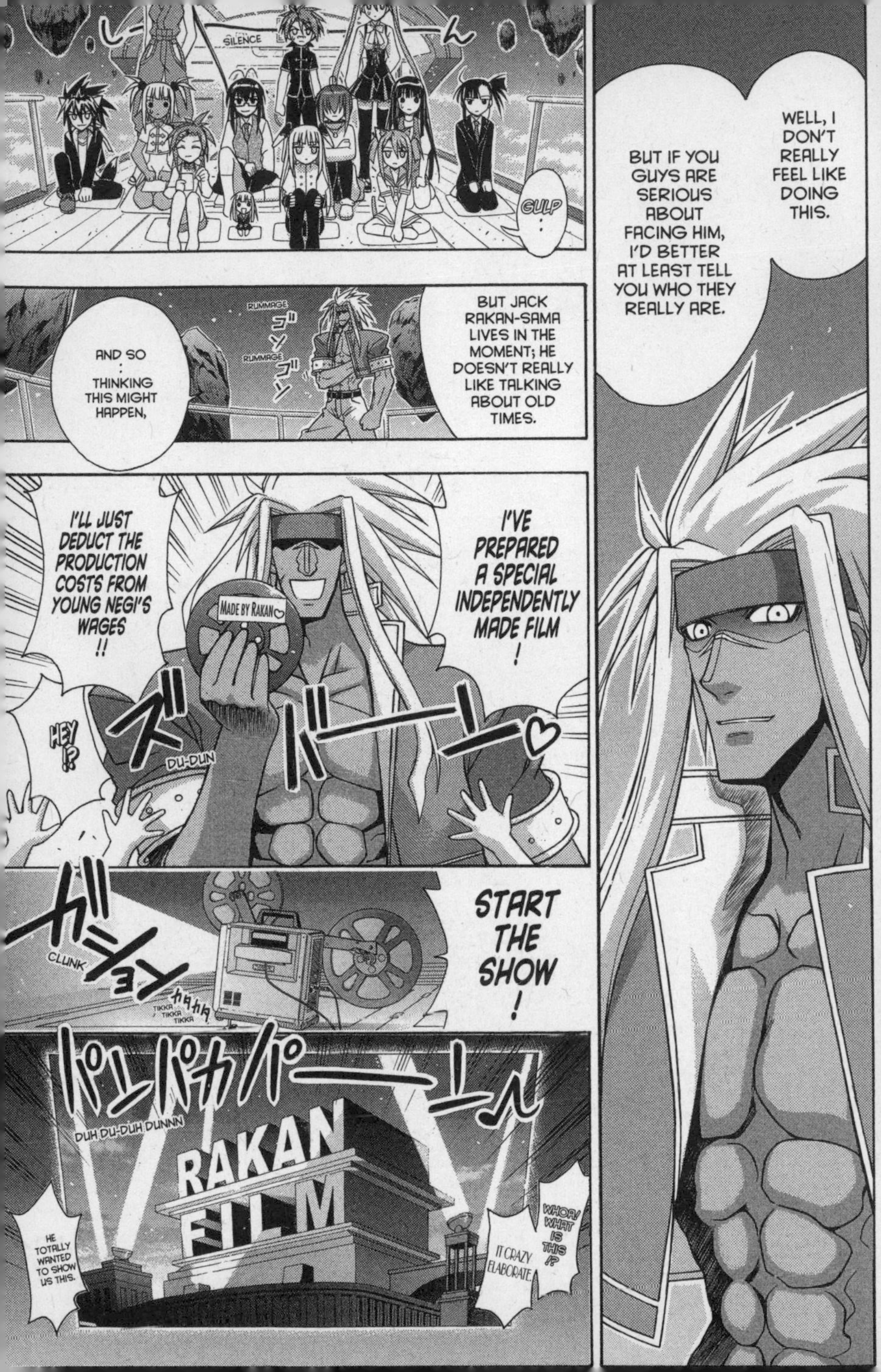
WELL, I DON'T REALLY FEEL LIKE DOING THIS.
BUT IF YOU GUYS ARE SERIOUS ABOUT FACING HIM, I'D BETTER AT LEAST TELL YOU WHO THEY REALLY ARE.
SILENCE
GULP
BUT JACK RAKAN-SAMA LIVES IN THE MOMENT; HE DOESN'T REALLY LIKE TALKING ABOUT OLD TIMES.
RUMMAGE
RUMMAGE
AND SO... THINKING THIS MIGHT HAPPEN,
I'VE PREPARED A SPECIAL INDEPENDENTLY MADE FILM!
MADE BY RAKAN
DU-DUN
I'LL JUST DEDUCT THE PRODUCTION COSTS FROM YOUNG NEGI'S WAGES!!
HEY!?
START THE SHOW!
CLUNK
TIKKA TIKKA TIKKA
DUH DU-DUH DUNNN
RAKAN FILM
WHOA! WHAT IS THIS!?
IT CRAZY ELABORATE.
HE TOTALLY WANTED TO SHOW US THIS.

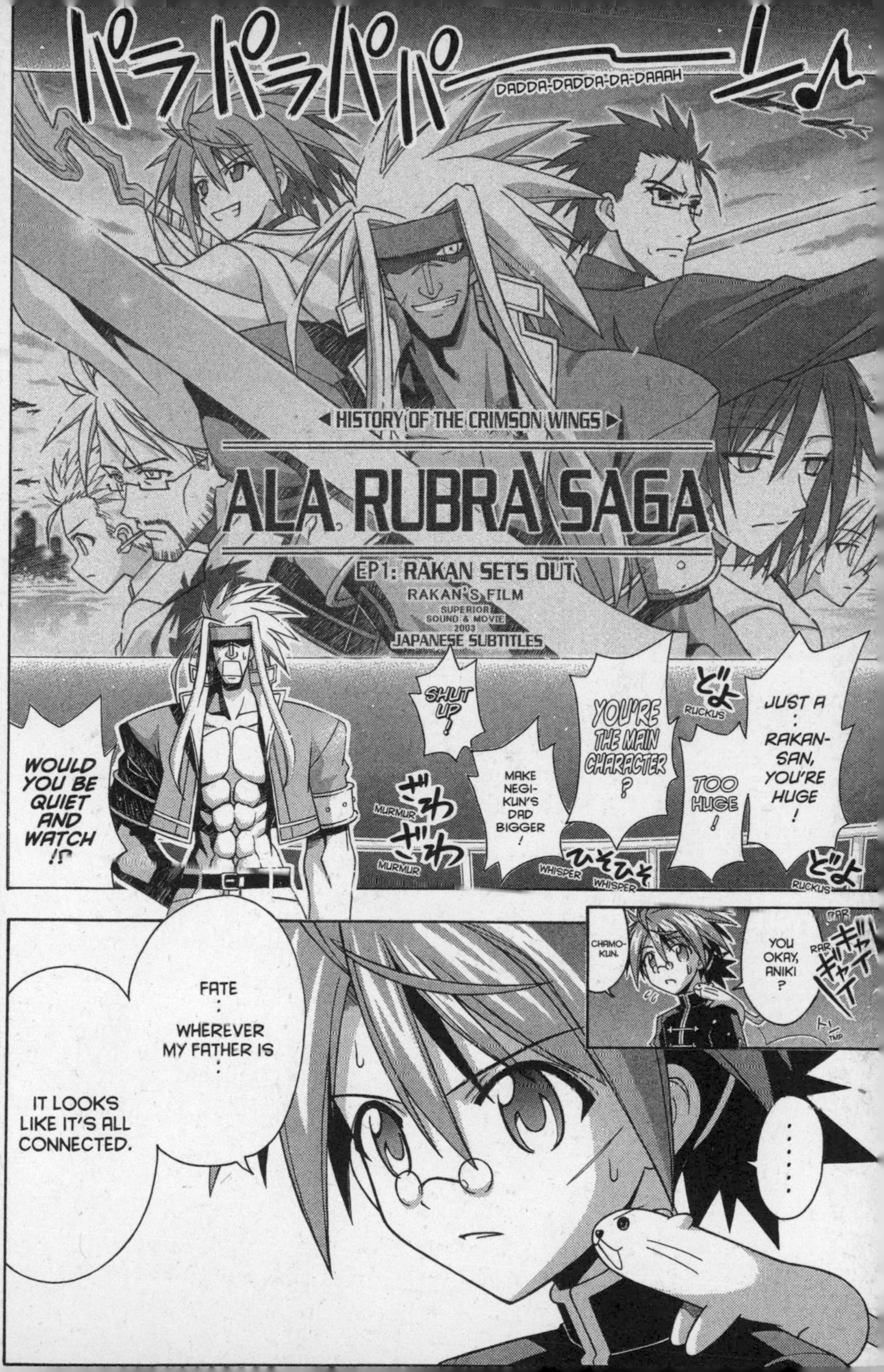
パラパラパーーーー!♪
DADDA-DADDA-DA-DAAAH
HISTORY OF THE CRIMSON WINGS
ALA RUBRA SAGA
EP1: RAKAN SETS OUT
RAKAN'S FILM
SUPERIOR SOUND & MOVIE 2003
JAPANESE SUBTITLES
どよ
RUCKUS
JUST A : RAKAN-SAN, YOU'RE HUGE!
どよ
RUCKUS
TOO HUGE!
YOU'RE THE MAIN CHARACTER?
ひそひそ
WHISPER WHISPER
MAKE NEGI-KUN'S DAD BIGGER!
SHUT UP!
ざわざわ
MURMUR MURMUR
WOULD YOU BE QUIET AND WATCH!?
ギャイギャイ
RAR RAR
YOU OKAY, ANIKI?
CHAMO-KUN.
トン
TMP
......
FATE : WHEREVER MY FATHER IS :
IT LOOKS LIKE IT'S ALL CONNECTED.

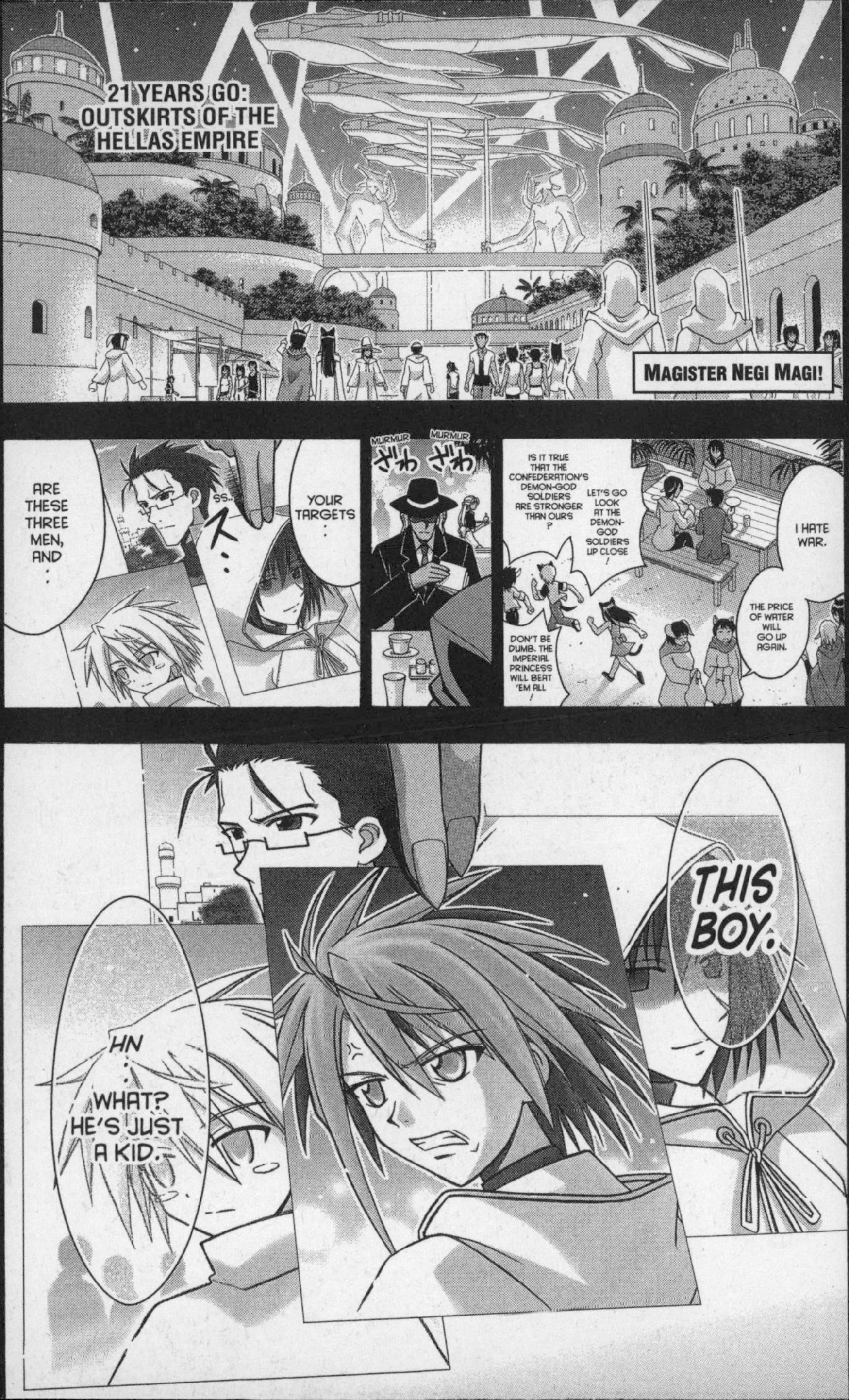
21 YEARS GO: OUTSKIRTS OF THE HELLAS EMPIRE
MAGISTER NEGI MAGI!
I HATE WAR.
IS IT TRUE THAT THE CONFEDERATION'S DEMON-GOD SOLDIERS ARE STRONGER THAN OURS?
LET'S GO LOOK AT THE DEMON-GOD SOLDIERS UP CLOSE!
THE PRICE OF WATER WILL GO UP AGAIN.
DON'T BE DUMB. THE IMPERIAL PRINCESS WILL BEAT 'EM ALL!
MURMUR MURMUR
ざわ ざわ
YOUR TARGETS...
SS...
ス...
ARE THESE THREE MEN, AND...
THIS BOY.
HN... WHAT? HE'S JUST A KID.

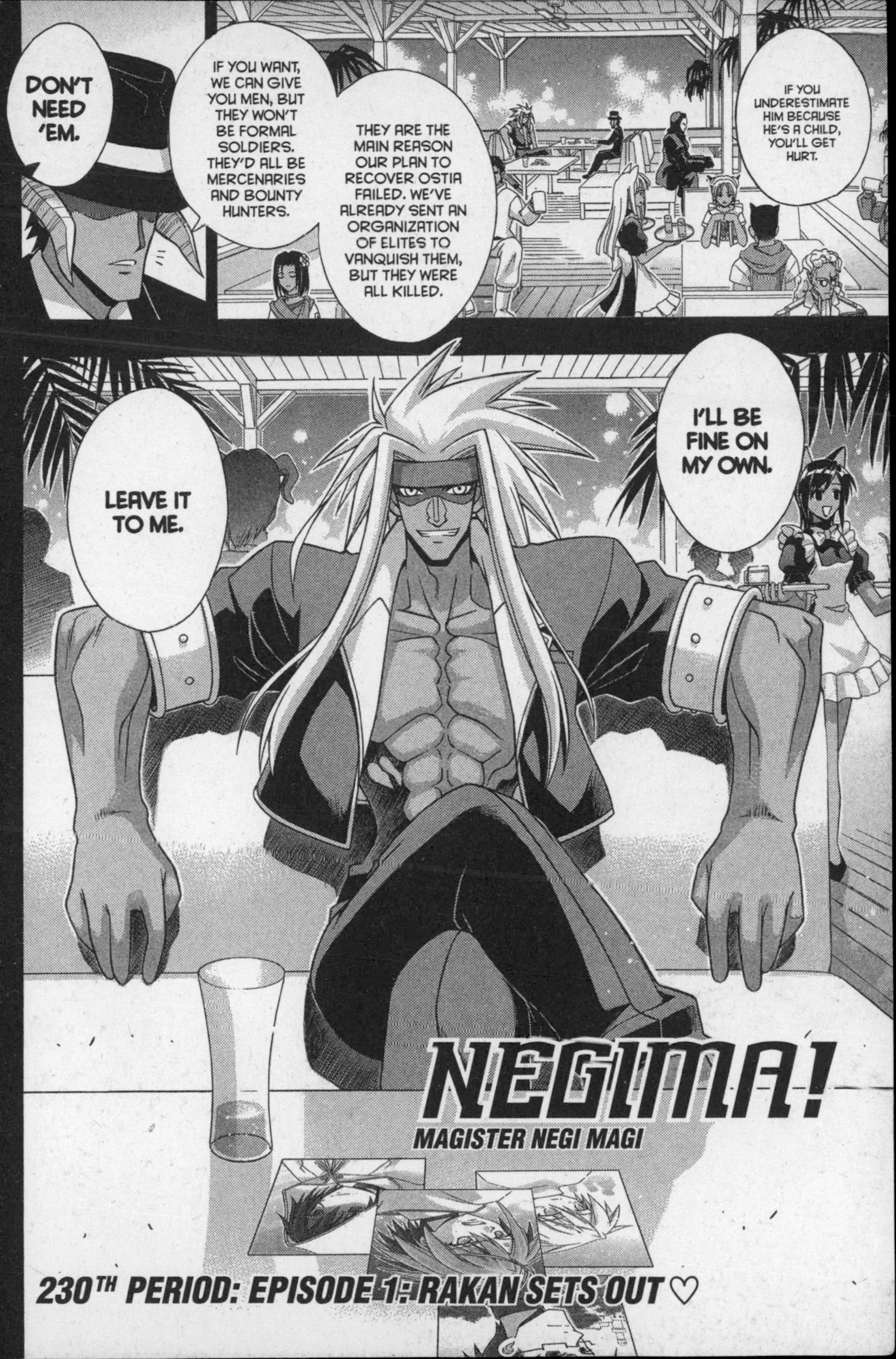
IF YOU UNDERESTIMATE HIM BECAUSE HE'S A CHILD, YOU'LL GET HURT.
IF YOU WANT, WE CAN GIVE YOU MEN, BUT THEY WON'T BE FORMAL SOLDIERS. THEY'D ALL BE MERCENARIES AND BOUNTY HUNTERS.
THEY ARE THE MAIN REASON OUR PLAN TO RECOVER OSTIA FAILED. WE'VE ALREADY SENT AN ORGANIZATION OF ELITES TO VANQUISH THEM, BUT THEY WERE ALL KILLED.
DON'T NEED 'EM.
I'LL BE FINE ON MY OWN.
LEAVE IT TO ME.
NEGIMA!
MAGISTER NEGI MAGI
230TH PERIOD: EPISODE 1: RAKAN SETS OUT ♡

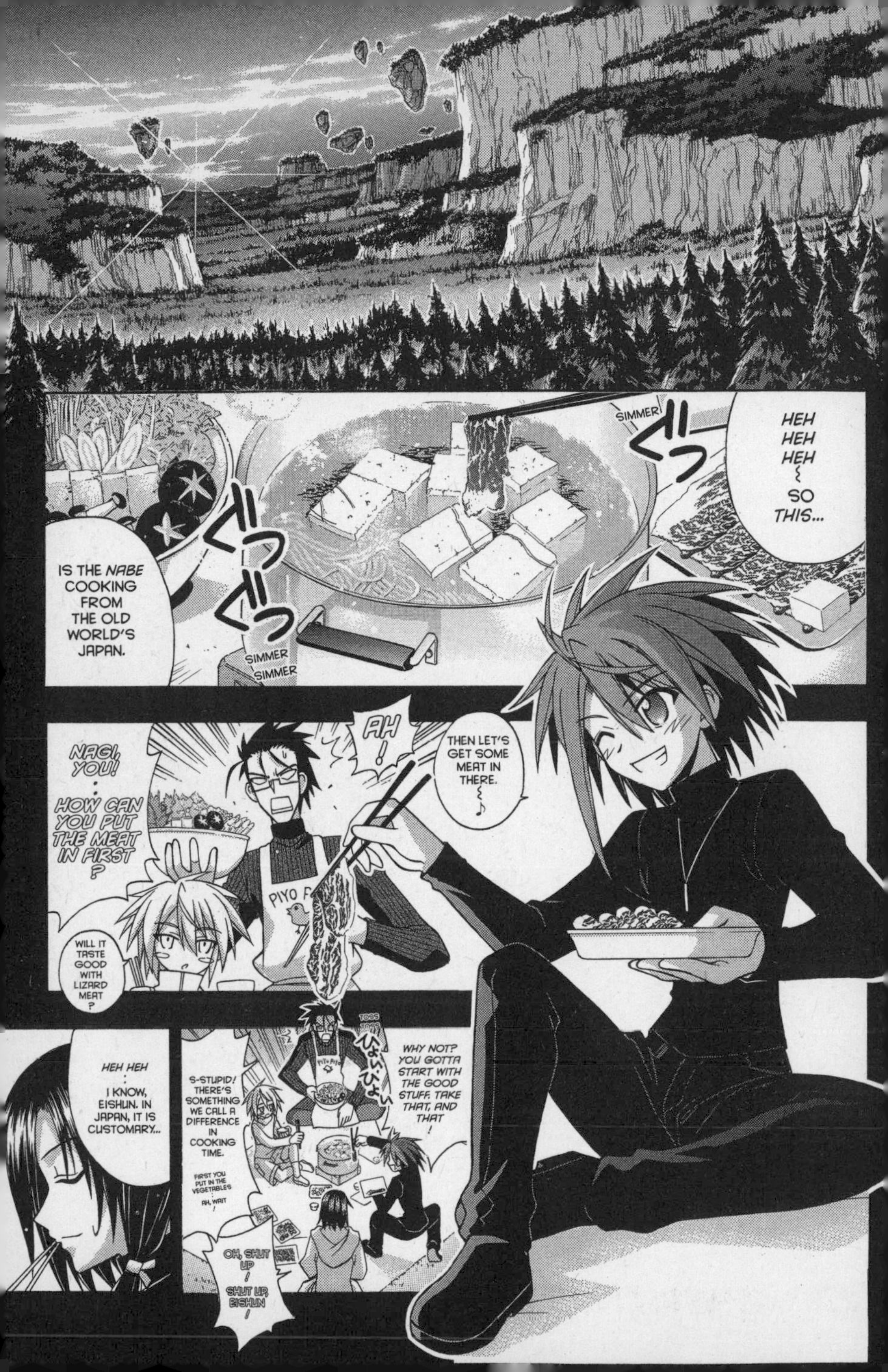
HEH HEH HEH ~ SO THIS...
SIMMER
IS THE NABE COOKING FROM THE OLD WORLD'S JAPAN.
SIMMER SIMMER
THEN LET'S GET SOME MEAT IN THERE. ~♪
AH!
NAGI, YOU! .. HOW CAN YOU PUT THE MEAT IN FIRST?
WILL IT TASTE GOOD WITH LIZARD MEAT?
TOSS
WHY NOT? YOU GOTTA START WITH THE GOOD STUFF, TAKE THAT, AND THAT!
S-STUPID! THERE'S SOMETHING WE CALL A DIFFERENCE IN COOKING TIME.
FIRST YOU PUT IN THE VEGETABLES
AH, WAIT!
OH, SHUT UP! SHUT UP, EISHUN!
HEH HEH .. I KNOW, EISHUN. IN JAPAN, IT IS CUSTOMARY...

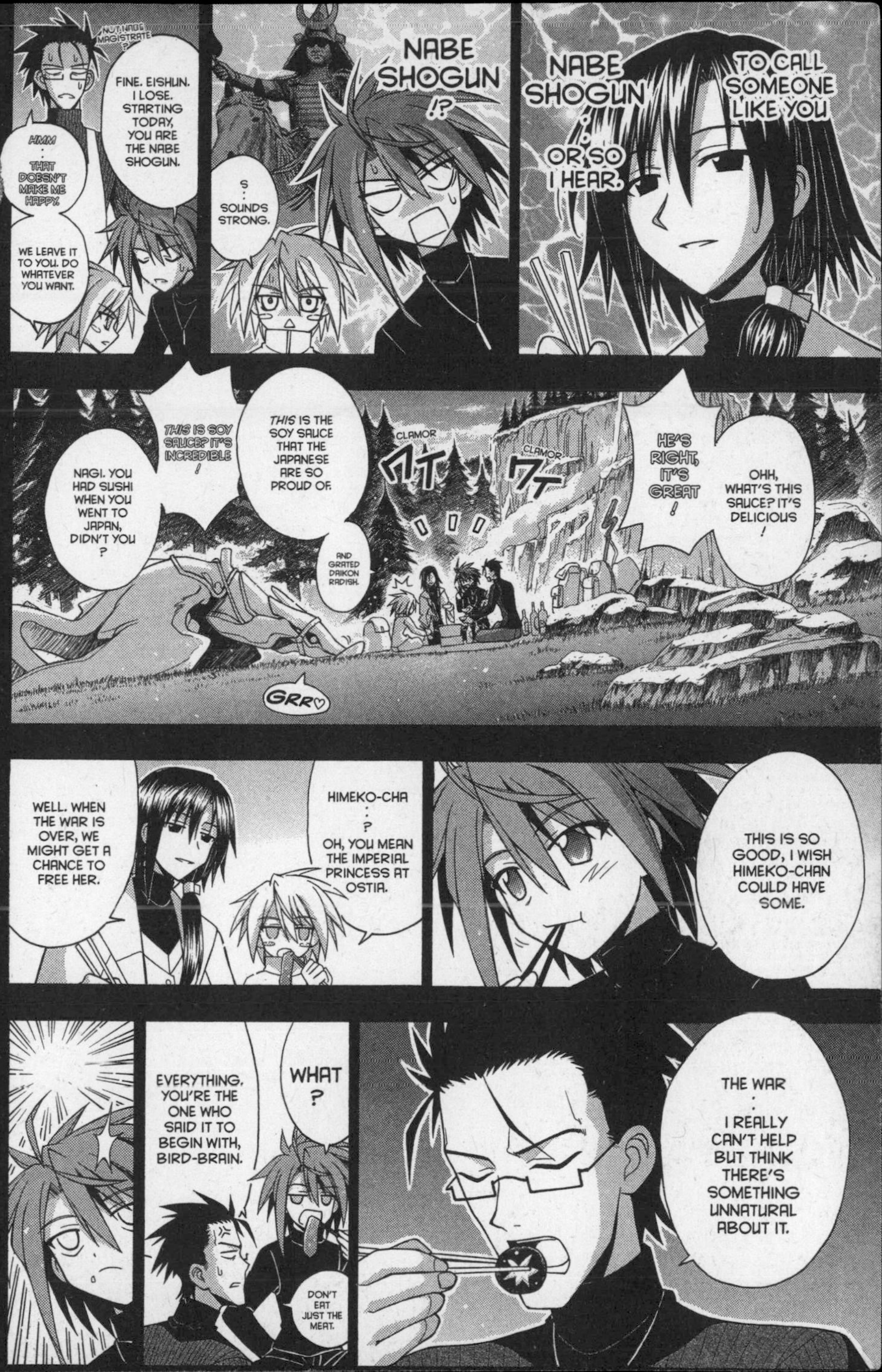
TO CALL SOMEONE LIKE YOU
NABE SHOGUN... OR SO I HEAR.
NABE SHOGUN !?
S... SOUNDS STRONG.
FINE. EISHUN. I LOSE. STARTING TODAY, YOU ARE THE NABE SHOGUN.
NOT NABE MAGISTRATE?
HMM... THAT DOESN'T MAKE ME HAPPY.
WE LEAVE IT TO YOU. DO WHATEVER YOU WANT.
OHH, WHAT'S THIS SAUCE? IT'S DELICIOUS!
HE'S RIGHT, IT'S GREAT!
CLAMOR
CLAMOR
AND GRATED DAIKON RADISH.
THIS IS THE SOY SAUCE THAT THE JAPANESE ARE SO PROUD OF.
THIS IS SOY SAUCE? IT'S INCREDIBLE!
NAGI. YOU HAD SUSHI WHEN YOU WENT TO JAPAN, DIDN'T YOU?
GRR♡
THIS IS SO GOOD, I WISH HIMEKO-CHAN COULD HAVE SOME.
HIMEKO-CHA... ? OH, YOU MEAN THE IMPERIAL PRINCESS AT OSTIA.
WELL. WHEN THE WAR IS OVER, WE MIGHT GET A CHANCE TO FREE HER.
THE WAR... I REALLY CAN'T HELP BUT THINK THERE'S SOMETHING UNNATURAL ABOUT IT.
WHAT?
EVERYTHING. YOU'RE THE ONE WHO SAID IT TO BEGIN WITH, BIRD-BRAIN.
DON'T EAT JUST THE MEAT.

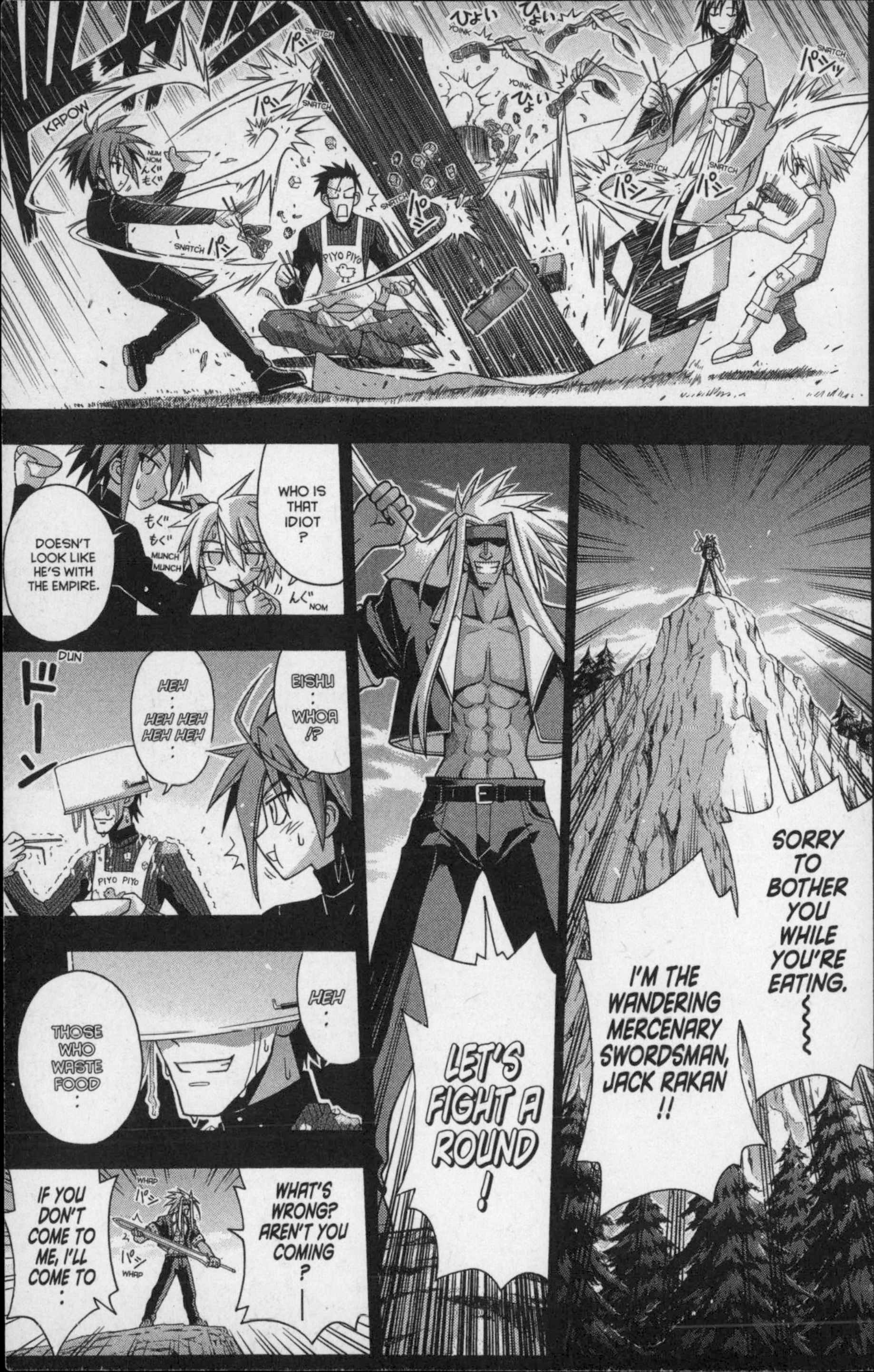
SNATCH
パンッ
YOINK
ひょい
YOINK
ひょい
SNATCH
パシ
SNATCH
パシ
SNATCH
パシ
YOINK
ひょい
SNATCH
パッ
SNATCH
パシ
KAPOW
NUM NOM
んぐ もぐ
SNATCH
パシ
PIYO PIYO
SORRY TO BOTHER YOU WHILE YOU'RE EATING.
I'M THE WANDERING MERCENARY SWORDSMAN, JACK RAKAN!!
LET'S FIGHT A ROUND!
WHO IS THAT IDIOT?
もぐ もぐ
MUNCH MUNCH
DOESN'T LOOK LIKE HE'S WITH THE EMPIRE.
んぐ
NOM
EISHU... WHOA!?
HEH... HEH HEH HEH HEH...
DUN
PIYO PIYO
HEH...
THOSE WHO WASTE FOOD...
WHAT'S WRONG? AREN'T YOU COMING?
WHAP
パシ
WHAP
パシ
IF YOU DON'T COME TO ME, I'LL COME TO...

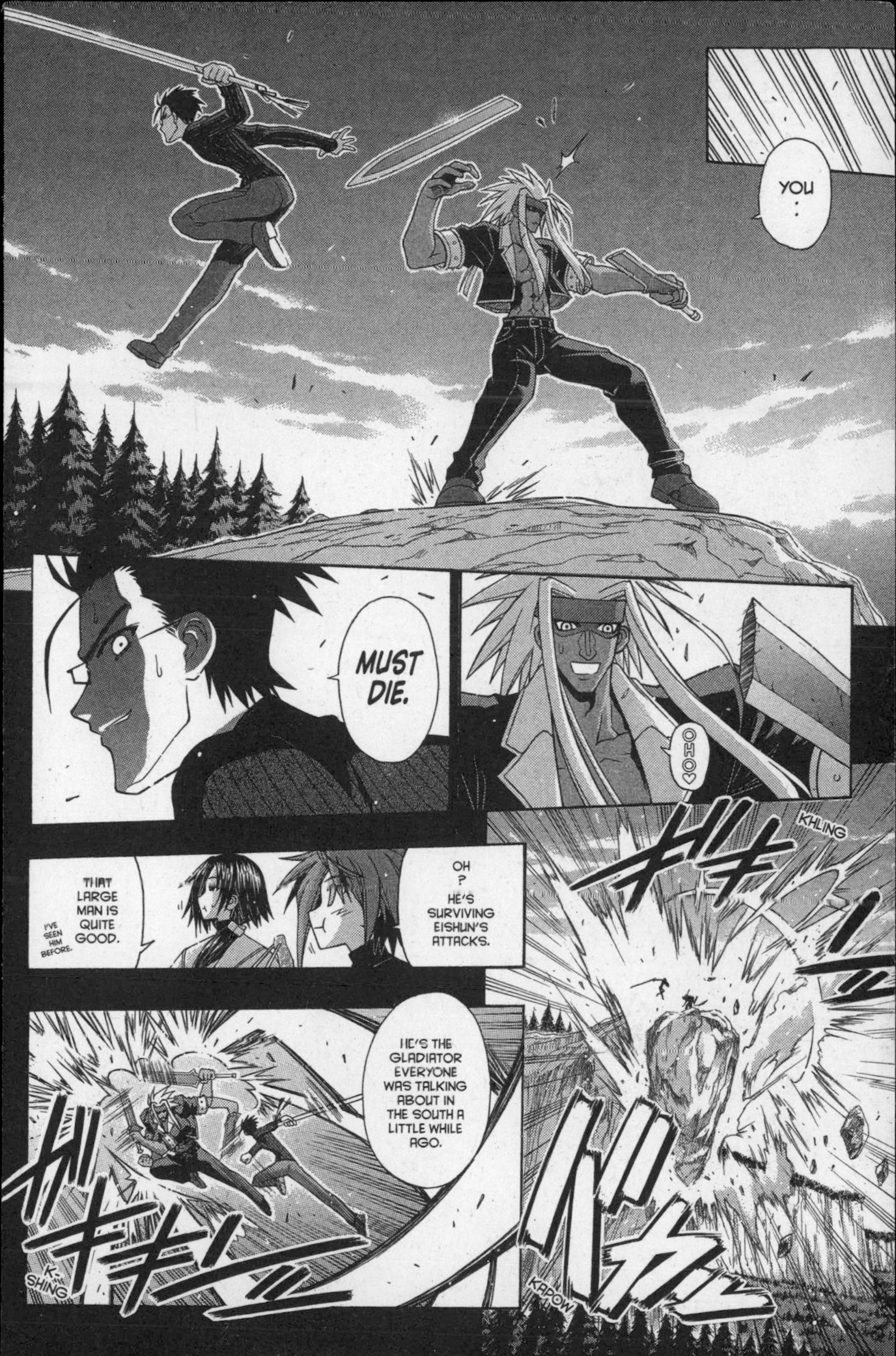
YOU...
OHO♥
MUST DIE.
KHLING
KAPOW
OH? HE'S SURVIVING EISHUN'S ATTACKS.
THAT LARGE MAN IS QUITE GOOD.
I'VE SEEN HIM BEFORE.
HE'S THE GLADIATOR EVERYONE WAS TALKING ABOUT IN THE SOUTH A LITTLE WHILE AGO.
K-SHING

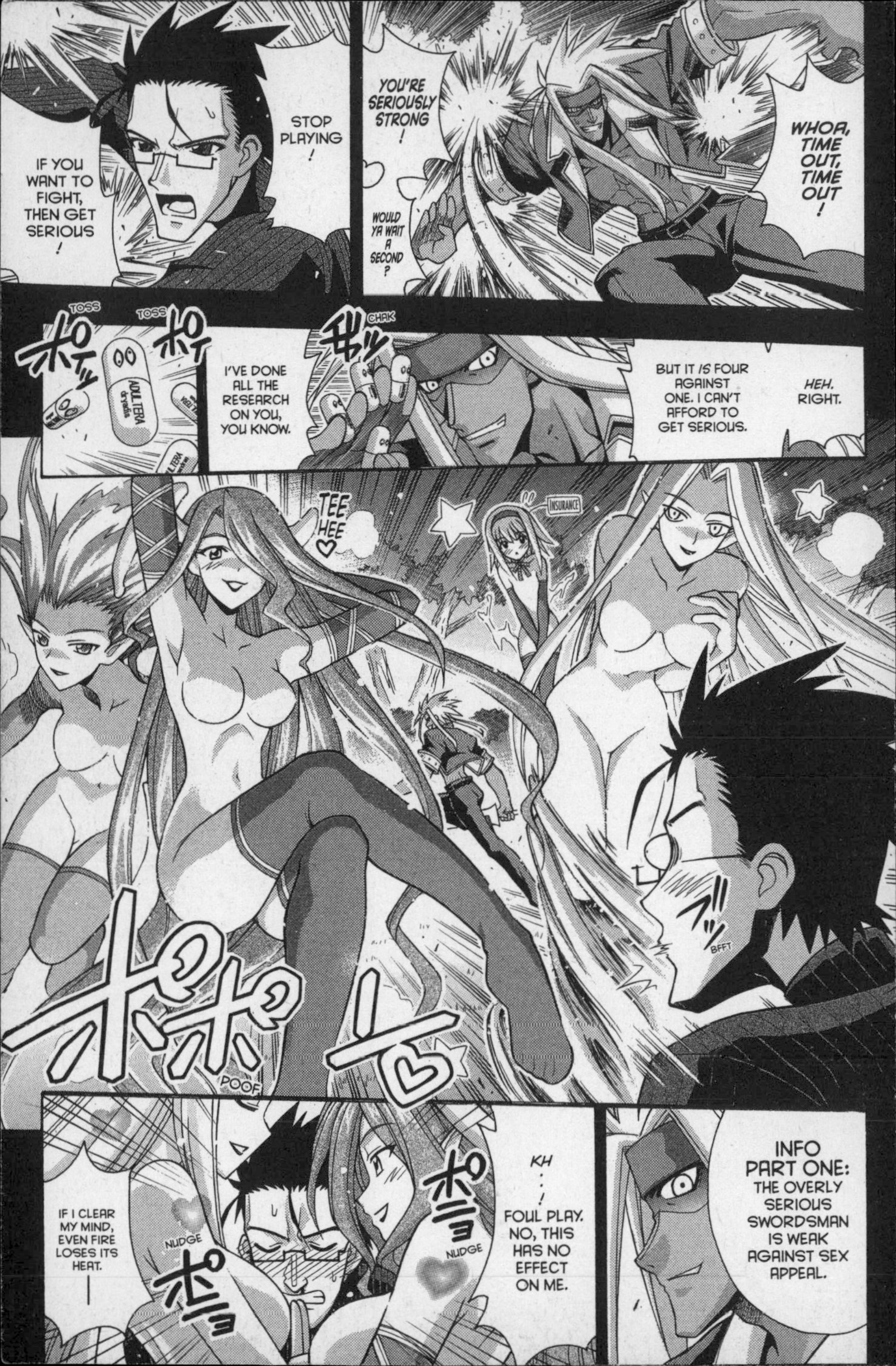
WHOA, TIME OUT, TIME OUT!
YOU'RE SERIOUSLY STRONG!
WOULD YA WAIT A SECOND?
STOP PLAYING!
IF YOU WANT TO FIGHT, THEN GET SERIOUS!
HEH. RIGHT.
BUT IT IS FOUR AGAINST ONE. I CAN'T AFFORD TO GET SERIOUS.
CHAK
I'VE DONE ALL THE RESEARCH ON YOU, YOU KNOW.
TOSS
TOSS
INSURANCE
TEE HEE
BFFT
POOF
INFO PART ONE: THE OVERLY SERIOUS SWORDSMAN IS WEAK AGAINST SEX APPEAL.
KH...!
FOUL PLAY. NO, THIS HAS NO EFFECT ON ME.
NUDGE
NUDGE
IF I CLEAR MY MIND, EVEN FIRE LOSES ITS HEAT.

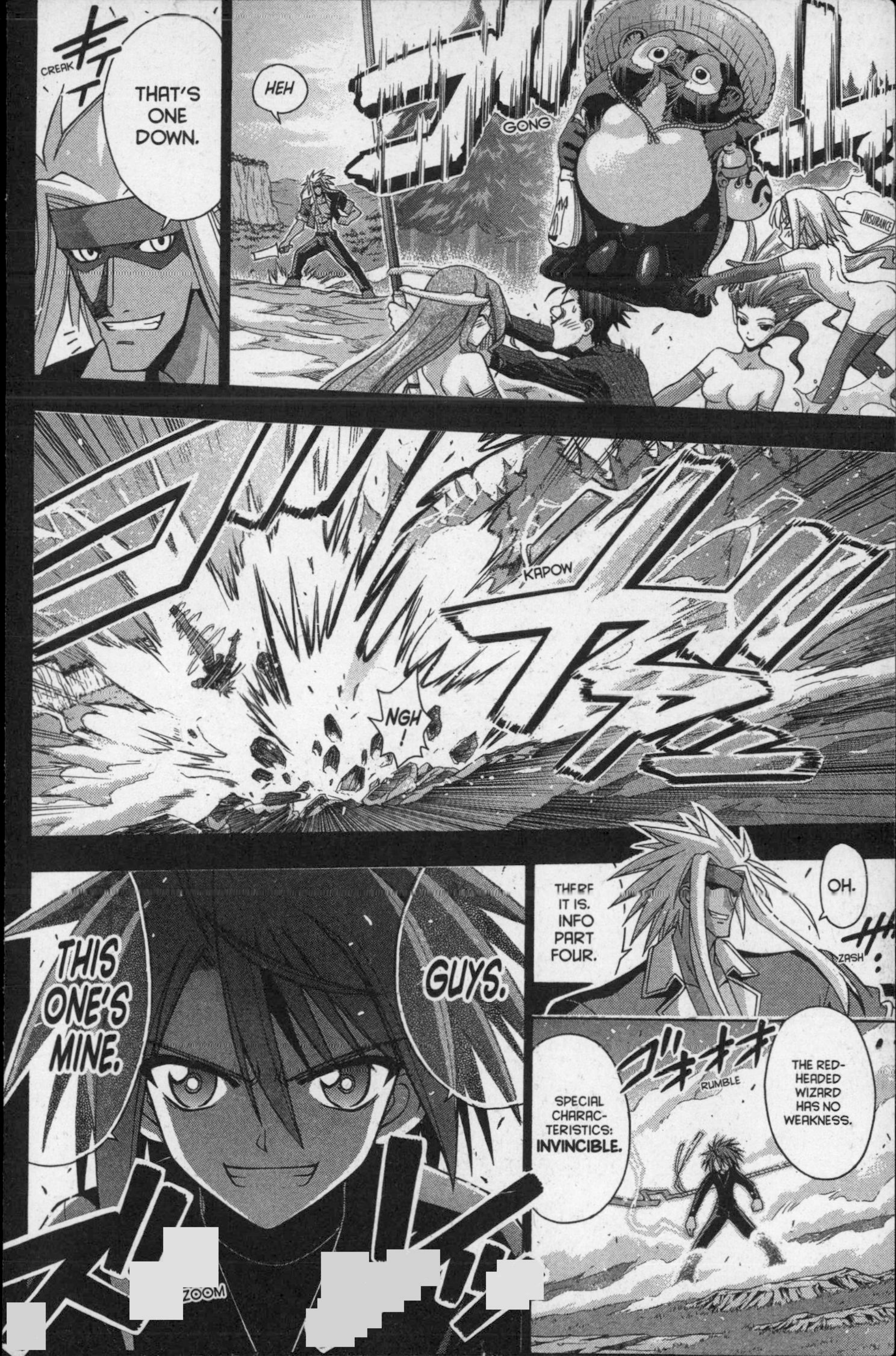
HEH
GONG
INSURANCE
CREAK
THAT'S ONE DOWN.
KAPOW
NGH!
OH.
ZASH
THERE IT IS. INFO PART FOUR.
THE RED-HEADED WIZARD HAS NO WEAKNESS.
RUMBLE
SPECIAL CHARACTERISTICS: INVINCIBLE.
GUYS.
THIS ONE'S MINE.
ZOOM

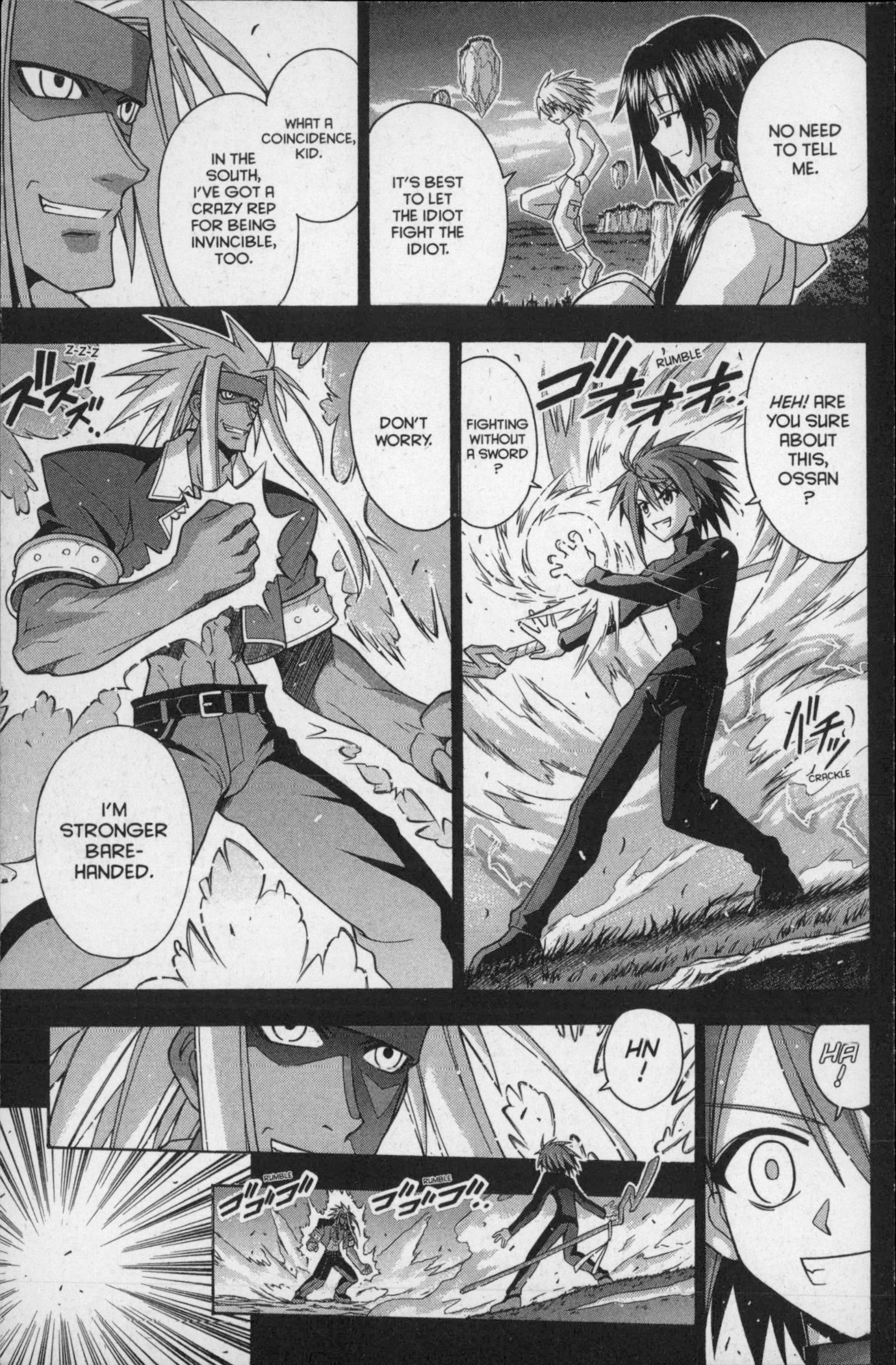
NO NEED TO TELL ME.
IT'S BEST TO LET THE IDIOT FIGHT THE IDIOT.
WHAT A COINCIDENCE, KID.
IN THE SOUTH, I'VE GOT A CRAZY REP FOR BEING INVINCIBLE, TOO.
HEH! ARE YOU SURE ABOUT THIS, OSSAN?
RUMBLE
FIGHTING WITHOUT A SWORD?
CRACKLE
Z-Z-Z
DON'T WORRY.
I'M STRONGER BARE-HANDED.
HA!
HN!
RUMBLE
RUMBLE

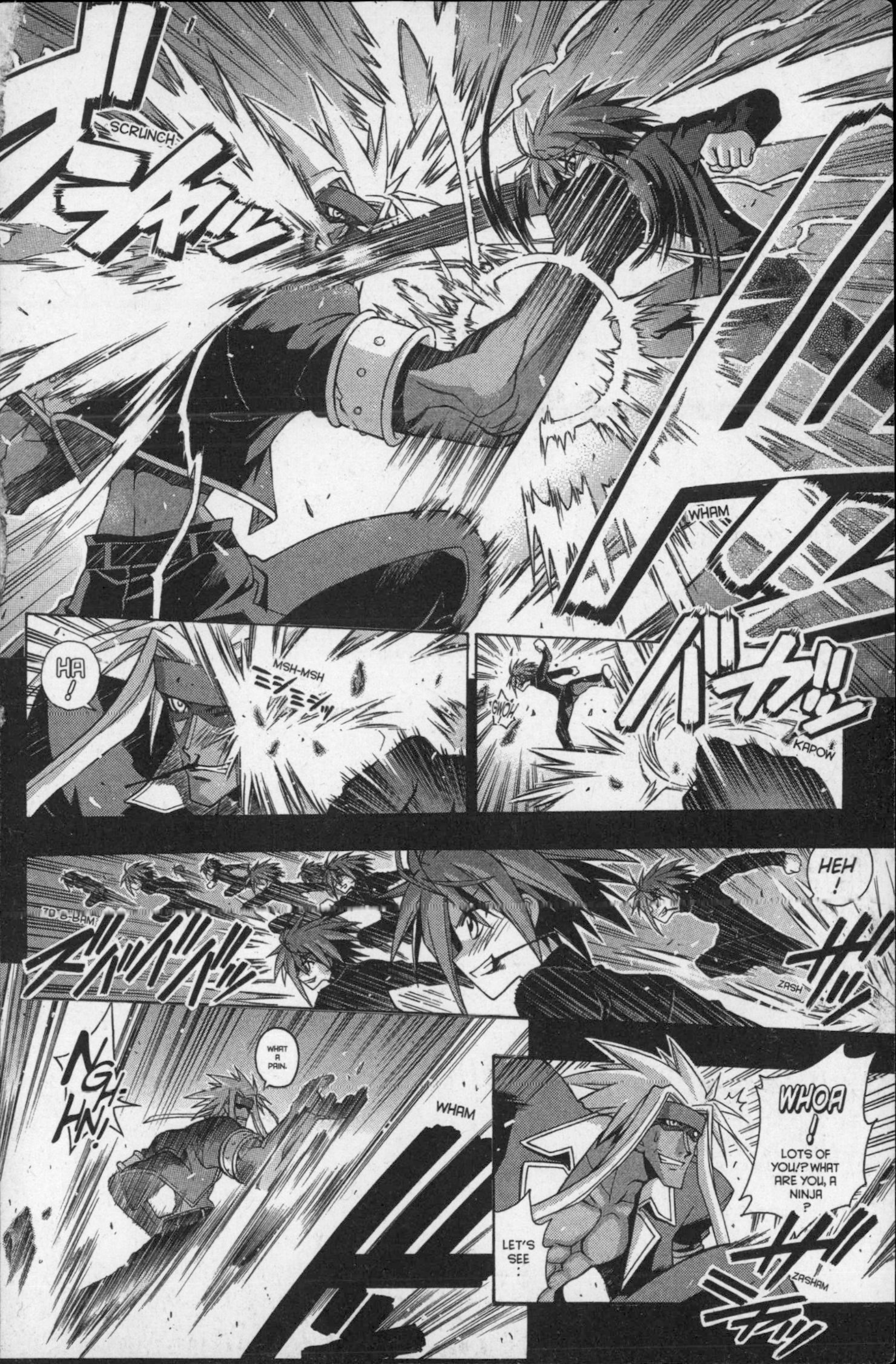
SCRUNCH
WHAM
GWOH
KAPOW
HA!
MSH-MSH
HEH!
ZASH
B-BAM
WHOA!
LOTS OF YOU!? WHAT ARE YOU, A NINJA?
LET'S SEE...
ZASHAM
WHAT A PAIN.
WHAM
NGH-HN!

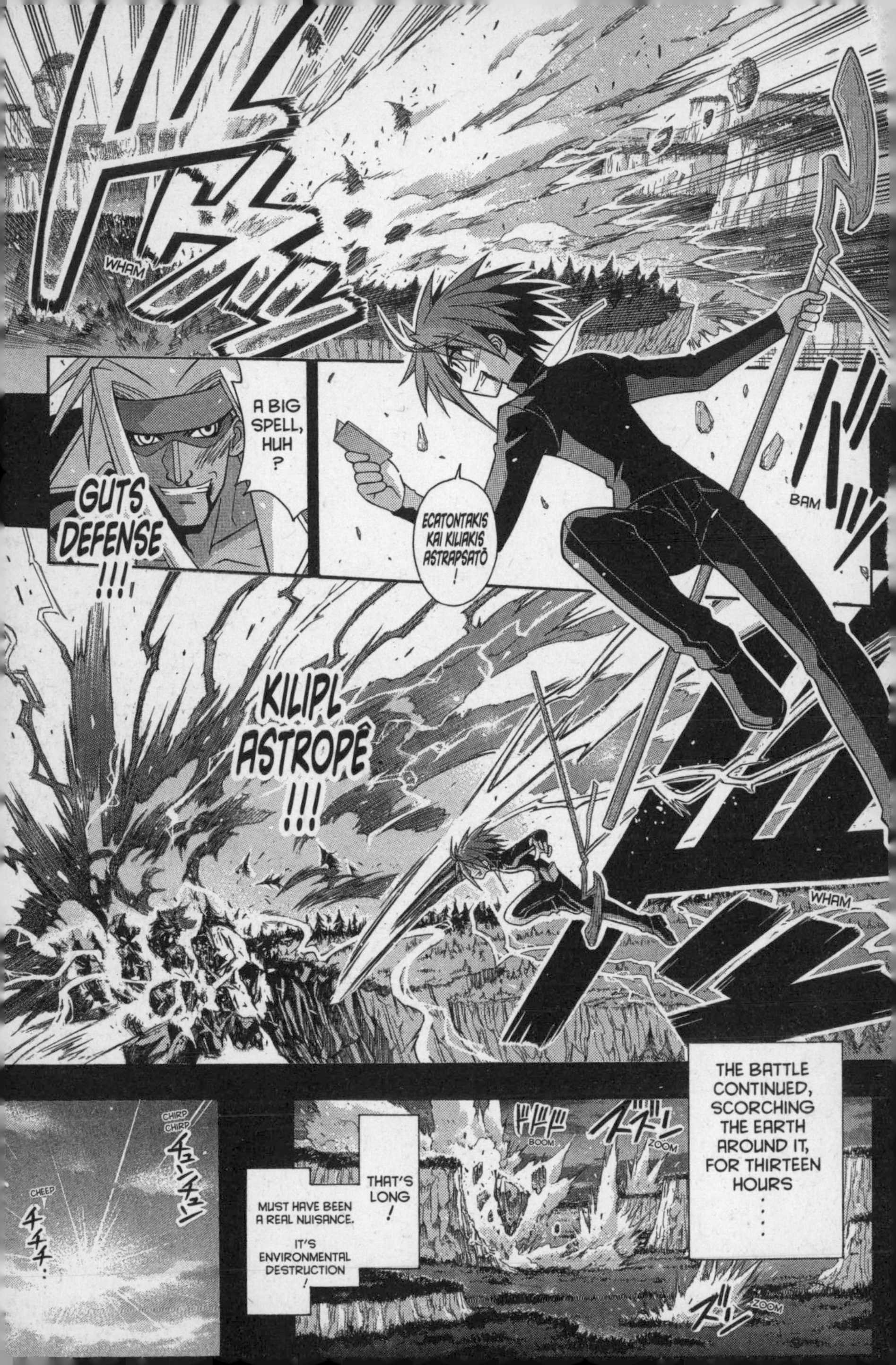
WHAM
ECATONTAKIS KAI KILIAKIS ASTRAPSATŌ!
BAM
A BIG SPELL, HUH?
GUTS DEFENSE!!!
KILIPL ASTROPÊ!!!
WHAM
THE BATTLE CONTINUED, SCORCHING THE EARTH AROUND IT, FOR THIRTEEN HOURS......
ズズン
ZOOM
ドドド
BOOM
THAT'S LONG!
MUST HAVE BEEN A REAL NUISANCE.
IT'S ENVIRONMENTAL DESTRUCTION!
ZOOM
チュンチュン
CHIRP CHIRP
チチチ
CHEEP

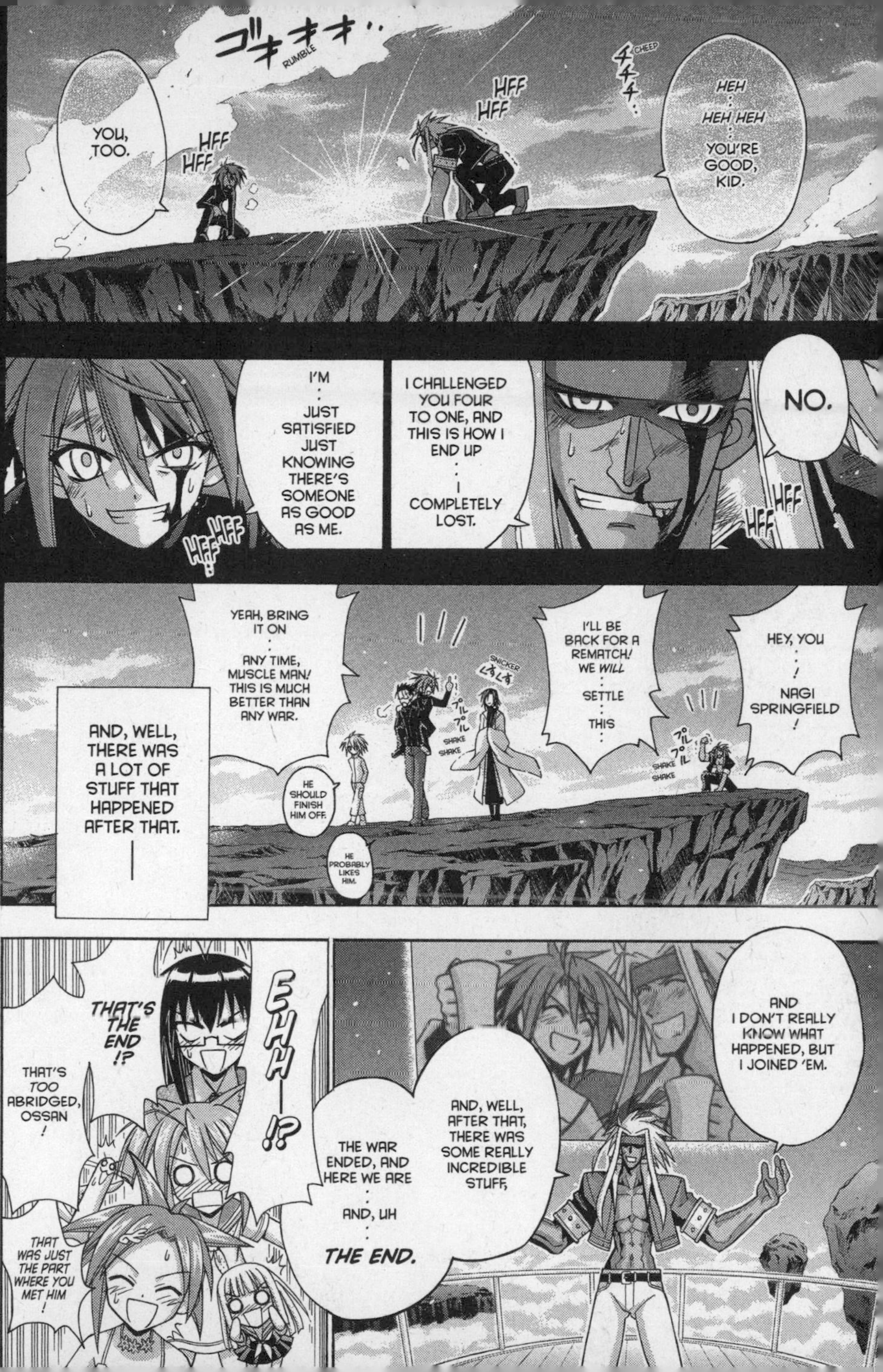

HEH... HEH HEH... YOU'RE GOOD, KID.
チチチ... CHEEP
HFF HFF
ゴオオオ.. RUMBLE
YOU, TOO.
HFF HFF
NO.
I CHALLENGED YOU FOUR TO ONE, AND THIS IS HOW I END UP... I COMPLETELY LOST.
HFF HFF
I'M... JUST SATISFIED JUST KNOWING THERE'S SOMEONE AS GOOD AS ME.
HFF HFF
HEY, YOU...! NAGI SPRINGFIELD!
プルプル SHAKE SHAKE
I'LL BE BACK FOR A REMATCH! WE *WILL*... SETTLE... THIS...
くすくす SNICKER
プルプル SHAKE SHAKE
YEAH, BRING IT ON... ANY TIME, MUSCLE MAN! THIS IS MUCH BETTER THAN ANY WAR.
HE SHOULD FINISH HIM OFF.
HE PROBABLY LIKES HIM.
AND, WELL, THERE WAS A LOT OF STUFF THAT HAPPENED AFTER THAT.
AND I DON'T REALLY KNOW WHAT HAPPENED, BUT I JOINED 'EM.
AND, WELL, AFTER THAT, THERE WAS SOME REALLY INCREDIBLE STUFF,
THE WAR ENDED, AND HERE WE ARE... AND, UH... ***THE END.***
EHH—!?
THAT'S THE END!?
THAT'S *TOO* ABRIDGED, OSSAN!
THAT WAS JUST THE PART WHERE YOU MET HIM!

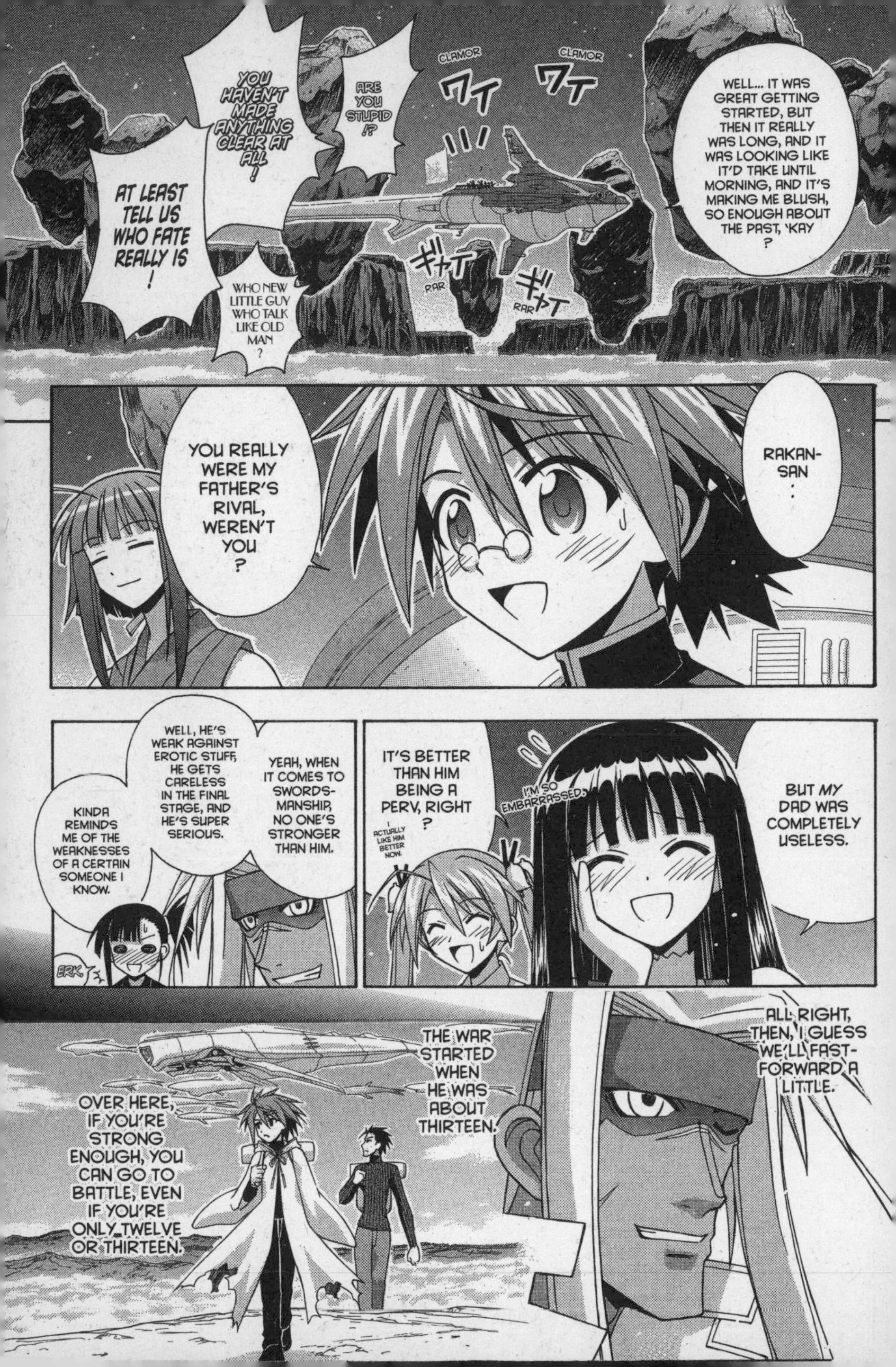
WELL... IT WAS GREAT GETTING STARTED, BUT THEN IT REALLY WAS LONG, AND IT WAS LOOKING LIKE IT'D TAKE UNTIL MORNING, AND IT'S MAKING ME BLUSH, SO ENOUGH ABOUT THE PAST, 'KAY?
CLAMOR ワイ
CLAMOR ワイ
ARE YOU STUPID!?
YOU HAVEN'T MADE ANYTHING CLEAR AT ALL!
AT LEAST TELL US WHO FATE REALLY IS!
WHO NEW LITTLE GUY WHO TALK LIKE OLD MAN?
ギャア RAR
ギャア RAR
RAKAN-SAN...
YOU REALLY WERE MY FATHER'S RIVAL, WEREN'T YOU?
BUT MY DAD WAS COMPLETELY USELESS.
I'M SO EMBARRASSED.
IT'S BETTER THAN HIM BEING A PERV, RIGHT?
I ACTUALLY LIKE HIM BETTER NOW.
YEAH, WHEN IT COMES TO SWORDSMANSHIP, NO ONE'S STRONGER THAN HIM.
WELL, HE'S WEAK AGAINST EROTIC STUFF, HE GETS CARELESS IN THE FINAL STAGE, AND HE'S SUPER SERIOUS.
KINDA REMINDS ME OF THE WEAKNESSES OF A CERTAIN SOMEONE I KNOW.
ERK.
ALL RIGHT, THEN, I GUESS WE'LL FAST-FORWARD A LITTLE.
THE WAR STARTED WHEN HE WAS ABOUT THIRTEEN.
OVER HERE, IF YOU'RE STRONG ENOUGH, YOU CAN GO TO BATTLE, EVEN IF YOU'RE ONLY TWELVE OR THIRTEEN.

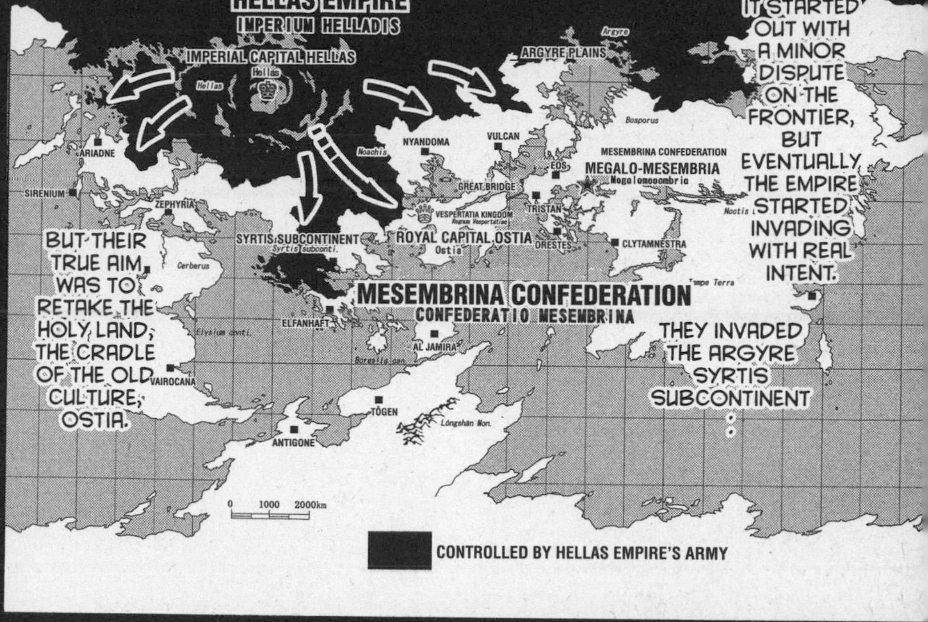
IT STARTED OUT WITH A MINOR DISPUTE ON THE FRONTIER, BUT EVENTUALLY THE EMPIRE STARTED INVADING WITH REAL INTENT.
THEY INVADED THE ARGYRE SYRTIS SUBCONTINENT
...
BUT THEIR TRUE AIM WAS TO RETAKE THE HOLY LAND, THE CRADLE OF THE OLD CULTURE, OSTIA.
HELLAS EMPIRE
IMPERIUM HELLADIS
IMPERIAL CAPITAL HELLAS
Hellas
Hellas
Argyre
ARGYRE PLAINS
Bosporus
ARIADNE
NYANDOMA
Noachis
VULCAN
MESEMBRINA CONFEDERATION
EOS
MEGALO-MESEMBRIA
Megalomesembria
GREAT BRIDGE
SIRENIUM
ZEPHYRIA
TRISTAN
VESPERTATIA KINGDOM
Regnum Vespertatiae
Noctis
SYRTIS SUBCONTINENT
Syrtis subconti.
ROYAL CAPITAL OSTIA
Ostia
ORESTES
CLYTAMNESTRA
Cerberus
Tempe Terra
MESEMBRINA CONFEDERATION
CONFEDERATIO MESEMBRINA
ELFANHAFT
Elysium conti.
AL JAMIRA
Borealis can.
VAIROCANA
TŌGEN
Lóngshān Mon.
ANTIGONE
0 1000 2000km
CONTROLLED BY HELLAS EMPIRE'S ARMY

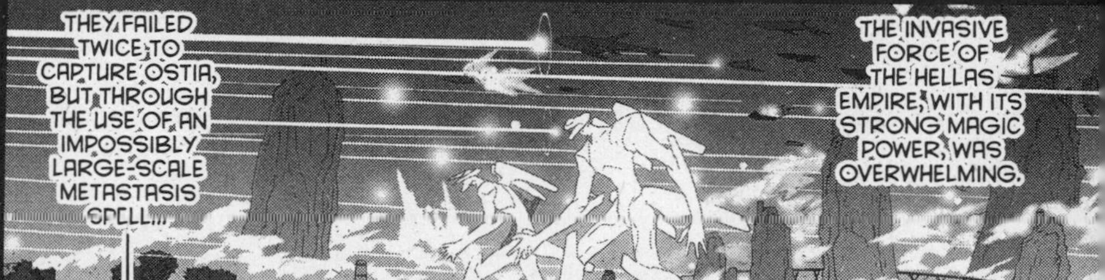
THE INVASIVE FORCE OF THE HELLAS EMPIRE, WITH ITS STRONG MAGIC POWER, WAS OVERWHELMING.
THEY FAILED TWICE TO CAPTURE OSTIA, BUT THROUGH THE USE OF AN IMPOSSIBLY LARGE-SCALE METASTASIS SPELL...

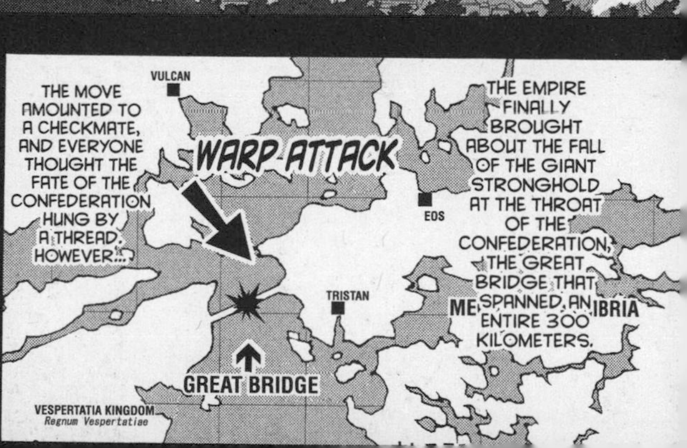
THE EMPIRE FINALLY BROUGHT ABOUT THE FALL OF THE GIANT STRONGHOLD AT THE THROAT OF THE CONFEDERATION, THE GREAT BRIDGE THAT SPANNED AN ENTIRE 300 KILOMETERS.
THE MOVE AMOUNTED TO A CHECKMATE, AND EVERYONE THOUGHT THE FATE OF THE CONFEDERATION HUNG BY A THREAD. HOWEVER...
VULCAN
WARP-ATTACK
EOS
TRISTAN
GREAT BRIDGE
VESPERTATIA KINGDOM
Regnum Vespertatiae

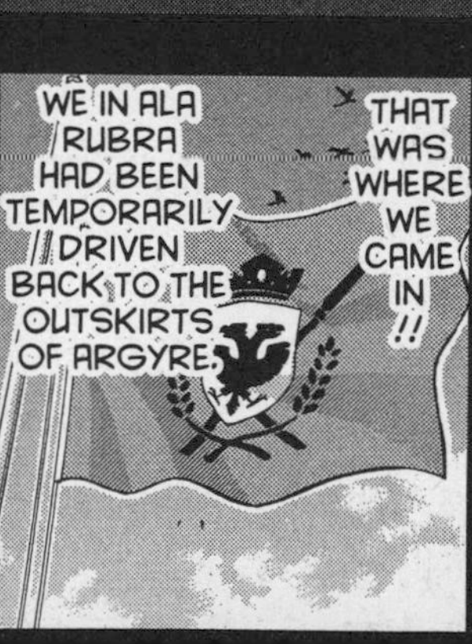
THAT WAS WHERE WE CAME IN!!
WE IN ALA RUBRA HAD BEEN TEMPORARILY DRIVEN BACK TO THE OUTSKIRTS OF ARGYRE.

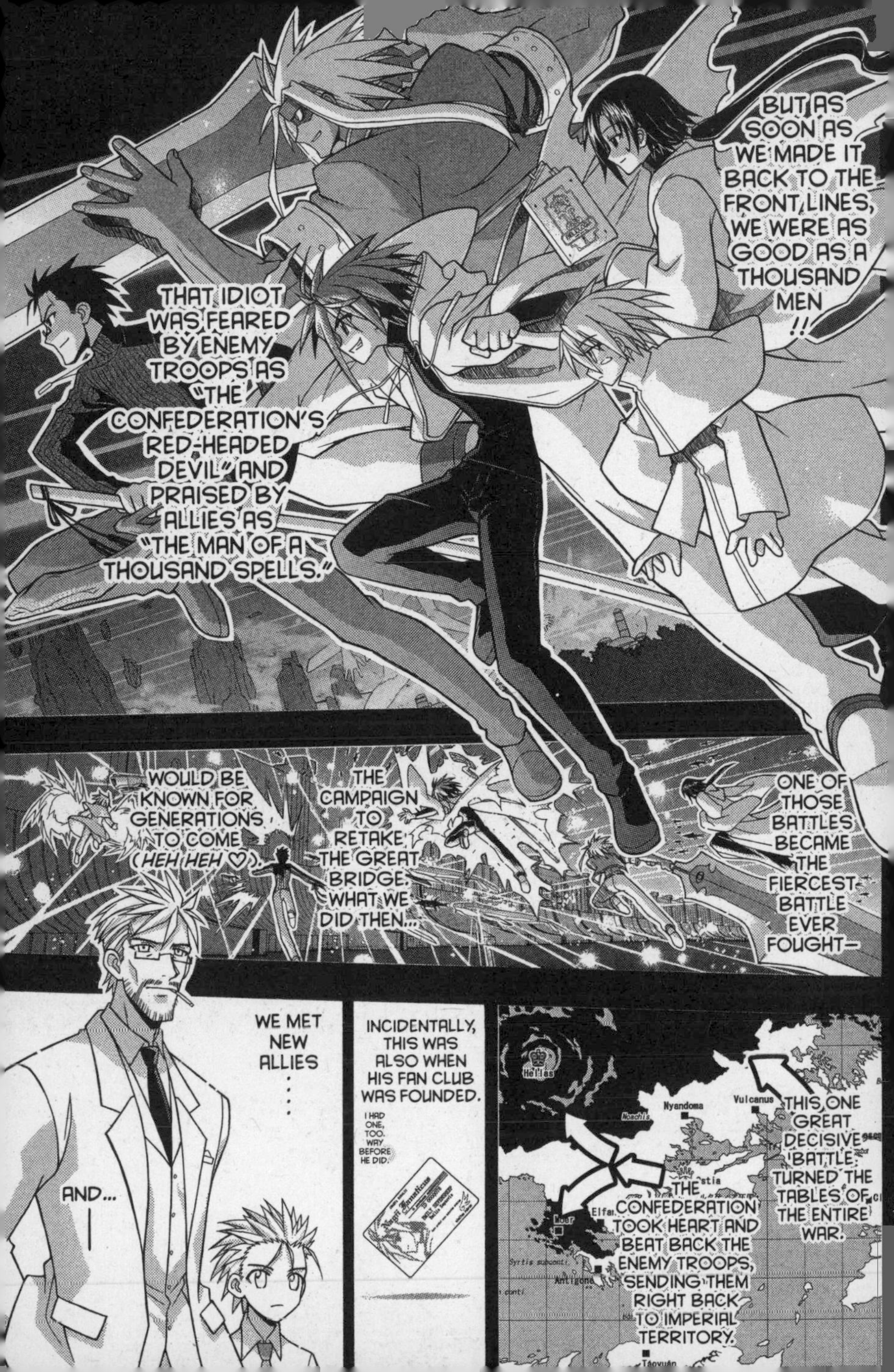
BUT AS SOON AS WE MADE IT BACK TO THE FRONT LINES, WE WERE AS GOOD AS A THOUSAND MEN!!
THAT IDIOT WAS FEARED BY ENEMY TROOPS AS "THE CONFEDERATION'S RED-HEADED DEVIL" AND PRAISED BY ALLIES AS "THE MAN OF A THOUSAND SPELLS."
ONE OF THOSE BATTLES BECAME THE FIERCEST BATTLE EVER FOUGHT—
THE CAMPAIGN TO RETAKE THE GREAT BRIDGE. WHAT WE DID THEN...
WOULD BE KNOWN FOR GENERATIONS TO COME (HEH HEH ♡).
THIS ONE GREAT DECISIVE BATTLE TURNED THE TABLES OF THE ENTIRE WAR.
Hellas
Nyandoma
Vulcanus
Antigone
THE CONFEDERATION TOOK HEART AND BEAT BACK THE ENEMY TROOPS, SENDING THEM RIGHT BACK TO IMPERIAL TERRITORY.
INCIDENTALLY, THIS WAS ALSO WHEN HIS FAN CLUB WAS FOUNDED.
I HAD ONE, TOO. WAY BEFORE HE DID.
WE MET NEW ALLIES...
AND...

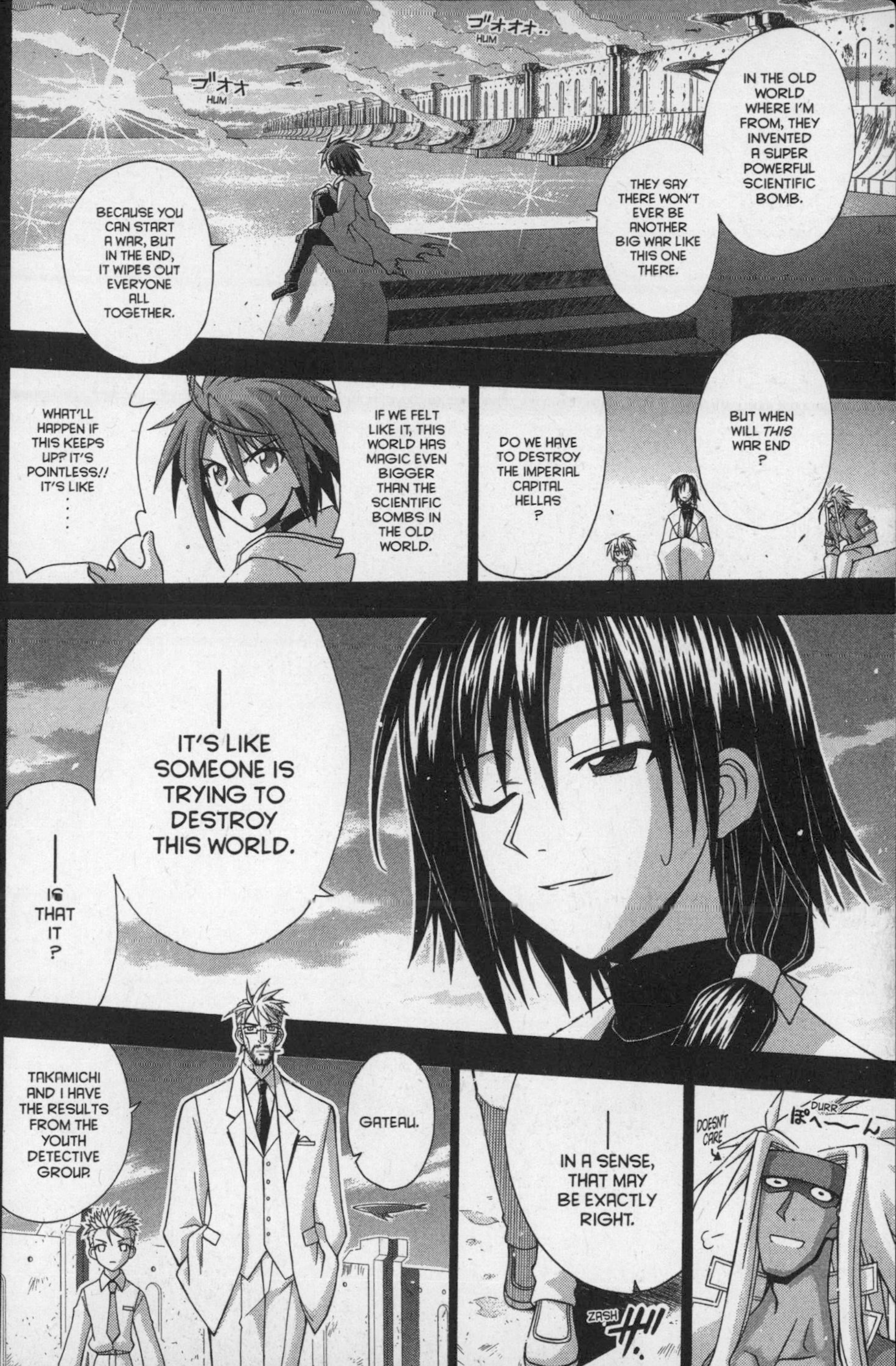
ゴオオ..
HUM
ゴオオ
HUM
IN THE OLD WORLD WHERE I'M FROM, THEY INVENTED A SUPER POWERFUL SCIENTIFIC BOMB.
THEY SAY THERE WON'T EVER BE ANOTHER BIG WAR LIKE THIS ONE THERE.
BECAUSE YOU CAN START A WAR, BUT IN THE END, IT WIPES OUT EVERYONE ALL TOGETHER.
BUT WHEN WILL *THIS* WAR END ?
DO WE HAVE TO DESTROY THE IMPERIAL CAPITAL HELLAS ?
IF WE FELT LIKE IT, THIS WORLD HAS MAGIC EVEN BIGGER THAN THE SCIENTIFIC BOMBS IN THE OLD WORLD.
WHAT'LL HAPPEN IF THIS KEEPS UP? IT'S POINTLESS!! IT'S LIKE ......
— IT'S LIKE SOMEONE IS TRYING TO DESTROY THIS WORLD.
— IS THAT IT ?
ぽへ～ん
DURR
DOESN'T CARE
— IN A SENSE, THAT MAY BE EXACTLY RIGHT.
ZASH
GATEAU.
TAKAMICHI AND I HAVE THE RESULTS FROM THE YOUTH DETECTIVE GROUP.

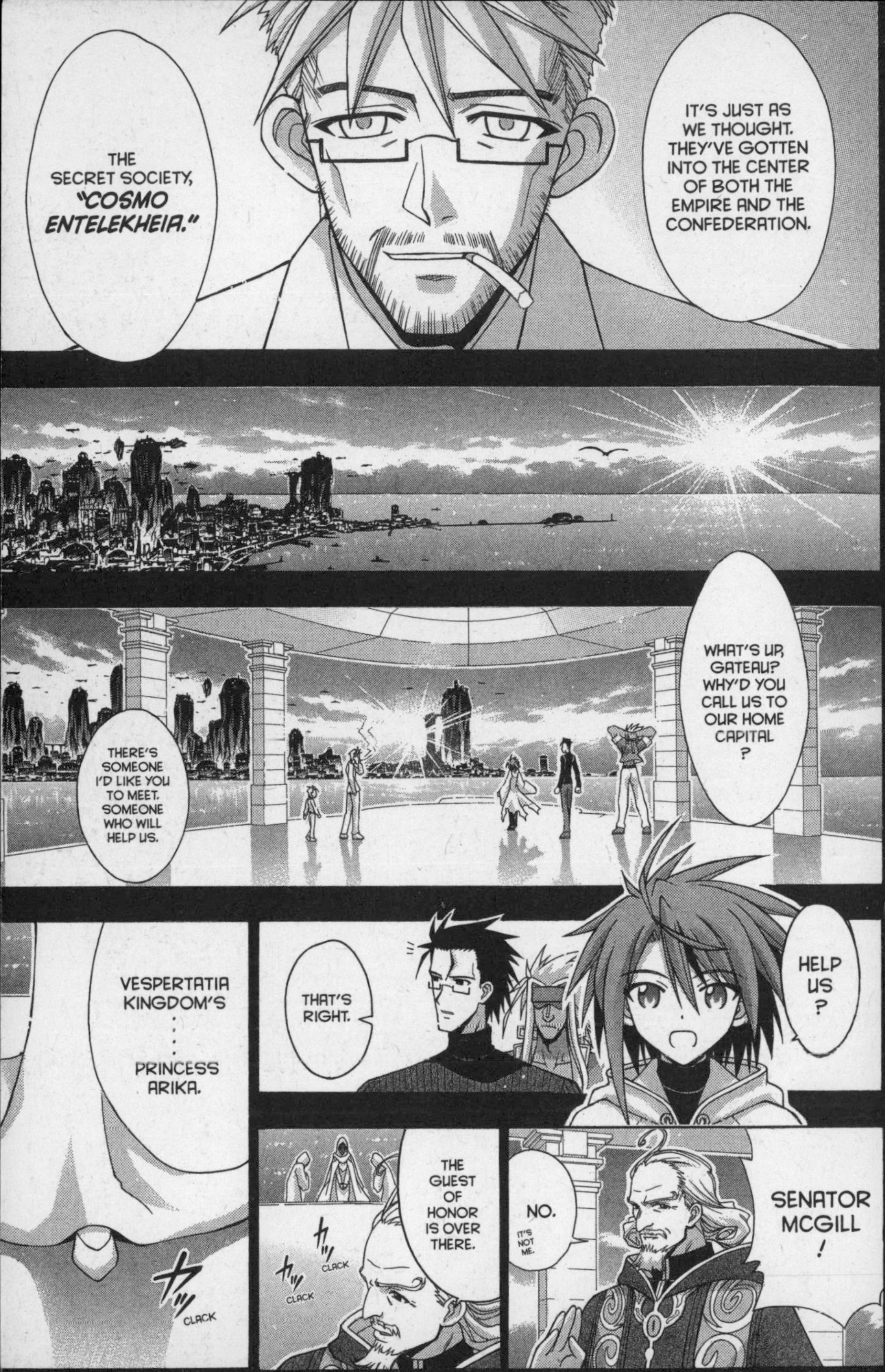
IT'S JUST AS WE THOUGHT. THEY'VE GOTTEN INTO THE CENTER OF BOTH THE EMPIRE AND THE CONFEDERATION.
THE SECRET SOCIETY, "COSMO ENTELEKHEIA."
WHAT'S UP, GATEAU? WHY'D YOU CALL US TO OUR HOME CAPITAL ?
THERE'S SOMEONE I'D LIKE YOU TO MEET. SOMEONE WHO WILL HELP US.
HELP US ?
THAT'S RIGHT.
SENATOR MCGILL !
NO.
IT'S NOT ME.
THE GUEST OF HONOR IS OVER THERE.
CLACK
CLACK
VESPERTATIA KINGDOM'S . . . PRINCESS ARIKA.
CLACK

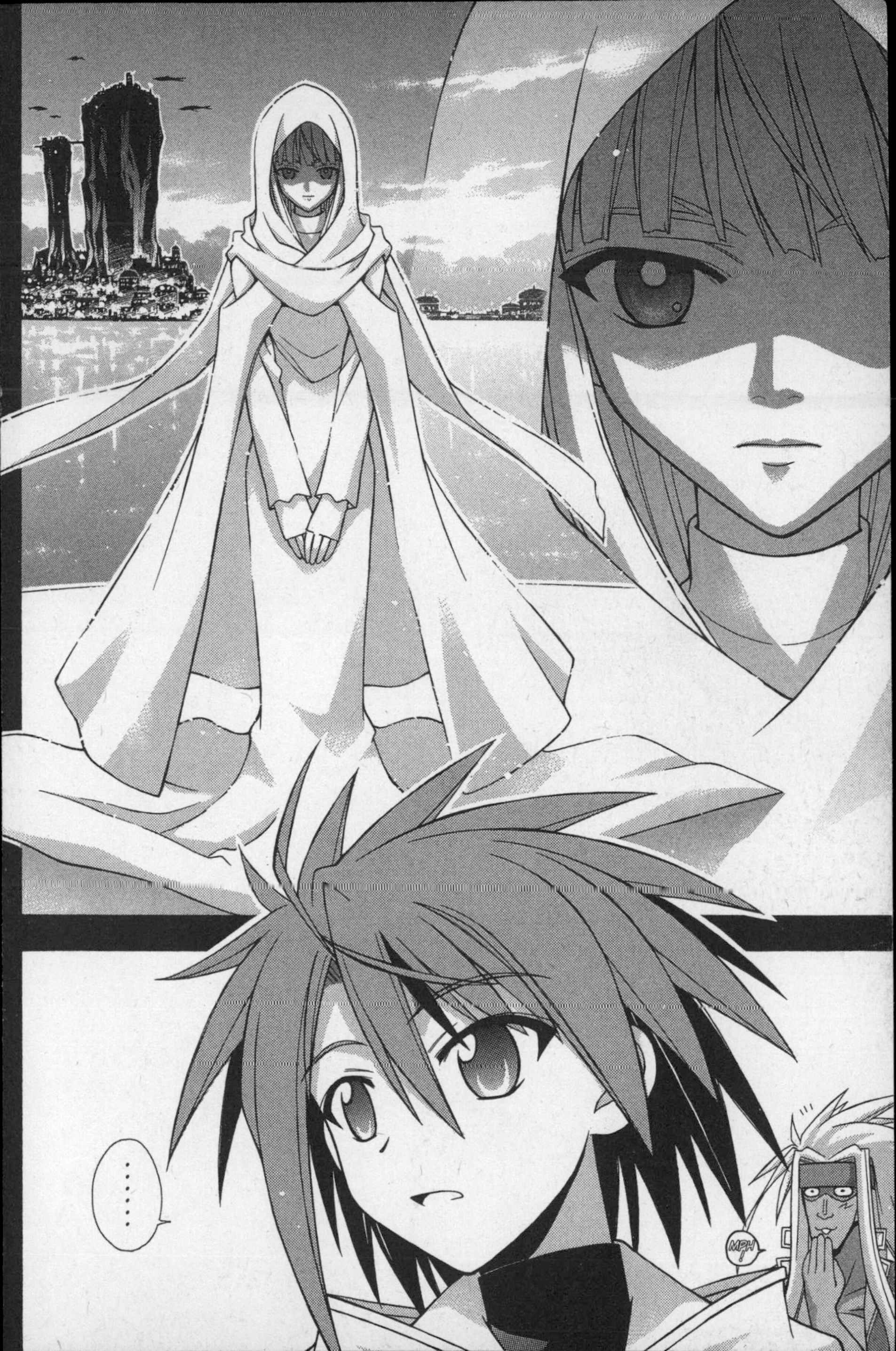
......
MPH!

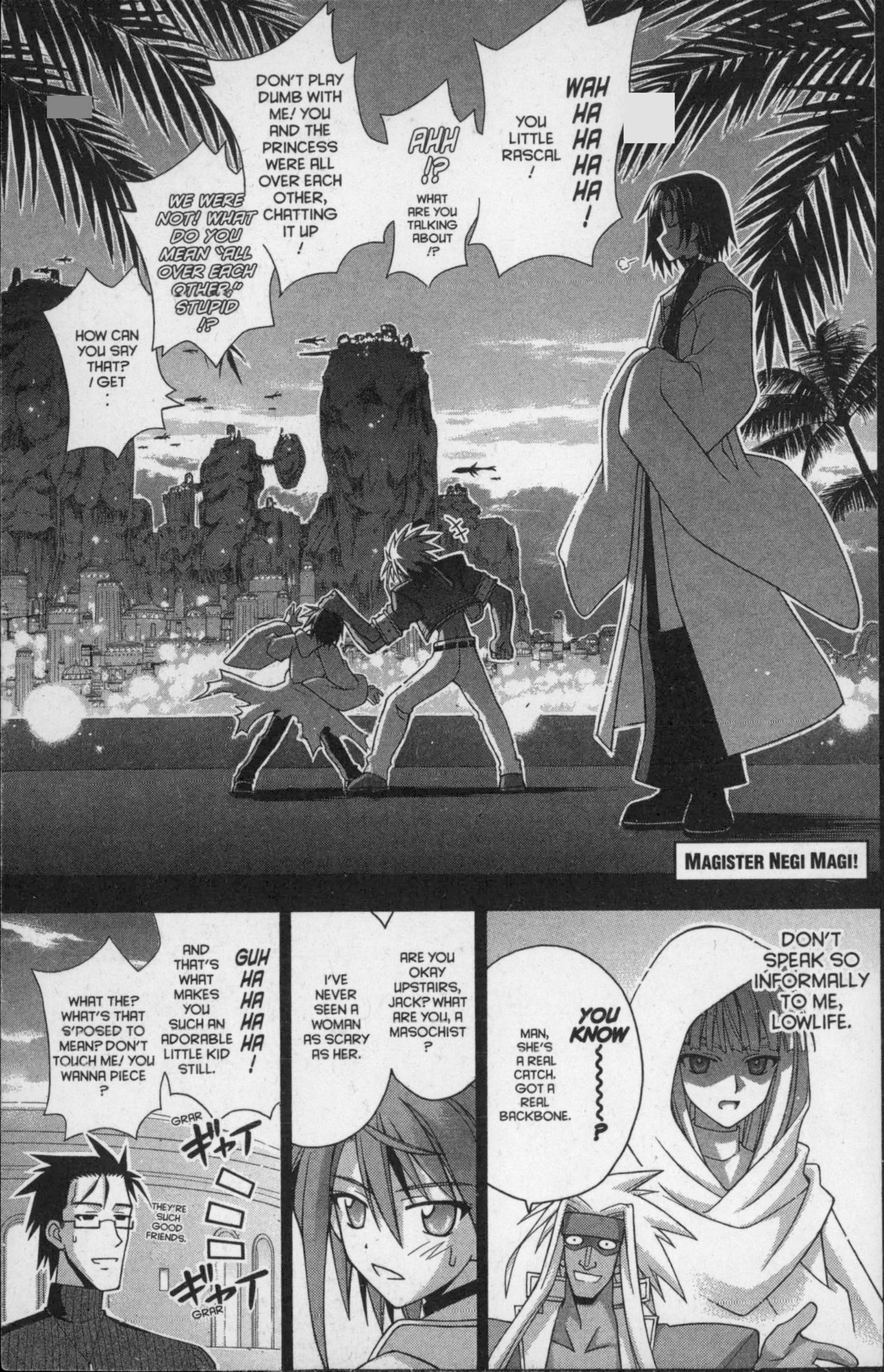
WAH HA HA HA HA!
YOU LITTLE RASCAL!
AHH!? WHAT ARE YOU TALKING ABOUT!?
DON'T PLAY DUMB WITH ME! YOU AND THE PRINCESS WERE ALL OVER EACH OTHER, CHATTING IT UP!
WE WERE NOT! WHAT DO YOU MEAN "ALL OVER EACH OTHER," STUPID!?
HOW CAN YOU SAY THAT? I GET:
MAGISTER NEGI MAGI!
DON'T SPEAK SO INFORMALLY TO ME, LOWLIFE.
YOU KNOW~~~?
MAN, SHE'S A REAL CATCH. GOT A REAL BACKBONE.
ARE YOU OKAY UPSTAIRS, JACK? WHAT ARE YOU, A MASOCHIST?
I'VE NEVER SEEN A WOMAN AS SCARY AS HER.
GUH HA HA HA HA!
AND THAT'S WHAT MAKES YOU SUCH AN ADORABLE LITTLE KID STILL.
WHAT THE? WHAT'S THAT S'POSED TO MEAN? DON'T TOUCH ME! YOU WANNA PIECE?
GRAR
ギャイ
THEY'RE SUCH GOOD FRIENDS.
ギャイ
GRAR

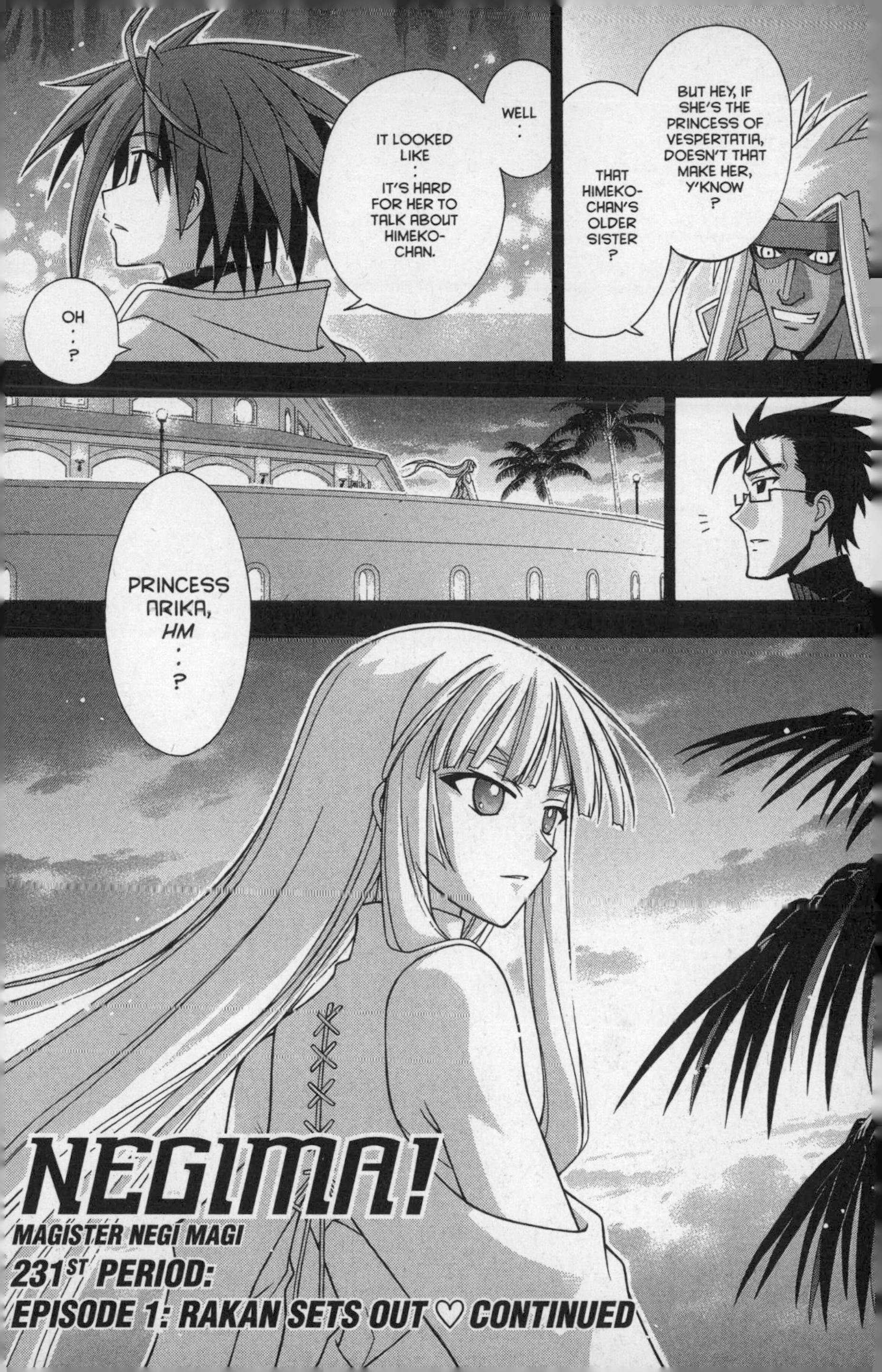
BUT HEY, IF SHE'S THE PRINCESS OF VESPERTATIA, DOESN'T THAT MAKE HER, Y'KNOW ?
THAT HIMEKO-CHAN'S OLDER SISTER ?
WELL . . .
IT LOOKED LIKE . . . IT'S HARD FOR HER TO TALK ABOUT HIMEKO-CHAN.
OH . . ?
PRINCESS ARIKA, HM . . ?
NEGIMA!
MAGISTER NEGI MAGI
231ST PERIOD:
EPISODE 1: RAKAN SETS OUT ♡ CONTINUED

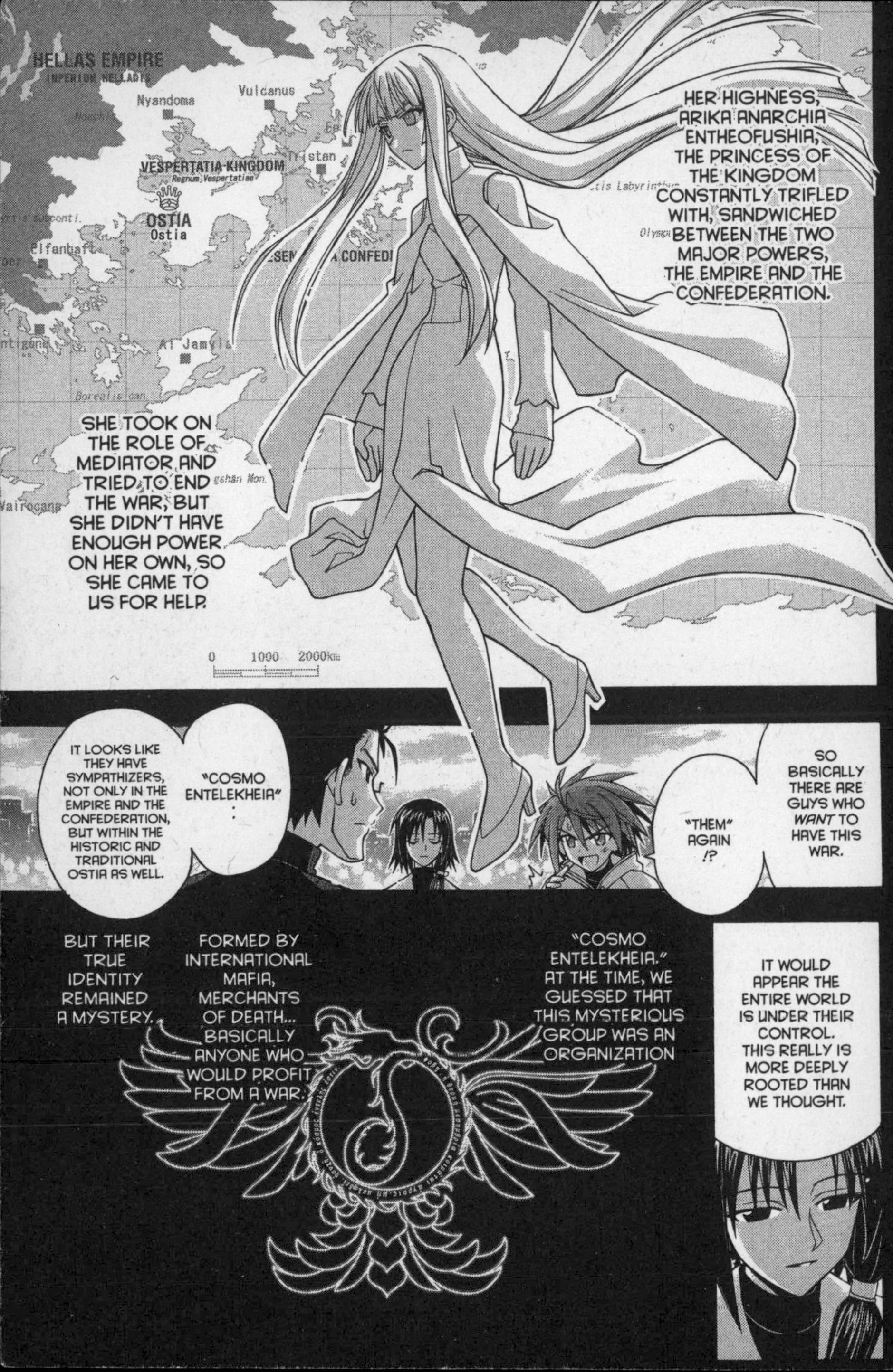
HELLAS EMPIRE
IMPERIUM HELLADIS
Vulcanus
Nyandoma
VESPERTATIA KINGDOM
Regnum Vespertatiae
OSTIA
Ostia
Tristan
Al Jamyla
0 1000 2000km
HER HIGHNESS, ARIKA ANARCHIA ENTHEOFUSHIA, THE PRINCESS OF THE KINGDOM CONSTANTLY TRIFLED WITH, SANDWICHED BETWEEN THE TWO MAJOR POWERS, THE EMPIRE AND THE CONFEDERATION.
SHE TOOK ON THE ROLE OF MEDIATOR AND TRIED TO END THE WAR, BUT SHE DIDN'T HAVE ENOUGH POWER ON HER OWN, SO SHE CAME TO US FOR HELP.
SO BASICALLY THERE ARE GUYS WHO *WANT* TO HAVE THIS WAR.
"THEM" AGAIN!?
"COSMO ENTELEKHEIA"...
IT LOOKS LIKE THEY HAVE SYMPATHIZERS, NOT ONLY IN THE EMPIRE AND THE CONFEDERATION, BUT WITHIN THE HISTORIC AND TRADITIONAL OSTIA AS WELL.
IT WOULD APPEAR THE ENTIRE WORLD IS UNDER THEIR CONTROL. THIS REALLY IS MORE DEEPLY ROOTED THAN WE THOUGHT.
"COSMO ENTELEKHEIA." AT THE TIME, WE GUESSED THAT THIS MYSTERIOUS GROUP WAS AN ORGANIZATION
FORMED BY INTERNATIONAL MAFIA, MERCHANTS OF DEATH... BASICALLY ANYONE WHO WOULD PROFIT FROM A WAR.
BUT THEIR TRUE IDENTITY REMAINED A MYSTERY.

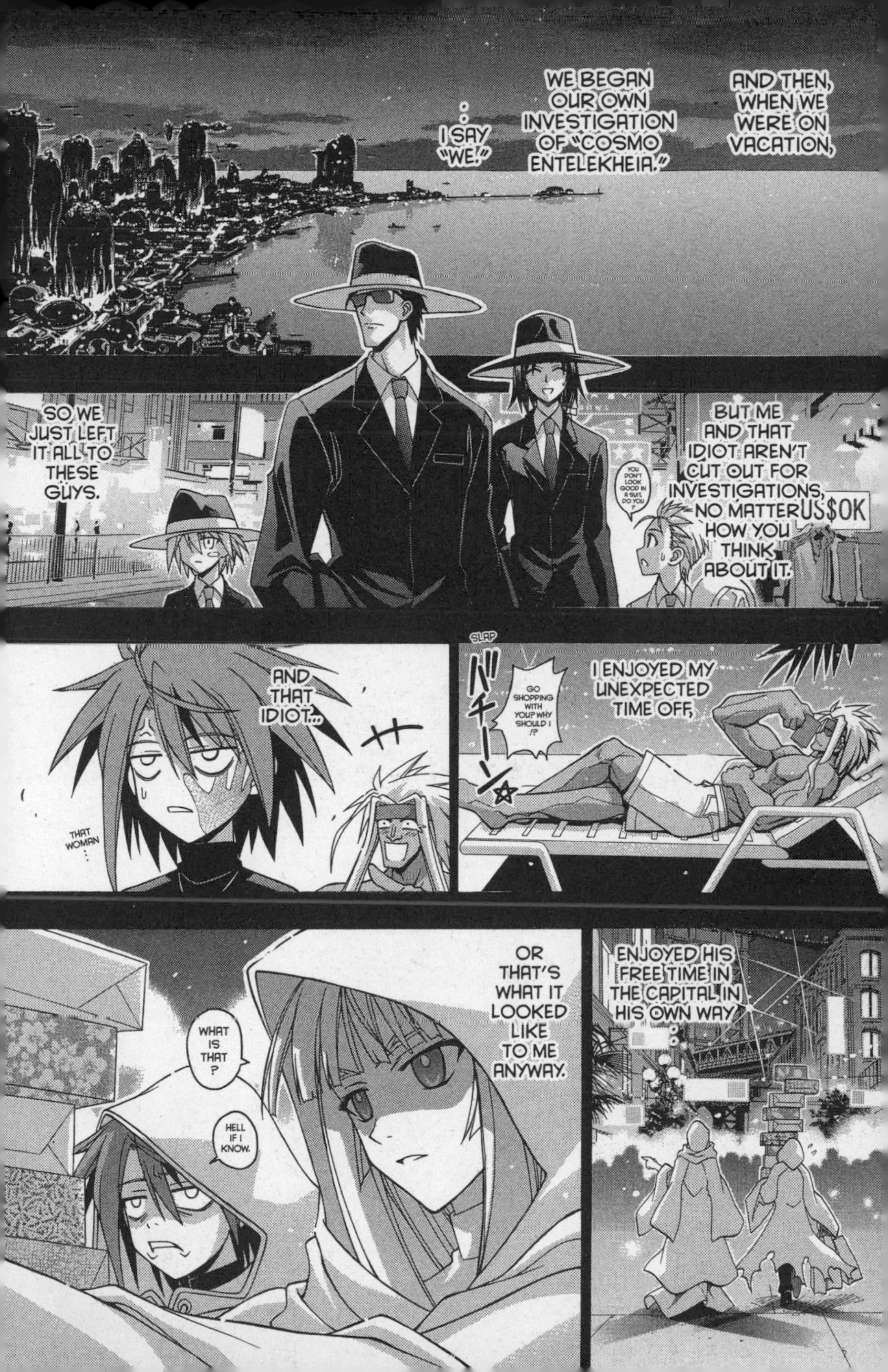
AND THEN, WHEN WE WERE ON VACATION,
WE BEGAN OUR OWN INVESTIGATION OF "COSMO ENTELEKHEIA."
...I SAY "WE."
BUT ME AND THAT IDIOT AREN'T CUT OUT FOR INVESTIGATIONS, NO MATTER HOW YOU THINK ABOUT IT.
US$0K
YOU DON'T LOOK GOOD IN A SUIT, DO YOU?
SO WE JUST LEFT IT ALL TO THESE GUYS.
I ENJOYED MY UNEXPECTED TIME OFF,
GO SHOPPING WITH YOU? WHY SHOULD I!?
SLAP
バチーン
AND THAT IDIOT...
THAT WOMAN...
ENJOYED HIS FREE TIME IN THE CAPITAL IN HIS OWN WAY...
OR THAT'S WHAT IT LOOKED LIKE TO ME ANYWAY.
WHAT IS THAT?
HELL IF I KNOW.

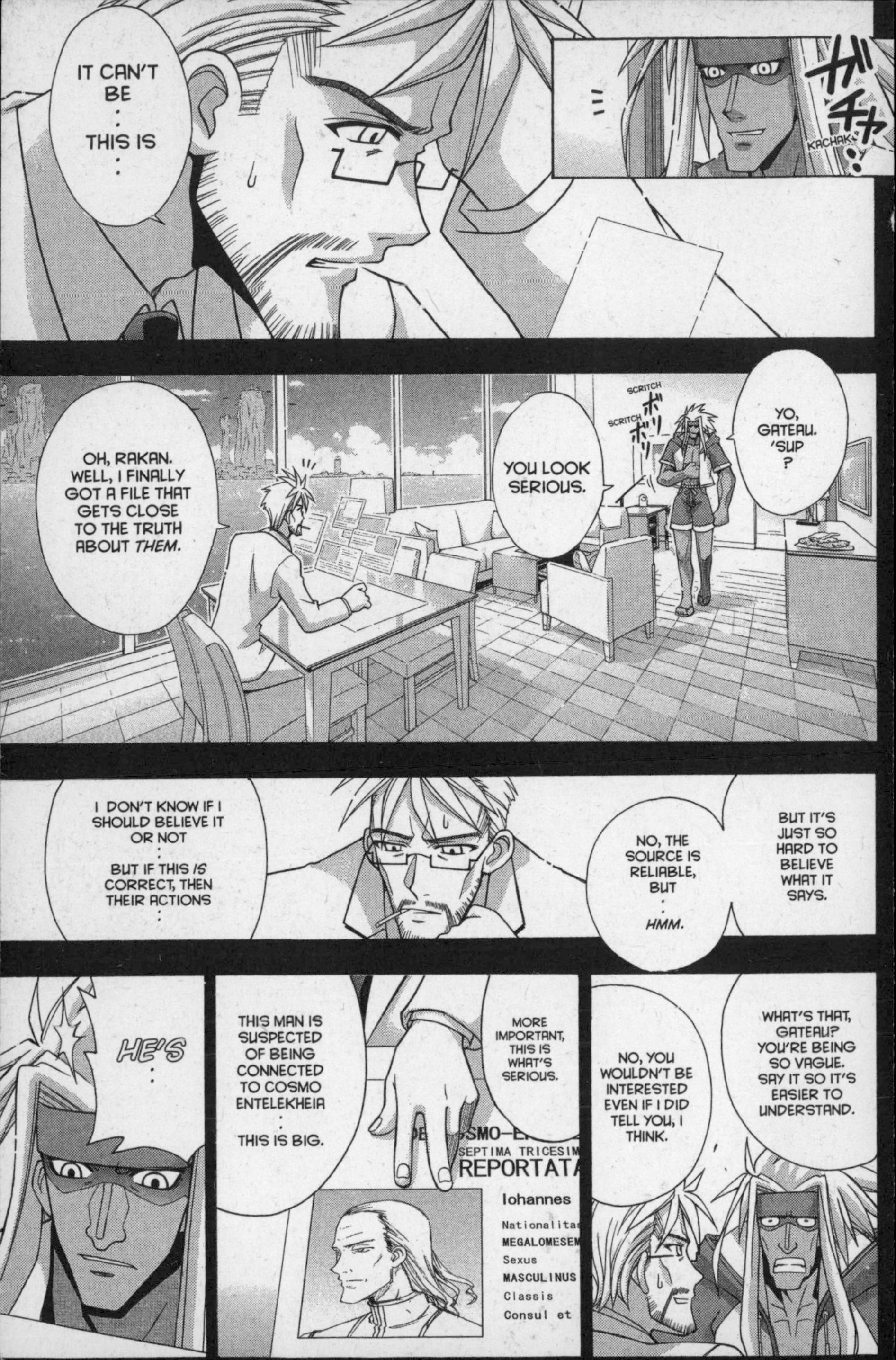
KACHAK!
IT CAN'T BE : THIS IS :
YO, GATEAU. 'SUP?
SCRITCH
SCRITCH
YOU LOOK SERIOUS.
OH, RAKAN. WELL, I FINALLY GOT A FILE THAT GETS CLOSE TO THE TRUTH ABOUT *THEM.*
BUT IT'S JUST SO HARD TO BELIEVE WHAT IT SAYS.
NO, THE SOURCE IS RELIABLE, BUT : *HMM.*
I DON'T KNOW IF I SHOULD BELIEVE IT OR NOT : BUT IF THIS *IS* CORRECT, THEN THEIR ACTIONS :
WHAT'S THAT, GATEAU? YOU'RE BEING SO VAGUE. SAY IT SO IT'S EASIER TO UNDERSTAND.
NO, YOU WOULDN'T BE INTERESTED EVEN IF I DID TELL YOU, I THINK.
MORE IMPORTANT, THIS IS WHAT'S SERIOUS.
THIS MAN IS SUSPECTED OF BEING CONNECTED TO COSMO ENTELEKHEIA : THIS IS BIG.
SEPTIMA TRICESIM
REPORTATA
Iohannes
Nationalitas
MEGALOMESEM
Sexus
MASCULINUS
Classis
Consul et
HE'S :

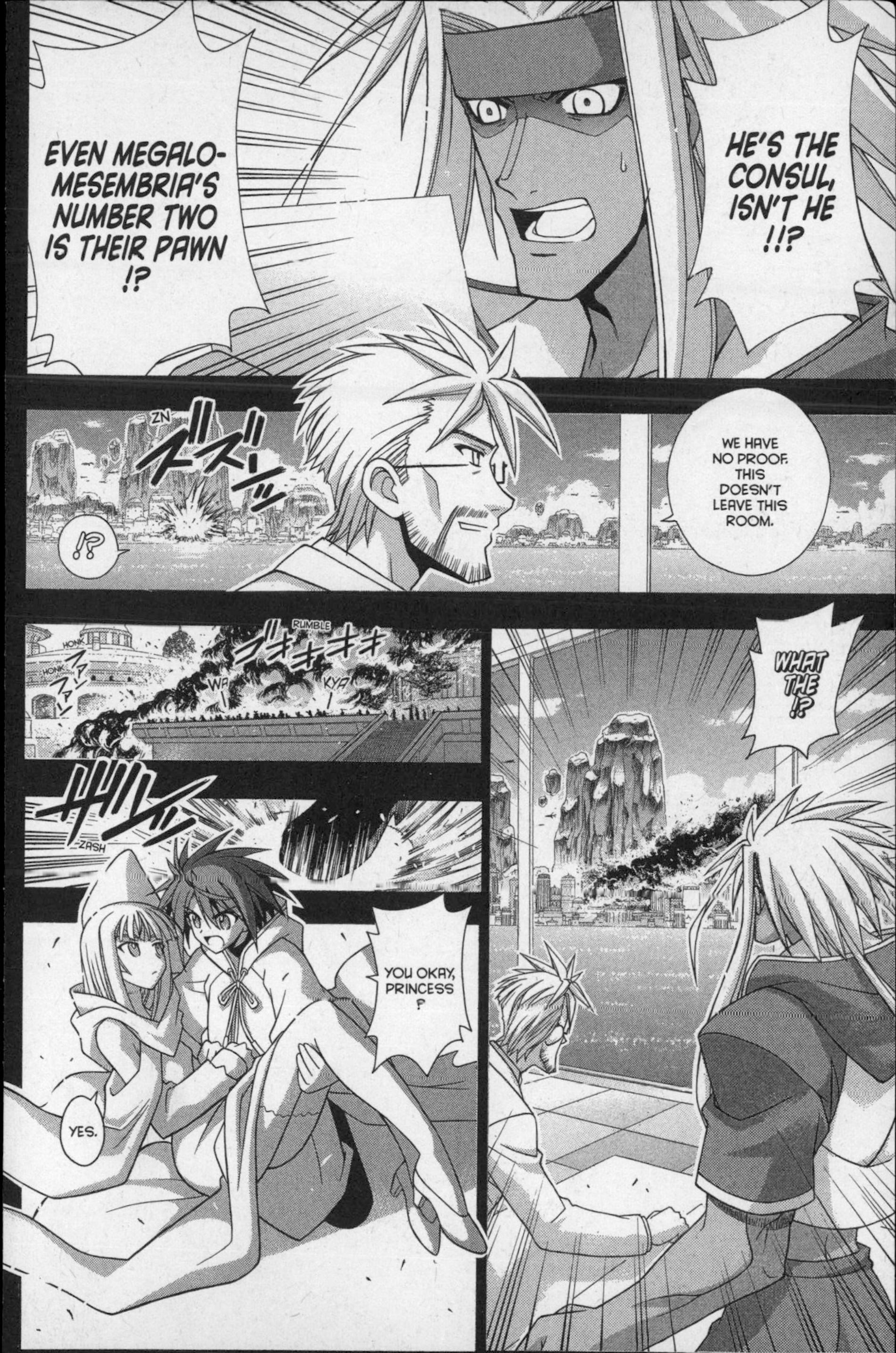
HE'S THE CONSUL, ISN'T HE !!?
EVEN MEGALO-MESEMBRIA'S NUMBER TWO IS THEIR PAWN !?
WE HAVE NO PROOF. THIS DOESN'T LEAVE THIS ROOM.
ZN
!?
WHAT THE !?
RUMBLE
HONK
HONK
WA
KYA
ZASH
YOU OKAY, PRINCESS !?
YES.

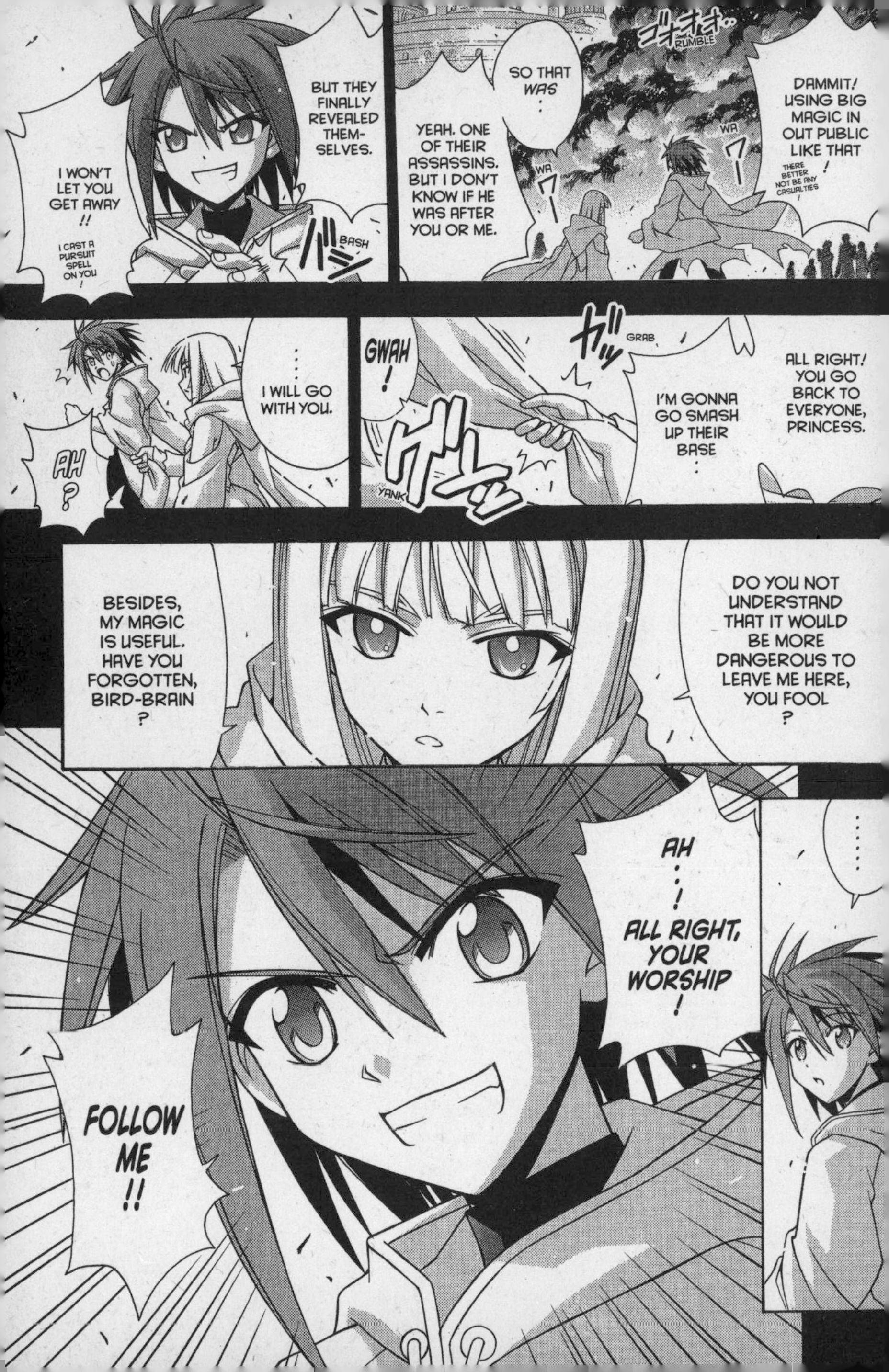
RUMBLE
DAMMIT! USING BIG MAGIC IN OUT PUBLIC LIKE THAT!
THERE BETTER NOT BE ANY CASUALTIES!
WA
WA
SO THAT WAS...
YEAH. ONE OF THEIR ASSASSINS. BUT I DON'T KNOW IF HE WAS AFTER YOU OR ME.
BUT THEY FINALLY REVEALED THEM-SELVES.
BASH
I WON'T LET YOU GET AWAY!!
I CAST A PURSUIT SPELL ON YOU!
ALL RIGHT! YOU GO BACK TO EVERYONE, PRINCESS.
I'M GONNA GO SMASH UP THEIR BASE...
GRAB
GWAH!
YANK
... I WILL GO WITH YOU.
AH?
DO YOU NOT UNDERSTAND THAT IT WOULD BE MORE DANGEROUS TO LEAVE ME HERE, YOU FOOL?
BESIDES, MY MAGIC IS USEFUL. HAVE YOU FORGOTTEN, BIRD-BRAIN?
......
AH...! ALL RIGHT, YOUR WORSHIP!
FOLLOW ME!!

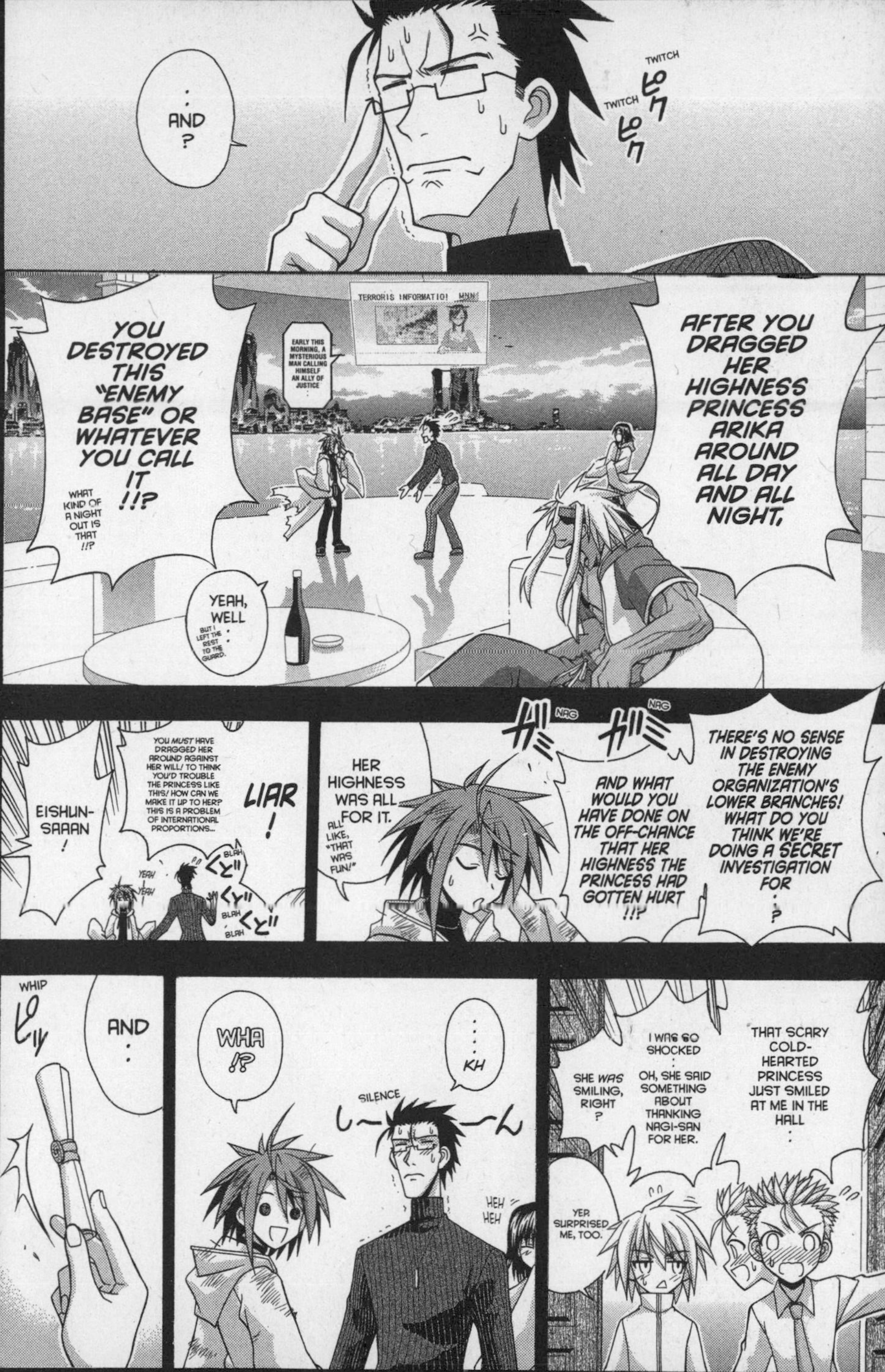

TWITCH
TWITCH
: AND ?
AFTER YOU DRAGGED HER HIGHNESS PRINCESS ARIKA AROUND ALL DAY AND ALL NIGHT,
YOU DESTROYED THIS "ENEMY BASE" OR WHATEVER YOU CALL IT !!?
TERRORIS INFORMATIO! WNN
EARLY THIS MORNING, A MYSTERIOUS MAN CALLING HIMSELF AN ALLY OF JUSTICE :
WHAT KIND OF A NIGHT OUT IS THAT !!?
YEAH, WELL :
BUT I LEFT THE REST TO THE GUARD.
NAG
NAG
THERE'S NO SENSE IN DESTROYING THE ENEMY ORGANIZATION'S LOWER BRANCHES! WHAT DO YOU THINK WE'RE DOING A SECRET INVESTIGATION FOR : ?
AND WHAT WOULD YOU HAVE DONE ON THE OFF-CHANCE THAT HER HIGHNESS THE PRINCESS HAD GOTTEN HURT !!?
HER HIGHNESS WAS ALL FOR IT.
ALL LIKE, "THAT WAS FUN!"
LIAR !
YOU MUST HAVE DRAGGED HER AROUND AGAINST HER WILL! TO THINK YOU'D TROUBLE THE PRINCESS LIKE THIS! HOW CAN WE MAKE IT UP TO HER? THIS IS A PROBLEM OF INTERNATIONAL PROPORTIONS...
EISHUN-SAAAN !
BLAH
YEAH YEAH
BLAH
BLAH
THAT SCARY COLD-HEARTED PRINCESS JUST SMILED AT ME IN THE HALL :
I WAS SO SHOCKED :
OH, SHE SAID SOMETHING ABOUT THANKING NAGI-SAN FOR HER.
SHE WAS SMILING, RIGHT ?
YER SURPRISED ME, TOO.
.... KH
WHA !?
SILENCE
HEH HEH
AND :
WHIP

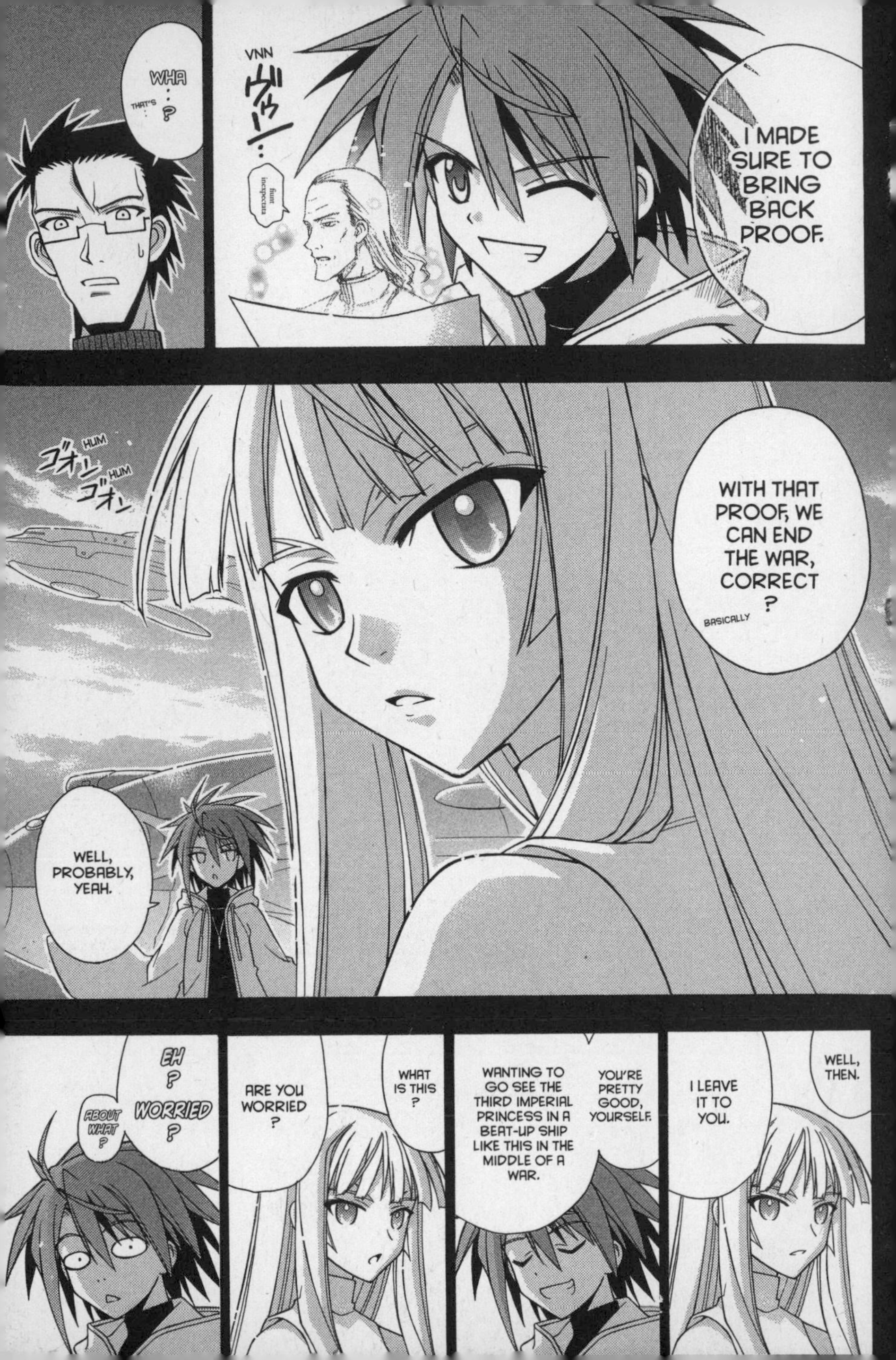
I MADE SURE TO BRING BACK PROOF.
VNN
fiunt inexpectata
WHA...
THAT'S...?
HUM
HUM
WITH THAT PROOF, WE CAN END THE WAR, CORRECT?
BASICALLY
WELL, PROBABLY, YEAH.
WELL, THEN.
I LEAVE IT TO YOU.
YOU'RE PRETTY GOOD, YOURSELF.
WANTING TO GO SEE THE THIRD IMPERIAL PRINCESS IN A BEAT-UP SHIP LIKE THIS IN THE MIDDLE OF A WAR.
WHAT IS THIS?
ARE YOU WORRIED?
EH? WORRIED?
ABOUT WHAT?

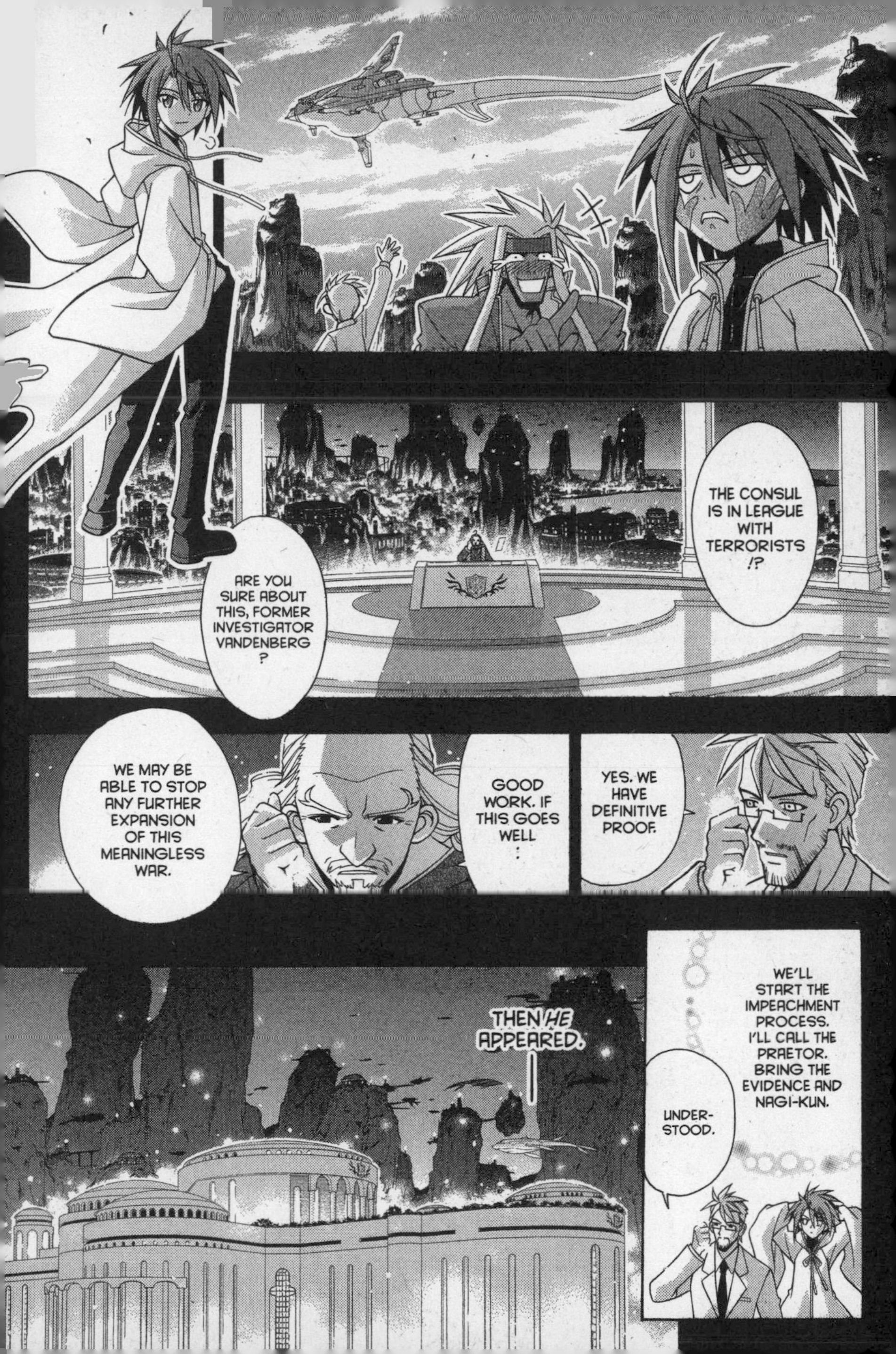
THE CONSUL IS IN LEAGUE WITH TERRORISTS!?
ARE YOU SURE ABOUT THIS, FORMER INVESTIGATOR VANDENBERG?
YES. WE HAVE DEFINITIVE PROOF.
GOOD WORK. IF THIS GOES WELL...
WE MAY BE ABLE TO STOP ANY FURTHER EXPANSION OF THIS MEANINGLESS WAR.
WE'LL START THE IMPEACHMENT PROCESS. I'LL CALL THE PRAETOR. BRING THE EVIDENCE AND NAGI-KUN.
UNDER-STOOD.
THEN *HE* APPEARED.

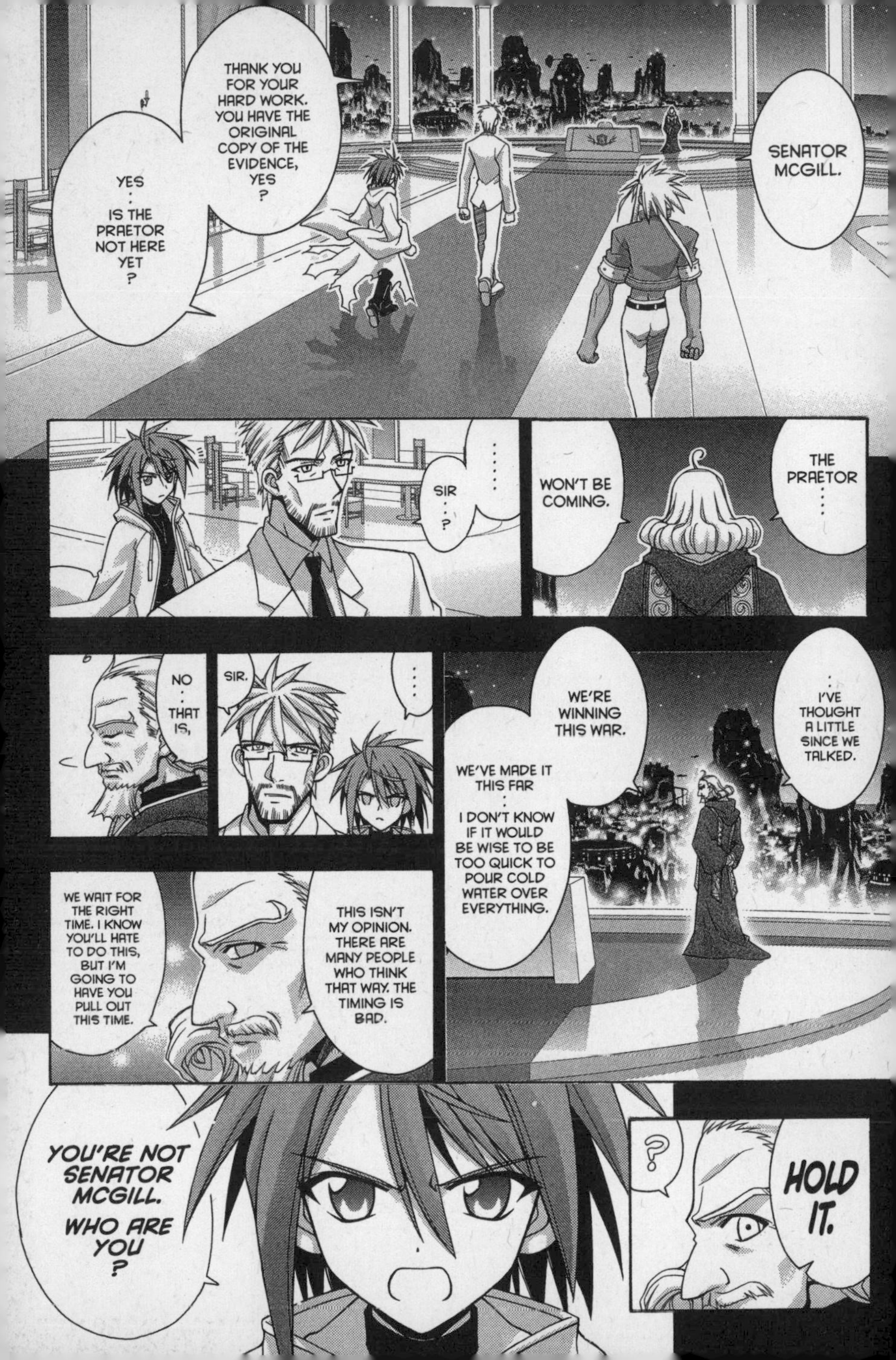
SENATOR MCGILL.
THANK YOU FOR YOUR HARD WORK. YOU HAVE THE ORIGINAL COPY OF THE EVIDENCE, YES?
YES... IS THE PRAETOR NOT HERE YET?
THE PRAETOR...
WON'T BE COMING.
......
SIR...?
...I'VE THOUGHT A LITTLE SINCE WE TALKED.
WE'RE WINNING THIS WAR.
WE'VE MADE IT THIS FAR... I DON'T KNOW IF IT WOULD BE WISE TO BE TOO QUICK TO POUR COLD WATER OVER EVERYTHING.
....
SIR.
NO... THAT IS,
THIS ISN'T MY OPINION. THERE ARE MANY PEOPLE WHO THINK THAT WAY. THE TIMING IS BAD.
WE WAIT FOR THE RIGHT TIME. I KNOW YOU'LL HATE TO DO THIS, BUT I'M GOING TO HAVE YOU PULL OUT THIS TIME.
HOLD IT.
?
YOU'RE NOT SENATOR MCGILL. WHO ARE YOU?

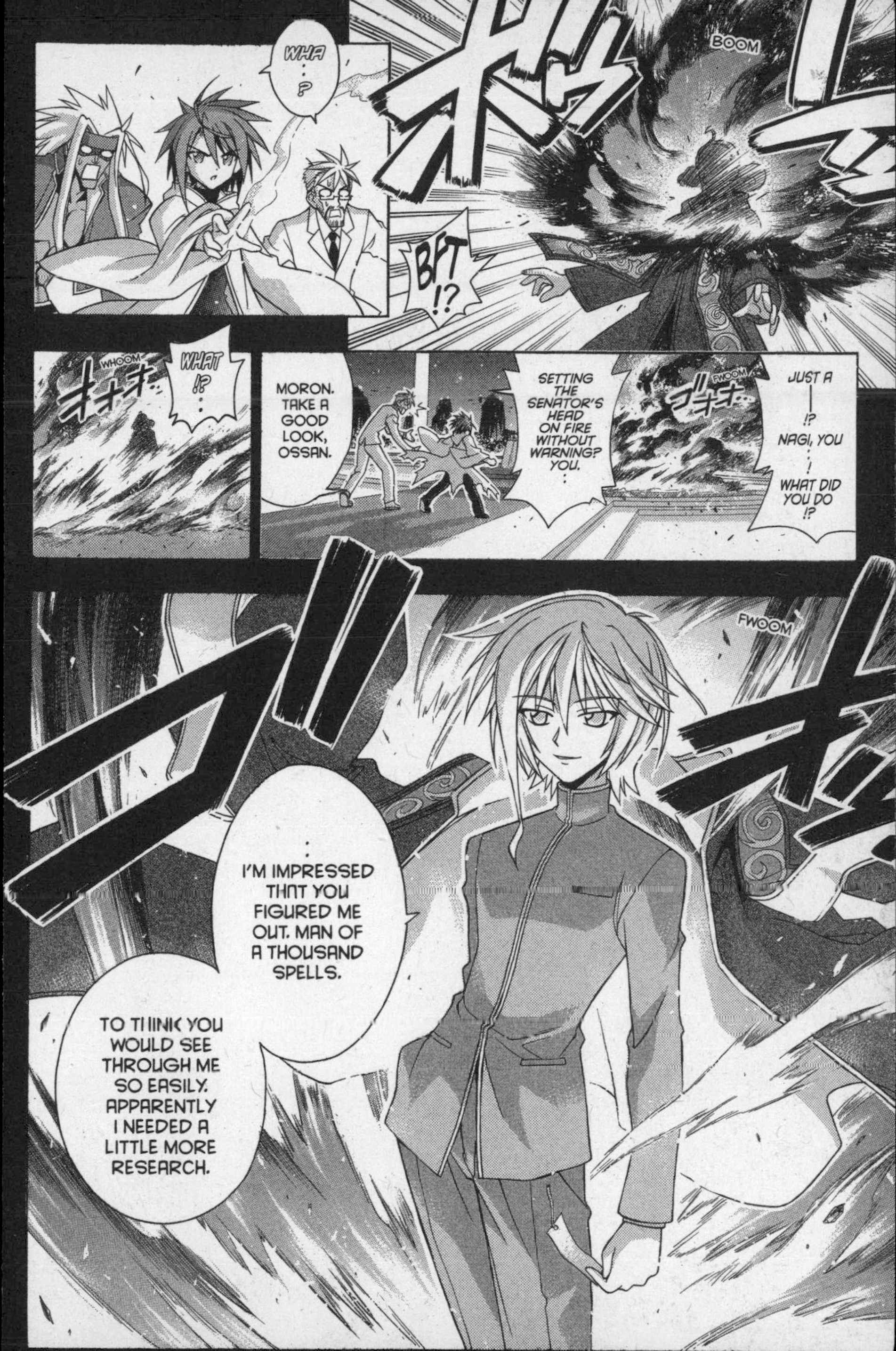
BOOM
BFT!?
WHA . . . ?
JUST A —— !? NAGI, YOU . . . ! WHAT DID YOU DO !?
FWOOM
SETTING THE SENATOR'S HEAD ON FIRE WITHOUT WARNING? YOU. . .
MORON. TAKE A GOOD LOOK, OSSAN.
WHAT !? . . .
WHOOM
FWOOM
: I'M IMPRESSED THAT YOU FIGURED ME OUT. MAN OF A THOUSAND SPELLS.
TO THINK YOU WOULD SEE THROUGH ME SO EASILY. APPARENTLY I NEEDED A LITTLE MORE RESEARCH.

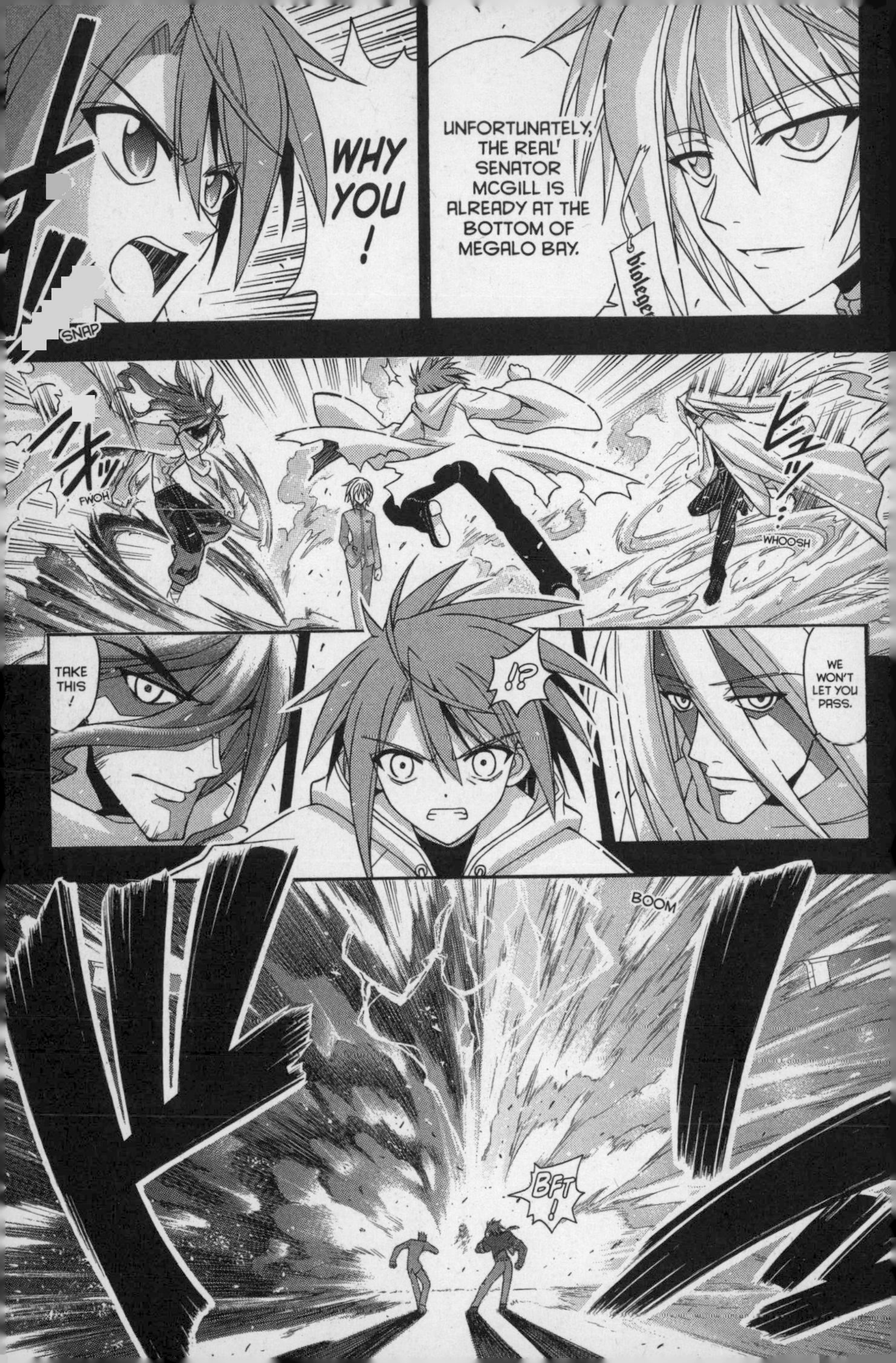
UNFORTUNATELY, THE REAL' SENATOR MCGILL IS ALREADY AT THE BOTTOM OF MEGALO BAY.
WHY YOU !
SNAP
WHOOSH
FWOH
WE WON'T LET YOU PASS.
!?
TAKE THIS !
BOOM
BFT !

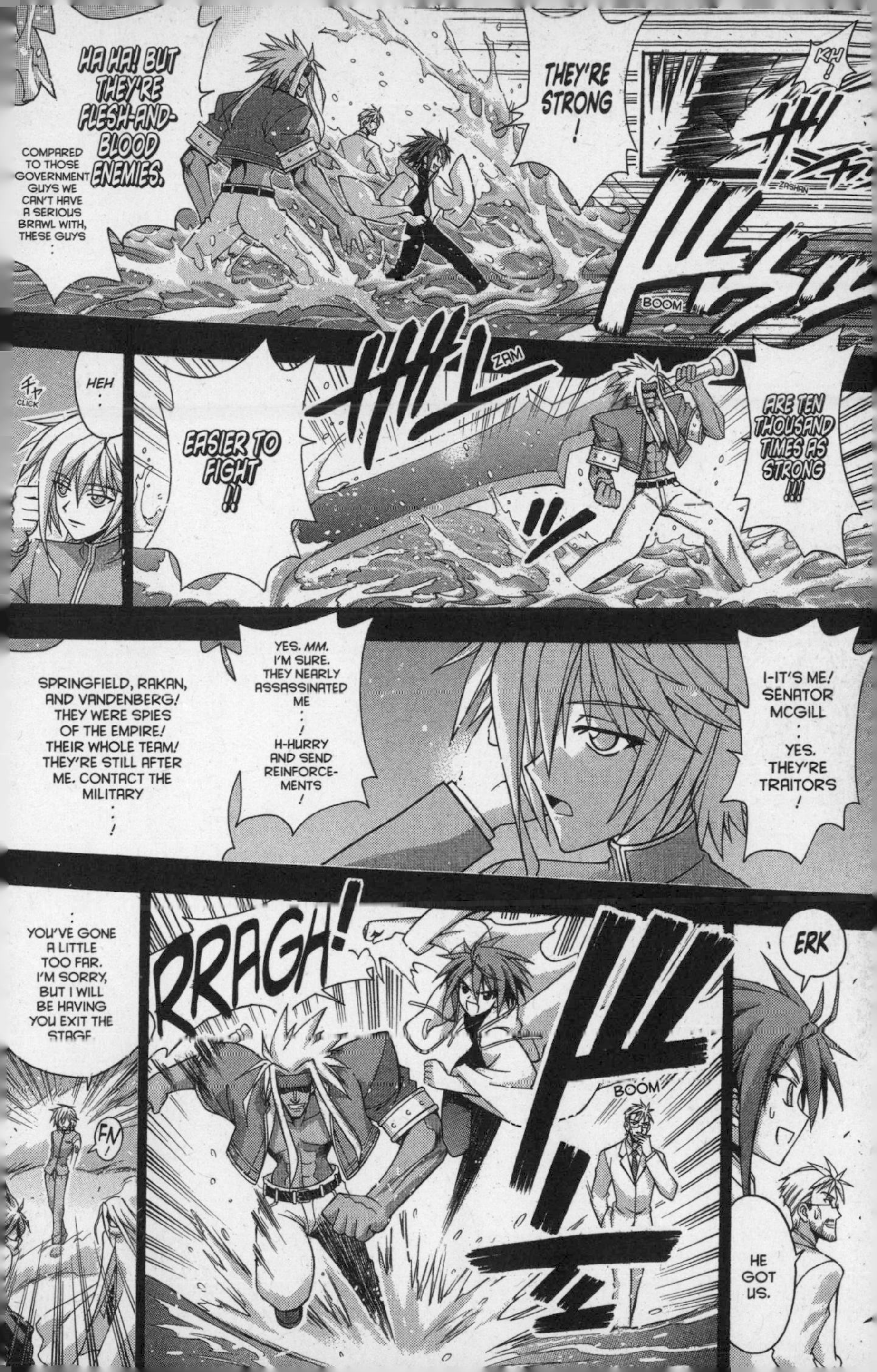

KH!
ZASHAN
BOOM
THEY'RE STRONG!
HA HA! BUT THEY'RE FLESH-AND-BLOOD ENEMIES.
COMPARED TO THOSE GOVERNMENT GUYS WE CAN'T HAVE A SERIOUS BRAWL WITH, THESE GUYS...
ARE TEN THOUSAND TIMES AS STRONG!!!
ZAM
EASIER TO FIGHT!!
HEH...
CLICK
I-IT'S ME! SENATOR MCGILL... YES. THEY'RE TRAITORS!
YES. MM. I'M SURE. THEY NEARLY ASSASSINATED ME...! H-HURRY AND SEND REINFORCEMENTS!
SPRINGFIELD, RAKAN, AND VANDENBERG! THEY WERE SPIES OF THE EMPIRE! THEIR WHOLE TEAM! THEY'RE STILL AFTER ME. CONTACT THE MILITARY...!
ERK
HE GOT US.
BOOM
RRAGH!
...YOU'VE GONE A LITTLE TOO FAR. I'M SORRY, BUT I WILL BE HAVING YOU EXIT THE STAGE.
FN

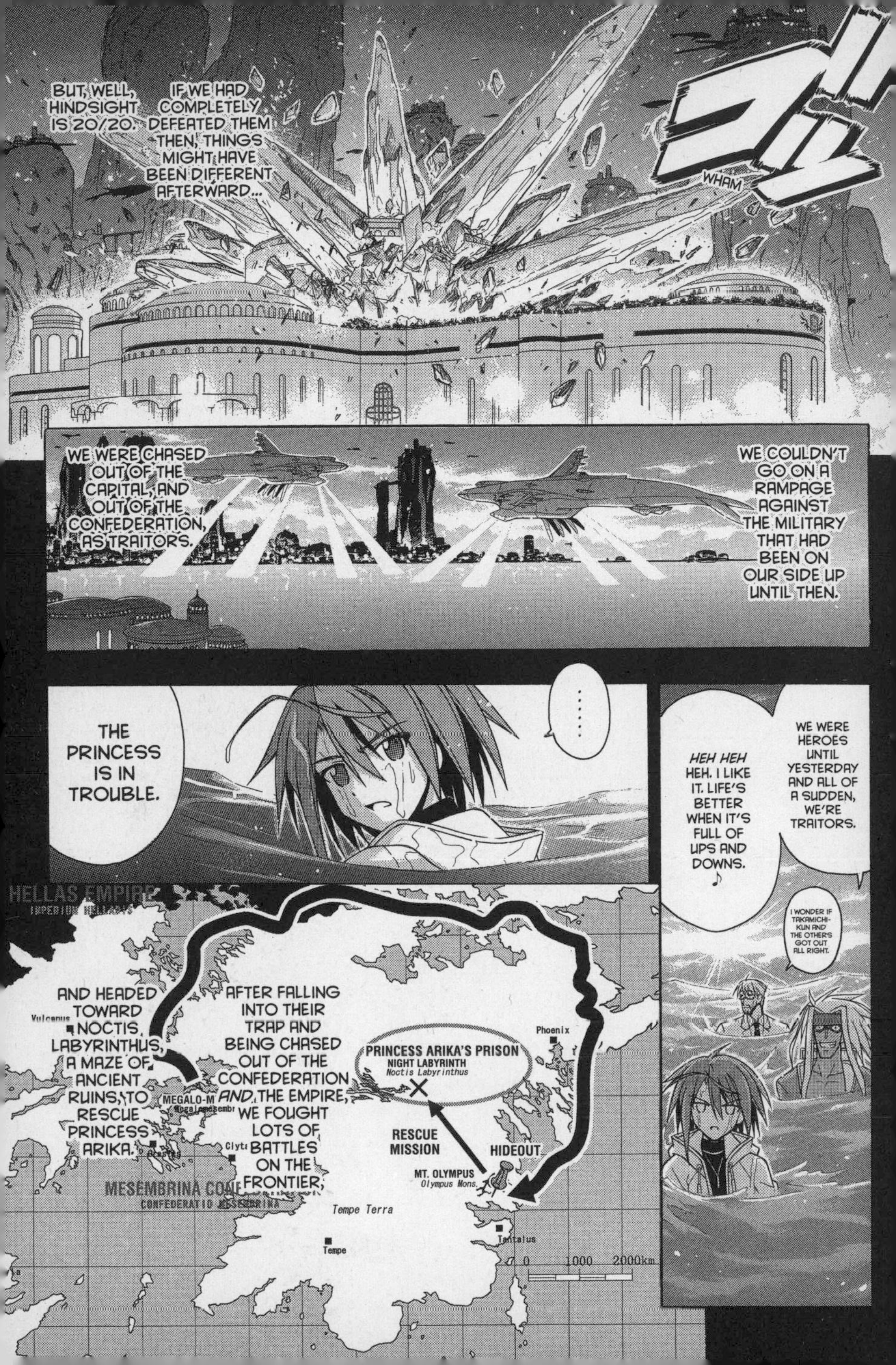
WHAM
IF WE HAD COMPLETELY DEFEATED THEM THEN, THINGS MIGHT HAVE BEEN DIFFERENT AFTERWARD...
BUT, WELL, HINDSIGHT IS 20/20.
WE COULDN'T GO ON A RAMPAGE AGAINST THE MILITARY THAT HAD BEEN ON OUR SIDE UP UNTIL THEN.
WE WERE CHASED OUT OF THE CAPITAL, AND OUT OF THE CONFEDERATION, AS TRAITORS.
WE WERE HEROES UNTIL YESTERDAY AND ALL OF A SUDDEN, WE'RE TRAITORS.
HEH HEH HEH. I LIKE IT. LIFE'S BETTER WHEN IT'S FULL OF UPS AND DOWNS. ♪
I WONDER IF TAKAMICHI-KUN AND THE OTHERS GOT OUT ALL RIGHT.
......
THE PRINCESS IS IN TROUBLE.
HELLAS EMPIRE
PRINCESS ARIKA'S PRISON
NIGHT LABYRINTH
Noctis Labyrinthus
Phoenix
RESCUE MISSION
HIDEOUT
MT. OLYMPUS
Olympus Mons.
Tempe Terra
Tempe
Tantalus
0 1000 2000km
AFTER FALLING INTO THEIR TRAP AND BEING CHASED OUT OF THE CONFEDERATION *AND* THE EMPIRE, WE FOUGHT LOTS OF BATTLES ON THE FRONTIER,
AND HEADED TOWARD NOCTIS LABYRINTHUS, A MAZE OF ANCIENT RUINS, TO RESCUE PRINCESS ARIKA.
Vulcanus
MEGALO-M
MESEMBRINA CONF
CONFEDERATIO MESEMBRINA

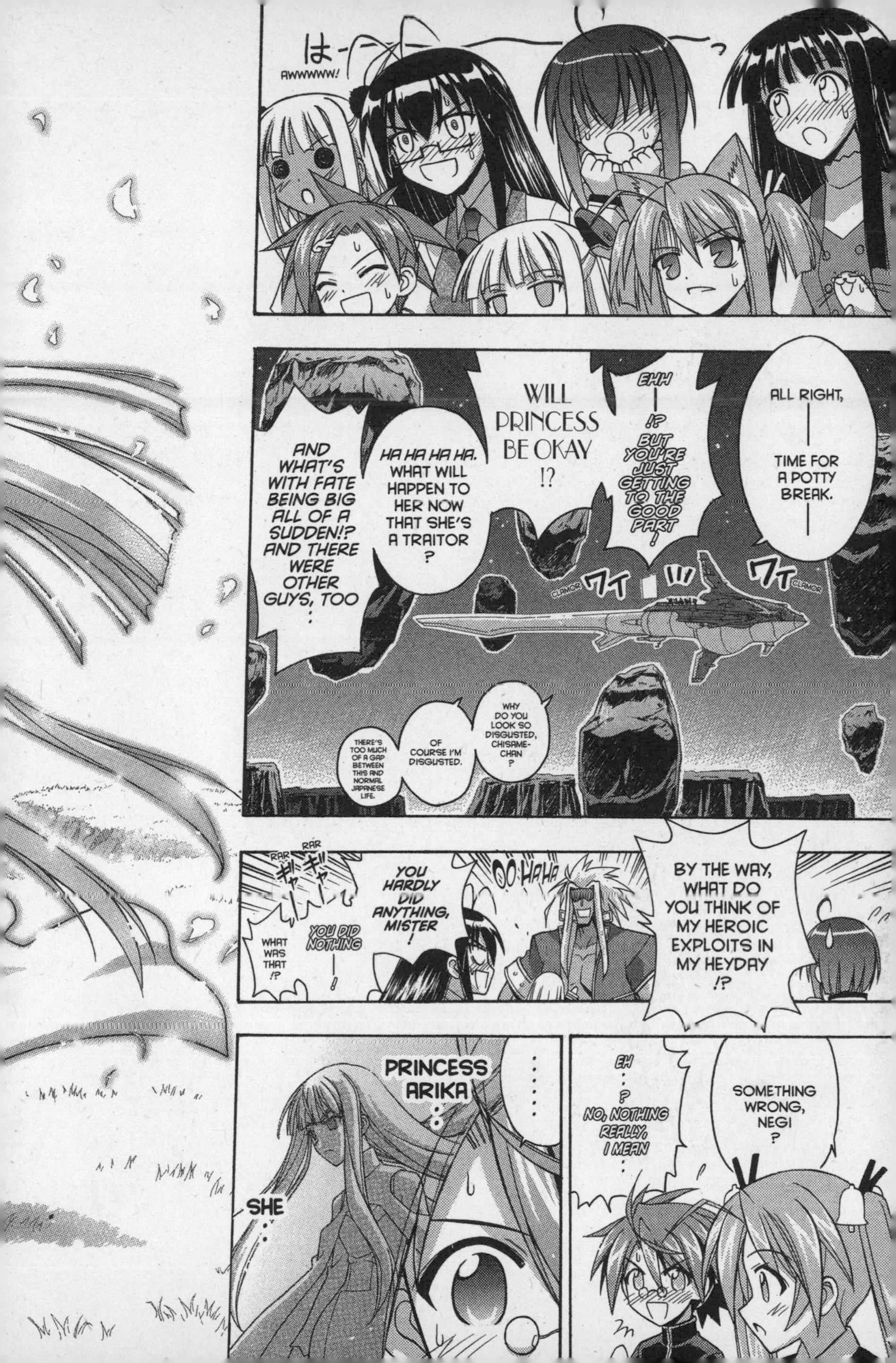

は—
AWWWWW!
ALL RIGHT, — TIME FOR A POTTY BREAK. —
EHH —!? BUT YOU'RE JUST GETTING TO THE GOOD PART!
WILL PRINCESS BE OKAY!?
HA HA HA HA. WHAT WILL HAPPEN TO HER NOW THAT SHE'S A TRAITOR?
AND WHAT'S WITH FATE BEING BIG ALL OF A SUDDEN!? AND THERE WERE OTHER GUYS, TOO...
ワイ CLAMOR
ワイ CLAMOR
WHY DO YOU LOOK SO DISGUSTED, CHISAME-CHAN?
OF COURSE I'M DISGUSTED.
THERE'S TOO MUCH OF A GAP BETWEEN THIS AND NORMAL JAPANESE LIFE.
BY THE WAY, WHAT DO YOU THINK OF MY HEROIC EXPLOITS IN MY HEYDAY!?
HAHA
YOU HARDLY DID ANYTHING, MISTER!
YOU DID NOTHING—!
RAR RAR
WHAT WAS THAT!?
SOMETHING WRONG, NEGI?
EH...? NO, NOTHING REALLY, I MEAN
......
PRINCESS ARIKA...
SHE...

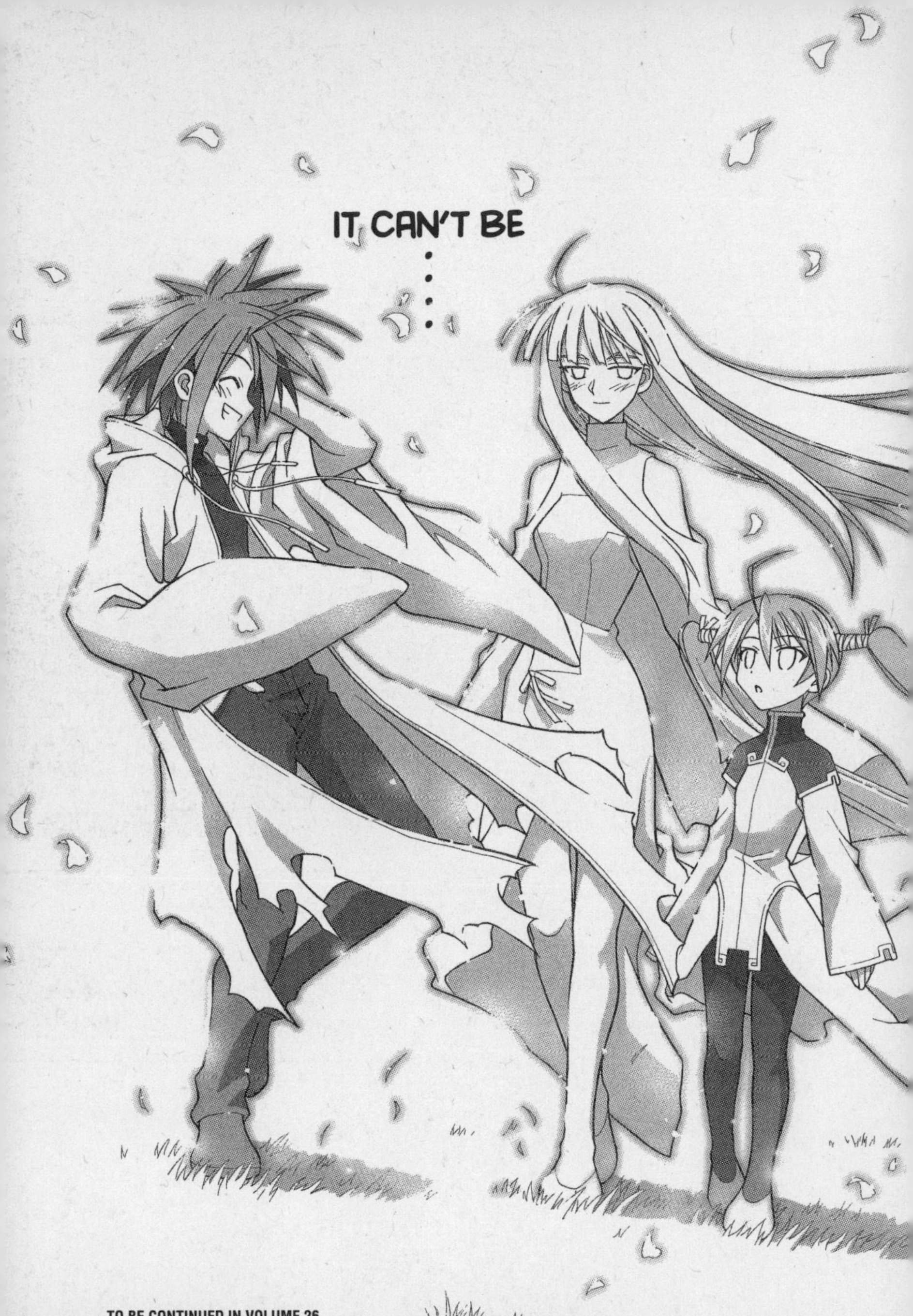
IT CAN'T BE
....

TO BE CONTINUED IN VOLUME 26

A Word from the Author

Presenting *Negima!* volume 26!

In the last volume, Fate defeated Negi yet again, but, provoked by Rakan's movie, Negi starts his training from hell. And on the last page of this volume, something shocking appears!...You'll just have to wait and see what it is. (^^)

Now then, starting with the limited edition of volume 27, the second OAD series will begin. The Magical World arc has gotten more intense and more interesting, so please watch the anime DVD!

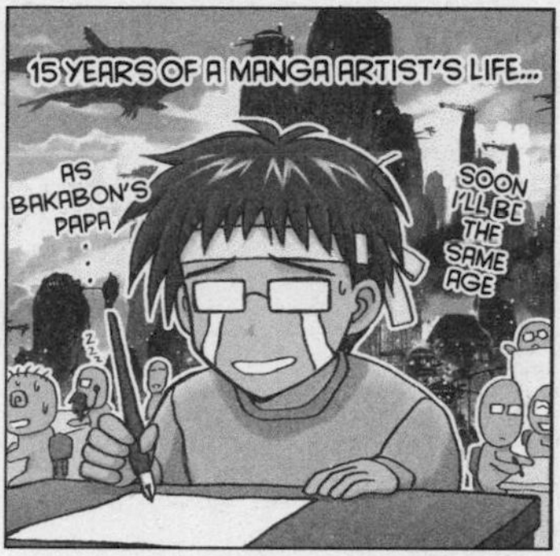
15 YEARS OF A MANGA ARTIST'S LIFE...
SOON I'LL BE THE SAME AGE
AS BAKABON'S PAPA...

As in the past, they'll all be sold through preorders. For details, check the official site or the flyer inside this book (in the Japanese version only).

Ken Akamatsu
www.ailove.net

26

赤松 健

Ken Akamatsu

魔法先生ネギま!

MAGISTER NEGI MAGI

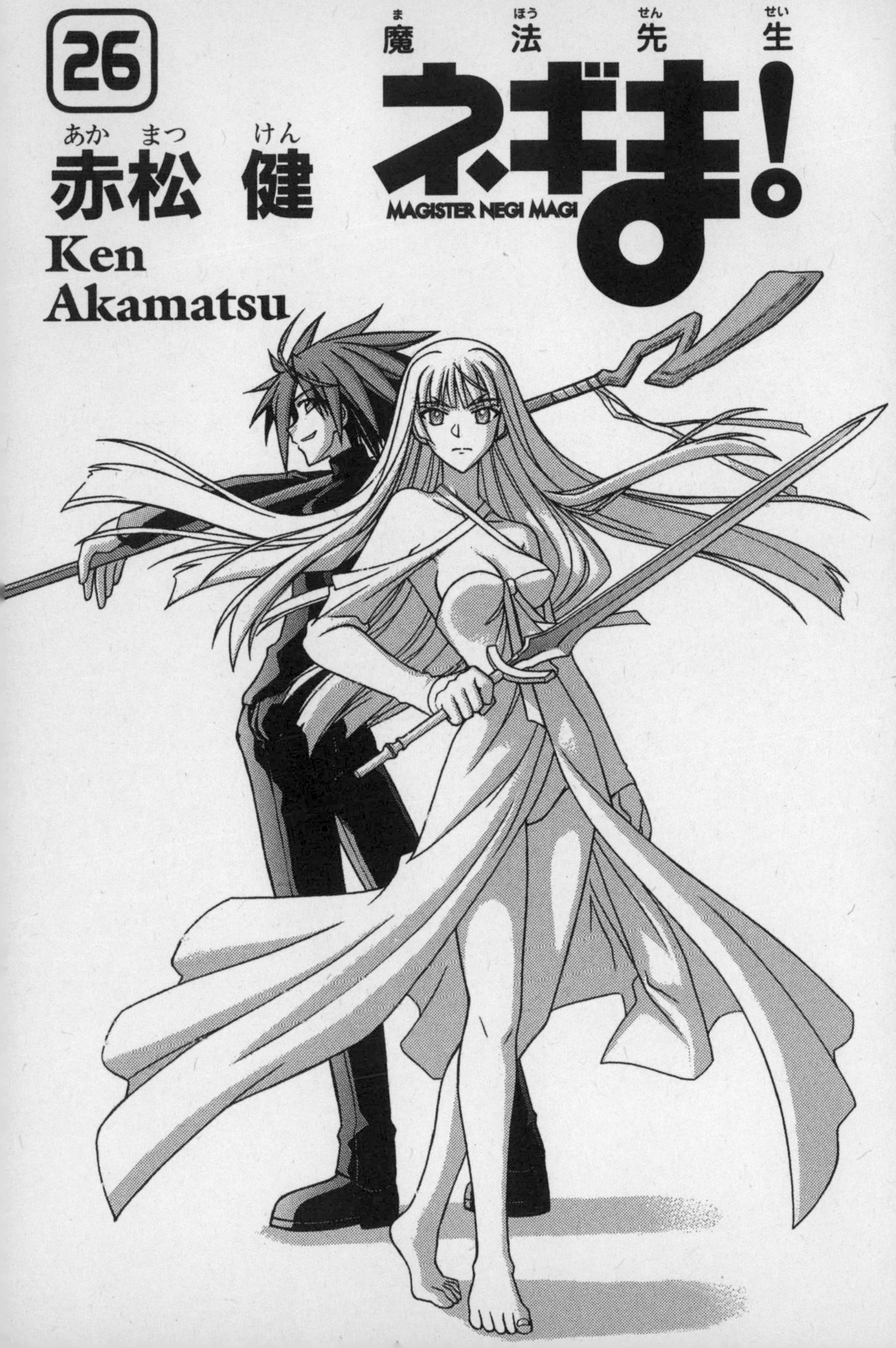

CONTENTS

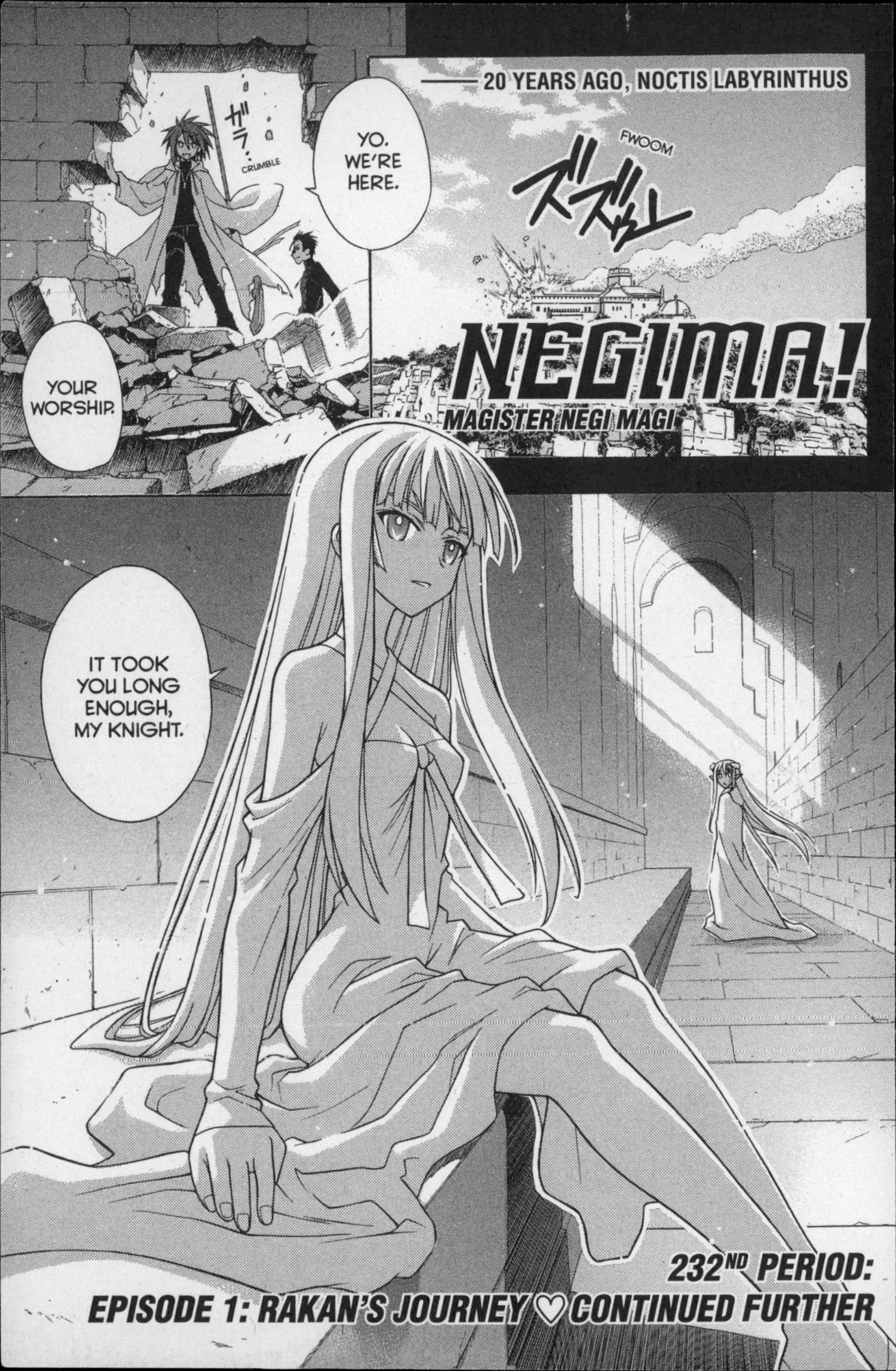
—20 YEARS AGO, NOCTIS LABYRINTHUS
FWOOM
NEGIMA!
MAGISTER NEGI MAGI
YO. WE'RE HERE.
ガラ…
CRUMBLE
YOUR WORSHIP.
IT TOOK YOU LONG ENOUGH, MY KNIGHT.
232ND PERIOD:
EPISODE 1: RAKAN'S JOURNEY ♡ CONTINUED FURTHER

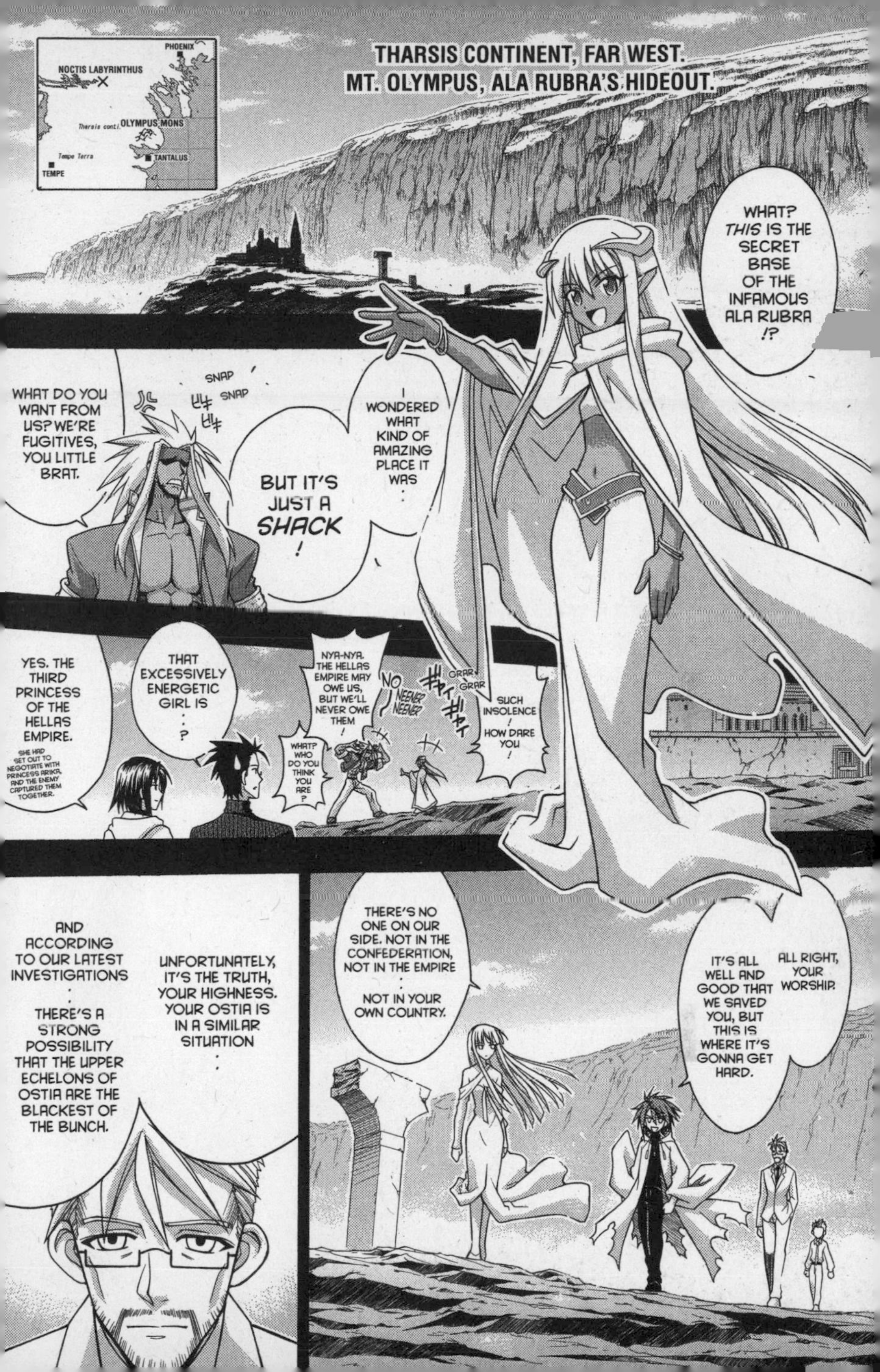
THARSIS CONTINENT, FAR WEST.
MT. OLYMPUS, ALA RUBRA'S HIDEOUT.
PHOENIX
NOCTIS LABYRINTHUS
Tharsis conti.
OLYMPUS MONS
Tempe Terra
TANTALUS
TEMPE
WHAT? THIS IS THE SECRET BASE OF THE INFAMOUS ALA RUBRA !?
I WONDERED WHAT KIND OF AMAZING PLACE IT WAS . . . BUT IT'S JUST A SHACK !
SNAP SNAP
WHAT DO YOU WANT FROM US? WE'RE FUGITIVES, YOU LITTLE BRAT.
SUCH INSOLENCE ! HOW DARE YOU !
GRAR GRAR
NO NEENER NEENER
NYA-NYA. THE HELLAS EMPIRE MAY OWE US, BUT WE'LL NEVER OWE THEM !
WHAT? WHO DO YOU THINK YOU ARE ?
THAT EXCESSIVELY ENERGETIC GIRL IS . . . ?
YES. THE THIRD PRINCESS OF THE HELLAS EMPIRE.
SHE HAD SET OUT TO NEGOTIATE WITH PRINCESS ARIKA, AND THE ENEMY CAPTURED THEM TOGETHER.
ALL RIGHT, YOUR WORSHIP.
IT'S ALL WELL AND GOOD THAT WE SAVED YOU, BUT THIS IS WHERE IT'S GONNA GET HARD.
THERE'S NO ONE ON OUR SIDE. NOT IN THE CONFEDERATION, NOT IN THE EMPIRE . . . NOT IN YOUR OWN COUNTRY.
UNFORTUNATELY, IT'S THE TRUTH, YOUR HIGHNESS. YOUR OSTIA IS IN A SIMILAR SITUATION . . .
AND ACCORDING TO OUR LATEST INVESTIGATIONS . . . THERE'S A STRONG POSSIBILITY THAT THE UPPER ECHELONS OF OSTIA ARE THE BLACKEST OF THE BUNCH.

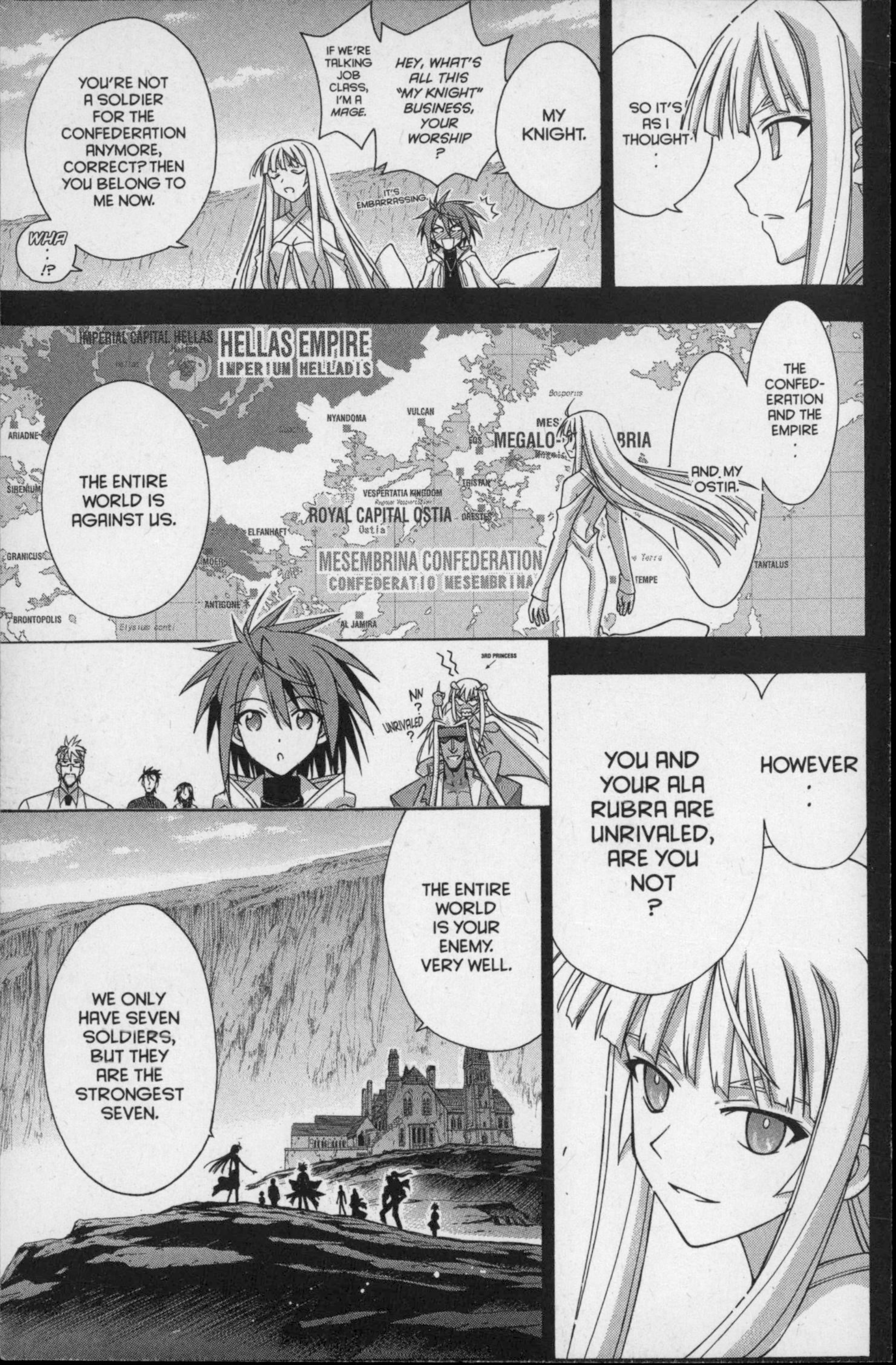
SO IT'S AS I THOUGHT...
MY KNIGHT.
HEY, WHAT'S ALL THIS "MY KNIGHT" BUSINESS, YOUR WORSHIP?
IF WE'RE TALKING JOB CLASS, I'M A MAGE.
IT'S EMBARRASSING
YOU'RE NOT A SOLDIER FOR THE CONFEDERATION ANYMORE, CORRECT? THEN YOU BELONG TO ME NOW.
WHA...!?
THE CONFEDERATION AND THE EMPIRE...
AND MY OSTIA.
HELLAS EMPIRE
IMPERIUM HELLADIS
IMPERIAL CAPITAL HELLAS
MEGALO-MESEMBRIA
ROYAL CAPITAL OSTIA
Ostia
MESEMBRINA CONFEDERATION
CONFEDERATIO MESEMBRINA
Bosporus
NYANDOMA
VULCAN
ARIADNE
SIRENIUM
VESPERTATIA KINGDOM
TRISTAN
ORESTES
ELFANHAFT
GRANICUS
MOER
ANTIGONE
BRONTOPOLIS
AL JAMIRA
TEMPE
TANTALUS
THE ENTIRE WORLD IS AGAINST US.
HOWEVER...
YOU AND YOUR ALA RUBRA ARE UNRIVALED, ARE YOU NOT?
3RD PRINCESS
NN?
UNRIVALED?
THE ENTIRE WORLD IS YOUR ENEMY. VERY WELL.
WE ONLY HAVE SEVEN SOLDIERS, BUT THEY ARE THE STRONGEST SEVEN.

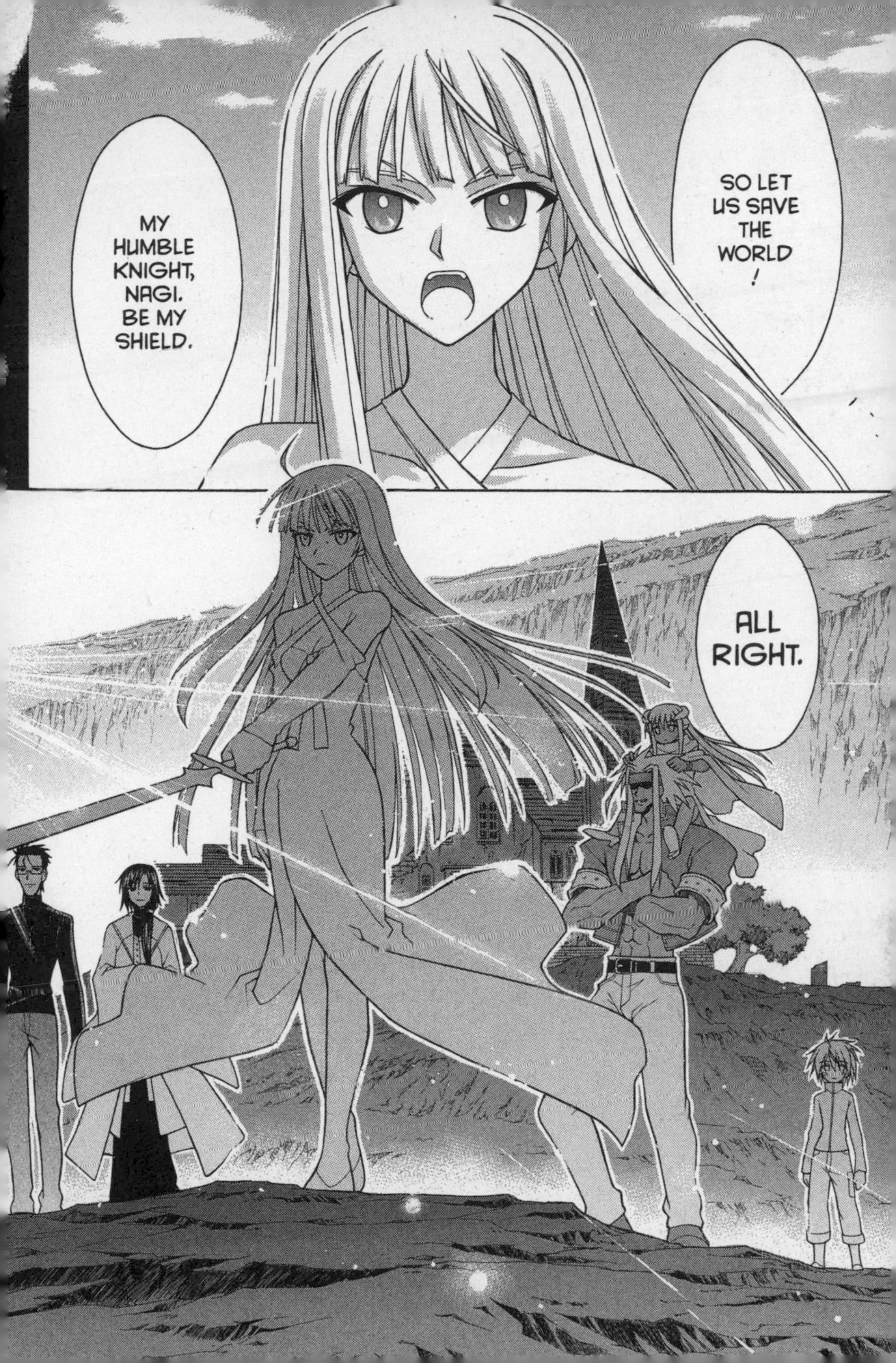

SO LET US SAVE THE WORLD!
MY HUMBLE KNIGHT, NAGI. BE MY SHIELD.
ALL RIGHT.

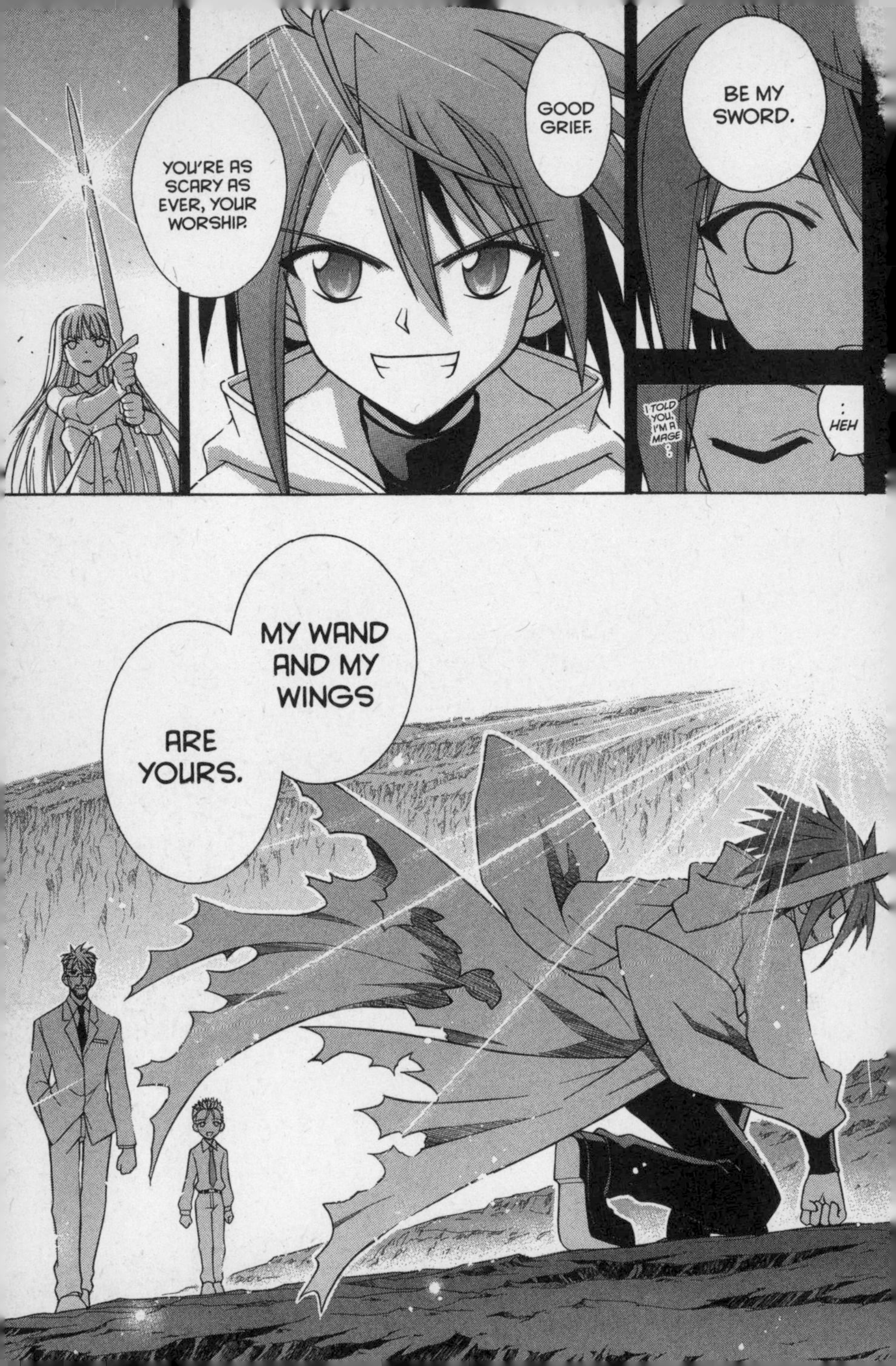
BE MY SWORD.
...HEH
I TOLD YOU, I'M A MAGE...
GOOD GRIEF.
YOU'RE AS SCARY AS EVER, YOUR WORSHIP.
MY WAND AND MY WINGS ARE YOURS.

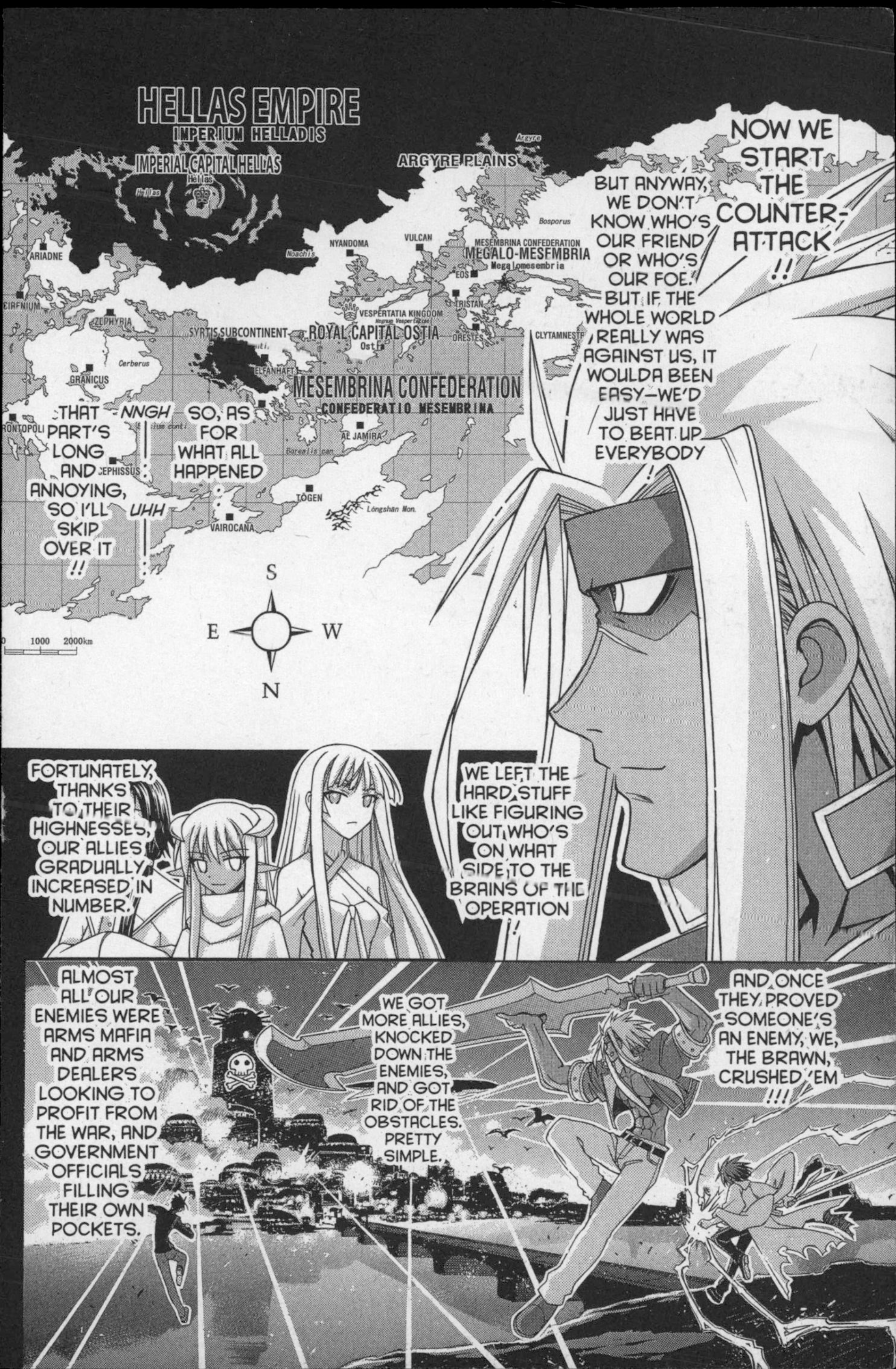
NOW WE START THE COUNTER-ATTACK!!
BUT ANYWAY, WE DON'T KNOW WHO'S OUR FRIEND OR WHO'S OUR FOE. BUT IF THE WHOLE WORLD REALLY WAS AGAINST US, IT WOULDA BEEN EASY—WE'D JUST HAVE TO BEAT UP EVERYBODY!
WE LEFT THE HARD STUFF LIKE FIGURING OUT WHO'S ON WHAT SIDE TO THE BRAINS OF THE OPERATION!
HELLAS EMPIRE
IMPERIUM HELLADIS
IMPERIAL CAPITAL HELLAS
Hellas
ARGYRE PLAINS
Argyre
Bosporus
NYANDOMA
VULCAN
Noachis
MESEMBRINA CONFEDERATION
MEGALO-MESEMBRIA
Megalomesembria
ARIADNE
EOS
TRISTAN
ZEPHYRIA
VESPERTATIA KINGDOM
SYRTIS SUBCONTINENT
ROYAL CAPITAL OSTIA
Ostia
ORESTES
Cerberus
GRANICUS
ELFANHAFT
MESEMBRINA CONFEDERATION
CONFEDERATIO MESEMBRINA
AL JAMIRA
TŌGEN
Longshan Mon.
VAIROCANA
S
E
W
N
0 1000 2000km
SO, AS FOR WHAT ALL HAPPENED
NNGH... UHH...
THAT PART'S LONG AND ANNOYING, SO I'LL SKIP OVER IT!!
FORTUNATELY, THANKS TO THEIR HIGHNESSES, OUR ALLIES GRADUALLY INCREASED IN NUMBER.
AND ONCE THEY PROVED SOMEONE'S AN ENEMY, WE, THE BRAWN, CRUSHED 'EM!!!
WE GOT MORE ALLIES, KNOCKED DOWN THE ENEMIES, AND GOT RID OF THE OBSTACLES. PRETTY SIMPLE.
ALMOST ALL OUR ENEMIES WERE ARMS MAFIA AND ARMS DEALERS LOOKING TO PROFIT FROM THE WAR, AND GOVERNMENT OFFICIALS FILLING THEIR OWN POCKETS.

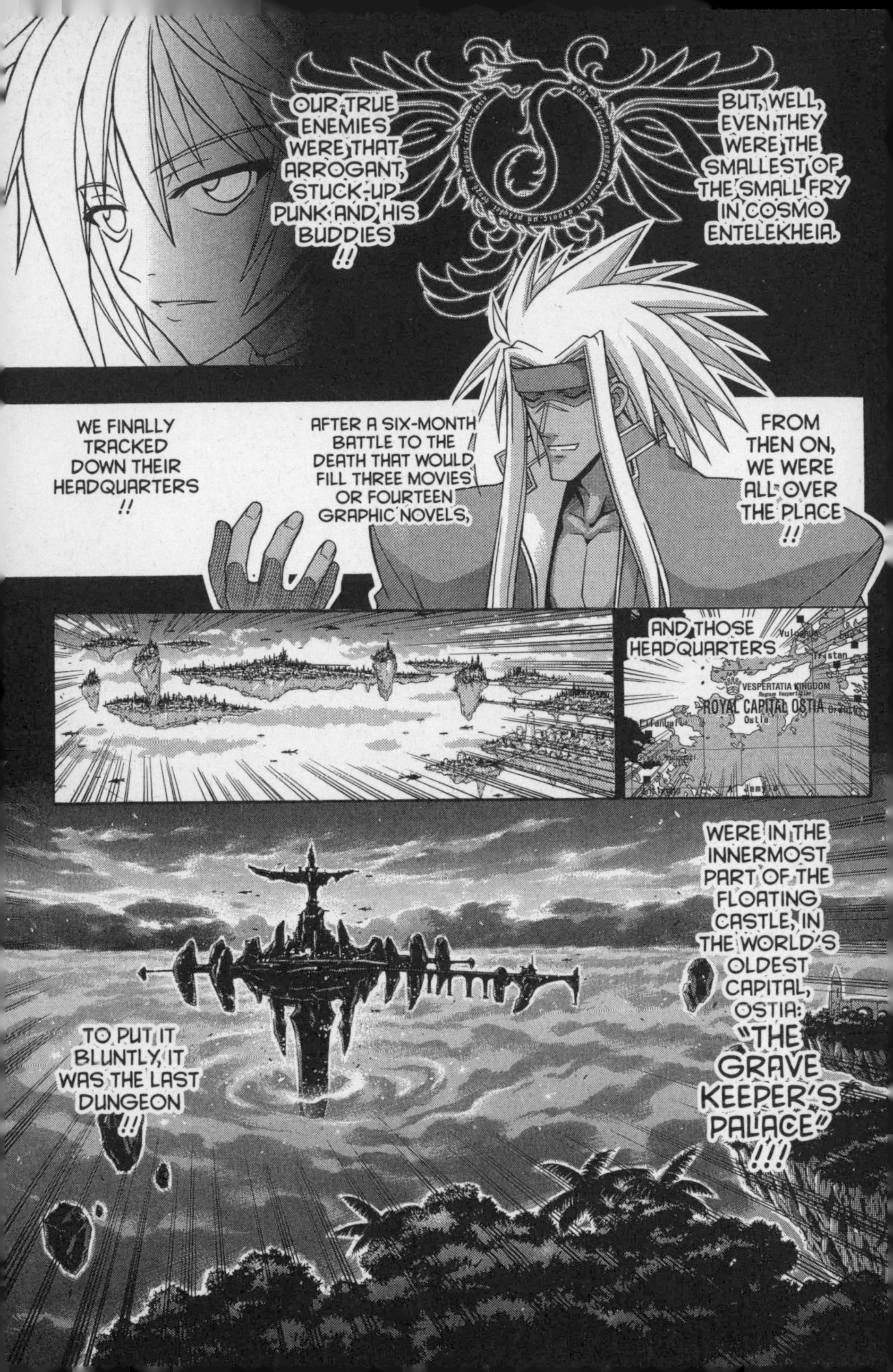
OUR TRUE ENEMIES WERE THAT ARROGANT, STUCK-UP PUNK AND HIS BUDDIES!!
BUT, WELL, EVEN THEY WERE THE SMALLEST OF THE SMALL FRY IN COSMO ENTELEKHEIA.
FROM THEN ON, WE WERE ALL OVER THE PLACE!!
AFTER A SIX-MONTH BATTLE TO THE DEATH THAT WOULD FILL THREE MOVIES OR FOURTEEN GRAPHIC NOVELS,
WE FINALLY TRACKED DOWN THEIR HEADQUARTERS!!
AND THOSE HEADQUARTERS
Tristan
VESPERTATIA KINGDOM
ROYAL CAPITAL OSTIA
Ostia
WERE IN THE INNERMOST PART OF THE FLOATING CASTLE, IN THE WORLD'S OLDEST CAPITAL, OSTIA: "THE GRAVE KEEPER'S PALACE"!!!
TO PUT IT BLUNTLY, IT WAS THE LAST DUNGEON!!

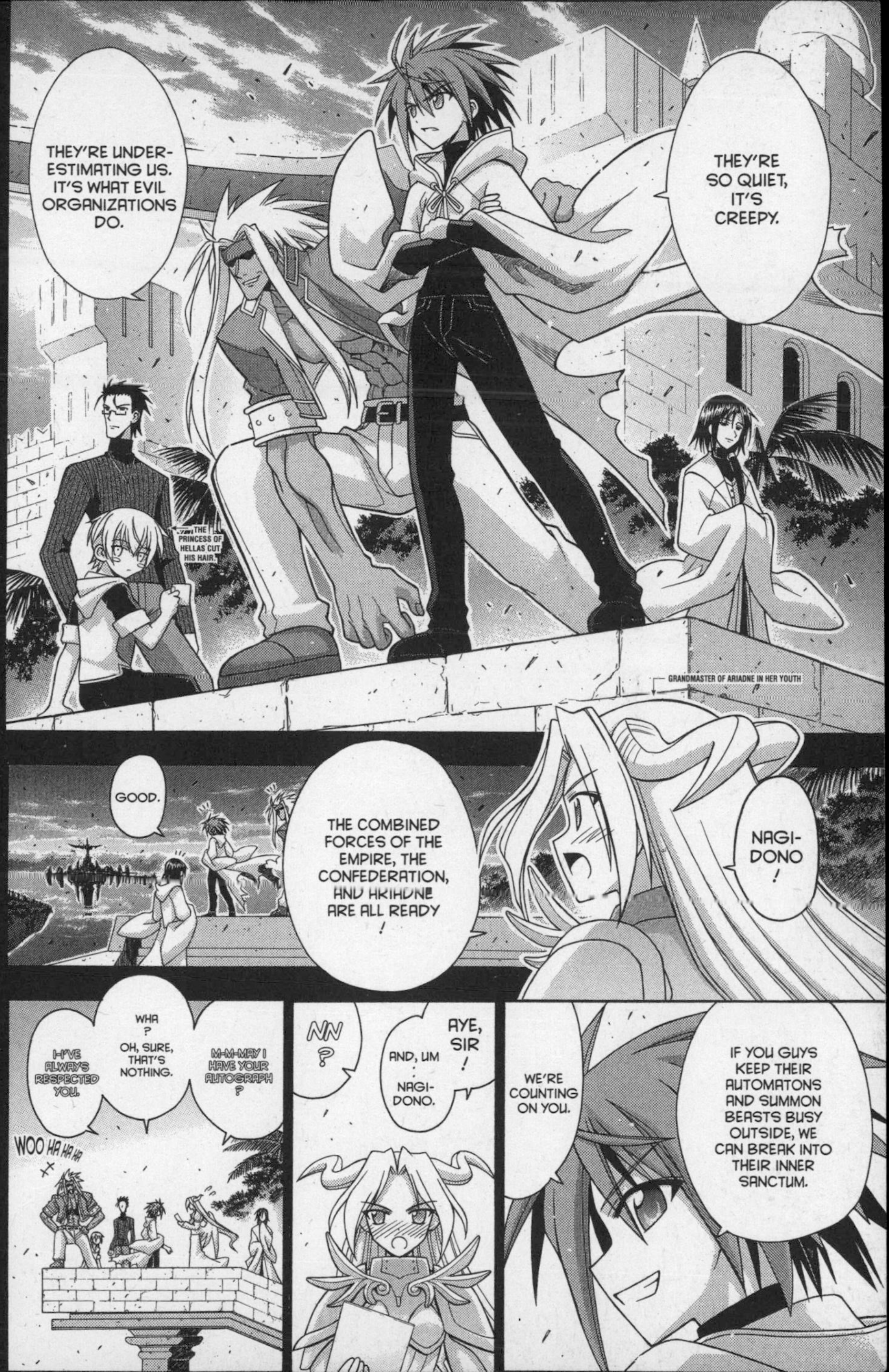
THEY'RE SO QUIET, IT'S CREEPY.
THEY'RE UNDER-ESTIMATING US. IT'S WHAT EVIL ORGANIZATIONS DO.
THE PRINCESS OF HELLAS CUT HIS HAIR.
GRANDMASTER OF ARIADNE IN HER YOUTH
NAGI-DONO!
THE COMBINED FORCES OF THE EMPIRE, THE CONFEDERATION, AND ARIADNE ARE ALL READY!
GOOD.
IF YOU GUYS KEEP THEIR AUTOMATONS AND SUMMON BEASTS BUSY OUTSIDE, WE CAN BREAK INTO THEIR INNER SANCTUM.
WE'RE COUNTING ON YOU.
AYE, SIR!
AND, UM
NAGI-DONO.
NN?
M-M-MAY I HAVE YOUR AUTOGRAPH?
WHA? OH, SURE, THAT'S NOTHING.
I-I'VE ALWAYS RESPECTED YOU.
WOO HA HA HA

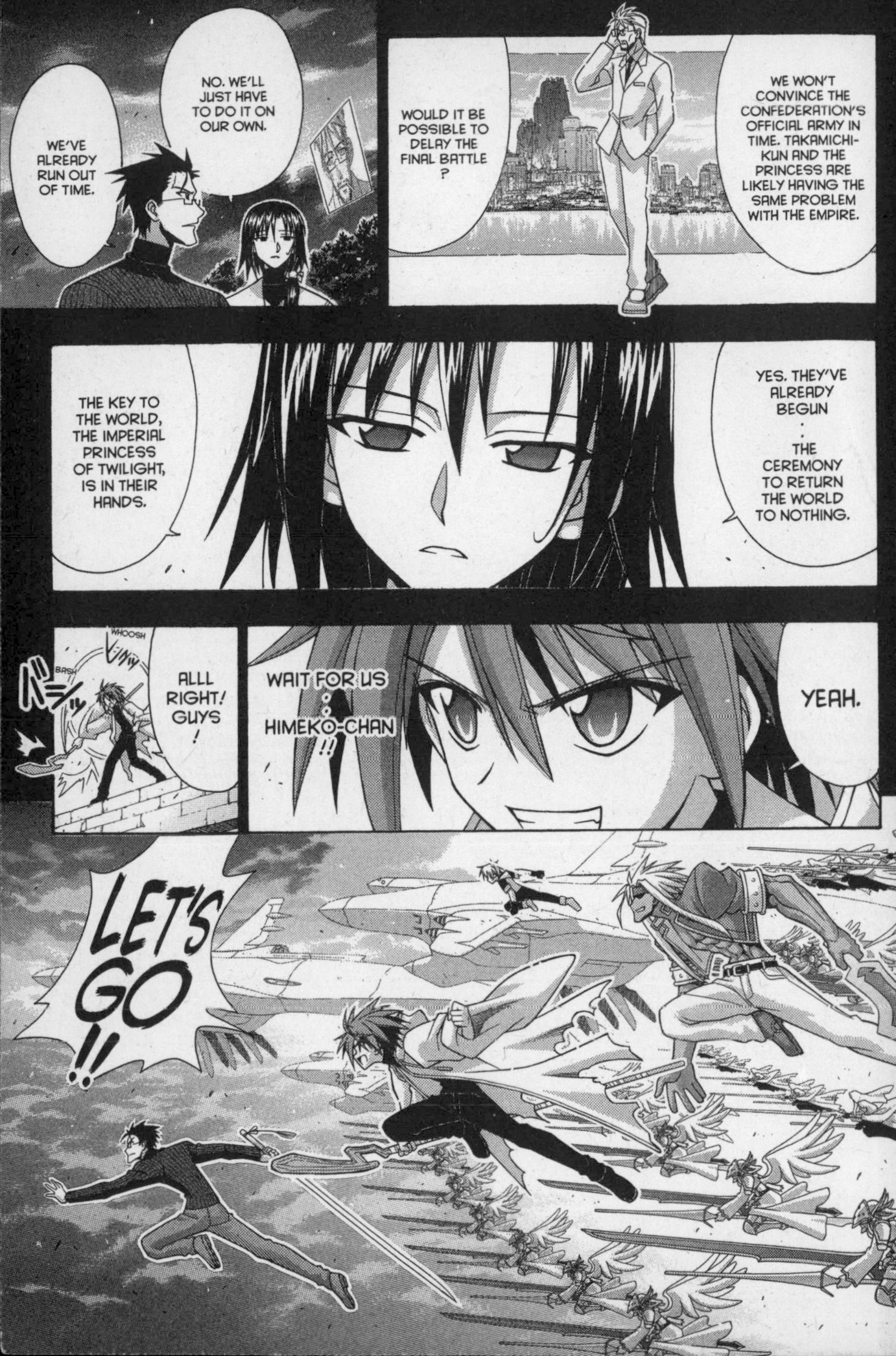
WE WON'T CONVINCE THE CONFEDERATION'S OFFICIAL ARMY IN TIME. TAKAMICHI-KUN AND THE PRINCESS ARE LIKELY HAVING THE SAME PROBLEM WITH THE EMPIRE.
WOULD IT BE POSSIBLE TO DELAY THE FINAL BATTLE?
NO. WE'LL JUST HAVE TO DO IT ON OUR OWN.
WE'VE ALREADY RUN OUT OF TIME.
YES. THEY'VE ALREADY BEGUN... THE CEREMONY TO RETURN THE WORLD TO NOTHING.
THE KEY TO THE WORLD, THE IMPERIAL PRINCESS OF TWILIGHT, IS IN THEIR HANDS.
YEAH.
WAIT FOR US... HIMEKO-CHAN!!
WHOOSH
BASH
ALLL RIGHT! GUYS!
LET'S GO!!

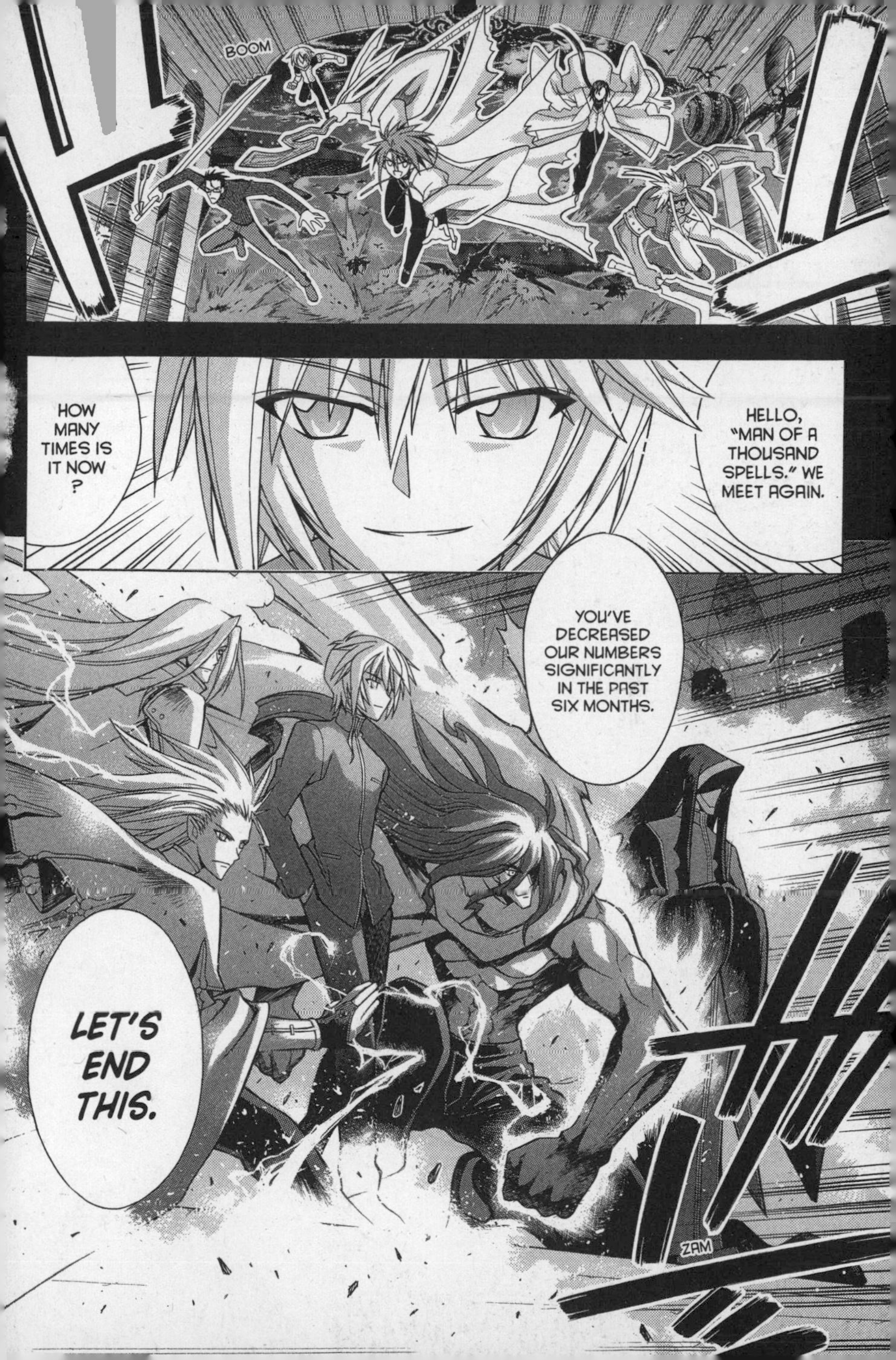
BOOM
HELLO, "MAN OF A THOUSAND SPELLS." WE MEET AGAIN.
HOW MANY TIMES IS IT NOW ?
YOU'VE DECREASED OUR NUMBERS SIGNIFICANTLY IN THE PAST SIX MONTHS.
LET'S END THIS.
ZAM

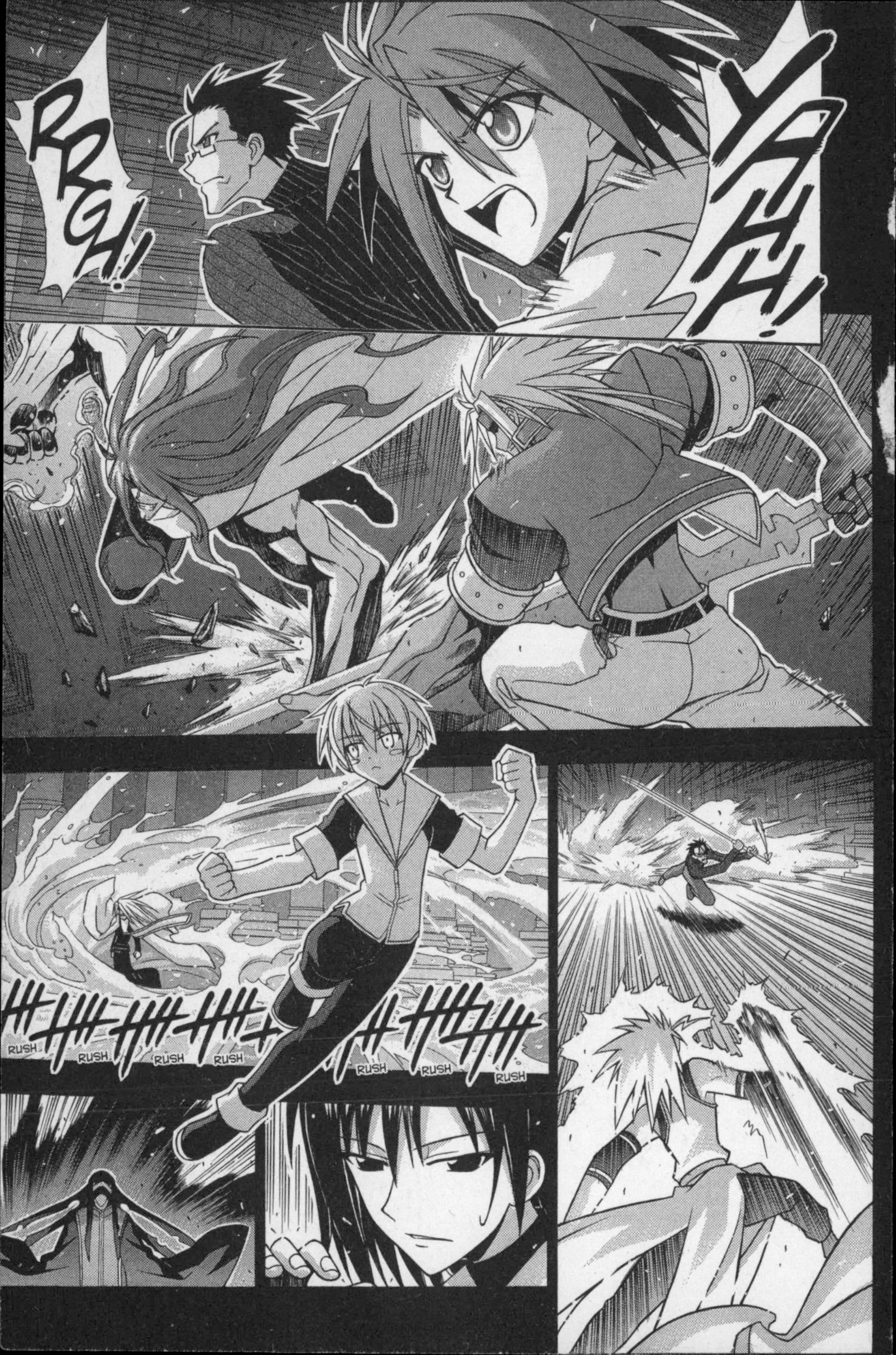
YAHH!
RRGH!
RUSH
RUSH
RUSH
RUSH
RUSH
RUSH
RUSH

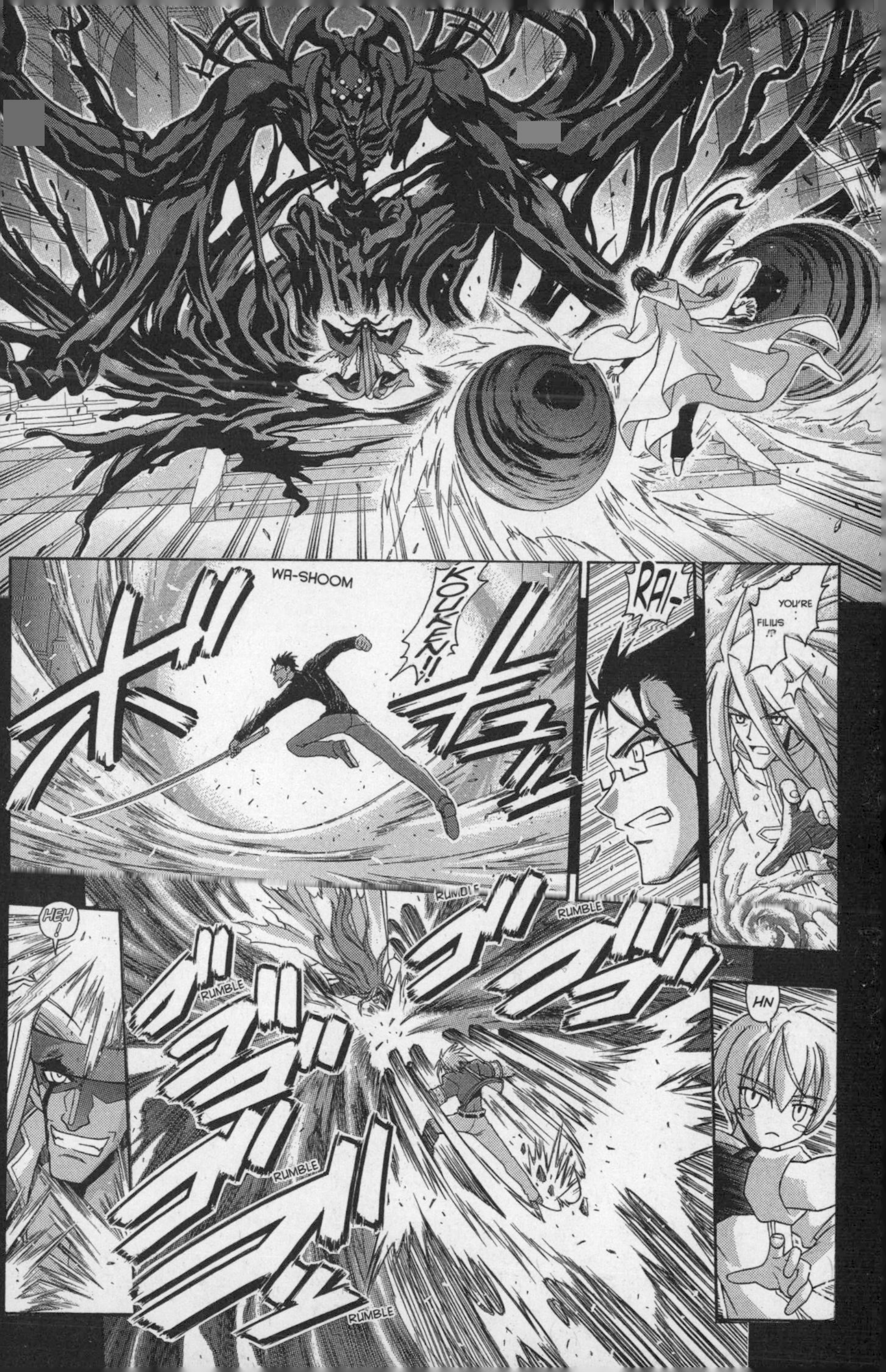
YOU'RE FILIUS !?
RAI-
KOUKEN!!
WA-SHOOM
HN
RUMBLE
RUMBLE
RUMBLE
RUMBLE
RUMBLE
HEH !

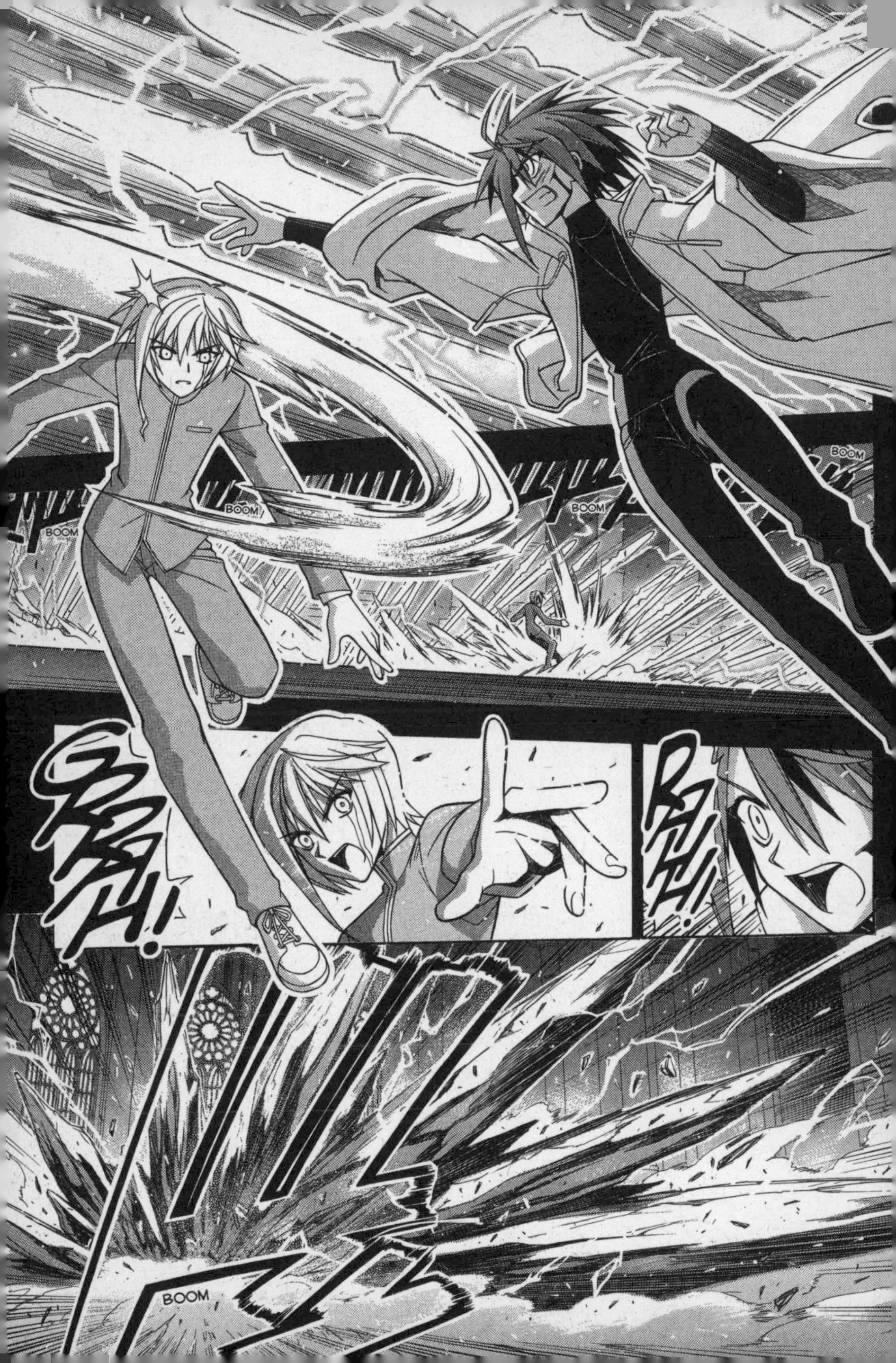
BOOM
BOOM
BOOM
BOOM
RAHH!
GRAAH!
BOOM

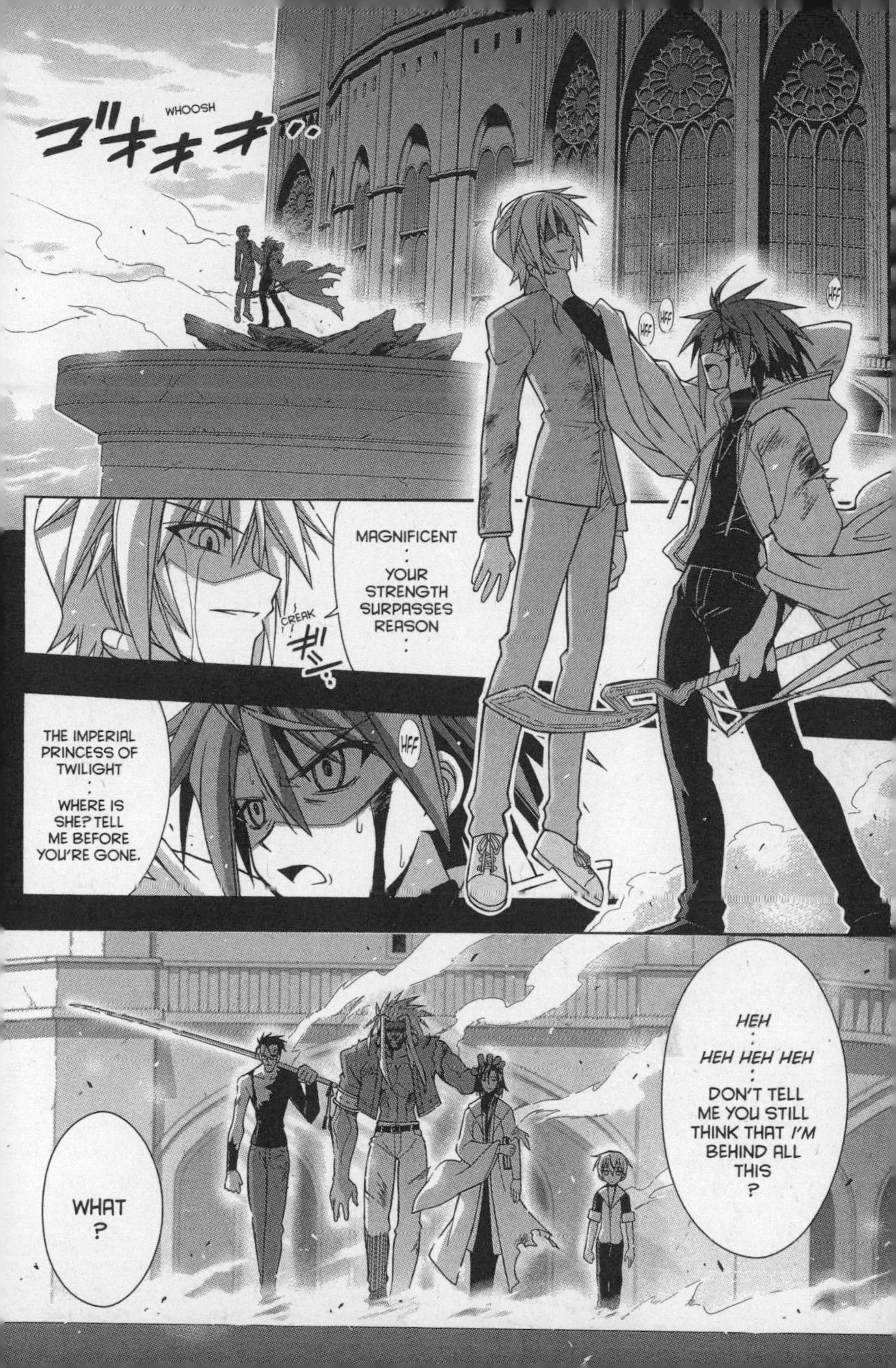
HFF
HFF
HFF
WHOOSH
MAGNIFICENT : YOUR STRENGTH SURPASSES REASON :
CREAK
THE IMPERIAL PRINCESS OF TWILIGHT : WHERE IS SHE? TELL ME BEFORE YOU'RE GONE.
HFF
HEH : HEH HEH HEH : DON'T TELL ME YOU STILL THINK THAT *I'M* BEHIND ALL THIS ?
WHAT ?

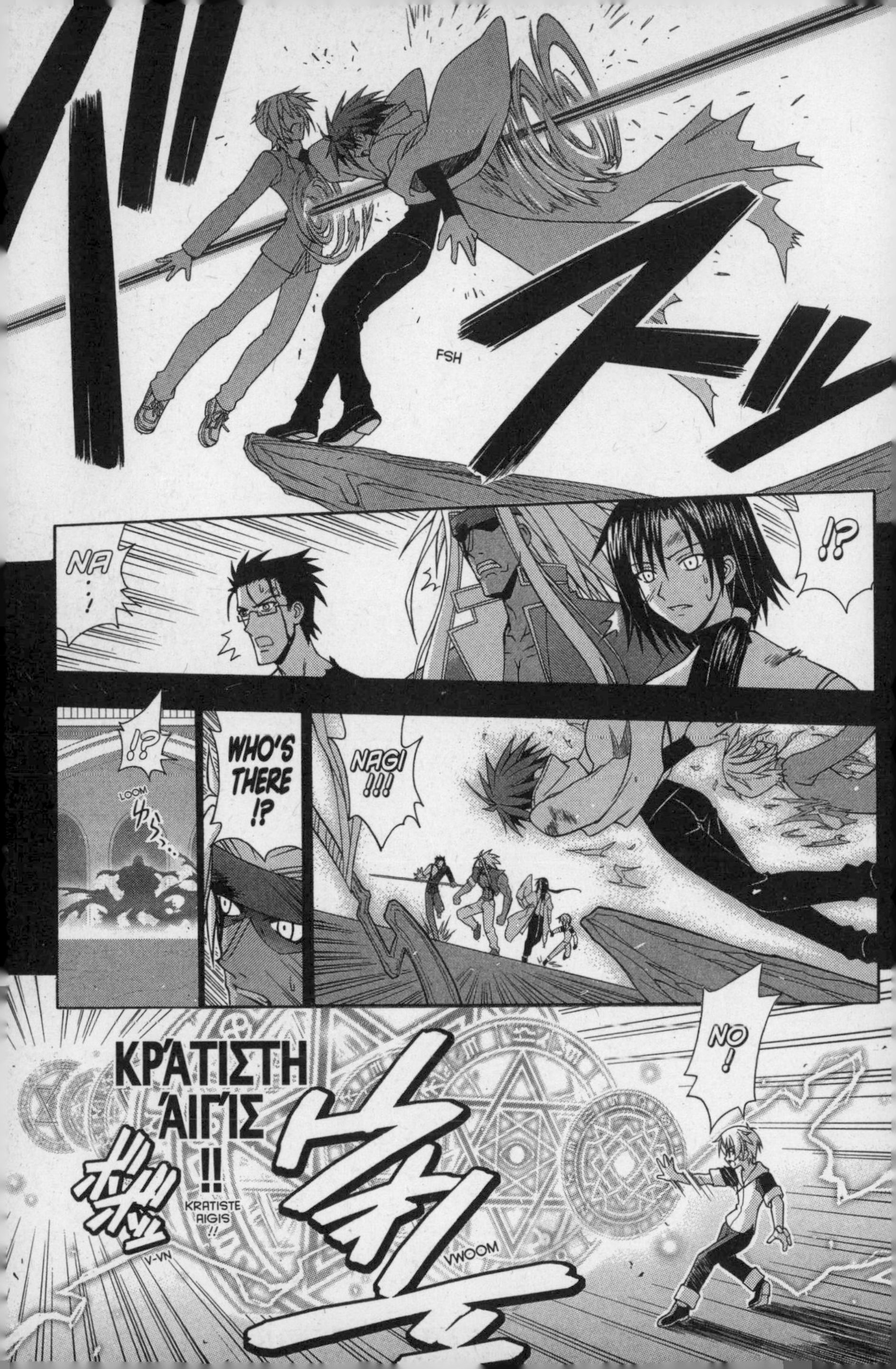
FSH
!?
NA...!
NAGI!!!
WHO'S THERE !?
!?
LOOM
NO!
ΚΡΆΤΙΣΤΗ ΆΙΓΊΣ !!
KRATISTE AIGIS !!
VWOOM
V-VN

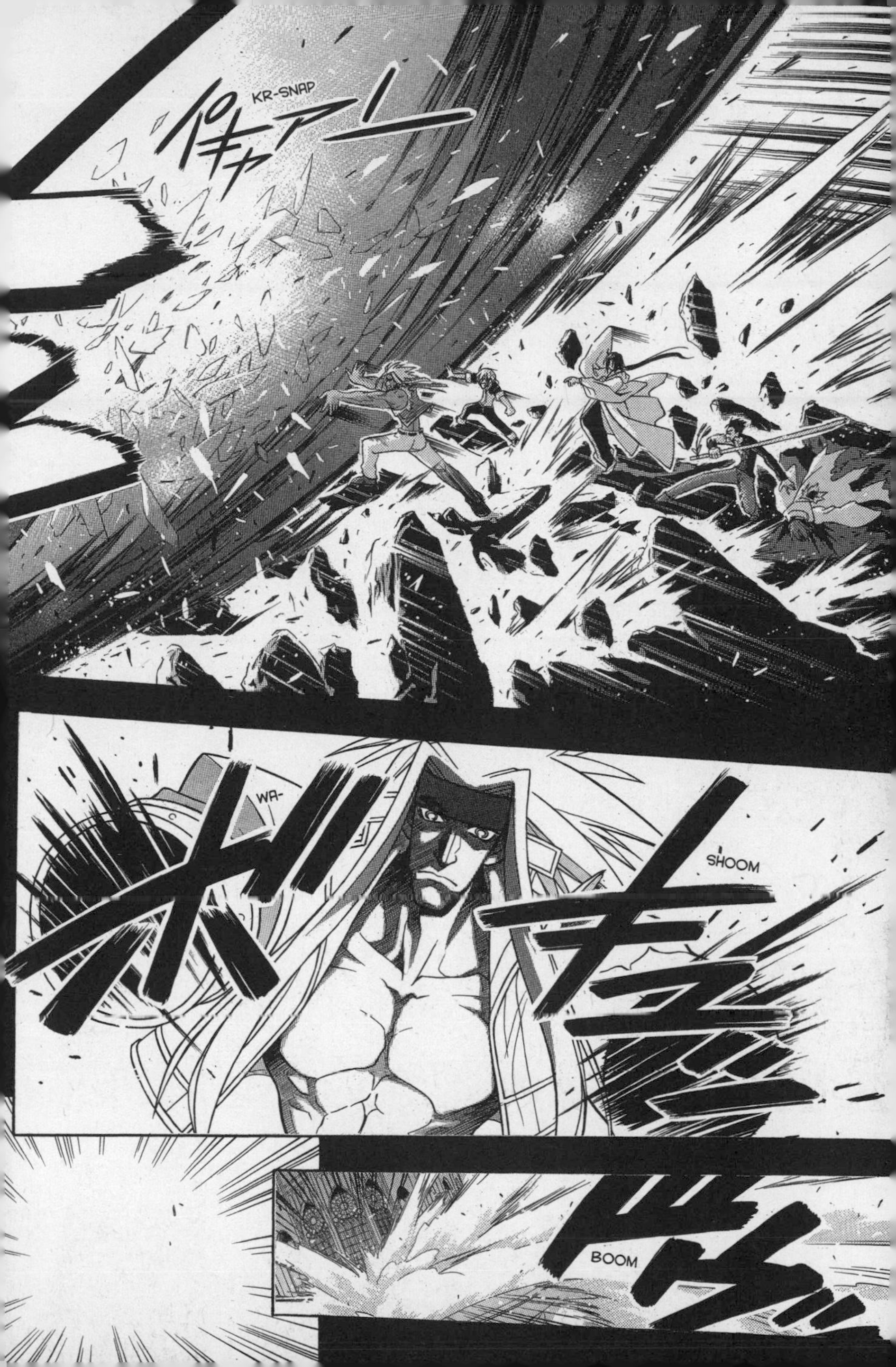
KR-SNAP
WA-
SHOOM
BOOM

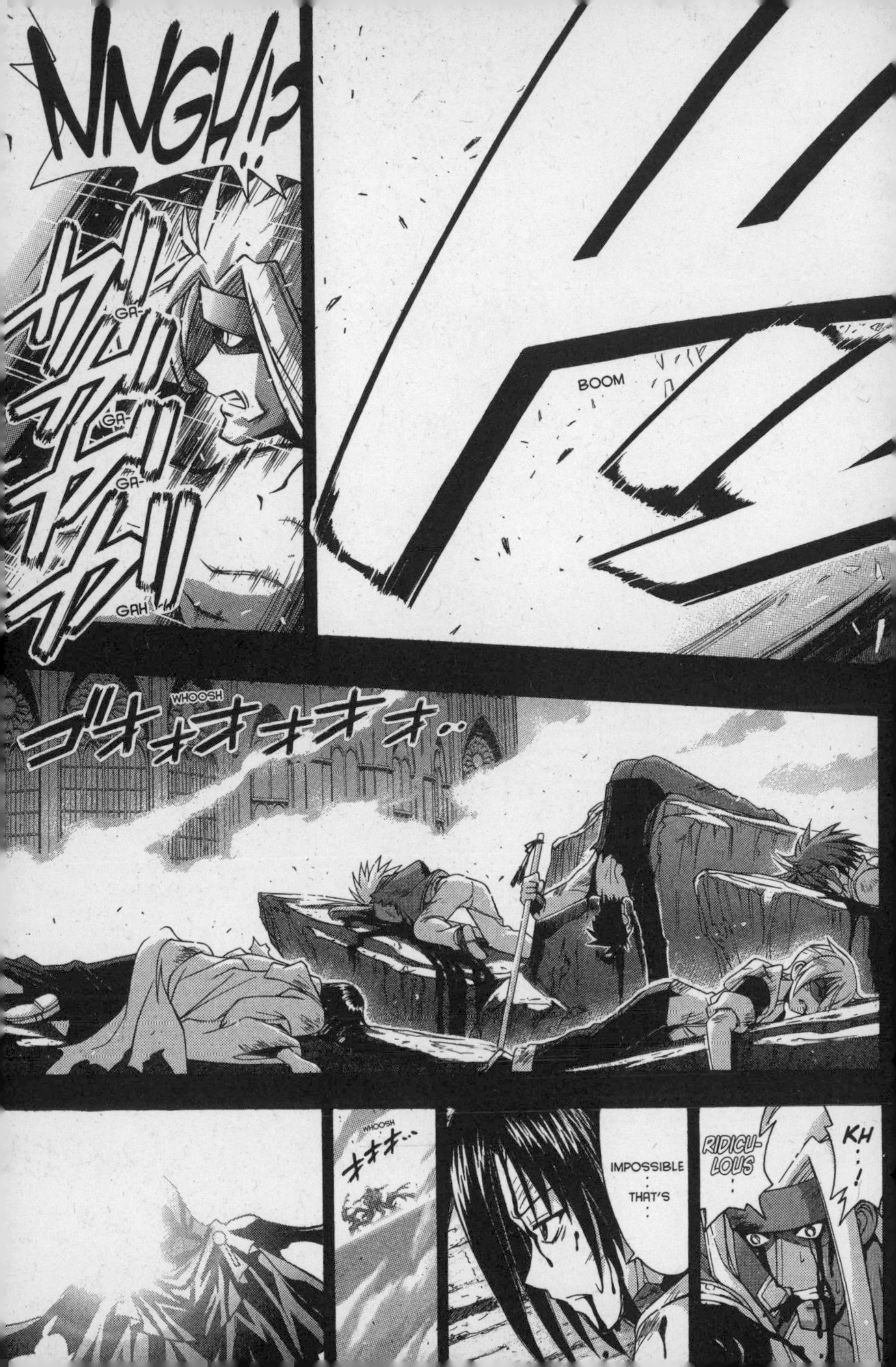
BOOM
NNGH!?
GA-
GA-
GA-
GAH
WHOOSH
KH...!
RIDICU-LOUS...
IMPOSSIBLE...
THAT'S...
WHOOSH

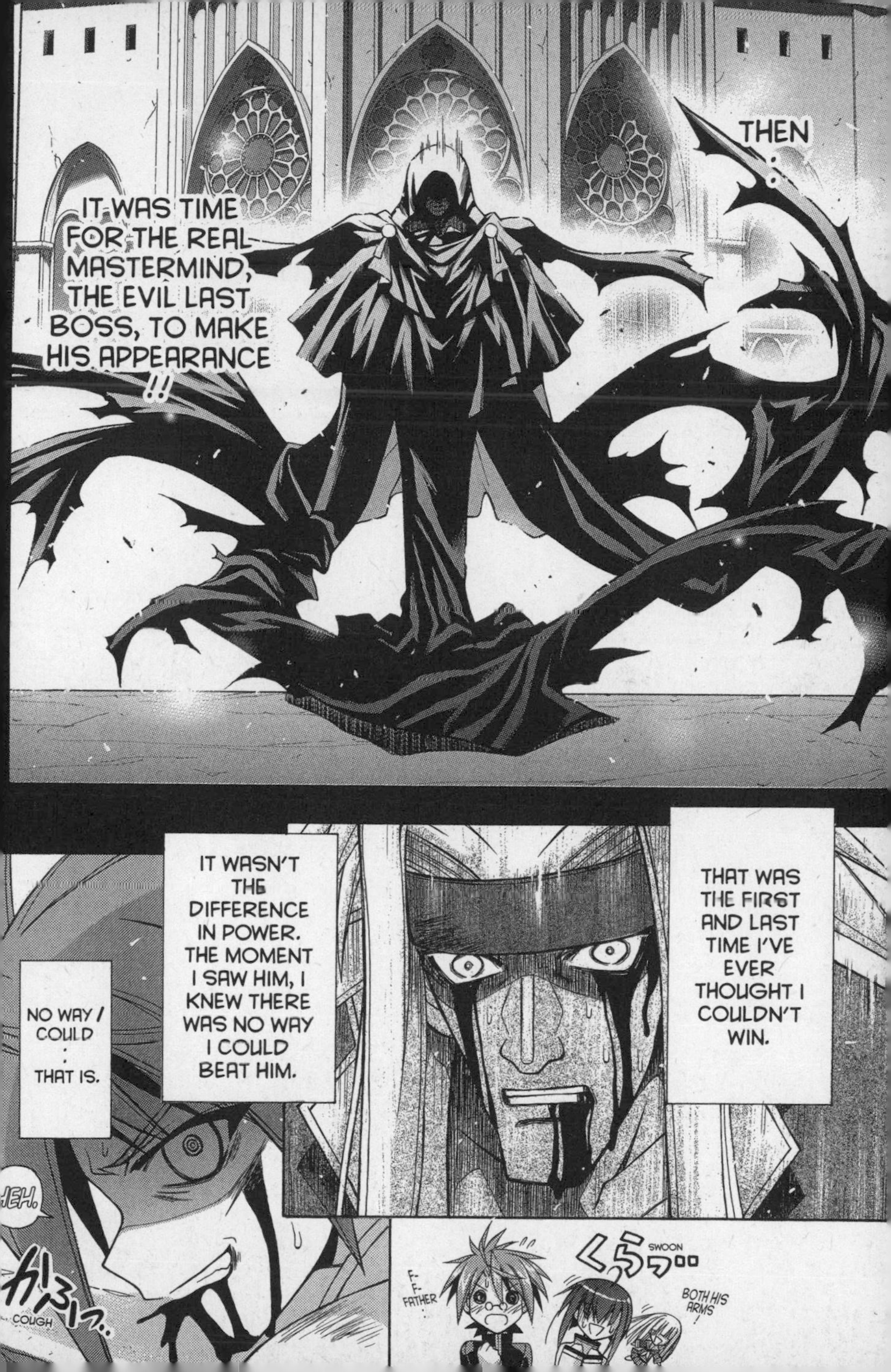
THEN :
IT WAS TIME FOR THE REAL MASTERMIND, THE EVIL LAST BOSS, TO MAKE HIS APPEARANCE !!
THAT WAS THE FIRST AND LAST TIME I'VE EVER THOUGHT I COULDN'T WIN.
IT WASN'T THE DIFFERENCE IN POWER. THE MOMENT I SAW HIM, I KNEW THERE WAS NO WAY I COULD BEAT HIM.
SWOON
F-F-FATHER :
BOTH HIS ARMS !
NO WAY / COULD : THAT IS.
HEH.
COUGH

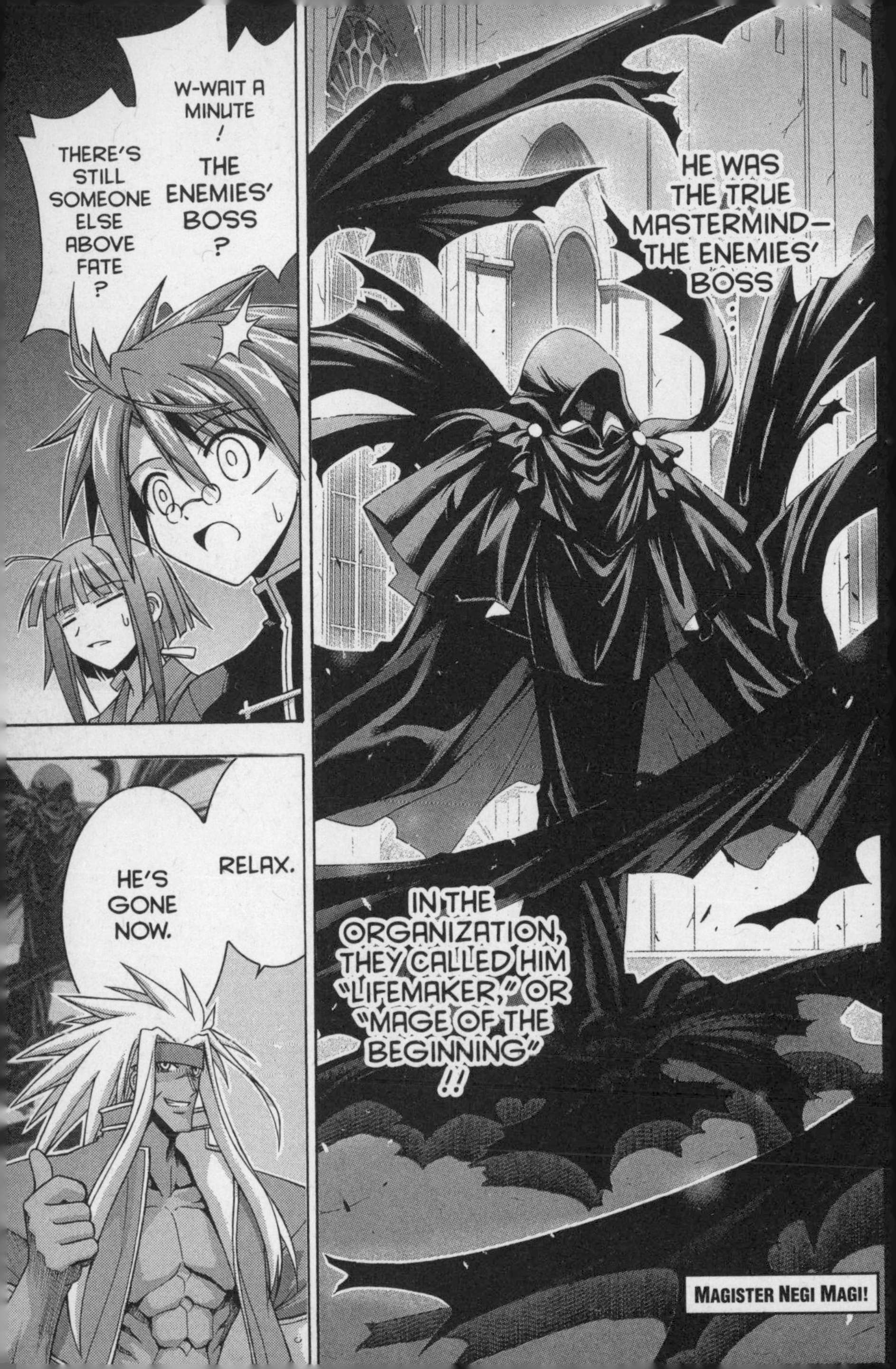
HE WAS THE TRUE MASTERMIND—THE ENEMIES' BOSS...
IN THE ORGANIZATION, THEY CALLED HIM "LIFEMAKER," OR "MAGE OF THE BEGINNING"!!
MAGISTER NEGI MAGI!
W-WAIT A MINUTE! THE ENEMIES' BOSS?
THERE'S STILL SOMEONE ELSE ABOVE FATE?
RELAX.
HE'S GONE NOW.

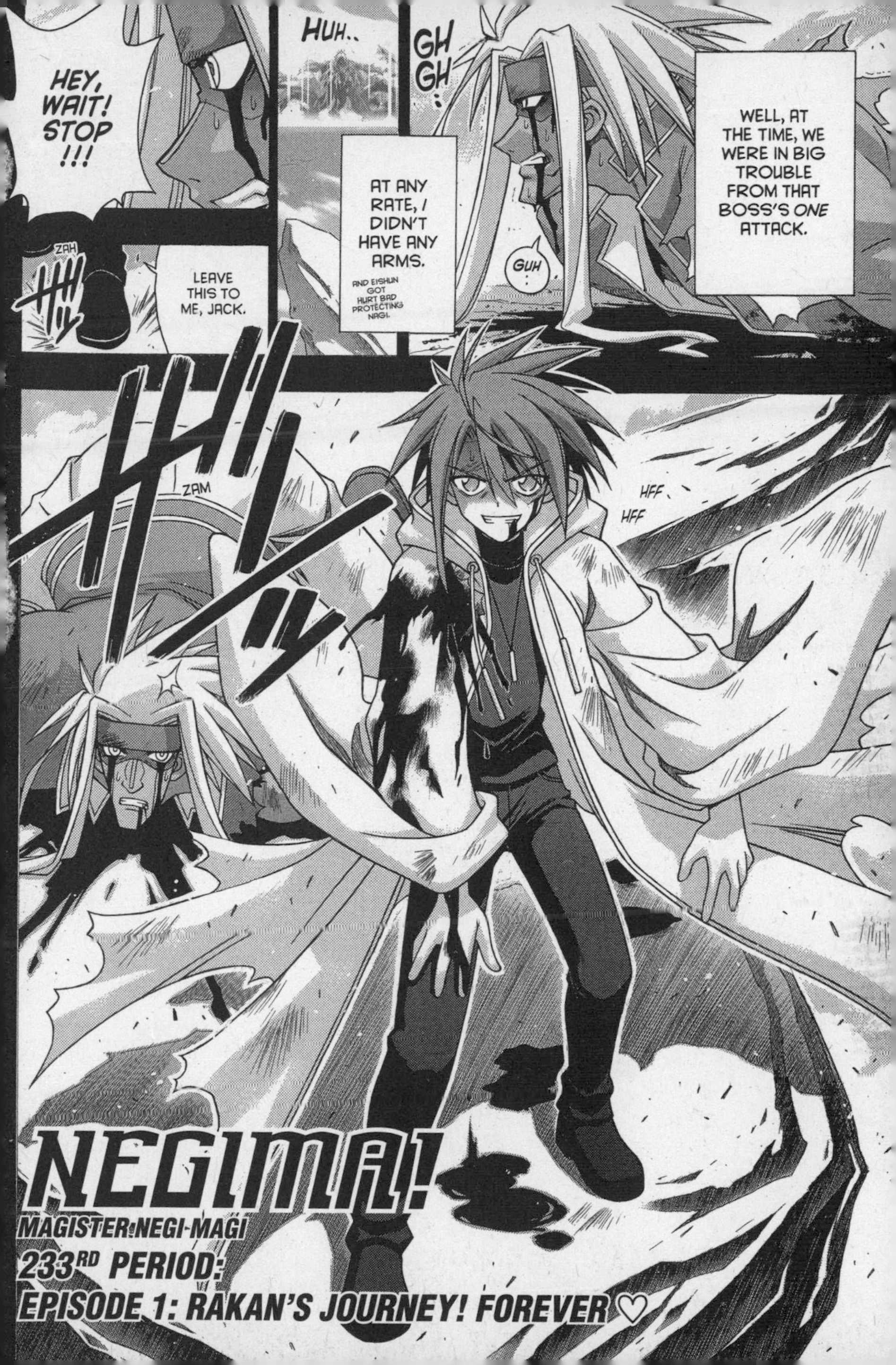
WELL, AT THE TIME, WE WERE IN BIG TROUBLE FROM THAT BOSS'S *ONE* ATTACK.
GH GH
GUH
AT ANY RATE, I DIDN'T HAVE ANY ARMS.
AND EISHUN GOT HURT BAD PROTECTING NAGI.
HUH..
HEY, WAIT! STOP!!!
LEAVE THIS TO ME, JACK.
ZAH
ZAM
HFF HFF
NEGIMA!
MAGISTER NEGI MAGI
233RD PERIOD:
EPISODE 1: RAKAN'S JOURNEY! FOREVER ♡

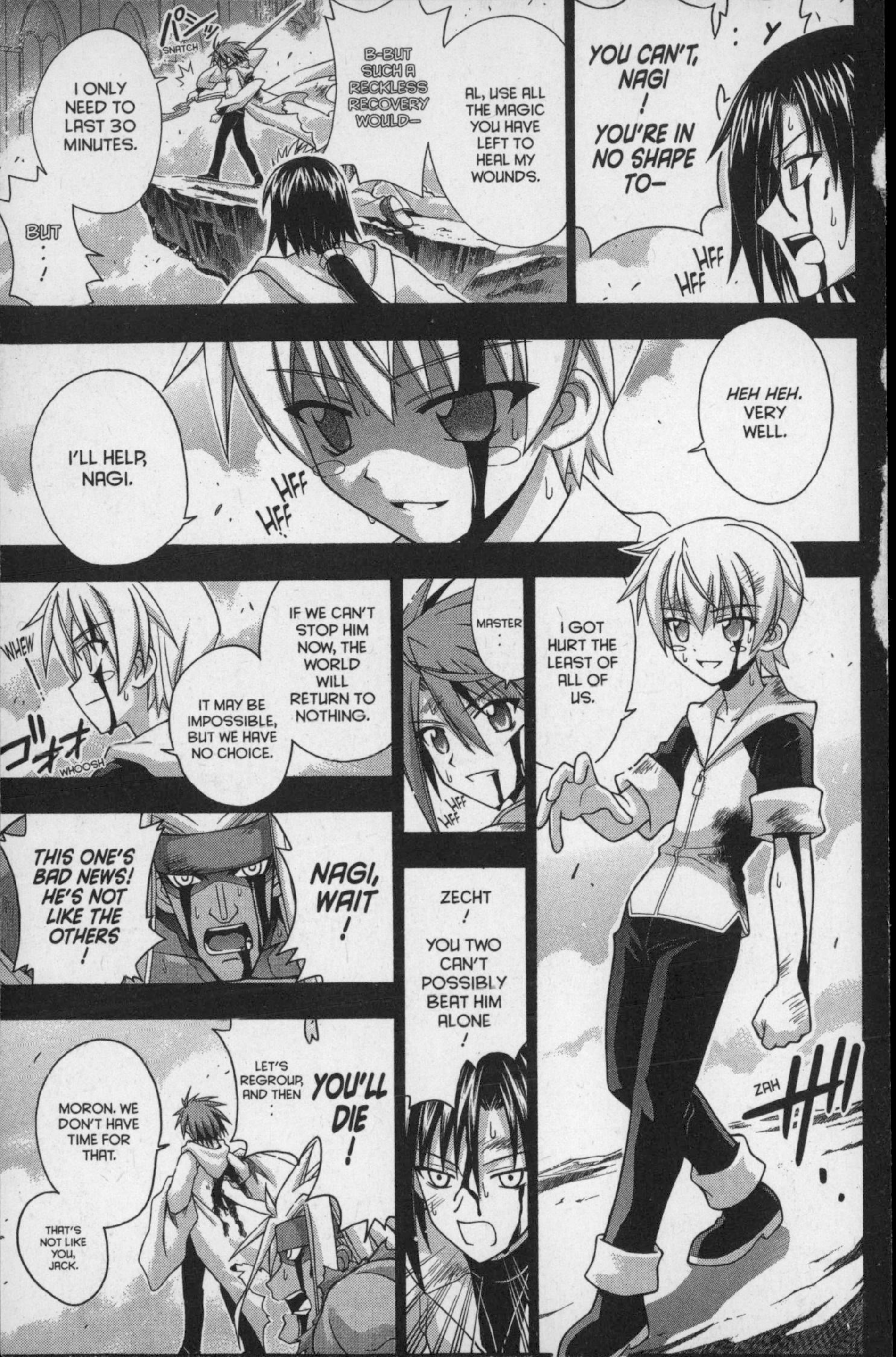
YOU CAN'T, NAGI! YOU'RE IN NO SHAPE TO—
HFF HFF
AL, USE ALL THE MAGIC YOU HAVE LEFT TO HEAL MY WOUNDS.
B-BUT SUCH A RECKLESS RECOVERY WOULD—
SNATCH
I ONLY NEED TO LAST 30 MINUTES.
BUT...!
HEH HEH. VERY WELL.
I'LL HELP, NAGI.
HFF HFF
I GOT HURT THE LEAST OF ALL OF US.
ZAH
MASTER...
HFF HFF
IF WE CAN'T STOP HIM NOW, THE WORLD WILL RETURN TO NOTHING.
IT MAY BE IMPOSSIBLE, BUT WE HAVE NO CHOICE.
WHEW
WHOOSH
ZECHT! YOU TWO CAN'T POSSIBLY BEAT HIM ALONE!
NAGI, WAIT!
THIS ONE'S BAD NEWS! HE'S NOT LIKE THE OTHERS!
YOU'LL DIE!
LET'S REGROUP, AND THEN...
MORON. WE DON'T HAVE TIME FOR THAT.
THAT'S NOT LIKE YOU, JACK.

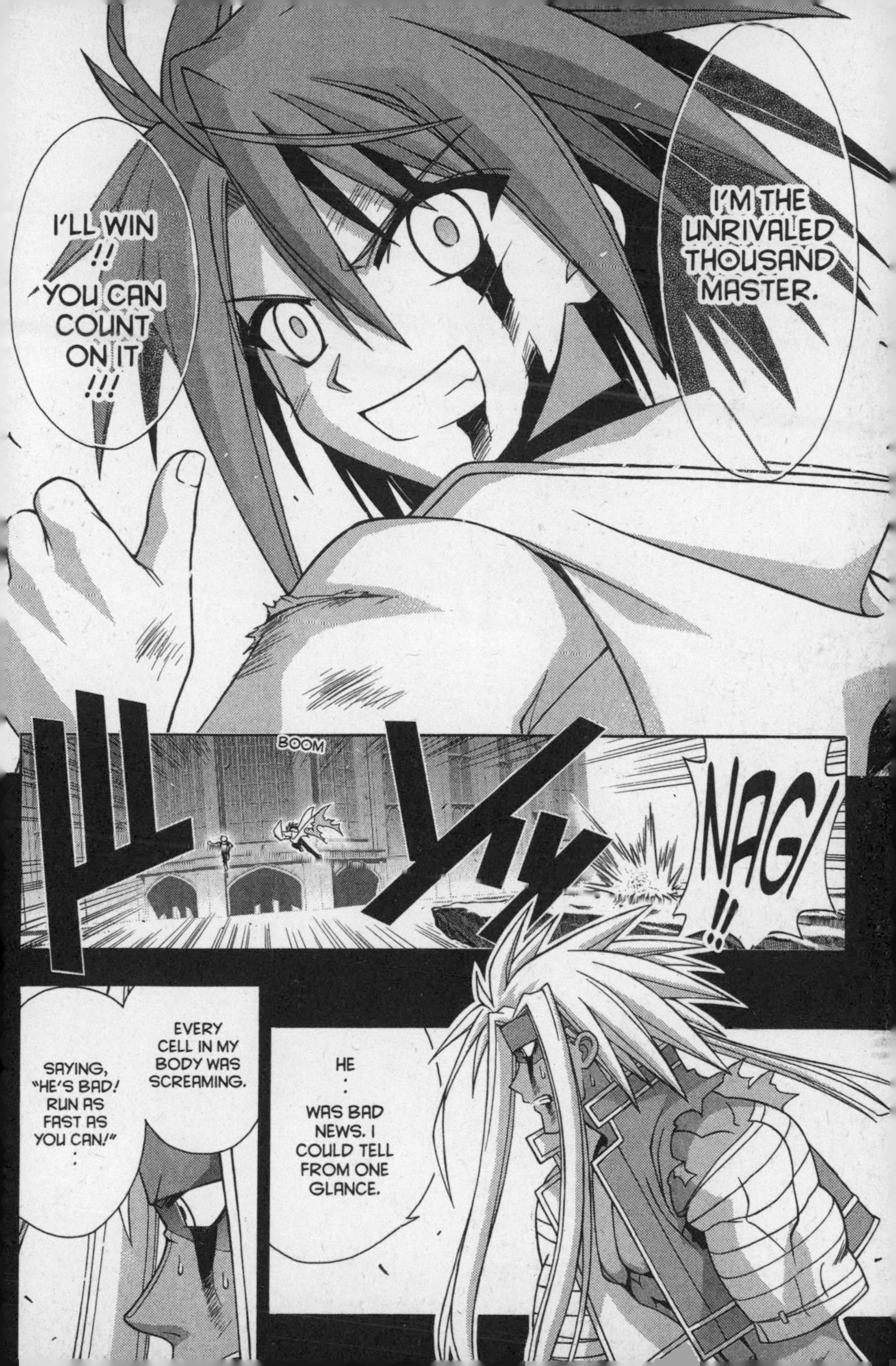

I'M THE UNRIVALED THOUSAND MASTER.
I'LL WIN !! YOU CAN COUNT ON IT !!!
NAGI !!
BOOM
HE : WAS BAD NEWS. I COULD TELL FROM ONE GLANCE.
EVERY CELL IN MY BODY WAS SCREAMING.
SAYING, "HE'S BAD! RUN AS FAST AS YOU CAN!" :

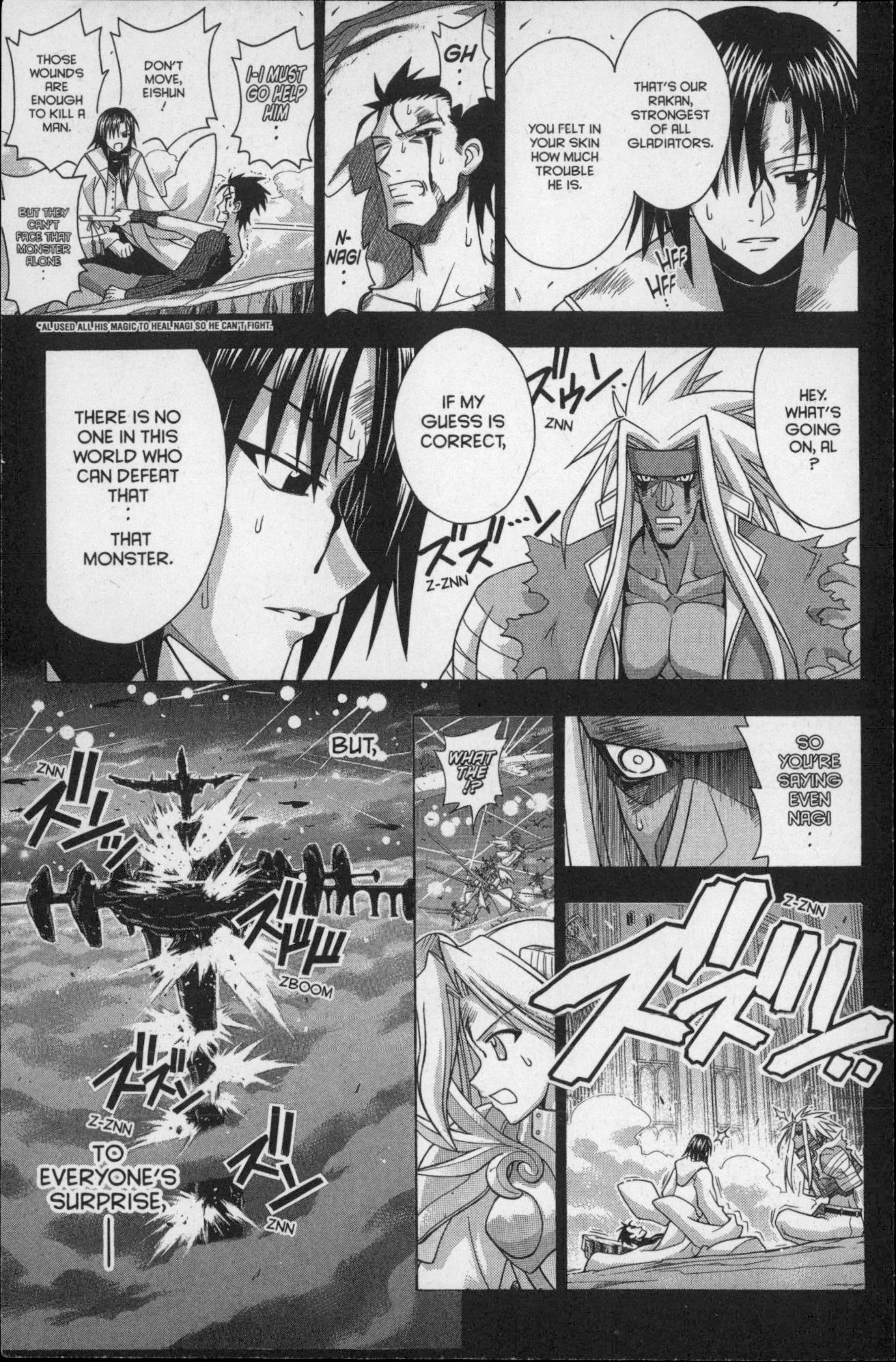
THAT'S OUR RAKAN, STRONGEST OF ALL GLADIATORS.
YOU FELT IN YOUR SKIN HOW MUCH TROUBLE HE IS.
HFF HFF
GH...
N-NAGI...
I-I MUST GO HELP HIM...
DON'T MOVE, EISHUN!
THOSE WOUNDS ARE ENOUGH TO KILL A MAN.
BUT THEY CAN'T FACE THAT MONSTER ALONE...
HEY. WHAT'S GOING ON, AL?
ZNN
IF MY GUESS IS CORRECT,
Z-ZNN
THERE IS NO ONE IN THIS WORLD WHO CAN DEFEAT THAT... THAT MONSTER.
SO YOU'RE SAYING EVEN NAGI...
Z-ZNN
WHAT THE!?
BUT,
ZNN
ZBOOM
Z-ZNN
ZNN
TO EVERYONE'S SURPRISE, —

*AL USED ALL HIS MAGIC TO HEAL NAGI SO HE CAN'T FIGHT.

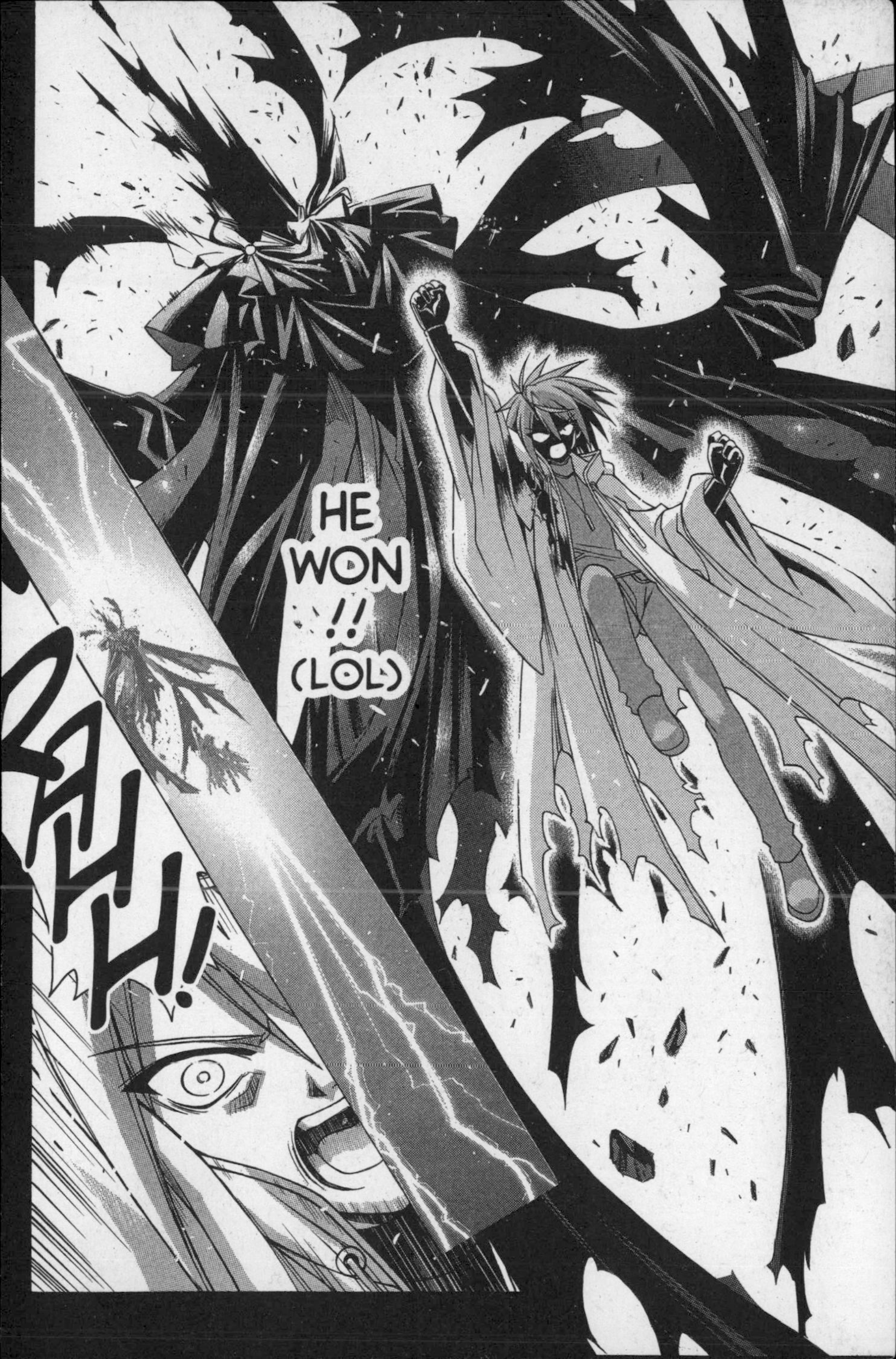
HE WON !! (LOL)
GAHH!

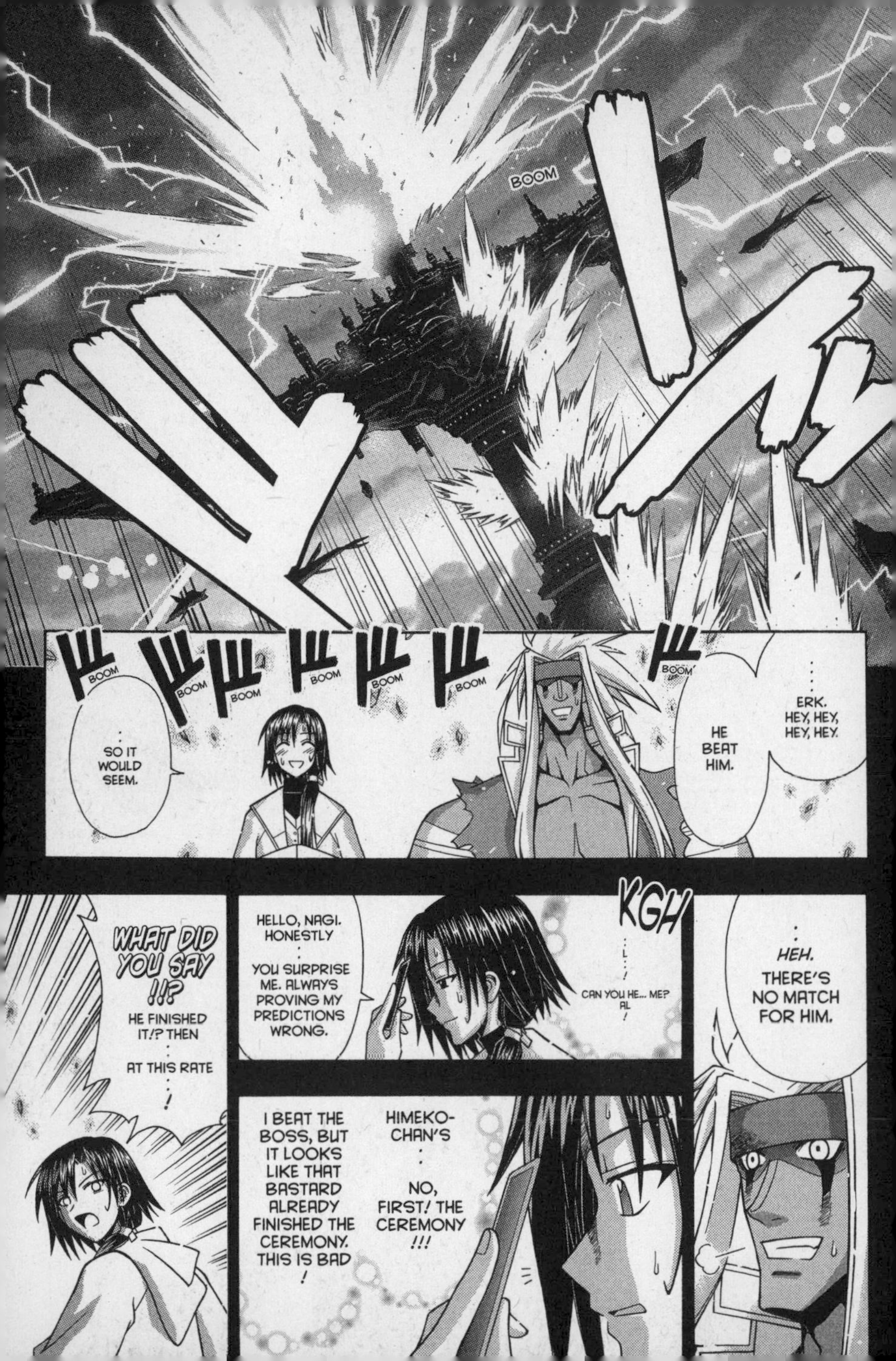
BOOM
BOOM
BOOM
BOOM
BOOM
BOOM
BOOM
... ERK. HEY, HEY, HEY, HEY.
HE BEAT HIM.
... SO IT WOULD SEEM.
... HEH. THERE'S NO MATCH FOR HIM.
KGH
...L...!
CAN YOU HE... ME? AL!
HELLO, NAGI. HONESTLY ... YOU SURPRISE ME. ALWAYS PROVING MY PREDICTIONS WRONG.
HIMEKO-CHAN'S ... NO, FIRST! THE CEREMONY!!!
I BEAT THE BOSS, BUT IT LOOKS LIKE THAT BASTARD ALREADY FINISHED THE CEREMONY. THIS IS BAD!
WHAT DID YOU SAY!!?
HE FINISHED IT!? THEN ... AT THIS RATE ...!

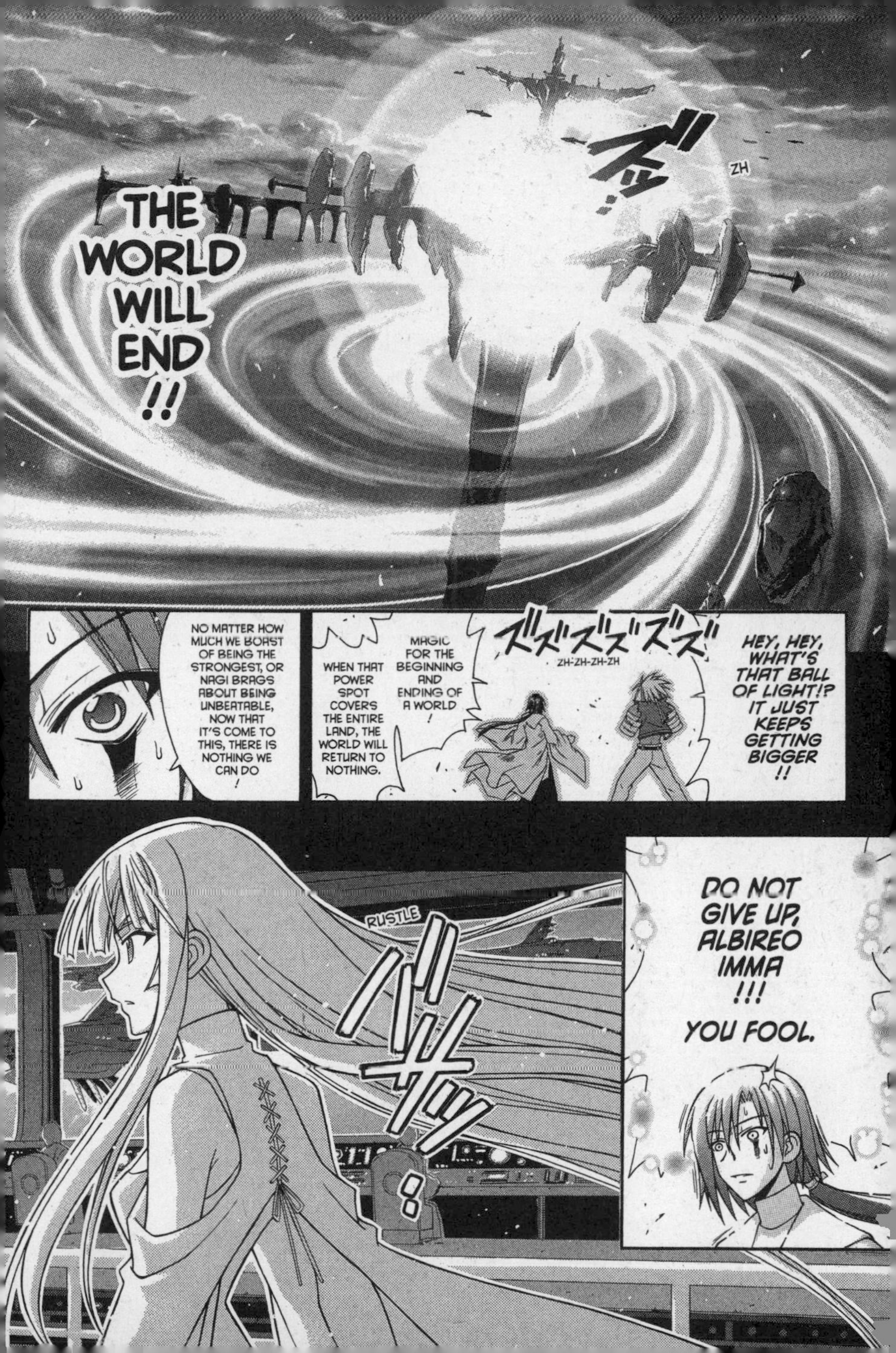

ZH
THE WORLD WILL END !!
HEY, HEY, WHAT'S THAT BALL OF LIGHT!? IT JUST KEEPS GETTING BIGGER !!
ZH-ZH-ZH-ZH
MAGIC FOR THE BEGINNING AND ENDING OF A WORLD !
WHEN THAT POWER SPOT COVERS THE ENTIRE LAND, THE WORLD WILL RETURN TO NOTHING.
NO MATTER HOW MUCH WE BOAST OF BEING THE STRONGEST, OR NAGI BRAGS ABOUT BEING UNBEATABLE, NOW THAT IT'S COME TO THIS, THERE IS NOTHING WE CAN DO !
DO NOT GIVE UP, ALBIREO IMMA !!!
YOU FOOL.
RUSTLE

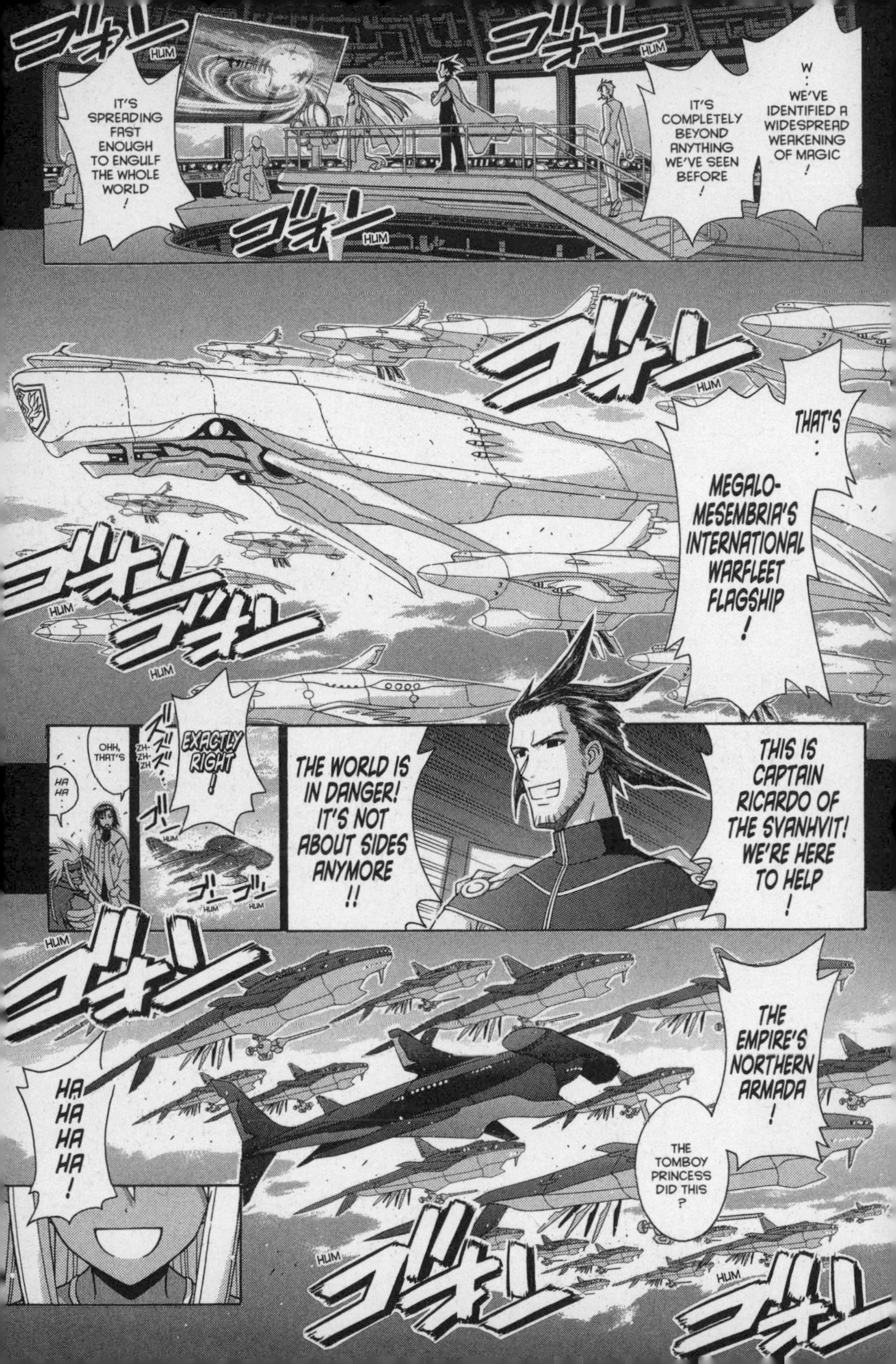
HUM
HUM
W... WE'VE IDENTIFIED A WIDESPREAD WEAKENING OF MAGIC!
IT'S COMPLETELY BEYOND ANYTHING WE'VE SEEN BEFORE!
IT'S SPREADING FAST ENOUGH TO ENGULF THE WHOLE WORLD!
HUM
HUM
THAT'S... MEGALO-MESEMBRIA'S INTERNATIONAL WARFLEET FLAGSHIP!
HUM
HUM
THIS IS CAPTAIN RICARDO OF THE SVANHVIT! WE'RE HERE TO HELP!
THE WORLD IS IN DANGER! IT'S NOT ABOUT SIDES ANYMORE!!
EXACTLY RIGHT!
ZH-ZH-ZH
HUM
HUM HUM
OHH, THAT'S...
HA HA
HUM
THE EMPIRE'S NORTHERN ARMADA!
THE TOMBOY PRINCESS DID THIS?
HA HA HA HA!
HUM
HUM

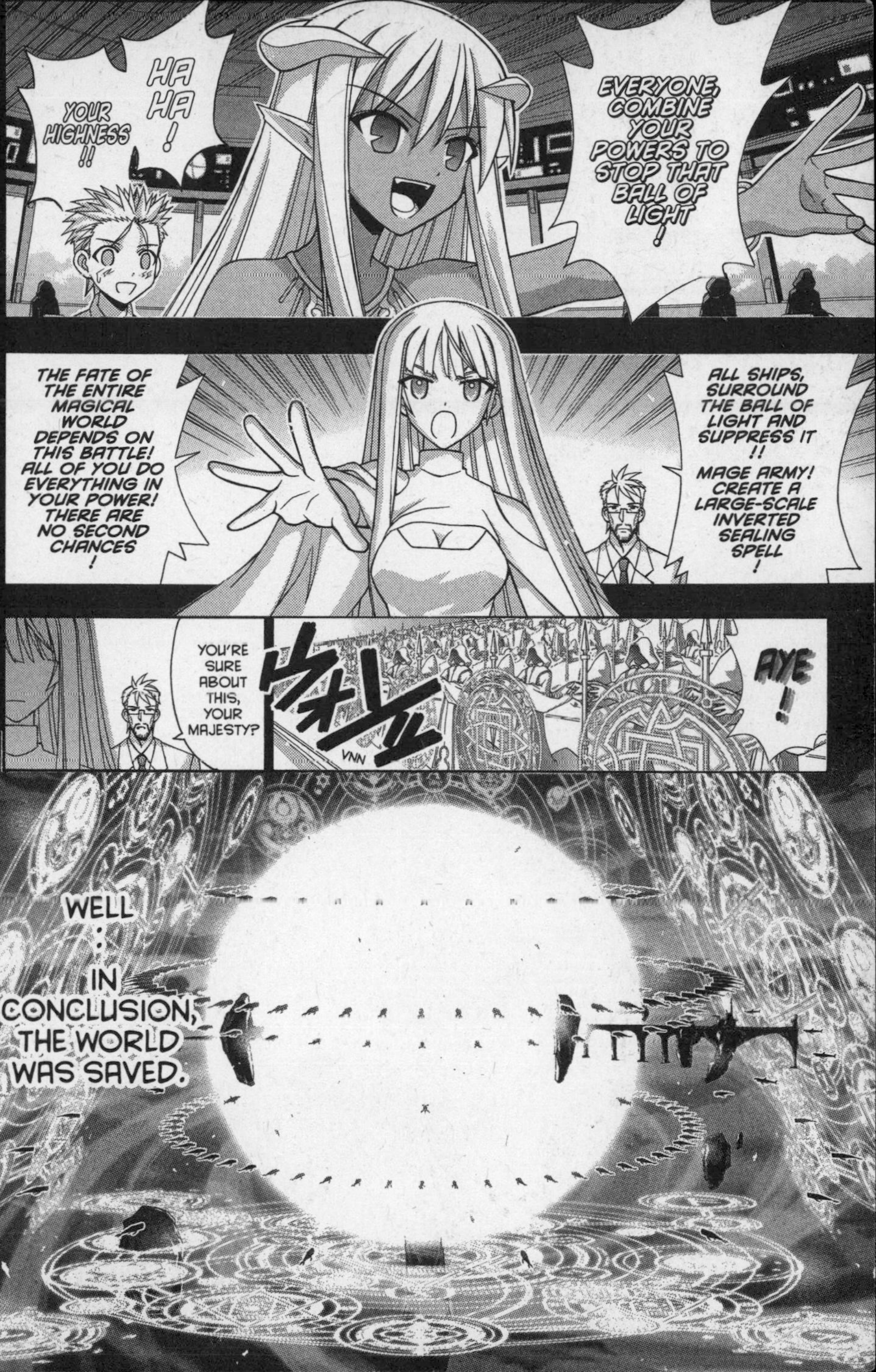
EVERYONE, COMBINE YOUR POWERS TO STOP THAT BALL OF LIGHT!
HA HA!
YOUR HIGHNESS!!
ALL SHIPS, SURROUND THE BALL OF LIGHT AND SUPPRESS IT!! MAGE ARMY! CREATE A LARGE-SCALE INVERTED SEALING SPELL!
THE FATE OF THE ENTIRE MAGICAL WORLD DEPENDS ON THIS BATTLE! ALL OF YOU DO EVERYTHING IN YOUR POWER! THERE ARE NO SECOND CHANCES!
AYE!
VNN
YOU'RE SURE ABOUT THIS, YOUR MAJESTY?
WELL... IN CONCLUSION, THE WORLD WAS SAVED.

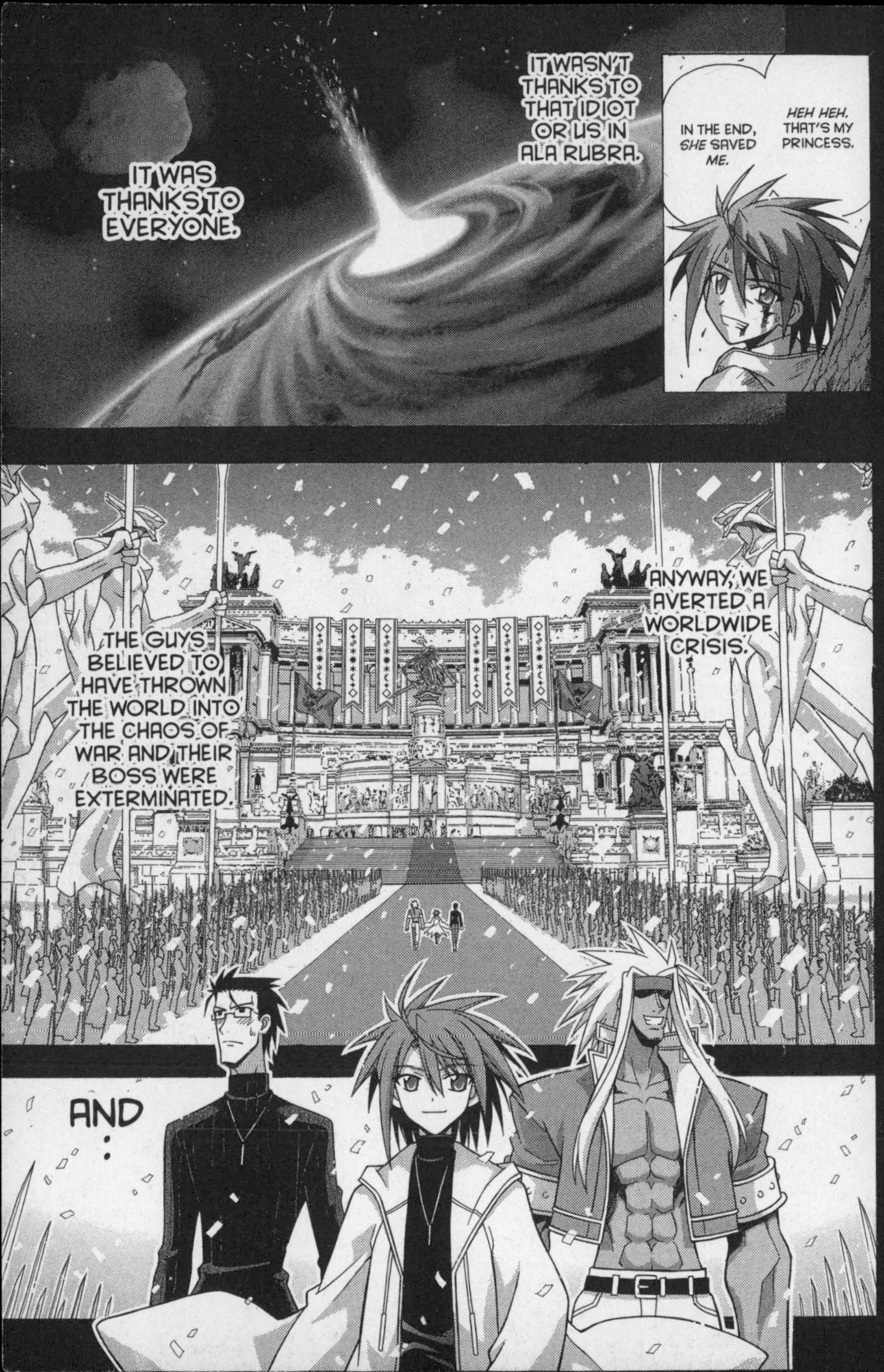
HEH HEH. THAT'S MY PRINCESS.
IN THE END, *SHE* SAVED ME.
IT WASN'T THANKS TO THAT IDIOT OR US IN ALA RUBRA.
IT WAS THANKS TO EVERYONE.
ANYWAY, WE AVERTED A WORLDWIDE CRISIS.
THE GUYS BELIEVED TO HAVE THROWN THE WORLD INTO THE CHAOS OF WAR AND THEIR BOSS WERE EXTERMINATED.
AND...

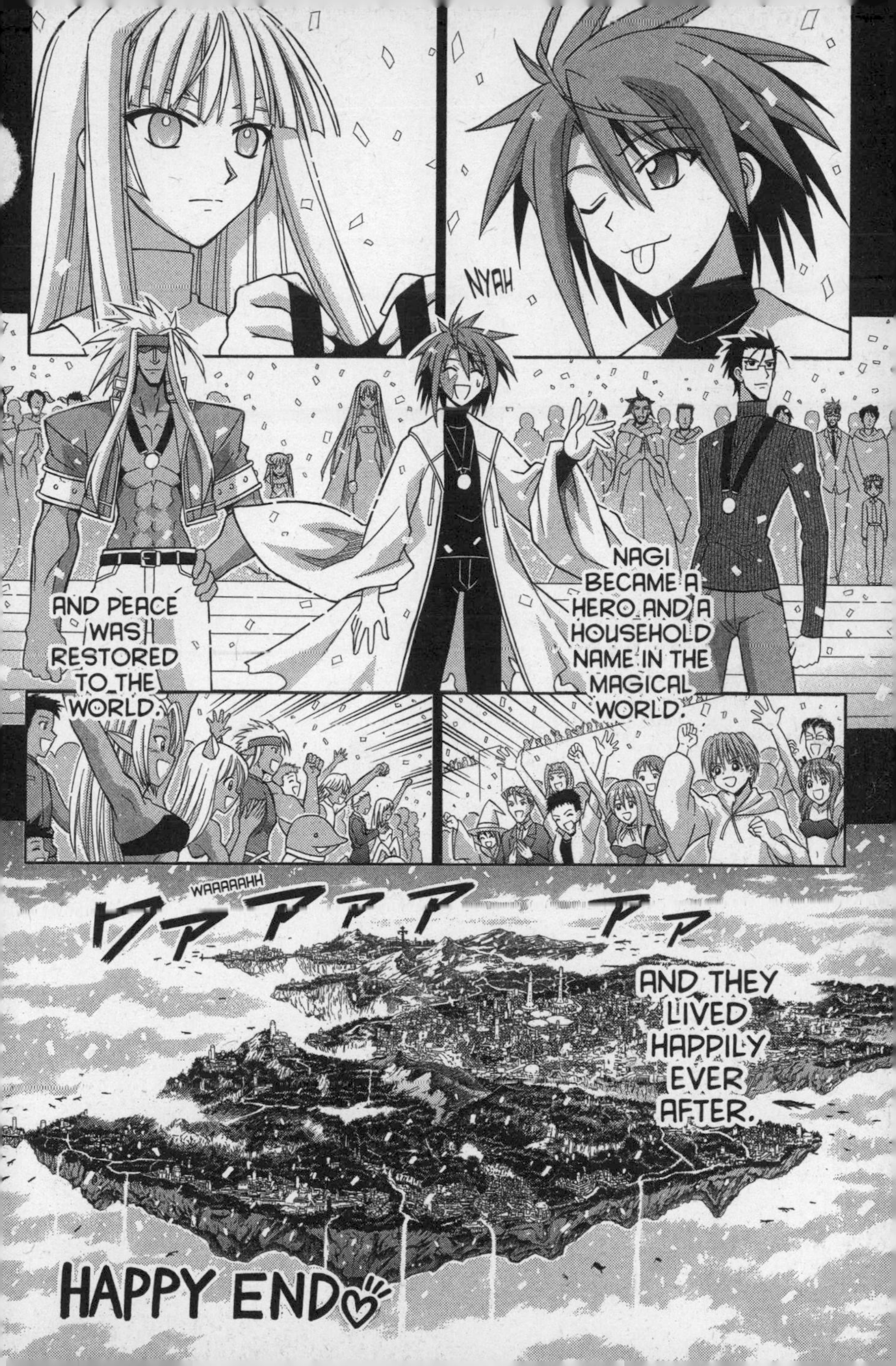
NYAH
NAGI BECAME A HERO AND A HOUSEHOLD NAME IN THE MAGICAL WORLD.
AND PEACE WAS RESTORED TO THE WORLD.
WAAAAAAH
ワァァァ ァァ
AND THEY LIVED HAPPILY EVER AFTER.
HAPPY END♡

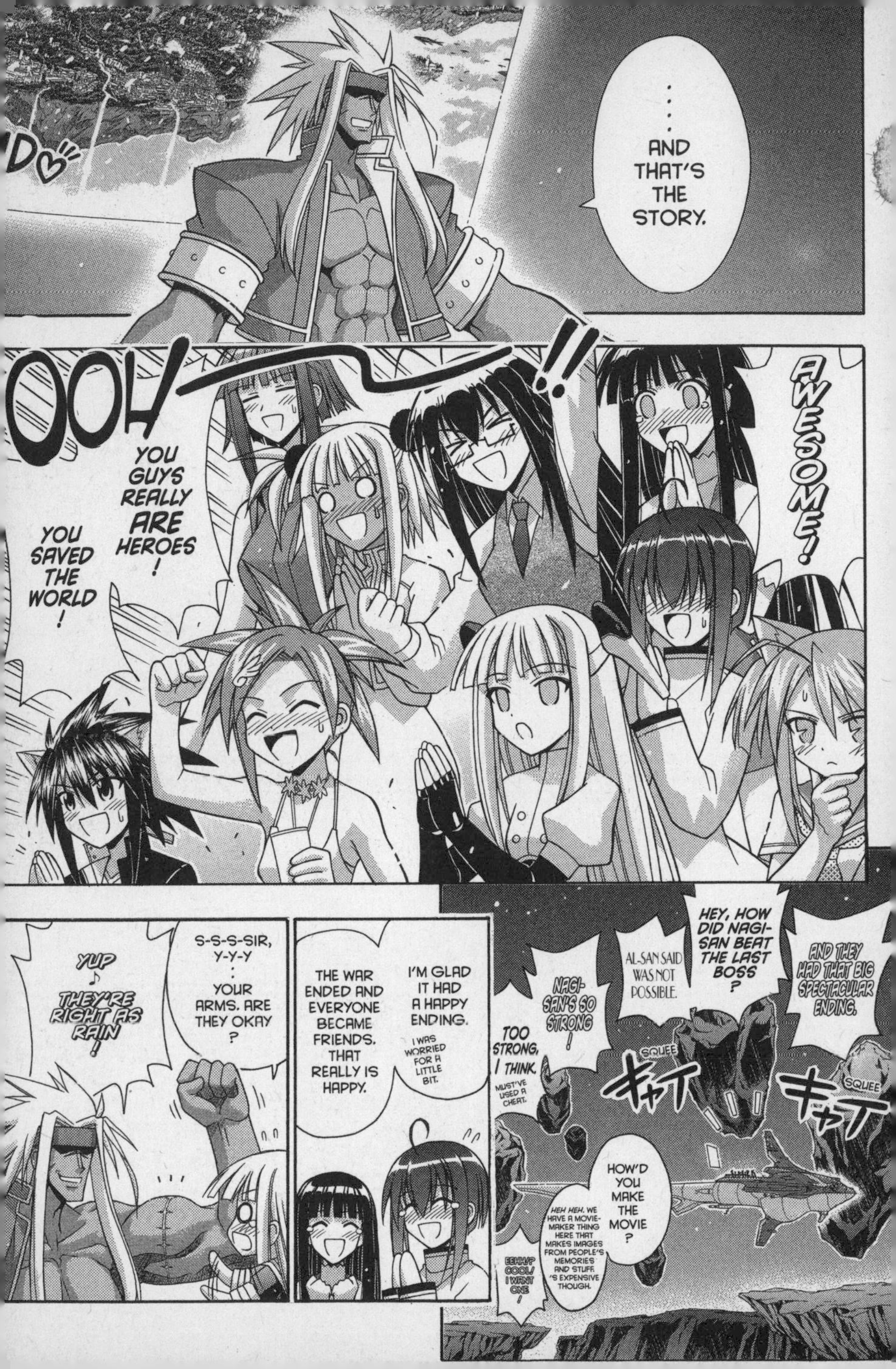
D♡
. . . AND THAT'S THE STORY.
AWESOME!
OOH—!!
YOU GUYS REALLY ARE HEROES!
YOU SAVED THE WORLD!
HEY, HOW DID NAGI-SAN BEAT THE LAST BOSS?
AND THEY HAD THAT BIG SPECTACULAR ENDING.
AL-SAN SAID WAS NOT POSSIBLE.
NAGI-SAN'S SO STRONG!
TOO STRONG, I THINK.
MUST'VE USED A CHEAT.
SQUEE
SQUEE
HOW'D YOU MAKE THE MOVIE?
HEH HEH. WE HAVE A MOVIE-MAKER THING HERE THAT MAKES IMAGES FROM PEOPLE'S MEMORIES AND STUFF. 'S EXPENSIVE THOUGH.
EEHH?! COOL! I WANT ONE!
I'M GLAD IT HAD A HAPPY ENDING.
I WAS WORRIED FOR A LITTLE BIT.
THE WAR ENDED AND EVERYONE BECAME FRIENDS. THAT REALLY IS HAPPY.
S-S-S-SIR, Y-Y-Y : YOUR ARMS. ARE THEY OKAY?
YUP♪ THEY'RE RIGHT AS RAIN!

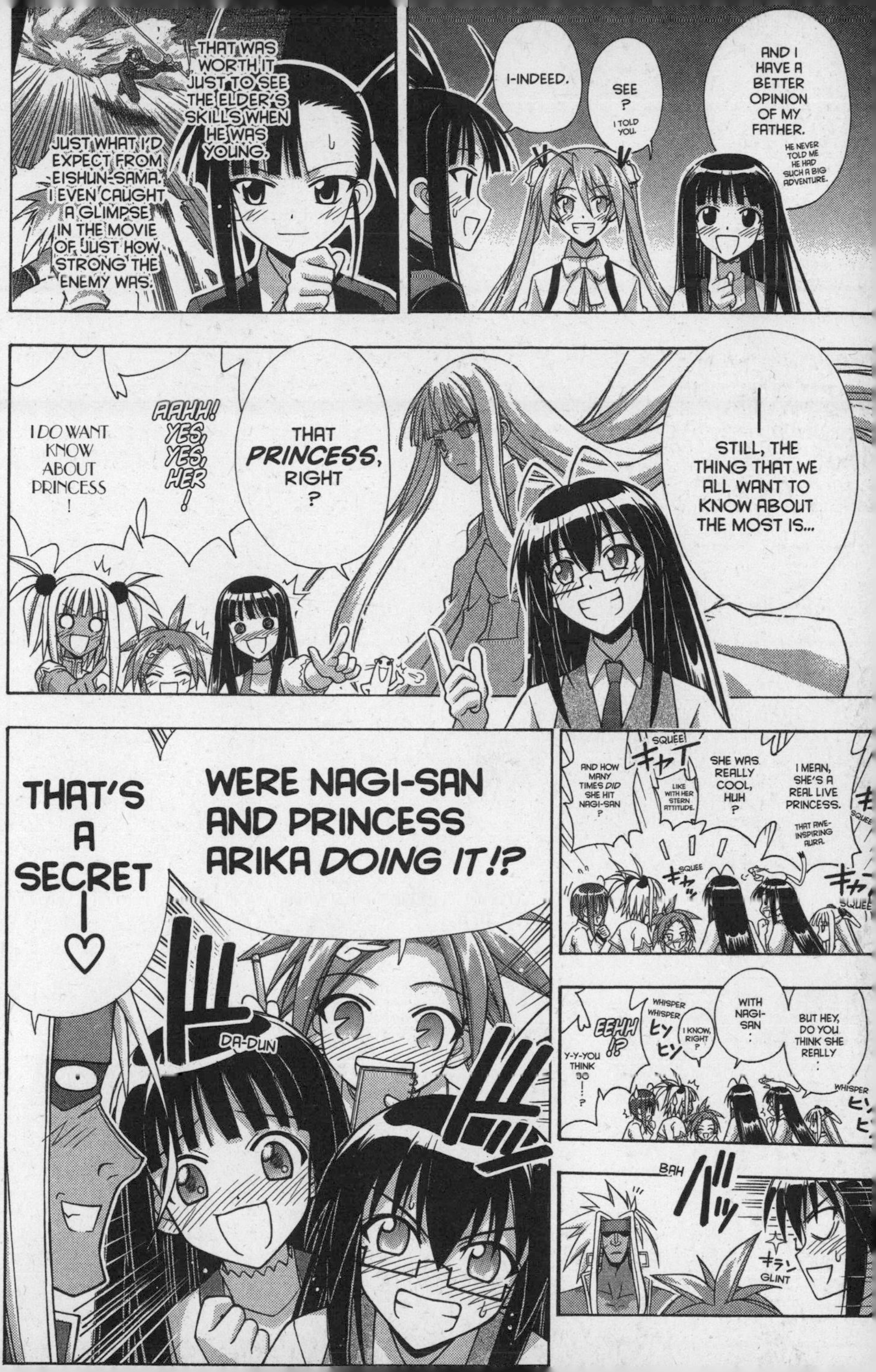

AND I HAVE A BETTER OPINION OF MY FATHER.
HE NEVER TOLD ME HE HAD SUCH A BIG ADVENTURE.
SEE? I TOLD YOU.
I-INDEED.
THAT WAS WORTH IT JUST TO SEE THE ELDER'S SKILLS WHEN HE WAS YOUNG.
JUST WHAT I'D EXPECT FROM EISHUN-SAMA. I EVEN CAUGHT A GLIMPSE IN THE MOVIE OF JUST HOW STRONG THE ENEMY WAS.
STILL, THE THING THAT WE ALL WANT TO KNOW ABOUT THE MOST IS...
THAT *PRINCESS*, RIGHT?
AAHH! YES, YES, HER!
I *DO* WANT KNOW ABOUT PRINCESS!
SQUEE
I MEAN, SHE'S A REAL LIVE PRINCESS.
THAT AWE-INSPIRING AURA.
SHE WAS REALLY COOL, HUH?
LIKE WITH HER STERN ATTITUDE.
AND HOW MANY TIMES *DID* SHE HIT NAGI-SAN?
SQUEE
SQUEE
WHISPER
BUT HEY, DO YOU THINK SHE REALLY...
WITH NAGI-SAN...
I KNOW, RIGHT?
WHISPER WHISPER
EEHH!?
Y-Y-YOU THINK SO...!?
BAH
GLINT
WERE NAGI-SAN AND PRINCESS ARIKA *DOING IT*!?
THAT'S A SECRET ♡
DA-DUN

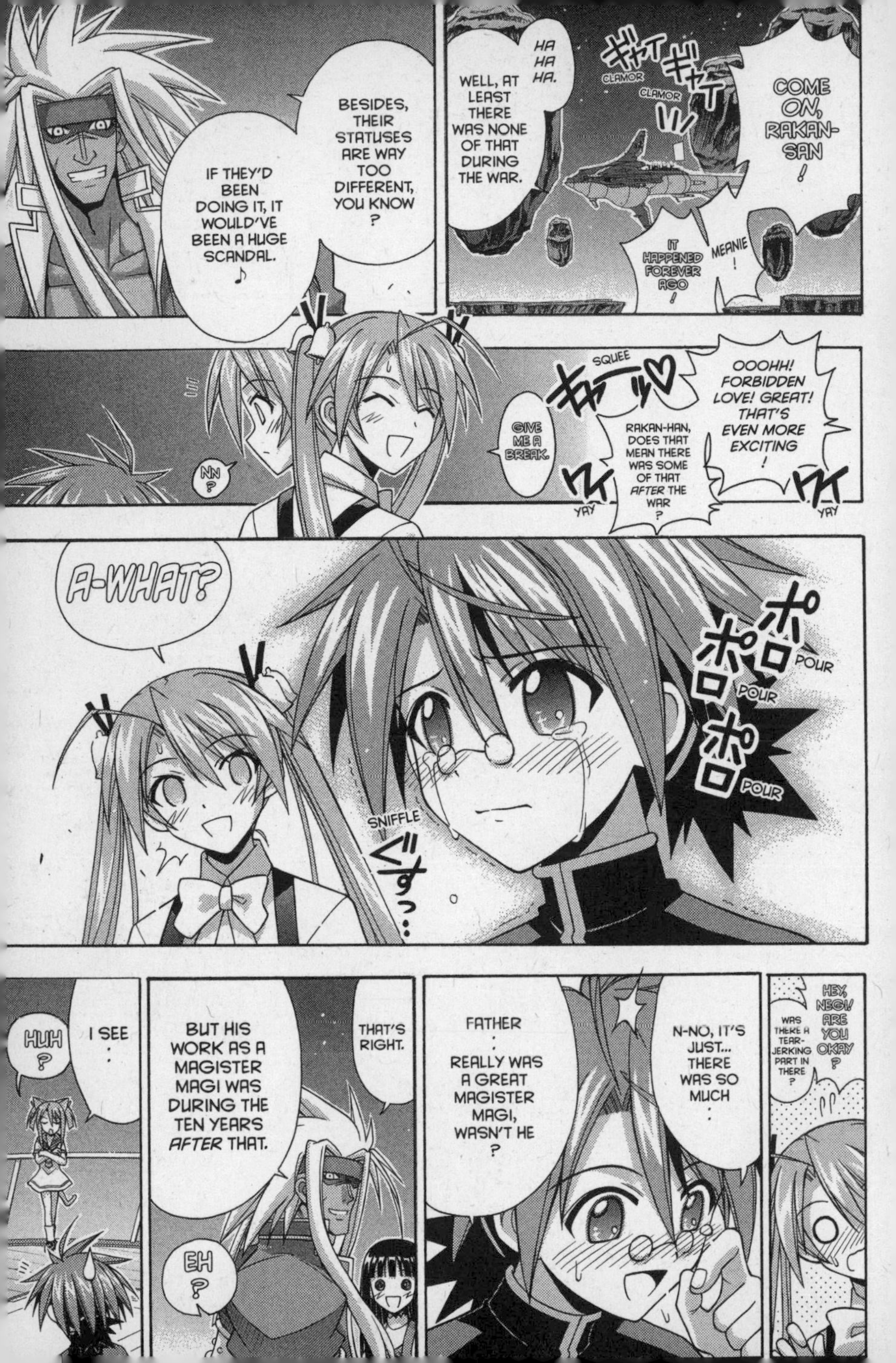
COME ON, RAKAN-SAN!
ギャイギャイ CLAMOR CLAMOR
IT HAPPENED FOREVER AGO!
MEANIE!
HA HA HA.
WELL, AT LEAST THERE WAS NONE OF THAT DURING THE WAR.
BESIDES, THEIR STATUSES ARE WAY TOO DIFFERENT, YOU KNOW?
IF THEY'D BEEN DOING IT, IT WOULD'VE BEEN A HUGE SCANDAL. ♪
OOOHH! FORBIDDEN LOVE! GREAT! THAT'S EVEN MORE EXCITING!
キャーッ♡ SQUEE
YAY
RAKAN-HAN, DOES THAT MEAN THERE WAS SOME OF THAT *AFTER* THE WAR?
YAY
GIVE ME A BREAK.
NN?
ポロポロポロ POUR POUR POUR
A-WHAT?
ぐすっ… SNIFFLE
HEY, NEGI! ARE YOU OKAY?
WAS THERE A TEAR-JERKING PART IN THERE?
N-NO, IT'S JUST... THERE WAS SO MUCH...
FATHER... REALLY WAS A GREAT MAGISTER MAGI, WASN'T HE?
THAT'S RIGHT.
BUT HIS WORK AS A MAGISTER MAGI WAS DURING THE TEN YEARS *AFTER* THAT.
EH?
I SEE...
HUH?

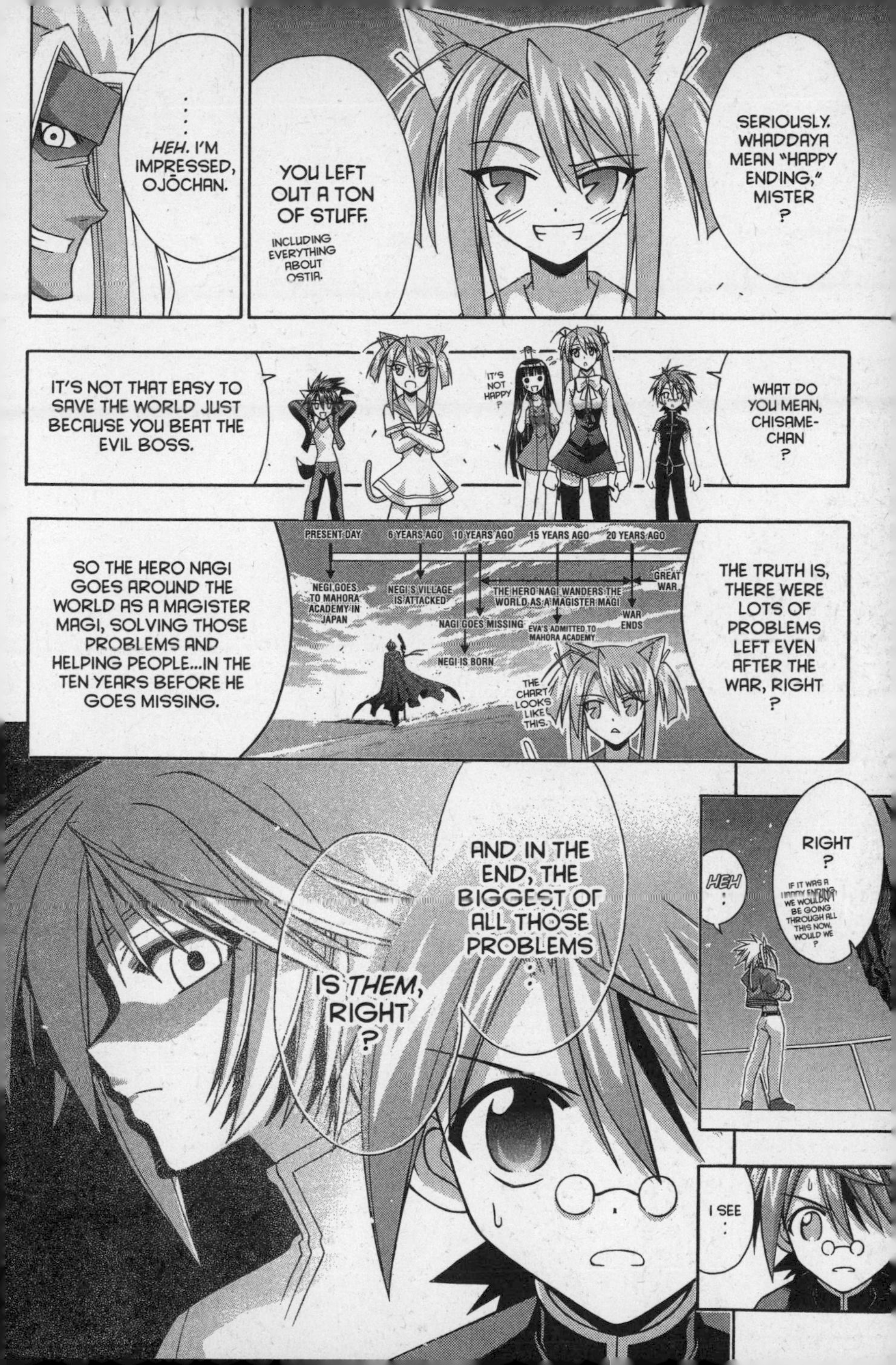
SERIOUSLY. WHADDAYA MEAN "HAPPY ENDING," MISTER ?
YOU LEFT OUT A TON OF STUFF.
INCLUDING EVERYTHING ABOUT OSTIA.
... HEH. I'M IMPRESSED, OJŌCHAN.
WHAT DO YOU MEAN, CHISAME-CHAN ?
IT'S NOT HAPPY ?
IT'S NOT THAT EASY TO SAVE THE WORLD JUST BECAUSE YOU BEAT THE EVIL BOSS.
THE TRUTH IS, THERE WERE LOTS OF PROBLEMS LEFT EVEN AFTER THE WAR, RIGHT ?
PRESENT DAY
6 YEARS AGO
10 YEARS AGO
15 YEARS AGO
20 YEARS AGO
GREAT WAR
THE HERO NAGI WANDERS THE WORLD AS A MAGISTER MAGI
WAR ENDS
EVA'S ADMITTED TO MAHORA ACADEMY
NAGI GOES MISSING
NEGI IS BORN
NEGI'S VILLAGE IS ATTACKED
NEGI GOES TO MAHORA ACADEMY IN JAPAN
THE CHART LOOKS LIKE THIS.
SO THE HERO NAGI GOES AROUND THE WORLD AS A MAGISTER MAGI, SOLVING THOSE PROBLEMS AND HELPING PEOPLE...IN THE TEN YEARS BEFORE HE GOES MISSING.
RIGHT ?
IF IT WAS A HAPPY ENDING, WE WOULDN'T BE GOING THROUGH ALL THIS NOW, WOULD WE ?
HEH !
I SEE ...
AND IN THE END, THE BIGGEST OF ALL THOSE PROBLEMS ...
IS THEM, RIGHT ?

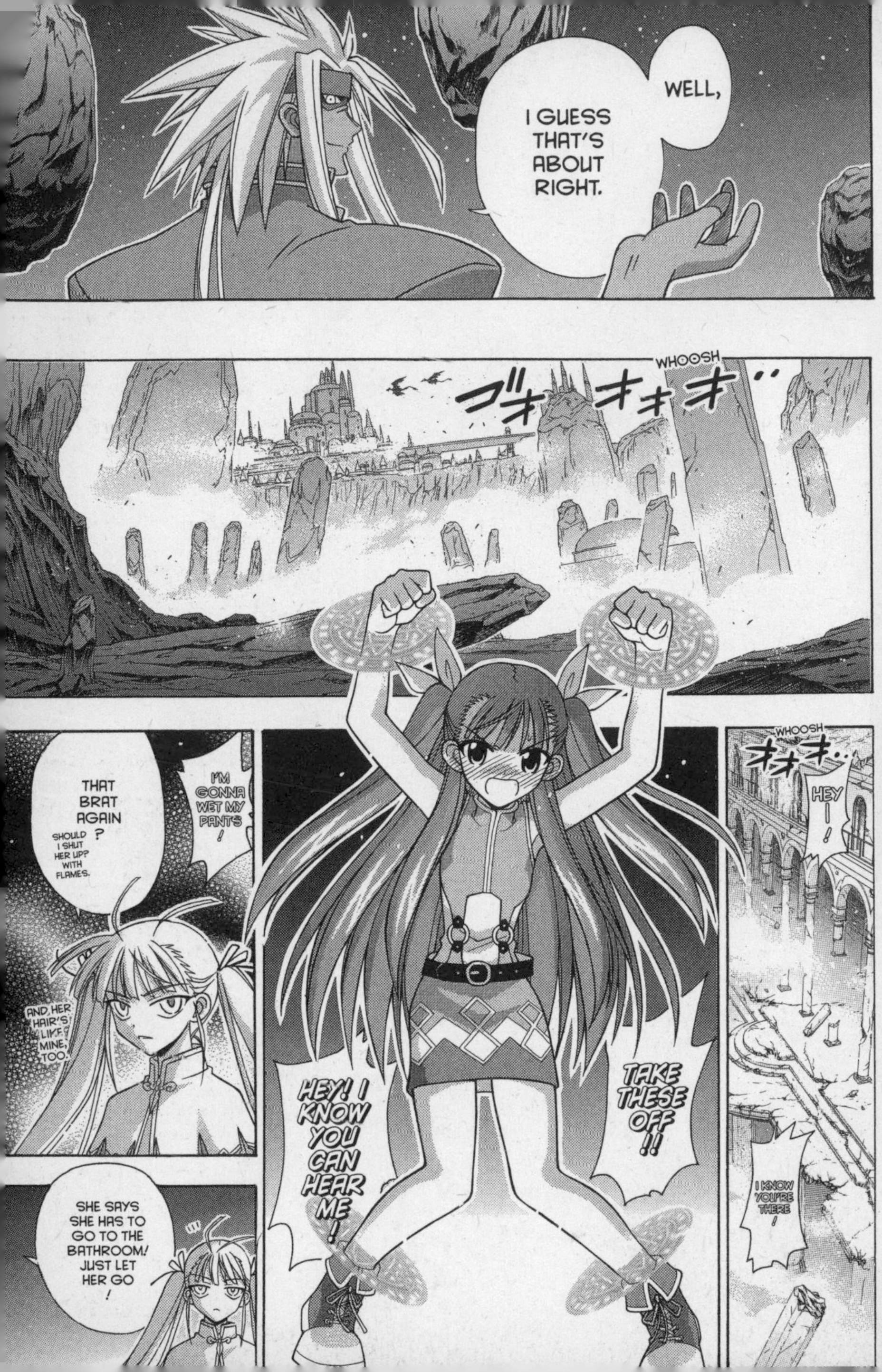
WELL,
I GUESS THAT'S ABOUT RIGHT.
WHOOSH
ゴオオオ
WHOOSH
オオオ…
HEY!
I KNOW YOU'RE THERE!
TAKE THESE OFF!!
HEY! I KNOW YOU CAN HEAR ME!
I'M GONNA WET MY PANTS!
THAT BRAT AGAIN?
SHOULD I SHUT HER UP? WITH FLAMES.
AND, HER HAIR'S LIKE MINE, TOO.
SHE SAYS SHE HAS TO GO TO THE BATHROOM! JUST LET HER GO!

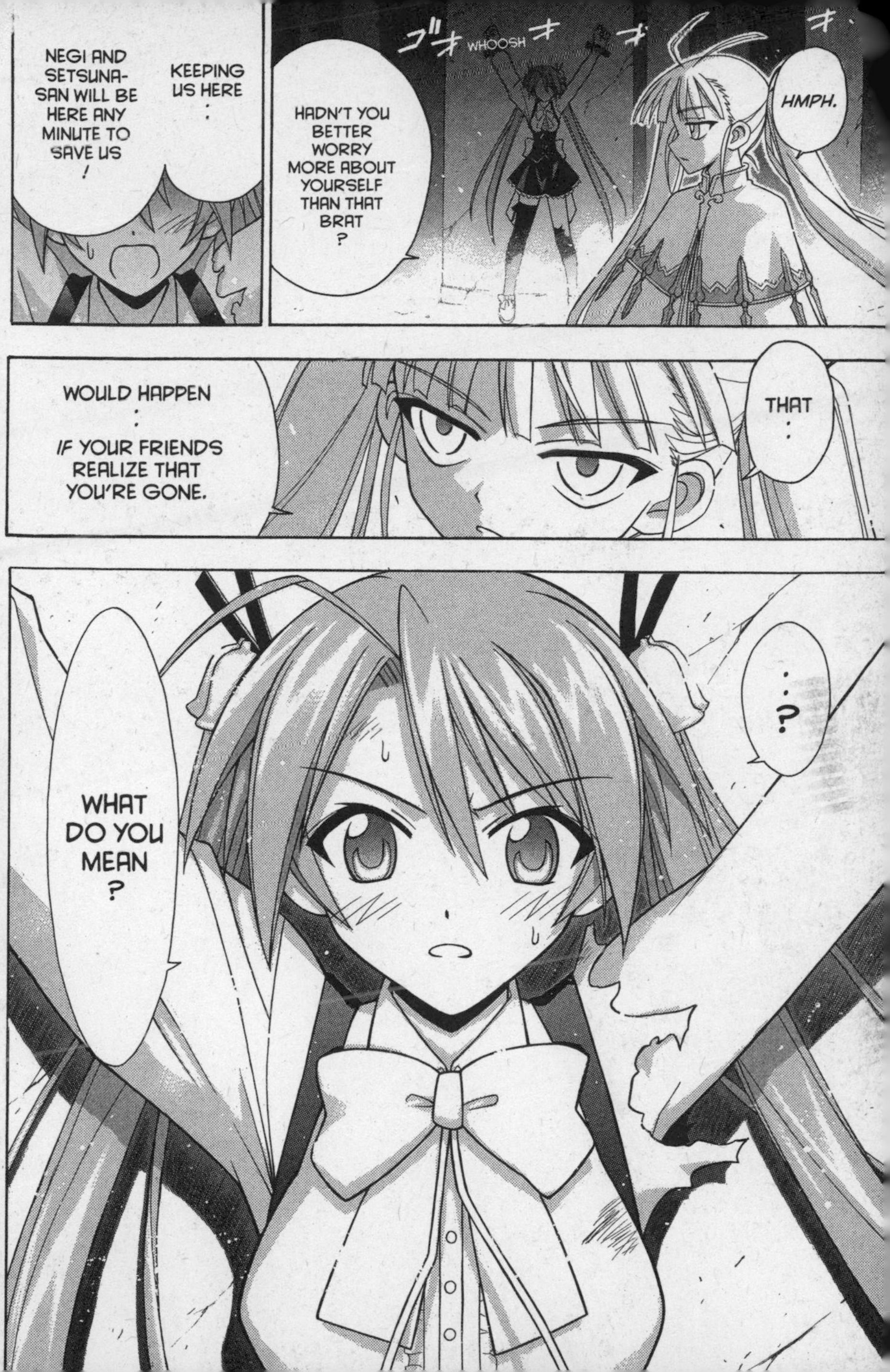
ゴオ WHOOSH オ オ オ
HMPH.
HADN'T YOU BETTER WORRY MORE ABOUT YOURSELF THAN THAT BRAT?
KEEPING US HERE...
NEGI AND SETSUNA-SAN WILL BE HERE ANY MINUTE TO SAVE US!
THAT...
WOULD HAPPEN... IF YOUR FRIENDS REALIZE THAT YOU'RE GONE.
..?
WHAT DO YOU MEAN?

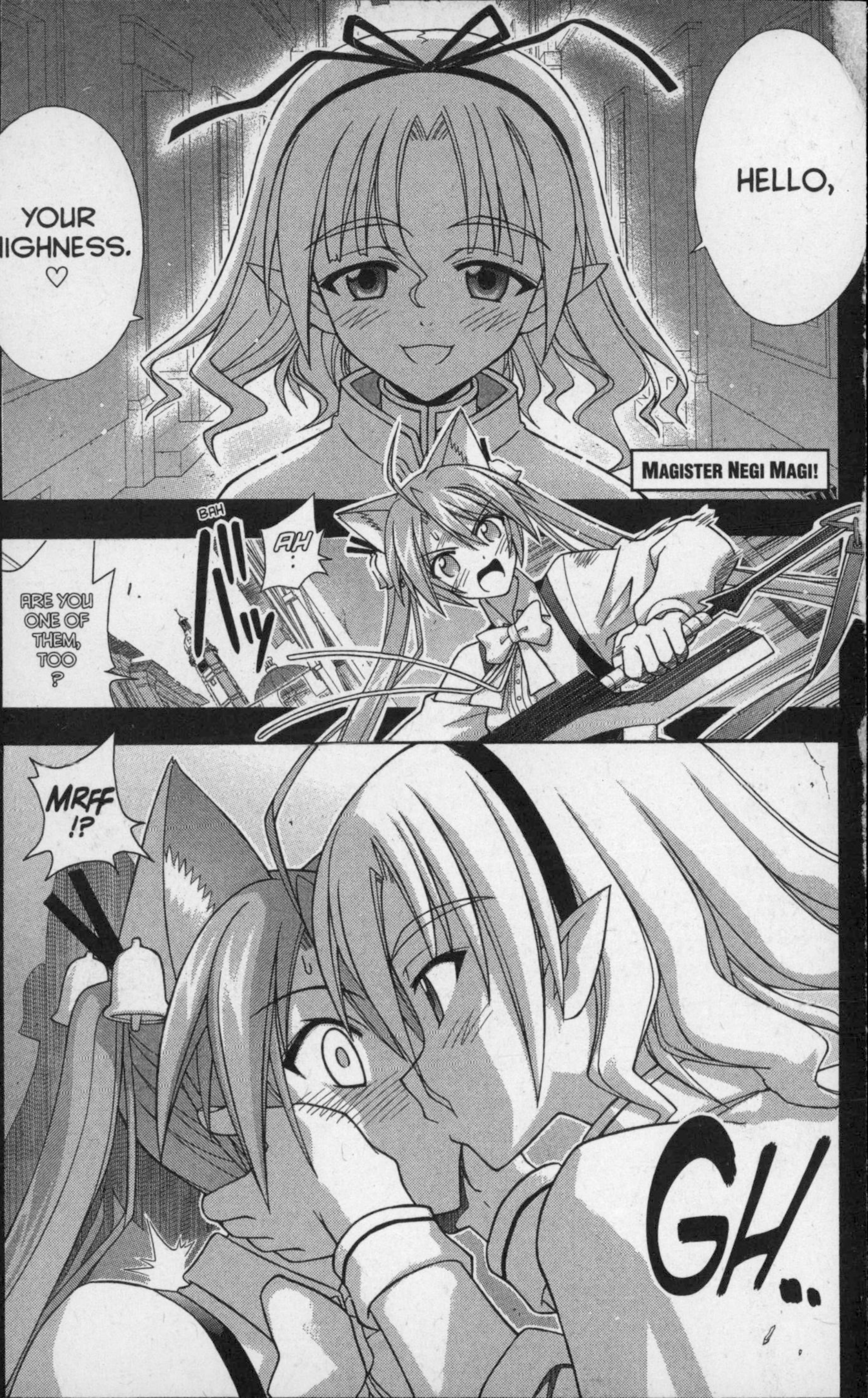
HELLO,
YOUR HIGHNESS. ♡
MAGISTER NEGI MAGI!
AH...
BAH
ARE YOU ONE OF THEM, TOO?
MRFF!?
GH..

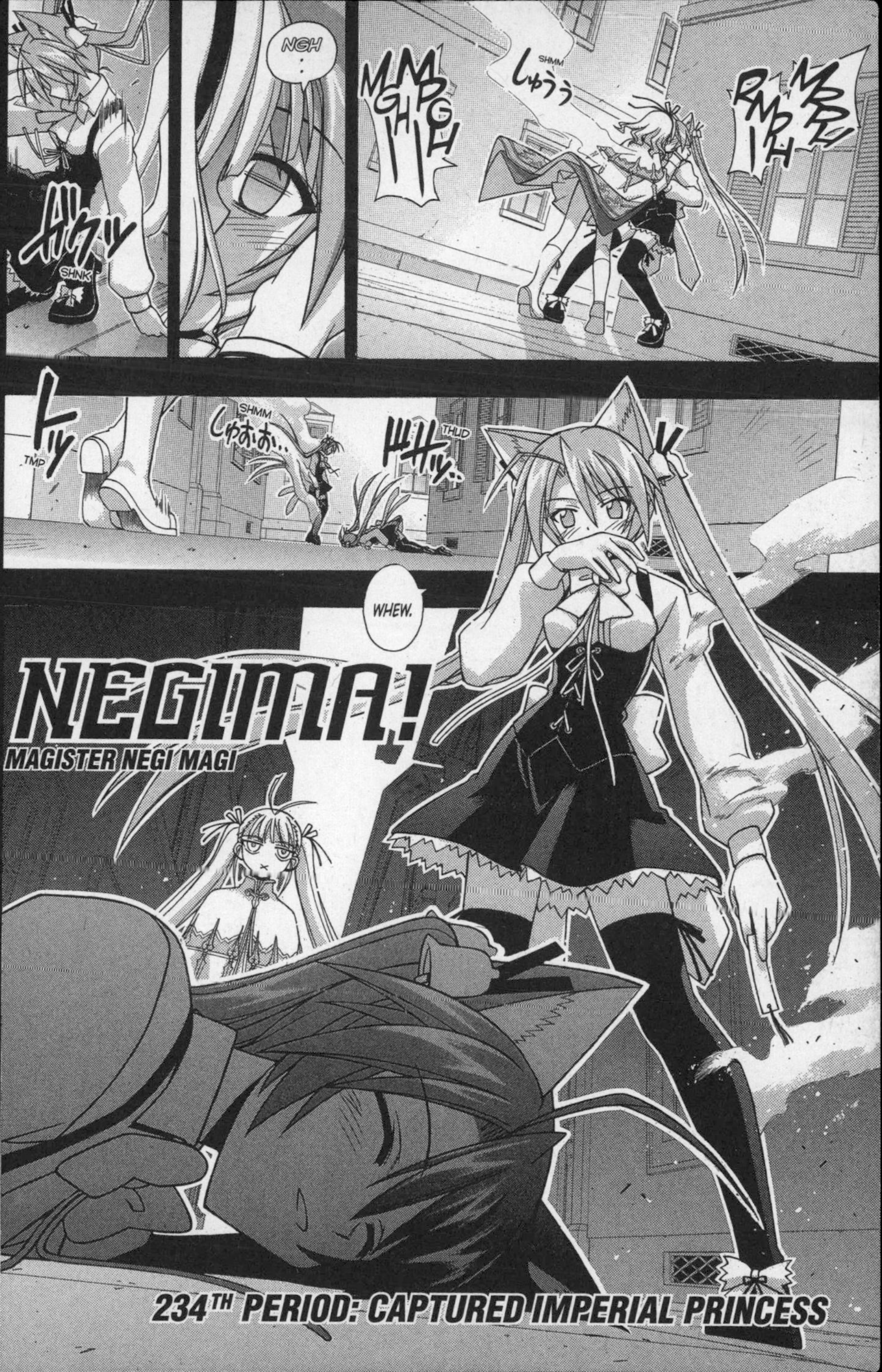

RMPH!
しゅううう
SHMM
MPGH!
MGH!
NGH
. . .
ガクッ
SHNK
ザザッ
THUD
しゅおぉ...
SHMM
トッ
TMP
WHEW.
NEGIMA!
MAGISTER NEGI MAGI
234TH PERIOD: CAPTURED IMPERIAL PRINCESS

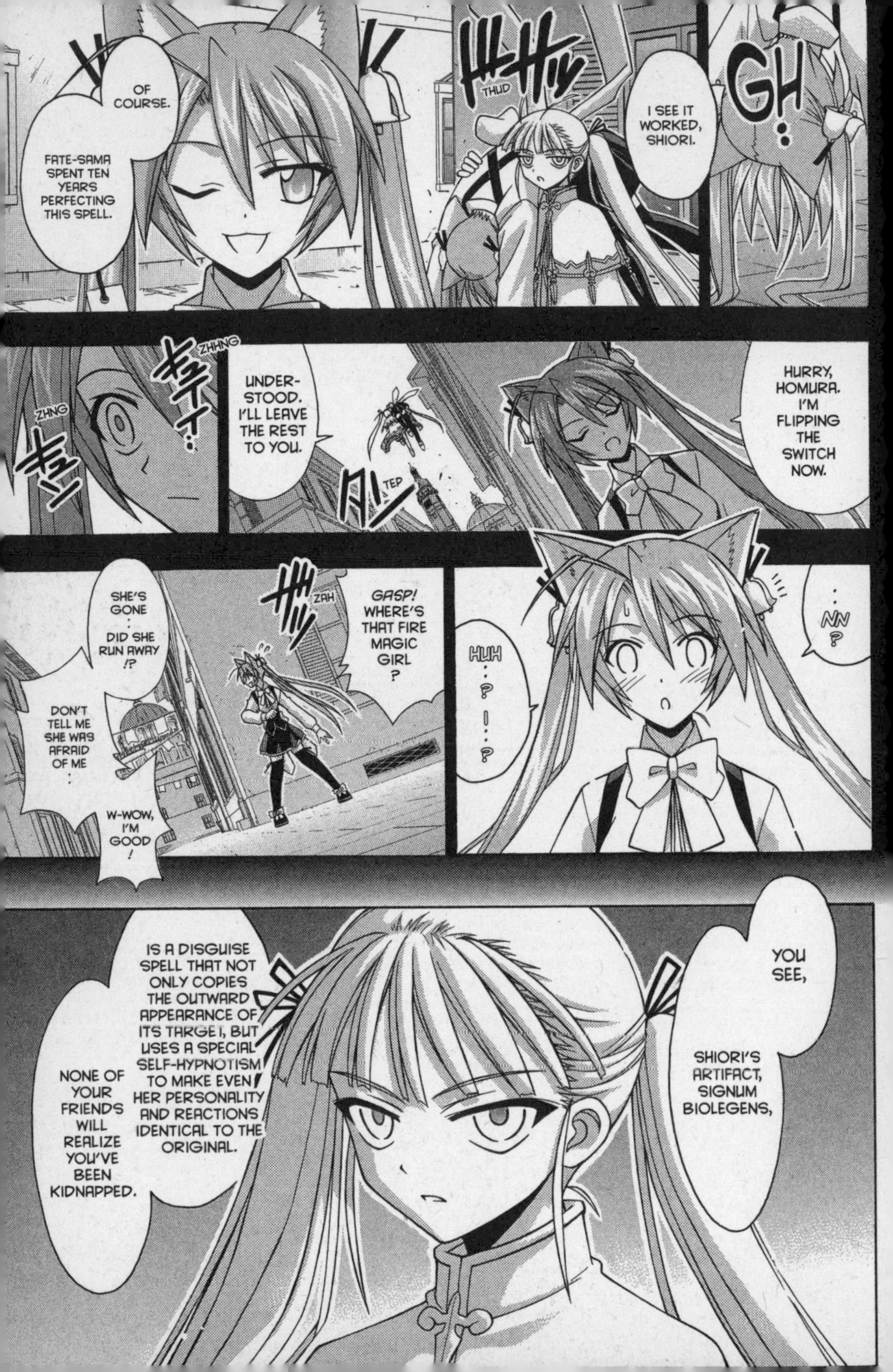
GH
THUD
I SEE IT WORKED, SHIORI.
OF COURSE.
FATE-SAMA SPENT TEN YEARS PERFECTING THIS SPELL.
HURRY, HOMURA. I'M FLIPPING THE SWITCH NOW.
UNDER-STOOD. I'LL LEAVE THE REST TO YOU.
TEP
ZHHNG
ZHNG
...NN?
HUH...? !...?
GASP! WHERE'S THAT FIRE MAGIC GIRL?
ZAH
SHE'S GONE... DID SHE RUN AWAY!?
DON'T TELL ME SHE WAS AFRAID OF ME...
W-WOW, I'M GOOD!
YOU SEE,
SHIORI'S ARTIFACT, SIGNUM BIOLEGENS,
IS A DISGUISE SPELL THAT NOT ONLY COPIES THE OUTWARD APPEARANCE OF ITS TARGET, BUT USES A SPECIAL SELF-HYPNOTISM TO MAKE EVEN HER PERSONALITY AND REACTIONS IDENTICAL TO THE ORIGINAL.
NONE OF YOUR FRIENDS WILL REALIZE YOU'VE BEEN KIDNAPPED.

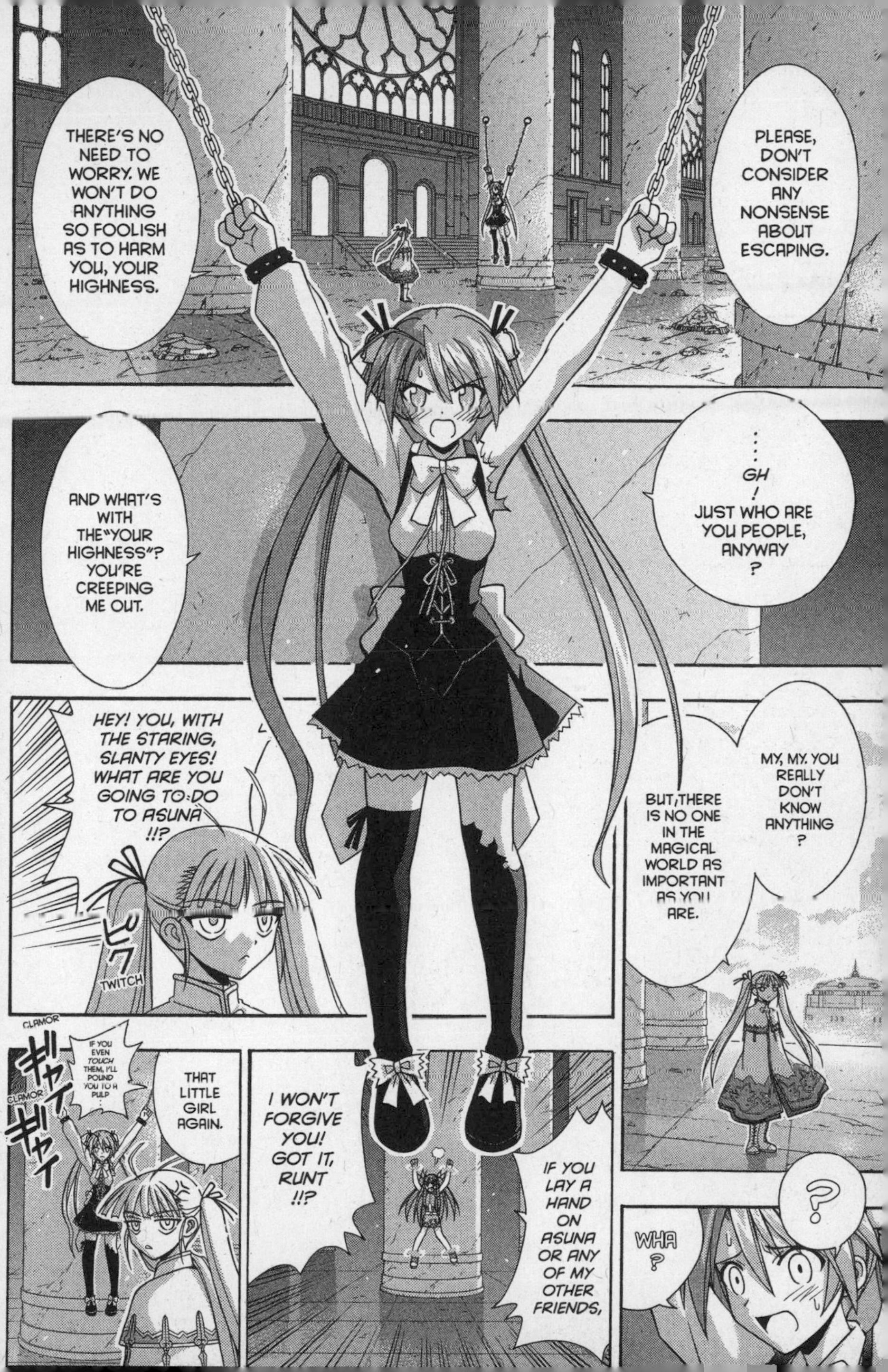
PLEASE, DON'T CONSIDER ANY NONSENSE ABOUT ESCAPING.
THERE'S NO NEED TO WORRY. WE WON'T DO ANYTHING SO FOOLISH AS TO HARM YOU, YOUR HIGHNESS.
...GH! JUST WHO ARE YOU PEOPLE, ANYWAY?
AND WHAT'S WITH THE "YOUR HIGHNESS"? YOU'RE CREEPING ME OUT.
MY, MY. YOU REALLY DON'T KNOW ANYTHING?
BUT, THERE IS NO ONE IN THE MAGICAL WORLD AS IMPORTANT AS YOU ARE.
HEY! YOU, WITH THE STARING, SLANTY EYES! WHAT ARE YOU GOING TO DO TO ASUNA!!?
ピク
TWITCH
?
WHA?
IF YOU LAY A HAND ON ASUNA OR ANY OF MY OTHER FRIENDS,
I WON'T FORGIVE YOU! GOT IT, RUNT!!?
THAT LITTLE GIRL AGAIN.
IF YOU EVEN TOUCH THEM, I'LL POUND YOU TO A PULP...
CLAMOR
ギャイ
CLAMOR
ギャイ

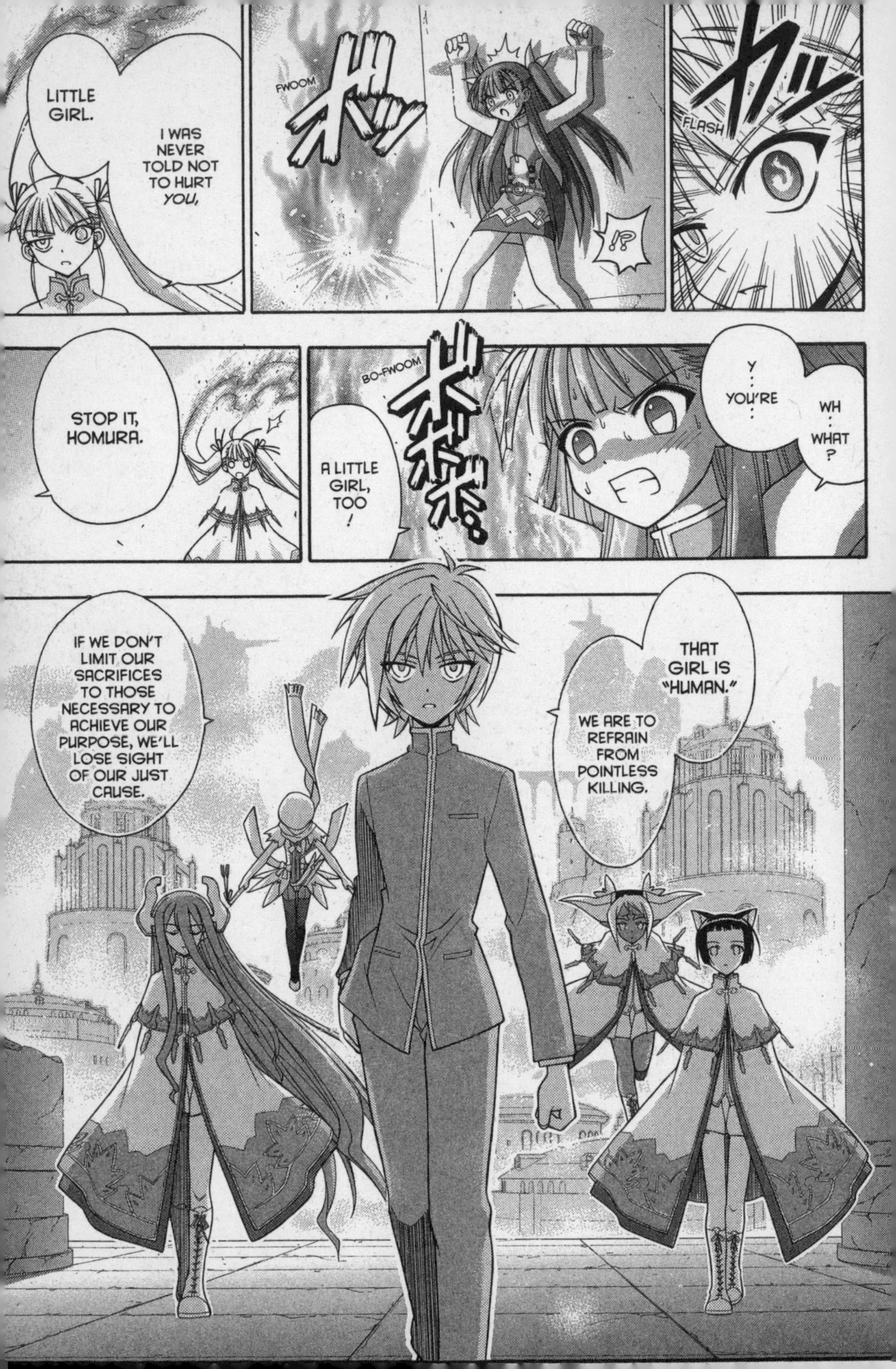
FLASH
FWOOM
!!?
LITTLE GIRL.
I WAS NEVER TOLD NOT TO HURT YOU,
WH... WHAT?
Y... YOU'RE
BO-FWOOM
A LITTLE GIRL, TOO!
STOP IT, HOMURA.
THAT GIRL IS "HUMAN."
WE ARE TO REFRAIN FROM POINTLESS KILLING.
IF WE DON'T LIMIT OUR SACRIFICES TO THOSE NECESSARY TO ACHIEVE OUR PURPOSE, WE'LL LOSE SIGHT OF OUR JUST CAUSE.

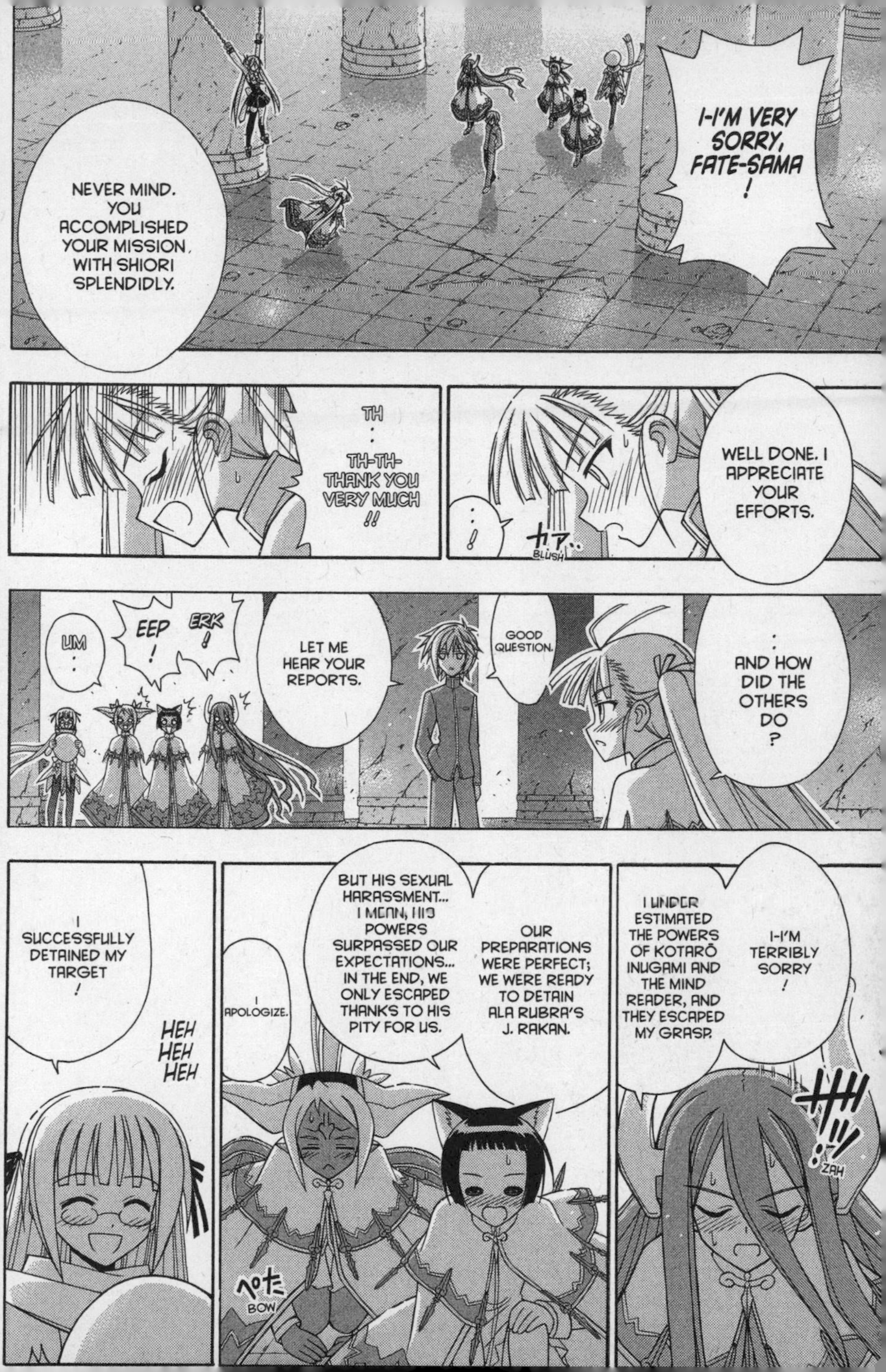

I-I'M VERY SORRY, FATE-SAMA!
NEVER MIND. YOU ACCOMPLISHED YOUR MISSION WITH SHIORI SPLENDIDLY.
WELL DONE. I APPRECIATE YOUR EFFORTS.
...!
BLUSH
TH... TH-TH-THANK YOU VERY MUCH!!
...AND HOW DID THE OTHERS DO?
GOOD QUESTION.
LET ME HEAR YOUR REPORTS.
ERK!
EEP!
UM...
I-I'M TERRIBLY SORRY!
I UNDERESTIMATED THE POWERS OF KOTARŌ INUGAMI AND THE MIND READER, AND THEY ESCAPED MY GRASP.
ZAH
OUR PREPARATIONS WERE PERFECT; WE WERE READY TO DETAIN ALA RUBRA'S J. RAKAN.
BUT HIS SEXUAL HARASSMENT... I MEAN, HIS POWERS SURPASSED OUR EXPECTATIONS... IN THE END, WE ONLY ESCAPED THANKS TO HIS PITY FOR US.
I APOLOGIZE.
BOW
I SUCCESSFULLY DETAINED MY TARGET!
HEH HEH HEH

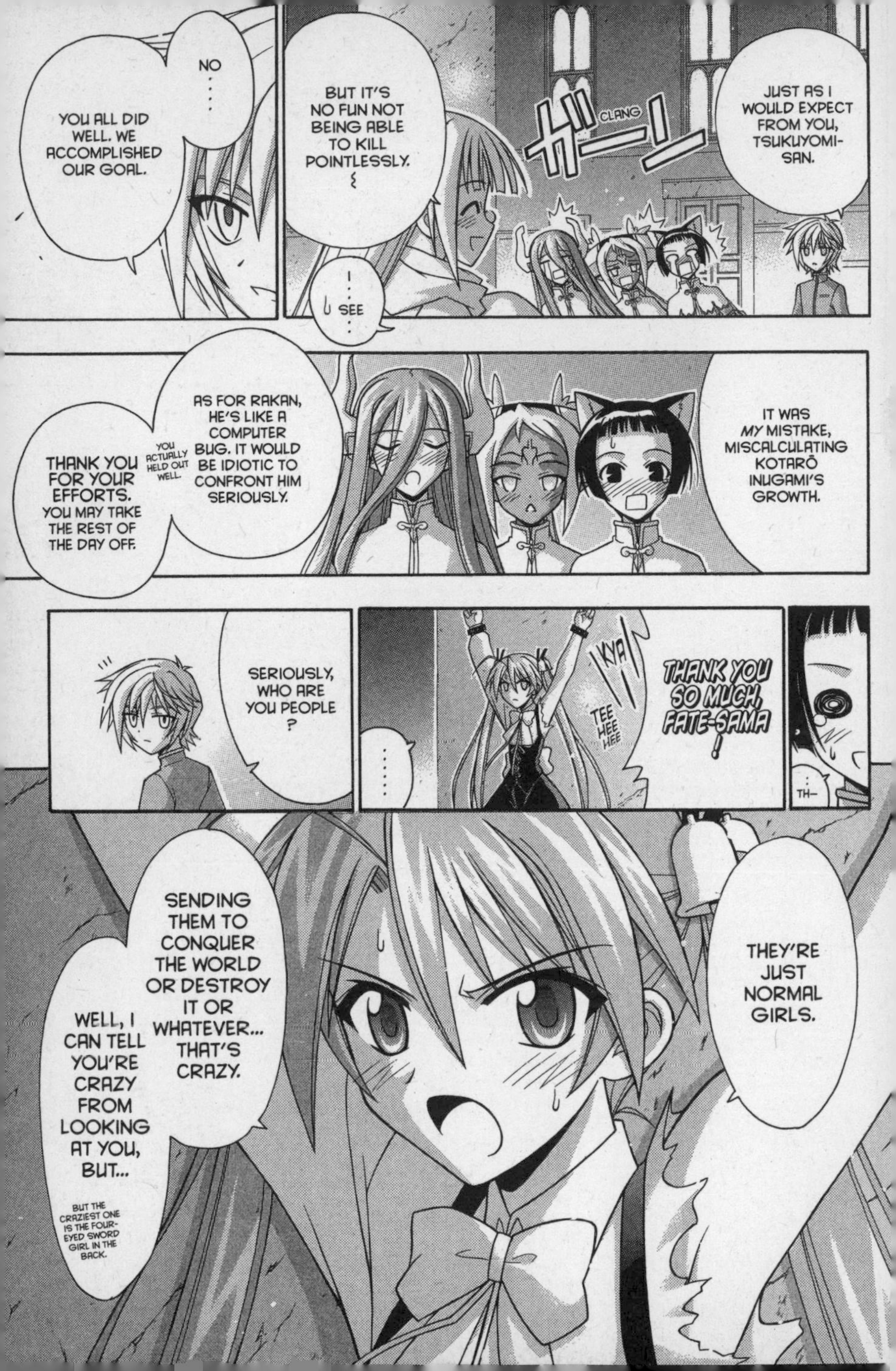
JUST AS I WOULD EXPECT FROM YOU, TSUKUYOMI-SAN.
CLANG
BUT IT'S NO FUN NOT BEING ABLE TO KILL POINTLESSLY.
I... SEE...
NO...
YOU ALL DID WELL. WE ACCOMPLISHED OUR GOAL.
IT WAS MY MISTAKE, MISCALCULATING KOTARŌ INUGAMI'S GROWTH.
AS FOR RAKAN, HE'S LIKE A COMPUTER BUG. IT WOULD BE IDIOTIC TO CONFRONT HIM SERIOUSLY.
YOU ACTUALLY HELD OUT WELL.
THANK YOU FOR YOUR EFFORTS. YOU MAY TAKE THE REST OF THE DAY OFF.
...TH—
THANK YOU SO MUCH, FATE-SAMA!
KYA!
TEE HEE HEE
......
SERIOUSLY, WHO ARE YOU PEOPLE?
THEY'RE JUST NORMAL GIRLS.
SENDING THEM TO CONQUER THE WORLD OR DESTROY IT OR WHATEVER... THAT'S CRAZY.
WELL, I CAN TELL YOU'RE CRAZY FROM LOOKING AT YOU, BUT...
BUT THE CRAZIEST ONE IS THE FOUR-EYED SWORD GIRL IN THE BACK.

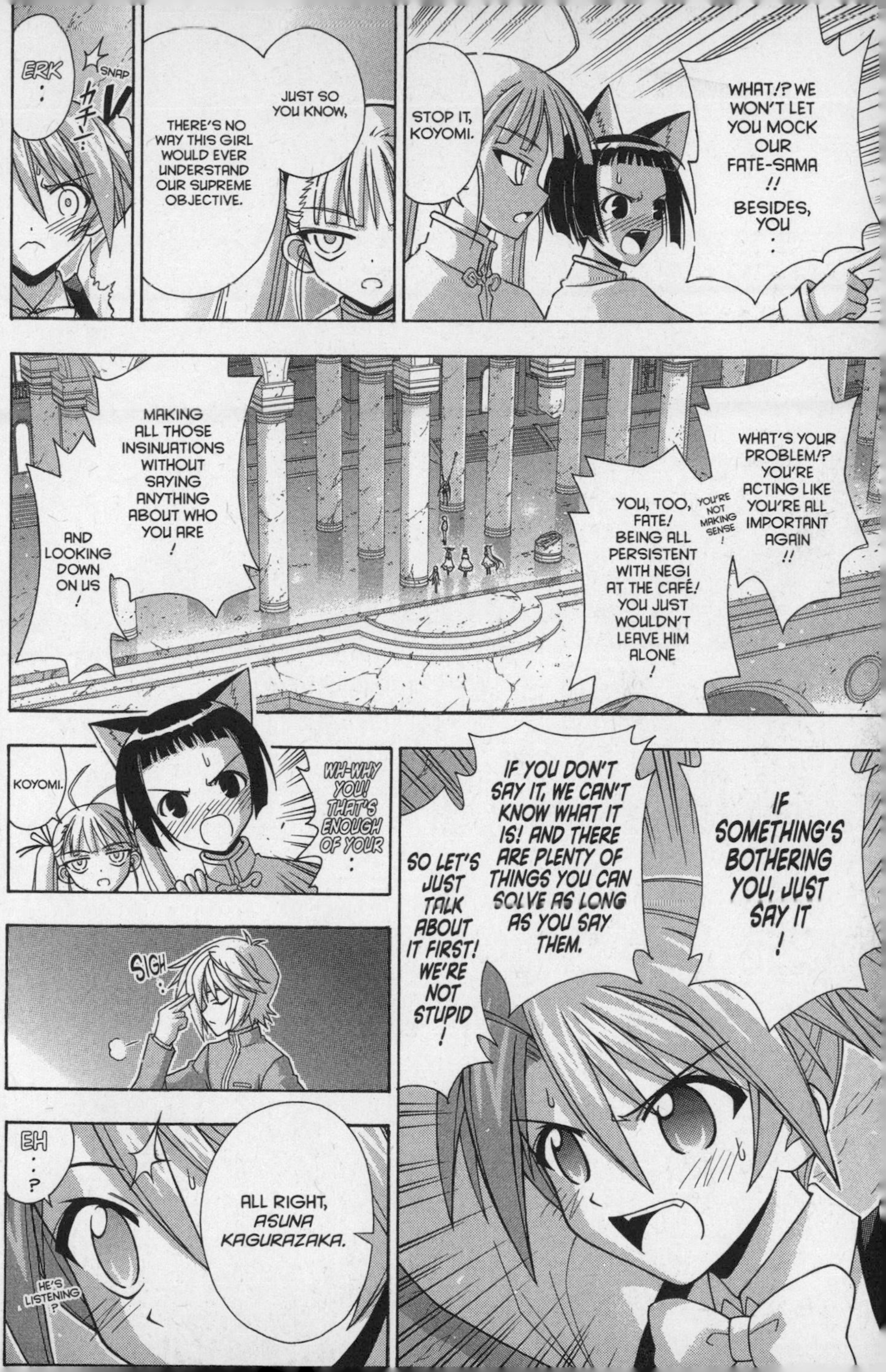
WHAT!? WE WON'T LET YOU MOCK OUR FATE-SAMA!! BESIDES, YOU...
STOP IT, KOYOMI.
JUST SO YOU KNOW,
THERE'S NO WAY THIS GIRL WOULD EVER UNDERSTAND OUR SUPREME OBJECTIVE.
ERK...
SNAP
WHAT'S YOUR PROBLEM!? YOU'RE ACTING LIKE YOU'RE ALL IMPORTANT AGAIN!!
YOU'RE NOT MAKING SENSE!
YOU, TOO, FATE! BEING ALL PERSISTENT WITH NEGI AT THE CAFÉ! YOU JUST WOULDN'T LEAVE HIM ALONE!
MAKING ALL THOSE INSINUATIONS WITHOUT SAYING ANYTHING ABOUT WHO YOU ARE!
AND LOOKING DOWN ON US!
IF SOMETHING'S BOTHERING YOU, JUST SAY IT!
IF YOU DON'T SAY IT, WE CAN'T KNOW WHAT IT IS! AND THERE ARE PLENTY OF THINGS YOU CAN SOLVE AS LONG AS YOU SAY THEM.
SO LET'S JUST TALK ABOUT IT FIRST! WE'RE NOT STUPID!
WH-WHY YOU! THAT'S ENOUGH OF YOUR...
KOYOMI.
SIGH...
ALL RIGHT, ASUNA KAGURAZAKA.
EH...?
HE'S LISTENING?

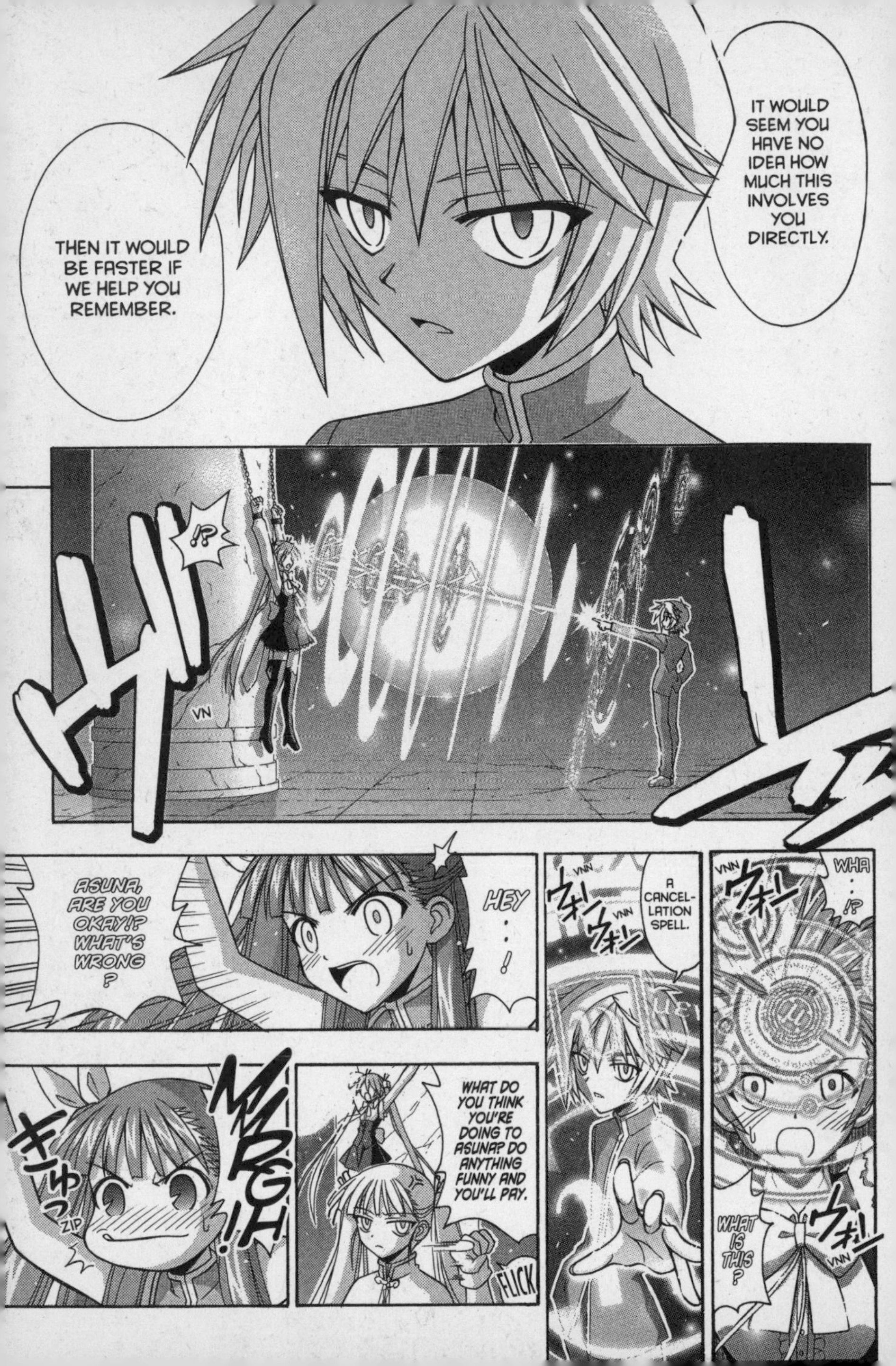
IT WOULD SEEM YOU HAVE NO IDEA HOW MUCH THIS INVOLVES YOU DIRECTLY.
THEN IT WOULD BE FASTER IF WE HELP YOU REMEMBER.
!?
VN
WHA...!?
VNN
WHAT IS THIS?
VNN
VNN
A CANCEL-LATION SPELL.
VNN
HEY...!
ASUNA, ARE YOU OKAY!? WHAT'S WRONG?
WHAT DO YOU THINK YOU'RE DOING TO ASUNA? DO ANYTHING FUNNY AND YOU'LL PAY.
FLICK
MMRGH!!
ZIP

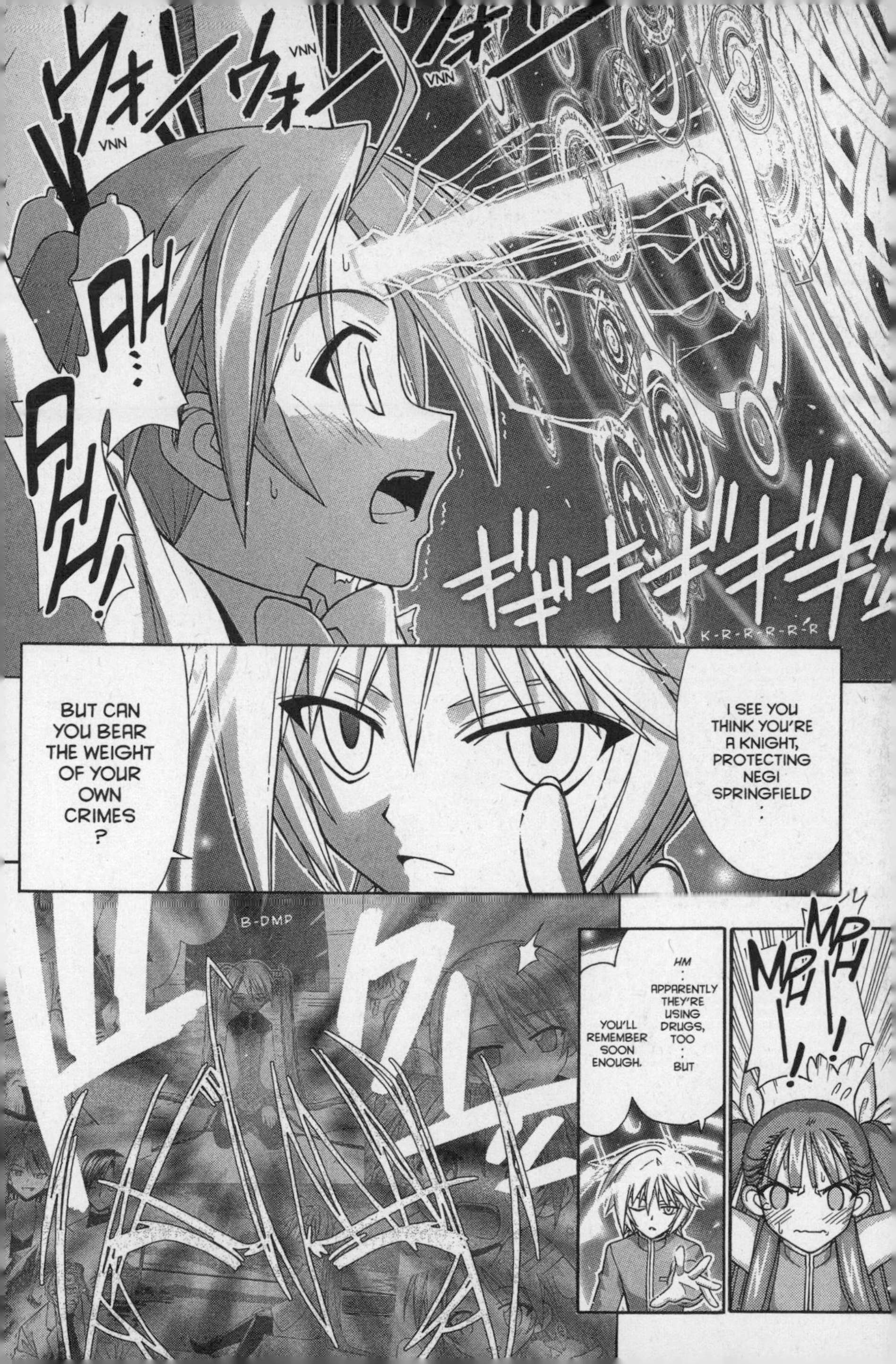
VNN
VNN
VNN
AH!...
AHH!
K-R-R-R-R-R
I SEE YOU THINK YOU'RE A KNIGHT, PROTECTING NEGI SPRINGFIELD...
BUT CAN YOU BEAR THE WEIGHT OF YOUR OWN CRIMES?
MPH MPH!!!
HM... APPARENTLY THEY'RE USING DRUGS, TOO... BUT
YOU'LL REMEMBER SOON ENOUGH.
B-DMP

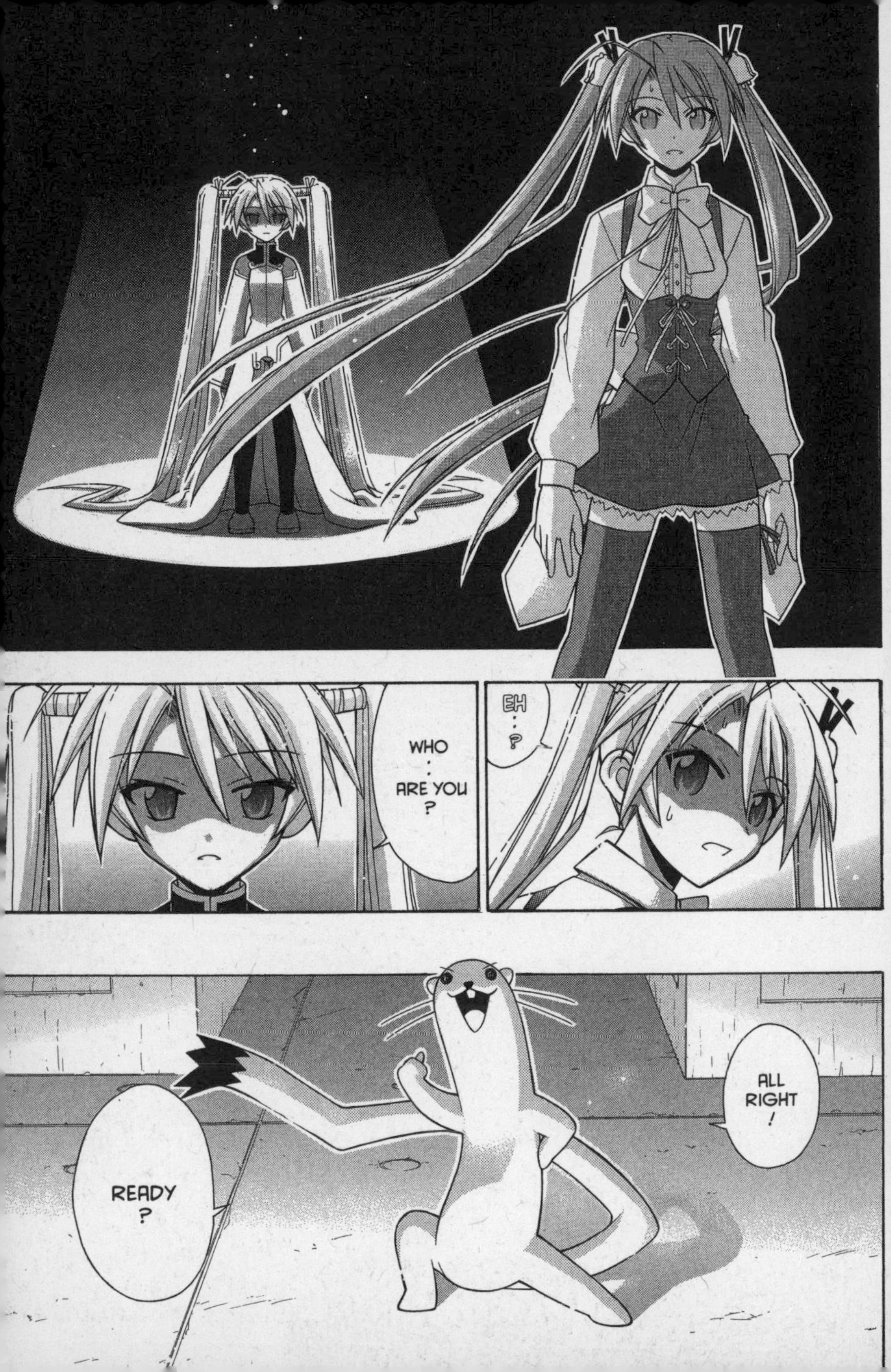
EH . . . ?
WHO . . . ARE YOU ?
ALL RIGHT !
READY ?

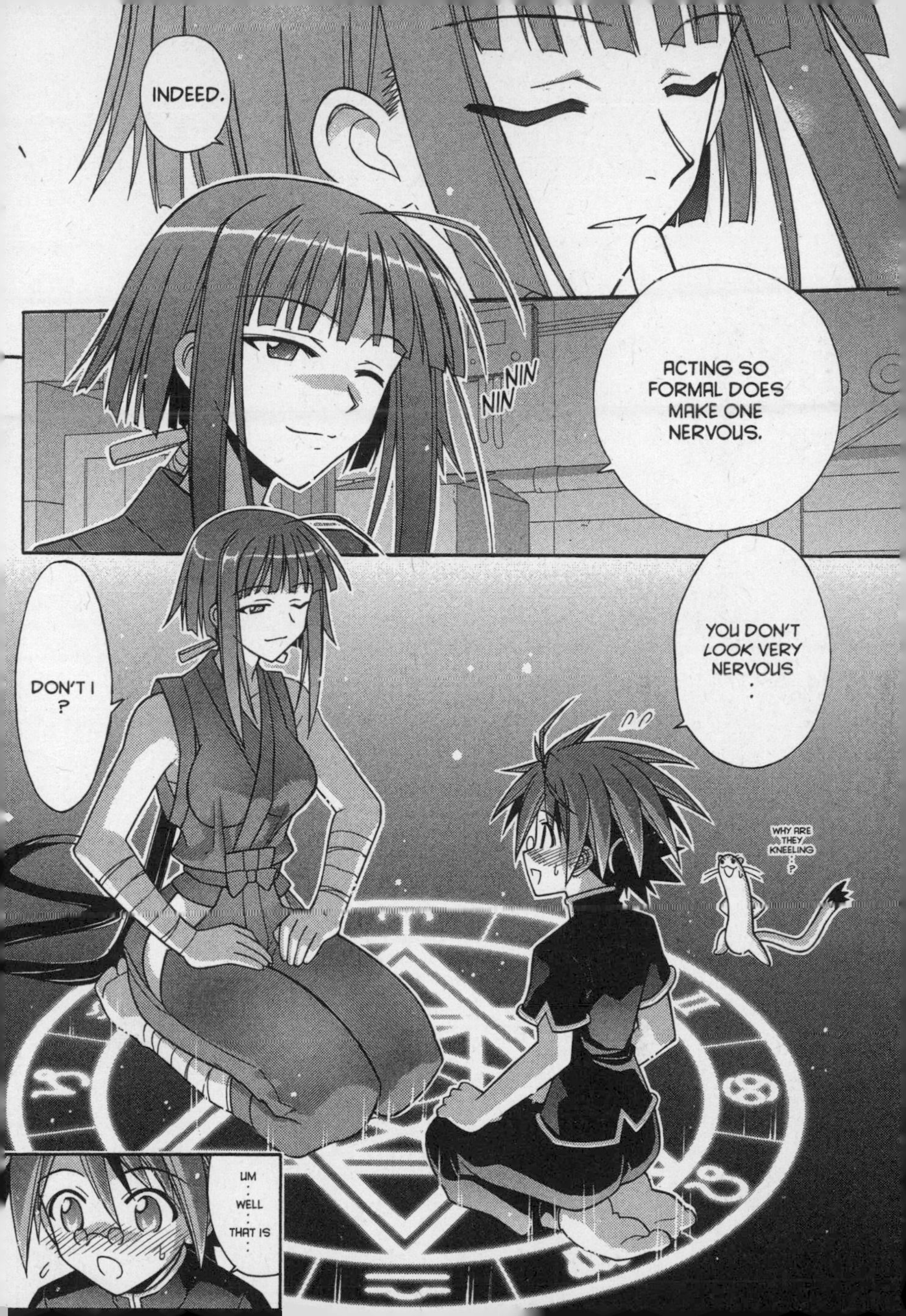
INDEED.
ACTING SO FORMAL DOES MAKE ONE NERVOUS.
NIN NIN
YOU DON'T *LOOK* VERY NERVOUS . .
DON'T I ?
WHY ARE THEY KNEELING . . ?
UM . . WELL . . THAT IS . . .

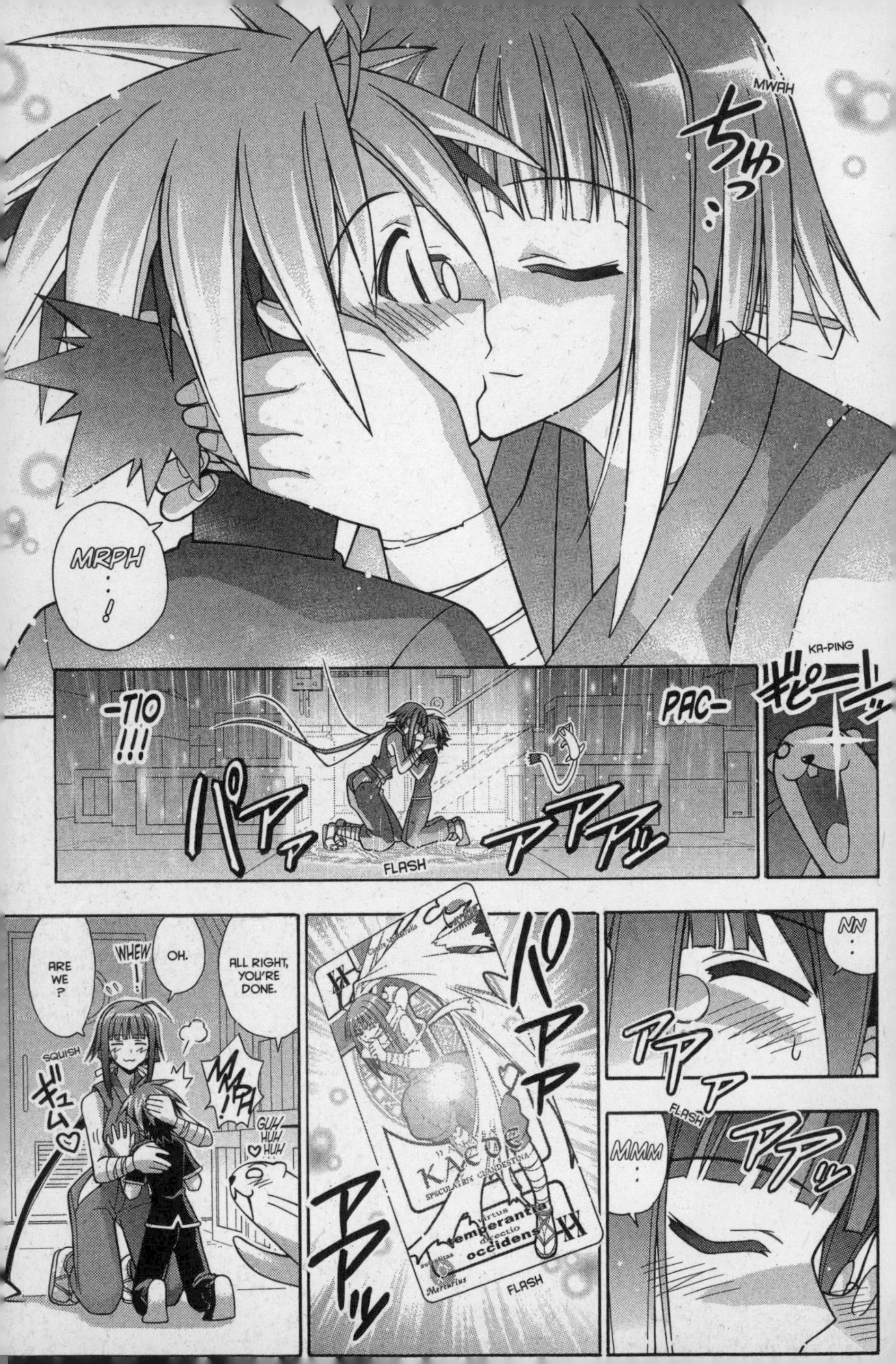

MWAH
ちゅっ
MRPH . . . !
KA-PING
PAC-
-TIO !!!
FLASH
NN . . .
FLASH
MMM . . .
KAEDE
SPECULATRIX CLANDESTINA
virtus temperantia directio occidens
XX
Mercurius
FLASH
ALL RIGHT, YOU'RE DONE.
OH.
WHEW!
ARE WE?
SQUISH
MRPH!
GUH HUH HUH

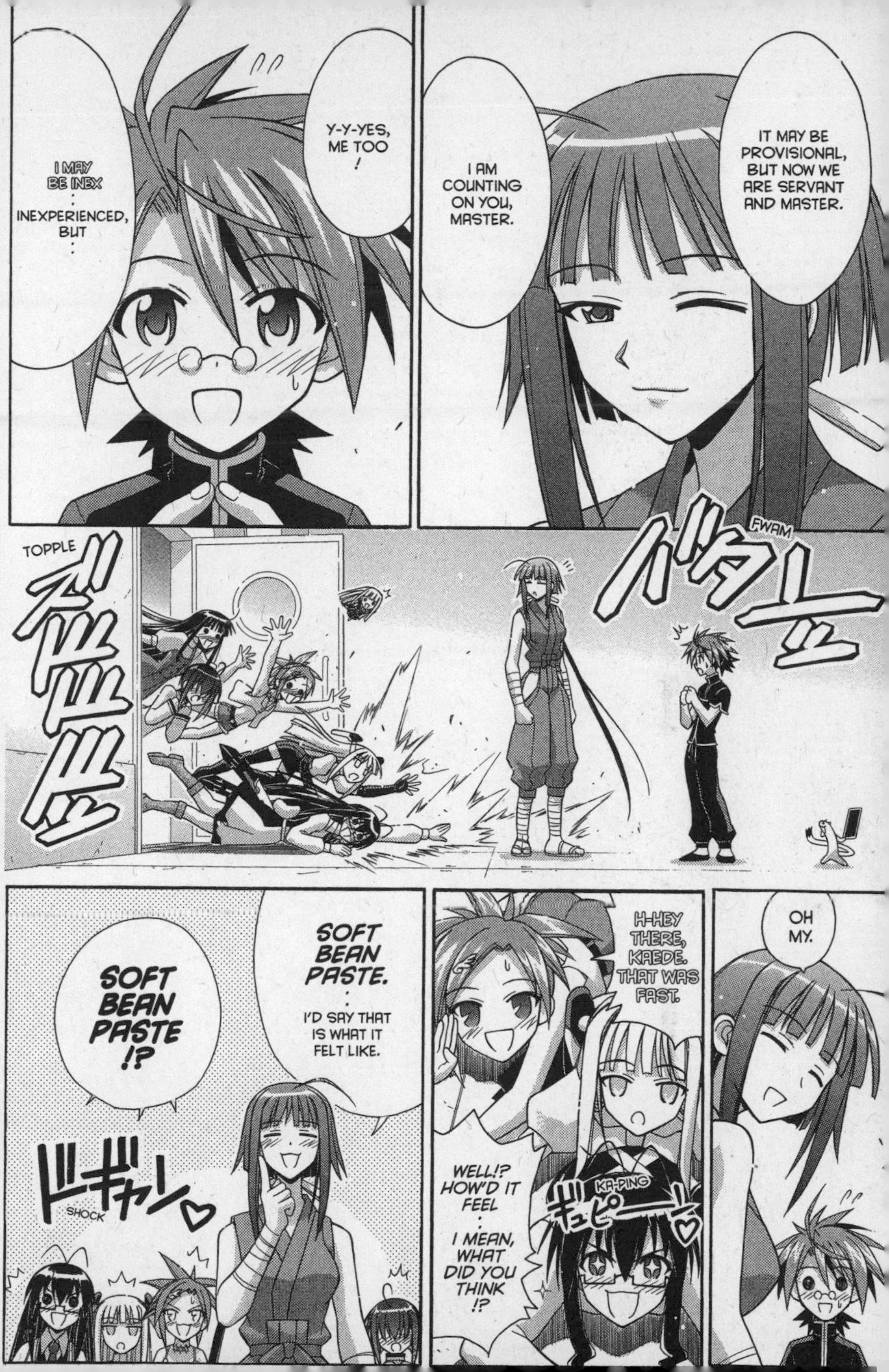
IT MAY BE PROVISIONAL, BUT NOW WE ARE SERVANT AND MASTER.
I AM COUNTING ON YOU, MASTER.
Y-Y-YES, ME TOO!
I MAY BE INEX... INEXPERIENCED, BUT...
FWAM
TOPPLE
OH MY.
H-HEY THERE, KAEDE. THAT WAS FAST.
KA-PING
WELL!? HOW'D IT FEEL... I MEAN, WHAT DID YOU THINK!?
SOFT BEAN PASTE... I'D SAY THAT IS WHAT IT FELT LIKE.
SOFT BEAN PASTE!?
SHOCK

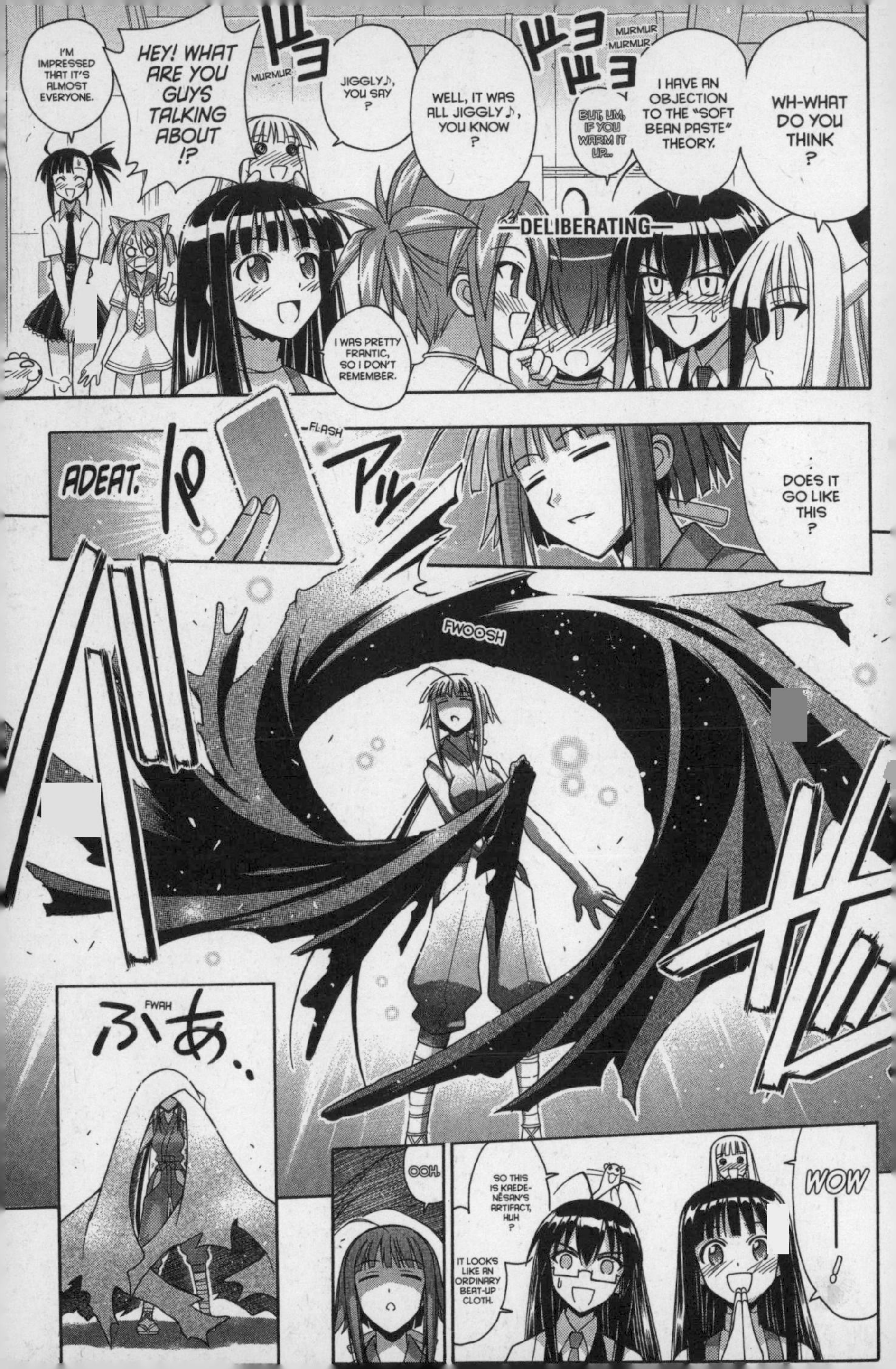
WH-WHAT DO YOU THINK?
I HAVE AN OBJECTION TO THE "SOFT BEAN PASTE" THEORY.
BUT, UM, IF YOU WARM IT UP...
MURMUR MURMUR
WELL, IT WAS ALL JIGGLY♪, YOU KNOW?
JIGGLY♪, YOU SAY?
MURMUR
DELIBERATING
I WAS PRETTY FRANTIC, SO I DON'T REMEMBER.
HEY! WHAT ARE YOU GUYS TALKING ABOUT!?
I'M IMPRESSED THAT IT'S ALMOST EVERYONE.
DOES IT GO LIKE THIS?
FLASH
ADEAT.
FWOOSH
WOW—!
SO THIS IS KAEDE-NÉSAN'S ARTIFACT, HUH?
IT LOOKS LIKE AN ORDINARY BEAT-UP CLOTH.
OOH
FWAH
ふあ..

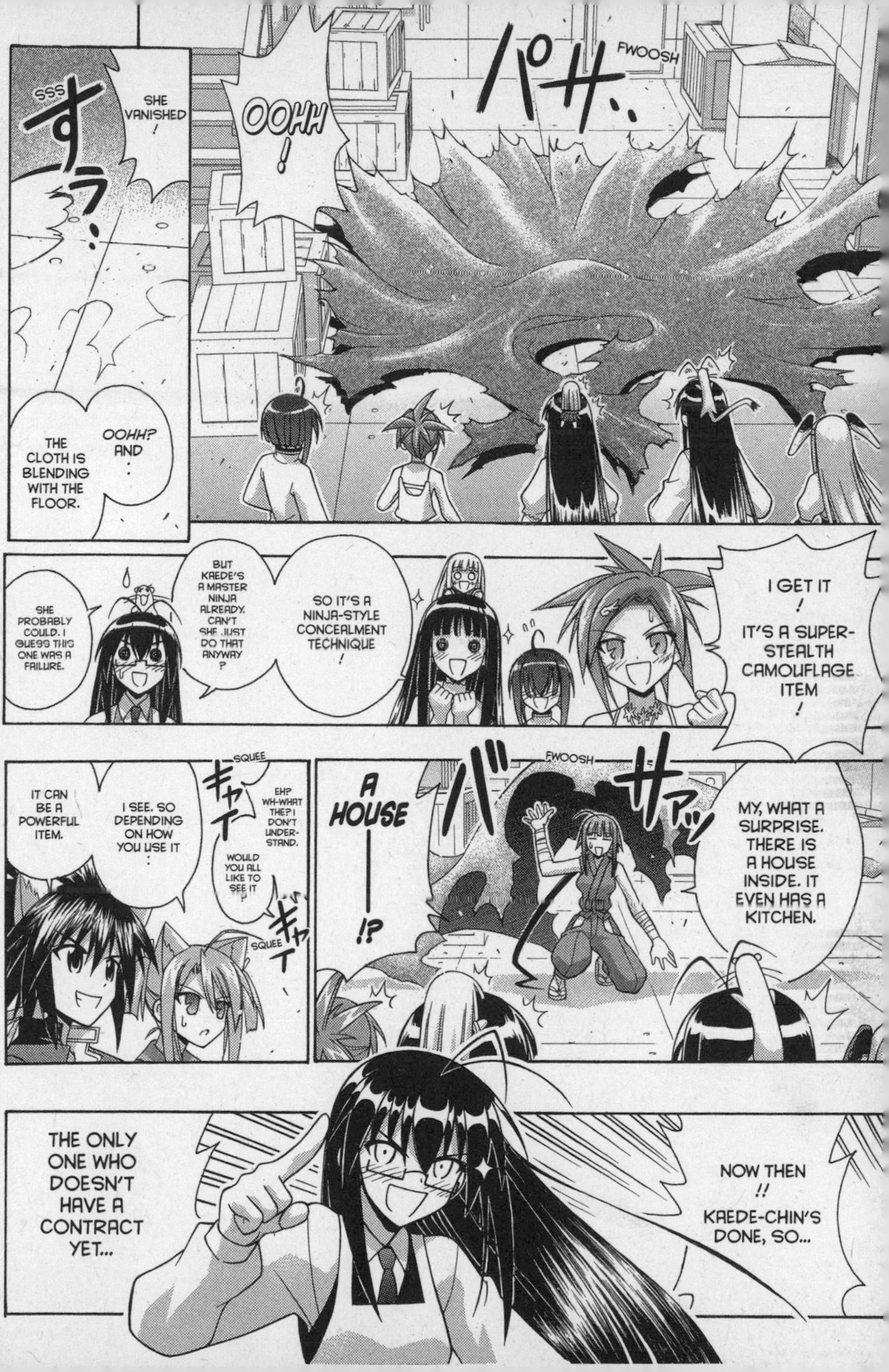

パサ..
FWOOSH
OOHH!
SSS
SHE VANISHED!
OOHH? AND...
THE CLOTH IS BLENDING WITH THE FLOOR.
I GET IT! IT'S A SUPER-STEALTH CAMOUFLAGE ITEM!
SO IT'S A NINJA-STYLE CONCEALMENT TECHNIQUE!
BUT KAEDE'S A MASTER NINJA ALREADY. CAN'T SHE JUST DO THAT ANYWAY?
SHE PROBABLY COULD. I GUESS THIS ONE WAS A FAILURE.
MY, WHAT A SURPRISE. THERE IS A HOUSE INSIDE. IT EVEN HAS A KITCHEN.
FWOOSH
A HOUSE——!?
EH? WH-WHAT THE?! I DON'T UNDERSTAND.
SQUEE
WOULD YOU ALL LIKE TO SEE IT?
SQUEE
I SEE. SO DEPENDING ON HOW YOU USE IT...
IT CAN BE A POWERFUL ITEM.
NOW THEN!! KAEDE-CHIN'S DONE, SO...
THE ONLY ONE WHO DOESN'T HAVE A CONTRACT YET...

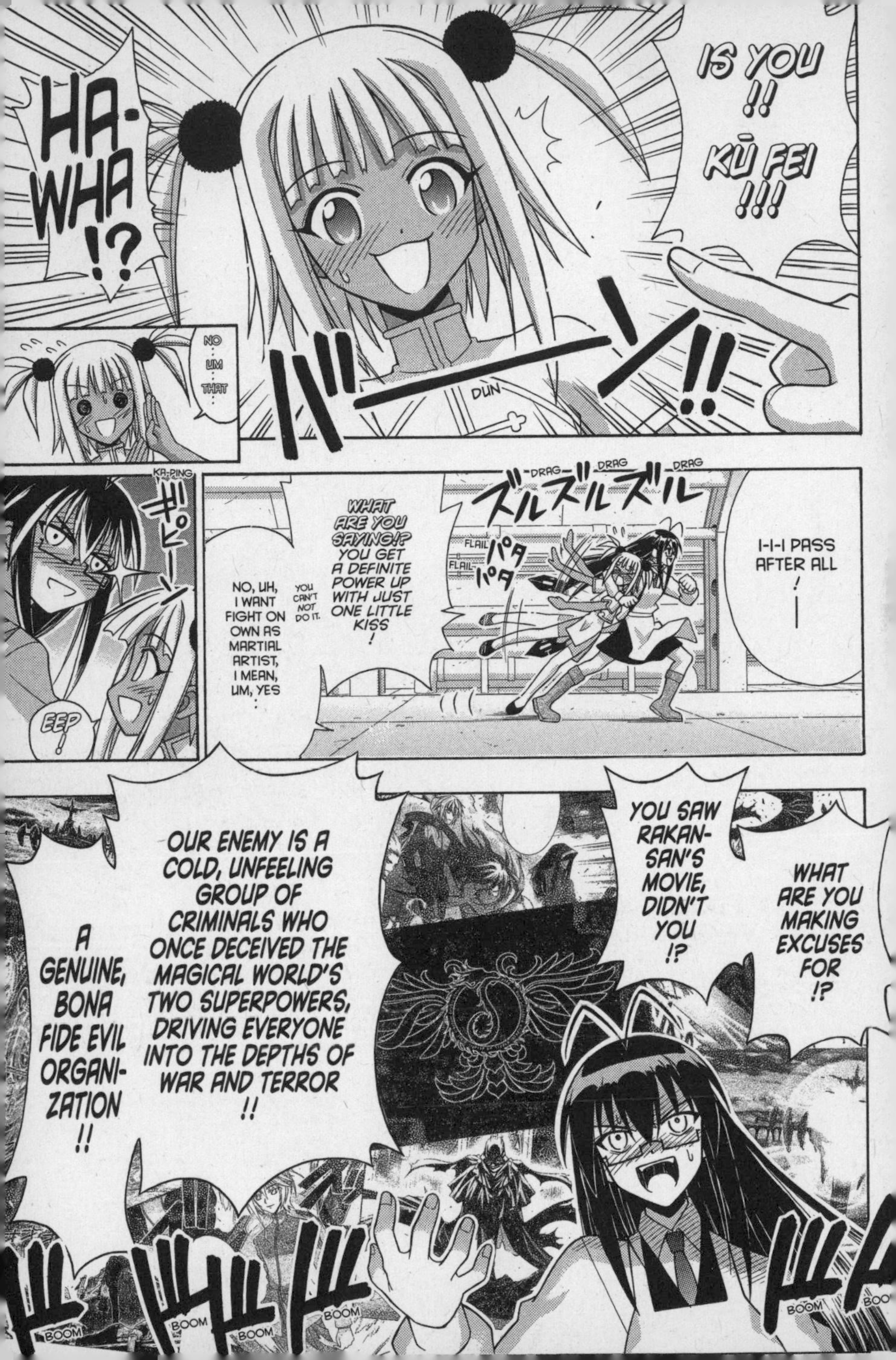
IS YOU!! KŪ FEI!!!
HA-WHA!?
DUN
NO... UM... THAT...
I-I-I PASS AFTER ALL!
DRAG DRAG DRAG
FLAIL FLAIL
WHAT ARE YOU SAYING!? YOU GET A DEFINITE POWER UP WITH JUST ONE LITTLE KISS!
YOU CAN'T NOT DO IT.
NO, UH, I WANT FIGHT ON OWN AS MARTIAL ARTIST, I MEAN, UM, YES...
KA-PING
EEP!
WHAT ARE YOU MAKING EXCUSES FOR!?
YOU SAW RAKAN-SAN'S MOVIE, DIDN'T YOU!?
OUR ENEMY IS A COLD, UNFEELING GROUP OF CRIMINALS WHO ONCE DECEIVED THE MAGICAL WORLD'S TWO SUPERPOWERS, DRIVING EVERYONE INTO THE DEPTHS OF WAR AND TERROR!!
A GENUINE, BONA FIDE EVIL ORGANIZATION!!
BOOM BOOM BOOM BOOM BOOM BOOM

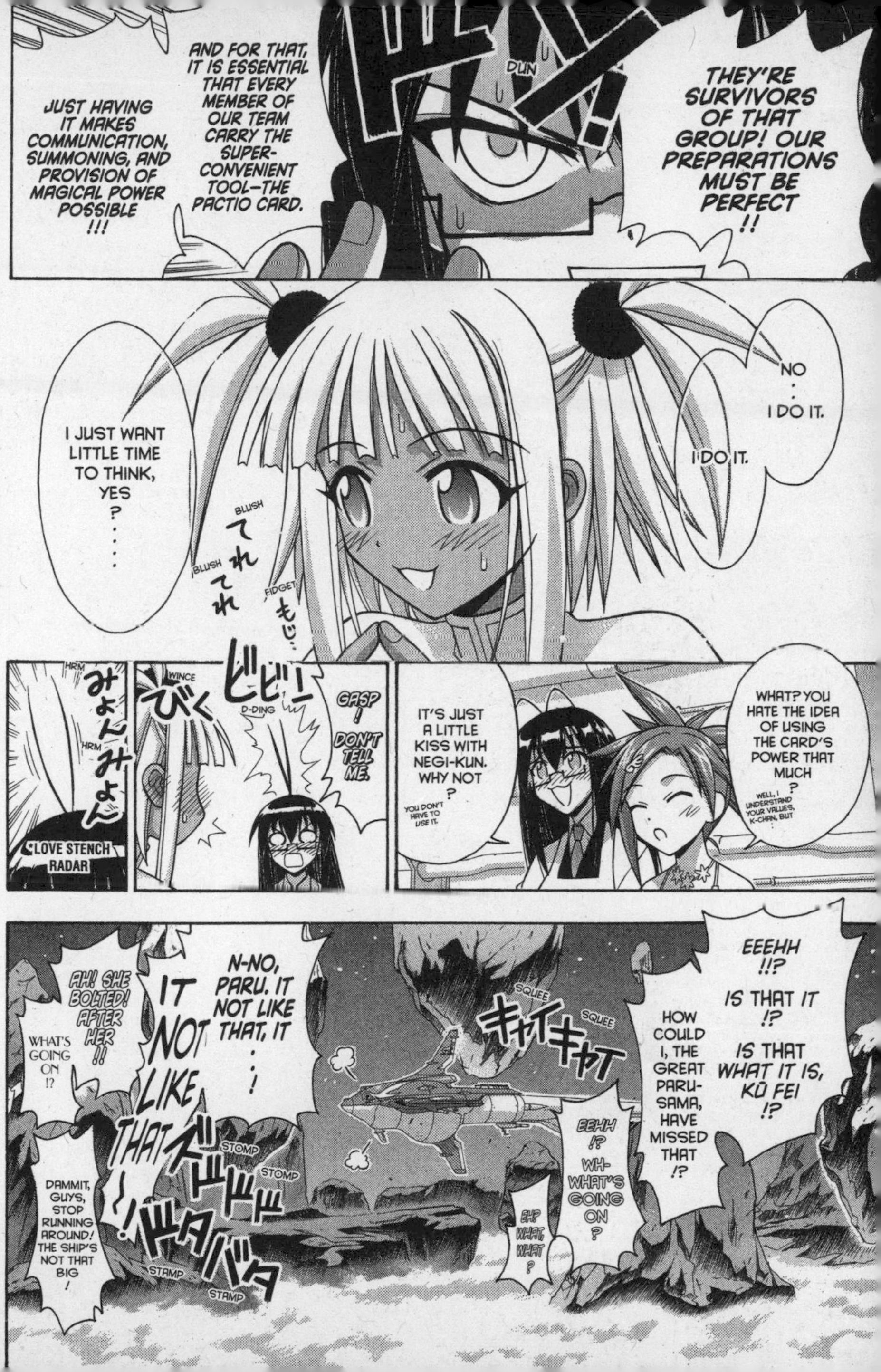
THEY'RE SURVIVORS OF THAT GROUP! OUR PREPARATIONS MUST BE PERFECT!!
DUN
AND FOR THAT, IT IS ESSENTIAL THAT EVERY MEMBER OF OUR TEAM CARRY THE SUPER-CONVENIENT TOOL—THE PACTIO CARD.
JUST HAVING IT MAKES COMMUNICATION, SUMMONING, AND PROVISION OF MAGICAL POWER POSSIBLE!!!
NO... I DO IT.
I DO IT.
I JUST WANT LITTLE TIME TO THINK, YES?.....
BLUSH てれ
BLUSH てれ
FIDGET もじ…
WHAT? YOU HATE THE IDEA OF USING THE CARD'S POWER THAT MUCH?
WELL, I UNDERSTAND YOUR VALUES, K-CHAN, BUT...
IT'S JUST A LITTLE KISS WITH NEGI-KUN. WHY NOT?
YOU DON'T HAVE TO USE IT.
GASP! DON'T TELL ME.
D-DING ビビーン
WINCE びく
HRM みょん
HRM みょん
LOVE STENCH RADAR
EEEHH!!? IS THAT IT!? IS THAT WHAT IT IS, KŪ FEI!?
HOW COULD I, THE GREAT PARU-SAMA, HAVE MISSED THAT!?
EEHH!? WH-WHAT'S GOING ON?
EH? WHAT, WHAT?
SQUEE キャイキャイ SQUEE
N-NO, PARU. IT NOT LIKE THAT, IT...!
IT NOT LIKE THAT~!
STOMP STOMP STAMP STAMP ドタバタ
AH! SHE BOLTED! AFTER HER!!
WHAT'S GOING ON!?
DAMMIT, GUYS, STOP RUNNING AROUND! THE SHIP'S NOT THAT BIG!

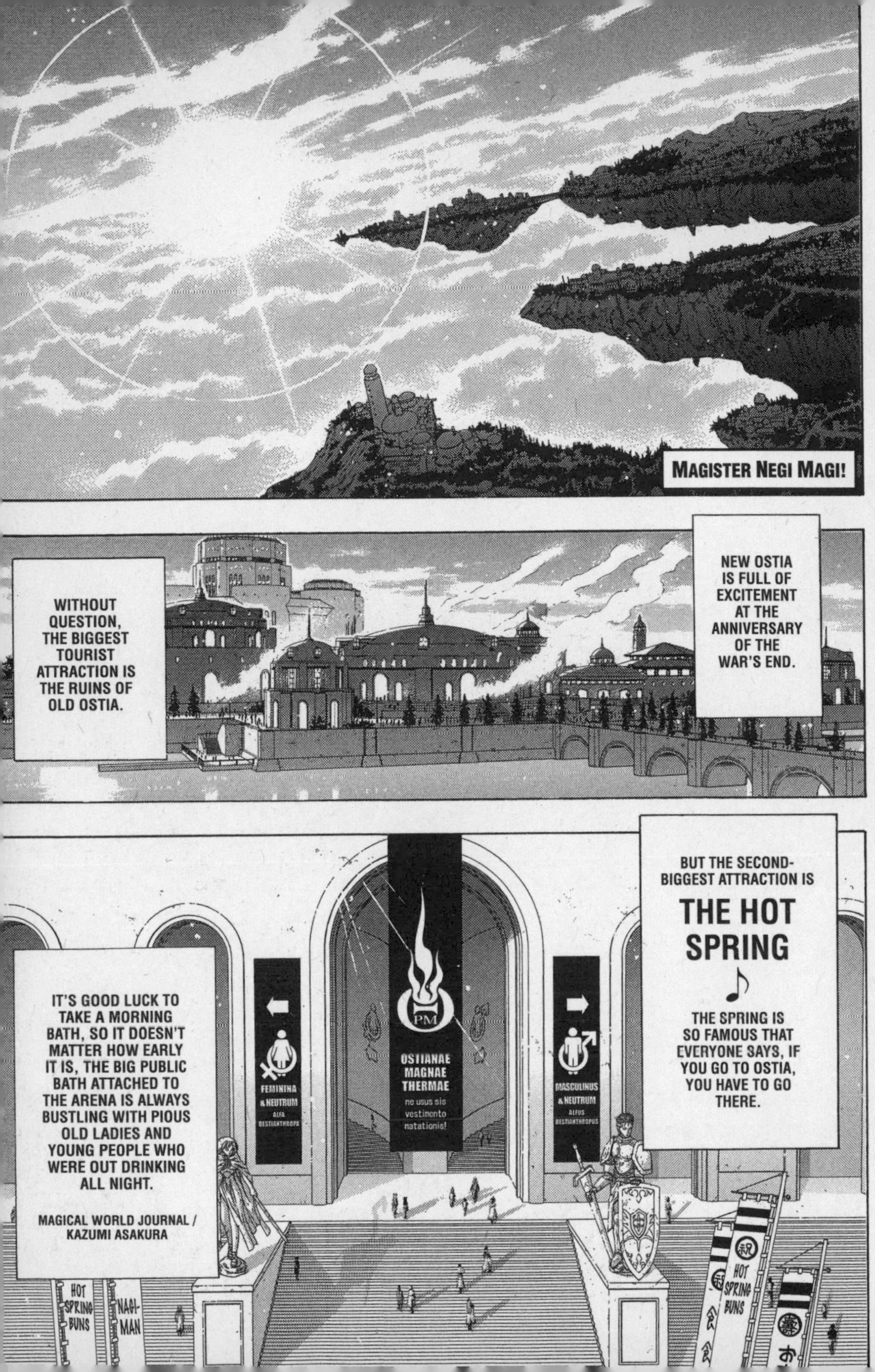
MAGISTER NEGI MAGI!
NEW OSTIA IS FULL OF EXCITEMENT AT THE ANNIVERSARY OF THE WAR'S END.
WITHOUT QUESTION, THE BIGGEST TOURIST ATTRACTION IS THE RUINS OF OLD OSTIA.
BUT THE SECOND-BIGGEST ATTRACTION IS
THE HOT SPRING ♪
THE SPRING IS SO FAMOUS THAT EVERYONE SAYS, IF YOU GO TO OSTIA, YOU HAVE TO GO THERE.
HOT SPRING BUNS
MASCULINUS & NEUTRUM ALFUS BESTIANTHROPUS
PM
OSTIANAE MAGNAE THERMAE
ne usus sis vestimento natationis!
FEMININA & NEUTRUM ALFA BESTIANTHROPA
IT'S GOOD LUCK TO TAKE A MORNING BATH, SO IT DOESN'T MATTER HOW EARLY IT IS, THE BIG PUBLIC BATH ATTACHED TO THE ARENA IS ALWAYS BUSTLING WITH PIOUS OLD LADIES AND YOUNG PEOPLE WHO WERE OUT DRINKING ALL NIGHT.
MAGICAL WORLD JOURNAL / KAZUMI ASAKURA
NAGI-MAN
HOT SPRING BUNS

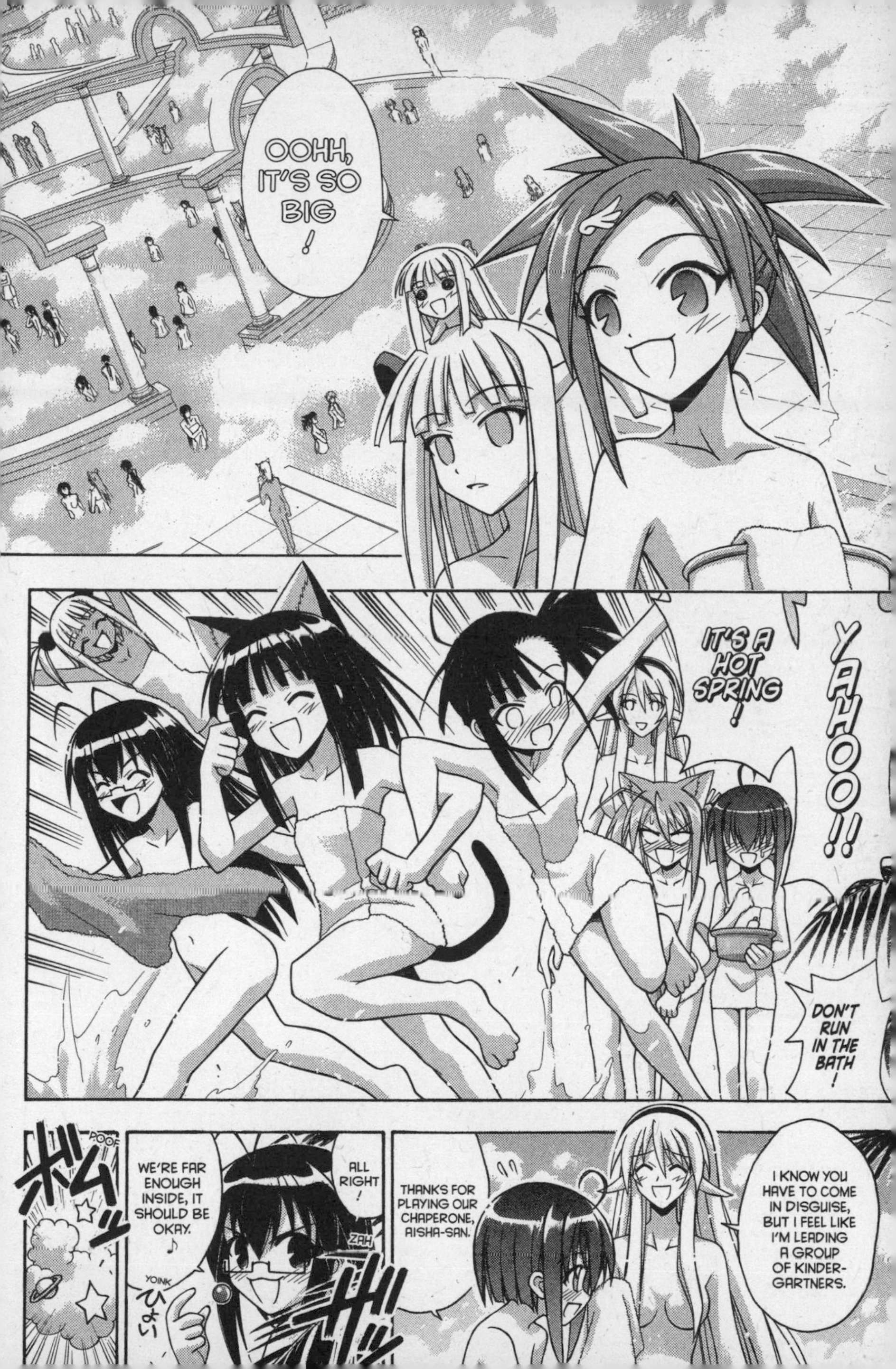
OOHH, IT'S SO BIG!
YAHOOO!!
IT'S A HOT SPRING!
DON'T RUN IN THE BATH!
I KNOW YOU HAVE TO COME IN DISGUISE, BUT I FEEL LIKE I'M LEADING A GROUP OF KINDER-GARTNERS.
THANKS FOR PLAYING OUR CHAPERONE, AISHA-SAN.
ALL RIGHT!
WE'RE FAR ENOUGH INSIDE, IT SHOULD BE OKAY. ♪
ZAH
YOINK
ひょい
POOF
ボムッ

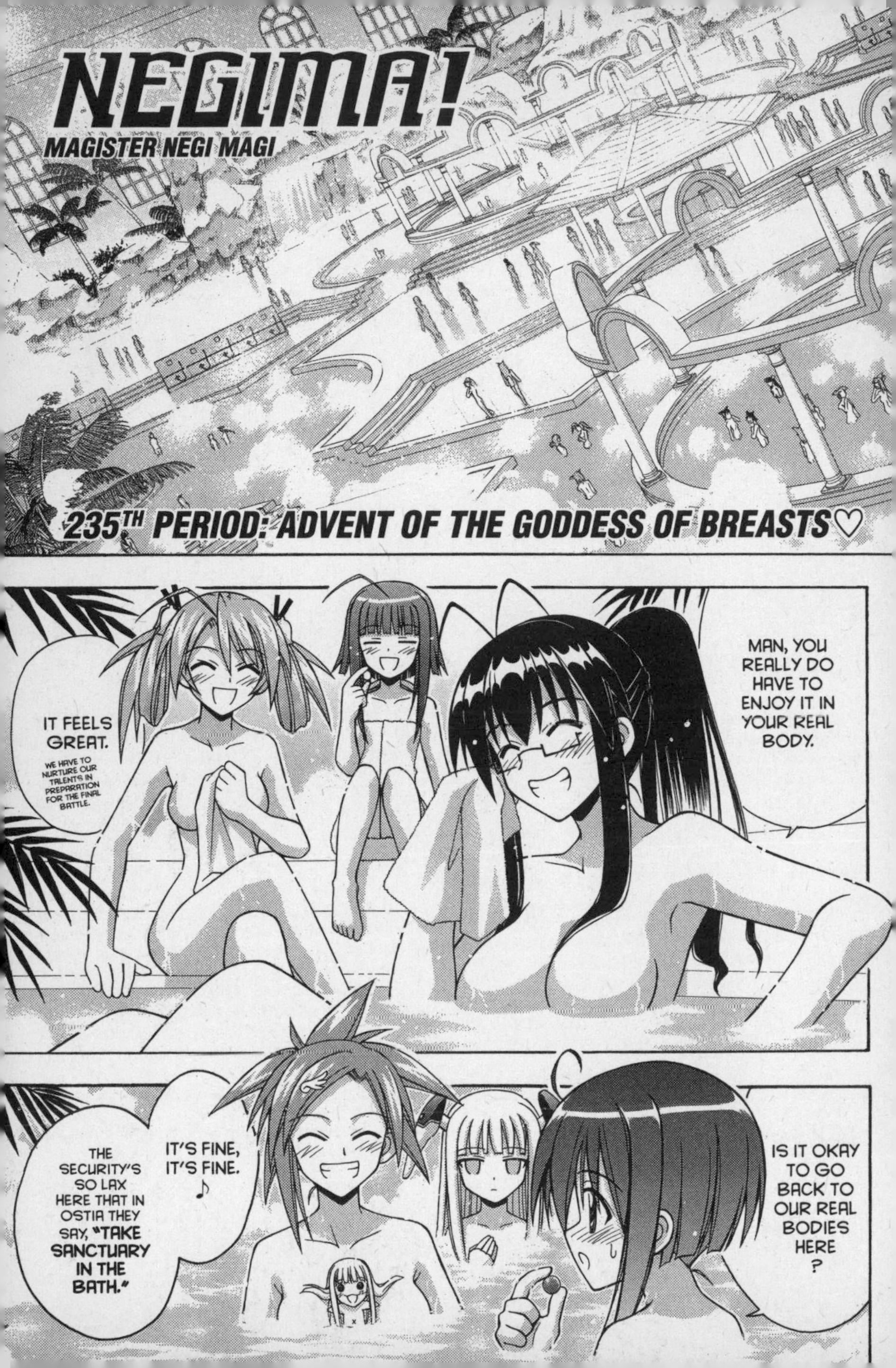
NEGIMA!
MAGISTER NEGI MAGI
235TH PERIOD: ADVENT OF THE GODDESS OF BREASTS♡
MAN, YOU REALLY DO HAVE TO ENJOY IT IN YOUR REAL BODY.
IT FEELS GREAT.
WE HAVE TO NURTURE OUR TALENTS IN PREPARATION FOR THE FINAL BATTLE.
IS IT OKAY TO GO BACK TO OUR REAL BODIES HERE?
IT'S FINE, IT'S FINE. ♪
THE SECURITY'S SO LAX HERE THAT IN OSTIA THEY SAY, "TAKE SANCTUARY IN THE BATH."

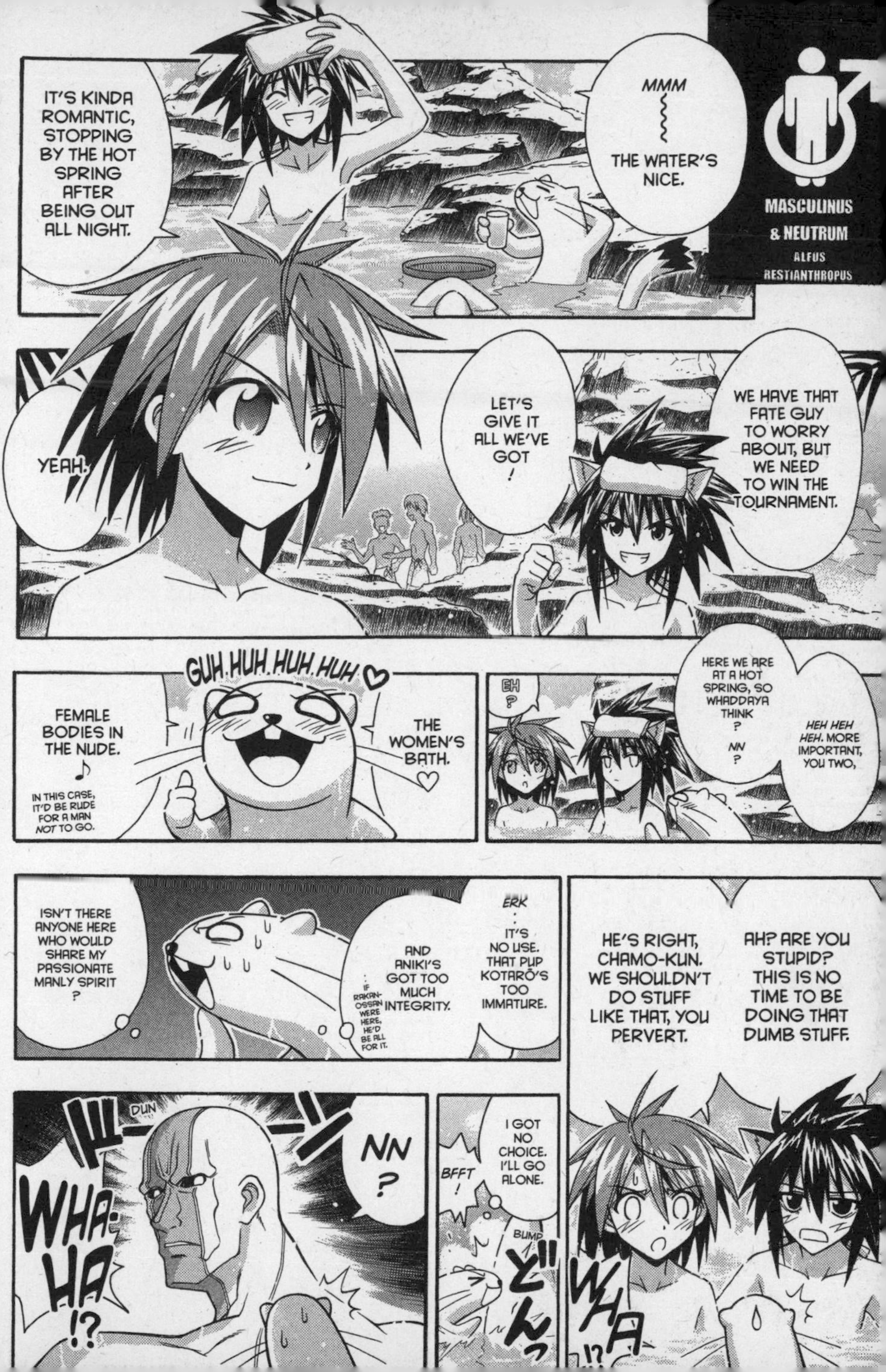
MASCULINUS
& NEUTRUM
ALFUS
RESTIANTHROPUS
MMM ~ THE WATER'S NICE.
IT'S KINDA ROMANTIC, STOPPING BY THE HOT SPRING AFTER BEING OUT ALL NIGHT.
WE HAVE THAT FATE GUY TO WORRY ABOUT, BUT WE NEED TO WIN THE TOURNAMENT.
LET'S GIVE IT ALL WE'VE GOT!
YEAH.
HEH HEH HEH. MORE IMPORTANT, YOU TWO,
HERE WE ARE AT A HOT SPRING, SO WHADDAYA THINK?
NN?
EH?
GUH HUH HUH HUH ♡
THE WOMEN'S BATH. ♡
FEMALE BODIES IN THE NUDE. ♪
IN THIS CASE, IT'D BE RUDE FOR A MAN NOT TO GO.
AH? ARE YOU STUPID? THIS IS NO TIME TO BE DOING THAT DUMB STUFF.
HE'S RIGHT, CHAMO-KUN. WE SHOULDN'T DO STUFF LIKE THAT, YOU PERVERT.
ERK...
IT'S NO USE. THAT PUP KOTARŌ'S TOO IMMATURE.
AND ANIKI'S GOT TOO MUCH INTEGRITY.
IF RAKAN-OSSAN WERE HERE, HE'D BE ALL FOR IT.
ISN'T THERE ANYONE HERE WHO WOULD SHARE MY PASSIONATE MANLY SPIRIT?
WHA!?
BUMP
どんっ
BFFT!
I GOT NO CHOICE. I'LL GO ALONE.
NN?
DUN
WHA-HA!?

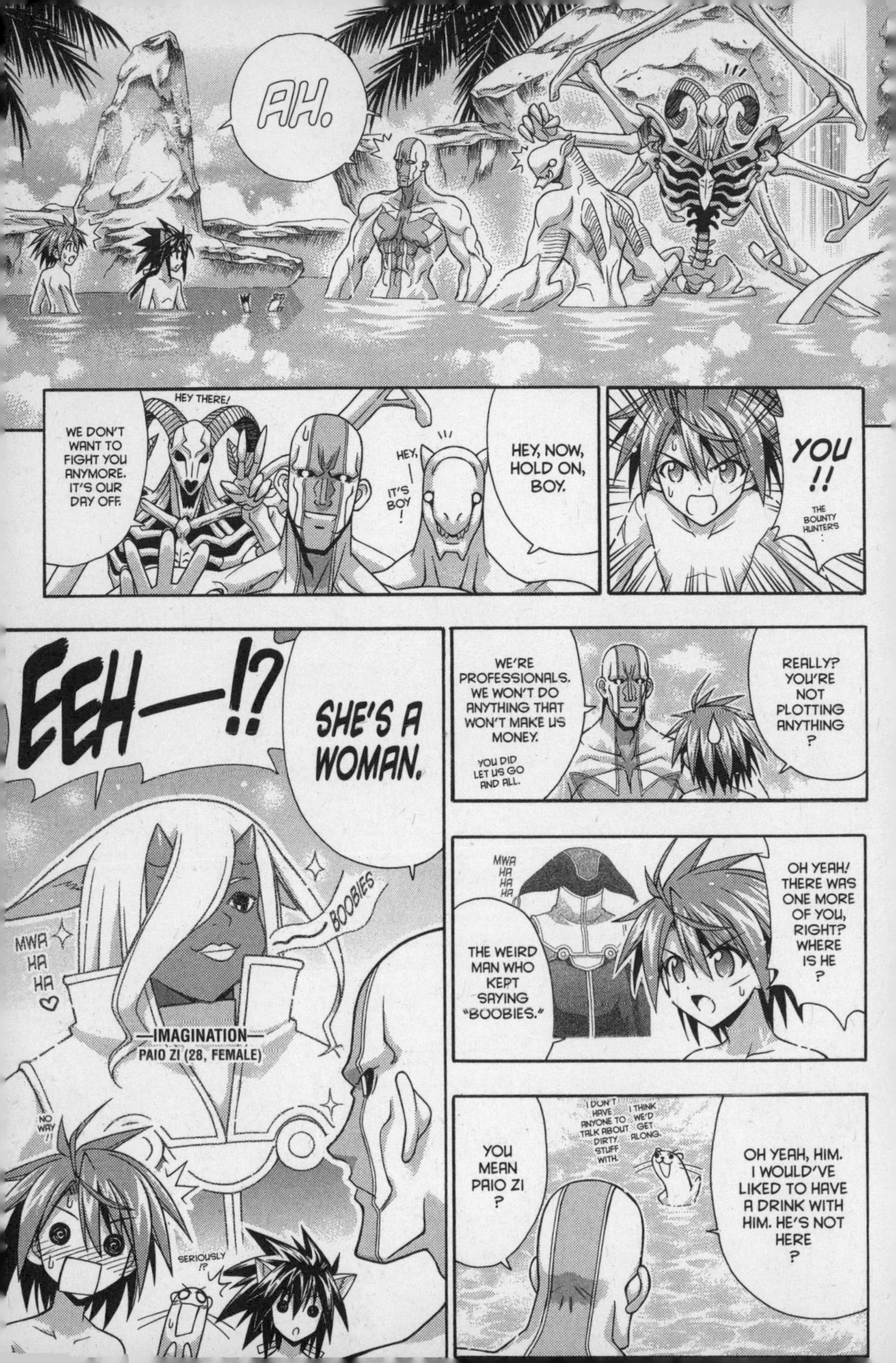
AH.
YOU !!
THE BOUNTY HUNTERS...
HEY, NOW, HOLD ON, BOY.
HEY, IT'S BOY!
HEY THERE!
WE DON'T WANT TO FIGHT YOU ANYMORE. IT'S OUR DAY OFF.
REALLY? YOU'RE NOT PLOTTING ANYTHING?
WE'RE PROFESSIONALS. WE WON'T DO ANYTHING THAT WON'T MAKE US MONEY.
YOU DID LET US GO AND ALL.
OH YEAH! THERE WAS ONE MORE OF YOU, RIGHT? WHERE IS HE?
MWA HA HA HA
THE WEIRD MAN WHO KEPT SAYING "BOOBIES."
OH YEAH, HIM. I WOULD'VE LIKED TO HAVE A DRINK WITH HIM. HE'S NOT HERE?
I THINK WE'D GET ALONG.
I DON'T HAVE ANYONE TO TALK ABOUT DIRTY STUFF WITH.
YOU MEAN PAIO ZI?
SHE'S A WOMAN.
EEH—!?
BOOBIES
MWA HA HA ♡
—IMAGINATION— PAIO ZI (28, FEMALE)
NO WAY!!
SERIOUSLY!?

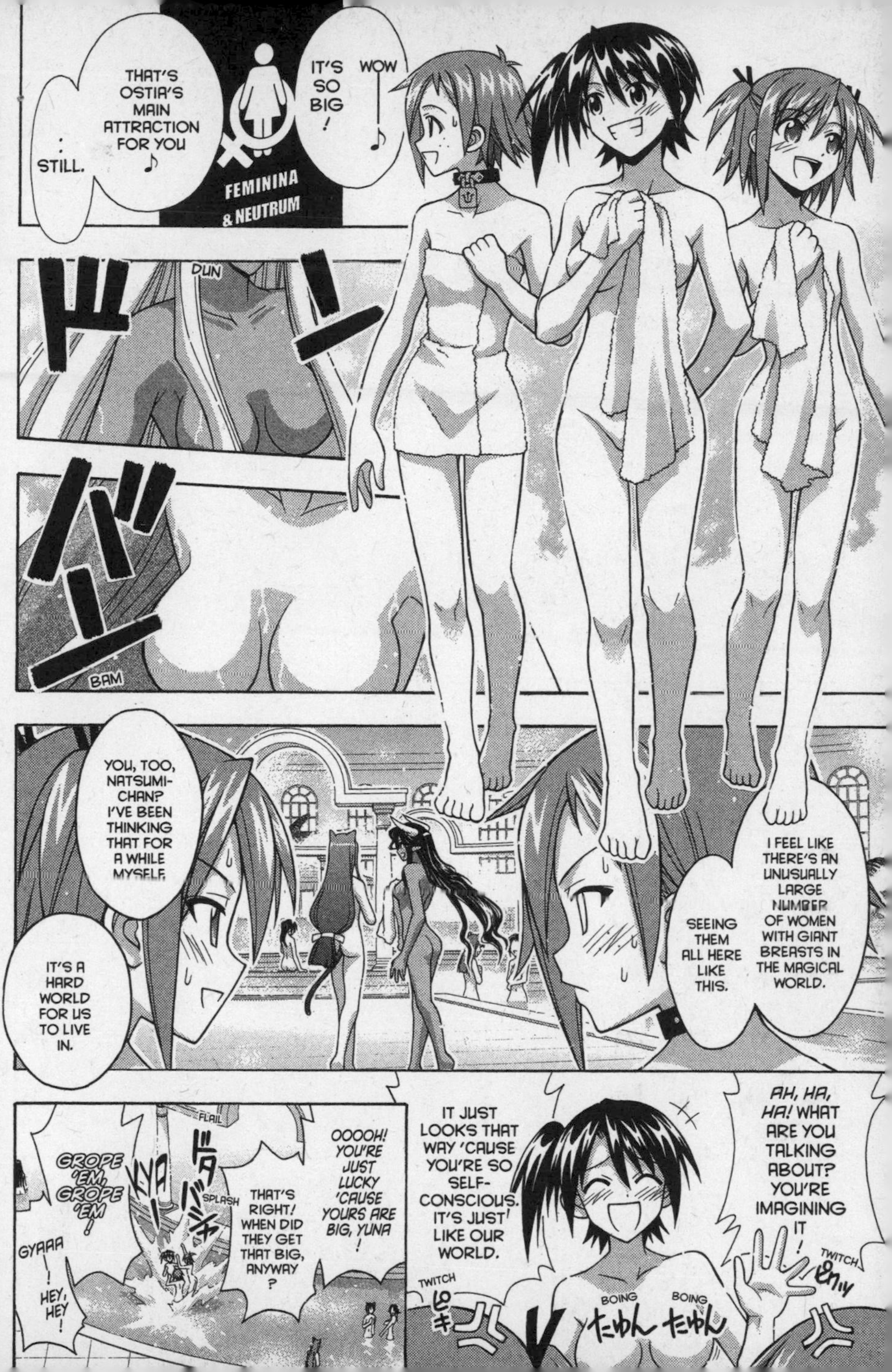
FEMININA & NEUTRUM
WOW ♪
IT'S SO BIG!
THAT'S OSTIA'S MAIN ATTRACTION FOR YOU ♪
: STILL.
DUN
BAM
I FEEL LIKE THERE'S AN UNUSUALLY LARGE NUMBER OF WOMEN WITH GIANT BREASTS IN THE MAGICAL WORLD.
SEEING THEM ALL HERE LIKE THIS.
YOU, TOO, NATSUMI-CHAN? I'VE BEEN THINKING THAT FOR A WHILE MYSELF.
IT'S A HARD WORLD FOR US TO LIVE IN.
AH, HA, HA! WHAT ARE YOU TALKING ABOUT? YOU'RE IMAGINING IT!
TWITCH
IT JUST LOOKS THAT WAY 'CAUSE YOU'RE SO SELF-CONSCIOUS. IT'S JUST LIKE OUR WORLD.
BOING たゆん BOING たゆん
TWITCH
OOOOH! YOU'RE JUST LUCKY 'CAUSE YOURS ARE BIG, YUNA!
THAT'S RIGHT! WHEN DID THEY GET THAT BIG, ANYWAY?
FLAIL
SPLASH
KYA!
GROPE 'EM, GROPE 'EM!
GYAAA!
HEY, HEY!

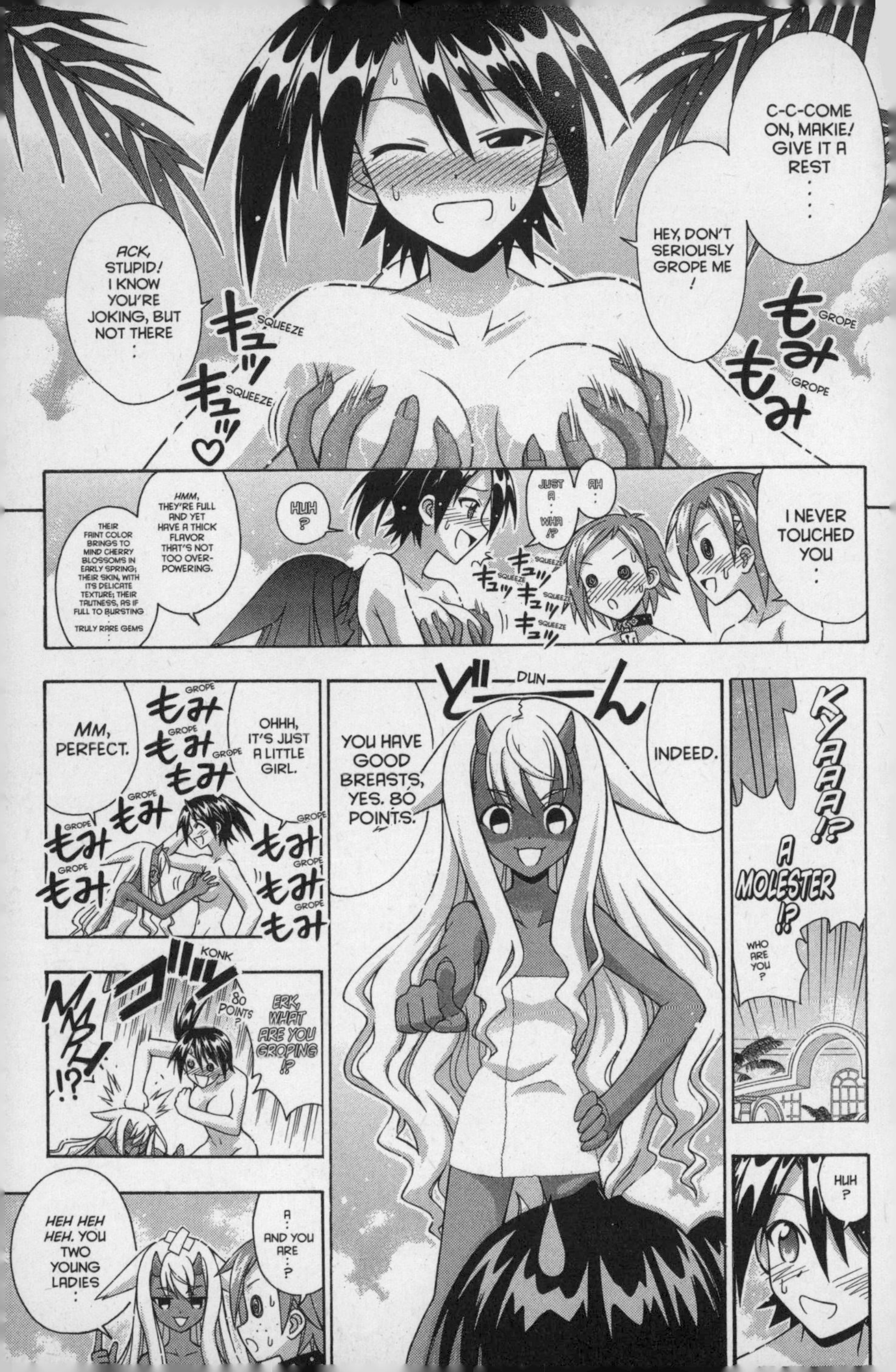

C-C-COME ON, MAKIE! GIVE IT A REST . . . .
HEY, DON'T SERIOUSLY GROPE ME !
もみ GROPE もみ GROPE
ACK, STUPID! I KNOW YOU'RE JOKING, BUT NOT THERE . . .
キュッ SQUEEZE キュッ SQUEEZE ♡
I NEVER TOUCHED YOU . . .
AH . . .
JUST A . . . WHA !?
キュッ SQUEEZE キュッ SQUEEZE キュッ SQUEEZE キュッ SQUEEZE
HUH ?
HMM, THEY'RE FULL AND YET HAVE A THICK FLAVOR THAT'S NOT TOO OVER-POWERING.
THEIR FAINT COLOR BRINGS TO MIND CHERRY BLOSSOMS IN EARLY SPRING; THEIR SKIN, WITH ITS DELICATE TEXTURE; THEIR TAUTNESS, AS IF FULL TO BURSTING
TRULY RARE GEMS
KYAAAA!?
A MOLESTER !?
WHO ARE YOU ?
HUH ?
どーーん DUN
INDEED.
YOU HAVE GOOD BREASTS, YES. 80 POINTS.
OHHH, IT'S JUST A LITTLE GIRL.
MM, PERFECT.
もみ GROPE もみ GROPE もみ GROPE もみ GROPE もみ GROPE もみ GROPE もみ GROPE もみ GROPE もみ GROPE もみ GROPE
ERK, WHAT ARE YOU GROPING !?
80 POINTS ?
ゴッ KONK
MMPH !?
A . . . AND YOU ARE . . . ?
HEH HEH HEH. YOU TWO YOUNG LADIES . . .

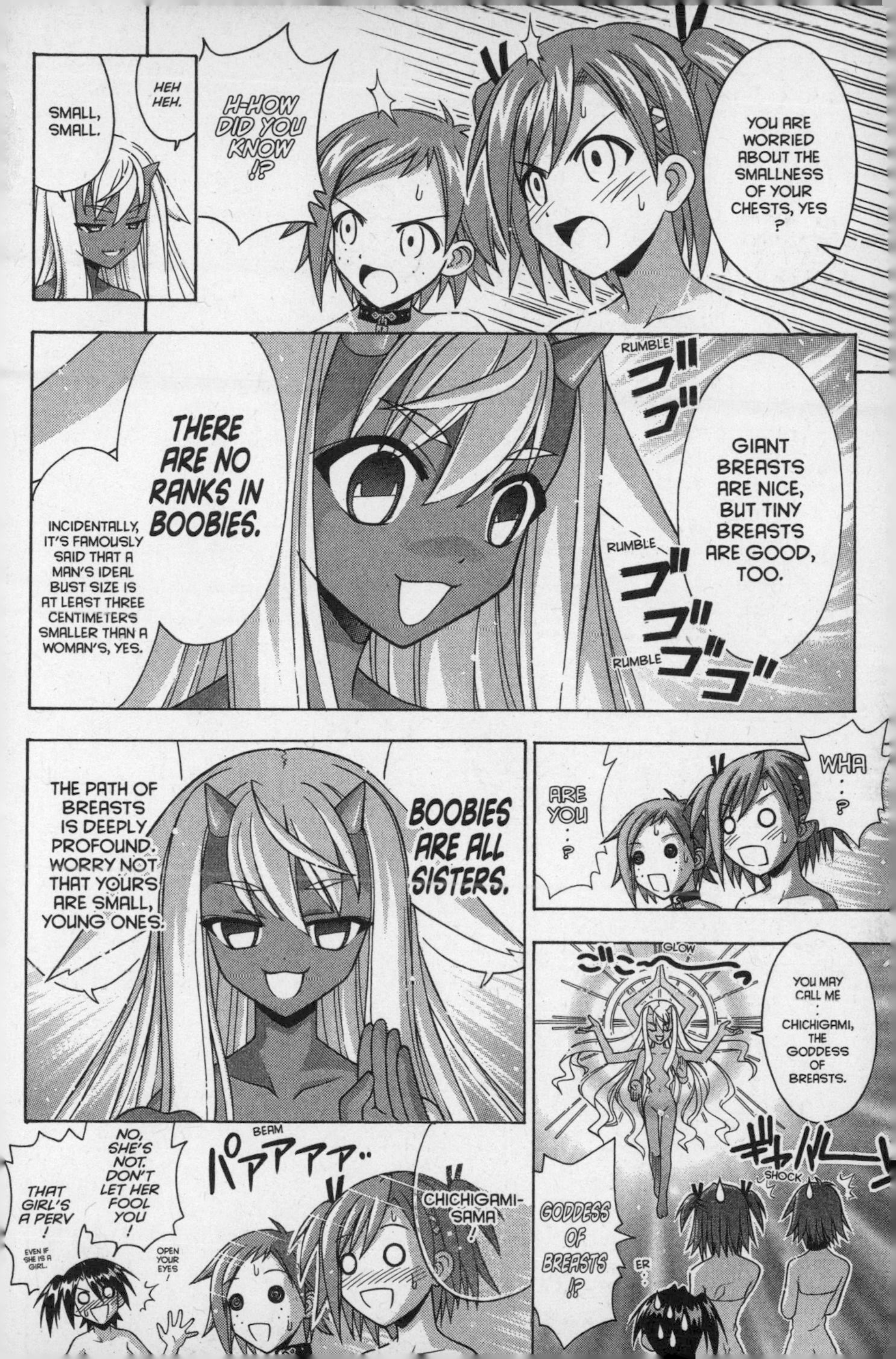
YOU ARE WORRIED ABOUT THE SMALLNESS OF YOUR CHESTS, YES?
H-HOW DID YOU KNOW!?
HEH HEH.
SMALL, SMALL.
RUMBLE
GIANT BREASTS ARE NICE, BUT TINY BREASTS ARE GOOD, TOO.
RUMBLE
RUMBLE
THERE ARE NO RANKS IN BOOBIES.
INCIDENTALLY, IT'S FAMOUSLY SAID THAT A MAN'S IDEAL BUST SIZE IS AT LEAST THREE CENTIMETERS SMALLER THAN A WOMAN'S, YES.
WHA...?
ARE YOU...?
GLOW
YOU MAY CALL ME: CHICHIGAMI, THE GODDESS OF BREASTS.
SHOCK
GODDESS OF BREASTS!?
ER
BOOBIES ARE ALL SISTERS.
THE PATH OF BREASTS IS DEEPLY PROFOUND. WORRY NOT THAT YOURS ARE SMALL, YOUNG ONES.
BEAM
CHICHIGAMI-SAMA!
NO, SHE'S NOT. DON'T LET HER FOOL YOU!
OPEN YOUR EYES!
THAT GIRL'S A PERV!
EVEN IF SHE IS A GIRL.

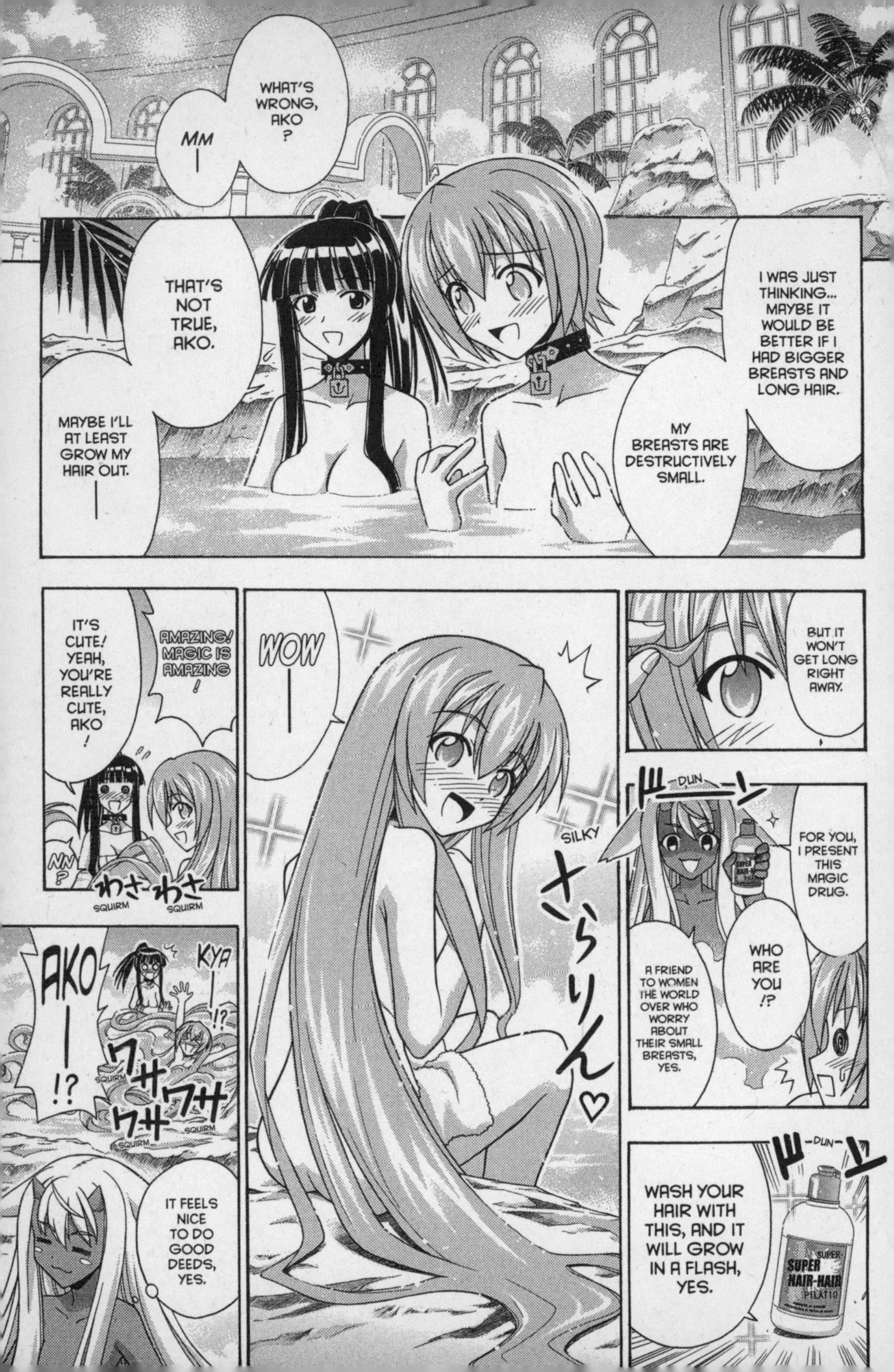

WHAT'S WRONG, AKO?
MM—
I WAS JUST THINKING... MAYBE IT WOULD BE BETTER IF I HAD BIGGER BREASTS AND LONG HAIR.
MY BREASTS ARE DESTRUCTIVELY SMALL.
THAT'S NOT TRUE, AKO.
MAYBE I'LL AT LEAST GROW MY HAIR OUT—
BUT IT WON'T GET LONG RIGHT AWAY.
DUN
FOR YOU, I PRESENT THIS MAGIC DRUG.
WHO ARE YOU!?
A FRIEND TO WOMEN THE WORLD OVER WHO WORRY ABOUT THEIR SMALL BREASTS, YES.
DUN
WASH YOUR HAIR WITH THIS, AND IT WILL GROW IN A FLASH, YES.
SUPER SUPER HAIR-HAIR PILATIO
WOW—
さらりん♡
SILKY
AMAZING! MAGIC IS AMAZING!
IT'S CUTE! YEAH, YOU'RE REALLY CUTE, AKO!
NN?
わさわさ
SQUIRM SQUIRM
KYA—!?
AKO—!?
ワサワサワサ
SQUIRM SQUIRM SQUIRM
IT FEELS NICE TO DO GOOD DEEDS, YES.

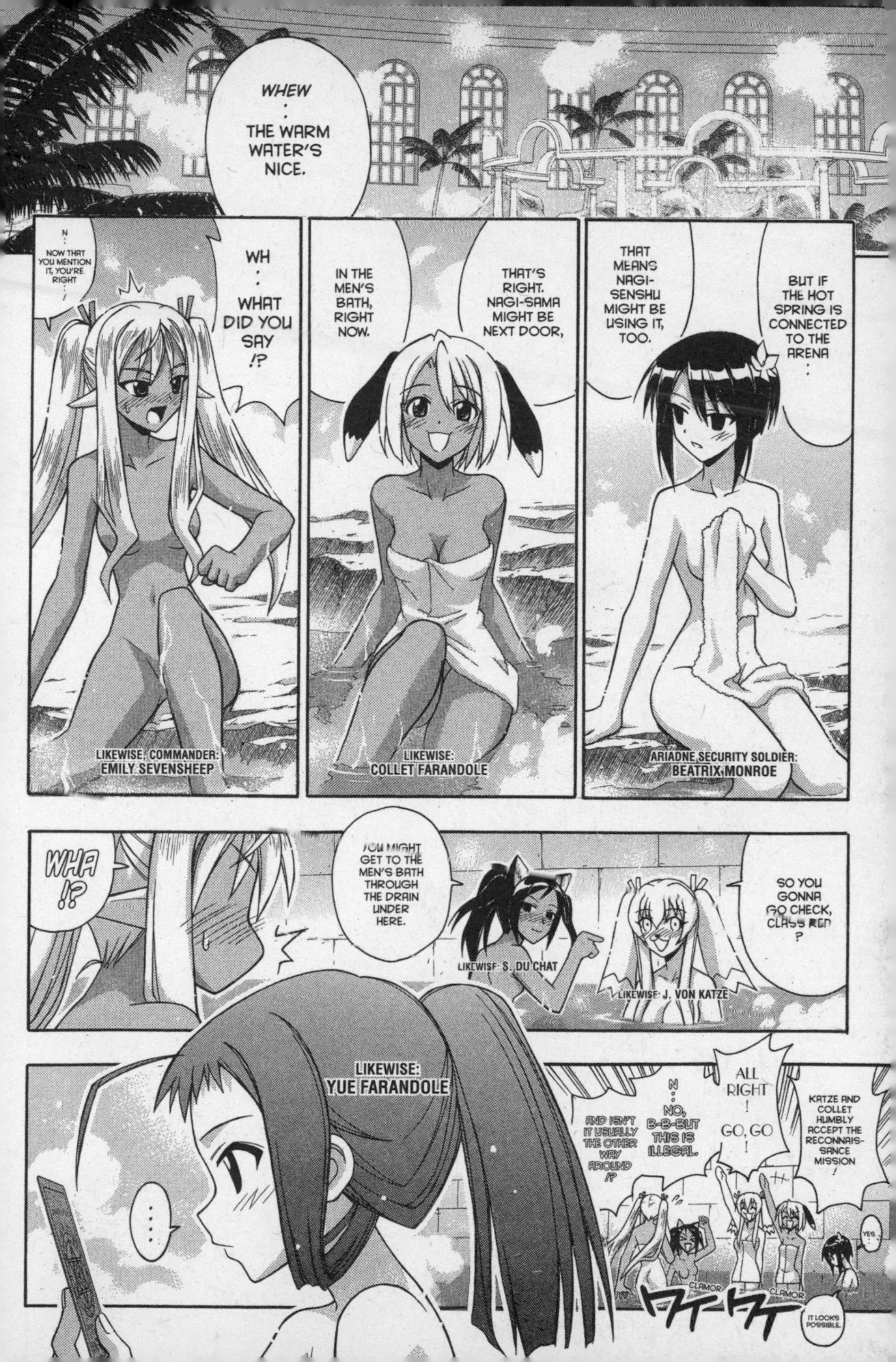

WHEW... THE WARM WATER'S NICE.
BUT IF THE HOT SPRING IS CONNECTED TO THE ARENA...
THAT MEANS NAGI-SENSHU MIGHT BE USING IT, TOO.
ARIADNE SECURITY SOLDIER: BEATRIX MONROE
THAT'S RIGHT. NAGI-SAMA MIGHT BE NEXT DOOR,
IN THE MEN'S BATH, RIGHT NOW.
LIKEWISE: COLLET FARANDOLE
WH... WHAT DID YOU SAY !?
N... NOW THAT YOU MENTION IT, YOU'RE RIGHT...!
LIKEWISE: COMMANDER: EMILY SEVENSHEEP
SO YOU GONNA GO CHECK, CLASS REP ?
LIKEWISE: J. VON KATZE
YOU MIGHT GET TO THE MEN'S BATH THROUGH THE DRAIN UNDER HERE.
LIKEWISE: S. DU CHAT
WHA !?
KATZE AND COLLET HUMBLY ACCEPT THE RECONNAISSANCE MISSION
ALL RIGHT! GO, GO!
N... NO, B-B-BUT THIS IS ILLEGAL.
AND ISN'T IT USUALLY THE OTHER WAY AROUND !?
YES...
CLAMOR CLAMOR
IT LOOKS POSSIBLE.
LIKEWISE: YUE FARANDOLE
....

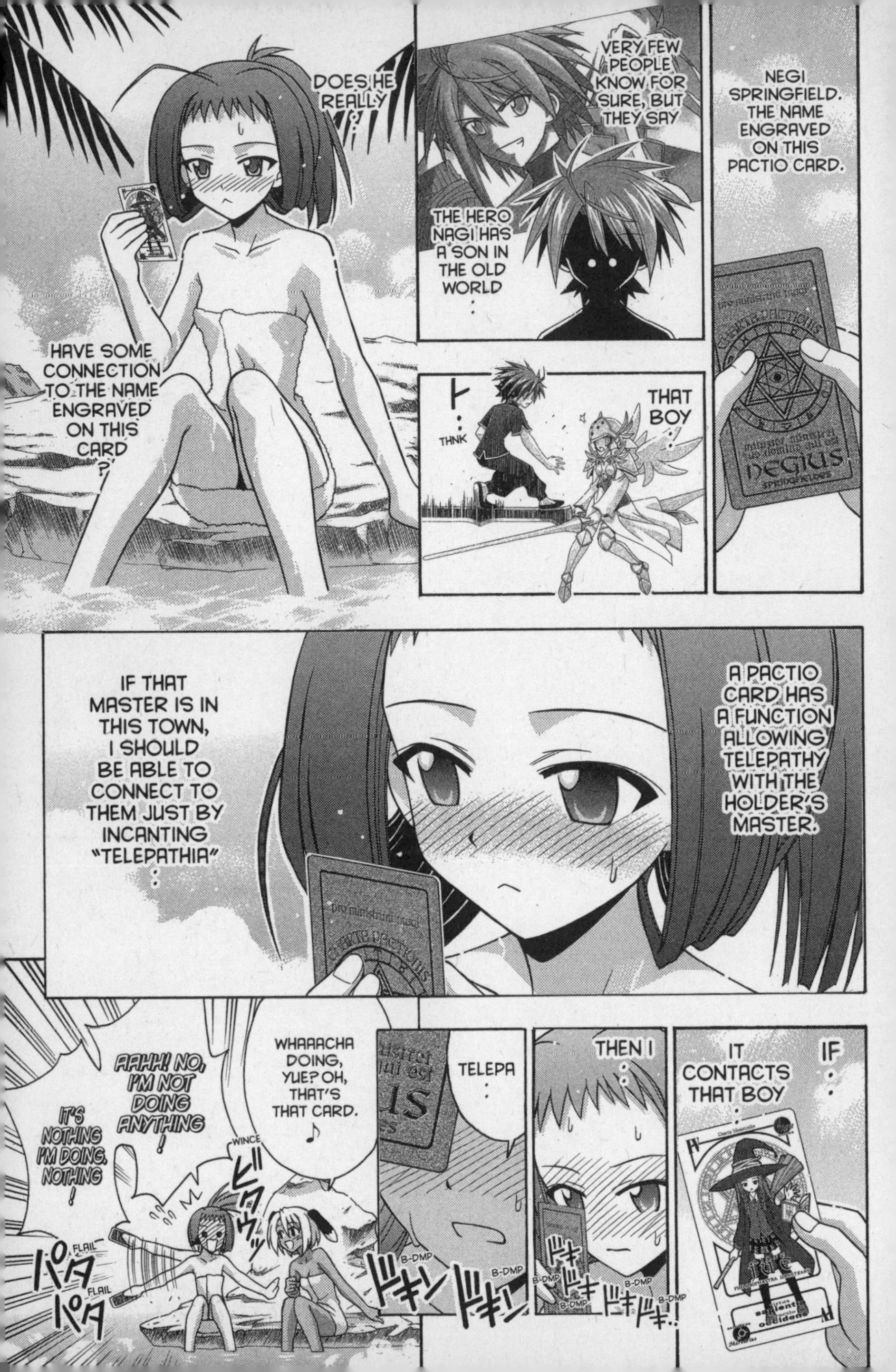
NEGI SPRINGFIELD. THE NAME ENGRAVED ON THIS PACTIO CARD.
VERY FEW PEOPLE KNOW FOR SURE, BUT THEY SAY
THE HERO NAGI HAS A SON IN THE OLD WORLD . .
THAT BOY . . .
THNK
DOES HE REALLY . . .
HAVE SOME CONNECTION TO THE NAME ENGRAVED ON THIS CARD?
A PACTIO CARD HAS A FUNCTION ALLOWING TELEPATHY WITH THE HOLDER'S MASTER.
IF THAT MASTER IS IN THIS TOWN, I SHOULD BE ABLE TO CONNECT TO THEM JUST BY INCANTING "TELEPATHIA" . .
IF . .
IT CONTACTS THAT BOY . .
THEN I . .
B-DMP
B-DMP
B-DMP
TELEPA . .
B-DMP
B-DMP
WHAAACHA DOING, YUE? OH, THAT'S THAT CARD. ♪
WINCE
AAHH! NO, I'M NOT DOING ANYTHING!
IT'S NOTHING I'M DOING, NOTHING!
FLAIL
FLAIL

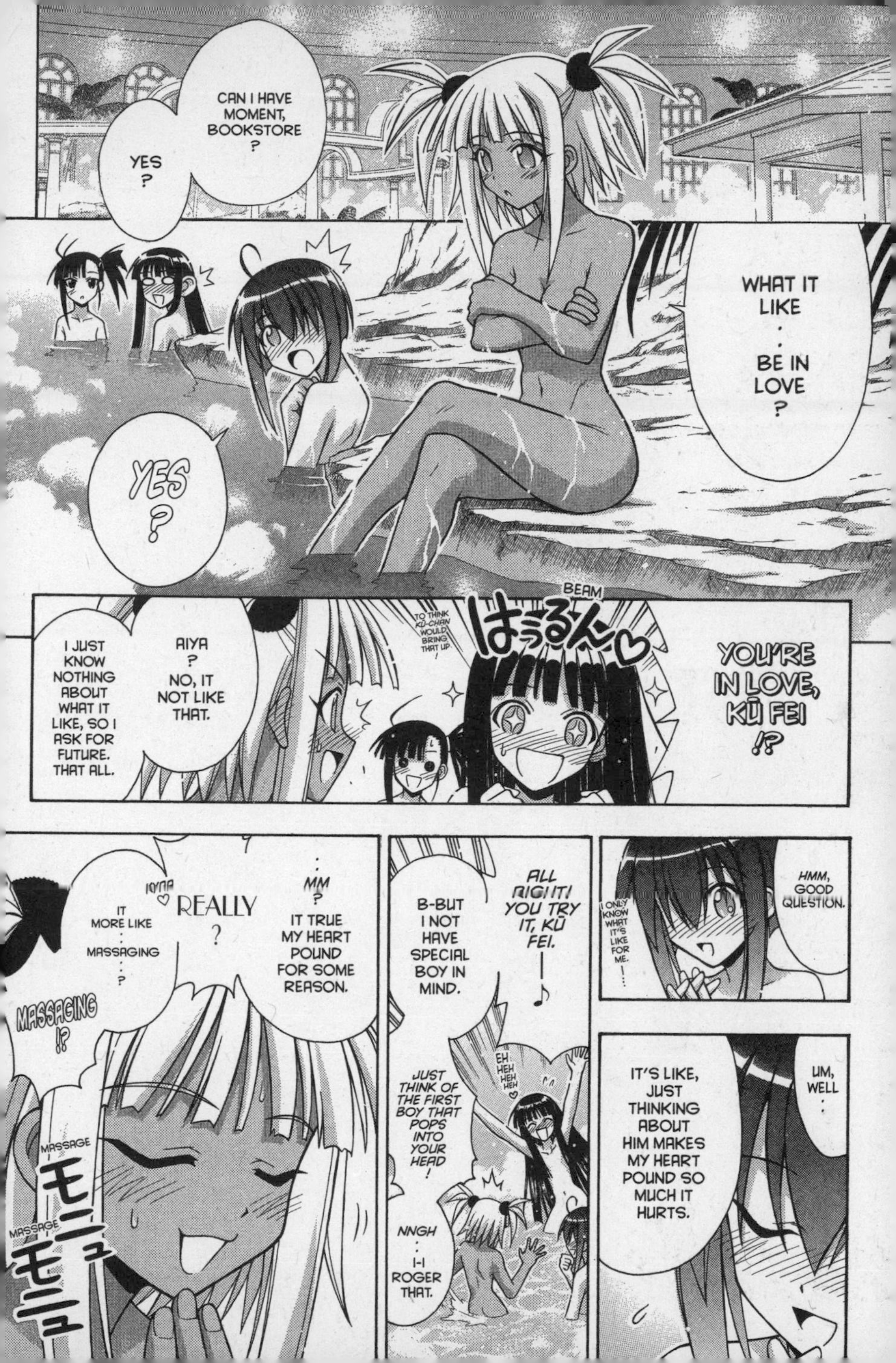
CAN I HAVE MOMENT, BOOKSTORE ?
YES ?
WHAT IT LIKE . . BE IN LOVE ?
YES ?
YOU'RE IN LOVE, KŪ FEI !?
BEAM
はぅるん♥
TO THINK KŪ-CHAN WOULD BRING THAT UP. !
AIYA ? NO, IT NOT LIKE THAT.
I JUST KNOW NOTHING ABOUT WHAT IT LIKE, SO I ASK FOR FUTURE. THAT ALL.
HMM, GOOD QUESTION.
I ONLY KNOW WHAT IT'S LIKE FOR ME. . . .
UM, WELL . .
IT'S LIKE, JUST THINKING ABOUT HIM MAKES MY HEART POUND SO MUCH IT HURTS.
ALL RIGHT! YOU TRY IT, KŪ FEI. ! ♪
B-BUT I NOT HAVE SPECIAL BOY IN MIND.
EH HEH HEH HEH
JUST THINK OF THE FIRST BOY THAT POPS INTO YOUR HEAD !
NNGH . . I-I ROGER THAT.
. . MM ? IT TRUE MY HEART POUND FOR SOME REASON.
REALLY ?
IT MORE LIKE . . . MASSAGING . . ?
MASSAGING !?
MASSAGE
モニュ
MASSAGE
モニュ

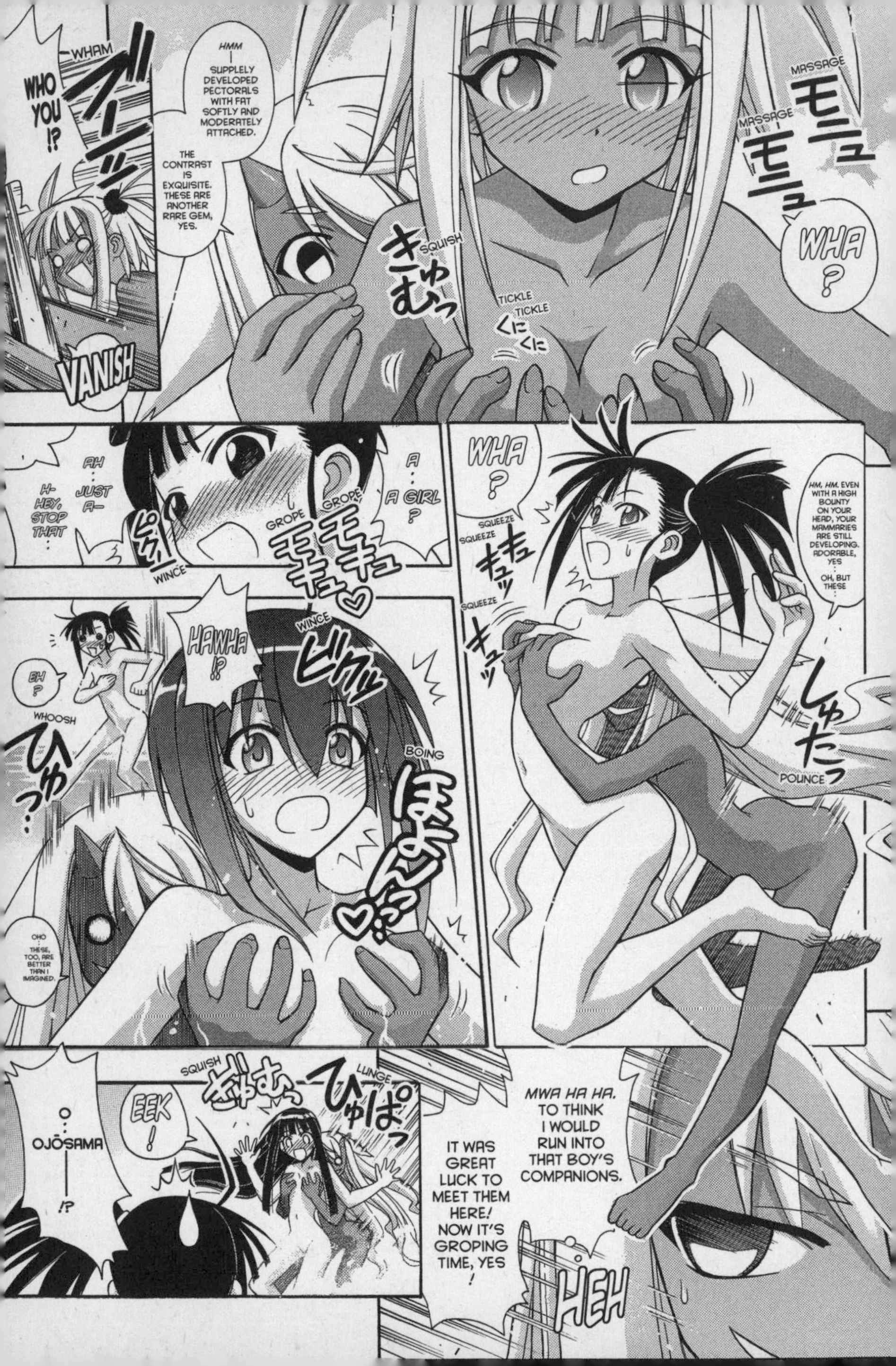
MASSAGE
MASSAGE
WHA ?
SQUISH
TICKLE TICKLE
HMM I SUPPLELY DEVELOPED PECTORALS WITH FAT SOFTLY AND MODERATELY ATTACHED.
THE CONTRAST IS EXQUISITE. THESE ARE ANOTHER RARE GEM, YES.
WHAM
WHO YOU !?
VANISH
WHA ?
HM, HM. EVEN WITH A HIGH BOUNTY ON YOUR HEAD, YOUR MAMMARIES ARE STILL DEVELOPING. ADORABLE, YES
OH, BUT THESE...
SQUEEZE
SQUEEZE
SQUEEZE
POUNCE
A... A GIRL ?
GROPE
GROPE
AH... JUST A–
H-HEY, STOP THAT...
WINCE
HAWHA !?
WINCE
BOING
EH ?
WHOOSH
OHO THESE, TOO, ARE BETTER THAN I IMAGINED.
MWA HA HA. TO THINK I WOULD RUN INTO THAT BOY'S COMPANIONS.
IT WAS GREAT LUCK TO MEET THEM HERE! NOW IT'S GROPING TIME, YES !
HEH
LUNGE
SQUISH
EEK !
O... OJŌSAMA —— !?

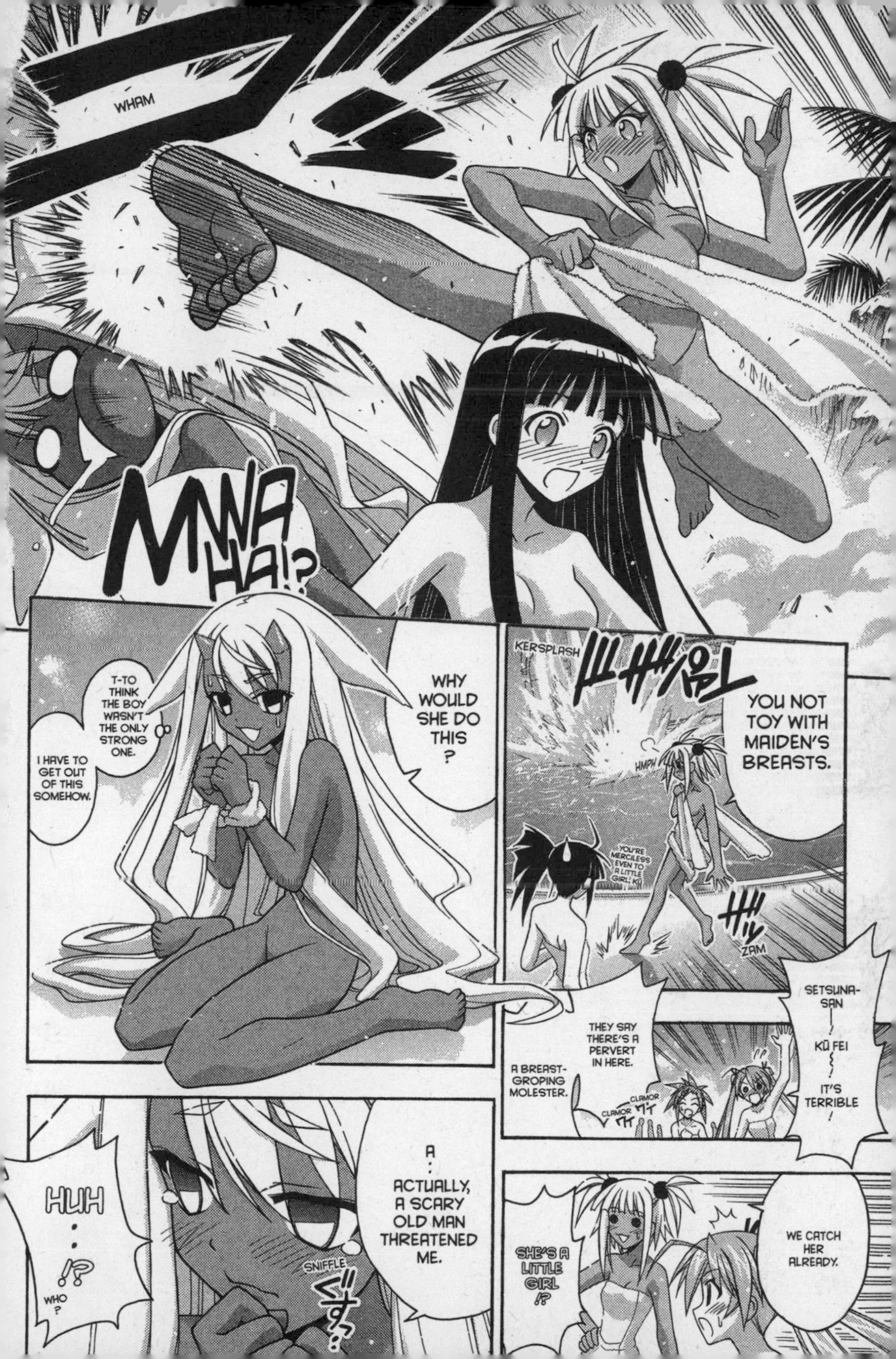
WHAM
MANA HA!?
KERSPLASH
YOU NOT TOY WITH MAIDEN'S BREASTS.
HMPH
YOU'RE MERCILESS EVEN TO A LITTLE GIRL! KI
ZAM
SETSUNA-SAN! KŪ FEI! IT'S TERRIBLE!
THEY SAY THERE'S A PERVERT IN HERE.
A BREAST-GROPING MOLESTER.
CLAMOR CLAMOR
WHY WOULD SHE DO THIS?
T-TO THINK THE BOY WASN'T THE ONLY STRONG ONE.
I HAVE TO GET OUT OF THIS SOMEHOW.
WE CATCH HER ALREADY.
SHE'S A LITTLE GIRL!?
A... ACTUALLY, A SCARY OLD MAN THREATENED ME.
SNIFFLE
HUH...!?
WHO?

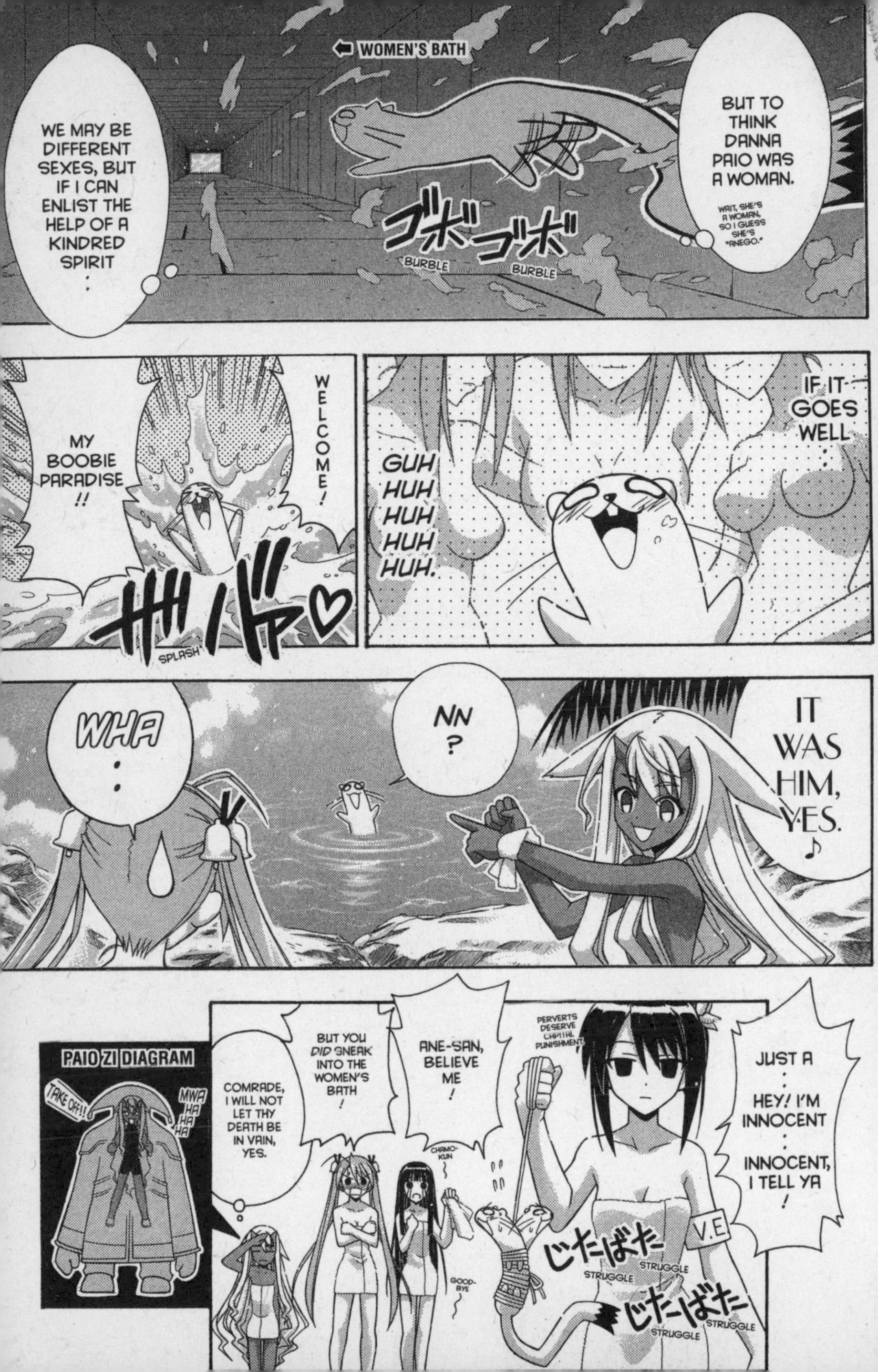
BUT TO THINK DANNA PAIO WAS A WOMAN.
WAIT, SHE'S A WOMAN, SO I GUESS SHE'S "ANEGO."
WOMEN'S BATH
ゴボゴボ
BURBLE BURBLE
WE MAY BE DIFFERENT SEXES, BUT IF I CAN ENLIST THE HELP OF A KINDRED SPIRIT
IF IT GOES WELL
GUH HUH HUH HUH HUH.
WELCOME!
MY BOOBIE PARADISE!!
ザバァ♡
SPLASH
IT WAS HIM, YES. ♪
NN?
WHA
JUST A
HEY! I'M INNOCENT
INNOCENT, I TELL YA!
PERVERTS DESERVE CAPITAL PUNISHMENT
V.E
じたばた
STRUGGLE STRUGGLE
じたばた
STRUGGLE STRUGGLE
ANE-SAN, BELIEVE ME!
CHAMO-KUN
BUT YOU DID SNEAK INTO THE WOMEN'S BATH!
GOOD-BYE
COMRADE, I WILL NOT LET THY DEATH BE IN VAIN, YES.
PAIO ZI DIAGRAM
MWA HA HA HA
TAKE OFF!!

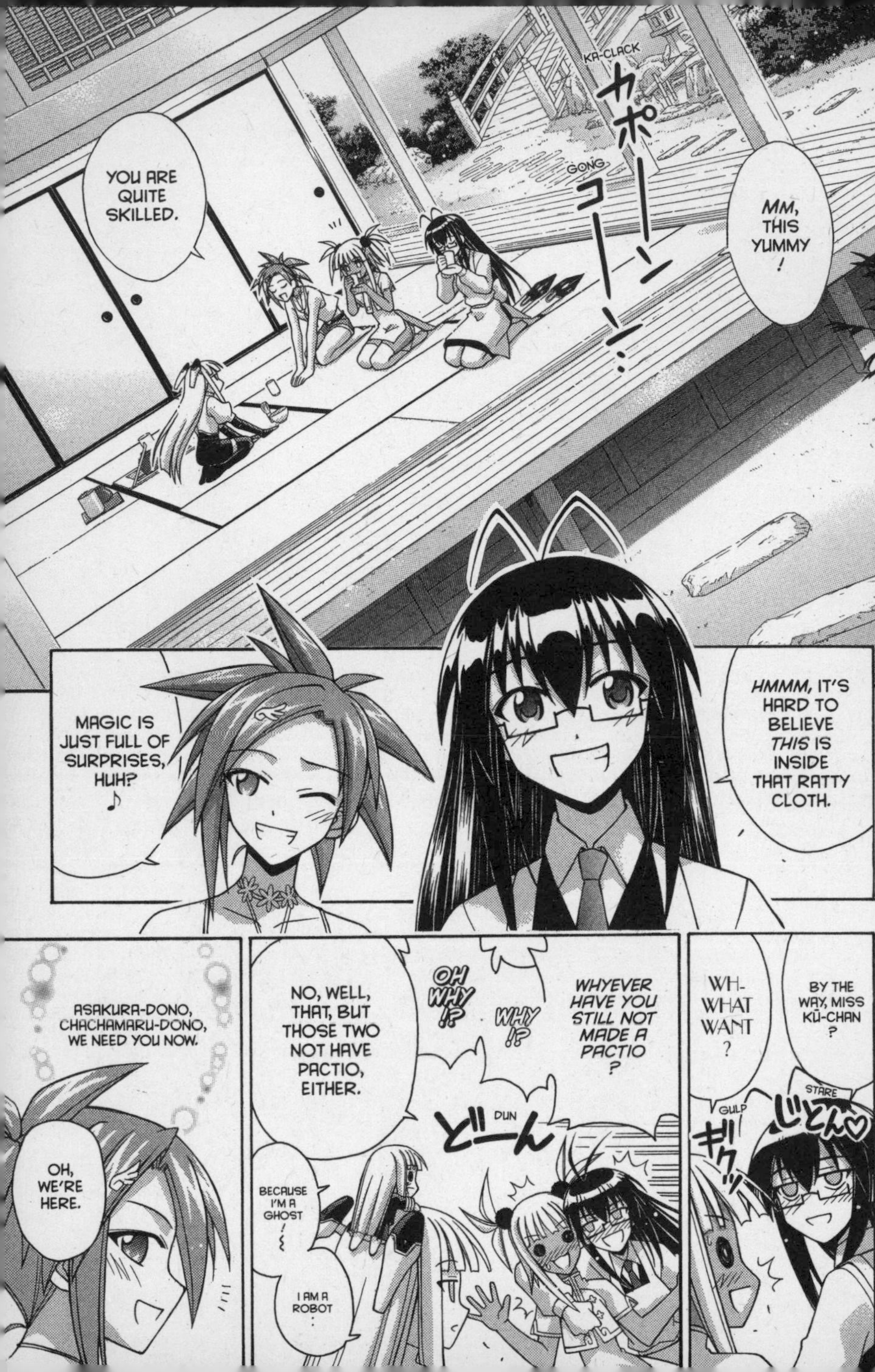
KA-CLACK
カポーン
GONG
コーン…
MM, THIS YUMMY!
YOU ARE QUITE SKILLED.
HMMM, IT'S HARD TO BELIEVE *THIS* IS INSIDE THAT RATTY CLOTH.
MAGIC IS JUST FULL OF SURPRISES, HUH? ♪
BY THE WAY, MISS KŪ-CHAN?
WH- WHAT WANT?
STARE
じとん♡
GULP
ギクッ
WHYEVER HAVE YOU STILL NOT MADE A PACTIO?
WHY!?
OH WHY!?
NO, WELL, THAT, BUT THOSE TWO NOT HAVE PACTIO, EITHER.
DUN
どーん
BECAUSE I'M A GHOST!
I AM A ROBOT
ASAKURA-DONO, CHACHAMARU-DONO, WE NEED YOU NOW.
OH, WE'RE HERE.

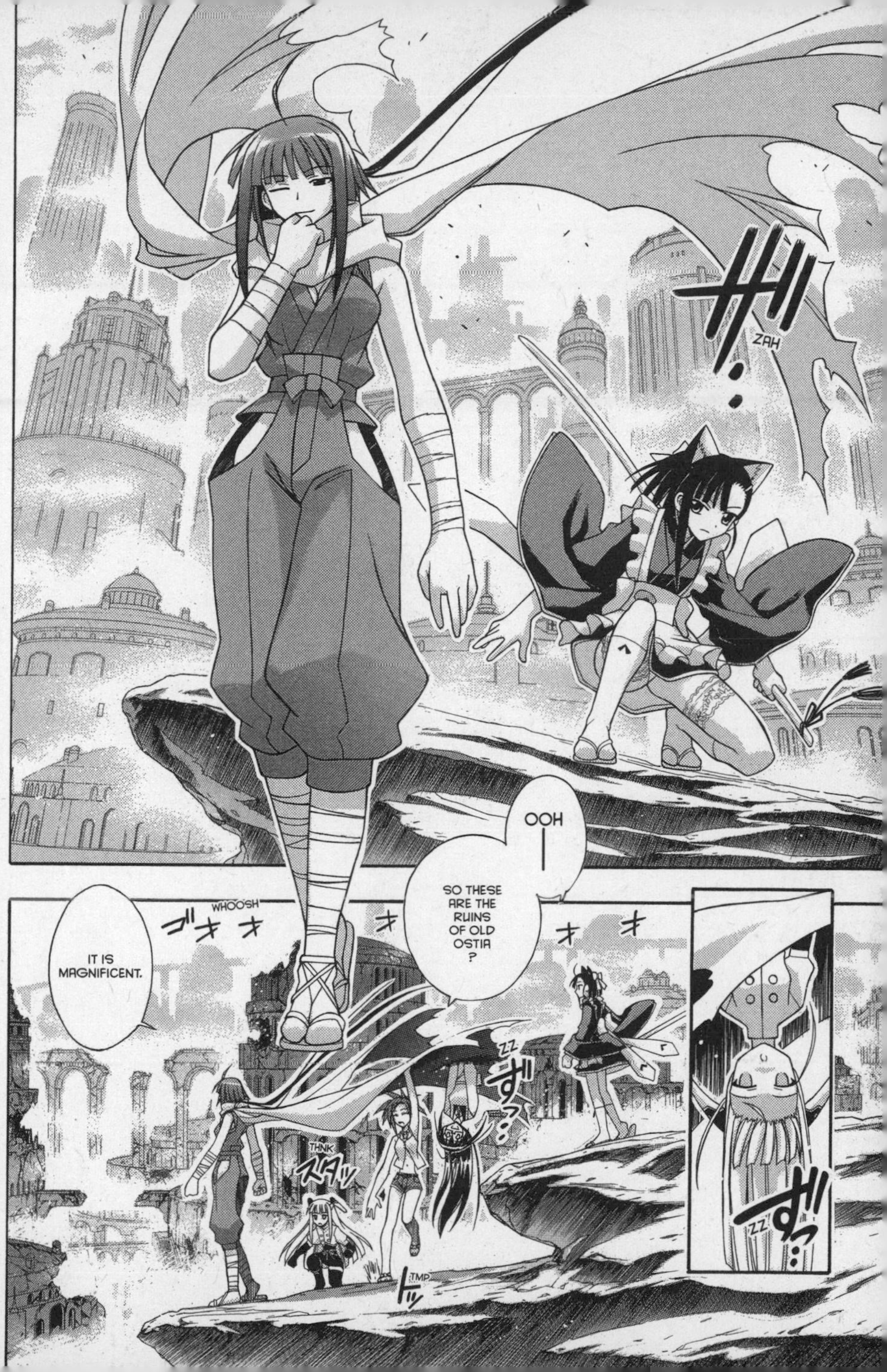
ZAH
ZZ
OOH —
SO THESE ARE THE RUINS OF OLD OSTIA?
WHOOSH
IT IS MAGNIFICENT.
ZZ
THNK
TMP

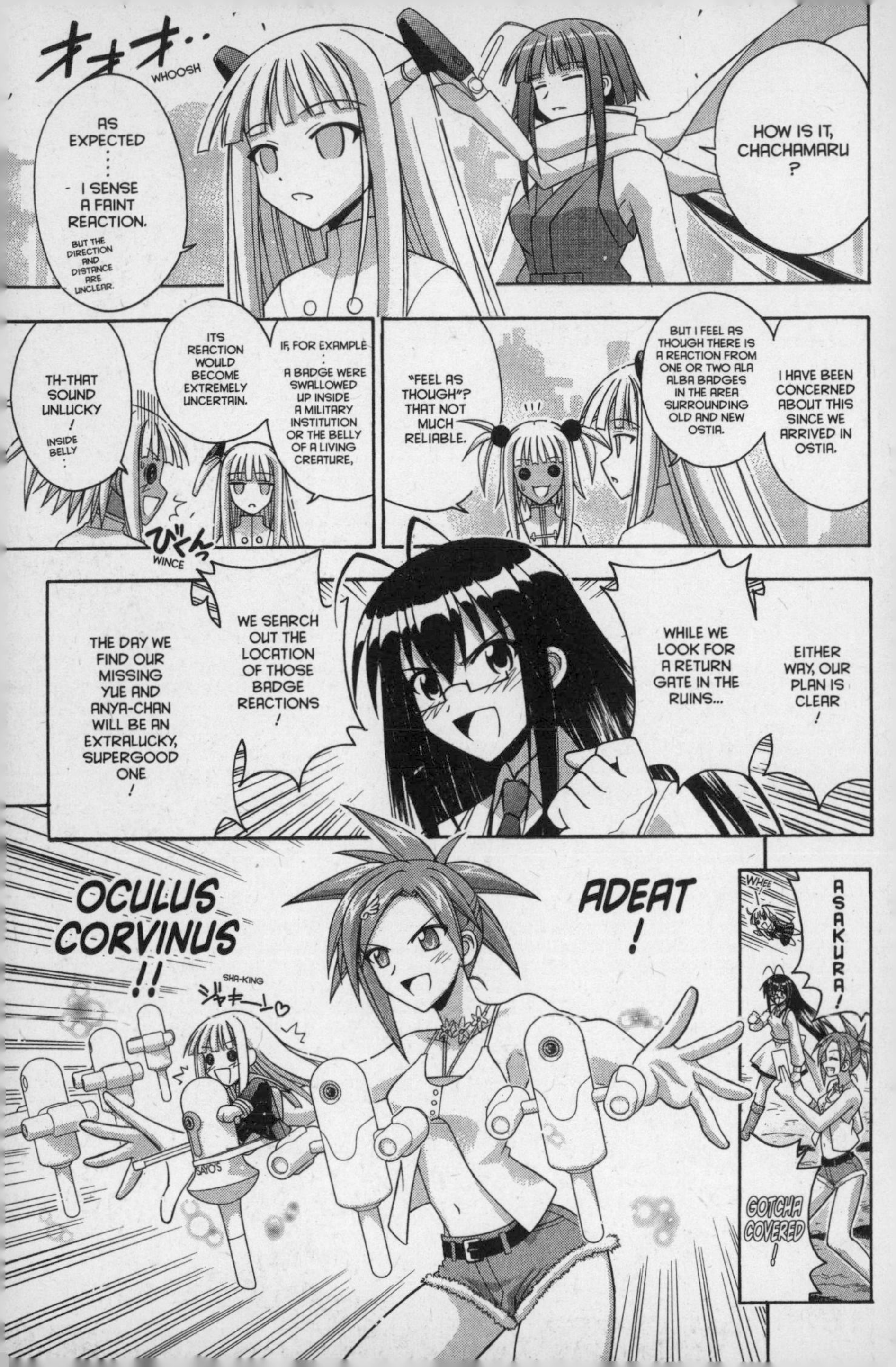
HOW IS IT, CHACHAMARU?
オォォ‥
WHOOSH
AS EXPECTED... I SENSE A FAINT REACTION.
BUT THE DIRECTION AND DISTANCE ARE UNCLEAR.
I HAVE BEEN CONCERNED ABOUT THIS SINCE WE ARRIVED IN OSTIA.
BUT I FEEL AS THOUGH THERE IS A REACTION FROM ONE OR TWO ALA ALBA BADGES IN THE AREA SURROUNDING OLD AND NEW OSTIA.
"FEEL AS THOUGH"? THAT NOT MUCH RELIABLE.
IF, FOR EXAMPLE: A BADGE WERE SWALLOWED UP INSIDE A MILITARY INSTITUTION OR THE BELLY OF A LIVING CREATURE,
ITS REACTION WOULD BECOME EXTREMELY UNCERTAIN.
TH-THAT SOUND UNLUCKY!
INSIDE BELLY...
びくんっ
WINCE
EITHER WAY, OUR PLAN IS CLEAR!
WHILE WE LOOK FOR A RETURN GATE IN THE RUINS...
WE SEARCH OUT THE LOCATION OF THOSE BADGE REACTIONS!
THE DAY WE FIND OUR MISSING YUE AND ANYA-CHAN WILL BE AN EXTRALUCKY, SUPERGOOD ONE!
WHEE
ASAKURA!
GOTCHA COVERED!
ADEAT!
OCULUS CORVINUS!!
SHA-KING
ジャキーン♡
SAYO'S

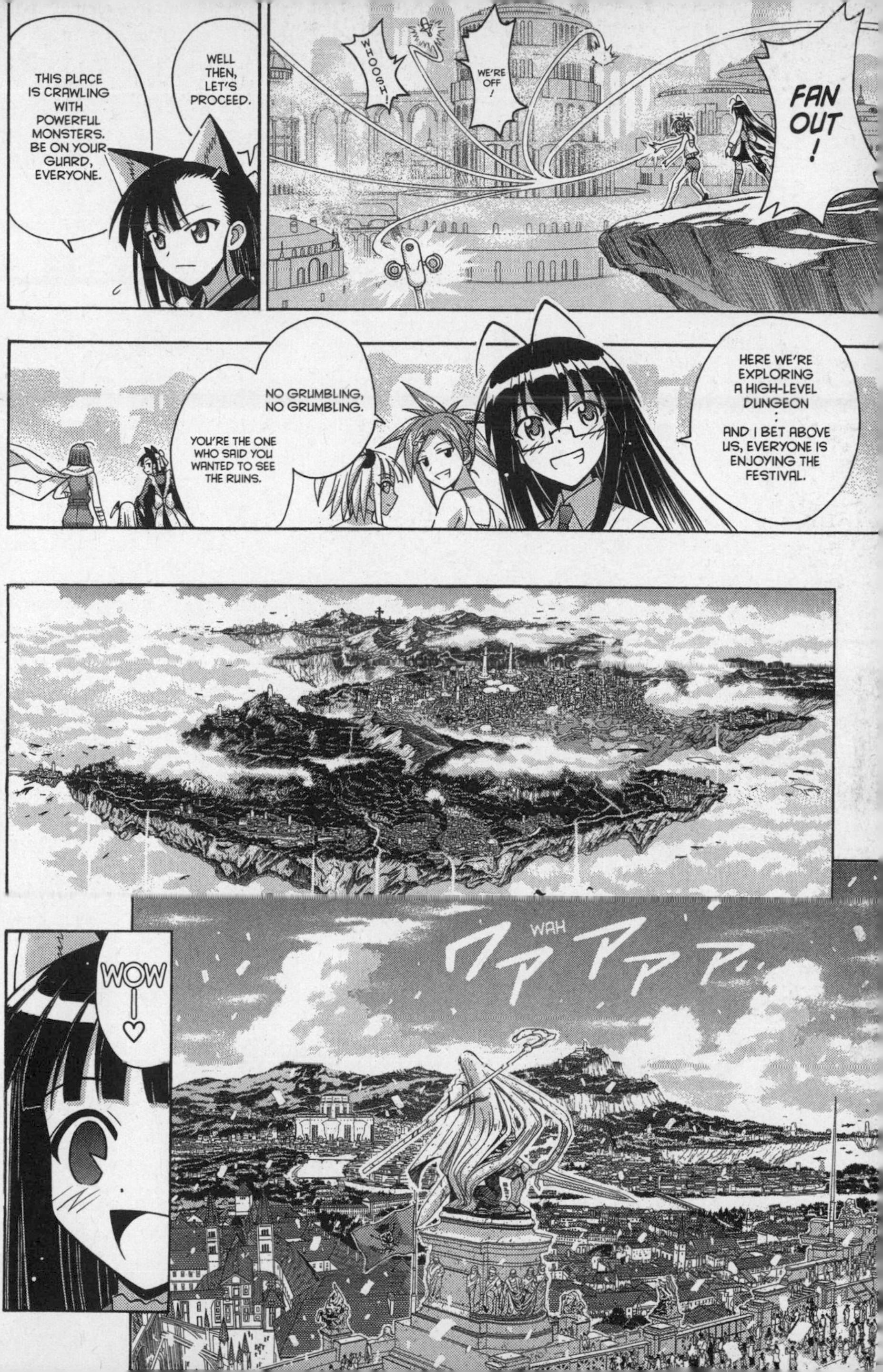
FAN OUT!
WE'RE OFF!
WHOOSH!
WELL THEN, LET'S PROCEED.
THIS PLACE IS CRAWLING WITH POWERFUL MONSTERS. BE ON YOUR GUARD, EVERYONE.
HERE WE'RE EXPLORING A HIGH-LEVEL DUNGEON: AND I BET ABOVE US, EVERYONE IS ENJOYING THE FESTIVAL.
NO GRUMBLING, NO GRUMBLING.
YOU'RE THE ONE WHO SAID YOU WANTED TO SEE THE RUINS.
WAH
ワアアア
WOW!♥

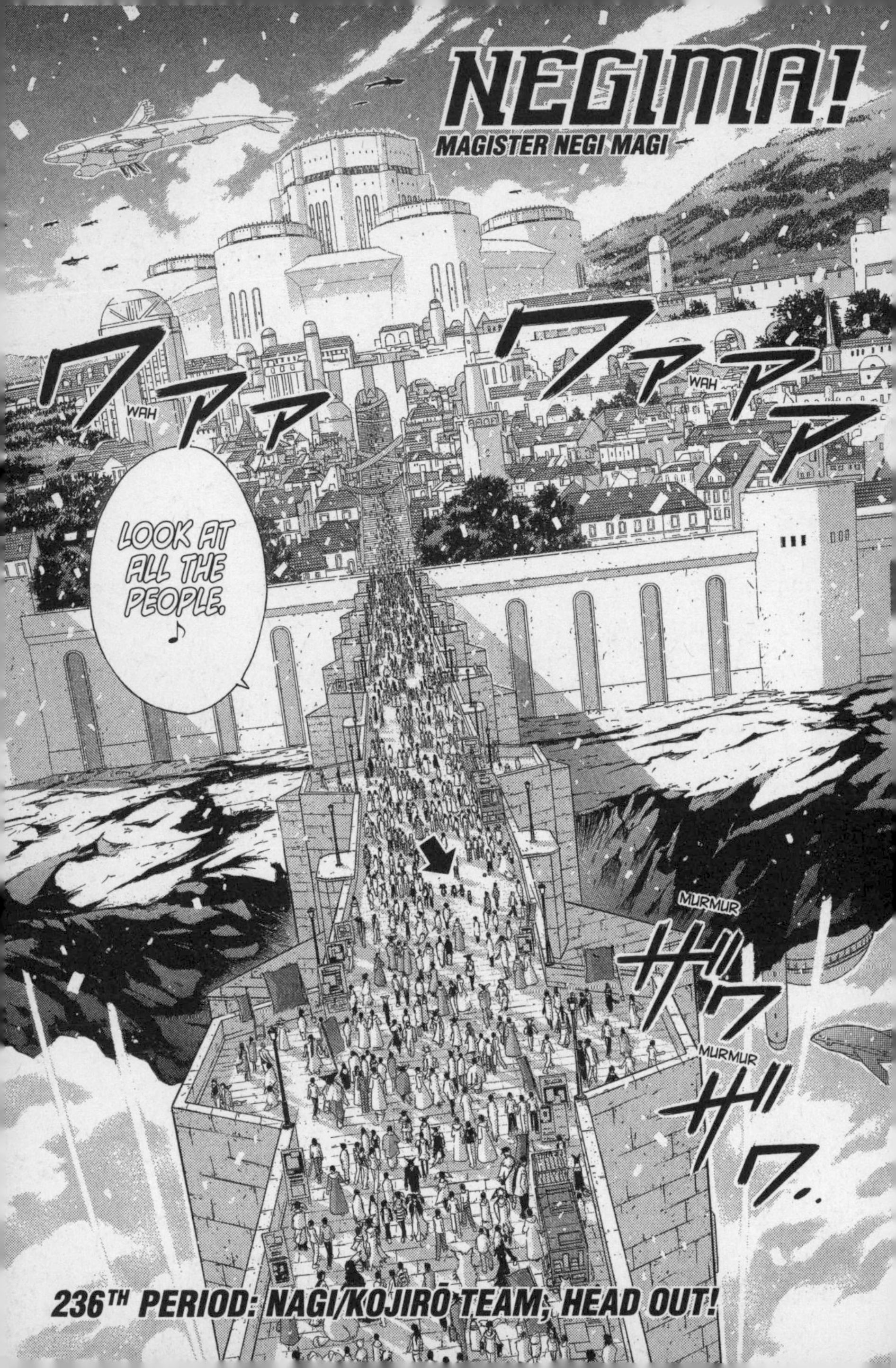
NEGIMA!
MAGISTER NEGI MAGI
WAH
WAH
LOOK AT ALL THE PEOPLE. ♪
MURMUR
MURMUR
236TH PERIOD: NAGI/KOJIRŌ TEAM, HEAD OUT!

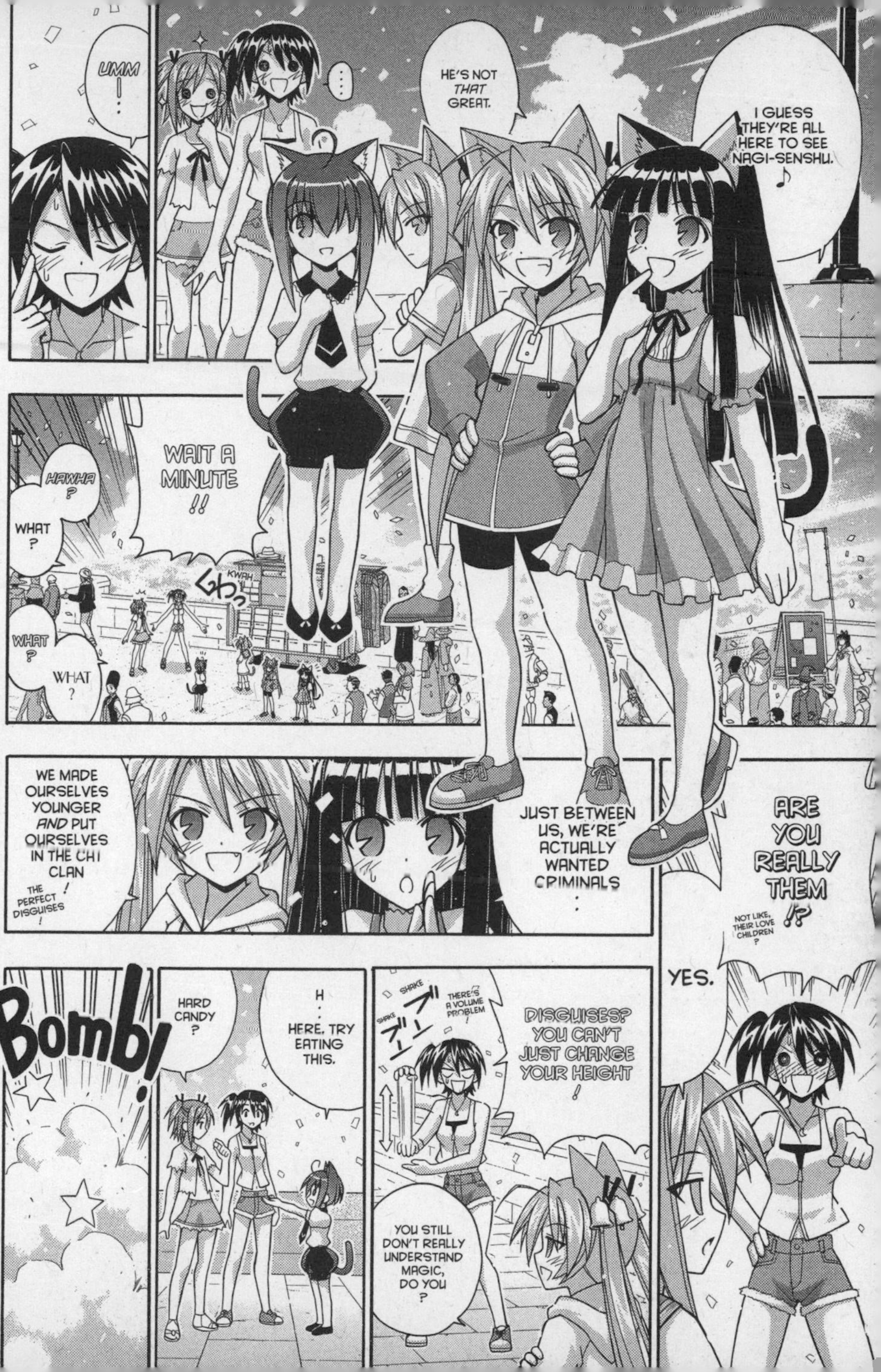

I GUESS THEY'RE ALL HERE TO SEE NAGI-SENSHU. ♪
HE'S NOT *THAT* GREAT.
...
UMM...!
WAIT A MINUTE!!
HAWHA?
WHAT?
KWAH
WHAT?
WHAT?
ARE YOU REALLY THEM!?
NOT LIKE, THEIR LOVE CHILDREN?
YES.
JUST BETWEEN US, WE'RE ACTUALLY WANTED CRIMINALS...
WE MADE OURSELVES YOUNGER *AND* PUT OURSELVES IN THE CHI CLAN!
THE PERFECT DISGUISES!
DISGUISES? YOU CAN'T JUST CHANGE YOUR HEIGHT!
SHAKE
SHAKE
THERE'S A VOLUME PROBLEM!
YOU STILL DON'T REALLY UNDERSTAND MAGIC, DO YOU?
H... HERE, TRY EATING THIS.
HARD CANDY?
Bomb!

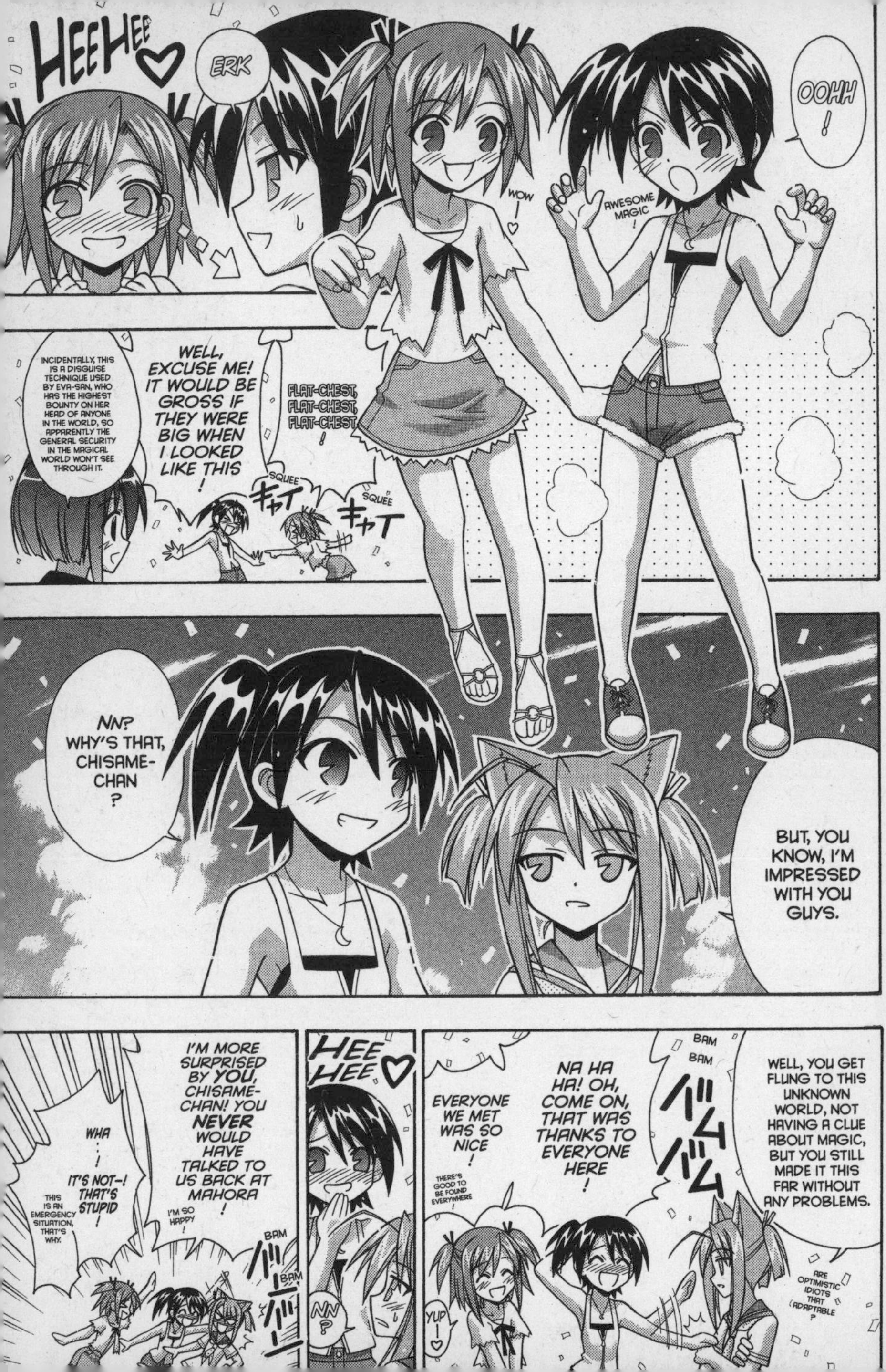

OOHH!
AWESOME MAGIC!
WOW! ♡
ERK
HEEHEE ♡
FLAT-CHEST, FLAT-CHEST, FLAT-CHEST!
WELL, EXCUSE ME! IT WOULD BE GROSS IF THEY WERE BIG WHEN I LOOKED LIKE THIS!
INCIDENTALLY, THIS IS A DISGUISE TECHNIQUE USED BY EVA-SAN, WHO HAS THE HIGHEST BOUNTY ON HER HEAD OF ANYONE IN THE WORLD, SO APPARENTLY THE GENERAL SECURITY IN THE MAGICAL WORLD WON'T SEE THROUGH IT.
SQUEE
キャイ
SQUEE
キャイ
BUT, YOU KNOW, I'M IMPRESSED WITH YOU GUYS.
NN? WHY'S THAT, CHISAME-CHAN?
WELL, YOU GET FLUNG TO THIS UNKNOWN WORLD, NOT HAVING A CLUE ABOUT MAGIC, BUT YOU STILL MADE IT THIS FAR WITHOUT ANY PROBLEMS.
BAM
BAM
バムバム
NA HA HA! OH, COME ON, THAT WAS THANKS TO EVERYONE HERE!
EVERYONE WE MET WAS SO NICE!
THERE'S GOOD TO BE FOUND EVERYWHERE
ARE OPTIMISTIC IDIOTS THAT ADAPTABLE?
YUP! ♡
HEE HEE ♡
NN?
BAM
BAM
バーバー
I'M MORE SURPRISED BY YOU, CHISAME-CHAN! YOU NEVER WOULD HAVE TALKED TO US BACK AT MAHORA!
I'M SO HAPPY!
WHA...!
IT'S NOT-! THAT'S STUPID!
THIS IS AN EMERGENCY SITUATION, THAT'S WHY.

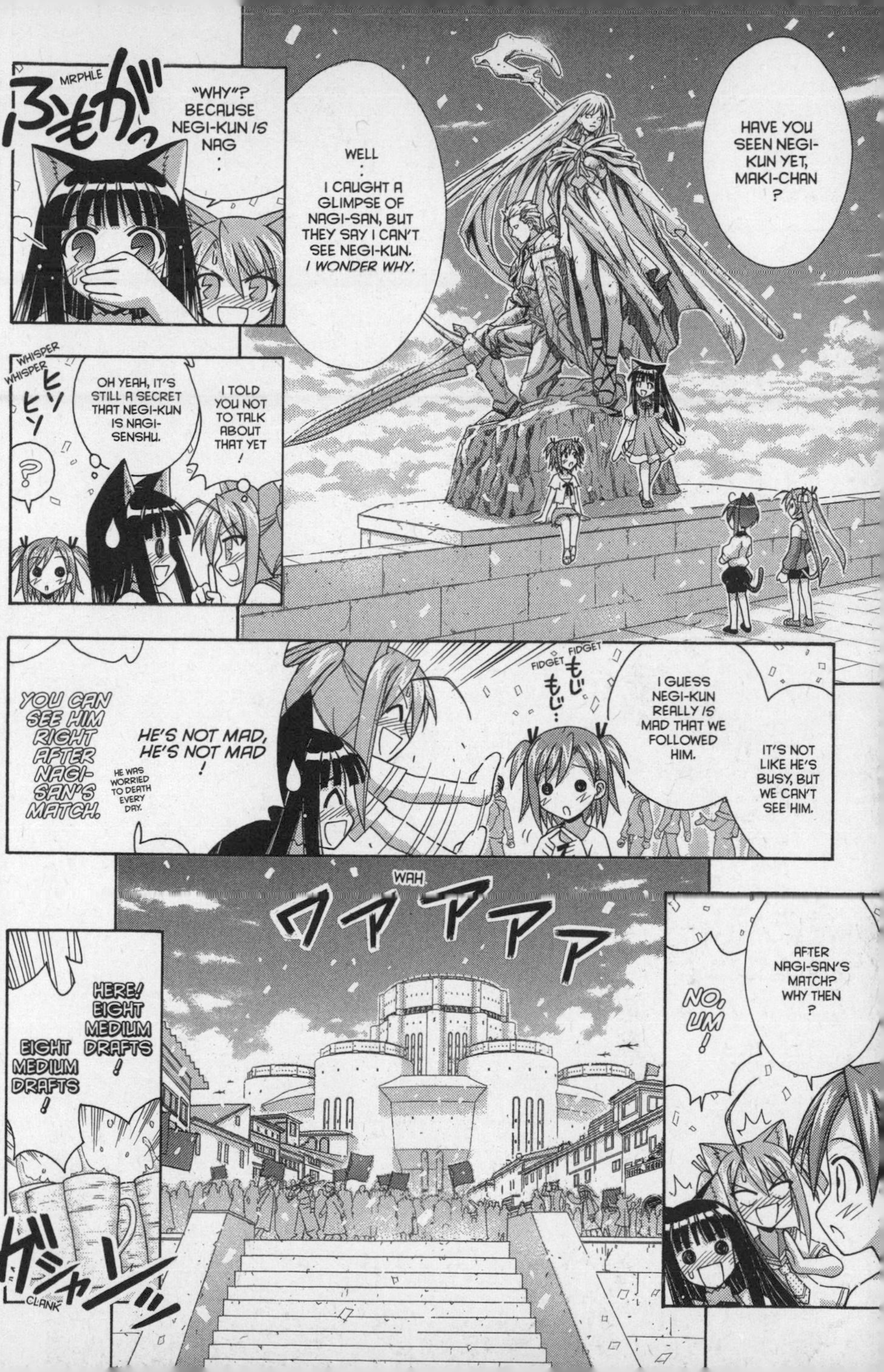

HAVE YOU SEEN NEGI-KUN YET, MAKI-CHAN?
WELL... I CAUGHT A GLIMPSE OF NAGI-SAN, BUT THEY SAY I CAN'T SEE NEGI-KUN. *I WONDER WHY.*
"WHY"? BECAUSE NEGI-KUN *IS* NAG...
MRPHLE
ふもがっ
I TOLD YOU NOT TO TALK ABOUT THAT YET!
OH YEAH, IT'S STILL A SECRET THAT NEGI-KUN IS NAGI-SENSHU.
WHISPER WHISPER
ヒソヒソ
?
IT'S NOT LIKE HE'S BUSY, BUT WE CAN'T SEE HIM.
I GUESS NEGI-KUN REALLY *IS* MAD THAT WE FOLLOWED HIM.
FIDGET FIDGET
もじもじ
HE'S NOT MAD, HE'S NOT MAD!
HE WAS WORRIED TO DEATH EVERY DAY.
YOU CAN SEE HIM RIGHT AFTER NAGI-SAN'S MATCH.
AFTER NAGI-SAN'S MATCH? WHY THEN?
NO, UM!
WAH
ワァァァ
HERE! EIGHT MEDIUM DRAFTS!
EIGHT MEDIUM DRAFTS!
ガシャーンッ
CLANK

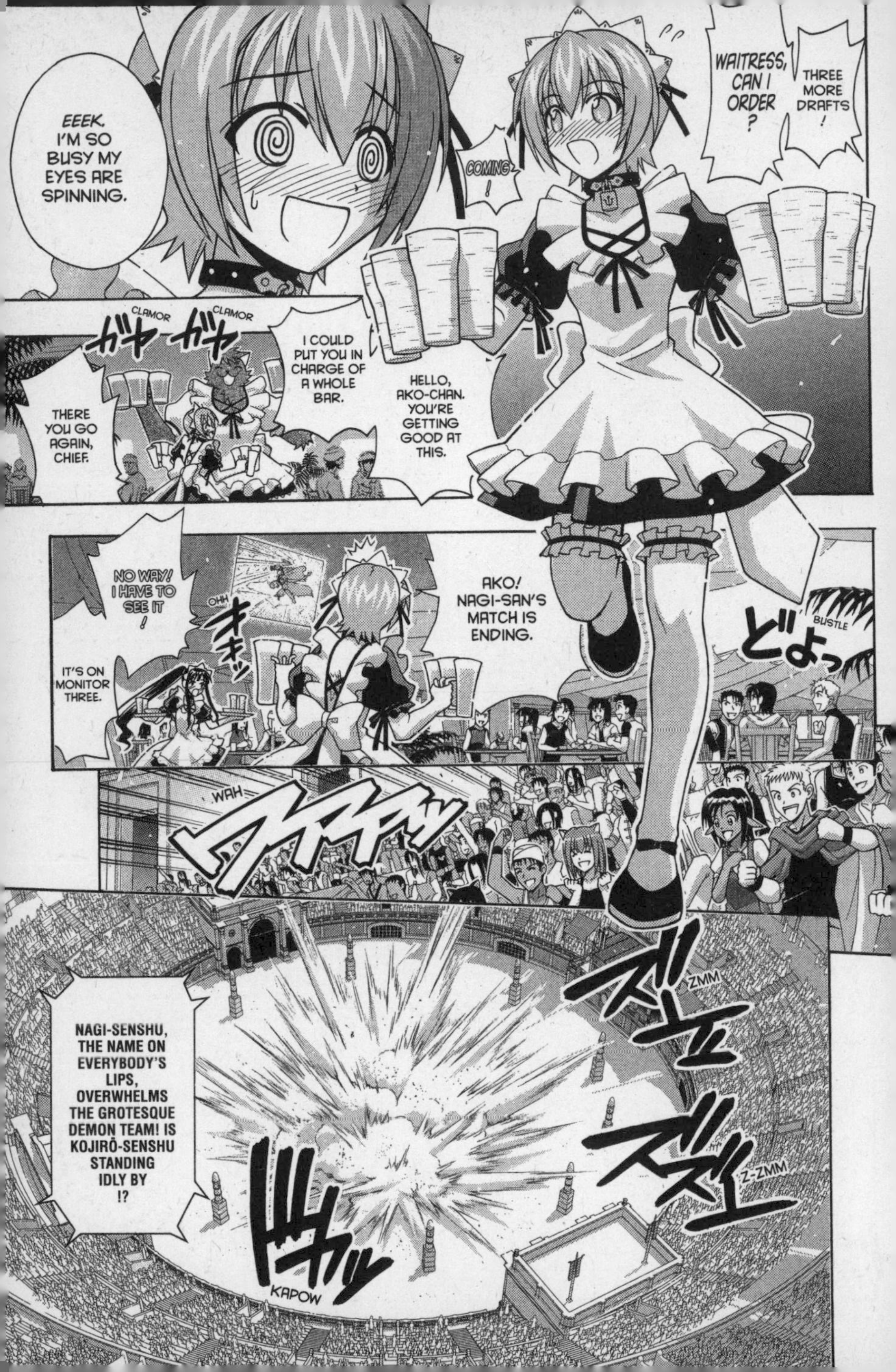
THREE MORE DRAFTS!
WAITRESS, CAN I ORDER?
COMING!
EEEK. I'M SO BUSY MY EYES ARE SPINNING.
ガヤ CLAMOR ガヤ CLAMOR
HELLO, AKO-CHAN. YOU'RE GETTING GOOD AT THIS.
I COULD PUT YOU IN CHARGE OF A WHOLE BAR.
THERE YOU GO AGAIN, CHIEF.
どよっ BUSTLE
AKO! NAGI-SAN'S MATCH IS ENDING.
NO WAY! I HAVE TO SEE IT!
オオッ OHH
IT'S ON MONITOR THREE.
WAH
ズズ ZMM
ズズ Z-ZMM
NAGI-SENSHU, THE NAME ON EVERYBODY'S LIPS, OVERWHELMS THE GROTESQUE DEMON TEAM! IS KOJIRŌ-SENSHU STANDING IDLY BY!?
ドカッ KAPOW

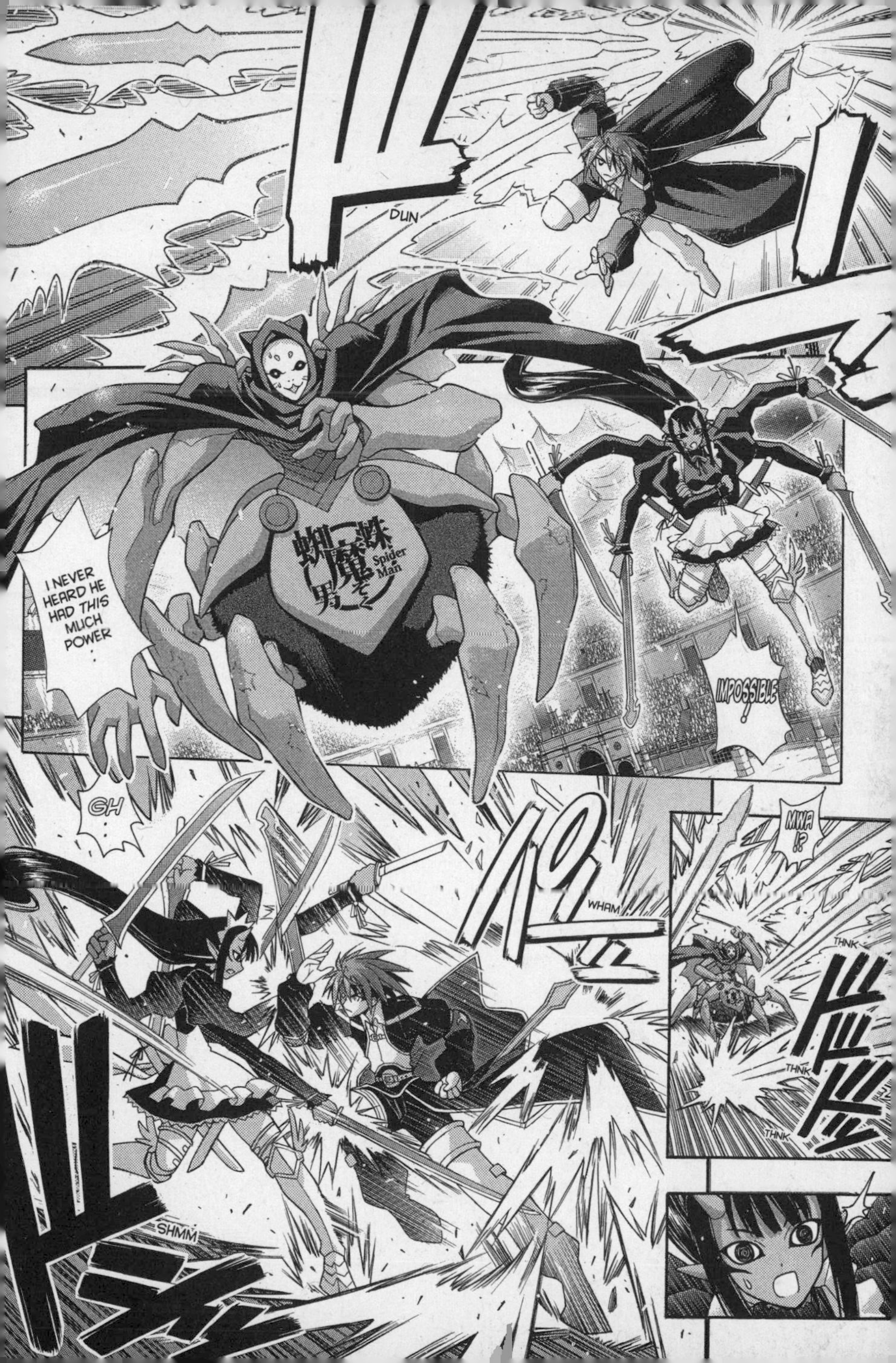
DUN
IMPOSSIBLE !
I NEVER HEARD HE HAD THIS MUCH POWER
Spider Man
MWA !?
THNK
THNK
THNK
WHAM
GH
SHMM

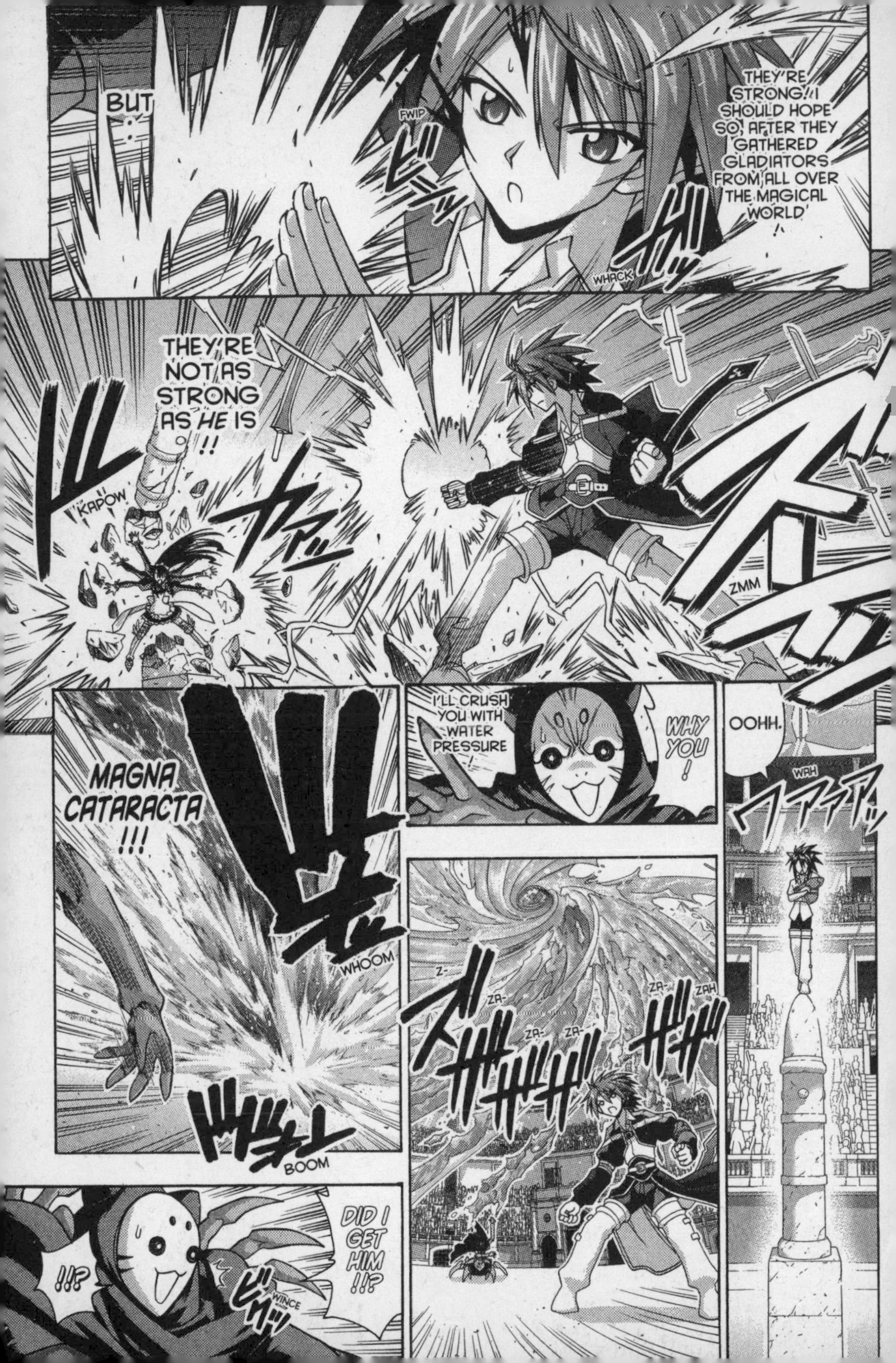
THEY'RE STRONG! I SHOULD HOPE SO, AFTER THEY GATHERED GLADIATORS FROM ALL OVER THE MAGICAL WORLD!
WHACK
FWIP
BUT...
ZMM
THEY'RE NOT AS STRONG AS HE IS!!
KAPOW
OOHH.
WAH
WHY YOU!
I'LL CRUSH YOU WITH WATER PRESSURE!
ZA- ZAH
ZA-
ZA-
ZA-
Z-
MAGNA CATARACTA!!!
WHOOM
BOOM
DID I GET HIM!!?
WINCE
!!?

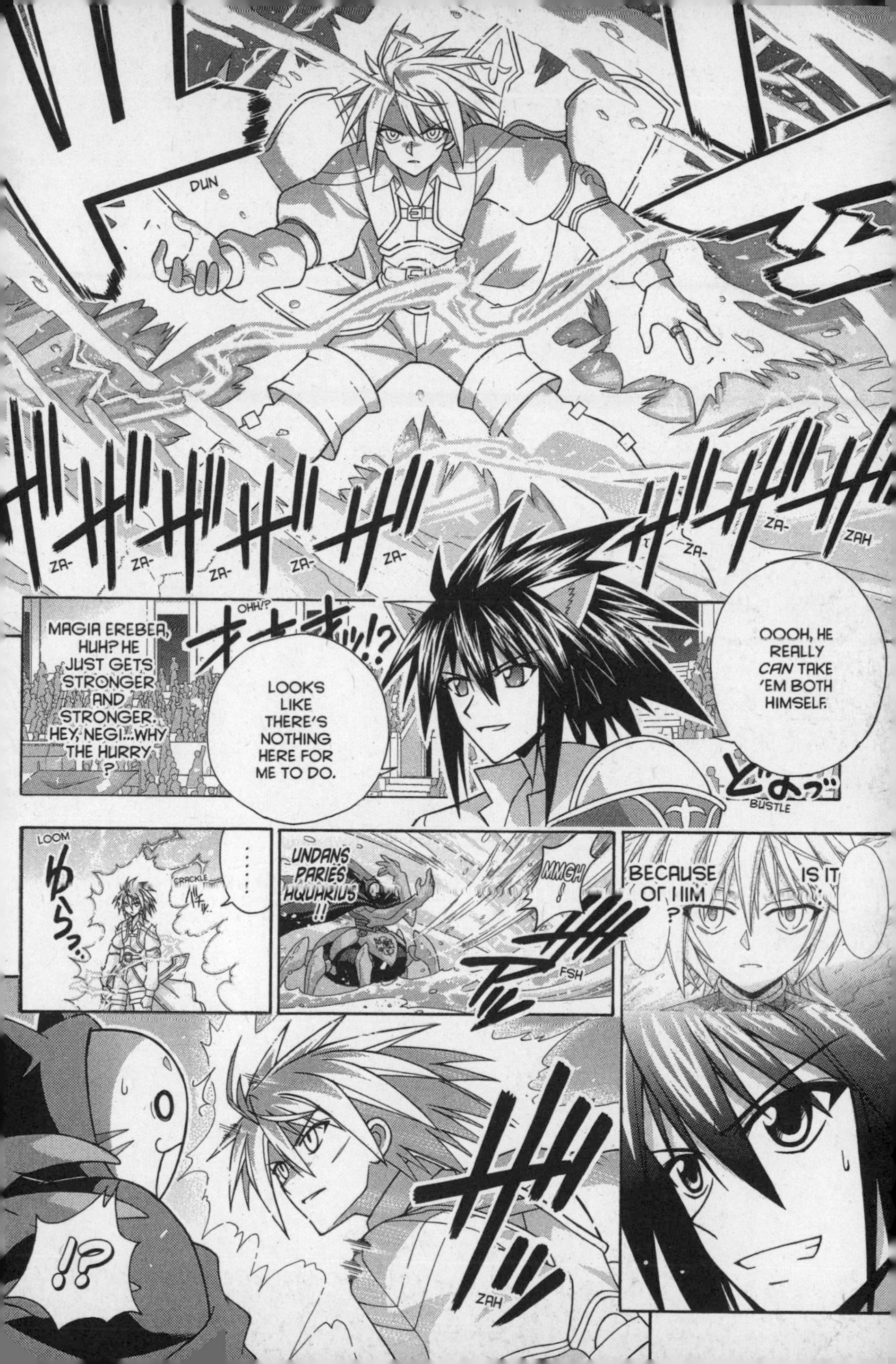

DUN
ZA-
ZA-
ZA-
ZA-
ZA-
ZA-
ZA-
ZAH
OOOH, HE REALLY *CAN* TAKE 'EM BOTH HIMSELF.
BUSTLE
LOOKS LIKE THERE'S NOTHING HERE FOR ME TO DO.
OHH!?
MAGIA EREBEA, HUH? HE JUST GETS STRONGER AND STRONGER. HEY, NEGI...WHY THE HURRY?
IS IT...
BECAUSE OF HIM?
MMGH!
UNDANS PARIES AQUARIUS!!
FSH
......!
CRACKLE
LOOM
ZAH
!?

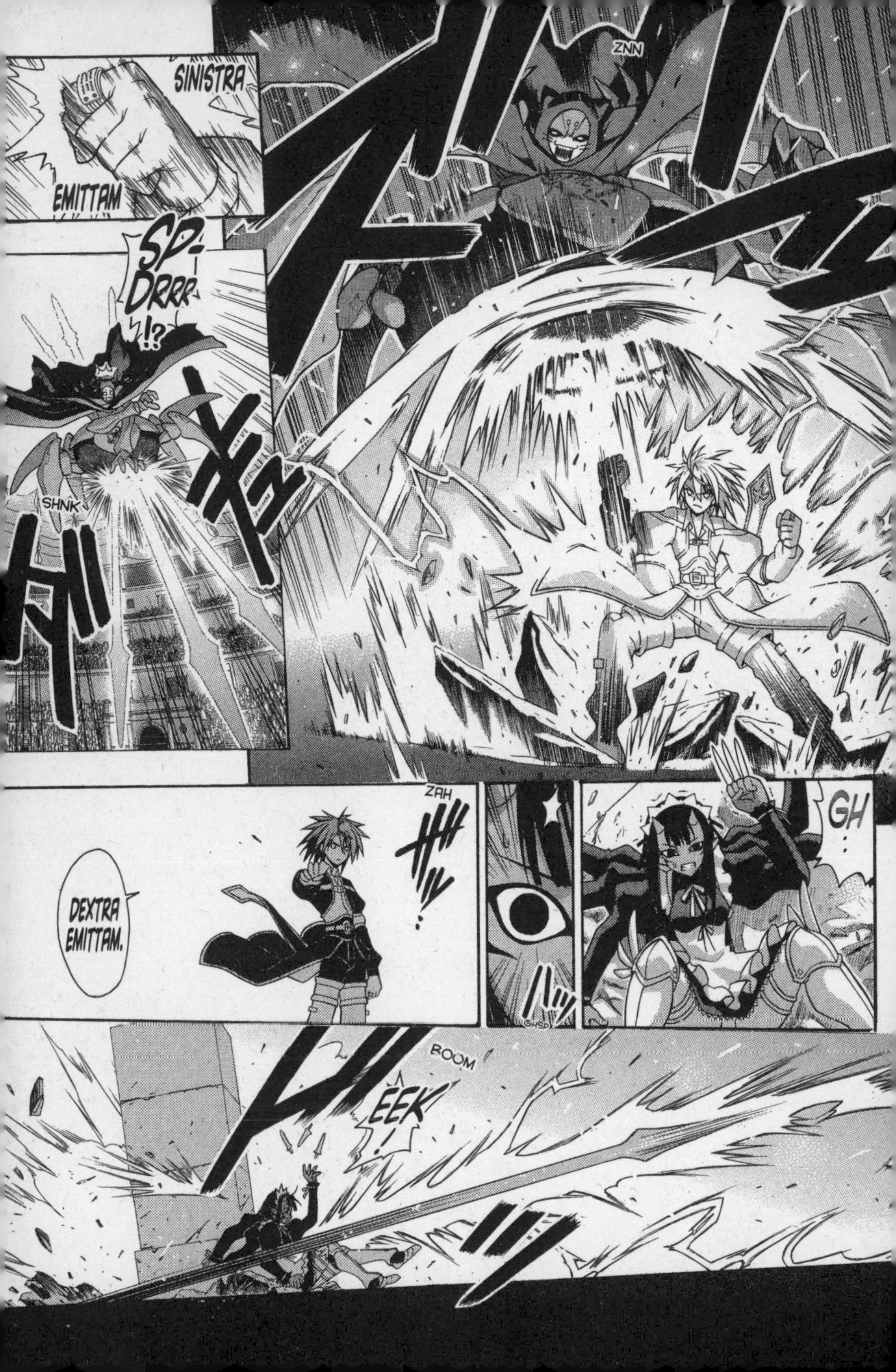
ZNN
SINISTRA
EMITTAM
SP-DRRR!?
SHNK
GH
GHSP
DEXTRA EMITTAM.
ZAH
BOOM
EEK!

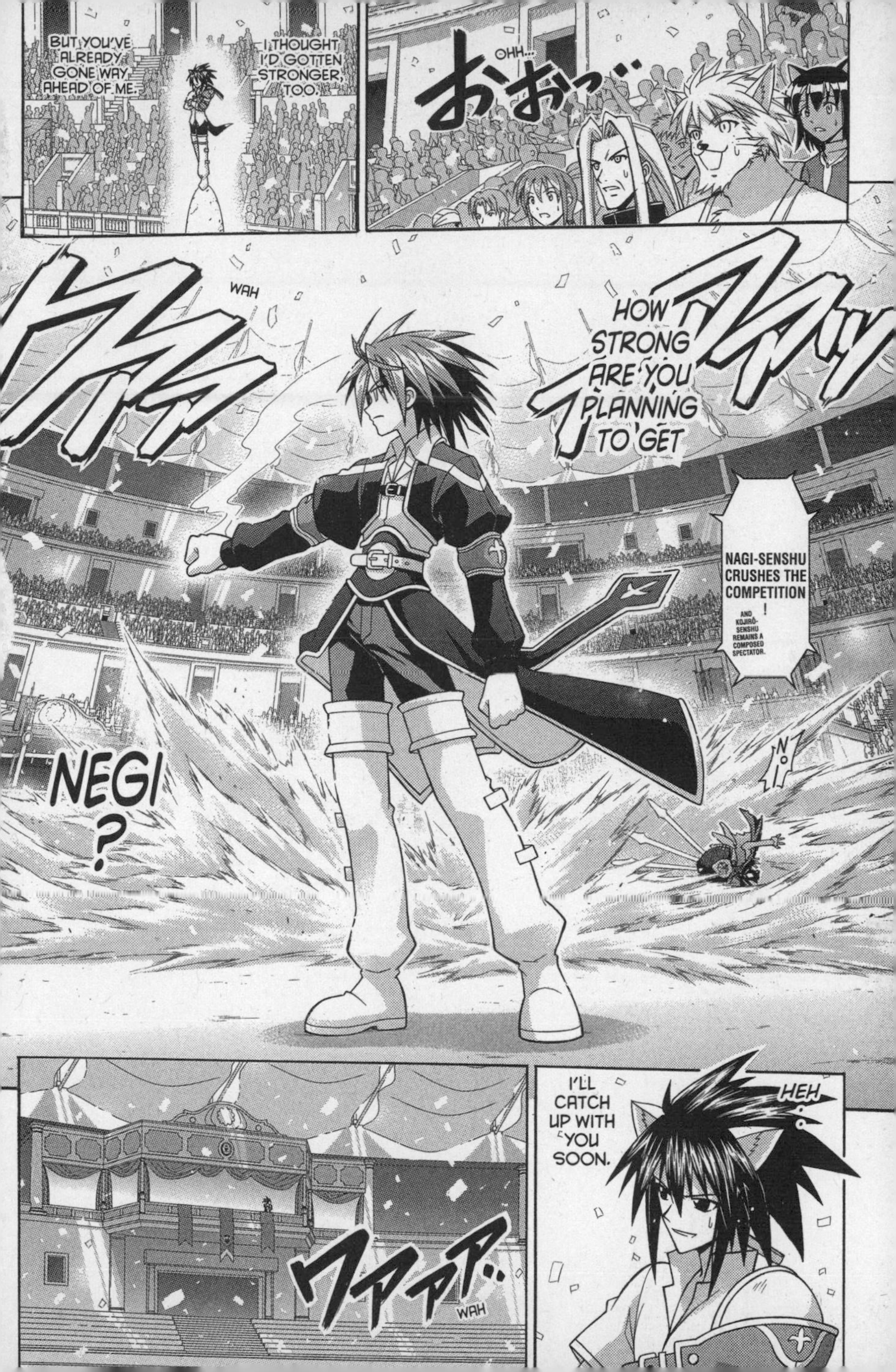
OHH...
おおっ
I THOUGHT I'D GOTTEN STRONGER, TOO.
BUT YOU'VE ALREADY GONE WAY AHEAD OF ME.
HOW STRONG ARE YOU PLANNING TO GET
NAGI-SENSHU CRUSHES THE COMPETITION!
AND KOJIRŌ-SENSHU REMAINS A COMPOSED SPECTATOR.
WAH
NEGI?
N...!
I'LL CATCH UP WITH YOU SOON.
HEH
ワァァ
WAH

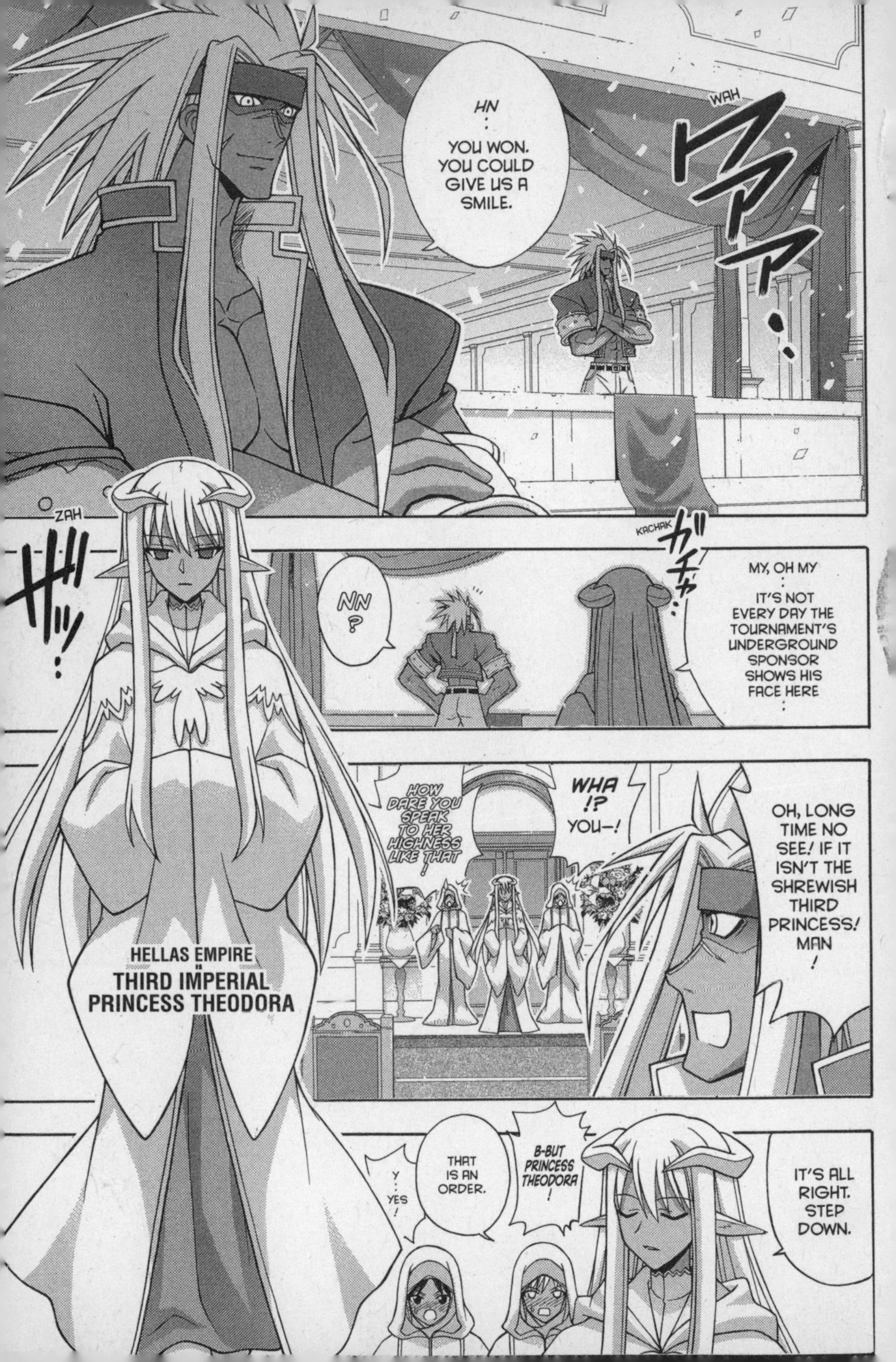

WAH
ワァァ…
HN: YOU WON. YOU COULD GIVE US A SMILE.
KACHAK
ガチャ…
MY, OH MY… IT'S NOT EVERY DAY THE TOURNAMENT'S UNDERGROUND SPONSOR SHOWS HIS FACE HERE…
NN?
OH, LONG TIME NO SEE! IF IT ISN'T THE SHREWISH THIRD PRINCESS! MAN!
WHA!? YOU—!
HOW DARE YOU SPEAK TO HER HIGHNESS LIKE THAT!
IT'S ALL RIGHT. STEP DOWN.
B-BUT PRINCESS THEODORA!
THAT IS AN ORDER.
Y…YES!
ZAH
ザッ
HELLAS EMPIRE
THIRD IMPERIAL PRINCESS THEODORA

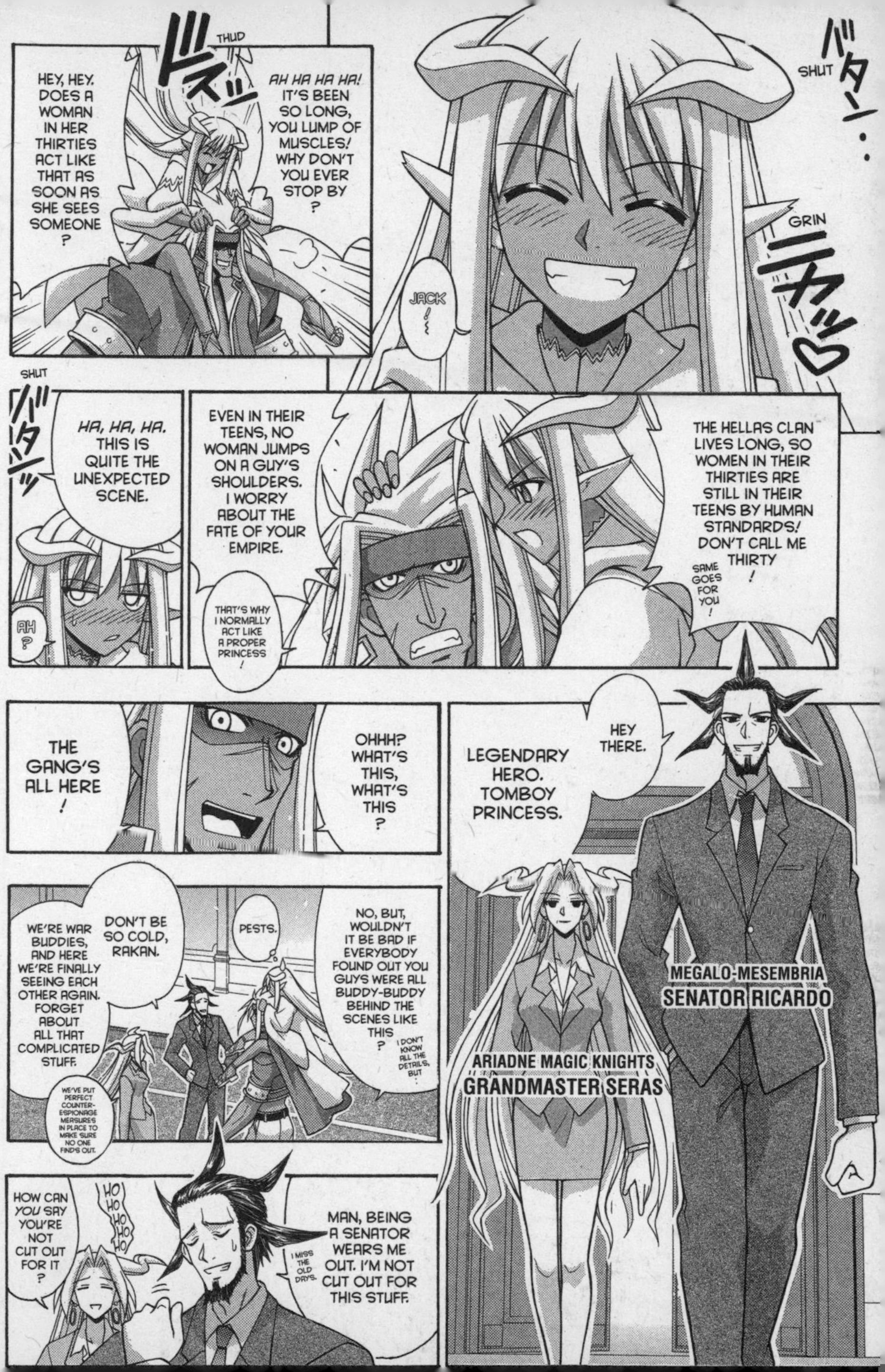SHUT
バタン・・
JACK!
GRIN
ニヤッ♡
THUD
ドスッ
AH HA HA HA! IT'S BEEN SO LONG, YOU LUMP OF MUSCLES! WHY DON'T YOU EVER STOP BY?
HEY, HEY. DOES A WOMAN IN HER THIRTIES ACT LIKE THAT AS SOON AS SHE SEES SOMEONE?
THE HELLAS CLAN LIVES LONG, SO WOMEN IN THEIR THIRTIES ARE STILL IN THEIR TEENS BY HUMAN STANDARDS! DON'T CALL ME THIRTY!
SAME GOES FOR YOU!
EVEN IN THEIR TEENS, NO WOMAN JUMPS ON A GUY'S SHOULDERS. I WORRY ABOUT THE FATE OF YOUR EMPIRE.
THAT'S WHY I NORMALLY ACT LIKE A PROPER PRINCESS!
SHUT
バタンッ
HA, HA, HA. THIS IS QUITE THE UNEXPECTED SCENE.
AH?
HEY THERE.
LEGENDARY HERO. TOMBOY PRINCESS.
MEGALO-MESEMBRIA
SENATOR RICARDO
ARIADNE MAGIC KNIGHTS
GRANDMASTER SERAS
OHHH? WHAT'S THIS, WHAT'S THIS?
THE GANG'S ALL HERE!
NO, BUT, WOULDN'T IT BE BAD IF EVERYBODY FOUND OUT YOU GUYS WERE ALL BUDDY-BUDDY BEHIND THE SCENES LIKE THIS?
I DON'T KNOW ALL THE DETAILS, BUT
PESTS.
DON'T BE SO COLD, RAKAN.
WE'RE WAR BUDDIES, AND HERE WE'RE FINALLY SEEING EACH OTHER AGAIN. FORGET ABOUT ALL THAT COMPLICATED STUFF.
WE'VE PUT PERFECT COUNTER-ESPIONAGE MEASURES IN PLACE TO MAKE SURE NO ONE FINDS OUT.
MAN, BEING A SENATOR WEARS ME OUT. I'M NOT CUT OUT FOR THIS STUFF.
I MISS THE OLD DAYS.
HO HO HO HO HO
HOW CAN YOU SAY YOU'RE NOT CUT OUT FOR IT?

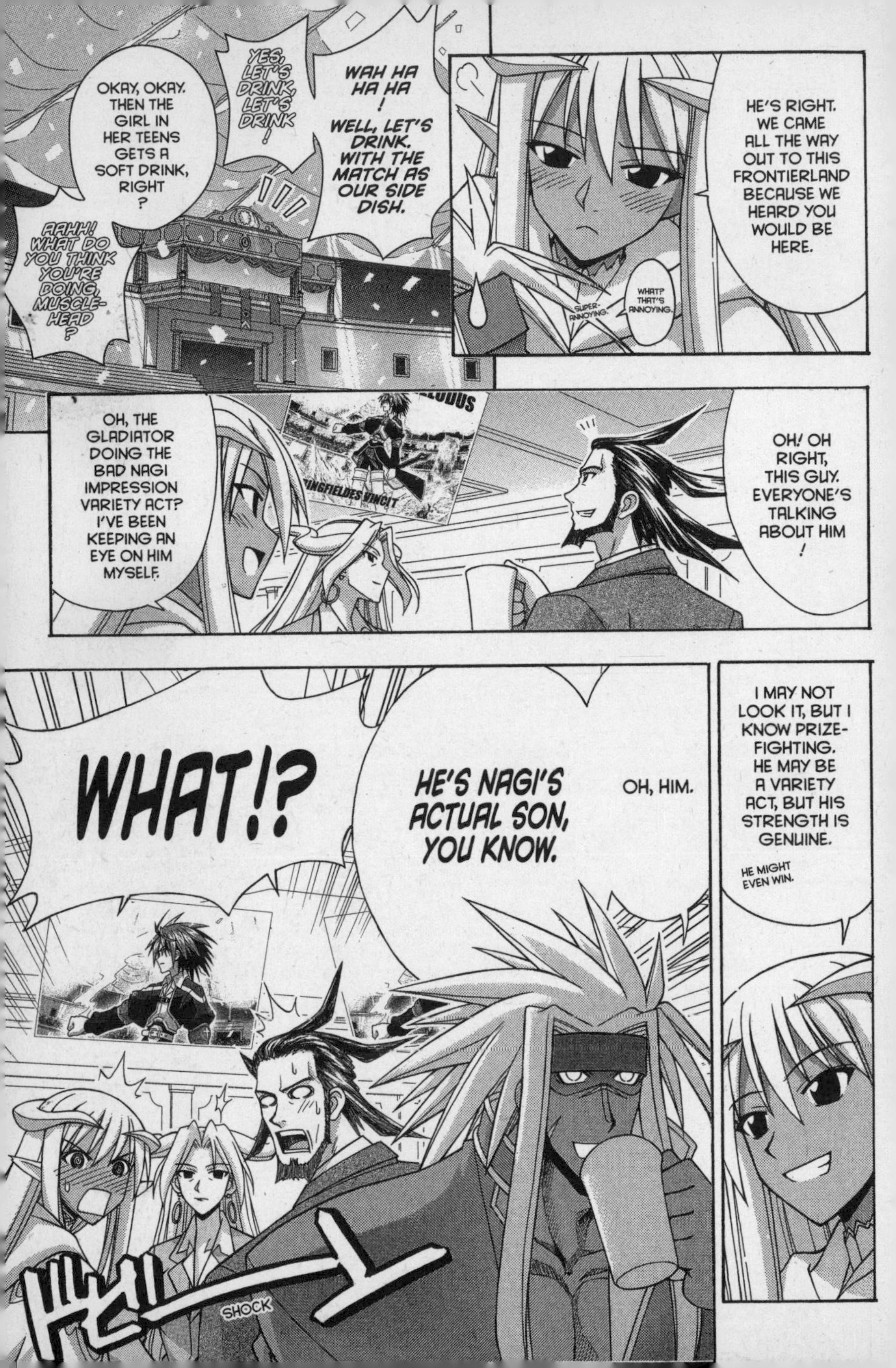
HE'S RIGHT. WE CAME ALL THE WAY OUT TO THIS FRONTIERLAND BECAUSE WE HEARD YOU WOULD BE HERE.
WHAT? THAT'S ANNOYING.
SUPER-ANNOYING.
WAH HA HA HA! WELL, LET'S DRINK. WITH THE MATCH AS OUR SIDE DISH.
YES, LET'S DRINK, LET'S DRINK!
OKAY, OKAY. THEN THE GIRL IN HER TEENS GETS A SOFT DRINK, RIGHT?
AAHH! WHAT DO YOU THINK YOU'RE DOING, MUSCLE-HEAD?
OH! OH RIGHT, THIS GUY. EVERYONE'S TALKING ABOUT HIM!
OH, THE GLADIATOR DOING THE BAD NAGI IMPRESSION VARIETY ACT? I'VE BEEN KEEPING AN EYE ON HIM MYSELF.
I MAY NOT LOOK IT, BUT I KNOW PRIZE-FIGHTING. HE MAY BE A VARIETY ACT, BUT HIS STRENGTH IS GENUINE.
HE MIGHT EVEN WIN.
OH, HIM.
HE'S NAGI'S ACTUAL SON, YOU KNOW.
WHAT!?
SHOCK

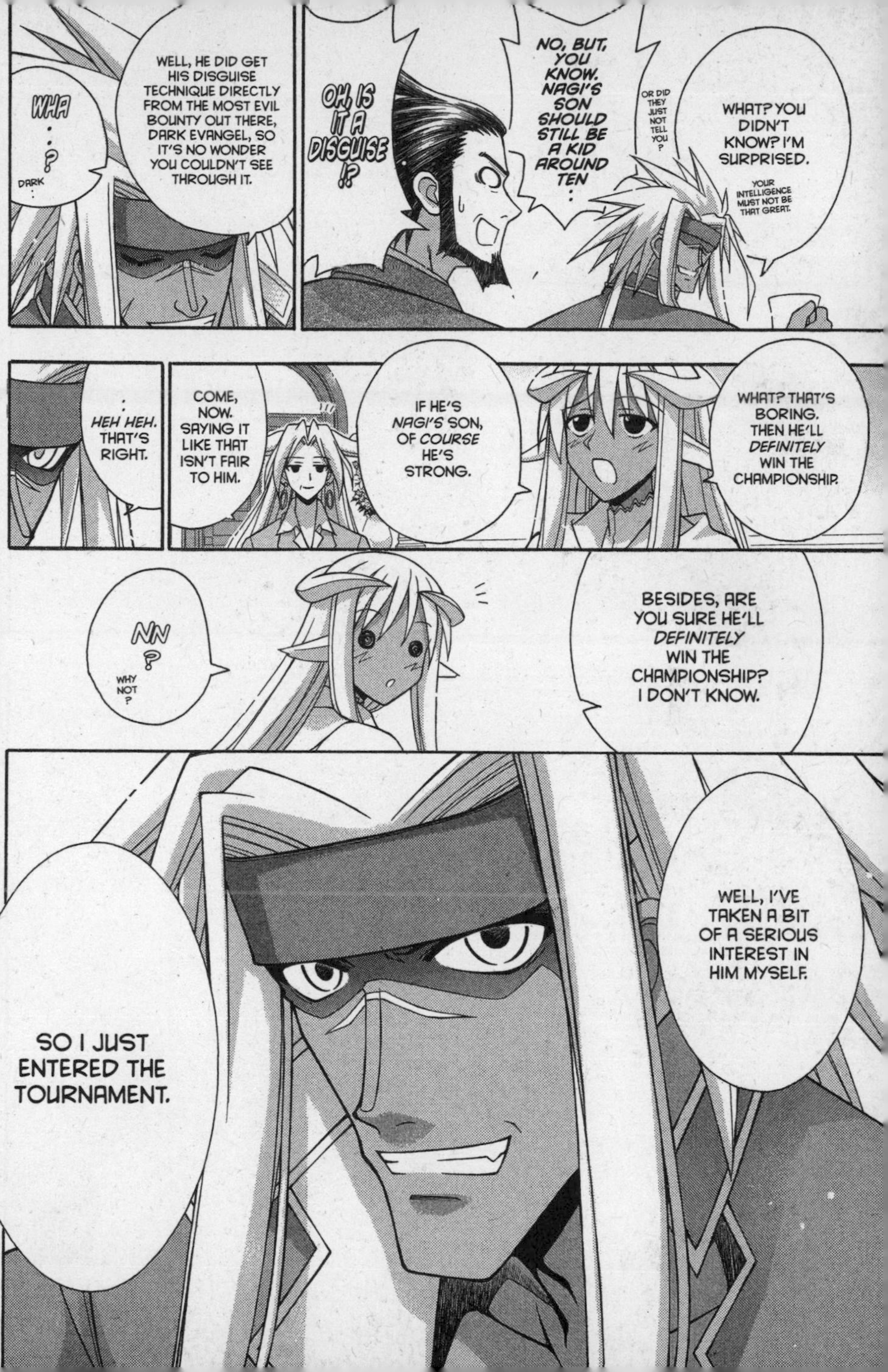
WHAT? YOU DIDN'T KNOW? I'M SURPRISED.
YOUR INTELLIGENCE MUST NOT BE THAT GREAT.
OR DID THEY JUST NOT TELL YOU?
NO, BUT, YOU KNOW. NAGI'S SON SHOULD STILL BE A KID AROUND TEN...
OH, IS IT A DISGUISE!?
WELL, HE DID GET HIS DISGUISE TECHNIQUE DIRECTLY FROM THE MOST EVIL BOUNTY OUT THERE, DARK EVANGEL, SO IT'S NO WONDER YOU COULDN'T SEE THROUGH IT.
WHA...?
DARK...
WHAT? THAT'S BORING. THEN HE'LL DEFINITELY WIN THE CHAMPIONSHIP.
IF HE'S NAGI'S SON, OF COURSE HE'S STRONG.
COME, NOW. SAYING IT LIKE THAT ISN'T FAIR TO HIM.
...HEH HEH. THAT'S RIGHT.
BESIDES, ARE YOU SURE HE'LL DEFINITELY WIN THE CHAMPIONSHIP? I DON'T KNOW.
NN?
WHY NOT?
WELL, I'VE TAKEN A BIT OF A SERIOUS INTEREST IN HIM MYSELF.
SO I JUST ENTERED THE TOURNAMENT.

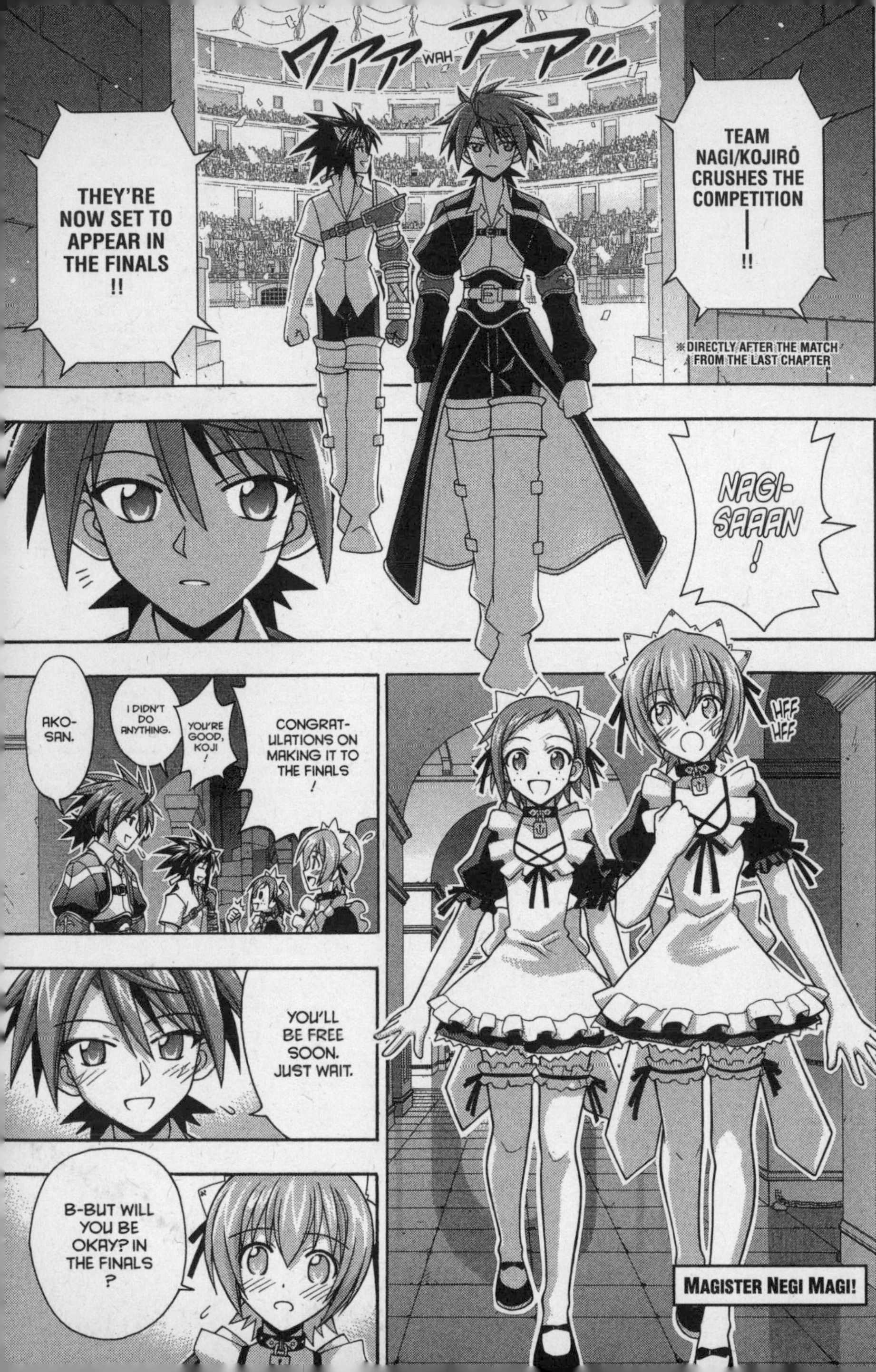
WAH
TEAM NAGI/KOJIRŌ CRUSHES THE COMPETITION — !!
THEY'RE NOW SET TO APPEAR IN THE FINALS !!
※DIRECTLY AFTER THE MATCH FROM THE LAST CHAPTER
NAGI-SAAAN!
HFF HFF
Magister Negi Magi!
CONGRAT-ULATIONS ON MAKING IT TO THE FINALS!
YOU'RE GOOD, KOJI!
I DIDN'T DO ANYTHING.
AKO-SAN.
YOU'LL BE FREE SOON. JUST WAIT.
B-BUT WILL YOU BE OKAY? IN THE FINALS?

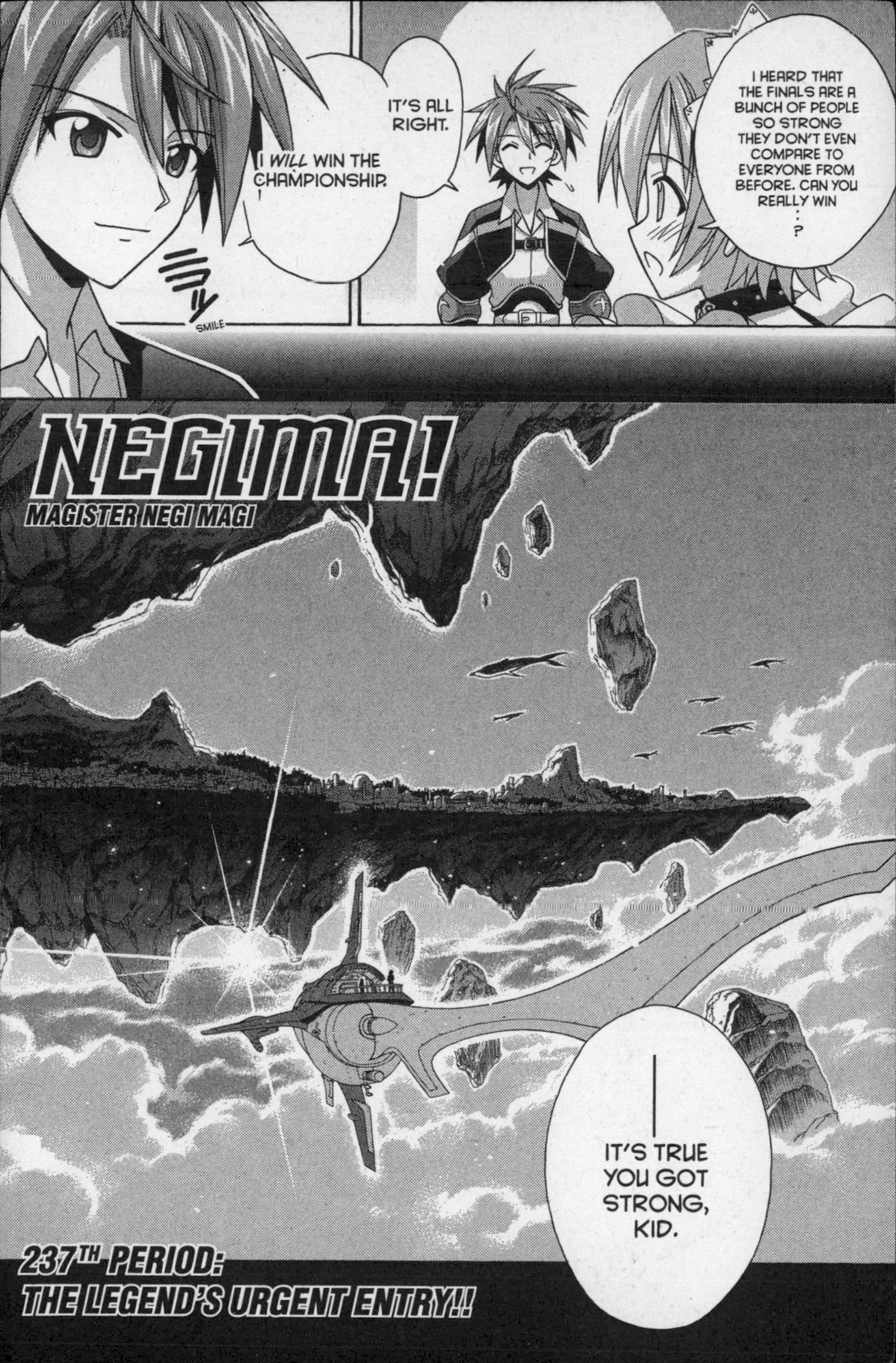
I HEARD THAT THE FINALS ARE A BUNCH OF PEOPLE SO STRONG THEY DON'T EVEN COMPARE TO EVERYONE FROM BEFORE. CAN YOU REALLY WIN . . . ?
IT'S ALL RIGHT.
I *WILL* WIN THE CHAMPIONSHIP.
SMILE
NEGIMA!
MAGISTER NEGI MAGI
— IT'S TRUE YOU GOT STRONG, KID.
237TH PERIOD: THE LEGEND'S URGENT ENTRY!!

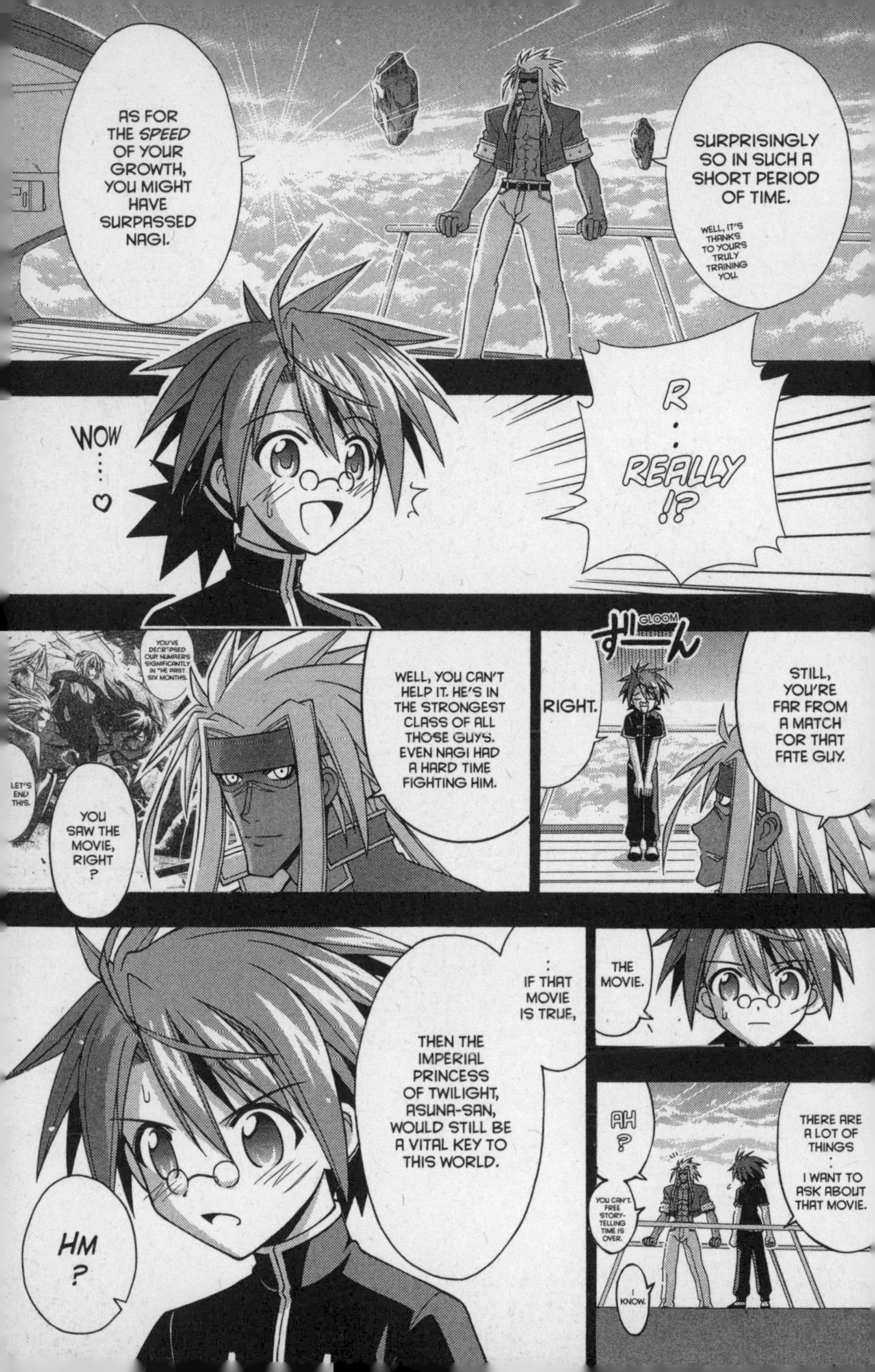
AS FOR THE *SPEED* OF YOUR GROWTH, YOU MIGHT HAVE SURPASSED NAGI.
SURPRISINGLY SO IN SUCH A SHORT PERIOD OF TIME.
WELL, IT'S THANKS TO YOURS TRULY TRAINING YOU.
R.. REALLY!?
WOW... ♡
GLOOM
ずーん
STILL, YOU'RE FAR FROM A MATCH FOR THAT FATE GUY.
RIGHT.
WELL, YOU CAN'T HELP IT. HE'S IN THE STRONGEST CLASS OF ALL THOSE GUYS. EVEN NAGI HAD A HARD TIME FIGHTING HIM.
YOU'VE DECREASED OUR NUMBERS SIGNIFICANTLY IN THE PAST SIX MONTHS.
LET'S END THIS.
YOU SAW THE MOVIE, RIGHT?
THE MOVIE.
THERE ARE A LOT OF THINGS... I WANT TO ASK ABOUT THAT MOVIE.
AH?
YOU CAN'T. FREE STORY-TELLING TIME IS OVER.
I KNOW.
: IF THAT MOVIE IS TRUE,
THEN THE IMPERIAL PRINCESS OF TWILIGHT, ASUNA-SAN, WOULD STILL BE A VITAL KEY TO THIS WORLD.
HM?

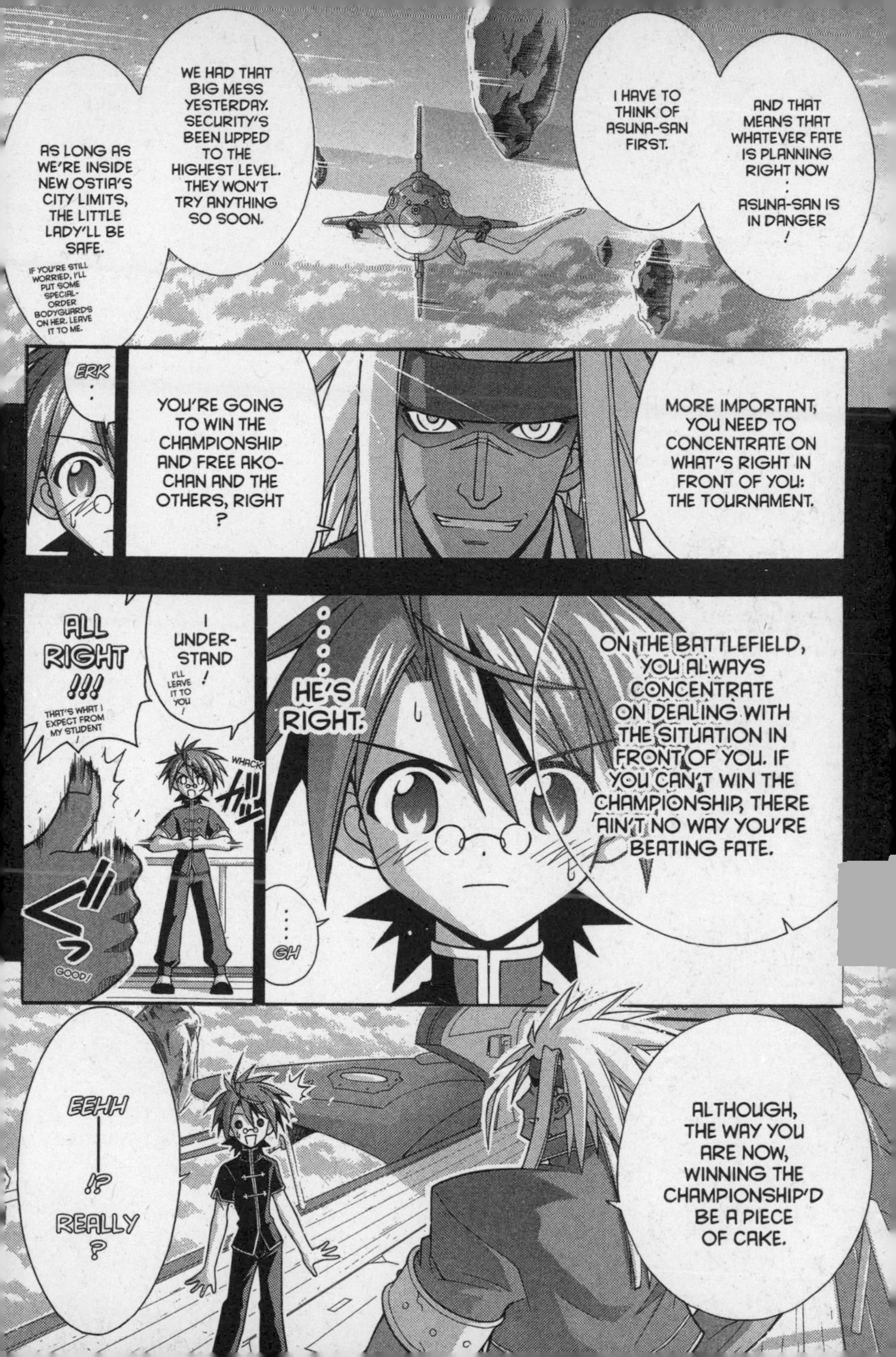

AND THAT MEANS THAT WHATEVER FATE IS PLANNING RIGHT NOW : ASUNA-SAN IS IN DANGER !
I HAVE TO THINK OF ASUNA-SAN FIRST.
WE HAD THAT BIG MESS YESTERDAY. SECURITY'S BEEN UPPED TO THE HIGHEST LEVEL. THEY WON'T TRY ANYTHING SO SOON.
AS LONG AS WE'RE INSIDE NEW OSTIA'S CITY LIMITS, THE LITTLE LADY'LL BE SAFE.
IF YOU'RE STILL WORRIED, I'LL PUT SOME SPECIAL-ORDER BODYGUARDS ON HER. LEAVE IT TO ME.
MORE IMPORTANT, YOU NEED TO CONCENTRATE ON WHAT'S RIGHT IN FRONT OF YOU: THE TOURNAMENT.
YOU'RE GOING TO WIN THE CHAMPIONSHIP AND FREE AKO-CHAN AND THE OTHERS, RIGHT ?
ERK . .
ON THE BATTLEFIELD, YOU ALWAYS CONCENTRATE ON DEALING WITH THE SITUATION IN FRONT OF YOU. IF YOU CAN'T WIN THE CHAMPIONSHIP, THERE AIN'T NO WAY YOU'RE BEATING FATE.
HE'S RIGHT.
. . . . GH
I UNDER-STAND !
I'LL LEAVE IT TO YOU !
ALL RIGHT !!!
THAT'S WHAT I EXPECT FROM MY STUDENT !
WHACK
GOOD!
ALTHOUGH, THE WAY YOU ARE NOW, WINNING THE CHAMPIONSHIP'D BE A PIECE OF CAKE.
EEHH —— !?
REALLY ?

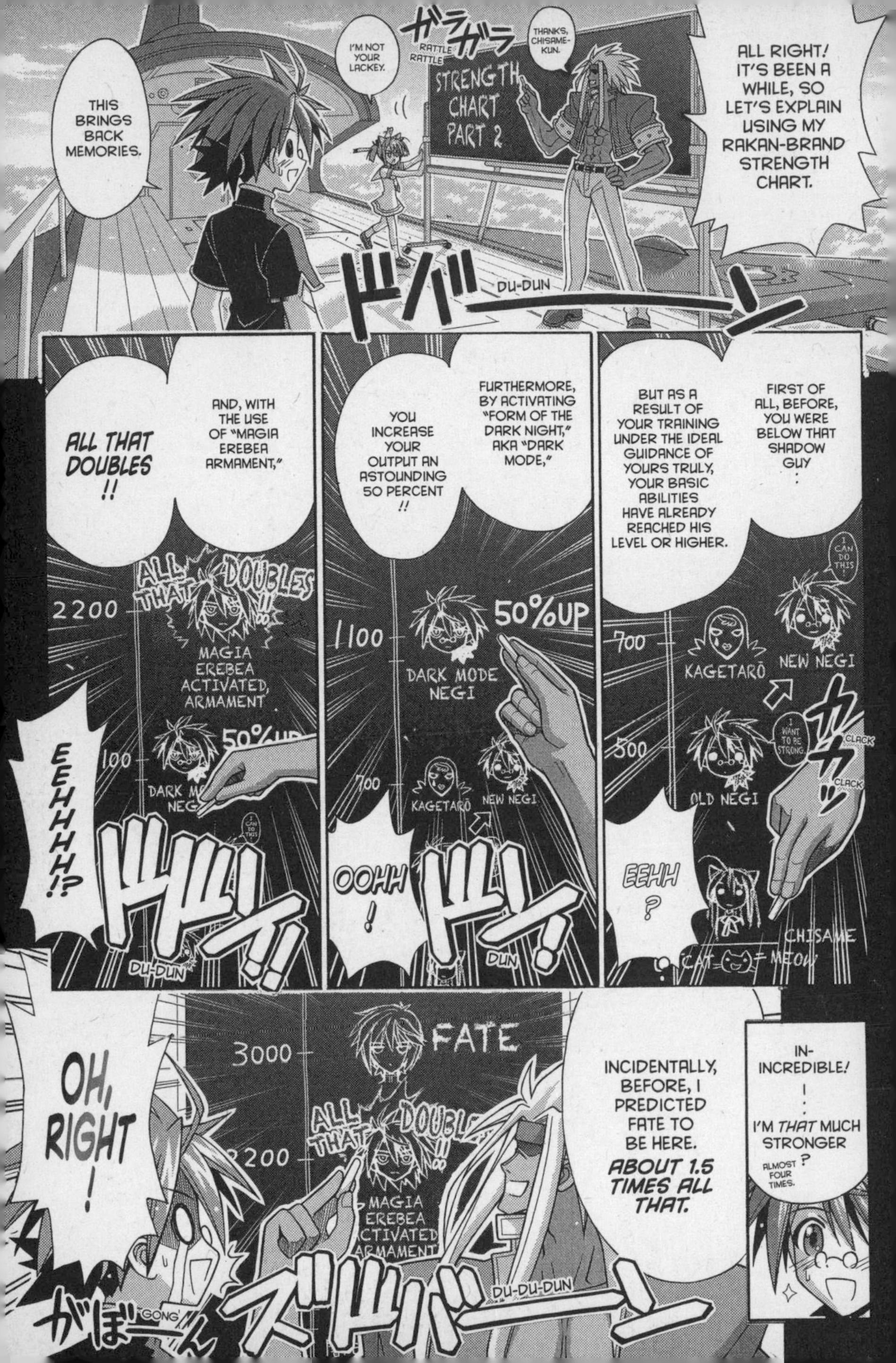

ALL RIGHT! IT'S BEEN A WHILE, SO LET'S EXPLAIN USING MY RAKAN-BRAND STRENGTH CHART.
THANKS, CHISAME-KUN.
RATTLE RATTLE
I'M NOT YOUR LACKEY.
STRENGTH CHART PART 2
THIS BRINGS BACK MEMORIES.
DU-DUN
FIRST OF ALL, BEFORE, YOU WERE BELOW THAT SHADOW GUY :
BUT AS A RESULT OF YOUR TRAINING UNDER THE IDEAL GUIDANCE OF YOURS TRULY, YOUR BASIC ABILITIES HAVE ALREADY REACHED HIS LEVEL OR HIGHER.
700
KAGETARŌ
I CAN DO THIS
NEW NEGI
500
I WANT TO BE STRONG.
OLD NEGI
CLACK
CLACK
EEHH ?
CHISAME
CAT = MEOW
FURTHERMORE, BY ACTIVATING "FORM OF THE DARK NIGHT," AKA "DARK MODE,"
YOU INCREASE YOUR OUTPUT AN ASTOUNDING 50 PERCENT !!
1100
50%UP
DARK MODE NEGI
700
KAGETARŌ
NEW NEGI
OOHH !
DUN
AND, WITH THE USE OF "MAGIA EREBEA ARMAMENT,"
ALL THAT DOUBLES !!
2200
ALL THAT DOUBLES !!
MAGIA EREBEA ACTIVATED, ARMAMENT
100
50%UP
DARK MODE NEGI
I CAN DO THIS
EEHHHHH!?
DU-DUN
IN-INCREDIBLE! : I'M THAT MUCH STRONGER ?
ALMOST FOUR TIMES.
INCIDENTALLY, BEFORE, I PREDICTED FATE TO BE HERE. ABOUT 1.5 TIMES ALL THAT.
FATE
3000
ALL THAT DOUBLES !!
2200
MAGIA EREBEA ACTIVATED ARMAMENT
OH, RIGHT !
DU-DU-DUN
GONG

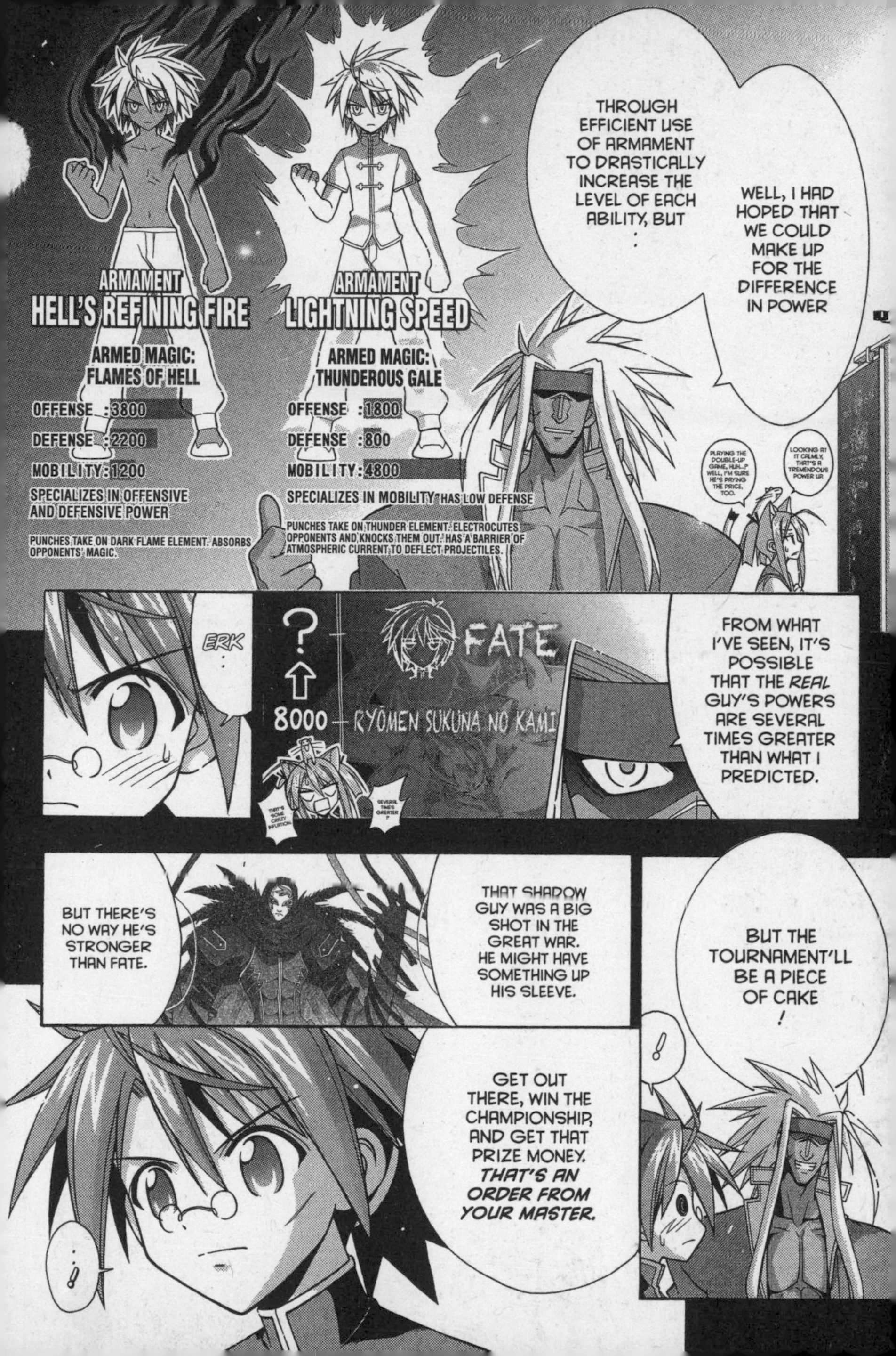

WELL, I HAD HOPED THAT WE COULD MAKE UP FOR THE DIFFERENCE IN POWER
THROUGH EFFICIENT USE OF ARMAMENT TO DRASTICALLY INCREASE THE LEVEL OF EACH ABILITY, BUT :
LOOKING AT IT CALMLY, THAT'S A TREMENDOUS POWER UP.
PLAYING THE DOUBLE-UP GAME, HUH...? WELL, I'M SURE HE'S PAYING THE PRICE, TOO.
ARMAMENT
LIGHTNING SPEED
ARMED MAGIC: THUNDEROUS GALE
OFFENSE : 1800
DEFENSE : 800
MOBILITY : 4800
SPECIALIZES IN MOBILITY HAS LOW DEFENSE
PUNCHES TAKE ON THUNDER ELEMENT. ELECTROCUTES OPPONENTS AND KNOCKS THEM OUT. HAS A BARRIER OF ATMOSPHERIC CURRENT TO DEFLECT PROJECTILES.
ARMAMENT
HELL'S REFINING FIRE
ARMED MAGIC: FLAMES OF HELL
OFFENSE : 3800
DEFENSE : 2200
MOBILITY : 1200
SPECIALIZES IN OFFENSIVE AND DEFENSIVE POWER
PUNCHES TAKE ON DARK FLAME ELEMENT. ABSORBS OPPONENTS' MAGIC.
FROM WHAT I'VE SEEN, IT'S POSSIBLE THAT THE *REAL* GUY'S POWERS ARE SEVERAL TIMES GREATER THAN WHAT I PREDICTED.
?
FATE
8000 — RYŌMEN SUKUNA NO KAMI
SEVERAL TIMES GREATER ?
THAT'S SOME CRAZY INFLATION.
ERK :
BUT THE TOURNAMENT'LL BE A PIECE OF CAKE !
!
THAT SHADOW GUY WAS A BIG SHOT IN THE GREAT WAR. HE MIGHT HAVE SOMETHING UP HIS SLEEVE.
BUT THERE'S NO WAY HE'S STRONGER THAN FATE.
GET OUT THERE, WIN THE CHAMPIONSHIP, AND GET THAT PRIZE MONEY. *THAT'S AN ORDER FROM YOUR MASTER.*
: !

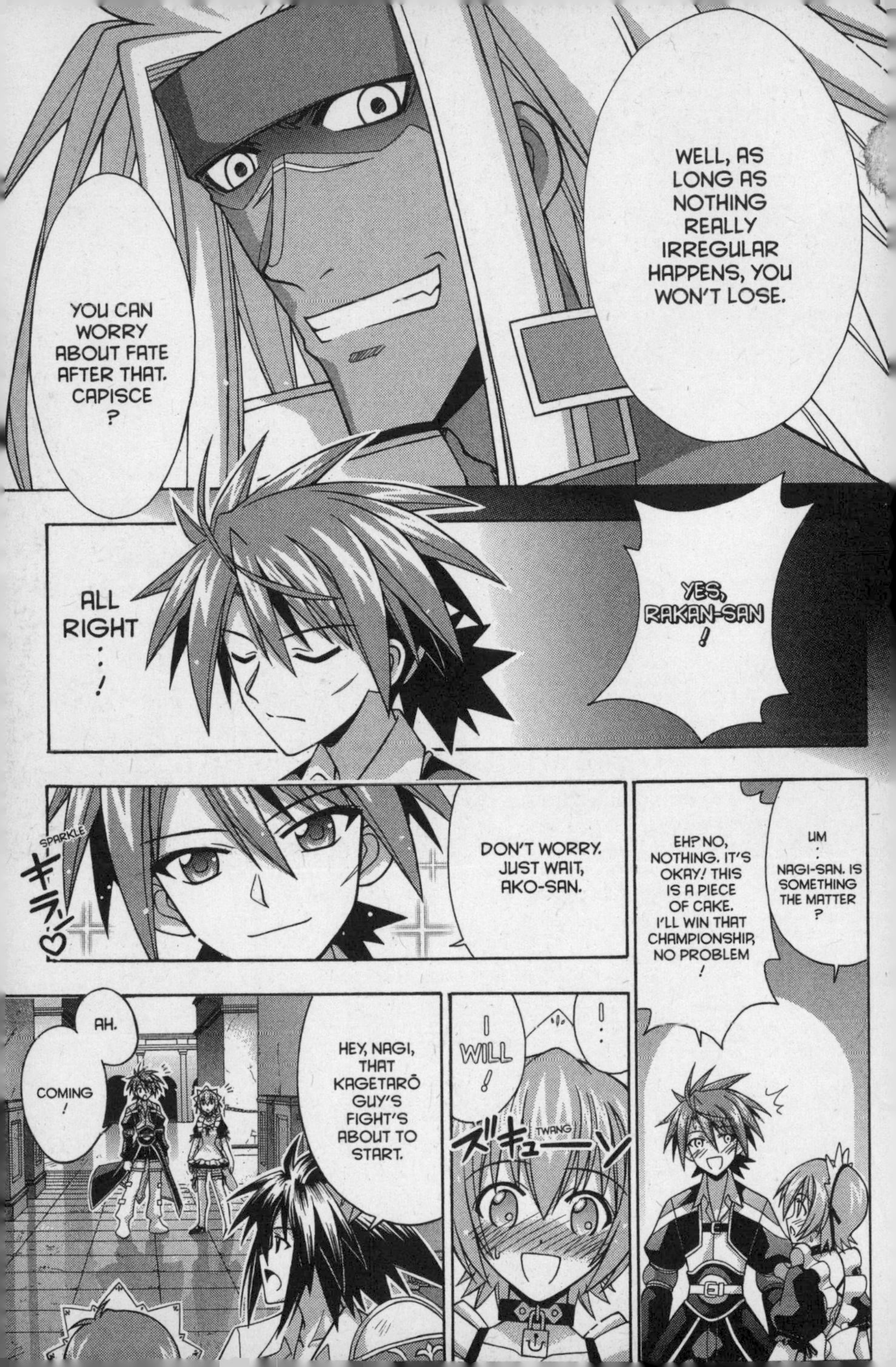

WELL, AS LONG AS NOTHING REALLY IRREGULAR HAPPENS, YOU WON'T LOSE.
YOU CAN WORRY ABOUT FATE AFTER THAT. CAPISCE?
YES, RAKAN-SAN!
ALL RIGHT...!
UM... NAGI-SAN. IS SOMETHING THE MATTER?
EH? NO, NOTHING. IT'S OKAY! THIS IS A PIECE OF CAKE. I'LL WIN THAT CHAMPIONSHIP, NO PROBLEM!
SPARKLE
DON'T WORRY. JUST WAIT, AKO-SAN.
!..
I WILL!
TWANG
HEY, NAGI, THAT KAGETARŌ GUY'S FIGHT'S ABOUT TO START.
AH.
COMING!

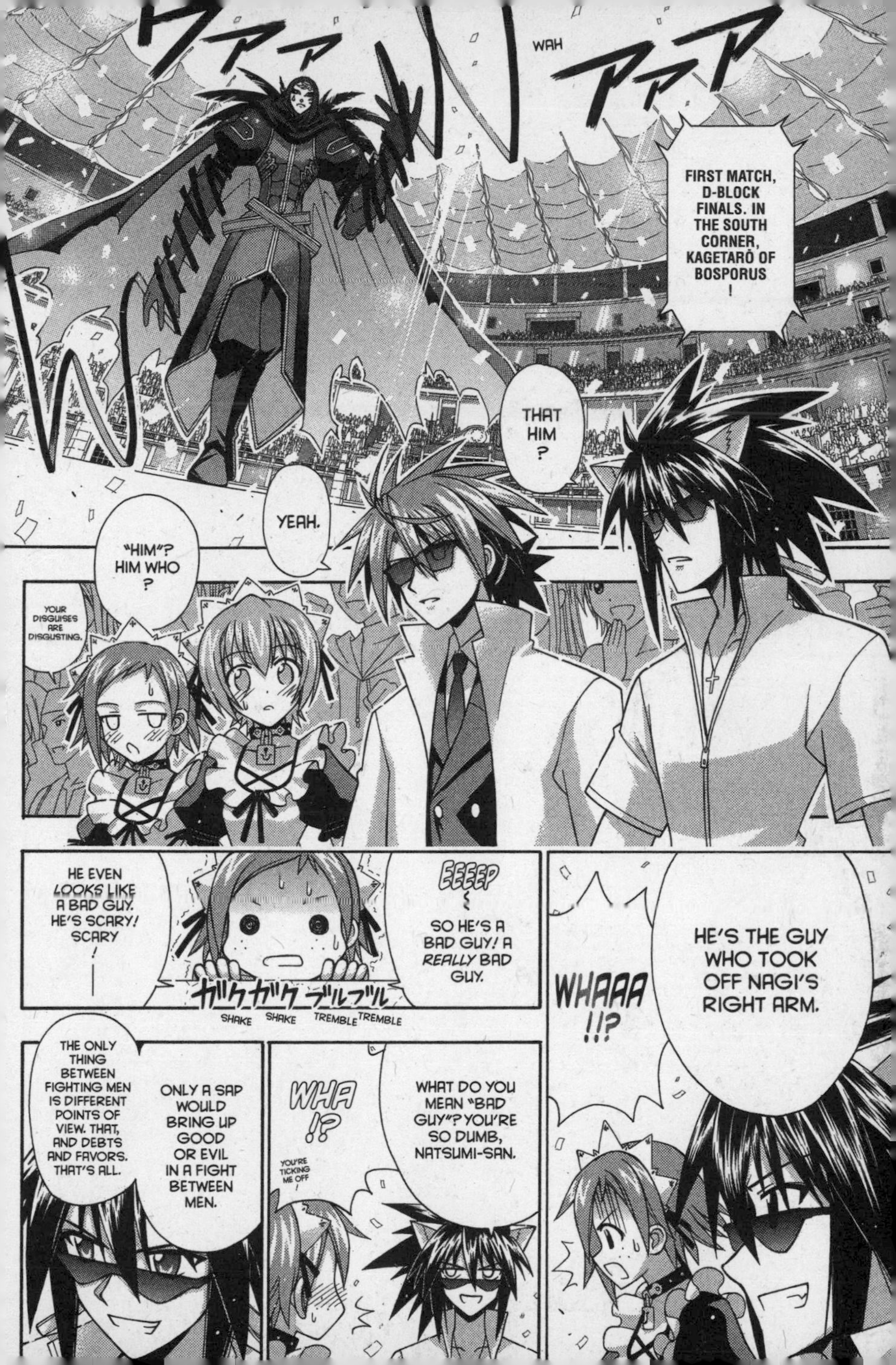
ワァァ
WAH
アァァ
FIRST MATCH, D-BLOCK FINALS. IN THE SOUTH CORNER, KAGETARŌ OF BOSPORUS!
THAT HIM?
YEAH.
"HIM"? HIM WHO?
YOUR DISGUISES ARE DISGUSTING.
HE'S THE GUY WHO TOOK OFF NAGI'S RIGHT ARM.
WHAAA!!?
EEEEP
SO HE'S A BAD GUY! A *REALLY* BAD GUY.
HE EVEN *LOOKS* LIKE A BAD GUY. HE'S SCARY! SCARY!
ガクガク ブルブル
SHAKE SHAKE TREMBLE TREMBLE
WHAT DO YOU MEAN "BAD GUY"? YOU'RE SO DUMB, NATSUMI-SAN.
WHA!?
YOU'RE TICKING ME OFF!
ONLY A SAP WOULD BRING UP GOOD OR EVIL IN A FIGHT BETWEEN MEN.
THE ONLY THING BETWEEN FIGHTING MEN IS DIFFERENT POINTS OF VIEW. THAT, AND DEBTS AND FAVORS. THAT'S ALL.

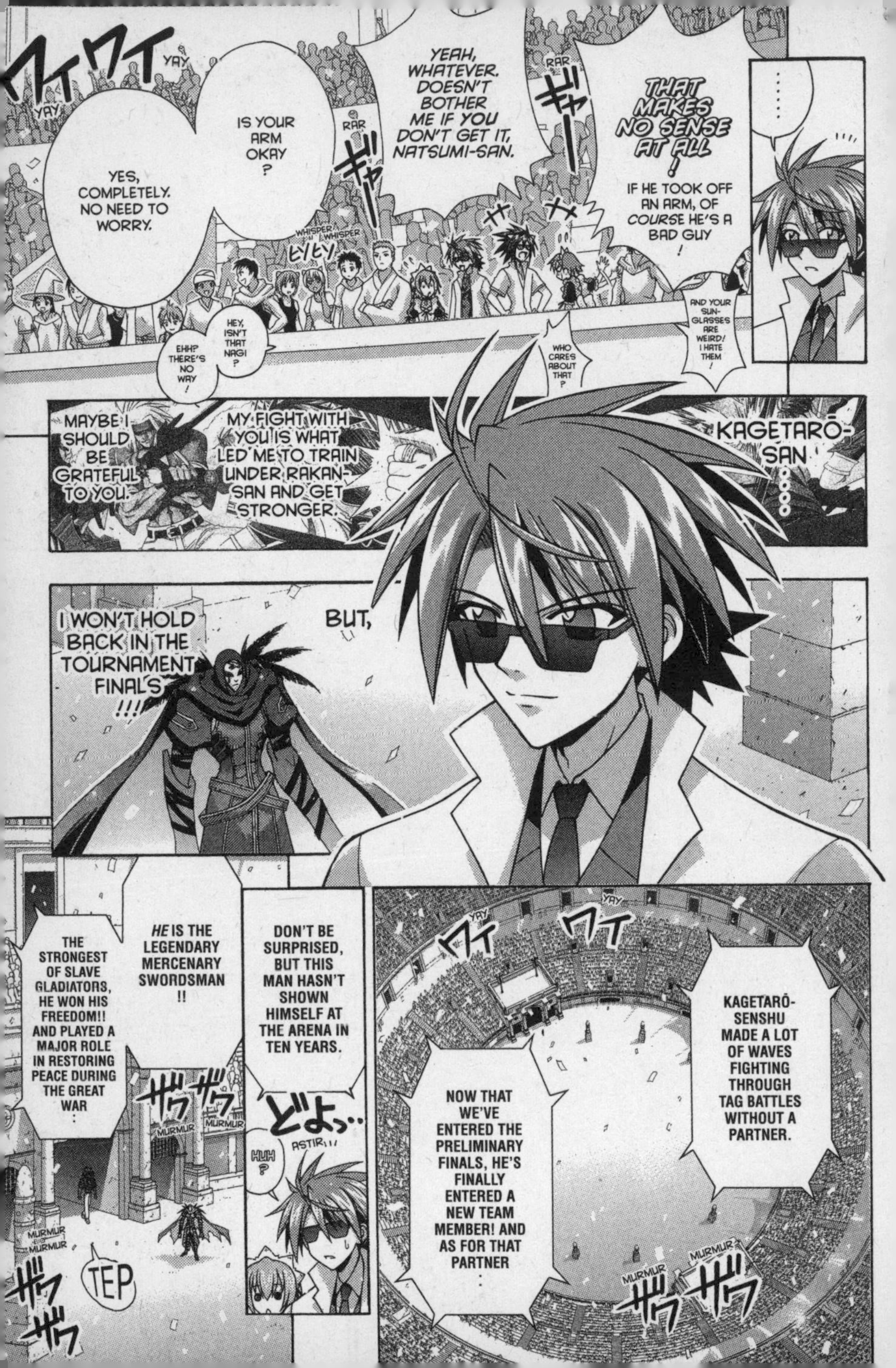
……
THAT MAKES NO SENSE AT ALL!
IF HE TOOK OFF AN ARM, OF COURSE HE'S A BAD GUY!
RAR ギャー
YEAH, WHATEVER. DOESN'T BOTHER ME IF YOU DON'T GET IT, NATSUMI-SAN.
RAR ギャ
IS YOUR ARM OKAY?
YES, COMPLETELY. NO NEED TO WORRY.
ワイワイ YAY YAY
AND YOUR SUNGLASSES ARE WEIRD! I HATE THEM!
WHO CARES ABOUT THAT?
WHISPER WHISPER ヒソヒソ
HEY, ISN'T THAT NAGI?
EHH? THERE'S NO WAY!
KAGETARŌ-SAN……
MY FIGHT WITH YOU IS WHAT LED ME TO TRAIN UNDER RAKAN-SAN AND GET STRONGER.
MAYBE I SHOULD BE GRATEFUL TO YOU.
BUT,
I WON'T HOLD BACK IN THE TOURNAMENT FINALS!!!
YAY ワイ YAY ワイ
KAGETARŌ-SENSHU MADE A LOT OF WAVES FIGHTING THROUGH TAG BATTLES WITHOUT A PARTNER.
NOW THAT WE'VE ENTERED THE PRELIMINARY FINALS, HE'S FINALLY ENTERED A NEW TEAM MEMBER! AND AS FOR THAT PARTNER:
MURMUR MURMUR ザワザワ
DON'T BE SURPRISED, BUT THIS MAN HASN'T SHOWN HIMSELF AT THE ARENA IN TEN YEARS.
ASTIR どよっ
HUH?
HE IS THE LEGENDARY MERCENARY SWORDSMAN!!
THE STRONGEST OF SLAVE GLADIATORS, HE WON HIS FREEDOM!! AND PLAYED A MAJOR ROLE IN RESTORING PEACE DURING THE GREAT WAR:
MURMUR MURMUR ザワザワ
TEP
MURMUR MURMUR ザワザワ

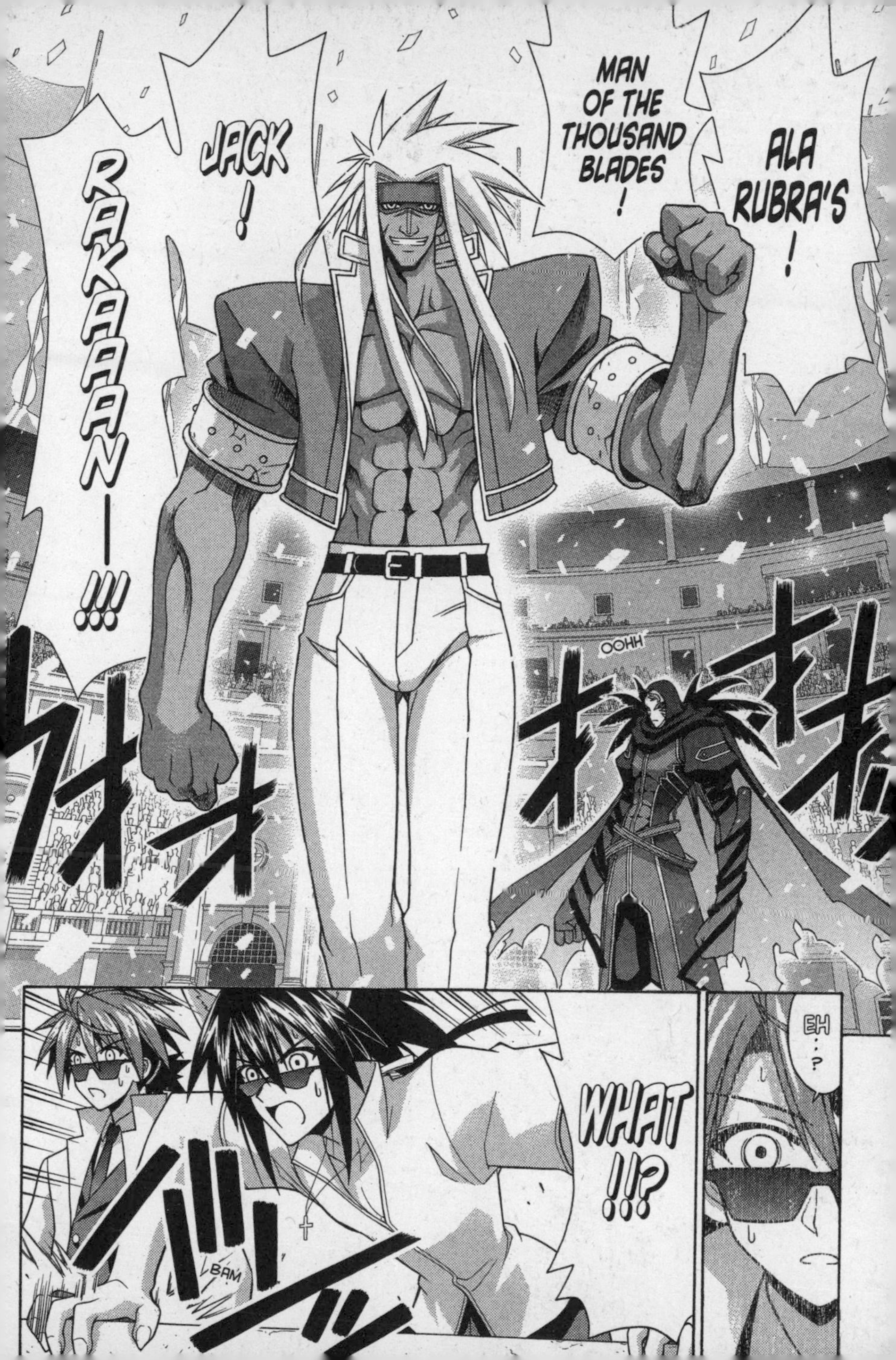
ALA RUBRA'S !
MAN OF THE THOUSAND BLADES !
JACK !
RAKAAAAAN—!!!
OOHH
EH...?
WHAT !!?
BAM

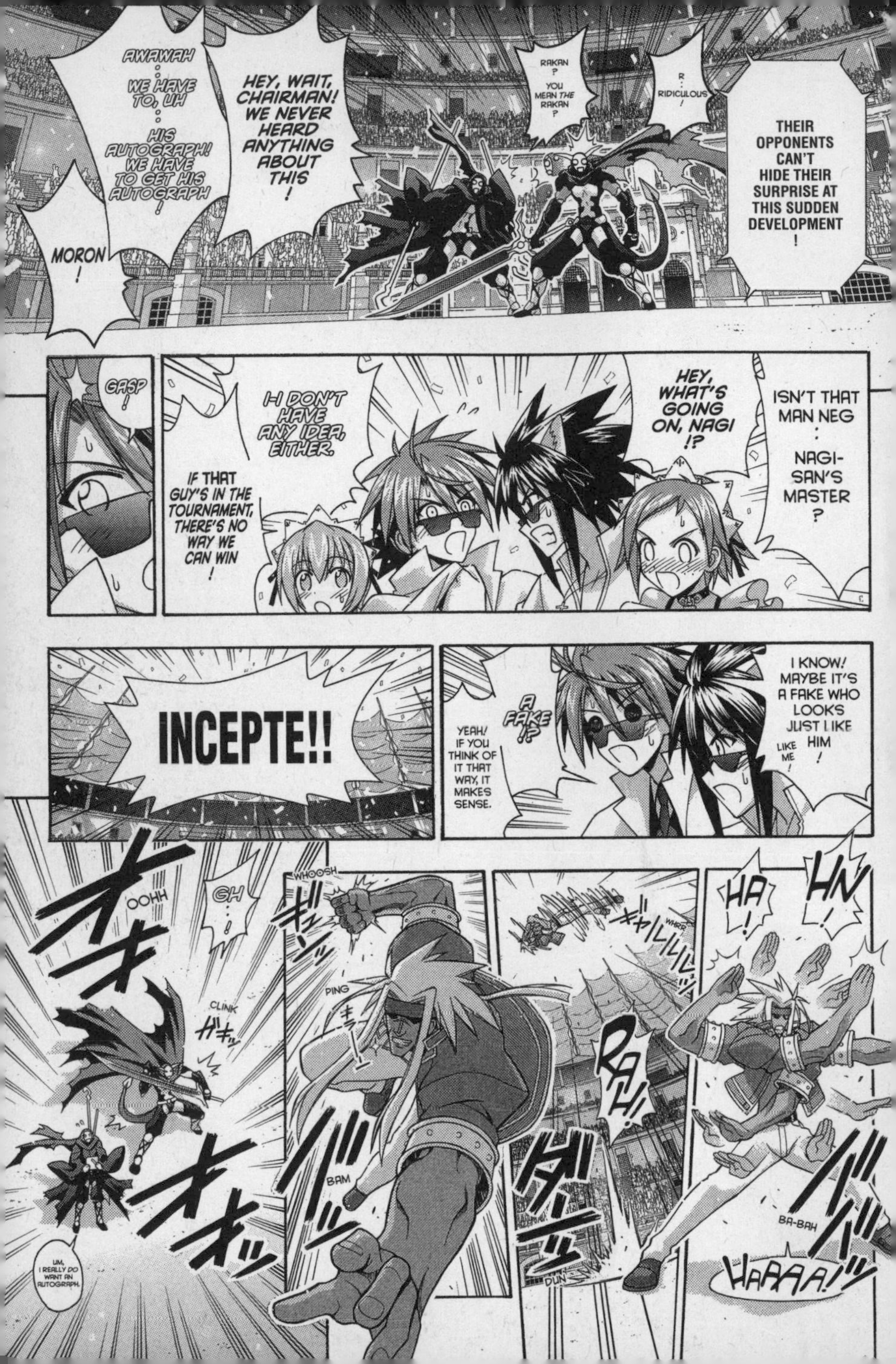
THEIR OPPONENTS CAN'T HIDE THEIR SURPRISE AT THIS SUDDEN DEVELOPMENT!
R... RIDICULOUS!
RAKAN? YOU MEAN THE RAKAN?
HEY, WAIT, CHAIRMAN! WE NEVER HEARD ANYTHING ABOUT THIS!
AWAWAH... WE HAVE TO, UH... HIS AUTOGRAPH! WE HAVE TO GET HIS AUTOGRAPH!
MORON!
ISN'T THAT MAN NEG: NAGI-SAN'S MASTER?
HEY, WHAT'S GOING ON, NAGI!?
I-I DON'T HAVE ANY IDEA, EITHER.
IF THAT GUY'S IN THE TOURNAMENT, THERE'S NO WAY WE CAN WIN!
GASP!
I KNOW! MAYBE IT'S A FAKE WHO LOOKS JUST LIKE HIM!
LIKE ME!
A FAKE!?
YEAH! IF YOU THINK OF IT THAT WAY, IT MAKES SENSE.
INCEPTE!!
HN!
HA!
RAH!
BA-BAH
HAAAAA!
WHRR
WHOOSH
PING
BAM
DUN
GH...!
OOHH
CLINK
UM, I REALLY DO WANT AN AUTOGRAPH.

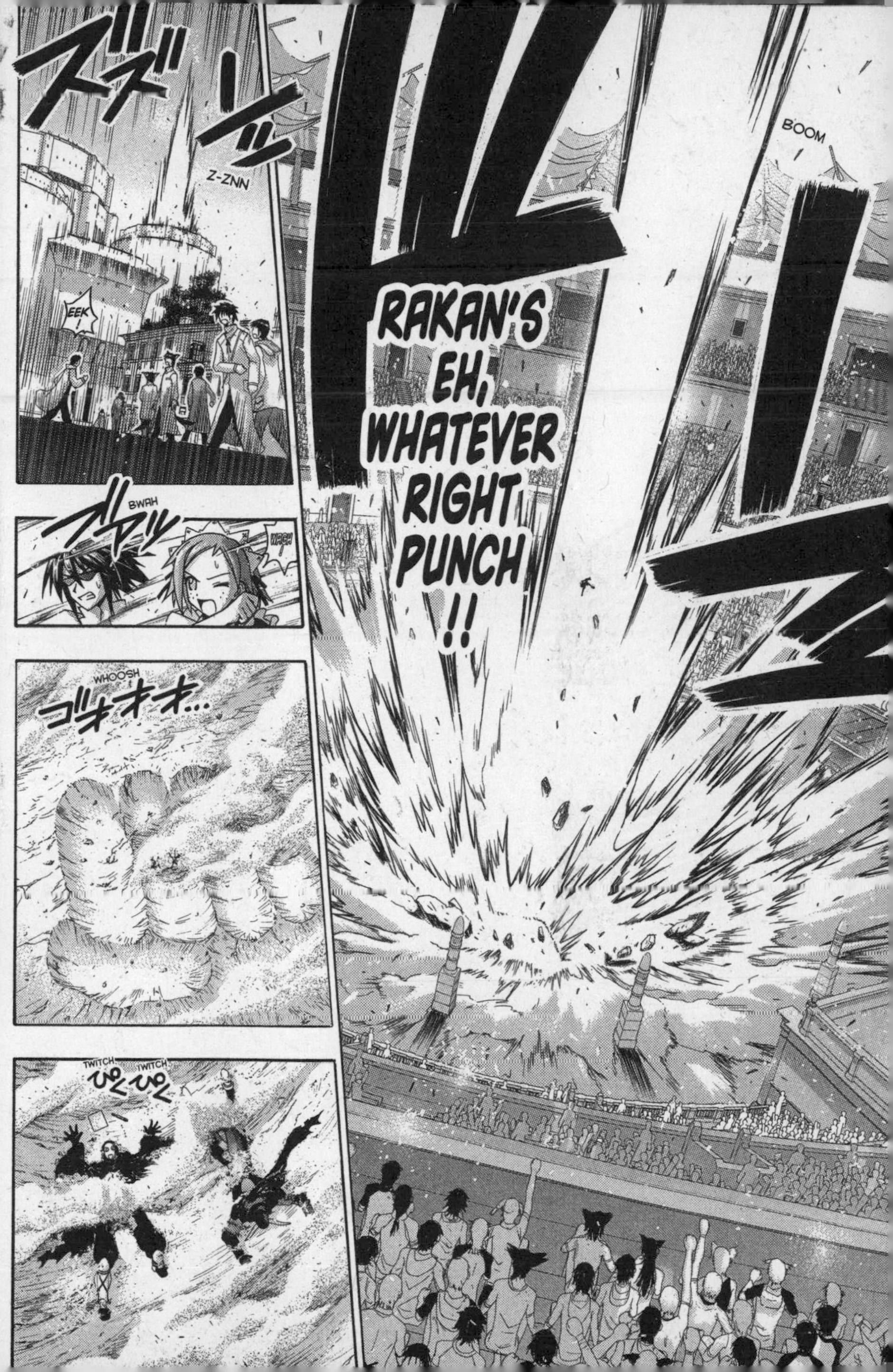

BOOM
RAKAN'S EH, WHATEVER RIGHT PUNCH!!
Z-ZNN
EEK!
BWAH
WAGH!
WHOOSH
TWITCH TWITCH

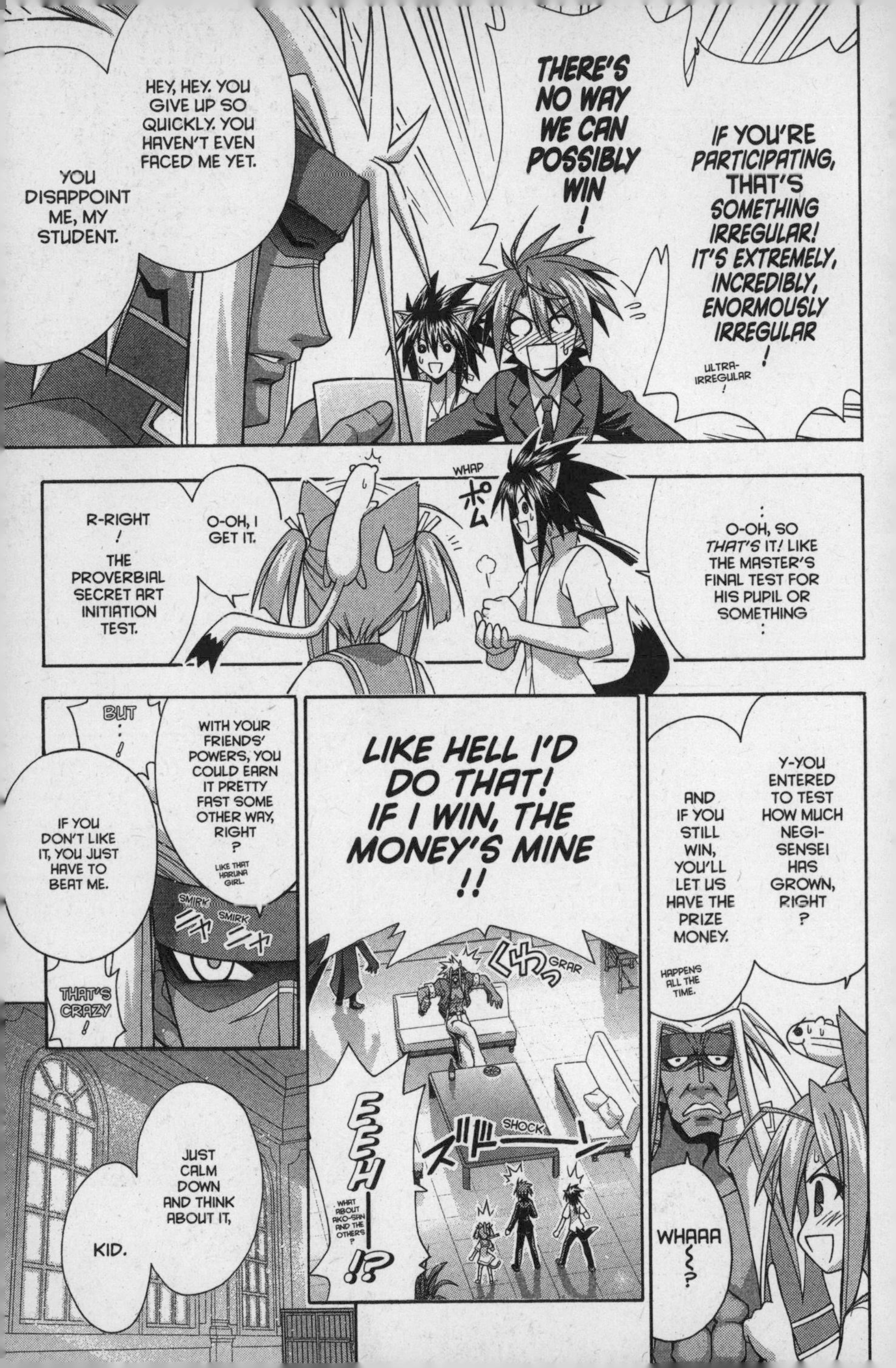
IF YOU'RE PARTICIPATING, THAT'S SOMETHING IRREGULAR! IT'S EXTREMELY, INCREDIBLY, ENORMOUSLY IRREGULAR!
ULTRA-IRREGULAR!
THERE'S NO WAY WE CAN POSSIBLY WIN!
HEY, HEY. YOU GIVE UP SO QUICKLY. YOU HAVEN'T EVEN FACED ME YET.
YOU DISAPPOINT ME, MY STUDENT.
...O-OH, SO THAT'S IT! LIKE THE MASTER'S FINAL TEST FOR HIS PUPIL OR SOMETHING...
WHAP
ポム
O-OH, I GET IT.
R-RIGHT! THE PROVERBIAL SECRET ART INITIATION TEST.
Y-YOU ENTERED TO TEST HOW MUCH NEGI-SENSEI HAS GROWN, RIGHT?
AND IF YOU STILL WIN, YOU'LL LET US HAVE THE PRIZE MONEY.
HAPPENS ALL THE TIME.
WHAAA~?
LIKE HELL I'D DO THAT! IF I WIN, THE MONEY'S MINE!!
くわっ
GRAR
EEEH!?
WHAT ABOUT AKO-SAN AND THE OTHERS?
ズドーン
SHOCK
BUT...!
WITH YOUR FRIENDS' POWERS, YOU COULD EARN IT PRETTY FAST SOME OTHER WAY, RIGHT?
LIKE THAT HARUNA GIRL.
IF YOU DON'T LIKE IT, YOU JUST HAVE TO BEAT ME.
SMIRK SMIRK
ニヤ ニヤ
THAT'S CRAZY!
JUST CALM DOWN AND THINK ABOUT IT, KID.

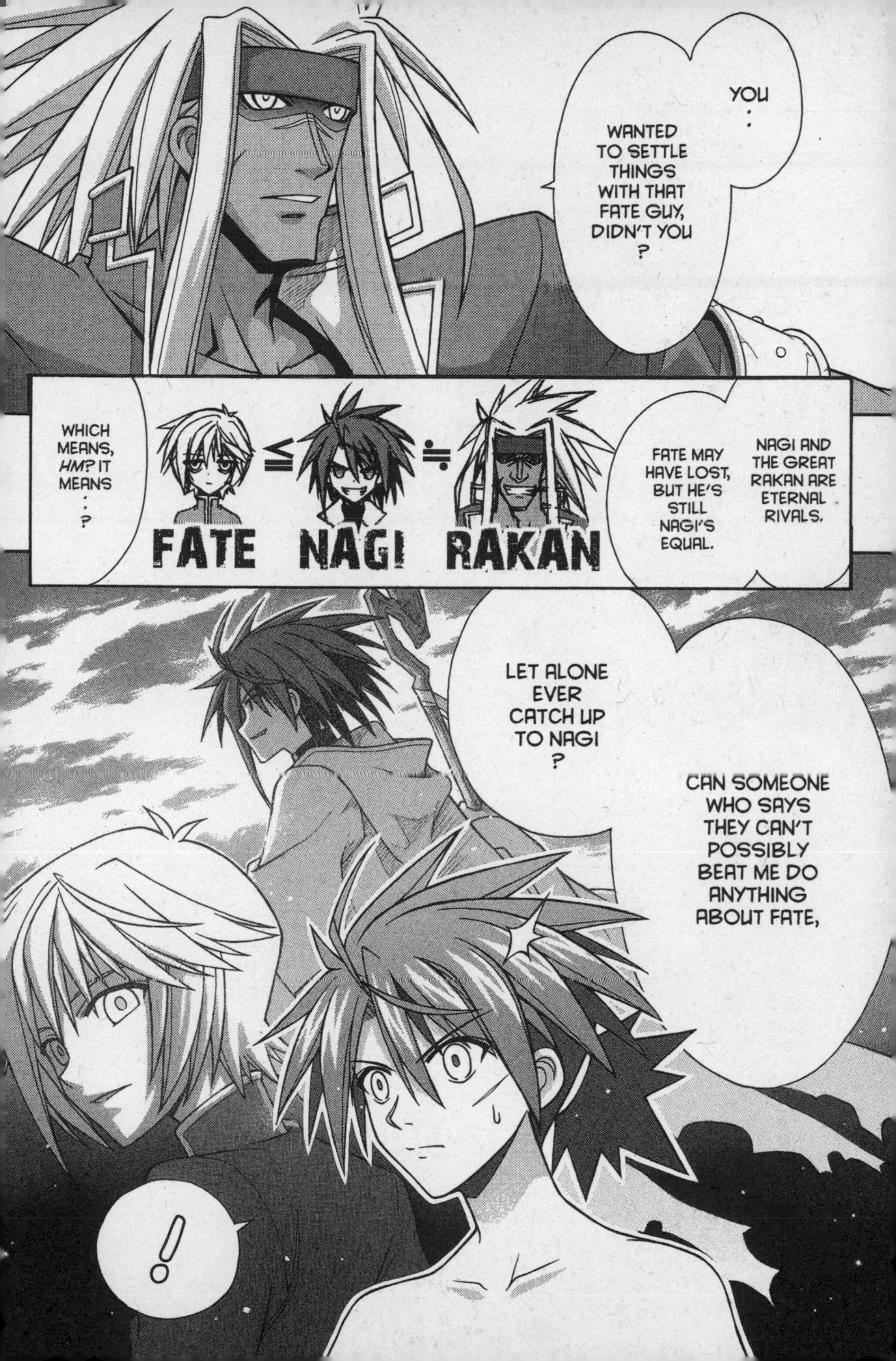
YOU . . . WANTED TO SETTLE THINGS WITH THAT FATE GUY, DIDN'T YOU ?
NAGI AND THE GREAT RAKAN ARE ETERNAL RIVALS.
FATE MAY HAVE LOST, BUT HE'S STILL NAGI'S EQUAL.
FATE ≦ NAGI ≒ RAKAN
WHICH MEANS, *HM?* IT MEANS . . . ?
CAN SOMEONE WHO SAYS THEY CAN'T POSSIBLY BEAT ME DO ANYTHING ABOUT FATE,
LET ALONE EVER CATCH UP TO NAGI ?
!

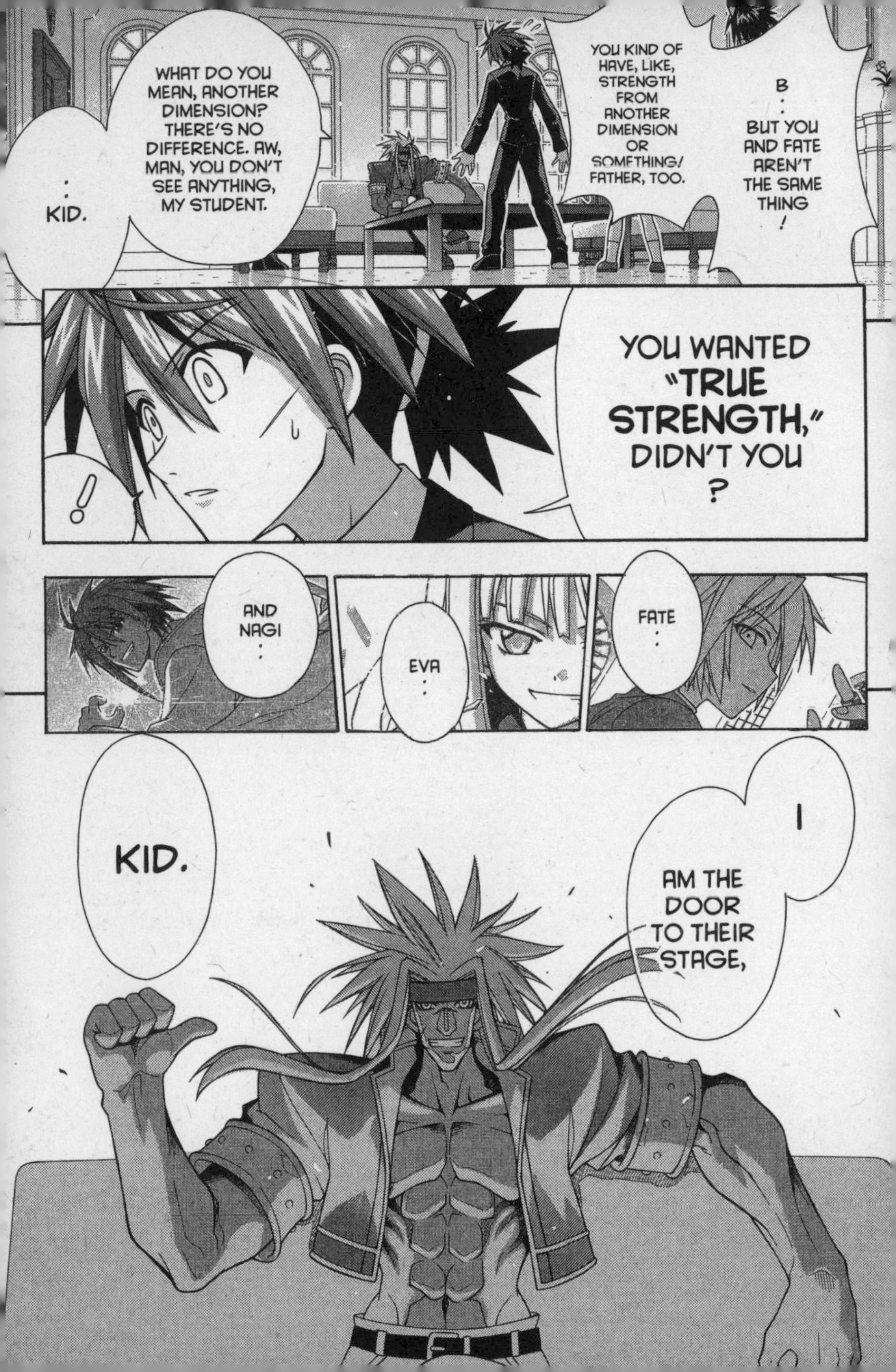
B. . BUT YOU AND FATE AREN'T THE SAME THING!
YOU KIND OF HAVE, LIKE, STRENGTH FROM ANOTHER DIMENSION OR SOMETHING! FATHER, TOO.
WHAT DO YOU MEAN, ANOTHER DIMENSION? THERE'S NO DIFFERENCE. AW, MAN, YOU DON'T SEE ANYTHING, MY STUDENT.
. . KID.
YOU WANTED "TRUE STRENGTH," DIDN'T YOU?
!
FATE . .
EVA . .
AND NAGI . .
I AM THE DOOR TO THEIR STAGE,
KID.

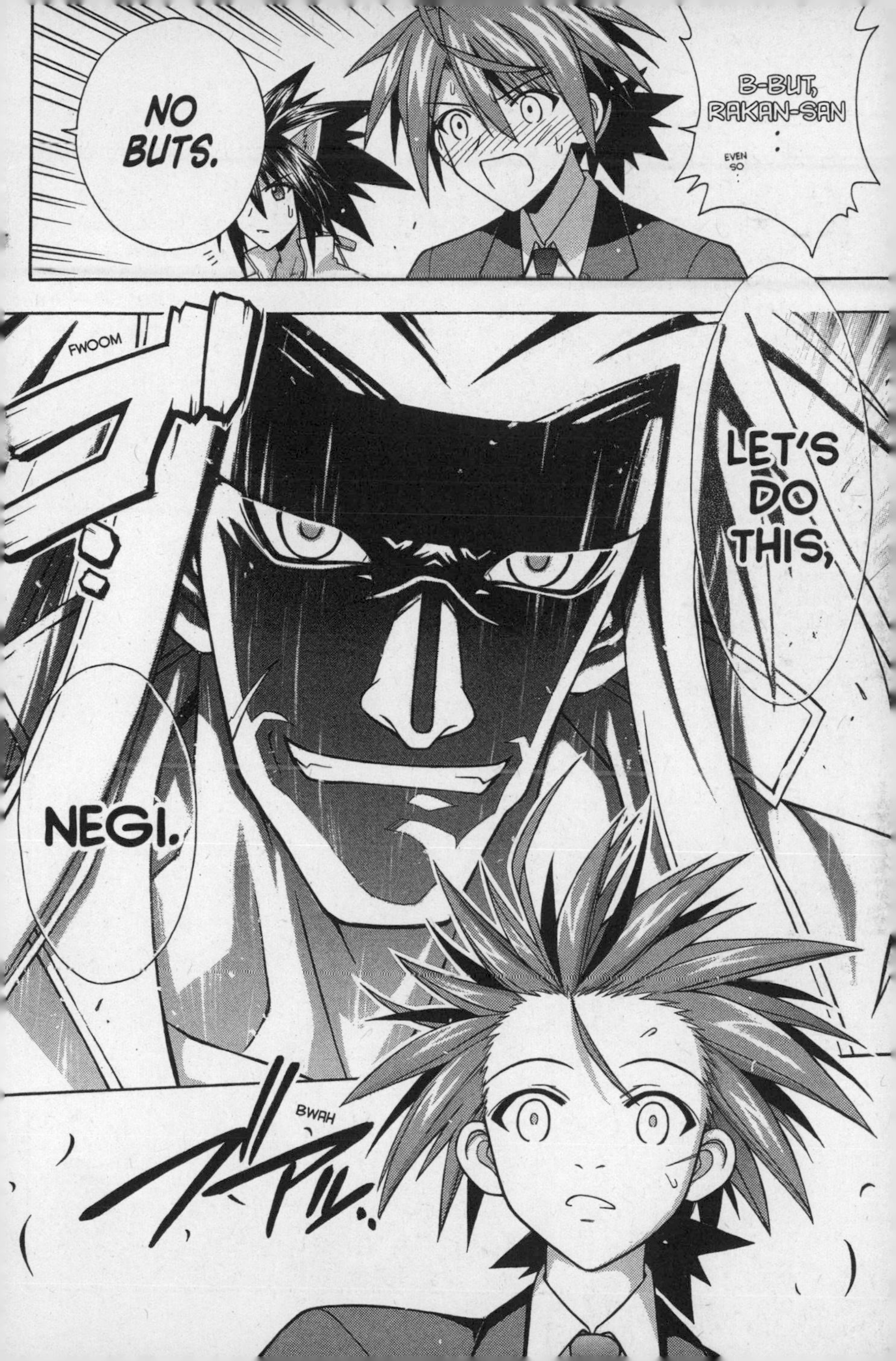
B-BUT, RAKAN-SAN
...
EVEN SO
...
NO BUTS.
LET'S DO THIS,
FWOOM
NEGI.
BWAH

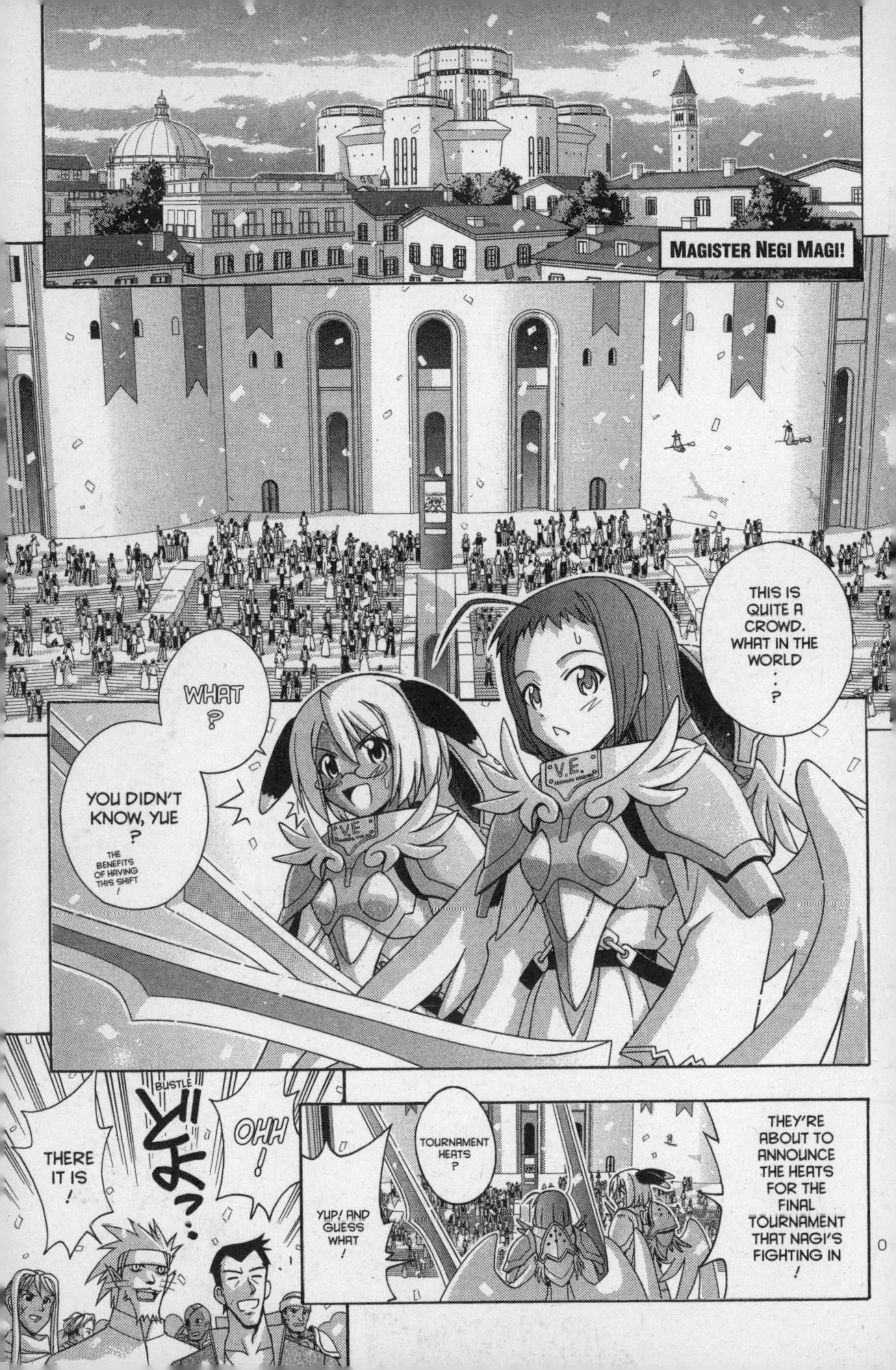
MAGISTER NEGI MAGI!
THIS IS QUITE A CROWD. WHAT IN THE WORLD . . ?
WHAT ?
YOU DIDN'T KNOW, YUE ?
THE BENEFITS OF HAVING THIS SHIFT !
THEY'RE ABOUT TO ANNOUNCE THE HEATS FOR THE FINAL TOURNAMENT THAT NAGI'S FIGHTING IN !
TOURNAMENT HEATS ?
YUP! AND GUESS WHAT !
OHH !
BUSTLE
THERE IT IS !

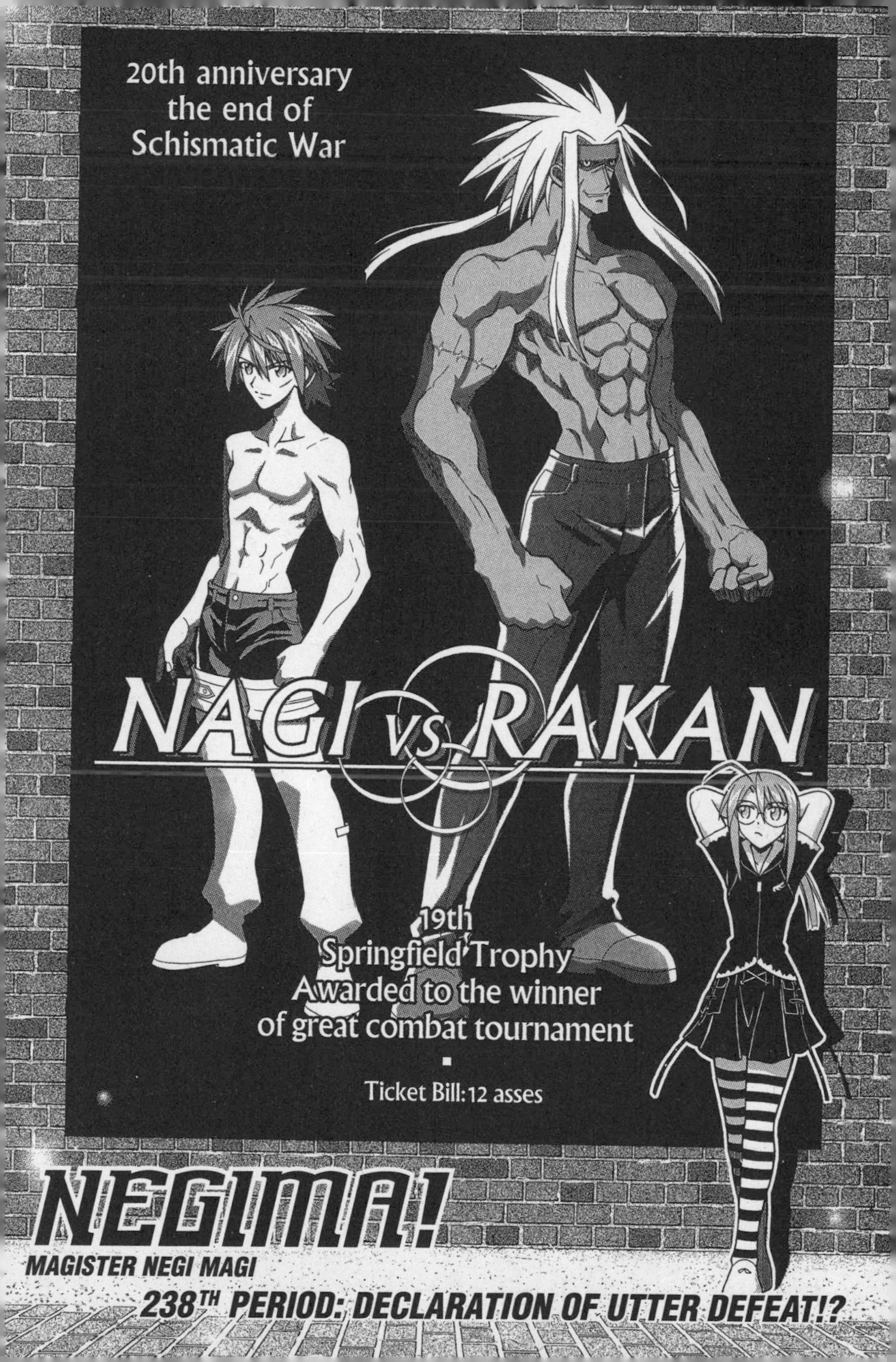

20th anniversary the end of Schismatic War
NAGI VS RAKAN
19th Springfield Trophy Awarded to the winner of great combat tournament
Ticket Bill: 12 asses
NEGIMA!
MAGISTER NEGI MAGI
238TH PERIOD: DECLARATION OF UTTER DEFEAT!?

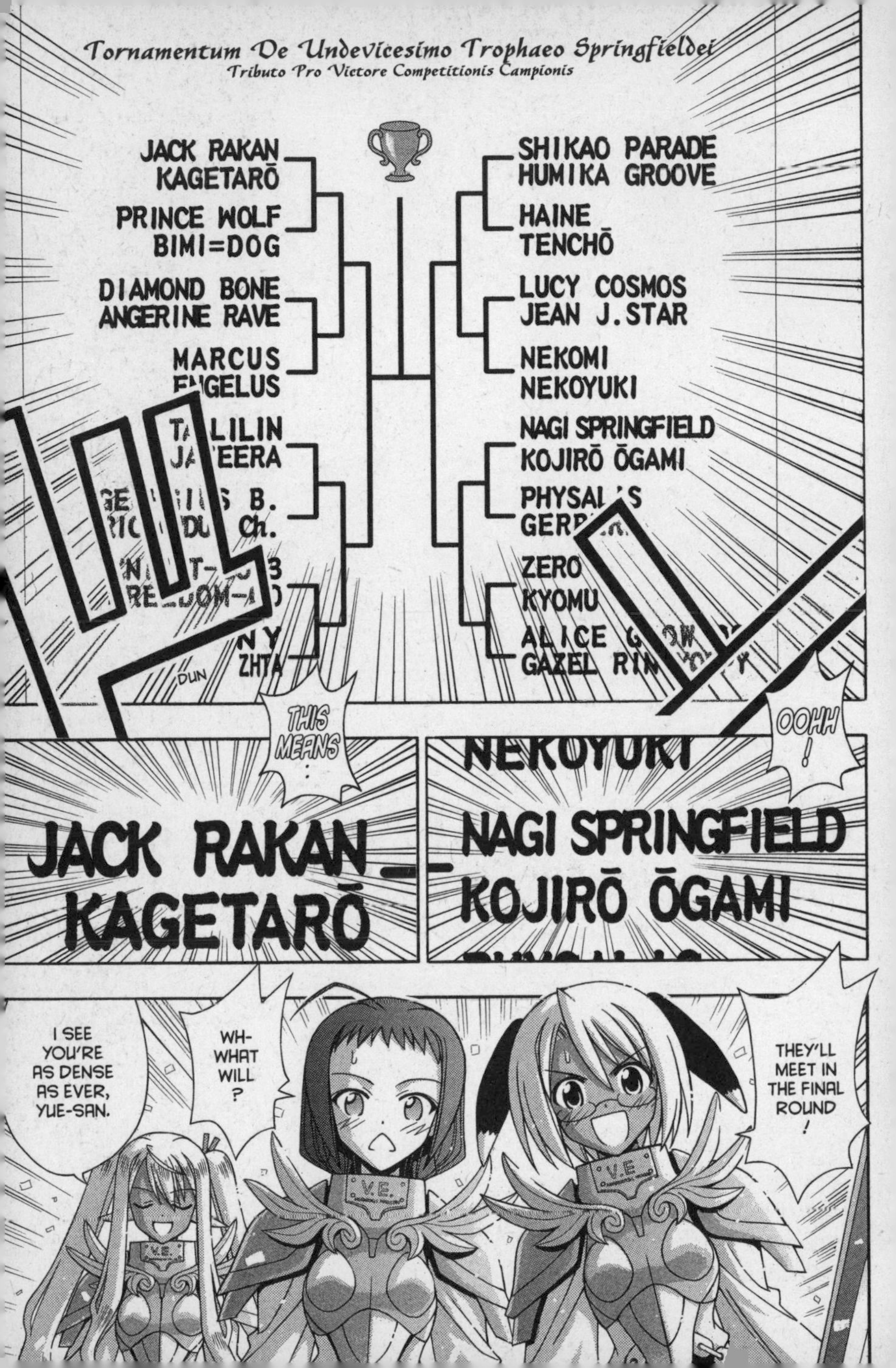
Tornamentum De Undevicesimo Trophaeo Springfieldei
Tributo Pro Victore Competitionis Campionis
SHIKAO PARADE
HUMIKA GROOVE
HAINE
TENCHŌ
LUCY COSMOS
JEAN J.STAR
NEKOMI
NEKOYUKI
NAGI SPRINGFIELD
KOJIRŌ ŌGAMI
ZERO
KYOMU
JACK RAKAN
KAGETARŌ
PRINCE WOLF
BIMI=DOG
DIAMOND BONE
ANGERINE RAVE
MARCUS
ENGELUS
DUN
OOHH!
NEKOYUKI
NAGI SPRINGFIELD
KOJIRŌ ŌGAMI
THIS MEANS...
JACK RAKAN
KAGETARŌ
THEY'LL MEET IN THE FINAL ROUND!
WH-WHAT WILL?
I SEE YOU'RE AS DENSE AS EVER, YUE-SAN.

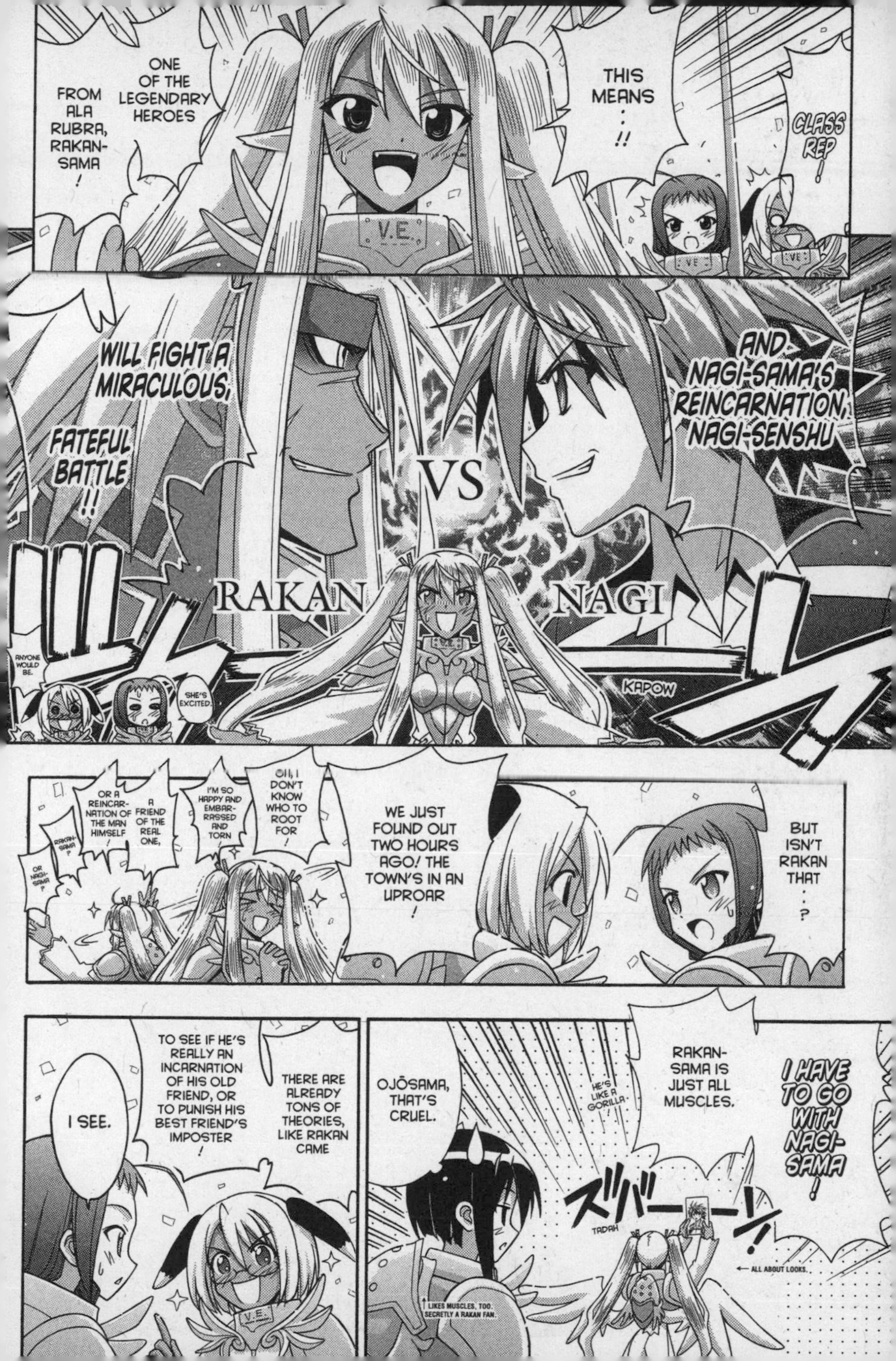
CLASS REP!
THIS MEANS...!!
ONE OF THE LEGENDARY HEROES
FROM ALA RUBRA, RAKAN-SAMA!
AND NAGI-SAMA'S REINCARNATION, NAGI-SENSHU
WILL FIGHT A MIRACULOUS,
FATEFUL BATTLE!!
VS
NAGI
RAKAN
KAPOW
SHE'S EXCITED.
ANYONE WOULD BE.
BUT ISN'T RAKAN THAT...?
WE JUST FOUND OUT TWO HOURS AGO! THE TOWN'S IN AN UPROAR!
OH, I DON'T KNOW WHO TO ROOT FOR!
I'M SO HAPPY AND EMBARRASSED AND TORN
A FRIEND OF THE REAL ONE,
OR A REINCARNATION OF THE MAN HIMSELF!
RAKAN-SAMA?
OR NAGI-SAMA?
I HAVE TO GO WITH NAGI-SAMA!
RAKAN-SAMA IS JUST ALL MUSCLES.
HE'S LIKE A GORILLA!
OJŌSAMA, THAT'S CRUEL.
ズバーーー!
TADAH
ALL ABOUT LOOKS.
LIKES MUSCLES, TOO. SECRETLY A RAKAN FAN.
THERE ARE ALREADY TONS OF THEORIES, LIKE RAKAN CAME
TO SEE IF HE'S REALLY AN INCARNATION OF HIS OLD FRIEND, OR TO PUNISH HIS BEST FRIEND'S IMPOSTER!
I SEE.

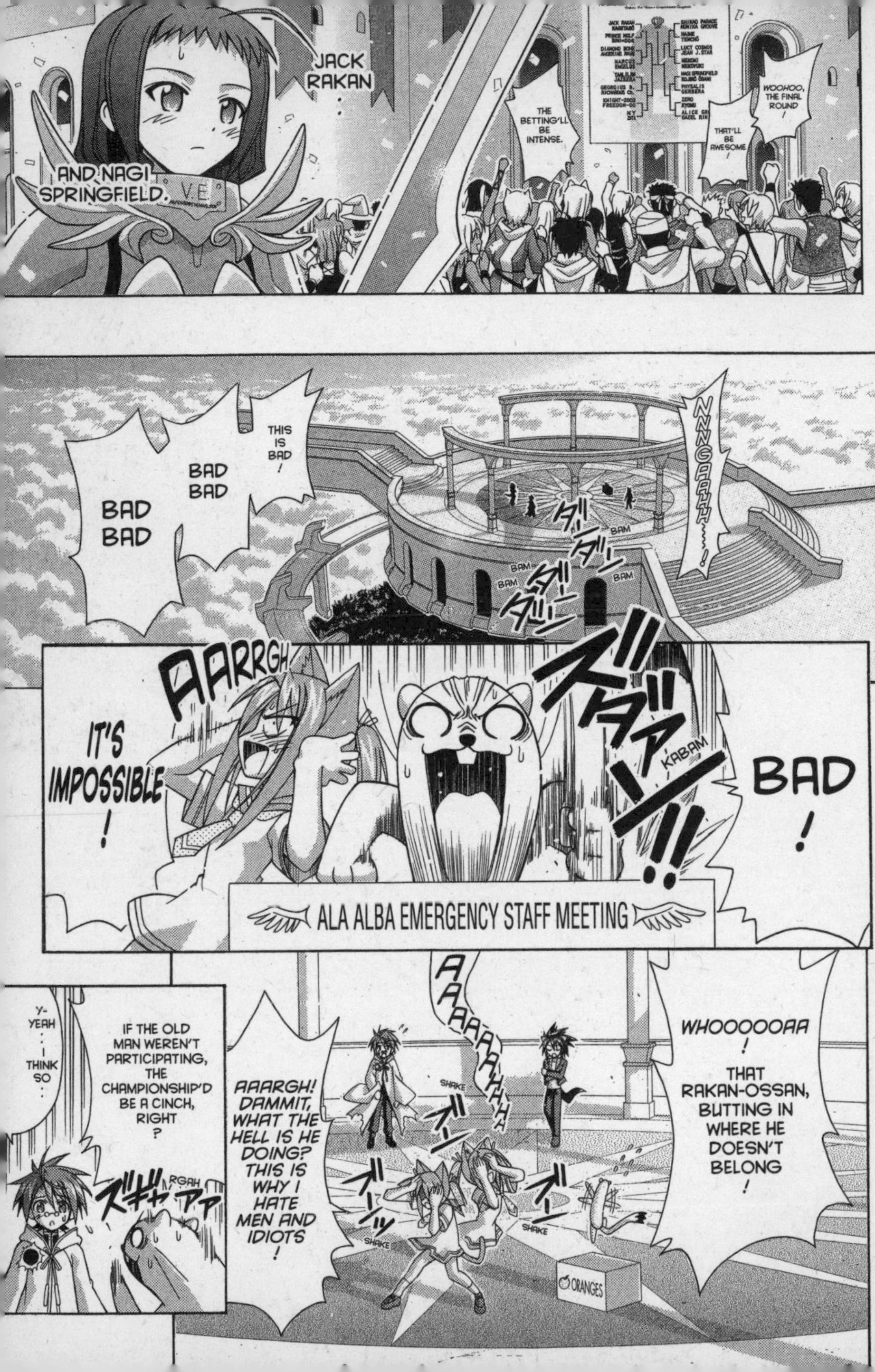

WOOHOO, THE FINAL ROUND!
THAT'LL BE AWESOME!
THE BETTING'LL BE INTENSE.
JACK RAKAN...
AND NAGI SPRINGFIELD.
NNNGAAAAH~~~!
BAM
BAM
BAM
BAM
THIS IS BAD!
BAD BAD
BAD BAD
BAD!
KABAM
AARRGH
IT'S IMPOSSIBLE!
ALA ALBA EMERGENCY STAFF MEETING
WHOOOOOAA! THAT RAKAN-OSSAN, BUTTING IN WHERE HE DOESN'T BELONG!
AAAAAAAAHHH
SHAKE
SHAKE
SHAKE
AAARGH! DAMMIT, WHAT THE HELL IS HE DOING? THIS IS WHY I HATE MEN AND IDIOTS!
ORANGES
IF THE OLD MAN WEREN'T PARTICIPATING, THE CHAMPIONSHIP'D BE A CINCH, RIGHT?
Y-YEAH... I THINK SO...
RGAH

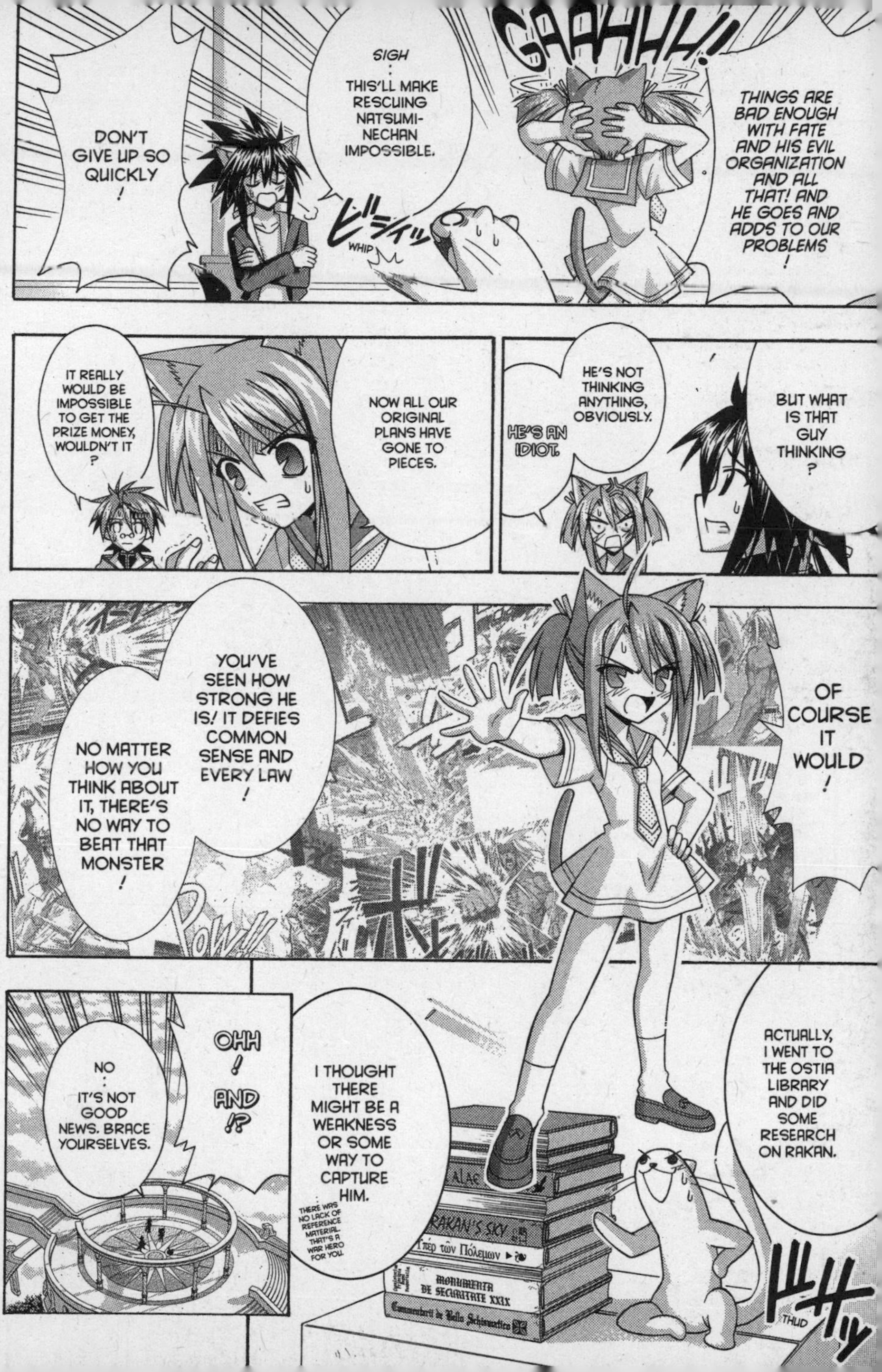
GAAHHH!!
THINGS ARE BAD ENOUGH WITH FATE AND HIS EVIL ORGANIZATION AND ALL THAT! AND HE GOES AND ADDS TO OUR PROBLEMS!
SIGH... THIS'LL MAKE RESCUING NATSUMI-NECHAN IMPOSSIBLE.
WHIP
DON'T GIVE UP SO QUICKLY!
BUT WHAT IS THAT GUY THINKING?
HE'S NOT THINKING ANYTHING, OBVIOUSLY.
HE'S AN IDIOT.
NOW ALL OUR ORIGINAL PLANS HAVE GONE TO PIECES.
IT REALLY WOULD BE IMPOSSIBLE TO GET THE PRIZE MONEY, WOULDN'T IT?
OF COURSE IT WOULD!
YOU'VE SEEN HOW STRONG HE IS! IT DEFIES COMMON SENSE AND EVERY LAW!
NO MATTER HOW YOU THINK ABOUT IT, THERE'S NO WAY TO BEAT THAT MONSTER!
POW!!
ACTUALLY, I WENT TO THE OSTIA LIBRARY AND DID SOME RESEARCH ON RAKAN.
THUD
I THOUGHT THERE MIGHT BE A WEAKNESS OR SOME WAY TO CAPTURE HIM.
THERE WAS NO LACK OF REFERENCE MATERIAL. THAT'S A WAR HERO FOR YOU.
RAKAN'S SKY
MONUMENTA DE SECURITATE XXIX
Commentarii de Bello Schismatico
OHH! AND!?
NO... IT'S NOT GOOD NEWS. BRACE YOURSELVES.

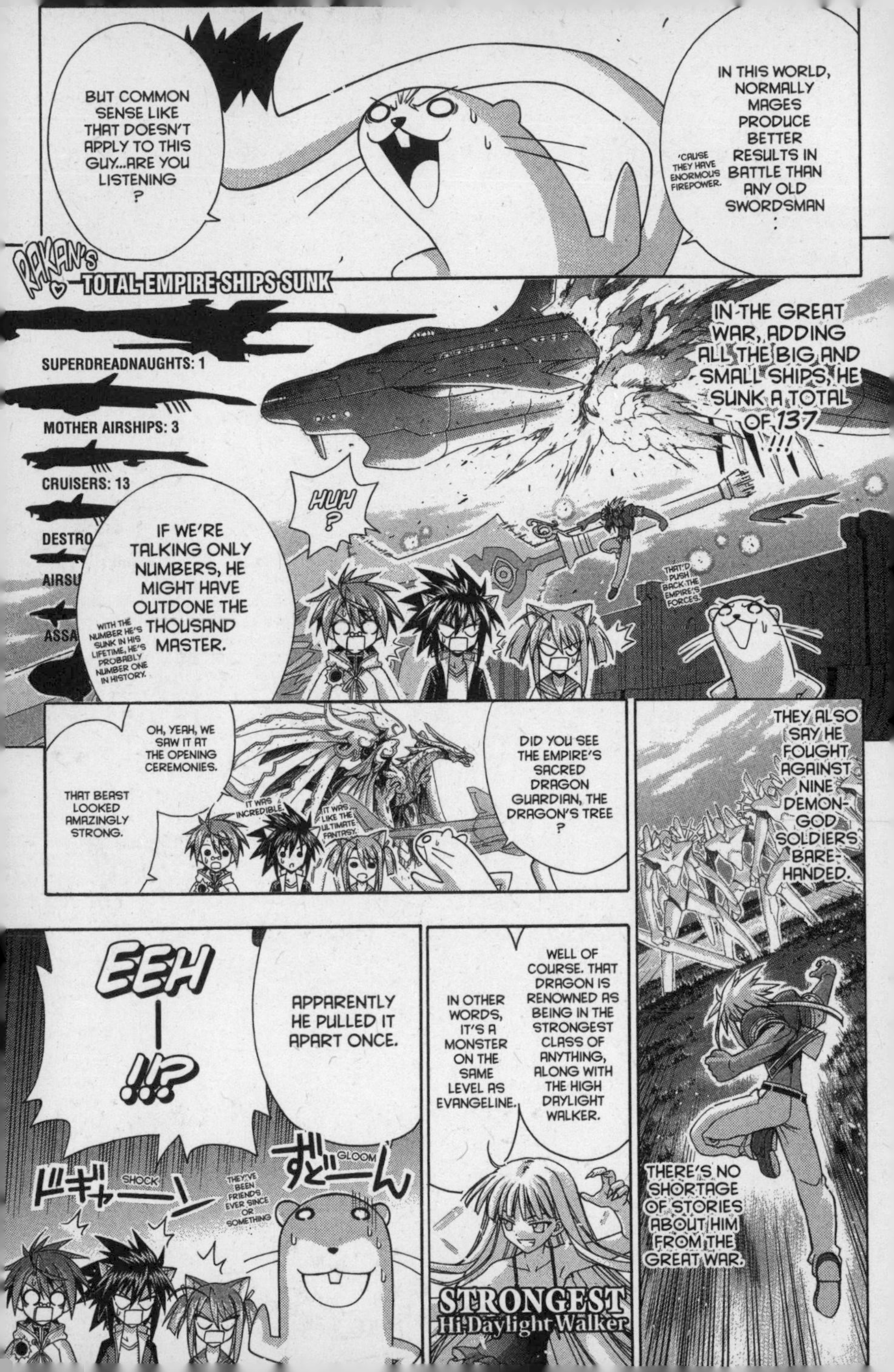
IN THIS WORLD, NORMALLY MAGES PRODUCE BETTER RESULTS IN BATTLE THAN ANY OLD SWORDSMAN
'CAUSE THEY HAVE ENORMOUS FIREPOWER.
BUT COMMON SENSE LIKE THAT DOESN'T APPLY TO THIS GUY...ARE YOU LISTENING ?
IN THE GREAT WAR, ADDING ALL THE BIG AND SMALL SHIPS, HE SUNK A TOTAL OF 137 !!!
RAKAN'S TOTAL EMPIRE SHIPS SUNK
SUPERDREADNAUGHTS: 1
MOTHER AIRSHIPS: 3
CRUISERS: 13
DESTRO
AIRSU
ASSA
HUH ?
THAT'D PUSH BACK THE EMPIRE'S FORCES.
IF WE'RE TALKING ONLY NUMBERS, HE MIGHT HAVE OUTDONE THE THOUSAND MASTER.
WITH THE NUMBER HE'S SUNK IN HIS LIFETIME, HE'S PROBABLY NUMBER ONE IN HISTORY.
THEY ALSO SAY HE FOUGHT AGAINST NINE DEMON-GOD SOLDIERS BARE-HANDED.
THERE'S NO SHORTAGE OF STORIES ABOUT HIM FROM THE GREAT WAR.
DID YOU SEE THE EMPIRE'S SACRED DRAGON GUARDIAN, THE DRAGON'S TREE ?
OH, YEAH, WE SAW IT AT THE OPENING CEREMONIES.
IT WAS INCREDIBLE.
IT WAS LIKE THE ULTIMATE FANTASY.
THAT BEAST LOOKED AMAZINGLY STRONG.
WELL OF COURSE. THAT DRAGON IS RENOWNED AS BEING IN THE STRONGEST CLASS OF ANYTHING, ALONG WITH THE HIGH DAYLIGHT WALKER.
IN OTHER WORDS, IT'S A MONSTER ON THE SAME LEVEL AS EVANGELINE.
STRONGEST
Hi-Daylight Walker
APPARENTLY HE PULLED IT APART ONCE.
EEH — !!?
ずどーん
GLOOM
THEY'VE BEEN FRIENDS EVER SINCE OR SOMETHING
ドギャーン
SHOCK

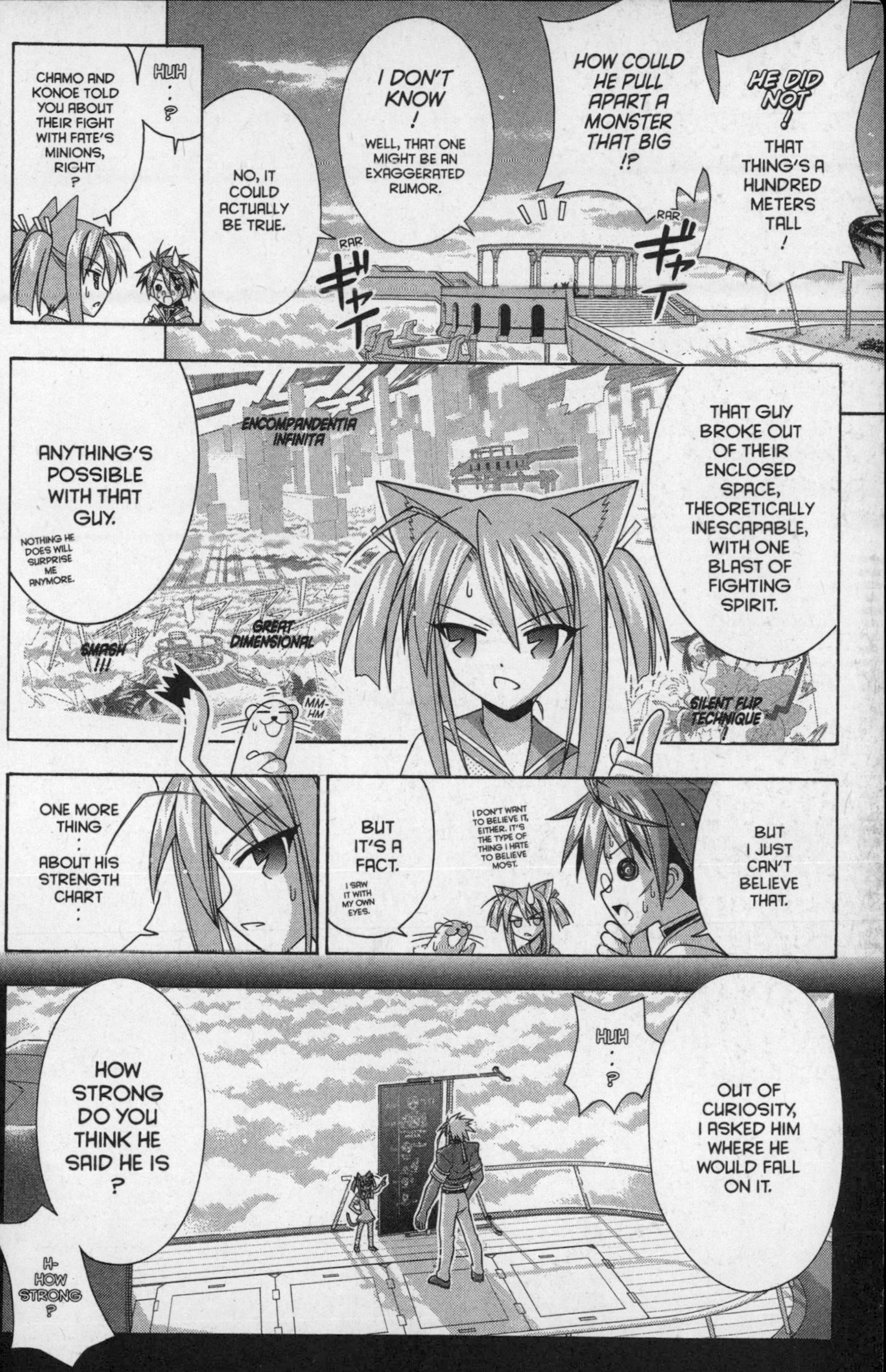
HE DID NOT! THAT THING'S A HUNDRED METERS TALL!
RAR
HOW COULD HE PULL APART A MONSTER THAT BIG!?
I DON'T KNOW! WELL, THAT ONE MIGHT BE AN EXAGGERATED RUMOR.
RAR
NO, IT COULD ACTUALLY BE TRUE.
HUH...?
CHAMO AND KONOE TOLD YOU ABOUT THEIR FIGHT WITH FATE'S MINIONS, RIGHT?
THAT GUY BROKE OUT OF THEIR ENCLOSED SPACE, THEORETICALLY INESCAPABLE, WITH ONE BLAST OF FIGHTING SPIRIT.
SILENT FLIP TECHNIQUE!
ENCOMPANDENTIA INFINITA
GREAT DIMENSIONAL
SMASH!!!
MM-HM
ANYTHING'S POSSIBLE WITH THAT GUY.
NOTHING HE DOES WILL SURPRISE ME ANYMORE.
BUT I JUST CAN'T BELIEVE THAT.
I DON'T WANT TO BELIEVE IT, EITHER. IT'S THE TYPE OF THING I HATE TO BELIEVE MOST.
BUT IT'S A FACT.
I SAW IT WITH MY OWN EYES.
ONE MORE THING: ABOUT HIS STRENGTH CHART:
OUT OF CURIOSITY, I ASKED HIM WHERE HE WOULD FALL ON IT.
HUH...?
HOW STRONG DO YOU THINK HE SAID HE IS?
H-HOW STRONG?

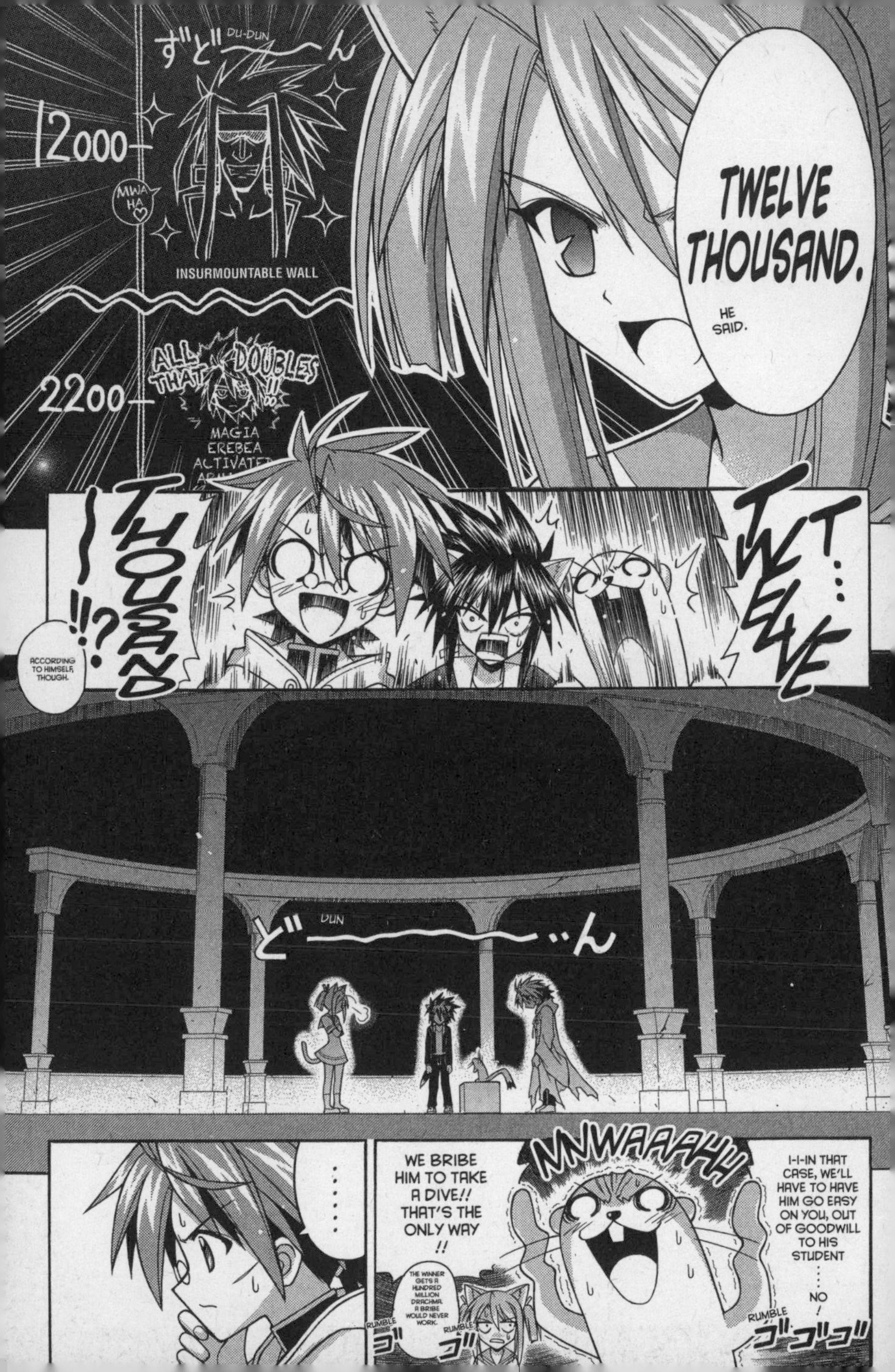

TWELVE THOUSAND.
HE SAID.
ずど〜〜ん
DU-DUN
12000
MWA HA ♡
INSURMOUNTABLE WALL
2200
ALL THAT DOUBLES!!
MAGIA EREBEA ACTIVATED
T... TWELVE
THOUSAND~~!!?
ACCORDING TO HIMSELF, THOUGH.
ど〜〜〜ん
DUN
I-I-IN THAT CASE, WE'LL HAVE TO HAVE HIM GO EASY ON YOU, OUT OF GOODWILL TO HIS STUDENT ...... NO!
MNWAAAAH
WE BRIBE HIM TO TAKE A DIVE!! THAT'S THE ONLY WAY!!
THE WINNER GETS A HUNDRED MILLION DRACHMA. A BRIBE WOULD NEVER WORK.
ゴゴゴ
RUMBLE
ゴ
RUMBLE
ゴ
RUMBLE
......

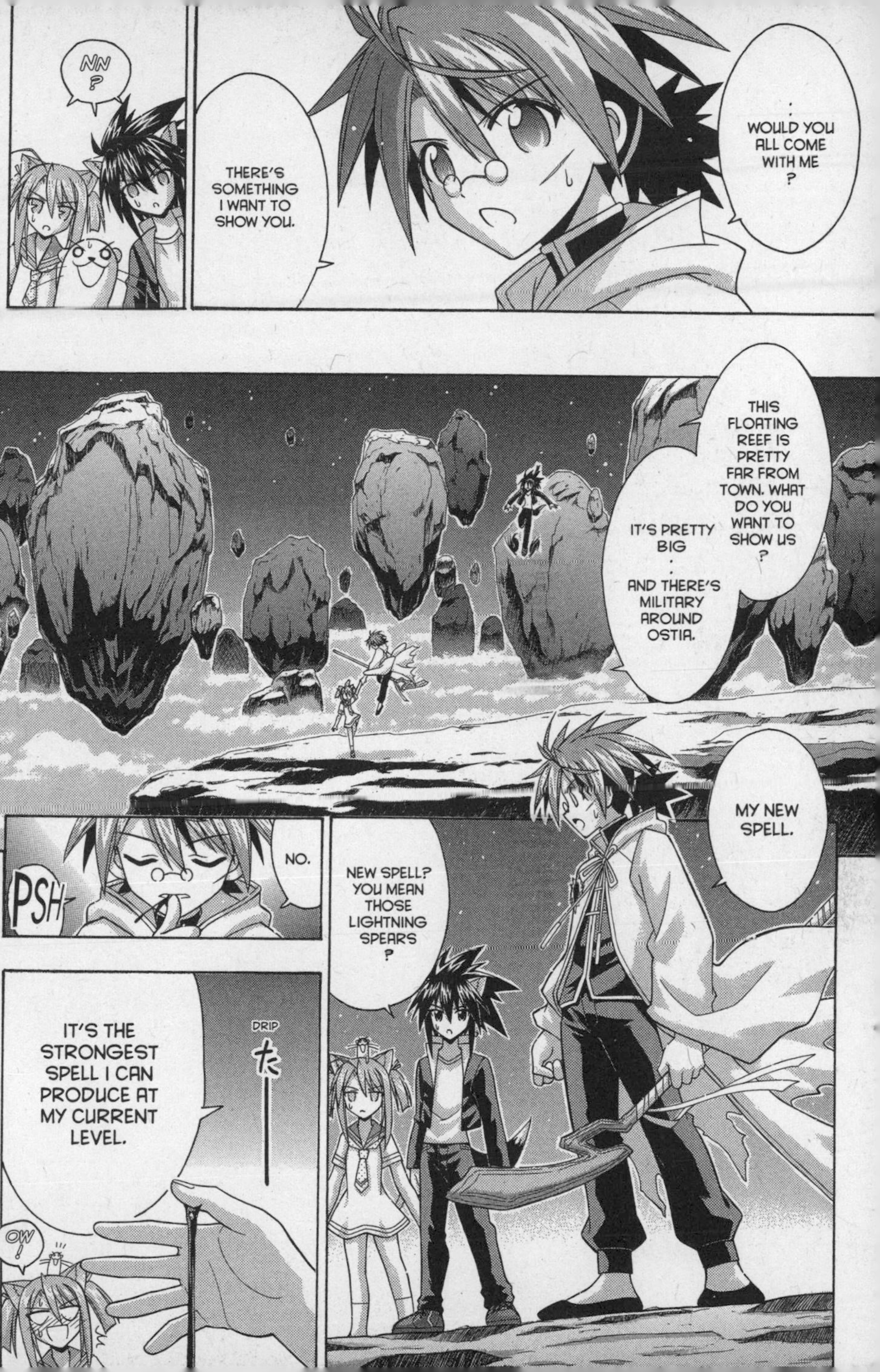

...WOULD YOU ALL COME WITH ME?
THERE'S SOMETHING I WANT TO SHOW YOU.
NN?
THIS FLOATING REEF IS PRETTY FAR FROM TOWN. WHAT DO YOU WANT TO SHOW US?
IT'S PRETTY BIG... AND THERE'S MILITARY AROUND OSTIA.
MY NEW SPELL.
NEW SPELL? YOU MEAN THOSE LIGHTNING SPEARS?
NO.
PSH
IT'S THE STRONGEST SPELL I CAN PRODUCE AT MY CURRENT LEVEL.
DRIP
たー
OW!

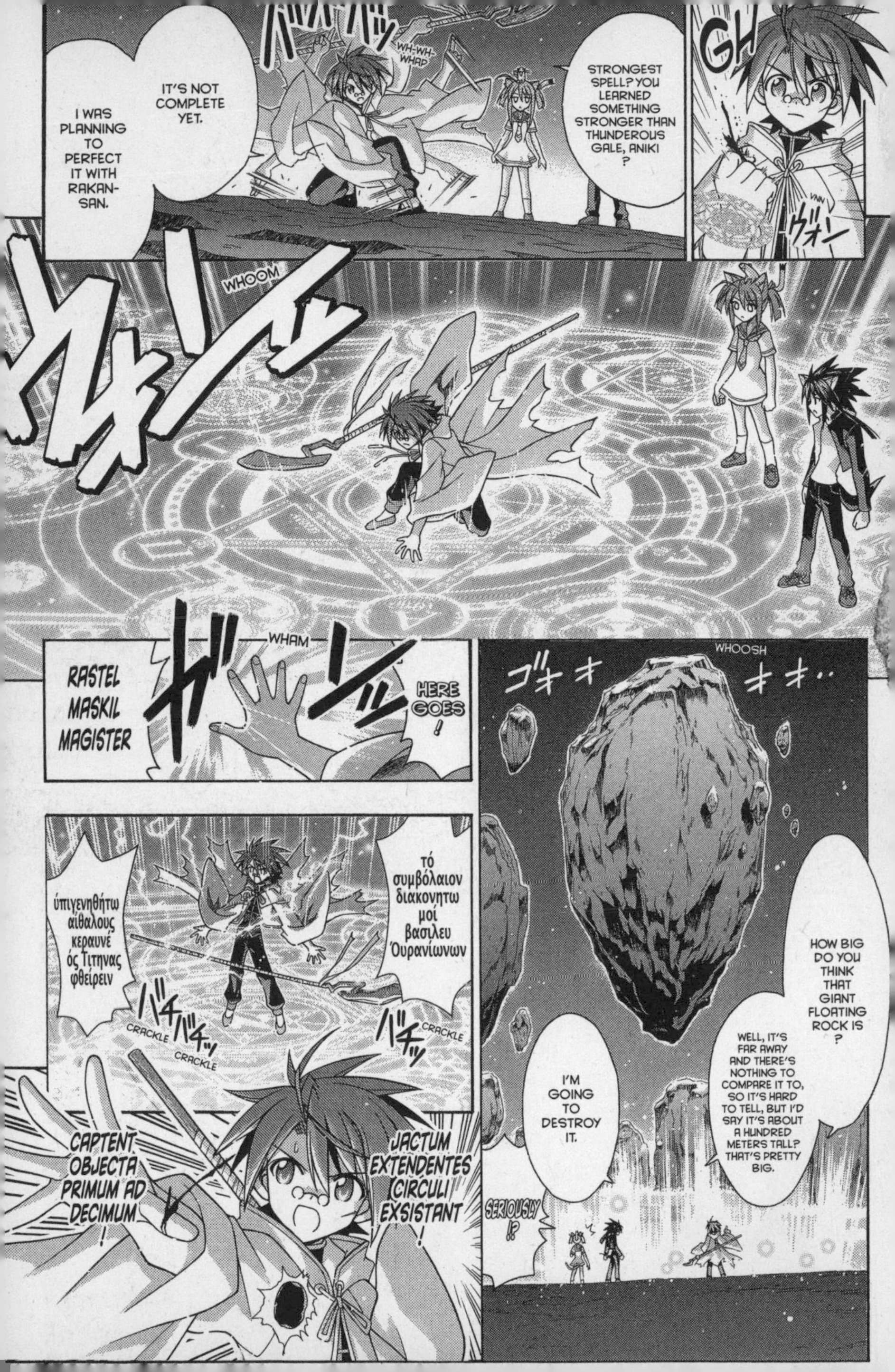
GH
VNN
WH-WH-WHAP
STRONGEST SPELL? YOU LEARNED SOMETHING STRONGER THAN THUNDEROUS GALE, ANIKI?
IT'S NOT COMPLETE YET.
I WAS PLANNING TO PERFECT IT WITH RAKAN-SAN.
WHOOM
WHOOSH
HOW BIG DO YOU THINK THAT GIANT FLOATING ROCK IS?
WELL, IT'S FAR AWAY AND THERE'S NOTHING TO COMPARE IT TO, SO IT'S HARD TO TELL, BUT I'D SAY IT'S ABOUT A HUNDRED METERS TALL? THAT'S PRETTY BIG.
I'M GOING TO DESTROY IT.
SERIOUSLY!?
WHAM
HERE GOES!
RASTEL MASKIL MAGISTER
τό συμβόλαιον διακονητω μοί βασιλευ Ούρανίωνων
ύπιγενηθήτω αίθαλους κεραυνέ ός Τιτηνας φθείρειν
CRACKLE
CRACKLE
CRACKLE
JACTUM EXTENDENTES CIRCULI EXSISTANT!
CAPTENT OBJECTA PRIMUM AD DECIMUM!

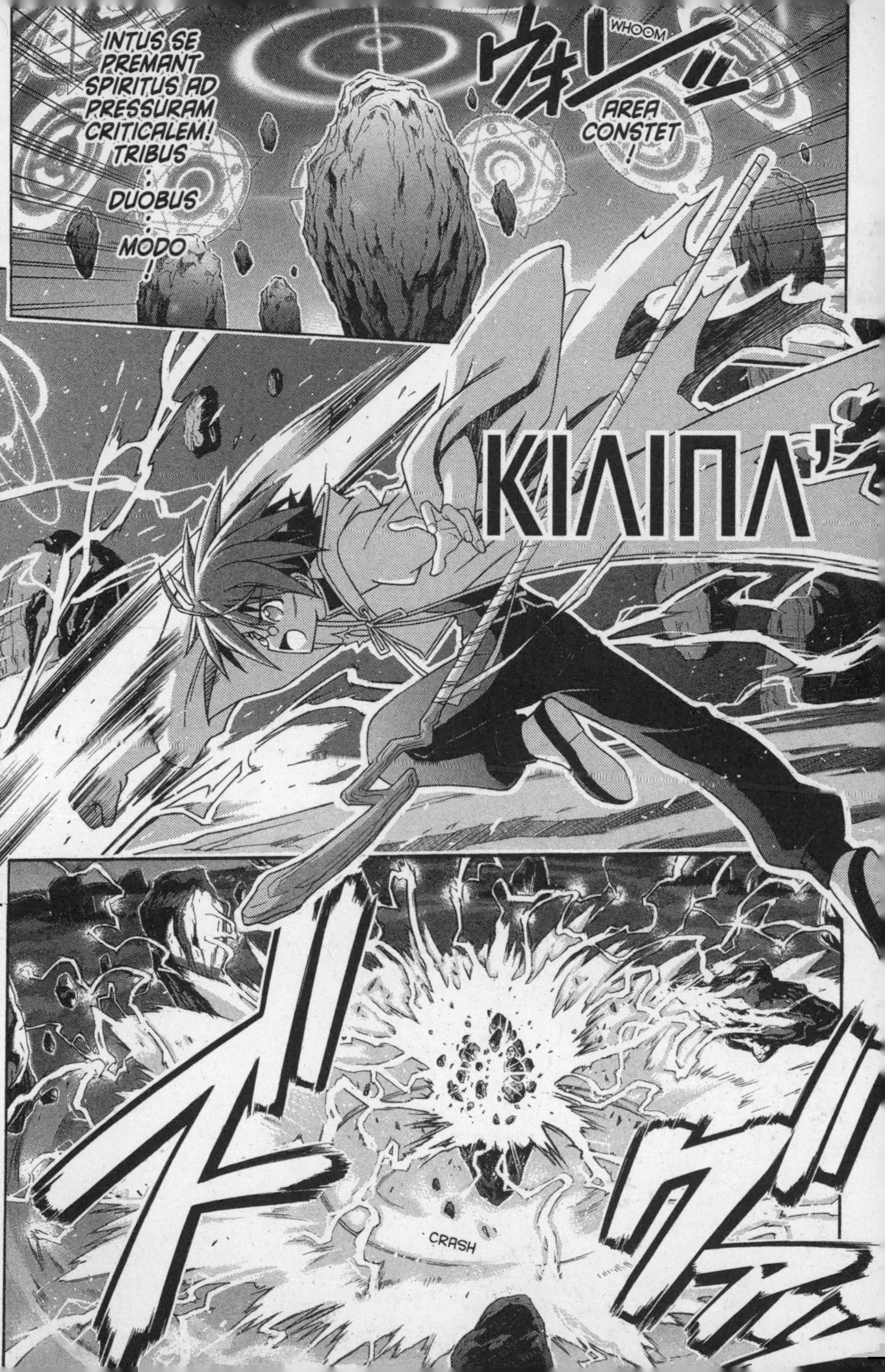
WHOOM
AREA CONSTET !
INTUS SE PREMANT SPIRITUS AD PRESSURAM CRITICALEM! TRIBUS
DUOBUS
MODO !
ΚΙΛΙΠΛ'
CRASH

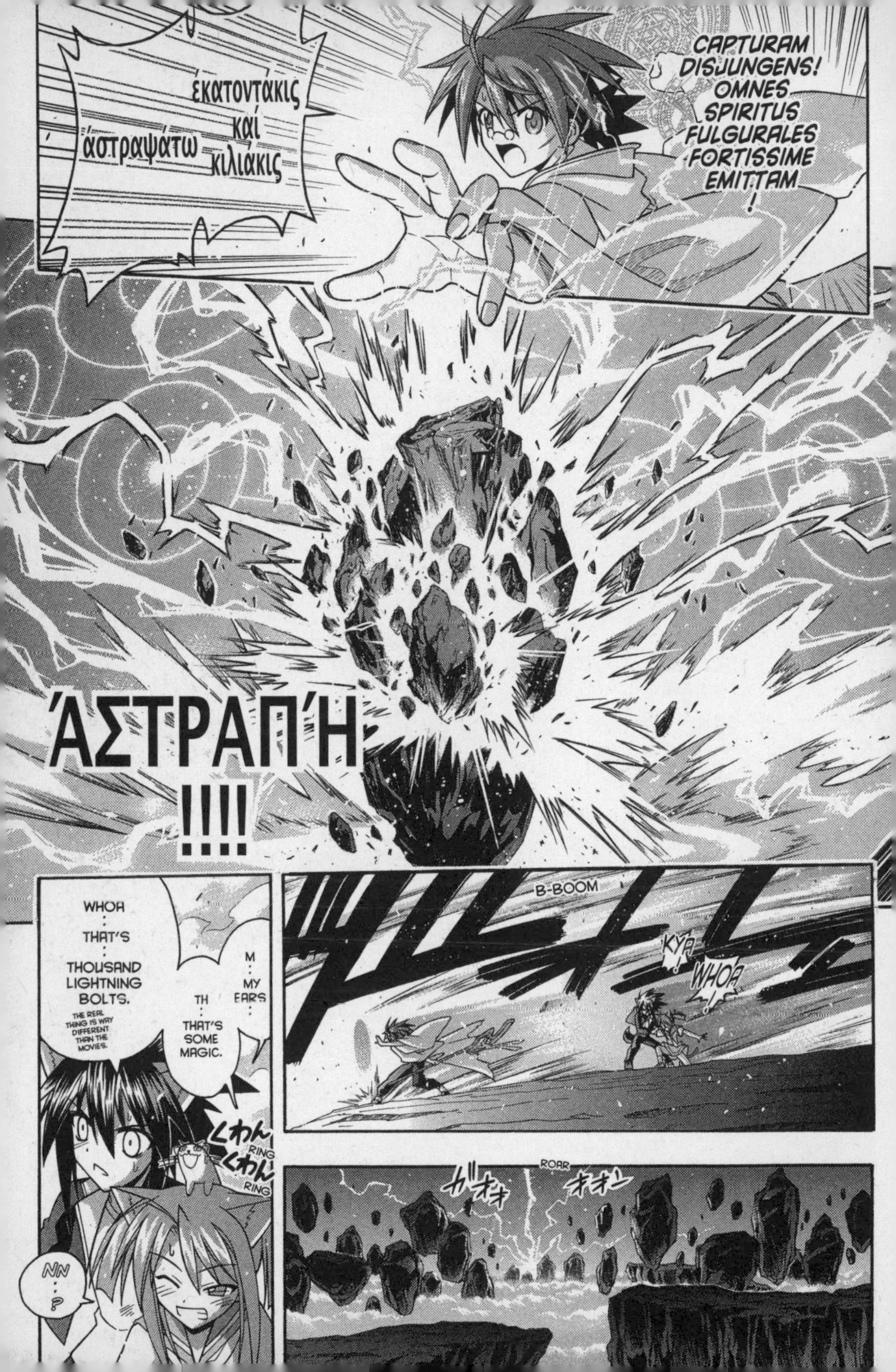
CAPTURAM DISJUNGENS! OMNES SPIRITUS FULGURALES FORTISSIME EMITTAM!
εκατοντάκις καί κιλιάκις άστραψάτω
ΆΣΤΡΑΠΉ !!!!
B-BOOM
KYA!
WHOA!
ROAR
M... MY EARS...
TH... THAT'S SOME MAGIC.
WHOA... THAT'S... THOUSAND LIGHTNING BOLTS.
THE REAL THING IS WAY DIFFERENT THAN THE MOVIES.
くわん RING
くわん RING
NN...?

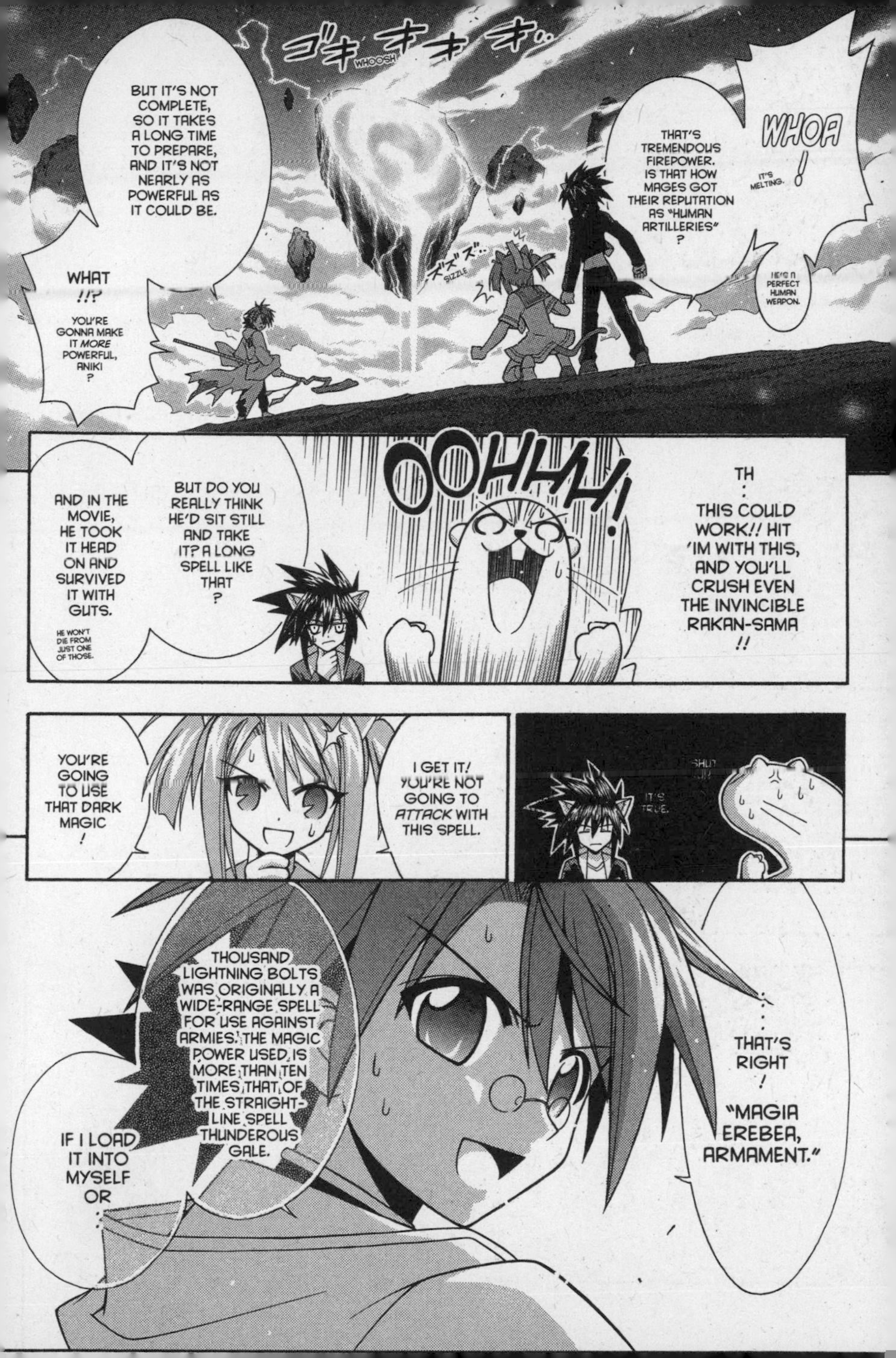

WHOOSH
WHOA!
IT'S MELTING.
THAT'S TREMENDOUS FIREPOWER. IS THAT HOW MAGES GOT THEIR REPUTATION AS "HUMAN ARTILLERIES"?
HE'S A PERFECT HUMAN WEAPON.
SIZZLE
BUT IT'S NOT COMPLETE, SO IT TAKES A LONG TIME TO PREPARE, AND IT'S NOT NEARLY AS POWERFUL AS IT COULD BE.
WHAT!!?
YOU'RE GONNA MAKE IT *MORE* POWERFUL, ANIKI?
TH... THIS COULD WORK!! HIT 'IM WITH THIS, AND YOU'LL CRUSH EVEN THE INVINCIBLE RAKAN-SAMA!!
OOHHH!
BUT DO YOU REALLY THINK HE'D SIT STILL AND TAKE IT? A LONG SPELL LIKE THAT?
AND IN THE MOVIE, HE TOOK IT HEAD ON AND SURVIVED IT WITH GUTS.
HE WON'T DIE FROM JUST ONE OF THOSE.
SHUT UP!
IT'S TRUE.
I GET IT! YOU'RE NOT GOING TO *ATTACK* WITH THIS SPELL.
YOU'RE GOING TO USE THAT DARK MAGIC!
...THAT'S RIGHT!
"MAGIA EREBEA, ARMAMENT."
THOUSAND LIGHTNING BOLTS WAS ORIGINALLY A WIDE-RANGE SPELL FOR USE AGAINST ARMIES. THE MAGIC POWER USED IS MORE THAN TEN TIMES THAT OF THE STRAIGHT-LINE SPELL THUNDEROUS GALE.
IF I LOAD IT INTO MYSELF OR...

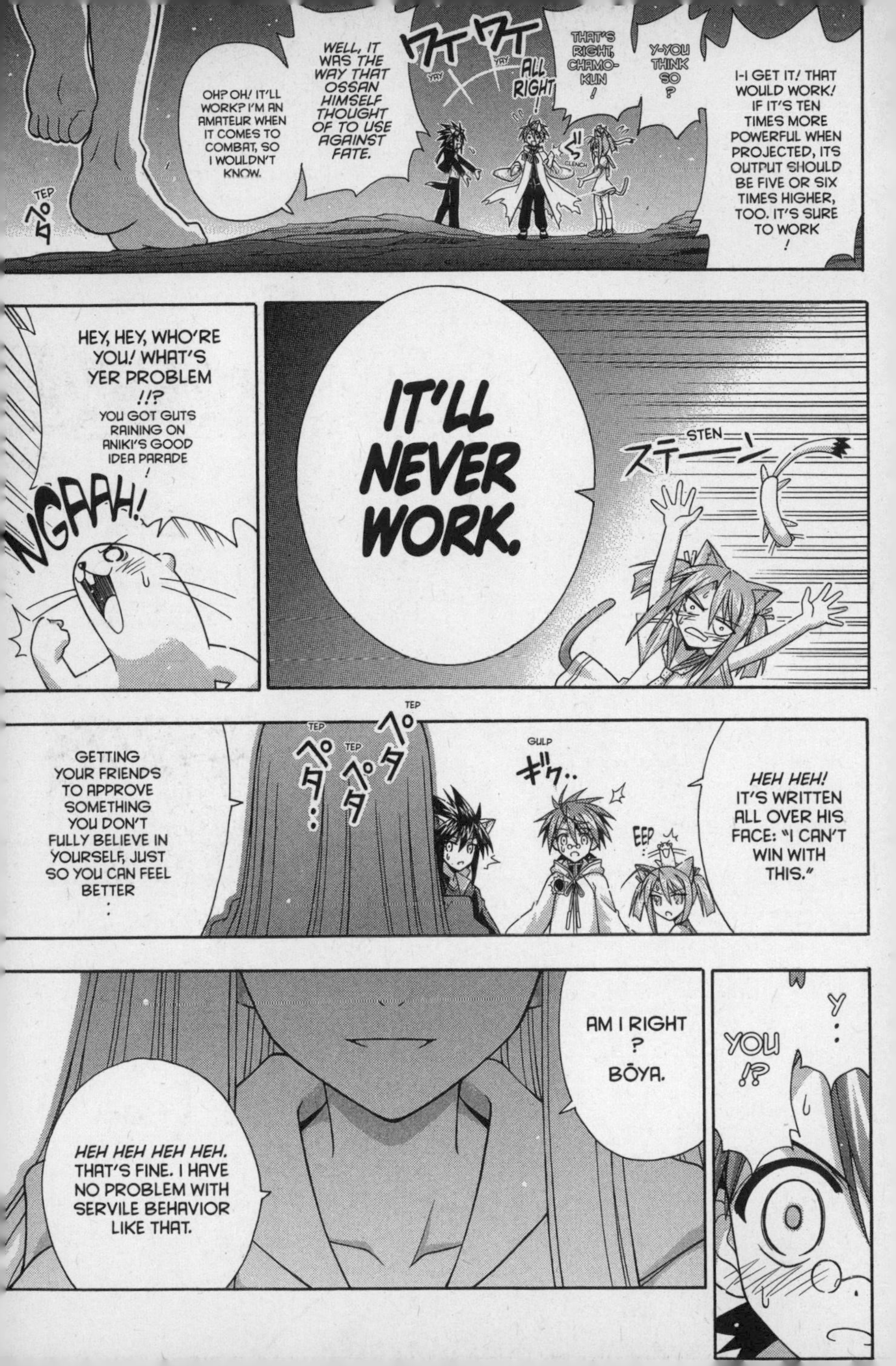

I-I GET IT! THAT WOULD WORK! IF IT'S TEN TIMES MORE POWERFUL WHEN PROJECTED, ITS OUTPUT SHOULD BE FIVE OR SIX TIMES HIGHER, TOO. IT'S SURE TO WORK!
Y-YOU THINK SO?
THAT'S RIGHT, CHAMO-KUN!
CLENCH
ワイワイ
YAY YAY
ALL RIGHT!
WELL, IT WAS THE WAY THAT OSSAN HIMSELF THOUGHT OF TO USE AGAINST FATE.
OH? OH! IT'LL WORK? I'M AN AMATEUR WHEN IT COMES TO COMBAT, SO I WOULDN'T KNOW.
TEP
STEN
ステーン
IT'LL NEVER WORK.
HEY, HEY, WHO'RE YOU! WHAT'S YER PROBLEM!!?
YOU GOT GUTS RAINING ON ANIKI'S GOOD IDEA PARADE!
NGAAH!
HEH HEH! IT'S WRITTEN ALL OVER HIS FACE: "I CAN'T WIN WITH THIS."
EEP
GULP
ギク..
TEP TEP TEP
GETTING YOUR FRIENDS TO APPROVE SOMETHING YOU DON'T FULLY BELIEVE IN YOURSELF, JUST SO YOU CAN FEEL BETTER...
Y... YOU!?
AM I RIGHT? BŌYA.
HEH HEH HEH HEH. THAT'S FINE. I HAVE NO PROBLEM WITH SERVILE BEHAVIOR LIKE THAT.

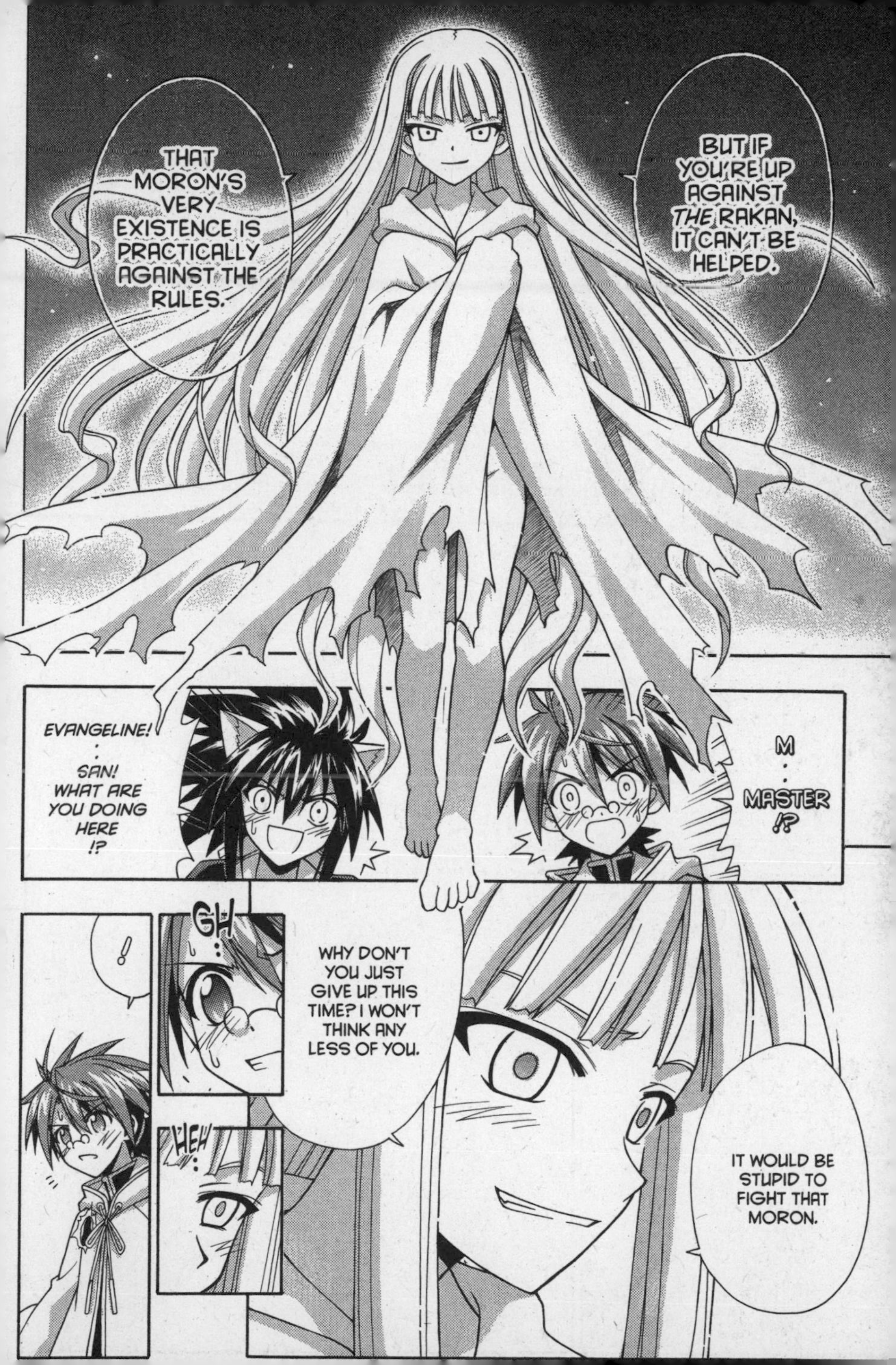
BUT IF YOU'RE UP AGAINST *THE* RAKAN, IT CAN'T BE HELPED.
THAT MORON'S VERY EXISTENCE IS PRACTICALLY AGAINST THE RULES.
M . . MASTER !?
EVANGELINE! . . SAN! WHAT ARE YOU DOING HERE !?
IT WOULD BE STUPID TO FIGHT THAT MORON.
WHY DON'T YOU JUST GIVE UP THIS TIME? I WON'T THINK ANY LESS OF YOU.
GH . .
HEH . .
!

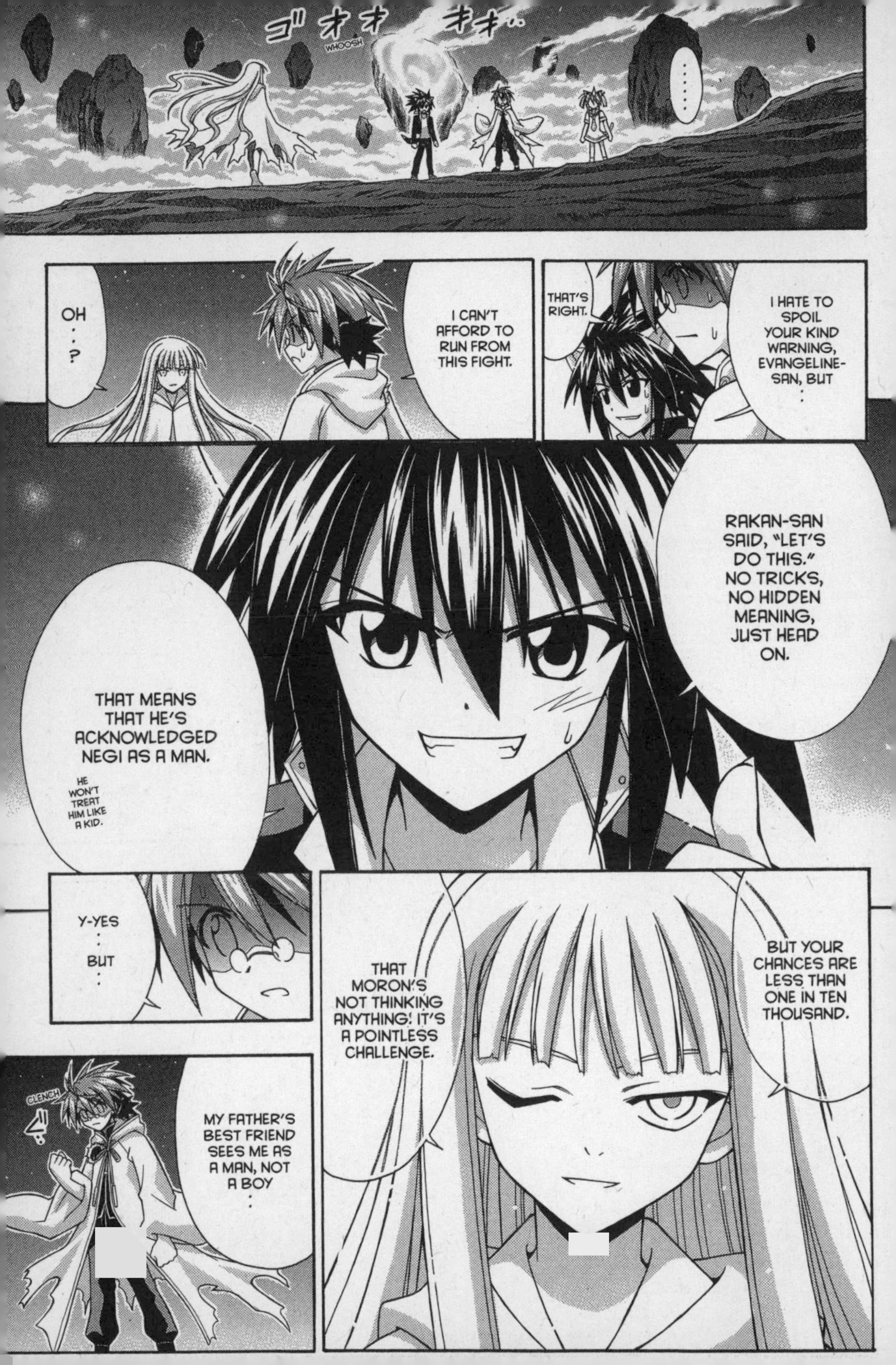
ゴオオ オオ..
WHOOSH
......
I HATE TO SPOIL YOUR KIND WARNING, EVANGELINE-SAN, BUT . . .
THAT'S RIGHT.
I CAN'T AFFORD TO RUN FROM THIS FIGHT.
OH . . ?
RAKAN-SAN SAID, "LET'S DO THIS." NO TRICKS, NO HIDDEN MEANING, JUST HEAD ON.
THAT MEANS THAT HE'S ACKNOWLEDGED NEGI AS A MAN.
HE WON'T TREAT HIM LIKE A KID.
BUT YOUR CHANCES ARE LESS THAN ONE IN TEN THOUSAND.
THAT MORON'S NOT THINKING ANYTHING! IT'S A POINTLESS CHALLENGE.
Y-YES . . BUT . .
CLENCH
MY FATHER'S BEST FRIEND SEES ME AS A MAN, NOT A BOY . .

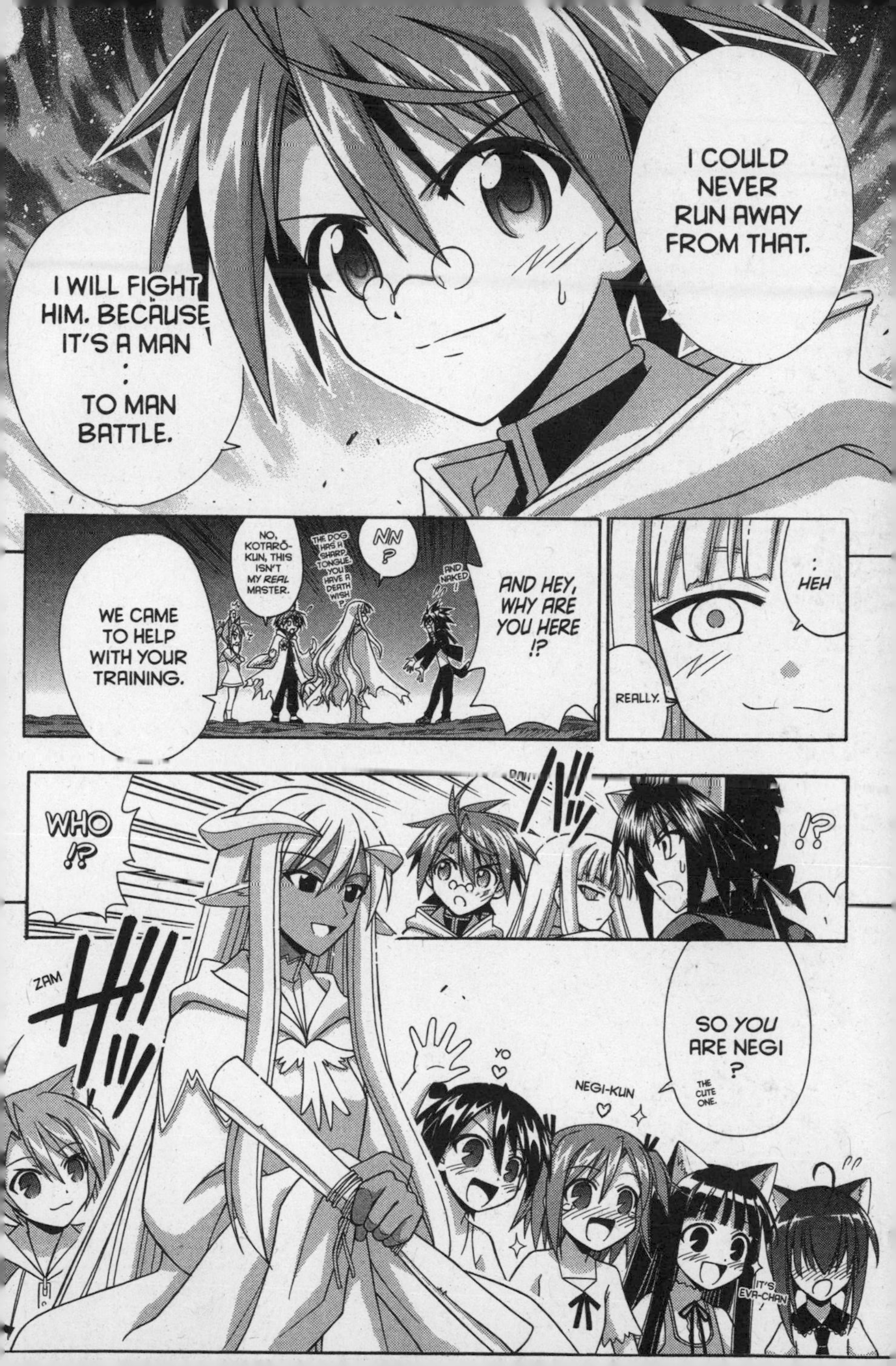
I COULD NEVER RUN AWAY FROM THAT.
I WILL FIGHT HIM. BECAUSE IT'S A MAN : TO MAN BATTLE.
: HEH
REALLY.
AND HEY, WHY ARE YOU HERE !?
AND NAKED !
NN ?
THE DOG HAS A SHARP TONGUE. YOU HAVE A DEATH WISH ?
NO, KOTARŌ-KUN, THIS ISN'T MY REAL MASTER.
WE CAME TO HELP WITH YOUR TRAINING.
!?
WHO !?
SO YOU ARE NEGI ?
THE CUTE ONE.
IT'S EVA-CHAN !
NEGI-KUN
YO
ZAM

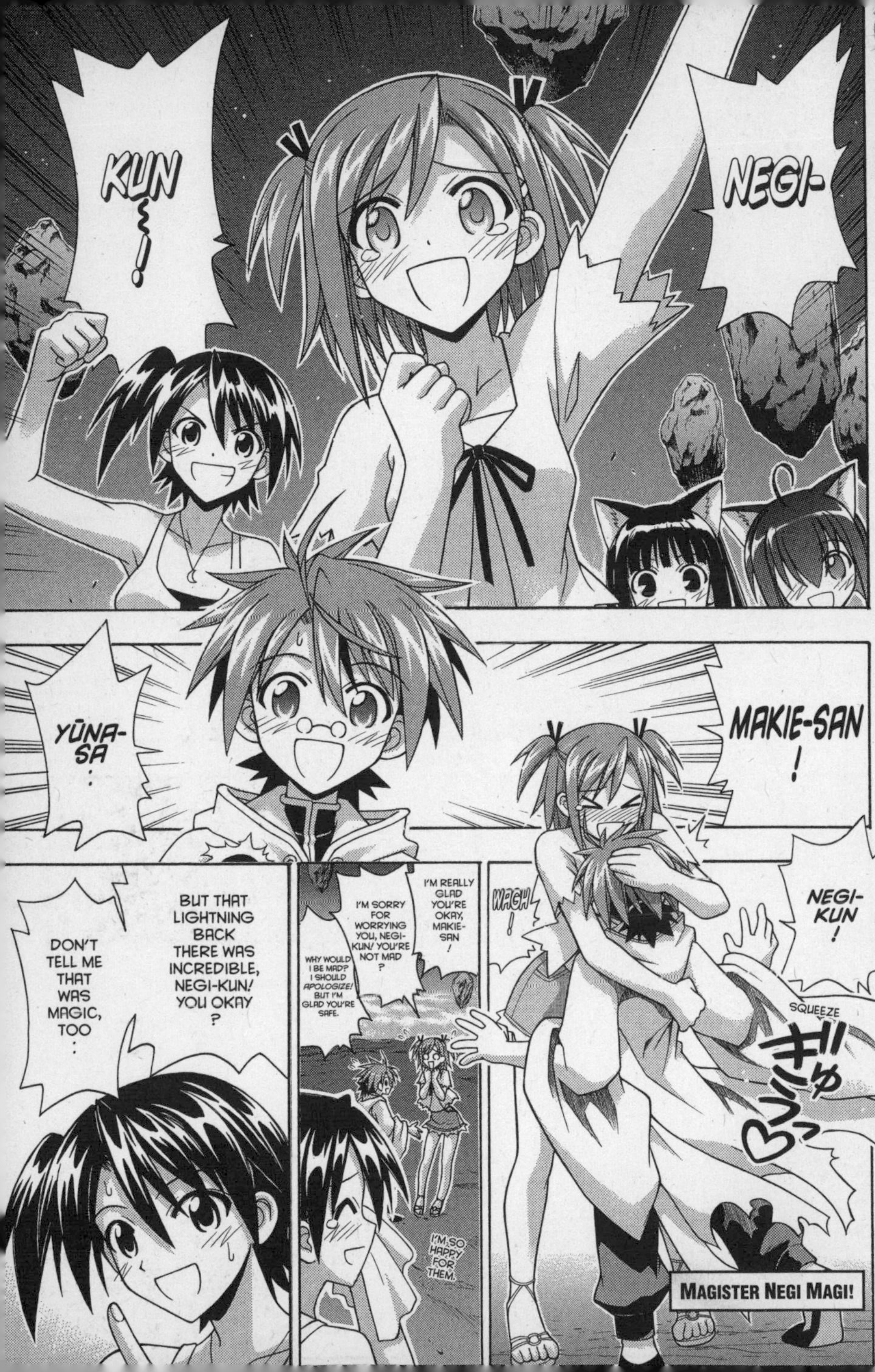
NEGI-
KUN~!
MAKIE-SAN!
YŪNA-SA...
NEGI-KUN!
WAGH!
SQUEEZE
ぎゅうっ
MAGISTER NEGI MAGI!
I'M REALLY GLAD YOU'RE OKAY, MAKIE-SAN!
I'M SORRY FOR WORRYING YOU, NEGI-KUN! YOU'RE NOT MAD?
WHY WOULD I BE MAD? I SHOULD APOLOGIZE! BUT I'M GLAD YOU'RE SAFE.
I'M SO HAPPY FOR THEM.
BUT THAT LIGHTNING BACK THERE WAS INCREDIBLE, NEGI-KUN! YOU OKAY?
DON'T TELL ME THAT WAS MAGIC, TOO...

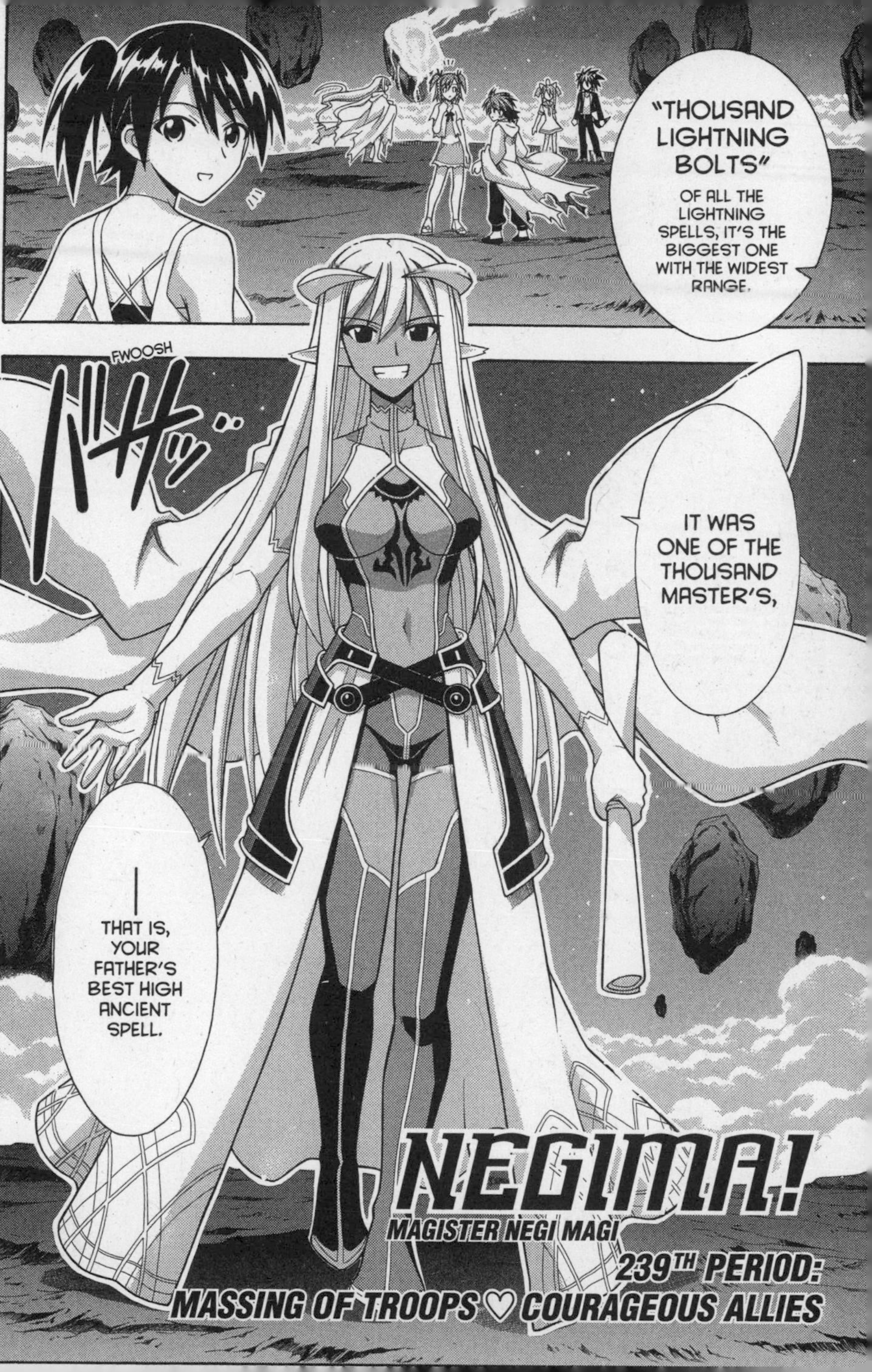
"THOUSAND LIGHTNING BOLTS" OF ALL THE LIGHTNING SPELLS, IT'S THE BIGGEST ONE WITH THE WIDEST RANGE.
FWOOSH
IT WAS ONE OF THE THOUSAND MASTER'S,
—THAT IS, YOUR FATHER'S BEST HIGH ANCIENT SPELL.
NEGIMA!
MAGISTER NEGI MAGI
239TH PERIOD: MASSING OF TROOPS ♡ COURAGEOUS ALLIES

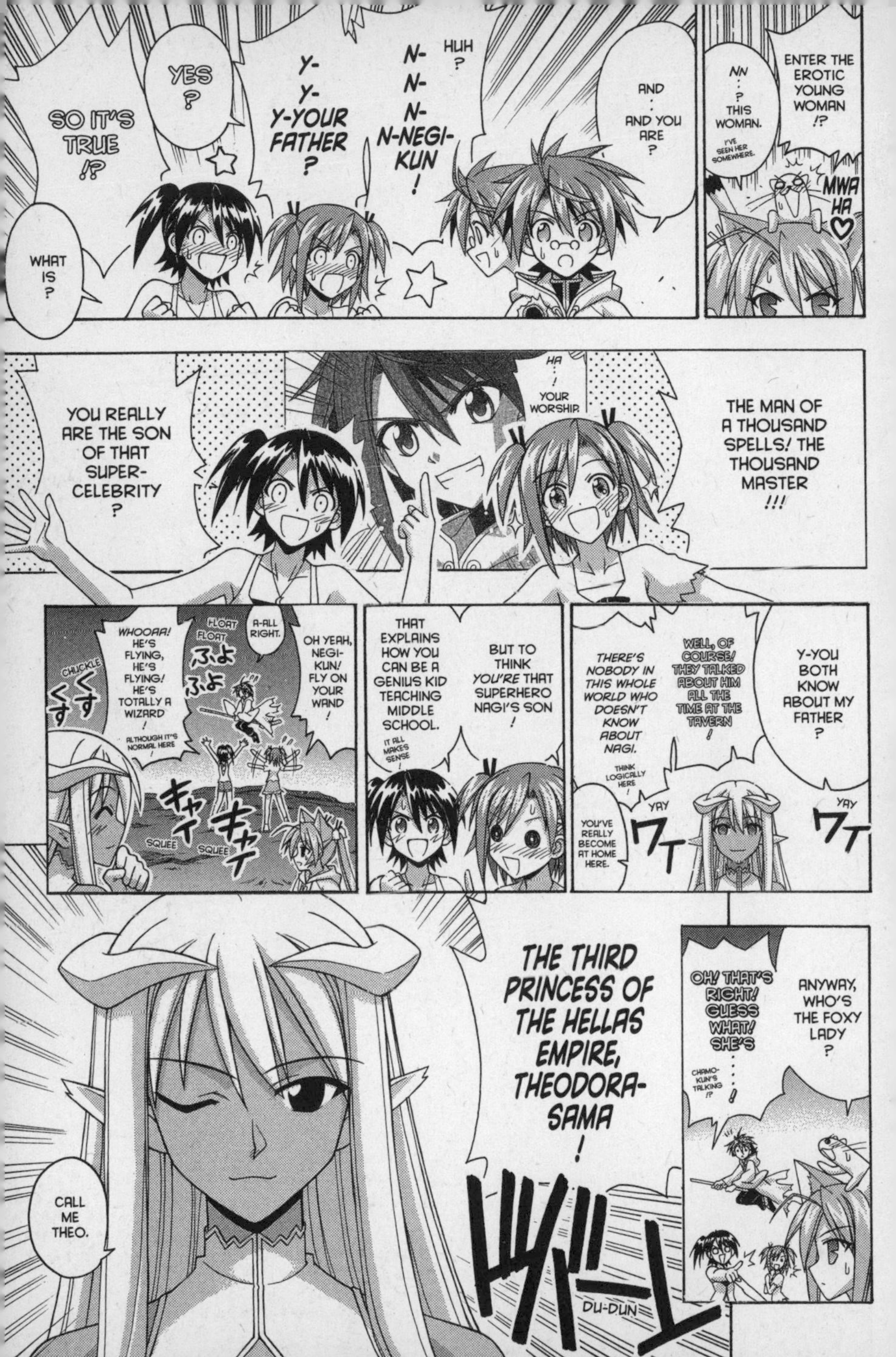

ENTER THE EROTIC YOUNG WOMAN !?
NN ... ? THIS WOMAN.
I'VE SEEN HER SOMEWHERE.
MWA HA ♡
AND ... AND YOU ARE ?
HUH ?
N-N-N-N-NEGI-KUN !
Y-Y-Y-YOUR FATHER ?
YES ?
SO IT'S TRUE !?
WHAT IS ?
THE MAN OF A THOUSAND SPELLS! THE THOUSAND MASTER !!!
HA ! YOUR WORSHIP.
YOU REALLY ARE THE SON OF THAT SUPER-CELEBRITY ?
Y-YOU BOTH KNOW ABOUT MY FATHER ?
YAY
WELL, OF COURSE! THEY TALKED ABOUT HIM ALL THE TIME AT THE TAVERN !
THERE'S NOBODY IN THIS WHOLE WORLD WHO DOESN'T KNOW ABOUT NAGI.
THINK LOGICALLY HERE !
YAY
YOU'VE REALLY BECOME AT HOME HERE.
BUT TO THINK YOU'RE THAT SUPERHERO NAGI'S SON !
THAT EXPLAINS HOW YOU CAN BE A GENIUS KID TEACHING MIDDLE SCHOOL.
IT ALL MAKES SENSE !
OH YEAH, NEGI-KUN! FLY ON YOUR WAND !
A-ALL RIGHT.
FLOAT FLOAT
WHOOAA! HE'S FLYING, HE'S FLYING! HE'S TOTALLY A WIZARD !
ALTHOUGH IT'S NORMAL HERE !
CHUCKLE
SQUEE SQUEE
ANYWAY, WHO'S THE FOXY LADY ?
OH! THAT'S RIGHT! GUESS WHAT! SHE'S ...... !
CHAMO-KUN'S TALKING !?
THE THIRD PRINCESS OF THE HELLAS EMPIRE, THEODORA-SAMA !
DU-DUN
CALL ME THEO.

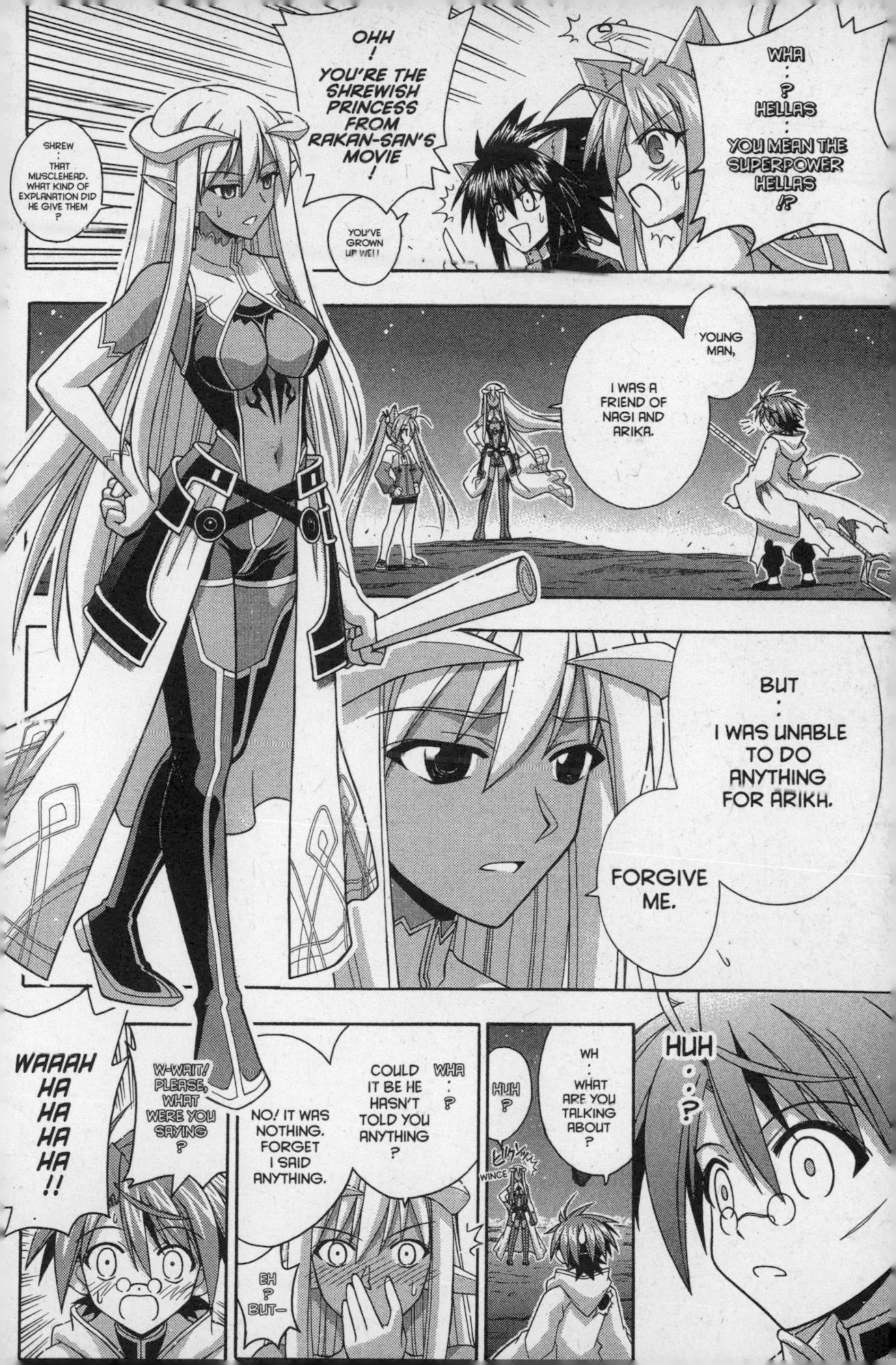

WHA... ? HELLAS... YOU MEAN THE SUPERPOWER HELLAS !?
YOU'VE GROWN UP WELL!
OHH! YOU'RE THE SHREWISH PRINCESS FROM RAKAN-SAN'S MOVIE!
SHREW... THAT MUSCLEHEAD. WHAT KIND OF EXPLANATION DID HE GIVE THEM?
YOUNG MAN,
I WAS A FRIEND OF NAGI AND ARIKA.
BUT... I WAS UNABLE TO DO ANYTHING FOR ARIKH.
FORGIVE ME.
HUH...?
WH... WHAT ARE YOU TALKING ABOUT?
HUH?
WINCE
WHA...?
COULD IT BE HE HASN'T TOLD YOU ANYTHING?
EH? BUT-
NO! IT WAS NOTHING. FORGET I SAID ANYTHING.
W-WAIT! PLEASE, WHAT WERE YOU SAYING?
WAAAH HA HA HA HA!!

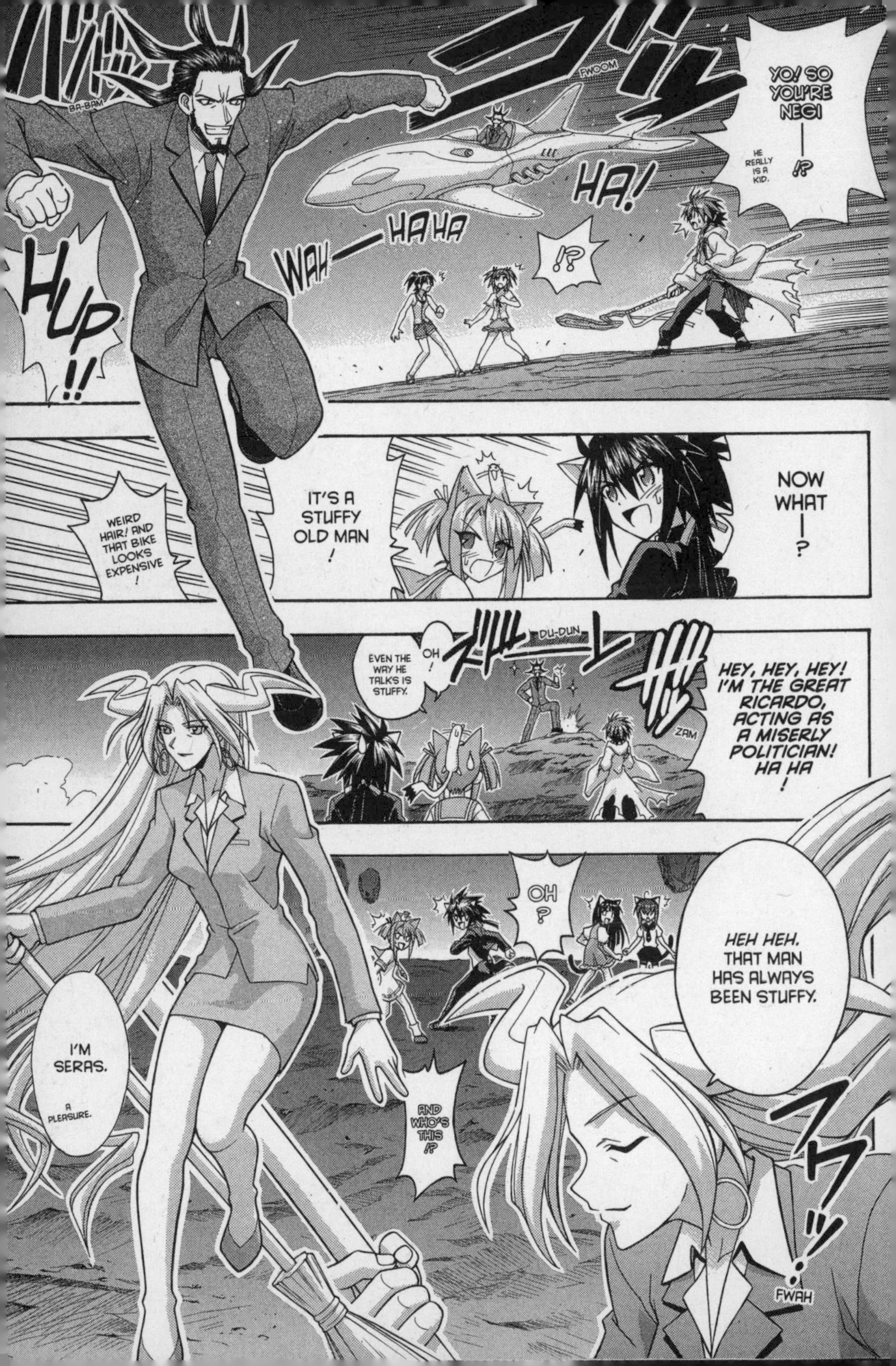
YO! SO YOU'RE NEGI—!?
HE REALLY IS A KID.
RWOOM
HA!
!?
WAH—HAHA
BA-BAM
HUP!!
NOW WHAT—?
IT'S A STUFFY OLD MAN!
WEIRD HAIR! AND THAT BIKE LOOKS EXPENSIVE!
HEY, HEY, HEY! I'M THE GREAT RICARDO, ACTING AS A MISERLY POLITICIAN! HA HA!
DU-DUN
ZAM
OH!
EVEN THE WAY HE TALKS IS STUFFY.
HEH HEH. THAT MAN HAS ALWAYS BEEN STUFFY.
FWAH
OH?
AND WHO'S THIS!?
I'M SERAS.
A PLEASURE.

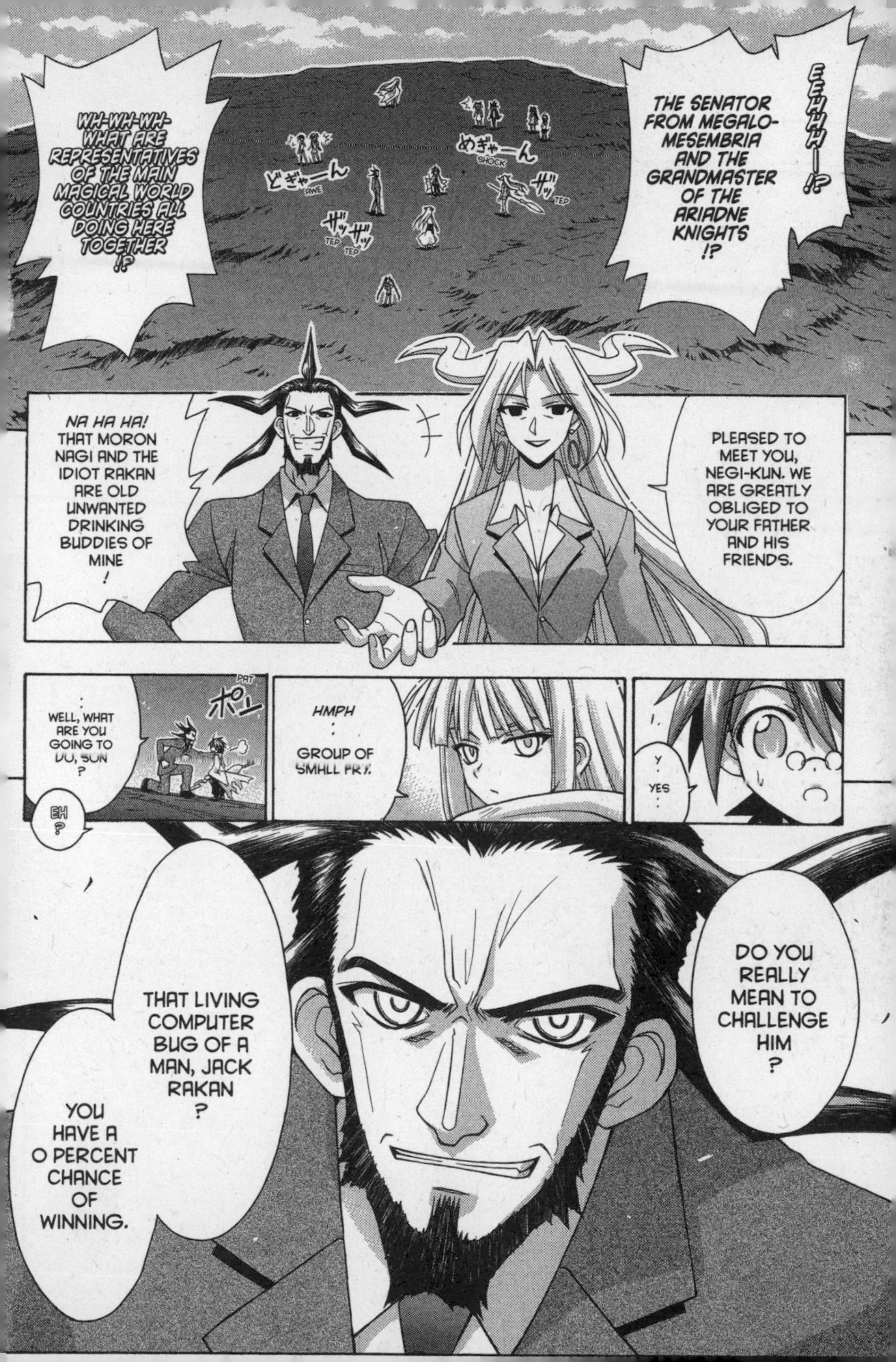
EEHHHH—!?
THE SENATOR FROM MEGALO-MESEMBRIA AND THE GRANDMASTER OF THE ARIADNE KNIGHTS !?
めぎゃーん SHOCK
ザッ TEP
WH-WH-WH-WHAT ARE REPRESENTATIVES OF THE MAIN MAGICAL WORLD COUNTRIES ALL DOING HERE TOGETHER !?
どぎゃーん AWE
ザッ ザッ TEP TEP
PLEASED TO MEET YOU, NEGI-KUN. WE ARE GREATLY OBLIGED TO YOUR FATHER AND HIS FRIENDS.
NA HA HA! THAT MORON NAGI AND THE IDIOT RAKAN ARE OLD UNWANTED DRINKING BUDDIES OF MINE !
Y... YES...
HMPH... GROUP OF SMALL FRY.
ポン PAT
...WELL, WHAT ARE YOU GOING TO DO, SON ?
EH ?
DO YOU REALLY MEAN TO CHALLENGE HIM ?
THAT LIVING COMPUTER BUG OF A MAN, JACK RAKAN ?
YOU HAVE A 0 PERCENT CHANCE OF WINNING.

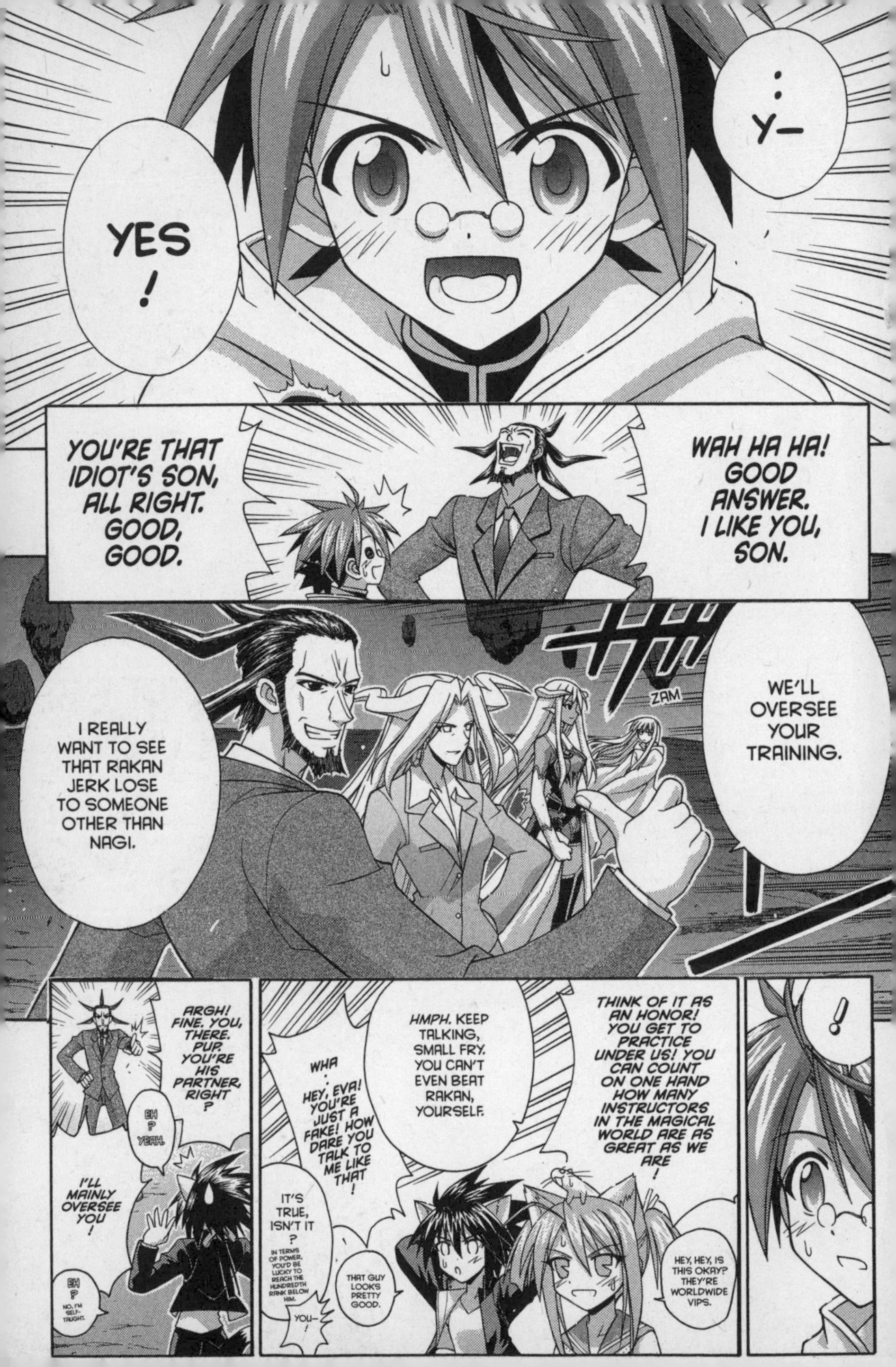
: Y—
YES!
WAH HA HA! GOOD ANSWER. I LIKE YOU, SON.
YOU'RE THAT IDIOT'S SON, ALL RIGHT. GOOD, GOOD.
WE'LL OVERSEE YOUR TRAINING.
ZAM
I REALLY WANT TO SEE THAT RAKAN JERK LOSE TO SOMEONE OTHER THAN NAGI.
!
THINK OF IT AS AN HONOR! YOU GET TO PRACTICE UNDER US! YOU CAN COUNT ON ONE HAND HOW MANY INSTRUCTORS IN THE MAGICAL WORLD ARE AS GREAT AS WE ARE!
HEY, HEY, IS THIS OKAY? THEY'RE WORLDWIDE VIPS.
HMPH. KEEP TALKING, SMALL FRY. YOU CAN'T EVEN BEAT RAKAN, YOURSELF.
WHA : HEY, EVA! YOU'RE JUST A FAKE! HOW DARE YOU TALK TO ME LIKE THAT!
THAT GUY LOOKS PRETTY GOOD.
IT'S TRUE, ISN'T IT?
IN TERMS OF POWER, YOU'D BE LUCKY TO REACH THE HUNDREDTH RANK BELOW HIM.
YOU—!
ARGH! FINE. YOU, THERE. PUP. YOU'RE HIS PARTNER, RIGHT?
EH? YEAH.
I'LL MAINLY OVERSEE YOU!
EH?
NO, I'M SELF-TAUGHT.

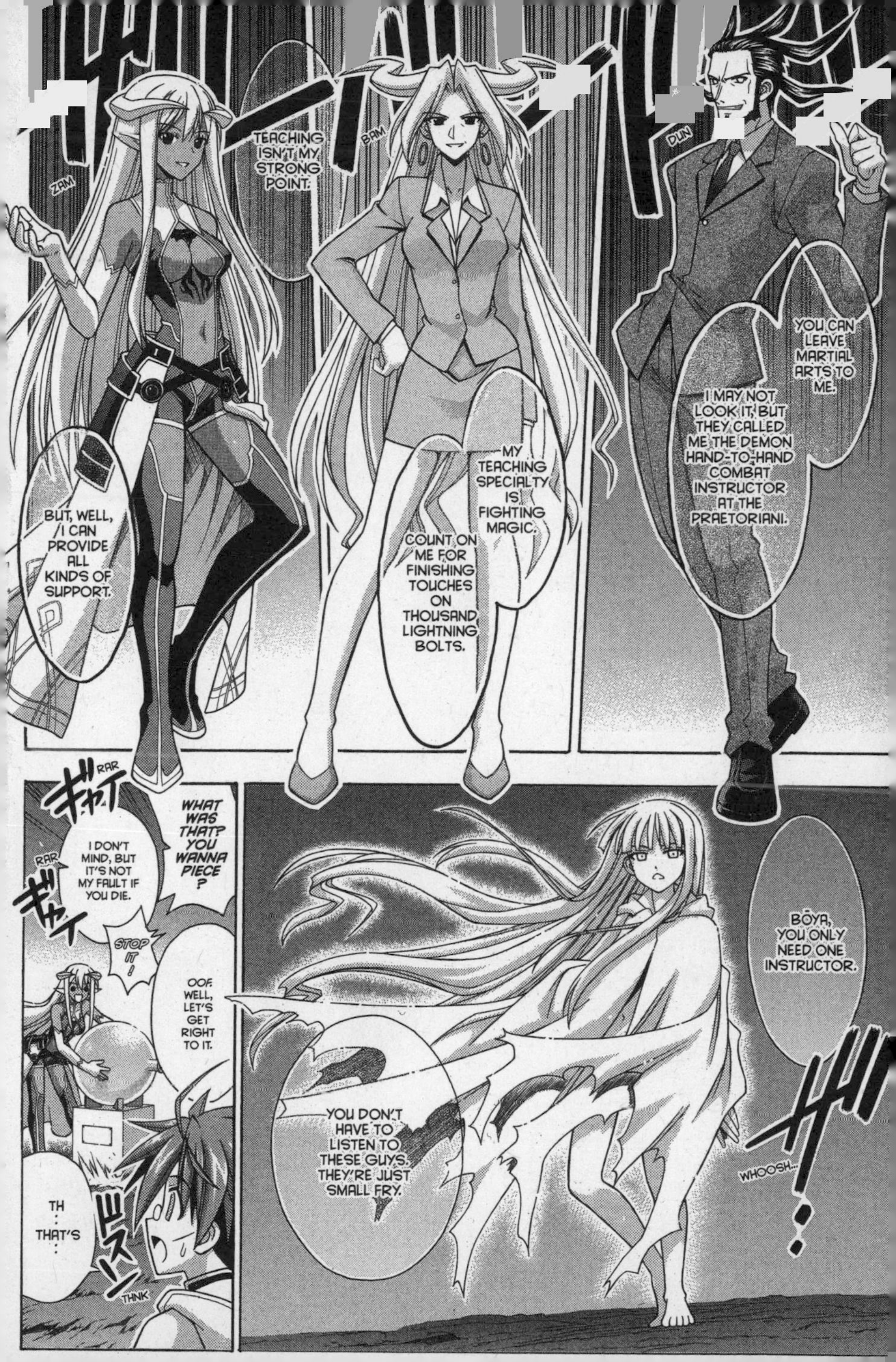
DUN
YOU CAN LEAVE MARTIAL ARTS TO ME.
I MAY NOT LOOK IT, BUT THEY CALLED ME THE DEMON HAND-TO-HAND COMBAT INSTRUCTOR AT THE PRAETORIANI.
BAM
MY TEACHING SPECIALTY IS FIGHTING MAGIC.
COUNT ON ME FOR FINISHING TOUCHES ON THOUSAND LIGHTNING BOLTS.
ZAM
TEACHING ISN'T MY STRONG POINT.
BUT, WELL, I CAN PROVIDE ALL KINDS OF SUPPORT.
BŌYA, YOU ONLY NEED ONE INSTRUCTOR.
WHOOSH...
YOU DON'T HAVE TO LISTEN TO THESE GUYS. THEY'RE JUST SMALL FRY.
WHAT WAS THAT? YOU WANNA PIECE?
RAR
I DON'T MIND, BUT IT'S NOT MY FAULT IF YOU DIE.
RAR
STOP IT!
OOF. WELL, LET'S GET RIGHT TO IT.
TH- THAT'S...
THNK

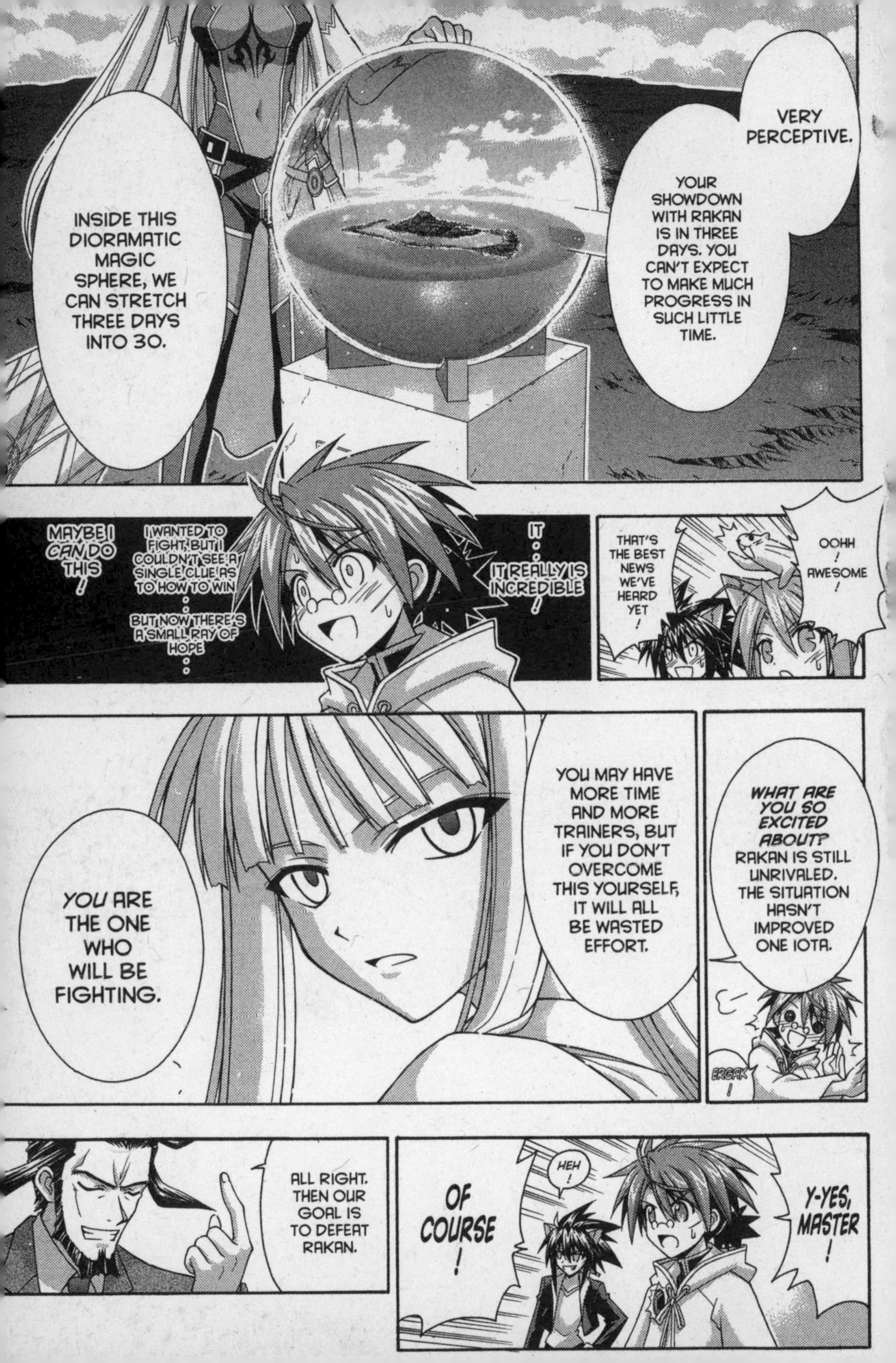
VERY PERCEPTIVE.
YOUR SHOWDOWN WITH RAKAN IS IN THREE DAYS. YOU CAN'T EXPECT TO MAKE MUCH PROGRESS IN SUCH LITTLE TIME.
INSIDE THIS DIORAMATIC MAGIC SPHERE, WE CAN STRETCH THREE DAYS INTO 30.
OOHH! AWESOME!
THAT'S THE BEST NEWS WE'VE HEARD YET!
IT... IT REALLY IS INCREDIBLE!
I WANTED TO FIGHT, BUT I COULDN'T SEE A SINGLE CLUE AS TO HOW TO WIN...
BUT NOW THERE'S A SMALL RAY OF HOPE...
MAYBE I CAN DO THIS!
WHAT ARE YOU SO EXCITED ABOUT? RAKAN IS STILL UNRIVALED. THE SITUATION HASN'T IMPROVED ONE IOTA.
ERGAK!
YOU MAY HAVE MORE TIME AND MORE TRAINERS, BUT IF YOU DON'T OVERCOME THIS YOURSELF, IT WILL ALL BE WASTED EFFORT.
YOU ARE THE ONE WHO WILL BE FIGHTING.
Y-YES, MASTER!
HEH!
OF COURSE!
ALL RIGHT. THEN OUR GOAL IS TO DEFEAT RAKAN.

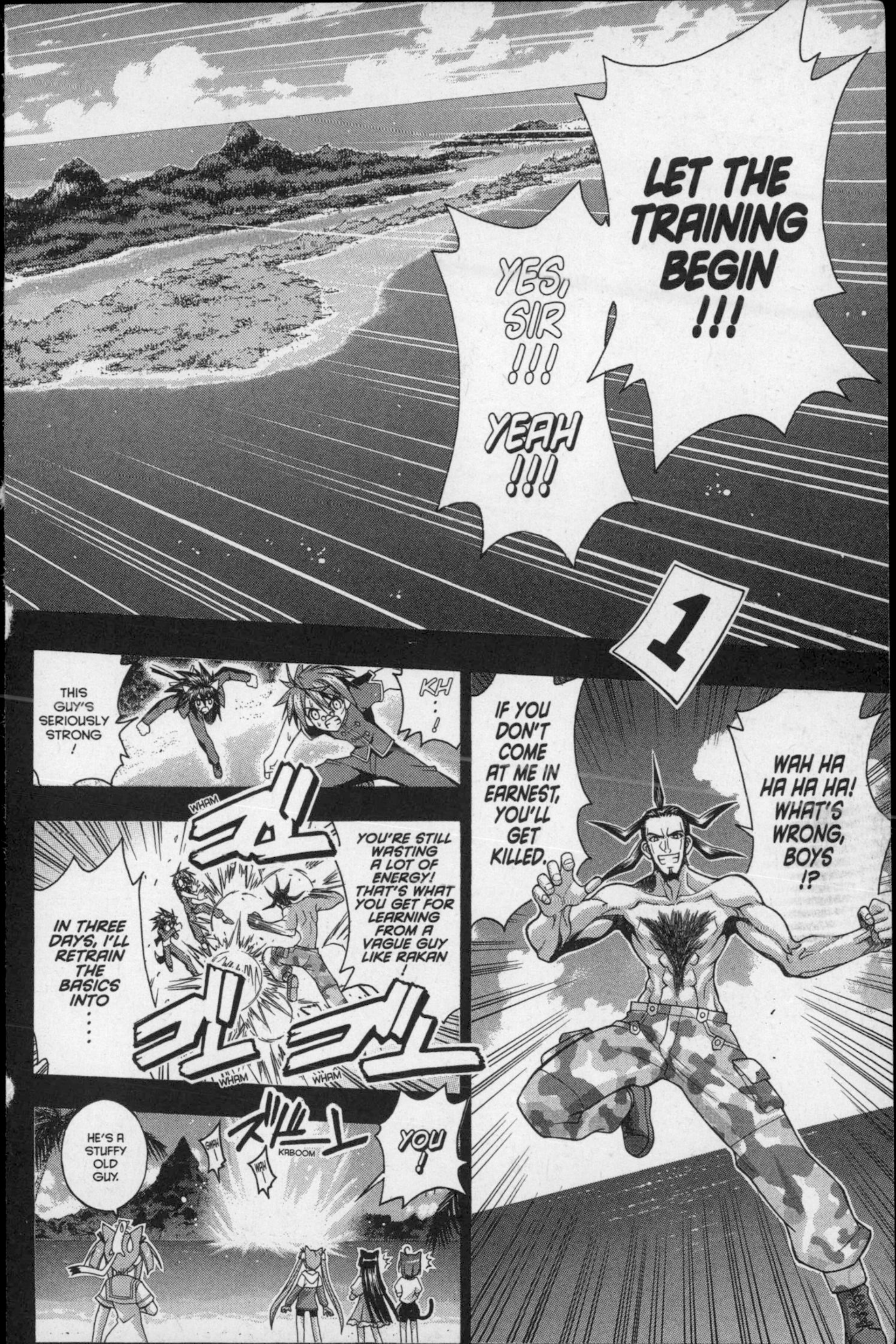
LET THE TRAINING BEGIN !!!
YES, SIR !!!
YEAH !!!
1
WAH HA HA HA HA! WHAT'S WRONG, BOYS !?
IF YOU DON'T COME AT ME IN EARNEST, YOU'LL GET KILLED.
KH...!
THIS GUY'S SERIOUSLY STRONG!
WHAM
YOU'RE STILL WASTING A LOT OF ENERGY! THAT'S WHAT YOU GET FOR LEARNING FROM A VAGUE GUY LIKE RAKAN!
IN THREE DAYS, I'LL RETRAIN THE BASICS INTO...
WHAM
WHAM
YOU!
KABOOM
GWAH!
WAH!
HE'S A STUFFY OLD GUY.

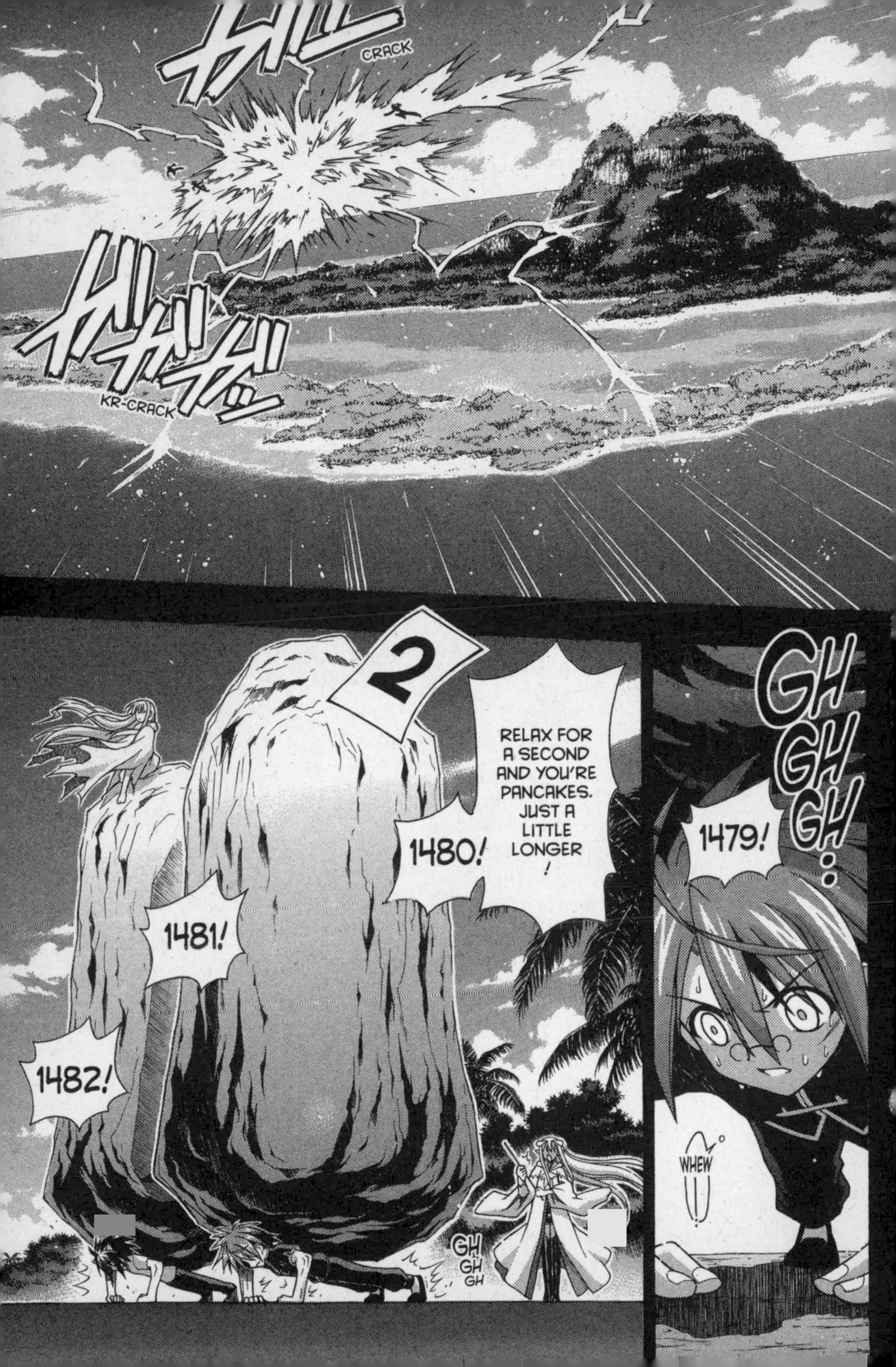
CRACK
KR-CRACK
GH GH GH..
1479!
WHEW
RELAX FOR A SECOND AND YOU'RE PANCAKES. JUST A LITTLE LONGER!
1480!
1481!
1482!
GH GH GH

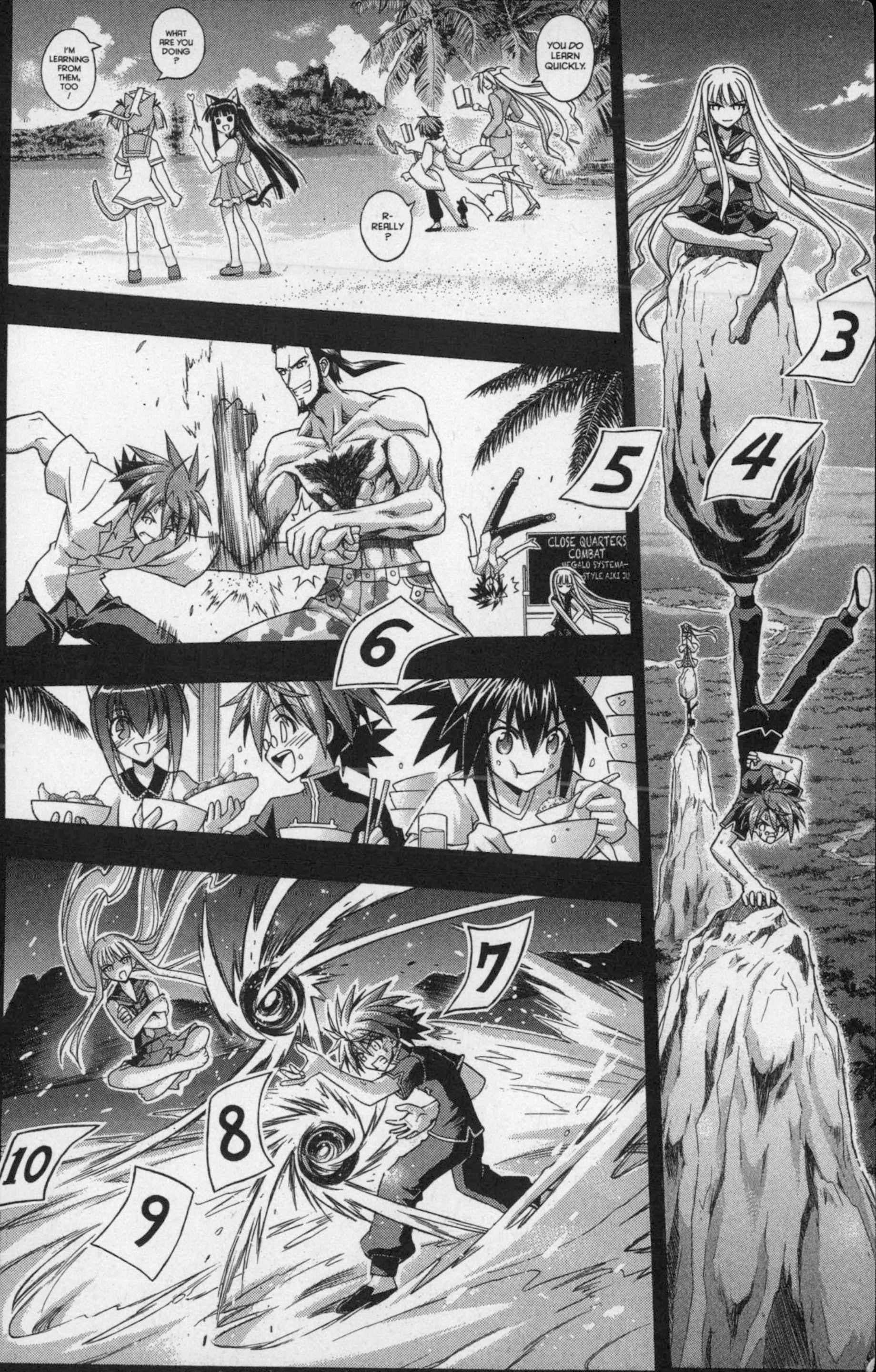
YOU DO LEARN QUICKLY.
R-REALLY?
WHAT ARE YOU DOING?
I'M LEARNING FROM THEM, TOO!
3
4
5
CLOSE QUARTERS COMBAT
6
7
8
9
10

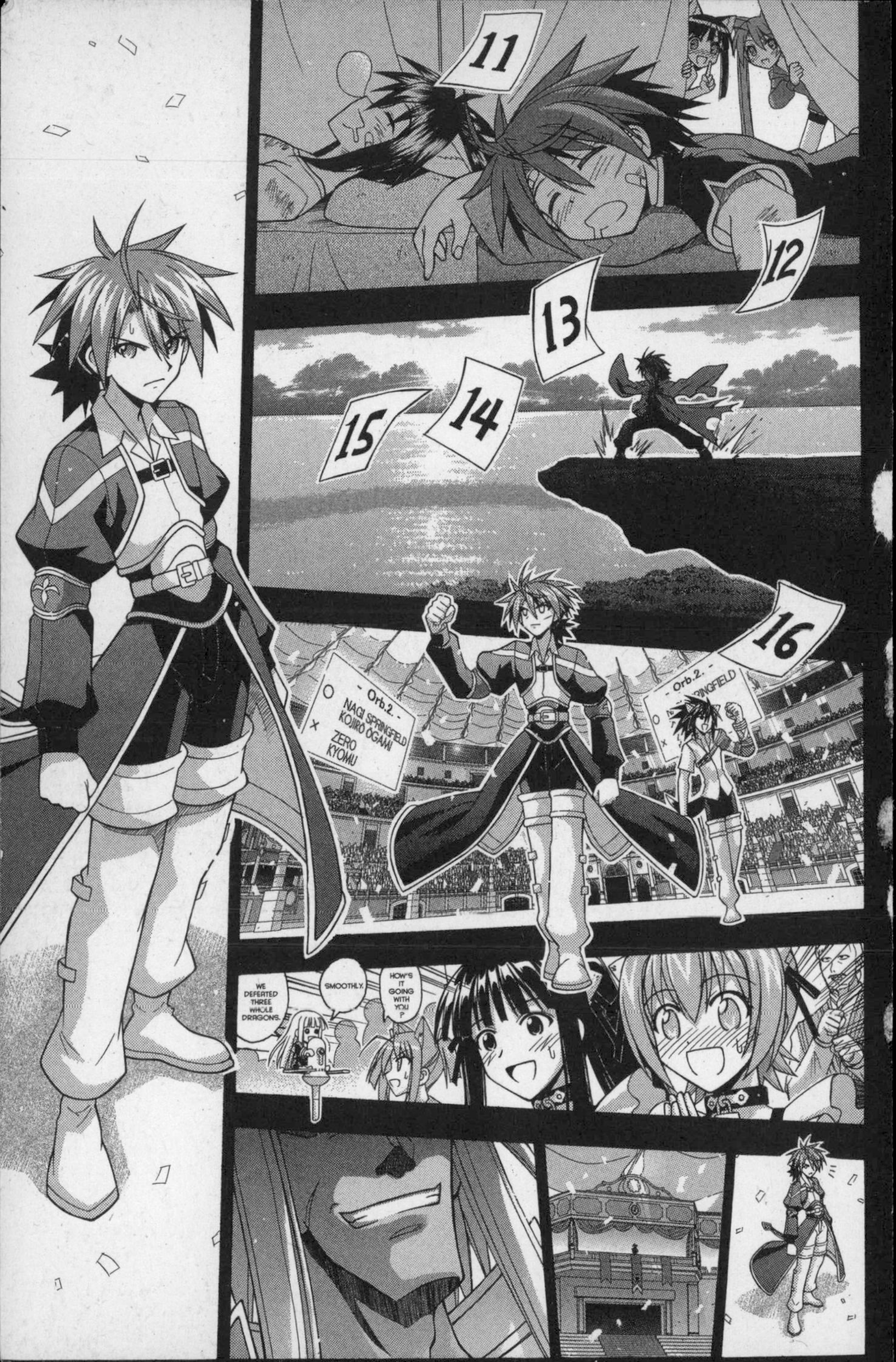
11
12
13
14
15
16
- Orb.2. -
- Orb.2. -
○ NAGI SPRINGFIELD KOJIRŌ ŌGAMI
× ZERO KYOMU
HOW'S IT GOING WITH YOU?
SMOOTHLY.
WE DEFEATED THREE WHOLE DRAGONS.

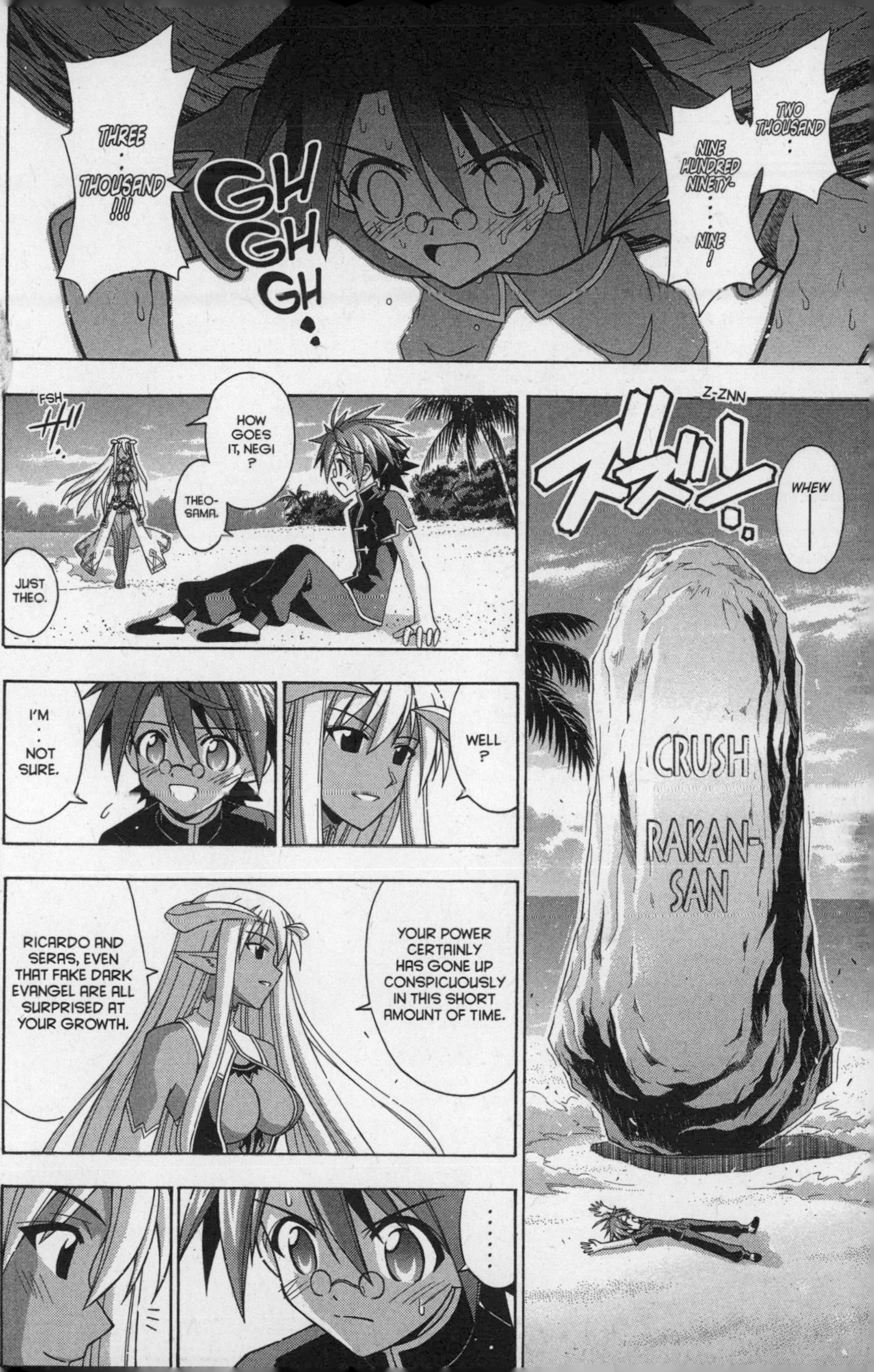
TWO THOUSAND . . . NINE HUNDRED NINETY- . . . NINE !
GH GH GH
THREE . . . THOUSAND !!!
Z-ZNN
WHEW
CRUSH RAKAN-SAN
FSH
HOW GOES IT, NEGI ?
THEO-SAMA.
JUST THEO.
WELL ?
I'M . . . NOT SURE.
YOUR POWER CERTAINLY HAS GONE UP CONSPICUOUSLY IN THIS SHORT AMOUNT OF TIME.
RICARDO AND SERAS, EVEN THAT FAKE DARK EVANGEL ARE ALL SURPRISED AT YOUR GROWTH.
. . . . . .

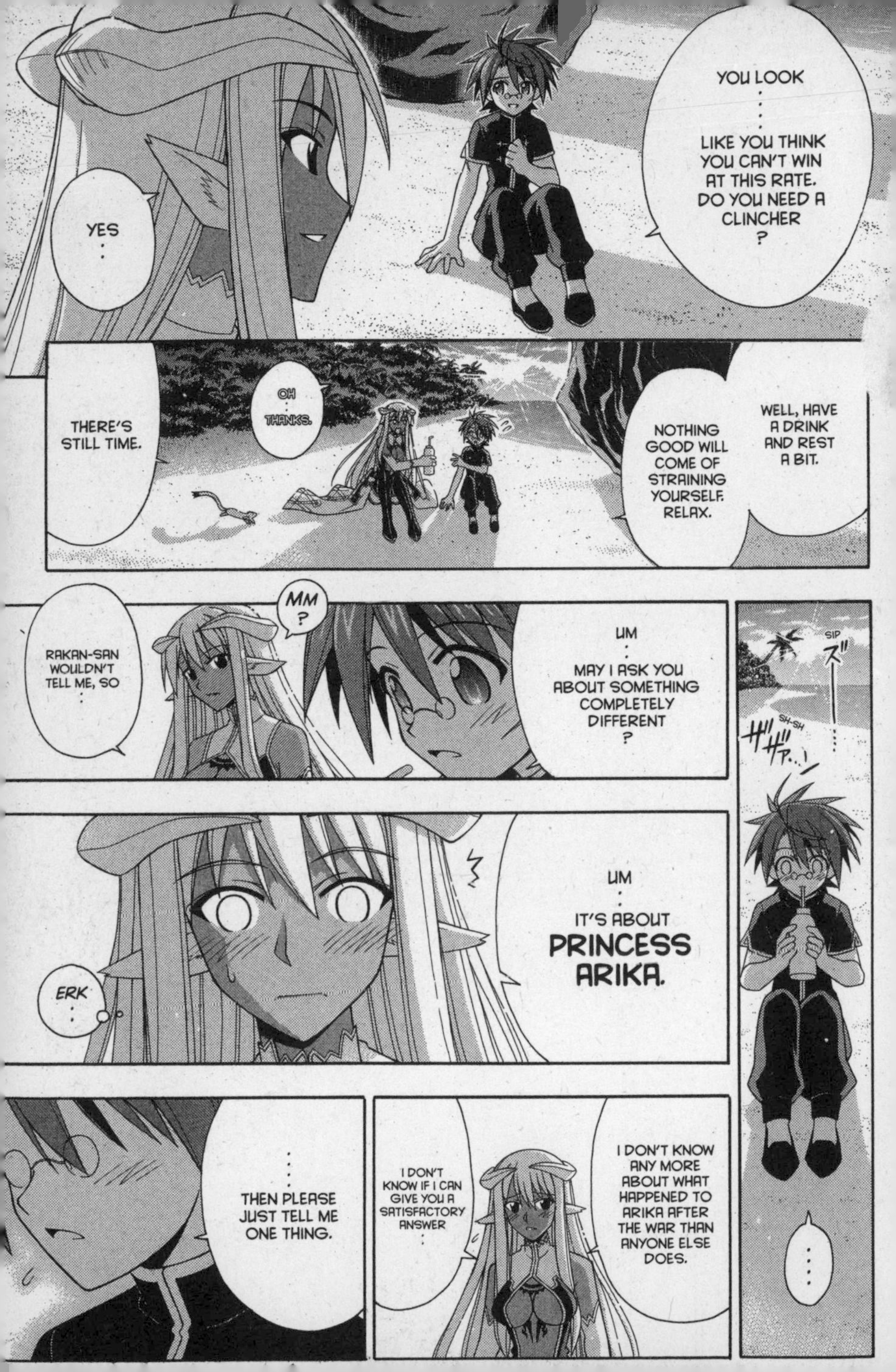

YOU LOOK ... LIKE YOU THINK YOU CAN'T WIN AT THIS RATE. DO YOU NEED A CLINCHER ?
YES ...
WELL, HAVE A DRINK AND REST A BIT.
NOTHING GOOD WILL COME OF STRAINING YOURSELF. RELAX.
OH ... THANKS.
THERE'S STILL TIME.
SIP
ズ ー ...
SH-SH
ザザァ...!
...
UM ... MAY I ASK YOU ABOUT SOMETHING COMPLETELY DIFFERENT ?
MM ?
RAKAN-SAN WOULDN'T TELL ME, SO ...
UM ... IT'S ABOUT PRINCESS ARIKA.
ERK ...
I DON'T KNOW ANY MORE ABOUT WHAT HAPPENED TO ARIKA AFTER THE WAR THAN ANYONE ELSE DOES.
I DON'T KNOW IF I CAN GIVE YOU A SATISFACTORY ANSWER ...
... THEN PLEASE JUST TELL ME ONE THING.

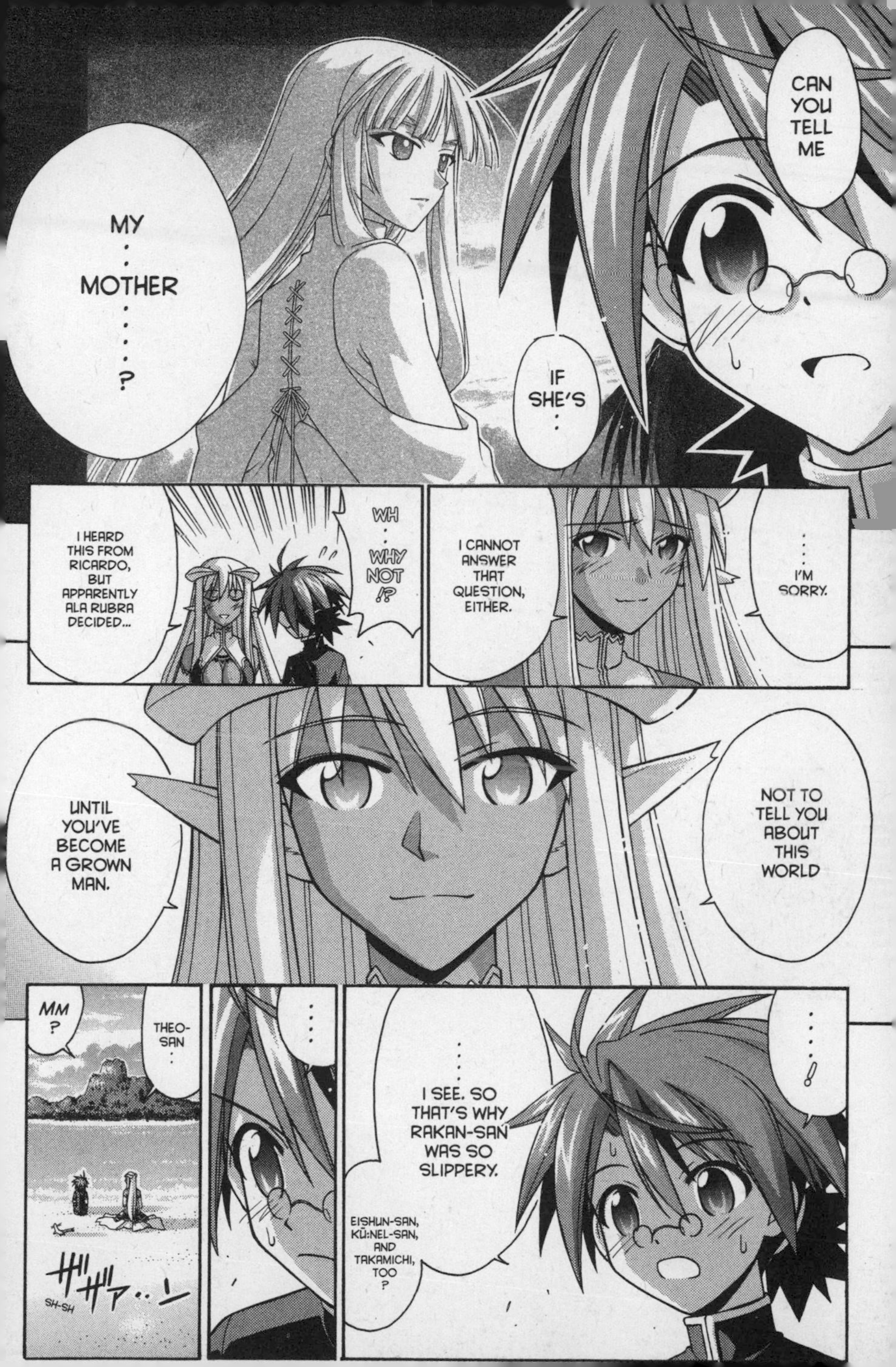
CAN YOU TELL ME
IF SHE'S . . .
MY . . MOTHER . . . . . ?
. . . I'M SORRY.
I CANNOT ANSWER THAT QUESTION, EITHER.
WH . . WHY NOT !?
I HEARD THIS FROM RICARDO, BUT APPARENTLY ALA RUBRA DECIDED...
NOT TO TELL YOU ABOUT THIS WORLD
UNTIL YOU'VE BECOME A GROWN MAN.
. . . . !
. . . . .
I SEE. SO THAT'S WHY RAKAN-SAN WAS SO SLIPPERY.
EISHUN-SAN, KÜ:NEL-SAN, AND TAKAMICHI, TOO ?
. . . .
THEO-SAN . . .
MM ?
SH-SH

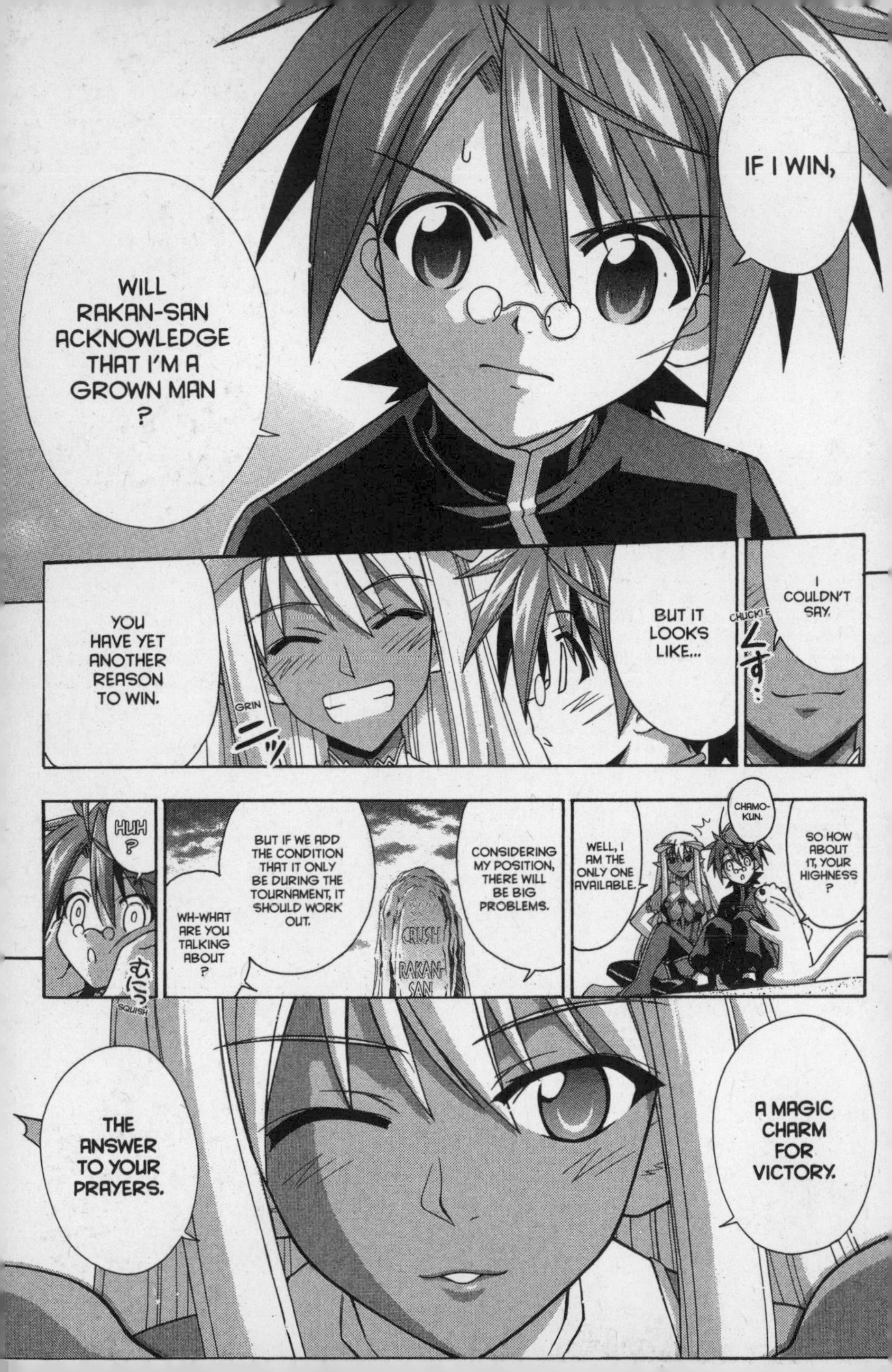

IF I WIN,
WILL RAKAN-SAN ACKNOWLEDGE THAT I'M A GROWN MAN ?
I COULDN'T SAY.
CHUCKLE
BUT IT LOOKS LIKE...
YOU HAVE YET ANOTHER REASON TO WIN.
GRIN
CHAMO-KUN.
SO HOW ABOUT IT, YOUR HIGHNESS ?
WELL, I AM THE ONLY ONE AVAILABLE.
CONSIDERING MY POSITION, THERE WILL BE BIG PROBLEMS.
BUT IF WE ADD THE CONDITION THAT IT ONLY BE DURING THE TOURNAMENT, IT SHOULD WORK OUT.
WH-WHAT ARE YOU TALKING ABOUT ?
CRUSH
RAKAN-SAN
HUH ?
SQUISH
A MAGIC CHARM FOR VICTORY.
THE ANSWER TO YOUR PRAYERS.

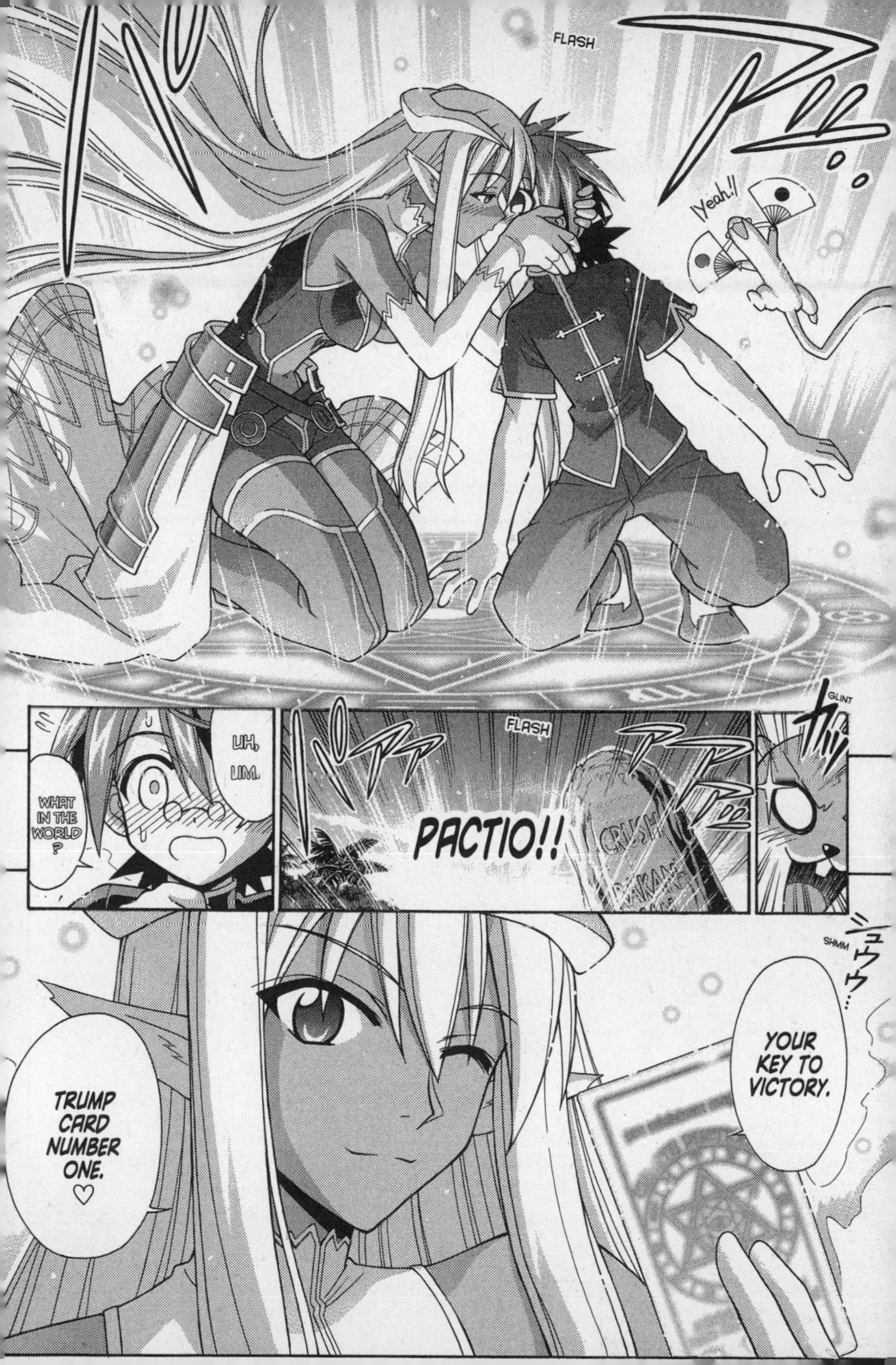

FLASH
Yeah!!
GLINT
FLASH
PACTIO!!
UH, UM.
WHAT IN THE WORLD?
SHMM
YOUR KEY TO VICTORY.
TRUMP CARD NUMBER ONE. ♡

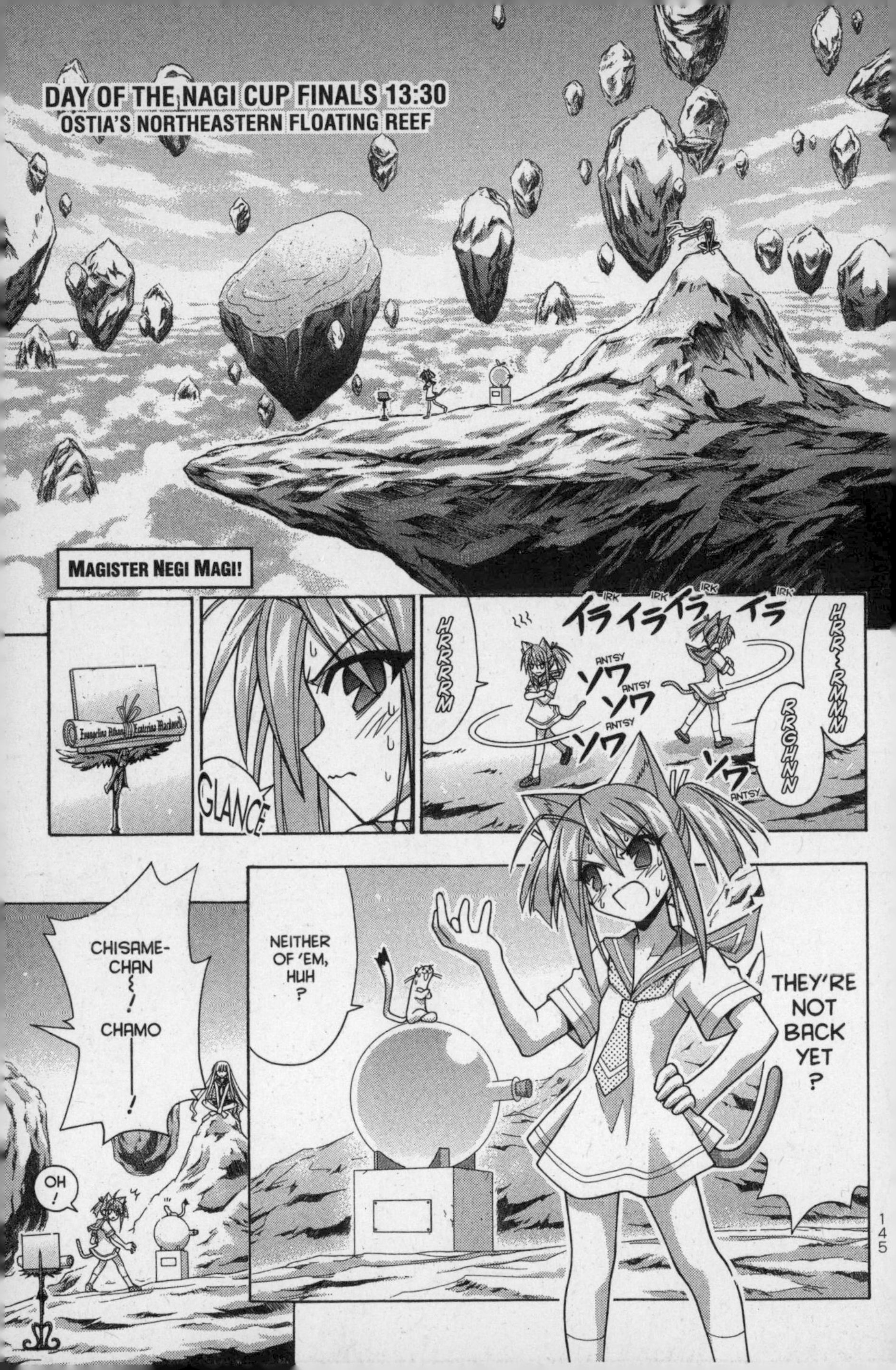
DAY OF THE NAGI CUP FINALS 13:30
OSTIA'S NORTHEASTERN FLOATING REEF
Magister Negi Magi!
IRK IRK IRK IRK
イラ イラ イラ イラ
HRR-RMMM
RRGHNN
ANTSY ANTSY ANTSY ANTSY
ソワ ソワ ソワ ソワ
HRRRRM
GLANCE
THEY'RE NOT BACK YET?
NEITHER OF 'EM, HUH?
CHISAME-CHAN~!
CHAMO—!
OH!

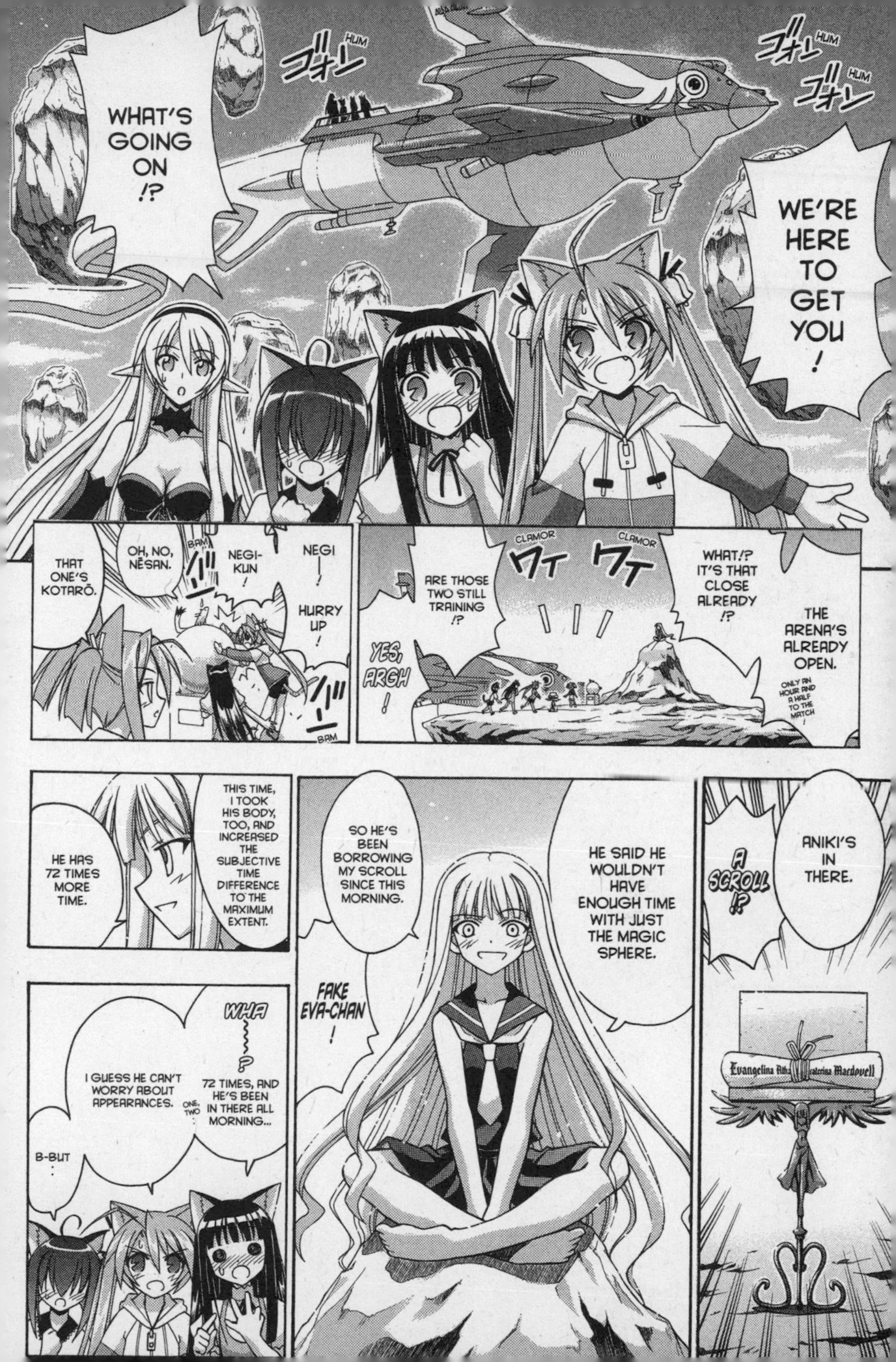

HUM
HUM
HUM
WE'RE HERE TO GET YOU!
WHAT'S GOING ON!?
THE ARENA'S ALREADY OPEN.
ONLY AN HOUR AND A HALF TO THE MATCH!
WHAT!? IT'S THAT CLOSE ALREADY!?
CLAMOR
CLAMOR
ARE THOSE TWO STILL TRAINING!?
YES, ARGH!
NEGI! HURRY UP!
NEGI-KUN!
BAM
OH, NO, NĒSAN.
THAT ONE'S KOTARŌ.
BAM
ANIKI'S IN THERE.
A SCROLL!?
HE SAID HE WOULDN'T HAVE ENOUGH TIME WITH JUST THE MAGIC SPHERE.
SO HE'S BEEN BORROWING MY SCROLL SINCE THIS MORNING.
FAKE EVA-CHAN!
THIS TIME, I TOOK HIS BODY, TOO, AND INCREASED THE SUBJECTIVE TIME DIFFERENCE TO THE MAXIMUM EXTENT.
HE HAS 72 TIMES MORE TIME.
WHA~~~?
72 TIMES, AND HE'S BEEN IN THERE ALL MORNING...
ONE, TWO:
I GUESS HE CAN'T WORRY ABOUT APPEARANCES.
B-BUT:

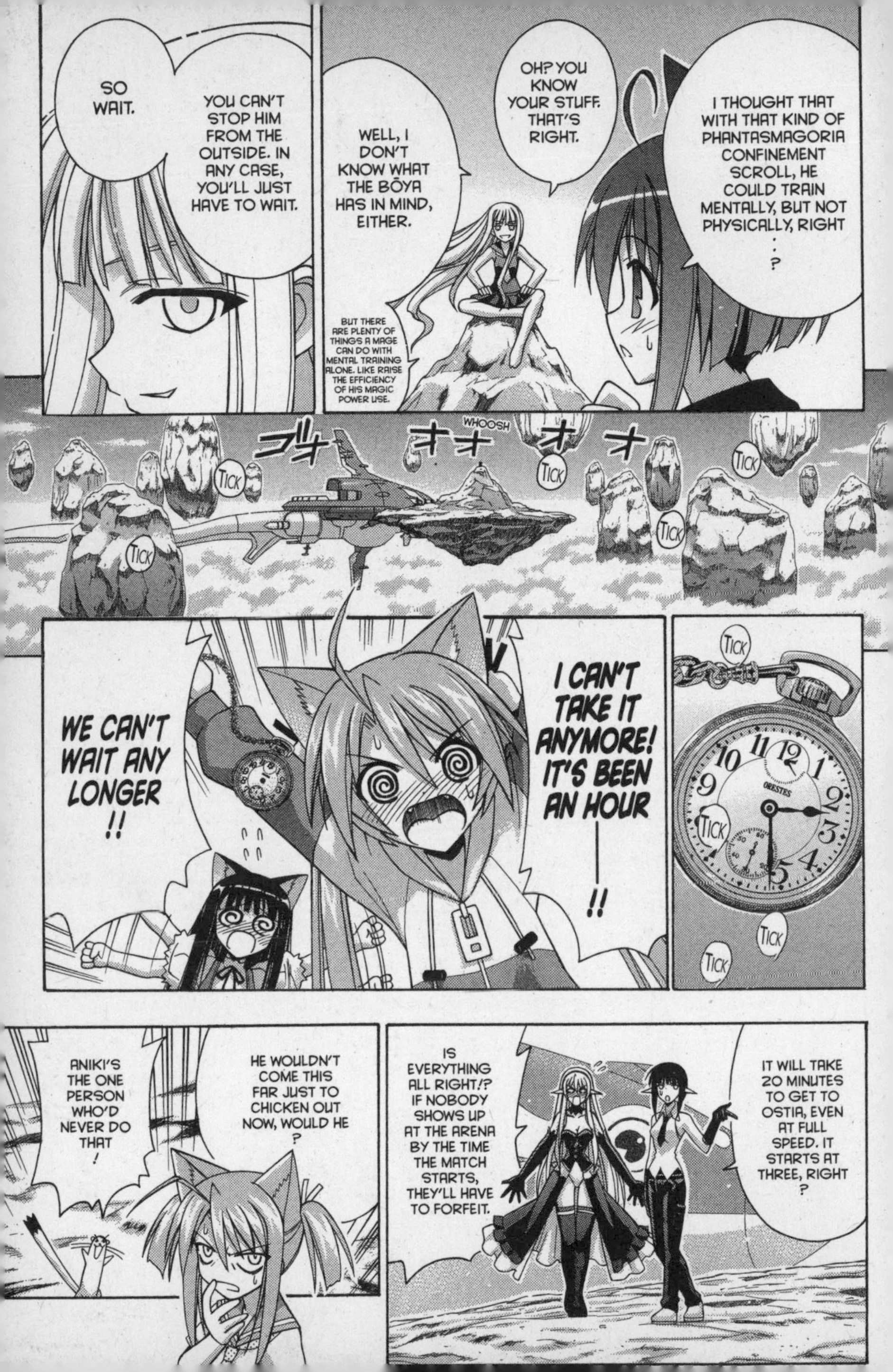
I THOUGHT THAT WITH THAT KIND OF PHANTASMAGORIA CONFINEMENT SCROLL, HE COULD TRAIN MENTALLY, BUT NOT PHYSICALLY, RIGHT...?
OH? YOU KNOW YOUR STUFF. THAT'S RIGHT.
WELL, I DON'T KNOW WHAT THE BŌYA HAS IN MIND, EITHER.
BUT THERE ARE PLENTY OF THINGS A MAGE CAN DO WITH MENTAL TRAINING ALONE. LIKE RAISE THE EFFICIENCY OF HIS MAGIC POWER USE.
YOU CAN'T STOP HIM FROM THE OUTSIDE. IN ANY CASE, YOU'LL JUST HAVE TO WAIT.
SO WAIT.
WHOOSH
TICK
TICK
TICK
TICK
TICK
TICK
TICK
TICK
TICK
I CAN'T TAKE IT ANYMORE! IT'S BEEN AN HOUR—!!
WE CAN'T WAIT ANY LONGER!!
IT WILL TAKE 20 MINUTES TO GET TO OSTIA, EVEN AT FULL SPEED. IT STARTS AT THREE, RIGHT?
IS EVERYTHING ALL RIGHT!? IF NOBODY SHOWS UP AT THE ARENA BY THE TIME THE MATCH STARTS, THEY'LL HAVE TO FORFEIT.
HE WOULDN'T COME THIS FAR JUST TO CHICKEN OUT NOW, WOULD HE?
ANIKI'S THE ONE PERSON WHO'D NEVER DO THAT!

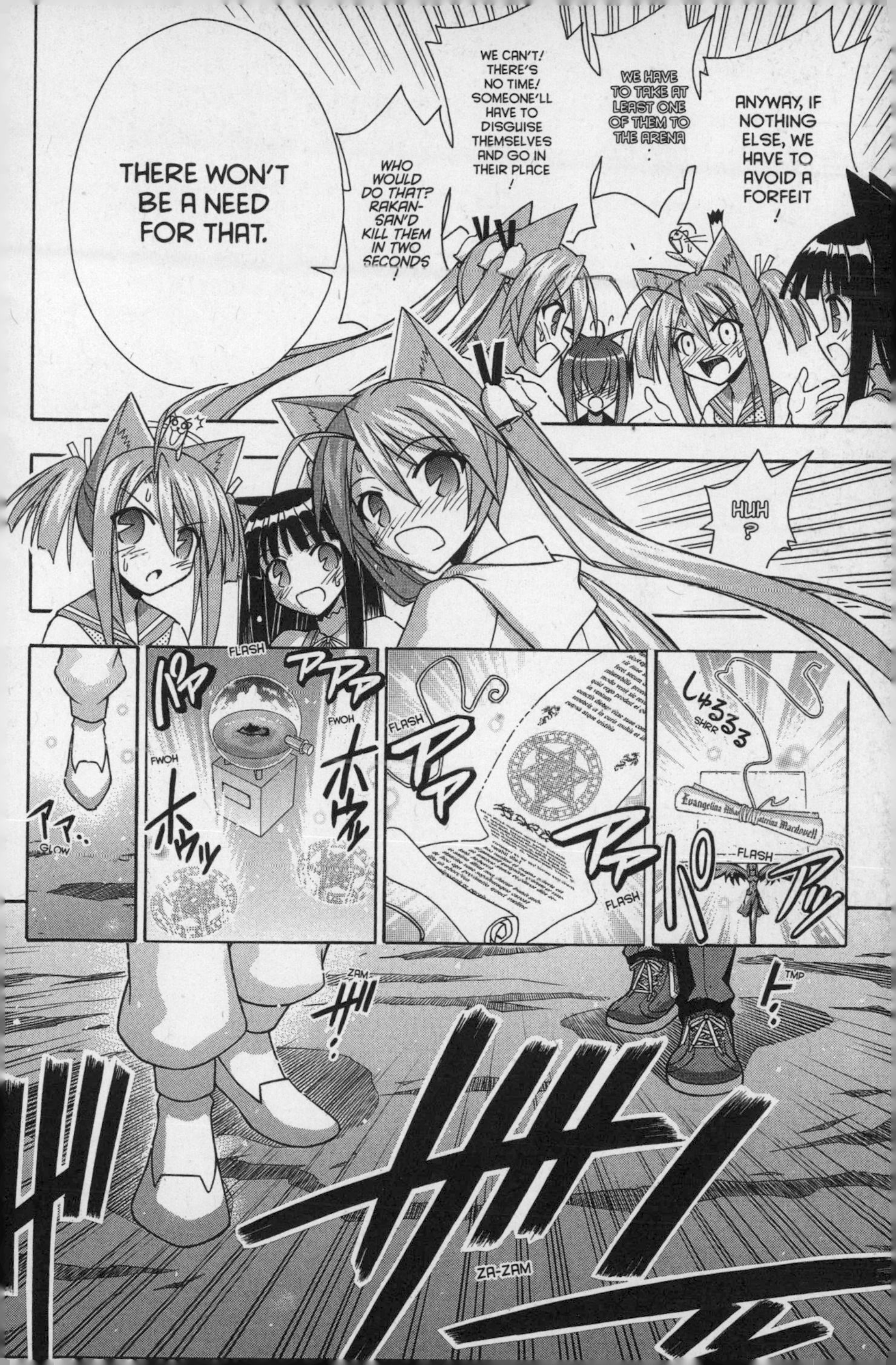
ANYWAY, IF NOTHING ELSE, WE HAVE TO AVOID A FORFEIT!
WE HAVE TO TAKE AT LEAST ONE OF THEM TO THE ARENA...
WE CAN'T! THERE'S NO TIME! SOMEONE'LL HAVE TO DISGUISE THEMSELVES AND GO IN THEIR PLACE!
WHO WOULD DO THAT? RAKAN-SAN'D KILL THEM IN TWO SECONDS!
THERE WON'T BE A NEED FOR THAT.
HUH?
SHRR
FLASH
FLASH
FLASH
FLASH
FWOH
FWOH
GLOW
TMP
ZAM
ZA-ZAM

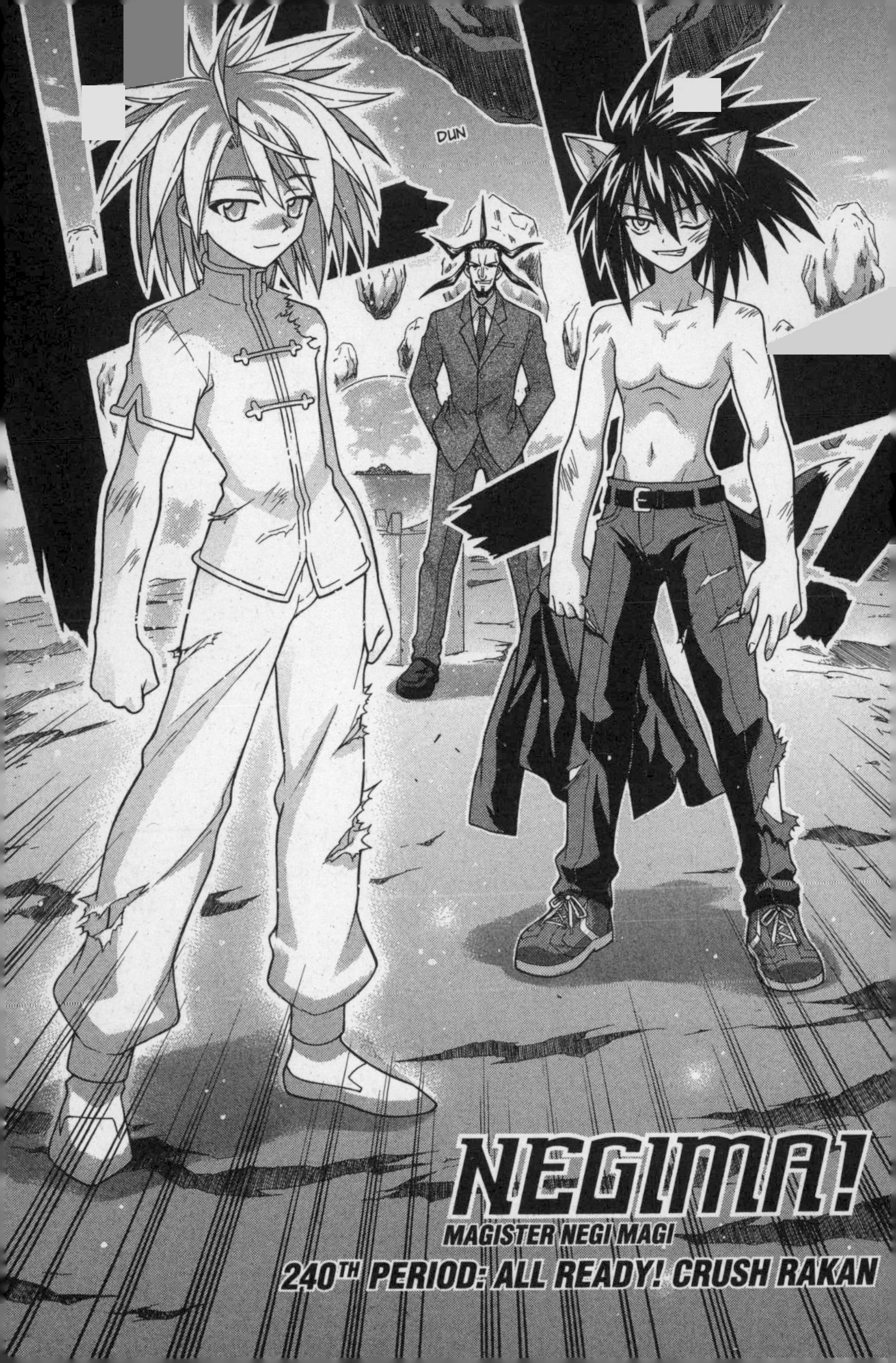
DUN
NEGIMA!
MAGISTER NEGI MAGI
240TH PERIOD: ALL READY! CRUSH RAKAN

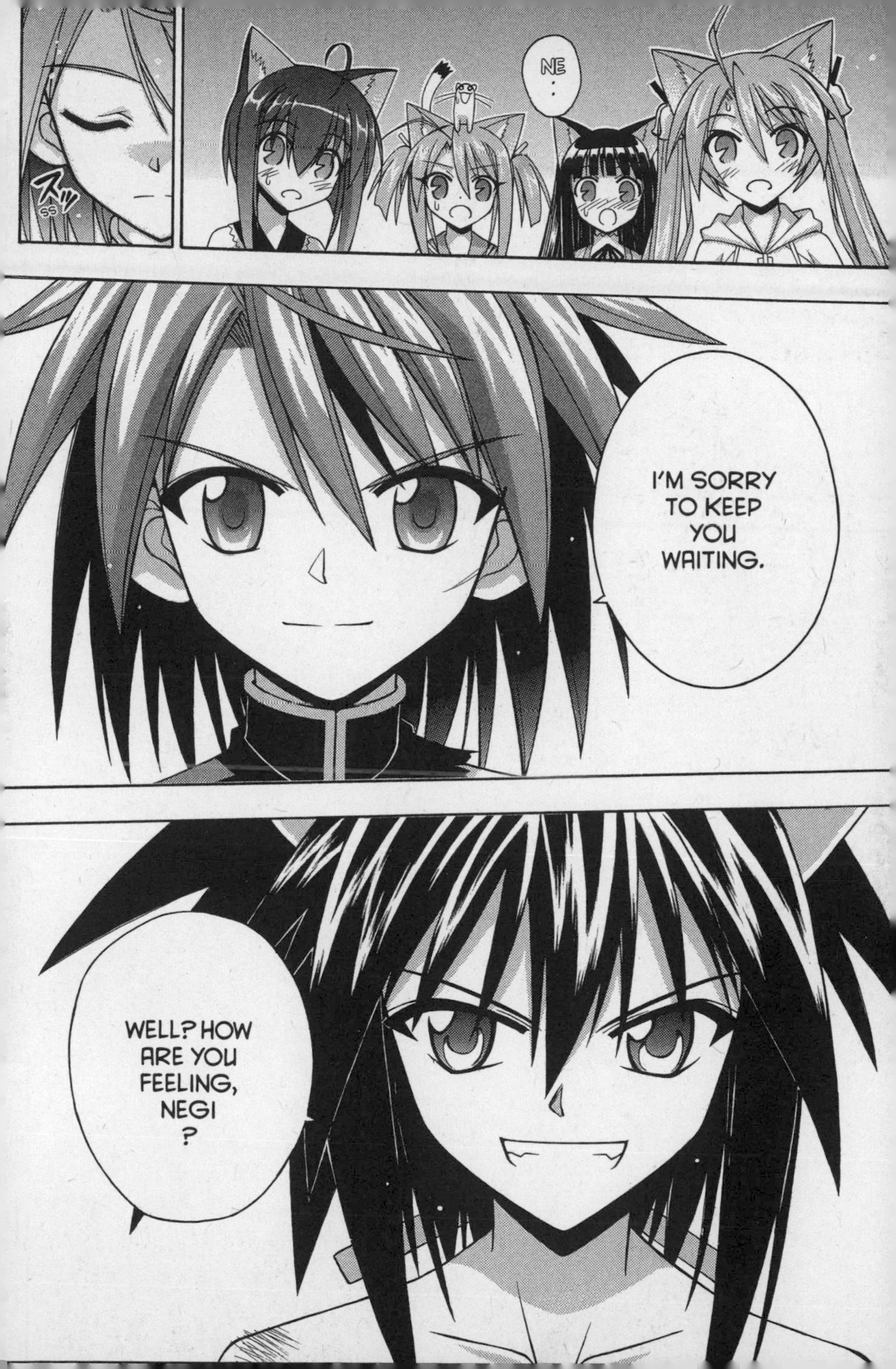
NE . .
スッ SS
I'M SORRY TO KEEP YOU WAITING.
WELL? HOW ARE YOU FEELING, NEGI ?

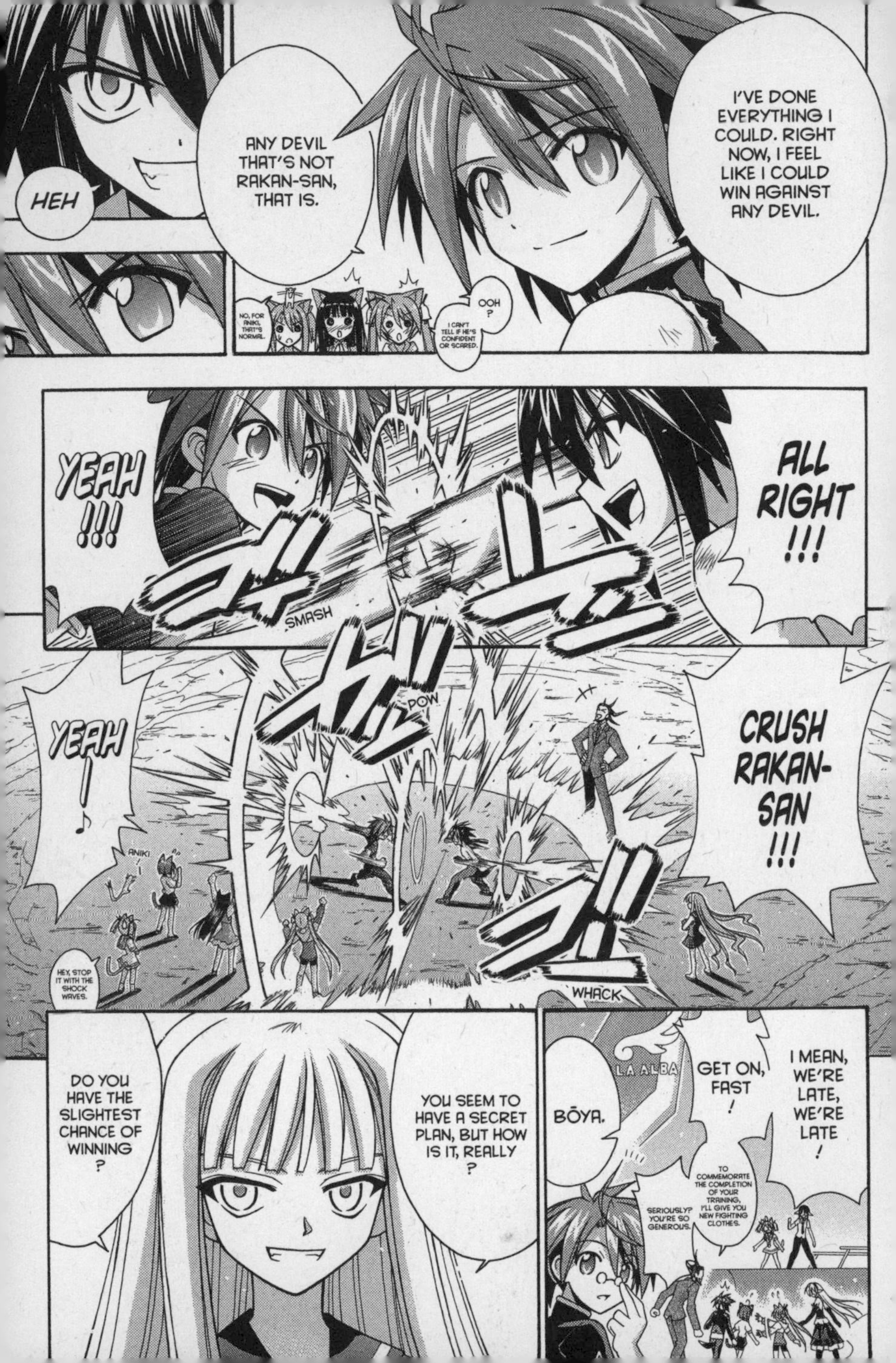
I'VE DONE EVERYTHING I COULD. RIGHT NOW, I FEEL LIKE I COULD WIN AGAINST ANY DEVIL.
OOH?
I CAN'T TELL IF HE'S CONFIDENT OR SCARED.
NO, FOR ANIKI, THAT'S NORMAL.
ANY DEVIL THAT'S NOT RAKAN-SAN, THAT IS.
HEH
ALL RIGHT!!!
YEAH!!!
SMASH
CRUSH RAKAN-SAN!!!
POW
WHACK
YEAH! ♪
ANIKI!
HEY, STOP IT WITH THE SHOCK WAVES.
I MEAN, WE'RE LATE, WE'RE LATE!
GET ON, FAST!
BŌYA.
LA ALBA
TO COMMEMORATE THE COMPLETION OF YOUR TRAINING, I'LL GIVE YOU NEW FIGHTING CLOTHES.
SERIOUSLY? YOU'RE SO GENEROUS.
YOU SEEM TO HAVE A SECRET PLAN, BUT HOW IS IT, REALLY?
DO YOU HAVE THE SLIGHTEST CHANCE OF WINNING?

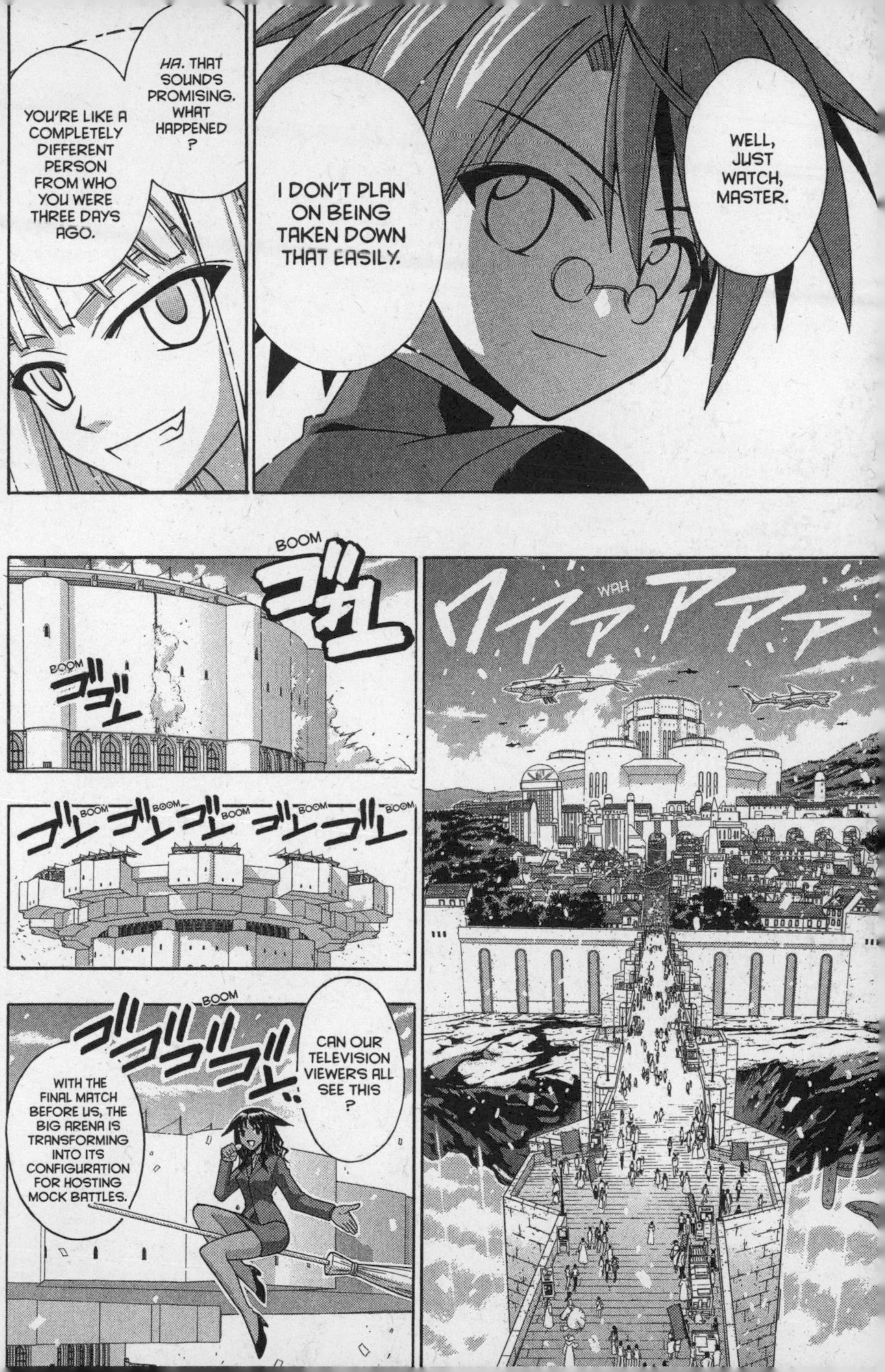
WELL, JUST WATCH, MASTER.
I DON'T PLAN ON BEING TAKEN DOWN THAT EASILY.
HA. THAT SOUNDS PROMISING. WHAT HAPPENED?
YOU'RE LIKE A COMPLETELY DIFFERENT PERSON FROM WHO YOU WERE THREE DAYS AGO.
WAH
BOOM
BOOM
BOOM
BOOM
BOOM
BOOM
BOOM
BOOM
CAN OUR TELEVISION VIEWERS ALL SEE THIS?
WITH THE FINAL MATCH BEFORE US, THE BIG ARENA IS TRANSFORMING INTO ITS CONFIGURATION FOR HOSTING MOCK BATTLES.

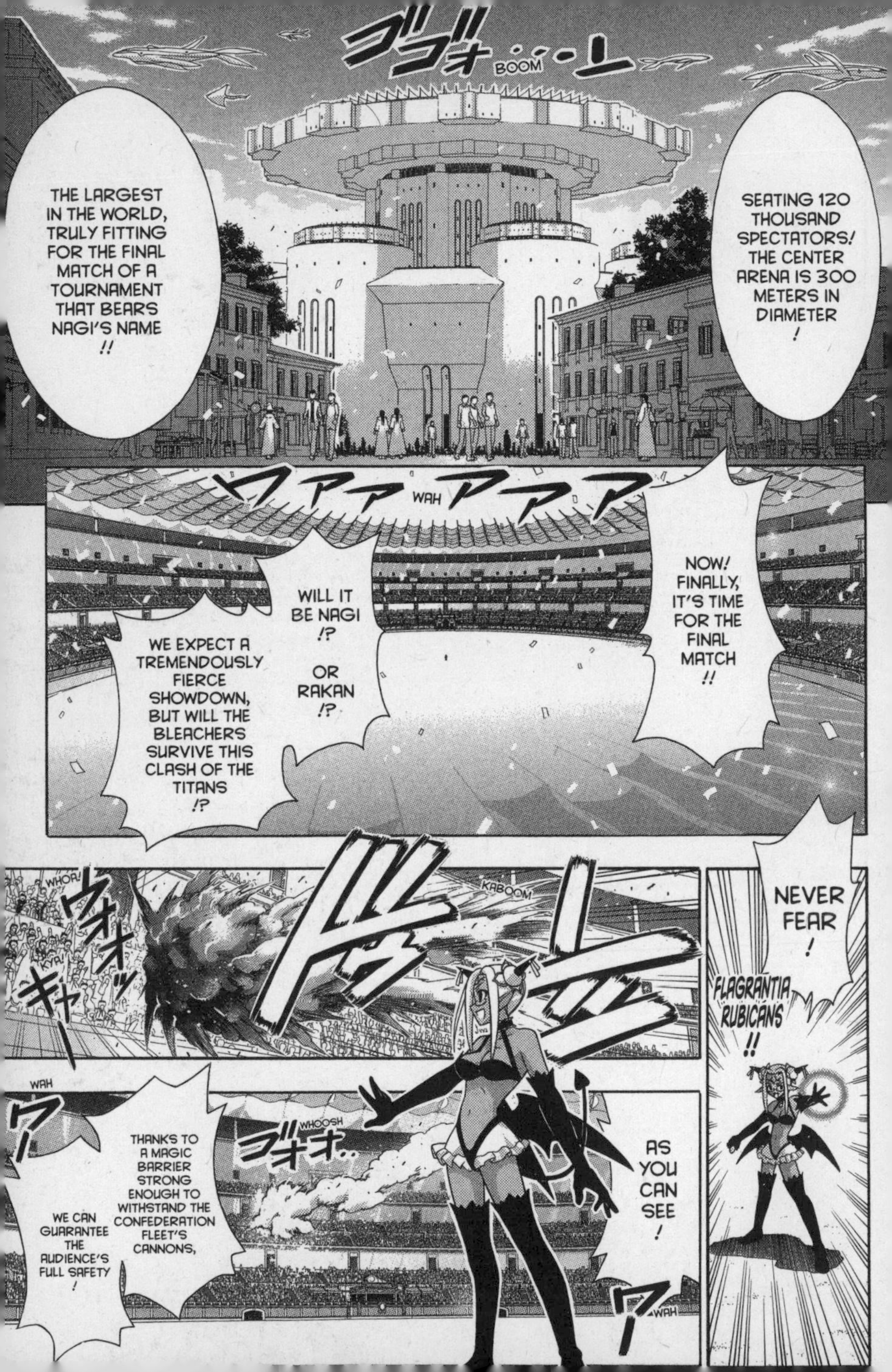
BOOM
SEATING 120 THOUSAND SPECTATORS! THE CENTER ARENA IS 300 METERS IN DIAMETER!
THE LARGEST IN THE WORLD, TRULY FITTING FOR THE FINAL MATCH OF A TOURNAMENT THAT BEARS NAGI'S NAME!!
WAH
NOW! FINALLY, IT'S TIME FOR THE FINAL MATCH!!
WILL IT BE NAGI!? OR RAKAN!?
WE EXPECT A TREMENDOUSLY FIERCE SHOWDOWN, BUT WILL THE BLEACHERS SURVIVE THIS CLASH OF THE TITANS!?
NEVER FEAR!
FLAGRANTIA RUBICANS!!
KABOOM
WHOA!
KYA!
AS YOU CAN SEE!
THANKS TO A MAGIC BARRIER STRONG ENOUGH TO WITHSTAND THE CONFEDERATION FLEET'S CANNONS,
WE CAN GUARANTEE THE AUDIENCE'S FULL SAFETY!
WHOOSH
WAH
WAH

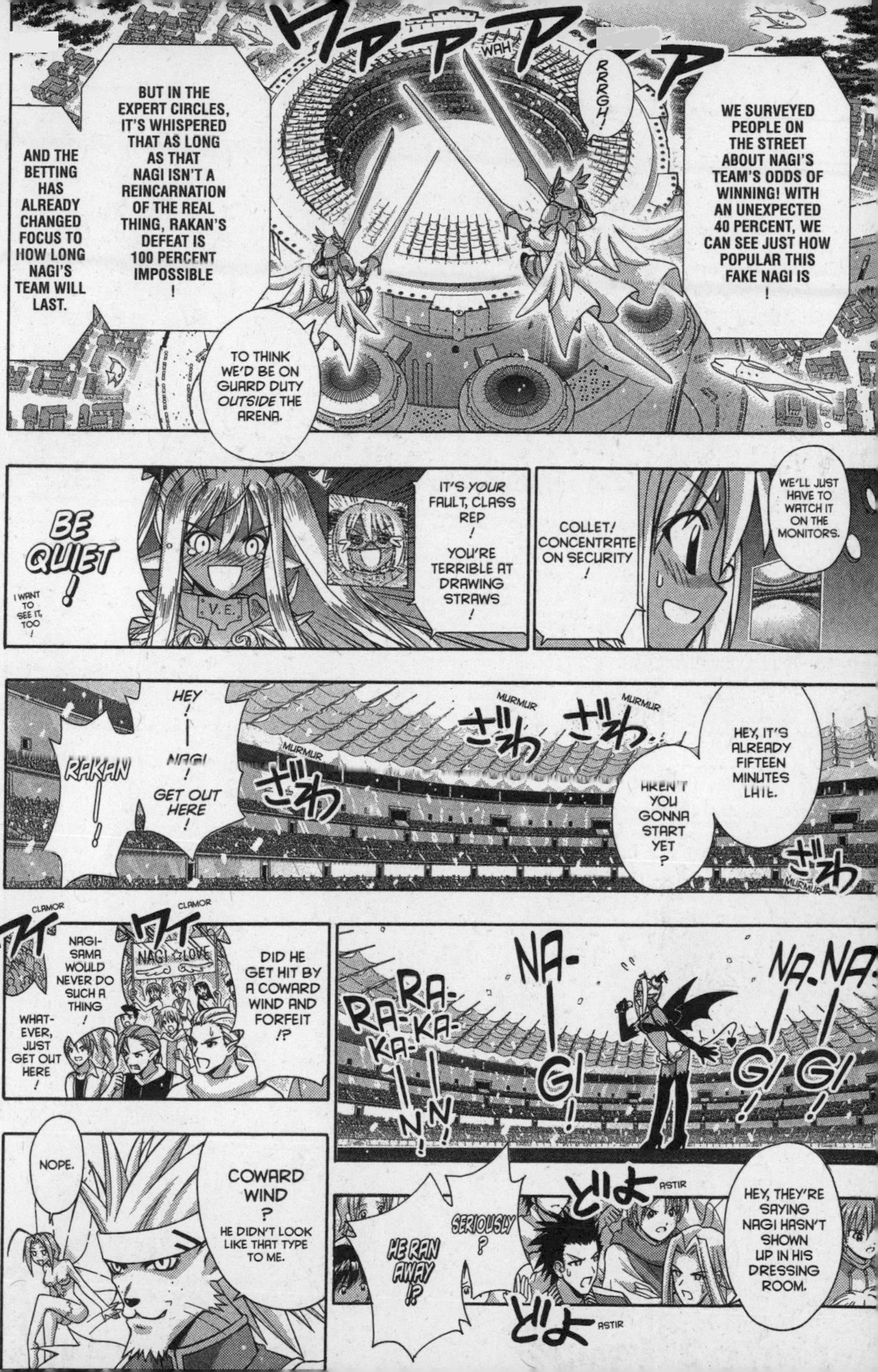
ワァァァ
WAH
RRRGH!
WE SURVEYED PEOPLE ON THE STREET ABOUT NAGI'S TEAM'S ODDS OF WINNING! WITH AN UNEXPECTED 40 PERCENT, WE CAN SEE JUST HOW POPULAR THIS FAKE NAGI IS!
BUT IN THE EXPERT CIRCLES, IT'S WHISPERED THAT AS LONG AS THAT NAGI ISN'T A REINCARNATION OF THE REAL THING, RAKAN'S DEFEAT IS 100 PERCENT IMPOSSIBLE!
AND THE BETTING HAS ALREADY CHANGED FOCUS TO HOW LONG NAGI'S TEAM WILL LAST.
TO THINK WE'D BE ON GUARD DUTY *OUTSIDE* THE ARENA.
WE'LL JUST HAVE TO WATCH IT ON THE MONITORS.
COLLET! CONCENTRATE ON SECURITY!
IT'S *YOUR* FAULT, CLASS REP! YOU'RE TERRIBLE AT DRAWING STRAWS!
BE QUIET!
I WANT TO SEE IT, TOO!
HEY, IT'S ALREADY FIFTEEN MINUTES LATE.
AREN'T YOU GONNA START YET?
ざわ
MURMUR
ざわ
MURMUR
ざわ
MURMUR
ざわ
MURMUR
HEY! NAGI! GET OUT HERE!
RAKAN!
NA-NA-GI! GI!
NA-GI!
RA-KA-N!
RA-KA-N!
ワイ
CLAMOR
ワイ
CLAMOR
DID HE GET HIT BY A COWARD WIND AND FORFEIT!?
NAGI☆LOVE
NAGI-SAMA WOULD NEVER DO SUCH A THING!
WHATEVER, JUST GET OUT HERE!
HEY, THEY'RE SAYING NAGI HASN'T SHOWN UP IN HIS DRESSING ROOM.
どよ
ASTIR
SERIOUSLY?
HE RAN AWAY!?
どよ
ASTIR
COWARD WIND? HE DIDN'T LOOK LIKE THAT TYPE TO ME.
NOPE.

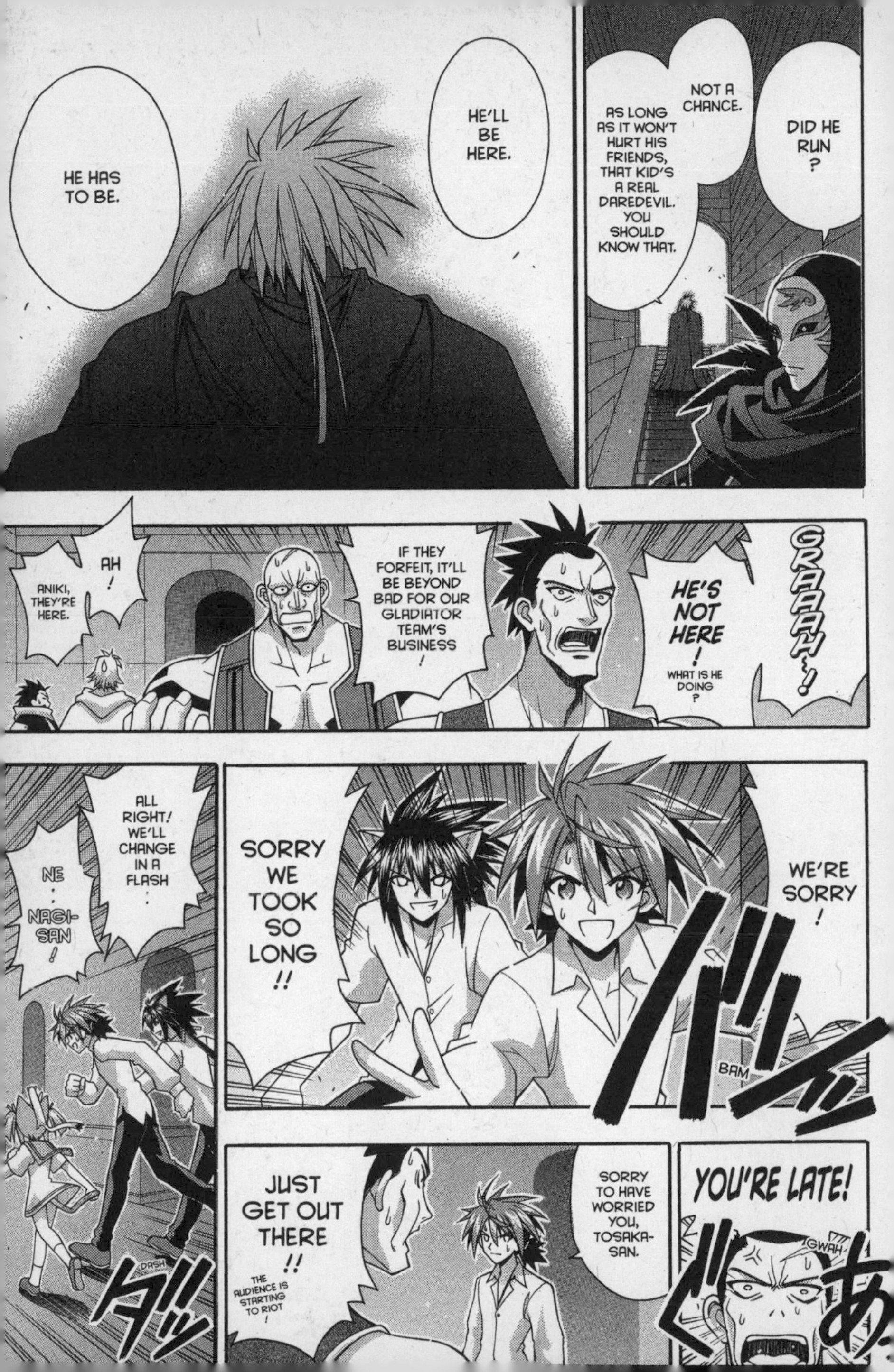
DID HE RUN?
NOT A CHANCE.
AS LONG AS IT WON'T HURT HIS FRIENDS, THAT KID'S A REAL DAREDEVIL. YOU SHOULD KNOW THAT.
HE'LL BE HERE.
HE HAS TO BE.
GRAAAH!
HE'S NOT HERE!
WHAT IS HE DOING?
IF THEY FORFEIT, IT'LL BE BEYOND BAD FOR OUR GLADIATOR TEAM'S BUSINESS!
AH!
ANIKI, THEY'RE HERE.
WE'RE SORRY!
SORRY WE TOOK SO LONG!!
BAM
YOU'RE LATE!
GWAH
SORRY TO HAVE WORRIED YOU, TOSAKA-SAN.
JUST GET OUT THERE!!
THE AUDIENCE IS STARTING TO RIOT
ALL RIGHT! WE'LL CHANGE IN A FLASH...
NE... NAGI-SAN!
DASH

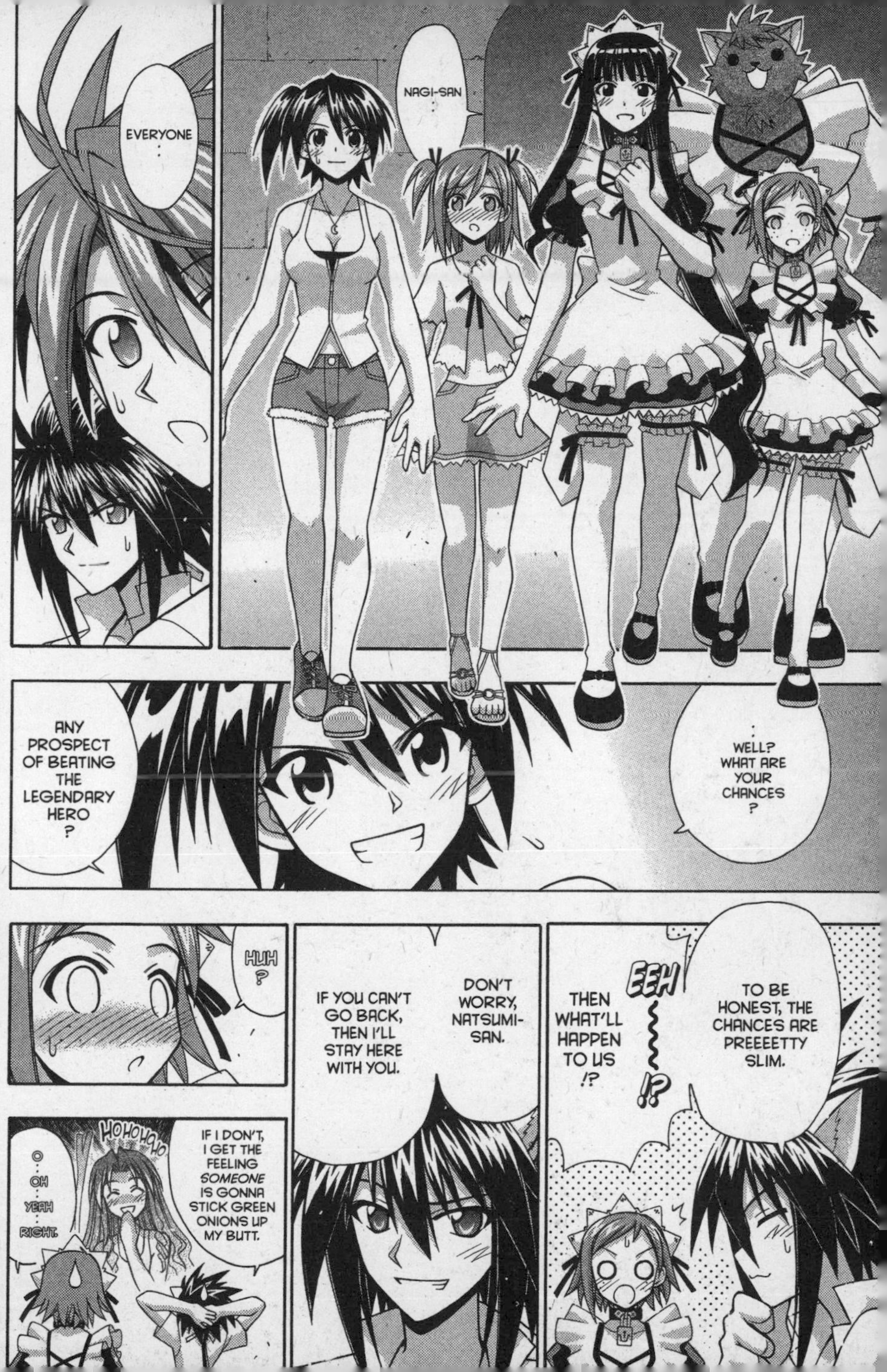

NAGI-SAN
:
EVERYONE
:
:
WELL? WHAT ARE YOUR CHANCES
?
ANY PROSPECT OF BEATING THE LEGENDARY HERO
?
TO BE HONEST, THE CHANCES ARE PREEEETTY SLIM.
EEH~!?
THEN WHAT'LL HAPPEN TO US
!?
DON'T WORRY, NATSUMI-SAN.
IF YOU CAN'T GO BACK, THEN I'LL STAY HERE WITH YOU.
HUH
?
IF I DON'T, I GET THE FEELING *SOMEONE* IS GONNA STICK GREEN ONIONS UP MY BUTT.
HOHOHOHO
O...OH YEAH...RIGHT.

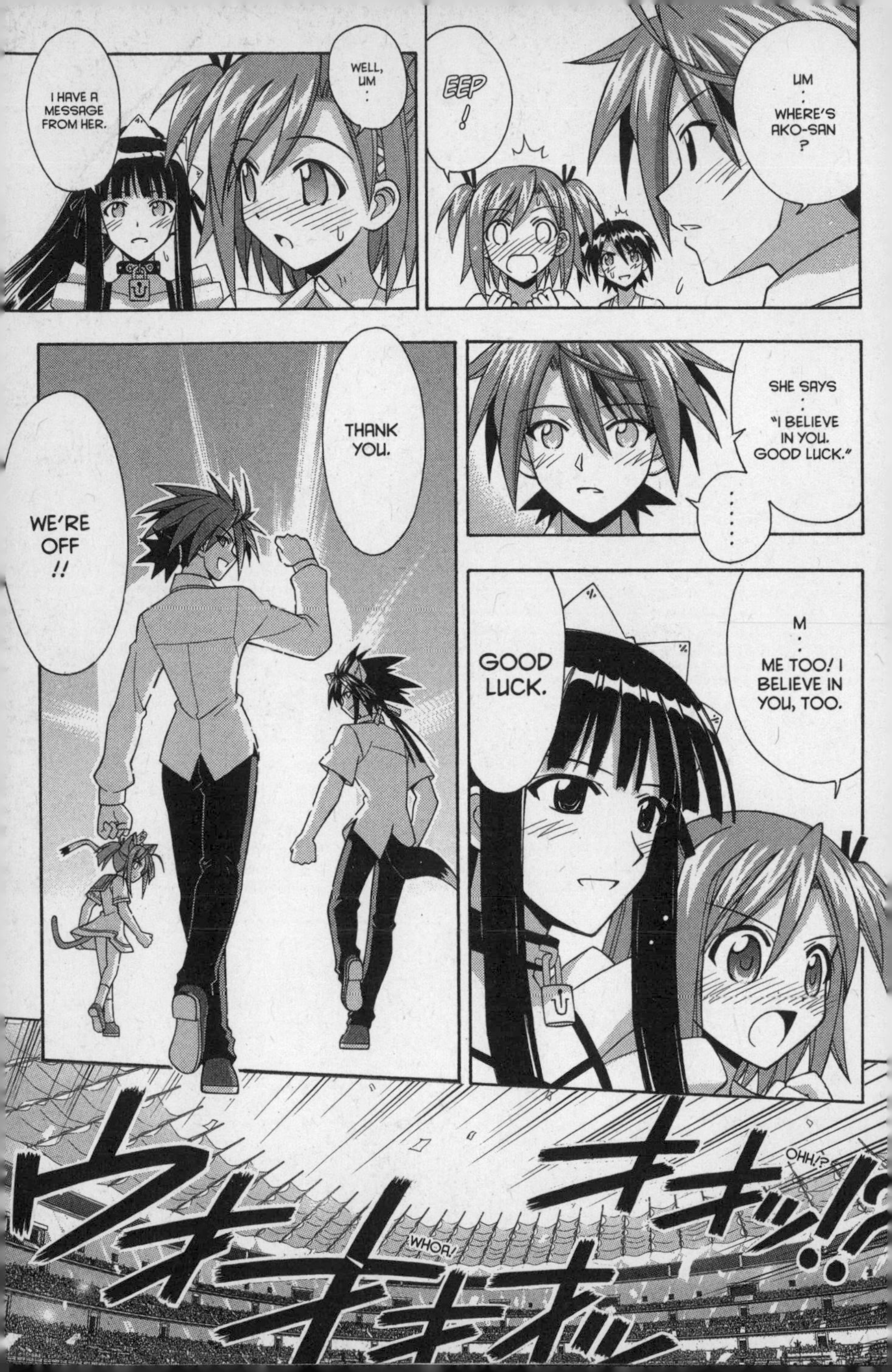
UM... WHERE'S AKO-SAN?
EEP!
WELL, UM...
I HAVE A MESSAGE FROM HER.
SHE SAYS: "I BELIEVE IN YOU. GOOD LUCK."
......
M... ME TOO! I BELIEVE IN YOU, TOO.
GOOD LUCK.
THANK YOU.
WE'RE OFF!!
OHH!?
WHOA!

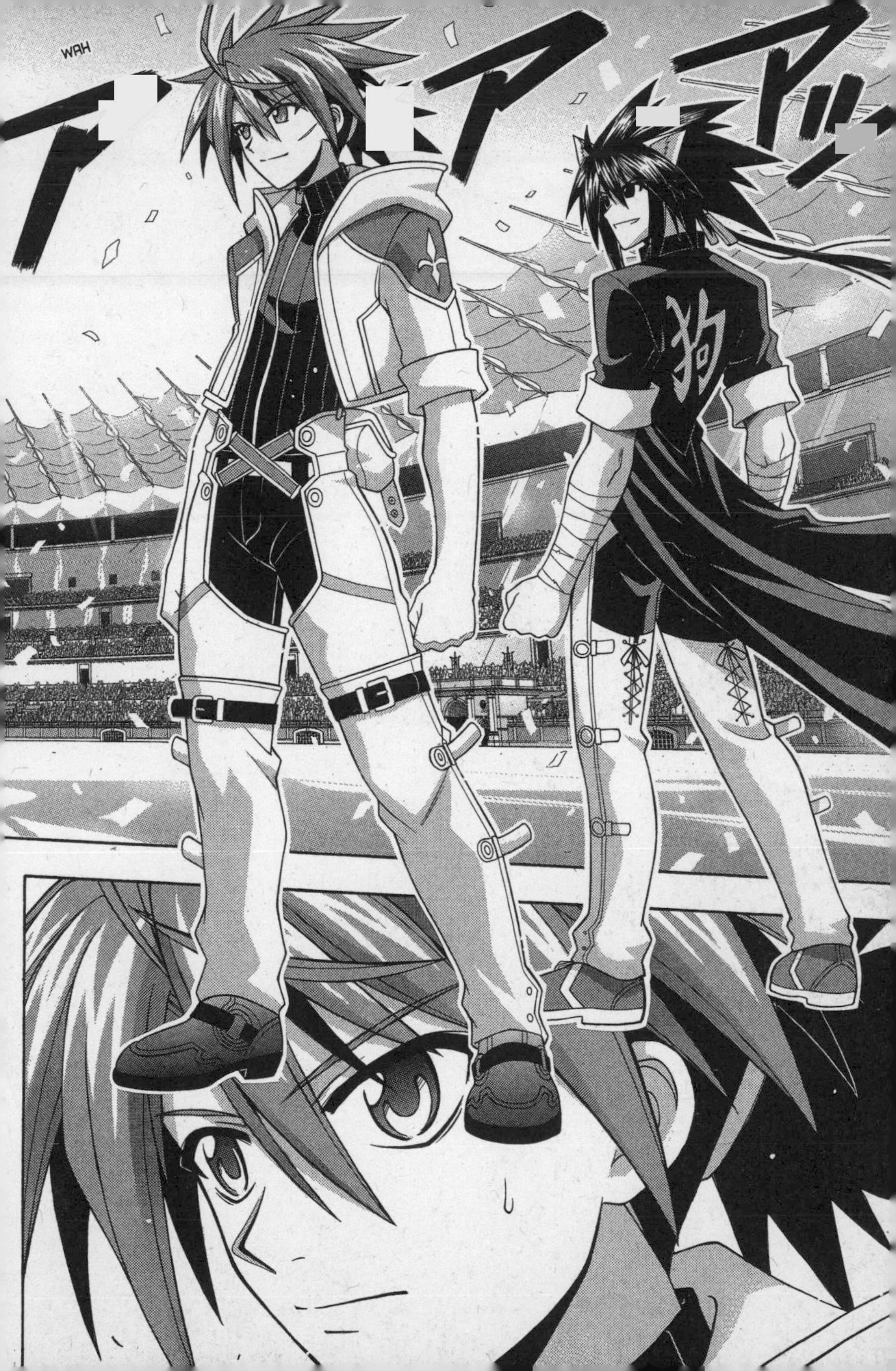
WAH

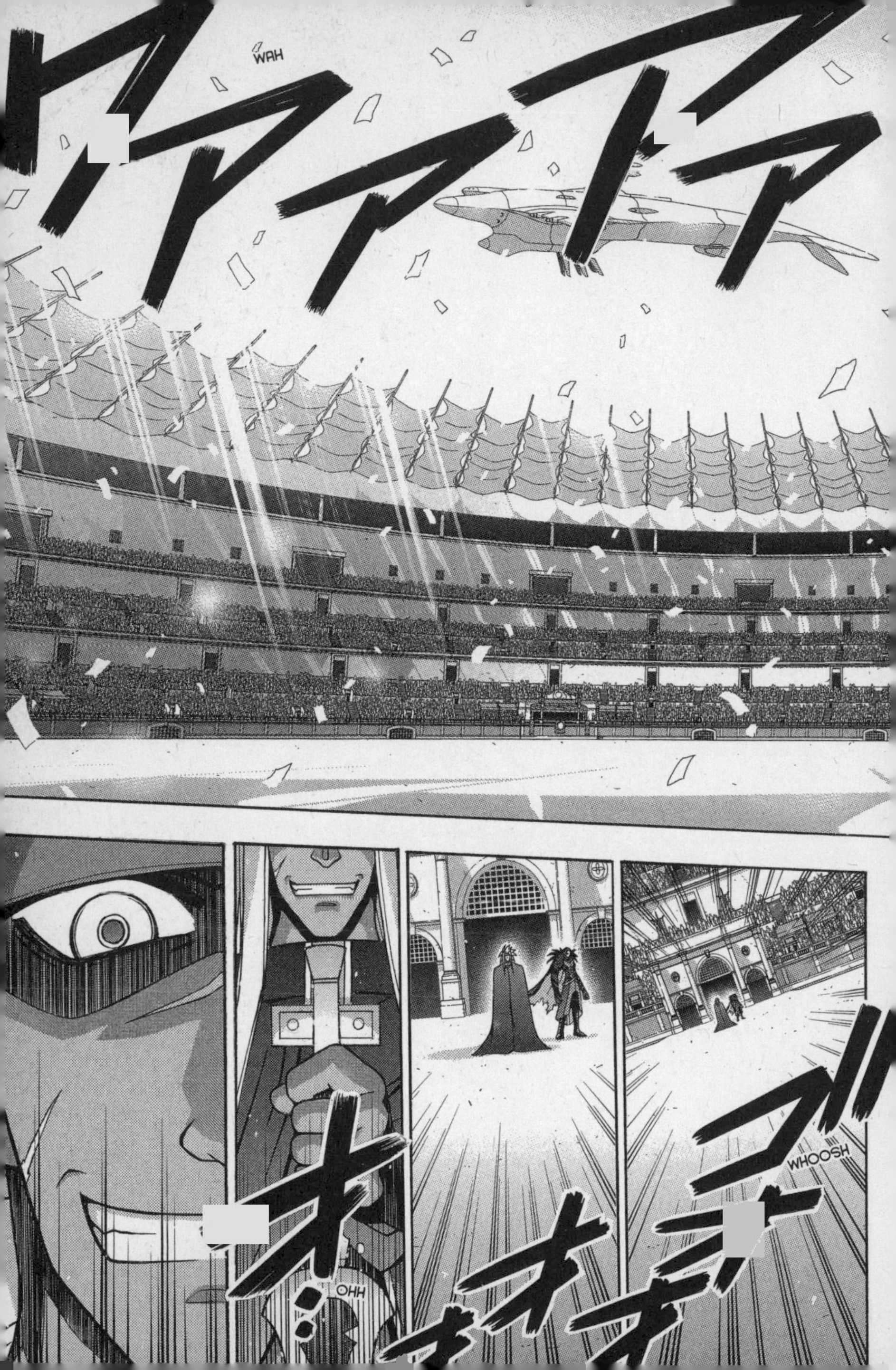
WAH
WHOOSH
OHH

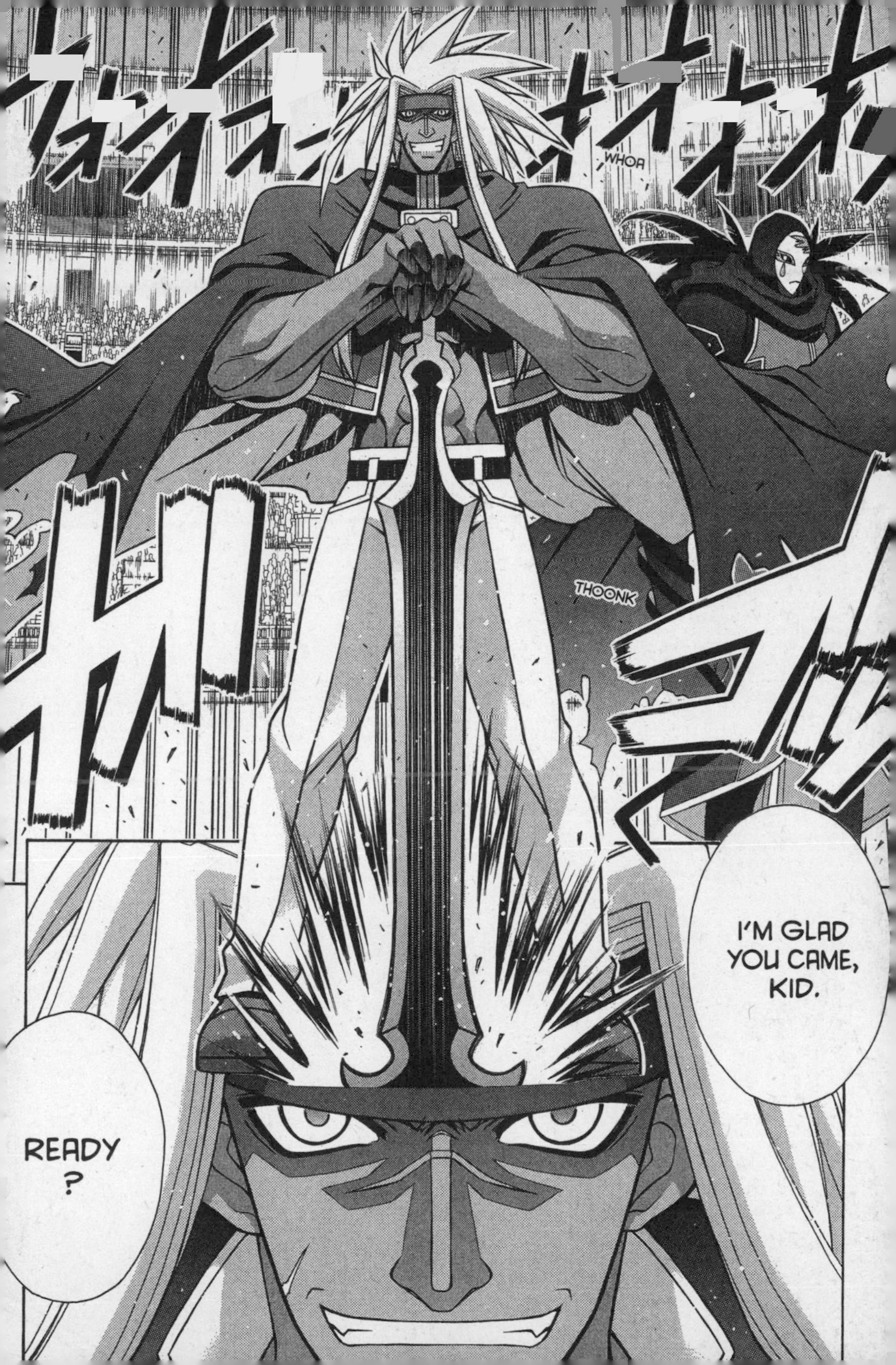
WHOA
THOONK
I'M GLAD YOU CAME, KID.
READY?

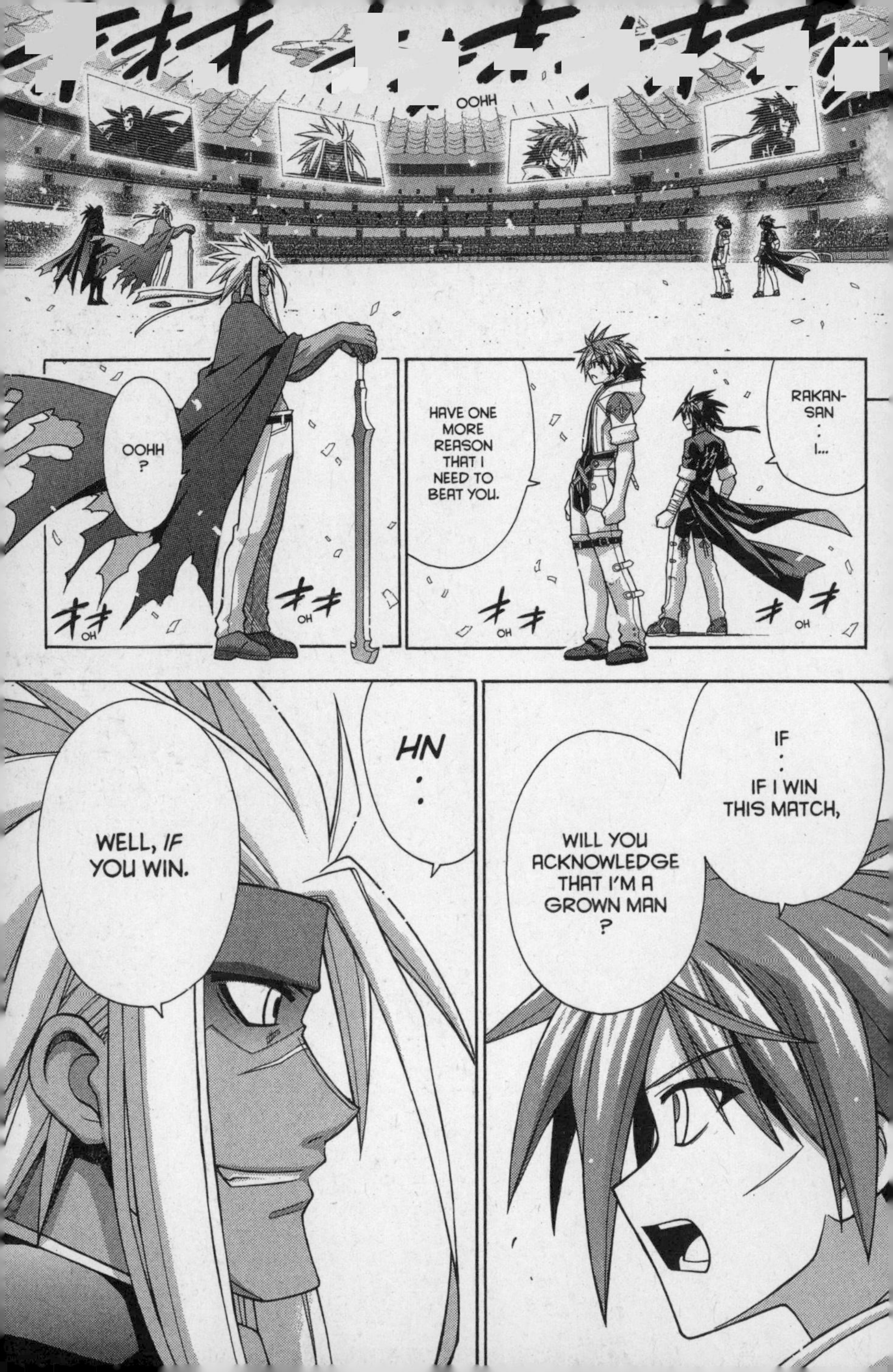
OOHH
RAKAN-SAN . . I...
HAVE ONE MORE REASON THAT I NEED TO BEAT YOU.
OH
OH
OOHH ?
OH
OH
IF . . IF I WIN THIS MATCH,
WILL YOU ACKNOWLEDGE THAT I'M A GROWN MAN ?
HN . .
WELL, *IF* YOU WIN.

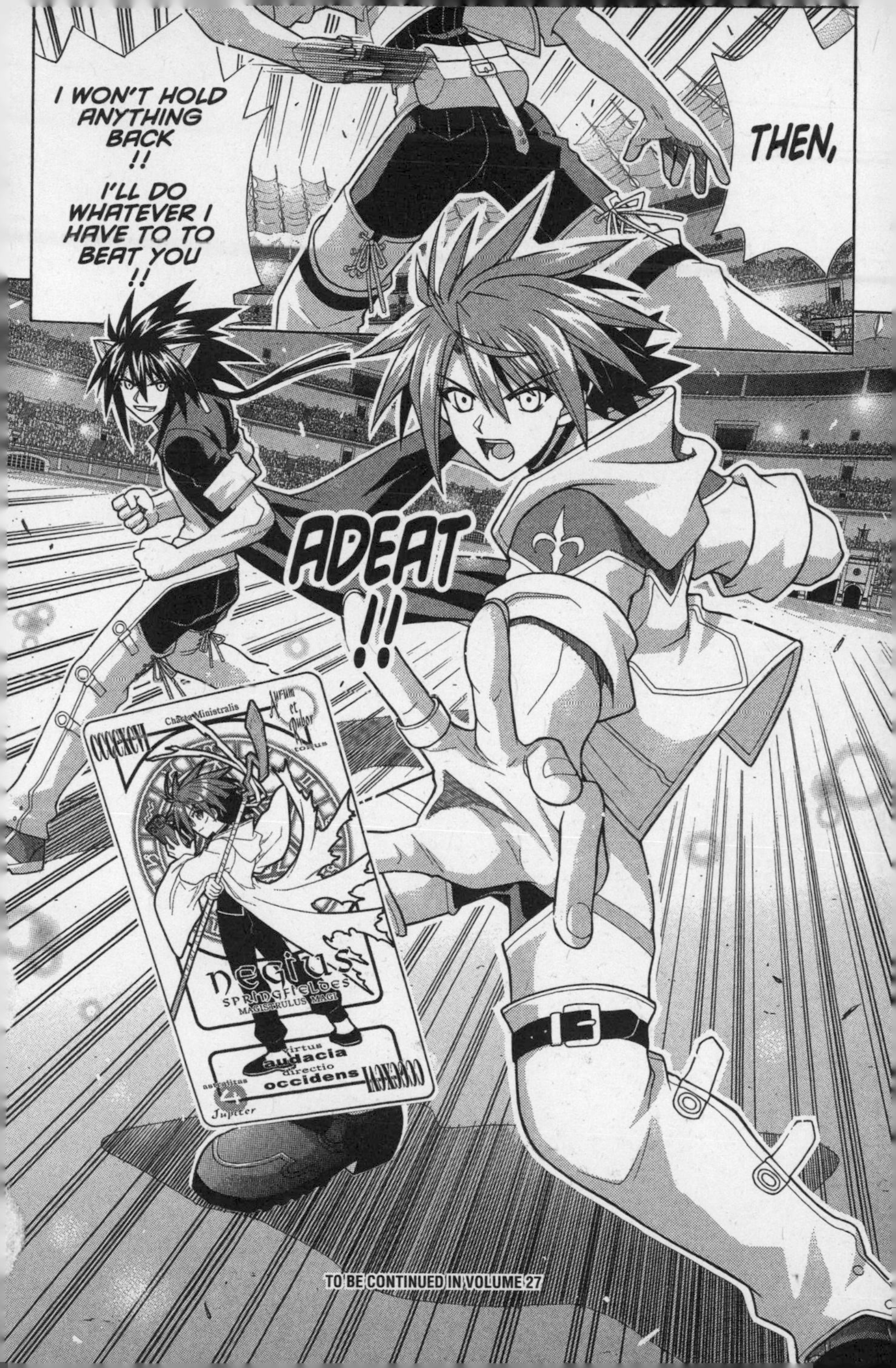
THEN,
I WON'T HOLD ANYTHING BACK !!
I'LL DO WHATEVER I HAVE TO TO BEAT YOU !!
ADEAT !!
Charta Ministralis
SPRINGFIELDES
MAGISTRULUS MAGI
virtus
audacia
directio
occidens
Jupiter
TO BE CONTINUED IN VOLUME 27

A Word from the Author

Sorry to have kept you waiting. I present *Negima!* volume 27! Shockingly, this entire volume is dedicated to the battle with Rakan!! A superbattle, fitting of a shounen manga, unfolds over nine chapters. It created a huge sensation in *Shonen Magazine*, too.

Negi's pactio card and artifact, which you could say are a special bonus for this battle only, drive his master Rakan up against a wall with their terrifying abilities.

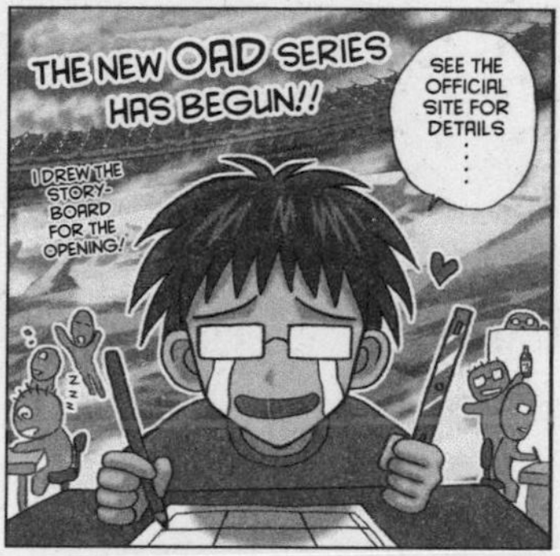
THE NEW OAD SERIES HAS BEGUN!!
SEE THE OFFICIAL SITE FOR DETAILS
...
I DREW THE STORY-BOARD FOR THE OPENING!

Negi or Rakan—who will come out the victor!?

...Incidentally, as a side effect of the battle, this time the classmates don't show up at all. m(_ _)m, Many apologies to their fans. They appear a lot in the next volume, so those of you who read for the classmates, please don't abandon me! (^^;)

Ken Akamatsu
www.ailove.net

CONTENTS

27

魔法先生ネギま!

MAGISTER NEGI MAGI

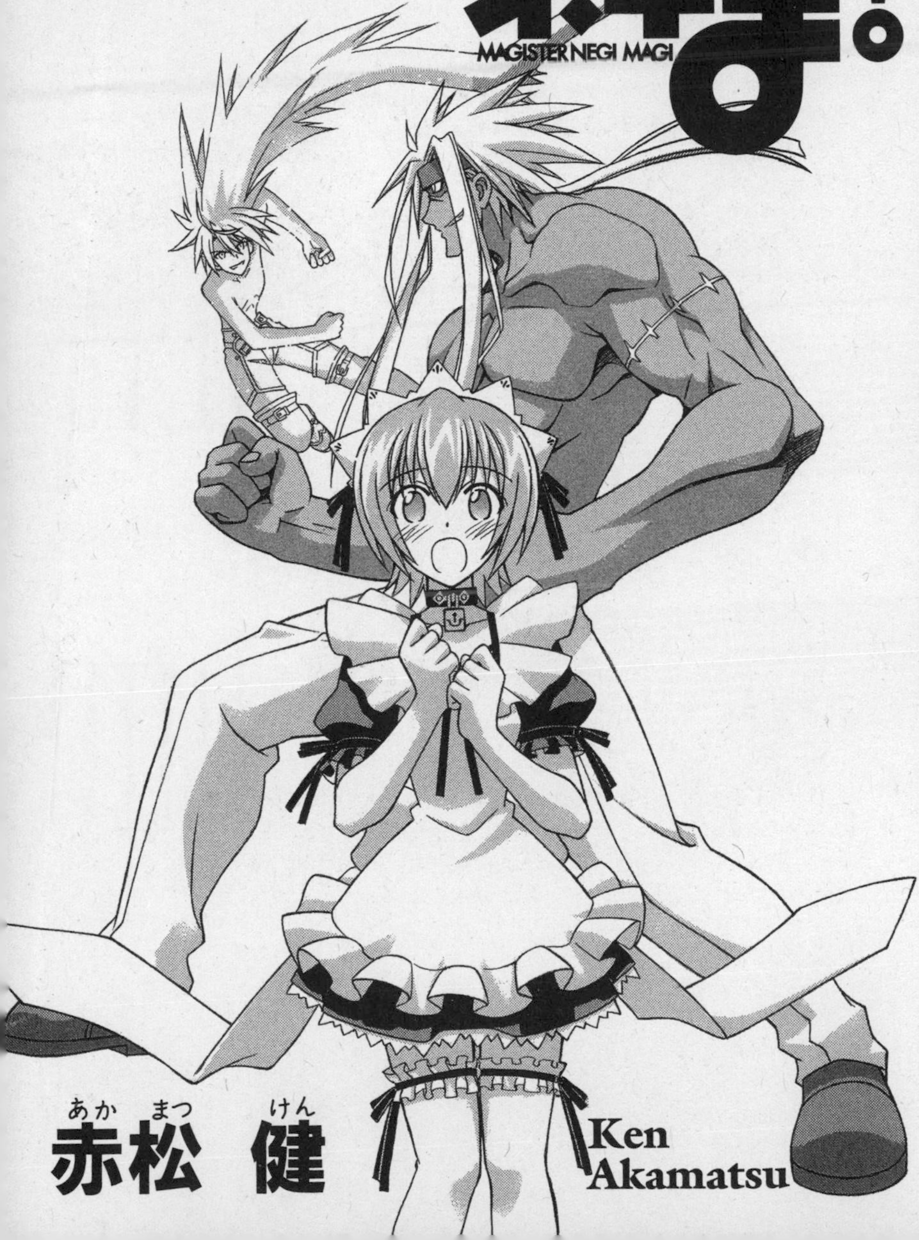

赤松 健

Ken Akamatsu

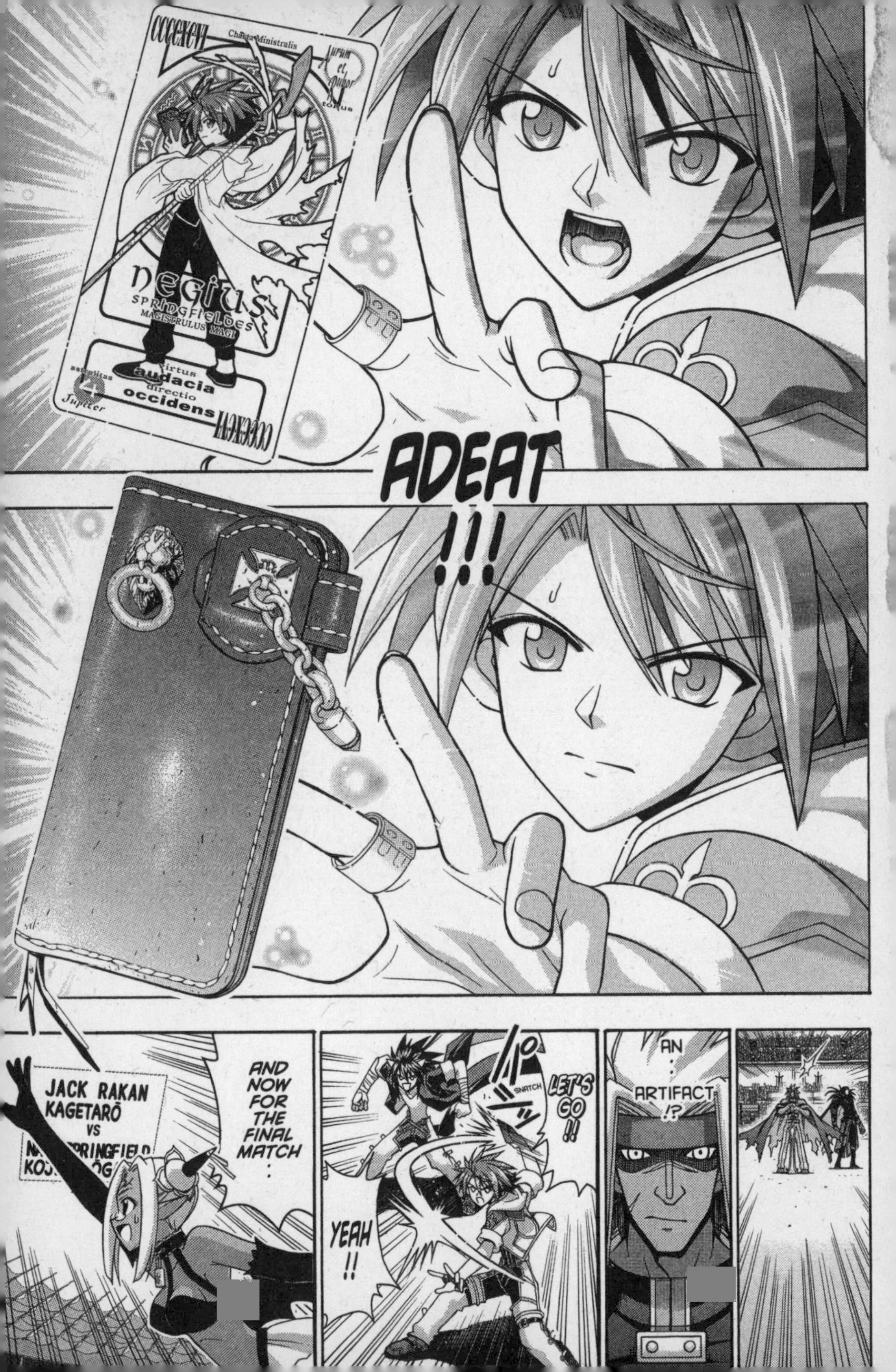

CCCCXCVI
Charta Ministralis
NEGIUS
SPRINGFIELDES
MAGISTRULUS MAGI
virtus
audacia
directio
occidens
Jupiter
ADEAT
!!!
AN...
ARTIFACT!?
LET'S GO!!
SNATCH
YEAH!!
AND NOW FOR THE FINAL MATCH:
JACK RAKAN KAGETARŌ
VS

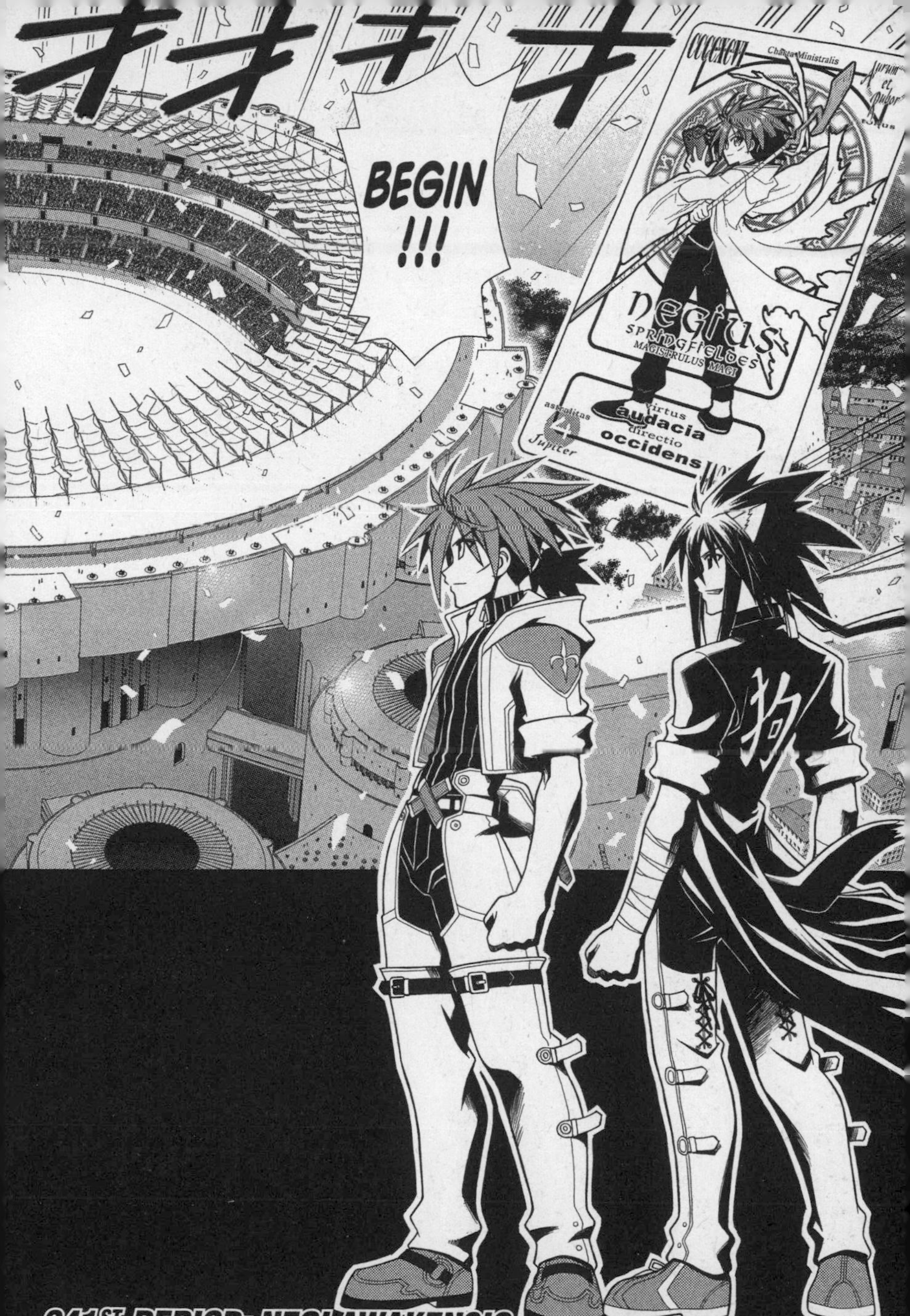
オオオオ
BEGIN !!!
CCCCXCVI
Charta Ministralis
NEGIUS SPRINGFIELDES
MAGISTRULUS MAGI
astralitas
4
Jupiter
virtus
audacia
directio
occidens

241ST PERIOD: NEGI AWAKENS!?

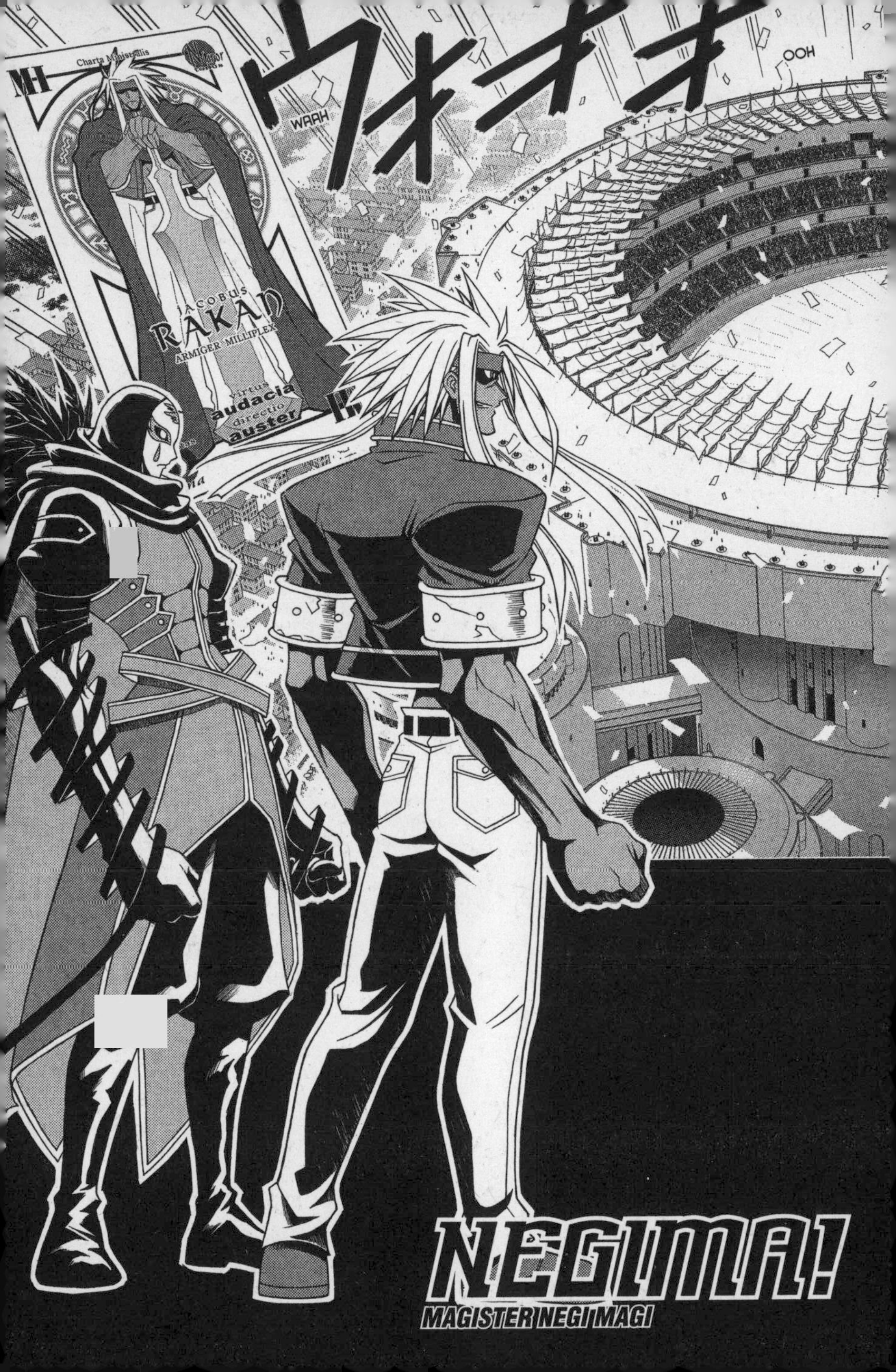
ウォオオ
WAAH
OOH
JACOBUS
RAKAN
ARMIGER MILLIPLEX
virtus
audacia
directio
auster
NEGIMA!
MAGISTER NEGI MAGI

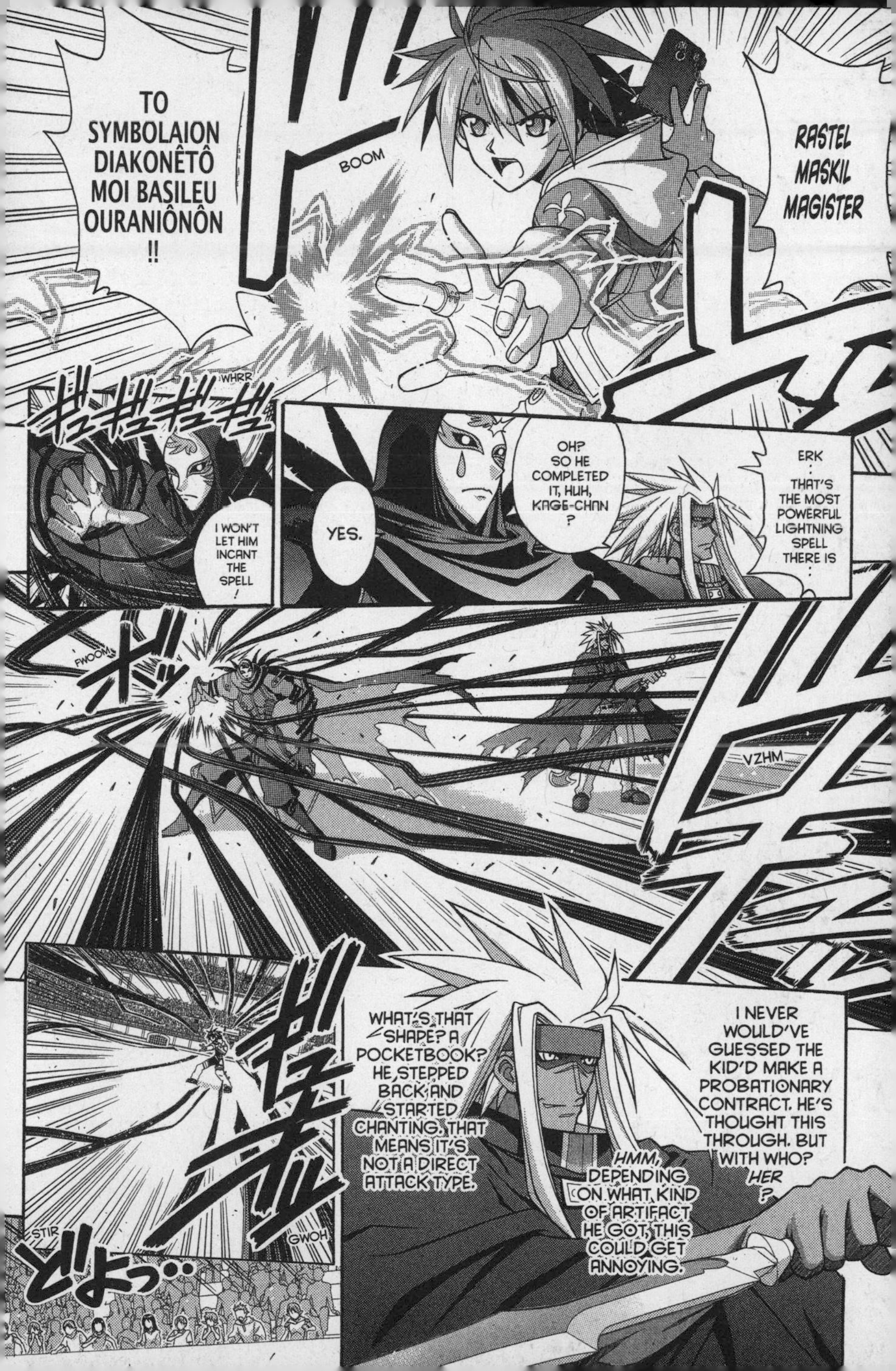
RASTEL MASKIL MAGISTER
TO SYMBOLAION DIAKONÊTÔ MOI BASILEU OURANIÔNÔN !!
BOOM
ERK : THAT'S THE MOST POWERFUL LIGHTNING SPELL THERE IS :
OH? SO HE COMPLETED IT, HUH, KAGE-CHAN ?
YES.
WHRR
I WON'T LET HIM INCANT THE SPELL !
FWOOM
VZHM
I NEVER WOULD'VE GUESSED THE KID'D MAKE A PROBATIONARY CONTRACT. HE'S THOUGHT THIS THROUGH. BUT WITH WHO? HER ?
HMM, DEPENDING ON WHAT KIND OF ARTIFACT HE GOT, THIS COULD GET ANNOYING.
WHAT'S THAT SHAPE? A POCKETBOOK? HE STEPPED BACK AND STARTED CHANTING. THAT MEANS IT'S NOT A DIRECT ATTACK TYPE.
GWOH
STIR
どよっ…

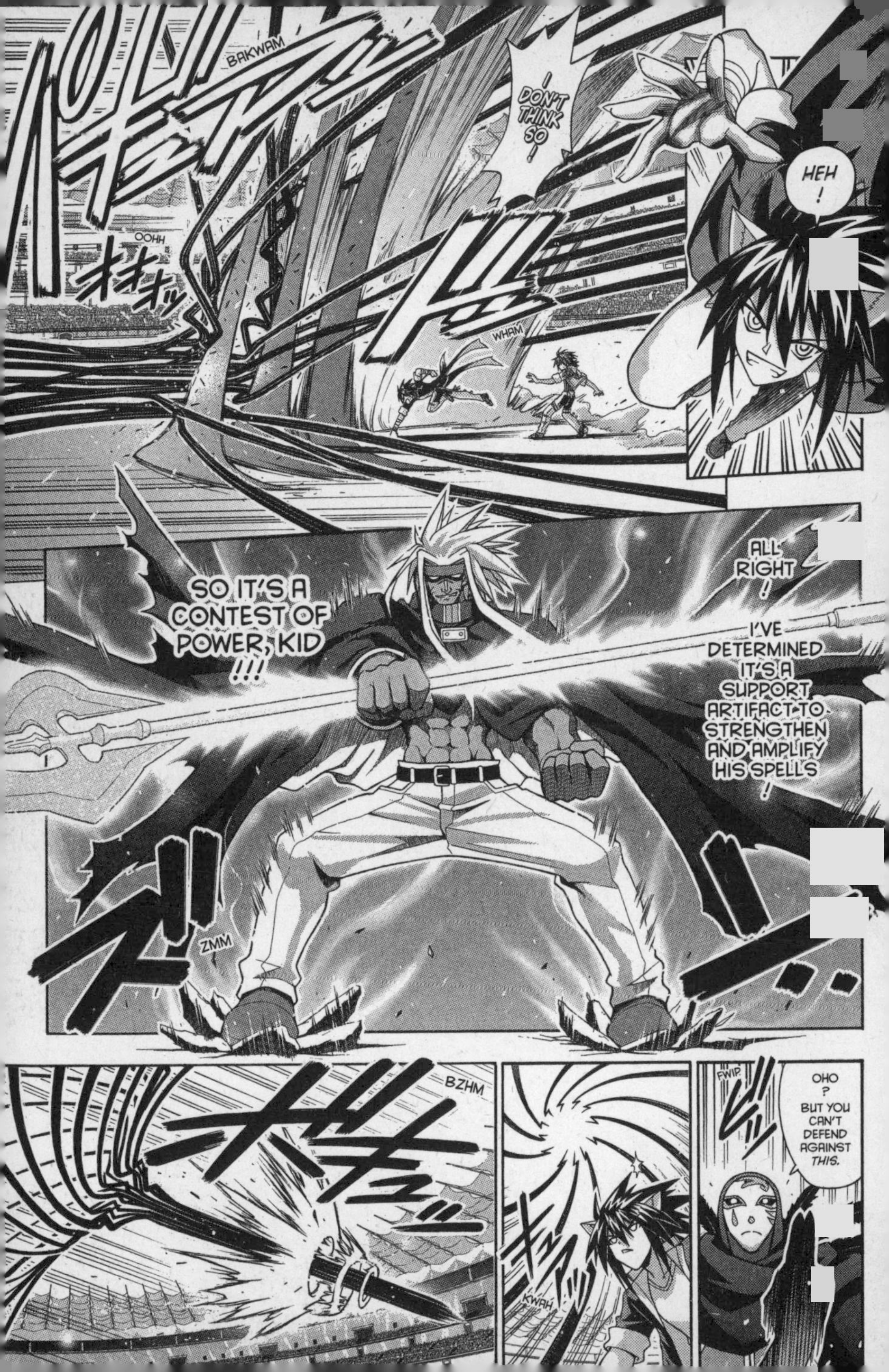
HEH!
I DON'T THINK SO!
BAKWAM
WHAM
OOHH
ALL RIGHT!
I'VE DETERMINED IT'S A SUPPORT ARTIFACT TO STRENGTHEN AND AMPLIFY HIS SPELLS!
SO IT'S A CONTEST OF POWER, KID!!!
ZMM
OHO? BUT YOU CAN'T DEFEND AGAINST *THIS*.
FWIP
KWAH
BZHM

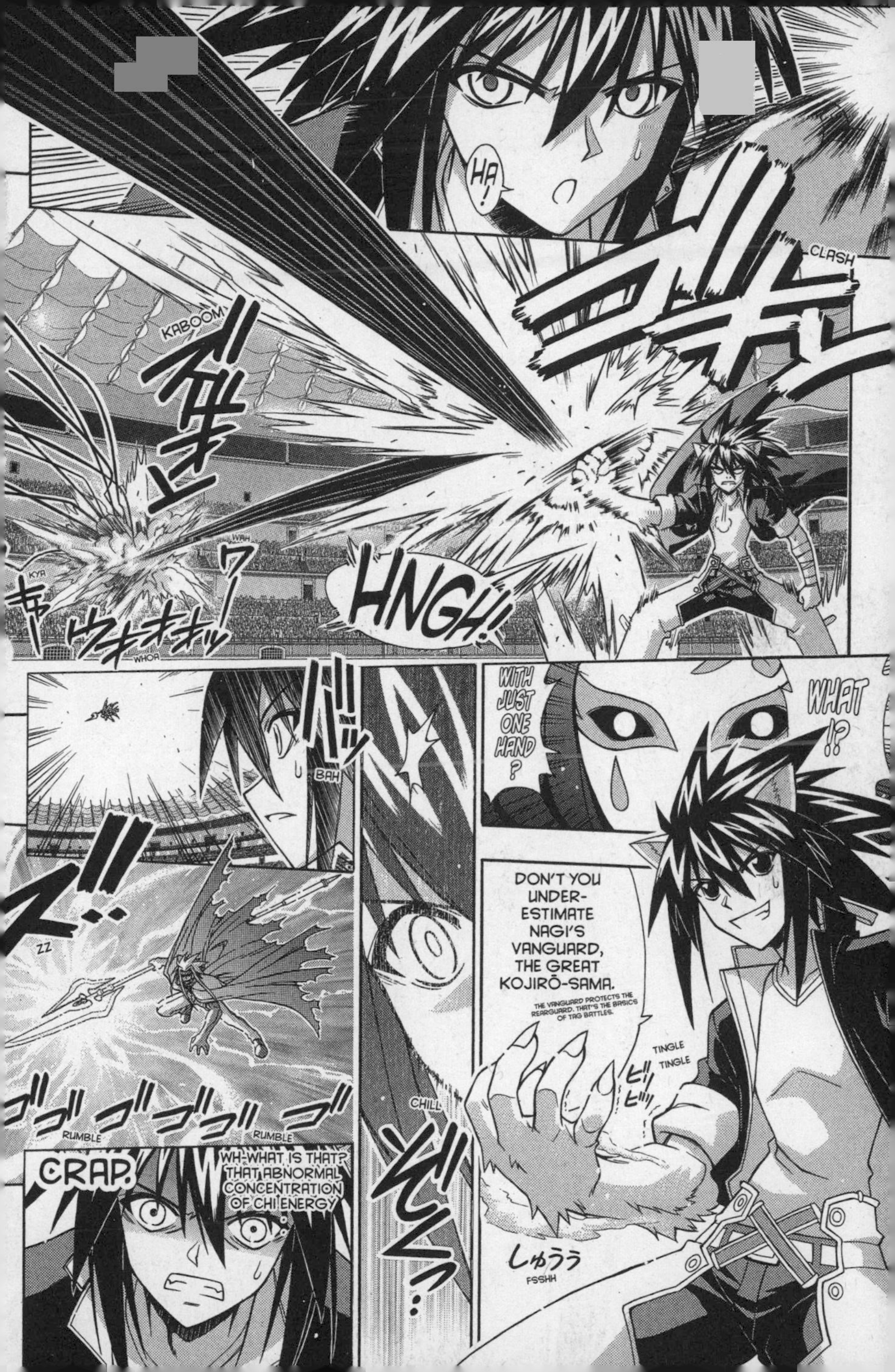
HA!
CLASH
HNGH!
WAH
KABOOM
KYA
WHOA
WHAT!?
WITH JUST ONE HAND?
DON'T YOU UNDER-ESTIMATE NAGI'S VANGUARD, THE GREAT KOJIRŌ-SAMA.
THE VANGUARD PROTECTS THE REARGUARD. THAT'S THE BASICS OF TAG BATTLES.
TINGLE TINGLE
FSSHH
CHILL
BAH
ZZ
RUMBLE
RUMBLE
WH-WHAT IS THAT? THAT ABNORMAL CONCENTRATION OF CHI ENERGY
CRAP.

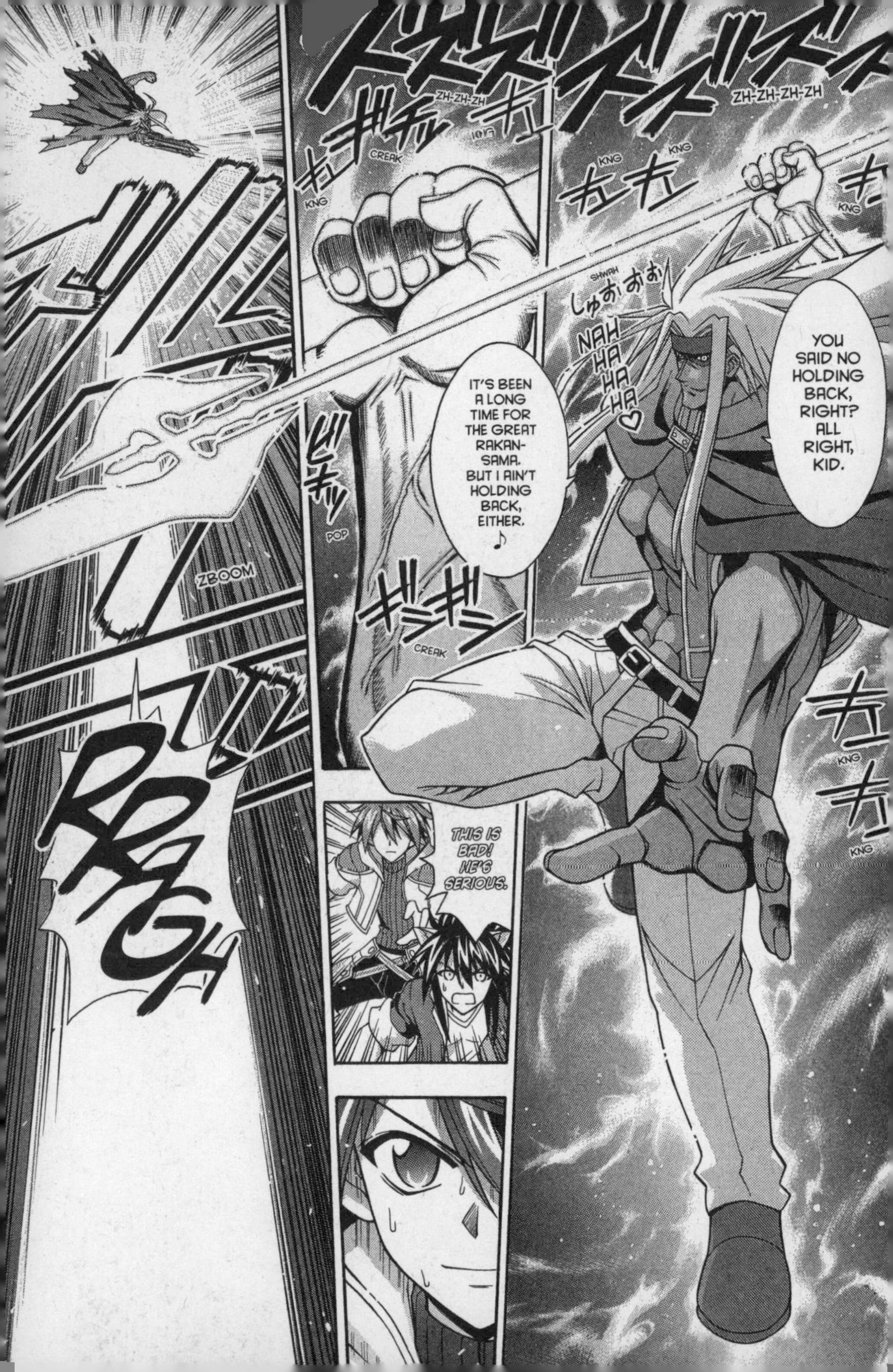

ZH-ZH-ZH-ZH
KNG
KNG
KNG
SHWAH
NAH HA HA HA ♡
YOU SAID NO HOLDING BACK, RIGHT? ALL RIGHT, KID.
IT'S BEEN A LONG TIME FOR THE GREAT RAKAN-SAMA. BUT I AIN'T HOLDING BACK, EITHER. ♪
KNG
KNG
ZH-ZH-ZH
CREAK
KNG
POP
CREAK
THIS IS BAD! HE'S SERIOUS.
ZBOOM
RRAGH

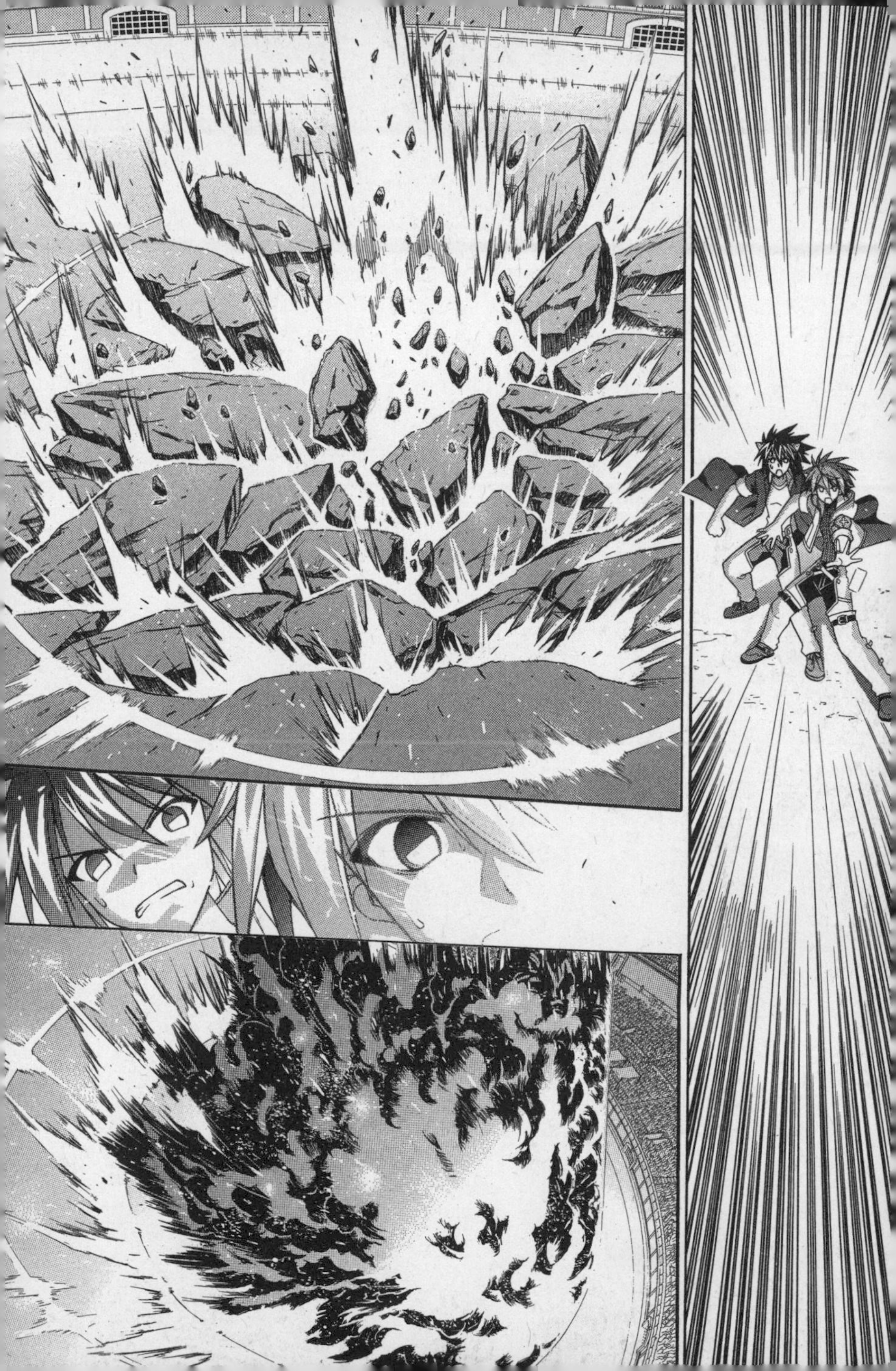

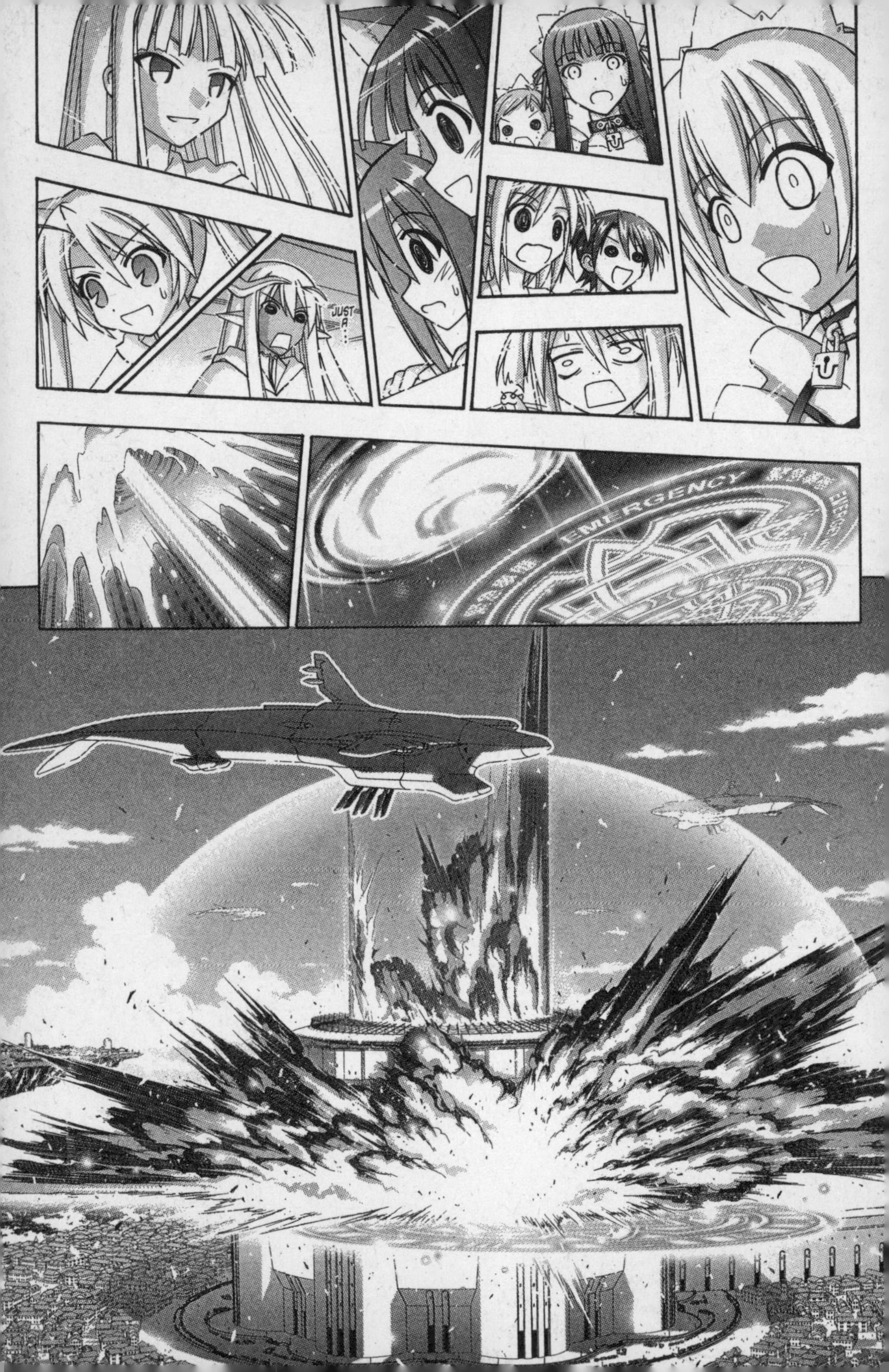
JUST A...
EMERGENCY

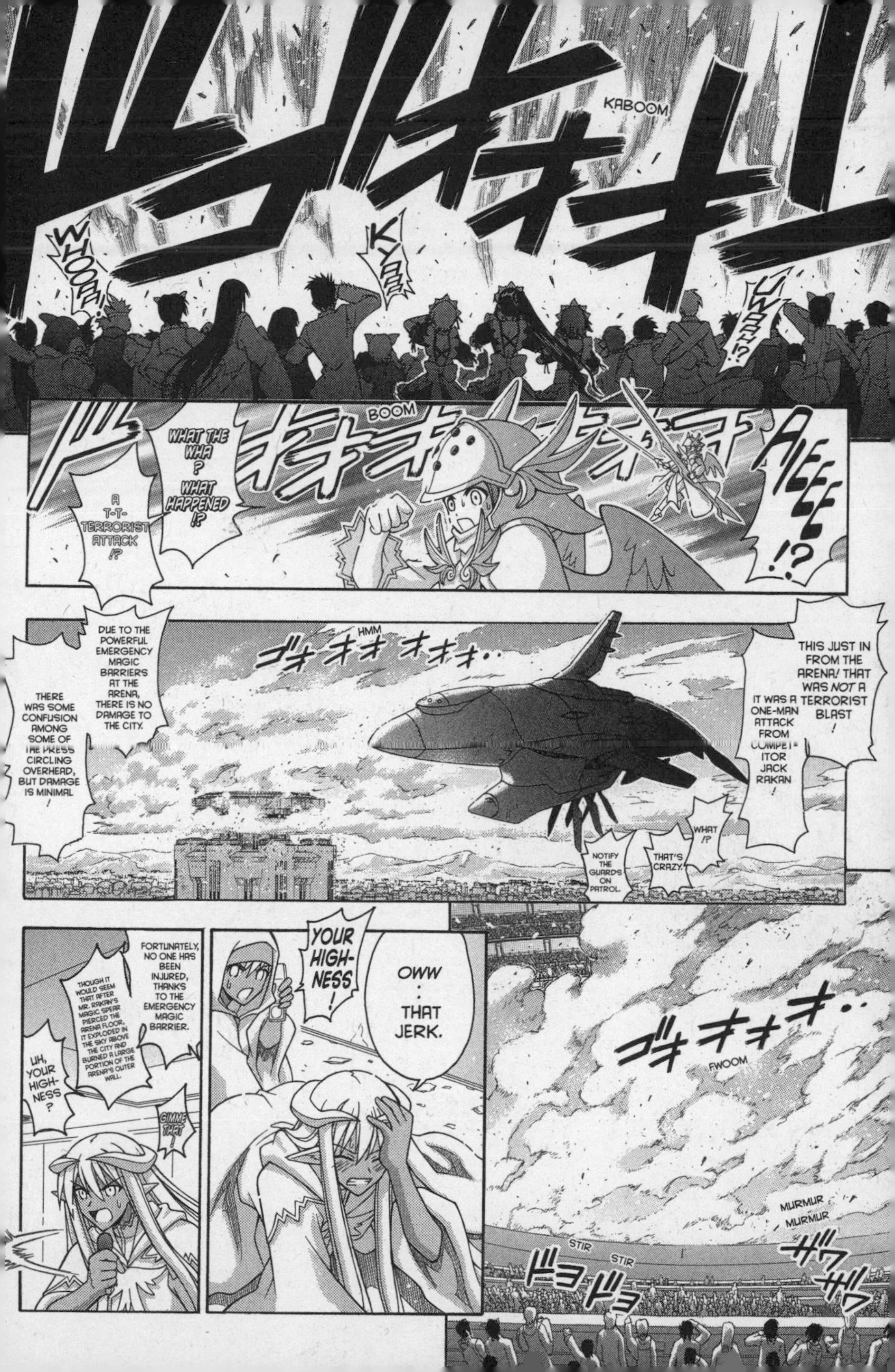
KABOOM
UWAAAH!?
KYAAA
WHOOAA!
BOOM
AIEEE!?
WHAT THE WHA? WHAT HAPPENED!?
A T-T-TERRORIST ATTACK!?
HMM
THIS JUST IN FROM THE ARENA! THAT WAS *NOT* A TERRORIST BLAST!
IT WAS A ONE-MAN ATTACK FROM COMPETITOR JACK RAKAN!
WHAT!?
THAT'S CRAZY.
NOTIFY THE GUARDS ON PATROL.
DUE TO THE POWERFUL EMERGENCY MAGIC BARRIERS AT THE ARENA, THERE IS NO DAMAGE TO THE CITY.
THERE WAS SOME CONFUSION AMONG SOME OF THE PRESS CIRCLING OVERHEAD, BUT DAMAGE IS MINIMAL!
FWOOM
MURMUR MURMUR
STIR STIR
YOUR HIGHNESS!
OWW... THAT JERK.
FORTUNATELY, NO ONE HAS BEEN INJURED, THANKS TO THE EMERGENCY MAGIC BARRIER.
THOUGH IT WOULD SEEM THAT AFTER MR. RAKAN'S MAGIC SPEAR PIERCED THE ARENA FLOOR, IT EXPLODED IN THE SKY ABOVE THE CITY AND BURNED A LARGE PORTION OF THE ARENA'S OUTER WALL.
UH, YOUR HIGHNESS?
GIMME THAT!

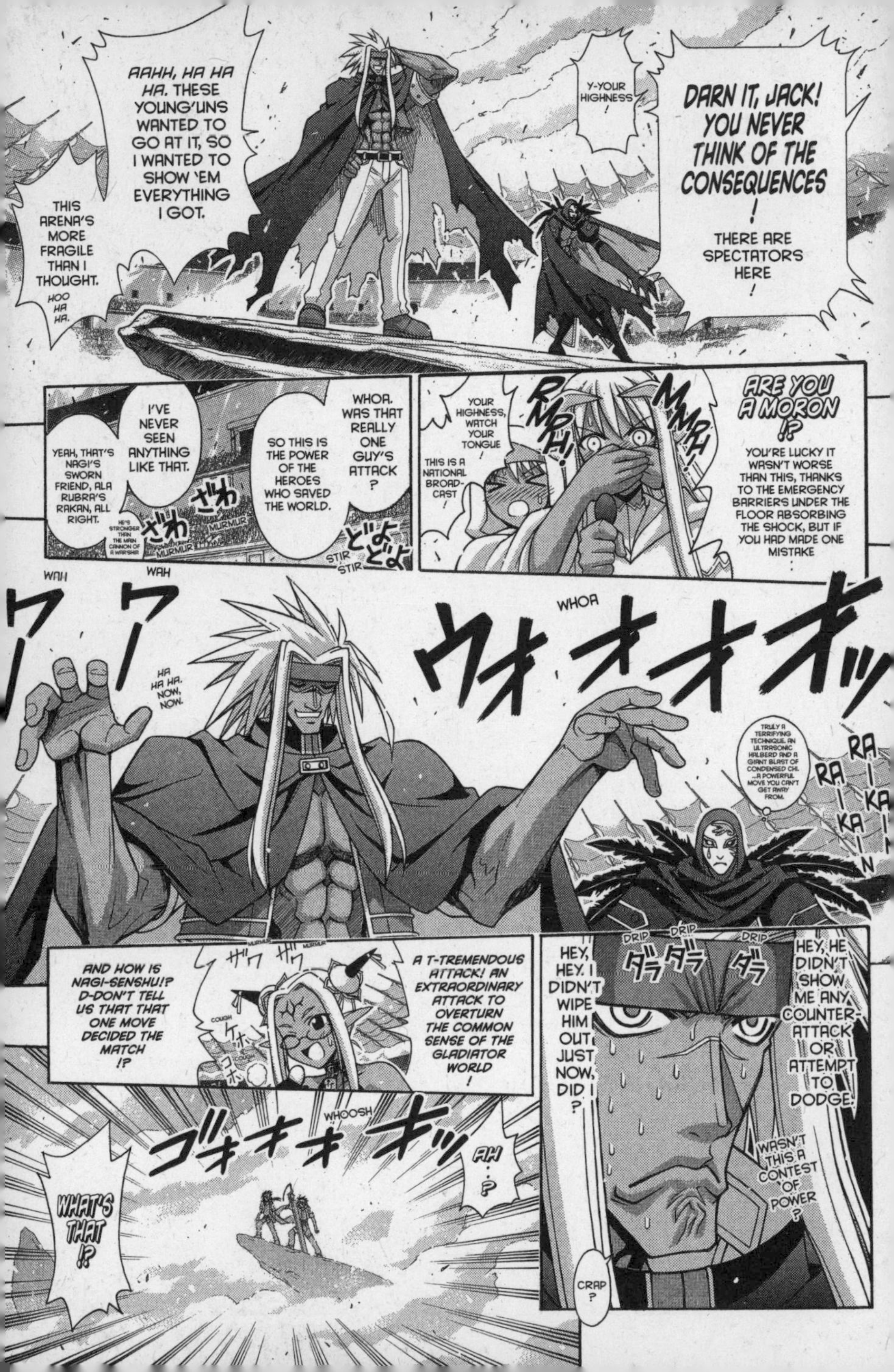
DARN IT, JACK! YOU NEVER THINK OF THE CONSEQUENCES!
THERE ARE SPECTATORS HERE!
Y-YOUR HIGHNESS
AAHH, HA HA HA. THESE YOUNG'UNS WANTED TO GO AT IT, SO I WANTED TO SHOW 'EM EVERYTHING I GOT.
THIS ARENA'S MORE FRAGILE THAN I THOUGHT.
HOO HA HA.
ARE YOU A MORON!?
YOU'RE LUCKY IT WASN'T WORSE THAN THIS, THANKS TO THE EMERGENCY BARRIERS UNDER THE FLOOR ABSORBING THE SHOCK, BUT IF YOU HAD MADE ONE MISTAKE!
MMMPH
RMPH!
YOUR HIGHNESS, WATCH YOUR TONGUE!
THIS IS A NATIONAL BROADCAST!
WHOA. WAS THAT REALLY ONE GUY'S ATTACK?
SO THIS IS THE POWER OF THE HEROES WHO SAVED THE WORLD.
I'VE NEVER SEEN ANYTHING LIKE THAT.
YEAH, THAT'S NAGI'S SWORN FRIEND, ALA RUBRA'S RAKAN, ALL RIGHT.
HE'S STRONGER THAN THE MAIN CANNON OF A WARSHIP
ざわ ざわ
MURMUR MURMUR
どよ どよ
STIR STIR
RA-I-KA-I-N
RA-I-KA-I-N
TRULY A TERRIFYING TECHNIQUE. AN ULTRASONIC HALBERD AND A GIANT BLAST OF CONDENSED CHI. ...A POWERFUL MOVE YOU CAN'T GET AWAY FROM.
ウォオオオッ
WHOA
HA HA HA. NOW, NOW.
ワ ワ
WAH WAH
DRIP DRIP DRIP
ダラ ダラ ダラ
HEY, HE DIDN'T SHOW ME ANY COUNTER-ATTACK OR ATTEMPT TO DODGE!
HEY, HEY. I DIDN'T WIPE HIM OUT JUST NOW, DID I?
WASN'T THIS A CONTEST OF POWER?
CRAP?
A T-TREMENDOUS ATTACK! AN EXTRAORDINARY ATTACK TO OVERTURN THE COMMON SENSE OF THE GLADIATOR WORLD!
ザワ ザワ
MURMUR MURMUR
AND HOW IS NAGI-SENSHU!? D-DON'T TELL US THAT THAT ONE MOVE DECIDED THE MATCH!?
ケホ コホ
COUGH COUGH
ゴォォォォッ
WHOOSH
AH..?
WHAT'S THAT!?

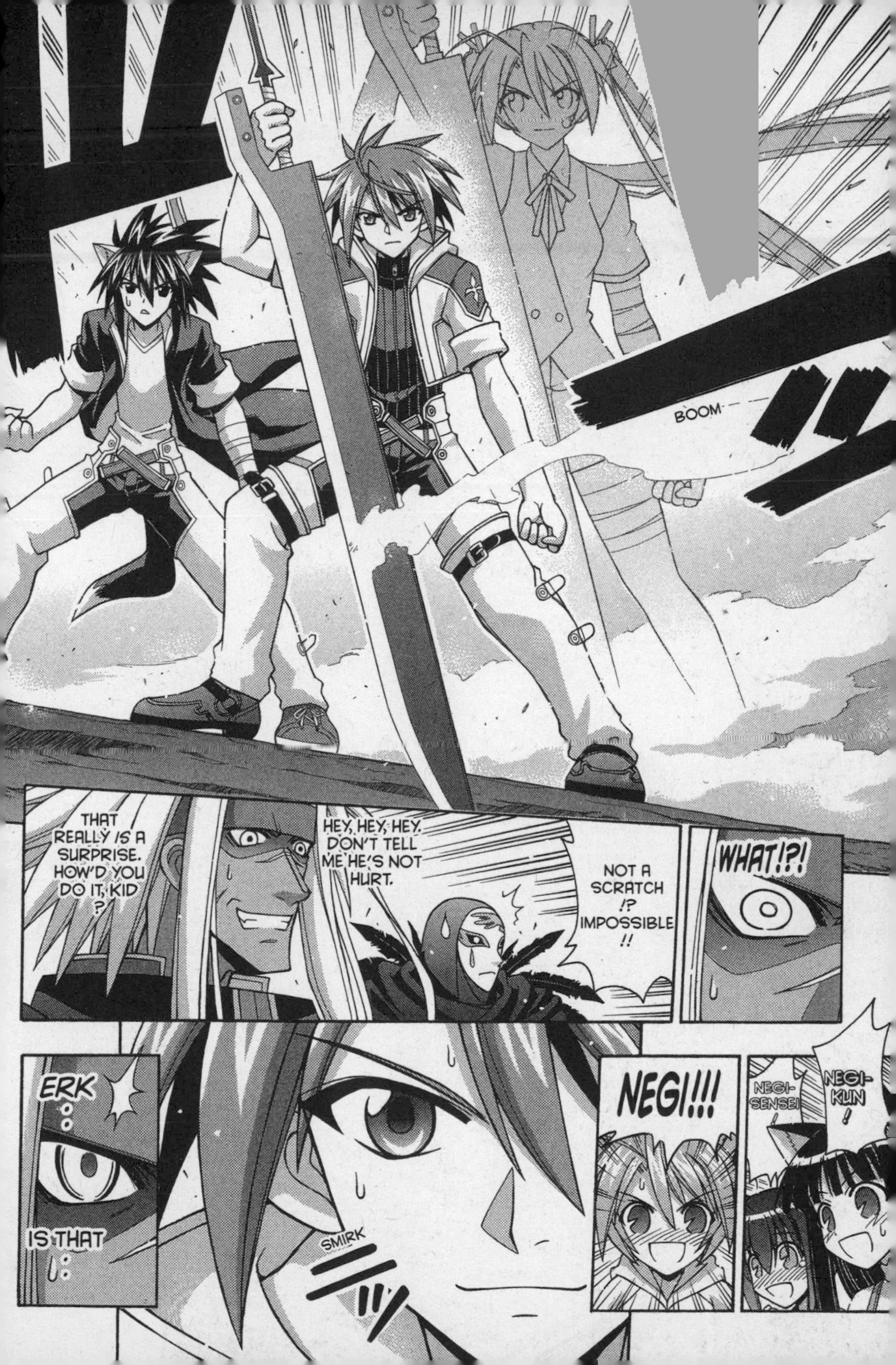
BOOM
WHAT!?!
NOT A SCRATCH!? IMPOSSIBLE!!
HEY, HEY, HEY. DON'T TELL ME HE'S NOT HURT.
THAT REALLY IS A SURPRISE. HOW'D YOU DO IT, KID?
NEGI-KUN!
NEGI-SENSEI!
NEGI!!!
SMIRK
ERK...
IS THAT...

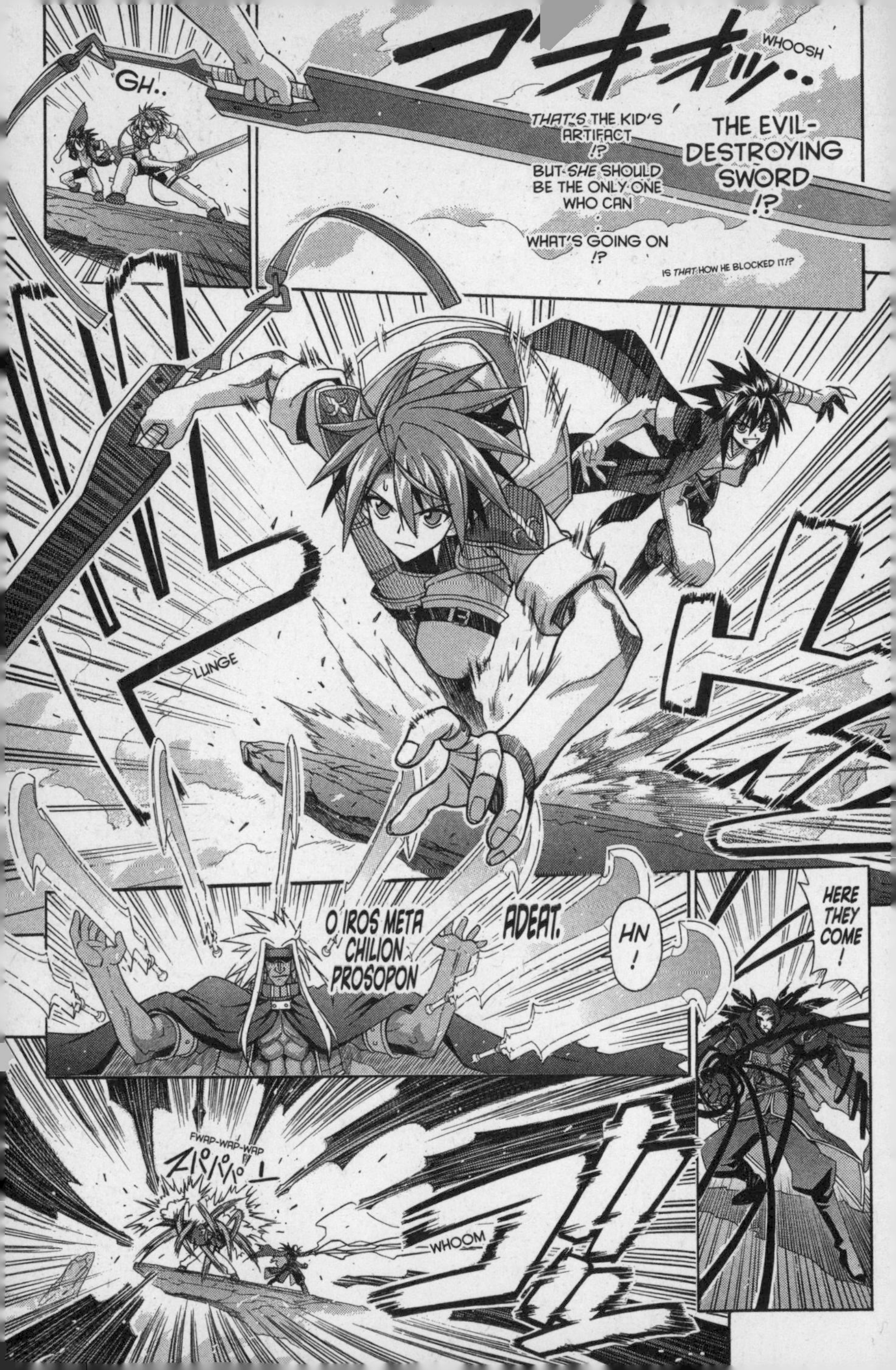
WHOOSH
THE EVIL-DESTROYING SWORD !?
THAT'S THE KID'S ARTIFACT !?
BUT SHE SHOULD BE THE ONLY ONE WHO CAN
WHAT'S GOING ON !?
IS THAT HOW HE BLOCKED IT!?
GH..
LUNGE
HERE THEY COME !
HN !
ADEAT.
O IROS META CHILION PROSOPON
WHOOM
FWAP-WAP-WAP

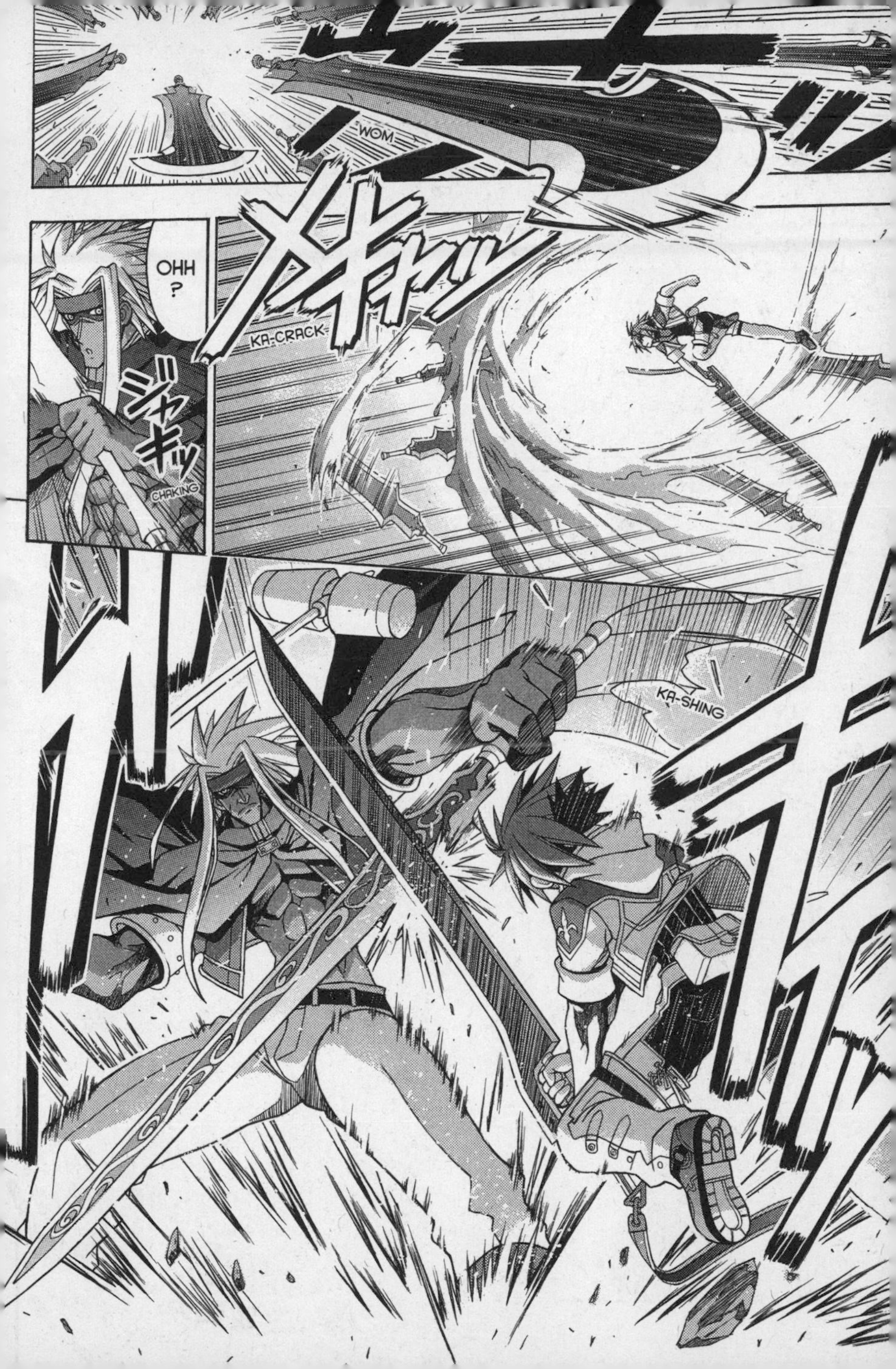
WOM
KA-CRACK
OHH ?
ジャキッ
CHAKING
KA-SHING

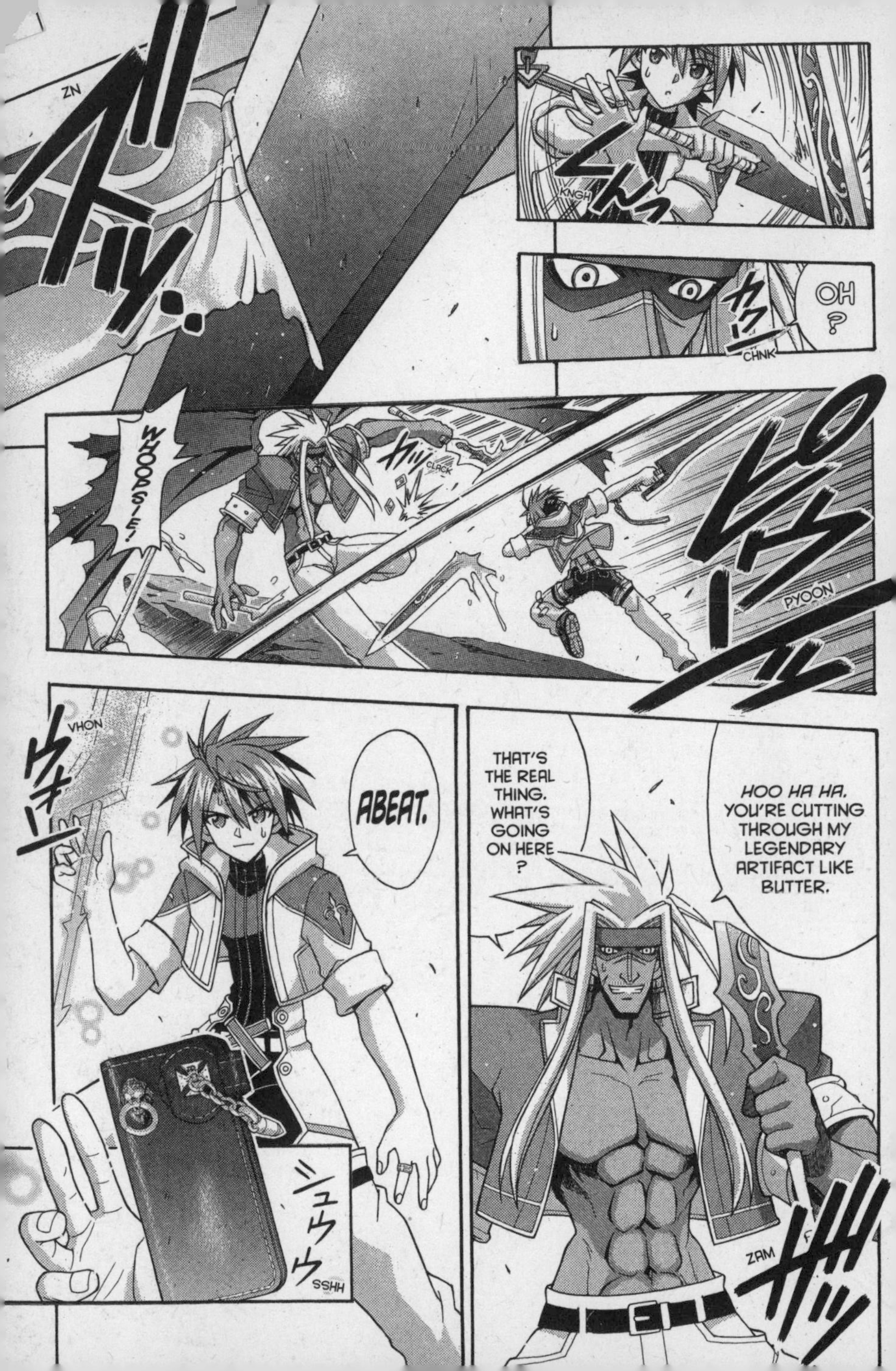
KNGH
OH?
CHNK
ZN
PYOON
CLACK
WHOOPSIE!
HOO HA HA. YOU'RE CUTTING THROUGH MY LEGENDARY ARTIFACT LIKE BUTTER.
THAT'S THE REAL THING. WHAT'S GOING ON HERE?
ZAM
VHON
ABEAT.
SSHH

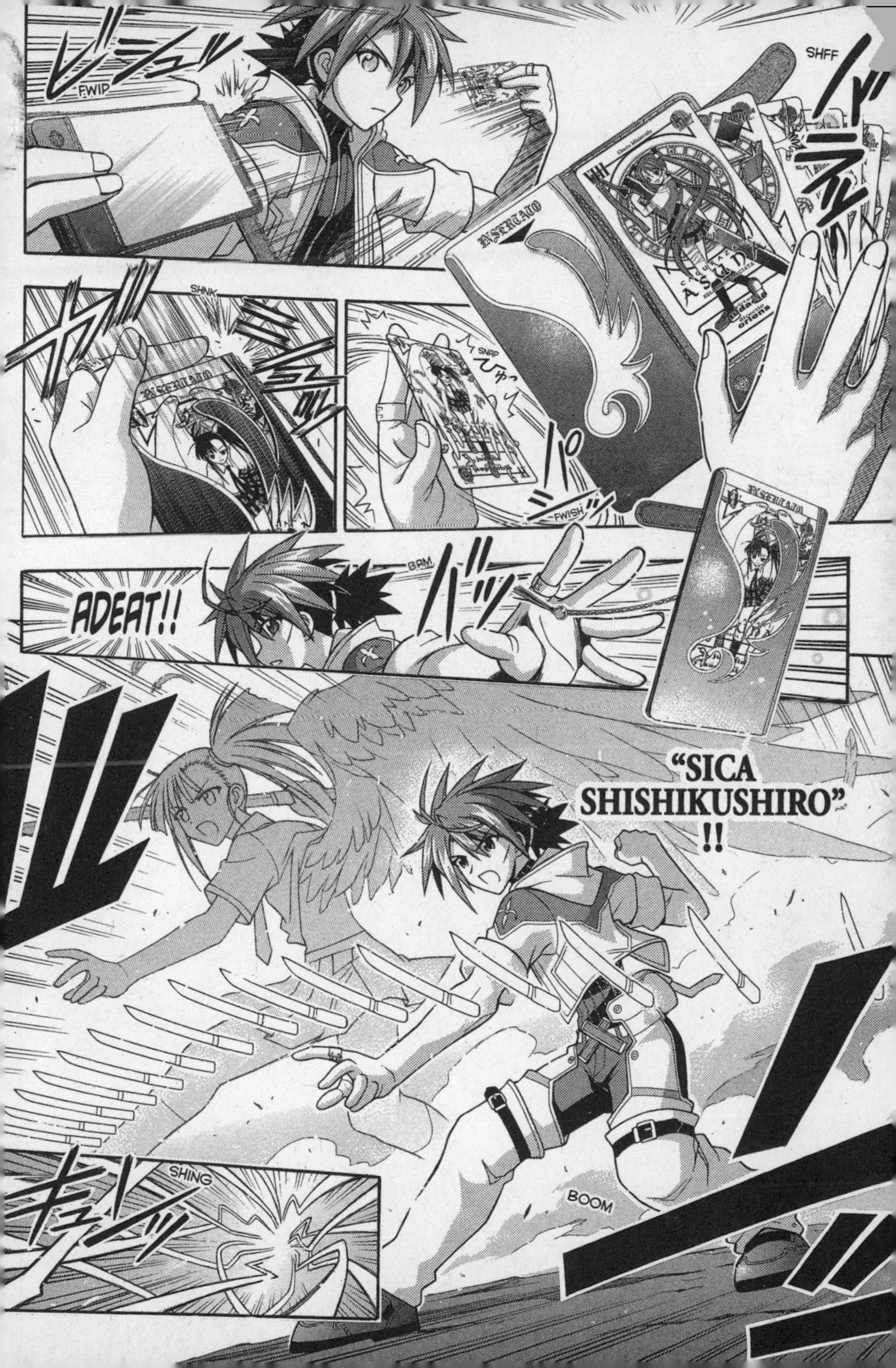
SHFF
FWISH
FWIP
SNAP
ぴゅっ
SHNK
BAM
ADEAT!!
"SICA SHISHIKUSHIRO"!!
BOOM
SHING

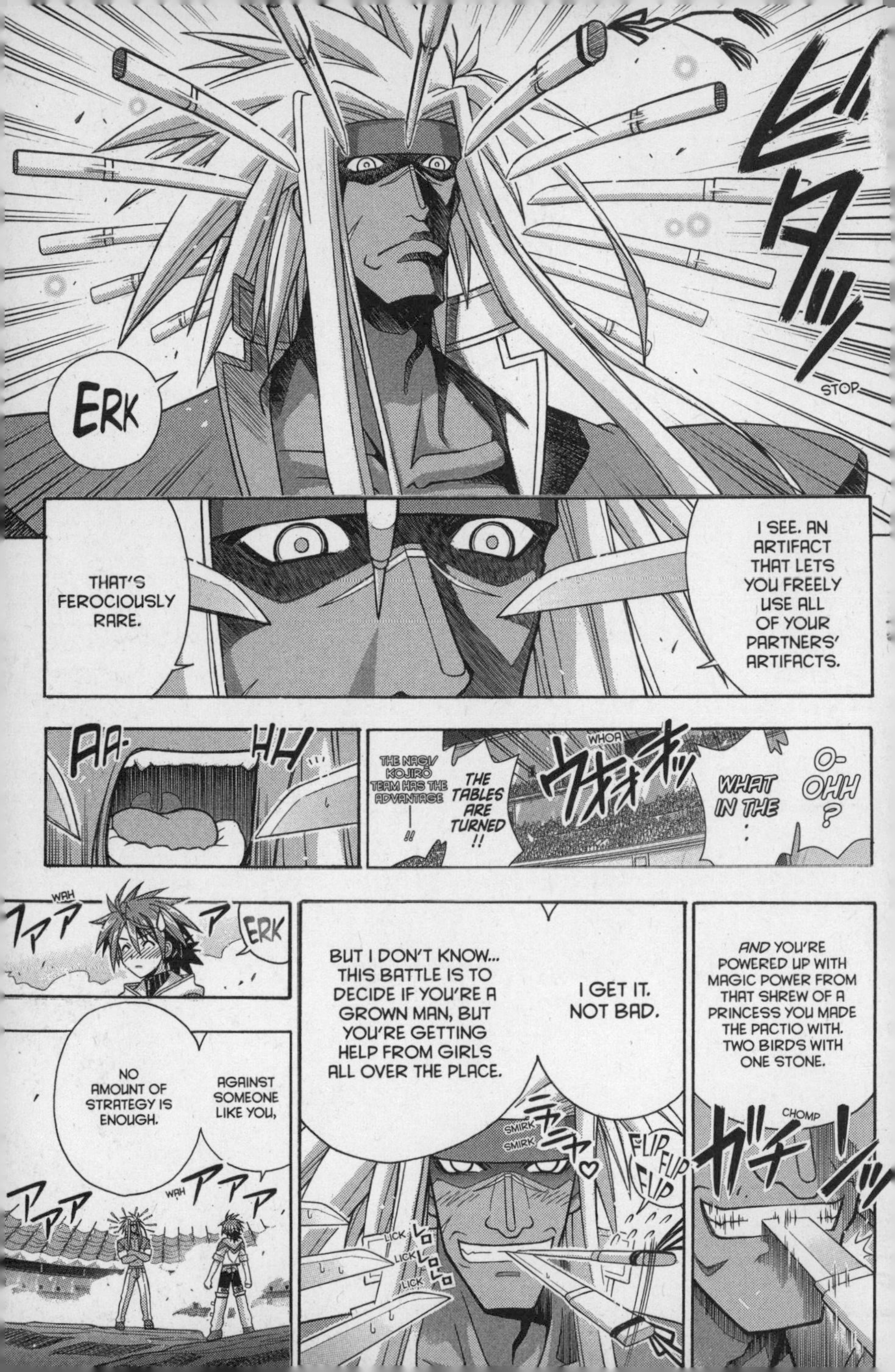
STOP
ERK
I SEE. AN ARTIFACT THAT LETS YOU FREELY USE ALL OF YOUR PARTNERS' ARTIFACTS.
THAT'S FEROCIOUSLY RARE.
O-OHH?
WHAT IN THE :
WHOA
THE TABLES ARE TURNED!!
THE NAGI/KOJIRO TEAM HAS THE ADVANTAGE —!!
AA-HH
AND YOU'RE POWERED UP WITH MAGIC POWER FROM THAT SHREW OF A PRINCESS YOU MADE THE PACTIO WITH. TWO BIRDS WITH ONE STONE.
CHOMP
I GET IT. NOT BAD.
BUT I DON'T KNOW... THIS BATTLE IS TO DECIDE IF YOU'RE A GROWN MAN, BUT YOU'RE GETTING HELP FROM GIRLS ALL OVER THE PLACE.
SMIRK SMIRK
FLIP FLIP FLIP
LICK LICK LICK
ERK
WAH
AGAINST SOMEONE LIKE YOU,
NO AMOUNT OF STRATEGY IS ENOUGH.
WAH

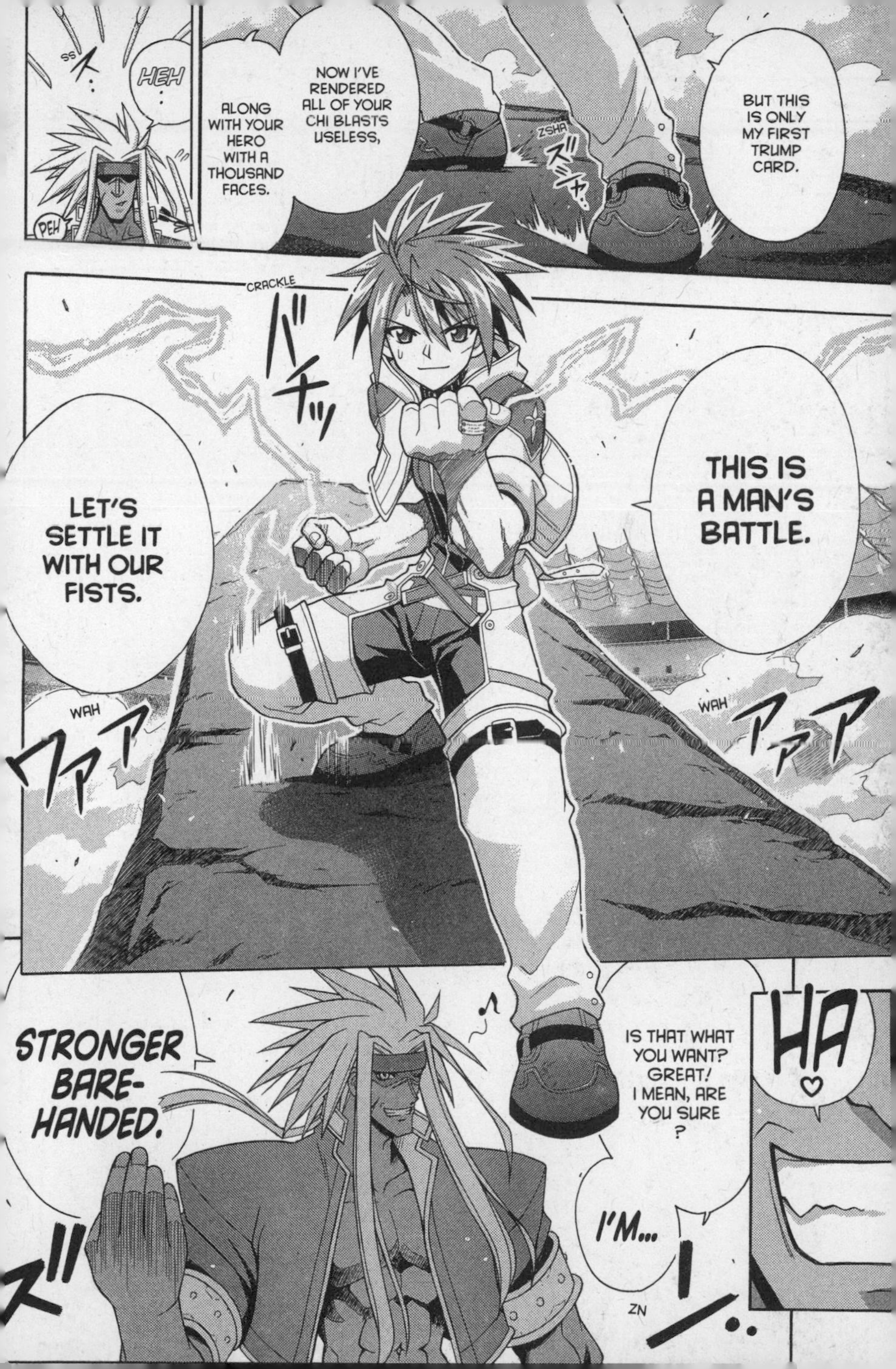
ZSHA
BUT THIS IS ONLY MY FIRST TRUMP CARD.
NOW I'VE RENDERED ALL OF YOUR CHI BLASTS USELESS,
ALONG WITH YOUR HERO WITH A THOUSAND FACES.
SS
HEH
PEH
CRACKLE
THIS IS A MAN'S BATTLE.
LET'S SETTLE IT WITH OUR FISTS.
WAH
WAH
HA ♥
IS THAT WHAT YOU WANT? GREAT! I MEAN, ARE YOU SURE?
I'M... !
ZN
STRONGER BARE-HANDED.

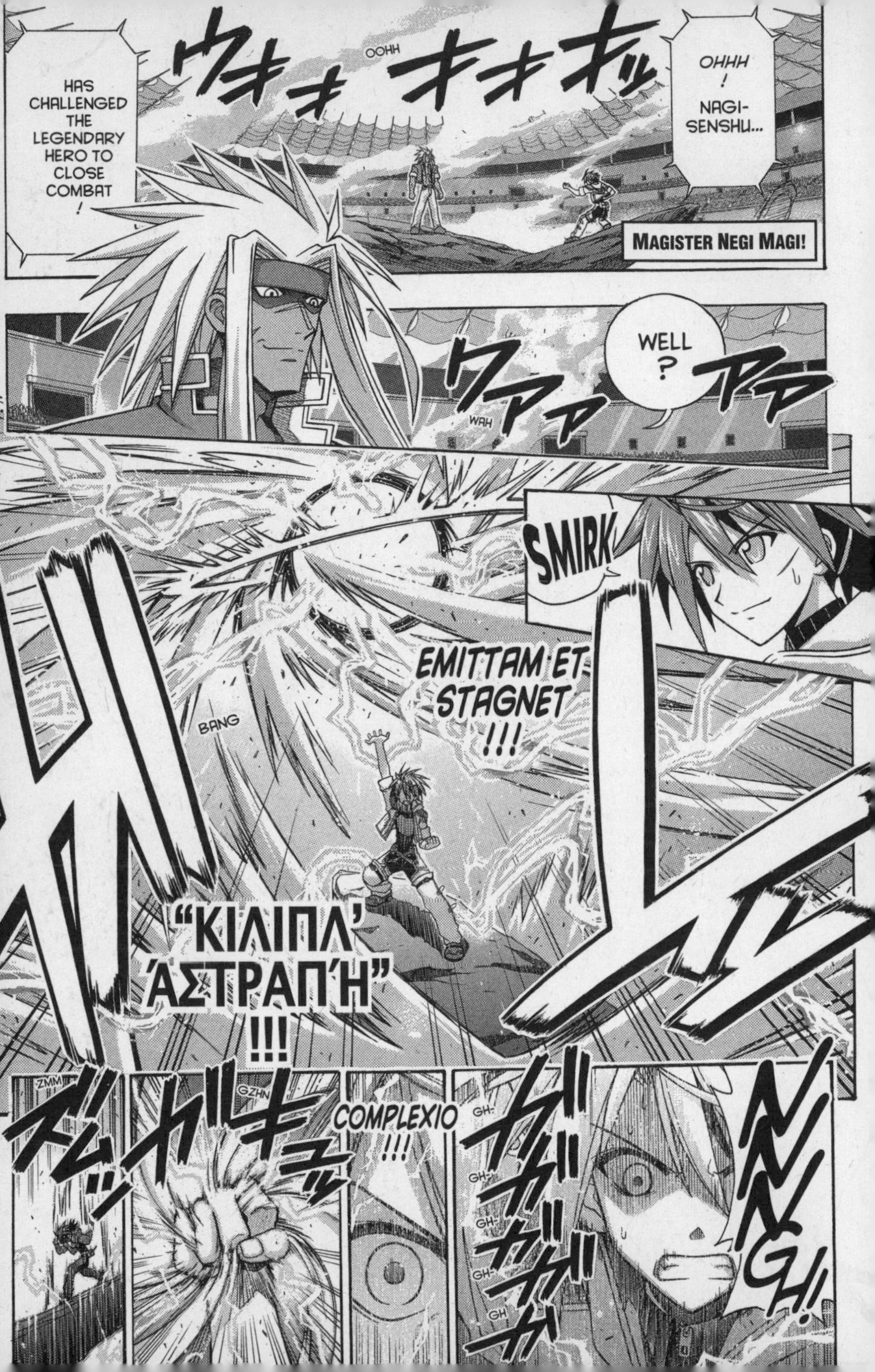
OHHH!
NAGI-SENSHU...
OOHH
HAS CHALLENGED THE LEGENDARY HERO TO CLOSE COMBAT!
MAGISTER NEGI MAGI!
WELL?
WAH
SMIRK
EMITTAM ET STAGNET!!!
BANG
"ΚΙΛΙΠΛ' ἈΣΤΡΑΠ'Η"!!!
NNNGH!!
GH-
GH-
GH-
GH-
GH
COMPLEXIO!!!
GZHN
ZMM

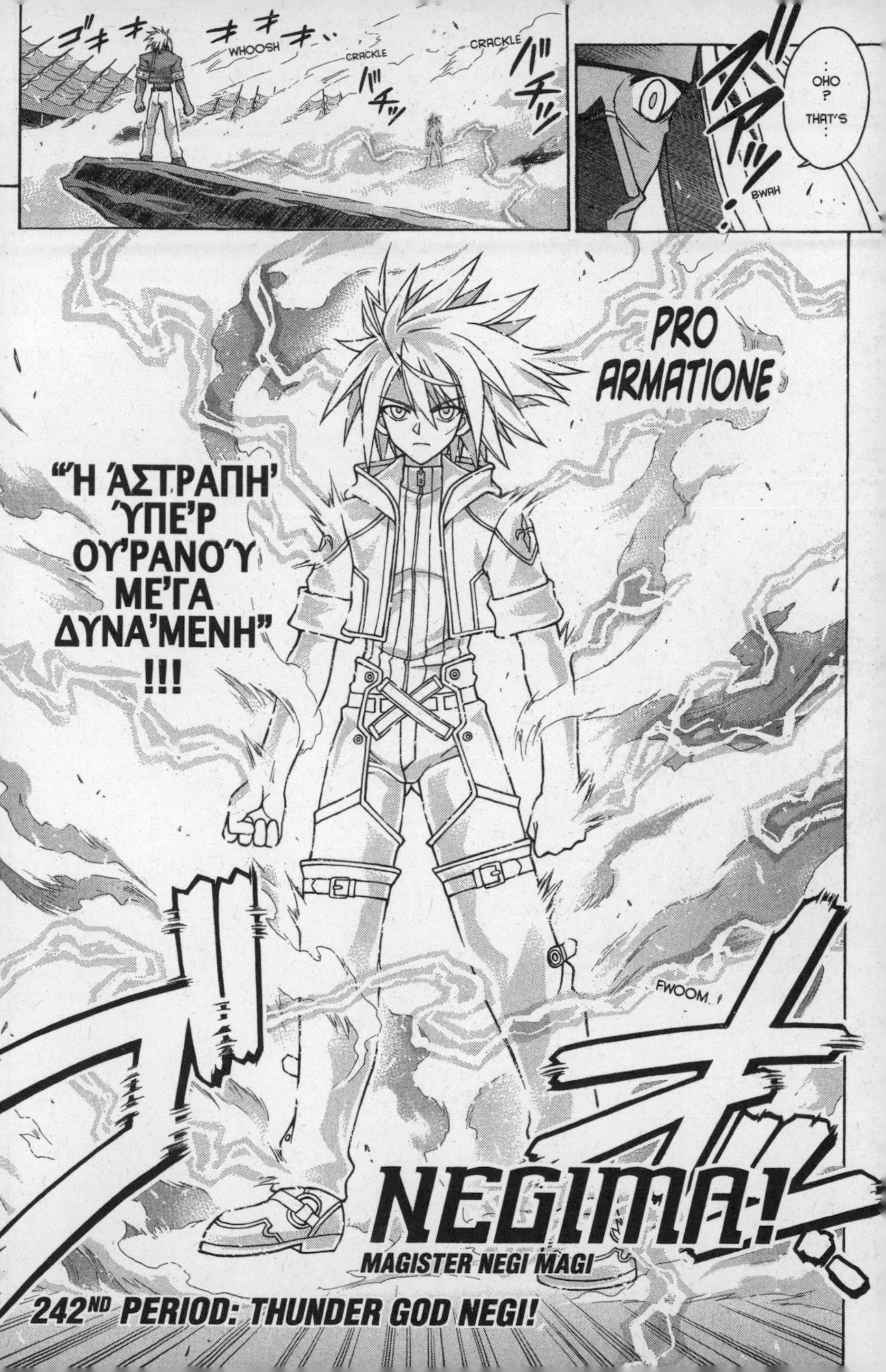
OHO ? THAT'S
BWAH
WHOOSH
CRACKLE
CRACKLE
PRO ARMATIONE
“Ή ΆΣΤΡΑΠΗ’ ΎΠΕ’Ρ ΟΥ’ΡΑΝΟ’Υ ΜΕ’ΓΑ ΔΥΝΑ’ΜΕΝΗ” !!!
FWOOM
NEGIMA!
MAGISTER NEGI MAGI
242ND PERIOD: THUNDER GOD NEGI!

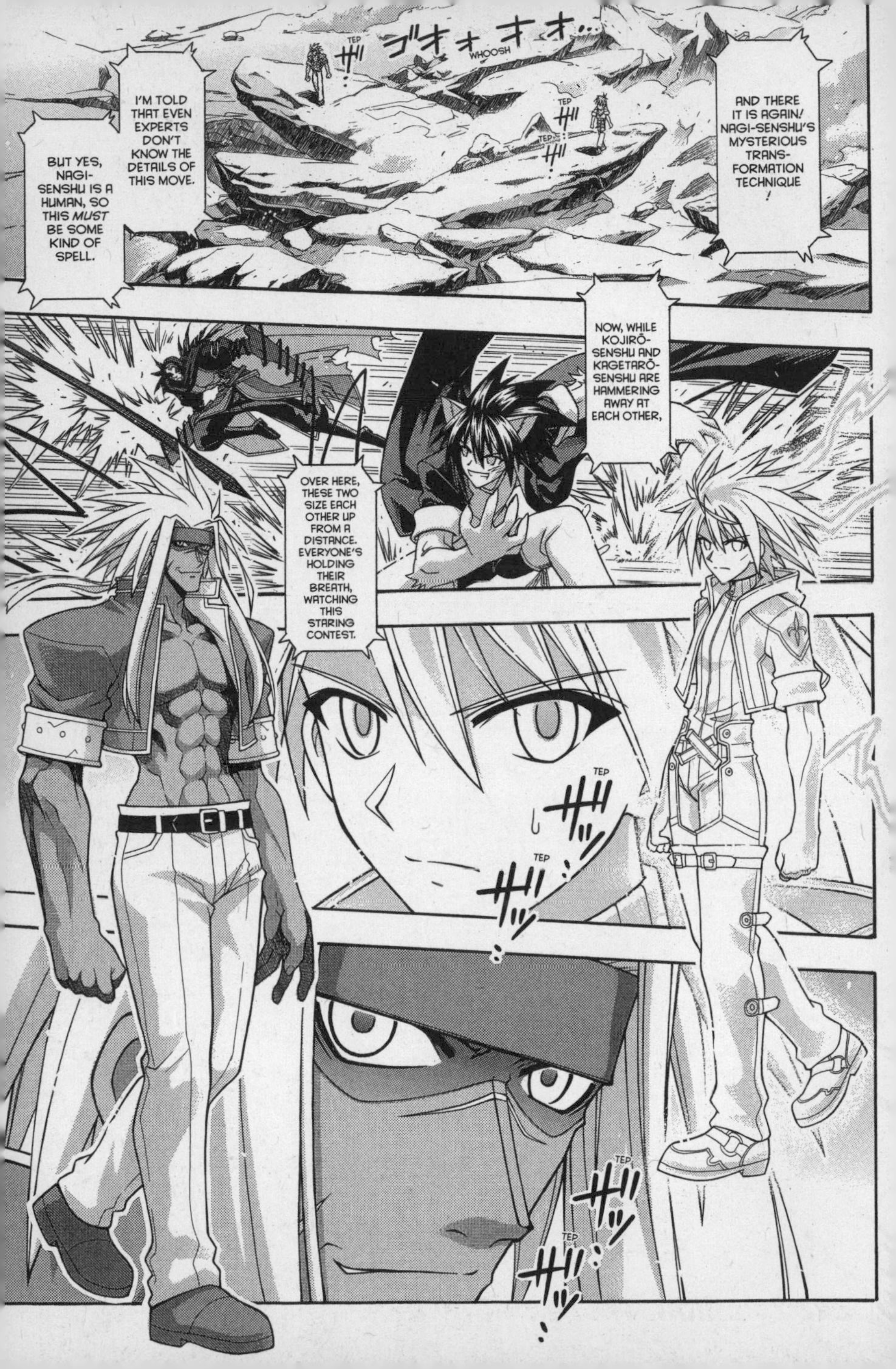
ゴオォオオ…
WHOOSH
TEP
ザッ
TEP
ザッ
TEP
ザッ
AND THERE IT IS AGAIN! NAGI-SENSHU'S MYSTERIOUS TRANS-FORMATION TECHNIQUE!
I'M TOLD THAT EVEN EXPERTS DON'T KNOW THE DETAILS OF THIS MOVE.
BUT YES, NAGI-SENSHU IS A HUMAN, SO THIS *MUST* BE SOME KIND OF SPELL.
NOW, WHILE KOJIRŌ-SENSHU AND KAGETARŌ-SENSHU ARE HAMMERING AWAY AT EACH OTHER,
OVER HERE, THESE TWO SIZE EACH OTHER UP FROM A DISTANCE. EVERYONE'S HOLDING THEIR BREATH, WATCHING THIS STARING CONTEST.
TEP
ザッ
TEP
ザッ
TEP
ザッ
TEP
ザッ

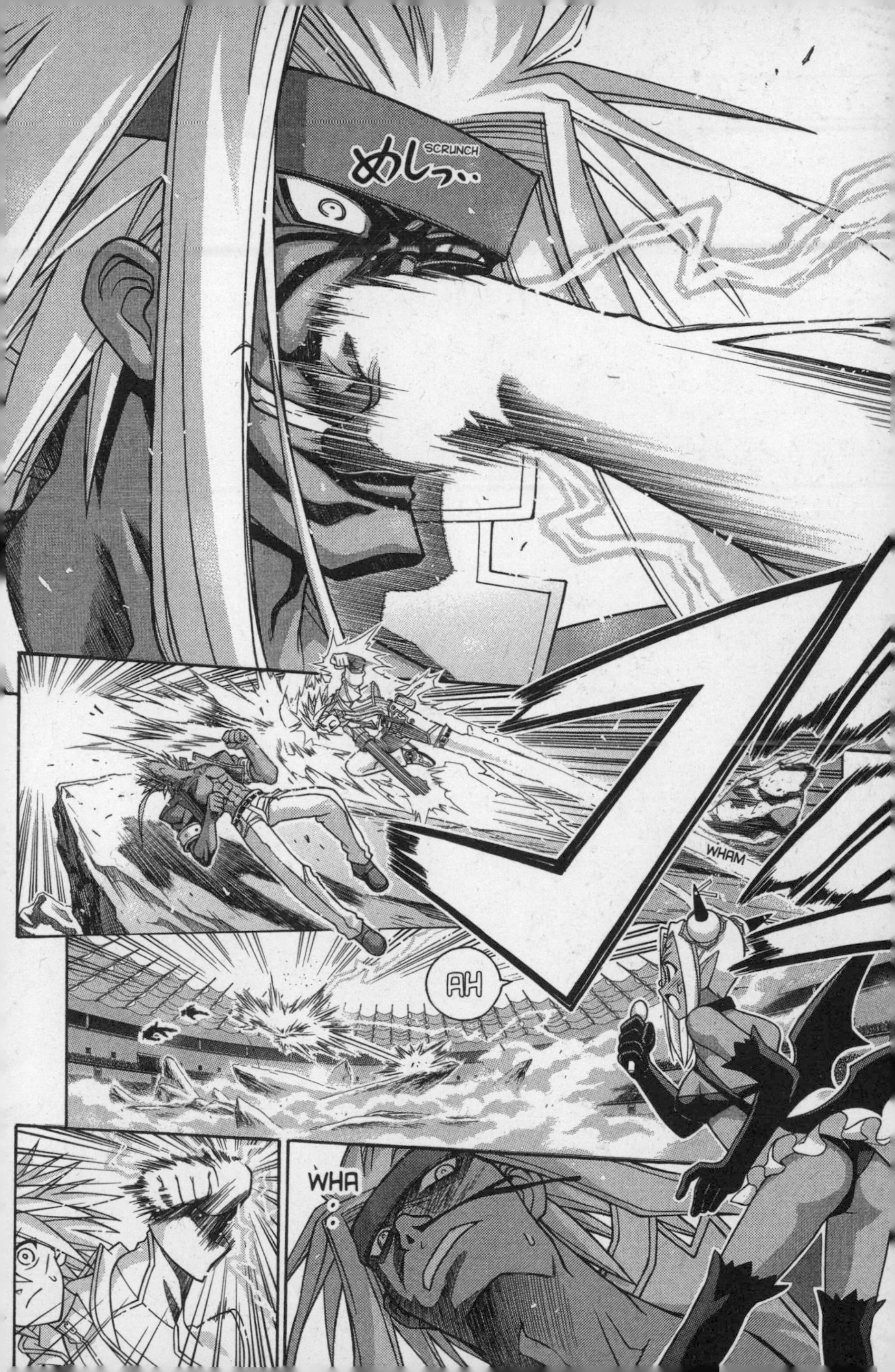
めしっ…
SCRUNCH
WHAM
AH
WHA...

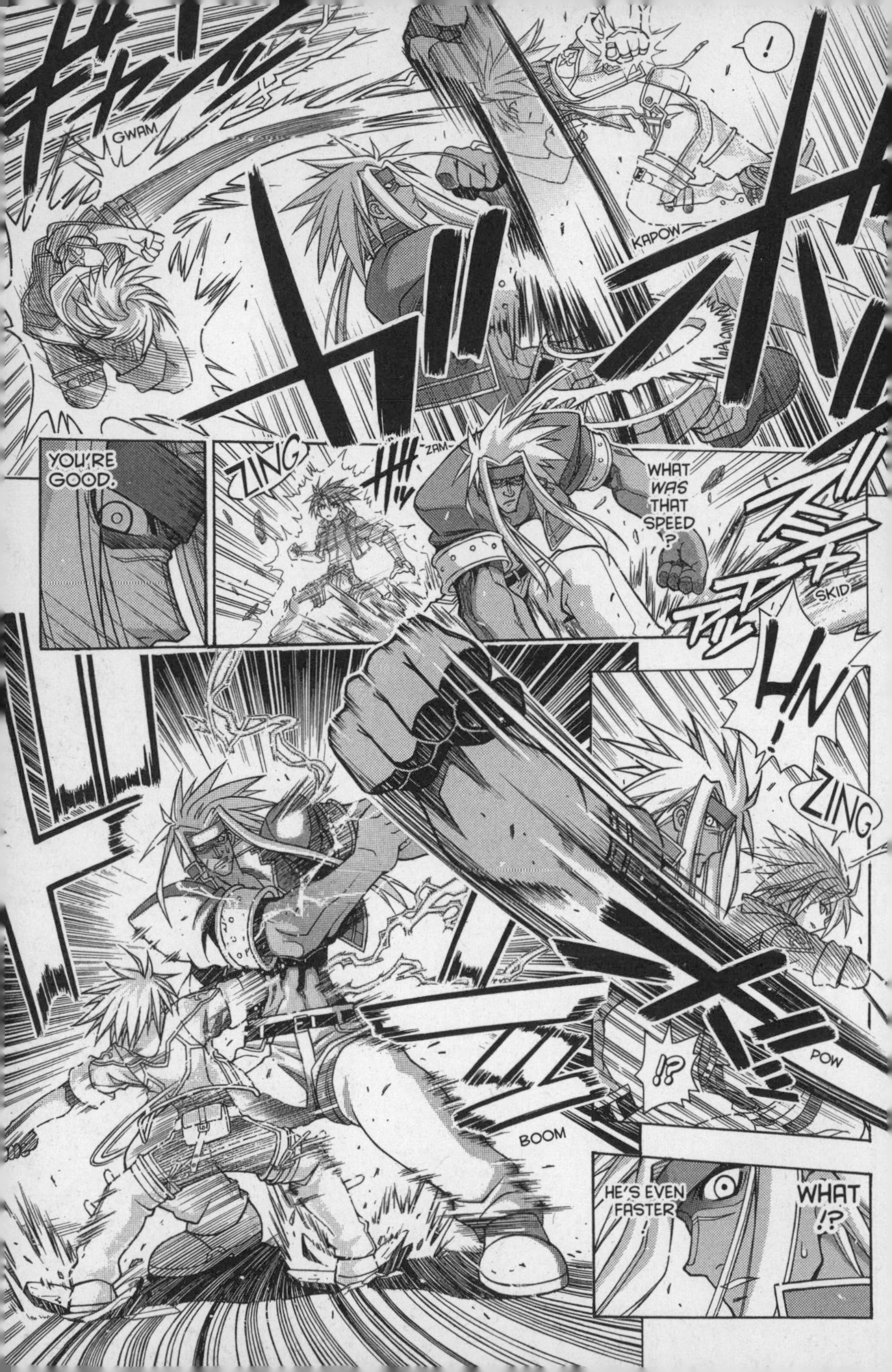

!
KAPOW
GWAM
WHAT WAS THAT SPEED?
SKID
ZAM
ZING
YOU'RE GOOD.
HN!
ZING
POW
!?
BOOM
WHAT!?
HE'S EVEN FASTER

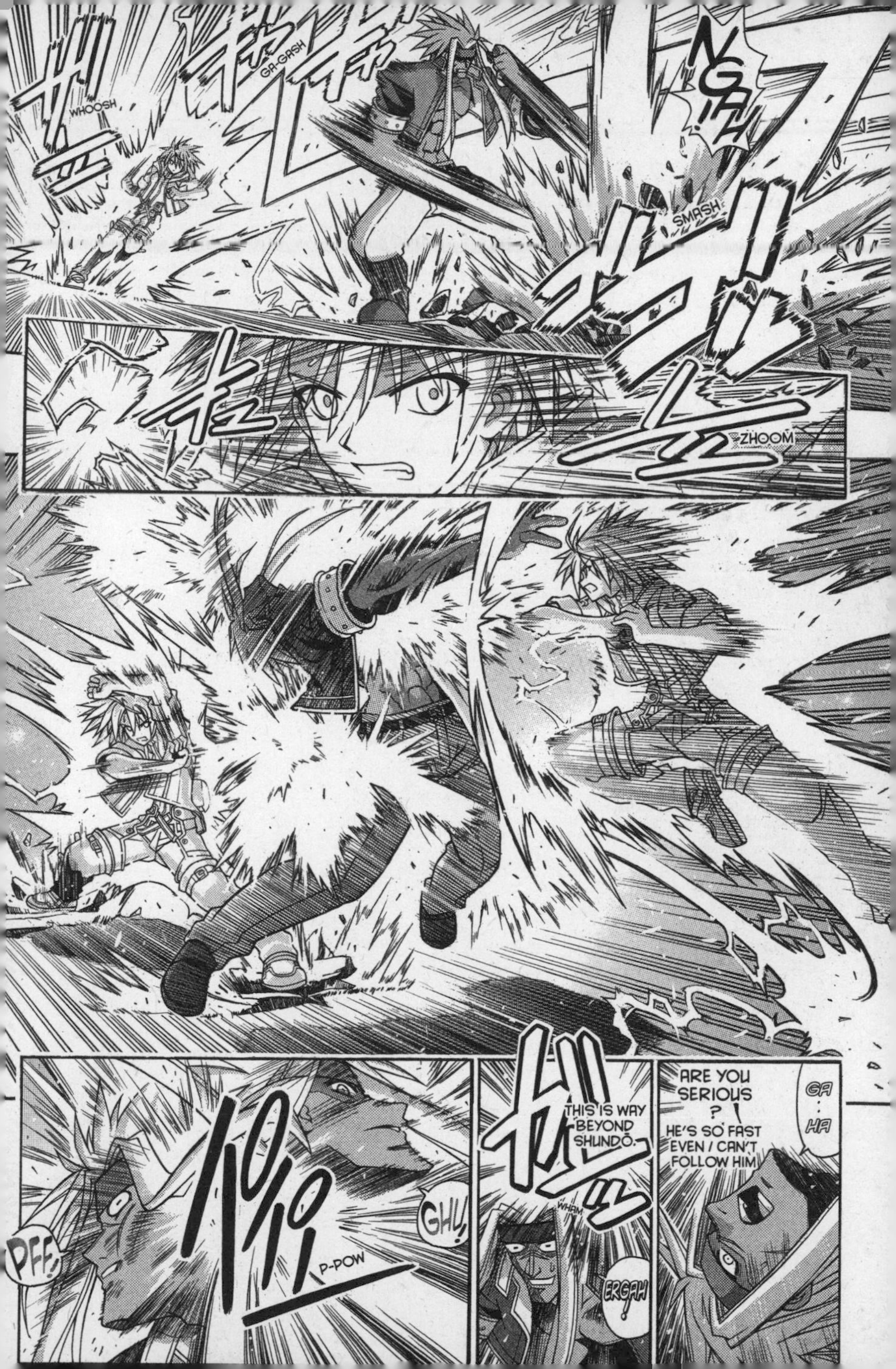
NGAH!
SMASH
GA-GASH
WHOOSH
ZHOOM
GA...HA
ARE YOU SERIOUS?!
HE'S SO FAST EVEN I CAN'T FOLLOW HIM
THIS IS WAY BEYOND SHUNDŌ.
WHAM
ERGAH!
GHU!
P-POW
PFF!

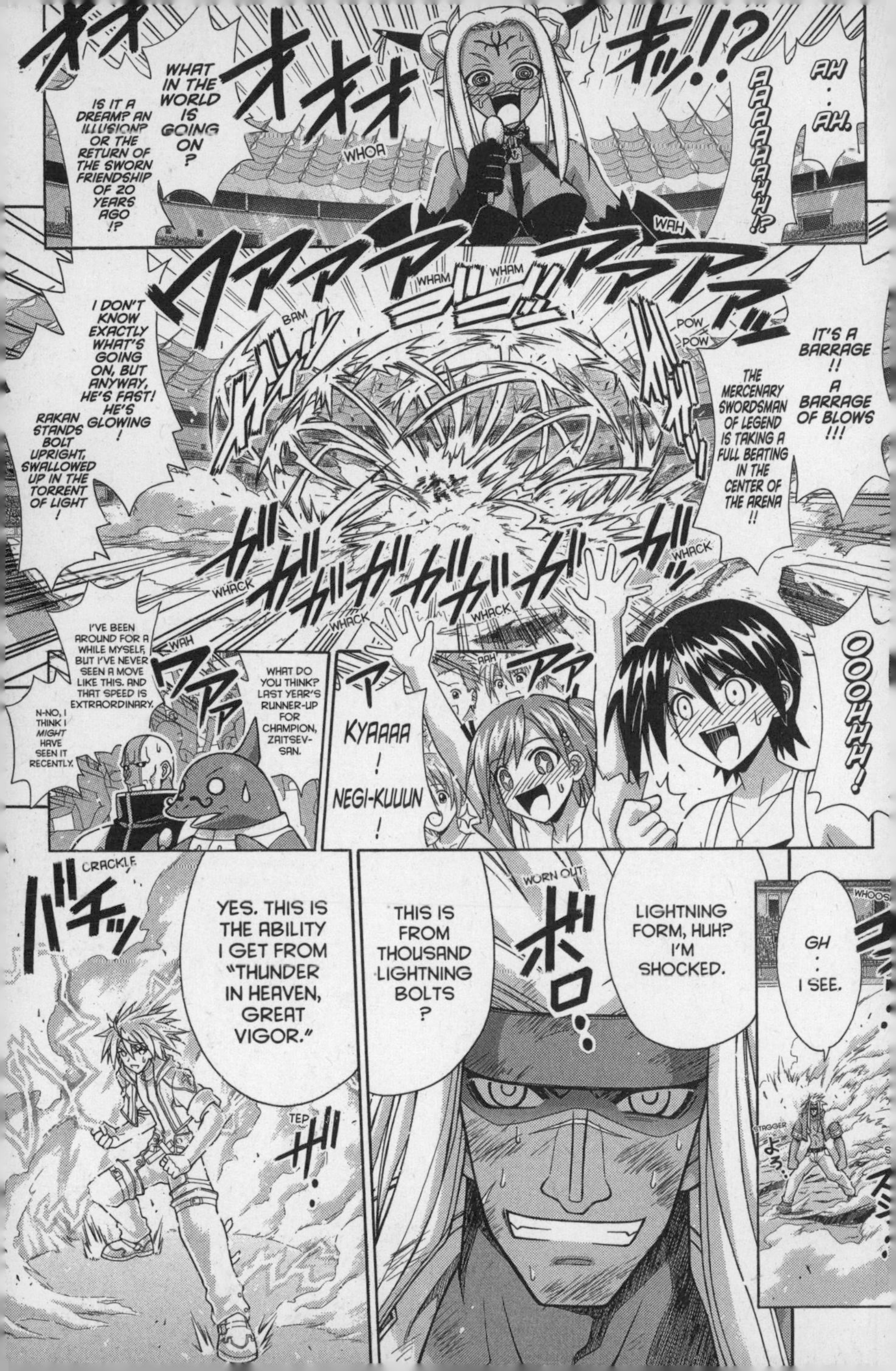
AH . . AH.
AAAAAAAAAH!?
WHAT IN THE WORLD IS GOING ON?
IS IT A DREAM? AN ILLUSION? OR THE RETURN OF THE SWORN FRIENDSHIP OF 20 YEARS AGO!?
WHOA
WAH
IT'S A BARRAGE!! A BARRAGE OF BLOWS!!!
THE MERCENARY SWORDSMAN OF LEGEND IS TAKING A FULL BEATING IN THE CENTER OF THE ARENA!!
POW
POW
WHAM
WHAM
BAM
I DON'T KNOW EXACTLY WHAT'S GOING ON, BUT ANYWAY, HE'S FAST! HE'S GLOWING!
RAKAN STANDS BOLT UPRIGHT, SWALLOWED UP IN THE TORRENT OF LIGHT!
WHACK
WHACK
WHACK
WHACK
OOOHHH!
AAH
KYAAAA! NEGI-KUUUN!
WHAT DO YOU THINK? LAST YEAR'S RUNNER-UP FOR CHAMPION, ZAITSEV-SAN.
I'VE BEEN AROUND FOR A WHILE MYSELF, BUT I'VE NEVER SEEN A MOVE LIKE THIS. AND THAT SPEED IS EXTRAORDINARY.
WAH
N-NO, I THINK I MIGHT HAVE SEEN IT RECENTLY.
GH . . I SEE.
STAGGER
LIGHTNING FORM, HUH? I'M SHOCKED.
WORN OUT
THIS IS FROM THOUSAND LIGHTNING BOLTS?
YES. THIS IS THE ABILITY I GET FROM "THUNDER IN HEAVEN, GREAT VIGOR."
CRACKLE
TEP

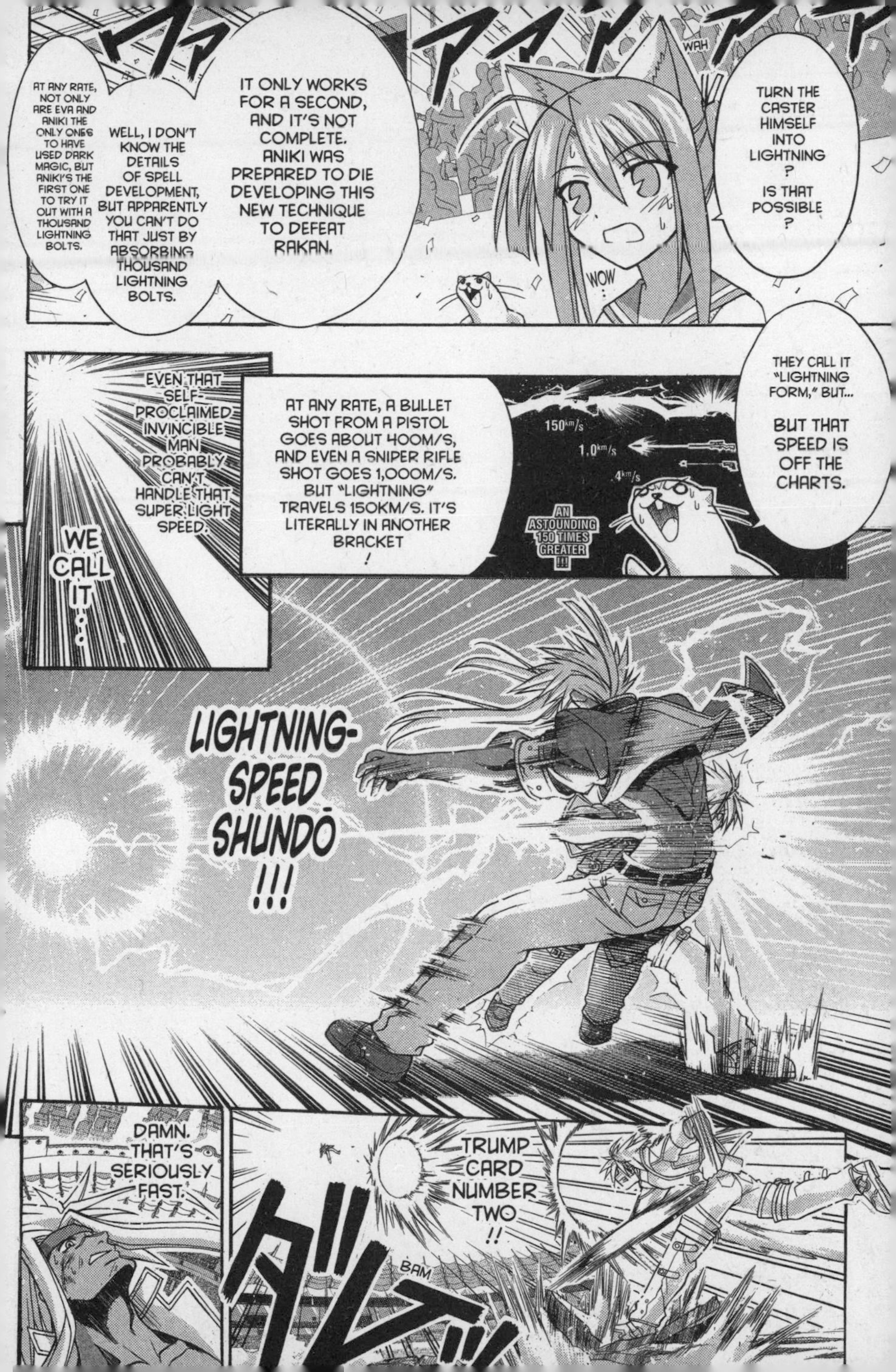
WAH
TURN THE CASTER HIMSELF INTO LIGHTNING? IS THAT POSSIBLE?
WOW...
IT ONLY WORKS FOR A SECOND, AND IT'S NOT COMPLETE. ANIKI WAS PREPARED TO DIE DEVELOPING THIS NEW TECHNIQUE TO DEFEAT RAKAN.
WELL, I DON'T KNOW THE DETAILS OF SPELL DEVELOPMENT, BUT APPARENTLY YOU CAN'T DO THAT JUST BY ABSORBING THOUSAND LIGHTNING BOLTS.
AT ANY RATE, NOT ONLY ARE EVA AND ANIKI THE ONLY ONES TO HAVE USED DARK MAGIC, BUT ANIKI'S THE FIRST ONE TO TRY IT OUT WITH A THOUSAND LIGHTNING BOLTS.
THEY CALL IT "LIGHTNING FORM," BUT...
BUT THAT SPEED IS OFF THE CHARTS.
150km/s
1,0km/s
4km/s
AN ASTOUNDING 150 TIMES GREATER!!!
AT ANY RATE, A BULLET SHOT FROM A PISTOL GOES ABOUT 400M/S, AND EVEN A SNIPER RIFLE SHOT GOES 1,000M/S. BUT "LIGHTNING" TRAVELS 150KM/S. IT'S LITERALLY IN ANOTHER BRACKET!
EVEN THAT SELF-PROCLAIMED INVINCIBLE MAN PROBABLY CAN'T HANDLE THAT SUPER LIGHT SPEED.
WE CALL IT...
LIGHTNING-SPEED SHUNDŌ!!!
TRUMP CARD NUMBER TWO!!
BAM
DAMN. THAT'S SERIOUSLY FAST.

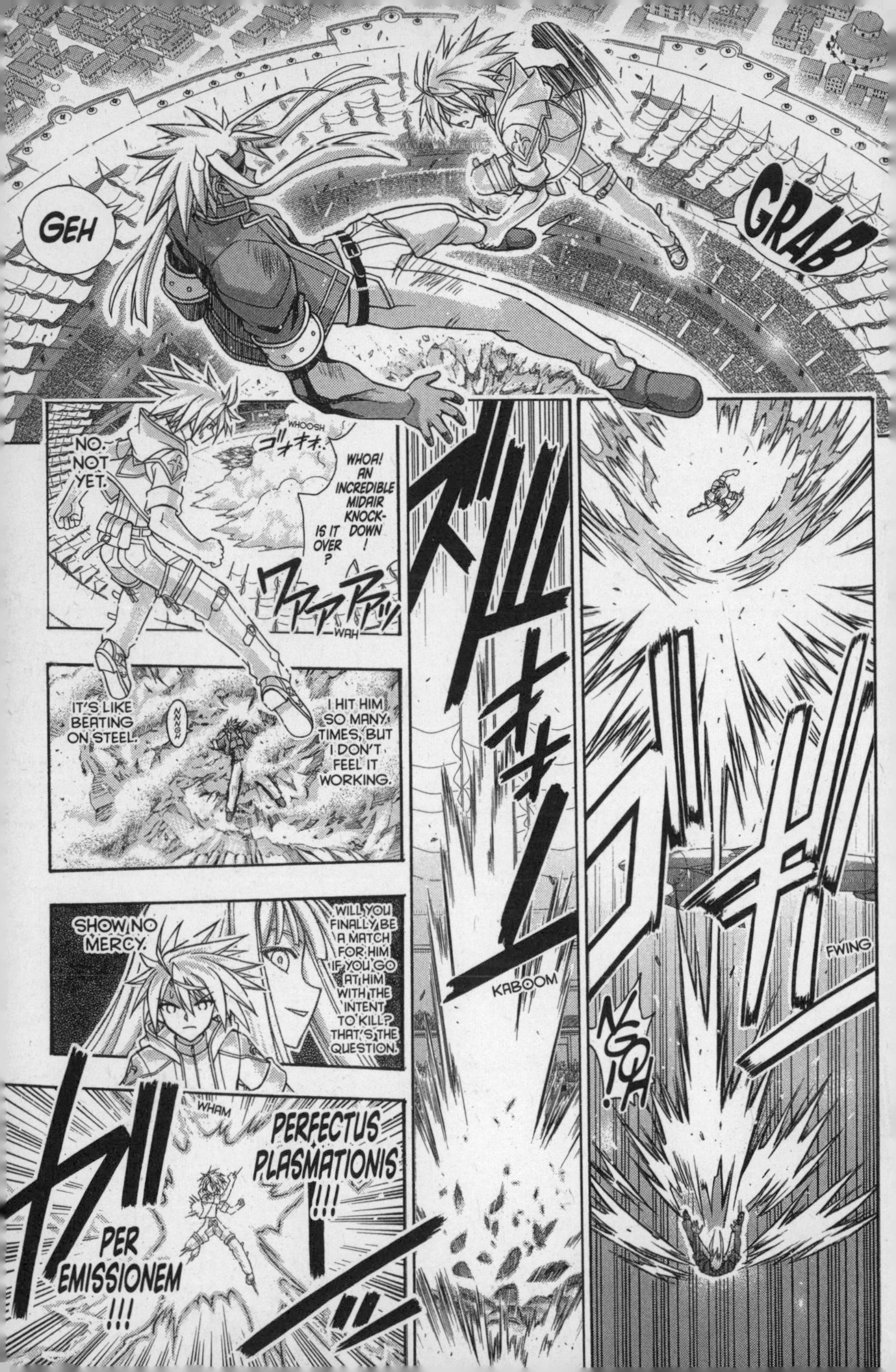
GRAB
GEH
FWING
NGGH!
KABOOM
WHOA! AN INCREDIBLE MIDAIR KNOCK-DOWN!
IS IT OVER?
WHOOSH
NO. NOT YET.
WAH
I HIT HIM SO MANY TIMES, BUT I DON'T FEEL IT WORKING.
NNGH
IT'S LIKE BEATING ON STEEL.
WILL YOU FINALLY BE A MATCH FOR HIM IF YOU GO AT HIM WITH THE INTENT TO KILL? THAT'S THE QUESTION.
SHOW NO MERCY.
PERFECTUS PLASMATIONIS!!!
WHAM
PER EMISSIONEM!!!

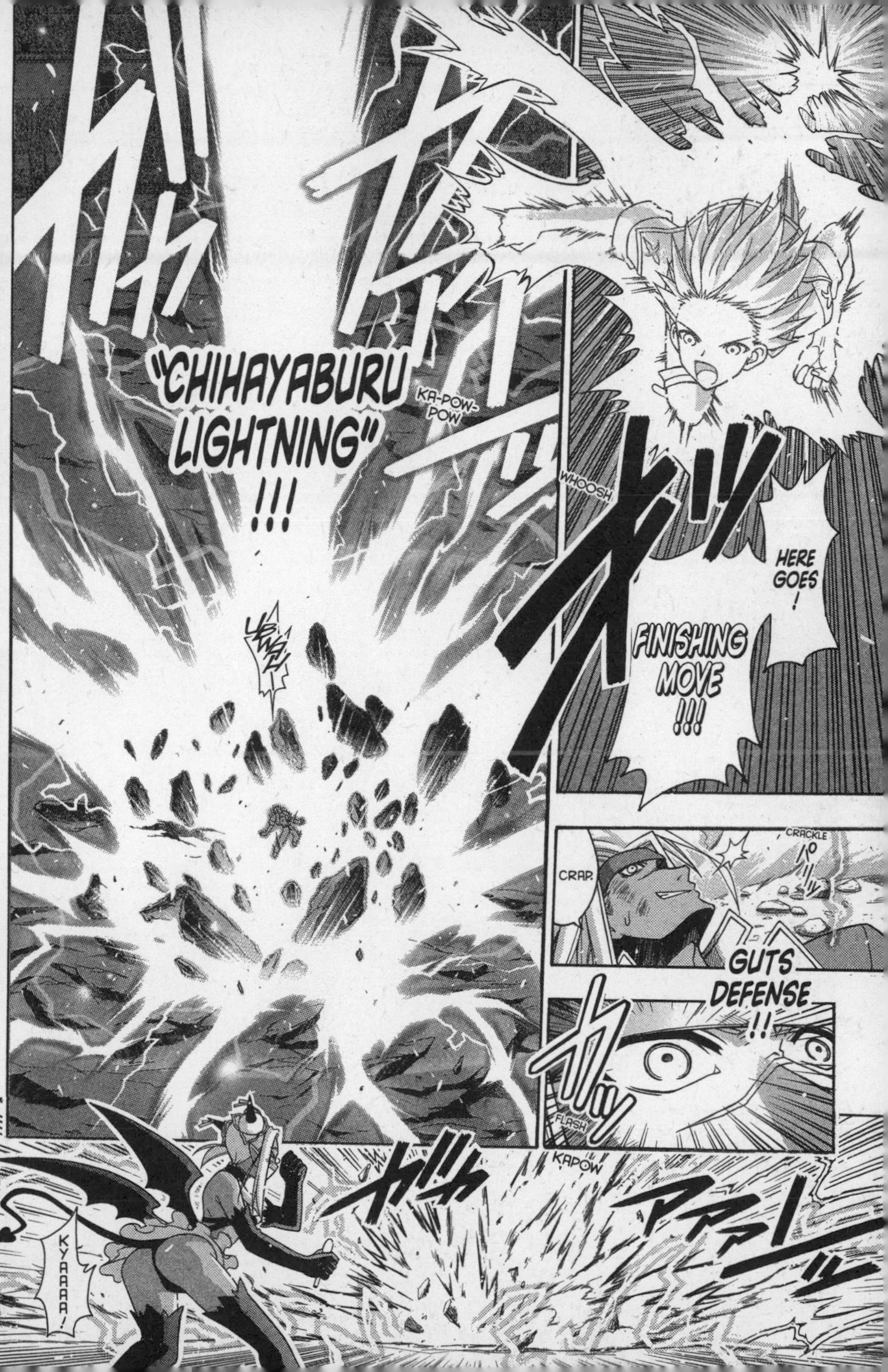
HERE GOES!
FINISHING MOVE!!!
WHOOSH
CRAP.
CRACKLE
GUTS DEFENSE!!
FLASH
"CHIHAYABURU LIGHTNING"!!!
KA-POW-POW
KAPOW
KYAAAA!

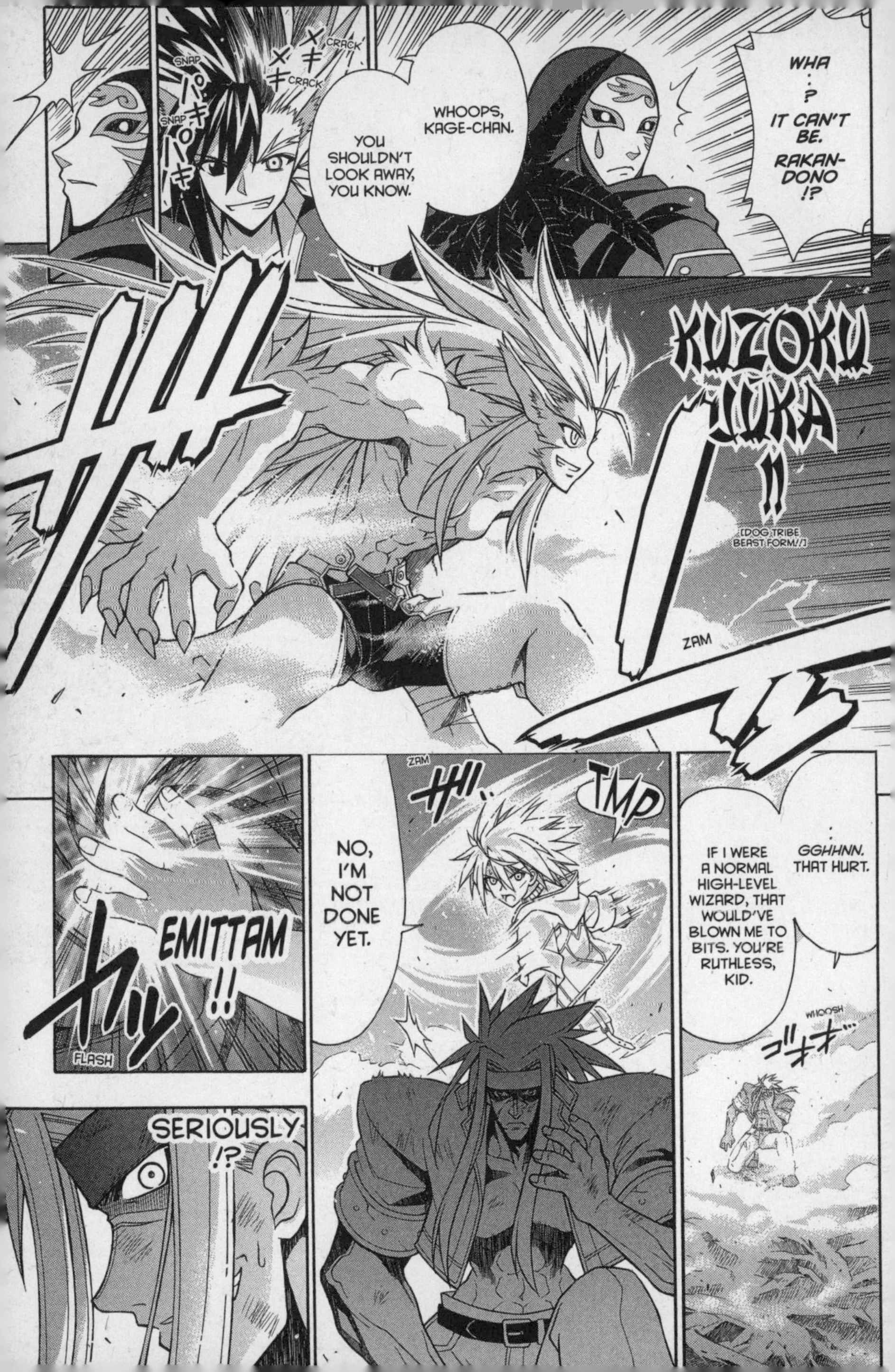
WHA . . ? IT CAN'T BE. RAKAN-DONO !?
WHOOPS, KAGE-CHAN.
YOU SHOULDN'T LOOK AWAY, YOU KNOW.
CRACK
CRACK
SNAP
SNAP
KUZOKU JUKA !!
[DOG TRIBE BEAST FORM!/]
ZAM
GGHHNN. THAT HURT.
IF I WERE A NORMAL HIGH-LEVEL WIZARD, THAT WOULD'VE BLOWN ME TO BITS. YOU'RE RUTHLESS, KID.
WHOOSH
ZAM
TMP
NO, I'M NOT DONE YET.
EMITTAM !!
FLASH
SERIOUSLY !?

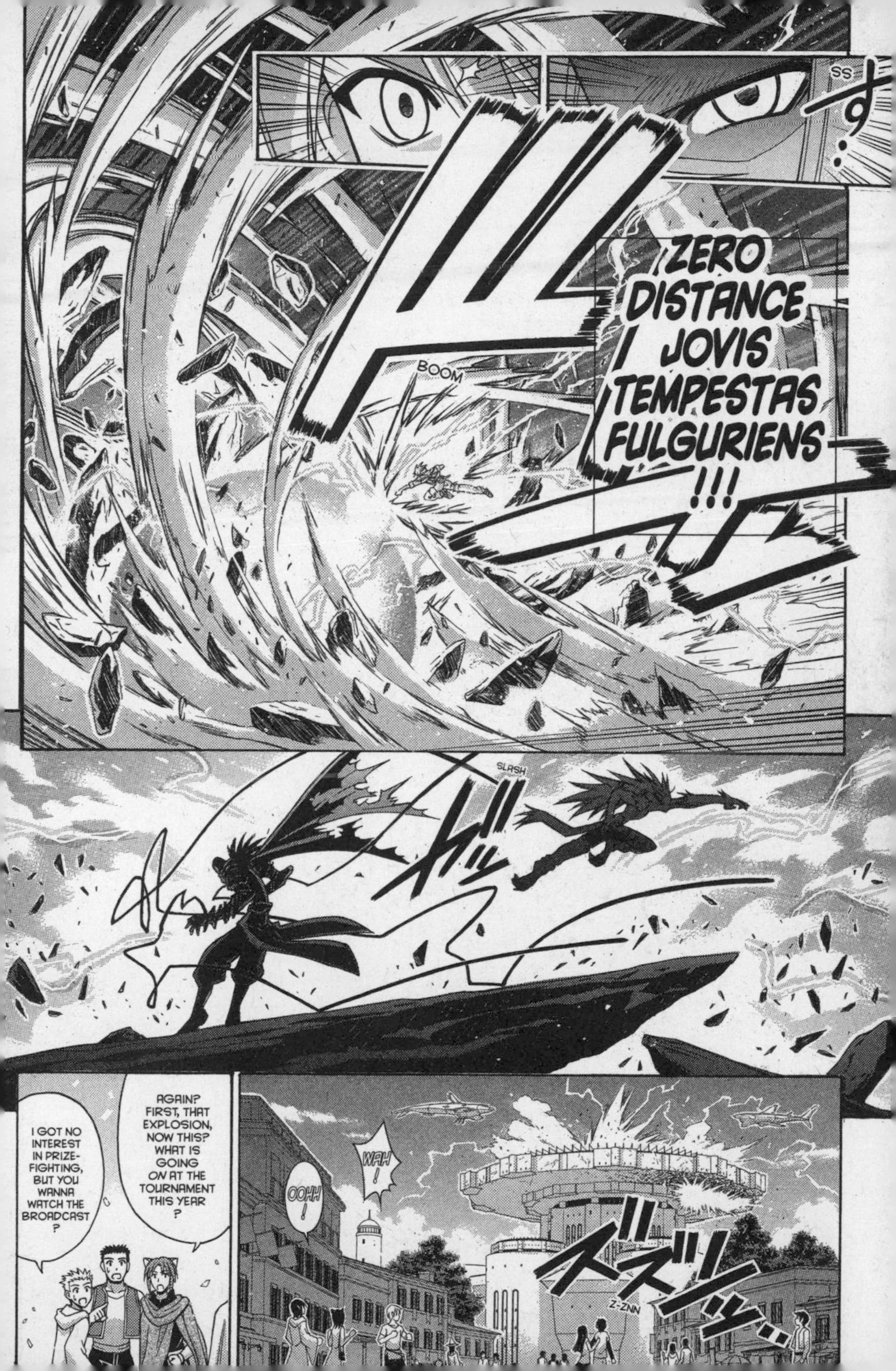
SS
ZERO DISTANCE JOVIS TEMPESTAS FULGURIENS !!!
BOOM
SLASH
WAH !
OOHH !
Z-ZNN
AGAIN? FIRST, THAT EXPLOSION, NOW THIS? WHAT IS GOING ON AT THE TOURNAMENT THIS YEAR ?
I GOT NO INTEREST IN PRIZE-FIGHTING, BUT YOU WANNA WATCH THE BROADCAST ?

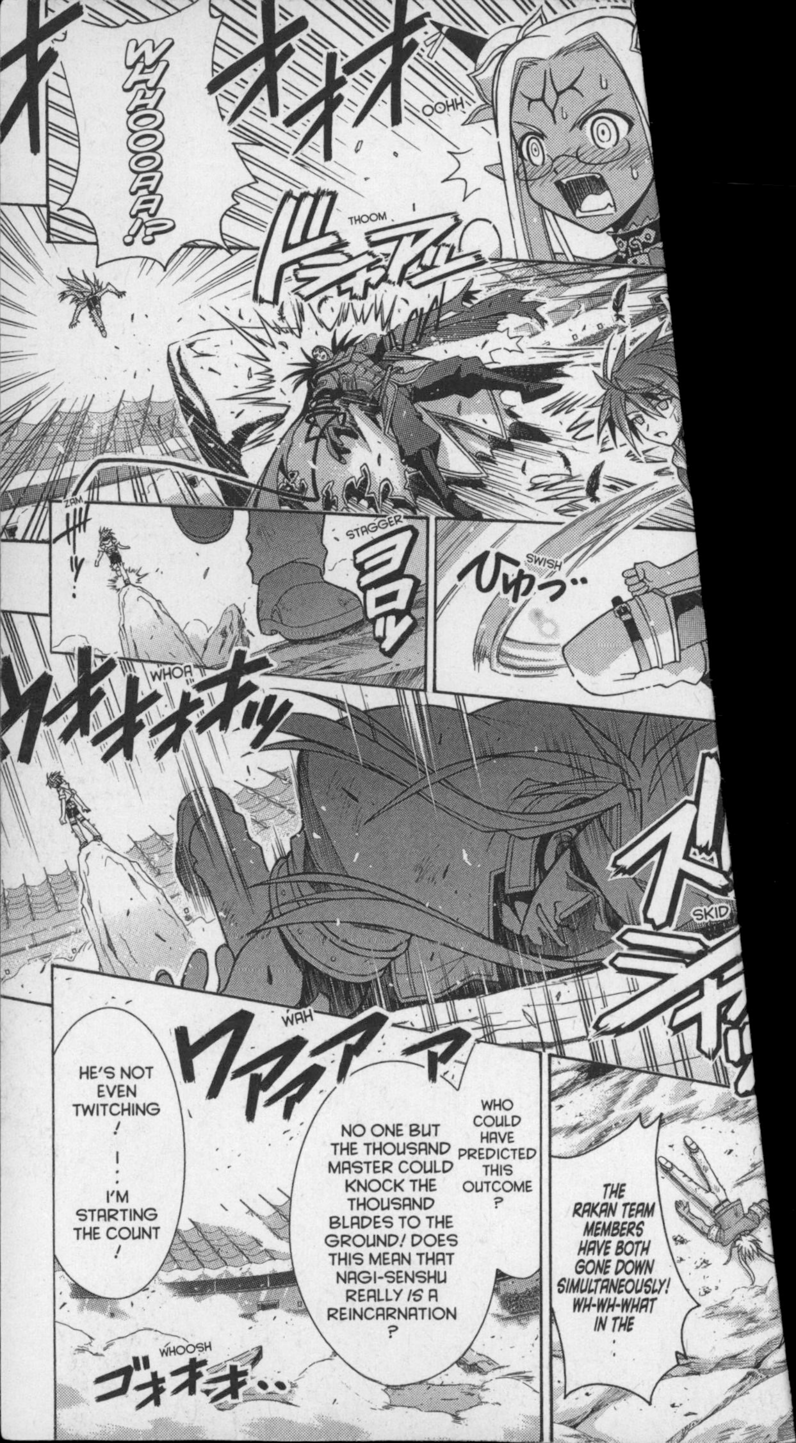
OOHH
WHHOOOAAA!?
THOOM
SWISH
STAGGER
ZAM
SKID
WHOA
THE RAKAN TEAM MEMBERS HAVE BOTH GONE DOWN SIMULTANEOUSLY! WH-WH-WHAT IN THE
WAH
WHO COULD HAVE PREDICTED THIS OUTCOME?
NO ONE BUT THE THOUSAND MASTER COULD KNOCK THE THOUSAND BLADES TO THE GROUND! DOES THIS MEAN THAT NAGI-SENSHU REALLY *IS* A REINCARNATION?
HE'S NOT EVEN TWITCHING!! ...I'M STARTING THE COUNT!
WHOOSH

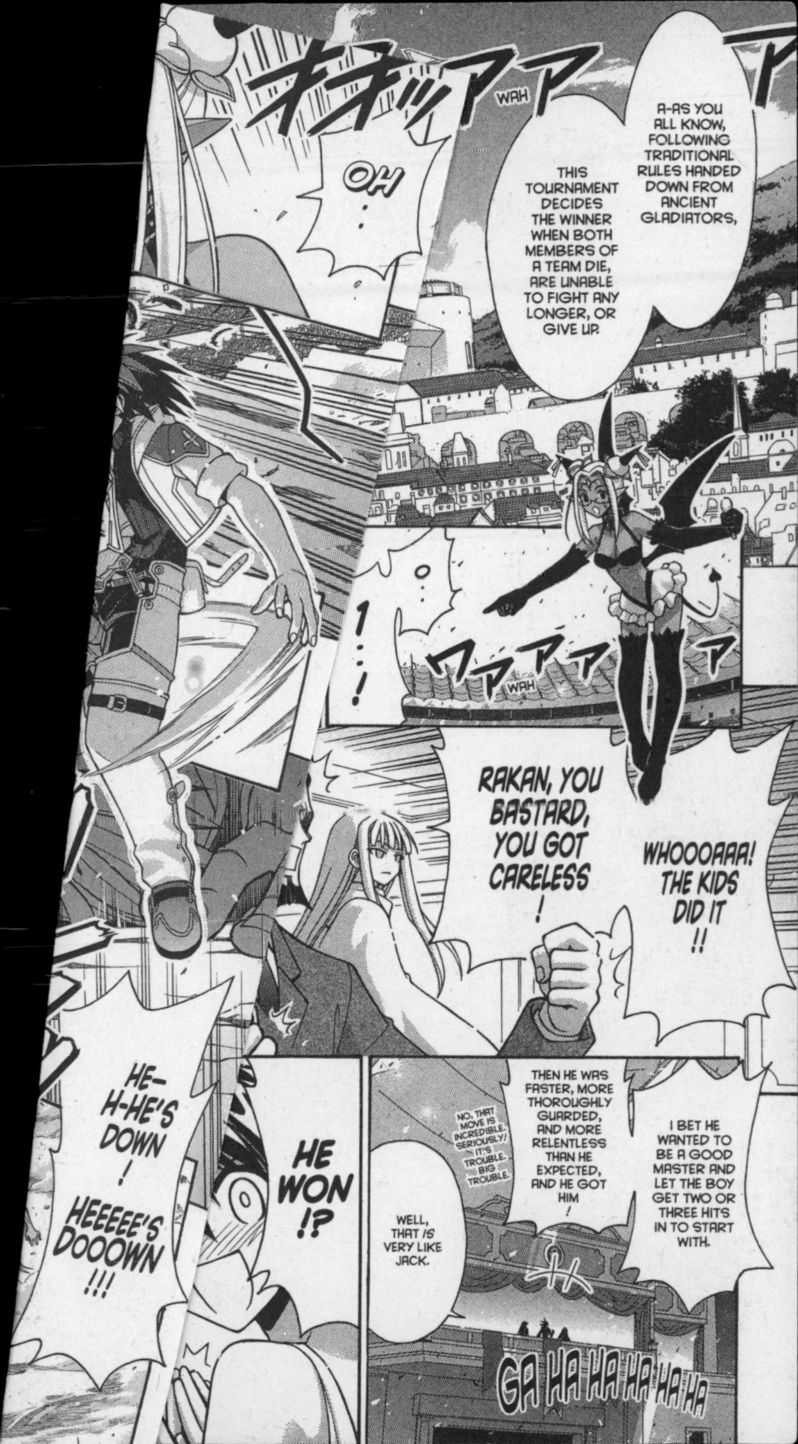
WAH
A-AS YOU ALL KNOW, FOLLOWING TRADITIONAL RULES HANDED DOWN FROM ANCIENT GLADIATORS,
THIS TOURNAMENT DECIDES THE WINNER WHEN BOTH MEMBERS OF A TEAM DIE, ARE UNABLE TO FIGHT ANY LONGER, OR GIVE UP.
OH...
WAH
WHOOOAAA! THE KIDS DID IT!!
RAKAN, YOU BASTARD, YOU GOT CARELESS!
I BET HE WANTED TO BE A GOOD MASTER AND LET THE BOY GET TWO OR THREE HITS IN TO START WITH.
THEN HE WAS FASTER, MORE THOROUGHLY GUARDED, AND MORE RELENTLESS THAN HE EXPECTED, AND HE GOT HIM!
NO, THAT MOVE IS INCREDIBLE. SERIOUSLY! IT'S TROUBLE. BIG TROUBLE.
WELL, THAT *IS* VERY LIKE JACK.
GA HA HA HA HA HA
HE WON!?
HE-H-HE'S DOWN! HEEEEE'S DOOOWN!!!

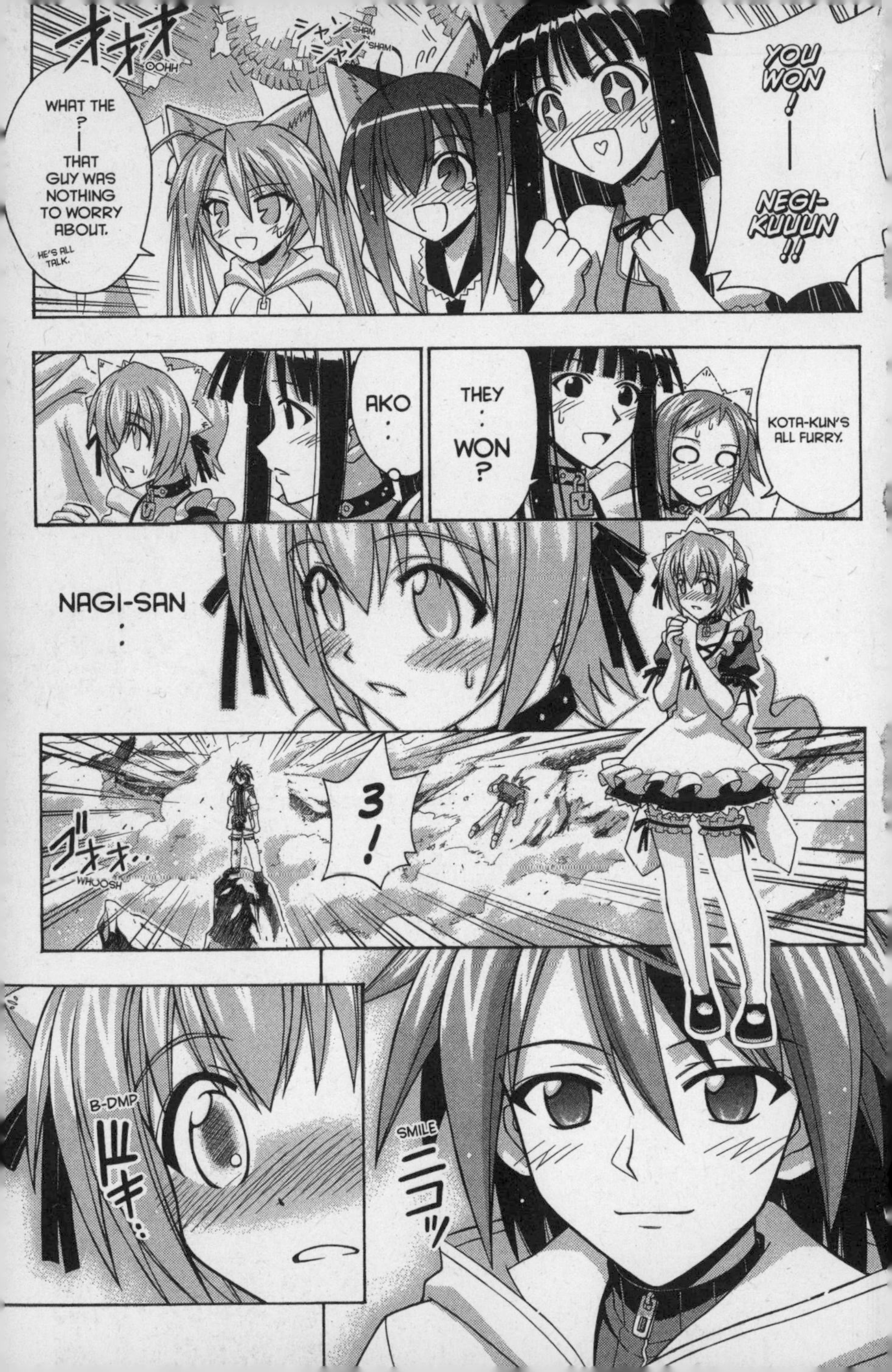
YOU WON!
—
NEGI-KUUUN!!
シャン SHAM
シャン SHAM
オオオ OOHH
WHAT THE?
—
THAT GUY WAS NOTHING TO WORRY ABOUT.
HE'S ALL TALK.
KOTA-KUN'S ALL FURRY.
THEY... WON?
AKO...
NAGI-SAN...
3!
ゴオオ.. WHUOSH
SMILE
ニコッ
B-DMP
ドキ...

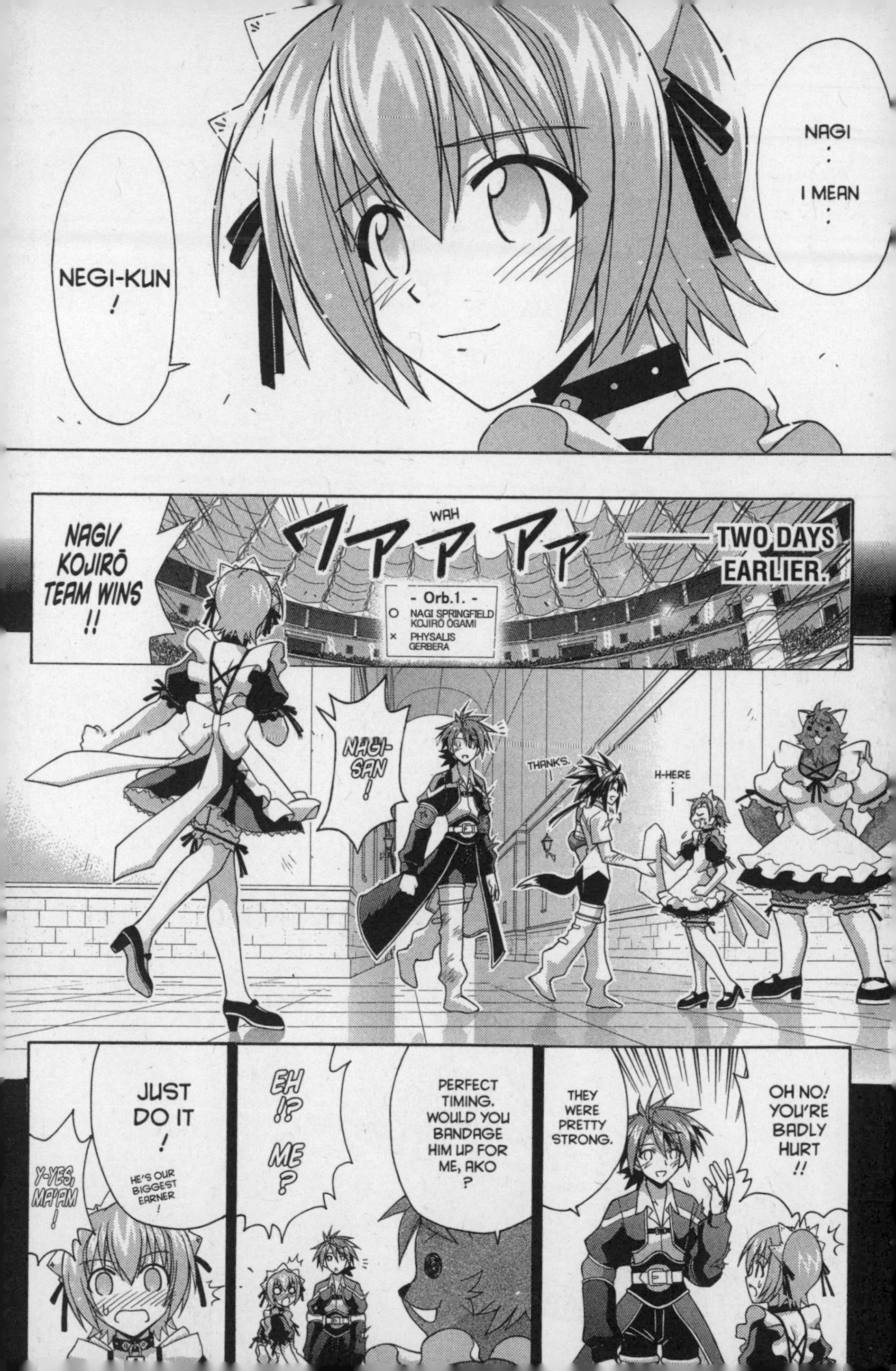
NAGI . . . I MEAN . . .
NEGI-KUN!
— TWO DAYS EARLIER.
WAH
- Orb.1. -
○ NAGI SPRINGFIELD KOJIRŌ ŌGAMI
× PHYSALIS GERBERA
NAGI/ KOJIRŌ TEAM WINS!!
H-HERE!
THANKS.
NAGI-SAN!
OH NO! YOU'RE BADLY HURT!!
THEY WERE PRETTY STRONG.
PERFECT TIMING. WOULD YOU BANDAGE HIM UP FOR ME, AKO?
EH!? ME?
JUST DO IT!
HE'S OUR BIGGEST EARNER!
Y-YES, MA'AM!

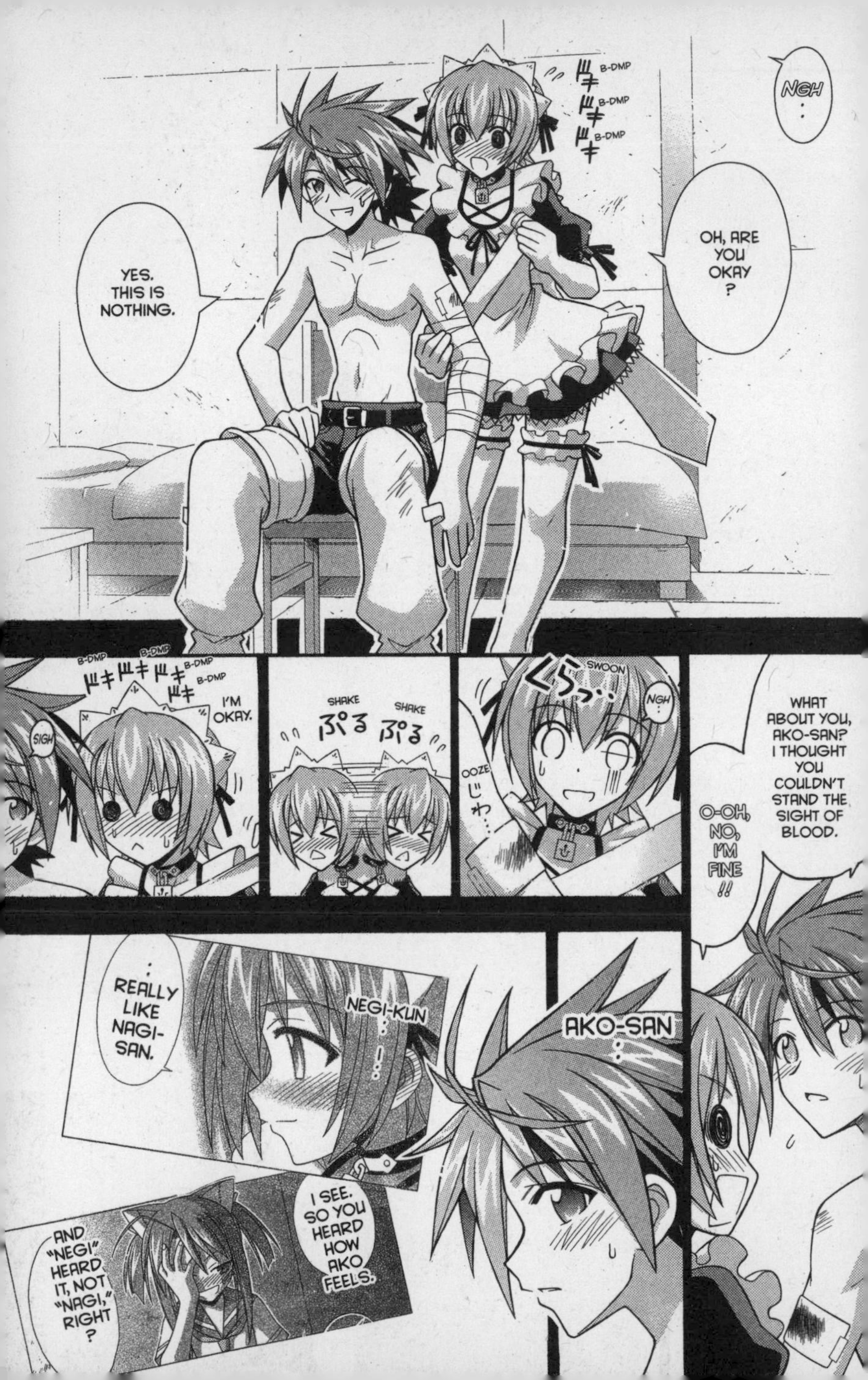
NGH
:
OH, ARE YOU OKAY?
ドキ B-DMP
ドキ B-DMP
ドキ B-DMP
YES. THIS IS NOTHING.
WHAT ABOUT YOU, AKO-SAN? I THOUGHT YOU COULDN'T STAND THE SIGHT OF BLOOD.
O-OH, NO, I'M FINE!!
くらっ SWOON
NGH
:
じわ OOZE
ぷる SHAKE
ぷる SHAKE
ドキドキドキドキ B-DMP B-DMP B-DMP B-DMP
I'M OKAY.
SIGH
AKO-SAN
:
NEGI-KUN
:!
:
REALLY LIKE NAGI-SAN.
I SEE. SO YOU HEARD HOW AKO FEELS.
AND "NEGI" HEARD IT, NOT "NAGI," RIGHT?

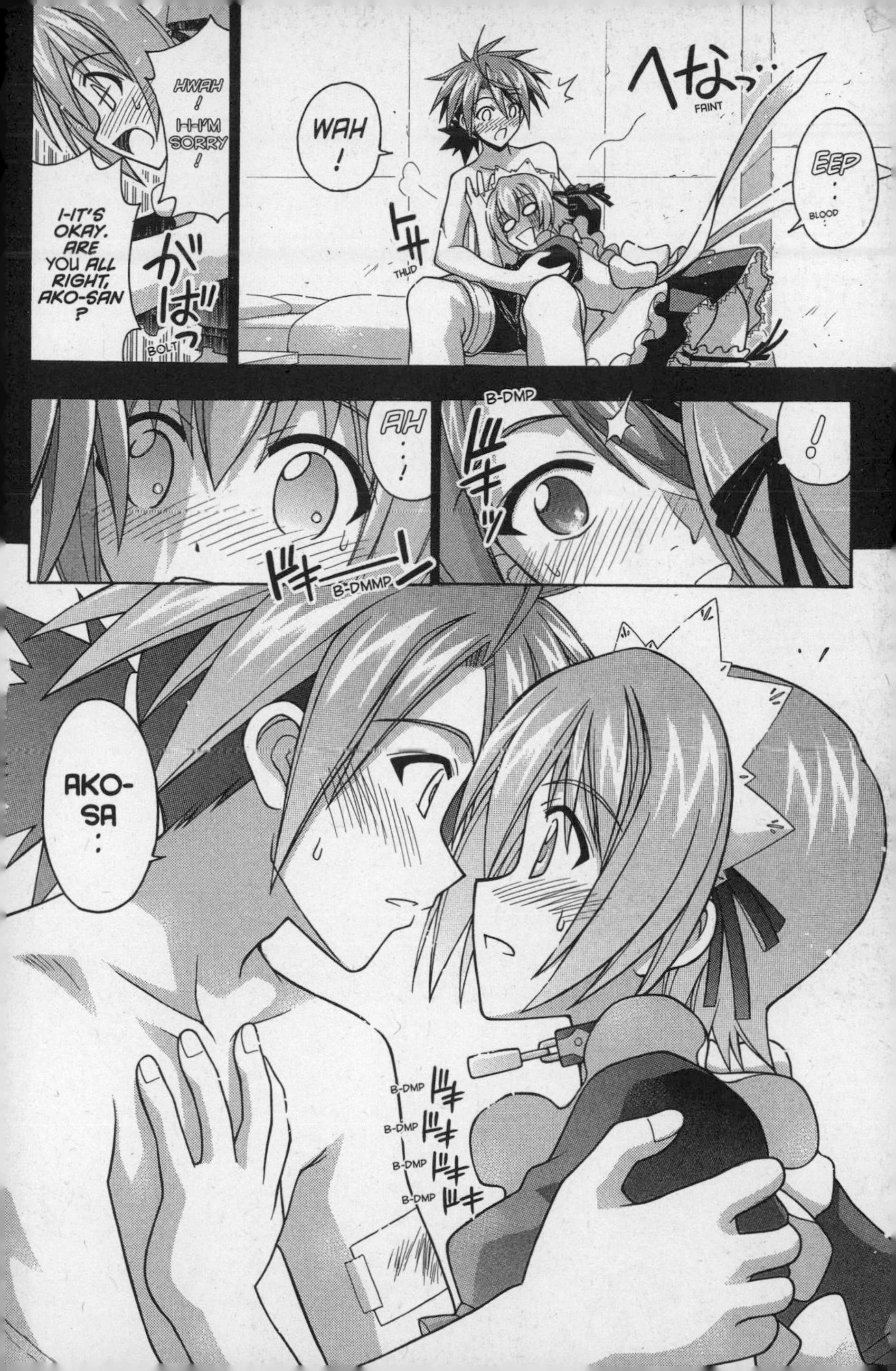

へなっ
FAINT
EEP... BLOOD...
WAH!
トサ
THUD
HWAH! I-I-I'M SORRY!
I-IT'S OKAY. ARE YOU ALL RIGHT, AKO-SAN?
がばっ
BOLT
!
ドキッ
B-DMP
AH...
ドキーーン
B-DMMP
AKO-SA...
ドキ
B-DMP
ドキ
B-DMP
ドキ
B-DMP
ドキ
B-DMP

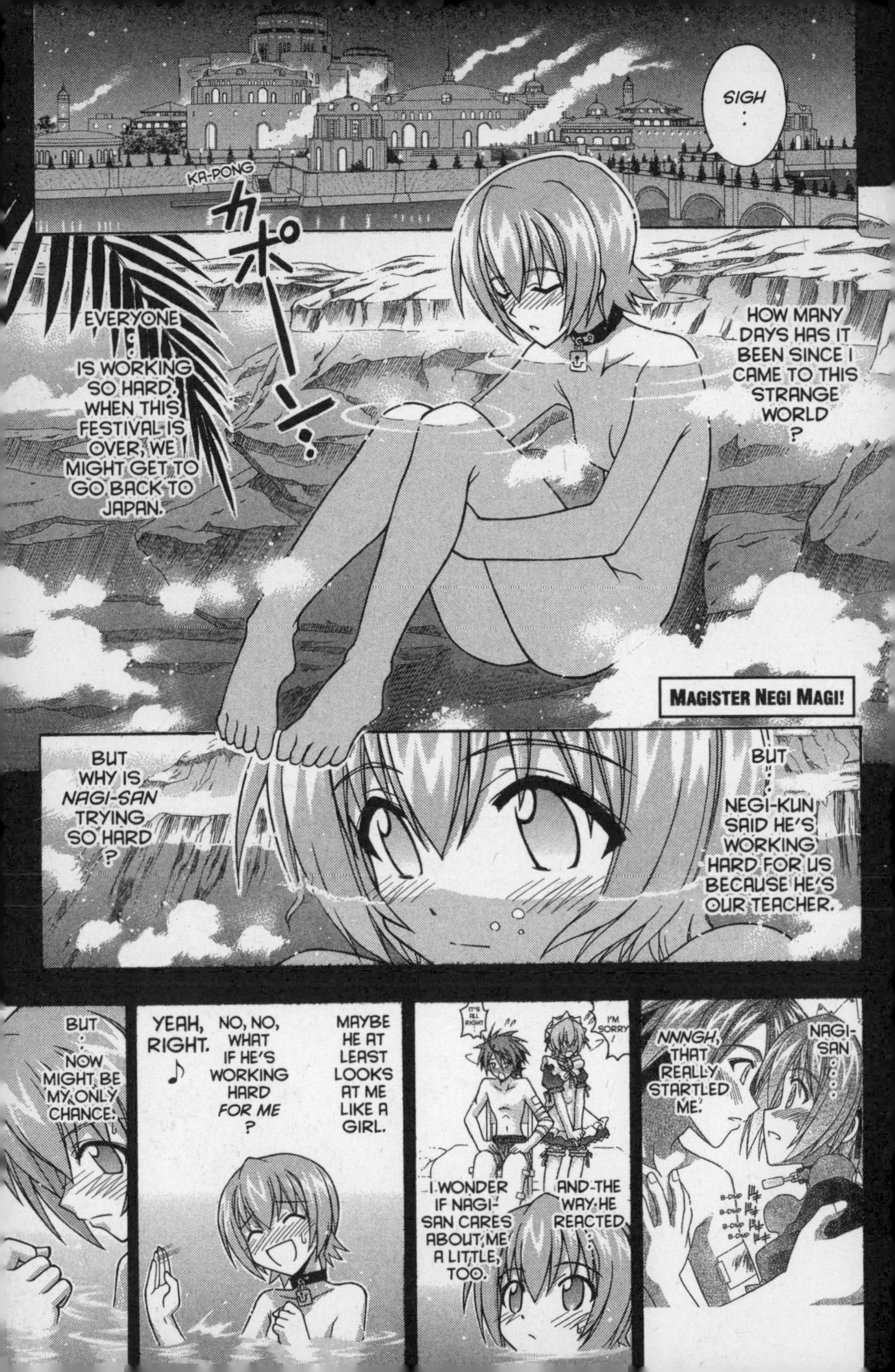
SIGH . . .
KA-PONG
カポーン
HOW MANY DAYS HAS IT BEEN SINCE I CAME TO THIS STRANGE WORLD?
EVERYONE . . . IS WORKING SO HARD. WHEN THIS FESTIVAL IS OVER, WE MIGHT GET TO GO BACK TO JAPAN.
MAGISTER NEGI MAGI!
BUT . . . NEGI-KUN SAID HE'S WORKING HARD FOR US BECAUSE HE'S OUR TEACHER.
BUT WHY IS *NAGI-SAN* TRYING SO HARD?
NAGI-SAN . . .
NNNGH, THAT REALLY STARTLED ME.
B-DMP
B-DMP
B-DMP
B-DMP
I'M SORRY!
IT'S ALL RIGHT
AND THE WAY HE REACTED . . .
I WONDER IF NAGI-SAN CARES ABOUT ME A LITTLE, TOO.
MAYBE HE AT LEAST LOOKS AT ME LIKE A GIRL.
NO, NO, WHAT IF HE'S WORKING HARD *FOR ME*?
YEAH, RIGHT. ♪
BUT . . . NOW MIGHT BE MY ONLY CHANCE.

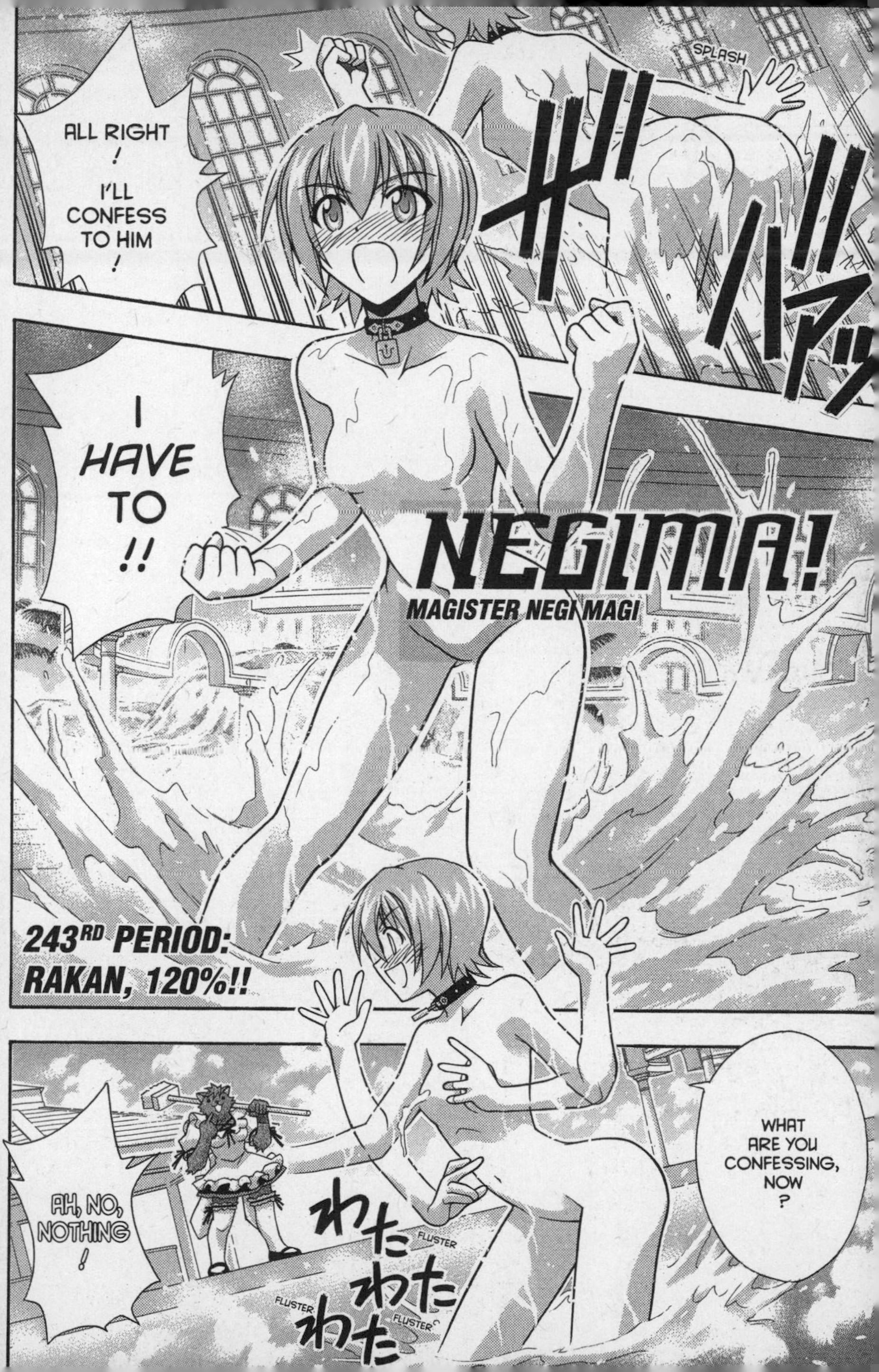
ザバァッ
SPLASH
ALL RIGHT! I'LL CONFESS TO HIM!
I HAVE TO!!
NEGIMA!
MAGISTER NEGI MAGI
243RD PERIOD: RAKAN, 120%!!
WHAT ARE YOU CONFESSING, NOW?
AH, NO, NOTHING!
わた
FLUSTER
わた
FLUSTER
わた
FLUSTER

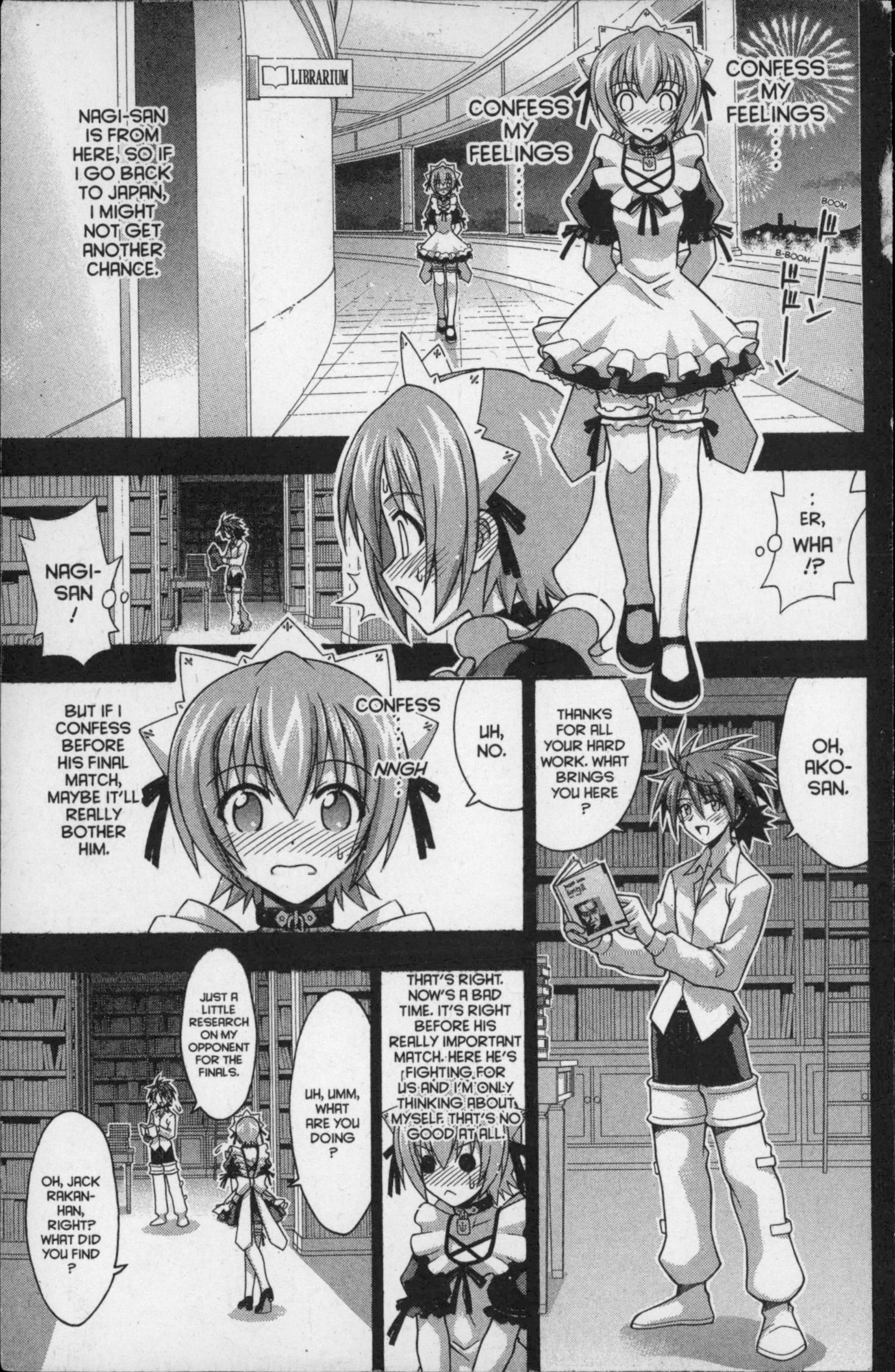
CONFESS MY FEELINGS......
BOOM
B-BOOM
CONFESS MY FEELINGS......
LIBRARIUM
NAGI-SAN IS FROM HERE, SO IF I GO BACK TO JAPAN, I MIGHT NOT GET ANOTHER CHANCE.
ER, WHA!?
NAGI-SAN!
OH, AKO-SAN.
THANKS FOR ALL YOUR HARD WORK. WHAT BRINGS YOU HERE?
UH, NO.
CONFESS
NNGH
BUT IF I CONFESS BEFORE HIS FINAL MATCH, MAYBE IT'LL REALLY BOTHER HIM.
THAT'S RIGHT. NOW'S A BAD TIME. IT'S RIGHT BEFORE HIS REALLY IMPORTANT MATCH. HERE HE'S FIGHTING FOR US AND I'M ONLY THINKING ABOUT MYSELF. THAT'S NO GOOD AT ALL.
UH, UMM, WHAT ARE YOU DOING?
JUST A LITTLE RESEARCH ON MY OPPONENT FOR THE FINALS.
OH, JACK RAKAN-HAN, RIGHT? WHAT DID YOU FIND?

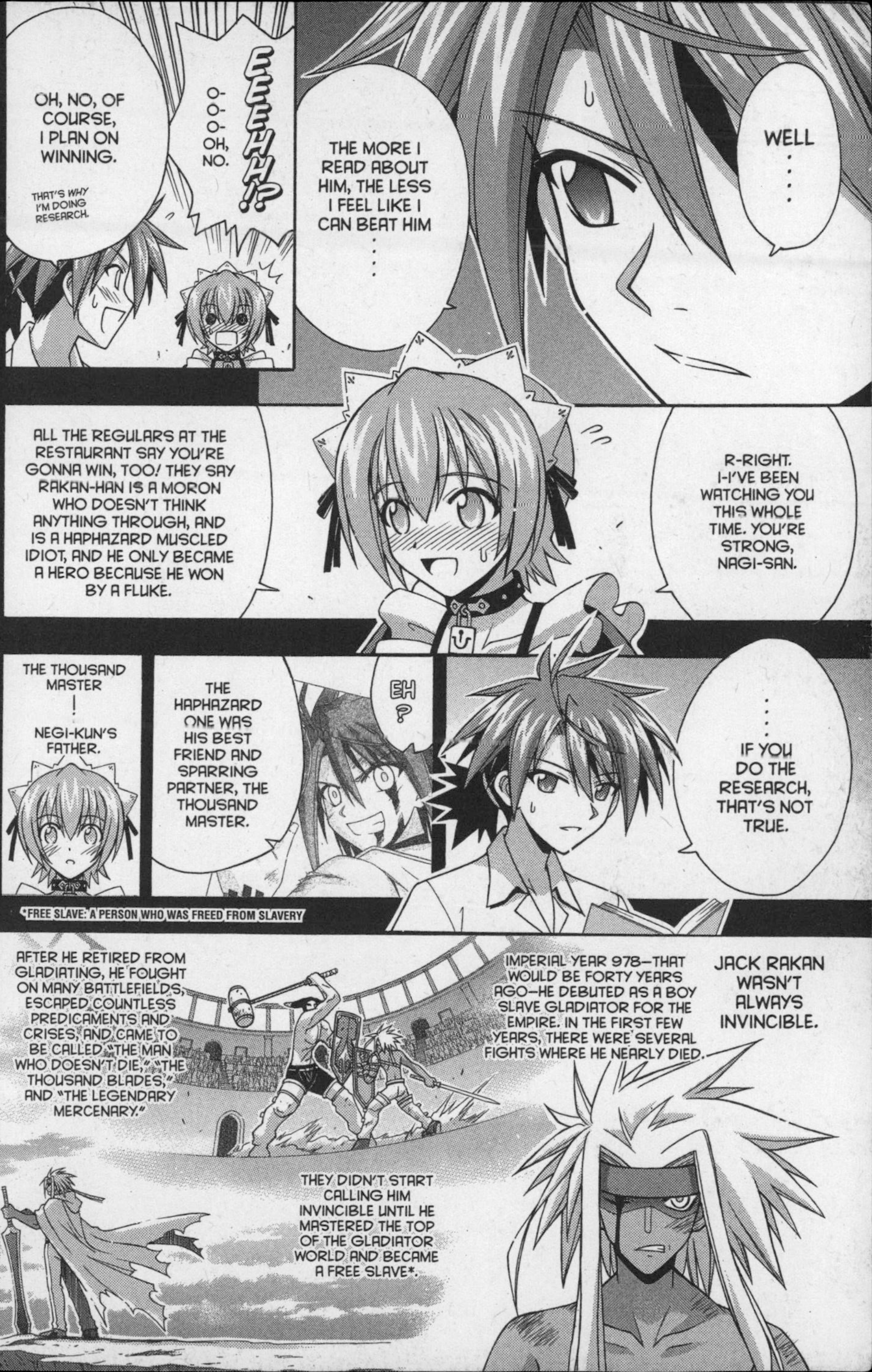
WELL . . . .
THE MORE I READ ABOUT HIM, THE LESS I FEEL LIKE I CAN BEAT HIM . . .
EEEHH!?
O-O-O-OH, NO.
OH, NO, OF COURSE, I PLAN ON WINNING.
THAT'S WHY I'M DOING RESEARCH.
R-RIGHT. I-I'VE BEEN WATCHING YOU THIS WHOLE TIME. YOU'RE STRONG, NAGI-SAN.
ALL THE REGULARS AT THE RESTAURANT SAY YOU'RE GONNA WIN, TOO! THEY SAY RAKAN-HAN IS A MORON WHO DOESN'T THINK ANYTHING THROUGH, AND IS A HAPHAZARD MUSCLED IDIOT, AND HE ONLY BECAME A HERO BECAUSE HE WON BY A FLUKE.
. . . IF YOU DO THE RESEARCH, THAT'S NOT TRUE.
EH?
THE HAPHAZARD ONE WAS HIS BEST FRIEND AND SPARRING PARTNER, THE THOUSAND MASTER.
THE THOUSAND MASTER ! NEGI-KUN'S FATHER.
JACK RAKAN WASN'T ALWAYS INVINCIBLE.
IMPERIAL YEAR 978—THAT WOULD BE FORTY YEARS AGO—HE DEBUTED AS A BOY SLAVE GLADIATOR FOR THE EMPIRE. IN THE FIRST FEW YEARS, THERE WERE SEVERAL FIGHTS WHERE HE NEARLY DIED.
AFTER HE RETIRED FROM GLADIATING, HE FOUGHT ON MANY BATTLEFIELDS, ESCAPED COUNTLESS PREDICAMENTS AND CRISES, AND CAME TO BE CALLED "THE MAN WHO DOESN'T DIE," "THE THOUSAND BLADES," AND "THE LEGENDARY MERCENARY."
THEY DIDN'T START CALLING HIM INVINCIBLE UNTIL HE MASTERED THE TOP OF THE GLADIATOR WORLD AND BECAME A FREE SLAVE*.
*FREE SLAVE: A PERSON WHO WAS FREED FROM SLAVERY

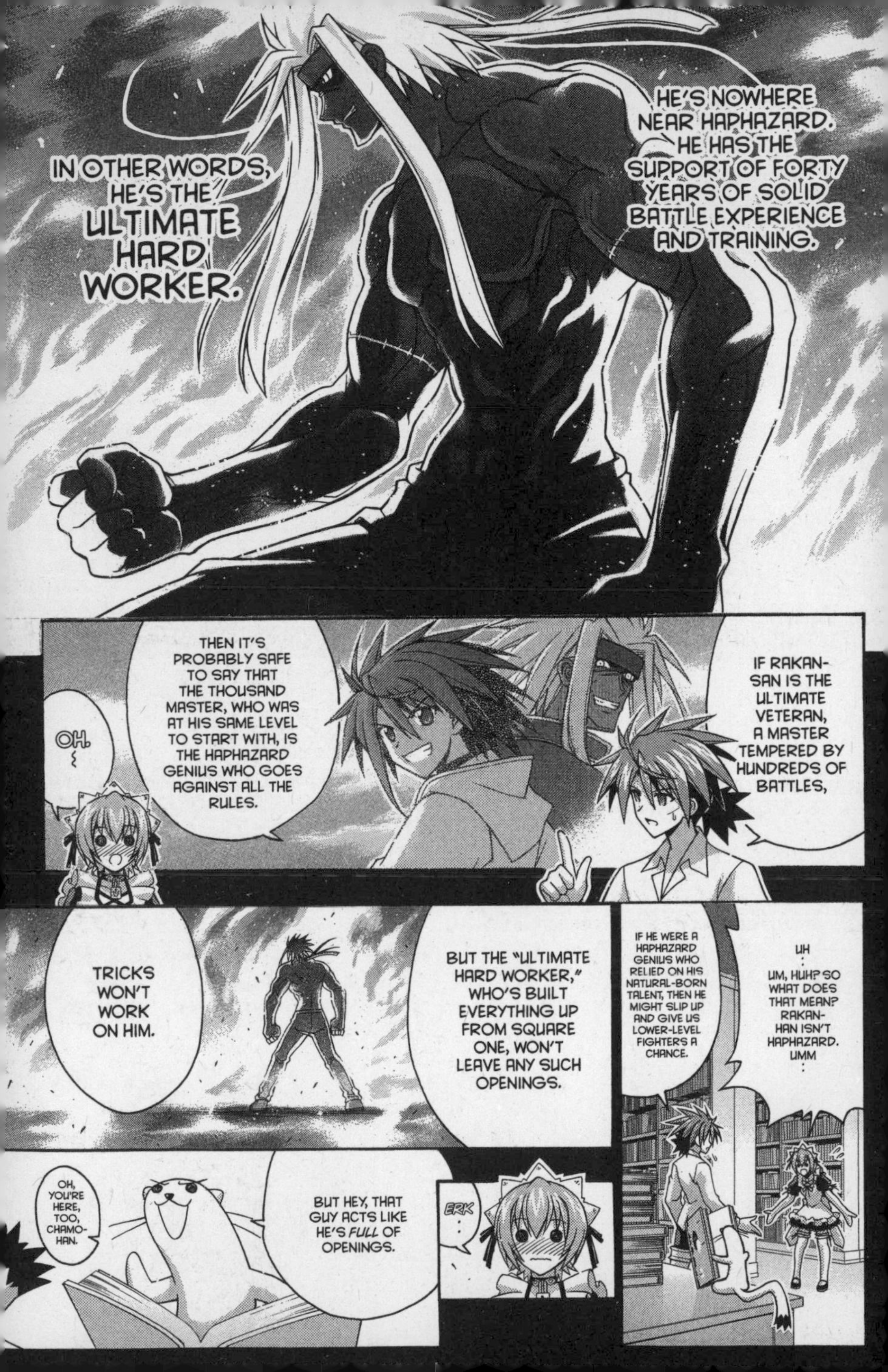

HE'S NOWHERE NEAR HAPHAZARD. HE HAS THE SUPPORT OF FORTY YEARS OF SOLID BATTLE EXPERIENCE AND TRAINING.
IN OTHER WORDS, HE'S THE ULTIMATE HARD WORKER.
IF RAKAN-SAN IS THE ULTIMATE VETERAN, A MASTER TEMPERED BY HUNDREDS OF BATTLES,
THEN IT'S PROBABLY SAFE TO SAY THAT THE THOUSAND MASTER, WHO WAS AT HIS SAME LEVEL TO START WITH, IS THE HAPHAZARD GENIUS WHO GOES AGAINST ALL THE RULES.
OH.
UH ... UM, HUH? SO WHAT DOES THAT MEAN? RAKAN-HAN ISN'T HAPHAZARD. UMM ...
IF HE WERE A HAPHAZARD GENIUS WHO RELIED ON HIS NATURAL-BORN TALENT, THEN HE MIGHT SLIP UP AND GIVE US LOWER-LEVEL FIGHTERS A CHANCE.
BUT THE "ULTIMATE HARD WORKER," WHO'S BUILT EVERYTHING UP FROM SQUARE ONE, WON'T LEAVE ANY SUCH OPENINGS.
TRICKS WON'T WORK ON HIM.
ERK ...
BUT HEY, THAT GUY ACTS LIKE HE'S *FULL* OF OPENINGS.
OH, YOU'RE HERE, TOO, CHAMO-HAN.

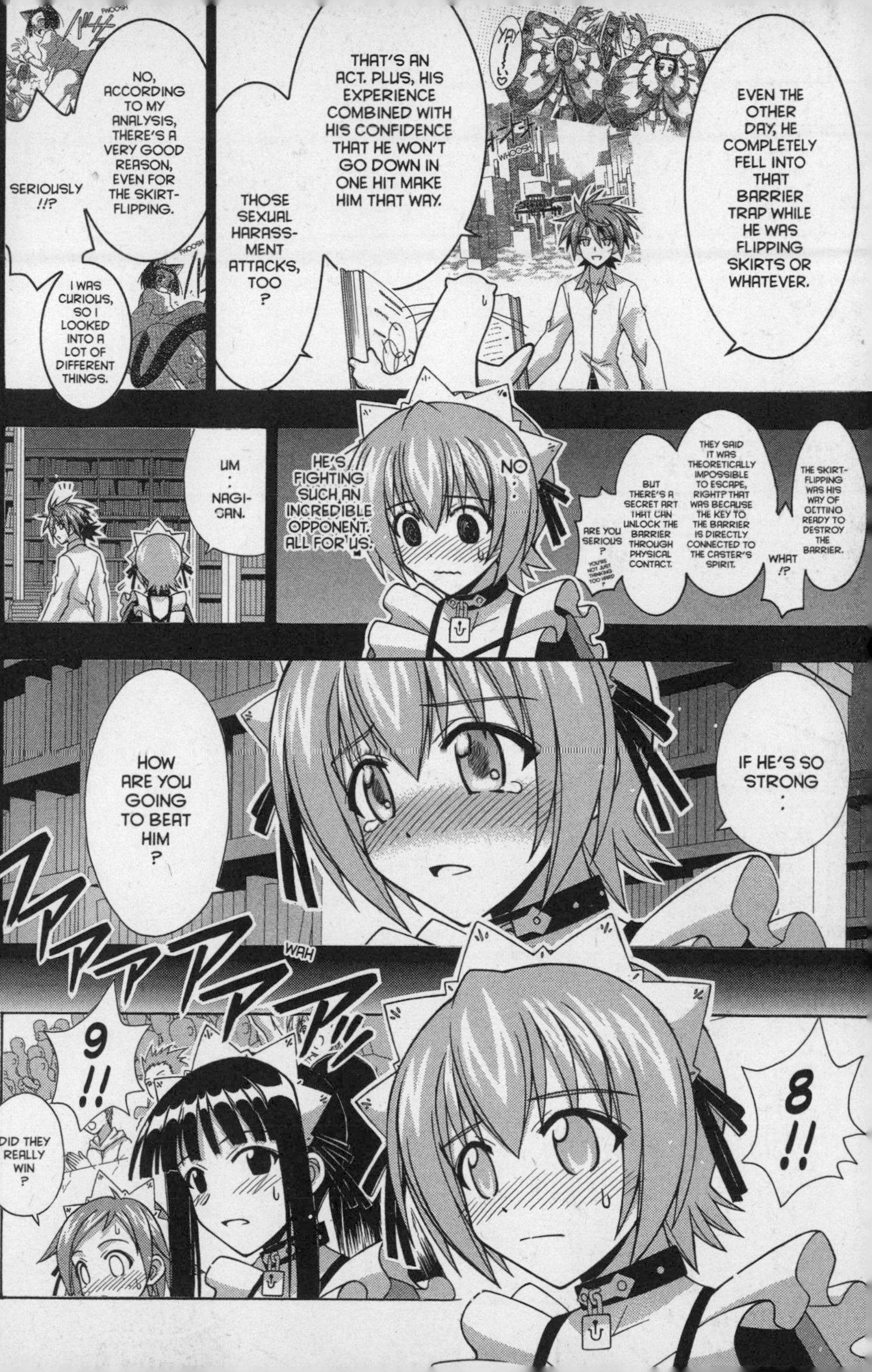
YAY!~♡
WHOOSH
EVEN THE OTHER DAY, HE COMPLETELY FELL INTO THAT BARRIER TRAP WHILE HE WAS FLIPPING SKIRTS OR WHATEVER.
THOSE SEXUAL HARASSMENT ATTACKS, TOO?
THAT'S AN ACT. PLUS, HIS EXPERIENCE COMBINED WITH HIS CONFIDENCE THAT HE WON'T GO DOWN IN ONE HIT MAKE HIM THAT WAY.
PWOOSH
NO, ACCORDING TO MY ANALYSIS, THERE'S A VERY GOOD REASON, EVEN FOR THE SKIRT-FLIPPING.
SERIOUSLY!!?
PWOOSH
I WAS CURIOUS, SO I LOOKED INTO A LOT OF DIFFERENT THINGS.
THE SKIRT-FLIPPING WAS HIS WAY OF GETTING READY TO DESTROY THE BARRIER.
WHAT!?
THEY SAID IT WAS THEORETICALLY IMPOSSIBLE TO ESCAPE, RIGHT? THAT WAS BECAUSE THE KEY TO THE BARRIER IS DIRECTLY CONNECTED TO THE CASTER'S SPIRIT.
BUT THERE'S A SECRET ART THAT CAN UNLOCK THE BARRIER THROUGH PHYSICAL CONTACT.
ARE YOU SERIOUS?
YOU'RE NOT JUST THINKING TOO HARD?
NO...
HE'S FIGHTING SUCH AN INCREDIBLE OPPONENT. ALL FOR US.
UM... NAGI-SAN.
IF HE'S SO STRONG...
HOW ARE YOU GOING TO BEAT HIM?
WAH
8!!
9!!
DID THEY REALLY WIN?

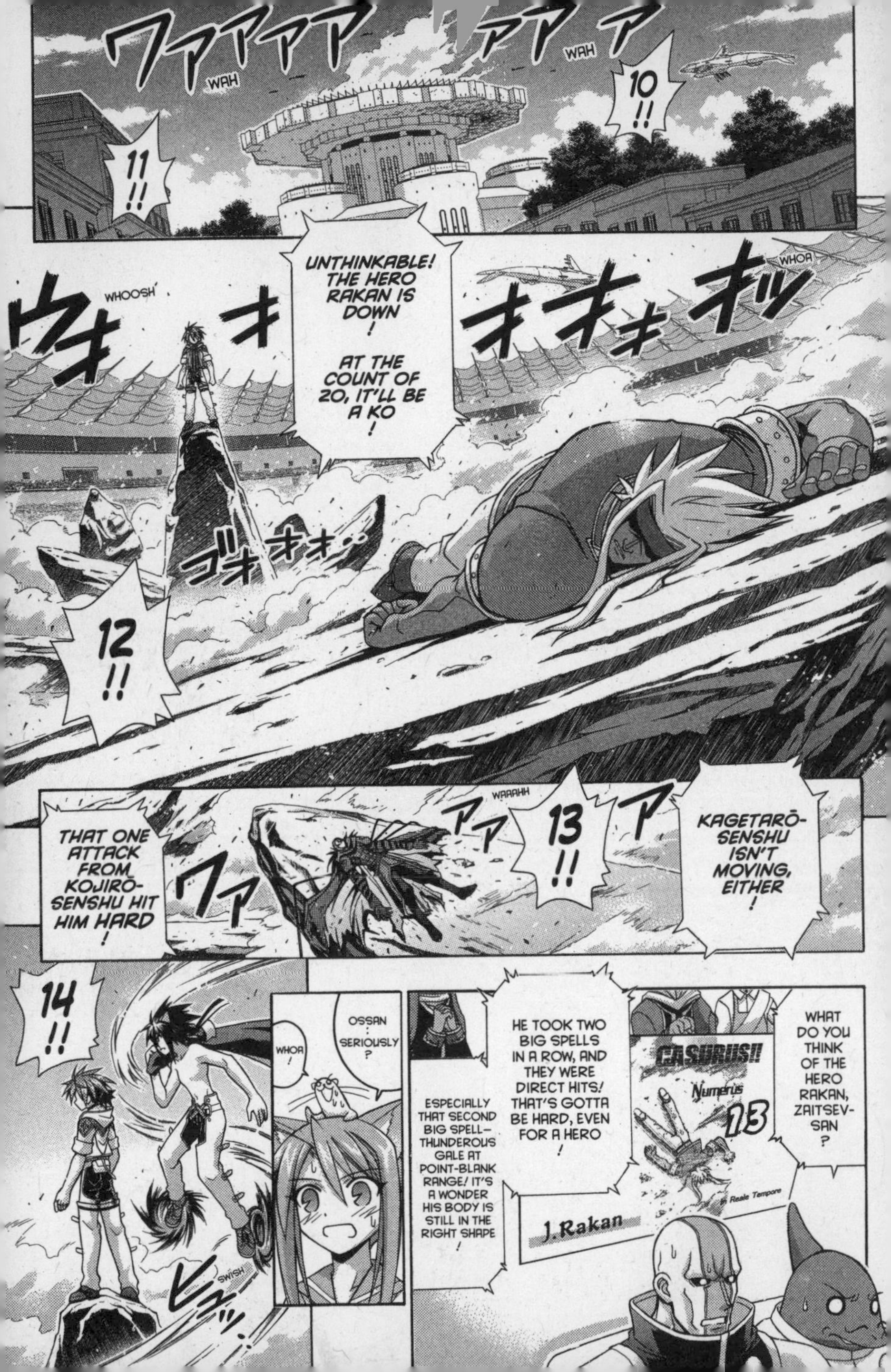
ワァァァァ ァア ア
WAH
WAH
10 !!
11 !!
UNTHINKABLE! THE HERO RAKAN IS DOWN! AT THE COUNT OF 20, IT'LL BE A KO!
ウォ オ オォォオッ
WHOOSH
WHOA
ゴオオオ
12 !!
KAGETARŌ-SENSHU ISN'T MOVING, EITHER!
13 !!
ワァ アァ ア
WAAAHH
THAT ONE ATTACK FROM KOJIRŌ-SENSHU HIT HIM HARD!
WHAT DO YOU THINK OF THE HERO RAKAN, ZAITSEV-SAN?
CASURUS!!
Numerus
13
Reale Tempore
J. Rakan
HE TOOK TWO BIG SPELLS IN A ROW, AND THEY WERE DIRECT HITS! THAT'S GOTTA BE HARD, EVEN FOR A HERO!
ESPECIALLY THAT SECOND BIG SPELL—THUNDEROUS GALE AT POINT-BLANK RANGE! IT'S A WONDER HIS BODY IS STILL IN THE RIGHT SHAPE!
OSSAN: SERIOUSLY?
WHOA!
14 !!
ヒュッ
SWISH

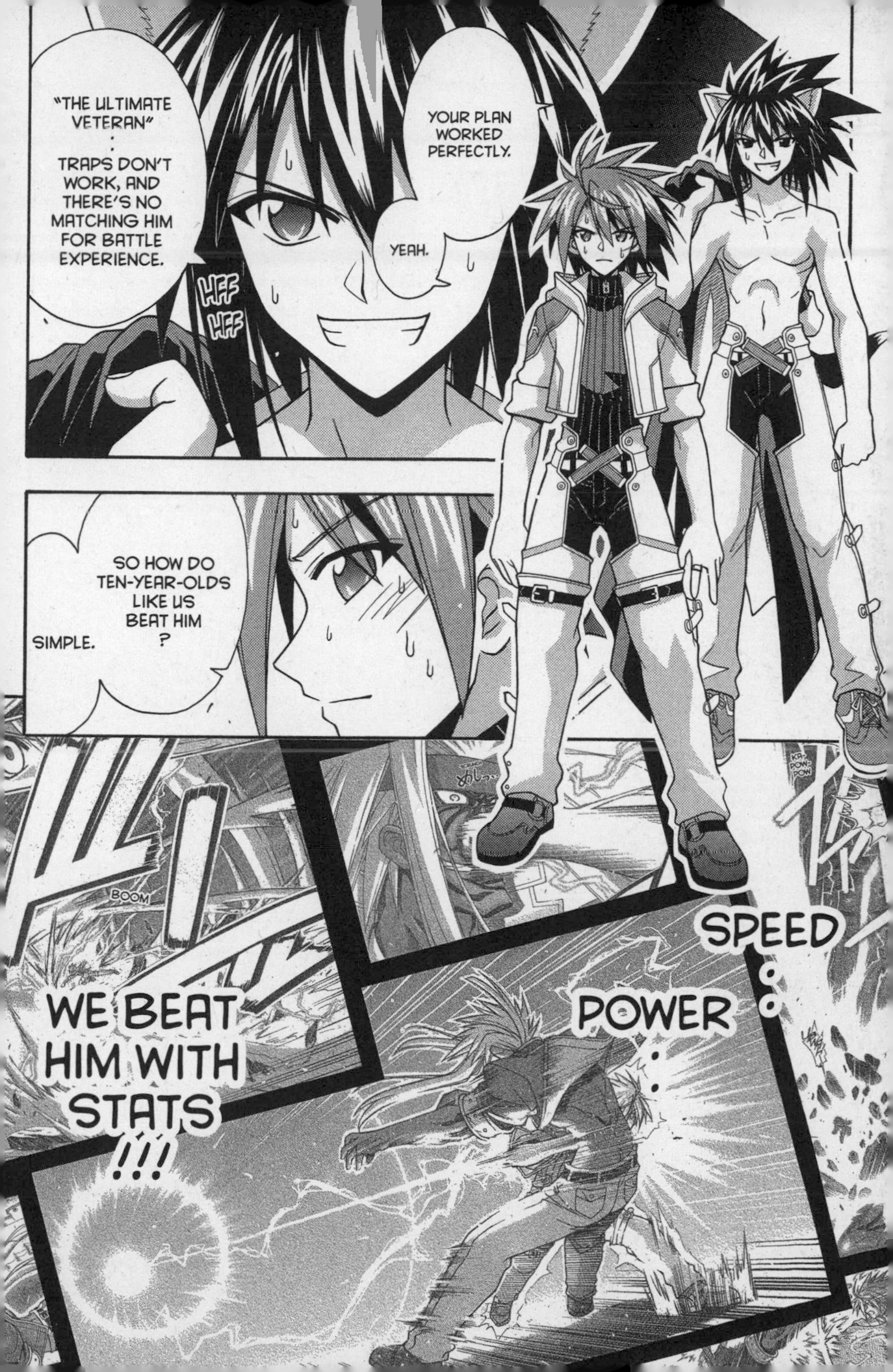
YOUR PLAN WORKED PERFECTLY.
YEAH.
"THE ULTIMATE VETERAN" : TRAPS DON'T WORK, AND THERE'S NO MATCHING HIM FOR BATTLE EXPERIENCE.
HFF HFF
SO HOW DO TEN-YEAR-OLDS LIKE US BEAT HIM ?
SIMPLE.
KA-POW-POW
BOOM
SPEED :
POWER :
WE BEAT HIM WITH STATS !!!

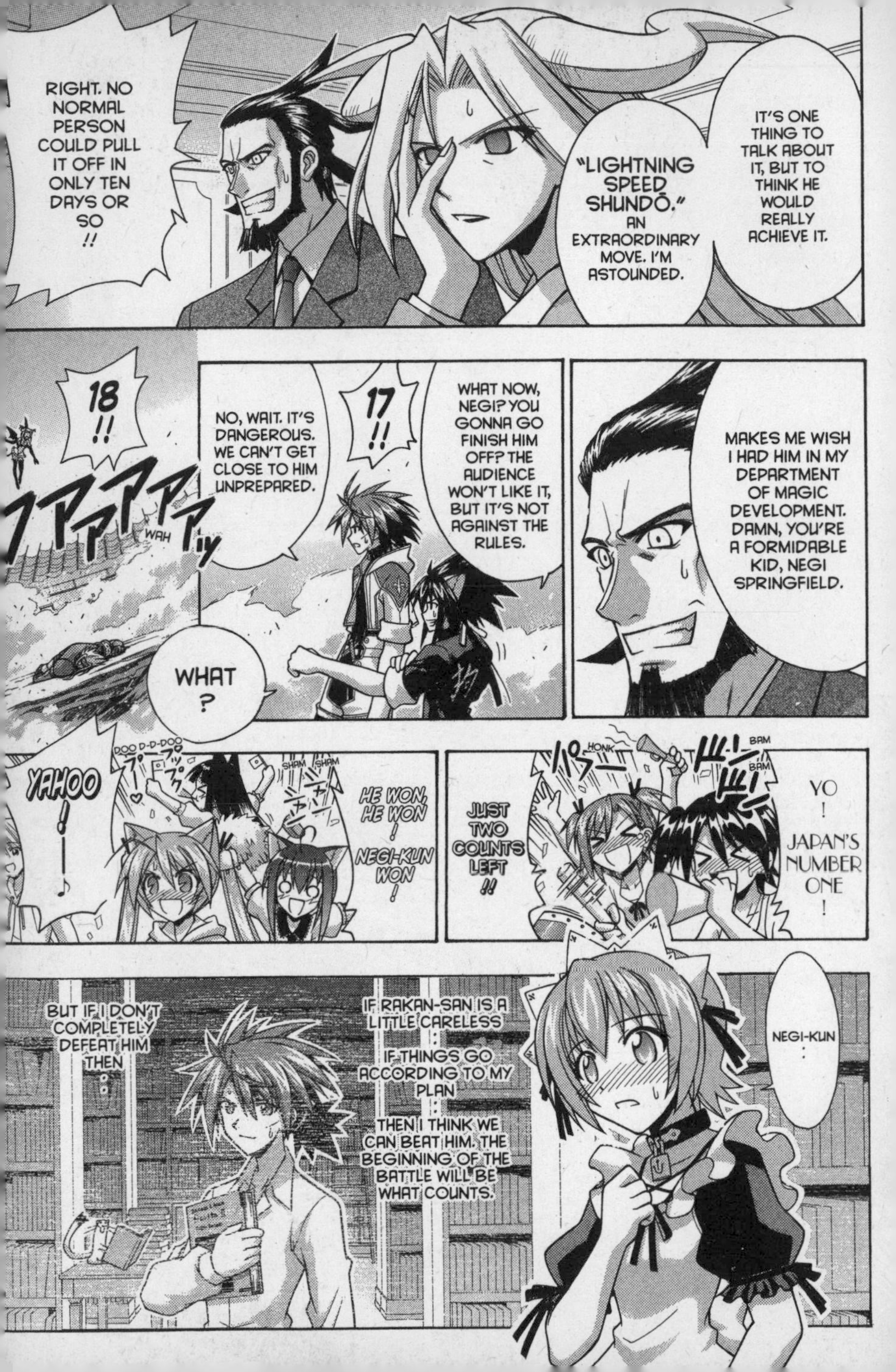
IT'S ONE THING TO TALK ABOUT IT, BUT TO THINK HE WOULD REALLY ACHIEVE IT.
"LIGHTNING SPEED SHUNDŌ." AN EXTRAORDINARY MOVE. I'M ASTOUNDED.
RIGHT. NO NORMAL PERSON COULD PULL IT OFF IN ONLY TEN DAYS OR SO !!
MAKES ME WISH I HAD HIM IN MY DEPARTMENT OF MAGIC DEVELOPMENT. DAMN, YOU'RE A FORMIDABLE KID, NEGI SPRINGFIELD.
WHAT NOW, NEGI? YOU GONNA GO FINISH HIM OFF? THE AUDIENCE WON'T LIKE IT, BUT IT'S NOT AGAINST THE RULES.
17 !!
NO, WAIT. IT'S DANGEROUS. WE CAN'T GET CLOSE TO HIM UNPREPARED.
WHAT ?
18 !!
WAH
YO ! JAPAN'S NUMBER ONE !
BAM
BAM
HONK
JUST TWO COUNTS LEFT !!
HE WON, HE WON ! NEGI-KUN WON !
SHAM
SHAM
DOO D-D-DOO
YAHOO !
NEGI-KUN . . .
IF RAKAN-SAN IS A LITTLE CARELESS . . .
IF THINGS GO ACCORDING TO MY PLAN . . .
THEN I THINK WE CAN BEAT HIM. THE BEGINNING OF THE BATTLE WILL BE WHAT COUNTS.
BUT IF I DON'T COMPLETELY DEFEAT HIM THEN . . .

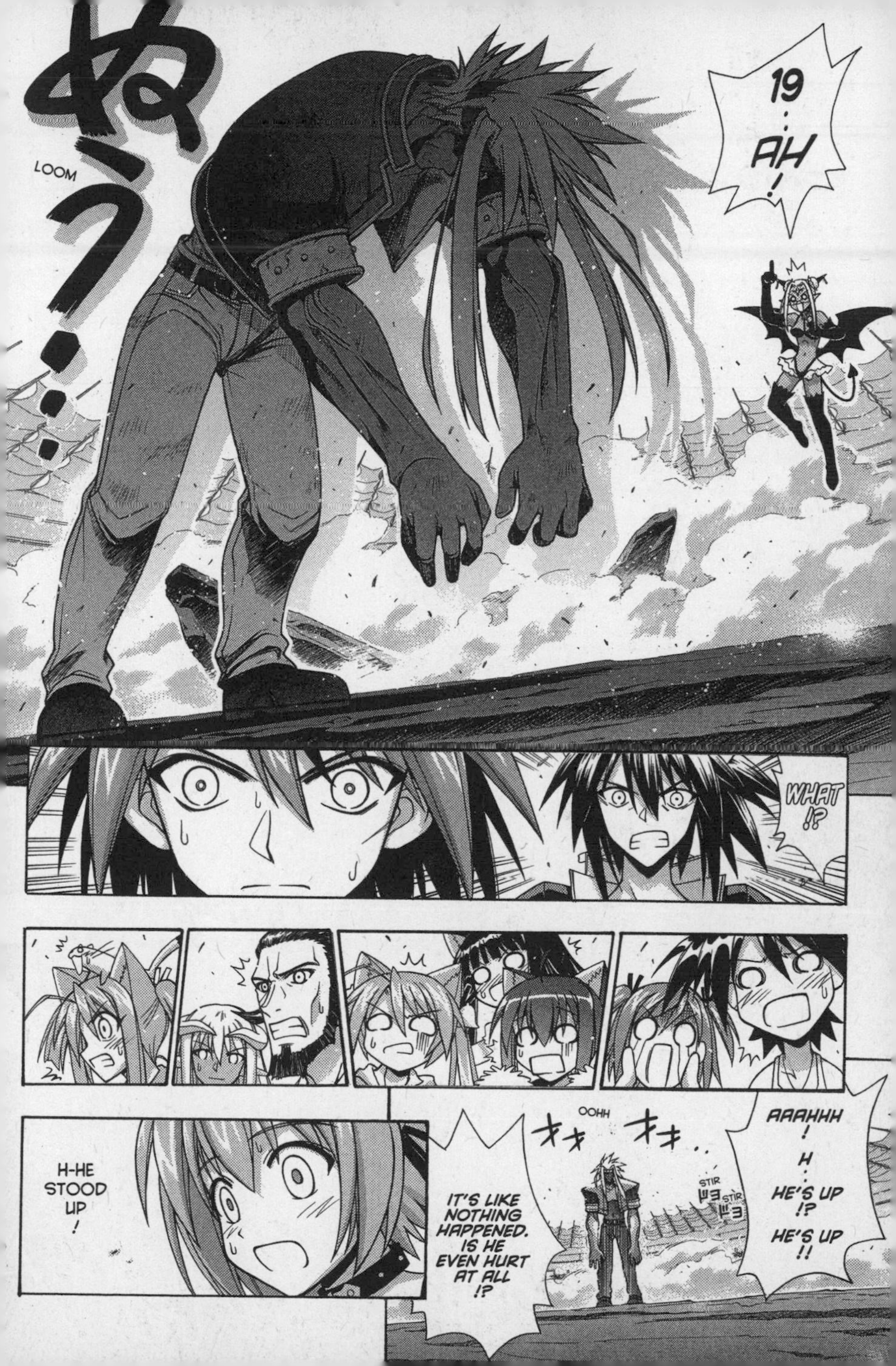
19 ... AH!
ぬう…
LOOM
WHAT!?
AAAHHH! H... HE'S UP!? HE'S UP!!
オォ オォ..
OOHH
ドヨ ドヨ
STIR STIR
IT'S LIKE NOTHING HAPPENED. IS HE EVEN HURT AT ALL!?
H-HE STOOD UP!

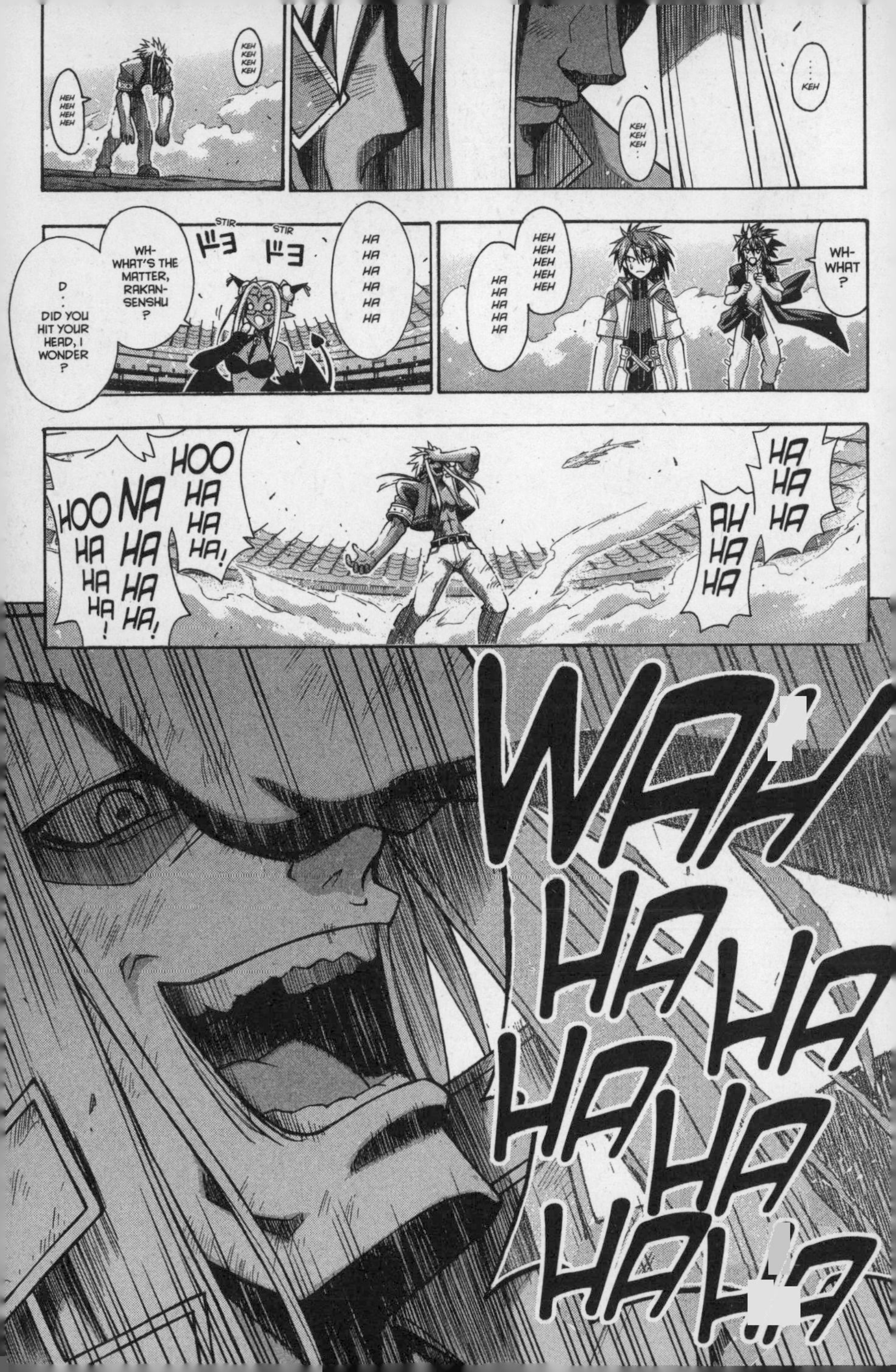
...KEH
KEH KEH KEH...
KEH KEH KEH KEH
HEH HEH HEH HEH
WH- WHAT?
HEH HEH HEH HEH HEH
HA HA HA HA HA
HA HA HA HA HA HA
STIR ドヨ
STIR ドヨ
WH- WHAT'S THE MATTER, RAKAN-SENSHU?
D... DID YOU HIT YOUR HEAD, I WONDER?
HA HA HA HA
AH HA HA HA
HOO HA HA HA!
NA HA HA HA HA!
HOO HA HA HA!
WAH HA HA HA HA HA HA HA

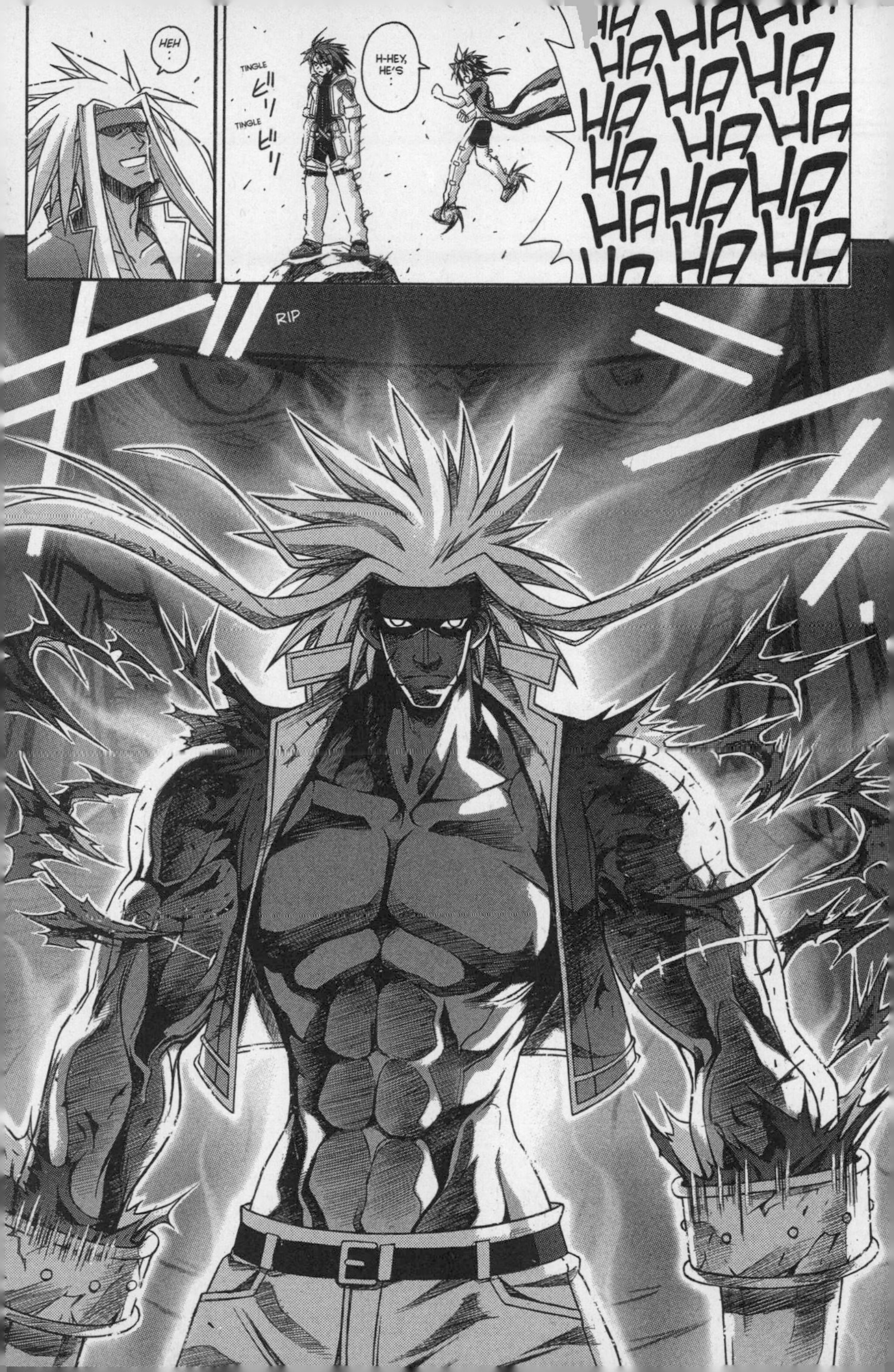
HA HAHA
HA HA HA
HA HA HA
HA HA HA
HA HA HA
HA HA HA
H-HEY, HE'S...
TINGLE
ビリ
TINGLE
ビリ
HEH...
RIP

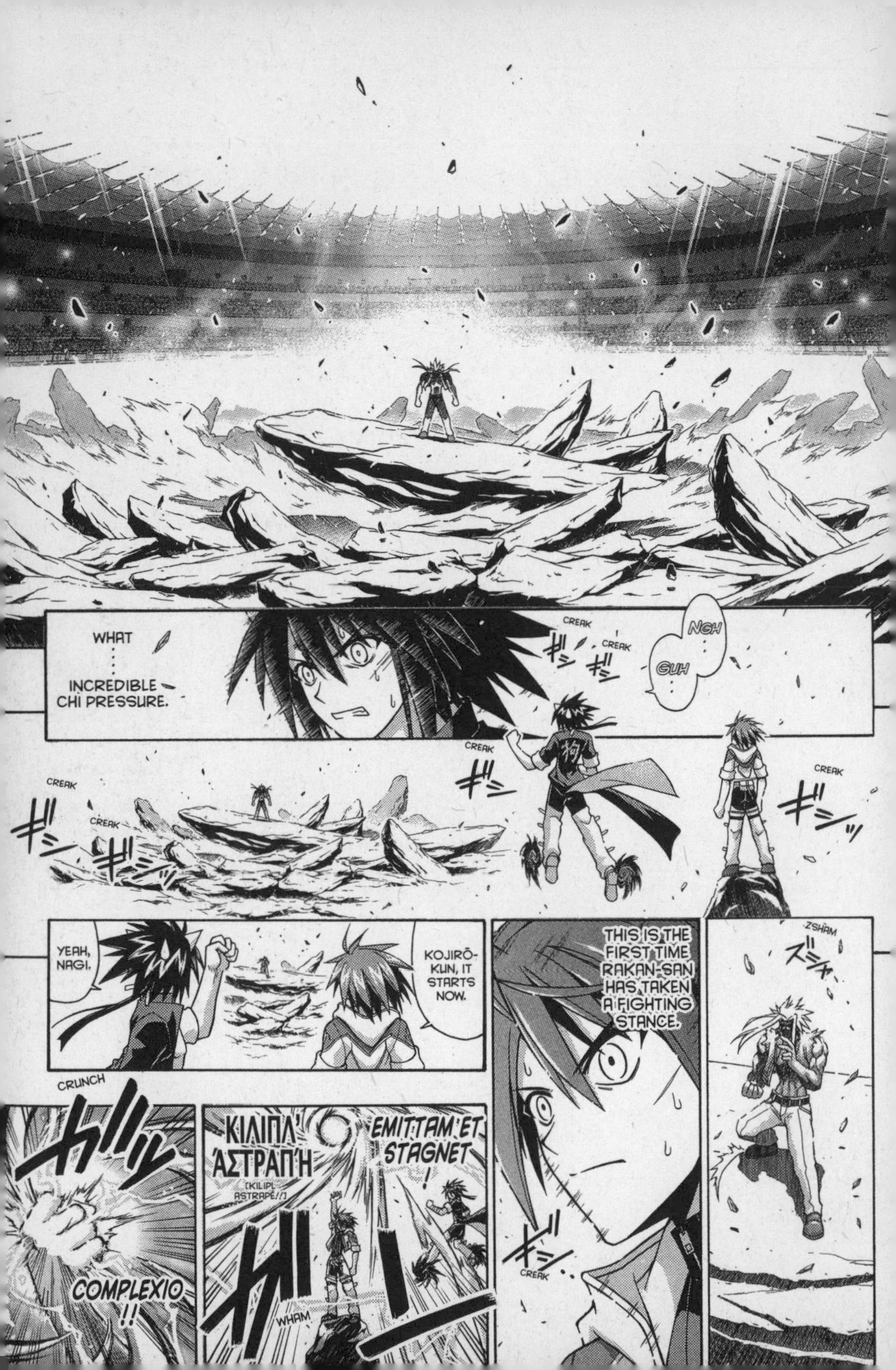
NGH... GUH...
CREAK
CREAK
WHAT... INCREDIBLE CHI PRESSURE.
CREAK
CREAK
CREAK
CREAK
Z'SHAM
THIS IS THE FIRST TIME RAKAN-SAN HAS TAKEN A FIGHTING STANCE.
CREAK
KOJIRŌ-KUN, IT STARTS NOW.
YEAH, NAGI.
EMITTAM ET STAGNET!
ΚΙΛΙΠΛ' ΆΣΤΡΑΠ'Η
[KILIPL ASTRAPĒ!!]
WHAM
CRUNCH
COMPLEXIO!!

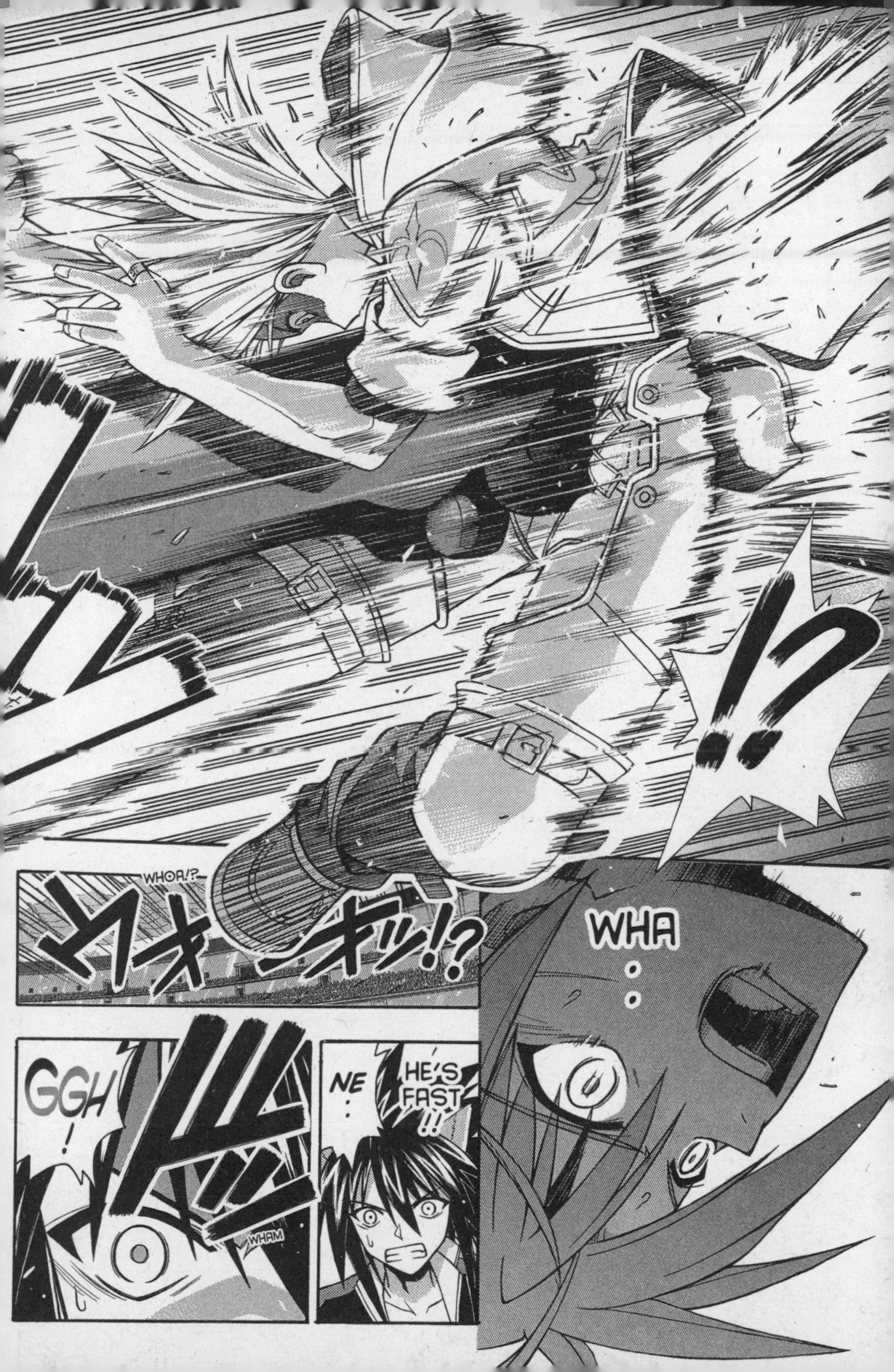

!?
WHA . . .
WHOA!?
NE . . .
HE'S FAST!!
GGH!
WHAM

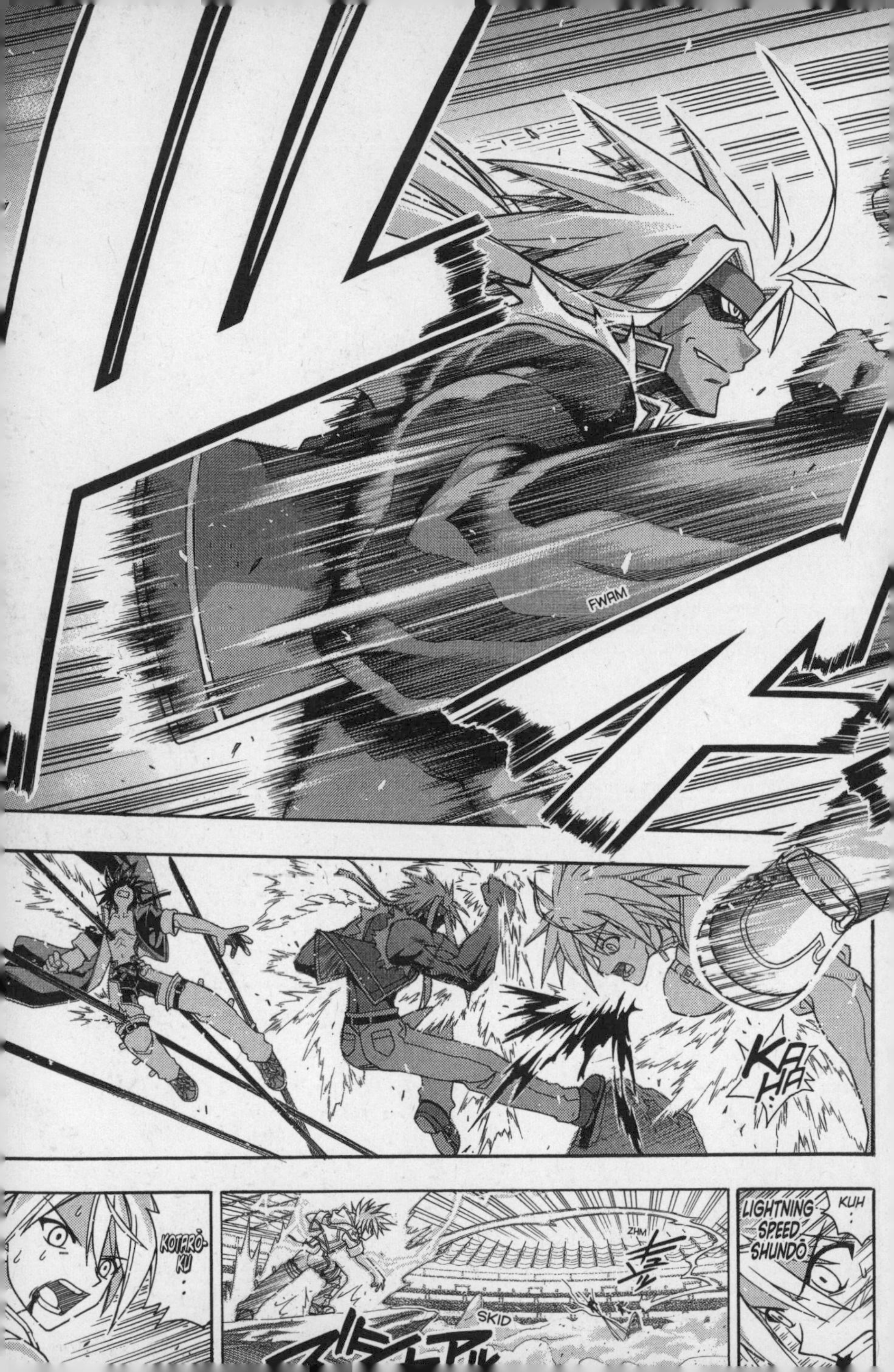
FWAM
KAHA
KUH
LIGHTNING SPEED SHUNDŌ
ZHM
SKID
KOTARŌ-KU...

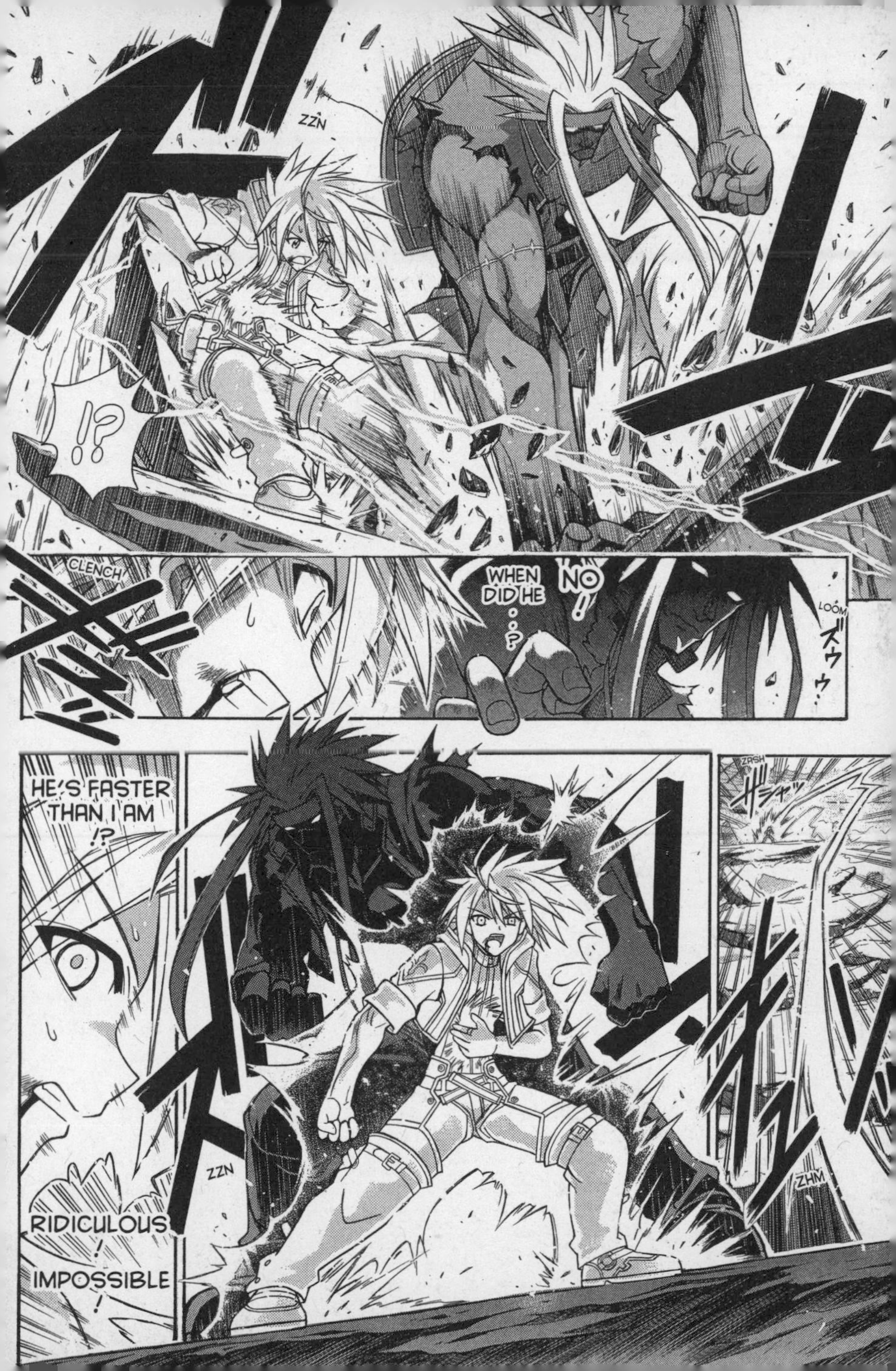
ZZN
!?
LOOM
ズウゥ…
NO!
WHEN DID HE...?
CLENCH
ZASH
ザシャッ
ZHM
HE'S FASTER THAN I AM!?
ZZN
RIDICULOUS!
IMPOSSIBLE!

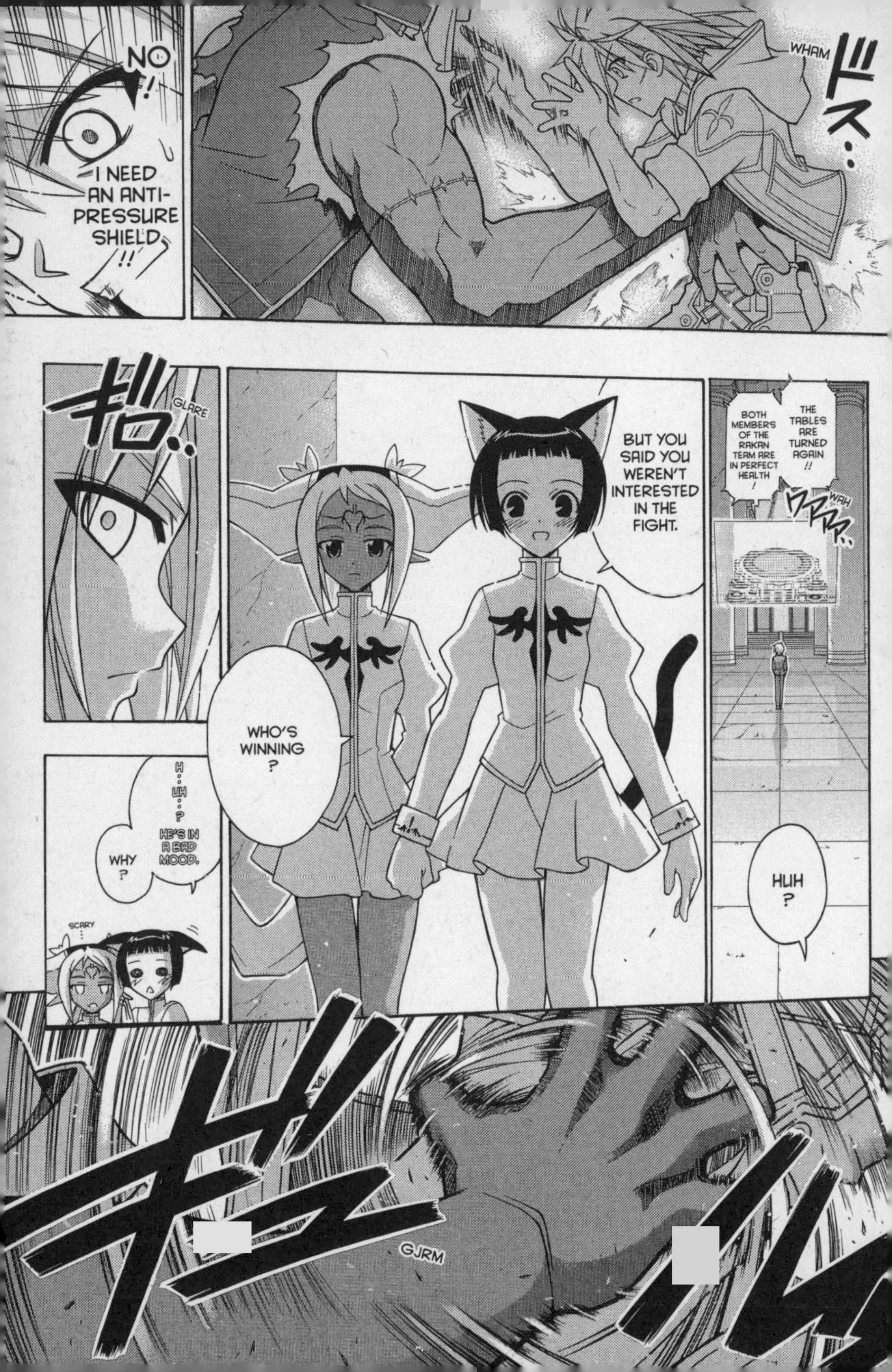

WHAM
ドス..
NO!
I NEED AN ANTI-PRESSURE SHIELD!!
THE TABLES ARE TURNED AGAIN!!
BOTH MEMBERS OF THE RAKAN TEAM ARE IN PERFECT HEALTH!
WAH
ワァァァ..
HUH?
BUT YOU SAID YOU WEREN'T INTERESTED IN THE FIGHT.
WHO'S WINNING?
GLARE
ギロ..
H.. UH..?
HE'S IN A BAD MOOD.
WHY?
SCARY...
GJRM

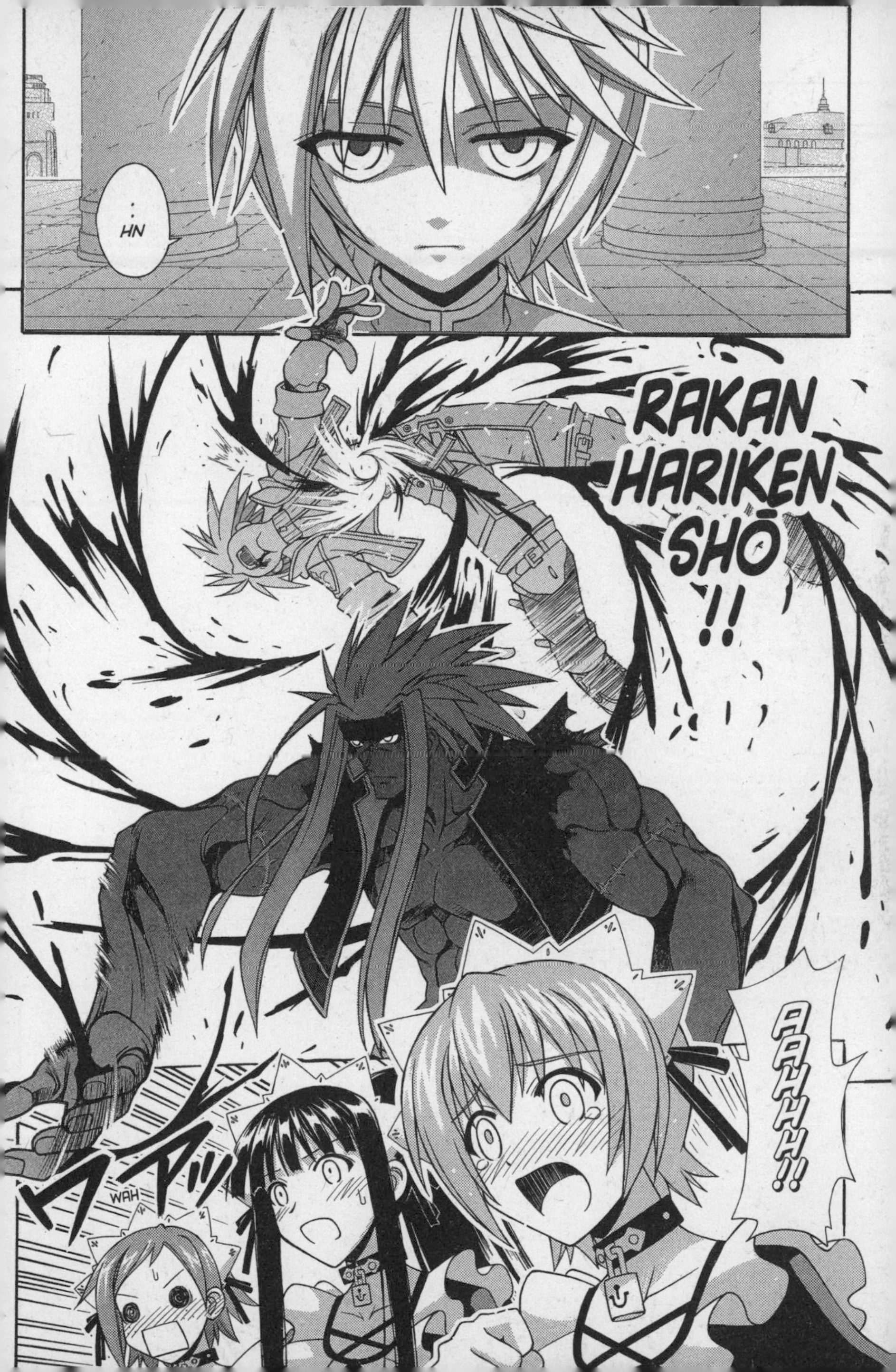

...HN
RAKAN HARIKEN SHŌ!!
AAHHH!!
WAH

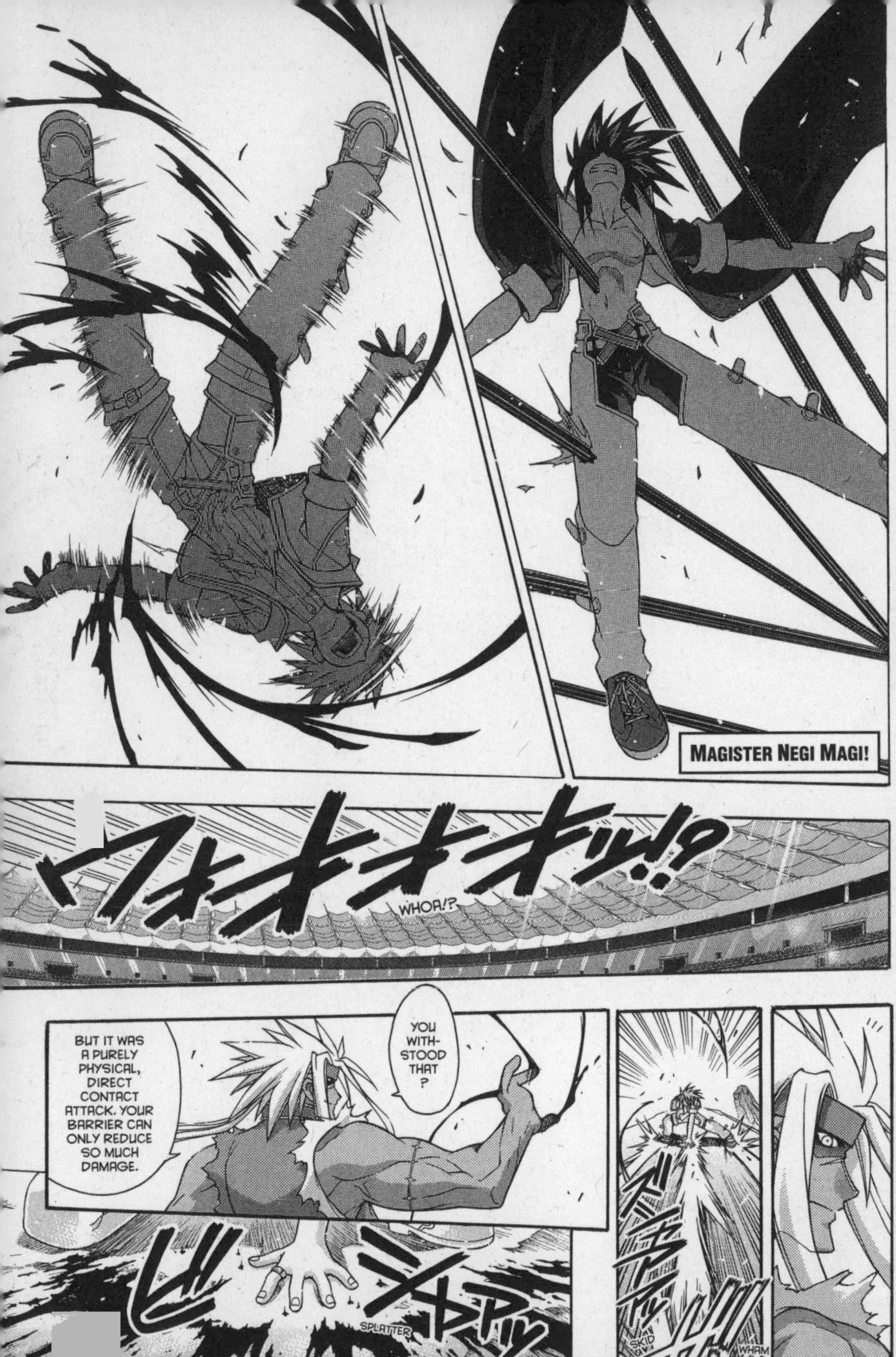
MAGISTER NEGI MAGI!
WHOA!?
WHAM
SKID
YOU WITH-STOOD THAT?
BUT IT WAS A PURELY PHYSICAL, DIRECT CONTACT ATTACK. YOUR BARRIER CAN ONLY REDUCE SO MUCH DAMAGE.
SPLATTER

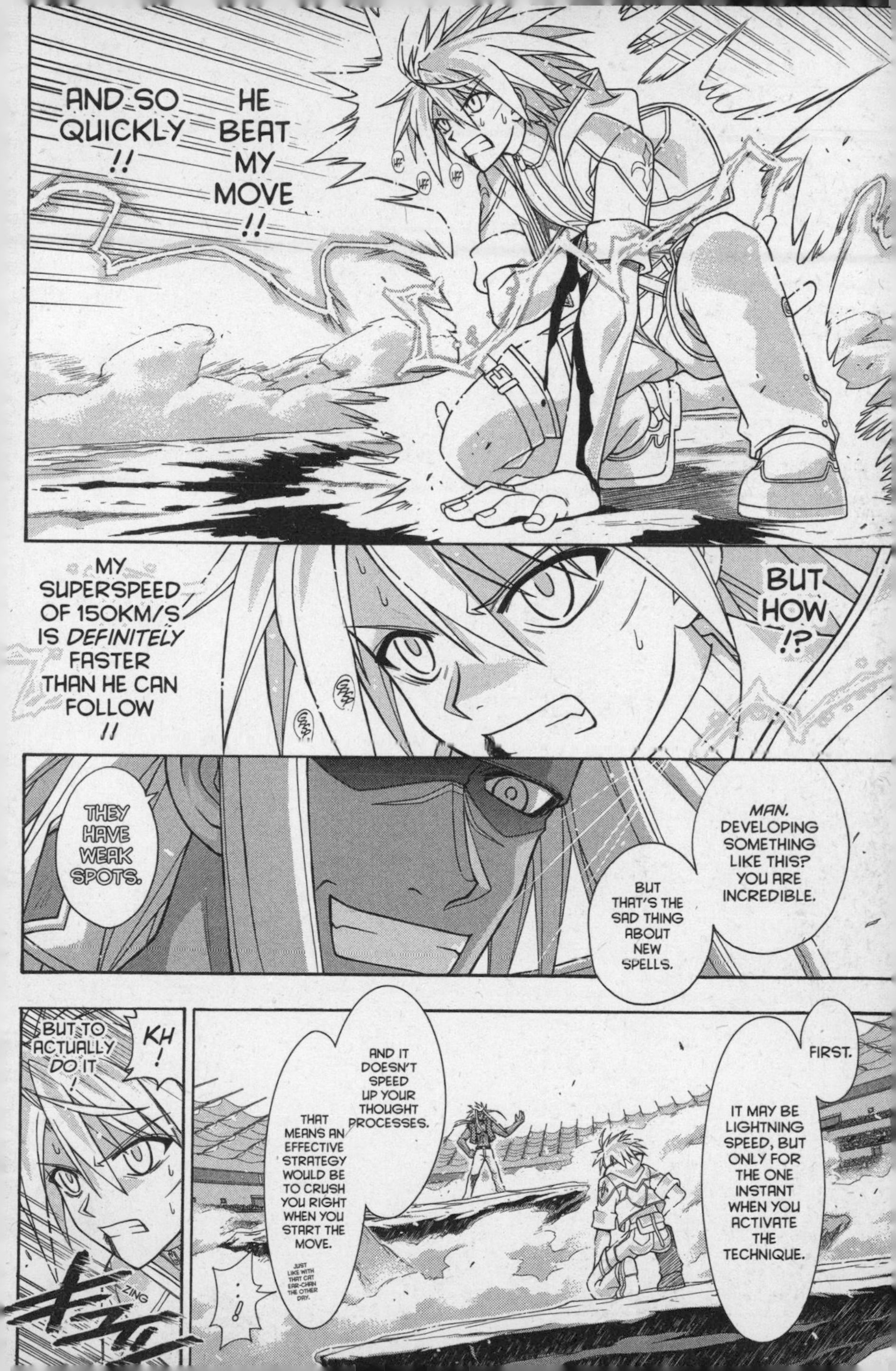
HE BEAT MY MOVE !!
AND SO QUICKLY !!
BUT HOW !?
MY SUPERSPEED OF 150KM/S IS *DEFINITELY* FASTER THAN HE CAN FOLLOW !!
MAN. DEVELOPING SOMETHING LIKE THIS? YOU ARE INCREDIBLE.
BUT THAT'S THE SAD THING ABOUT NEW SPELLS.
THEY HAVE WEAK SPOTS.
FIRST.
IT MAY BE LIGHTNING SPEED, BUT ONLY FOR THE ONE INSTANT WHEN YOU ACTIVATE THE TECHNIQUE.
AND IT DOESN'T SPEED UP YOUR THOUGHT PROCESSES.
THAT MEANS AN EFFECTIVE STRATEGY WOULD BE TO CRUSH YOU RIGHT WHEN YOU START THE MOVE.
JUST LIKE WITH THAT CAT EAR-CHAN THE OTHER DAY.
!
KH!
BUT TO ACTUALLY *DO IT*!
ZING

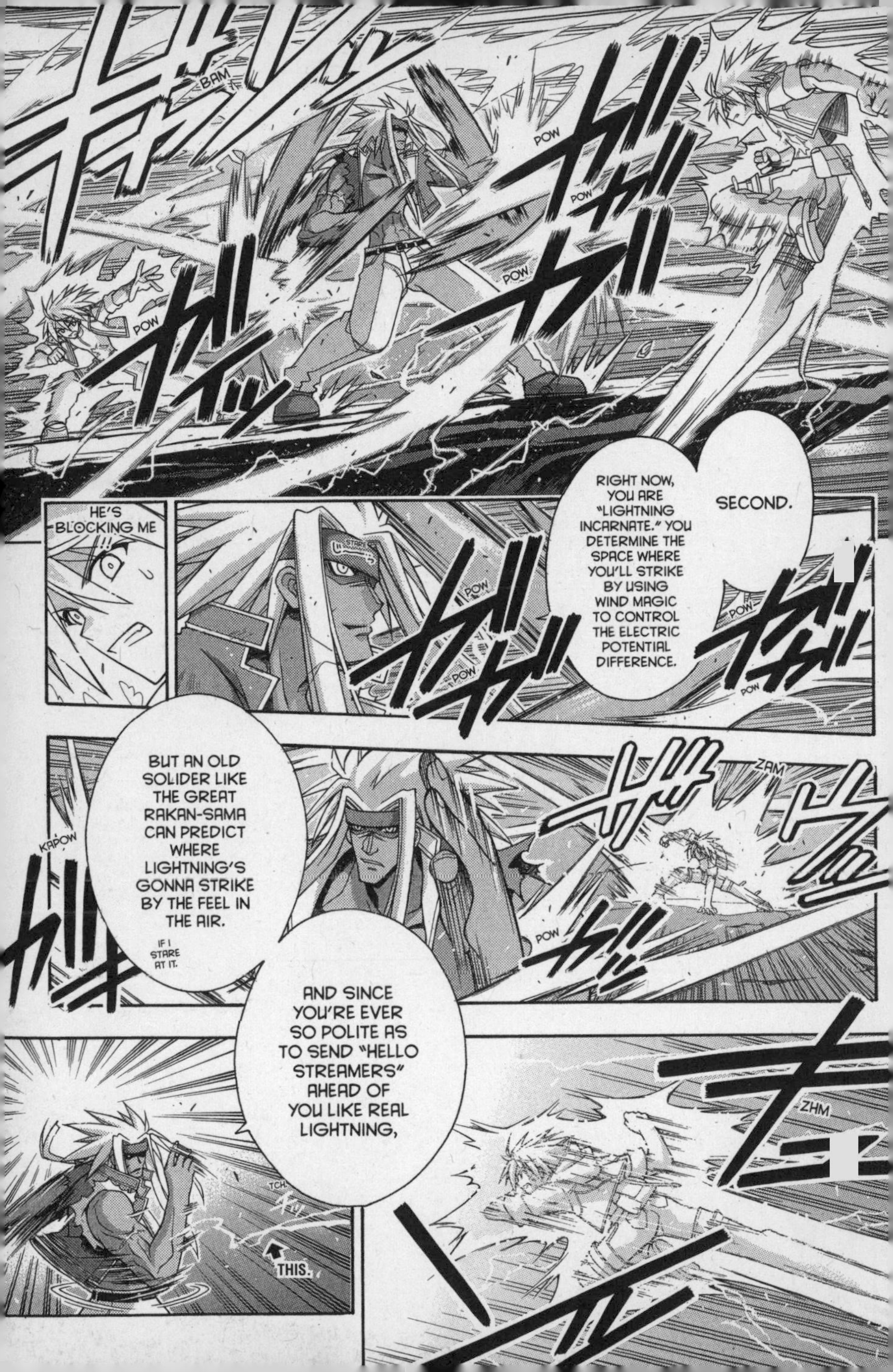

POW
POW
POW
BAM
POW
SECOND.
RIGHT NOW, YOU ARE "LIGHTNING INCARNATE." YOU DETERMINE THE SPACE WHERE YOU'LL STRIKE BY USING WIND MAGIC TO CONTROL THE ELECTRIC POTENTIAL DIFFERENCE.
POW
POW
POW
POW
STARE
HE'S BLOCKING ME!!!
ZAM
POW
BUT AN OLD SOLIDER LIKE THE GREAT RAKAN-SAMA CAN PREDICT WHERE LIGHTNING'S GONNA STRIKE BY THE FEEL IN THE AIR.
IF I STARE AT IT.
KAPOW
ZHM
AND SINCE YOU'RE EVER SO POLITE AS TO SEND "HELLO STREAMERS" AHEAD OF YOU LIKE REAL LIGHTNING,
TCH
THIS.

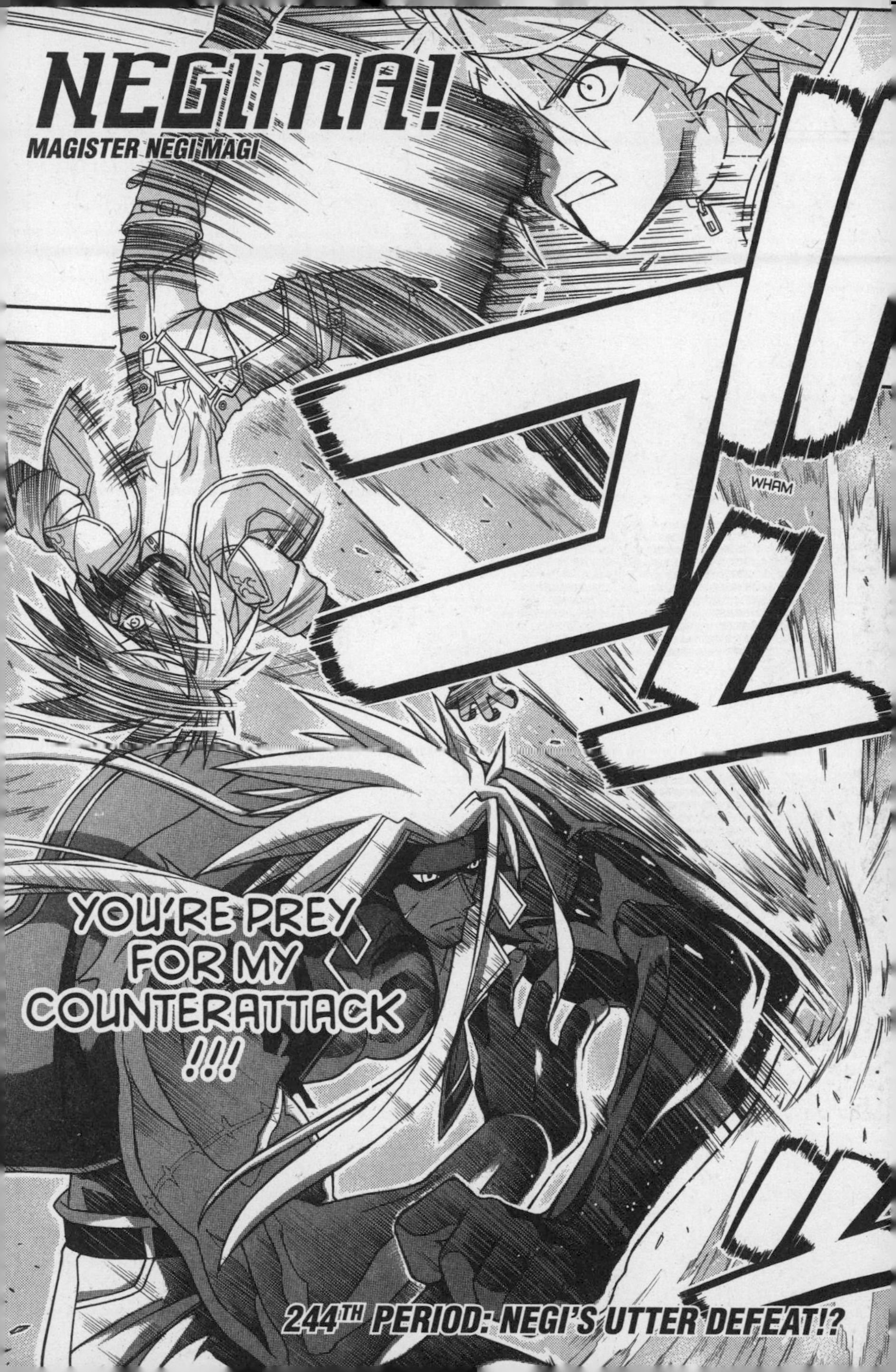
NEGIMA!
MAGISTER NEGI MAGI
WHAM
YOU'RE PREY FOR MY COUNTERATTACK !!!
244TH PERIOD: NEGI'S UTTER DEFEAT!?

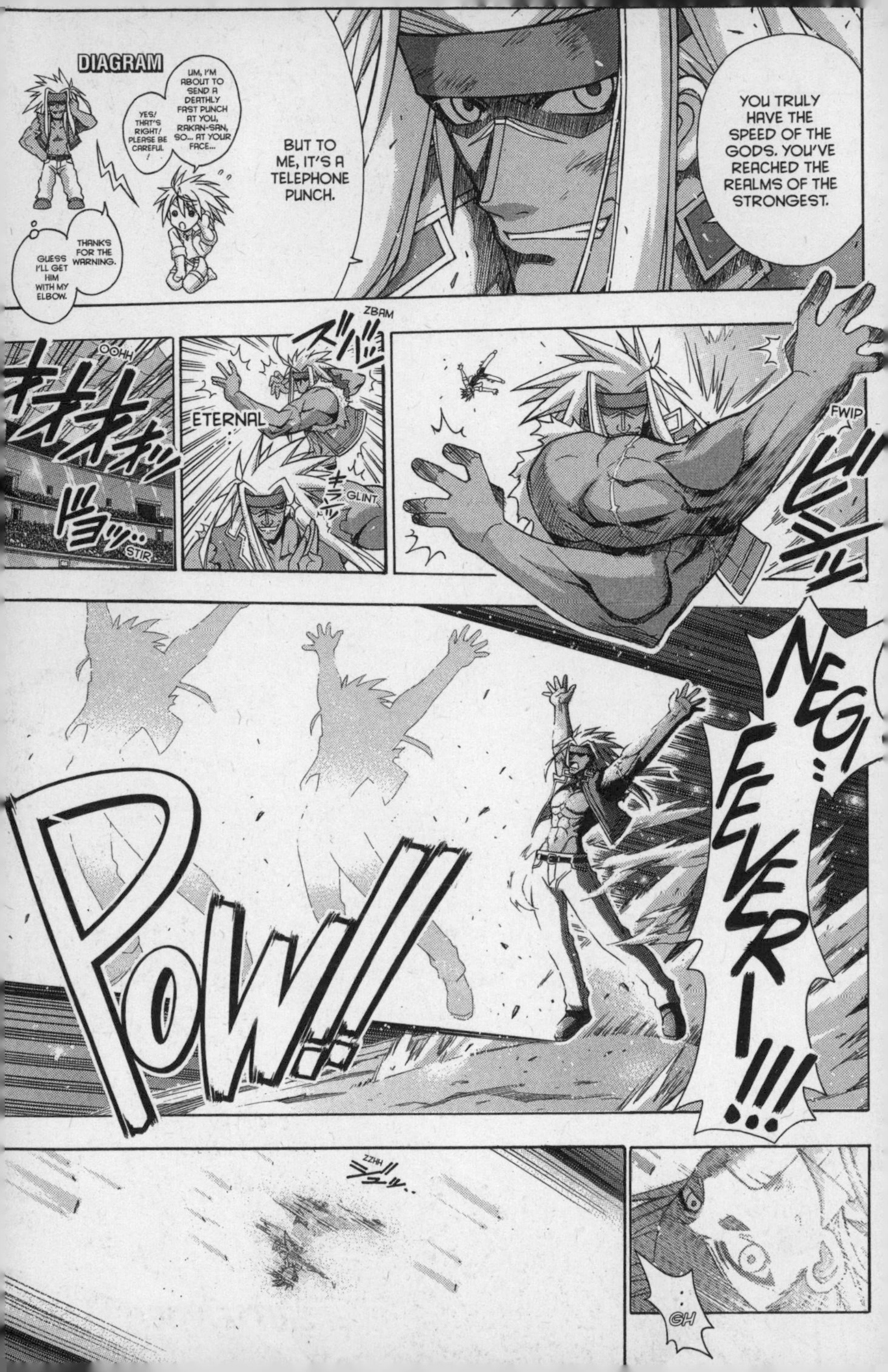

YOU TRULY HAVE THE SPEED OF THE GODS. YOU'VE REACHED THE REALMS OF THE STRONGEST.
BUT TO ME, IT'S A TELEPHONE PUNCH.
DIAGRAM
UM, I'M ABOUT TO SEND A DEATHLY FAST PUNCH AT YOU, RAKAN-SAN, SO... AT YOUR FACE...
YES! THAT'S RIGHT! PLEASE BE CAREFUL!
THANKS FOR THE WARNING.
GUESS I'LL GET HIM WITH MY ELBOW.
FWIP
ZBAM
ETERNAL
GLINT
OOHH
STIR
NEGI FEVER!!!
POW!!
GH
ZZHH

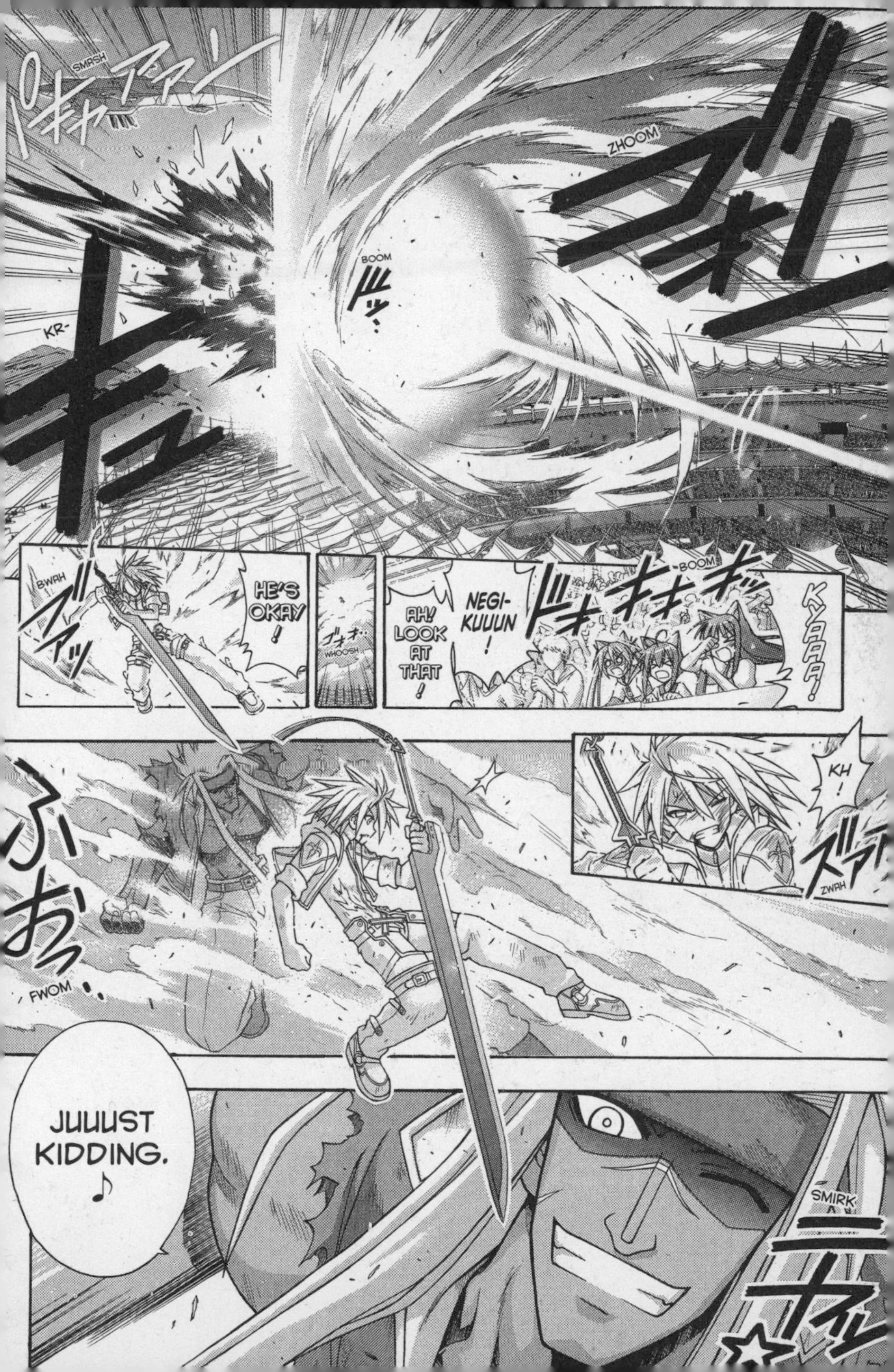
ZHOOM
BOOM
SMASH
KR-
KYAAAA!
BOOM
NEGI-KUUUN!
AH! LOOK AT THAT!
WHOOSH
HE'S OKAY!
BWAH
KH!
ZWAH
FWOM
JUUUST KIDDING. ♪
SMIRK

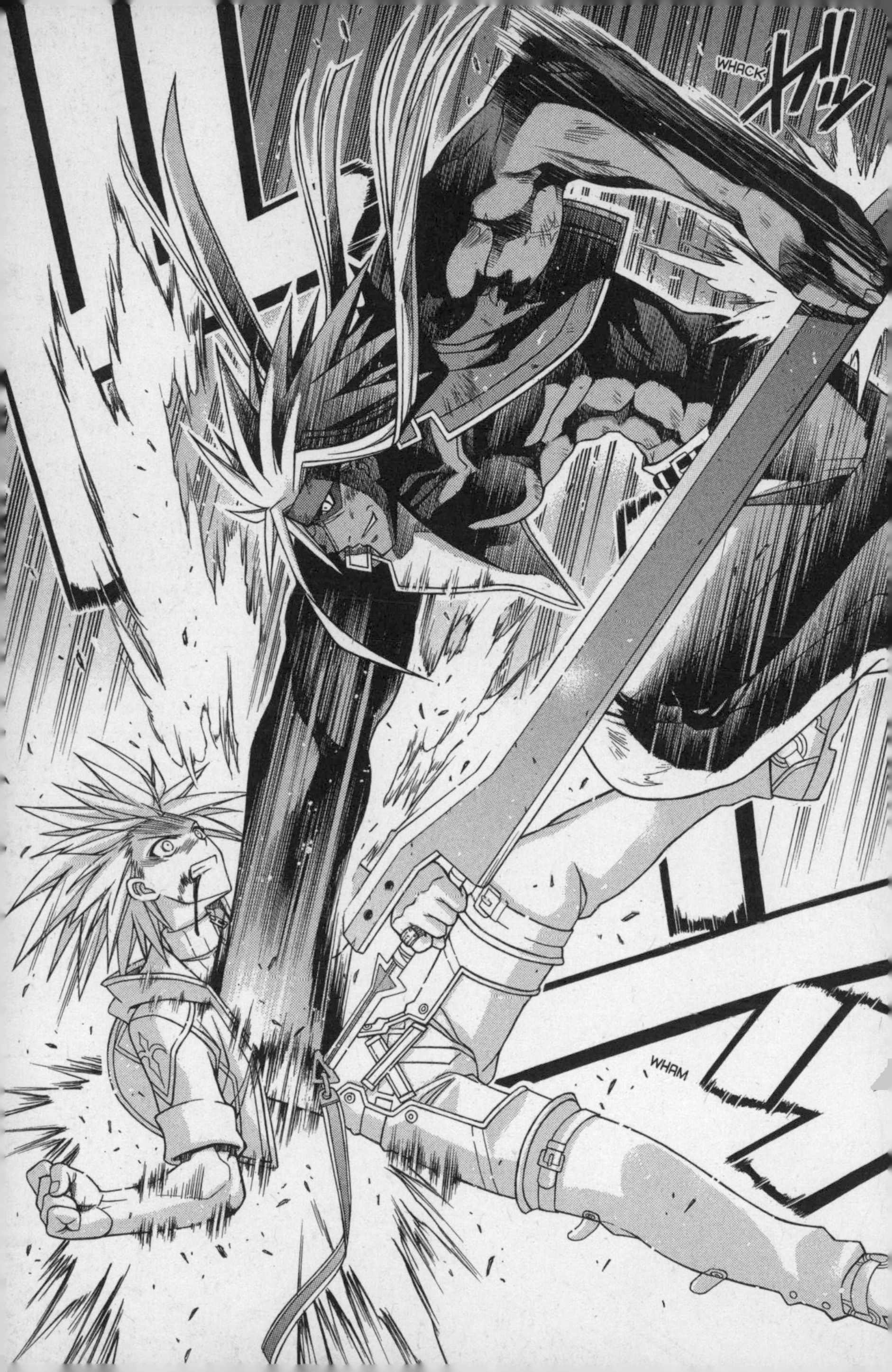

WHACK
ズガッ
WHAM

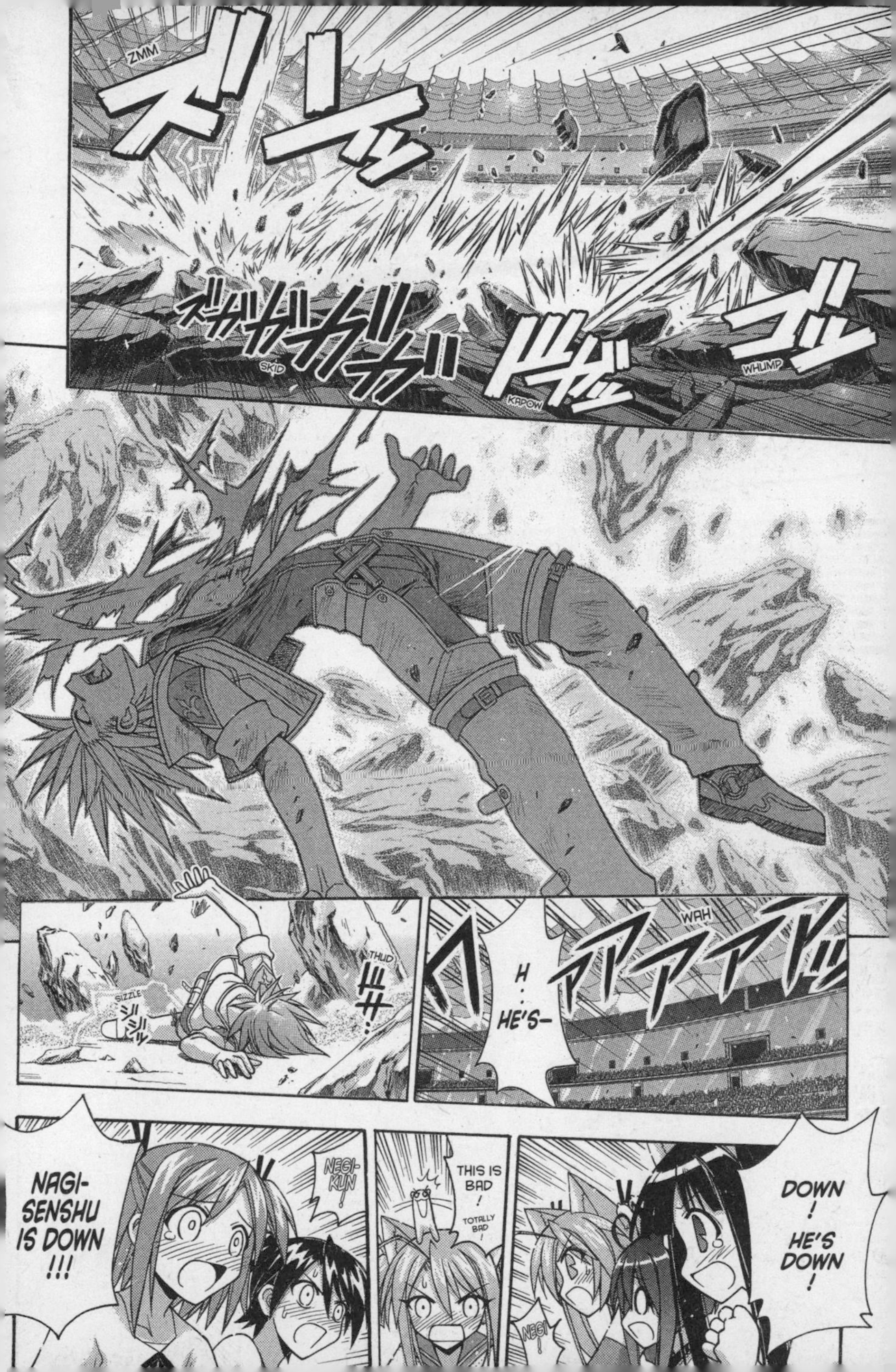
ZMM
WHUMP
KAPOW
SKID
WAH
H... HE'S–
THUD
SIZZLE
DOWN! HE'S DOWN!
NEGI!
THIS IS BAD!
TOTALLY BAD!
NEGI-KUN!
NAGI-SENSHU IS DOWN!!!

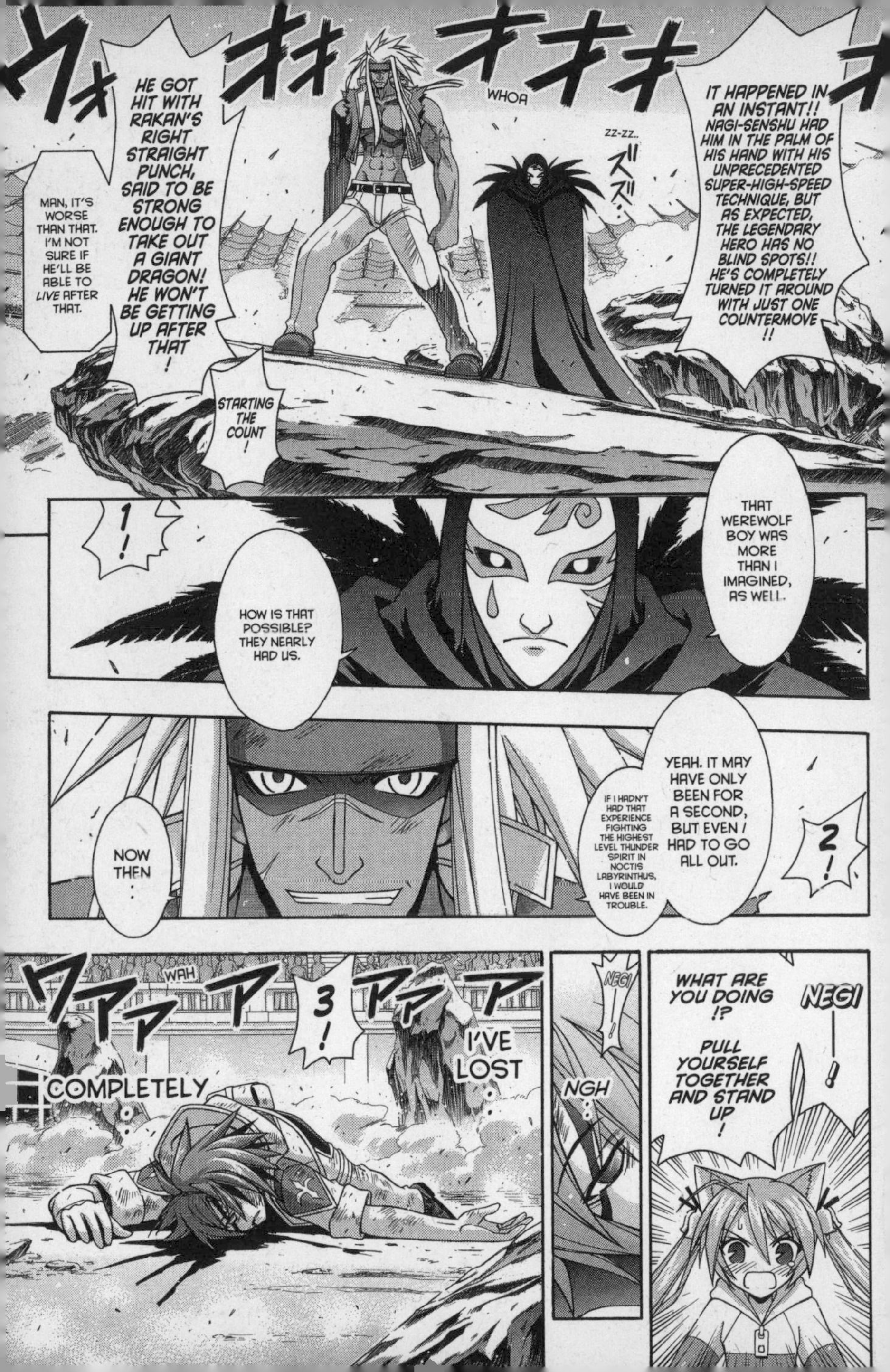
WHOA
IT HAPPENED IN AN INSTANT!! NAGI-SENSHU HAD HIM IN THE PALM OF HIS HAND WITH HIS UNPRECEDENTED SUPER-HIGH-SPEED TECHNIQUE, BUT AS EXPECTED, THE LEGENDARY HERO HAS NO BLIND SPOTS!! HE'S COMPLETELY TURNED IT AROUND WITH JUST ONE COUNTERMOVE!!
ZZ-ZZ..
HE GOT HIT WITH RAKAN'S RIGHT STRAIGHT PUNCH, SAID TO BE STRONG ENOUGH TO TAKE OUT A GIANT DRAGON! HE WON'T BE GETTING UP AFTER THAT!
MAN, IT'S WORSE THAN THAT. I'M NOT SURE IF HE'LL BE ABLE TO *LIVE* AFTER THAT.
STARTING THE COUNT!
THAT WEREWOLF BOY WAS MORE THAN I IMAGINED, AS WELL.
HOW IS THAT POSSIBLE? THEY NEARLY HAD US.
1!
2!
YEAH. IT MAY HAVE ONLY BEEN FOR A SECOND, BUT EVEN I HAD TO GO ALL OUT.
IF I HADN'T HAD THAT EXPERIENCE FIGHTING THE HIGHEST LEVEL THUNDER SPIRIT IN NOCTIS LABYRINTHUS, I WOULD HAVE BEEN IN TROUBLE.
NOW THEN...
NEGI!
WHAT ARE YOU DOING!? PULL YOURSELF TOGETHER AND STAND UP!
NEGI!
NGH...
WAH
3!
I'VE LOST
COMPLETELY...

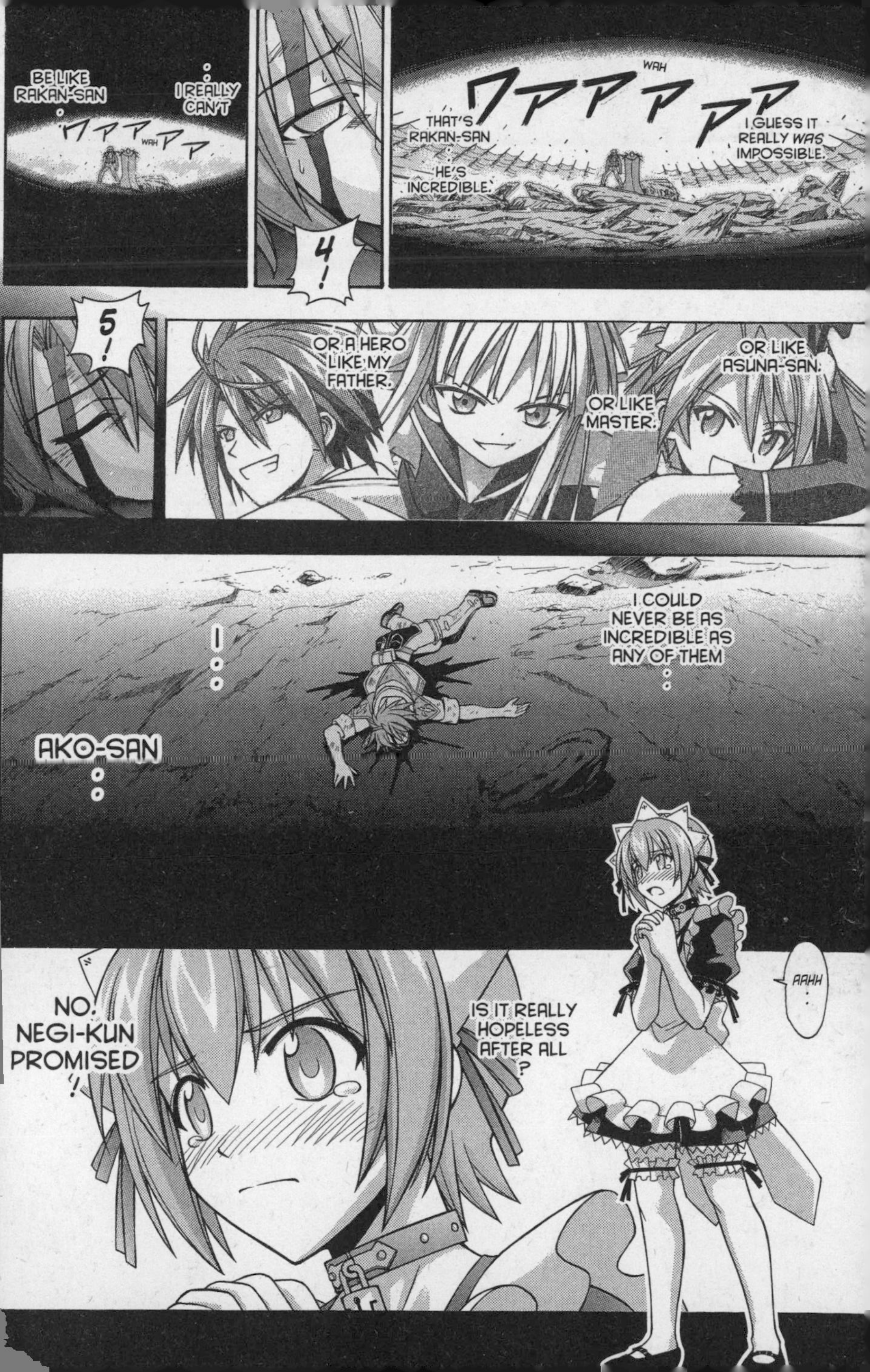
WAH
ワァァァァァ
I GUESS IT REALLY *WAS* IMPOSSIBLE.
THAT'S RAKAN-SAN...
HE'S INCREDIBLE.
4!
...I REALLY CAN'T
BE LIKE RAKAN-SAN.
ワァァァ WAH ァァ
OR LIKE ASUNA-SAN.
OR LIKE MASTER.
OR A HERO LIKE MY FATHER.
5!
I COULD NEVER BE AS INCREDIBLE AS ANY OF THEM...
I...
AKO-SAN...
AAHH...
IS IT REALLY HOPELESS AFTER ALL?
NO. NEGI-KUN PROMISED!

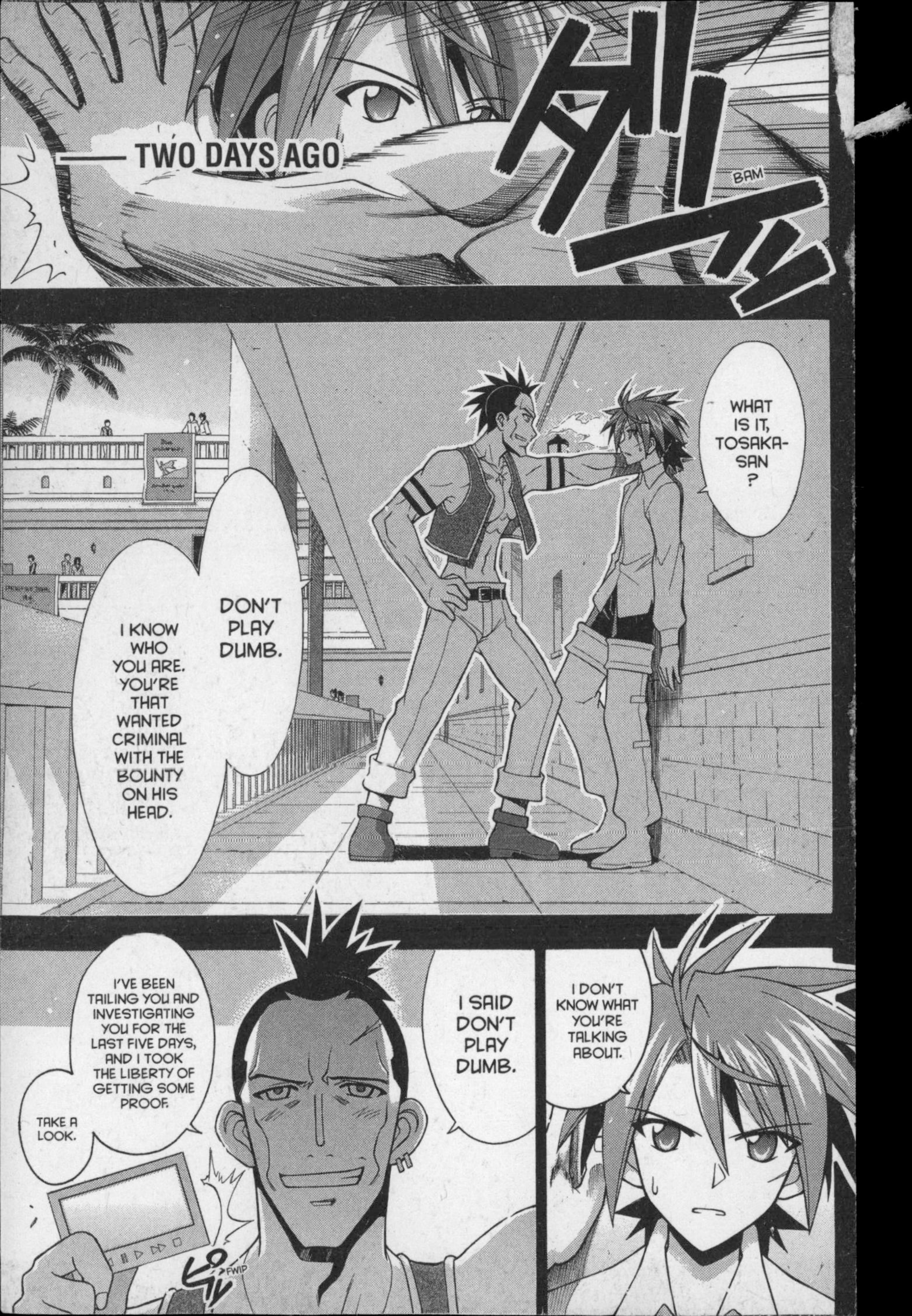
BAM
—— TWO DAYS AGO
WHAT IS IT, TOSAKA-SAN?
DON'T PLAY DUMB.
I KNOW WHO YOU ARE. YOU'RE THAT WANTED CRIMINAL WITH THE BOUNTY ON HIS HEAD.
I DON'T KNOW WHAT YOU'RE TALKING ABOUT.
I SAID DON'T PLAY DUMB.
I'VE BEEN TAILING YOU AND INVESTIGATING YOU FOR THE LAST FIVE DAYS, AND I TOOK THE LIBERTY OF GETTING SOME PROOF.
TAKE A LOOK.
FWIP

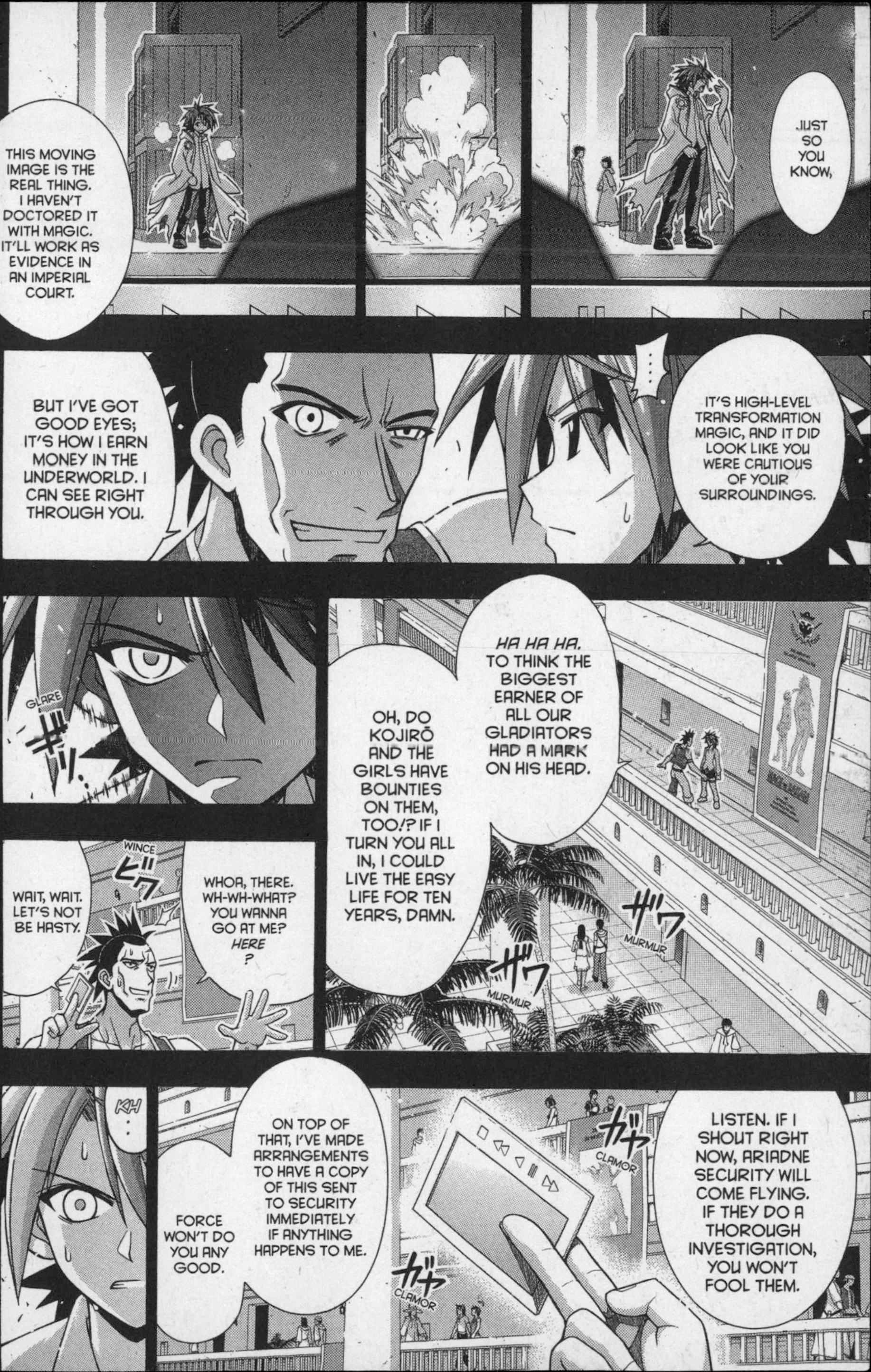
JUST SO YOU KNOW,
THIS MOVING IMAGE IS THE REAL THING. I HAVEN'T DOCTORED IT WITH MAGIC. IT'LL WORK AS EVIDENCE IN AN IMPERIAL COURT.
IT'S HIGH-LEVEL TRANSFORMATION MAGIC, AND IT DID LOOK LIKE YOU WERE CAUTIOUS OF YOUR SURROUNDINGS.
...!
BUT I'VE GOT GOOD EYES; IT'S HOW I EARN MONEY IN THE UNDERWORLD. I CAN SEE RIGHT THROUGH YOU.
HA HA HA. TO THINK THE BIGGEST EARNER OF ALL OUR GLADIATORS HAD A MARK ON HIS HEAD.
OH, DO KOJIRŌ AND THE GIRLS HAVE BOUNTIES ON THEM, TOO!? IF I TURN YOU ALL IN, I COULD LIVE THE EASY LIFE FOR TEN YEARS, DAMN.
MURMUR
MURMUR
GLARE
WHOA, THERE. WH-WH-WHAT? YOU WANNA GO AT ME? *HERE* ?
WINCE
WAIT, WAIT. LET'S NOT BE HASTY.
LISTEN. IF I SHOUT RIGHT NOW, ARIADNE SECURITY WILL COME FLYING. IF THEY DO A THOROUGH INVESTIGATION, YOU WON'T FOOL THEM.
CLAMOR
ON TOP OF THAT, I'VE MADE ARRANGEMENTS TO HAVE A COPY OF THIS SENT TO SECURITY IMMEDIATELY IF ANYTHING HAPPENS TO ME.
FORCE WON'T DO YOU ANY GOOD.
CLAMOR
KH...

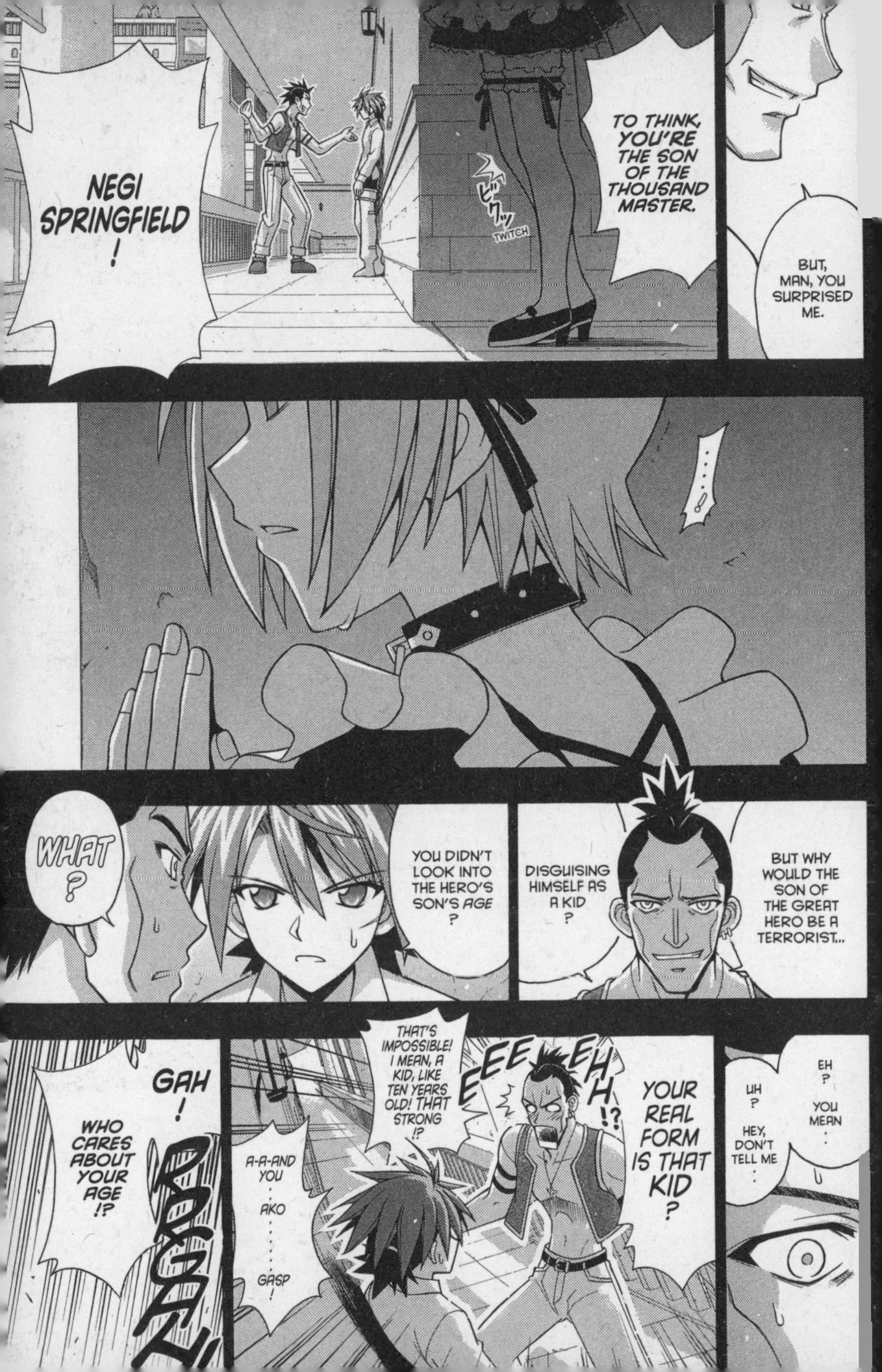
BUT, MAN, YOU SURPRISED ME.
TO THINK, YOU'RE THE SON OF THE THOUSAND MASTER.
TWITCH
NEGI SPRINGFIELD !
. . . !
BUT WHY WOULD THE SON OF THE GREAT HERO BE A TERRORIST...
DISGUISING HIMSELF AS A KID ?
YOU DIDN'T LOOK INTO THE HERO'S SON'S AGE ?
WHAT ?
EH ? YOU MEAN . . .
UH ? HEY, DON'T TELL ME . . .
YOUR REAL FORM IS THAT KID ?
EEEEEH !?
THAT'S IMPOSSIBLE! I MEAN, A KID, LIKE TEN YEARS OLD! THAT STRONG !?
A-A-AND YOU . . . AKO . . . GASP !
GAH !
WHO CARES ABOUT YOUR AGE !?

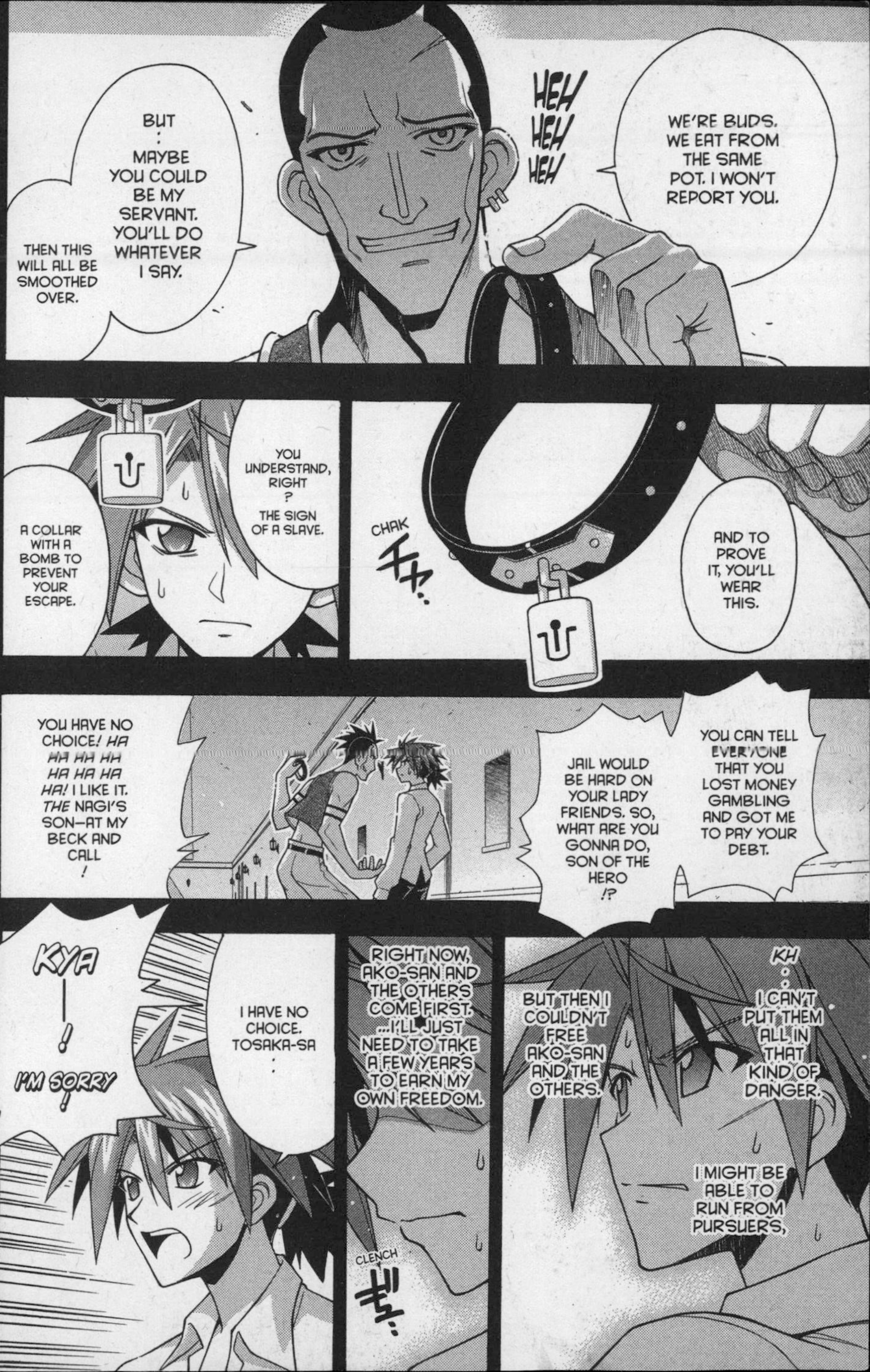
WE'RE BUDS. WE EAT FROM THE SAME POT. I WON'T REPORT YOU.
HEH HEH HEH
BUT : MAYBE YOU COULD BE MY SERVANT. YOU'LL DO WHATEVER I SAY.
THEN THIS WILL ALL BE SMOOTHED OVER.
AND TO PROVE IT, YOU'LL WEAR THIS.
CHAK
YOU UNDERSTAND, RIGHT? THE SIGN OF A SLAVE.
A COLLAR WITH A BOMB TO PREVENT YOUR ESCAPE.
YOU CAN TELL EVERYONE THAT YOU LOST MONEY GAMBLING AND GOT ME TO PAY YOUR DEBT.
JAIL WOULD BE HARD ON YOUR LADY FRIENDS. SO, WHAT ARE YOU GONNA DO, SON OF THE HERO!?
YOU HAVE NO CHOICE! HA HA HA HA HA HA HA HA! I LIKE IT. THE NAGI'S SON—AT MY BECK AND CALL!
KH.. I CAN'T PUT THEM ALL IN THAT KIND OF DANGER.
I MIGHT BE ABLE TO RUN FROM PURSUERS,
BUT THEN I COULDN'T FREE AKO-SAN AND THE OTHERS.
RIGHT NOW, AKO-SAN AND THE OTHERS COME FIRST. ...I'LL JUST NEED TO TAKE A FEW YEARS TO EARN MY OWN FREEDOM.
CLENCH
I HAVE NO CHOICE. TOSAKA-SA :
KYA—!
I'M SORRY!

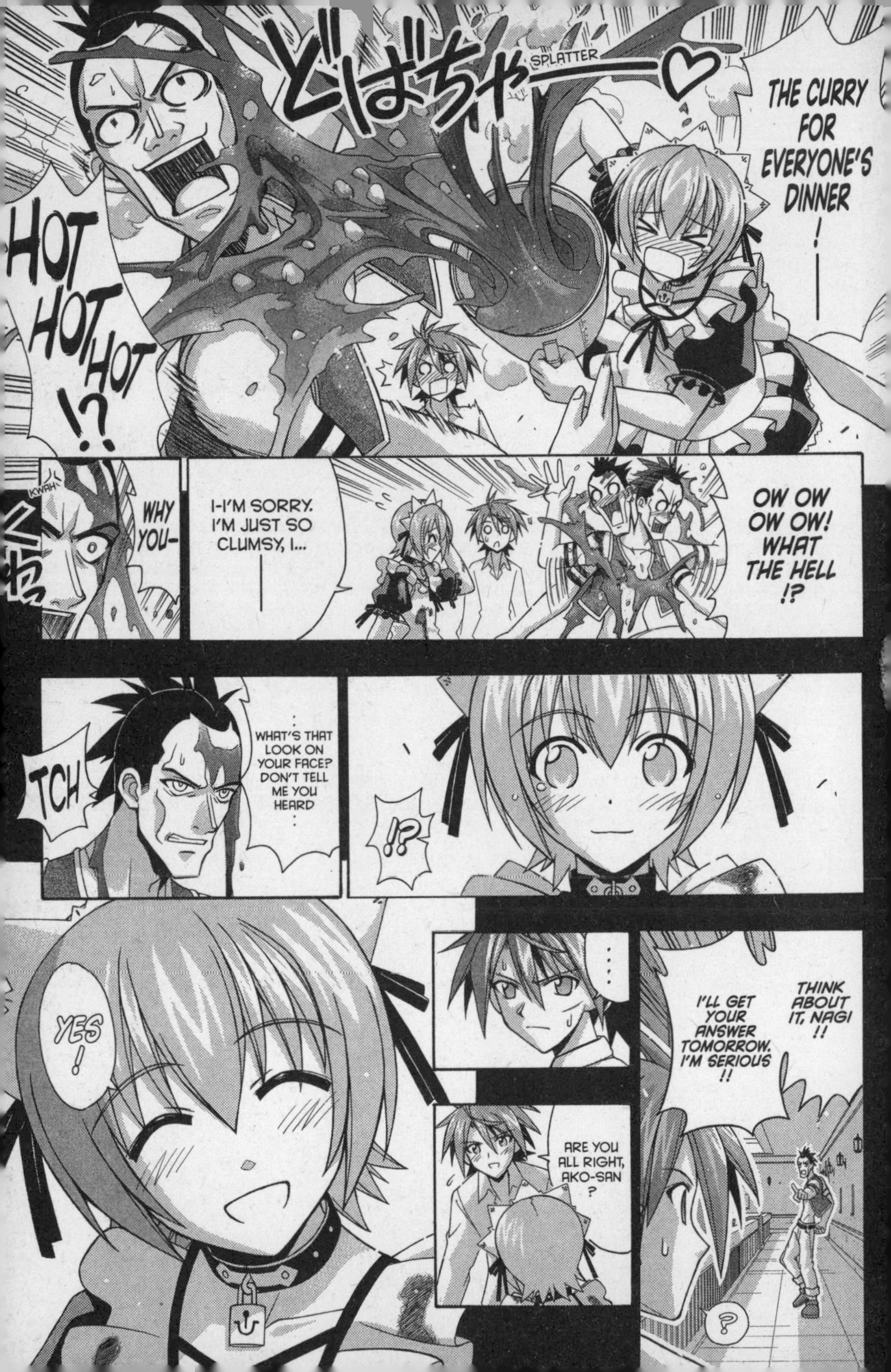
THE CURRY FOR EVERYONE'S DINNER!
どばちゃー♡
SPLATTER
HOT HOT HOT HOT!?
OW OW OW OW! WHAT THE HELL!?
I-I'M SORRY. I'M JUST SO CLUMSY, I...
WHY YOU-
くわっ
KWAH
!?
...WHAT'S THAT LOOK ON YOUR FACE? DON'T TELL ME YOU HEARD...
TCH
THINK ABOUT IT, NAGI!!
I'LL GET YOUR ANSWER TOMORROW. I'M SERIOUS!!
?
...
ARE YOU ALL RIGHT, AKO-SAN?
YES!

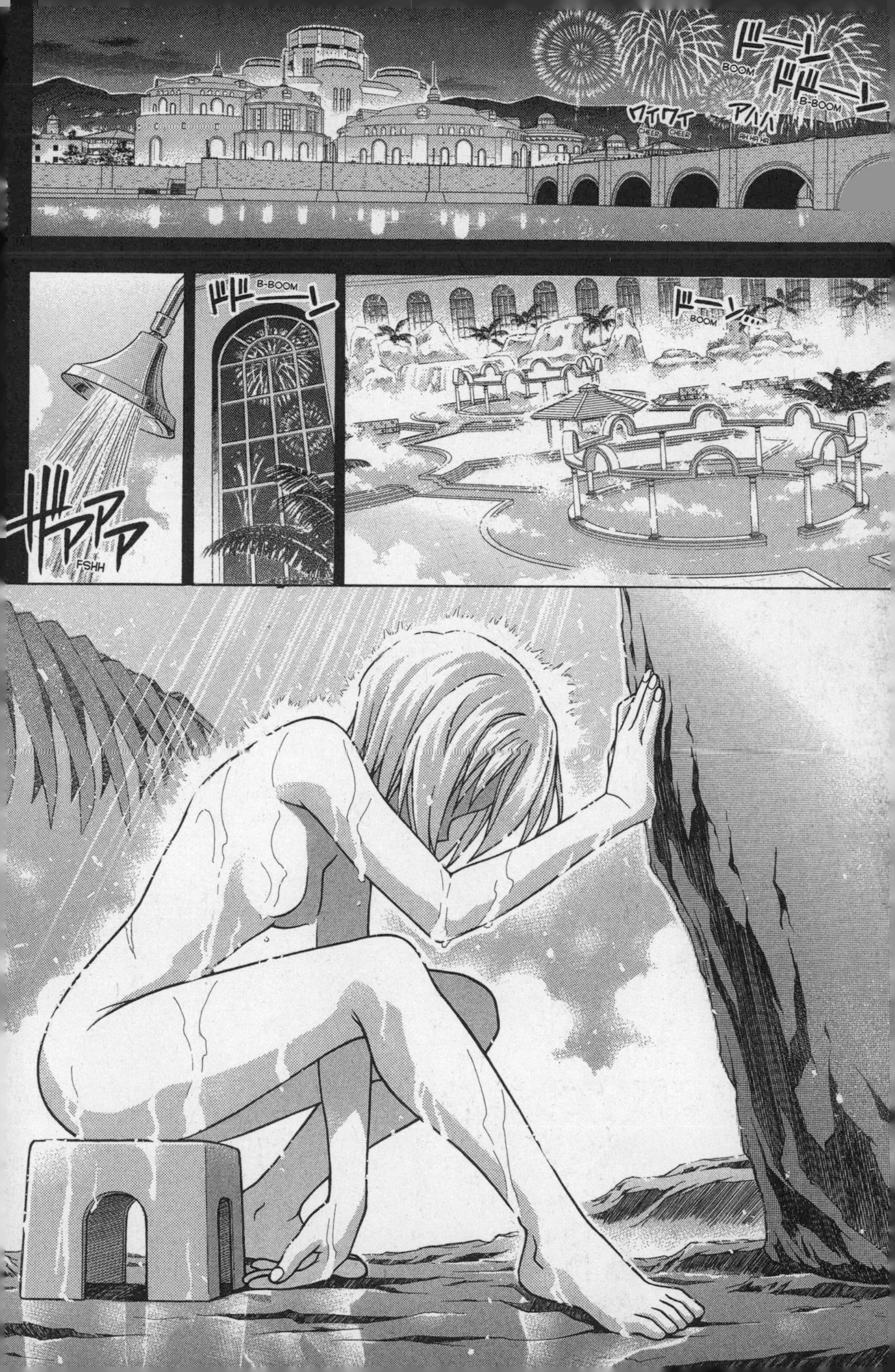
ドーン
BOOM
ドドーーン
B-BOOM
アハハ
AH HA HA
ワイワイ
CHEER CHEER
ドーン…
BOOM
ドドーーン
B-BOOM
ザァァァ
FSHH

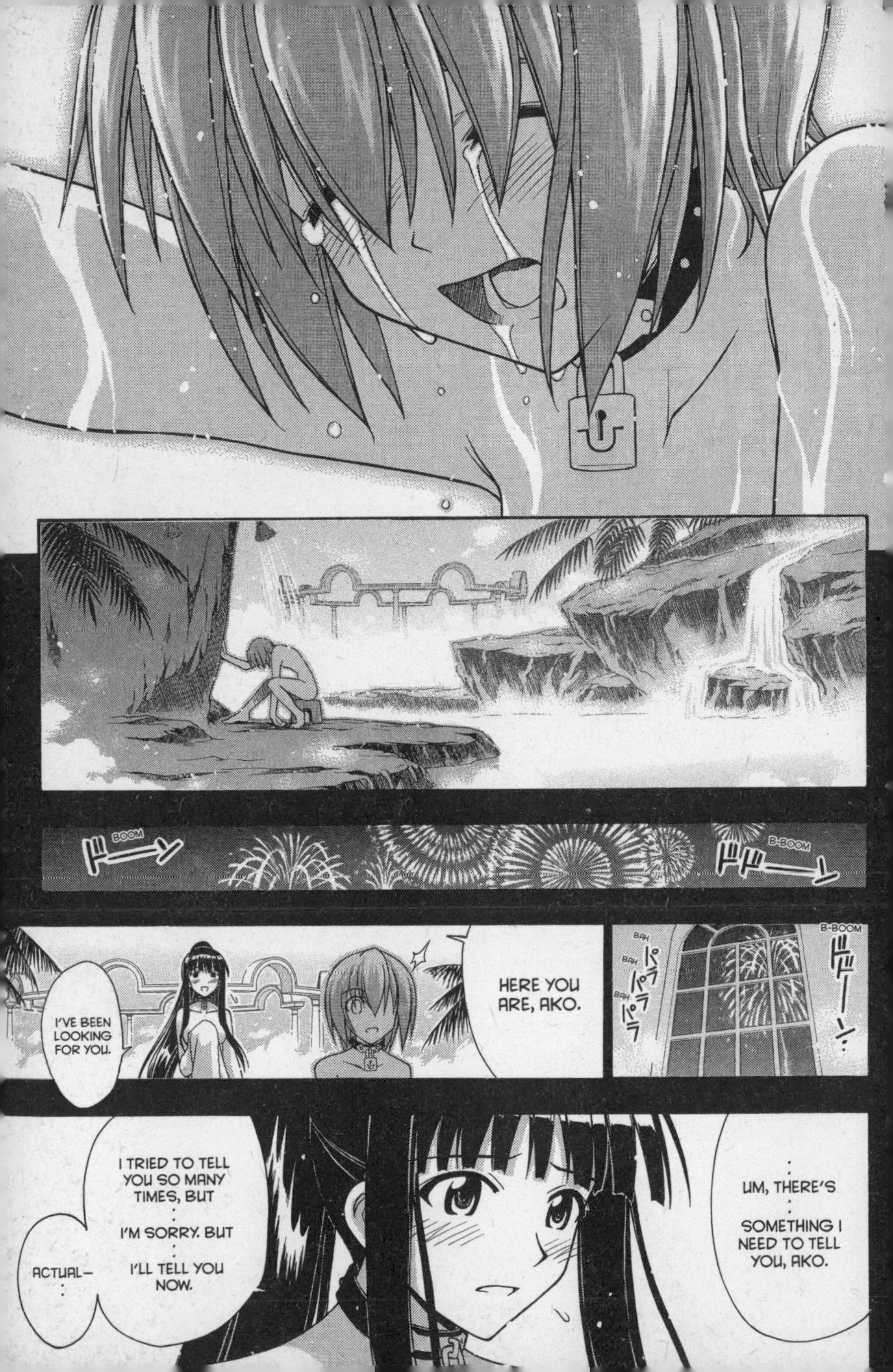
B-BOOM
ドドーン
BOOM
ドーン
B-BOOM
ドドーン
BAH BAH BAH
パラパラパラ
HERE YOU ARE, AKO.
I'VE BEEN LOOKING FOR YOU.
UM, THERE'S... SOMETHING I NEED TO TELL YOU, AKO.
I TRIED TO TELL YOU SO MANY TIMES, BUT... I'M SORRY. BUT... I'LL TELL YOU NOW.
ACTUAL—...

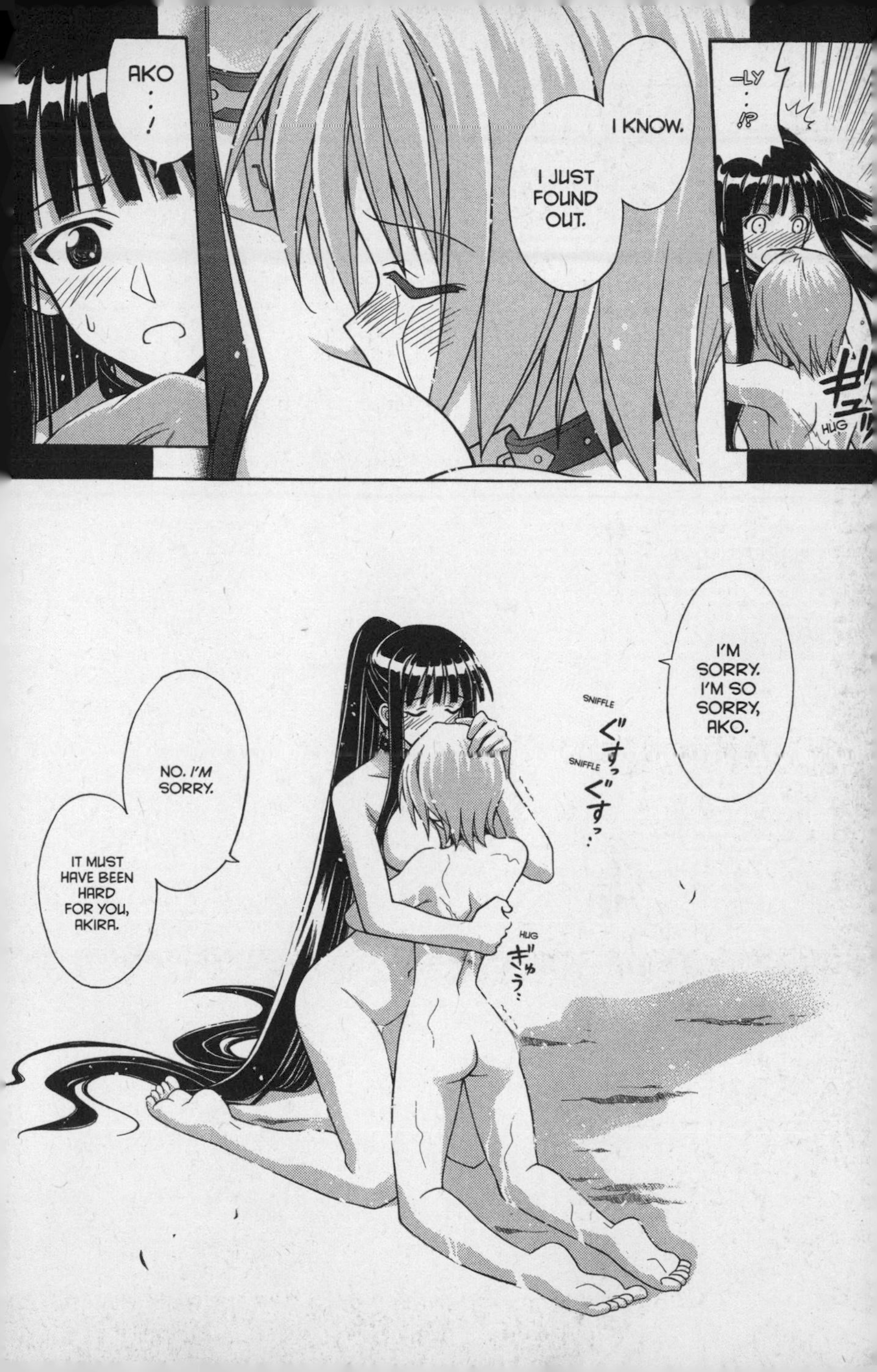

—LY . . !?
HUG
I KNOW.
I JUST FOUND OUT.
AKO . . . !
I'M SORRY. I'M SO SORRY, AKO.
SNIFFLE
ぐすっ
SNIFFLE
ぐすっ
HUG
ぎゅう
NO. I'M SORRY.
IT MUST HAVE BEEN HARD FOR YOU, AKIRA.

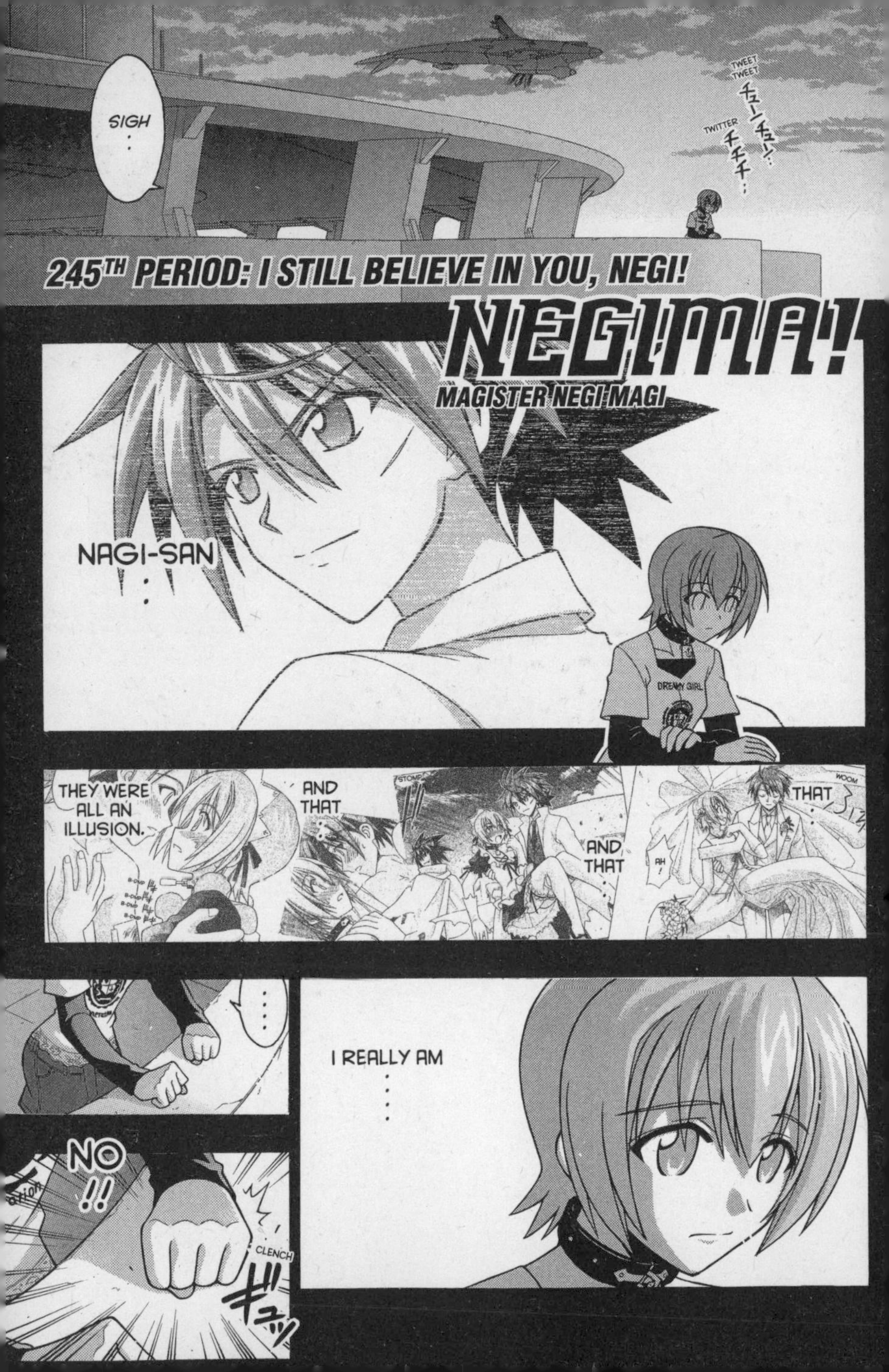
TWEET TWEET
TWITTER
SIGH . .
245TH PERIOD: I STILL BELIEVE IN YOU, NEGI!
NEGIMA!
MAGISTER NEGI MAGI
NAGI-SAN . .
WOOM
THAT . .
AH !
AND THAT . .
STOMP
AND THAT
THEY WERE ALL AN ILLUSION.
I REALLY AM . . .
. . . .
NO !!
CLENCH

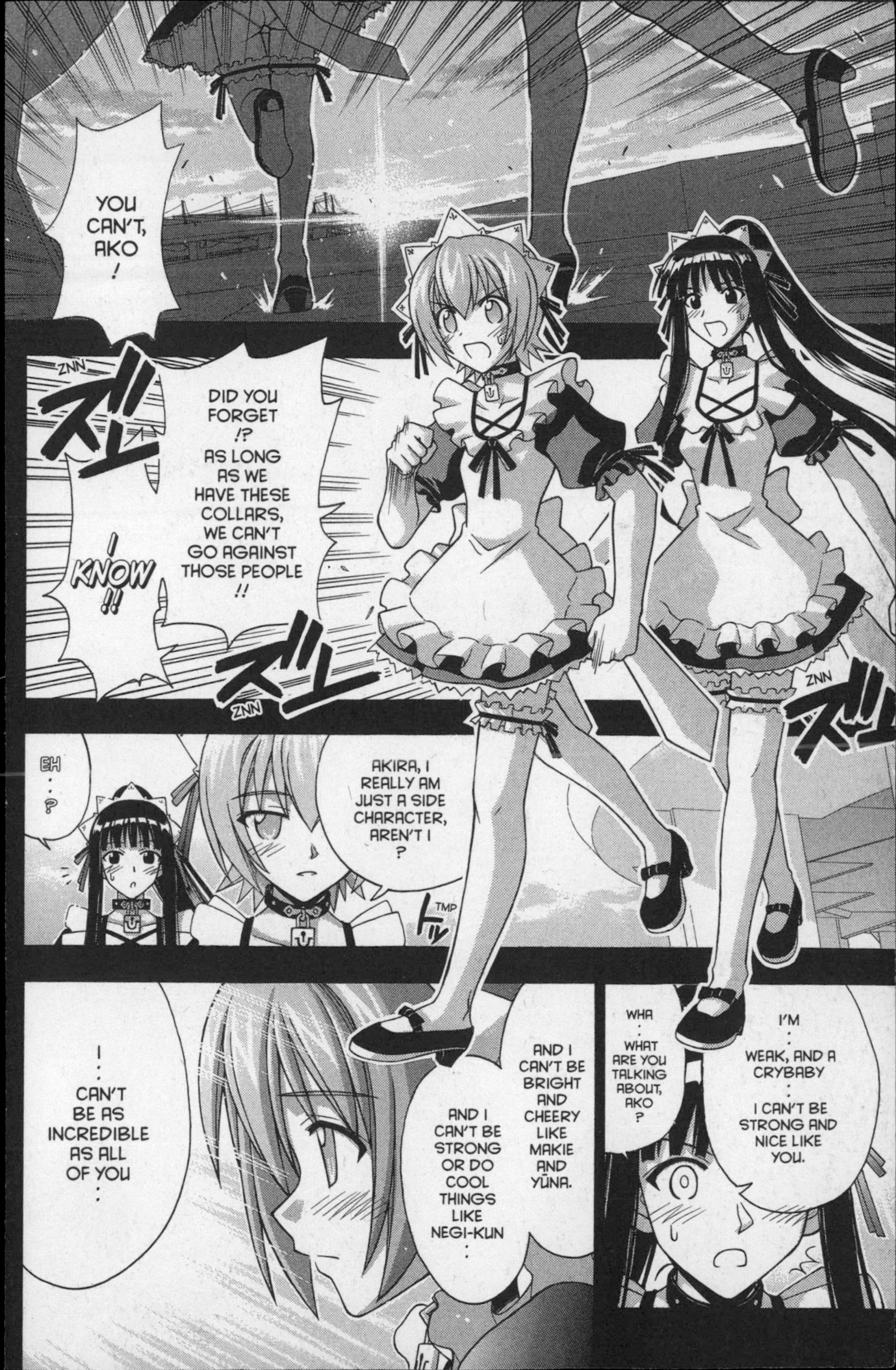

YOU CAN'T, AKO!
DID YOU FORGET!? AS LONG AS WE HAVE THESE COLLARS, WE CAN'T GO AGAINST THOSE PEOPLE!!
I KNOW!!
ZNN
ZNN
ZNN
AKIRA, I REALLY AM JUST A SIDE CHARACTER, AREN'T I?
EH...?
TMP
WHA... WHAT ARE YOU TALKING ABOUT, AKO?
I'M... WEAK, AND A CRYBABY... I CAN'T BE STRONG AND NICE LIKE YOU.
AND I CAN'T BE BRIGHT AND CHEERY LIKE MAKIE AND YŪNA.
AND I CAN'T BE STRONG OR DO COOL THINGS LIKE NEGI-KUN...
I... CAN'T BE AS INCREDIBLE AS ALL OF YOU...

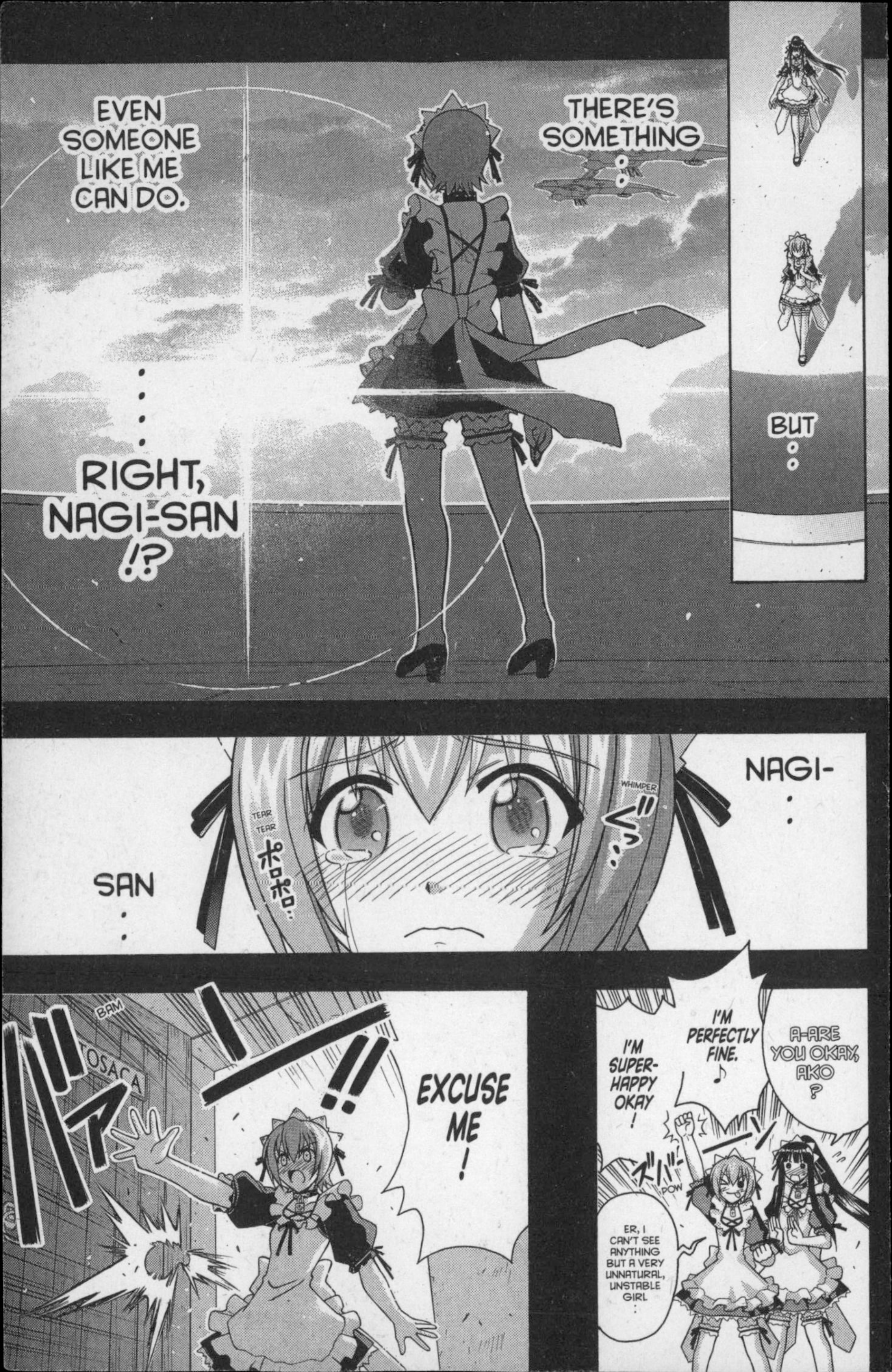

BUT...
THERE'S SOMETHING...
EVEN SOMEONE LIKE ME CAN DO.
...RIGHT, NAGI-SAN!?
NAGI-...
WHIMPER
TEAR TEAR
SAN...
A-ARE YOU OKAY, AKO?
I'M PERFECTLY FINE. ♪
I'M SUPER-HAPPY OKAY!
POW
ER, I CAN'T SEE ANYTHING BUT A VERY UNNATURAL, UNSTABLE GIRL...
EXCUSE ME!
BAM
TOSACA

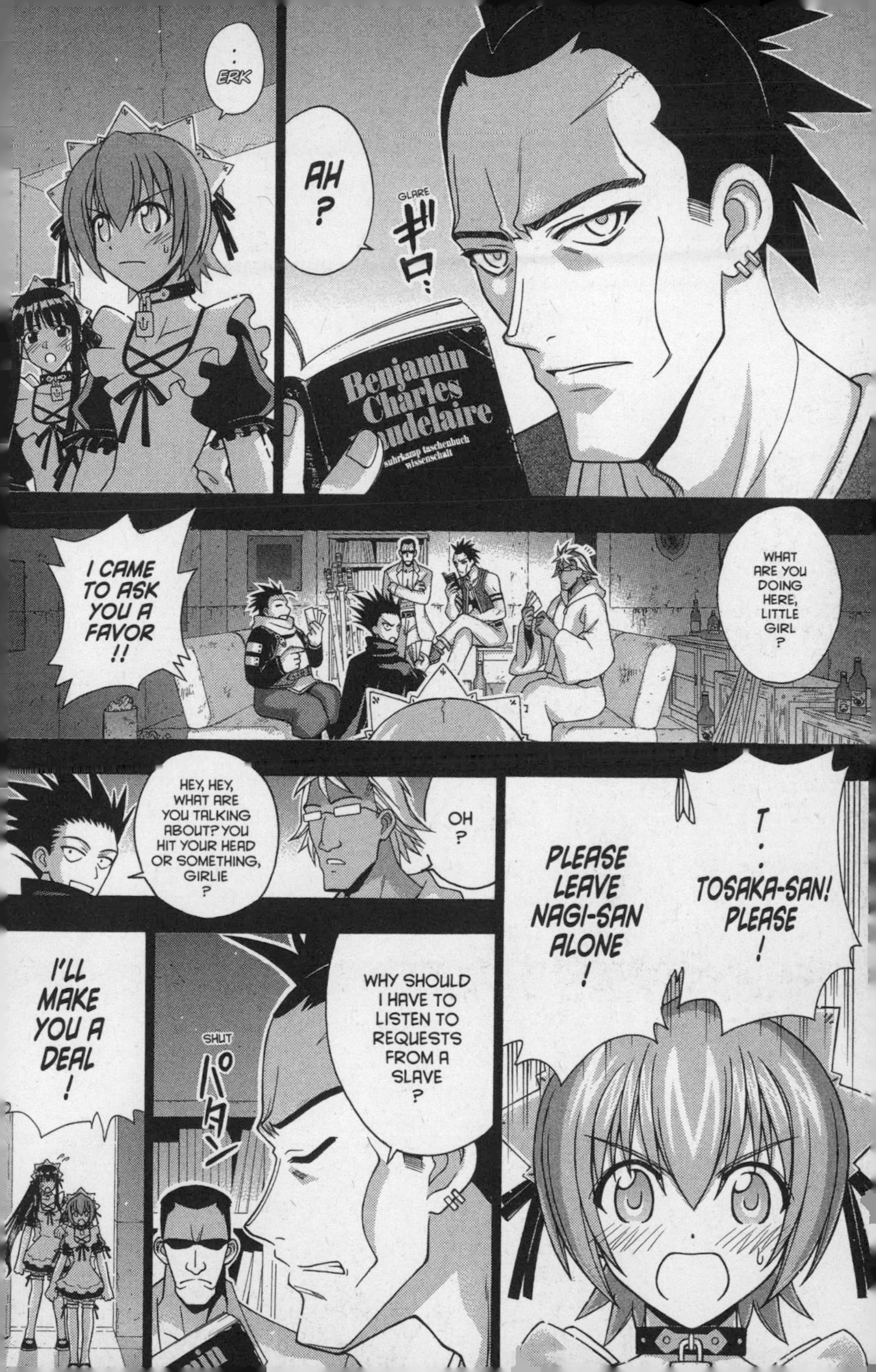
GLARE
AH ?
Benjamin Charles udelaire
suhrkamp taschenbuch wissenschaft
. . ERK
WHAT ARE YOU DOING HERE, LITTLE GIRL ?
I CAME TO ASK YOU A FAVOR !!
T . . TOSAKA-SAN! PLEASE !
PLEASE LEAVE NAGI-SAN ALONE !
OH ?
HEY, HEY, WHAT ARE YOU TALKING ABOUT? YOU HIT YOUR HEAD OR SOMETHING, GIRLIE ?
WHY SHOULD I HAVE TO LISTEN TO REQUESTS FROM A SLAVE ?
SHUT
I'LL MAKE YOU A DEAL !

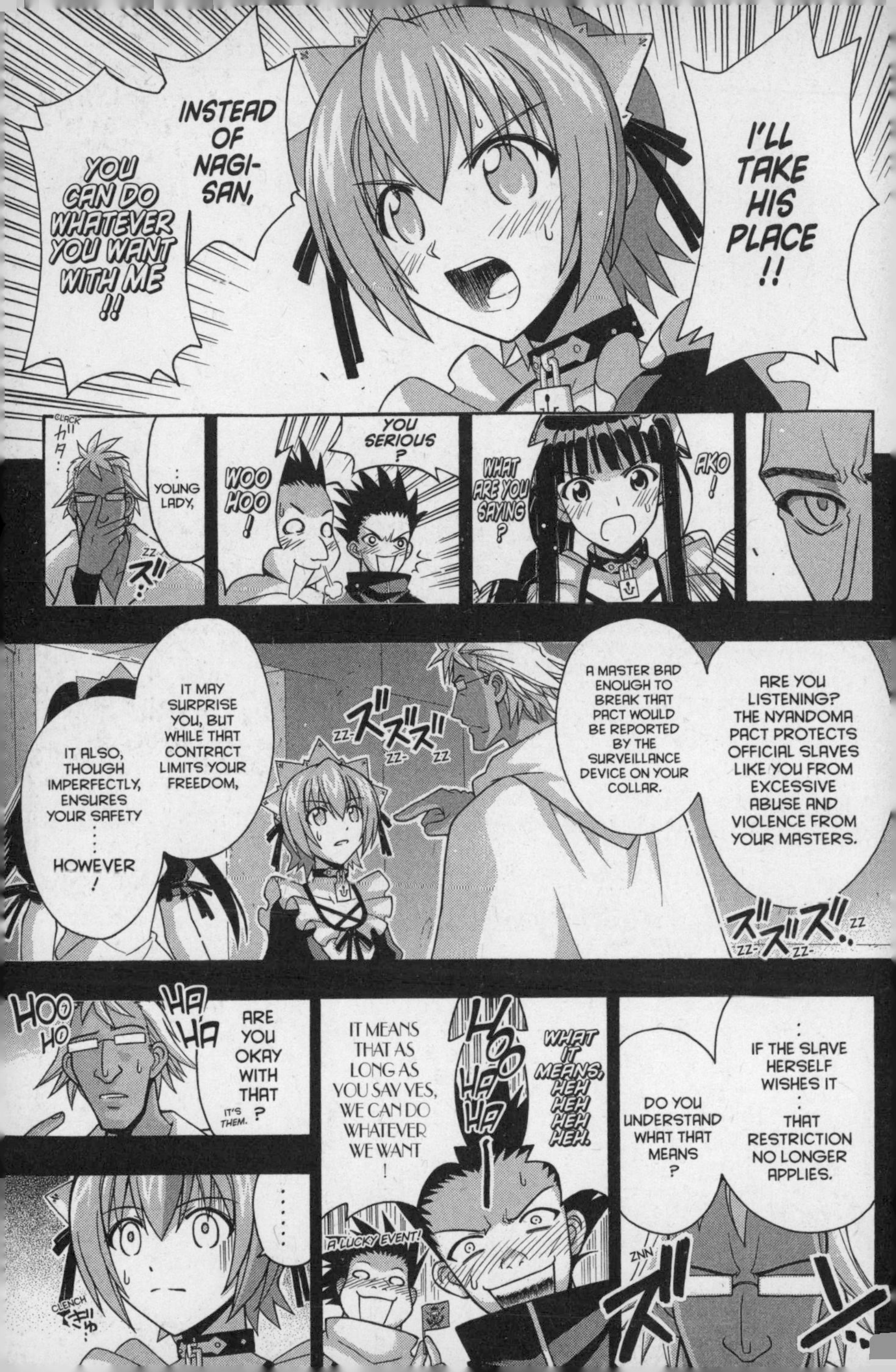
I'LL TAKE HIS PLACE!!
INSTEAD OF NAGI-SAN,
YOU CAN DO WHATEVER YOU WANT WITH ME!!
AKO!
WHAT ARE YOU SAYING?
YOU SERIOUS?
WOO HOO!
...YOUNG LADY,
CLACK
ZZ
ARE YOU LISTENING? THE NYANDOMA PACT PROTECTS OFFICIAL SLAVES LIKE YOU FROM EXCESSIVE ABUSE AND VIOLENCE FROM YOUR MASTERS.
A MASTER BAD ENOUGH TO BREAK THAT PACT WOULD BE REPORTED BY THE SURVEILLANCE DEVICE ON YOUR COLLAR.
ZZ- ZZ- ZZ
IT MAY SURPRISE YOU, BUT WHILE THAT CONTRACT LIMITS YOUR FREEDOM,
IT ALSO, THOUGH IMPERFECTLY, ENSURES YOUR SAFETY...... HOWEVER!
ZZ- ZZ- ZZ
...IF THE SLAVE HERSELF WISHES IT... THAT RESTRICTION NO LONGER APPLIES.
DO YOU UNDERSTAND WHAT THAT MEANS?
ZNN
WHAT IT MEANS, HEH HEH HEH HEH.
HOO HA HA
IT MEANS THAT AS LONG AS YOU SAY YES, WE CAN DO WHATEVER WE WANT!
A LUCKY EVENT!
HA HA
ARE YOU OKAY WITH THAT?
IT'S THEM.
HOO HO
......
CLENCH

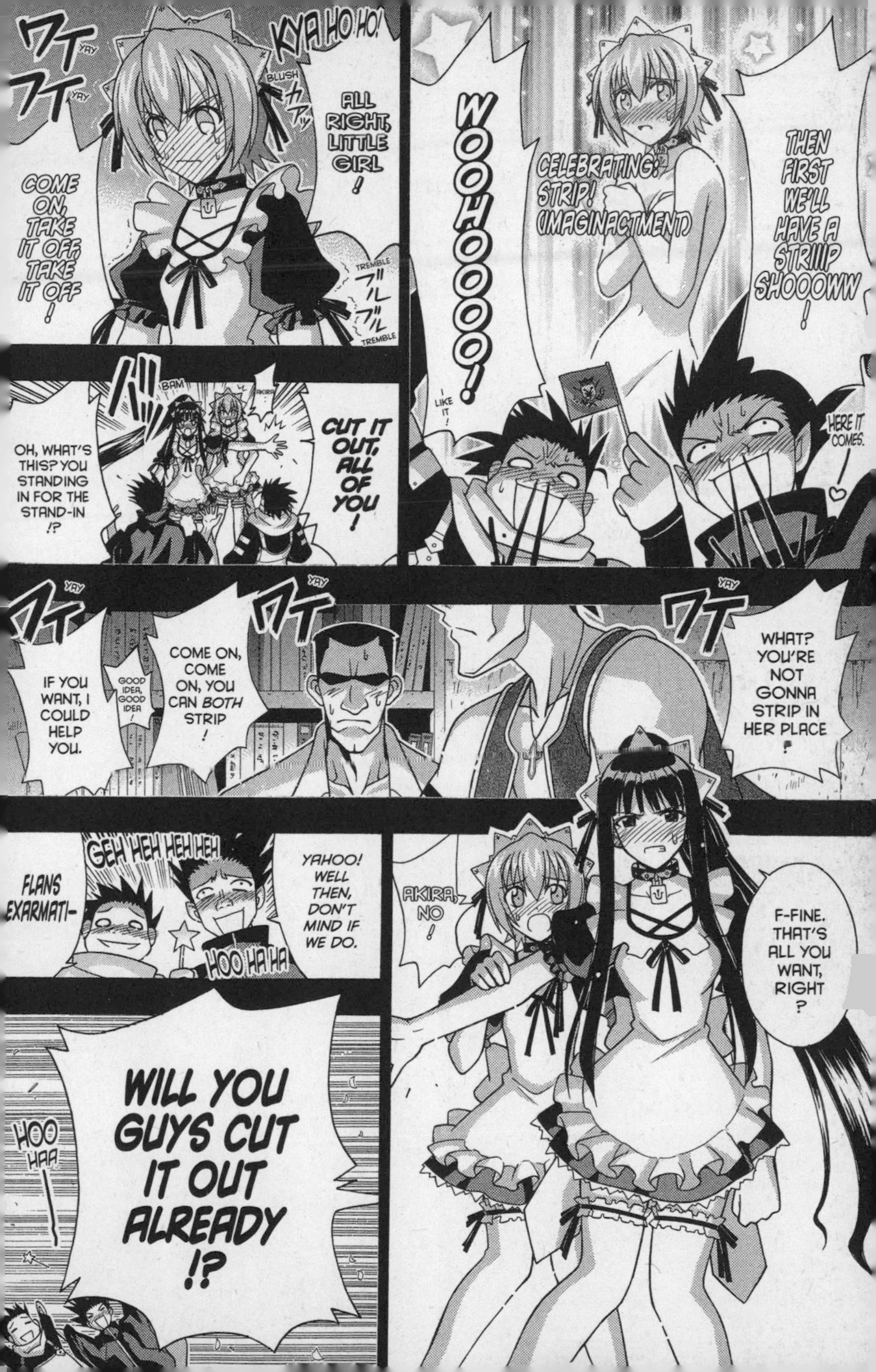
THEN FIRST WE'LL HAVE A STRIIIP SHOOOWW!
CELEBRATING: STRIP! (IMAGINACTMENT)
WOOHOOOOOO!
I LIKE IT!
HERE IT COMES. ♥
KYA HO HO!
ALL RIGHT, LITTLE GIRL!
BLUSH
YAY
YAY
COME ON, TAKE IT OFF, TAKE IT OFF!
TREMBLE
TREMBLE
CUT IT OUT, ALL OF YOU!
AKIRA!
BAM
OH, WHAT'S THIS? YOU STANDING IN FOR THE STAND-IN!?
YAY
WHAT? YOU'RE NOT GONNA STRIP IN HER PLACE!?
YAY
COME ON, COME ON, YOU CAN BOTH STRIP!
GOOD IDEA, GOOD IDEA!
YAY
IF YOU WANT, I COULD HELP YOU.
F-FINE. THAT'S ALL YOU WANT, RIGHT?
AKIRA, NO!
YAHOO! WELL THEN, DON'T MIND IF WE DO.
GEH HEH HEH HEH
HOO HA HA
FLANS EXARMATI-
WILL YOU GUYS CUT IT OUT ALREADY!?
HOO HAA—

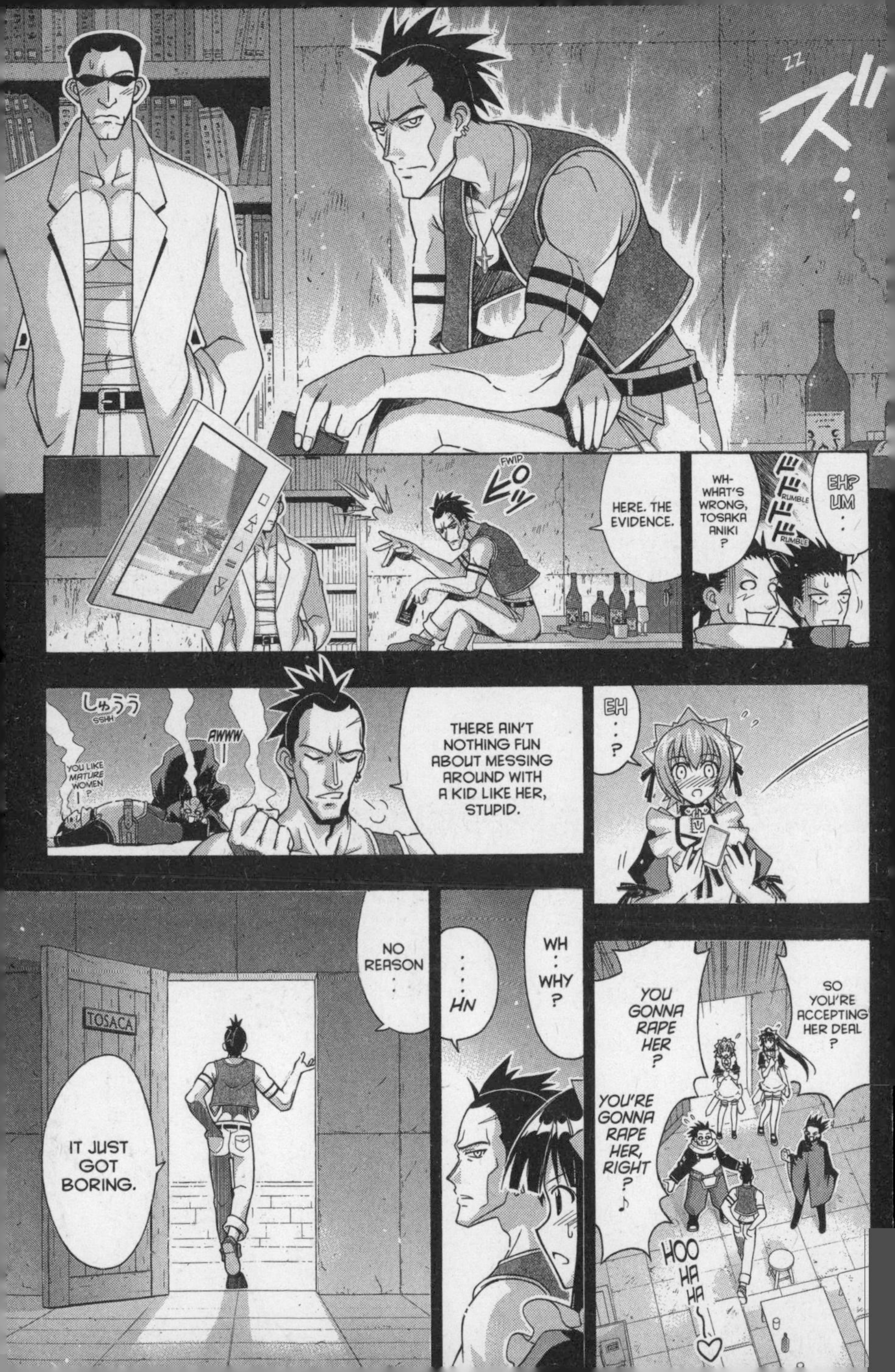
ZZ
ズ…
EH? UM . . .
WH- WHAT'S WRONG, TOSAKA ANIKI ?
RUMBLE RUMBLE
HERE. THE EVIDENCE.
FWIP
EH . . . ?
THERE AIN'T NOTHING FUN ABOUT MESSING AROUND WITH A KID LIKE HER, STUPID.
AWWW
YOU LIKE MATURE WOMEN ?
SSHH
SO YOU'RE ACCEPTING HER DEAL ?
YOU GONNA RAPE HER ?
YOU'RE GONNA RAPE HER, RIGHT ?♪
HOO HA HA ~ ♥
WH . . WHY ?
. . . . HN
NO REASON . . .
TOSACA
IT JUST GOT BORING.

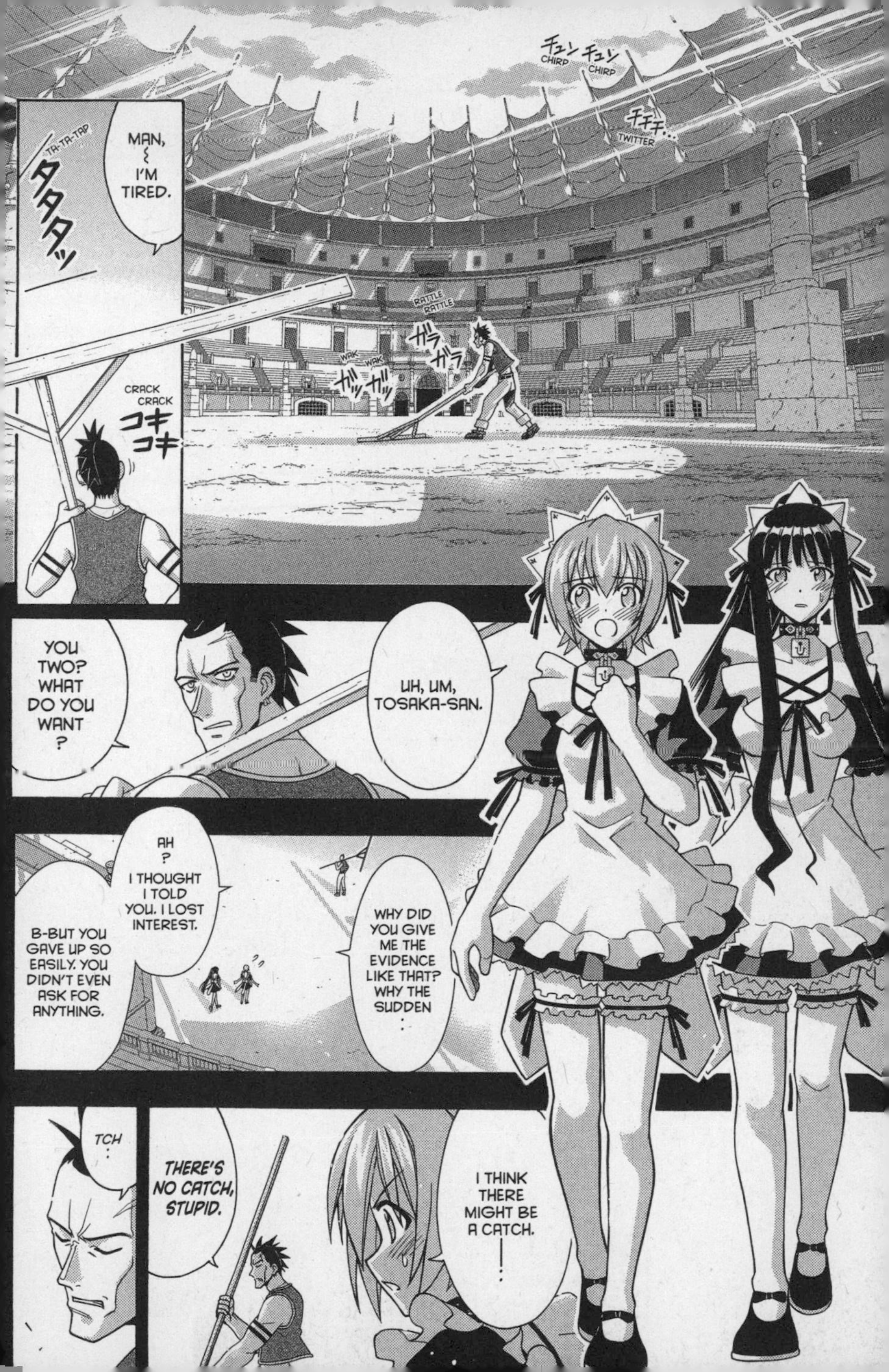

チュン チュン
CHIRP CHIRP
チチチ…
TWITTER
RATTLE RATTLE
ガラ ガラ
WAK WAK
ガッガッ
MAN, ~ I'M TIRED.
TA-TA-TAP
タタタッ
CRACK CRACK
コキ コキ
UH, UM, TOSAKA-SAN.
YOU TWO? WHAT DO YOU WANT?
WHY DID YOU GIVE ME THE EVIDENCE LIKE THAT? WHY THE SUDDEN …
AH? I THOUGHT I TOLD YOU. I LOST INTEREST.
B-BUT YOU GAVE UP SO EASILY. YOU DIDN'T EVEN ASK FOR ANYTHING.
I THINK THERE MIGHT BE A CATCH …!
THERE'S NO CATCH, STUPID.
TCH …

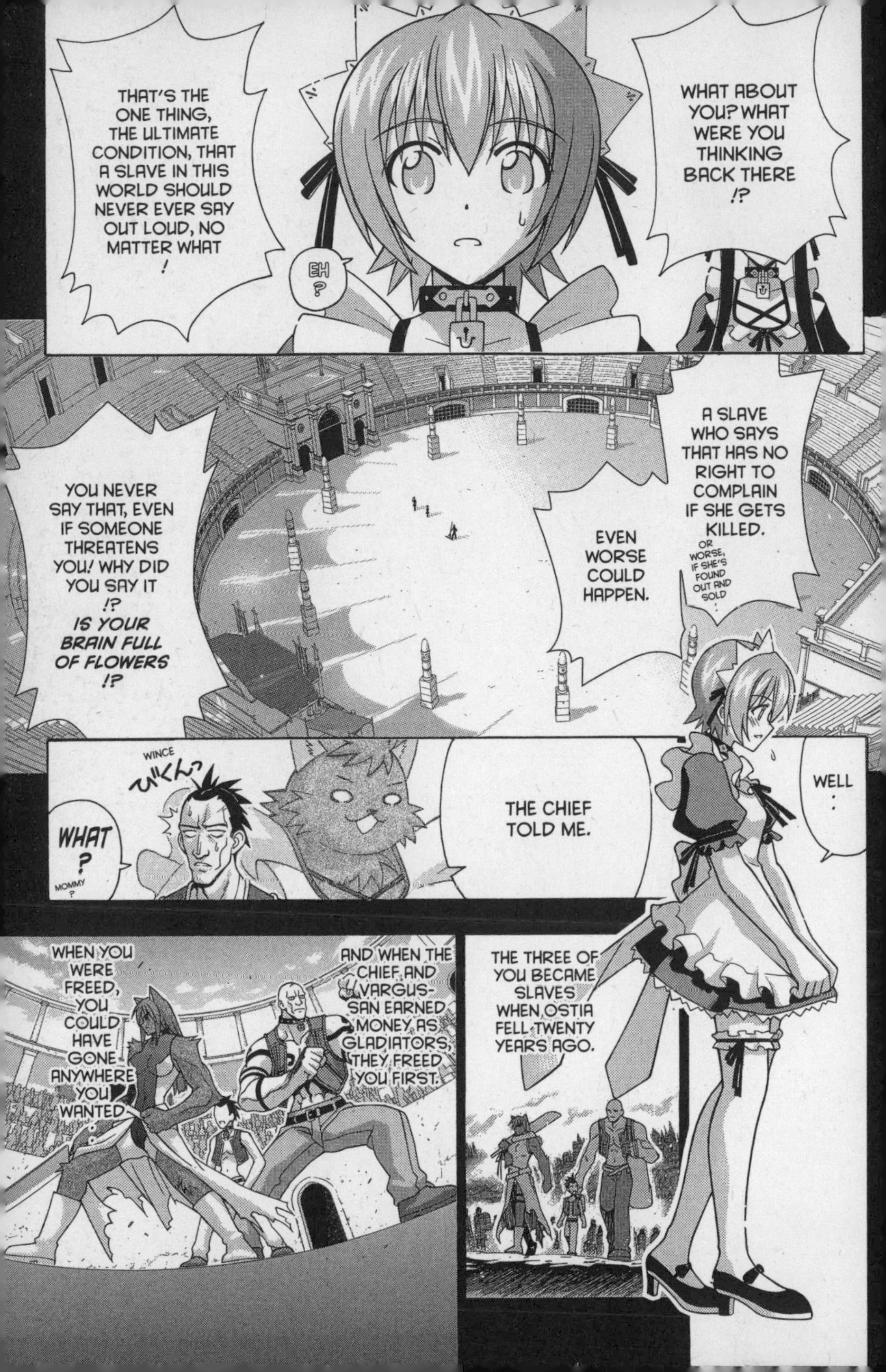
WHAT ABOUT YOU? WHAT WERE YOU THINKING BACK THERE !?
THAT'S THE ONE THING, THE ULTIMATE CONDITION, THAT A SLAVE IN THIS WORLD SHOULD NEVER EVER SAY OUT LOUD, NO MATTER WHAT !
EH ?
A SLAVE WHO SAYS THAT HAS NO RIGHT TO COMPLAIN IF SHE GETS KILLED.
OR WORSE, IF SHE'S FOUND OUT AND SOLD
EVEN WORSE COULD HAPPEN.
YOU NEVER SAY THAT, EVEN IF SOMEONE THREATENS YOU! WHY DID YOU SAY IT !? *IS YOUR BRAIN FULL OF FLOWERS !?*
WELL :
THE CHIEF TOLD ME.
WINCE
びくんっ
WHAT ?
MOMMY ?
THE THREE OF YOU BECAME SLAVES WHEN OSTIA FELL TWENTY YEARS AGO.
AND WHEN THE CHIEF AND VARGUS-SAN EARNED MONEY AS GLADIATORS, THEY FREED YOU FIRST.
WHEN YOU WERE FREED, YOU COULD HAVE GONE ANYWHERE YOU WANTED

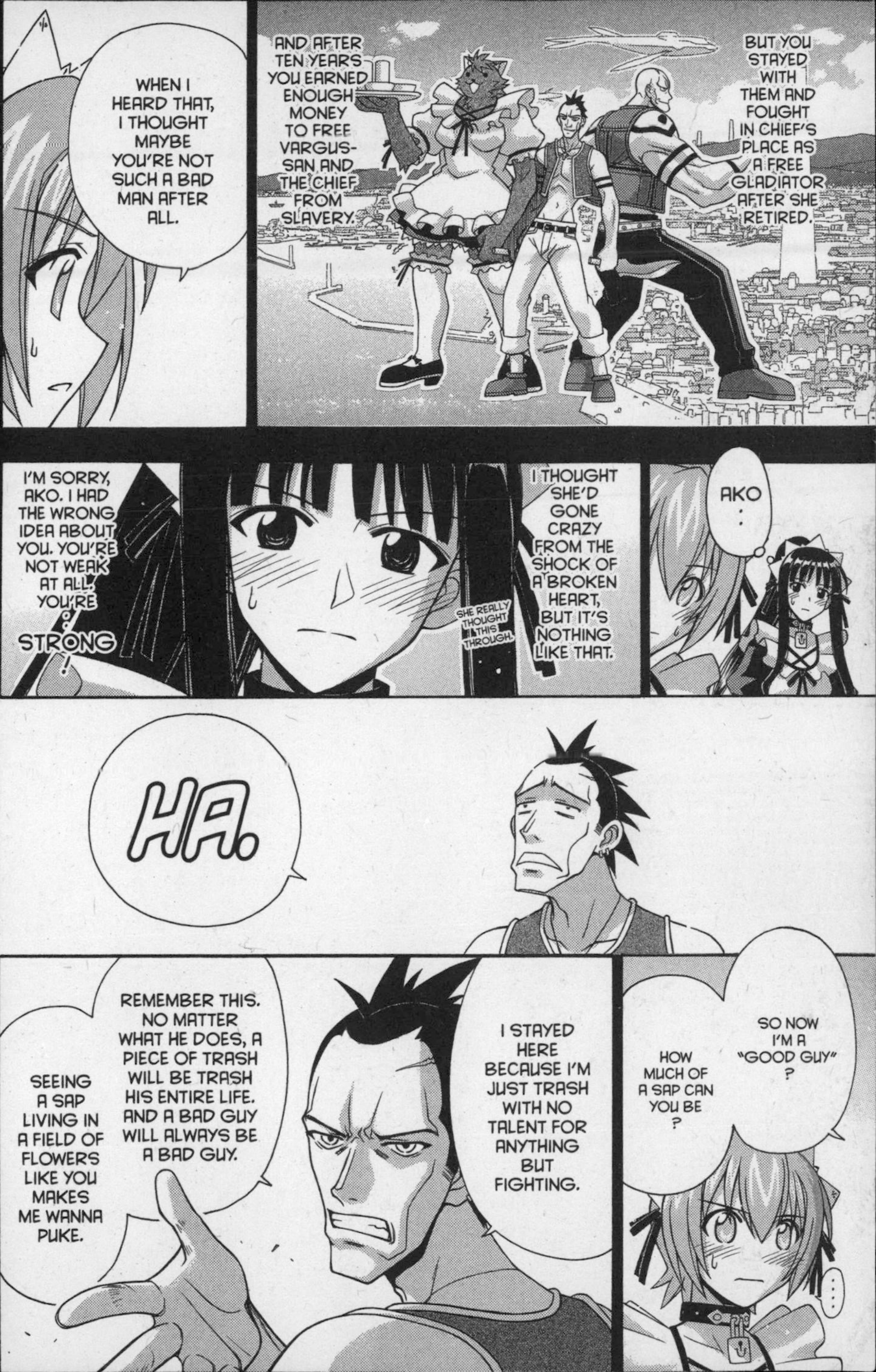

AND AFTER TEN YEARS YOU EARNED ENOUGH MONEY TO FREE VARGUS-SAN AND THE CHIEF FROM SLAVERY.
BUT YOU STAYED WITH THEM AND FOUGHT IN CHIEF'S PLACE AS A FREE GLADIATOR AFTER SHE RETIRED.
WHEN I HEARD THAT, I THOUGHT MAYBE YOU'RE NOT SUCH A BAD MAN AFTER ALL.
AKO...
I THOUGHT SHE'D GONE CRAZY FROM THE SHOCK OF A BROKEN HEART, BUT IT'S NOTHING LIKE THAT.
SHE REALLY THOUGHT THIS THROUGH.
I'M SORRY, AKO. I HAD THE WRONG IDEA ABOUT YOU. YOU'RE NOT WEAK AT ALL. YOU'RE... STRONG!
HA.
SO NOW I'M A "GOOD GUY"?
HOW MUCH OF A SAP CAN YOU BE?
...
I STAYED HERE BECAUSE I'M JUST TRASH WITH NO TALENT FOR ANYTHING BUT FIGHTING.
REMEMBER THIS. NO MATTER WHAT HE DOES, A PIECE OF TRASH WILL BE TRASH HIS ENTIRE LIFE. AND A BAD GUY WILL ALWAYS BE A BAD GUY.
SEEING A SAP LIVING IN A FIELD OF FLOWERS LIKE YOU MAKES ME WANNA PUKE.

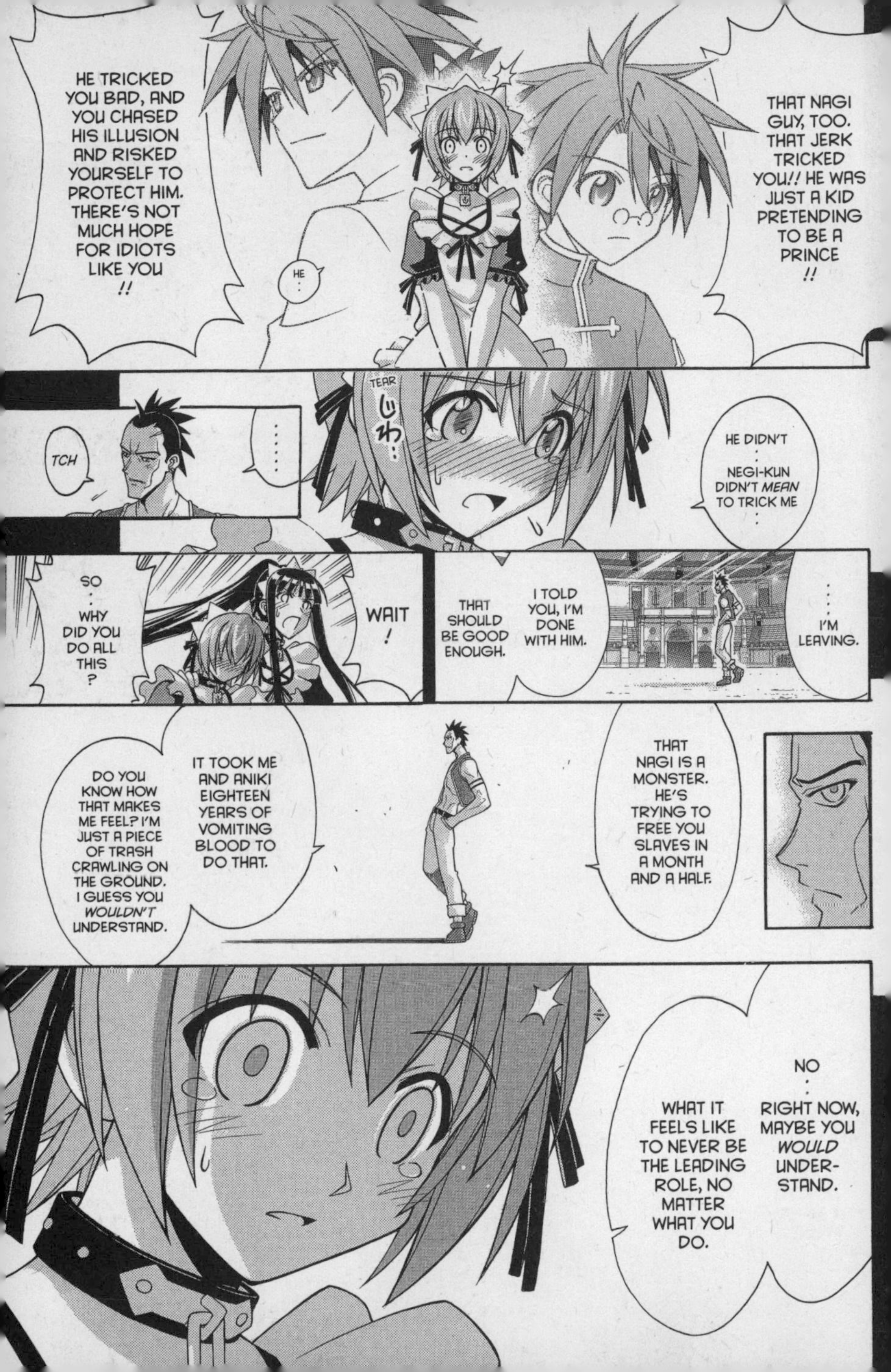

THAT NAGI GUY, TOO. THAT JERK TRICKED YOU!! HE WAS JUST A KID PRETENDING TO BE A PRINCE!!
HE TRICKED YOU BAD, AND YOU CHASED HIS ILLUSION AND RISKED YOURSELF TO PROTECT HIM. THERE'S NOT MUCH HOPE FOR IDIOTS LIKE YOU!!
HE...
TEAR
じわ...
HE DIDN'T... NEGI-KUN DIDN'T *MEAN* TO TRICK ME...
......
TCH
......
I'M LEAVING.
I TOLD YOU, I'M DONE WITH HIM.
THAT SHOULD BE GOOD ENOUGH.
WAIT!
SO... WHY DID YOU DO ALL THIS?
THAT NAGI IS A MONSTER. HE'S TRYING TO FREE YOU SLAVES IN A MONTH AND A HALF.
IT TOOK ME AND ANIKI EIGHTEEN YEARS OF VOMITING BLOOD TO DO THAT.
DO YOU KNOW HOW THAT MAKES ME FEEL? I'M JUST A PIECE OF TRASH CRAWLING ON THE GROUND. I GUESS YOU *WOULDN'T* UNDERSTAND.
NO... RIGHT NOW, MAYBE YOU *WOULD* UNDER-STAND.
WHAT IT FEELS LIKE TO NEVER BE THE LEADING ROLE, NO MATTER WHAT YOU DO.

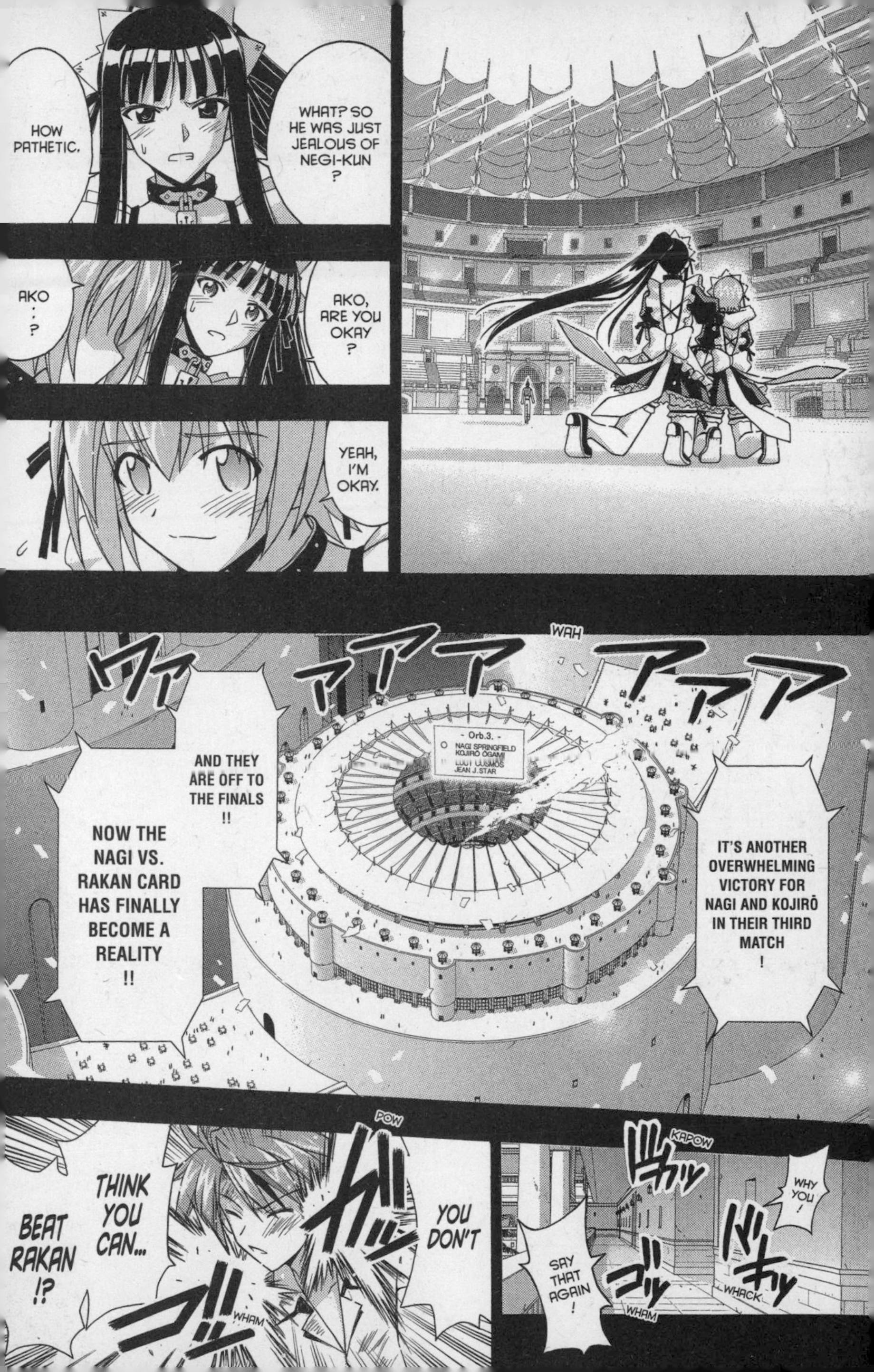
WHAT? SO HE WAS JUST JEALOUS OF NEGI-KUN?
HOW PATHETIC.
AKO, ARE YOU OKAY?
AKO...?
YEAH, I'M OKAY.
WAH
- Orb.3. -
NAGI SPRINGFIELD
KOJIRŌ ŌGAMI
JEAN J. STAR
IT'S ANOTHER OVERWHELMING VICTORY FOR NAGI AND KOJIRŌ IN THEIR THIRD MATCH!
AND THEY ARE OFF TO THE FINALS!!
NOW THE NAGI VS. RAKAN CARD HAS FINALLY BECOME A REALITY!!
KAPOW
WHY YOU!
WHACK
SAY THAT AGAIN!
WHAM
POW
YOU DON'T
THINK YOU CAN...
BEAT RAKAN!?
WHAM

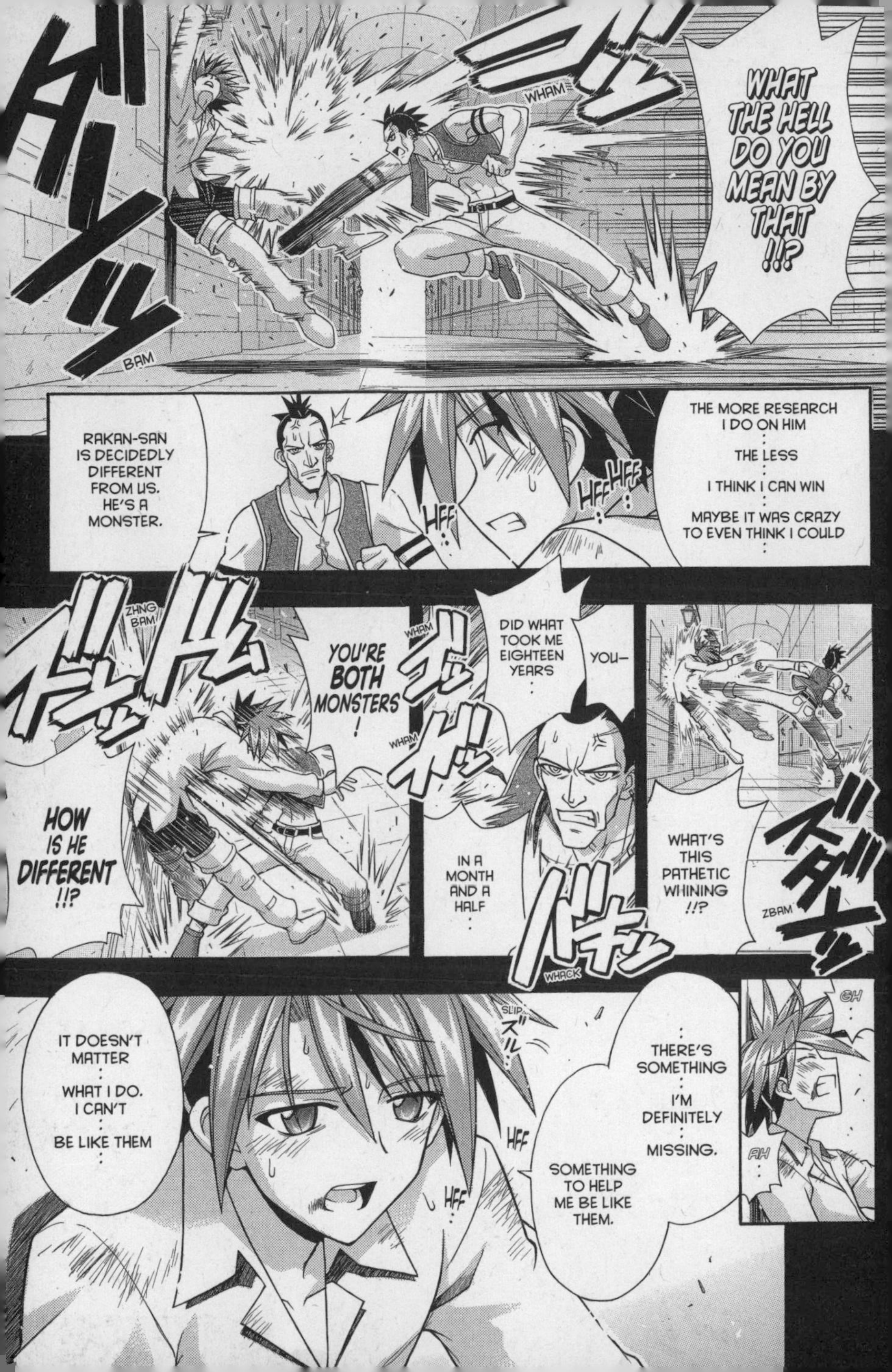
WHAM
WHAT THE HELL DO YOU MEAN BY THAT !!?
BAM
THE MORE RESEARCH I DO ON HIM
...THE LESS
...I THINK I CAN WIN
MAYBE IT WAS CRAZY TO EVEN THINK I COULD...
HFF HFF
HFF
RAKAN-SAN IS DECIDEDLY DIFFERENT FROM US. HE'S A MONSTER.
WHAT'S THIS PATHETIC WHINING !!?
ZBAM
YOU—
DID WHAT TOOK ME EIGHTEEN YEARS...
IN A MONTH AND A HALF...
WHAM
WHAM
WHACK
YOU'RE BOTH MONSTERS!
ZHNG BAM
HOW IS HE DIFFERENT !!?
GH
AH...
...THERE'S SOMETHING... I'M DEFINITELY... MISSING.
SOMETHING TO HELP ME BE LIKE THEM.
SLIP ズル...
HFF
HFF
IT DOESN'T MATTER... WHAT I DO. I CAN'T... BE LIKE THEM...

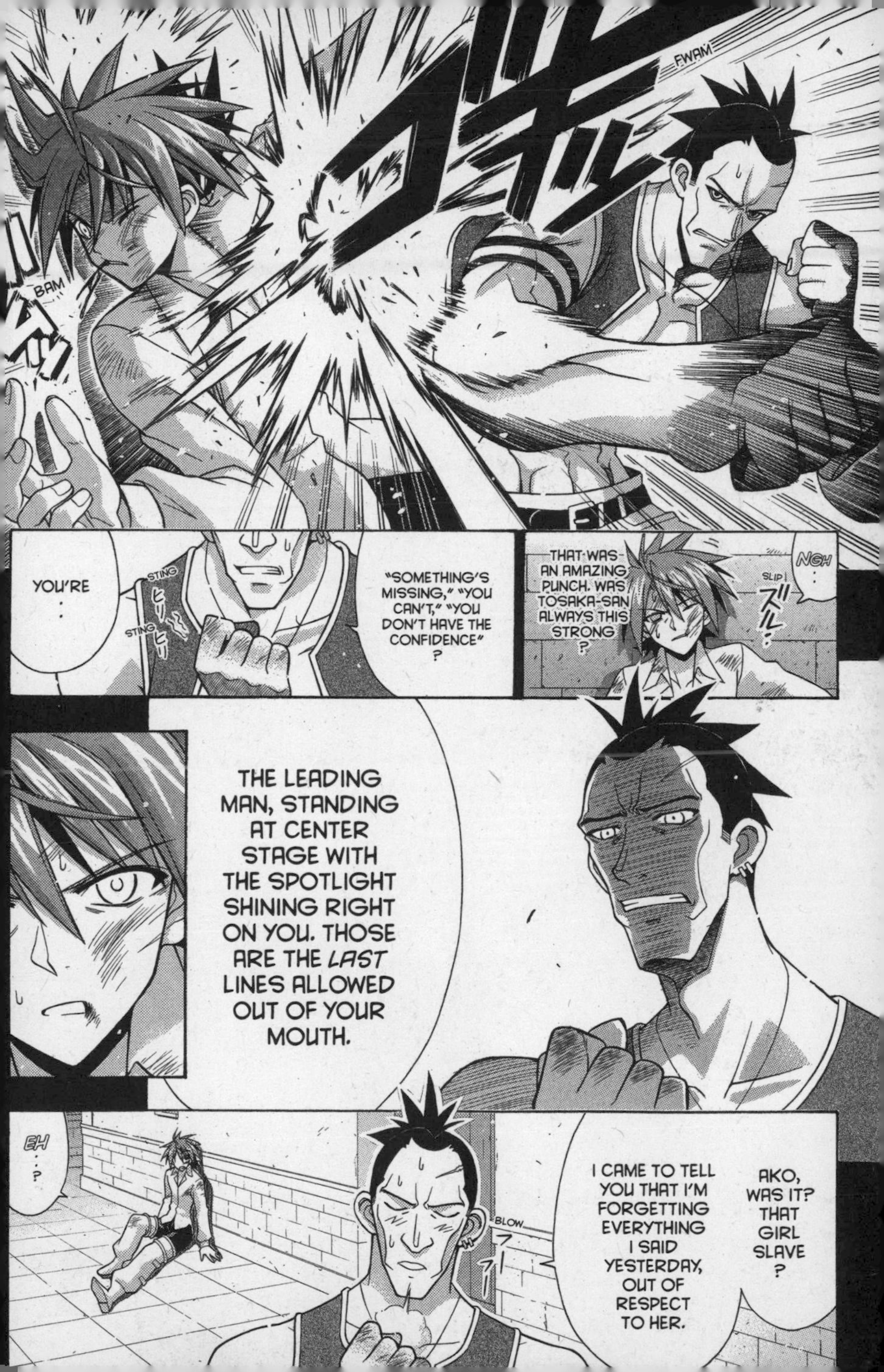

FWAM
BAM
NGH...
SLIP
THAT WAS AN AMAZING PUNCH. WAS TOSAKA-SAN ALWAYS THIS STRONG?
"SOMETHING'S MISSING," "YOU CAN'T," "YOU DON'T HAVE THE CONFIDENCE"?
STING STING
YOU'RE...
THE LEADING MAN, STANDING AT CENTER STAGE WITH THE SPOTLIGHT SHINING RIGHT ON YOU. THOSE ARE THE *LAST* LINES ALLOWED OUT OF YOUR MOUTH.
AKO, WAS IT? THAT GIRL SLAVE?
I CAME TO TELL YOU THAT I'M FORGETTING EVERYTHING I SAID YESTERDAY, OUT OF RESPECT TO HER.
BLOW
EH...?

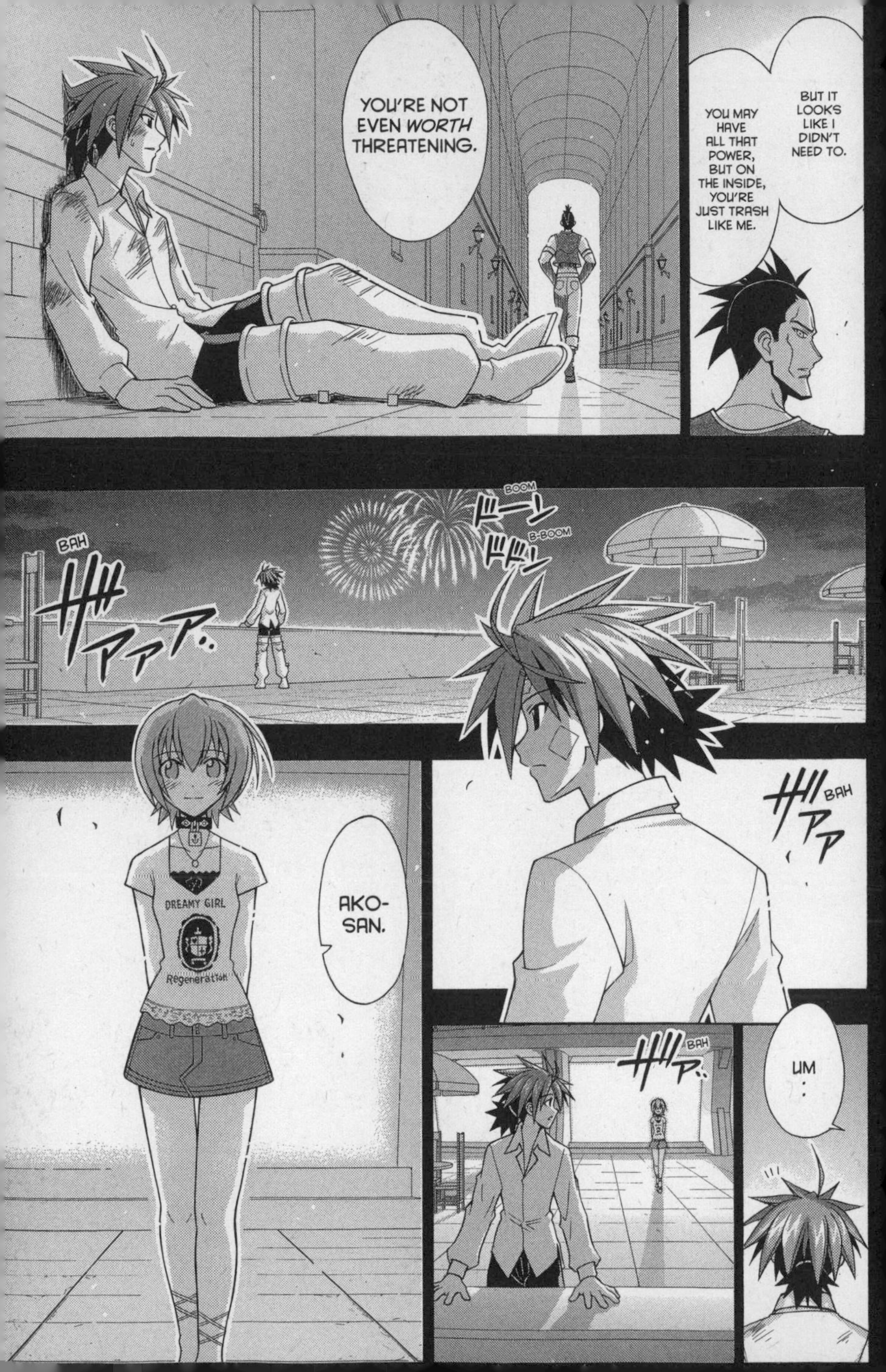
BUT IT LOOKS LIKE I DIDN'T NEED TO.
YOU MAY HAVE ALL THAT POWER, BUT ON THE INSIDE, YOU'RE JUST TRASH LIKE ME.
YOU'RE NOT EVEN WORTH THREATENING.
BOOM
ドーン
B-BOOM
ドドン
BAH
ザァァア..
BAH
ザァァ
UM..
BAH
ザァ..
AKO-SAN.
DREAMY GIRL
Regeneration

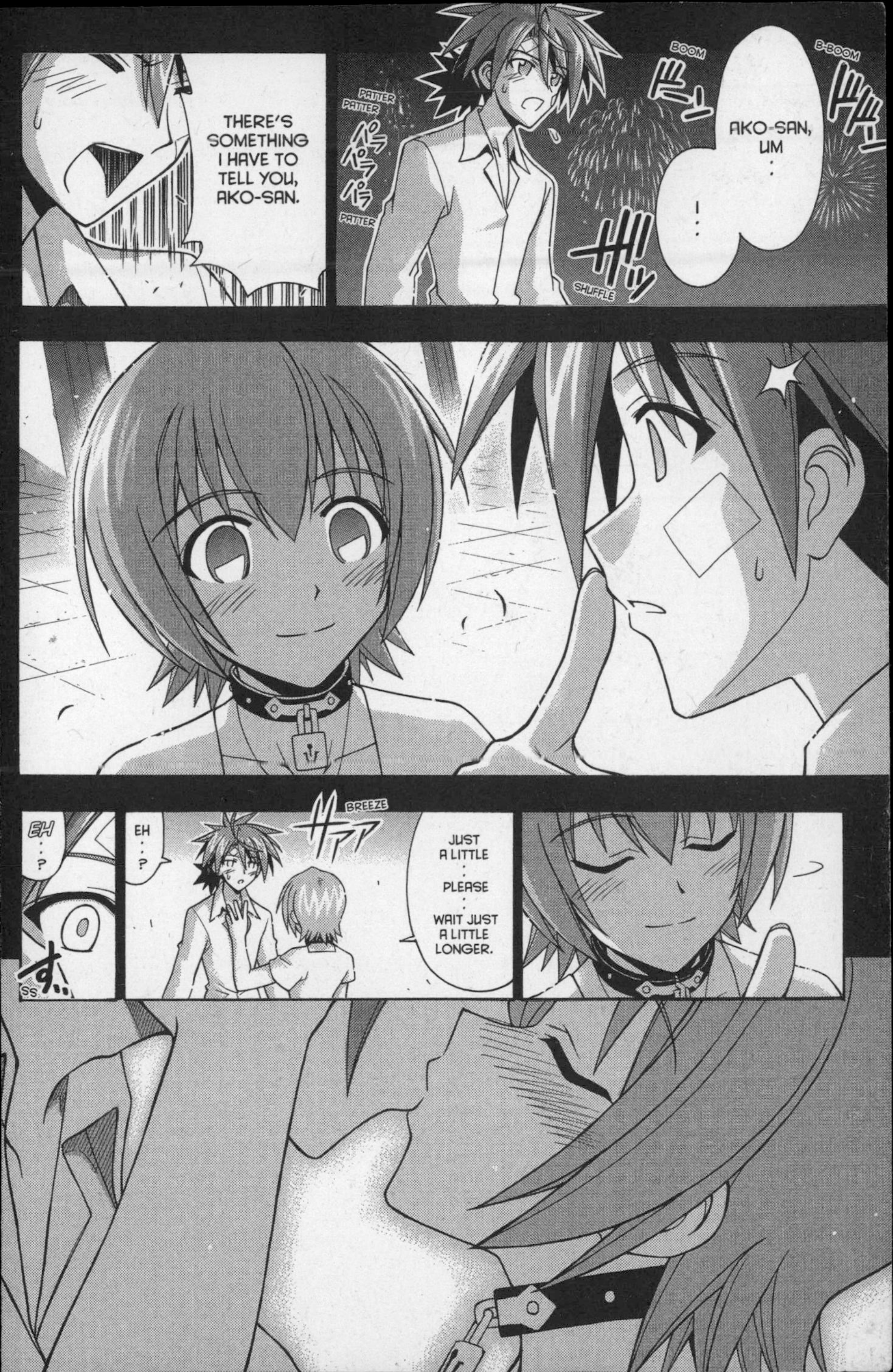
B-BOOM
BOOM
AKO-SAN, UM . . . ! . .
PATTER PATTER
PATTER
SHUFFLE
THERE'S SOMETHING I HAVE TO TELL YOU, AKO-SAN.
BREEZE
JUST A LITTLE . . . PLEASE . . . WAIT JUST A LITTLE LONGER.
EH . . . ?
EH . . . ?
SS . .

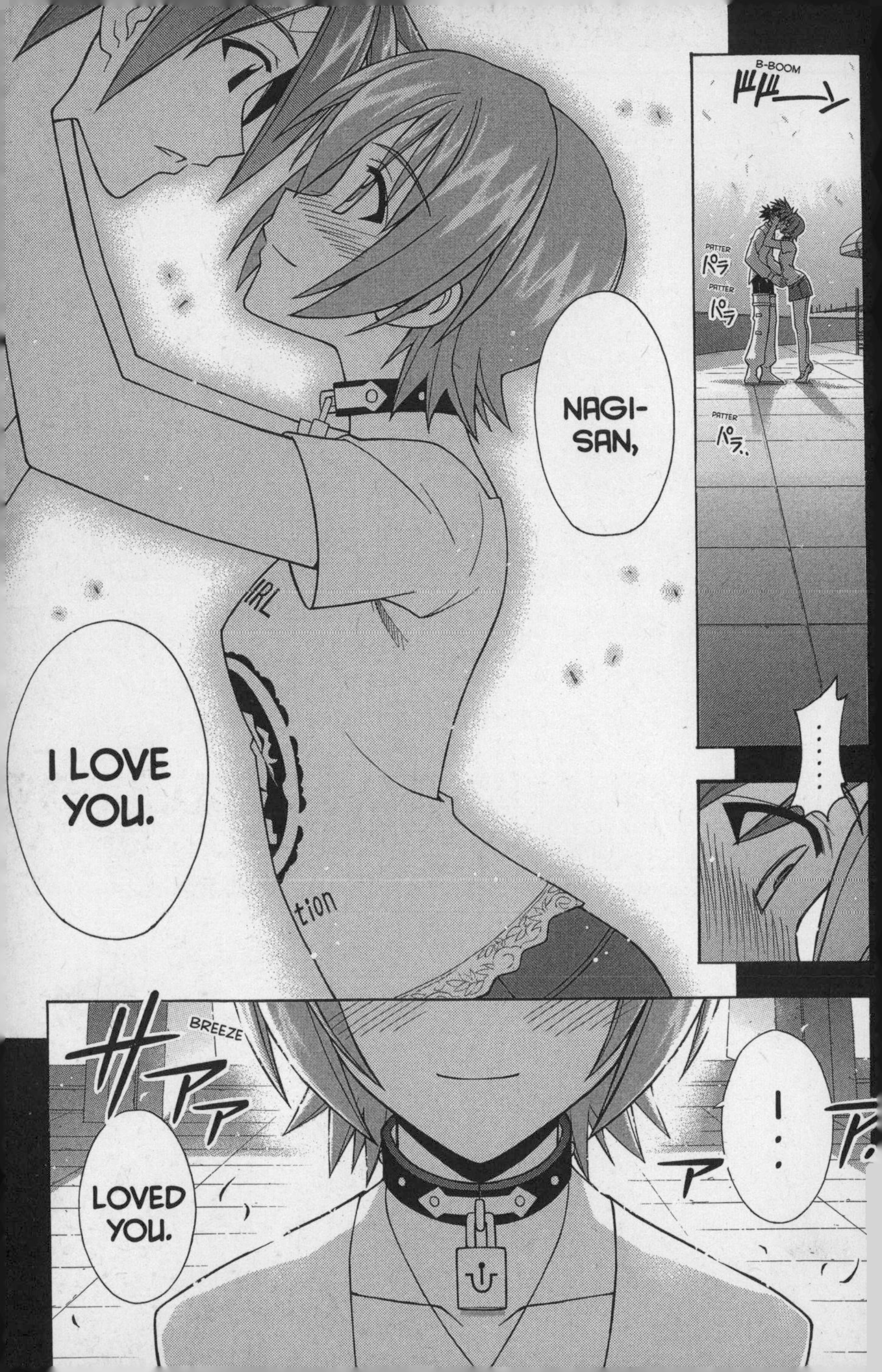
B-BOOM
PATTER
PATTER
PATTER
......
NAGI-SAN,
I LOVE YOU.
!..
BREEZE
LOVED YOU.

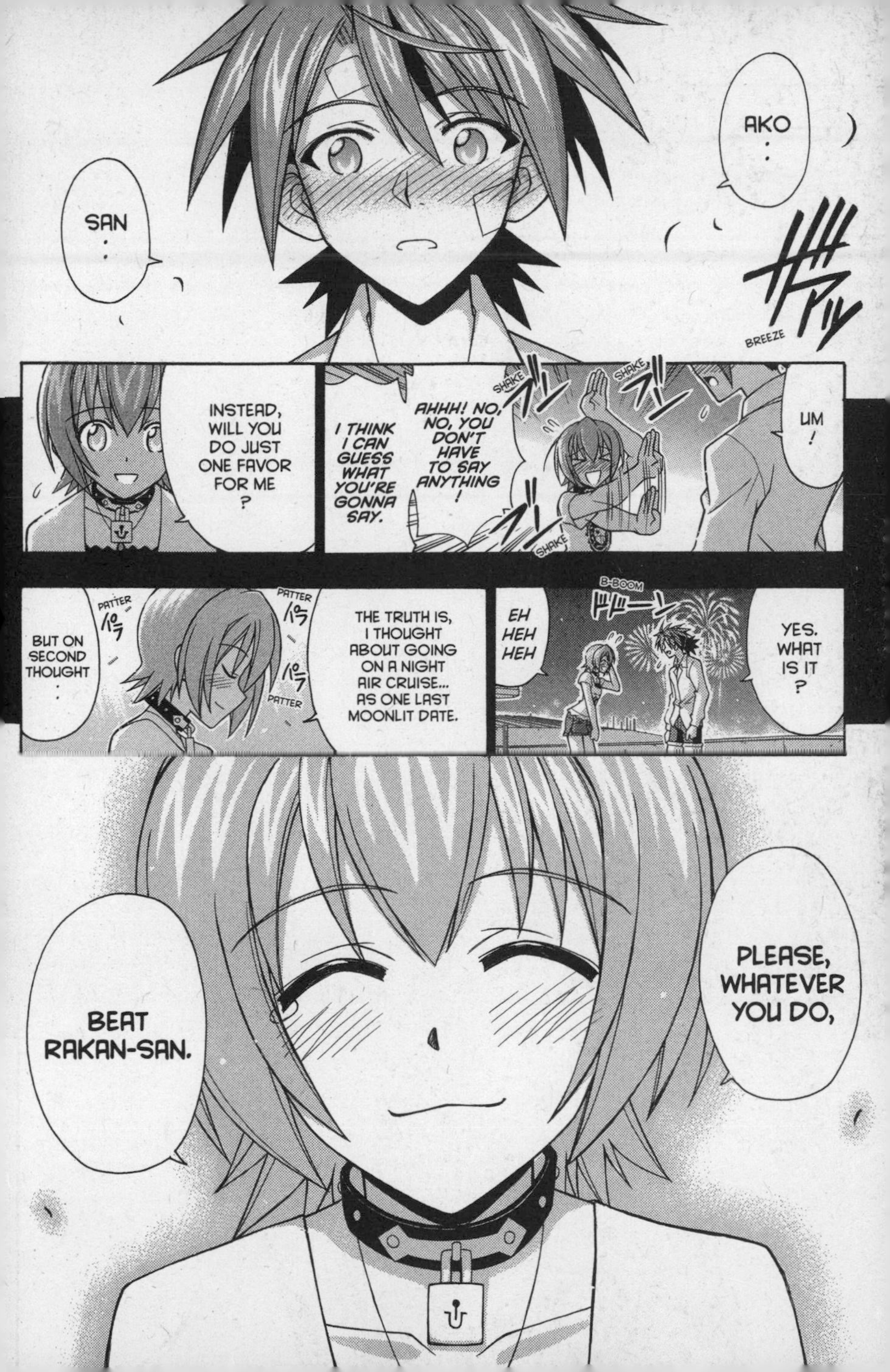
AKO :
SAN :
BREEZE
UM !
SHAKE
SHAKE
AHHH! NO, NO, YOU DON'T HAVE TO SAY ANYTHING !
SHAKE
I THINK I CAN GUESS WHAT YOU'RE GONNA SAY.
INSTEAD, WILL YOU DO JUST ONE FAVOR FOR ME ?
YES. WHAT IS IT ?
B-BOOM
EH HEH HEH
THE TRUTH IS, I THOUGHT ABOUT GOING ON A NIGHT AIR CRUISE... AS ONE LAST MOONLIT DATE.
PATTER
PATTER
PATTER
BUT ON SECOND THOUGHT :
PLEASE, WHATEVER YOU DO,
BEAT RAKAN-SAN.

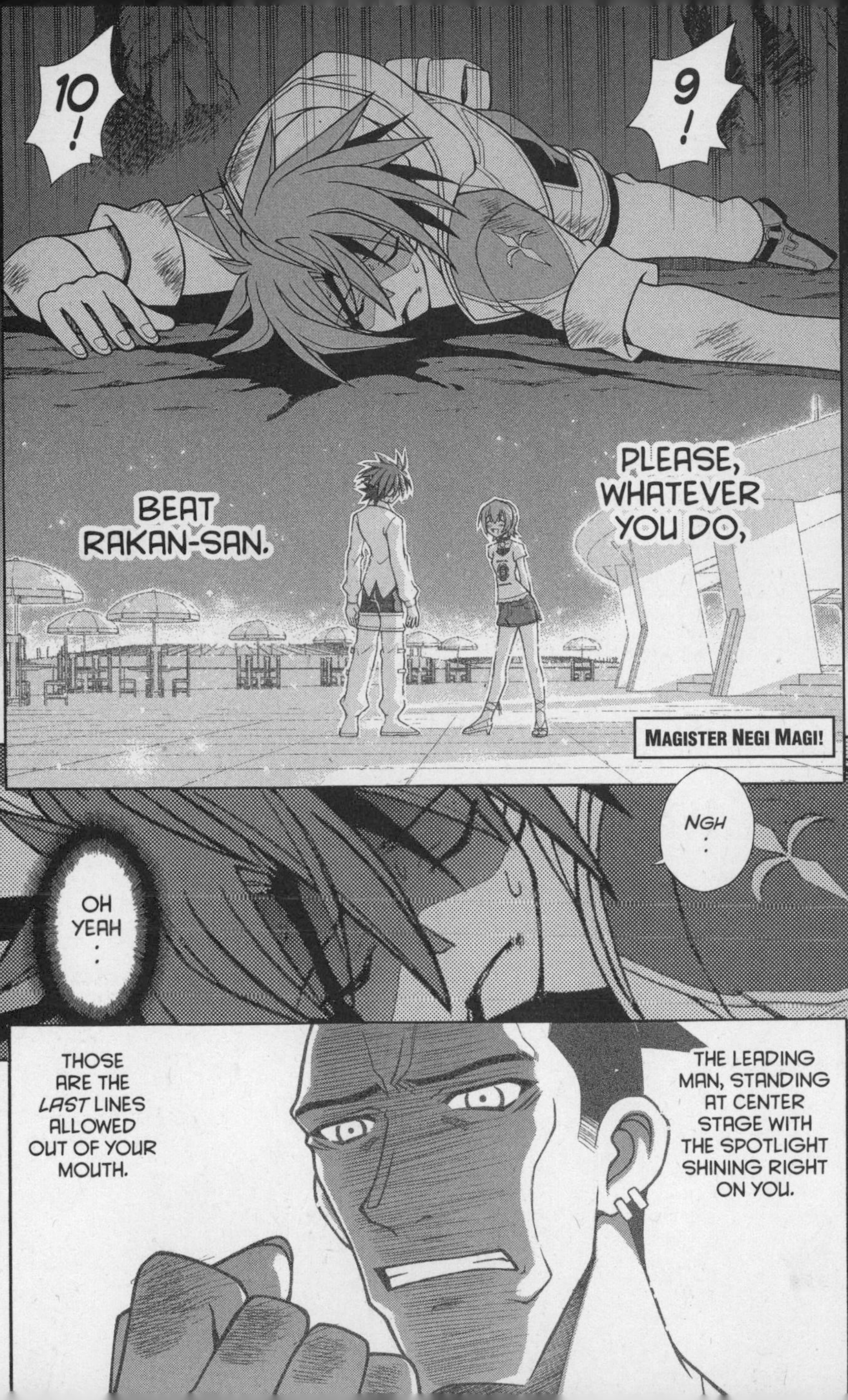
9!
10!
PLEASE, WHATEVER YOU DO,
BEAT RAKAN-SAN.
MAGISTER NEGI MAGI!
NGH...
OH YEAH...
THE LEADING MAN, STANDING AT CENTER STAGE WITH THE SPOTLIGHT SHINING RIGHT ON YOU.
THOSE ARE THE *LAST* LINES ALLOWED OUT OF YOUR MOUTH.

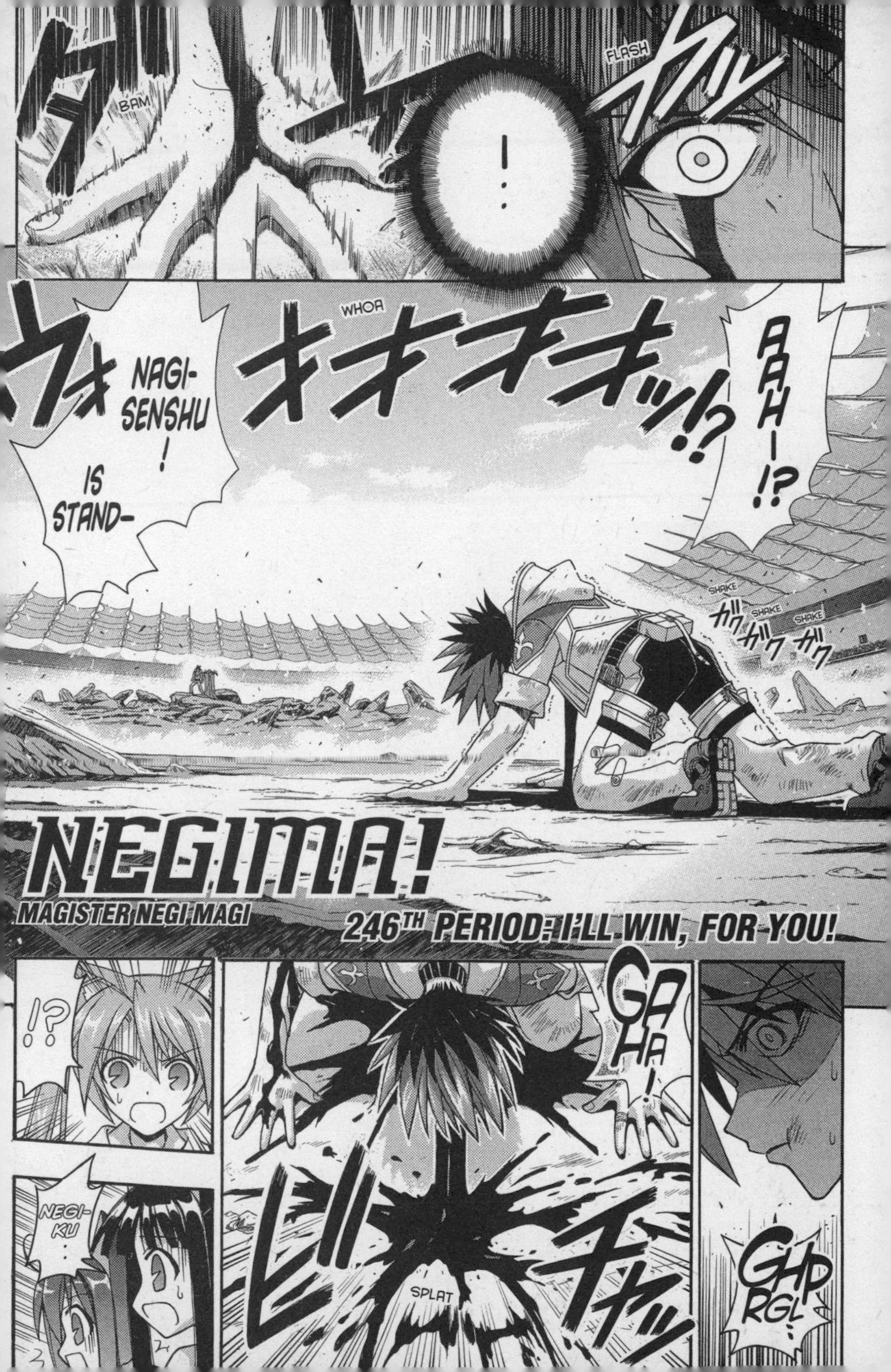

FLASH
!..
BAM
AAH-!?
WHOA
NAGI-SENSHU!
IS STAND-
SHAKE
SHAKE
SHAKE
NEGIMA!
MAGISTER NEGI MAGI
246TH PERIOD: I'LL WIN, FOR YOU!
GHPRGL!
GAHA-!
SPLAT
!?
NEGI-KU

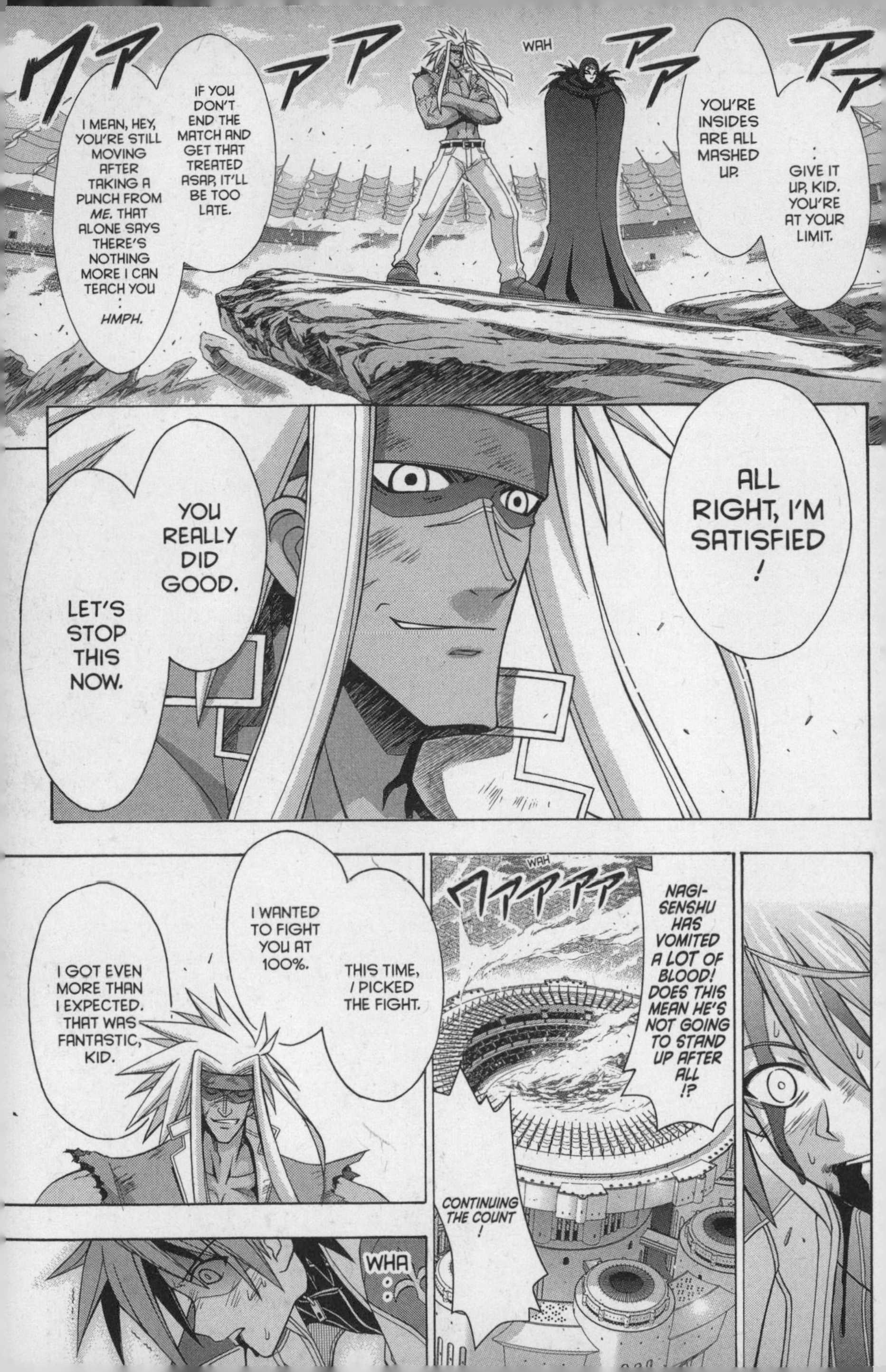
WAH
YOU'RE INSIDES ARE ALL MASHED UP. : GIVE IT UP, KID. YOU'RE AT YOUR LIMIT.
I MEAN, HEY, YOU'RE STILL MOVING AFTER TAKING A PUNCH FROM *ME*. THAT ALONE SAYS THERE'S NOTHING MORE I CAN TEACH YOU : *HMPH.* IF YOU DON'T END THE MATCH AND GET THAT TREATED ASAP, IT'LL BE TOO LATE.
ALL RIGHT, I'M SATISFIED!
YOU REALLY DID GOOD. LET'S STOP THIS NOW.
WAH
NAGI-SENSHU HAS VOMITED A LOT OF BLOOD! DOES THIS MEAN HE'S NOT GOING TO STAND UP AFTER ALL!?
CONTINUING THE COUNT!
I WANTED TO FIGHT YOU AT 100%. THIS TIME, I PICKED THE FIGHT.
I GOT EVEN MORE THAN I EXPECTED. THAT WAS FANTASTIC, KID.
WHA...

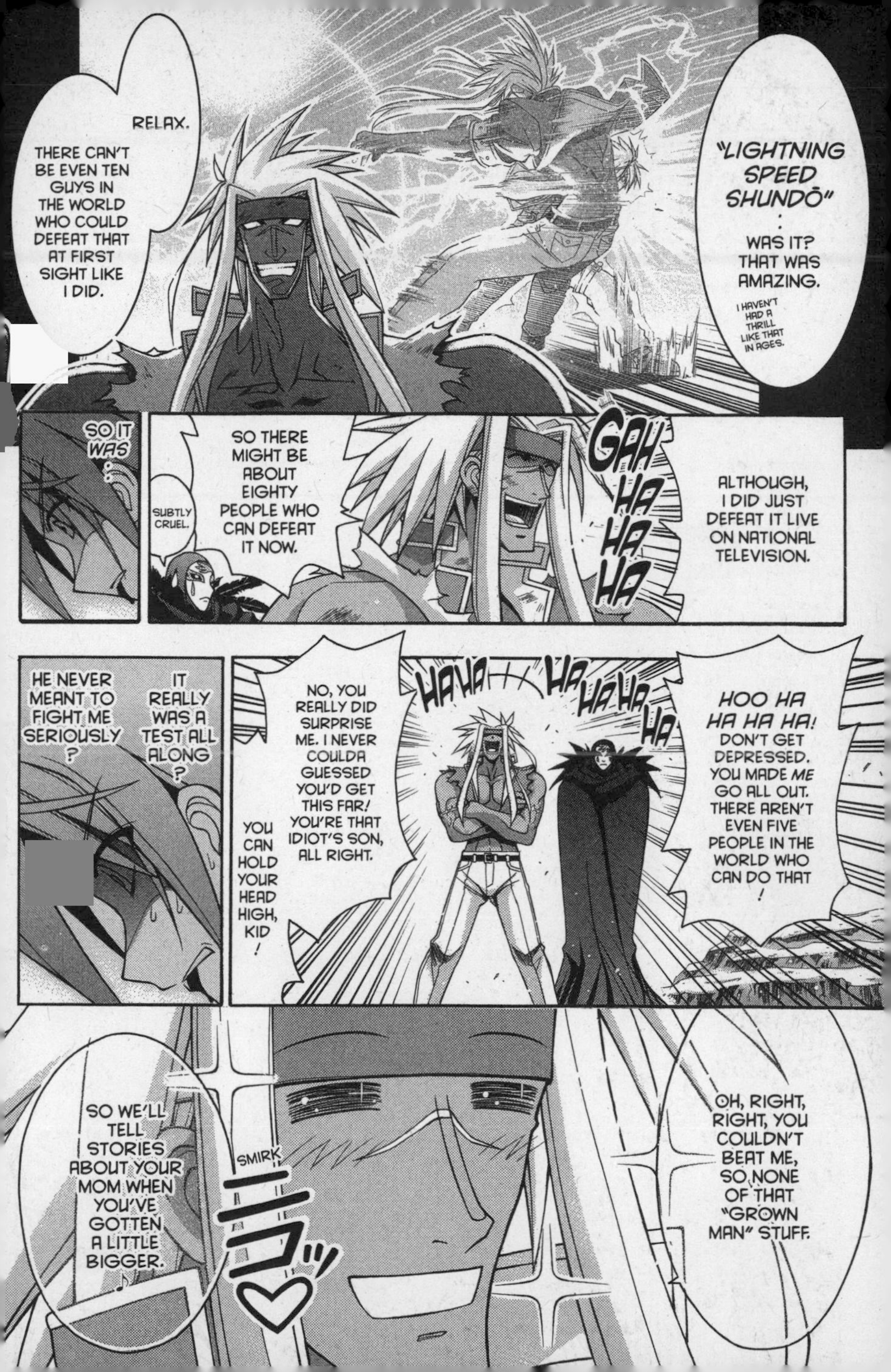

"LIGHTNING SPEED SHUNDŌ"...
WAS IT? THAT WAS AMAZING.
I HAVEN'T HAD A THRILL LIKE THAT IN AGES.
RELAX.
THERE CAN'T BE EVEN TEN GUYS IN THE WORLD WHO COULD DEFEAT THAT AT FIRST SIGHT LIKE I DID.
ALTHOUGH, I DID JUST DEFEAT IT LIVE ON NATIONAL TELEVISION.
GAH HA HA HA HA
SO THERE MIGHT BE ABOUT EIGHTY PEOPLE WHO CAN DEFEAT IT NOW.
SUBTLY CRUEL.
SO IT WAS...
HOO HA HA HA HA! DON'T GET DEPRESSED. YOU MADE ME GO ALL OUT. THERE AREN'T EVEN FIVE PEOPLE IN THE WORLD WHO CAN DO THAT!
HA HA HA HA HA HA HA
NO, YOU REALLY DID SURPRISE ME. I NEVER COULDA GUESSED YOU'D GET THIS FAR! YOU'RE THAT IDIOT'S SON, ALL RIGHT.
YOU CAN HOLD YOUR HEAD HIGH, KID!
IT REALLY WAS A TEST ALL ALONG?
HE NEVER MEANT TO FIGHT ME SERIOUSLY?
OH, RIGHT, RIGHT, YOU COULDN'T BEAT ME, SO NONE OF THAT "GROWN MAN" STUFF.
SMIRK
SO WE'LL TELL STORIES ABOUT YOUR MOM WHEN YOU'VE GOTTEN A LITTLE BIGGER.

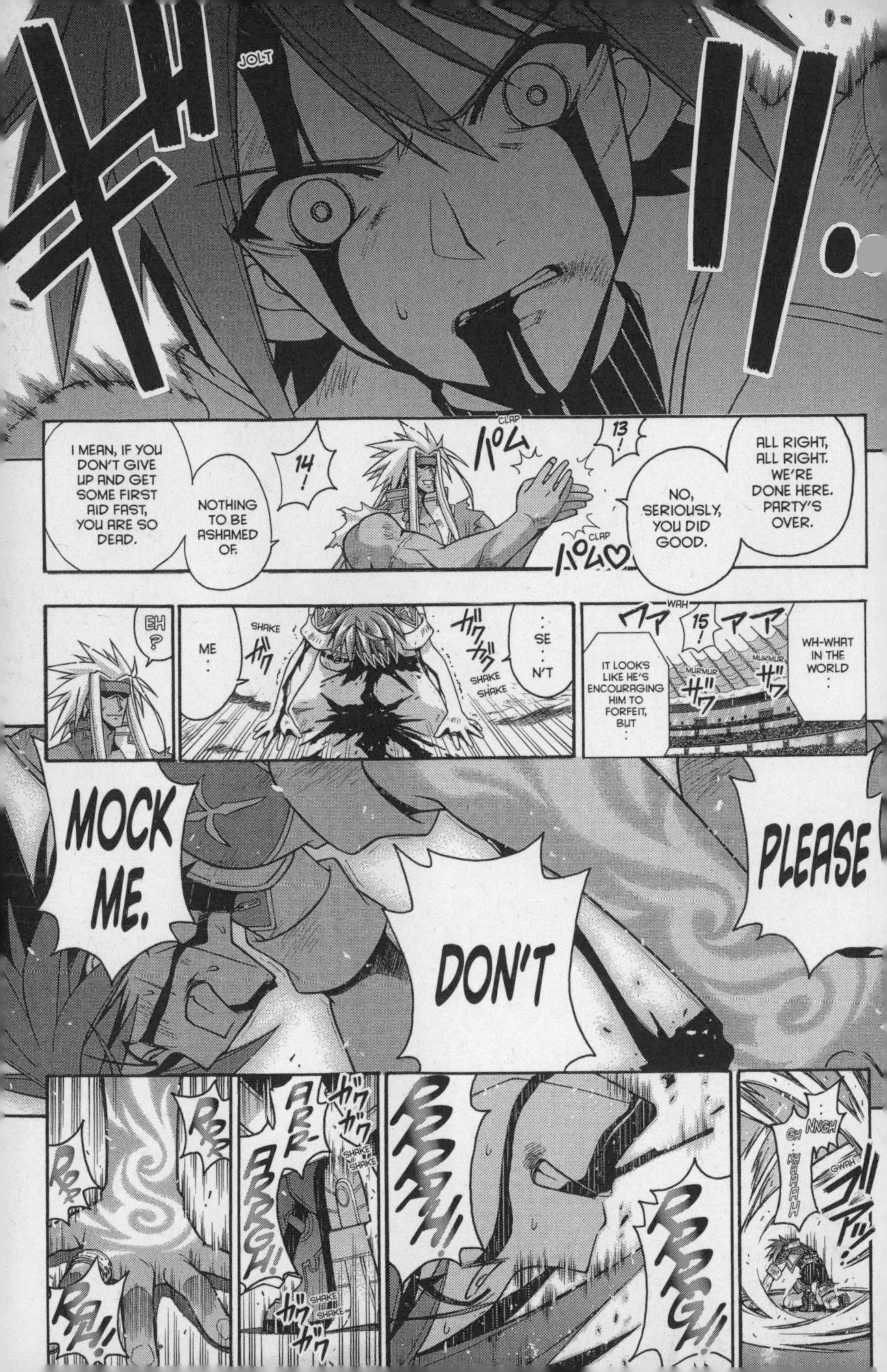
JOLT
ALL RIGHT, ALL RIGHT. WE'RE DONE HERE. PARTY'S OVER.
13!
NO, SERIOUSLY, YOU DID GOOD.
CLAP
CLAP
14!
NOTHING TO BE ASHAMED OF.
I MEAN, IF YOU DON'T GIVE UP AND GET SOME FIRST AID FAST, YOU ARE SO DEAD.
WH-WHAT IN THE WORLD...
MURMUR
MURMUR
WAH
15!
IT LOOKS LIKE HE'S ENCOURAGING HIM TO FORFEIT, BUT...
...SE...N'T
SHAKE SHAKE
SHAKE
ME...
EH?
PLEASE
DON'T
MOCK ME.
...NNGH
GH... KWAAAAH
GWAH
ARR-
SHAKE SHAKE
SHAKE SHAKE
RAH!!

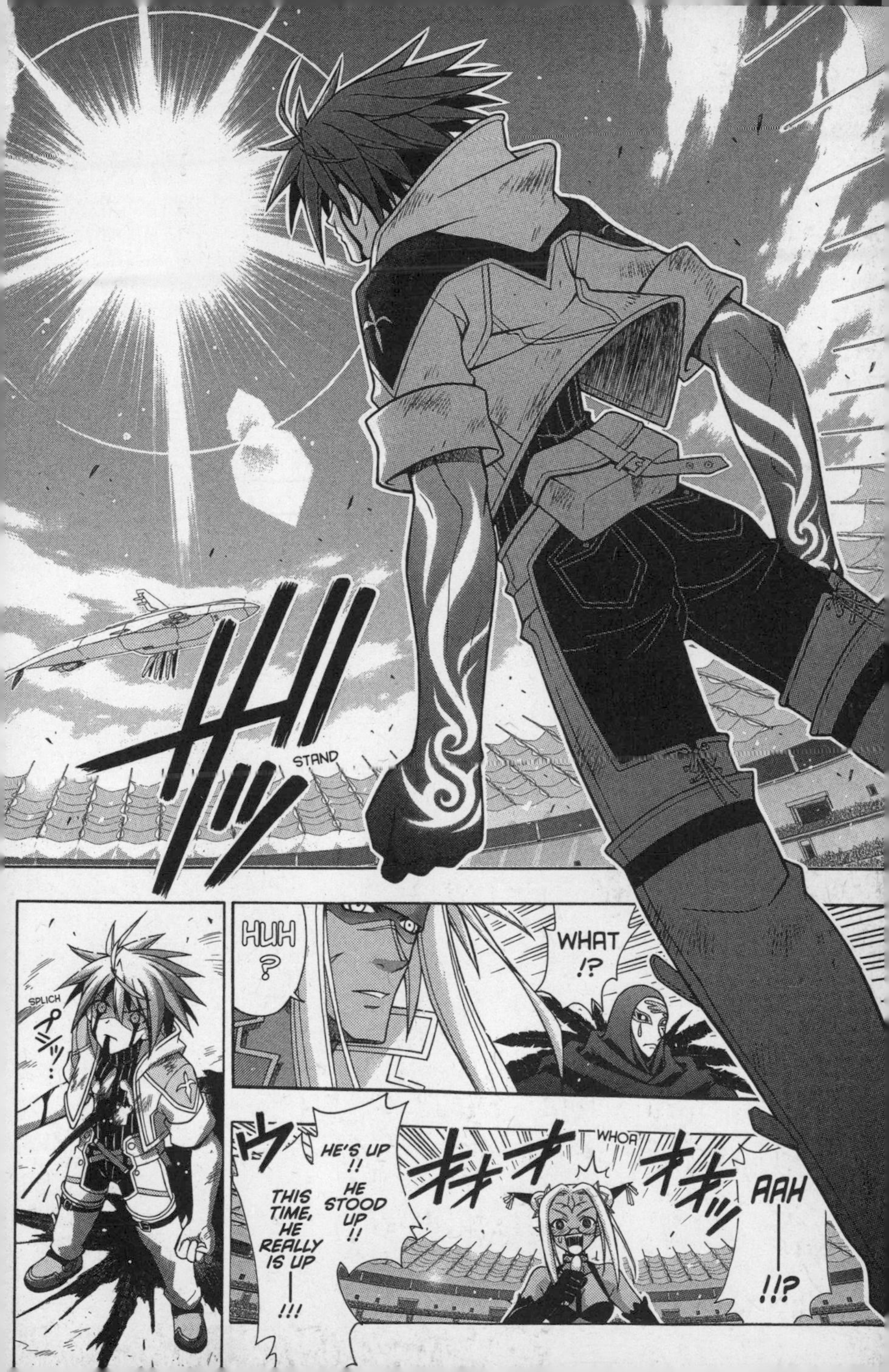
STAND
WHAT !?
HUH ?
AAH—!!?
WHOA
HE'S UP !!
HE STOOD UP !!
THIS TIME, HE REALLY IS UP—!!!
SPLICH

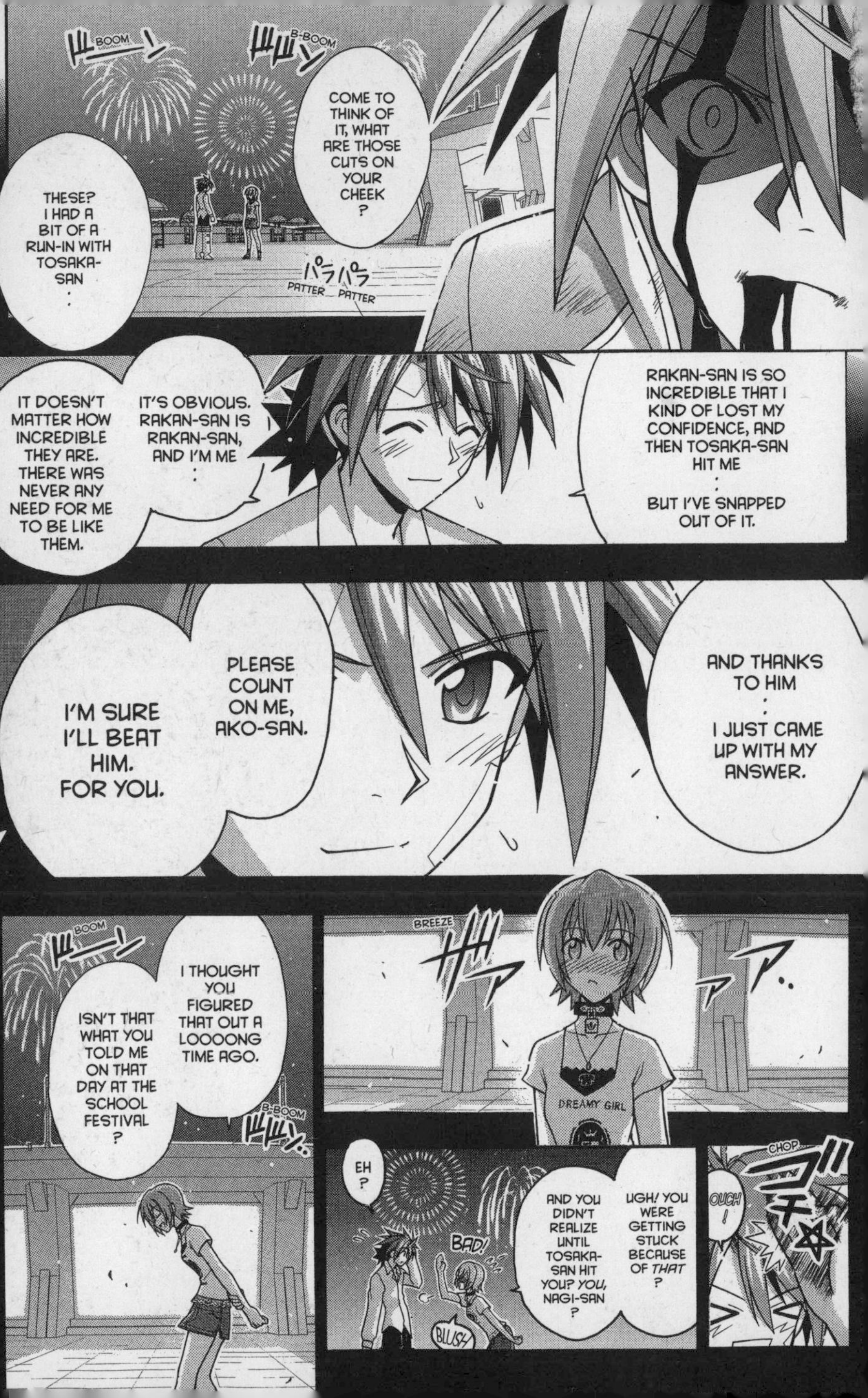
B-BOOM
BOOM
COME TO THINK OF IT, WHAT ARE THOSE CUTS ON YOUR CHEEK ?
THESE? I HAD A BIT OF A RUN-IN WITH TOSAKA-SAN :
PATTER PATTER
RAKAN-SAN IS SO INCREDIBLE THAT I KIND OF LOST MY CONFIDENCE, AND THEN TOSAKA-SAN HIT ME : BUT I'VE SNAPPED OUT OF IT.
IT'S OBVIOUS. RAKAN-SAN IS RAKAN-SAN, AND I'M ME :
IT DOESN'T MATTER HOW INCREDIBLE THEY ARE. THERE WAS NEVER ANY NEED FOR ME TO BE LIKE THEM.
AND THANKS TO HIM : I JUST CAME UP WITH MY ANSWER.
PLEASE COUNT ON ME, AKO-SAN.
I'M SURE I'LL BEAT HIM. FOR YOU.
BREEZE
CHOP
OUCH!
UGH! YOU WERE GETTING STUCK BECAUSE OF THAT ?
AND YOU DIDN'T REALIZE UNTIL TOSAKA-SAN HIT YOU? YOU, NAGI-SAN ?
EH ?
BAD!
BLUSH
BOOM
I THOUGHT YOU FIGURED THAT OUT A LOOOONG TIME AGO.
ISN'T THAT WHAT YOU TOLD ME ON THAT DAY AT THE SCHOOL FESTIVAL ?
B-BOOM

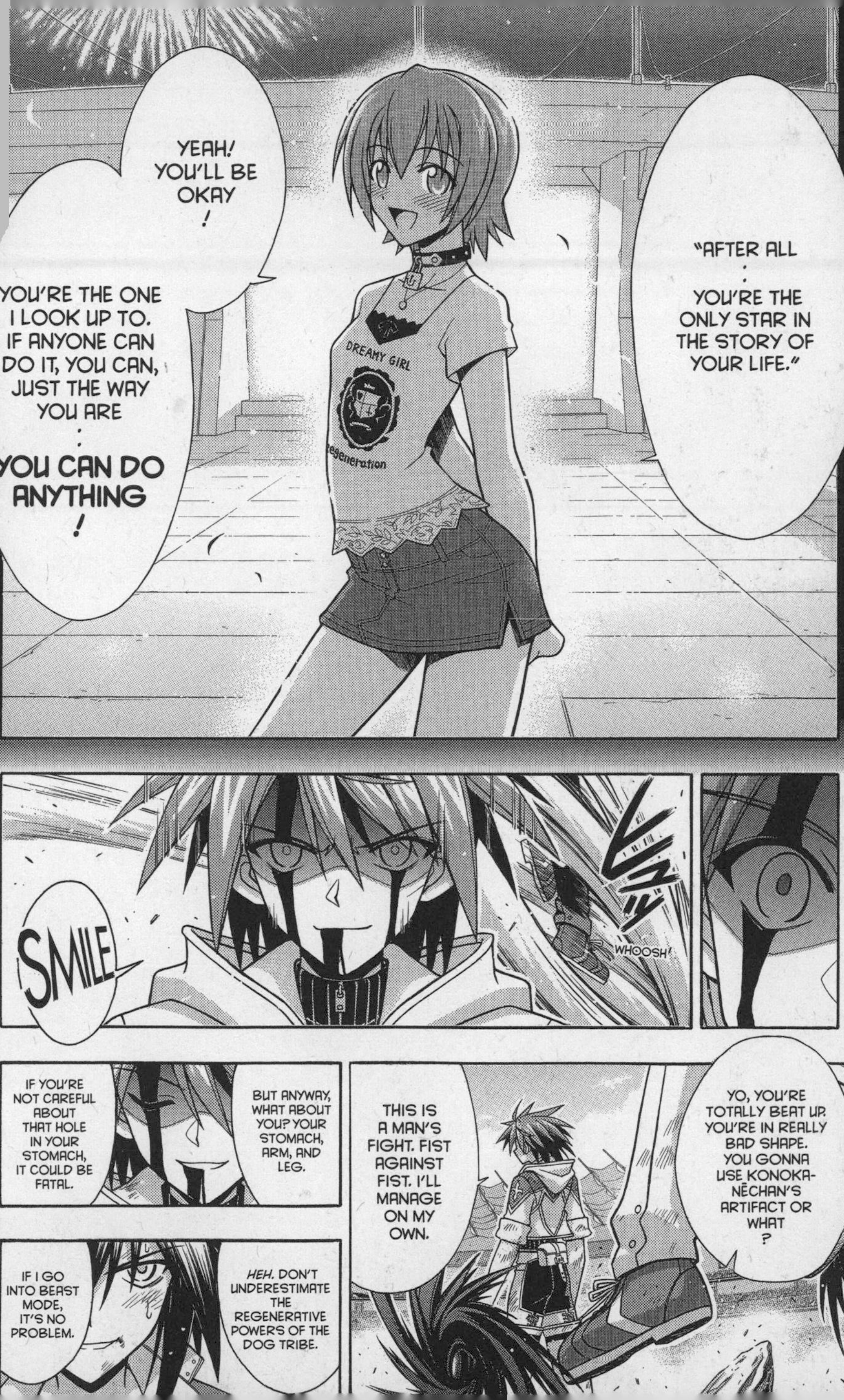
"AFTER ALL . . . YOU'RE THE ONLY STAR IN THE STORY OF YOUR LIFE."
YEAH! YOU'LL BE OKAY!
YOU'RE THE ONE I LOOK UP TO. IF ANYONE CAN DO IT, YOU CAN, JUST THE WAY YOU ARE . . . YOU CAN DO ANYTHING!
DREAMY GIRL
WHOOSH!
SMILE
YO, YOU'RE TOTALLY BEAT UP. YOU'RE IN REALLY BAD SHAPE. YOU GONNA USE KONOKA-NĔCHAN'S ARTIFACT OR WHAT?
THIS IS A MAN'S FIGHT. FIST AGAINST FIST. I'LL MANAGE ON MY OWN.
BUT ANYWAY, WHAT ABOUT YOU? YOUR STOMACH, ARM, AND LEG.
IF YOU'RE NOT CAREFUL ABOUT THAT HOLE IN YOUR STOMACH, IT COULD BE FATAL.
HEH. DON'T UNDERESTIMATE THE REGENERATIVE POWERS OF THE DOG TRIBE.
IF I GO INTO BEAST MODE, IT'S NO PROBLEM.

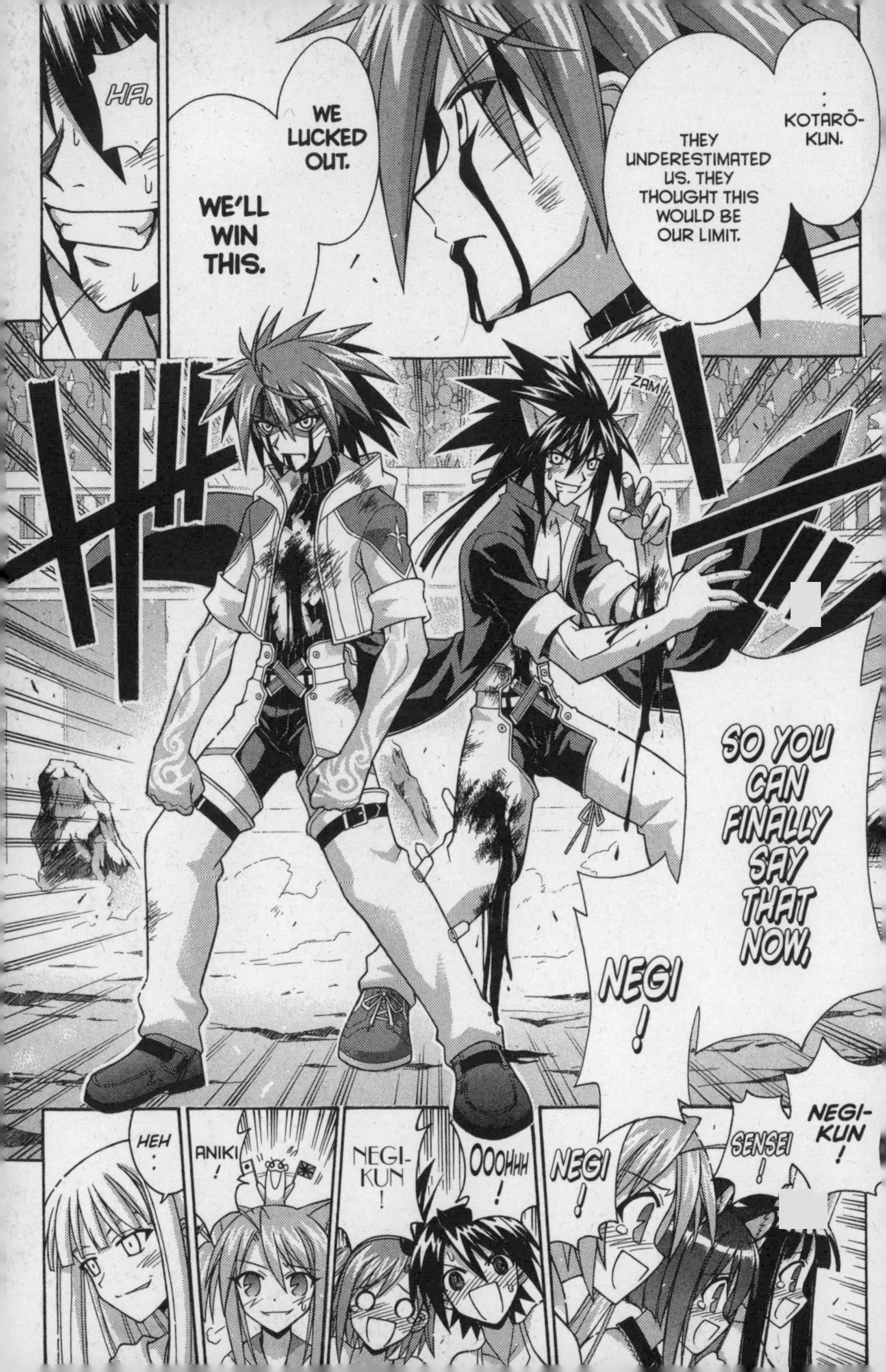
KOTARŌ-KUN.
THEY UNDERESTIMATED US. THEY THOUGHT THIS WOULD BE OUR LIMIT.
WE LUCKED OUT.
WE'LL WIN THIS.
HA.
ZAM
SO YOU CAN FINALLY SAY THAT NOW, NEGI!
NEGI-KUN!
SENSEI!
NEGI!
OOOHHH!
NEGI-KUN!
ANIKI!
HEH...

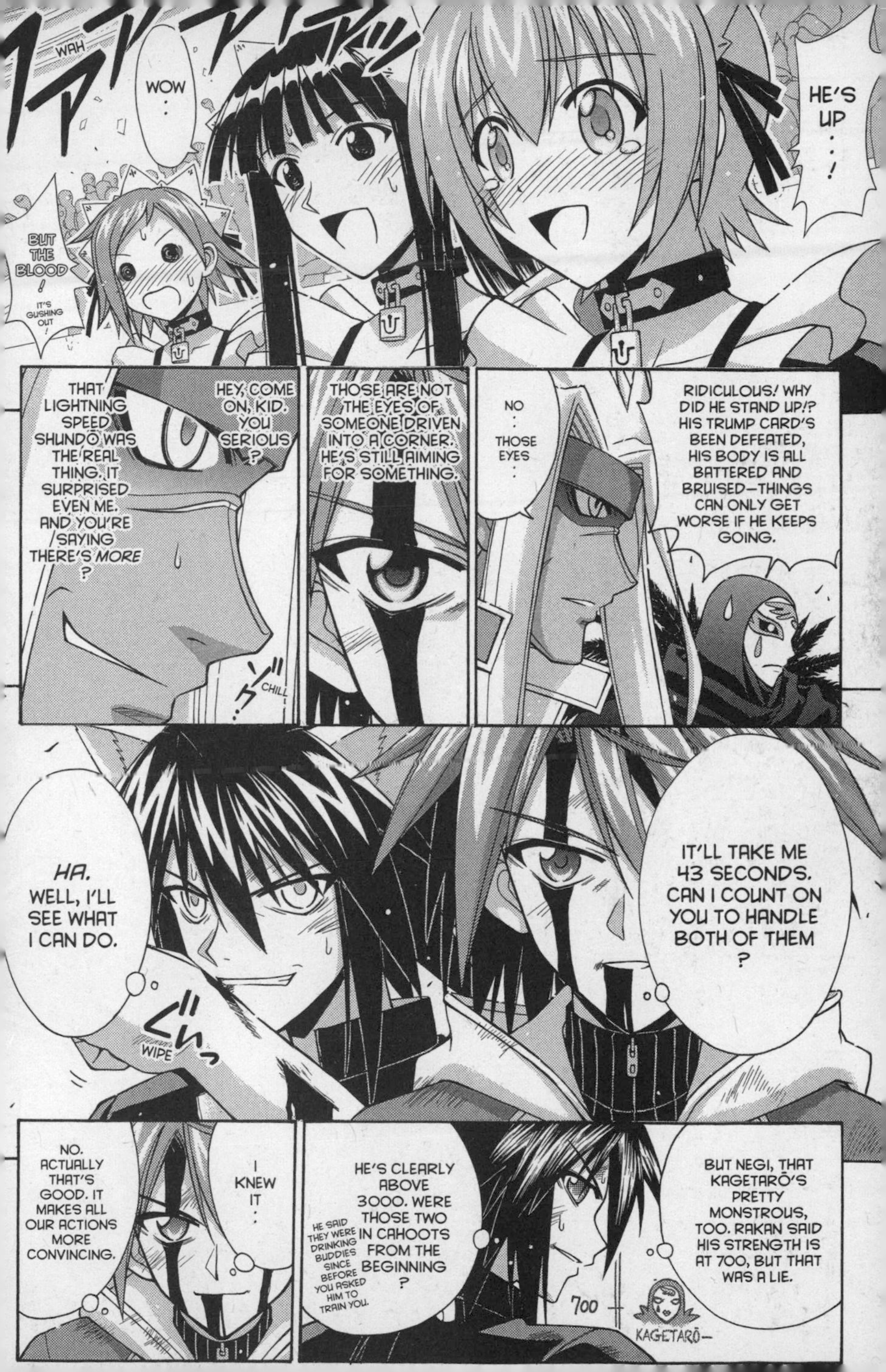
HE'S UP...!
WAH
WOW...
BUT THE BLOOD!
IT'S GUSHING OUT!
RIDICULOUS! WHY DID HE STAND UP!? HIS TRUMP CARD'S BEEN DEFEATED, HIS BODY IS ALL BATTERED AND BRUISED—THINGS CAN ONLY GET WORSE IF HE KEEPS GOING.
NO... THOSE EYES...
THOSE ARE NOT THE EYES OF SOMEONE DRIVEN INTO A CORNER. HE'S STILL AIMING FOR SOMETHING.
HEY, COME ON, KID. YOU SERIOUS?
THAT LIGHTNING SPEED SHUNDŌ WAS THE REAL THING. IT SURPRISED EVEN ME. AND YOU'RE SAYING THERE'S *MORE*?
CHILL
IT'LL TAKE ME 43 SECONDS. CAN I COUNT ON YOU TO HANDLE BOTH OF THEM?
HA. WELL, I'LL SEE WHAT I CAN DO.
WIPE
BUT NEGI, THAT KAGETARŌ'S PRETTY MONSTROUS, TOO. RAKAN SAID HIS STRENGTH IS AT 700, BUT THAT WAS A LIE.
HE'S CLEARLY ABOVE 3000. WERE THOSE TWO IN CAHOOTS FROM THE BEGINNING?
HE SAID THEY WERE DRINKING BUDDIES SINCE BEFORE YOU ASKED HIM TO TRAIN YOU.
700
KAGETARŌ—
I KNEW IT...
NO. ACTUALLY THAT'S GOOD. IT MAKES ALL OUR ACTIONS MORE CONVINCING.

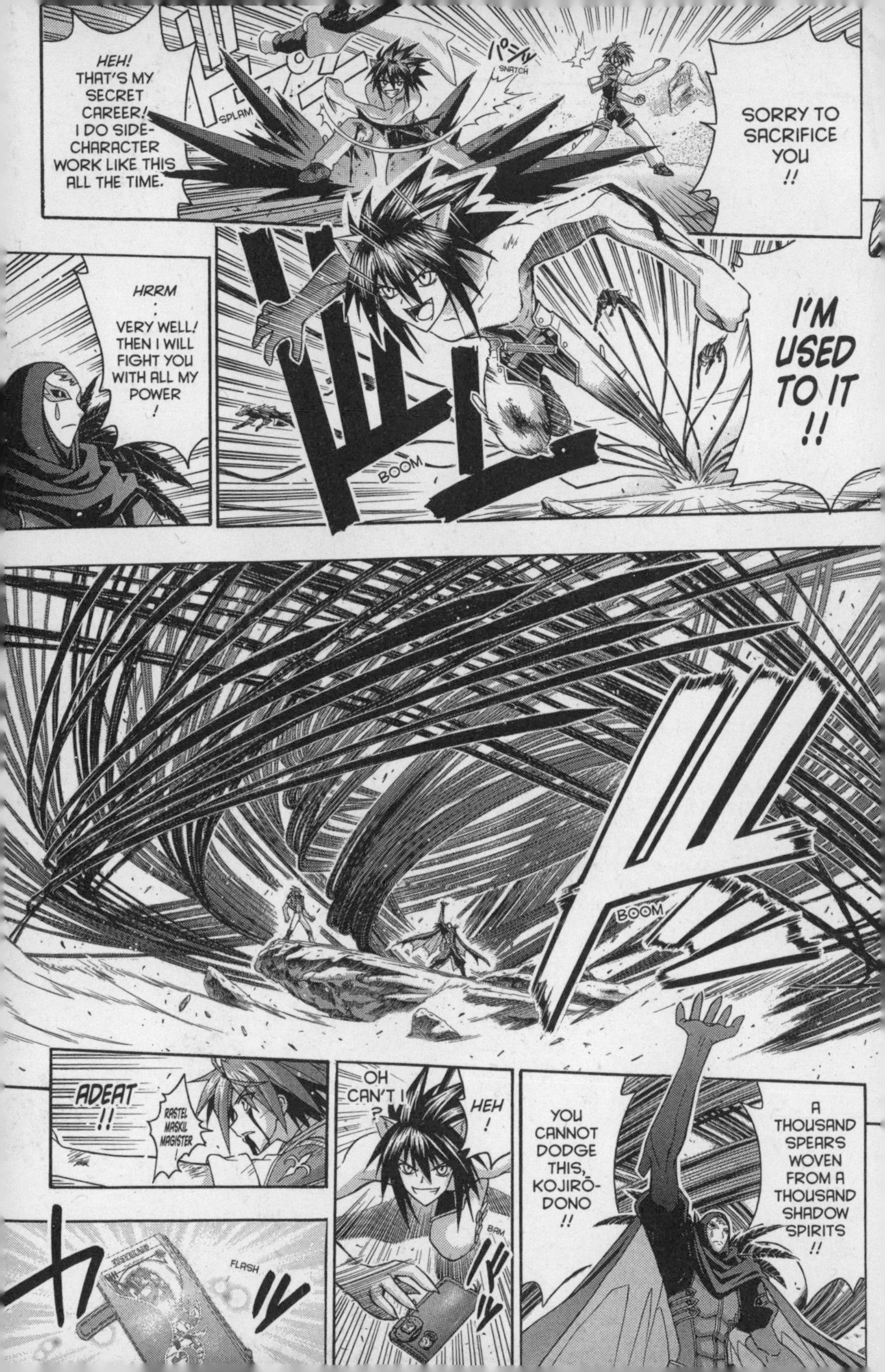
SORRY TO SACRIFICE YOU !!
SNATCH
SPLAM
HEH! THAT'S MY SECRET CAREER! I DO SIDE-CHARACTER WORK LIKE THIS ALL THE TIME.
I'M USED TO IT !!
BOOM
HRRM : VERY WELL! THEN I WILL FIGHT YOU WITH ALL MY POWER !
BOOM
A THOUSAND SPEARS WOVEN FROM A THOUSAND SHADOW SPIRITS !!
YOU CANNOT DODGE THIS, KOJIRŌ-DONO !!
HEH !
OH CAN'T I ?
BAM
ADEAT !!
RASTEL MASKIL MAGISTER !
FLASH

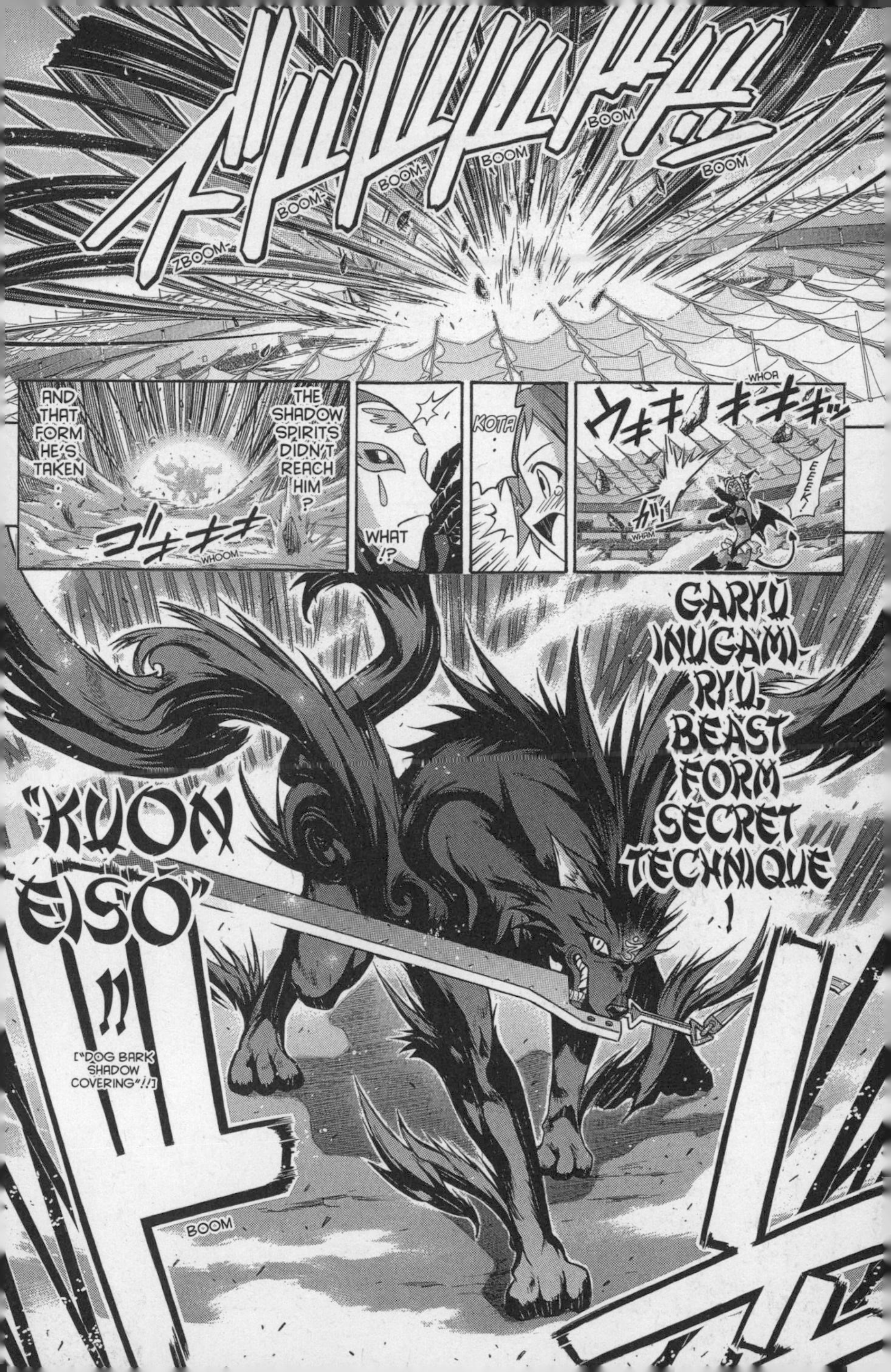
ZBOOM-
BOOM-
BOOM-
BOOM
BOOM
BOOM
-WHOA
EEEK!
ガッ
WHAM
KOTA
WHAT!?
THE SHADOW SPIRITS DIDN'T REACH HIM?
AND THAT FORM HE'S TAKEN
WHOOM
GARYŪ INUGAMI RYŪ, BEAST FORM SECRET TECHNIQUE!
"KUON EISŌ"!!
["DOG BARK SHADOW COVERING"!!]
BOOM

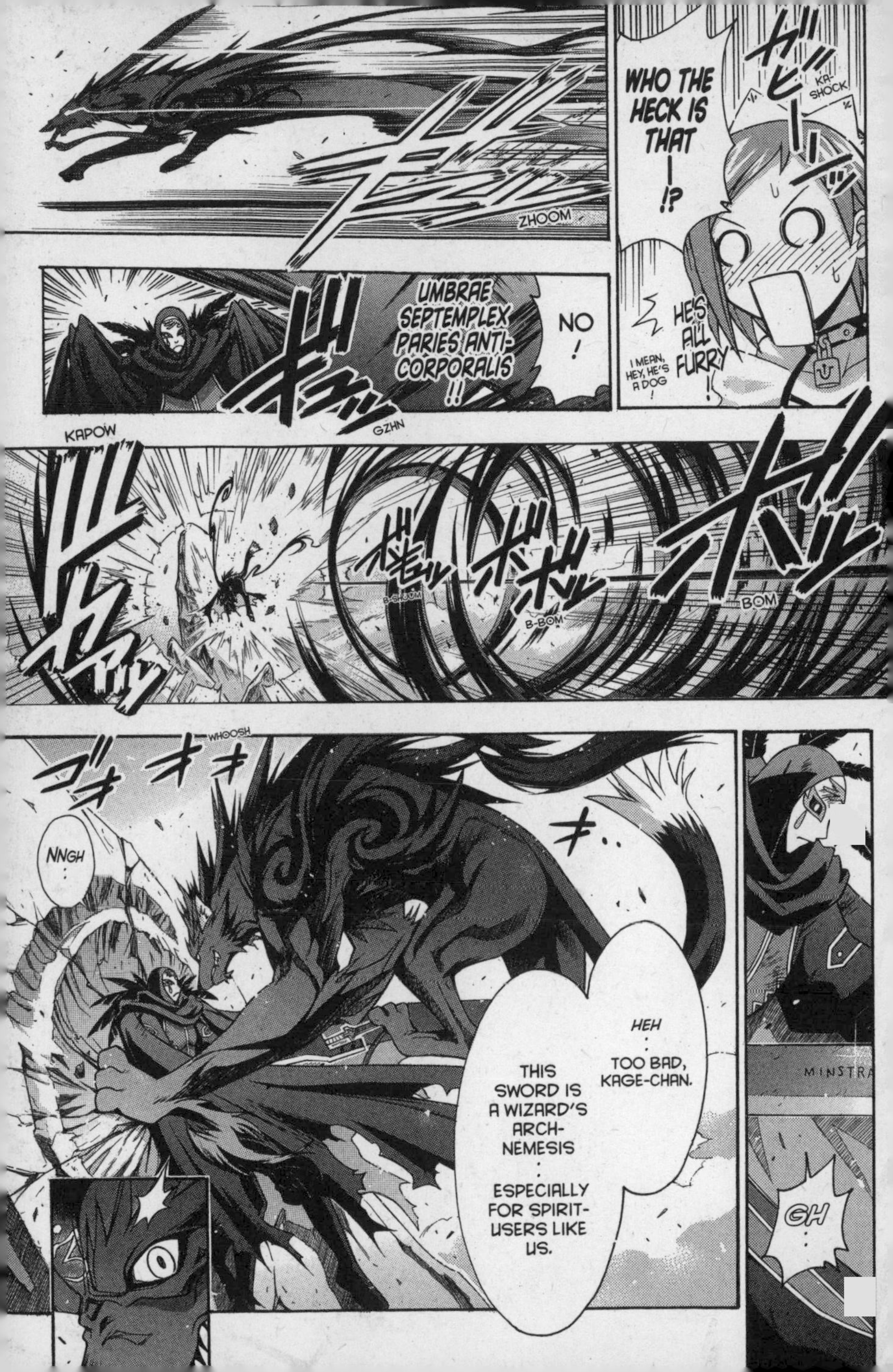
KA-SHOCK
WHO THE HECK IS THAT—!?
HE'S ALL FURRY!
I MEAN, HEY, HE'S A DOG!
ZHOOM
NO!
UMBRAE SEPTEMPLEX PARIES ANTI-CORPORALIS!!
GZHN
BOM
B-BOM
B-SHOOM
KAPOW
GH...
HEH... TOO BAD, KAGE-CHAN.
THIS SWORD IS A WIZARD'S ARCH-NEMESIS...
ESPECIALLY FOR SPIRIT-USERS LIKE US.
WHOOSH
NNGH...

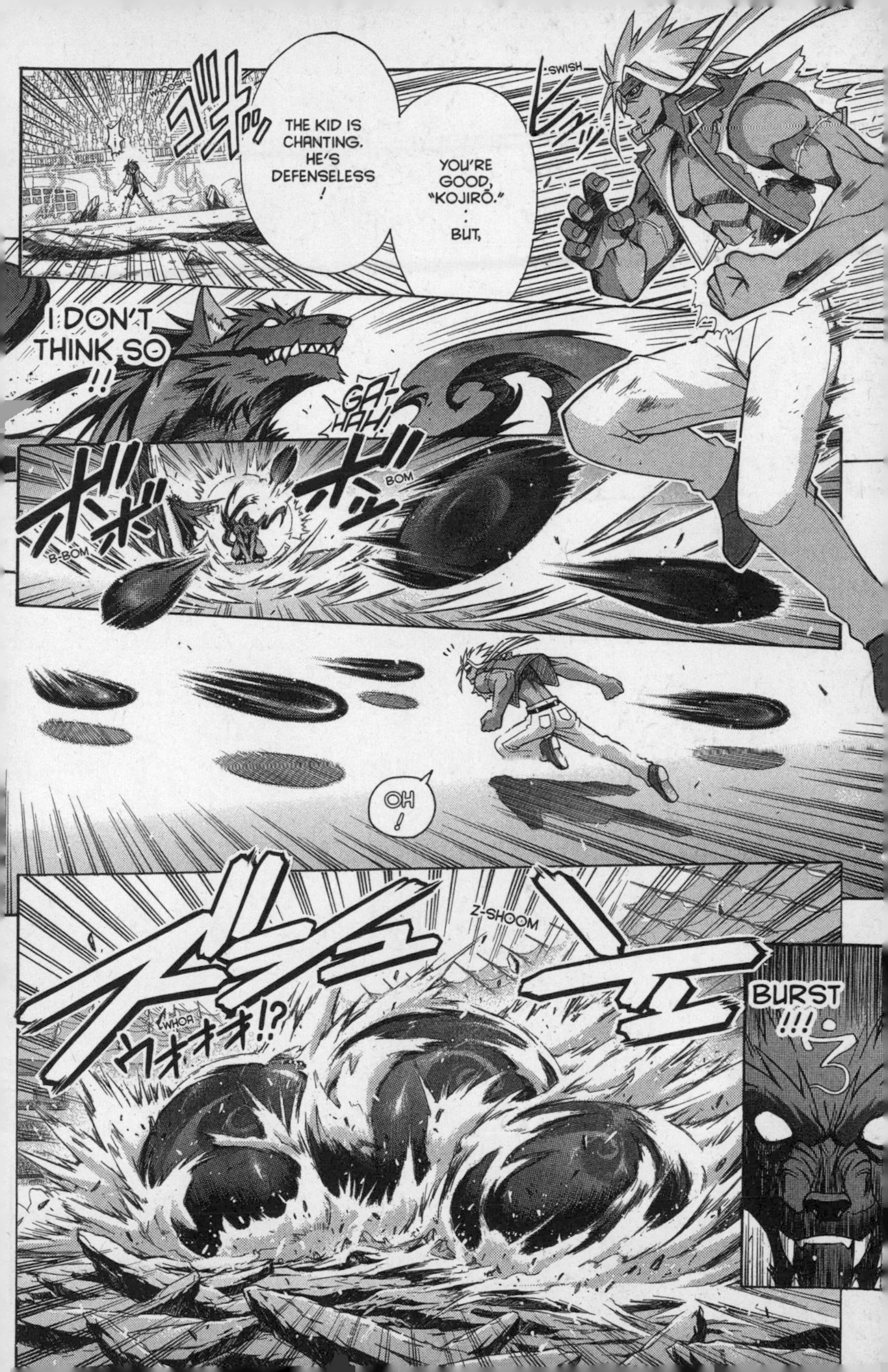
WHOOSH
THE KID IS CHANTING. HE'S DEFENSELESS!
SWISH
YOU'RE GOOD, "KOJIRŌ." BUT,
I DON'T THINK SO!!
GA-HAH!
BOM
B-BOM
OH!
Z-SHOOM
WHOA
BURST!!!

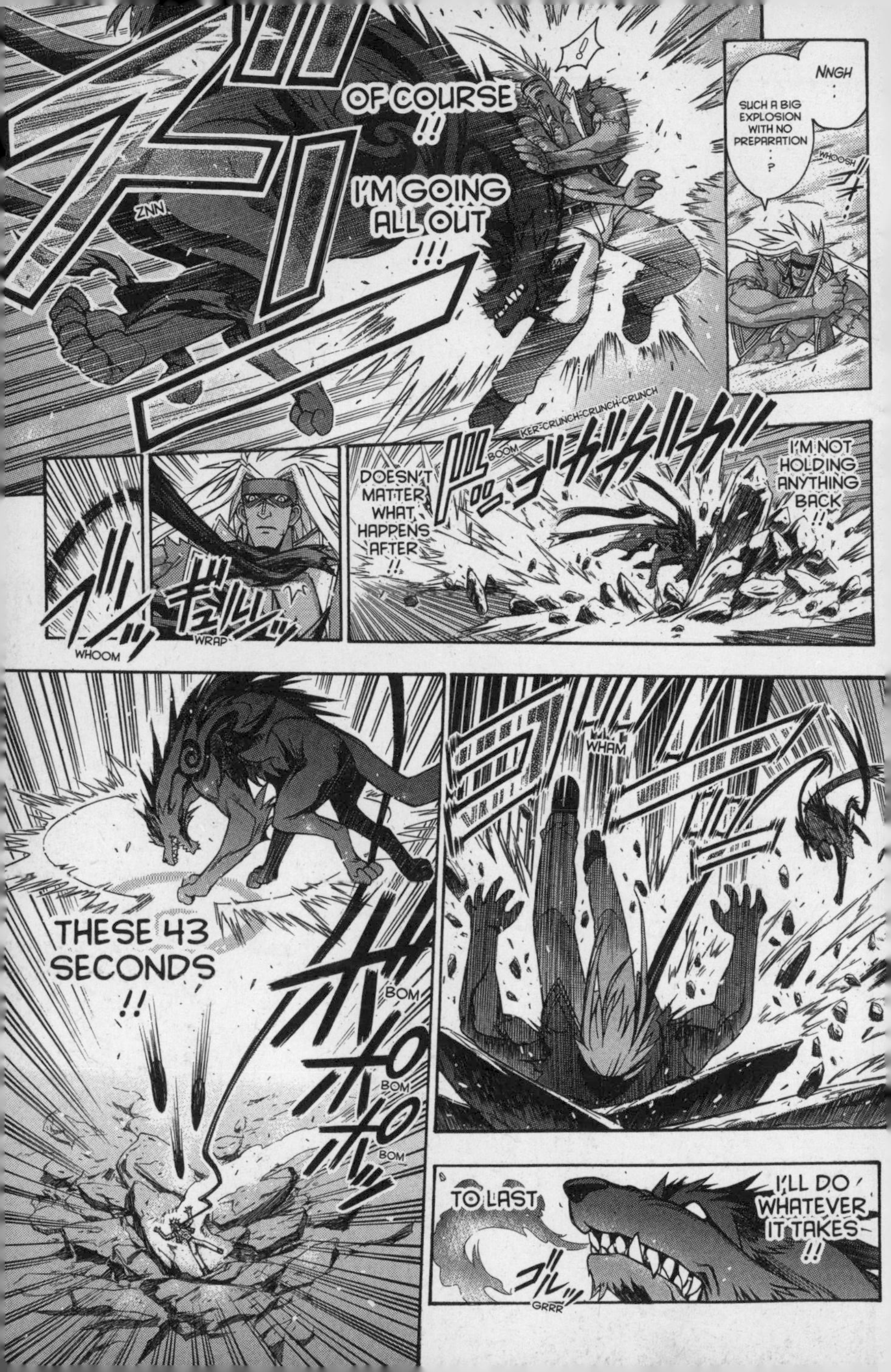
NNGH
SUCH A BIG EXPLOSION WITH NO PREPARATION . . . ?
WHOOSH
!
OF COURSE!!
I'M GOING ALL OUT!!!
ZNN
I'M NOT HOLDING ANYTHING BACK!!
KER-CRUNCH-CRUNCH-CRUNCH
BOOM
DOESN'T MATTER WHAT HAPPENS AFTER!!
WRAP
WHOOM
WHAM
I'LL DO WHATEVER IT TAKES!!
TO LAST
GRRR
THESE 43 SECONDS!!
BOM
BOM
BOM

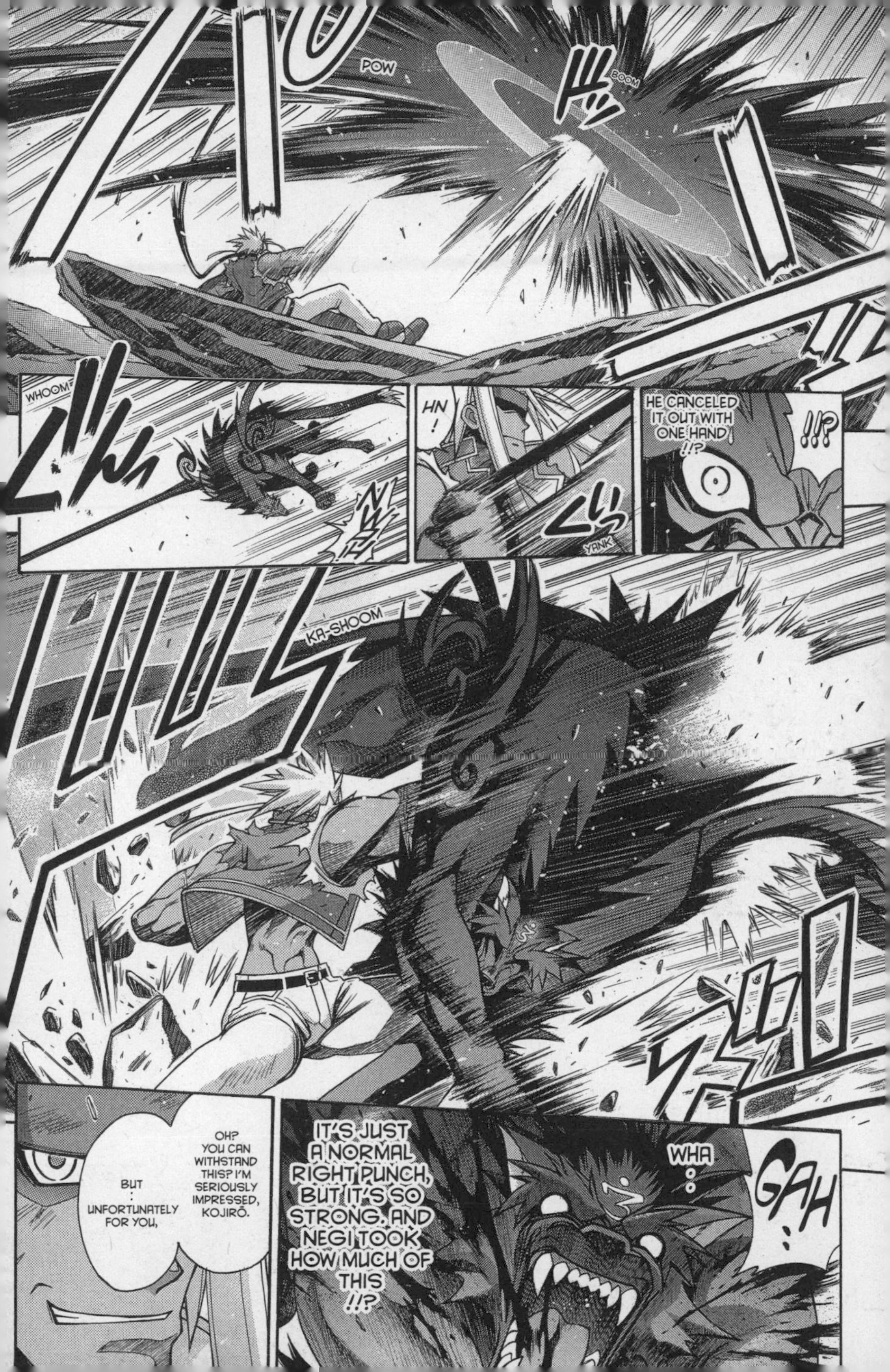
BOOM
POW
HE CANCELED IT OUT WITH ONE HAND !!?
!!?
HN !
YANK
WHOOM
KA-SHOOM
GAH
WHA . . .
IT'S JUST A NORMAL RIGHT PUNCH, BUT IT'S SO STRONG. AND NEGI TOOK HOW MUCH OF THIS !!?
OH? YOU CAN WITHSTAND THIS? I'M SERIOUSLY IMPRESSED, KOJIRŌ.
BUT : UNFORTUNATELY FOR YOU,

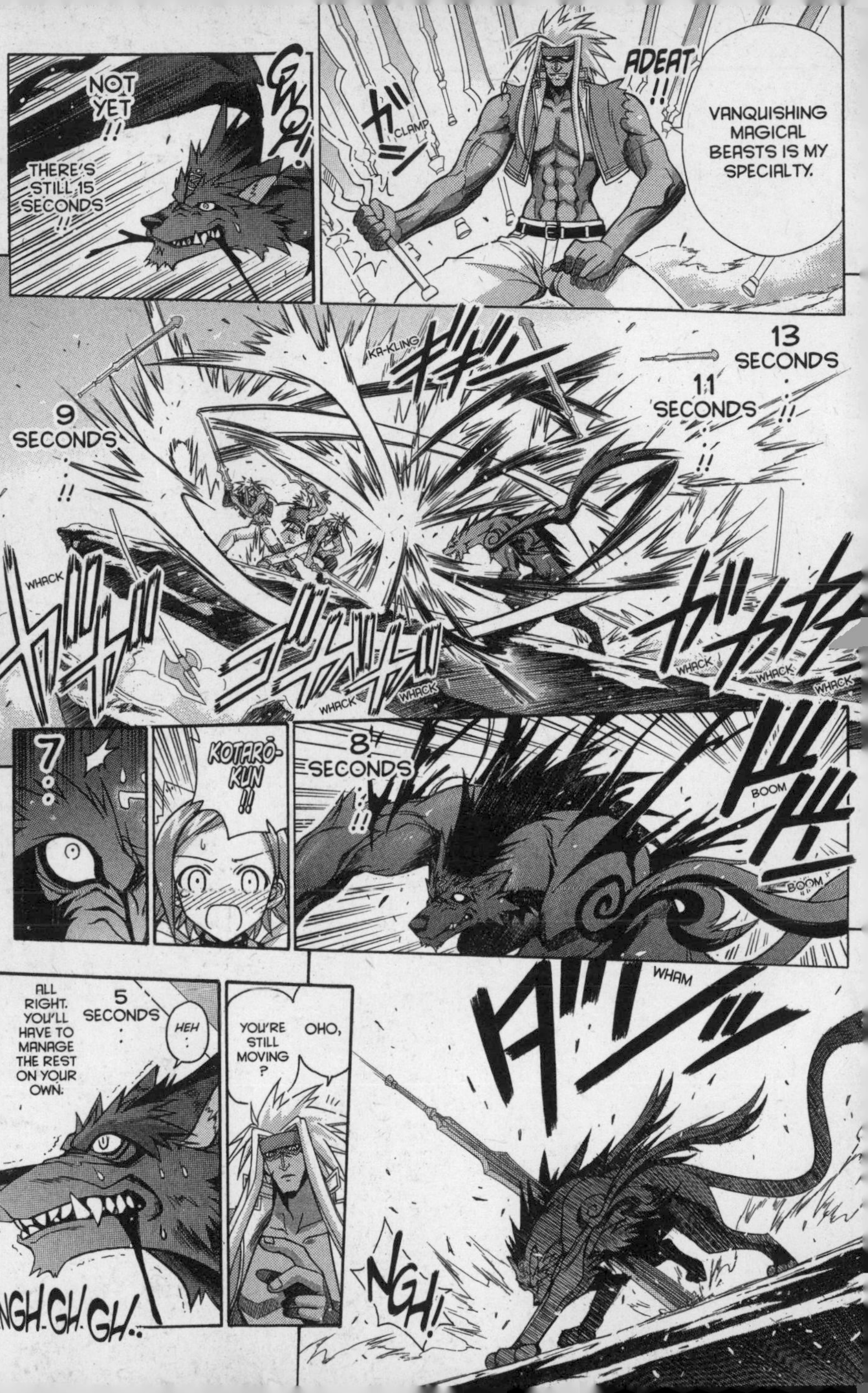
VANQUISHING MAGICAL BEASTS IS MY SPECIALTY.
ADEAT!!
CLAMP
GWOH!
NOT YET!!
THERE'S STILL 15 SECONDS!!
13 SECONDS...!!
11 SECONDS...!!
KA-KLING
9 SECONDS...!!
WHACK
WHACK
WHACK
WHACK
WHACK
WHACK
BOOM
BOOM
8 SECONDS...!!
KOTARŌ-KUN!!
7...
WHAM
NGH!
OHO,
YOU'RE STILL MOVING?
HEH...
5 SECONDS...
ALL RIGHT. YOU'LL HAVE TO MANAGE THE REST ON YOUR OWN.
NGH..GH..GH..

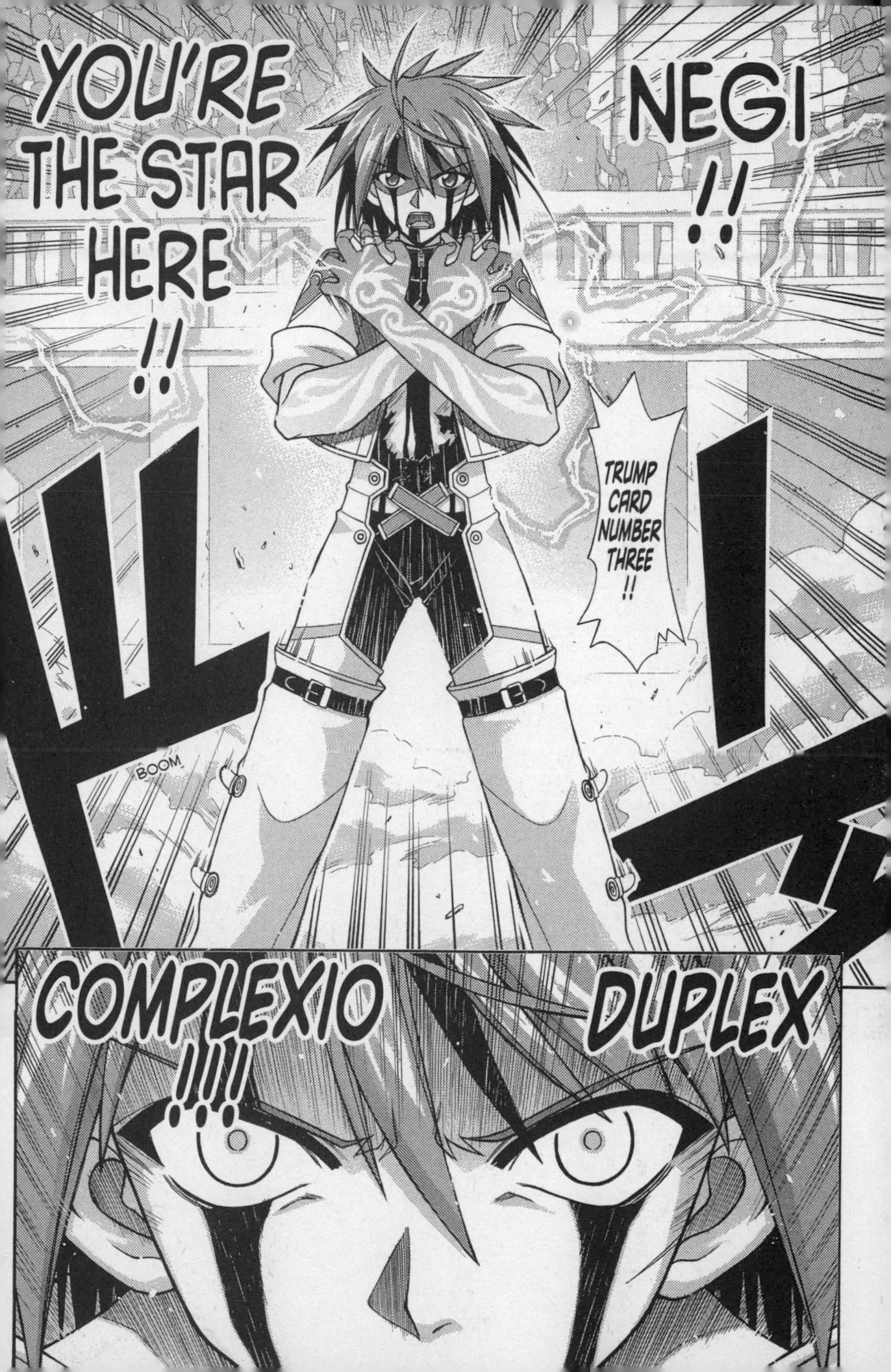
NEGI !!
YOU'RE THE STAR HERE !!
TRUMP CARD NUMBER THREE !!
BOOM
COMPLEXIO
DUPLEX !!!!

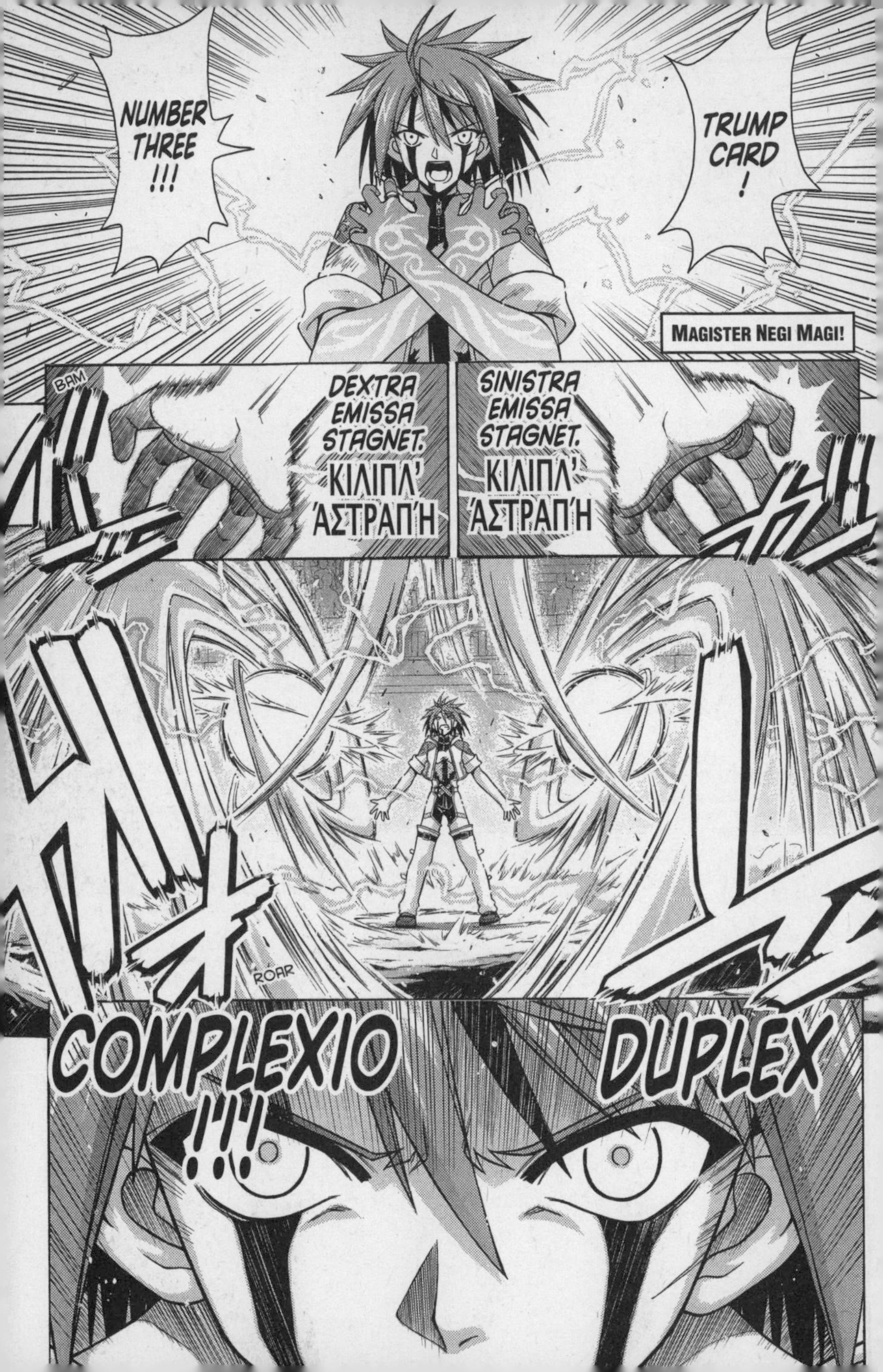
TRUMP CARD !
NUMBER THREE !!!
MAGISTER NEGI MAGI!
SINISTRA EMISSA STAGNET. ΚΙΛΙΠΛ’ ΆΣΤΡΑΠ’Η
DEXTRA EMISSA STAGNET. ΚΙΛΙΠΛ’ ΆΣΤΡΑΠ’Η
BAM
ROAR
COMPLEXIO DUPLEX !!!!

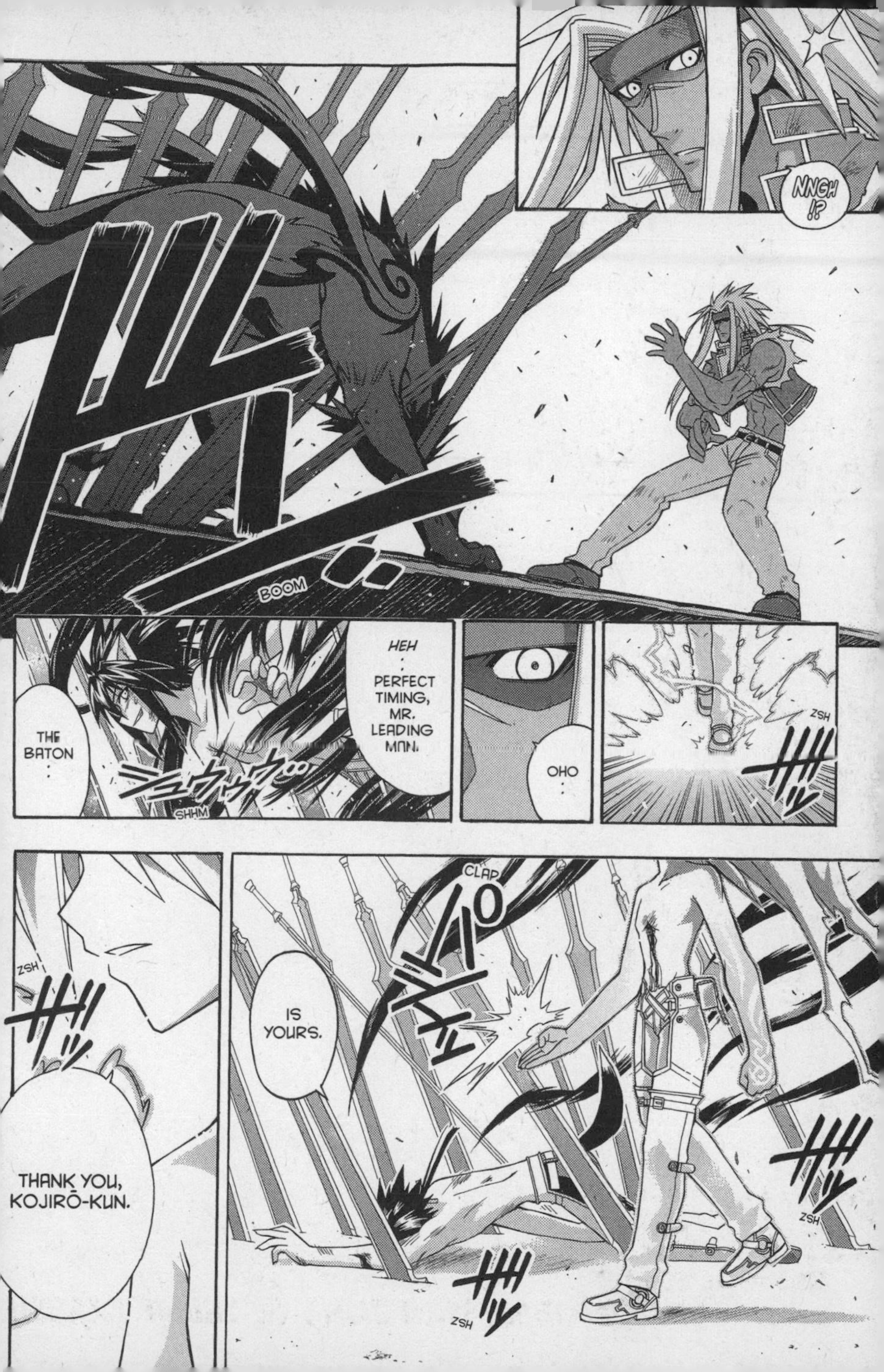
NNGH !?
BOOM
ZSH
OHO :
HEH : PERFECT TIMING, MR. LEADING MAN.
THE BATON :
SHHM
CLAP
IS YOURS.
ZSH
ZSH
ZSH
THANK YOU, KOJIRŌ-KUN.

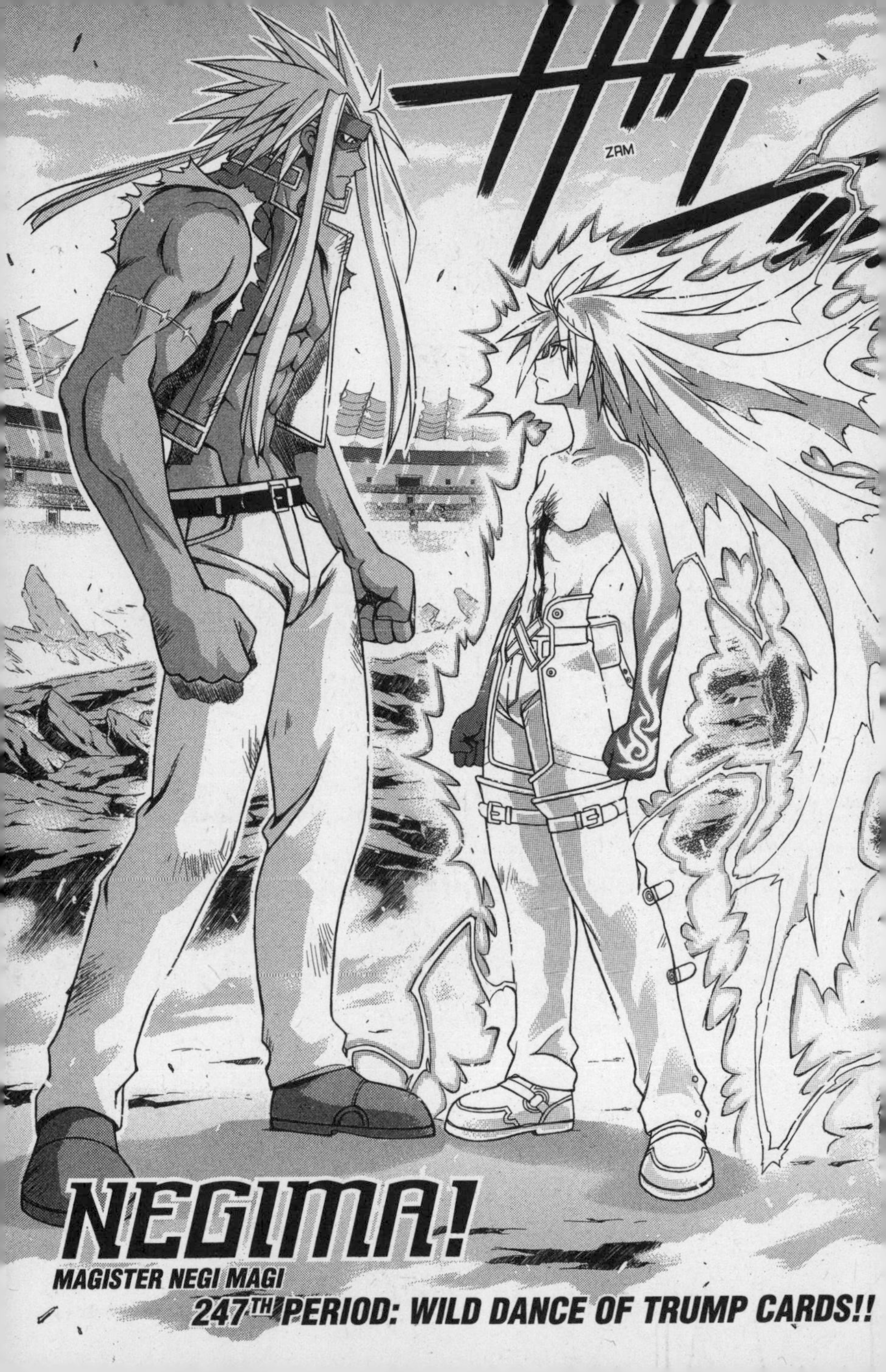
ZAM
NEGIMA!
MAGISTER NEGI MAGI
247TH PERIOD: WILD DANCE OF TRUMP CARDS!!

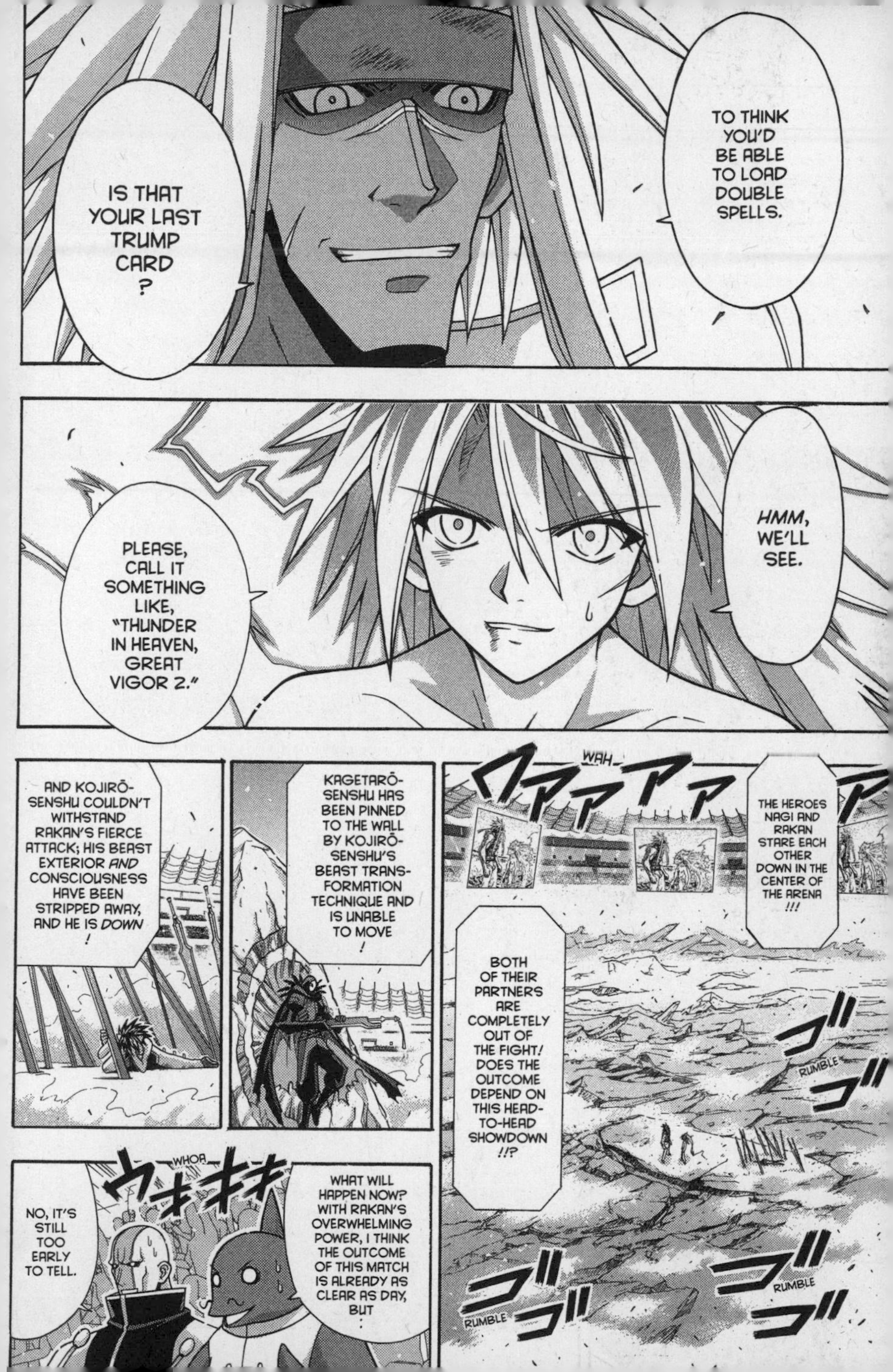
TO THINK YOU'D BE ABLE TO LOAD DOUBLE SPELLS.
IS THAT YOUR LAST TRUMP CARD ?
HMM, WE'LL SEE.
PLEASE, CALL IT SOMETHING LIKE, "THUNDER IN HEAVEN, GREAT VIGOR 2."
WAH
THE HEROES NAGI AND RAKAN STARE EACH OTHER DOWN IN THE CENTER OF THE ARENA !!!
BOTH OF THEIR PARTNERS ARE COMPLETELY OUT OF THE FIGHT! DOES THE OUTCOME DEPEND ON THIS HEAD-TO-HEAD SHOWDOWN !!?
RUMBLE
RUMBLE
RUMBLE
KAGETARŌ-SENSHU HAS BEEN PINNED TO THE WALL BY KOJIRŌ-SENSHU'S BEAST TRANSFORMATION TECHNIQUE AND IS UNABLE TO MOVE !
AND KOJIRŌ-SENSHU COULDN'T WITHSTAND RAKAN'S FIERCE ATTACK; HIS BEAST EXTERIOR *AND* CONSCIOUSNESS HAVE BEEN STRIPPED AWAY, AND HE IS *DOWN* !
WHOA
WHAT WILL HAPPEN NOW? WITH RAKAN'S OVERWHELMING POWER, I THINK THE OUTCOME OF THIS MATCH IS ALREADY AS CLEAR AS DAY, BUT
NO, IT'S STILL TOO EARLY TO TELL.

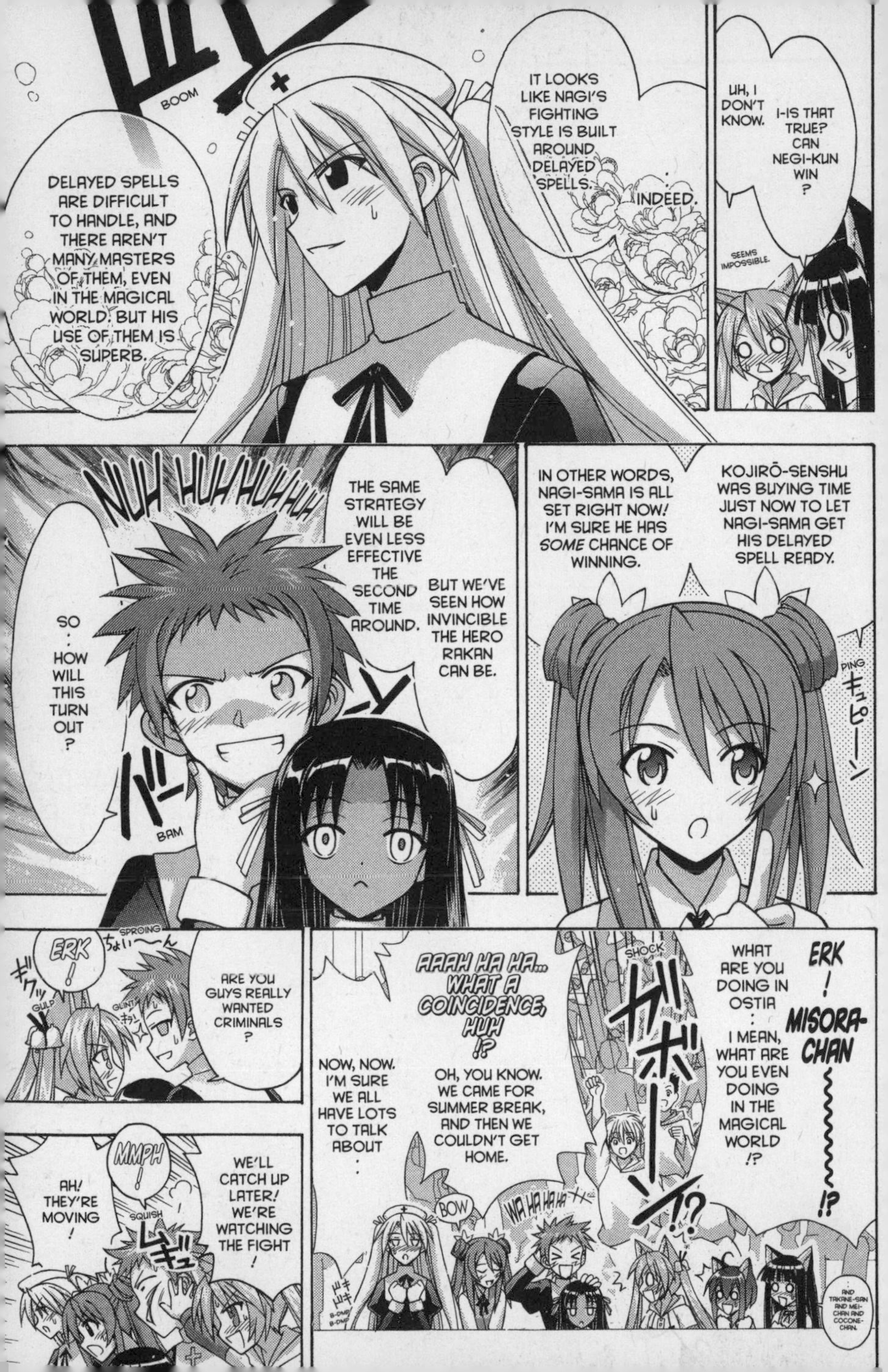
I-IS THAT TRUE? CAN NEGI-KUN WIN?
UH, I DON'T KNOW.
SEEMS IMPOSSIBLE.
BOOM
IT LOOKS LIKE NAGI'S FIGHTING STYLE IS BUILT AROUND DELAYED SPELLS.
: INDEED.
DELAYED SPELLS ARE DIFFICULT TO HANDLE, AND THERE AREN'T MANY MASTERS OF THEM, EVEN IN THE MAGICAL WORLD. BUT HIS USE OF THEM IS SUPERB.
KOJIRŌ-SENSHU WAS BUYING TIME JUST NOW TO LET NAGI-SAMA GET HIS DELAYED SPELL READY.
IN OTHER WORDS, NAGI-SAMA IS ALL SET RIGHT NOW! I'M SURE HE HAS *SOME* CHANCE OF WINNING.
PING
キュピーン
THE SAME STRATEGY WILL BE EVEN LESS EFFECTIVE THE SECOND TIME AROUND.
BUT WE'VE SEEN HOW INVINCIBLE THE HERO RAKAN CAN BE.
NUH HUHUHUHUH
SO : HOW WILL THIS TURN OUT?
BAM
ERK! MISORA-CHAN ~~~!?
WHAT ARE YOU DOING IN OSTIA : I MEAN, WHAT ARE YOU EVEN DOING IN THE MAGICAL WORLD!?
SHOCK
AAAH HA HA... WHAT A COINCIDENCE, HUH!?
OH, YOU KNOW. WE CAME FOR SUMMER BREAK, AND THEN WE COULDN'T GET HOME.
NOW, NOW. I'M SURE WE ALL HAVE LOTS TO TALK ABOUT :
WA HA HA HA
BOW
B-DMP B-DMP
AND TAKANE-SAN AND MEI-CHAN AND COCONE-CHAN.
SPROING
ちょい〜ん
ARE YOU GUYS REALLY WANTED CRIMINALS?
ERK!
GLINT
GULP
WE'LL CATCH UP LATER! WE'RE WATCHING THE FIGHT
MMPH!
SQUISH
AH! THEY'RE MOVING

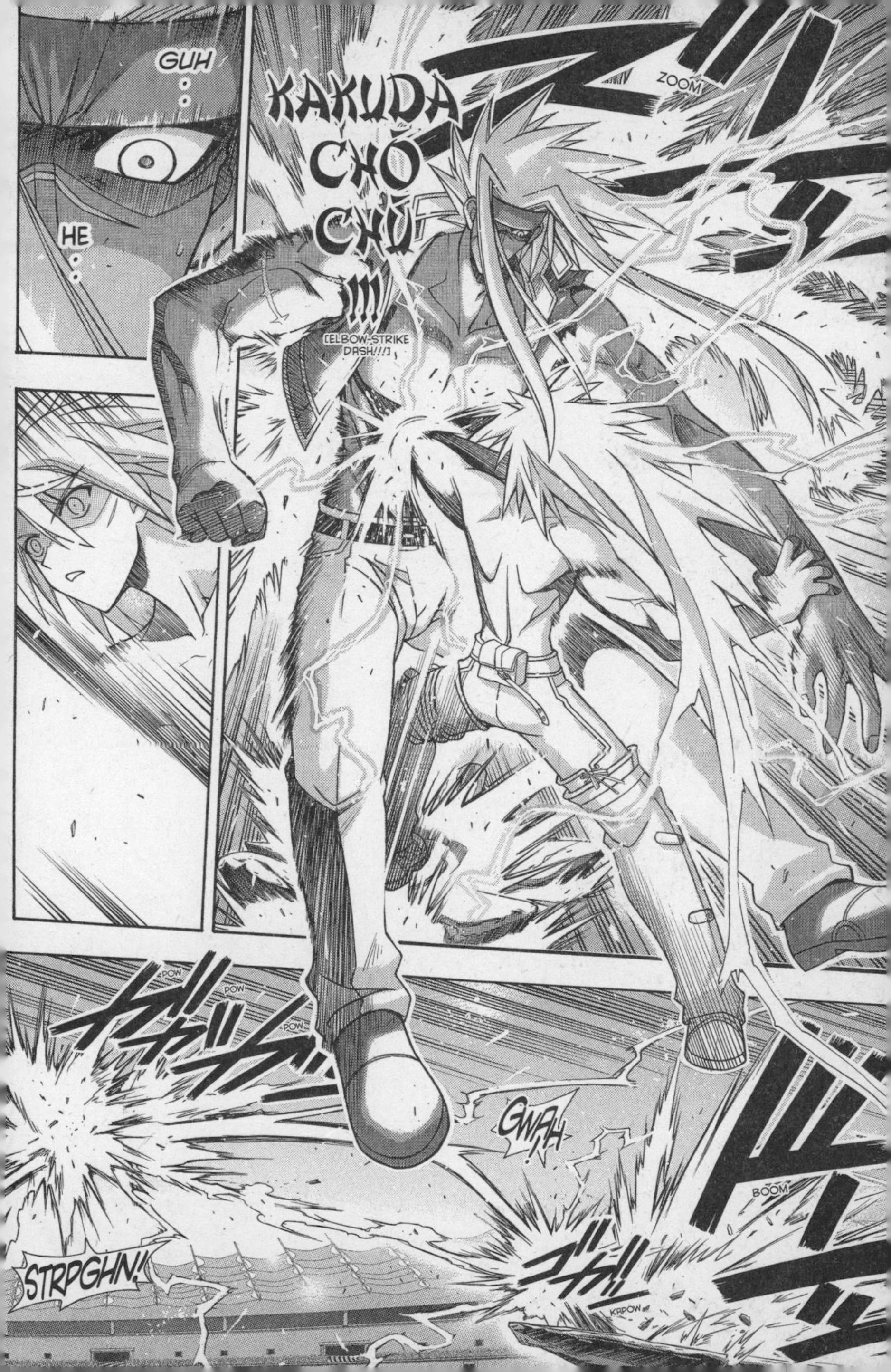
ZOOM
KAKUDA CHŌ CHŪ !!!
[ELBOW-STRIKE DASH!!!]
GUH...
HE...
BOOM
GWAH!
KAPOW
POW
POW
POW
STRPGHN!!

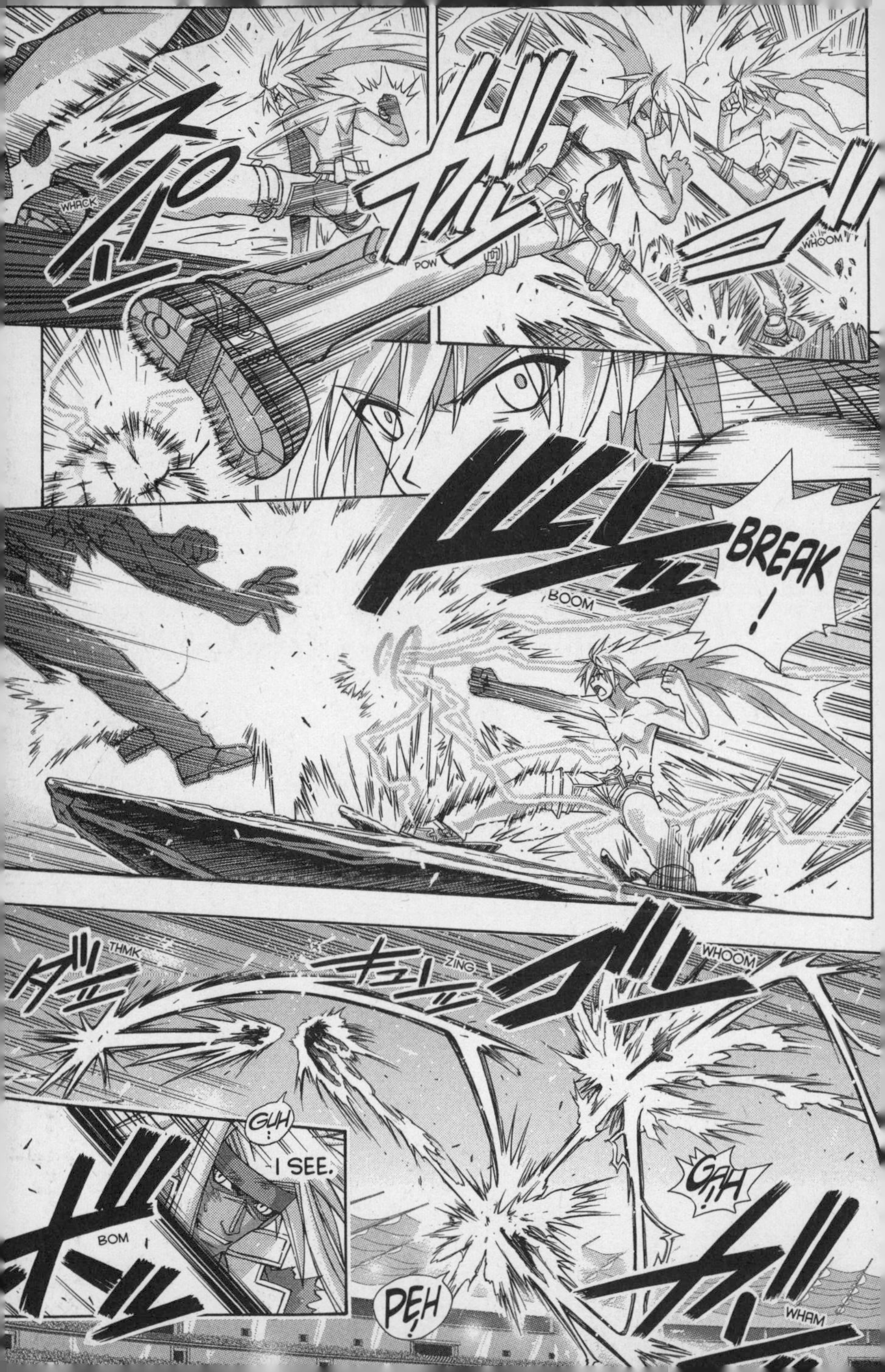
WHOOM
POW
WHACK
BREAK!
BOOM
WHOOM
ZING
THMK
GAH!
GUH...
I SEE.
BOM
PEH!
WHAM

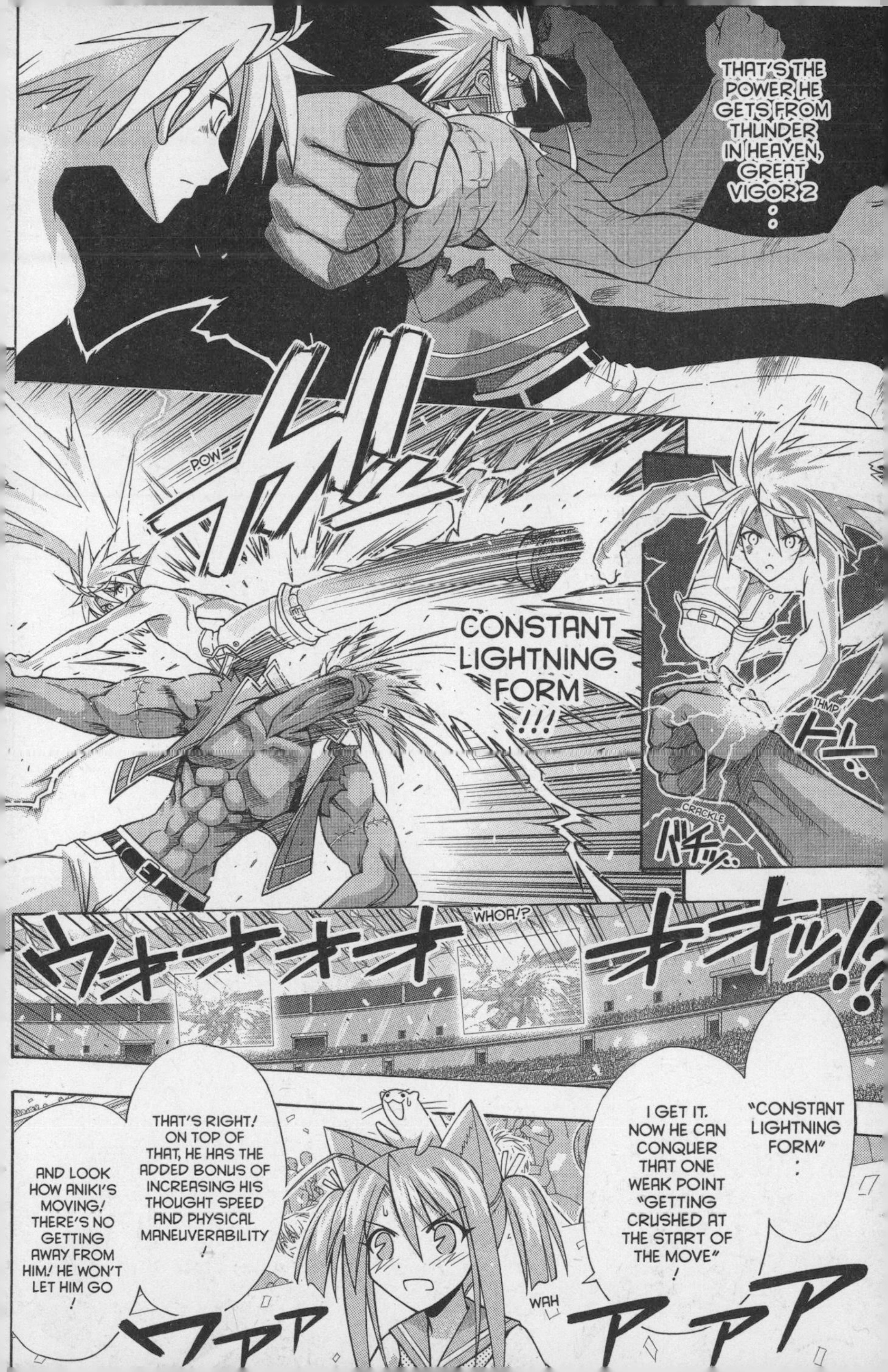
THAT'S THE POWER HE GETS FROM THUNDER IN HEAVEN, GREAT VIGOR 2 : :
THMP
CRACKLE
POW
CONSTANT LIGHTNING FORM !!!
WHOA!?
ウォオオオ オオオッ!?
"CONSTANT LIGHTNING FORM" :
I GET IT. NOW HE CAN CONQUER THAT ONE WEAK POINT "GETTING CRUSHED AT THE START OF THE MOVE" !
THAT'S RIGHT! ON TOP OF THAT, HE HAS THE ADDED BONUS OF INCREASING HIS THOUGHT SPEED AND PHYSICAL MANEUVERABILITY !
AND LOOK HOW ANIKI'S MOVING! THERE'S NO GETTING AWAY FROM HIM! HE WON'T LET HIM GO !
WAH

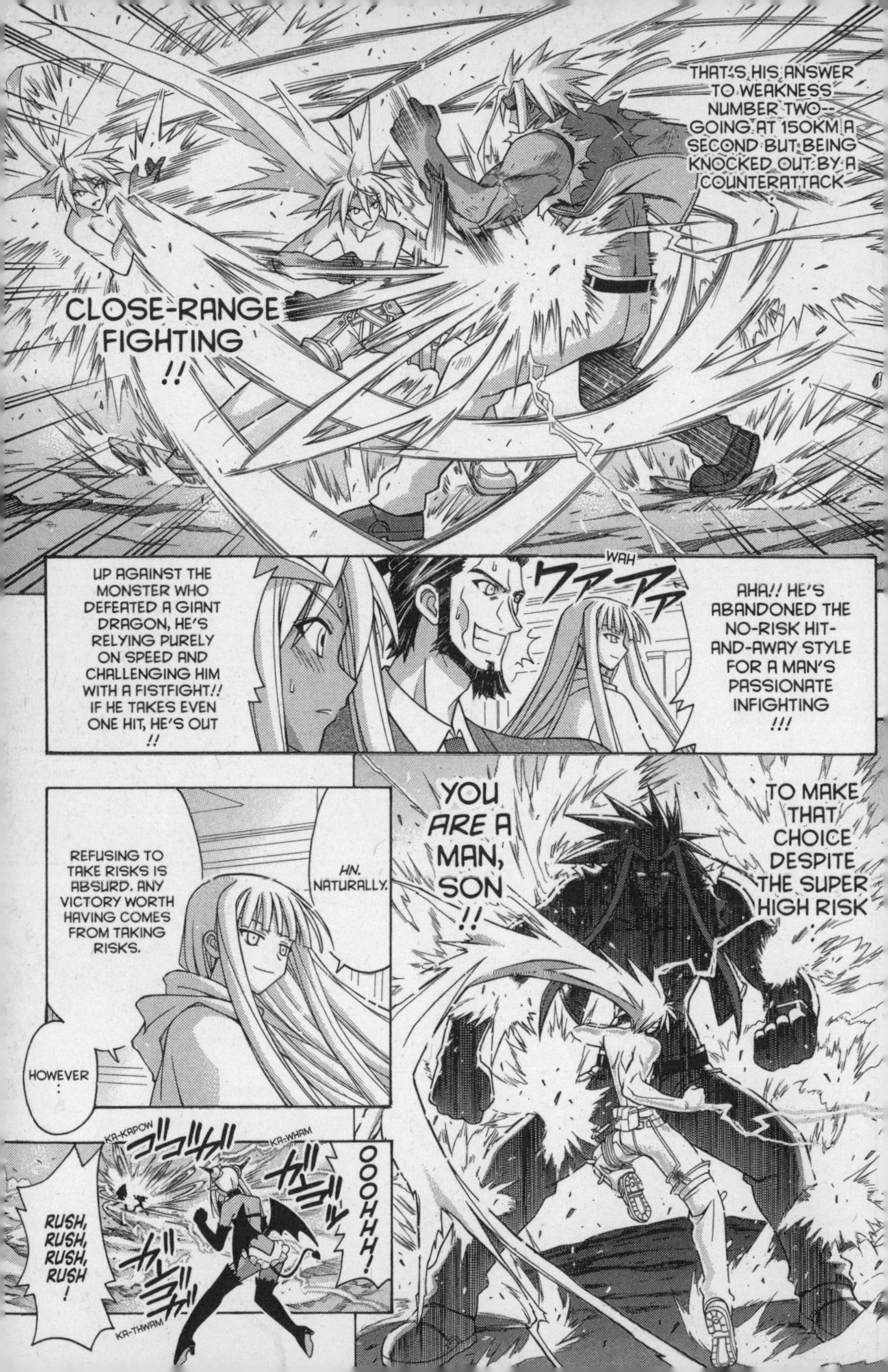
THAT'S HIS ANSWER TO WEAKNESS NUMBER TWO-- GOING AT 150KM A SECOND BUT BEING KNOCKED OUT BY A COUNTERATTACK
CLOSE-RANGE FIGHTING !!
AHA!! HE'S ABANDONED THE NO-RISK HIT-AND-AWAY STYLE FOR A MAN'S PASSIONATE INFIGHTING !!!
ワァァ
WAH
UP AGAINST THE MONSTER WHO DEFEATED A GIANT DRAGON, HE'S RELYING PURELY ON SPEED AND CHALLENGING HIM WITH A FISTFIGHT!! IF HE TAKES EVEN ONE HIT, HE'S OUT !!
TO MAKE THAT CHOICE DESPITE THE SUPER HIGH RISK
YOU ARE A MAN, SON !!
HN. NATURALLY.
REFUSING TO TAKE RISKS IS ABSURD. ANY VICTORY WORTH HAVING COMES FROM TAKING RISKS.
HOWEVER
OOOHHHH!
KA-WHAM
KA-KAPOW
RUSH, RUSH, RUSH, RUSH!
KA-THWAM

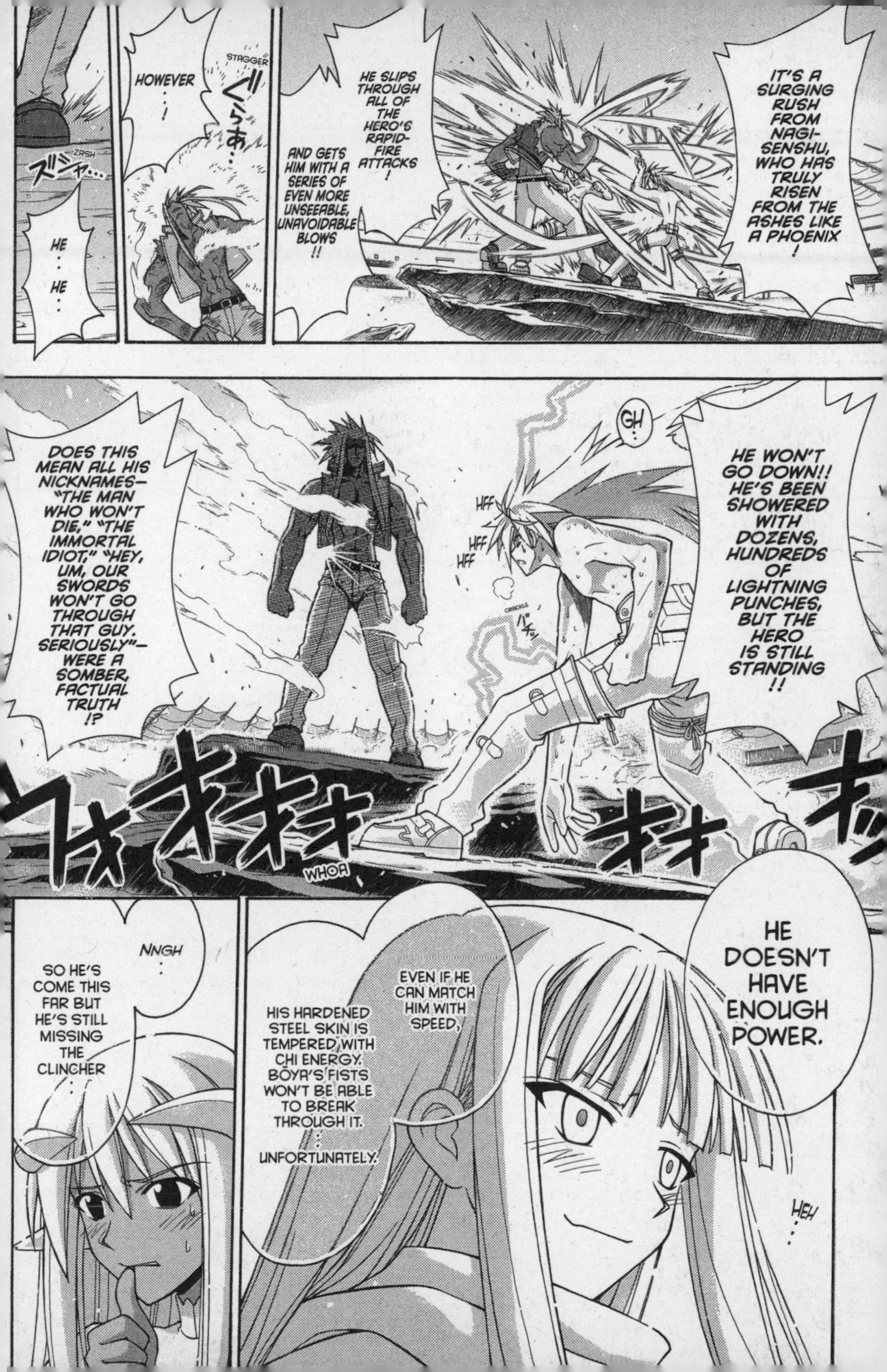
IT'S A SURGING RUSH FROM NAGI-SENSHU, WHO HAS TRULY RISEN FROM THE ASHES LIKE A PHOENIX!
HE SLIPS THROUGH ALL OF THE HERO'S RAPID-FIRE ATTACKS!
AND GETS HIM WITH A SERIES OF EVEN MORE UNSEEABLE, UNAVOIDABLE BLOWS!!
HOWEVER..!
STAGGER
ぐらぁ…
HE... HE...
ZASH
ズシャ…
GH...
HE WON'T GO DOWN!! HE'S BEEN SHOWERED WITH DOZENS, HUNDREDS OF LIGHTNING PUNCHES, BUT THE HERO IS STILL STANDING!!
HFF
HFF
HFF
CRACKLE
DOES THIS MEAN ALL HIS NICKNAMES—"THE MAN WHO WON'T DIE," "THE IMMORTAL IDIOT," "HEY, UM, OUR SWORDS WON'T GO THROUGH THAT GUY. SERIOUSLY"—WERE A SOMBER, FACTUAL TRUTH!?
WHOA
HE DOESN'T HAVE ENOUGH POWER.
HEH...
EVEN IF HE CAN MATCH HIM WITH SPEED,
HIS HARDENED STEEL SKIN IS TEMPERED WITH CHI ENERGY. BŌYA'S FISTS WON'T BE ABLE TO BREAK THROUGH IT.
...UNFORTUNATELY.
NNGH...
SO HE'S COME THIS FAR BUT HE'S STILL MISSING THE CLINCHER...

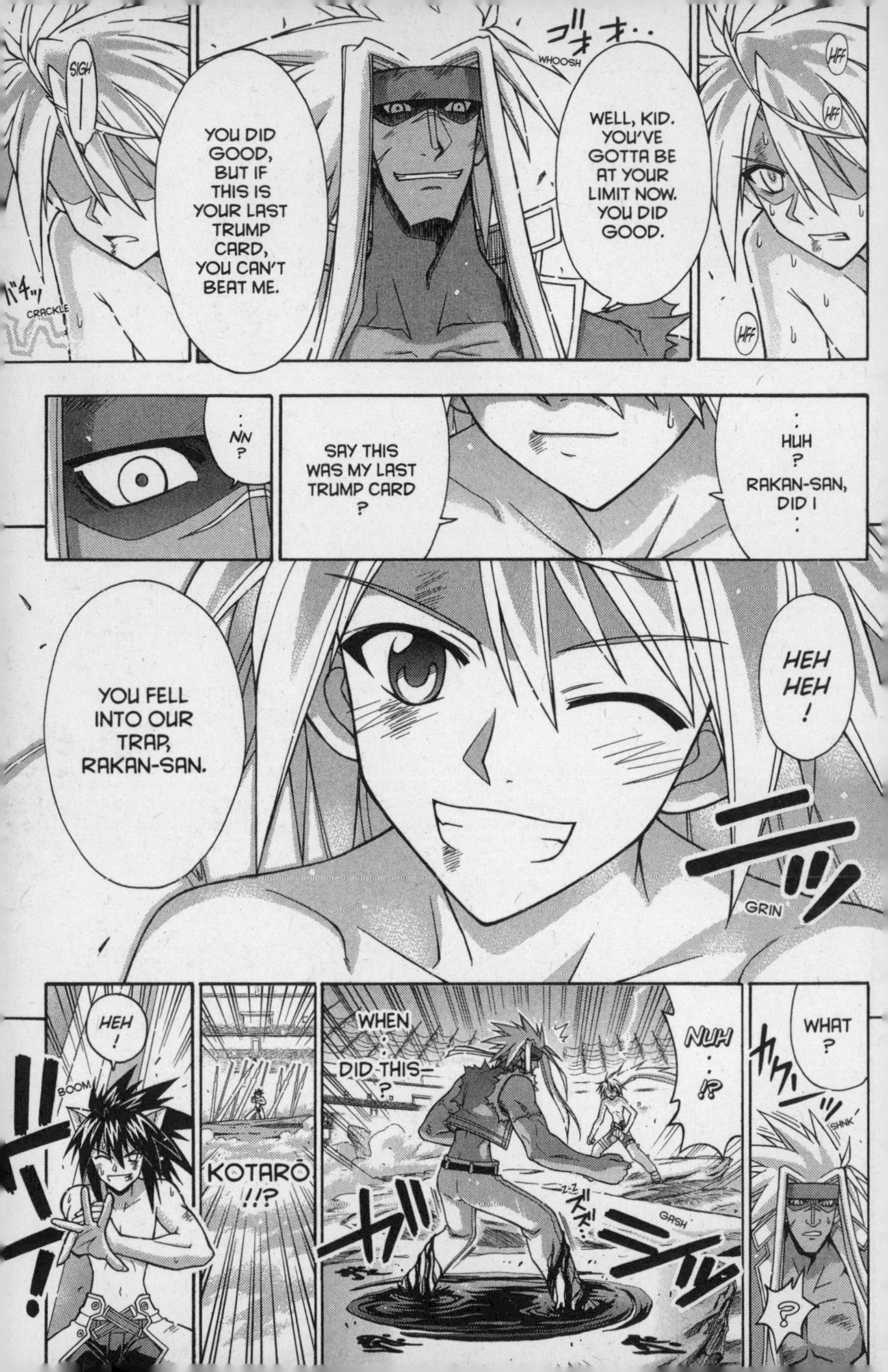
HFF
HFF
HFF
ゴォォ‥
WHOOSH
WELL, KID. YOU'VE GOTTA BE AT YOUR LIMIT NOW. YOU DID GOOD.
YOU DID GOOD, BUT IF THIS IS YOUR LAST TRUMP CARD, YOU CAN'T BEAT ME.
SIGH
バチッ
CRACKLE
...HUH? RAKAN-SAN, DID I...
SAY THIS WAS MY LAST TRUMP CARD?
...NN?
HEH HEH!
ニッ
GRIN
YOU FELL INTO OUR TRAP, RAKAN-SAN.
WHAT?
SHNK
?
NUH...!?
WHEN... DID THIS-?
Z-Z
GASH
KOTARŌ!!?
HEH!
BOOM

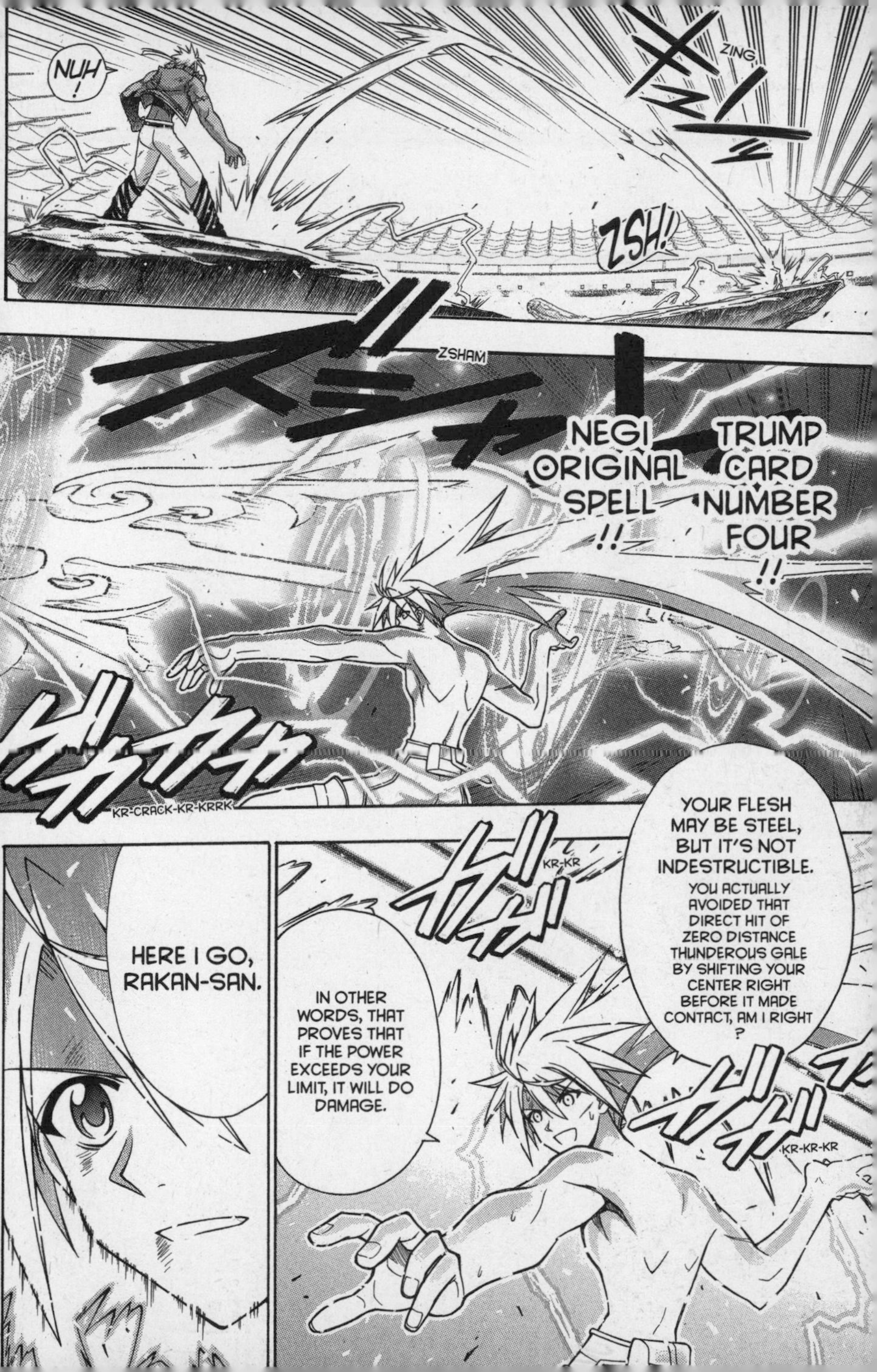
ZING
ZSH!
NUH!
ZSHAM
TRUMP CARD NUMBER FOUR!!
NEGI ORIGINAL SPELL!!
KR-CRACK-KR-KRRK
YOUR FLESH MAY BE STEEL, BUT IT'S NOT INDESTRUCTIBLE.
YOU ACTUALLY AVOIDED THAT DIRECT HIT OF ZERO DISTANCE THUNDEROUS GALE BY SHIFTING YOUR CENTER RIGHT BEFORE IT MADE CONTACT, AM I RIGHT?
KR-KR
IN OTHER WORDS, THAT PROVES THAT IF THE POWER EXCEEDS YOUR LIMIT, IT WILL DO DAMAGE.
KR-KR-KR
HERE I GO, RAKAN-SAN.

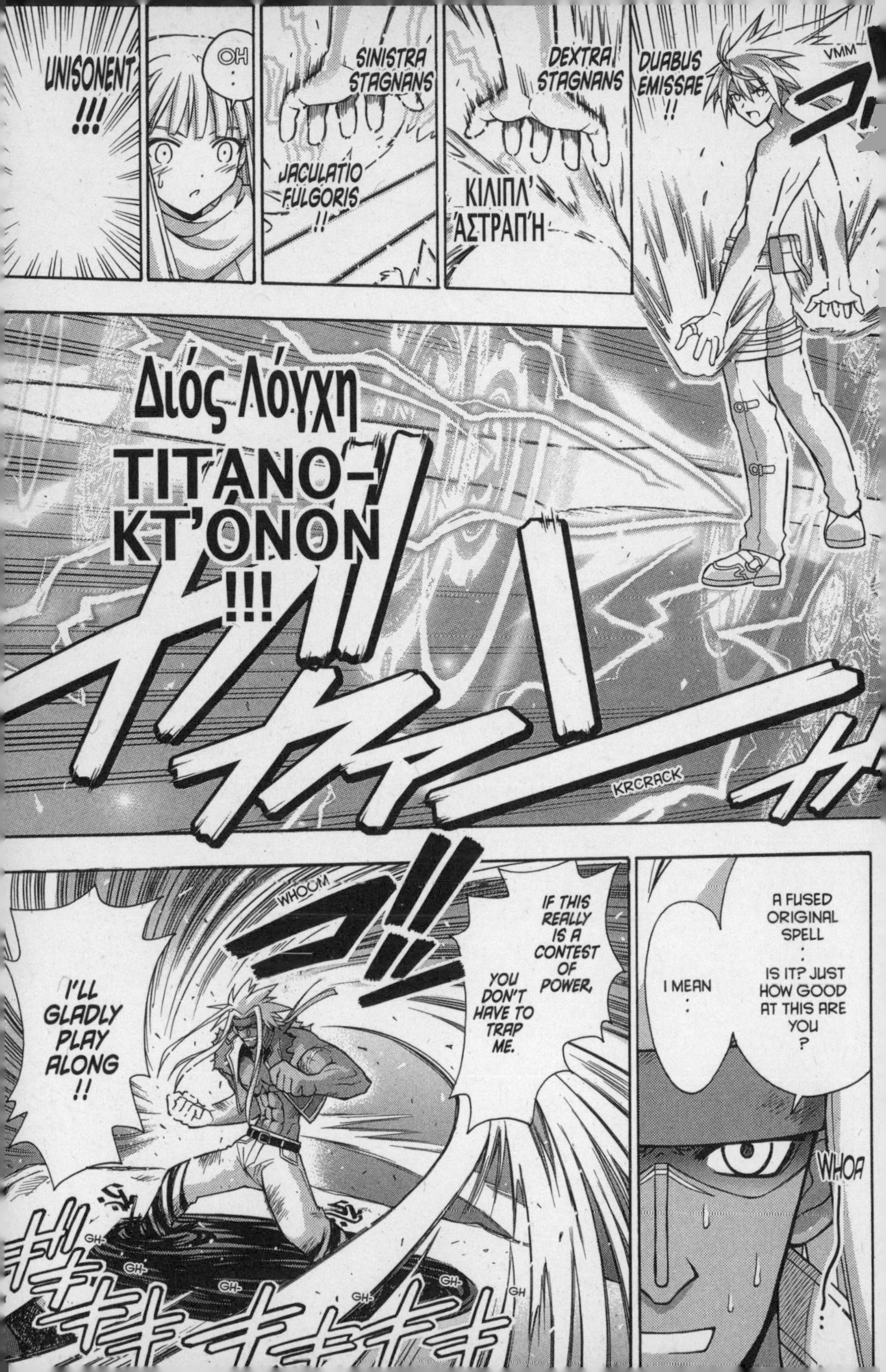
VMM
DUABUS EMISSAE !!
DEXTRA STAGNANS
ΚΙΛΙΠΛ' ΆΣΤΡΑΠ'Η
SINISTRA STAGNANS
JACULATIO FULGORIS !!
OH . .
UNISONENT !!!
Διός Λόγχη
ΤΙΤΑΝΟ-ΚΤ'ΌΝΟΝ !!!
KRCRACK
A FUSED ORIGINAL SPELL . . IS IT? JUST HOW GOOD AT THIS ARE YOU ?
I MEAN . .
WHOA
IF THIS REALLY IS A CONTEST OF POWER,
YOU DON'T HAVE TO TRAP ME.
WHOOM
I'LL GLADLY PLAY ALONG !!
GH- GH- GH- GH- GH

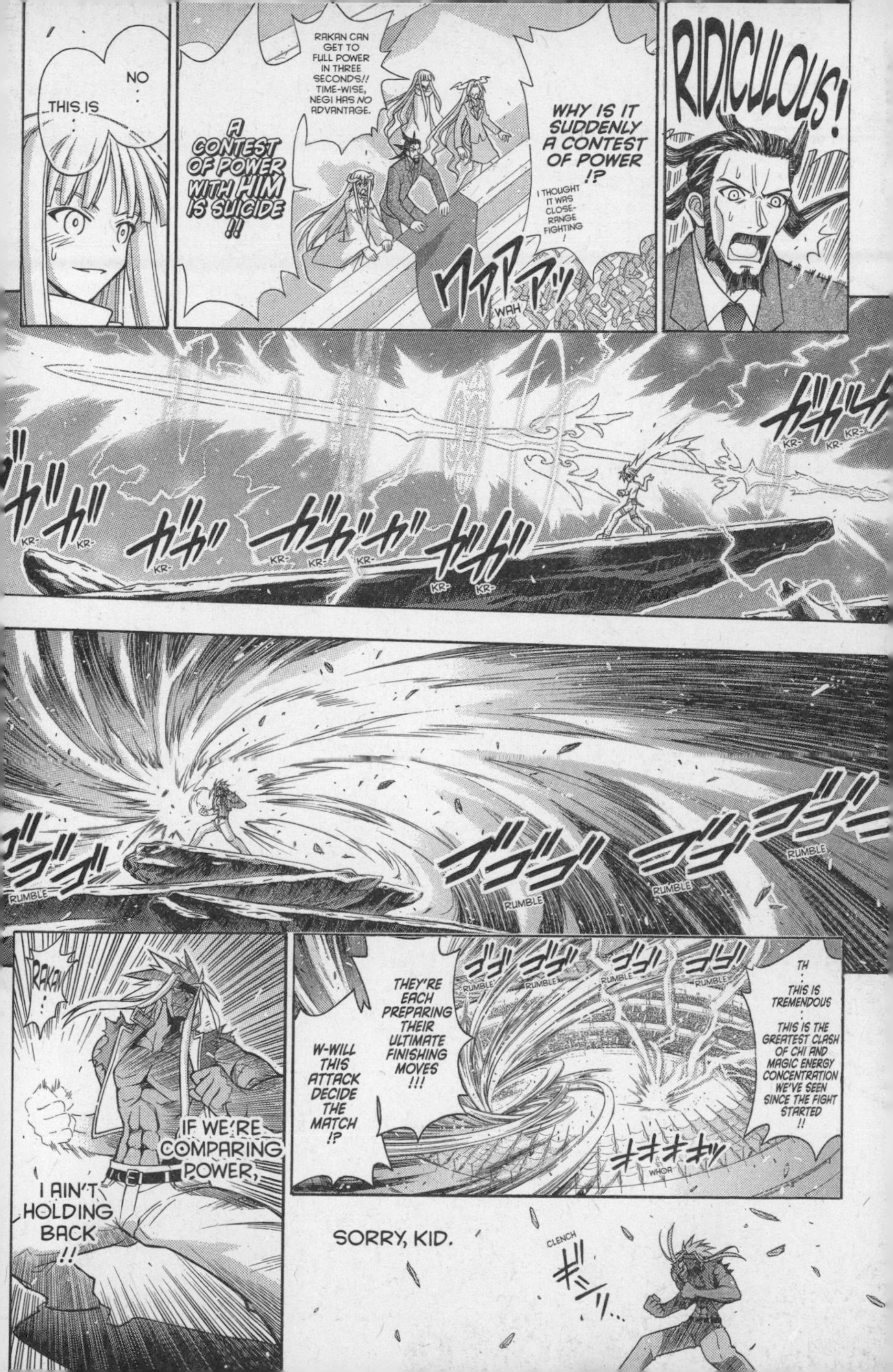

RIDICULOUS!
WHY IS IT SUDDENLY A CONTEST OF POWER !?
I THOUGHT IT WAS CLOSE-RANGE FIGHTING!
RAKAN CAN GET TO FULL POWER IN THREE SECONDS!! TIME-WISE, NEGI HAS NO ADVANTAGE.
A CONTEST OF POWER WITH HIM IS SUICIDE !!
WAH
NO...
THIS IS
KR- KR- KR-
KR- KR- KR- KR- KR- KR- KR-
RUMBLE RUMBLE RUMBLE RUMBLE
TH... THIS IS TREMENDOUS... THIS IS THE GREATEST CLASH OF CHI AND MAGIC ENERGY CONCENTRATION WE'VE SEEN SINCE THE FIGHT STARTED !!
RUMBLE RUMBLE RUMBLE RUMBLE
THEY'RE EACH PREPARING THEIR ULTIMATE FINISHING MOVES !!!
W-WILL THIS ATTACK DECIDE THE MATCH !?
WHOA
CLENCH
SORRY, KID.
RAKAN...!
IF WE'RE COMPARING POWER,
I AIN'T HOLDING BACK !!

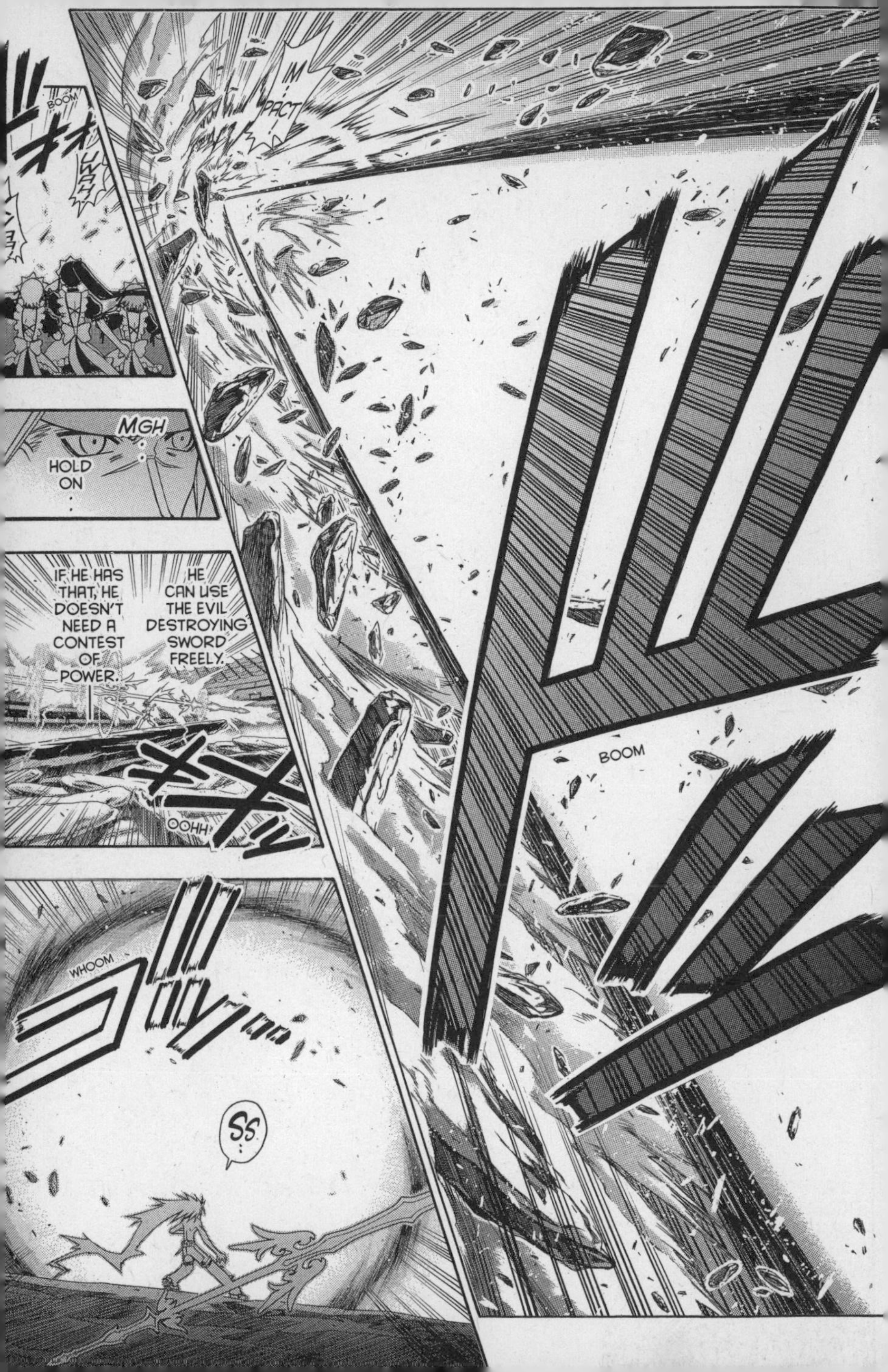

IMPACT
BOOM
BOOM
UWAH
MGH
HOLD ON
HE CAN USE THE EVIL DESTROYING SWORD FREELY.
IF HE HAS THAT, HE DOESN'T NEED A CONTEST OF POWER.
OOHH
WHOOM
SS

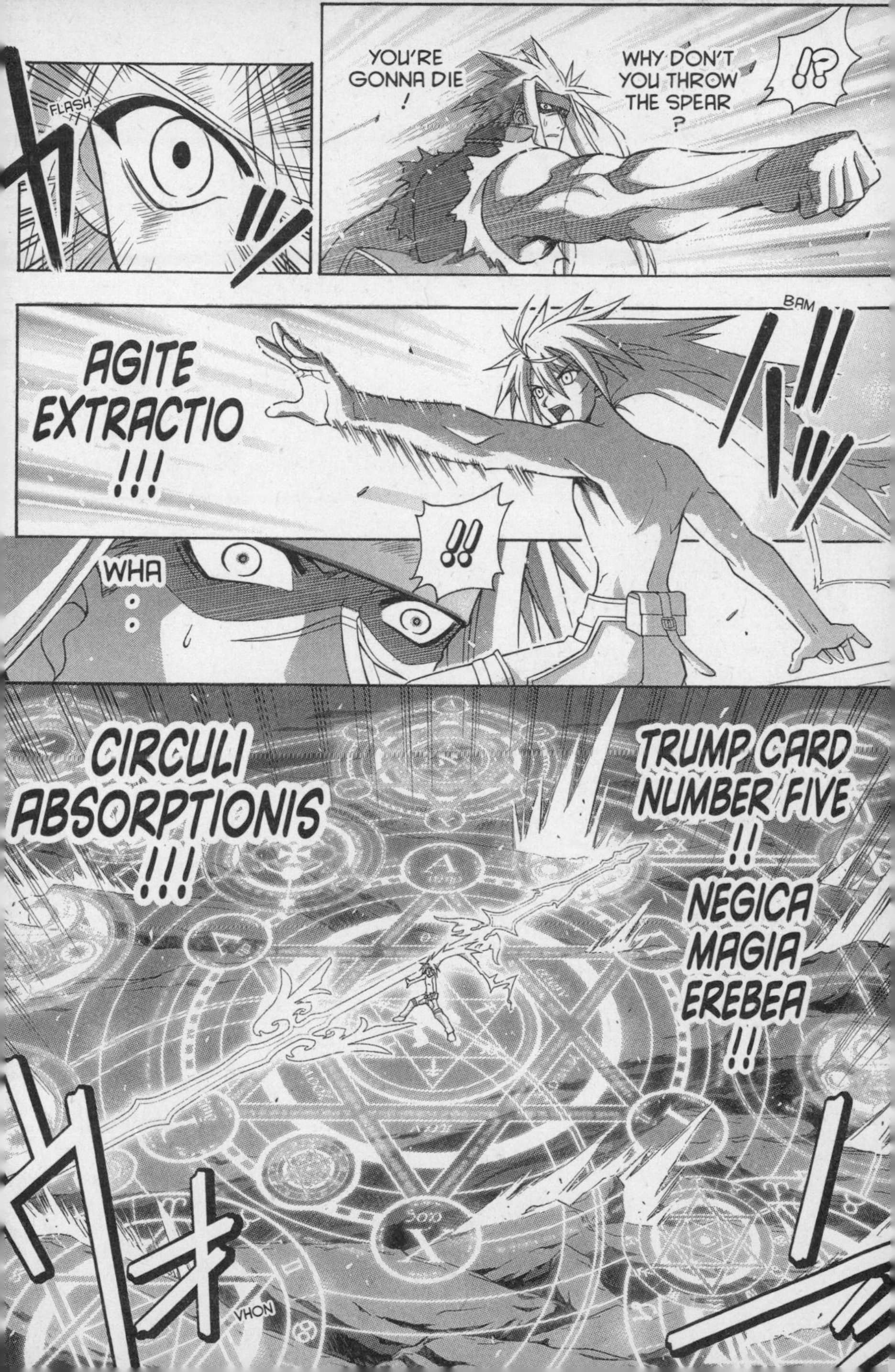
!?
WHY DON'T YOU THROW THE SPEAR?
YOU'RE GONNA DIE!
FLASH
BAM
AGITE EXTRACTIO!!!
!!
WHA..
TRUMP CARD NUMBER FIVE!!
NEGICA MAGIA EREBEA!!
CIRCULI ABSORPTIONIS!!!
VHON

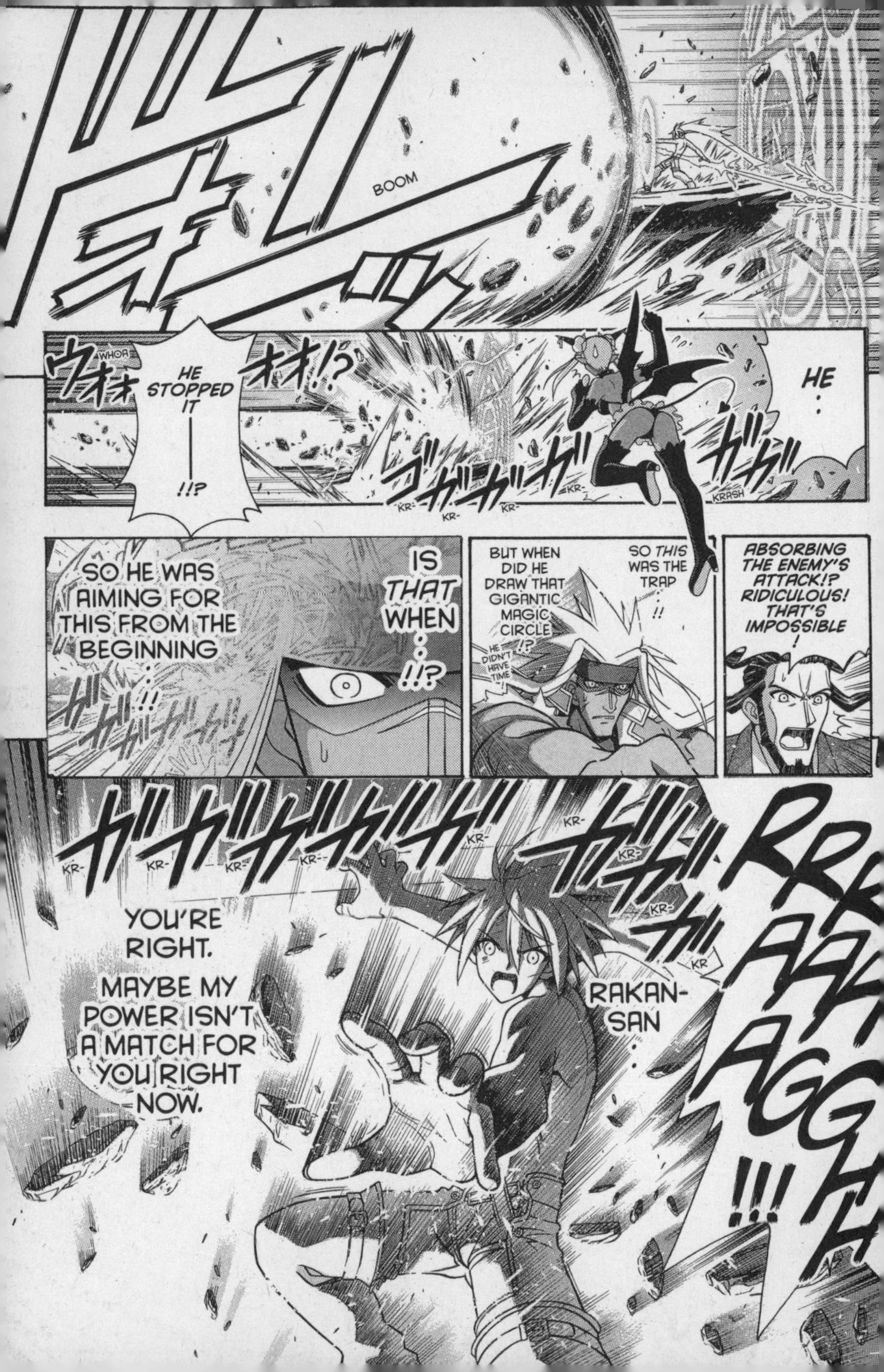
BOOM
HE...
KRASH
KR-
HE STOPPED IT——!!?
WHOA
ABSORBING THE ENEMY'S ATTACK!? RIDICULOUS! THAT'S IMPOSSIBLE!
SO THIS WAS THE TRAP...!!
BUT WHEN DID HE DRAW THAT GIGANTIC MAGIC CIRCLE...!?
HE DIDN'T HAVE TIME...!
IS THAT WHEN...!!?
SO HE WAS AIMING FOR THIS FROM THE BEGINNING...!!
RRAAAGGHH!!!
KR-
RAKAN-SAN...
YOU'RE RIGHT.
MAYBE MY POWER ISN'T A MATCH FOR YOU RIGHT NOW.

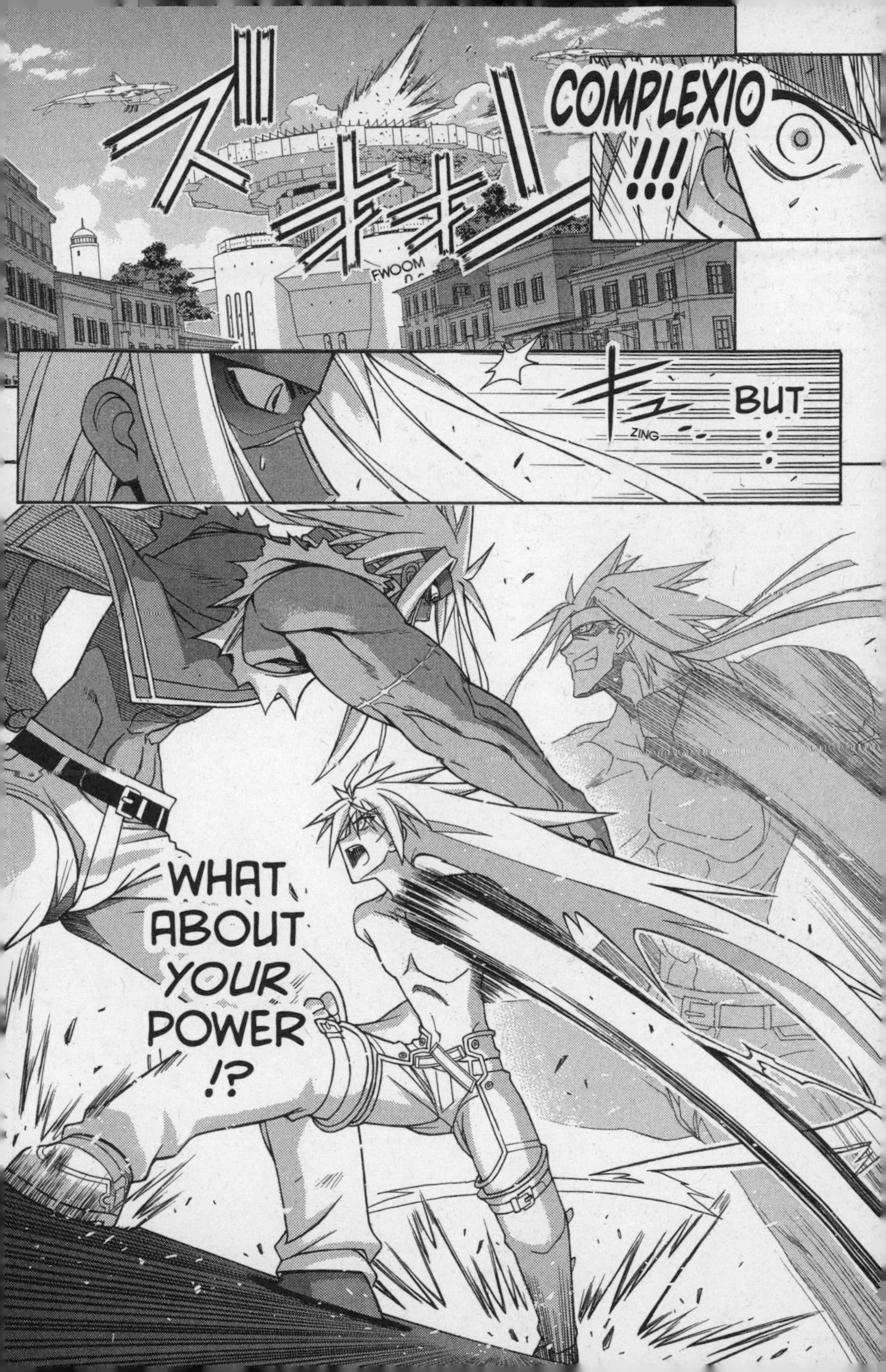
COMPLEXIO !!!
FWOOM
BUT...
ZING
WHAT ABOUT YOUR POWER !?

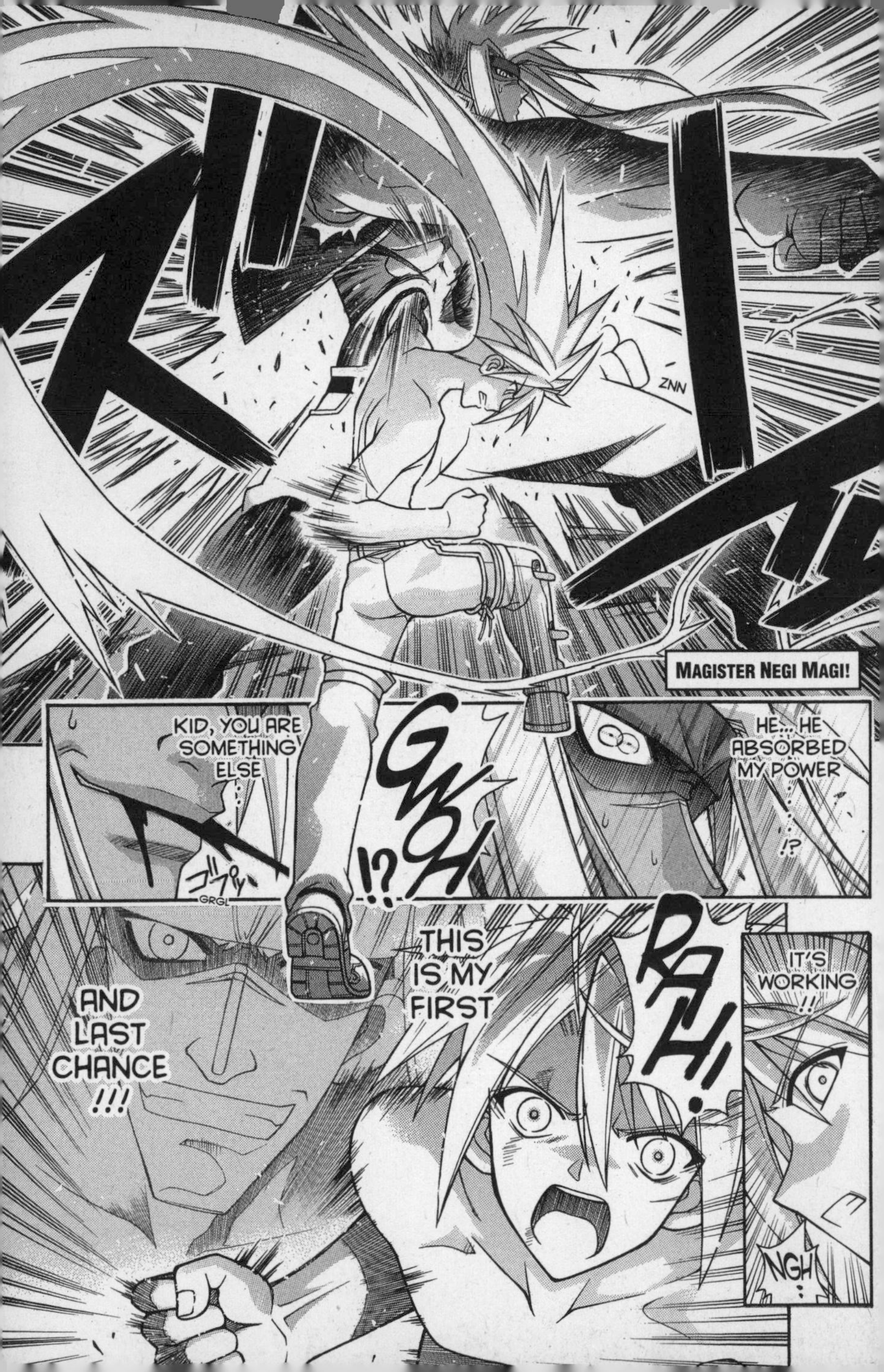
ZNN
MAGISTER NEGI MAGI!
HE... HE ABSORBED MY POWER ...!?
GWOH !?
KID, YOU ARE SOMETHING ELSE...
ゴプッ
GRGL
IT'S WORKING !!
NGH...
RAH!
THIS IS MY FIRST
AND LAST CHANCE !!!

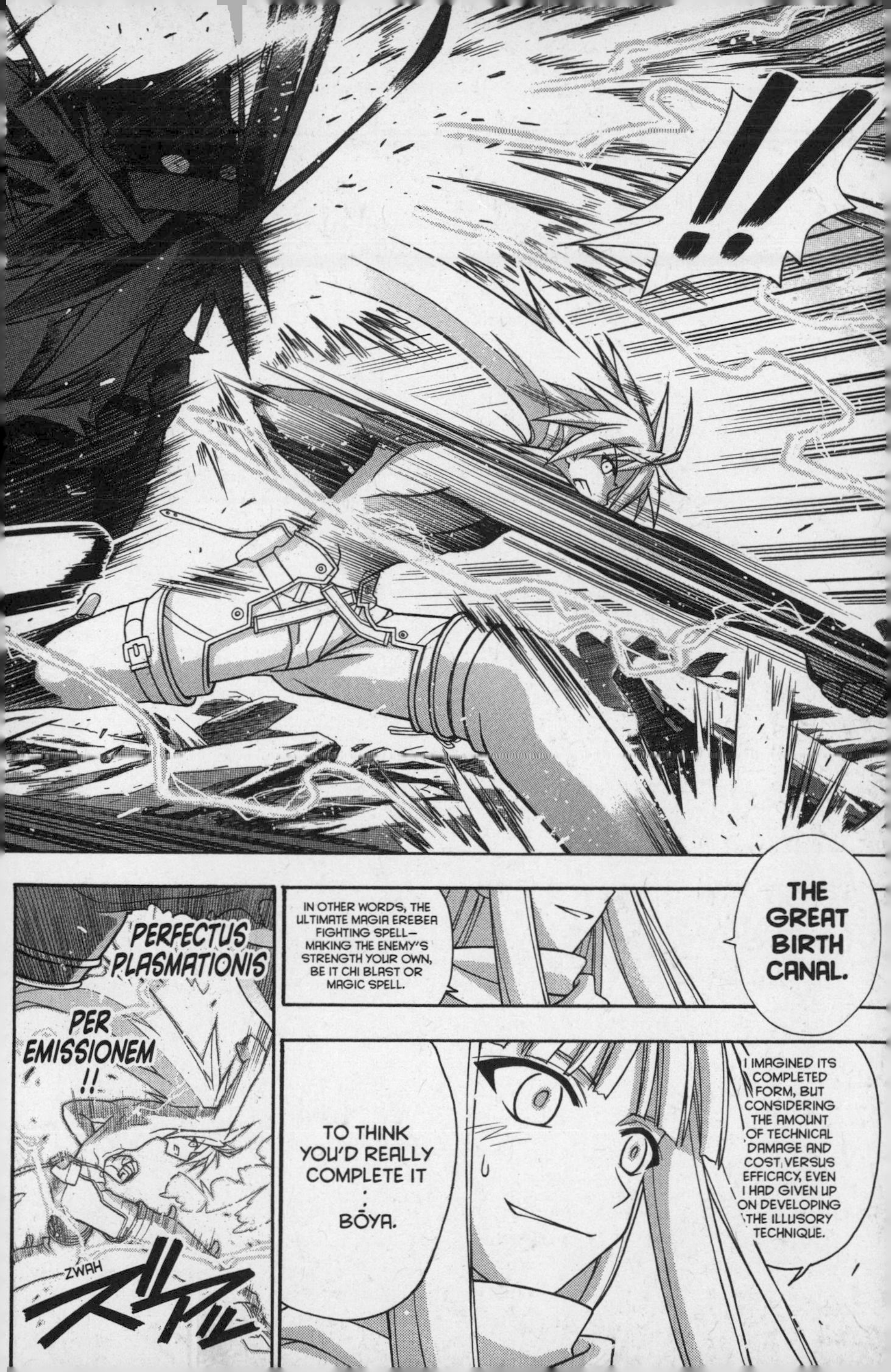
!!
THE GREAT BIRTH CANAL.
IN OTHER WORDS, THE ULTIMATE MAGIA EREBEA FIGHTING SPELL— MAKING THE ENEMY'S STRENGTH YOUR OWN, BE IT CHI BLAST OR MAGIC SPELL.
I IMAGINED ITS COMPLETED FORM, BUT CONSIDERING THE AMOUNT OF TECHNICAL DAMAGE AND COST VERSUS EFFICACY, EVEN I HAD GIVEN UP ON DEVELOPING THE ILLUSORY TECHNIQUE.
TO THINK YOU'D REALLY COMPLETE IT
BÔYA.
PERFECTUS PLASMATIONIS
PER EMISSIONEM !!
ZWAH

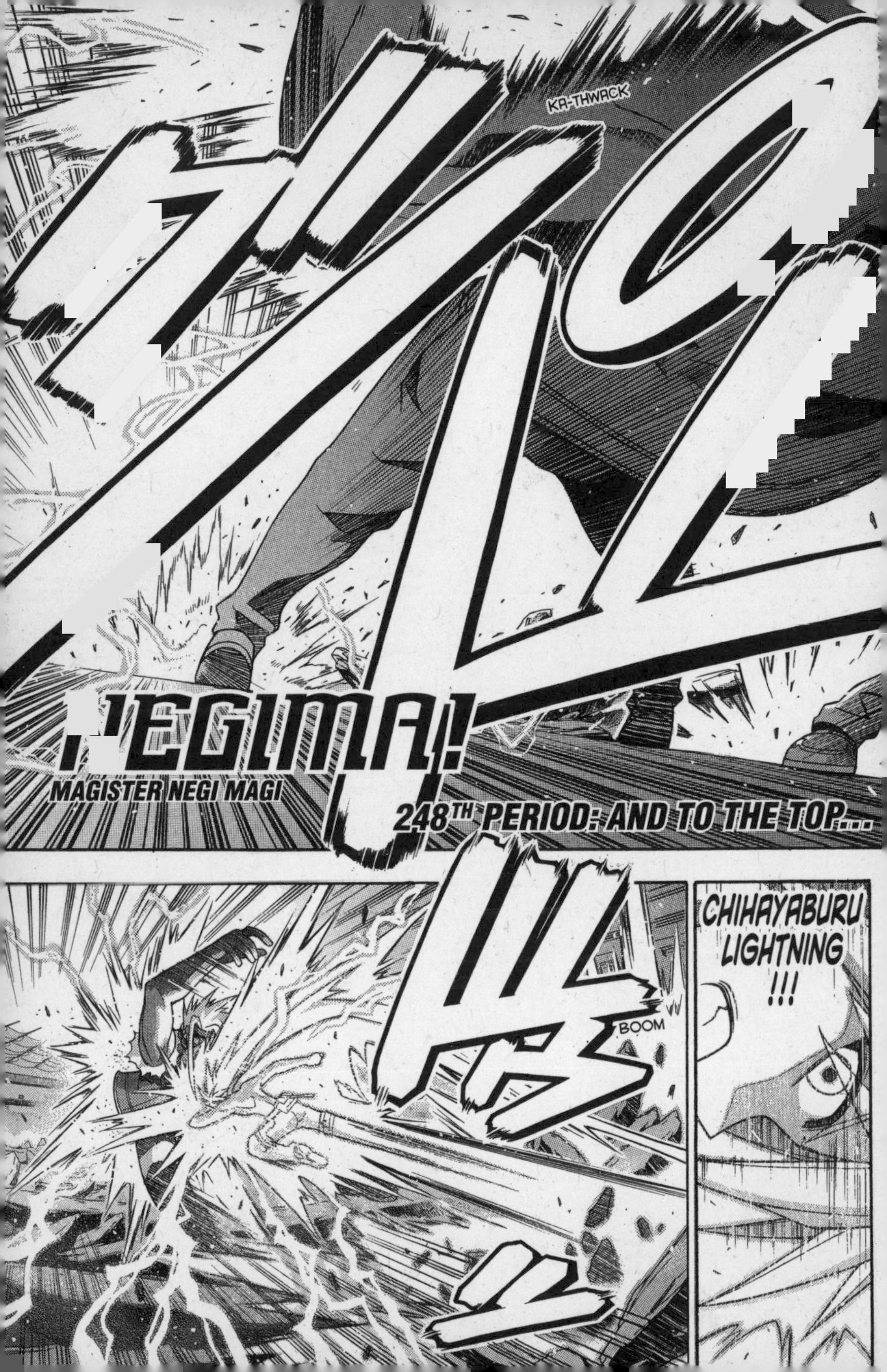
KA-THWACK
EGIMA!
MAGISTER NEGI MAGI
248TH PERIOD: AND TO THE TOP...
CHIHAYABURU LIGHTNING !!!
BOOM

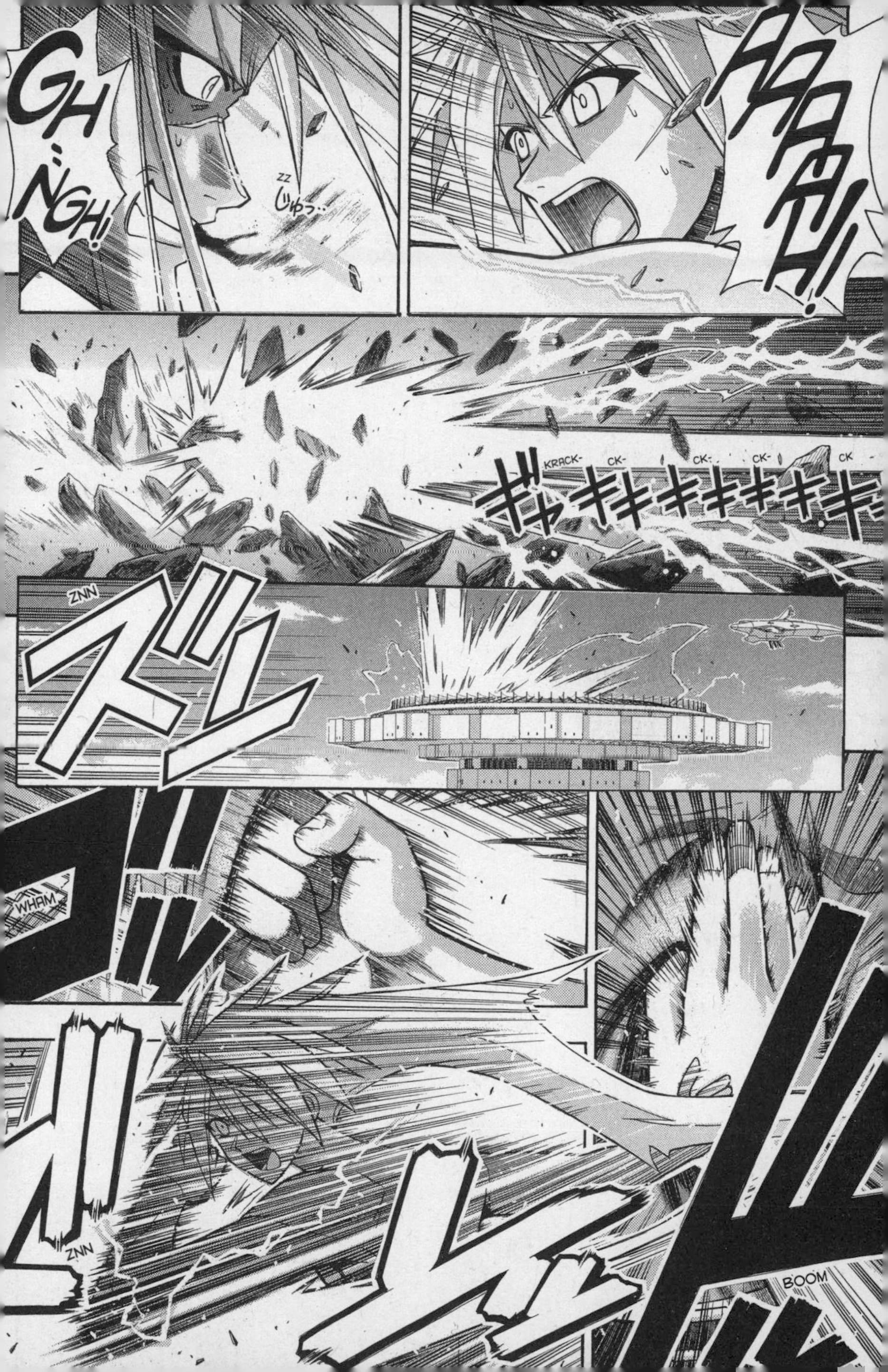
AAAAH!!
GH... NGH!
ZZ じゅっ...
KRACK- CK- CK- CK- CK
ギャキキキキキキキ
ZNN
ズゾン
WHAM
ZNN
BOOM

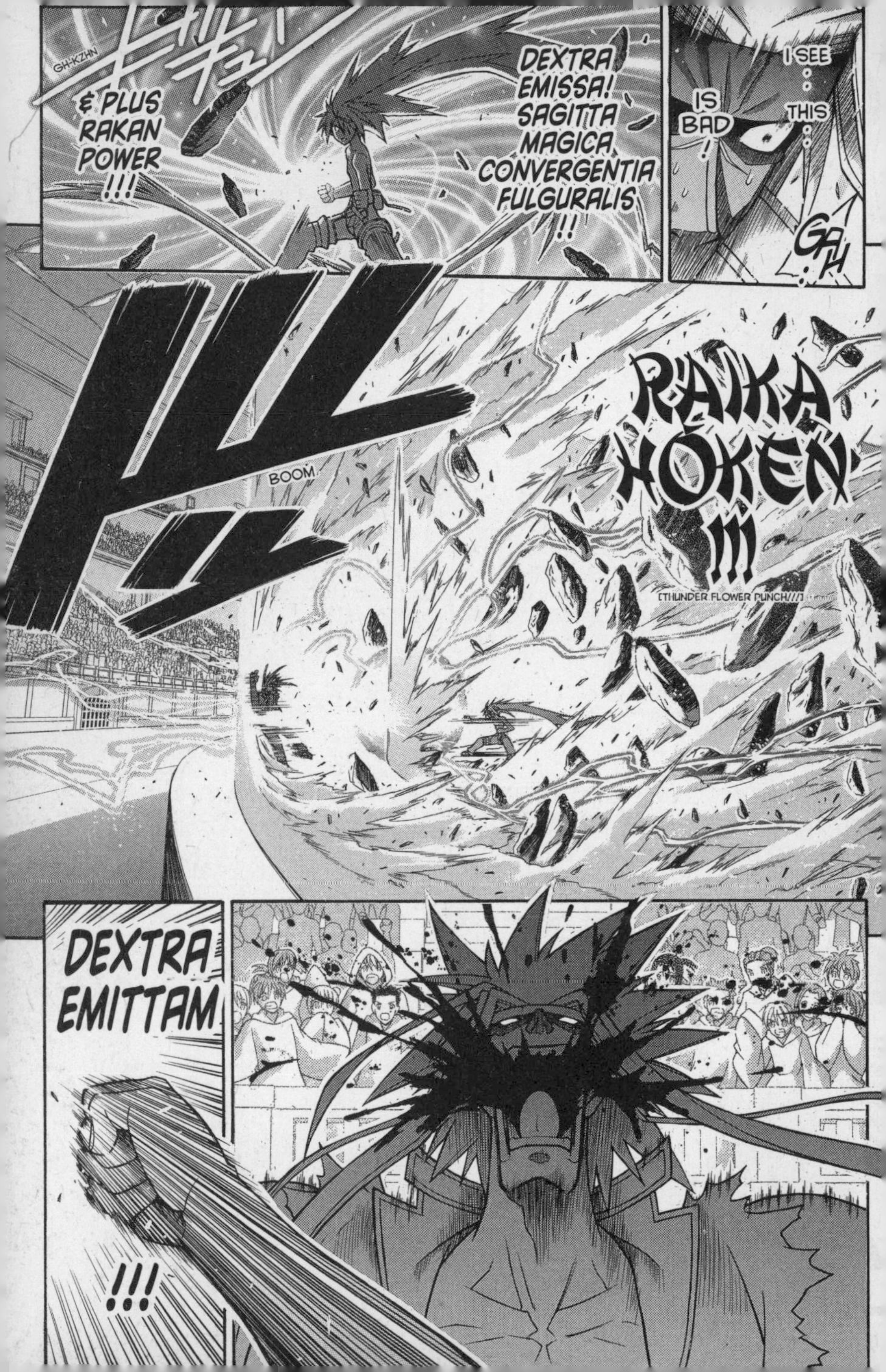
I SEE...
THIS...
IS BAD!
GAH
DEXTRA EMISSA! SAGITTA MAGICA CONVERGENTIA FULGURALIS!!
GH-KZHN
& PLUS RAKAN POWER!!!
RAIKA HOKEN!!!
[THUNDER FLOWER PUNCH!!!]
BOOM
DEXTRA EMITTAM
!!!

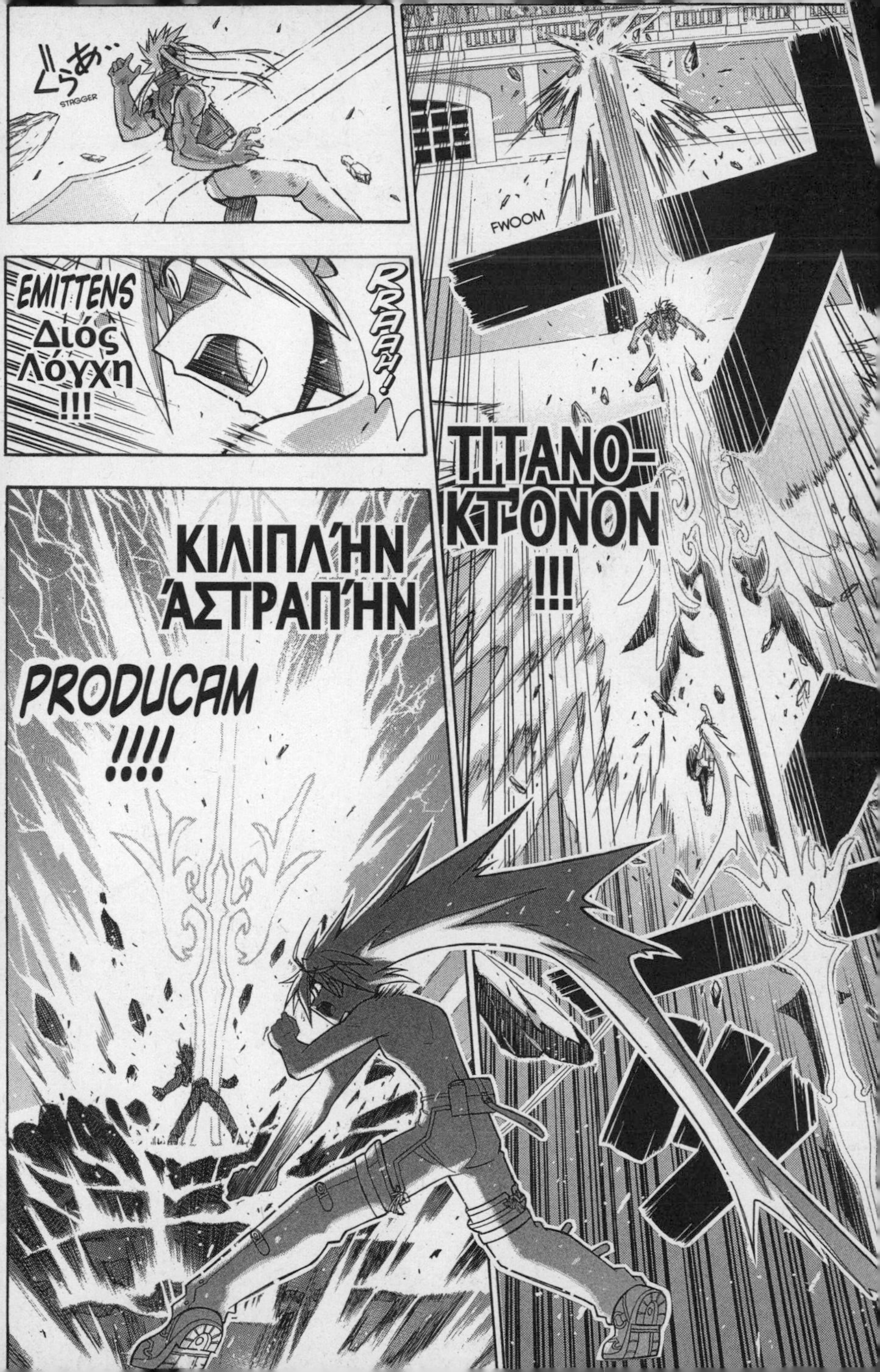
FWOOM
ΤΙΤΑΝΟ-
ΚΤΌΝΟΝ
!!!
くらあ
STAGGER
RRAAH!
EMITTENS
Διός
Λόγχη
!!!
ΚΙΛΙΠΛΉΗΝ
ΆΣΤΡΑΠΉΗΝ
PRODUCAM
!!!!

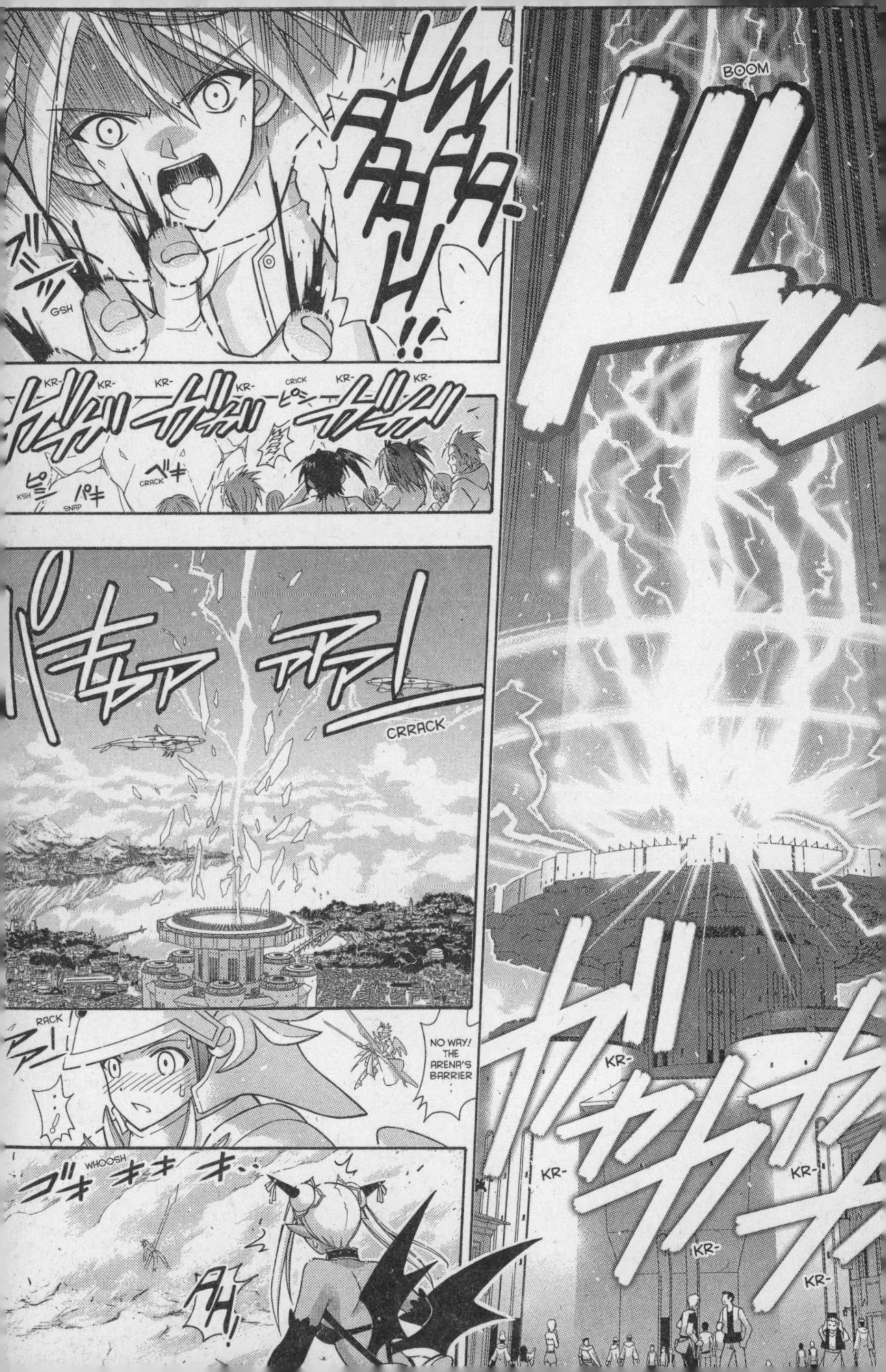
BOOM
KR-
KR-
KR-
KR-
UWAAAAA-H!!
GSH
KR-
KR-
KR-
KR-
CRICK
KR-
KR-
CRACK
KSH
SNAP
CRRACK
RACK
NO WAY! THE ARENA'S BARRIER
WHOOSH
AH!

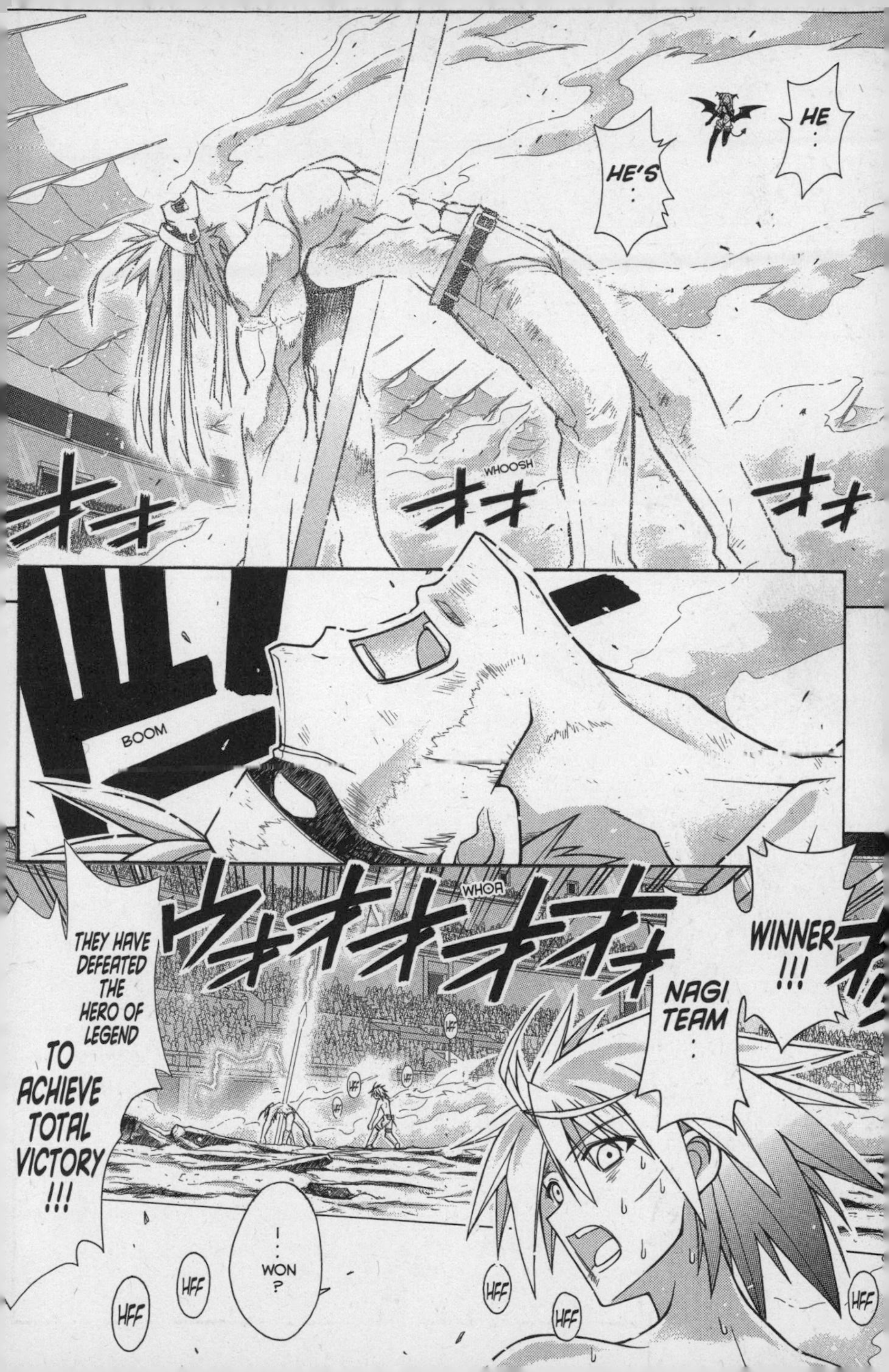
HE . . .
HE'S . . .
WHOOSH
BOOM
WINNER!!!
NAGI TEAM . . .
WHOA
THEY HAVE DEFEATED THE HERO OF LEGEND
TO ACHIEVE TOTAL VICTORY!!!
HFF
HFF
HFF
HFF
HFF
! . . WON?
HFF
HFF

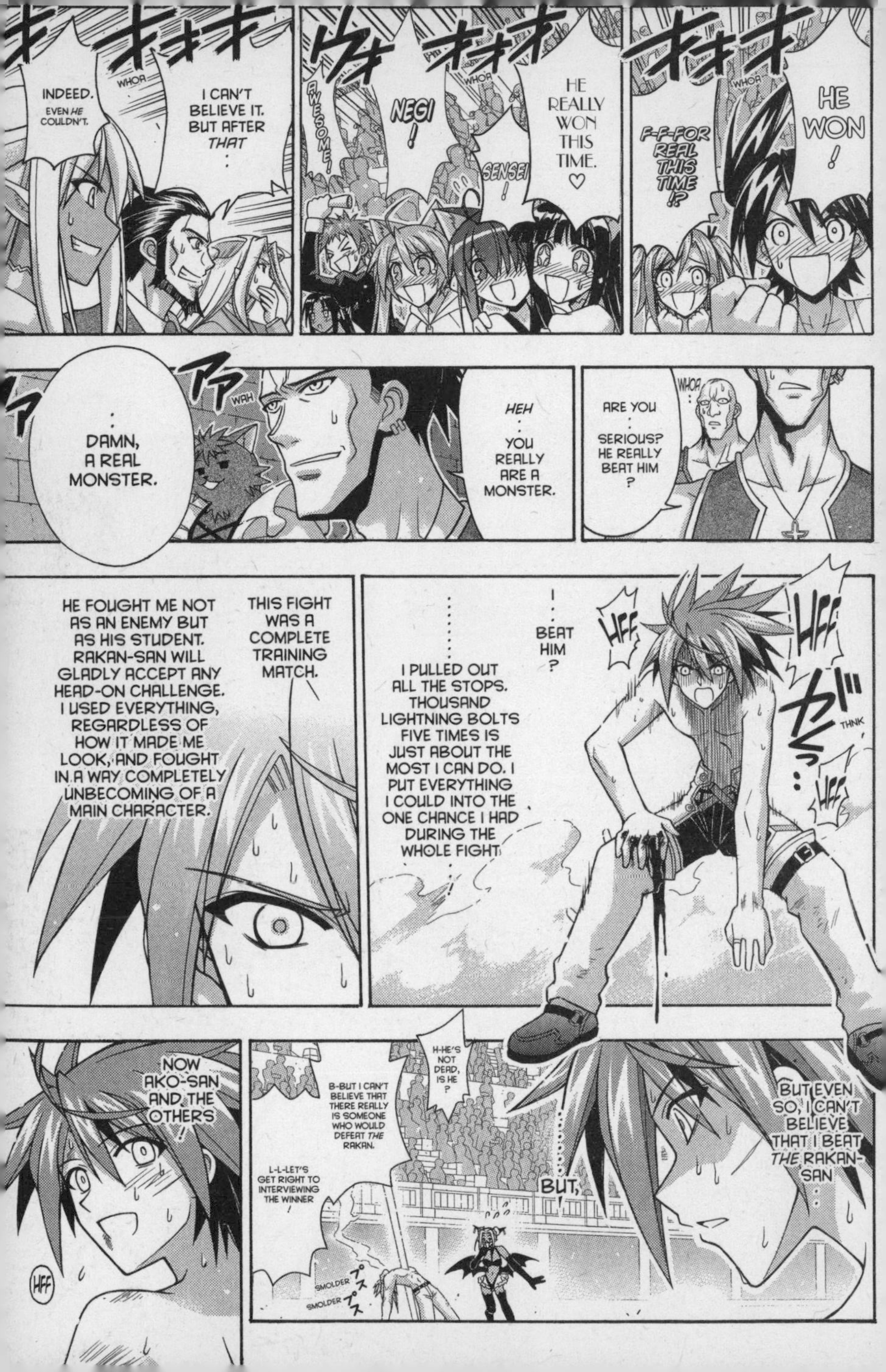
WHOA
HE WON!
F-F-FOR REAL THIS TIME!?
WHOA
HE REALLY WON THIS TIME. ♡
SENSEI!
NEGI!
AWESOME!
WHOA
I CAN'T BELIEVE IT. BUT AFTER *THAT*...
INDEED. EVEN *HE* COULDN'T.
WHOA
ARE YOU... SERIOUS? HE REALLY BEAT HIM?
HEH... YOU REALLY ARE A MONSTER.
WAH
...DAMN, A REAL MONSTER.
HFF
HFF
THNK
HFF
...BEAT HIM?
......I PULLED OUT ALL THE STOPS. THOUSAND LIGHTNING BOLTS FIVE TIMES IS JUST ABOUT THE MOST I CAN DO. I PUT EVERYTHING I COULD INTO THE ONE CHANCE I HAD DURING THE WHOLE FIGHT.
THIS FIGHT WAS A COMPLETE TRAINING MATCH.
HE FOUGHT ME NOT AS AN ENEMY BUT AS HIS STUDENT. RAKAN-SAN WILL GLADLY ACCEPT ANY HEAD-ON CHALLENGE. I USED EVERYTHING, REGARDLESS OF HOW IT MADE ME LOOK, AND FOUGHT IN A WAY COMPLETELY UNBECOMING OF A MAIN CHARACTER.
BUT EVEN SO, I CAN'T BELIEVE THAT I BEAT *THE* RAKAN-SAN...
BUT,!
H-HE'S NOT DEAD, IS HE?
B-BUT I CAN'T BELIEVE THAT THERE REALLY IS SOMEONE WHO WOULD DEFEAT *THE* RAKAN.
L-L-LET'S GET RIGHT TO INTERVIEWING THE WINNER!
SMOLDER
SMOLDER
NOW AKO-SAN AND THE OTHERS!
HFF

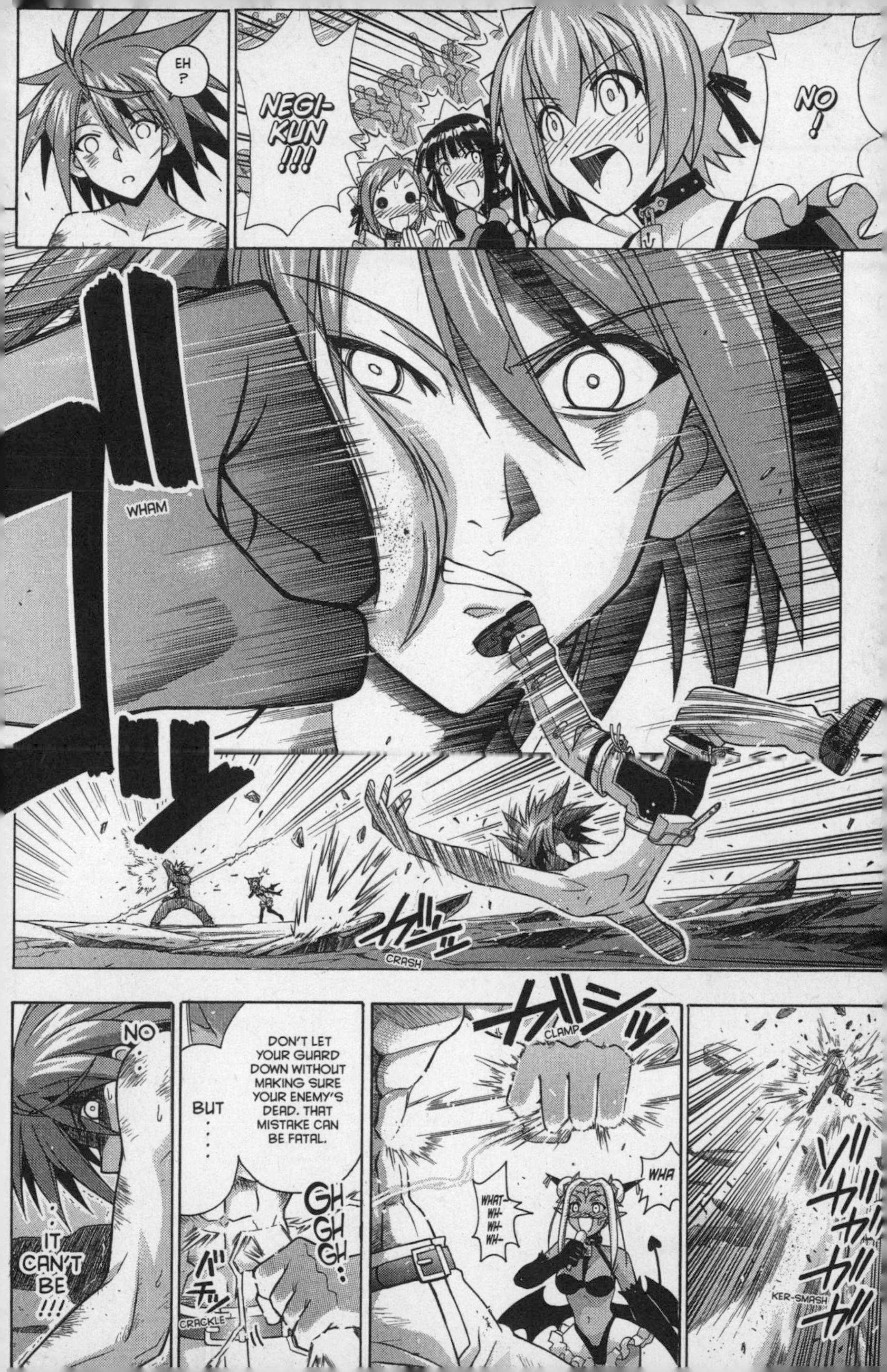
NO!
NEGI-KUN!!!
EH?
WHAM
CRASH
KER-SMASH
CLAMP
WHA...
WHAT-WH-WH-WH-
DON'T LET YOUR GUARD DOWN WITHOUT MAKING SURE YOUR ENEMY'S DEAD. THAT MISTAKE CAN BE FATAL.
BUT...
GH GH GH...
CRACKLE
NO...
...IT CAN'T BE!!!

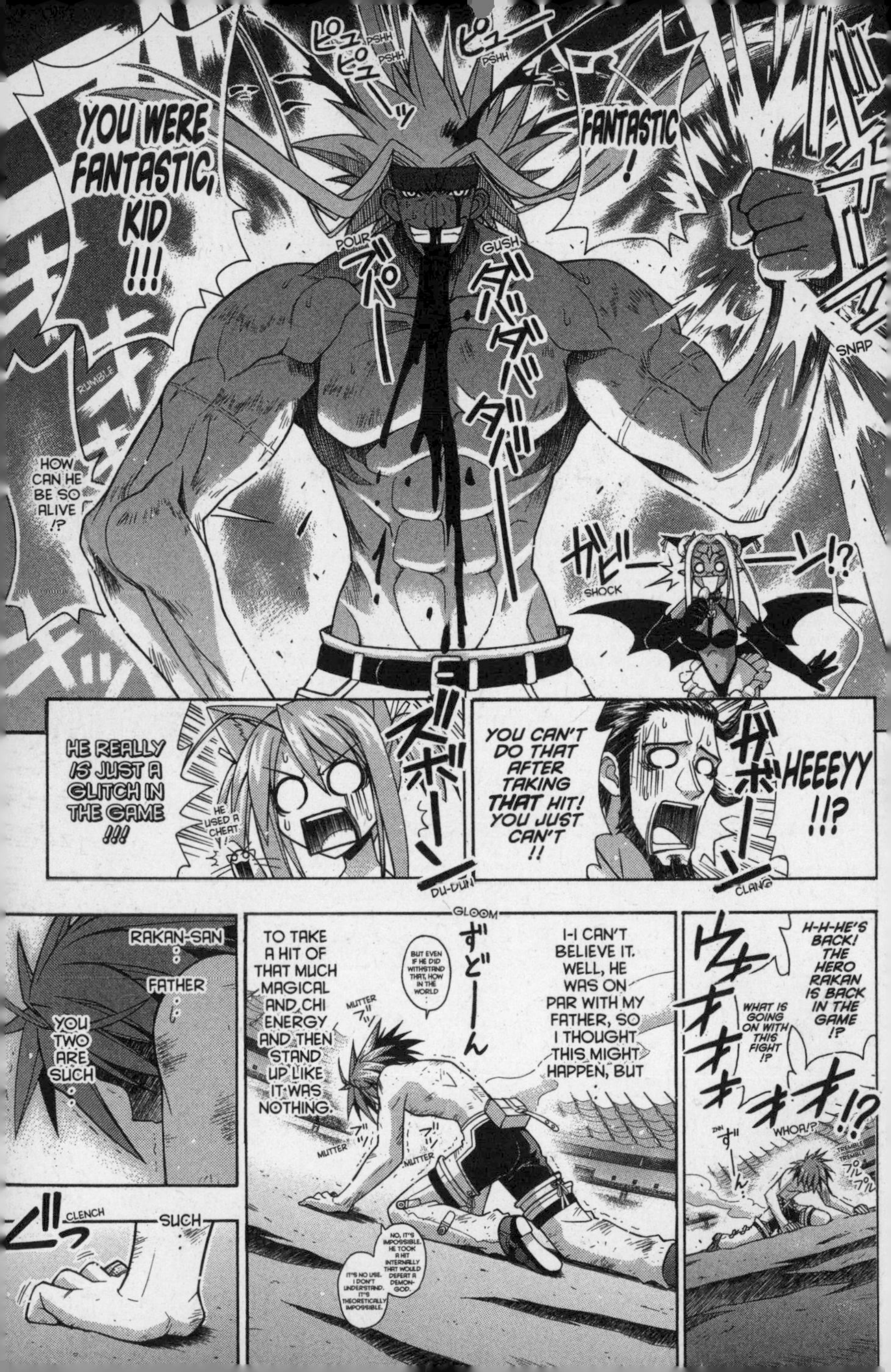
PSHH
PSHH
PSHH
FANTASTIC !
YOU WERE FANTASTIC, KID !!!
POUR
GUSH
SNAP
RUMBLE
HOW CAN HE BE SO ALIVE !?
SHOCK
HEEEYY !!?
YOU CAN'T DO THAT AFTER TAKING THAT HIT! YOU JUST CAN'T !!
CLANG
HE REALLY IS JUST A GLITCH IN THE GAME !!!
HE USED A CHEAT
DU-DUN
H-H-HE'S BACK! THE HERO RAKAN IS BACK IN THE GAME !?
WHAT IS GOING ON WITH THIS FIGHT !?
WHOA!?
ZNN
TREMBLE TREMBLE
GLOOM
I-I CAN'T BELIEVE IT. WELL, HE WAS ON PAR WITH MY FATHER, SO I THOUGHT THIS MIGHT HAPPEN, BUT
BUT EVEN IF HE DID WITHSTAND THAT, HOW IN THE WORLD . . .
TO TAKE A HIT OF THAT MUCH MAGICAL AND CHI ENERGY AND THEN STAND UP LIKE IT WAS NOTHING.
MUTTER
MUTTER
MUTTER
NO, IT'S IMPOSSIBLE. HE TOOK A HIT INTERNALLY THAT WOULD DEFEAT A DEMON-GOD.
IT'S NO USE. I DON'T UNDERSTAND. IT'S THEORETICALLY IMPOSSIBLE.
RAKAN-SAN . . .
FATHER . . .
YOU TWO ARE SUCH . . .
CLENCH
SUCH

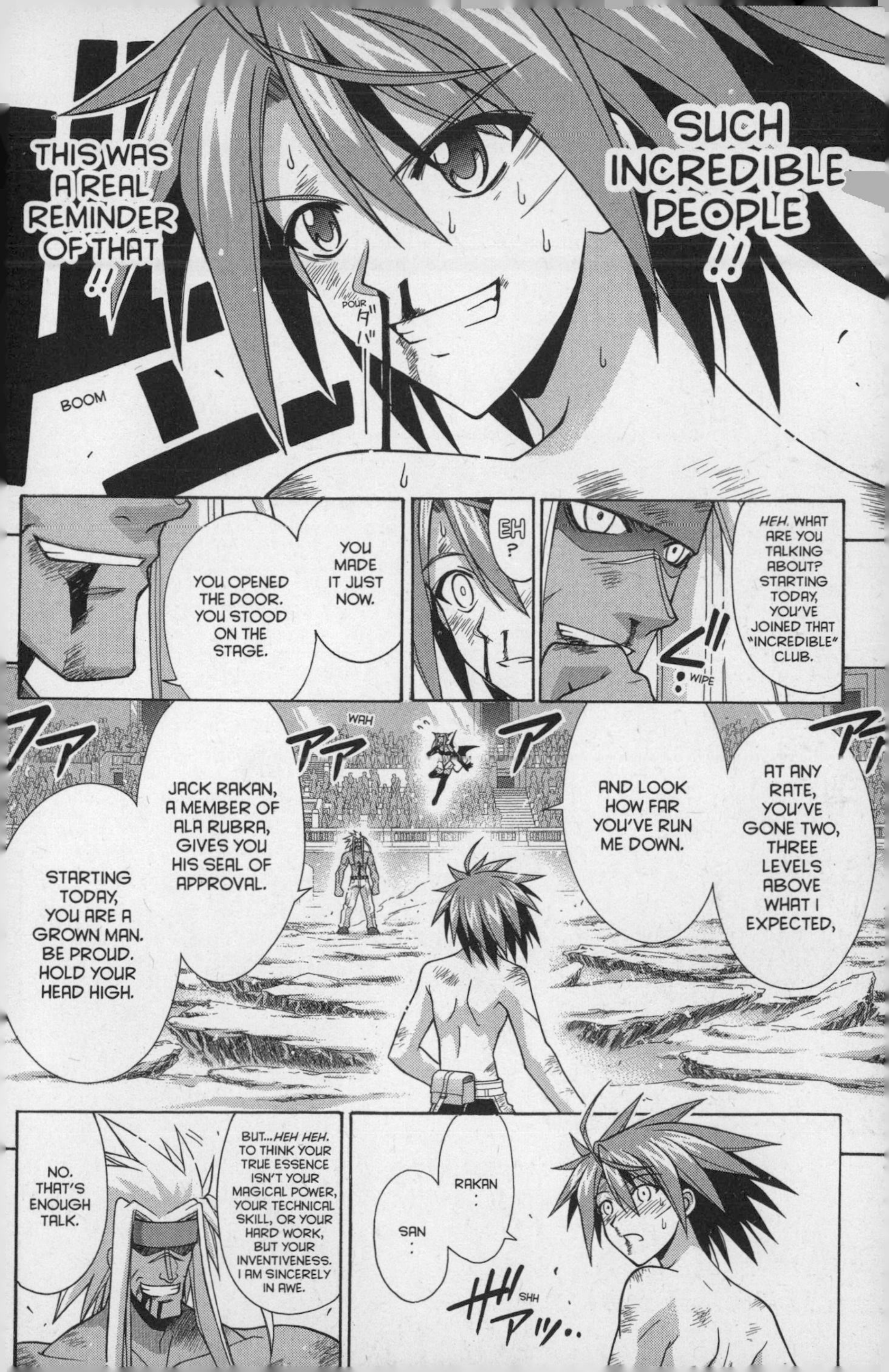
SUCH INCREDIBLE PEOPLE!!
THIS WAS A REAL REMINDER OF THAT!!
POUR
BOOM
HEH. WHAT ARE YOU TALKING ABOUT? STARTING TODAY, YOU'VE JOINED THAT "INCREDIBLE" CLUB.
WIPE
EH?
YOU MADE IT JUST NOW.
YOU OPENED THE DOOR. YOU STOOD ON THE STAGE.
AT ANY RATE, YOU'VE GONE TWO, THREE LEVELS ABOVE WHAT I EXPECTED,
AND LOOK HOW FAR YOU'VE RUN ME DOWN.
WAH
JACK RAKAN, A MEMBER OF ALA RUBRA, GIVES YOU HIS SEAL OF APPROVAL.
STARTING TODAY, YOU ARE A GROWN MAN. BE PROUD. HOLD YOUR HEAD HIGH.
RAKAN...
SAN...
SHH
BUT...*HEH HEH.* TO THINK YOUR TRUE ESSENCE ISN'T YOUR MAGICAL POWER, YOUR TECHNICAL SKILL, OR YOUR HARD WORK, BUT YOUR INVENTIVENESS. I AM SINCERELY IN AWE.
NO. THAT'S ENOUGH TALK.

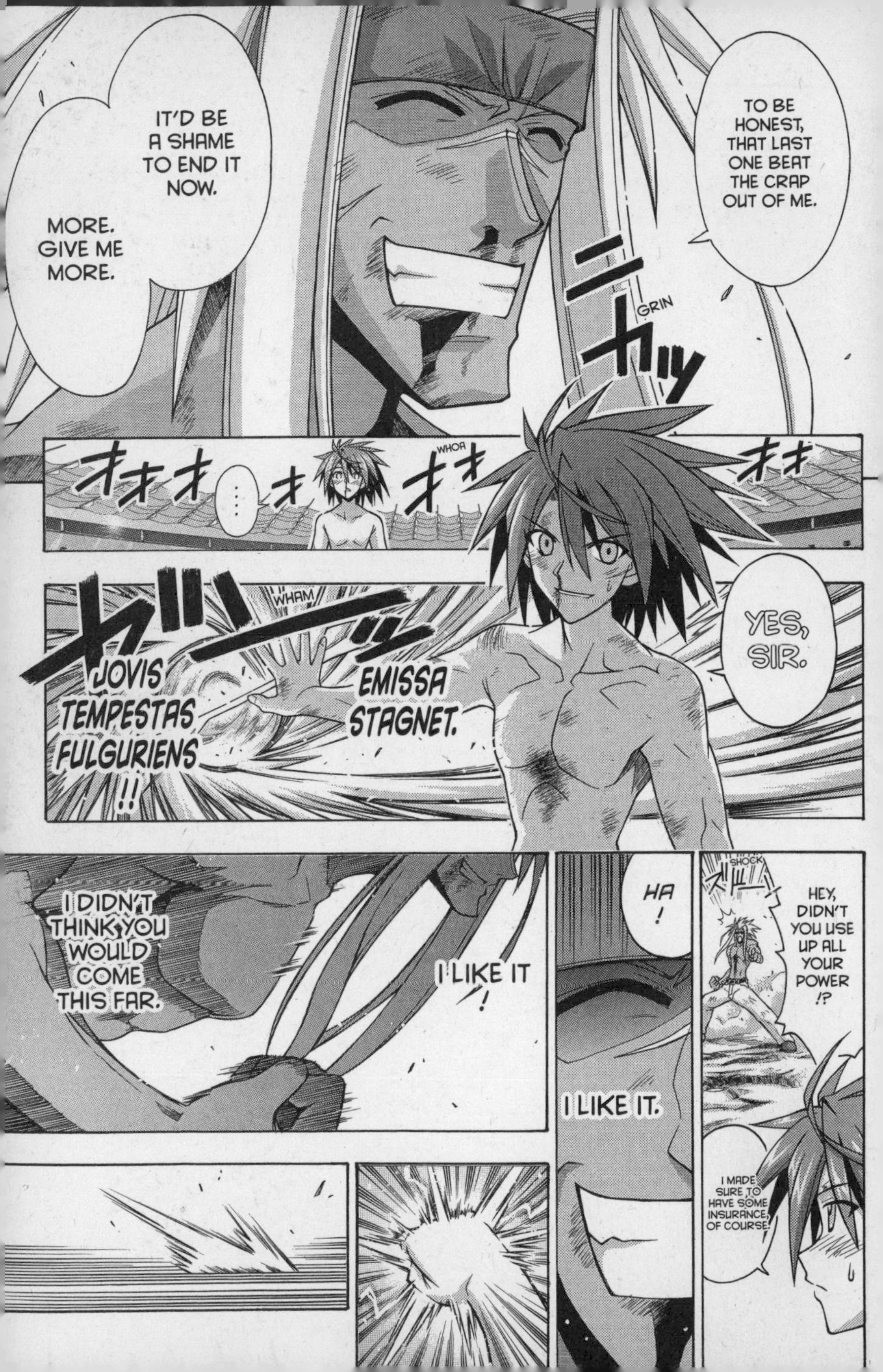
TO BE HONEST, THAT LAST ONE BEAT THE CRAP OUT OF ME.
IT'D BE A SHAME TO END IT NOW.
MORE. GIVE ME MORE.
GRIN
WHOA
....
YES, SIR.
WHAM
EMISSA STAGNET.
JOVIS TEMPESTAS FULGURIENS!!
SHOCK
HEY, DIDN'T YOU USE UP ALL YOUR POWER!?
I MADE SURE TO HAVE SOME INSURANCE, OF COURSE.
HA!
I LIKE IT.
I LIKE IT!
I DIDN'T THINK YOU WOULD COME THIS FAR.

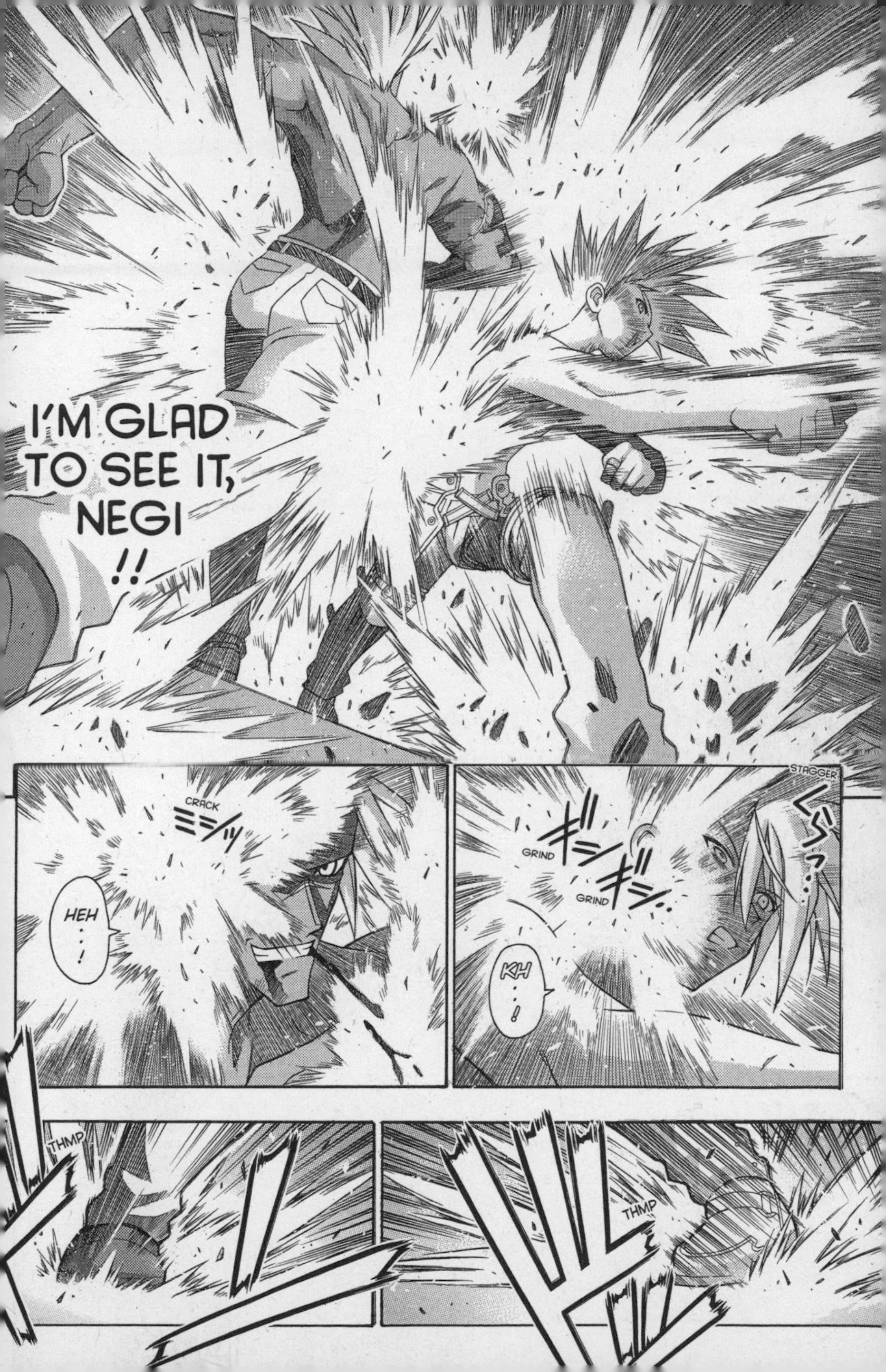
I'M GLAD TO SEE IT, NEGI!!
STAGGER
GRIND
GRIND
KH...!
CRACK
HEH...!
THMP
THMP

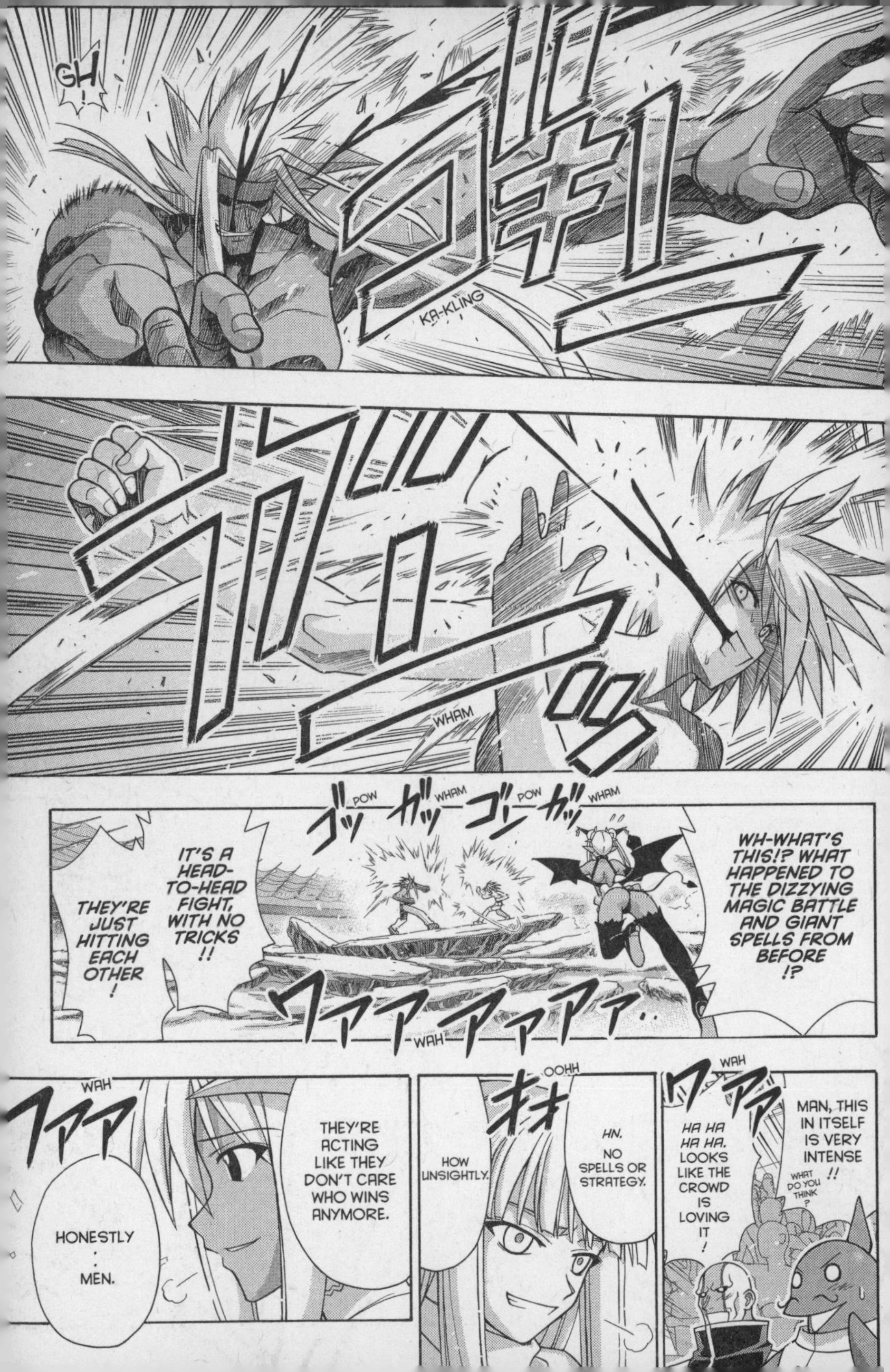
GH!
KA-KLING
WHAM
POW
WHAM
POW
WHAM
WH-WHAT'S THIS!? WHAT HAPPENED TO THE DIZZYING MAGIC BATTLE AND GIANT SPELLS FROM BEFORE!?
IT'S A HEAD-TO-HEAD FIGHT, WITH NO TRICKS!!
THEY'RE JUST HITTING EACH OTHER!
WAH
WAH
MAN, THIS IN ITSELF IS VERY INTENSE!!
WHAT DO YOU THINK?
HA HA HA HA. LOOKS LIKE THE CROWD IS LOVING IT!
OOHH
HN. NO SPELLS OR STRATEGY.
HOW UNSIGHTLY.
THEY'RE ACTING LIKE THEY DON'T CARE WHO WINS ANYMORE.
WAH
HONESTLY... MEN.

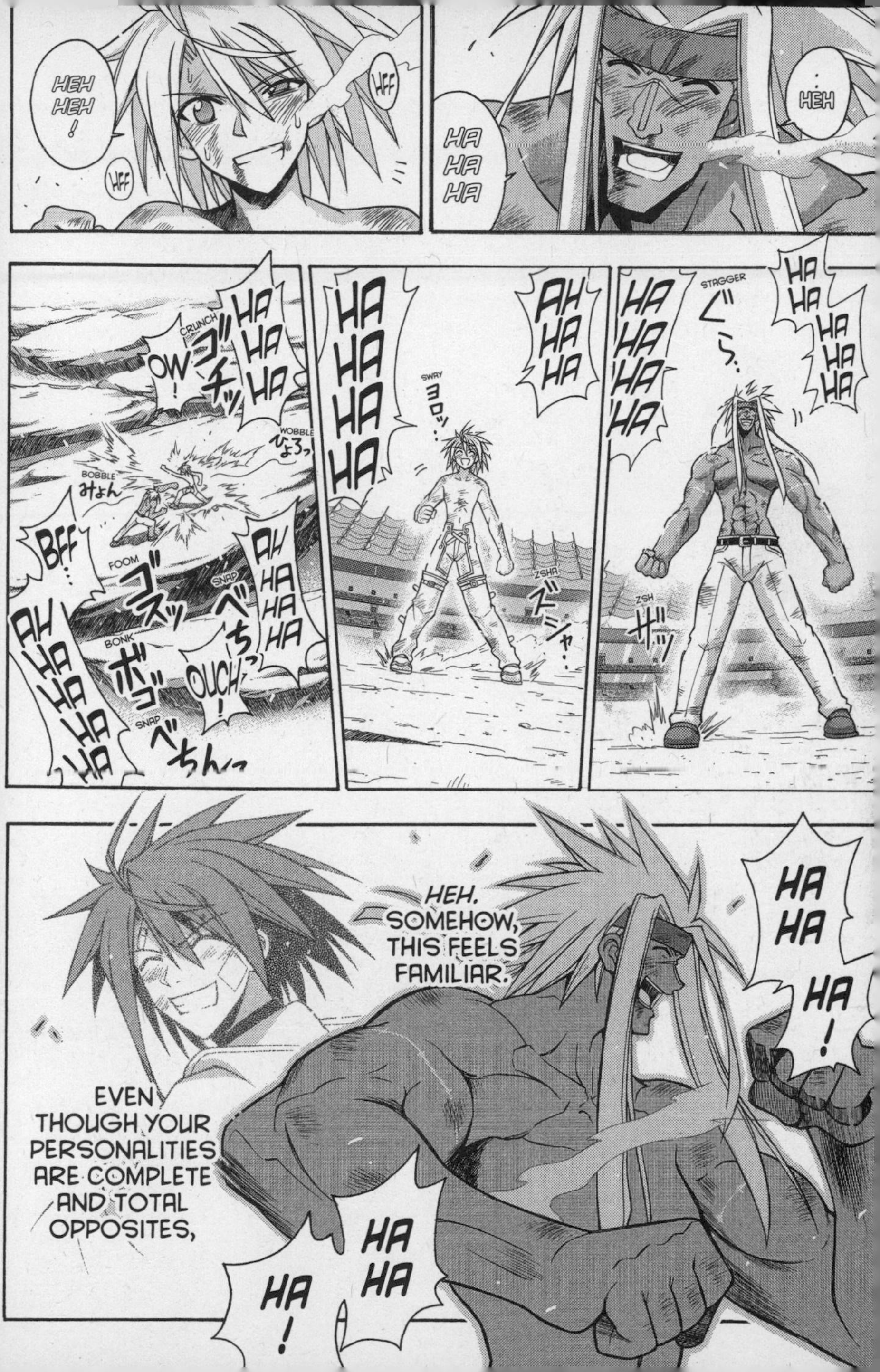

...HEH
HA HA HA
HEH HEH!
HFF
HFF
HA HA HA HA HA
STAGGER
ぐら…
HA HA HA HA
ZSH
ザッ
AH HA HA
HA HA HA HA
SWAY
ヨロッ…
ZSHA
ズシャ…
HA HA HA
CRUNCH
ゴチッ
OW!
WOBBLE
ひょろっ
BOBBLE
みょん
AH HA HA HA HA
BFF…
FOOM
ゴスッ
SNAP
べちっ
OUCH!
BONK
ボゴ
SNAP
べちんっ
AH HA HA HA HA HA
HA HA HA!
HEH. SOMEHOW, THIS FEELS FAMILIAR.
EVEN THOUGH YOUR PERSONALITIES ARE COMPLETE AND TOTAL OPPOSITES,
HA HA HA!

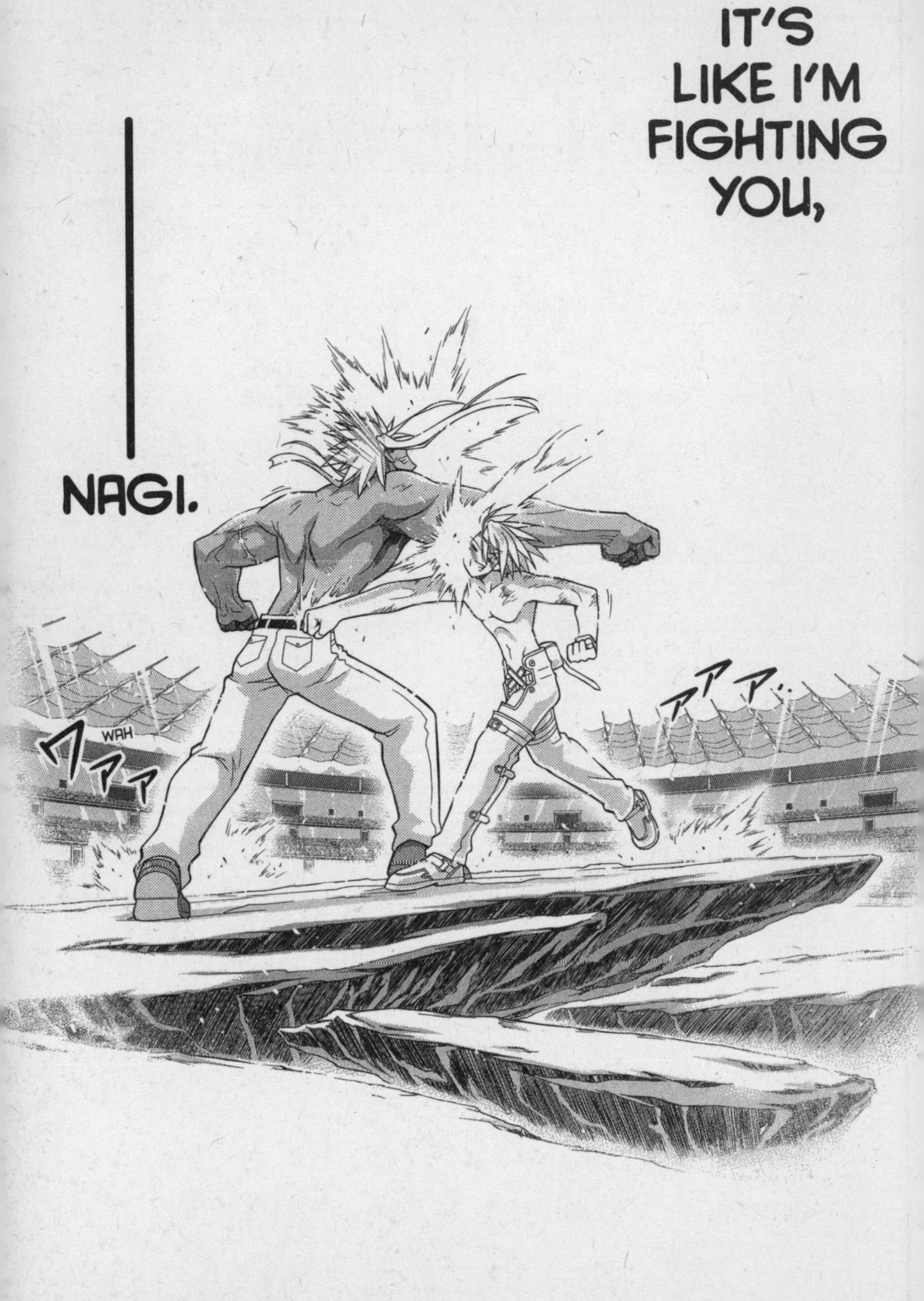
IT'S LIKE I'M FIGHTING YOU,
NAGI.
アアア..
WAH
ワァァ

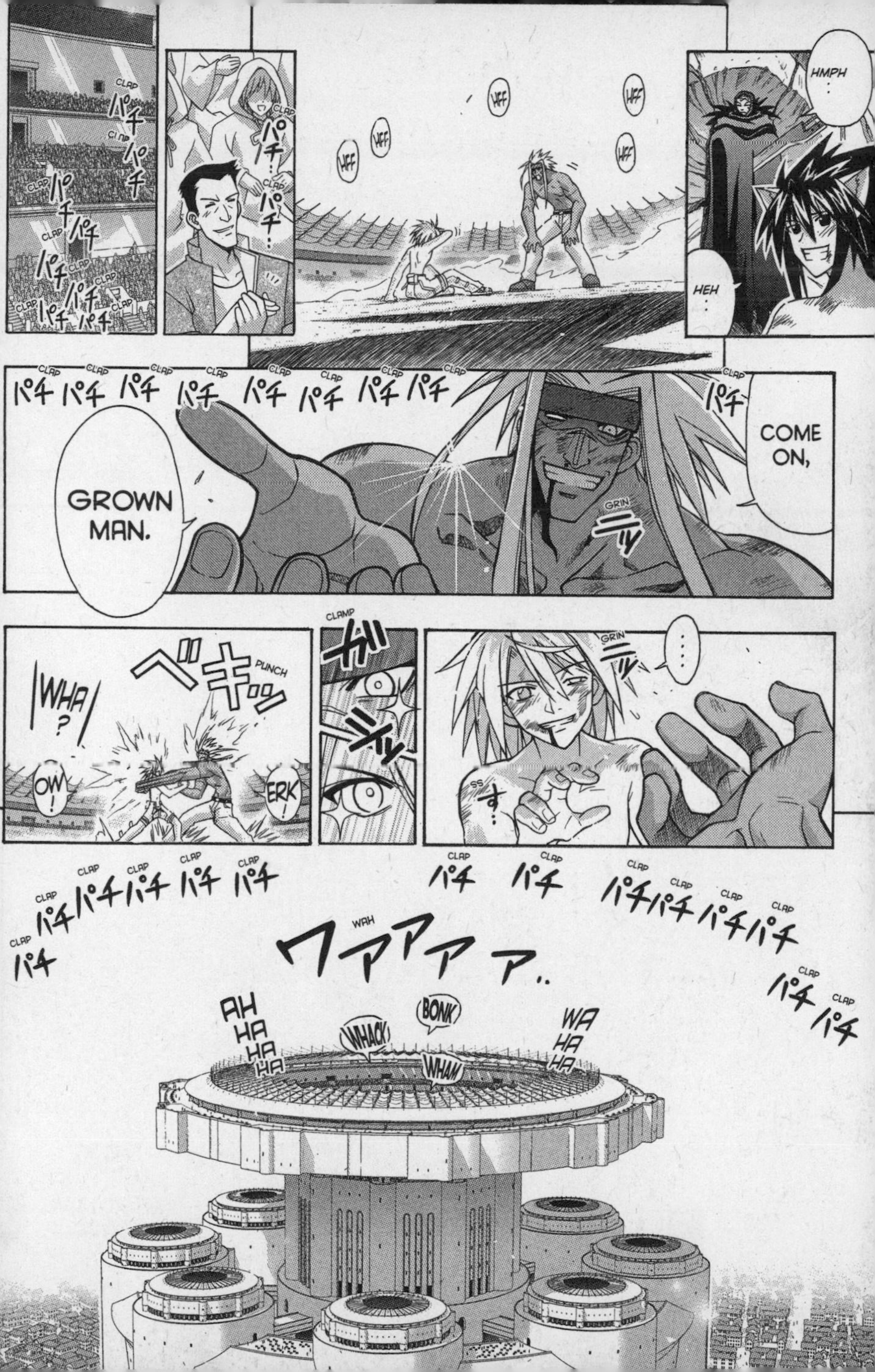
HMPH...
HEH...
HFF
HFF
HFF
HFF
HFF
CLAP パチ... CLAP パチ...
CLAP パチ CLAP パチ CLAP パチ CLAP パチ CLAP パチ CLAP パチ
CLAP パチ
COME ON,
GROWN MAN.
GRIN ニッ
CLAP パチ CLAP パチ CLAP パチ CLAP パチ CLAP パチ CLAP パチ CLAP パチ CLAP パチ
...
GRIN ニッ
SS す...
CLAMP ガッ
PUNCH ベキッ
WHA?
OW!
ERK!
CLAP パチ CLAP パチ CLAP パチ CLAP パチ CLAP パチ CLAP パチ CLAP パチ CLAP パチ
WAH ワアアア..
CLAP パチ CLAP パチ CLAP パチ CLAP パチ CLAP パチ CLAP パチ
WA HA HA HA
BONK
WHAM
WHACK
AH HA HA HA

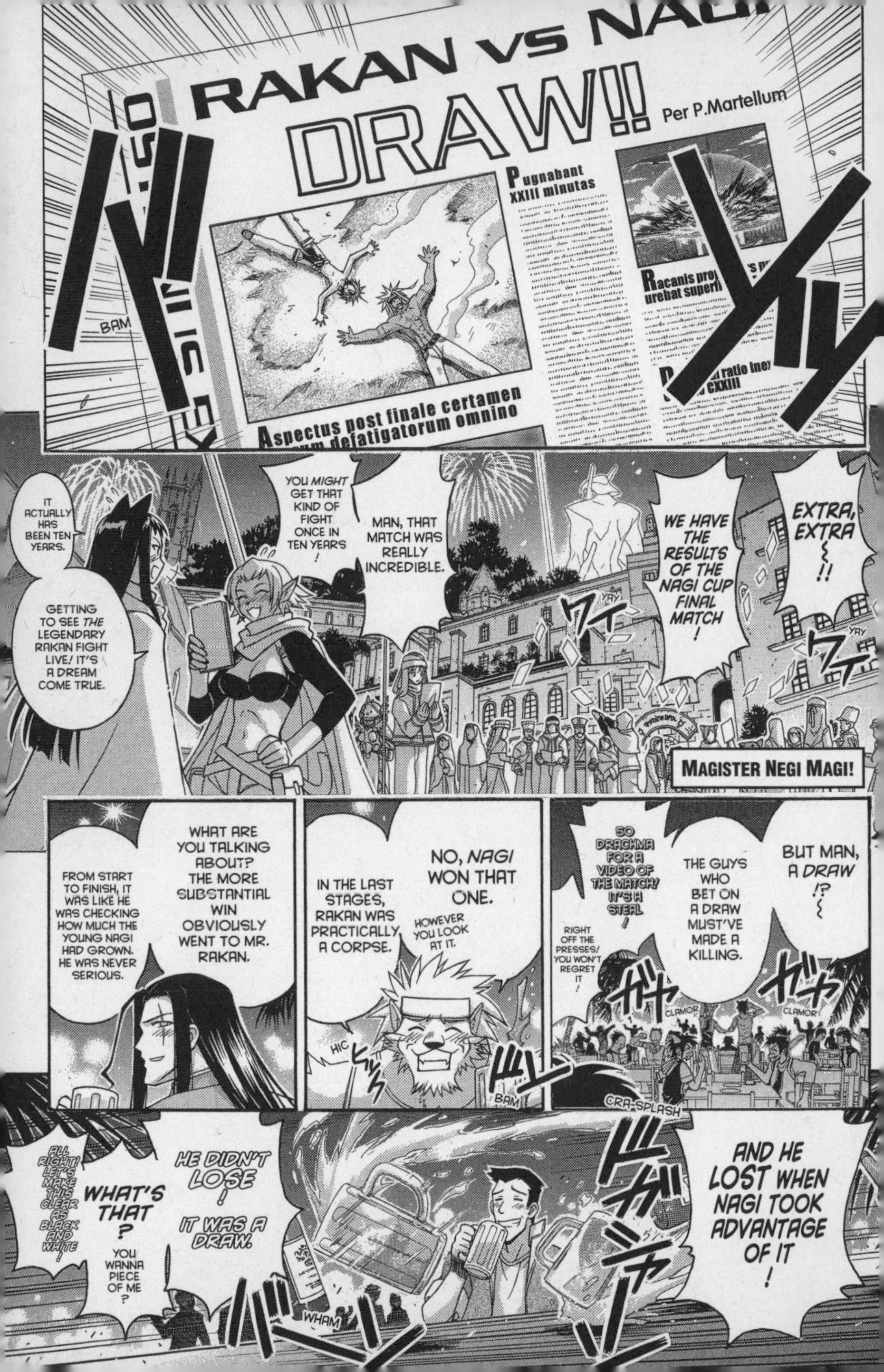
RAKAN VS NAG
DRAW!!
Per P.Martellum
Pugnabant XXIII minutas
Aspectus post finale certamen
defatigatorum omnino
BAM
EXTRA, EXTRA~!!
WE HAVE THE RESULTS OF THE NAGI CUP FINAL MATCH!
YAY
YAY
MAN, THAT MATCH WAS REALLY INCREDIBLE.
YOU MIGHT GET THAT KIND OF FIGHT ONCE IN TEN YEARS!
IT ACTUALLY HAS BEEN TEN YEARS.
GETTING TO SEE THE LEGENDARY RAKAN FIGHT LIVE! IT'S A DREAM COME TRUE.
MAGISTER NEGI MAGI!
BUT MAN, A DRAW!?~
THE GUYS WHO BET ON A DRAW MUST'VE MADE A KILLING.
50 DRACHMA FOR A VIDEO OF THE MATCH! IT'S A STEAL!
RIGHT OFF THE PRESSES! YOU WON'T REGRET IT!
CLAMOR
CLAMOR
NO, NAGI WON THAT ONE.
IN THE LAST STAGES, RAKAN WAS PRACTICALLY A CORPSE.
HOWEVER YOU LOOK AT IT.
HIC
BAM
WHAT ARE YOU TALKING ABOUT? THE MORE SUBSTANTIAL WIN OBVIOUSLY WENT TO MR. RAKAN.
FROM START TO FINISH, IT WAS LIKE HE WAS CHECKING HOW MUCH THE YOUNG NAGI HAD GROWN. HE WAS NEVER SERIOUS.
CRA-SPLASH
AND HE LOST WHEN NAGI TOOK ADVANTAGE OF IT!
HE DIDN'T LOSE! IT WAS A DRAW.
WHAT'S THAT?
YOU WANNA PIECE OF ME?
ALL RIGHT! LET'S MAKE THIS CLEAR AS BLACK AND WHITE!
WHAM

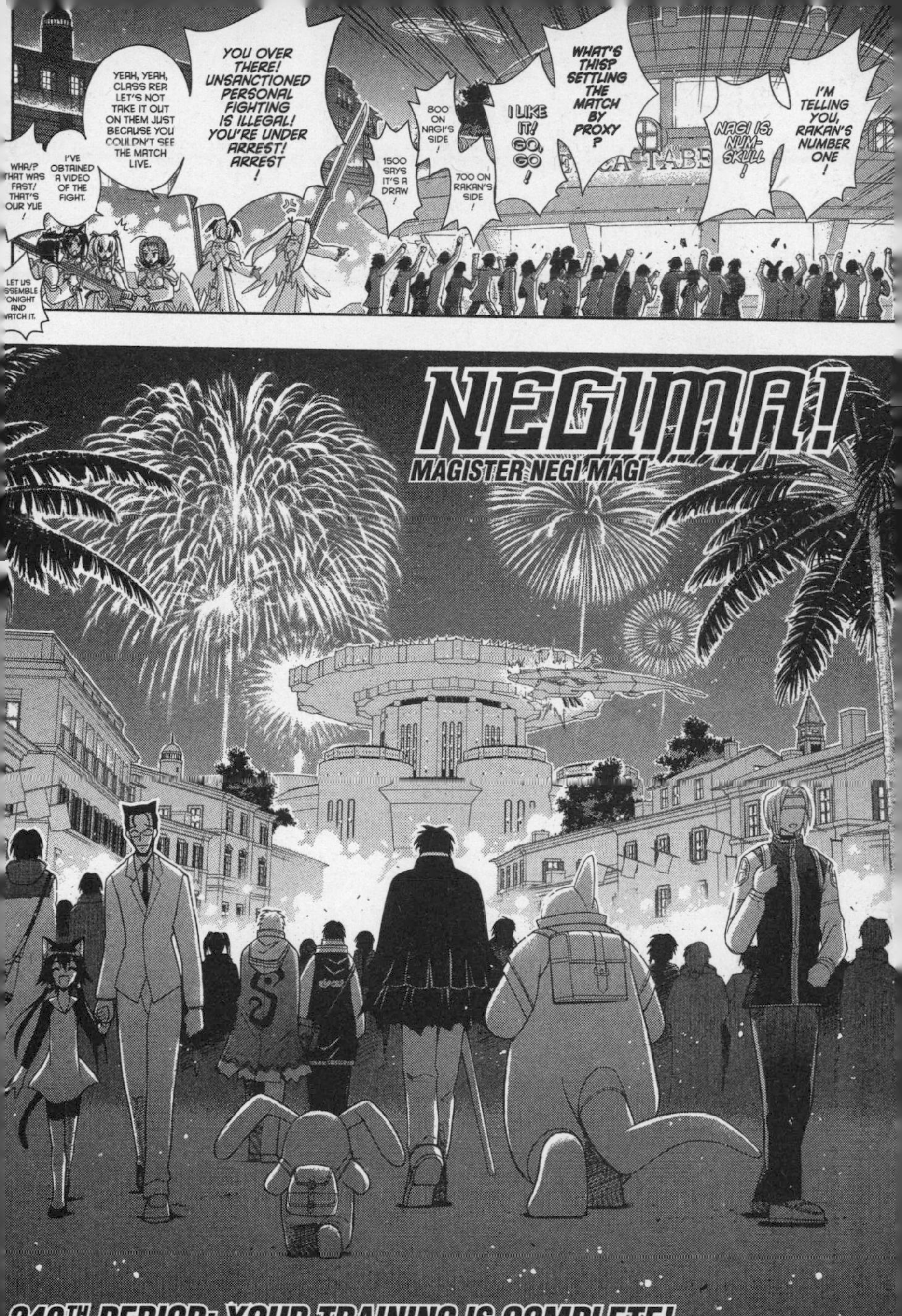

I'M TELLING YOU, RAKAN'S NUMBER ONE!
NAGI IS, NUM-SKULL!
WHAT'S THIS? SETTLING THE MATCH BY PROXY?
I LIKE IT! GO, GO!
700 ON RAKAN'S SIDE!
800 ON NAGI'S SIDE!
1500 SAYS IT'S A DRAW!
YOU OVER THERE! UNSANCTIONED PERSONAL FIGHTING IS ILLEGAL! YOU'RE UNDER ARREST! ARREST!
YEAH, YEAH, CLASS REP. LET'S NOT TAKE IT OUT ON THEM JUST BECAUSE YOU COULDN'T SEE THE MATCH LIVE.
I'VE OBTAINED A VIDEO OF THE FIGHT.
WHA!? THAT WAS FAST! THAT'S OUR YUE!
LET US SSEMBLE ONIGHT AND WATCH IT.
NEGIMA!
MAGISTER NEGI MAGI
249TH PERIOD: YOUR TRAINING IS COMPLETE!

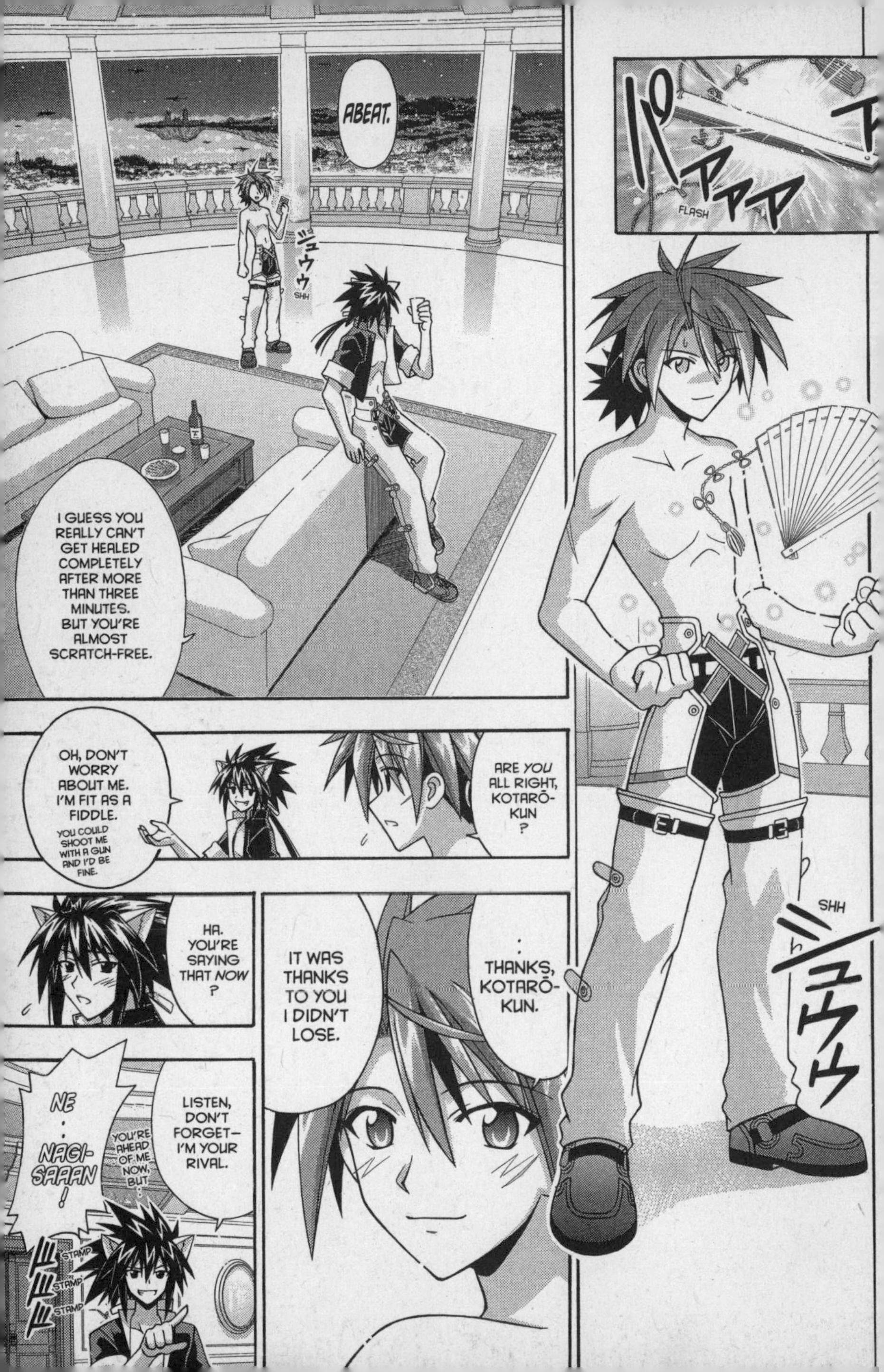
パァァァ
FLASH
シュウウ
SHH
ABEAT.
ジュウウ
SHH
I GUESS YOU REALLY CAN'T GET HEALED COMPLETELY AFTER MORE THAN THREE MINUTES. BUT YOU'RE ALMOST SCRATCH-FREE.
ARE *YOU* ALL RIGHT, KOTARŌ-KUN?
OH, DON'T WORRY ABOUT ME. I'M FIT AS A FIDDLE.
YOU COULD SHOOT ME WITH A GUN AND I'D BE FINE.
: THANKS, KOTARŌ-KUN.
IT WAS THANKS TO YOU I DIDN'T LOSE.
HA. YOU'RE SAYING THAT *NOW*?
LISTEN, DON'T FORGET— I'M YOUR RIVAL.
YOU'RE AHEAD OF ME NOW, BUT...
NE... NAGI-SAAAN!
STAMP
STAMP
STAMP

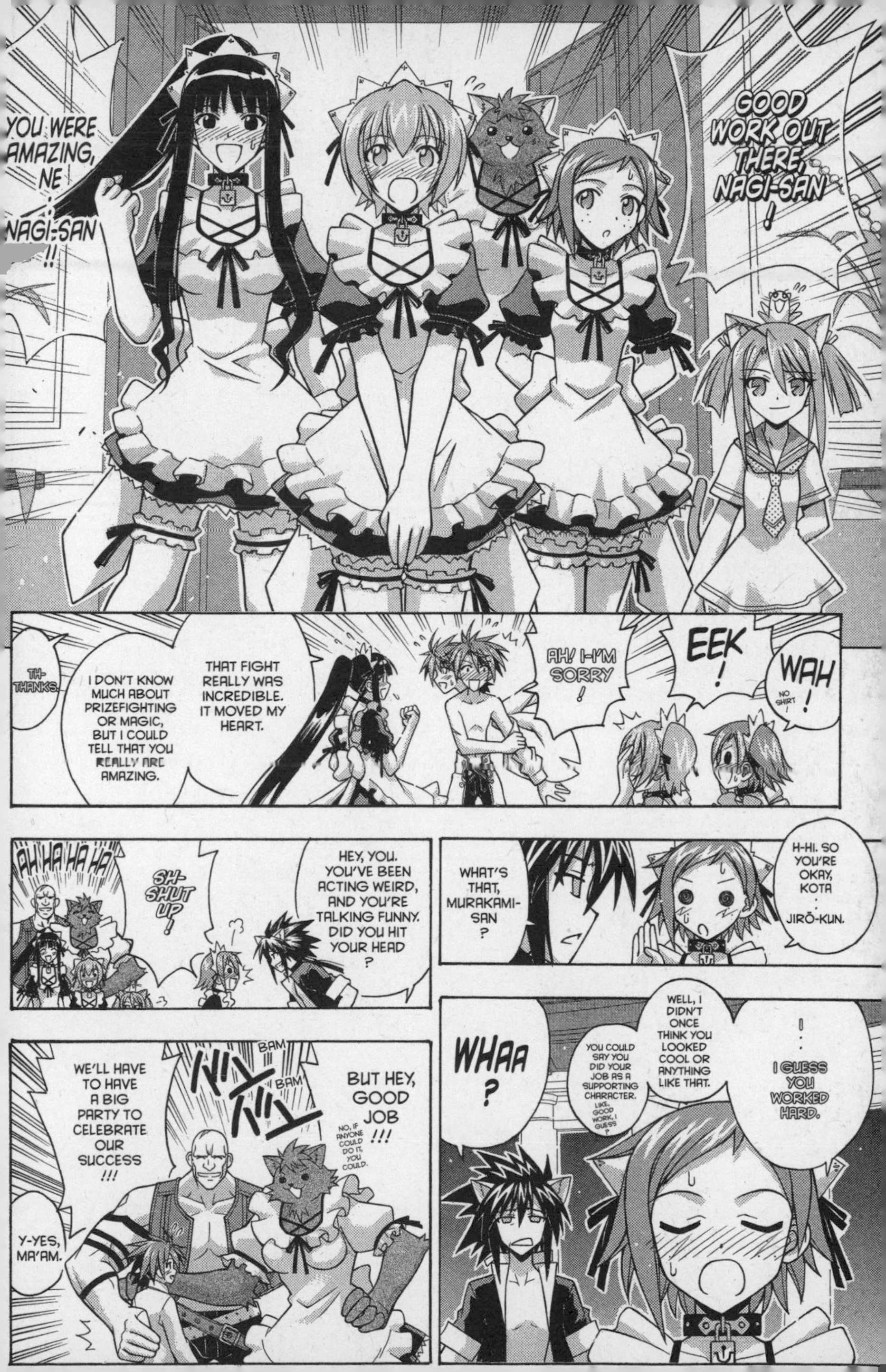
GOOD WORK OUT THERE, NAGI-SAN!
YOU WERE AMAZING, NE NAGI-SAN!!
WAH! NO SHIRT!
EEK!
AH! I-I'M SORRY!
THAT FIGHT REALLY WAS INCREDIBLE. IT MOVED MY HEART.
I DON'T KNOW MUCH ABOUT PRIZEFIGHTING OR MAGIC, BUT I COULD TELL THAT YOU REALLY ARE AMAZING.
TH-THANKS.
H-HI. SO YOU'RE OKAY, KOTA JIRŌ-KUN.
WHAT'S THAT, MURAKAMI-SAN?
HEY, YOU. YOU'VE BEEN ACTING WEIRD, AND YOU'RE TALKING FUNNY. DID YOU HIT YOUR HEAD?
SH-SHUT UP!
AH HA HA HA
I GUESS YOU WORKED HARD.
WELL, I DIDN'T ONCE THINK YOU LOOKED COOL OR ANYTHING LIKE THAT.
YOU COULD SAY YOU DID YOUR JOB AS A SUPPORTING CHARACTER. LIKE, GOOD WORK, I GUESS?
WHAA?
BUT HEY, GOOD JOB!!!
NO, IF ANYONE COULD DO IT, YOU COULD.
BAM
BAM
WE'LL HAVE TO HAVE A BIG PARTY TO CELEBRATE OUR SUCCESS!!!
Y-YES, MA'AM.

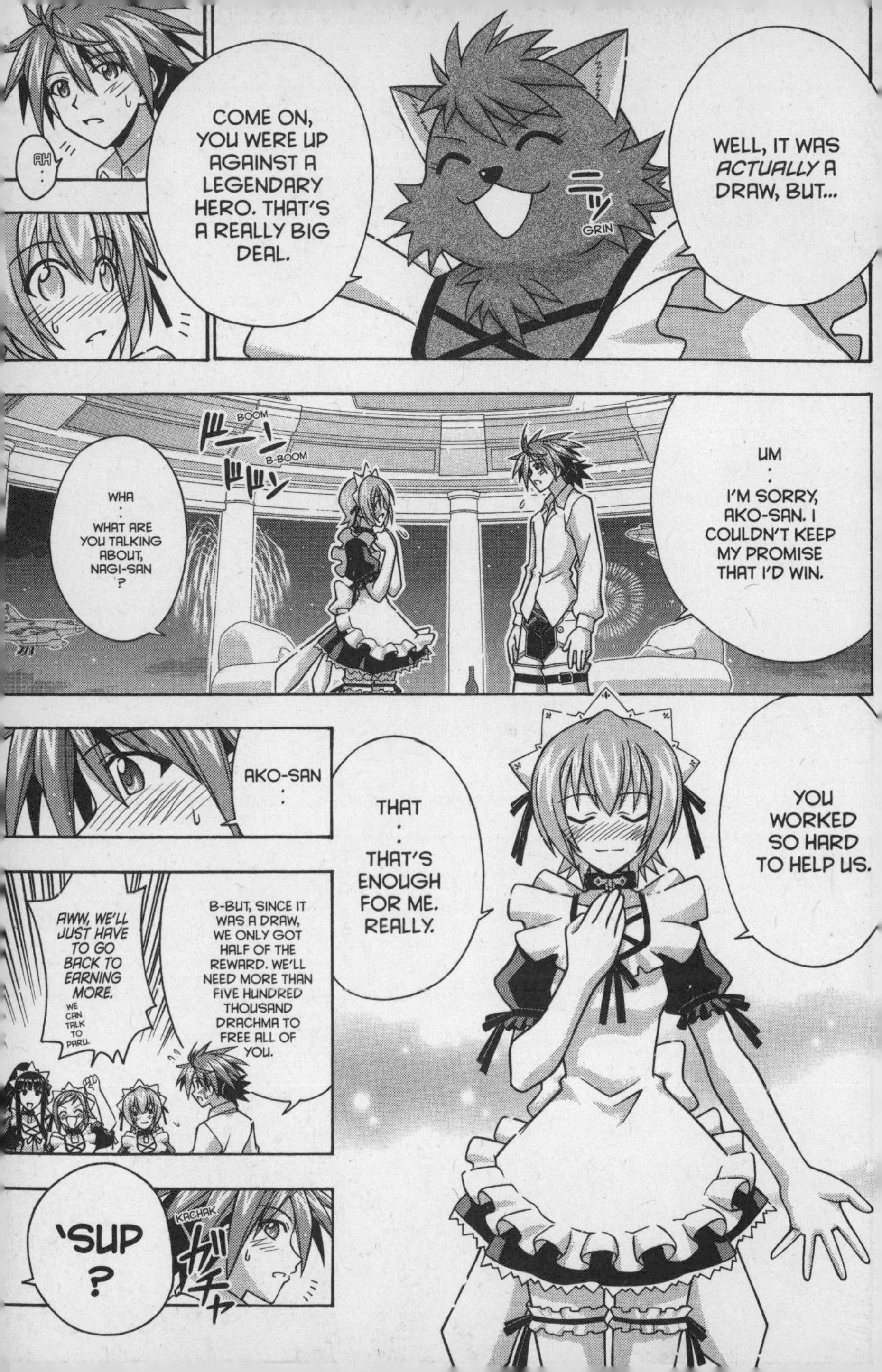
WELL, IT WAS *ACTUALLY* A DRAW, BUT...
GRIN
COME ON, YOU WERE UP AGAINST A LEGENDARY HERO. THAT'S A REALLY BIG DEAL.
AH
:
BOOM
B-BOOM
UM
:
I'M SORRY, AKO-SAN. I COULDN'T KEEP MY PROMISE THAT I'D WIN.
WHA
:
WHAT ARE YOU TALKING ABOUT, NAGI-SAN
?
YOU WORKED SO HARD TO HELP US.
THAT
:
THAT'S ENOUGH FOR ME. REALLY.
AKO-SAN
:
B-BUT, SINCE IT WAS A DRAW, WE ONLY GOT HALF OF THE REWARD. WE'LL NEED MORE THAN FIVE HUNDRED THOUSAND DRACHMA TO FREE ALL OF YOU.
AWW, WE'LL JUST HAVE TO GO BACK TO EARNING MORE.
WE CAN TALK TO PARU.
KACHAK
'SUP
?

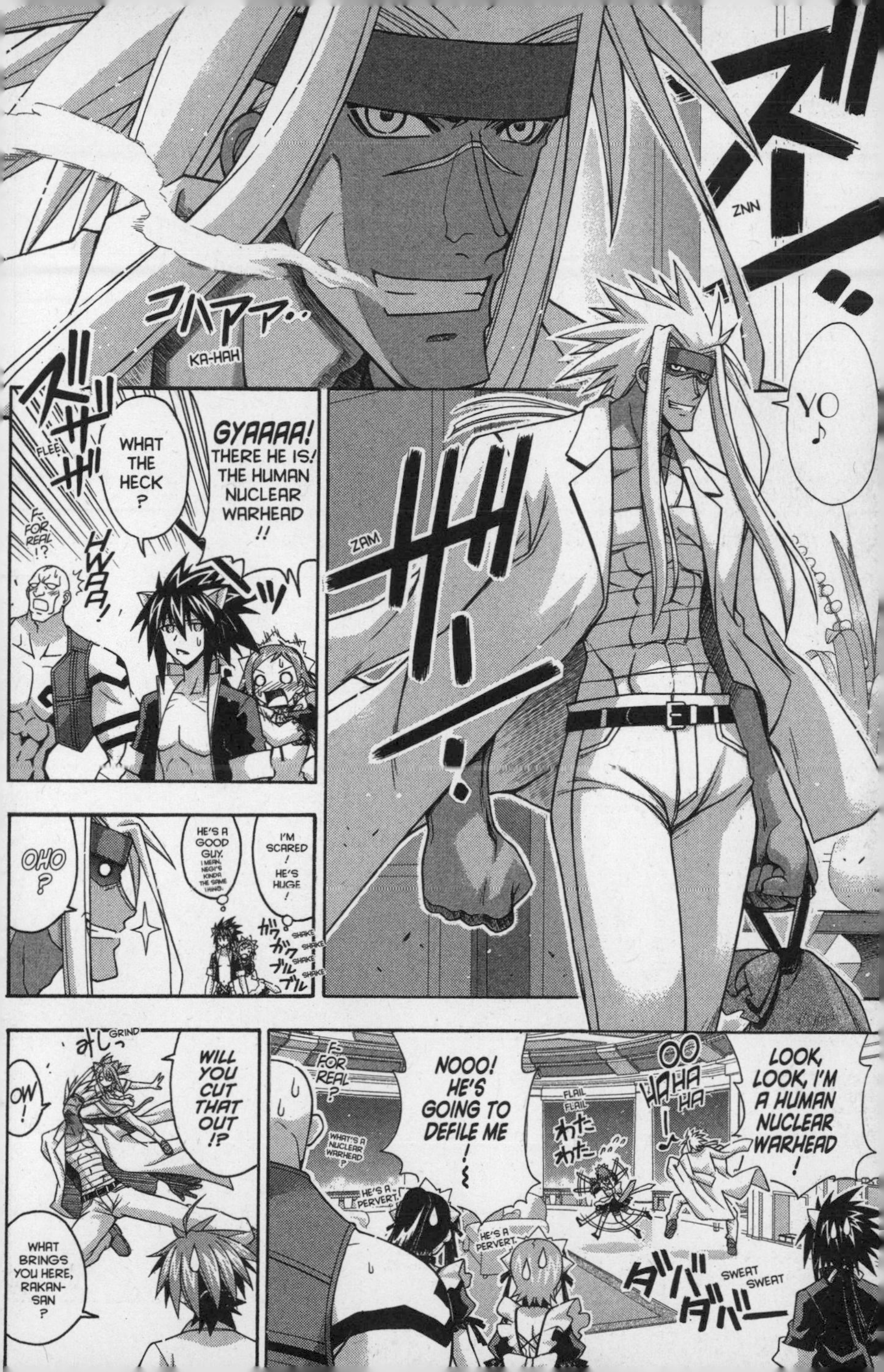
ZNN
KA-HAH
YO ♪
ZAM
GYAAAA! THERE HE IS! THE HUMAN NUCLEAR WARHEAD!!
WHAT THE HECK?
FLEE
F-FOR REAL!?
HWAA!
I'M SCARED! HE'S HUGE!
HE'S A GOOD GUY. I MEAN, NEGI'S KINDA THE SAME THING.
SHAKE SHAKE SHAKE SHAKE
OHO?
LOOK, LOOK, I'M A HUMAN NUCLEAR WARHEAD!
HA HA HA
FLAIL FLAIL
NOOO! HE'S GOING TO DEFILE ME!
F-FOR REAL?
WHAT'S A NUCLEAR WARHEAD?
HE'S A PERVERT.
HE'S A PERVERT.
SWEAT SWEAT
WILL YOU CUT THAT OUT!?
GRIND
OW!
WHAT BRINGS YOU HERE, RAKAN-SAN?

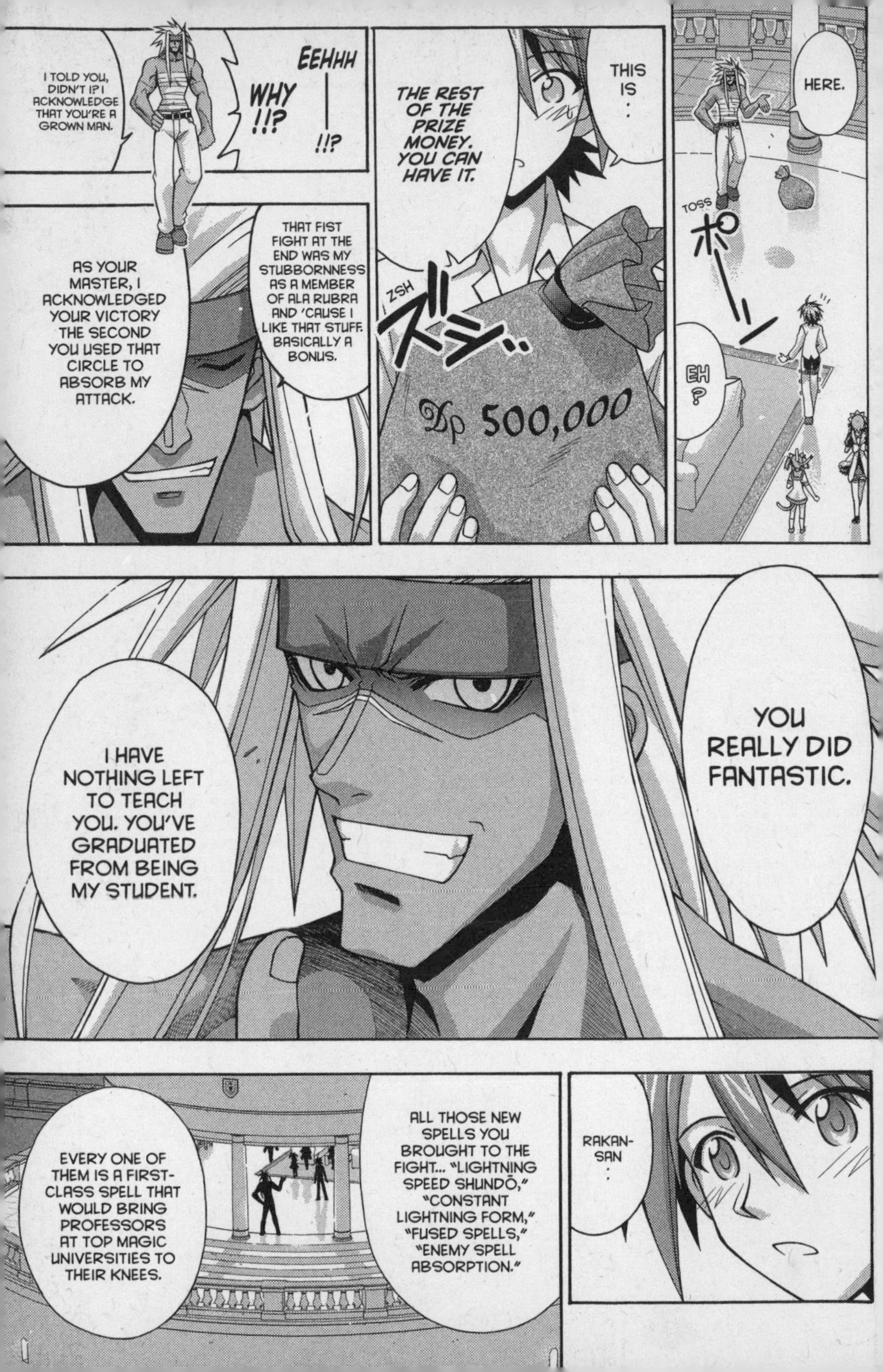
HERE.
TOSS
EH ?
THIS IS :
THE REST OF THE PRIZE MONEY. YOU CAN HAVE IT.
ZSH
Dp 500,000
EEHHH —!!?
WHY !!?
I TOLD YOU, DIDN'T I?! I ACKNOWLEDGE THAT YOU'RE A GROWN MAN.
THAT FIST FIGHT AT THE END WAS MY STUBBORNNESS AS A MEMBER OF ALA RUBRA AND 'CAUSE I LIKE THAT STUFF. BASICALLY A BONUS.
AS YOUR MASTER, I ACKNOWLEDGED YOUR VICTORY THE SECOND YOU USED THAT CIRCLE TO ABSORB MY ATTACK.
YOU REALLY DID FANTASTIC.
I HAVE NOTHING LEFT TO TEACH YOU. YOU'VE GRADUATED FROM BEING MY STUDENT.
RAKAN-SAN :
ALL THOSE NEW SPELLS YOU BROUGHT TO THE FIGHT... "LIGHTNING SPEED SHUNDŌ," "CONSTANT LIGHTNING FORM," "FUSED SPELLS," "ENEMY SPELL ABSORPTION."
EVERY ONE OF THEM IS A FIRST-CLASS SPELL THAT WOULD BRING PROFESSORS AT TOP MAGIC UNIVERSITIES TO THEIR KNEES.

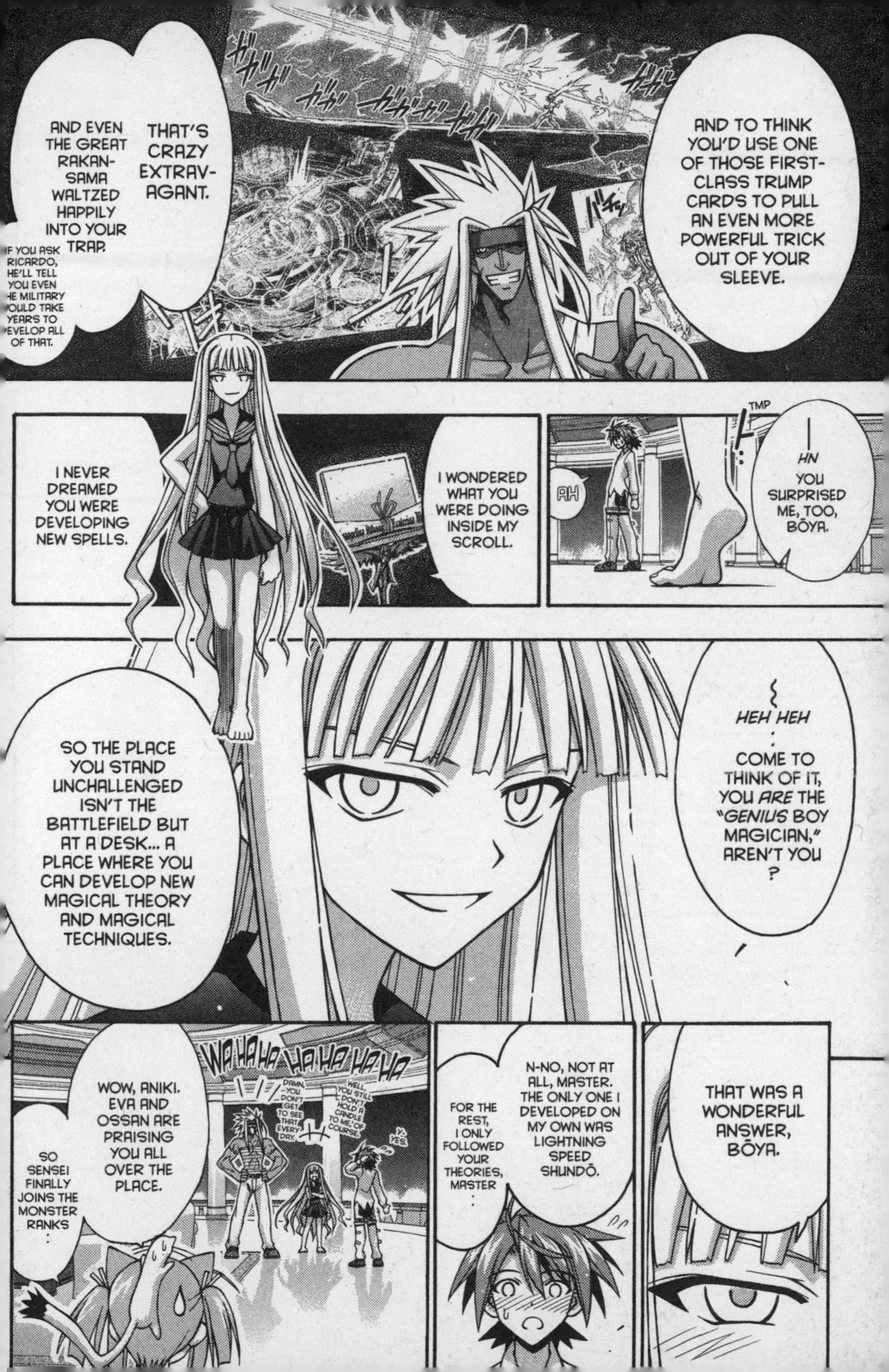
AND TO THINK YOU'D USE ONE OF THOSE FIRST-CLASS TRUMP CARDS TO PULL AN EVEN MORE POWERFUL TRICK OUT OF YOUR SLEEVE.
THAT'S CRAZY EXTRAV-AGANT.
AND EVEN THE GREAT RAKAN-SAMA WALTZED HAPPILY INTO YOUR TRAP.
F YOU ASK RICARDO, HE'LL TELL YOU EVEN HE MILITARY OULD TAKE YEARS TO EVELOP ALL OF THAT.
TMP
HN
YOU SURPRISED ME, TOO, BŌYA.
AH
I WONDERED WHAT YOU WERE DOING INSIDE MY SCROLL.
I NEVER DREAMED YOU WERE DEVELOPING NEW SPELLS.
HEH HEH
COME TO THINK OF IT, YOU *ARE* THE "*GENIUS* BOY MAGICIAN," AREN'T YOU?
SO THE PLACE YOU STAND UNCHALLENGED ISN'T THE BATTLEFIELD BUT AT A DESK... A PLACE WHERE YOU CAN DEVELOP NEW MAGICAL THEORY AND MAGICAL TECHNIQUES.
THAT WAS A WONDERFUL ANSWER, BŌYA.
N-NO, NOT AT ALL, MASTER. THE ONLY ONE I DEVELOPED ON MY OWN WAS LIGHTNING SPEED SHUNDŌ.
FOR THE REST, I ONLY FOLLOWED YOUR THEORIES, MASTER
WA HA HA HA HA HA HA HA
Y-YES.
WELL, YOU STILL DON'T HOLD A CANDLE TO ME, OF COURSE.
DAMN, YOU DON'T GET TO SEE THAT EVERY DAY.
WOW, ANIKI. EVA AND OSSAN ARE PRAISING YOU ALL OVER THE PLACE.
SO SENSEI FINALLY JOINS THE MONSTER RANKS

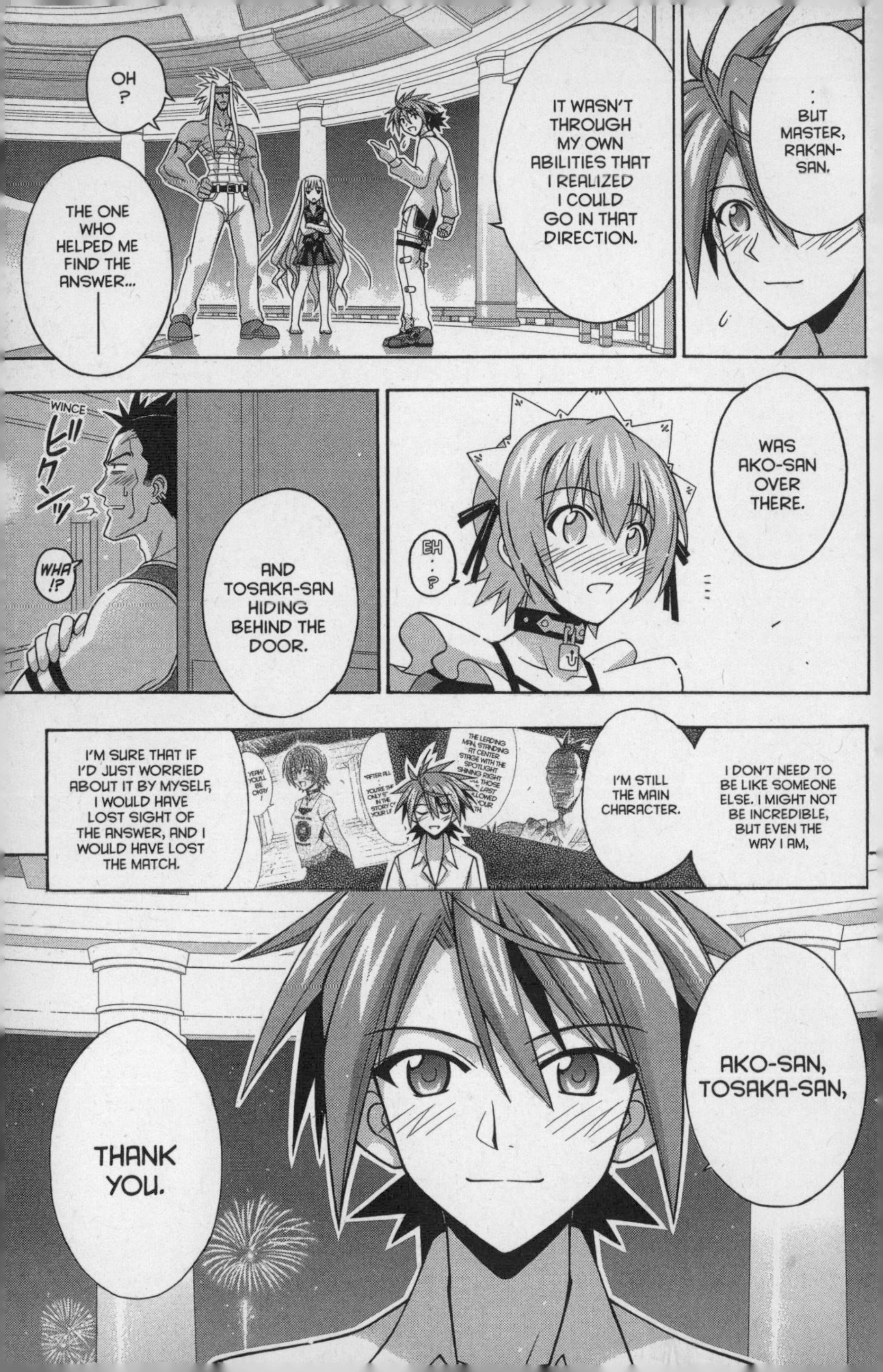

...BUT MASTER, RAKAN-SAN.
IT WASN'T THROUGH MY OWN ABILITIES THAT I REALIZED I COULD GO IN THAT DIRECTION.
OH?
THE ONE WHO HELPED ME FIND THE ANSWER...—
WAS AKO-SAN OVER THERE.
EH..?
AND TOSAKA-SAN HIDING BEHIND THE DOOR.
WINCE
WHA!?
I DON'T NEED TO BE LIKE SOMEONE ELSE. I MIGHT NOT BE INCREDIBLE, BUT EVEN THE WAY I AM,
I'M STILL THE MAIN CHARACTER.
I'M SURE THAT IF I'D JUST WORRIED ABOUT IT BY MYSELF, I WOULD HAVE LOST SIGHT OF THE ANSWER, AND I WOULD HAVE LOST THE MATCH.
AKO-SAN, TOSAKA-SAN,
THANK YOU.

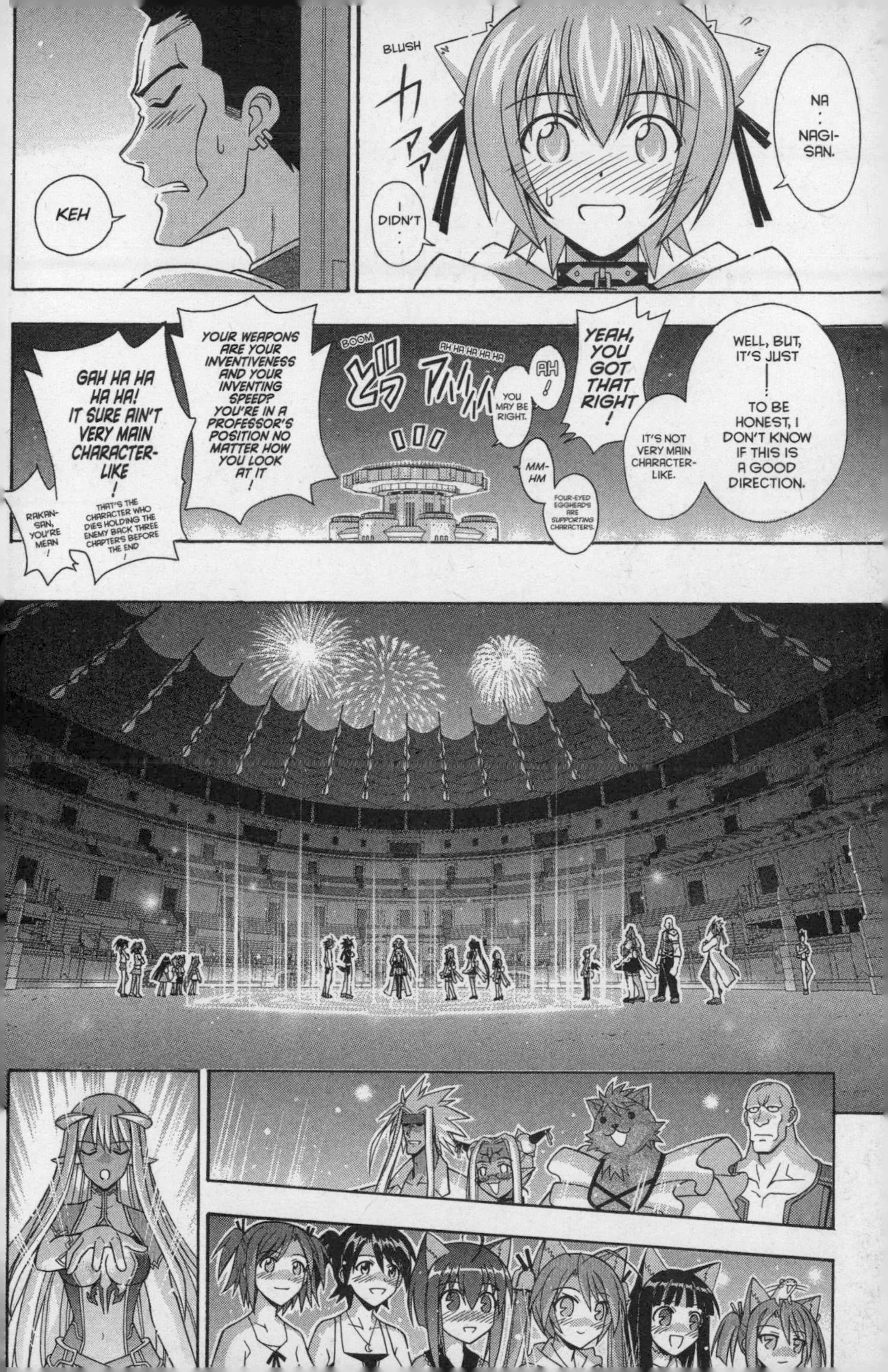
NA : NAGI-SAN.
BLUSH
I DIDN'T : :
KEH
WELL, BUT, IT'S JUST !
TO BE HONEST, I DON'T KNOW IF THIS IS A GOOD DIRECTION.
IT'S NOT VERY MAIN CHARACTER-LIKE.
YEAH, YOU GOT THAT RIGHT!
AH!
YOU MAY BE RIGHT.
MM-HM
FOUR-EYED EGGHEADS ARE SUPPORTING CHARACTERS.
AH HA HA HA HA
BOOM
YOUR WEAPONS ARE YOUR INVENTIVENESS AND YOUR INVENTING SPEED? YOU'RE IN A PROFESSOR'S POSITION NO MATTER HOW YOU LOOK AT IT!
GAH HA HA HA HA! IT SURE AIN'T VERY MAIN CHARACTER-LIKE!
THAT'S THE CHARACTER WHO DIES HOLDING THE ENEMY BACK THREE CHAPTERS BEFORE THE END!
RAKAN-SAN, YOU'RE MEAN!

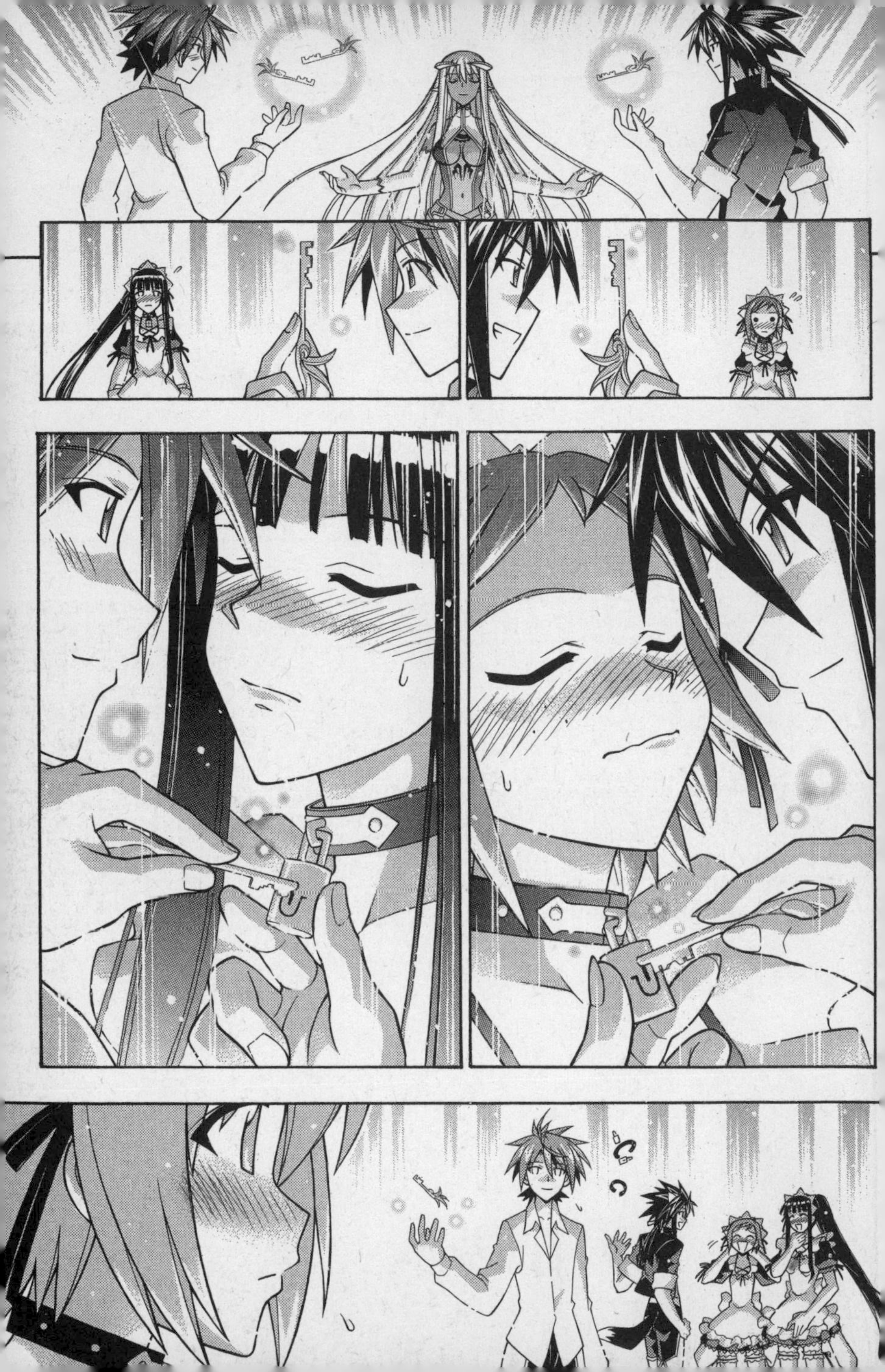

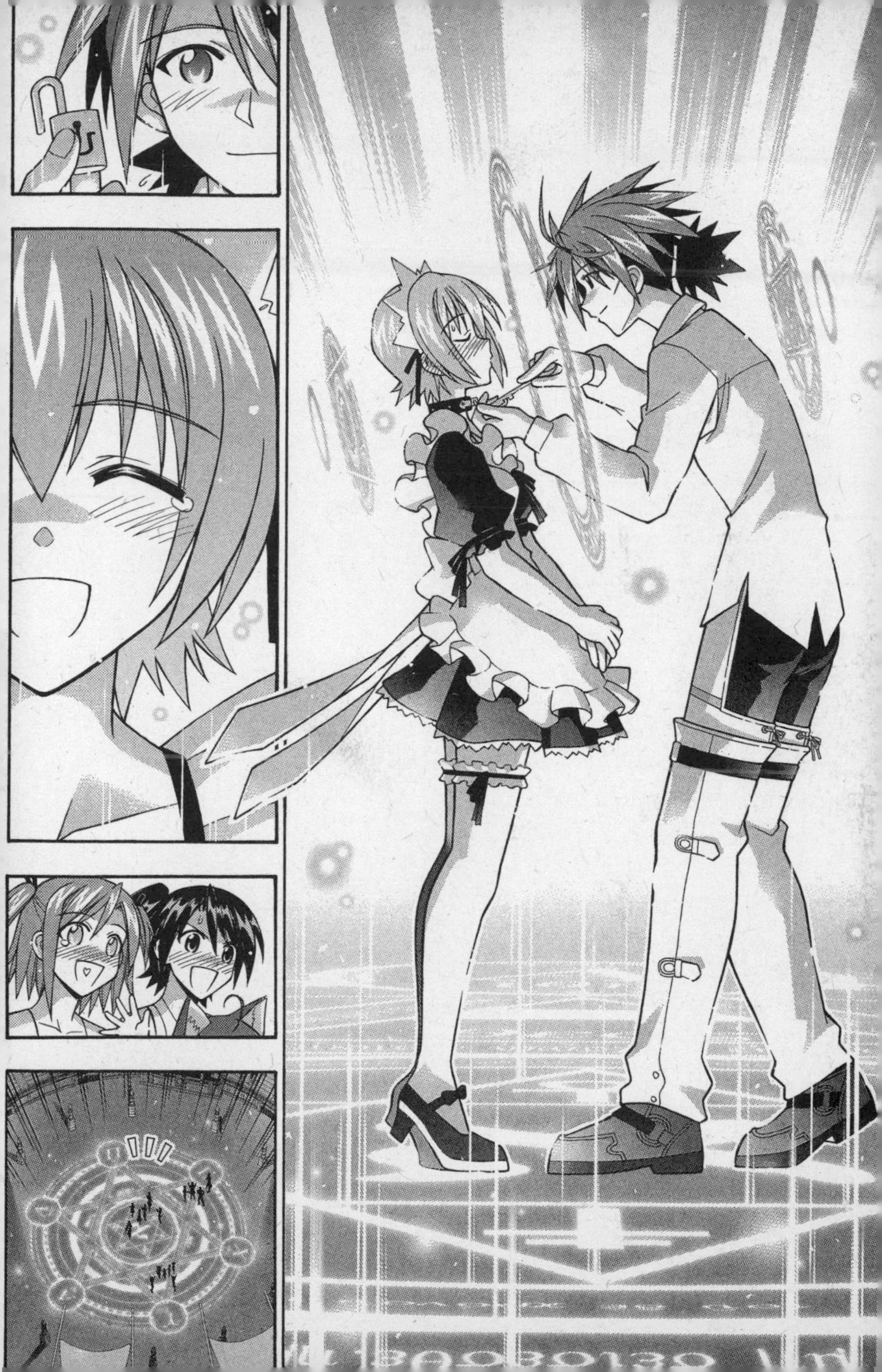

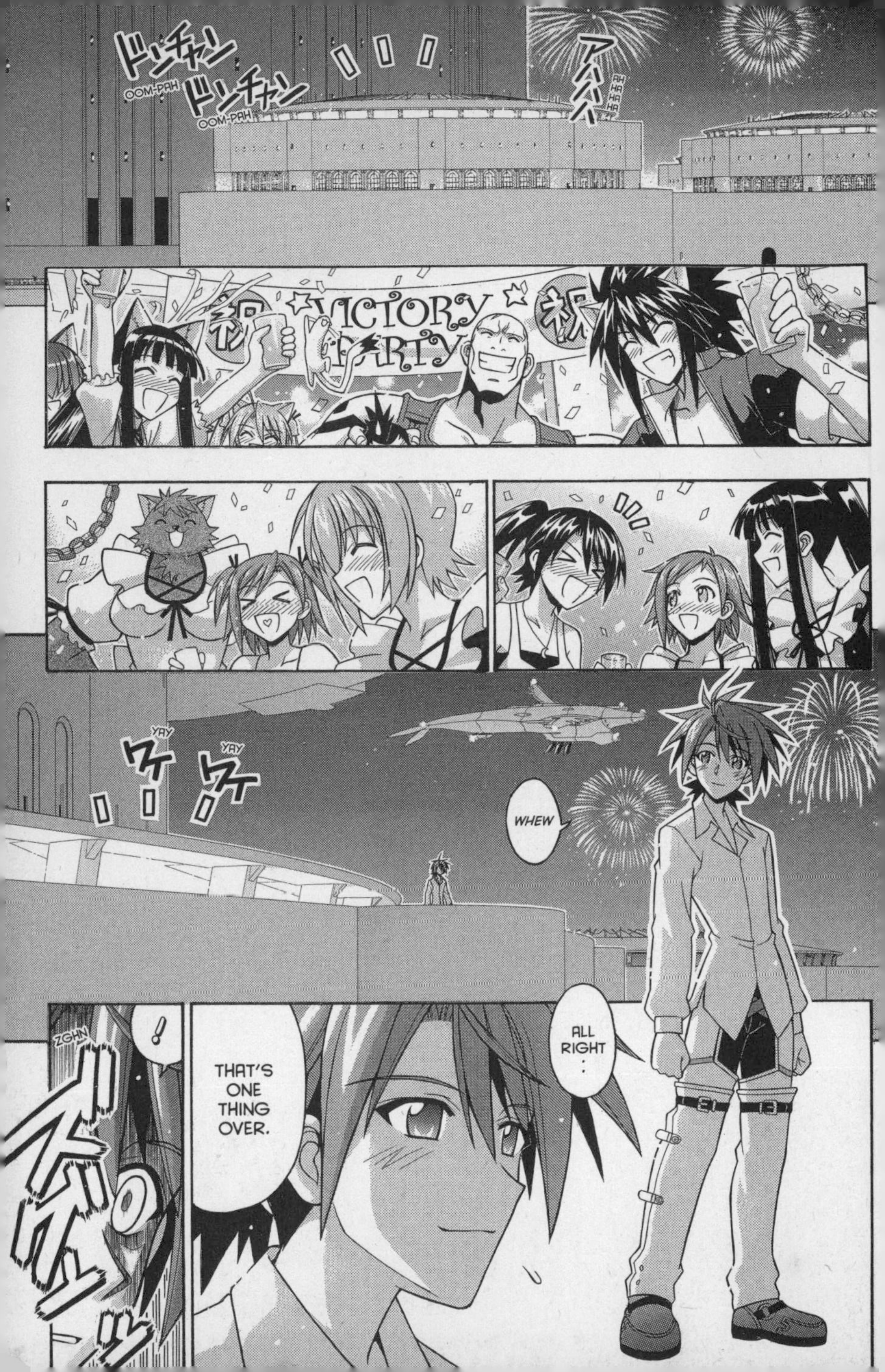

アハハハ
AH HA HA HA
ドンチャン
OOM-PAH
ドンチャン
OOM-PAH
祝
VICTORY PARTY
祝
WHEW
ALL RIGHT
:
ワイ
YAY
ワイ
YAY
THAT'S ONE THING OVER.
!
ZGHN

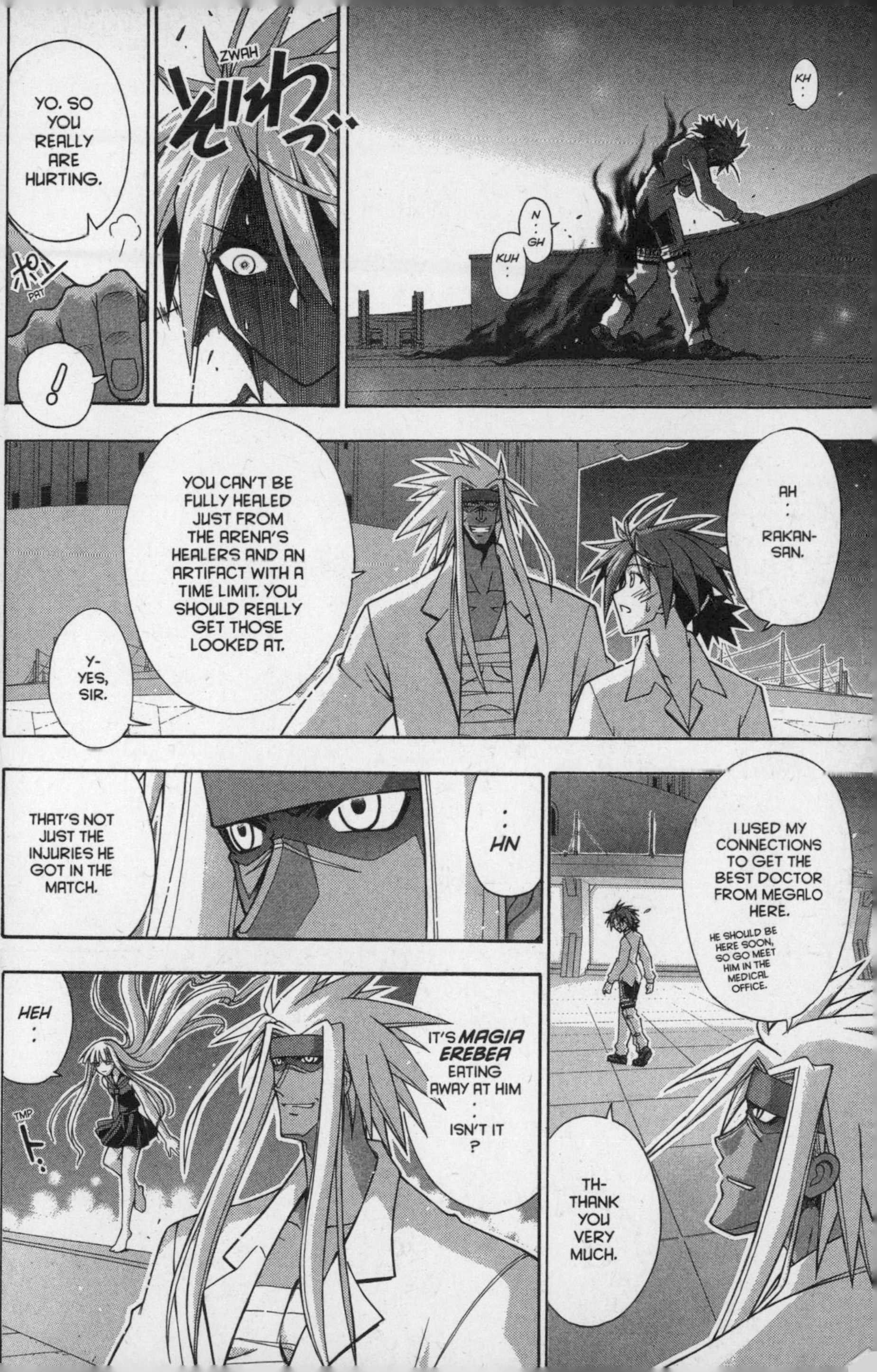
KH...
N-GH
KUH...
ZWAH
ぞわっ
YO. SO YOU REALLY ARE HURTING.
PAT
!
AH... RAKAN-SAN.
YOU CAN'T BE FULLY HEALED JUST FROM THE ARENA'S HEALERS AND AN ARTIFACT WITH A TIME LIMIT. YOU SHOULD REALLY GET THOSE LOOKED AT.
Y-YES, SIR.
I USED MY CONNECTIONS TO GET THE BEST DOCTOR FROM MEGALO HERE.
HE SHOULD BE HERE SOON, SO GO MEET HIM IN THE MEDICAL OFFICE.
TH-THANK YOU VERY MUCH.
...HN
THAT'S NOT JUST THE INJURIES HE GOT IN THE MATCH.
IT'S MAGIA EREBEA EATING AWAY AT HIM... ISN'T IT?
HEH...
TMP

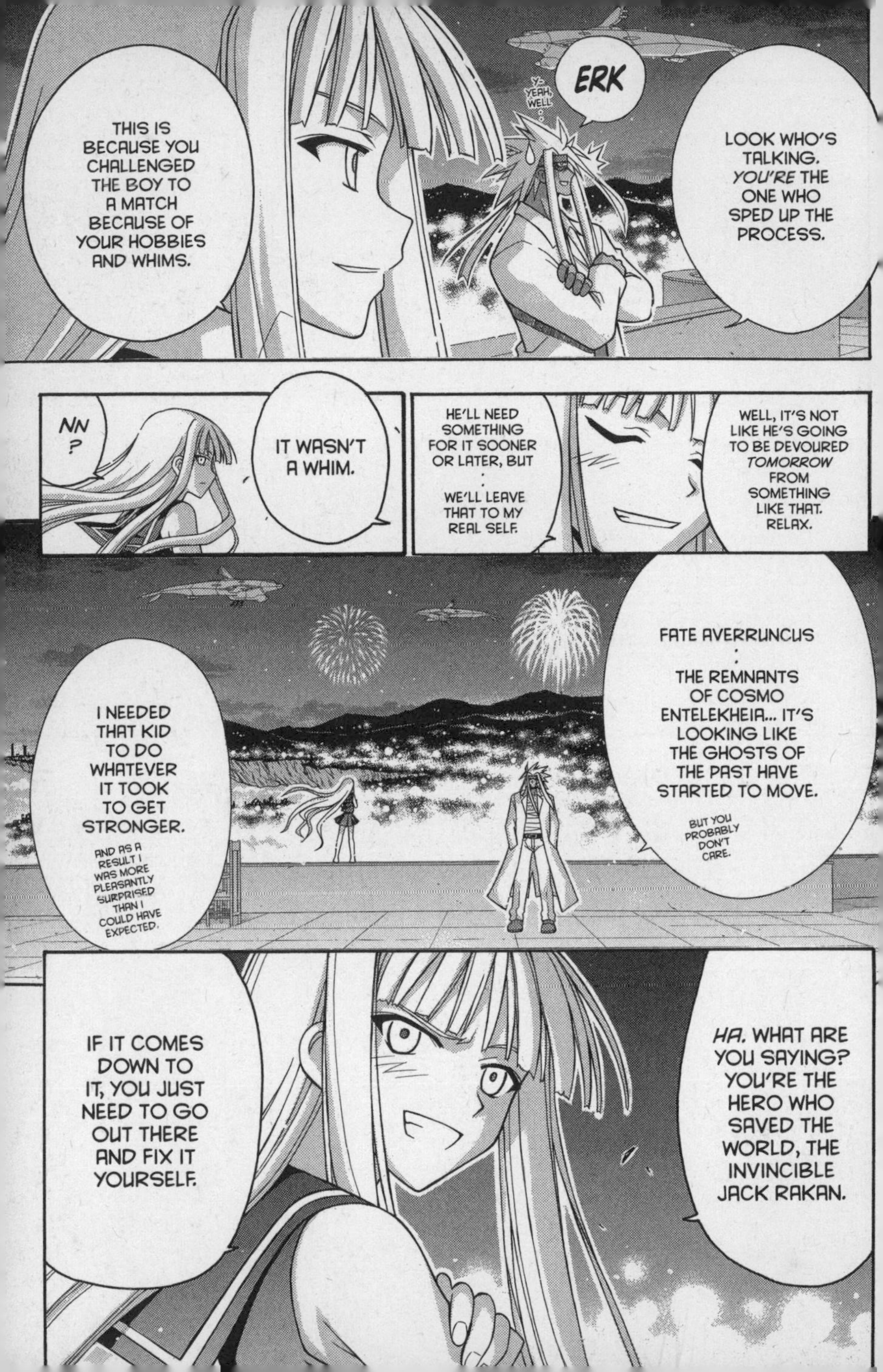
LOOK WHO'S TALKING. *YOU'RE* THE ONE WHO SPED UP THE PROCESS.
ERK
Y-YEAH, WELL...
THIS IS BECAUSE YOU CHALLENGED THE BOY TO A MATCH BECAUSE OF YOUR HOBBIES AND WHIMS.
WELL, IT'S NOT LIKE HE'S GOING TO BE DEVOURED *TOMORROW* FROM SOMETHING LIKE THAT. RELAX.
HE'LL NEED SOMETHING FOR IT SOONER OR LATER, BUT : WE'LL LEAVE THAT TO MY REAL SELF.
IT WASN'T A WHIM.
NN?
FATE AVERRUNCUS : THE REMNANTS OF COSMO ENTELEKHEIA... IT'S LOOKING LIKE THE GHOSTS OF THE PAST HAVE STARTED TO MOVE.
BUT YOU PROBABLY DON'T CARE.
I NEEDED THAT KID TO DO WHATEVER IT TOOK TO GET STRONGER.
AND AS A RESULT I WAS MORE PLEASANTLY SURPRISED THAN I COULD HAVE EXPECTED.
HA. WHAT ARE YOU SAYING? YOU'RE THE HERO WHO SAVED THE WORLD, THE INVINCIBLE JACK RAKAN.
IF IT COMES DOWN TO IT, YOU JUST NEED TO GO OUT THERE AND FIX IT YOURSELF.

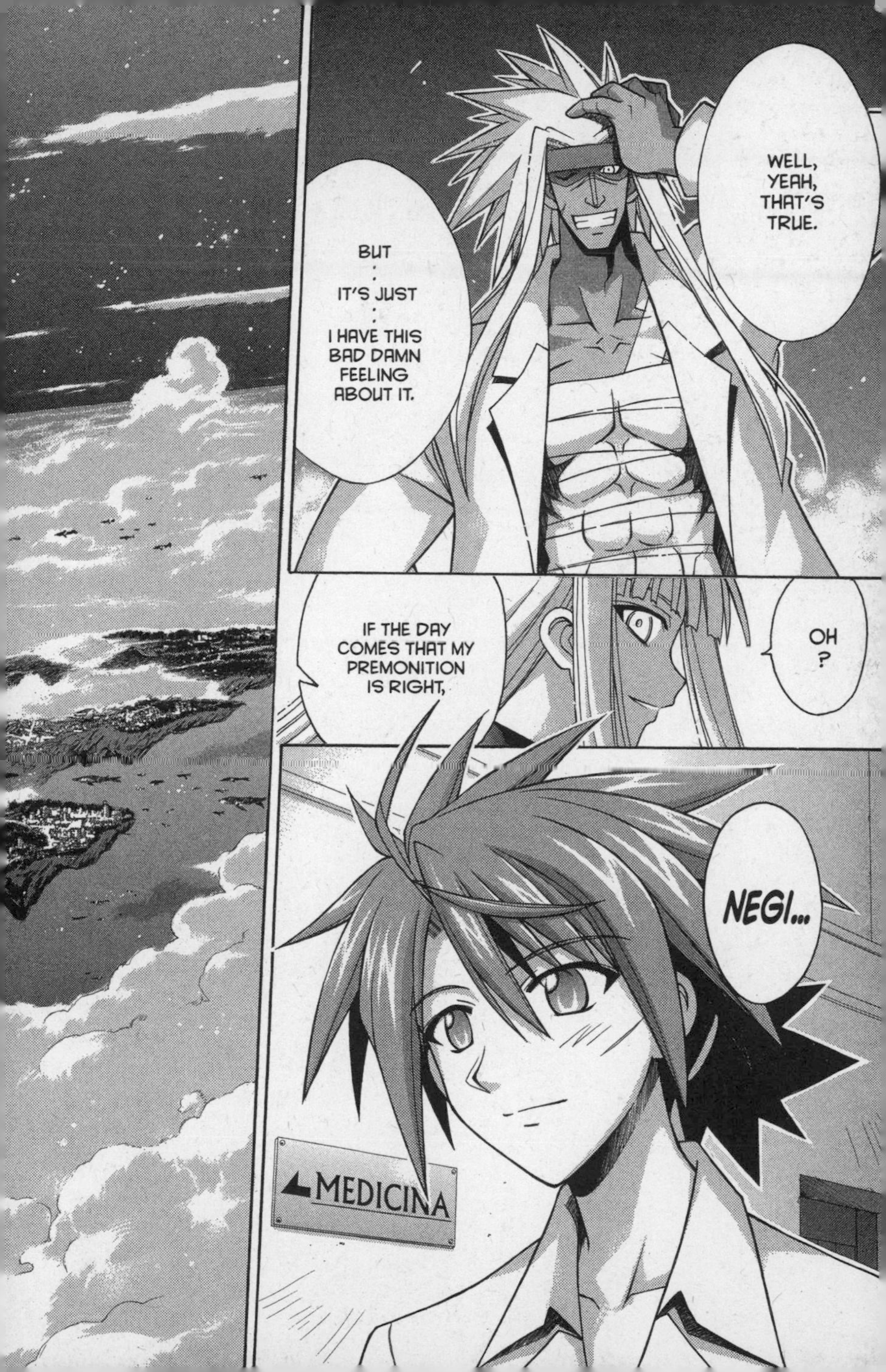
WELL, YEAH, THAT'S TRUE.
BUT . . . IT'S JUST . . . I HAVE THIS BAD DAMN FEELING ABOUT IT.
OH?
IF THE DAY COMES THAT MY PREMONITION IS RIGHT,
NEGI...
MEDICINA

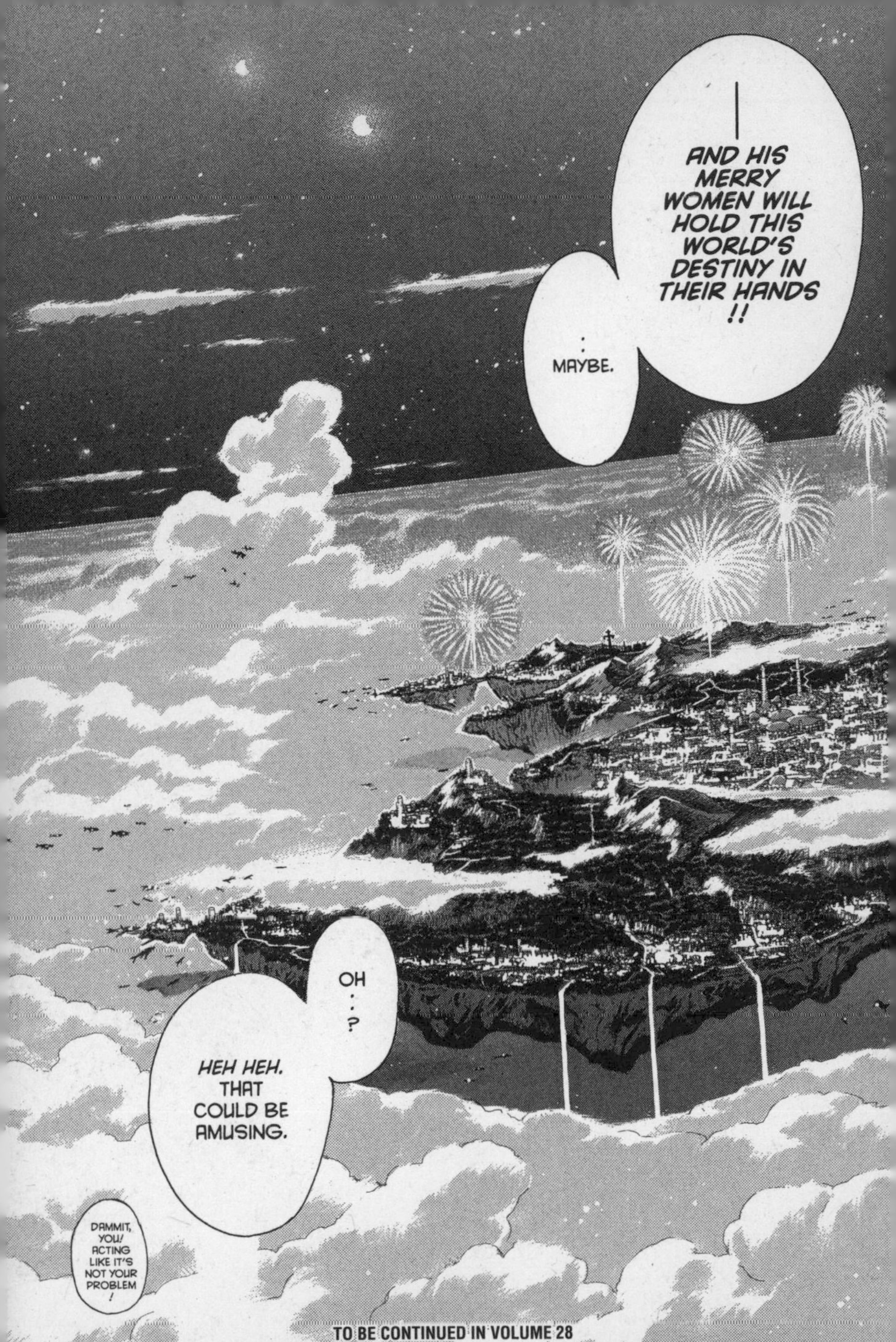
—AND HIS MERRY WOMEN WILL HOLD THIS WORLD'S DESTINY IN THEIR HANDS !!
...MAYBE.
OH...?
HEH HEH. THAT COULD BE AMUSING.
DAMMIT, YOU! ACTING LIKE IT'S NOT YOUR PROBLEM!

TO BE CONTINUED IN VOLUME 28

-STAFF-

Ken Akamatsu
Takashi Takemoto
Kenichi Nakamura
Masaki Ohyama
Keiichi Yamashita
Tadashi Maki
Tohru Mitsuhashi
Yuichi Yoshida

Thanks to
Ran Ayanaga

LEXICON NEGIMARIUM

[*Negima!* 223rd Period Lexicon Negimarium]

■ Lunatic Fiddle
(fidicula lunatica)

The girl known as Shirabe is awarded this item for her use by the power of the pactio with the white-haired boy. "Fidicula" is Latin for a small, stringed instruments, and, in this case, refers to a violin. In the Middle Ages, stringed instruments played with bows were all called violas ("viola" in Latin, also). For small violas, they attached the diminutive "-ina" to "viola," and called them "violina," and thus the modern name "violin" was born.

Objects showered in the strong sound waves emitted from Fidicula Lunatica are blasted into dust. But because these sound waves have directivity, merely listening to the sound will not expose one to its destructive powers. Otherwise, we would be mincemeat before we could comment on the poor quality of Shirabe's playing, and more than anything, Shirabe herself would fall victim to her own performance.

[*Negima!* 224th Period Lexicon Negimarium]

■ Song of Saving Mercy
(cantus elemosynes)

An omnidirectional attack using the sound waves of Fidicula Lunatica. How waves sent from a single source can become an omnidirectional attack remains a mystery. "Cantus" is Latin for "song," and "elemosynes" is the genitive case of "elemosyne." "Elemosyne" is a Latinized version of ἐλημοσύνη (elêmosynê), Ancient Greek for "mercy."

■ Infinite Embrace
(encompandentia infinita)

The girl known as Tamaki is awarded this item for her use by the power of the pactio with the white-haired boy. She uses a finite amount of magic power to develop and control a barrier space of infinite expanse around herself.

■ Randgrid
(Randgríð)

The flying patrol ship of the Ariadne Magic Knights. It is equipped with a long cruising range and superior ability to search out enemies. However, its firepower is minimal, and its ability to bombard other ships in battle is low. Patrol ships of the same model are widely used in the Mesembrina Confederation city-states.

Randgríð is the name of a page in Odin's hall, who appears in "The Ballad

of Grimnir," recorded in the *Elder Edda*. The name means "shield hall" in Old Norse. According to later-written *Snorri's Edda*, Randgríð was counted as one of the Valkyries, but this is no more than Snorri Sturluson's (1178-1241) interpretation, and it is not made clear in the *Elder Edda* whether or not she was a Valkyrie.

[*Negima!* 225th Period Lexicon Negimarium]

■ "Hell's Refining Fire"

(sim fabricatus ab incendio)

One of the practical uses of dark magic, it takes the magic power from "Flames of Hell (Incendium Gehennae)" into one's flesh and fuses it with the spirit. In doing so, the caster's flesh gains powerful hardness and resistance to heat, and is imbued with a sinister spiritual power that steals magical power from any living thing it touches. But if it fails, not only is there a danger that the blaze of "Flames of Hell" will damage the caster's flesh, but there are also cases when the fire spirits (spritus) violate the caster's mind (spiritus) and make him go mad.

[*Negima!* 226th Period Lexicon Negimarium]

■ Left Arm Release

(sinistra emittam)

"Sinistra" is a Latin ablative meaning "left hand." An "ablative" indicates a placc or a method. *"Emittam"* is in the first person singular present active subjunctive mood. Therefore, this phrase means "may I release from my left hand." This spell is incanted in order to release delayed magic and the like from the left hand.

■ Time Corridor

(horaria porticus)

The girl known as Koyomi is awarded this item for her use by the power of the pactio with the white-haired boy. It creates a sphere of effect in which physical phenomena and mental phenomena are delayed. The user can determine the extent of the phenomena's delay at her pleasure, and can cancel the delay whenever she likes.

To persons outside the sphere of effect created by the Horaria Porticus, phenomena inside the sphere become abnormally slow, while to those inside the sphere, phenomena outside become abnormally fast. For that reason, once captured inside the sphere of effect, even relatively quick actions will be no more than lagging movements as long as they are viewed from outside. Even the artifact's user is not exempt from this.

That being the case, even an attack with projectiles from outside the sphere, whether they be arrows or bullets, will lag once it enters the sphere, so it is not effective for direct offensive battle. If she is to use it in battle, it would be most suitable for such uses as setting traps outside the sphere, as depicted in the story, or moving to places where it would be easier to fight.

■ Great Dimensional Smash (named just now)

(magna confractio dimensionis [modo nomino])

Using gravity magic learned by watching others, it warps four-dimensional worlds and destroys them.

In a vacuum, when light (electromagnetic waves, to be precise) moves from one point to another, the course the light follows is the shortest distance between those two points. To put it in classical physics terms, light "moves linearly." However, when gravity is at work (no matter how small), the course the light follows becomes a "curved line." This is because in space (space-time to be precise) where gravity is at work, the shortest distance between two points is not a straight line. This is the "warping of space-time."

The curvature of space-time doesn't only *look* bent; it actually is bent. For that reason, space-time warping regulates not only the behavior of light, but also of matter. The reason gravity attracts matter is precisely that space-time is warped. Therefore, it can be said that space-time warping generates gravity, and it can also be said that gravity generates warping of space-time.

Objects with mass or energy (especially heavenly bodies) pull the matter and electromagnetic waves around them toward their gravitational center. In most cases, these objects do not cause any special phenomena. However, special cases do occur when the object is contained within the radius r_g created by this equation,

$$r_g = 2GM \div c^2$$

where M is the mass of the object, G is the gravitational constant, and c is the speed of light. The r_g created in the above formula is called the "Schwarzschild radius." In this Schwarzschild radius, because the force of gravity is so strong, and therefore space-time is curved so greatly, the course light takes is not only "curved," but the light "falls" toward the center (as for what happens to objects other than light, that is better left unsaid). When likened to three-dimensional formations, these objects are called "black holes."

The Schwarzschild radius is inversely proportional to the speed of light squared, so it tends to be an extremely small value. For example, the Schwarzschild radius for an object with the same mass as the moon is approximately 0.11mm. However, gravity magic can create gravity even in places where no objects with mass exist. In other words, gravity magic is the creating of curves in space-time without interposing an object with mass. Furthermore, the strength of a gravitational force F of a source of gravity is

$$F = GMm \div r^2$$

where G is the gravitational constant, M is the mass of the source of gravity, m is the mass of the object pulled by the gravity, and r is the distance between the two. As long as the gravity magic is functioning, gravity will exist there, and F will not equal zero. As long as the left side of the equation does not equal zero, then the right side will not equal zero, either, and (even without an object) the mass M in the formula will not equal zero (however, $r \neq \infty$).

From the above equation, when powerful gravity magic is at work, the value of M becomes great, and in proportion, the Schwarzschild radius becomes great as well. Gravity magic does not require a wide space to create immense gravitational force. For that reason, if one uses powerful energy to exercise gravity magic, in

the end, they generate the required value M, within the Schwarzschild radius, to generate a black hole.

At the center of a black hole, gravity is infinite, and therefore the warping of space-time, or the curvature of space-time, is infinitely large, and the density of matter is infinite as well. Therefore, in regard to such unique "points" as these, (traditional) laws of physics cannot be applied. Tamaki's artifact, Encompandentia Infinita, functions to develop and control a barrier space. But that function is designed based, more than anything, on ideas of space from a system of magical culture that came at least before the Theory of Relativity, and certainly before modern physics. Ergo, it was not supposed that a warping of space-time and density of matter of infinitely high value would exist inside a barrier space that she created herself.*

Furthermore, Encompandentia Infinita uses a limited amount of magic to develop and control an infinite expanse. But its magic is too weak to control infinitely great density and space-time warp as well as the infinite expanse. In contrast, an infinite amount of gravity or magic power is not required to create a black hole. This is because, while the speed of light is a great physical quantity, it is in fact finite, and therefore the amount of gravity required to prevent light escaping is also finite. And if enough gravity to trap light is at work, from geometric inevitabilities, the center of the black hole will generate infinitely large gravity on its own. However, the extremely superior function to control infinity is Encompandentia Infinita's basic function. Therefore, as long as there are no abnormalities in its user's mental state, the artifact will work to maintain the barrier space.

Nevertheless, that does not change the fact that there is a large difference in the magical burden of controlling a barrier with a black hole inside it and that of using gravity magic to create a black hole. For this reason, powerful gravity magic is the natural enemy of magic for controlling barriers. Gravity magic has an extremely wide range of applications. Perhaps Rakan once saw Kūnel use gravity magic to destroy a similar trap. Furthermore, a black hole only needs to exist for an instant in order to destroy the barrier, and the danger of injuring surrounding people with a wave of powerful gravity magic is minimal.

*The classical physics concept of "space" is quite different from the modern physics idea of "place." But as an exception, the concept of space in Euclidean geometry and that in modern physics are very similar.

[*Negima!* 228th Period Lexicon Negimarium]

■ Eternal Petrification

Aionion Petrosis

(ʾΑΙΩΝΙΟΝ ΠΕΤΡΩΣΙΣ)

A spell that emits a beam from the fingertips, which petrifies its targets. It is an extremely powerful and dangerous spell, and is incanted in Ancient Greek. But, while petrification from spells such as Pnoe Petras (Breath of Stone) and Kakon Omma Petroseos (Evil Eye of Petrifaction) can be undone with a certain extent of strong magic, petrification from this spell is semipermanent. For that reason, without power emitted from extremely unique and high-ranking spiritual capacity (power from a persona great enough among all the various spirits to be called a "god"), this petrification will not be undone. However, whatever damage it may

take, Nodoka's artifact can recover if she only returns it to her card, so she did not get a taste of the true terror of this spell.

[*Negima!* 229th Period Lexicon Negimarium]

■ Phoenix Law Imperial Seal

Ennomos Aetosphragis

(ἔννομος ἀετοσφραγίς)

A magical seal modeled as an eagle holding scales. This seal uses powerful magic to force its target to strictly honor his word.

The eagle and the scales of this magical item's design represent power and justice, respectively.

The eagle as a symbol of power comes from the eagle being the bird sacred to the chief Greek/Roman god, Zeus/Jupiter. The ancient Roman poet P. Ovidius N. (B.C.43 - A.D.17(18)) relates the following. "Once, high and mighty lord [Jupiter] burned with the flames of love for Ganymede of Troy. Now Jupiter looked around for something he could change himself into. Jupiter must have wanted to change into something other than himself. But the one known as Jupiter would never become any bird other than one that could carry his thunderbolts. He took to the sky with his false wings and stole away the Trojan youth." (*Metamorphoses*, 10,155-160) It is not specified here, but according to Apollodoros (B.C.1C?), this bird that carries Jupiter's thunderbolts was none other than the eagle (ἀετός) (*Bibliotheca [Βιβλιοθήκη]*, 3,12,2).

Thus, the bird known as the eagle is a sacred bird with supreme divine authority. For that reason, it became the symbol of the Roman Empire, the Roman Emperor, and the Roman Empire's military. Even after the fall of the ancient Roman Empire, the western German Empire (the Holy Roman Empire) and the eastern Russian Empire each used the eagle as their national symbol, and the eagle continued to signify the highest authority (in connection with the ancient Roman Empire).

The design of the scales representing justice comes from conventions of Renaissance art. Since that time, the Roman goddess Justitia, who has become the personification of the virtue of justice, has been represented as a statue holding a sword and scales (or a book of law), and the scales are a symbol of the justice of law.

This design of power and justice is precisely what signifies the compelling force of the contract.

[*Negima!* 230th Period Lexicon Negimarium]

■ ADULTERA

The characters inscribed on the magic capsules that summon half-human, half-spirit beings such as undina. "Adultera" is a Latin word meaning "lascivious woman," and this magic item is used (mainly) to satisfy the sexual desires of men. The capsules Rakan had in 230th Period were a wood spirit (Dryas) capsule, a fire spirit (salamandra) capsule, a wind spirit (sylpha) capsule, and, for insurance, a water spirit (undina) capsule.

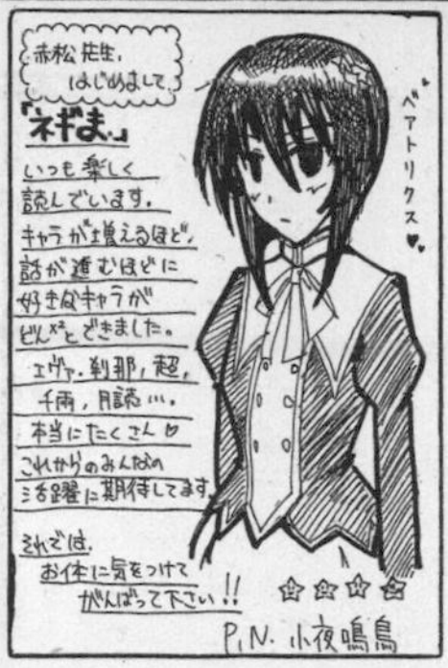
赤松先生、はじめまして。
「ネギま」
いつも楽しく読んでいます。
キャラが増えるほど、話が進むほどに好きなキャラがどんどんできました。
エヴァ、刹那、超、千雨、月詠…。
本当にたくさん♡
これからのみんなの活躍に期待してます。
それでは、お体に気をつけてがんばって下さい!!
ベアトリクス♥
P.N. 小夜鳴鳥

▲ OHH, IT'S BEATRIX.

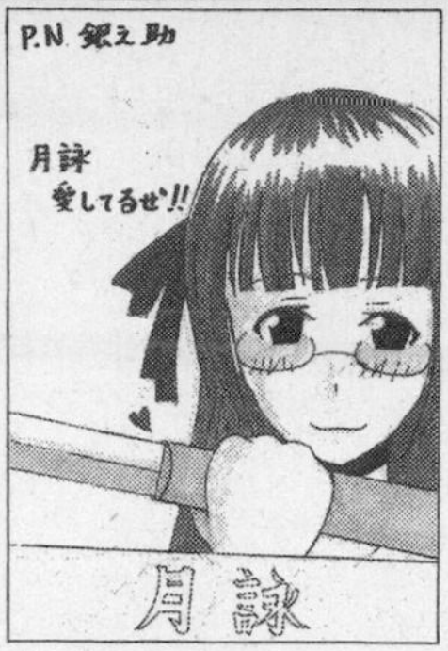
P.N.
月詠 愛してるぜ!!
月詠

▲ WE DON'T SEE TSUKUYOMI VERY OFTEN.

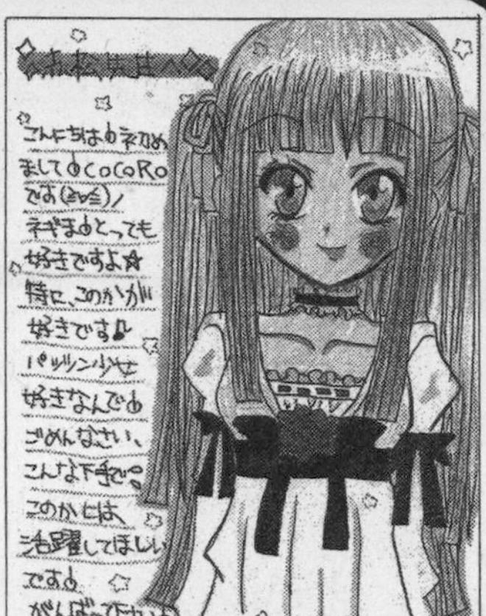
赤松先生へ
こんにちは♪ はじめまして♪COCORO です(^^)ノ
ネギま♪とっても好きですよ☆
特に、このかが!! 好きです♪
パッツン少女好きなんで♪
ごめんなさい、こんな下手で。
このかには活躍してほしいです♪
がんばってください♪
PN COCORO
このか

HOW FASHIONABLE. ▶

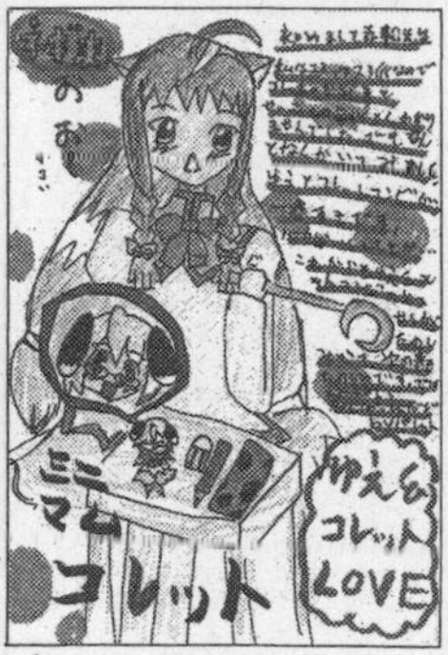
ミニマム コレット
ゆえ&コレット LOVE

▲ COLLET SHRANK?

NEGIMA!
FAN ART CORNER

HELLO! THE CHARACTERS IN THE STORY HAVE INCREASED, AND WE'RE GETTING SUBMISSIONS OF ALL KINDS OF CHARACTERS★ ON THE OTHER HAND, WE'RE ALSO GETTING CHARACTERS THAT AREN'T IN THE STORY MUCH (LAUGH). PLEASE, SHINE LIGHT ON THEM, TOO! (^○^) (LAUGH). WELL THEN, LET'S TAKE A LOOK.♪

TEXT BY MAX

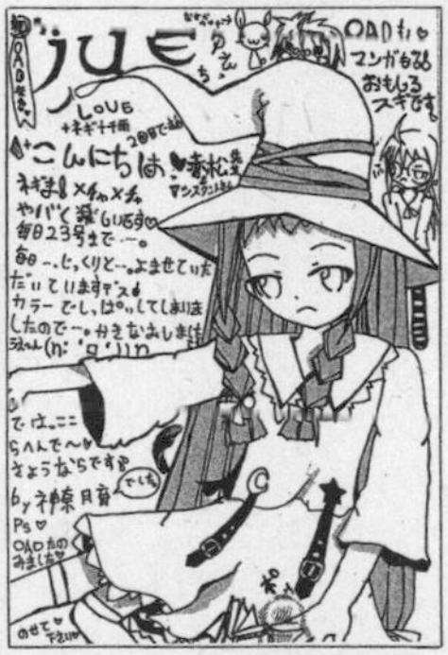
YUE
LOVE
こんにちは!♥赤松先生
では、ここらへんで～ さようならです

▲ YUE, WITH A MYSTERIOUS EXPRESSION.

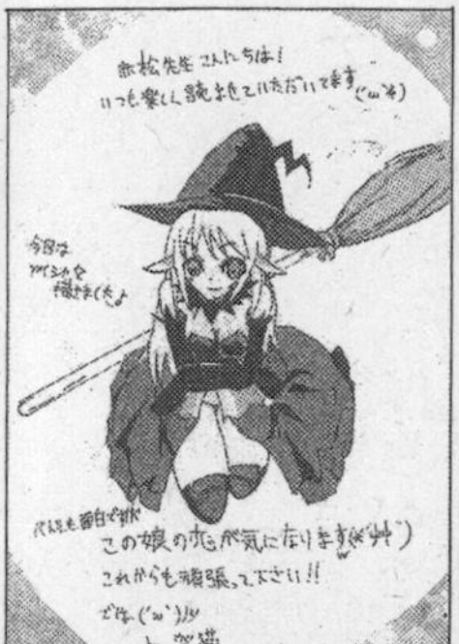
赤松先生 こんにちは!
いつも楽しく読ませていただいてます
この娘の出番が気になります
これからも頑張って下さい!!
by 空猫

▲ TO THINK WE'D GET AISHA. (LAUGH)

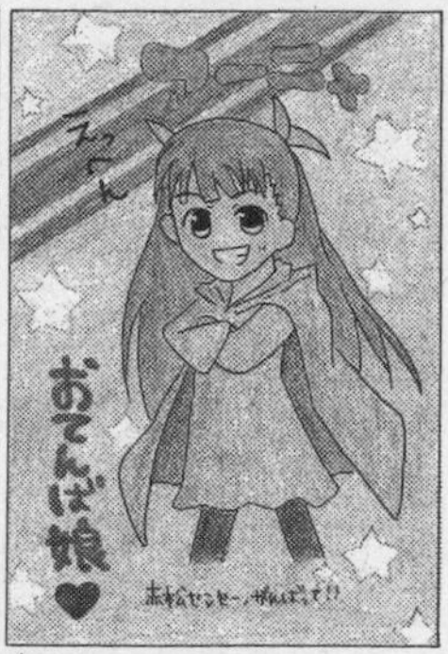
おてんば娘♥
赤松センセー、がんばって!!

▲ SO ENERGETIC.

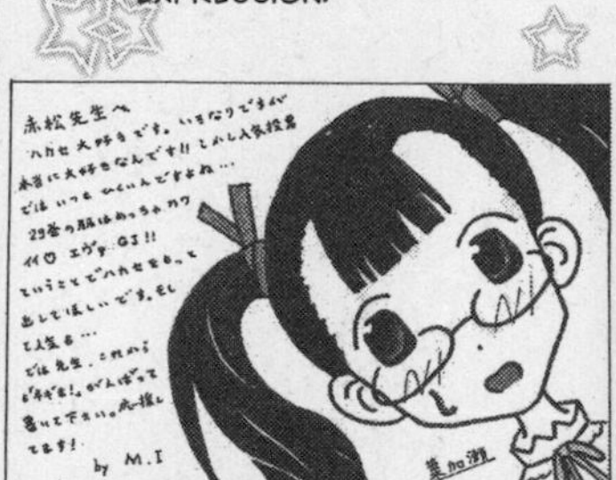
赤松先生へ
by M.I

▲ PLEASE KEEP SUPPORTING HAKASE.♪

NEGI MA!

NEGI MAGI

MAGISTER

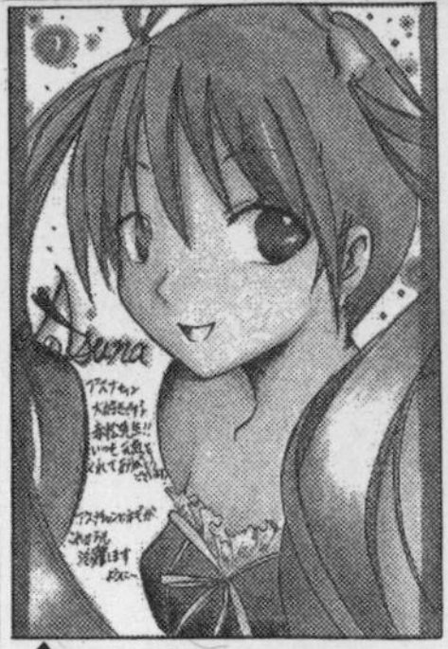

▲ SO SEXY.

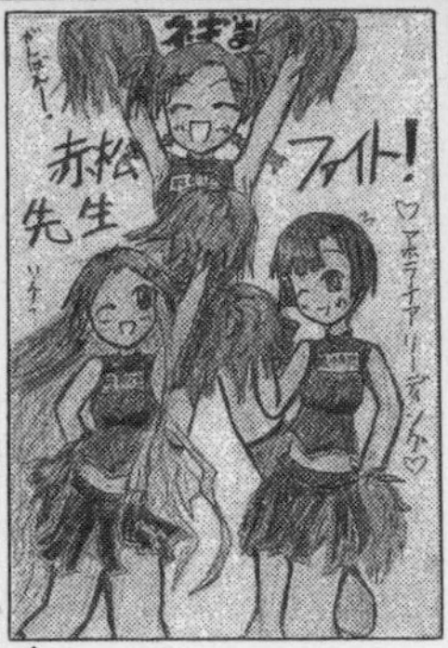
ネギま！
赤松先生
ファイト！

▲ THE CHEER SQUAD IS LOOKING WELL.♪

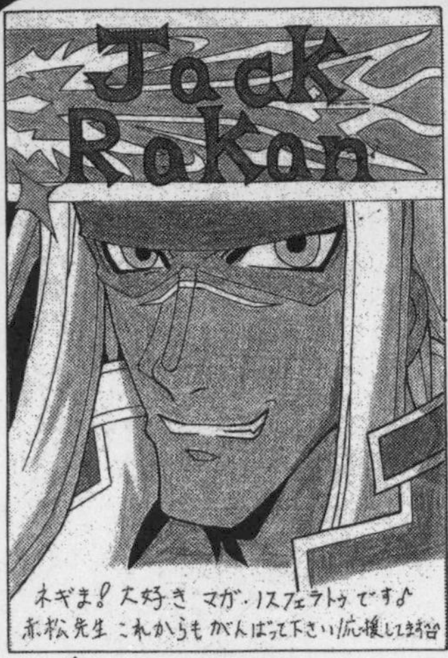
Jack Rakan

▲ AND HERE'S RAKAN.

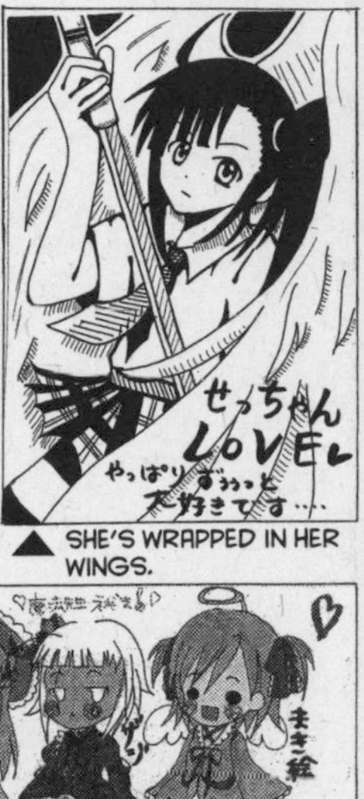
せっちゃん LOVE
やっぱりずっと大好きです…

▲ SHE'S WRAPPED IN HER WINGS.

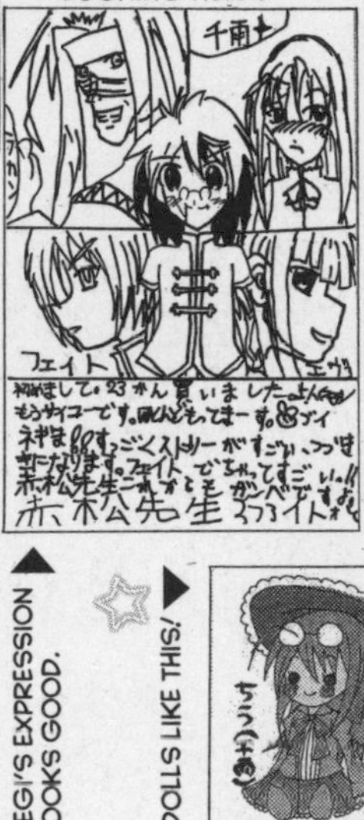
千雨
フェイト
赤松先生ファイト

▲ NEGI'S EXPRESSION LOOKS GOOD.

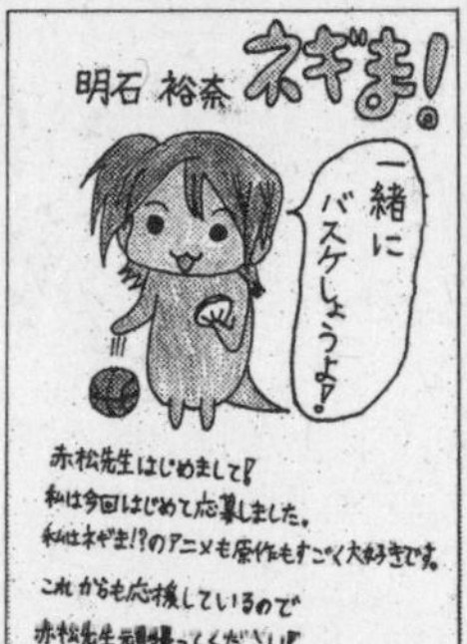
明石 裕奈 ネギま！
一緒にバスケしょうよ！
赤松先生はじめまして！
私は今回はじめて応募しました。
私はネギま！？のアニメも原作もすごく大好きです。
これからも応援しているので
赤松先生頑張ってください！

▲ SHE HAS A TAIL.

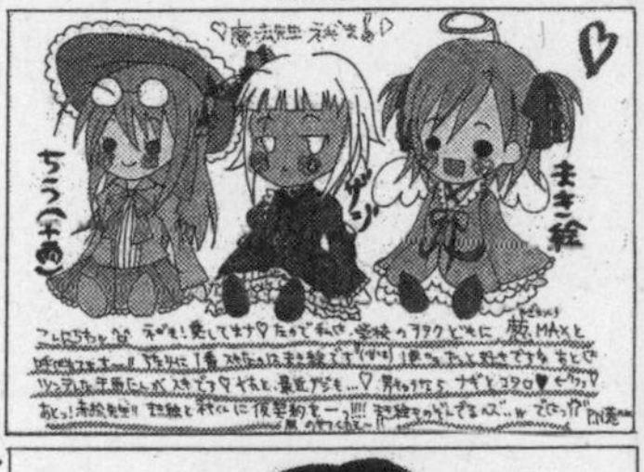

▲ I WANT DOLLS LIKE THIS!

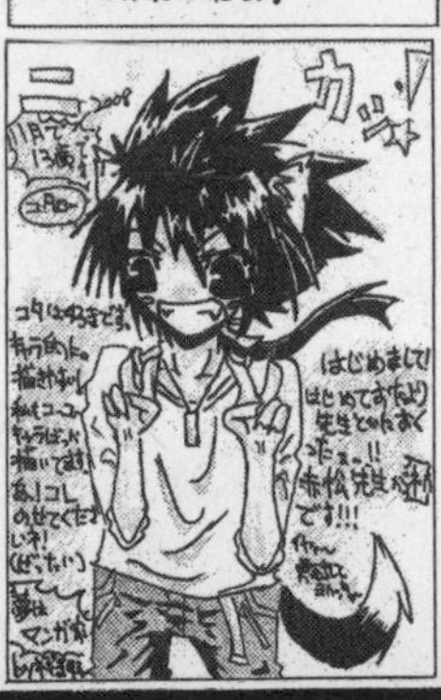
はじめまして！
赤松先生
です!!!

▲ HE LOOKS MISCHIEVOUS.

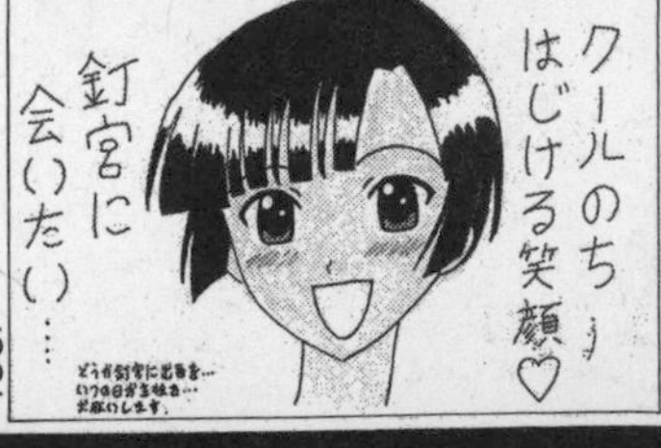
クールのちはじける笑顔♡
釘宮に会いたい…

▲ KUGIMIYA'S POPULAR, TOO.

NEGI MA!

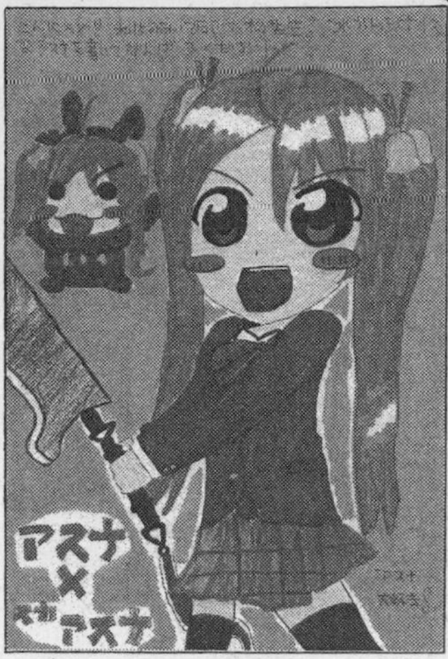
アスナ
×
アスナ

▲ ADORABLE♪ ASUNA

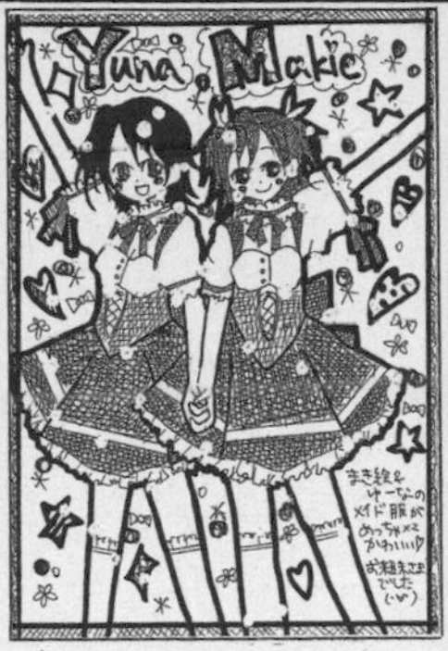
Yuna
Makie

▲ IT'S BLACK AND WHITE, BUT VERY VIBRANT.

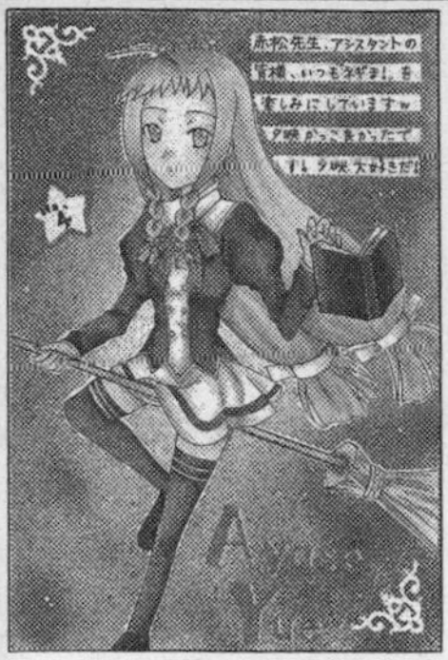

▲ THIS IS A VERY PRETTY DRAWING.

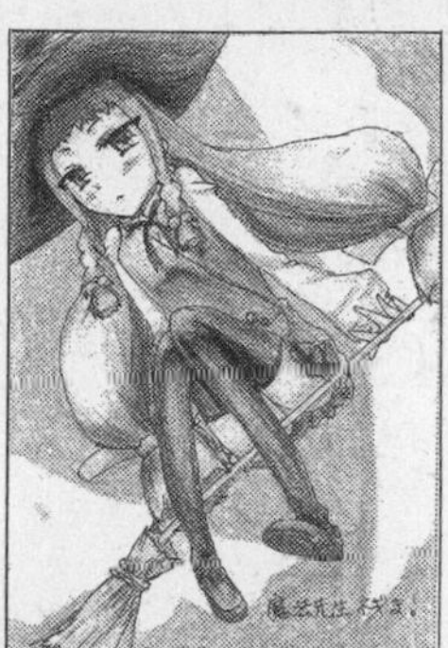

▲ YOU HAVE A DELICATE TOUCH.

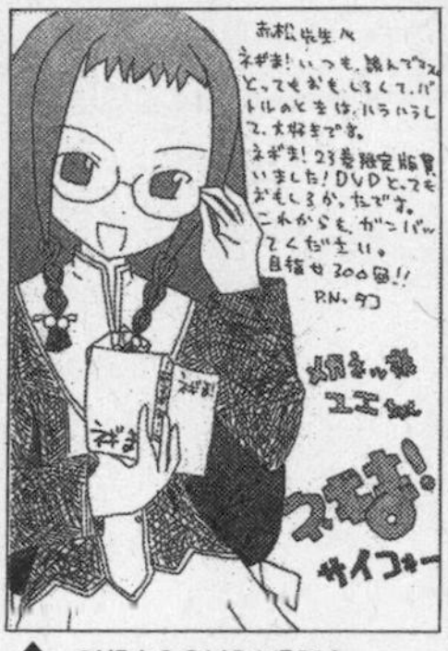

▲ SHE LOOKS VERY INTELLECTUAL.

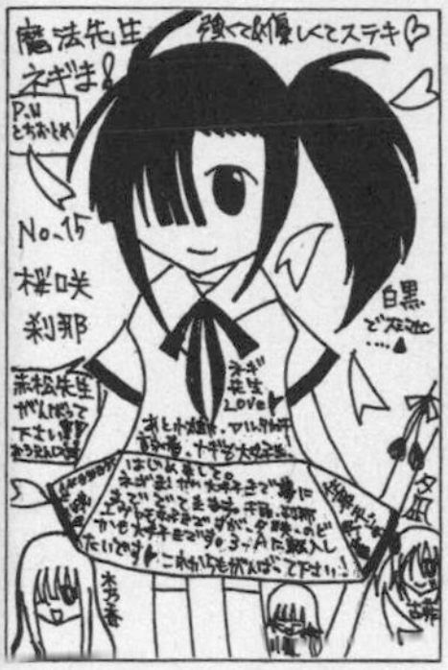
魔法先生
ネギま!
No.15
桜咲
刹那

▲ SHE LOOKS LIKE A KINDERGARTNER.

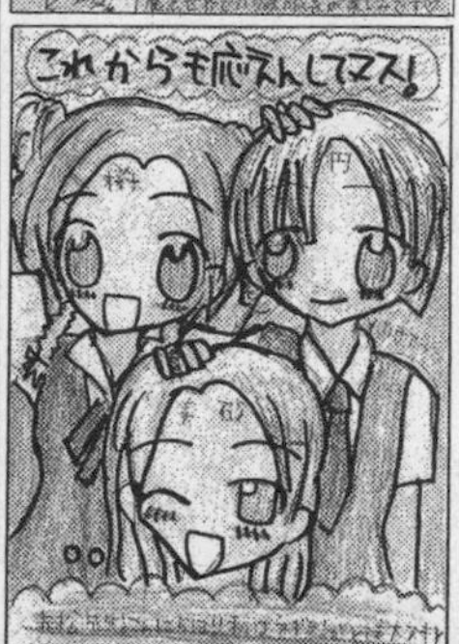
これからも応えんしてマス!

▲ THEIR NAMES ARE ON THEIR FOREHEADS. (LAUGH)

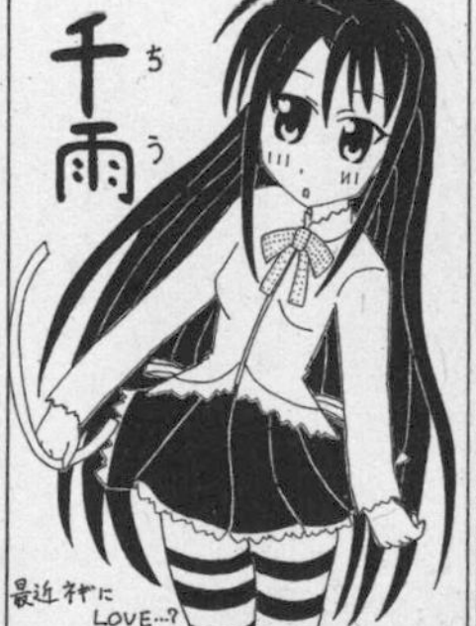
千雨
最近ネギに
LOVE…?

▲ IT'S LOLI CHISAME. (LAUGH)

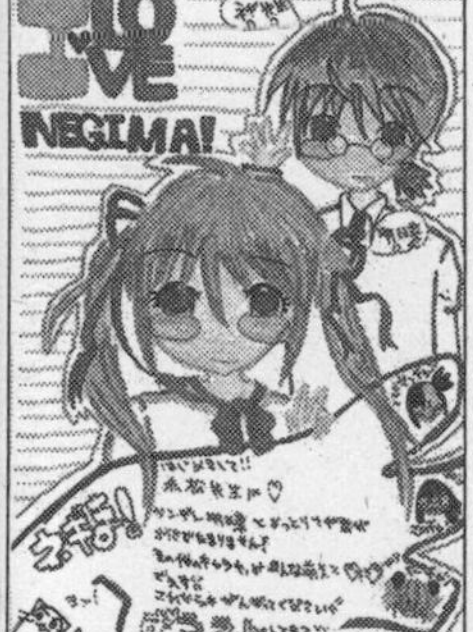
I LOVE
NEGIMA!

▲ THEY'VE BECOME SUPER CUTE.

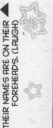

THIS VOLUME'S FEATURED CHARACTER

NODOKA MIYAZAKI RANKING

FIRST PLACE

初カラーに挑戦したものの、やはり下手×。ハマりまきた。のどか◎。1000%♥

のどか

この本、(マジで)オススメです！

こんにちは～。赤松先生、スタッフのみなさま、のどかの本、オススメ、です！私に言われて神本！の本を出されたら、最高だなー！て！！（どうでもいい？！）私ならな感じ、出来って●ちまう位、神本も大変ですが、がんばって下さい。おうえん、くれます☆

(リターンズ) 5年生

神本！って言うんです♥

そうだ！シリーズ累計1000万部！

A-ANOTHER AKAMATSU-SAN DREW THIS? THE SHAPE OF THE EYES IS VERY GOOD. HER EXPRESSION IS REALLY ALIVE; IT'S VERY WELL DRAWN. ～♡

(AKAMATSU)

NEGI MAGI

MAGISTER

white NODOKA by ネコ

SECOND PLACE

OHH! THIS IS A BEAUTIFUL BOOKSTORE...SHE LOOKS LIKE A PRINCESS. ♡

YOU WONDER WHAT HAPPENS NEXT? (LAUGH) THAT *IS* SOMETHING I'M ALWAYS CONCERNED ABOUT. THIS BOOKSTORE'S EYES ARE GOOD, TOO.

THIRD PLACE

初めまして！うーろん☆です。

毎回「ネギ！」を見て赤松先生の絵のうまさに感動しています！マンガの終わり方など、死ぬほど気になるようになっていて、尊敬するばかりです！この子も個性的でとても可愛いです。これから先頑張って下さい！

のどか

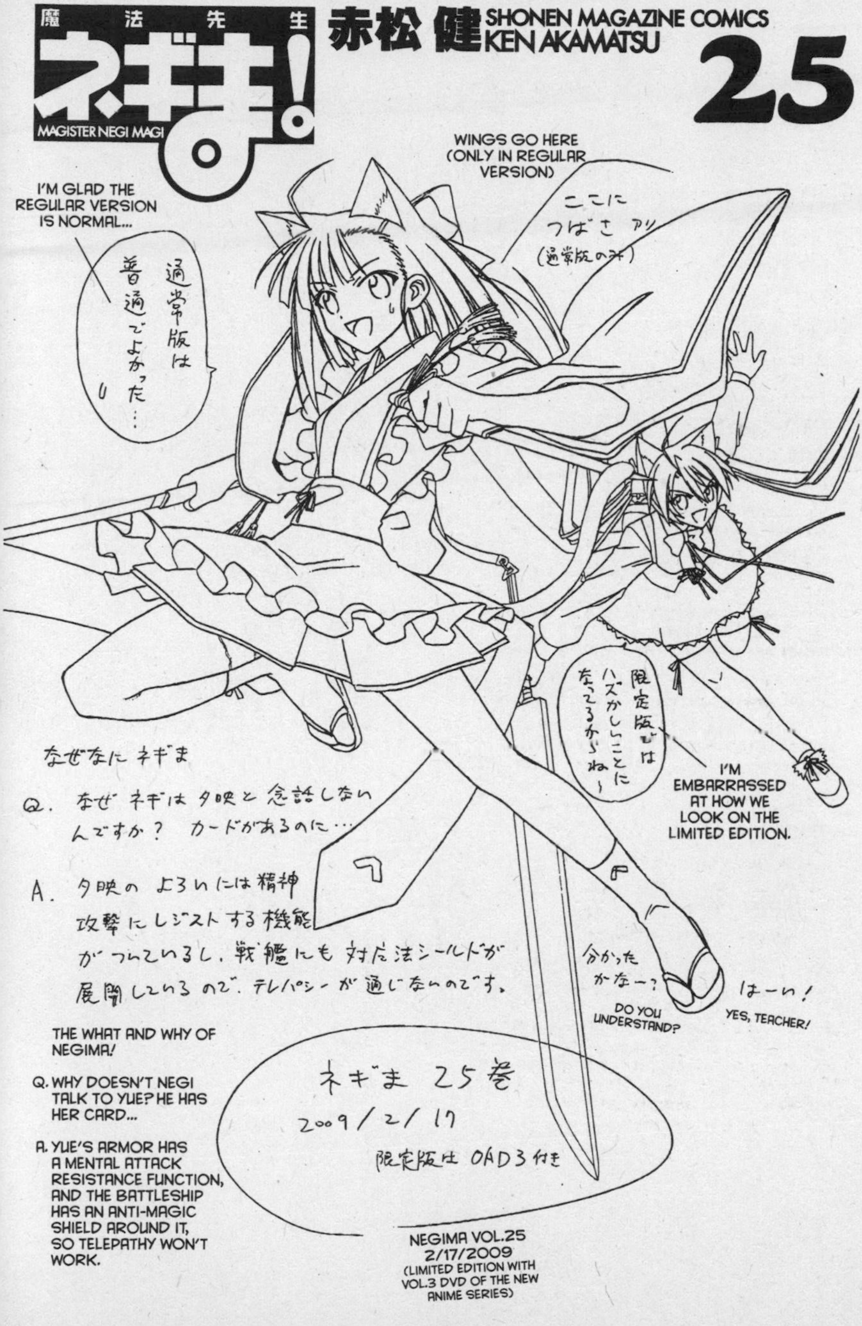

魔法先生
ネギま！
MAGISTER NEGI MAGI
赤松 健
SHONEN MAGAZINE COMICS
KEN AKAMATSU
25
ここに つばさ アリ (通常版のみ)
WINGS GO HERE (ONLY IN REGULAR VERSION)
通常版は普通でよかった…
I'M GLAD THE REGULAR VERSION IS NORMAL...
限定版ではハズかしいことになってるからね～
I'M EMBARRASSED AT HOW WE LOOK ON THE LIMITED EDITION.
なぜなにネギま
Q. なぜネギは夕映と念話しないんですか？ カードがあるのに…
A. 夕映のよろいには精神攻撃にレジストする機能がついているし、戦艦にも対魔法シールドが展開しているので、テレパシーが通じないのです。
分かったかなー？
DO YOU UNDERSTAND?
はーい！
YES, TEACHER!
THE WHAT AND WHY OF NEGIMA!
Q. WHY DOESN'T NEGI TALK TO YUE? HE HAS HER CARD...
A. YUE'S ARMOR HAS A MENTAL ATTACK RESISTANCE FUNCTION, AND THE BATTLESHIP HAS AN ANTI-MAGIC SHIELD AROUND IT, SO TELEPATHY WON'T WORK.
ネギま 25巻
2009/2/17
限定版は OAD3付き
NEGIMA VOL.25
2/17/2009
(LIMITED EDITION WITH VOL.3 DVD OF THE NEW ANIME SERIES)

キャラ解説

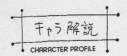

CHARACTER PROFILE

㉓ 鳴滝史伽

㉓ FUMIKA NARUTAKI

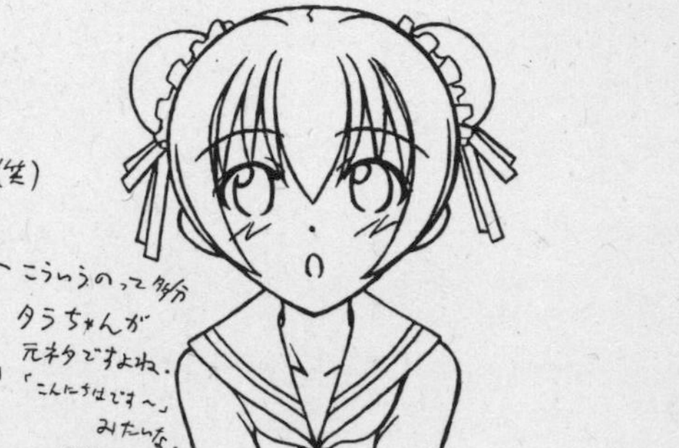

双子ちゃんの弱気な方です。(笑)

THE TIMID ONE OF THE TWINS. (LAUGH)

夕映と同じく丁寧語です。← こういうのって多分タラちゃんが元ネタですよね。「こんにちはです～」みたいな。

SHE SPEAKS WITH POLITE LANGUAGE, LIKE YUE.

I THINK THIS IS BASED ON TARA-CHAN. LIKE "HELLO DESU."

姉よりタレ目なのは、おそらく

I THINK THAT THE REASON HER EYES DROOP DOWN MORE THAN

性格的なものが表情に出ている

HER SISTER'S IS PROBABLY JUST THAT HER PERSONALITY

だけで、パーツ的にはうりふたつ

SHOWS UP IN HER EXPRESSIONS; THE BODY PARTS OF THE SIS-

なんだと思いますよ。(一卵性だから)

TER'S ARE AN EXACT MATCH. (SINCE THEY'RE IDENTICAL TWINS.)

姉と同じく、大人になった姿を想像できない…し

LIKE WITH HER SISTER, I CAN'T IMAGINE HER HAVING GROWN UP...

でもきっと美人になるんじゃないかな。(^^) なんとなく。

BUT I'M SURE SHE'LL BE BEAUTIFUL. (^^) JUST A HUNCH.

アニメ版CVは狩野茉莉さん。

IN THE ANIME, SHE IS VOICED BY MARI KANŌ-SAN. SHE'S A

ライブイベントなどの打ち上げで、いつも

LOVELY PERSON WHO ALWAYS BAWLS

号泣しちゃうかわいらしい人です。

WHEN WE LAUNCH LIVE EVENTS.

守ってあげたくなっちゃう。(笑)

I JUST WANT TO PROTECT HER. (LAUGH)

ドラマ版はまなちゃこと山本真菜香ちゃん。

IN THE DRAMA, SHE IS PLAYED BY MANAKA YAMAMOTO-CHAN, AKA

だまってると美少女なんですが、その中身は…

MANACHI. WHEN SHE'S QUIET, SHE'S A BEAUTIFUL YOUNG LADY, BUT ON

私をはるかに超えるオタクです!(笑)

THE INSIDE... SHE FAR SURPASSES ME AS AN OTAKU! (LAUGH) WHEN I

ブログ読んでても7割くらいしか分からない…し

READ HER BLOG, I ONLY UNDERSTAND ABOUT 70% OF IT...

赤松

AKAMATSU

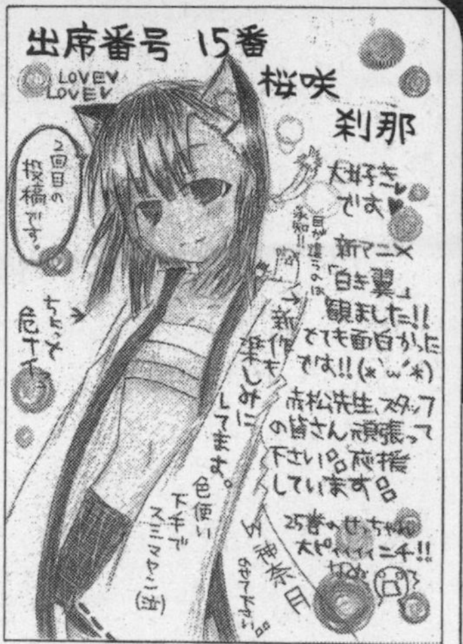
出席番号 15番
桜咲
刹那
LOVE♥
LOVE♥
大好きです♥

I LIKE THE BANDAGE.

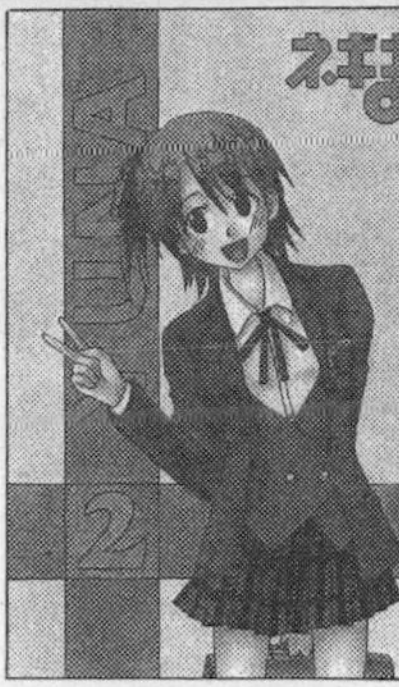
ネギま!

SHE LOOKS LIKE A PRETTY ORTHODOX SCHOOLGIRL.

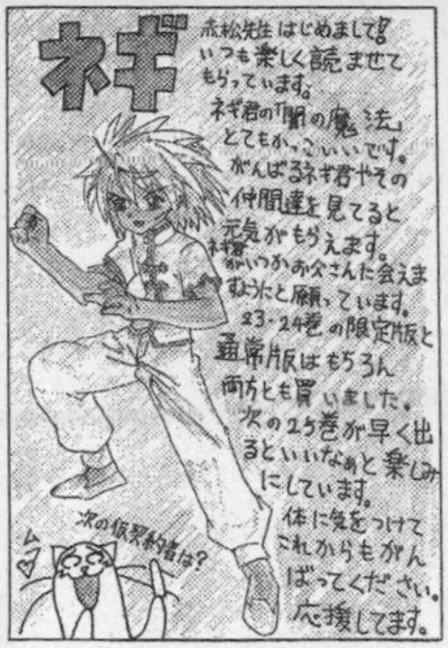
ネギ

IT'S A WHITE-COLORED NEGI.

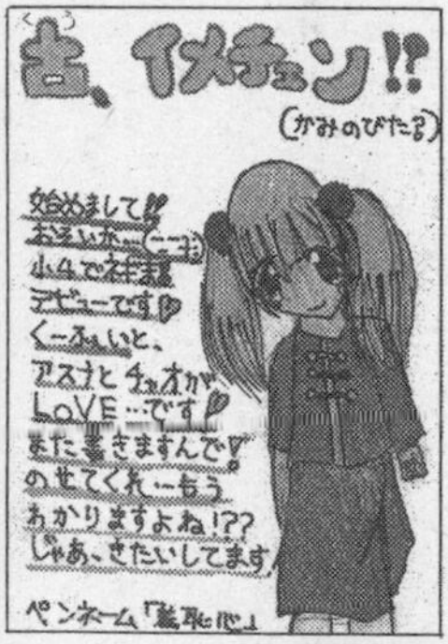
古、イメチェン!!

WHAT AN ADORABLE KŪ.

NEGIMA! FAN ART CORNER

THANK YOU FOR ALWAYS SENDING PICTURES AND LETTERS. I ALWAYS HAVE A HARD TIME CHOOSING PICTURES, AND THIS TIME THE SELECTION WAS FIERCE. I REALLY AM FEELING THE POWER OF MIDDLE AND ELEMENTARY SCHOOLGIRLS ★ I GET THE FEELING THAT FATE AND NEGI SUBMISSIONS ARE GRADUALLY INCREASING, AND THERE'S LESS VARIATION ON THE FEMALE CHARACTERS. NOW THEN, LET'S TAKE A LOOK (^^)

TEXT BY MOI

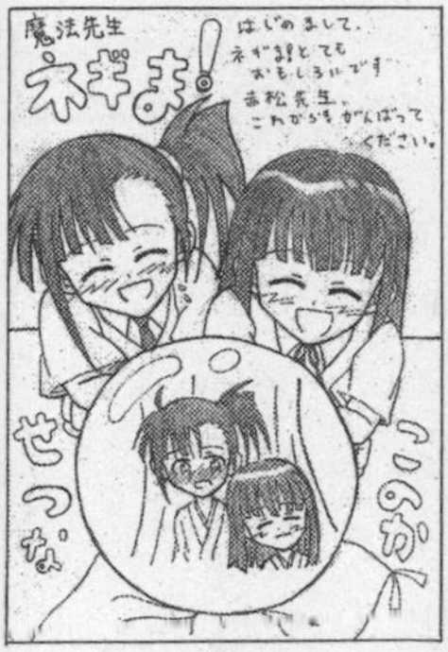
魔法先生
ネギま!

HEARTWARMING☆

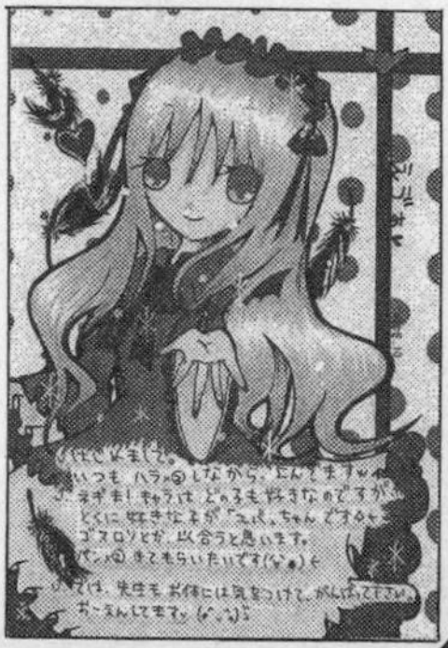
I GET A SENSE OF HER STYLE!

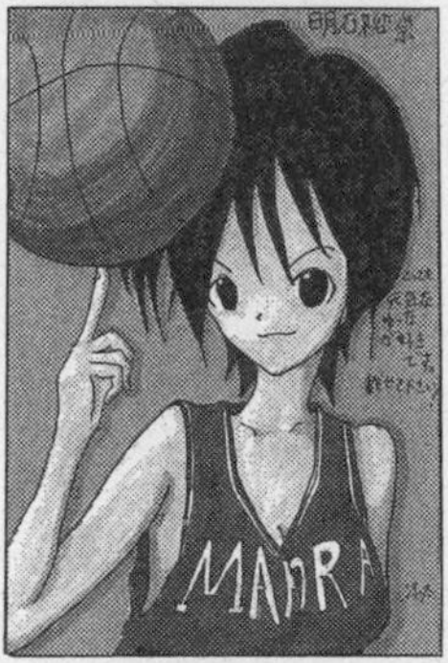
MAHORA

SHE'S COOL AND CUTE IN HER BASKETBALL UNIFORM.

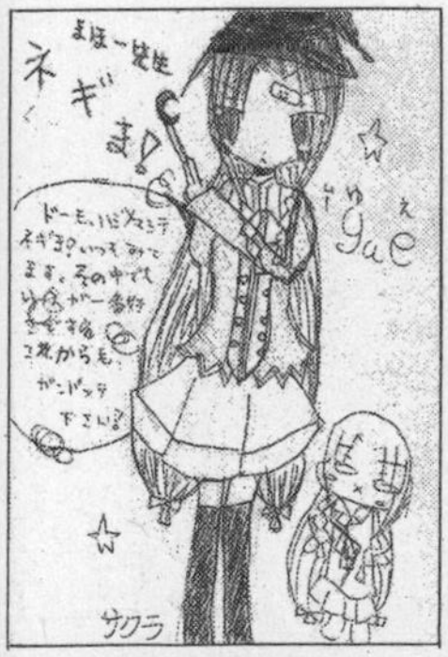
ネギま!

THE BAND-AID IS ADORABLE.

MAGISTER NEGI MAGI

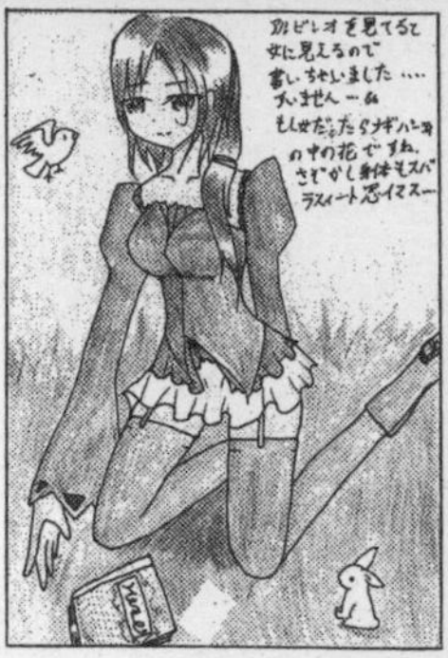

YUNA

▲ A FEMALE KŪ:NEL. (LAUGH)

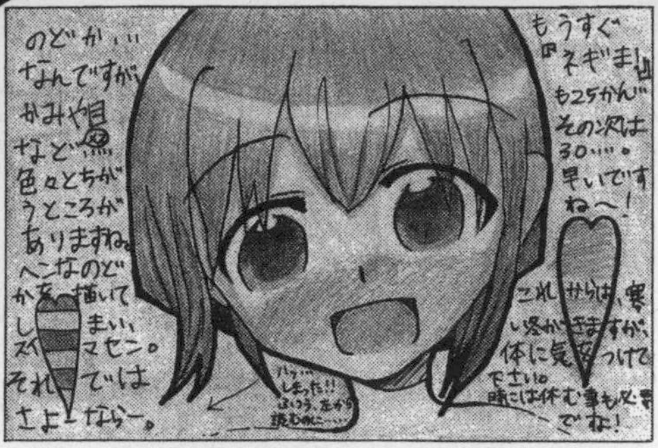

もうすぐ『ネギま!』も25かんで

▲ WHAT A BIG SMILE!

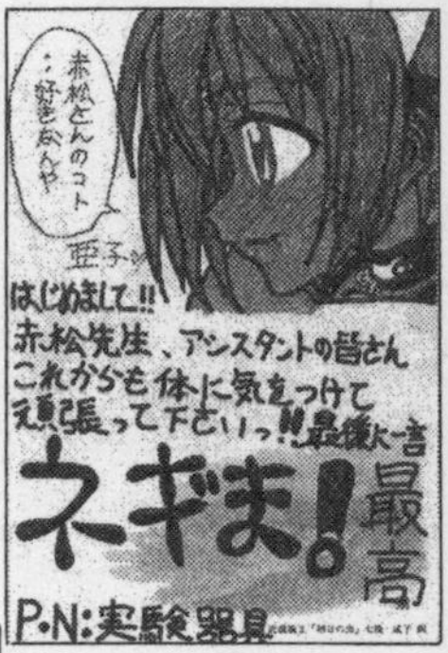

亜子
はじめまして!!
赤松先生、アシスタントの皆さん
これからも体に気をつけて
頑張って下さいっ!!最後に一言
ネギま!最高
P・N:実験器具

▲ NICE DRAWING.

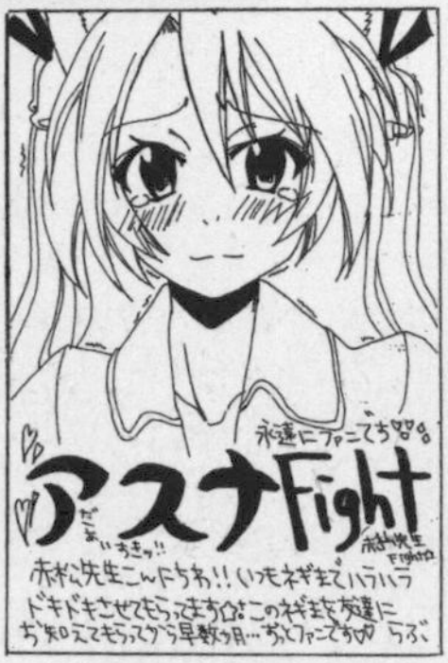

永遠にファンです。
アスナFight
赤松先生こんにちわ!!

▲ HER FEELINGS ARE GOING TO OVERFLOW.

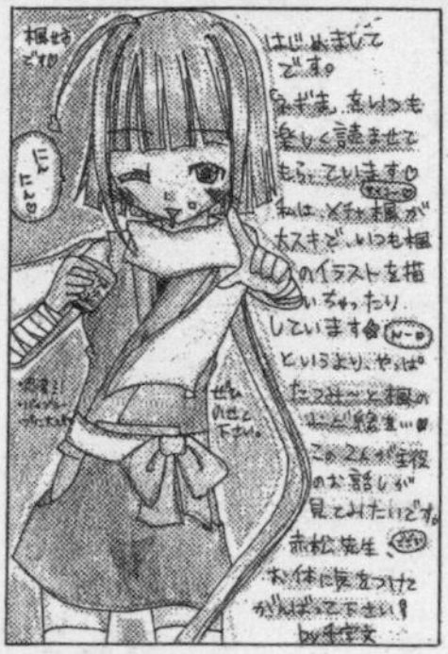

▲ KAEDE'S GOTTEN MORE POPULAR LATELY.

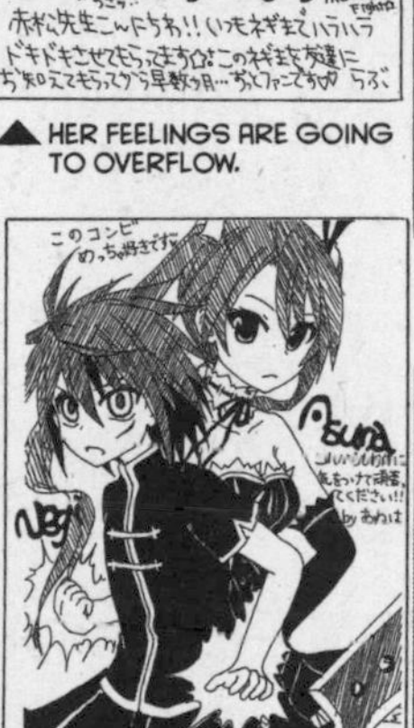

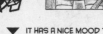

Asuna
NEGI

▲ THEY LOOK IN SYNC♪

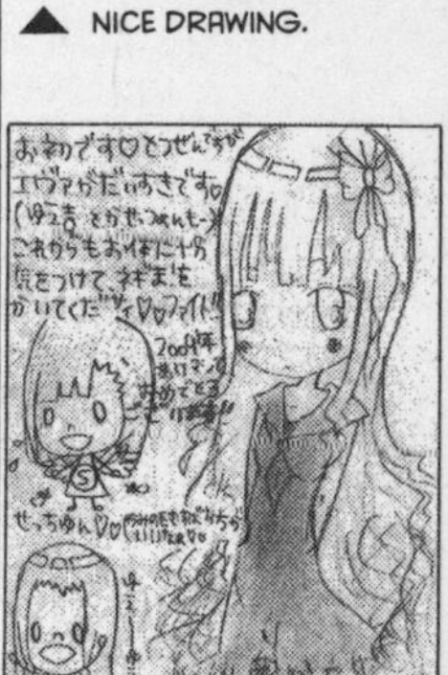

▲ IT'S A GIRLY EVA. I LIKE IT.

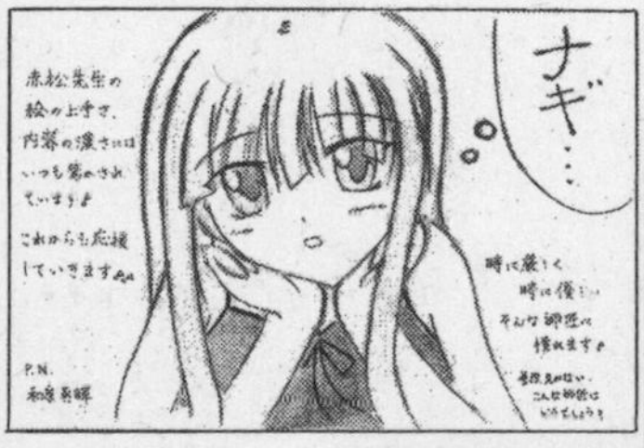

ナギ…

▼ IT HAS A NICE MOOD TO IT.

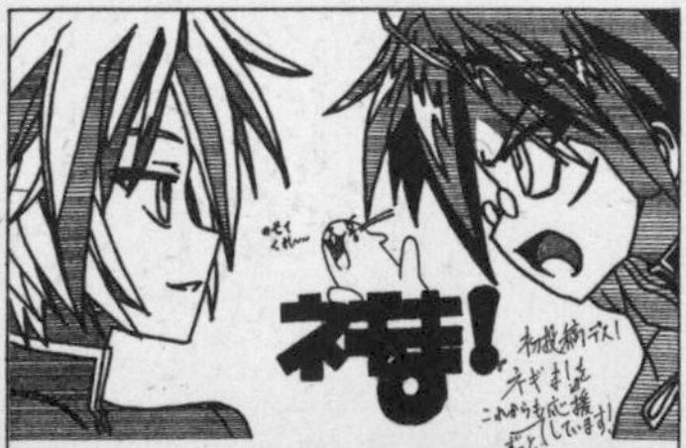

ネギま!

◀ A MANLY PAIR.

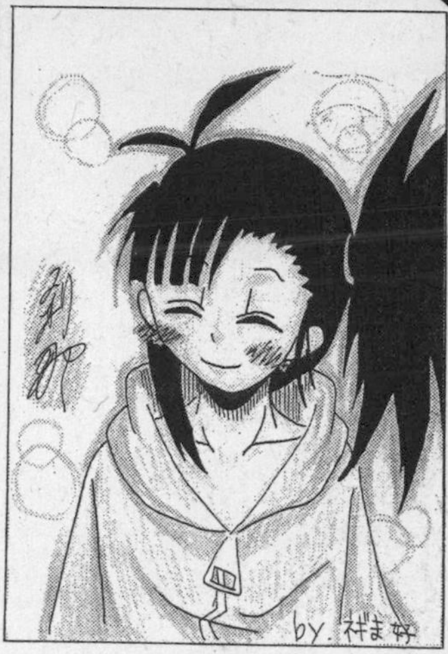

by.

L-LIKE A BODHISATTVA, A BUDDHIST SAINT. ▶

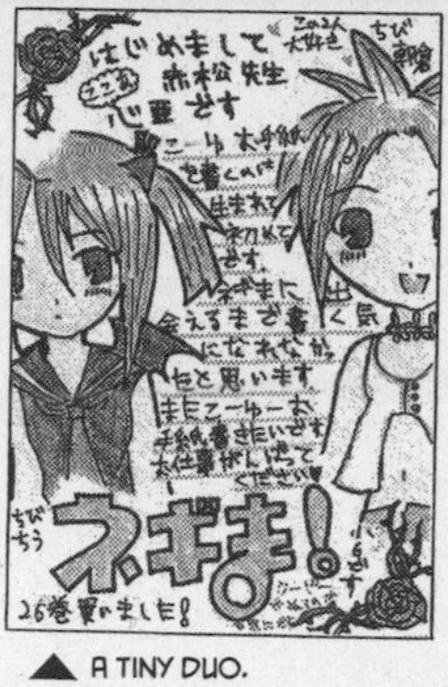

はじめまして
赤松先生
ネギま!
26巻買いました!

▲ A TINY DUO.

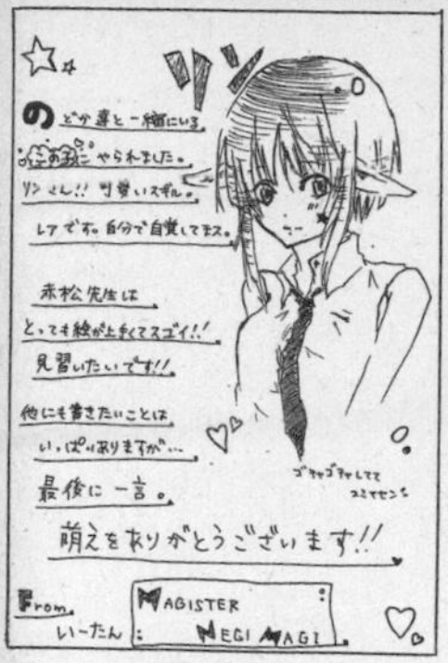

リン
リンさん!! 可愛いスギル。
赤松先生は
とっても絵が上手くてスゴイ!!
見習いたいです!!
他にも書きたいことは、
いっぱいありますが…
最後に一言。
萌えをありがとうございます!!
From.
いーたん
MAGISTER
NEGI MAGI

▲ IT'S TRUE; LYNN IS CUTE.

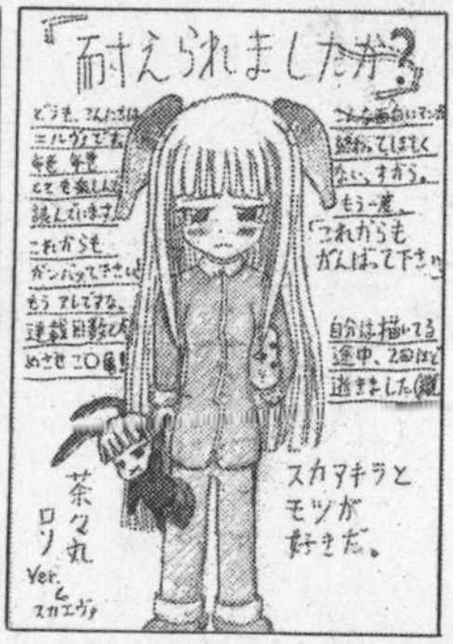

耐えられましたか?

◀ HOW LOL.

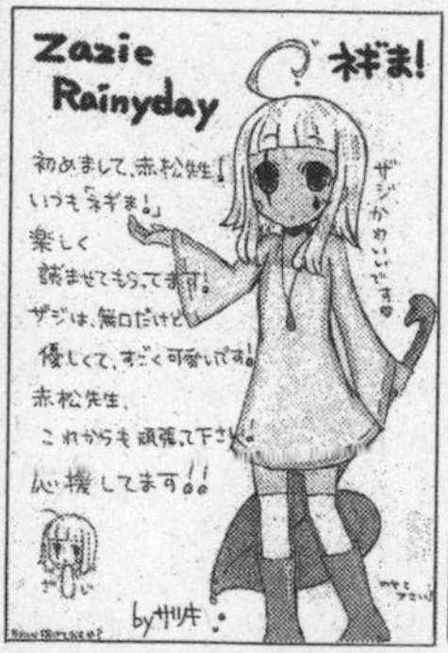

Zazie
Rainyday
ネギま!
初めまして、赤松先生!
いつも「ネギま!」
楽しく
読ませてもらってます!
ザジは、無口だけど
優しくて、すごく可愛いです!
赤松先生、
これからも頑張って下さい!
応援してます!!
byサツキ

▲ THIS ZAZIE IS SOOOO CUUUTE☆

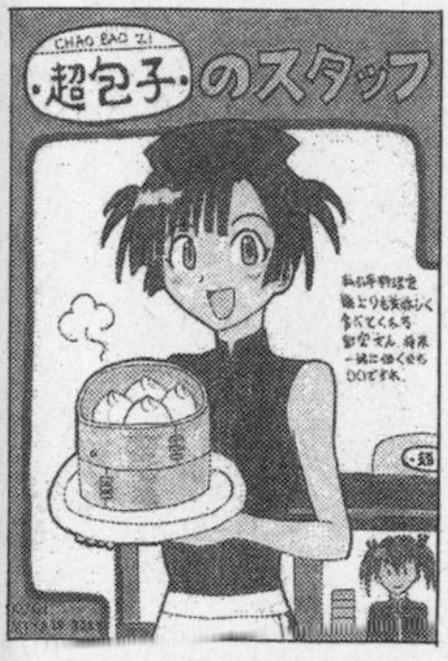

CHAO BAO ZI
・超包子・のスタッフ

▲ LOOKS DELICIOUS☆

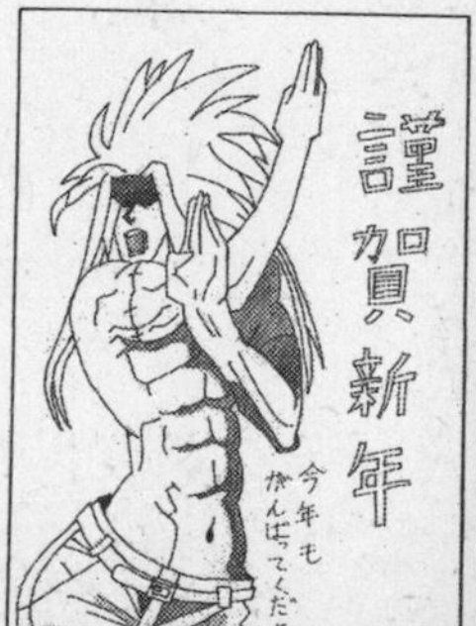

謹賀新年
今年もがんばってください

THIS ONE'S GOOD. ▶

▼ A SEXY♪ ASUNA (^^)

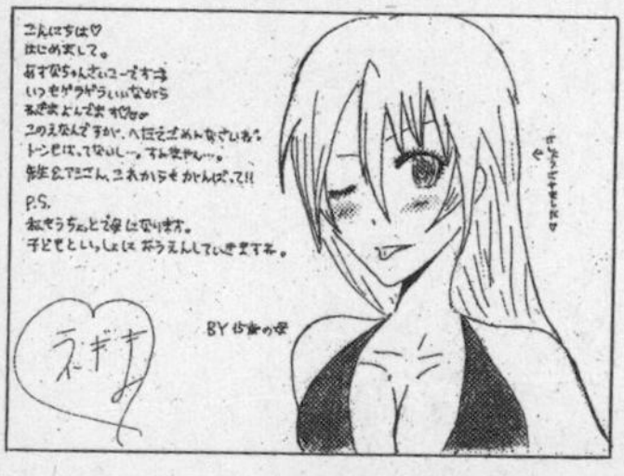

ネギま

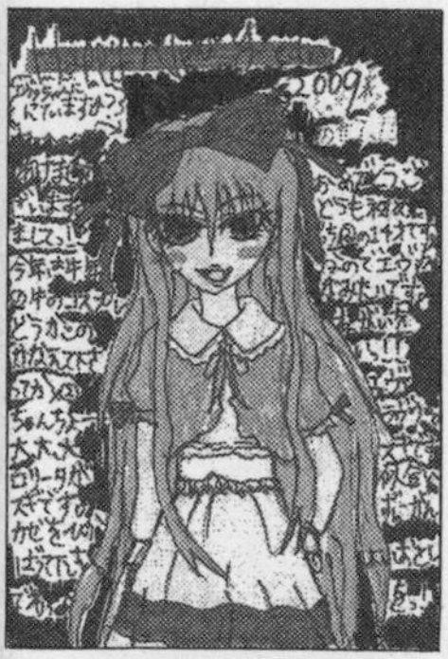

▲ THE RIBBON LEAVES A BIG IMPRESSION.

NEGI MA!

THIS VOLUME'S
FEATURED CHARACTER
FATE AVERRUNCUS
RANKING

FIRST PLACE ▶

「世界を救う」

一生ついていこうと思った…(ﾉ∀`)
フェイトには萌えようぞをまにさいなのでは?!!

フェイト・アーウェルンクス

あけましておめでとうございます!!
前をみつめて、現実を受け入れるフェイトが
大好きです♡ 25巻もフェイトがたあーくさんかつやく
してくれるコトをねがっています♡
2009年もがんばってネギま!かいて下さい♡ P.N さかえり

APPARENTLY THE FATE GIRLS (THOSE FIVE GIRLS) WANT TO FOLLOW HIM FOR THE REST OF THEIR LIVES, LIKE YOU DO. (LAUGH) HE SURE IS POPULAR (^^;)

(AKAMATSU)

IF YOU LIKE THEM BOTH, THEN HOW ABOUT A FATE X NAGI PAIRING? (LAUGH) (HUH? WOULD IT BE NAGI X FATE?)

フェイト

アーウェルンクス
By 雅歩

フェイト最強ーーー!
大人(!?)フェイトも
めっちゃカッコイイです♡
櫥れましたww
私はフェイトを応援
します←(笑)

THIRD PLACE

ネギま!

お姫様を
渡して
もらおう

どうだ…?

フェイト・
アーウェルンクス

P.N てぃはる

はじめまして、赤松先生!!。いっつも
ネギま!楽しく読ませてもらってます♪前
まではナギとか好きだったんですが、この
24巻、この一言でフェイトにおちてしまいました♡
めっちゃかっこいいです♡ 女の子では、アスナ
とかセツナ、このふたりが好きです!本当、はやく
アスナの過去が知りたいです♡(次巻持ちどおしい♡)
では、お体に気をつけてずっと応援してます!!!

SECOND PLACE

I BET AKIRA ISHIDA-SAN'S VOICE WOULD WORK EVEN BETTER FOR ADULT FATE!

LEXICON NEGIMARIUM

[*Negima!* 232nd Period Lexicon Negimarium]

■ "Strongest Protection"

(kratistê aigis)
(ΚΡΑ'ΤΙΣΤΗ ' ΑΙΓΙ'Σ)

A spell that creates multiple wide-range magic circles equipped with extremely powerful anti-physical and anti-magical defense. It is extremely high-level magic, so the spell is incanted in Ancient Greek. The wind defense spell that Negi uses is derived from the defense magic with the *aigis* name used by Nagi's master Zecht. This is because it is believed that the true nature of *aigis* (αἰγίς, "aegis" in Latin and English) is a power that makes up storms and weather.

κράτιστη (kratistê) is the superlative feminine singular nominative case of the adjective κρατύ (kratu), meaning "strong." And—according to dictionaries such as Oxford's Liddell & Scott—it is the shield of the king of the gods, Zeus, as well as Athena, in Greek mythology. However, it is commonly accepted in modern studies of the classics that the *aigis* is not a shield. According to the legendary poet Homer (8C BC?), the *aigis* takes the following form:

"Meanwhile, Athena, daughter of *aigis*-bearing Zeus (...) placed the dreaded tasseled *aigis* about her shoulders. All around, the *aigis* was wrapped in fear, and in its center (...) was affixed the dreaded ill omen of the Gorgon's head, terrible to look upon, portent of the *aigis*-bearing Zeus." (The *Iliad*, 5.733-742)

Take note that Athena wrapped the aigis around her shoulders. The passage does not depict the equipping of a shield. The interpretation that the *aigis* is a shield comes from the depiction of the Gorgon's head being affixed to its center. For example, as written in Apollodorus' (1C BC) record, "[Perseus] (...) gave the Gorgon's head to Athena. Then (...) Athena placed the Gorgon's head in the center of the shield (αἰγίς)," (*Bibliotheca [Βιβλιοθήκη]*, 2,4,3), there was a myth in Ancient Greece in which the hero Perseus slays one of the three Gorgon sisters, the goddess Athena accepts her head, and places it on her shield. Based on this myth, one can logically come to the conclusion that the *aigis* is the shield with the Gorgon's head affixed onto it.

However, the Father of History, Herodotus (5C BC?), leaves the following record: "The Greeks used the dress of Libyan women as the basis for the clothing and *aigis* of the statue of Athena. This is determined because everything is fashioned in the same manner, excepting that Libyan women's clothing is made of leather, and their tassels are of leather cords and not of snakes. The name, too, is evidence that the attire of the Athena statue came from Libya. Libyan women wear over their clothes an *aigea*

(αἰγέα), or goatskin with the hair plucked, decorated with tassels, and dyed red. The Greeks took the name *aigis* from this *aigea*." (*The Histories,* 4.189)

Herodotus' linguistic theory here is mistaken. Nevertheless, his record of the Athena statue's attire was written at the time of its construction, and there is no room for doubt. Thus, the *aigis* is of course nothing like a shield, nor is it anything resembling armor.

The *aigis* is in the form of a cloak worn over one's clothing. Also, according to Herodotus' record, the *aigis* worn by the Athena statue had tassel decorations in the shape of snakes. This coincides with Homer's poem describing the *aigis* as being decorated by the Gorgon's head.

The reason such a cloak would be a priceless treasure in battle is that the *aigis* had the Gorgon's head affixed to it. Various archaeological research lends credence to this fact. For example, in a mosaic found at the Pompeii excavation site in Italy (now in the Naples National Archaeological Museum), the Gorgon's head was depicted on the breast of Alexander the Great at the Battle of Issus. From these evidences, we see that the Gorgon is no mere monster. The Gorgon is a guardian deity in a grotesque form. This is a commonality with the gargoyles of Europe and the *onigawara* of Japan, who ward off evil despite their monstrous appearances.

The name of the Gorgon slain by Perseus and offered to Athena is Medusa. The name Medusa (Μέδουσα) is the present participle active aspect of the feminine singular form of the verb μέδειν (medein, to protect) and means "protector." As the name suggests, the Gorgon's head placed on the *aigis* has the power of a protective charm. The basic-level superstitious practice of wearing a grotesque Gorgon as a protective charm came first, and it was from this practice that the statue of armed Athena came to be ornamented with a Gorgon. This begs the question: Why would a statue of Athena wear a Gorgon? The myth that Medusa had offended Athena and was changed into an ugly creature was born later, in answer to that question (e.g., *Metamorphoses* 4.791–804). Thus, Medusa would have had a terrifying appearance even before the myth was created. This is because if she were not grotesque, she could not serve as a guardian deity, or a "protector (Medusa)."

There is suspicion that Athena is associated with the *aigis* imbued with the Gorgon's magic, because of the popularity of the myth about Perseus slaying Medusa. However, the *aigis* originally belonged to Zeus. This is expressed in the epithets (ἐπίθετον) characteristic of Ancient Greek literary works. For example, Zeus is called "Zeus the *aigis*-bearing (αἰγίοχον, *aigiochon*), son of Kronos" (*The Iliad,* 2.375), and the epithet "*aigis*-bearing" is attached to Zeus, but never to Athena (Athena's epithets are "bright-eyed," etc.). Zeus' other epithets include "high-thundering" (ibid. 1.354), "cloud-gatherer" (ibid. 1.511), "lightning-wielder" (ibid. 1.580), and "loud-thundering" (ibid. 5.672), all fitting of a god who controls storms and weather. That being the case, we can guess that the epithet "*aigis*-bearing" also refers to phenomena relating to weather. The works of Aeschylus (525/524–456/455 BC), one of the three great Greek tragedians, provide the following:

"Indeed, the land nurtures a multitude of terrible things, of pains of fear. Both hands of the sea are filled with defiant beasts. The burning light hung

in the sky approaches. Those with wings, those who walk the earth, all tell of the blowing rage of the *aigis*" (*The Libation Bearers*, 585–593).

The "rage of the *aigis*" is described as "blowing" (ἠνεμόεν). In other words, the rage of the *aigis* is a violent storm. Birds and other animals are all sensitive to changes in the weather. That is exactly why it is said that they can tell us of the rage of the *aigis*—the arrival of a storm. Thus, the "burning light hung in the sky" mentioned before would be flashes of lightning (though some interpret it as a falling star). Based on these examples, the *aigis* refers to something like the power of the weather, which takes the form of a storm when enraged. It is extremely appropriate that Zeus, the god of storms and weather, would have the epithet of "*aigis*-bearer."

That being the case, the Gorgon, who lends her magic to the *aigis*, would have a strong connection to the power of storms and weather. In *The Iliad*, cited above, the Gorgon's head is described as a "portent of Zeus." The Gorgon and Zeus are connected through the medium of the *aigis* symbol. We can also see this in the myth about Pegasus. "When Perseus cut off the head [of Medusa], from her neck (...) sprung the horse Pegasus. (...) And Pegasus leapt from the earth and flew to the immortal gods. He now carries the thunder and lightning to the wise Zeus and lives in Zeus' palace." (Hesiod's *Theogony*, 280–286)

According to Hesiod, Pegasus was born from the neck of the Gorgon, Medusa. And this Pegasus fulfills the duty of carrying Zeus' lightning. In fact, the word "pegasus" is said to come from "*pihassas*," a word from Luwian, one of the Indo-European Anatolian languages, meaning "lightning." Like the Zeus-*Aigis*-Gorgon formula, the Zeus-Pegasus-Gorgon formula, too, connects the Gorgon to Zeus.

[*Negima!* 234th Period Lexicon Negimarium]

■ Life-Stealing Signet

(signum biolegens)

The girl known as Shiori is awarded this item for her use by the power of the pactio with the white-haired boy. Through the sharing of a kiss with a human or humanoid life-form, it reconstructs the target's physical and mental characteristics inside the body and actions of the user.

Signum is Latin for "mark" or "symbol" (the origin of the English "sign"); "biolegens" is an adjective formed from a combination of the Ancient Greek βίος (bios), meaning "life," and the Latin *legere*, meaning "to read," and means "life-stealing." The word *legere* means "to read," but also means "to steal." This artifact steals the target's life (βίος) through a kiss.

[*Negima!* 236th Period Lexicon Negimarium]

■ "Water Spirit's Great Deluge"

(MAGNA CATARACTA)

Magic that produces a large quantity of water. It can quench the thirst of many living things. When generating water from a high place, the potential energy of the great mass will cause great destruction where the water lands, so use with care.

■ "Water Current Barrier"

(UNDANS PARIES AQUARIUS)

It is normal for a wizard to surround himself with a magical wall to protect himself from physical damage. That is why, in First Period, the blackboard eraser that fell on Negi's head floated in the air.

"Undans paries aquarius" means "wall of surging water" in Latin and is a barrier spell in the same category as "flans paries aerialis," which means "wall of blowing air." Both have enough defensive power to guard against the impact of a ten-ton truck. "Water Current Barrier" is also excellent against heat and dryness.

[*Negima!* 238th Period Lexicon Negimarium]

■ "Upon our pact, do my bidding, O Lord of the Heavens. Come forth, blazing bolts that overthrow Titans. Let hundreds and thousands combine; run forth, lightning. Thousand Lightning Bolts."

(To symbolaion diakonêtô moi basileu Ouraniônôn. Epigenêthêtô aithalous keraune os Titênas phtheirein. Êcatontakis kai kiliakis astrapsatô. KILIPL ASTRAPÊ)

Nagi used this superwide-range lightning annihilation magic back in *Negima!* volume 19, 169th Period. The spell is incanted in Ancient Greek. The full incantation appeared in the 238th Period, so it is now being listed here.

■ "Spread forth, extended aide magic circle. Capture targets one through ten. Lock on. Increase spirit pressure inside range to maximum. 3...2...critical pressure. Remove restraints. All lightning spirits, release full power."

(jactum extendentes circuli existant, captent objecta primum ad decimum. area constet. intus se premant spiritus ad pressuram criticalem. tribus...duobus...modo. capturam disjungens. omnes spiritus fulgurales fortissime emittam.)

A spell that generates a magic circle that expands and corrects the distance and effective range of magical abilities used in the physical world. In the story, Negi's Kilipl Astrapê (Thousand Lightning Bolts) was incomplete, so he demonstrated near-perfect results through the use of a support spell.

3-D BACKGROUNDS EXPLANATION CORNER

THIS TIME WE'RE CHANGING THE IDEA A BIT AND TALKING ABOUT THE PRACTICAL APPLICATIONS OF 3D CG.

LATELY, 3D BACKGROUNDS HAVE BEEN INCREASING LITTLE BY LITTLE, AND THIS TIME I WILL TALK ABOUT MAKING FINISHING TOUCHES WITH CG. I HAD BEEN CREATING LINE DRAWINGS FOR SOME OF THE *NEGIMA!* BACKGROUNDS WITH CG FOR SOME TIME NOW, BUT I HAD BEEN FINISHING THEM UP, AS ALWAYS, WITH THE OLD-FASHIONED, NON-DIGITAL TECHNIQUES OF SPREADING SCREENTONE ON THOSE LINE DRAWINGS. BUT WHEN THE BACKGROUNDS ARE MADE WITH 3D GRAPHICS, THEN SOMETIMES IT'S MORE CONVENIENT TO FINISH THEM UP WITH COMPUTER GRAPHICS, TOO, SO RECENTLY THE CG TOUCH-UPS HAVE BEEN GRADUALLY INCREASING. NOW I WOULD LIKE TO EXPLAIN THE TECHNIQUES FOR COMBINING THE 3D BACKGROUNDS WITH CG FINISHING TOUCHES.

- CASE 1: DROPPING SHADOWS -

I INTRODUCED THIS METHOD BEFORE, BUT THIS TIME, I WOULD LIKE TO GO THROUGH THE PROCESS STEP BY STEP. 3D GRAPHIC SOFTWARE HAS A FUNCTION THAT ALLOWS YOU TO SET A LIGHT SOURCE, THEN CALCULATES WHERE THE OBJECTS' SHADOWS WOULD FALL, AND WITH IT, WE CAN DROP SHADOWS ACCURATELY AND EASILY. NOW THEN, LET'S TAKE A LOOK AT THE PROCESS USING A SPECIFIC EXAMPLE.

• GRAVE KEEPER'S PALACE

SCENE NAME: DARK PALACE   POLYGON COUNT: 32,925

THE SCENE OF THE FINAL BATTLE BETWEEN NAGI'S PARTY AND THE BIG BOSS (MAGE OF THE BEGINNING). THE LINE DRAWING IS 3D, OF COURSE, BUT THERE WAS A NEED FOR REALISTIC SHADOWS, SO THEY WERE MADE IN 3D, TOO. I USED PHOTOSHOP FOR THE FINISHING TOUCHES, MAKING THEM CG AS WELL.

- STEP 1: CREATING THE LINE DRAWING -

FIRST, I CREATE THE LINES FOR THE 3D SECTIONS. THIS IS THE SAME AS ALWAYS.

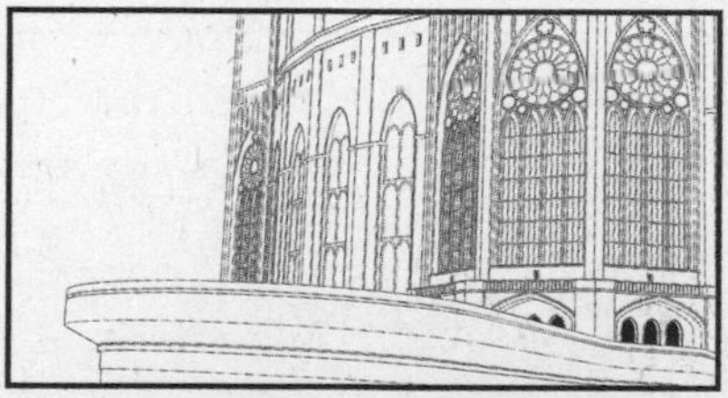

- STEP 2: CREATING THE SHADOW IMAGES -

NEXT, I MAKE THE IMAGE FOR THE SHADOWS SEPARATELY FROM THE LINE DRAWING. I DO MORE BRIGHTNESS ADJUSTING IN PHOTOSHOP, SO THIS IMAGE IS TEMPORARY.

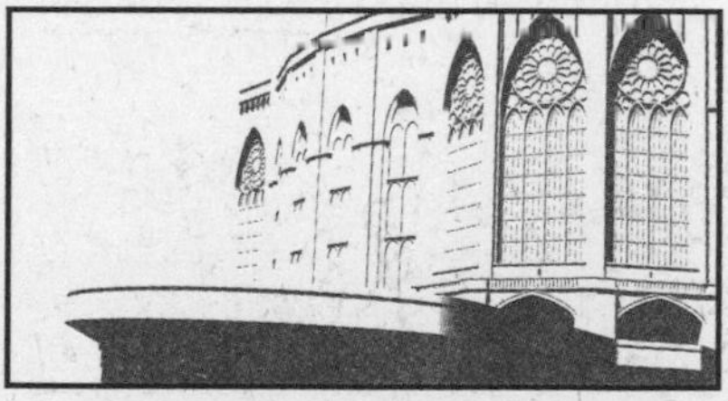

- STEP 3: ADJUSTING THE SHADOW BRIGHTNESS -

HERE, I MADE THE SHADOWS BLACK TO CREATE A SENSE OF TENSION. WHEN I COMBINE IT WITH THE LINE DRAWING AND HAND-DRAWN ELEMENTS, LIKE THE CHARACTERS, IT LOOKS LIKE THE PICTURE BELOW.

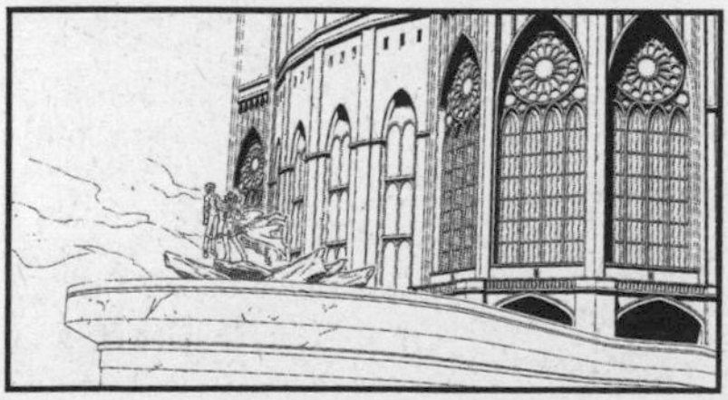

- STEP 4: FINISHING TOUCHES -

I TOUCH UP EVERYTHING ELSE. DROPPING THE SHADOWS IS A SNAP, SO ACTUALLY THIS IS WHERE THE REAL WORK STARTS (^_^;) BELOW IS THE FINISHED DRAWING. CHARACTERS WILL BE ADDED TO THE LOWER RIGHT.

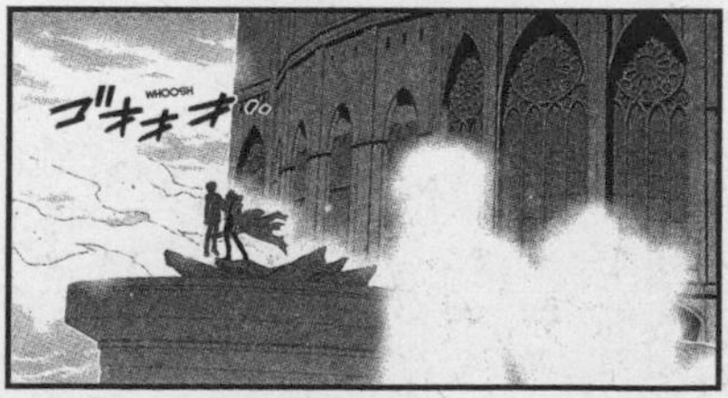
WHOOSH

- CASE 2: BACKGROUND REFLECTIONS -

3D CG SOFTWARE ALSO HAS A FUNCTION TO RE-CREATE THE PHENOMENON OF PICTURES REFLECTING OFF OF SURFACES SUCH AS WATER. THIS PHENOMENON IS VERY DIFFICULT TO REPRODUCE ACCURATELY BY HAND, BUT WITH 3D CG, IT'S SIMPLE. NOW THEN, I HAVE AN EXAMPLE REPRESENTING THE USE OF THAT TECHNIQUE, SO I WILL PROVIDE IT HERE.

• OSTIA'S BRICK BRIDGE

SCENE NAME: BRICK BRIDGE   POLYGON COUNT: 862,826

THIS IS THE PART OF OSTIA WHERE NEGI AND FATE HAVE THEIR STREET FIGHT IN VOLUME 25. I HAD A REQUEST TO MAKE THE WATER SURFACE IN THIS PANEL REALISTIC, SO I USED 3D CG TO RE-CREATE THE REFLECTION OF THE TOWN AND THE BRIDGE ON THE WATER.

- STEP 1: CREATING THE LINE DRAWING -

FIRST, I CREATE THE 3D LINE DRAWING. I MAKE ADJUSTMENTS USING PHOTOSHOP.

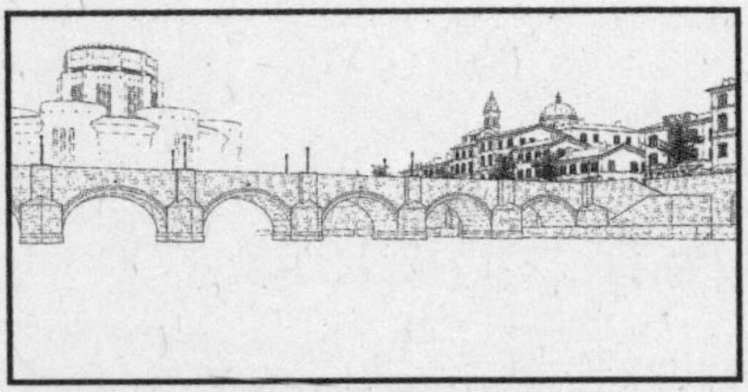

- STEP 2: CREATING THE REFLECTED IMAGE -

I CREATE A PICTURE TO BE USED FOR THE REFLECTION. SHADOWS ARE ADDED AS WELL. BUT THE WATER SURFACE IN THIS PICTURE IS TOO REAL, AND NOT VERY MANGA-LIKE, SO I ADJUST IT FROM HERE.

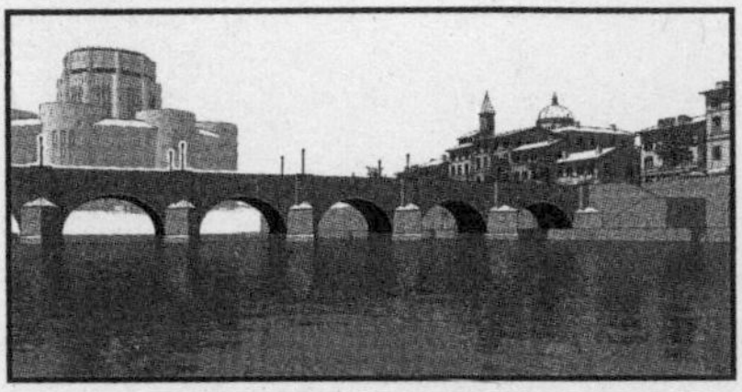

- STEP 3: CORRECTING COLOR TONE IN PHOTOSHOP -

I USE THE COLOR CORRECTION FUNCTION TO DECREASE THE NUMBER OF COLORS ON THE WATER'S SURFACE, SIMPLIFYING IT. BUT IT'S STILL REALISTIC, RIGHT? FROM HERE, I FIX IT BY HAND.

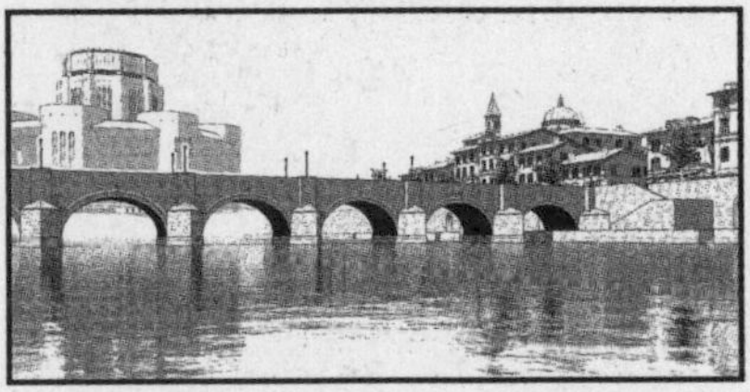

- STEP 4: ALTERING THE SHAPE -

I BLOT OUT THE PARTS WITH TOO MUCH DETAIL AND MAKE THEM MORE VAGUE. I STILL FEEL LIKE IT'S TOO REALISTIC, BUT THIS TIME WE'LL SAY IT'S GOOD ENOUGH...

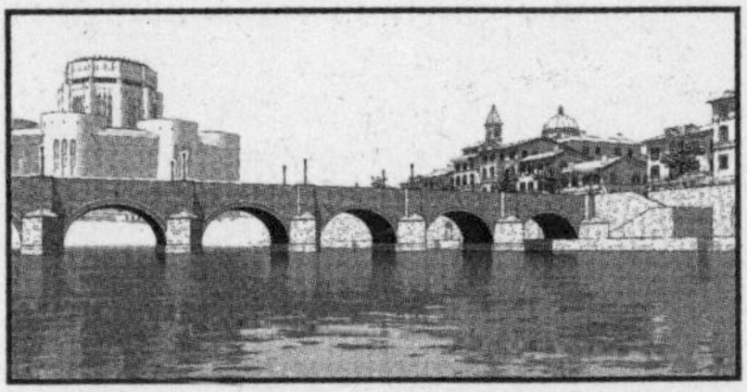

- STEP 5: TOUCHING UP THE WATER'S SURFACE -

I PUT THE CHARACTERS IN THE PICTURE AND ADD THEIR REFLECTIONS BY HAND. I ADD SOME MORE FLAVOR WITH DETAILS LIKE THE SHADOWS UNDER THE BRIDGE, THE RIPPLES, AND OTHER TONE-ERASING EFFECTS, AND THE WATER'S SURFACE IS COMPLETE.

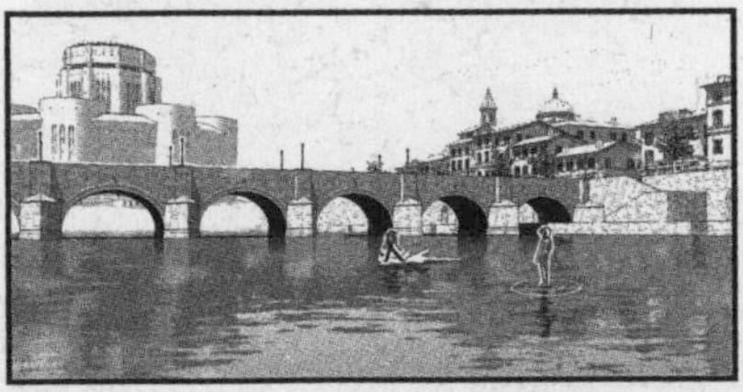

- STEP 6: TOUCHING UP EVERYTHING ELSE -

I FINISH UP THE TOWN, THE SKY, AND EVERYTHING ELSE. I GET THE FEELING THEY DON'T QUITE BLEND WITH THE WATER, BUT WE'LL MAKE THAT OUR ASSIGNMENT FOR NEXT TIME (^_^;) AT ANY RATE, IT'S COMPLETE.

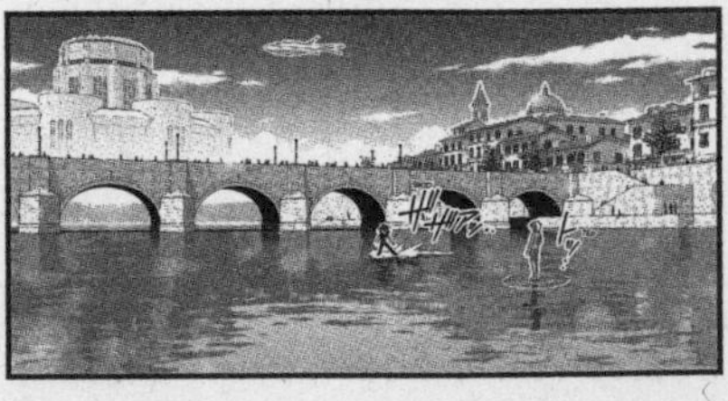

魔法先生

ネギま!

MAGISTER NEGI MAGI

赤松 健 SHONEN MAGAZINE COMICS
KEN AKAMATSU

26

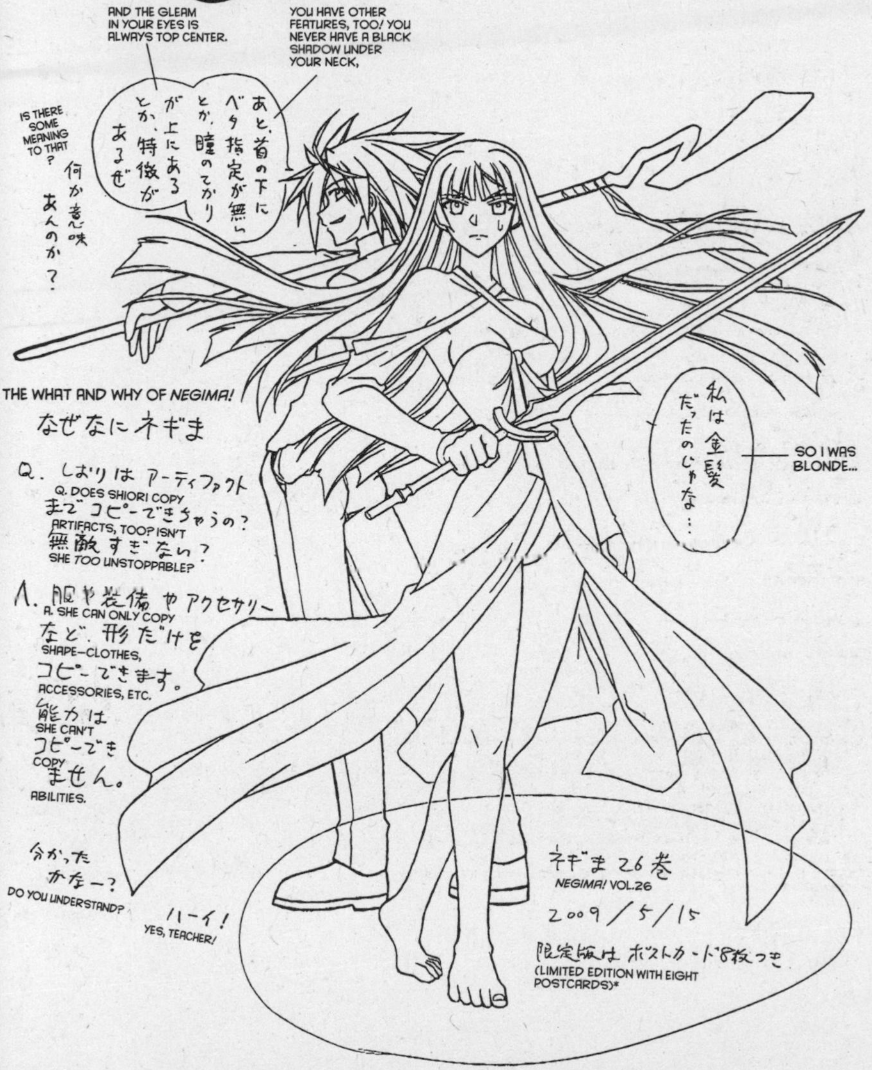

あと、首の下にベタ指定が無いとか、瞳のてかりが上にあるとか、特徴があるぜ
YOU HAVE OTHER FEATURES, TOO! YOU NEVER HAVE A BLACK SHADOW UNDER YOUR NECK,
AND THE GLEAM IN YOUR EYES IS ALWAYS TOP CENTER.
何か意味あんのか?
IS THERE SOME MEANING TO THAT?
私は金髪だったのじゃな…
SO I WAS BLONDE...
THE WHAT AND WHY OF *NEGIMA!*
なぜなにネギま
Q. しおりはアーティファクトまでコピーできちゃうの? 無敵すぎない?
Q. DOES SHIORI COPY ARTIFACTS, TOO? ISN'T SHE *TOO* UNSTOPPABLE?
A. 服や装備やアクセサリーなど、形だけをコピーできます。能力はコピーできません。
A. SHE CAN ONLY COPY SHAPE—CLOTHES, ACCESSORIES, ETC. SHE CAN'T COPY ABILITIES.
分かったかなー?
DO YOU UNDERSTAND?
ハーイ!
YES, TEACHER!
ネギま26巻
NEGIMA! VOL.26
2009/5/15
限定版はポストカード8枚つき
(LIMITED EDITION WITH EIGHT POSTCARDS)*

*LIMITED EDITION AVAILABLE ONLY IN JAPAN

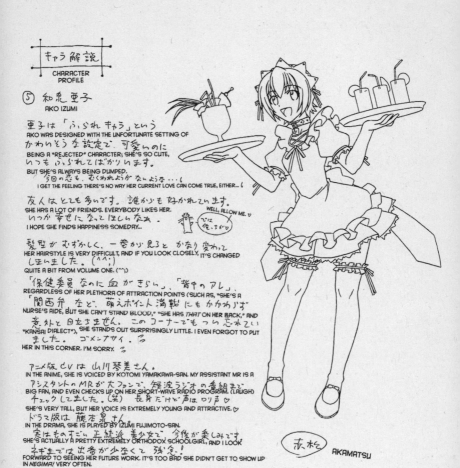

キャラ解説
CHARACTER PROFILE

⑤ 知泉 亜子
AKO IZUMI

亜子は「ふられキャラ」という
AKO WAS DESIGNED WITH THE UNFORTUNATE SETTING OF
かわいそうな設定で、可愛いのに
BEING A "REJECTED" CHARACTER; SHE'S SO CUTE,
いつも ふられてばかりいます。
BUT SHE'S ALWAYS BEING DUMPED.
今回の恋も、むくわれないがなんとなる…(
I GET THE FEELING THERE'S NO WAY HER CURRENT LOVE CAN COME TRUE, EITHER... (

友人はとても多いです。誰からも好かれています。
SHE HAS A LOT OF FRIENDS. EVERYBODY LIKES HER.
いつか 幸せに なってほしいなあ。
I HOPE SHE FINDS HAPPINESS SOMEDAY...

WELL, ALLOW ME. ♡

髪型がむずかしく、一巻が見ると かなり変わって
HER HAIRSTYLE IS VERY DIFFICULT, AND IF YOU LOOK CLOSELY, IT'S CHANGED
しまいました。(^^;)
QUITE A BIT FROM VOLUME ONE. (^^)

「保健委員 なのに血がきらい、「背中のアレ」、
REGARDLESS OF HER PLETHORA OF ATTRACTION POINTS (SUCH AS, "SHE'S A
「関西弁 など、萌えポイント満載にもかかわらず
NURSE'S AIDE, BUT SHE CAN'T STAND BLOOD," "SHE HAS THAT ON HER BACK," AND
意外と目立ちません。このコーナーでもつい忘れてい
"KANSAI DIALECT"), SHE STANDS OUT SURPRISINGLY LITTLE. I EVEN FORGOT TO PUT
ました。ゴメンナサイ。
HER IN THIS CORNER. I'M SORRY.

アニメ版 CVは 山川琴美さん。MY ASSISTANT MR IS A
IN THE ANIME, SHE IS VOICED BY KOTOMI YAMAKAWA-SAN. MY ASSISTANT MR IS A
アシスタントのMRが大ファンで、短波ラジオの番組まで
BIG FAN, AND EVEN CHECKS UP ON HER SHORT-WAVE RADIO PROGRAM. (LAUGH)
チェックしてました。(笑) 長身だけど声はロリ声♡
SHE'S VERY TALL, BUT HER VOICE IS EXTREMELY YOUNG AND ATTRACTIVE. ♡
ドラマ版は 藤本泉さん。
IN THE DRAMA, SHE IS PLAYED BY IZUMI FUJIMOTO-SAN.
実はものすごい正統派美少女で、今後が楽しみです
SHE'S ACTUALLY A PRETTY EXTREMELY ORTHODOX SCHOOLGIRL, AND I LOOK
ネギまでは出番が少なくて残念!
FORWARD TO SEEING HER FUTURE WORK. IT'S TOO BAD SHE DIDN'T GET TO SHOW UP
IN NEGIMA! VERY OFTEN.

赤松 AKAMATSU

About the Creator

Negima! is only Ken Akamatsu's third manga, although he started working in the field in 1994 with *AI Ga Tomaranai* (released in the United States with the title *A.I. Love You*). Like all of Akamatsu's work to date, it was published in Kodansha's *Shonen Magazine*. *AI Ga Tomaranai* ran for five years before concluding in 1999. In 1998, however, Akamatsu began the work that would make him one of the most popular manga artists in Japan: *Love Hina*. *Love Hina* ran for four years, and before its conclusion in 2002, it would cause Akamatsu to be granted the prestigious Manga of the Year award from Kodansha, as well as going on to become one of the bestselling manga in the United States.

LEXICON NEGIMARIUM

■ "Thunder in Heaven, Great Vigor"

Ê ASTRAPÊ UPER OURANOU MEGA DUNAMENÊ

(ʿΗ ʾΑΣΤΡΑΠΗ΄ ʾΥΠΕʾΡ ΟΥʾΡΑΝΟʾΥ ΜΕʾΓΑ ΔΥΝΑʹΜΕΝΗ)

One of the practical uses of dark magic, it takes the magic power from "Thousand Lightning Bolts (Kilipl Astrapê)" into one's flesh and fuses it with the spirit. In doing so, the caster becomes a mass of electrically charged particles.

"Thunder in Heaven, Great Vigor" is the aesthetic name of "Great Vigor," one of the hexagrams of I Ching divination. It gets the name because the zhèn (shake) trigram, symbolizing thunder, is placed above the qián (force) trigram, symbolizing heaven. The "Great Vigor" *Hsiang Chuan* of I Ching states, "Thunder is above the heavens, there will be great vigor," and the *T'uan Chuan* states, "Great vigor, greatness is vigor. It moves by means of strength, therefore it is vigor." Thus, the "Great Vigor" hexagram signifies strong, fierce mobility. In keeping with that, ʿΗ ʾΑΣΤΡΑΠΗʾ ʾΥΠΕʾΡ ΟΥʾΡΑΝΟʾΥ ΜΕΓΑ ΔΥΝΑʹΜΕΝΗ [ΕΣΤΙʾΝ] (Ê ASTRAPÊ UPER OURANOU MEGA DUNAMENÊ [ESTIN]) is ancient Greek meaning, "the lightning above heaven is greatly powerful."

Once the caster has become a mass of charged particles, he separates positively charged particles from his body and positions them to create a certain extent of an electrical field. The charged particles and electrical field can be changed at will from a latent state to an active one, and vice versa, by the caster, who has taken the lightning magic into himself. When the electrical field becomes active, its powerful electric potential difference draws the negatively charged particles that make up the caster's body toward the positively charged particles of the field with tremendous force. Thus, the caster can move at high speeds via the electrical discharge (In the story, Chamo says that he travels at 150km per second, because that is the average progression velocity of the advance discharge when lightning strikes. The main lightning strike occurs after the electrical path is opened, so it is even faster. For example, in a simple calculation, to ionize a nitrogen atom, a single electrical particle flying inside a discharge path needs to go at a speed greater than 2,260km/s. Either way, electrical discharge in the atmosphere is controlled by outside conditions such as temperature, pressure, and medium, so we can't expect an accurate figure).

During this time, the negatively charged particles of the caster's body collide with various molecules and atoms in the air, bringing with them tremendous kinetic energy. Because this kinetic energy becomes ionization energy, impact ionization occurs repeatedly along the discharge path followed by the caster, creating an enormous amount of charged particles and sending out giant flashes of lightning.

However, due to the repeated impact ionization, almost all of the negatively charged particles that made up the caster's body combine with the newly generated positively charged particles inside the discharge path. Therefore, the negatively charged particles making up the caster's body can't simply continue to move at high speeds in the direction of the positioned positively charged particles. This magic is not as simple as merely moving with the speed of lightning.

It was first proven that lightning is an electrical discharge in the air by an experiment conducted in 1752 by the American statesman B. Franklin (1706–90), using a kite and an electric condenser.

However, before modern times, lightning was considered to be *fire* in the sky. The ancient Greek philosopher Aristotle (384 BC–322 BC) states: "The compressed breath is frequently burnt by weak, small fire. This is what we call lightning. At the origin of this lightning, it appears just as though the breath has taken on color." (*Meteorologica*, 369B) In the age of mythology, too, lightning was fire. Hesiod (eighth century BC) states, "From his powerful arms sprang several bolts, bringing with them thunder and lightning. Whirling up the sacred flame (ἱερή φλόξ, ieri flox)." (*Theogony*, 690–693) In that case, to put it in magical terms, "becoming a mass of electrically charged particles" means "turning one's body into fire."

Based on this, the spell "Thunder in Heaven, Great Vigor" would be magic that re-creates the caster's body of flesh and blood into a body of fire, changing him into a genie (ينّ‎). We can say this because a genie is an entity that has been given a body of fire. For example, in the *Qur'an*, it is stated, "Which of the blessings of your Lord will you decline? The Lord created man from the dry earth. Just as one creates earthen vessels. And the Lord created the genies from fire." (55:13–15).

Genies are a paranormal life-form famous in Middle Eastern folklore, such as the spirit in the lamp in *Aladdin*. While their bodies are made of burning fire, they never burn out (this is similar to how living things are not injured by their metabolism). By changing into a genie's body like this, even after losing the charged particles (his fire element) from the early stages of the spell, he regenerates by absorbing the charged particles in the discharge path, thus maintaining his body and continuing to exist.

■ "Spell Emission, Complete Lightning Form"
(perfectus plasmationis per emissionem)

A spell that uses all of the electric attacks taken inside the caster to expand the electrical field that was made active through "Thunder in Heaven, Great Vigor (Ê Astrapê Uper Ouranou Mega Dunamenê)." The electric potential difference expanded through this spell becomes extremely large, and the impact ionization generated in the discharge path becomes enormous. The electrical attack from this enormous impact ionization is "Chihayaburu Lightning." *"Chihayaburu"* is an ancient Japanese adjective describing forceful strength. It has been represented in ancient Japanese text with characters such as "千早振 (thousand fast tremors)," "知波夜夫流 (waves of knowledge, night man flow)," etc., but the ones used here, "千磐破 (thousand boulder smash)," are believed to give it the meaning "crushing as many as a thousand boulders."

[*Negima!* 246th Period Lexicon Negimarium]

■ "Shadow Cloth Sevenfold, Anti-Physical Wall"
(umbrae septemplex paries anti-corporalis)

A spell that sets up multiple layers of magical barriers made of shadow to defend against physical attacks.

[*Negima!* 247th Period Lexicon Negimarium]

■ "Left Arm Release Stabilize 'Thousand Thunder Bolts.' Right Arm Release Stabilize 'Thousand Thunder Bolts.' Double Load Magic."
(sinistra emissa stagnet KILIPL ASTRAPÊ. dextra emissa stagnet KILIPL ASTRAPÊ. DUPLEX COMPLEXIO)

A spell that first releases two delayed spells of Thousand Lightning Bolts, then takes them into one's flesh and fuses them with the spirit. It exercises double the power of "Thunder in Heaven, Great Vigor." When "Thunder in Heaven, Great Vigor" is only used once, the caster cannot travel at high speeds via the discharge path until after he has separated the positively charged particles from himself and formed the electrical field. But when exercising two "Thunder in Heaven, Great Vigor" spells, the caster can position a new set of positively charged particles while traveling at high speeds, so he can create his next discharge path while in transit. As he repeatedly secures a discharge path mid-motion, it becomes possible for the caster to constantly travel at high speeds.

■ "Dual Arm Release, Right Arm Stabilize 'Thousand Lightning Bolts,' Left Arm Stabilize 'Throwing Thunder,' Spells Unite. Thunder Deity Spear, 'Titan Slayer.'"

(duabus emissae, dextra stagnans *ΚΙΛΙΠΛ' 'ΑΣΤΡΑΠ'Η*, sinistra stagnans JACULATIO FULGORIS, unisonent. *Διὸς Λόγχη. ΤΙΤΑΝΟ-ΚΤ'ΟΝΟΝ.*)

A spell that releases the delayed spells, "Thousand Lightning Bolts" and "Throwing Thunder," and breathes the enormous magical power from "Thousand Lightning Bolts" into the magic spear created by "Throwing Thunder," creating a gigantic thunder spear. Because it focuses the power of super-wide-range extermination lightning magic into a single point, the sparks created by a direct attack from the spear are limitlessly intense.

■ "Spell Thaw. Negi-style Dark Magic. 'Enemy Spell Absorption Circle.'"

(agite extractio. Negica Magia Erebea. CIRCULI ABSOPTIONES.)

A spell that draws out a magical-power-absorbing circle that had been drawn and hidden beforehand. The circle that absorbs the magical power is joined directly to Negi's body and soul. For that reason, the magic (or chi energy) absorbed by the circle is activated by dark magic.

[*Negima!* 248th Period Lexicon Negimarium]

■ "The Great Birth Canal"

(sinus magnus)

In Latin, "sinus magnus" means "great birth canal." The birth canal is the path to the great womb, through which life is born and to which life returns. Like the dolmens in Ireland and the tortoise-shell tombs in Okinawa, the tombs seen in various regions are modeled after the womb and birth canal. This is because they were considered to be part of the refrain in which one returns to the source of life through death and is born again. The process of death and rebirth, in which the caster takes the phenomena before his eyes into the bosom of death and gives new life to them is the deepest secret of dark magic.

■ "Release, Thunder Deity Spear, Bring Thousand Thunder Bolts"

(emittens, dios lonchi, KILIPLÊN ASTRAPÊN producam)

The spell that releases the "Thousand Lightning Bolts" electrical attack breathed into the magic spear created by the fusion of "Throwing Thunder" and "Thousand Lightning Bolts."

NEGIMA!
FAN ART CORNER

HELLO, HELLO! I FEEL LIKE THERE WERE A LOT OF KIND OF INTENSE DRAWINGS THIS TIME (IMPRESSED). (^^)♪ OF COURSE I MEAN THAT IN A GOOD WAY (LAUGH). STILL, SETSUNA SURE IS POPULAR, HUH? (LAUGH) WELL, LET'S TAKE A LOOK. ☆

TEXT BY MAX

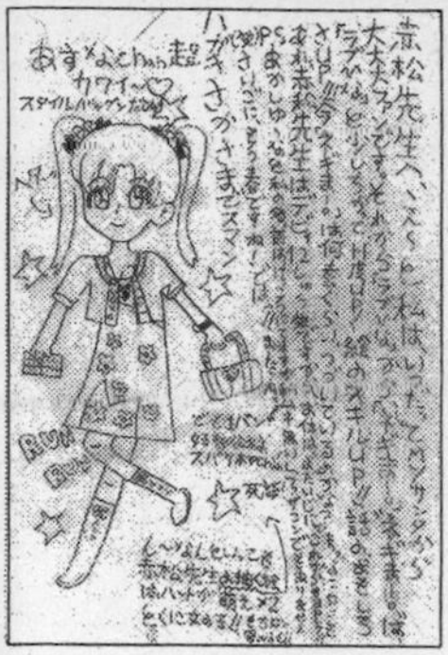

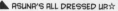

▲ ASUNA'S ALL DRESSED UP.☆

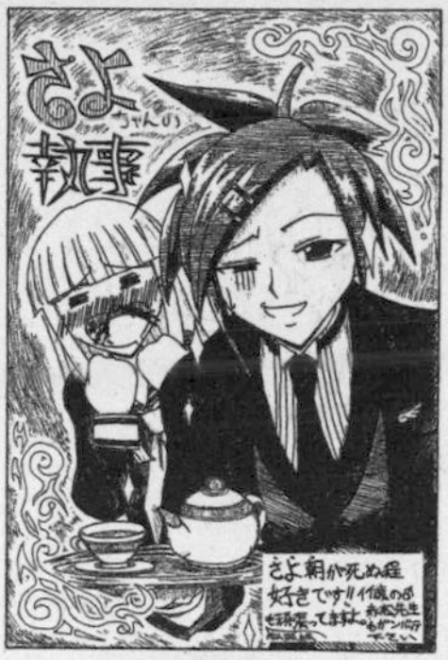

▲ HANDSOME! KAZUMI ☆

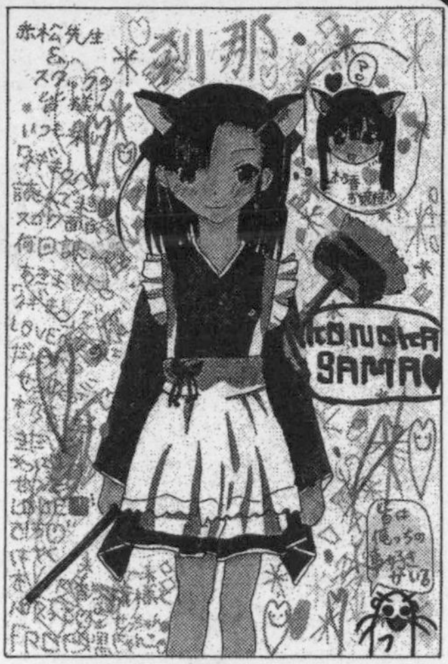

I FEEL HOW OVERFLOWING WITH LOVE IT IS. ▶

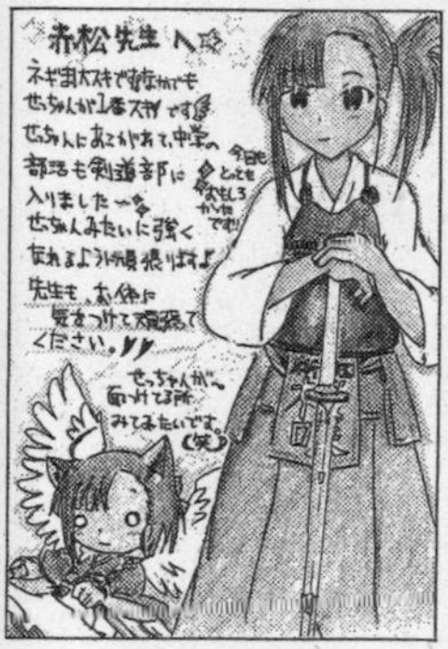

▲ SHE LOOKS SO GALLANT.☆

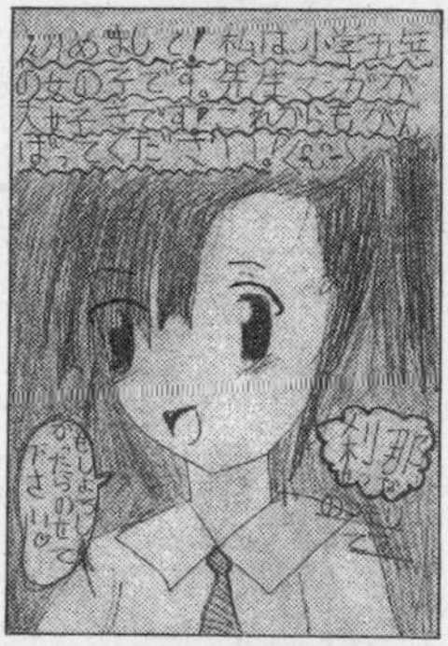

▶ SUCH A KIND-LOOKING SETSUNA.

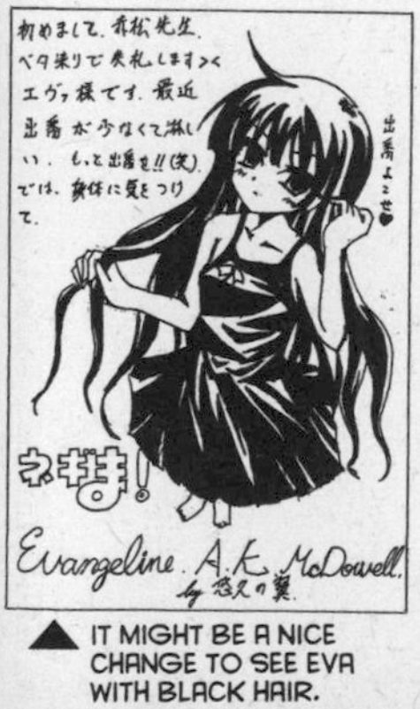
ネギま!
Evangeline. A.K. McDowell.

▲ IT MIGHT BE A NICE CHANGE TO SEE EVA WITH BLACK HAIR.

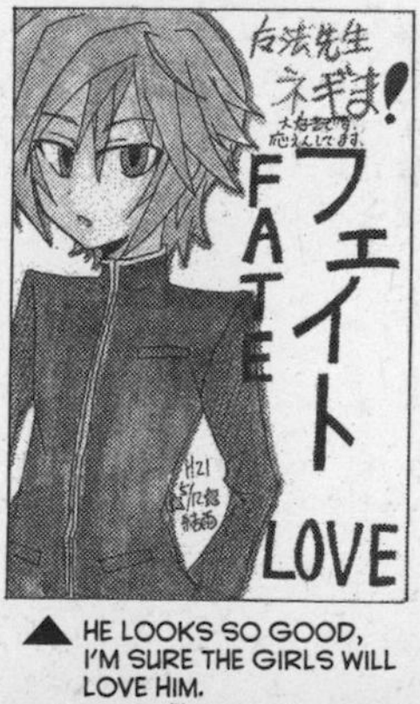
ネギま!
フェイト
FATE
LOVE

▲ HE LOOKS SO GOOD, I'M SURE THE GIRLS WILL LOVE HIM.

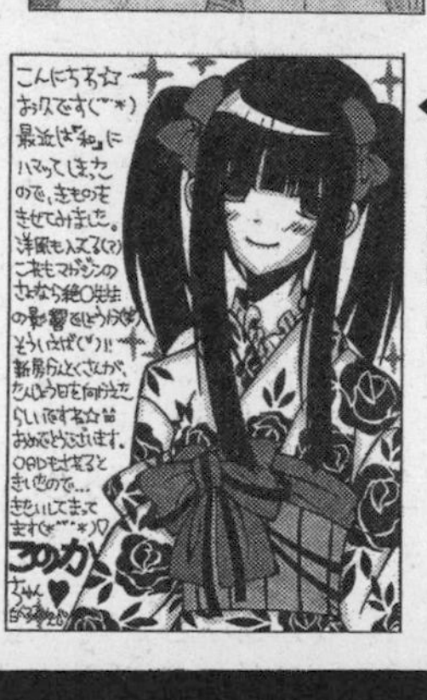

▶ SO REFRESHING.

NEGI MAGI MAGISTER

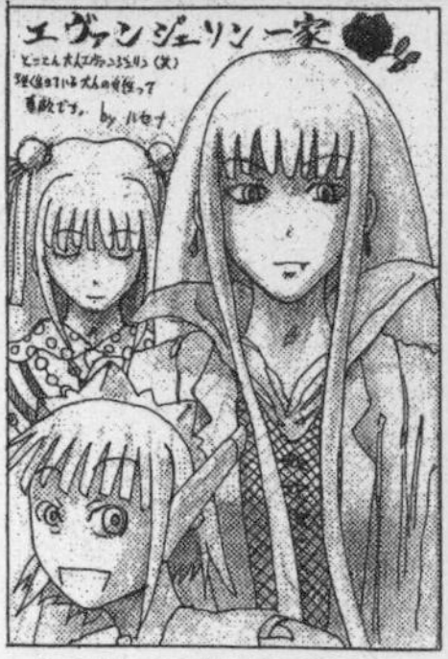
エヴァンジェリン一家

THEY MAKE A DIGNIFIED FAMILY, DON'T THEY?

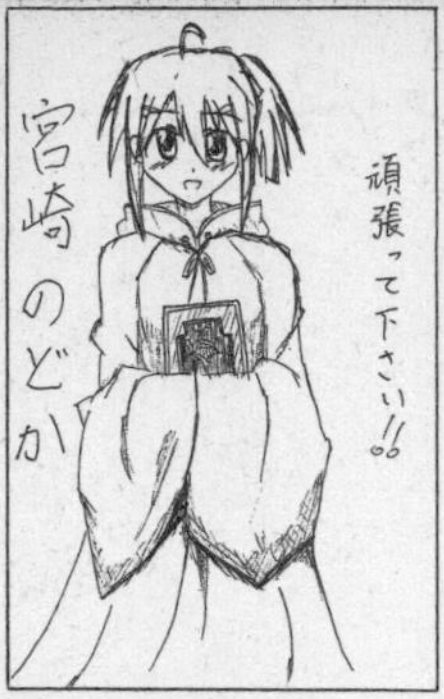
宮崎のどか
頑張って下さい!!

BOOKSTORE'S PERSONALITY FILLS THIS DRAWING.

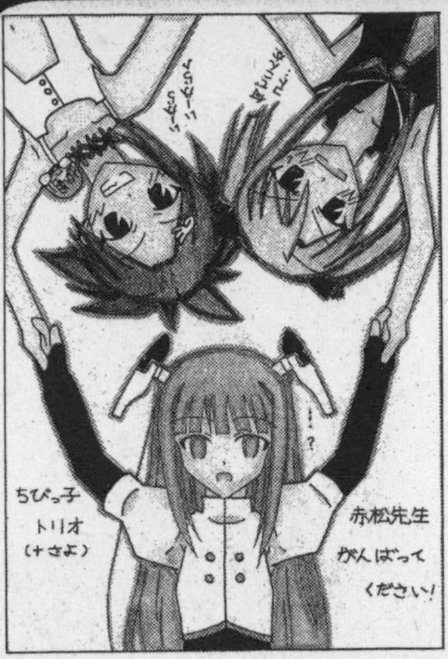
ちびっ子トリオ (+さよ)
赤松先生 がんばってください!

KIND OF A NICE TRIO.

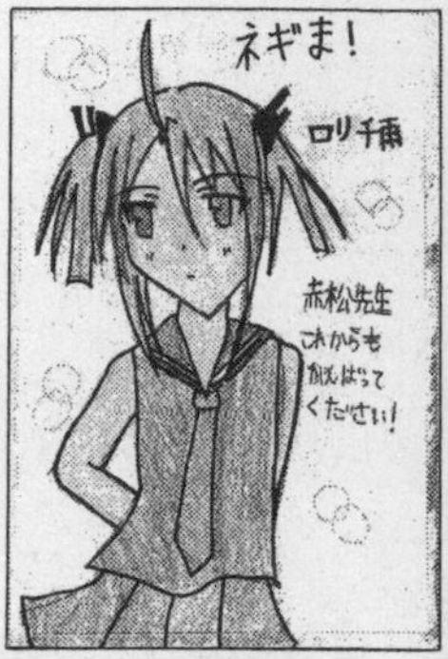
ネギま!
ロリ千雨
赤松先生 これからも頑張ってください!

CHISAME WITH A MELANCHOLY EXPRESSION.

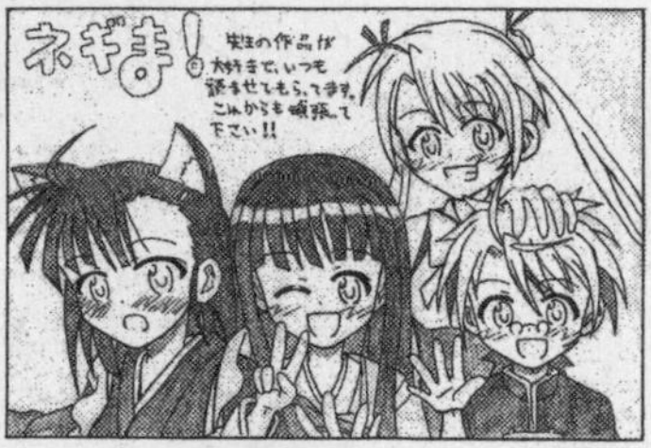
ネギま!
先生の作品が大好きで、いつも読ませてもらってます。これからも頑張って下さい!!

THEIR EYES ARE SO ROUND AND CUTE.☆

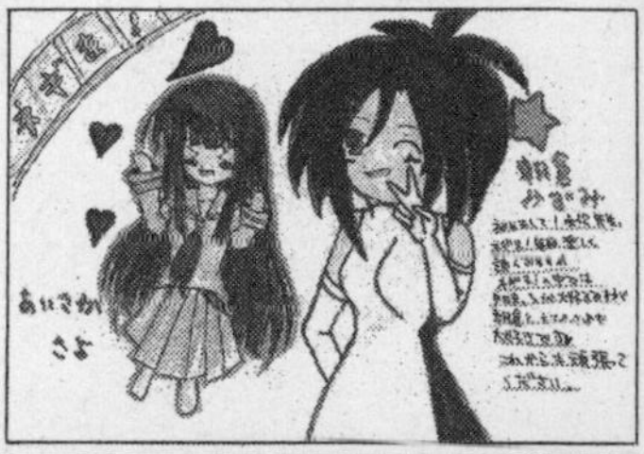
あいさかさよ

SAYO LOOKS SO HAPPY.

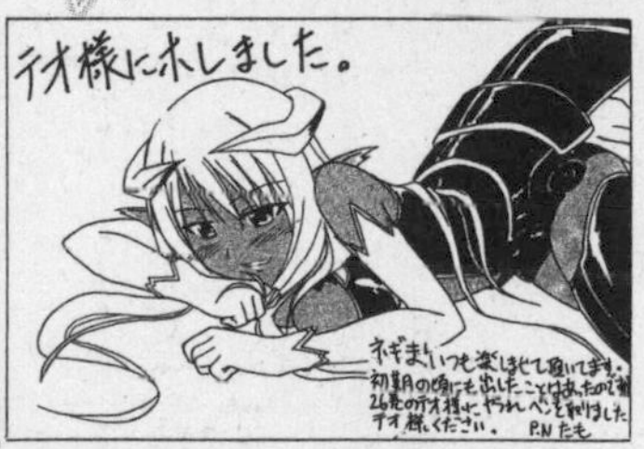
テオ様にホレしました。

SHE MAKES ME SWOON. (LAUGH)

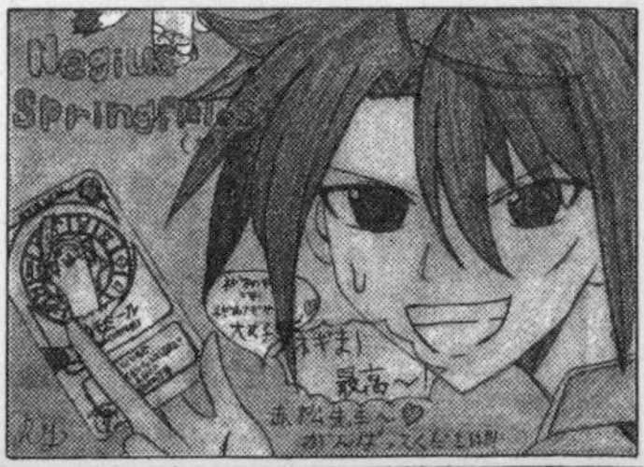

THAT CHAMO CARD IS EXCELLENT.☆

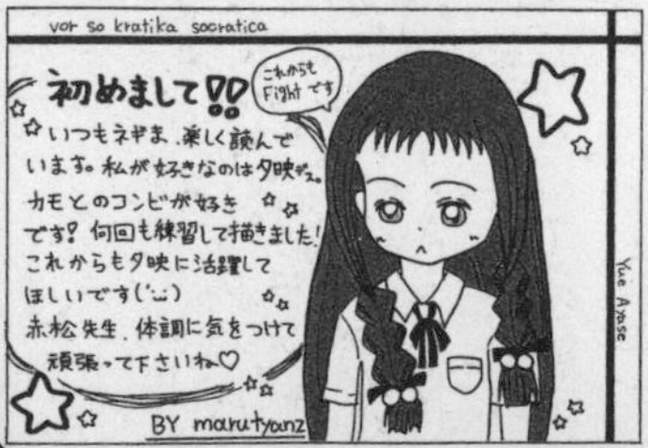
vor so kratika socratica
初めまして!!
これからもFightです
いつもネギま、楽しく読んでいます。私が好きなのは夕映ちゃん。カモとのコンビが好きです?何回も練習して描きました!これからも夕映に活躍してほしいです(^_^)
赤松先生、体調に気をつけて頑張って下さいね♡
BY marutyanz
Yue Ayase

I LIKE HER SERIOUS ATMOSPHERE.

NEGI MA!

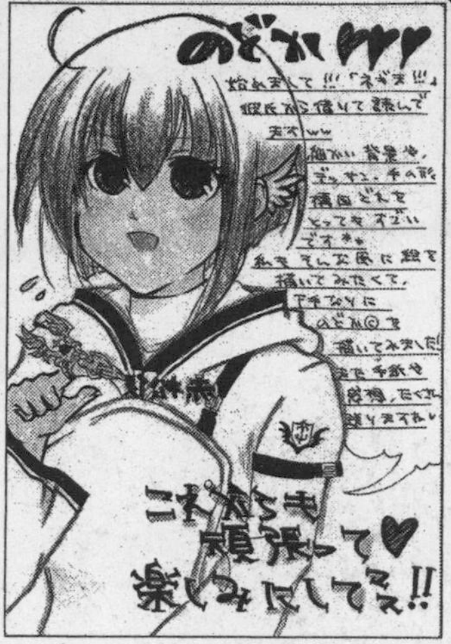

これからも
頑張って♥
楽しみにしてます!!

▲ A VERY CALM NODOKA.

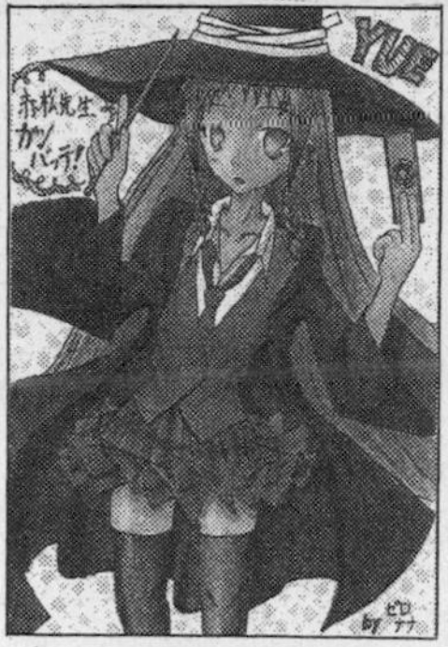

YUE

▲ A SLENDER AND BEAUTIFUL YUECCHI.

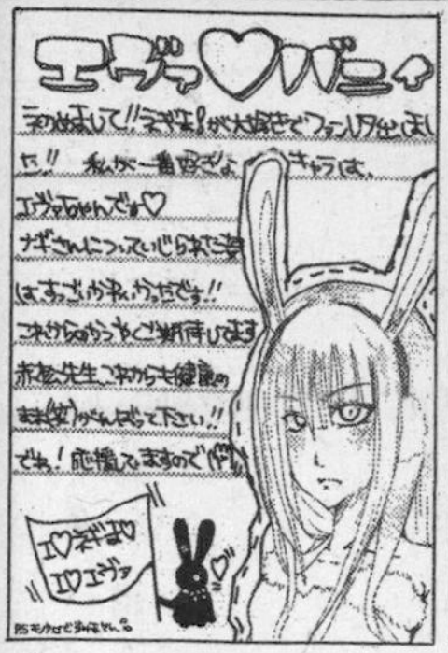

エヴァ♡バニィ

▲ COOL BUNNY EARS.

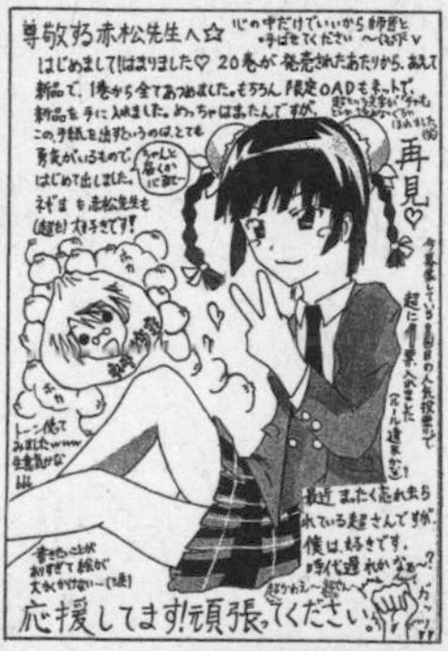

再見
応援してます!頑張ってください。

▲ THIS IS NICE CHAO. ♪

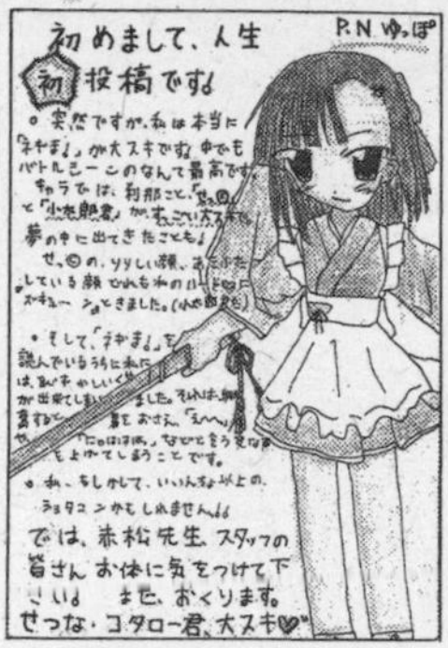

初めまして、人生
初投稿です。
では、赤松先生、スタッフの
皆さん お体に気をつけて下さいね。 また、おくります。
せつな・コタロー君、大スキ♥

▲ THIS MADE MY HEART SKIP A BEAT.

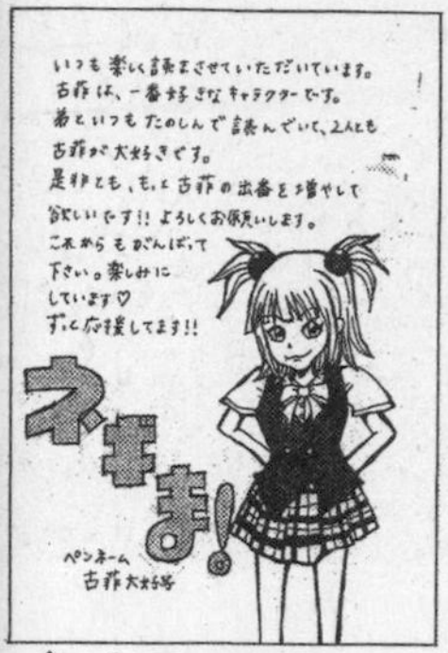

いつも楽しく読ませていただいています。
古菲は、一番好きなキャラクターです。
ネギま!

▲ KŪ FEI IN A UNIFORM. THAT'S ALMOST A NOSTALGIA TRIP.

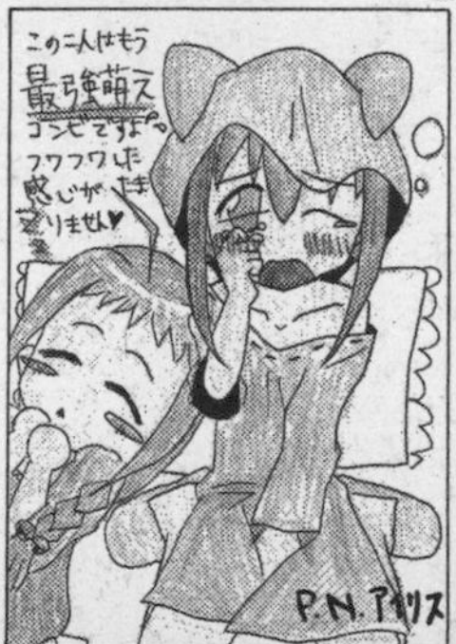

この二人はもう
最強萌え
コンビですよ~
フワフワした
感じがたまりません♥
P.N.アイリス

▲ THEY SHARE A PILLOW. ☆

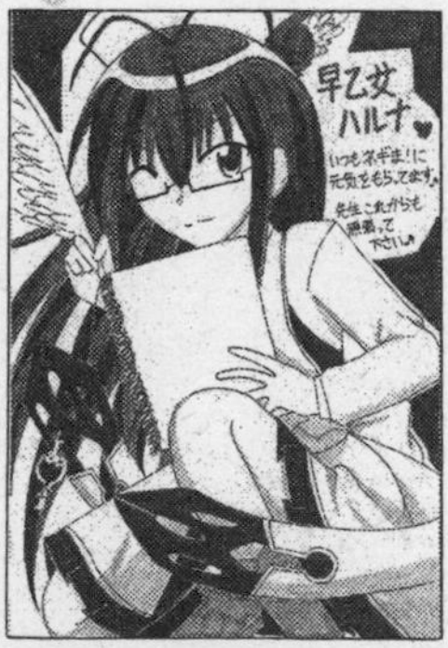

早乙女
ハルナ

▲ PARU-SAMAAA ☆

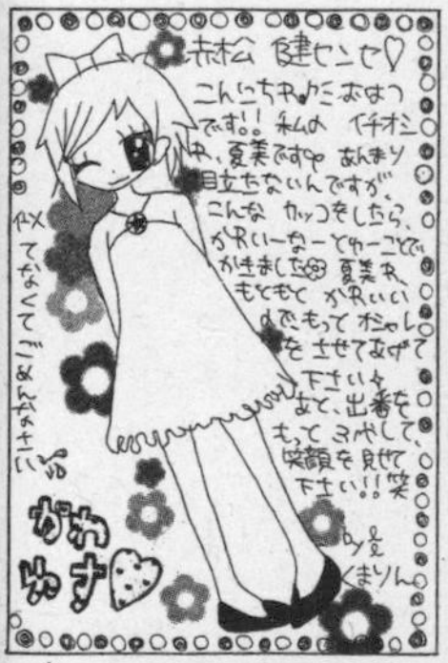

赤松 健センセ♡

▲ VERY CUTE NATSUMI ♪

THIS VOLUME'S FEATURED CHARACTER MAKIE SASAKI RANKING

FIRST PLACE

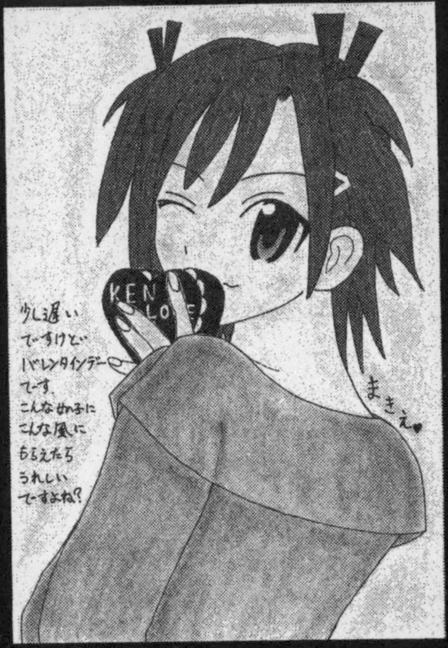
KEN LOVE
少し遅いですけどバレンタインデーです。こんな女の子にこんな風にもらえたらうれしいですよね?
まきえ♥

I'VE NEVER GOTTEN ONE LIKE THIS. (LAUGH) THE CHOCOLATE SAYS "KEN LOVE" ON IT, SO IS SHE GONNA GIVE IT TO ME!? THANK YOU ♡

(AKAMATSU)

SECOND PLACE

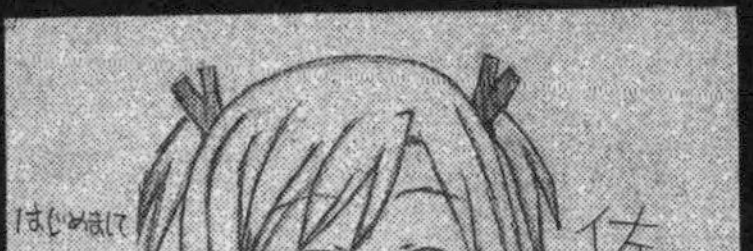
はじめまして カイカイです。
3月7日は 佐々木まき絵さんの誕生日でしたね。
赤松 健さん
お体に気をつけてがんばってください。
だしてください♡
佐々木まき絵
HAPPY

SHE'LL BE IN THE NEXT VOLUME A LOT. PLEASE BE PATIENT! ~

THIRD PLACE

YOUR SISTER GETS A NOSEBLEED WHEN SHE SEES SETSUNA? WHAT IN THE WORLD? (LAUGH) I'VE ALREADY DONE THE DESIGN FOR MAKIE'S CARD, AND I WANT TO BRING IT OUT SOON, BUT... SO MANY REASONS...

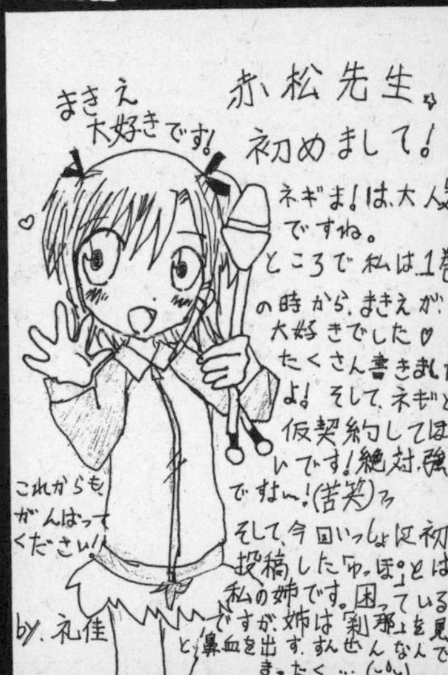
まきえ大好きです!
赤松先生、初めまして!
ネギま!は、大人気ですね。ところで私は、1巻の時から、まきえが、大好きでした♡ たくさん書きましたよ! そして、ネギと、仮契約してほしいです! 絶対、強いですよ~!(苦笑)
そして、今回いっしょに初投稿した「ゆっぽ」とは、私の姉です。困っているんですが、姉は「刹那」を見ると、鼻血を出す、すんせんなんです。まったく…。
これからも、がんばってください!!
by. 礼佳

MAGISTER NEGI MAGI

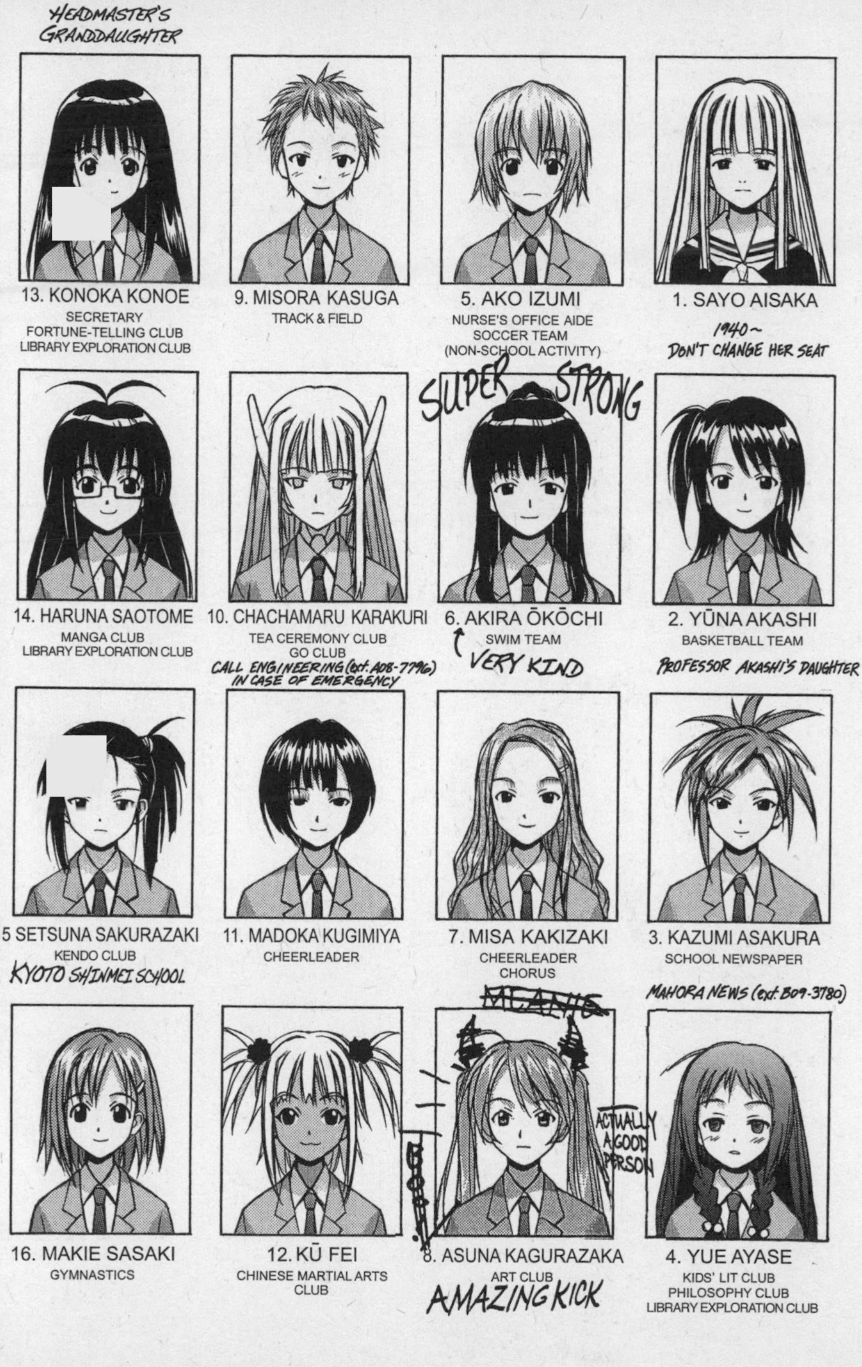
1. SAYO AISAKA
1940~
DON'T CHANGE HER SEAT
5. AKO IZUMI
NURSE'S OFFICE AIDE
SOCCER TEAM
(NON-SCHOOL ACTIVITY)
9. MISORA KASUGA
TRACK & FIELD
HEADMASTER'S GRANDDAUGHTER
13. KONOKA KONOE
SECRETARY
FORTUNE-TELLING CLUB
LIBRARY EXPLORATION CLUB
2. YŪNA AKASHI
BASKETBALL TEAM
PROFESSOR AKASHI'S DAUGHTER
SUPER STRONG
6. AKIRA ŌKŌCHI
SWIM TEAM
VERY KIND
10. CHACHAMARU KARAKURI
TEA CEREMONY CLUB
GO CLUB
CALL ENGINEERING (ext. A08-7796) IN CASE OF EMERGENCY
14. HARUNA SAOTOME
MANGA CLUB
LIBRARY EXPLORATION CLUB
3. KAZUMI ASAKURA
SCHOOL NEWSPAPER
MAHORA NEWS (ext. B09-3780)
7. MISA KAKIZAKI
CHEERLEADER
CHORUS
11. MADOKA KUGIMIYA
CHEERLEADER
15 SETSUNA SAKURAZAKI
KENDO CLUB
KYOTO SHINMEI SCHOOL
4. YUE AYASE
KIDS' LIT CLUB
PHILOSOPHY CLUB
LIBRARY EXPLORATION CLUB
MEANIE
ACTUALLY A GOOD PERSON
8. ASUNA KAGURAZAKA
ART CLUB
AMAZING KICK
12. KŪ FEI
CHINESE MARTIAL ARTS CLUB
16. MAKIE SASAKI
GYMNASTICS

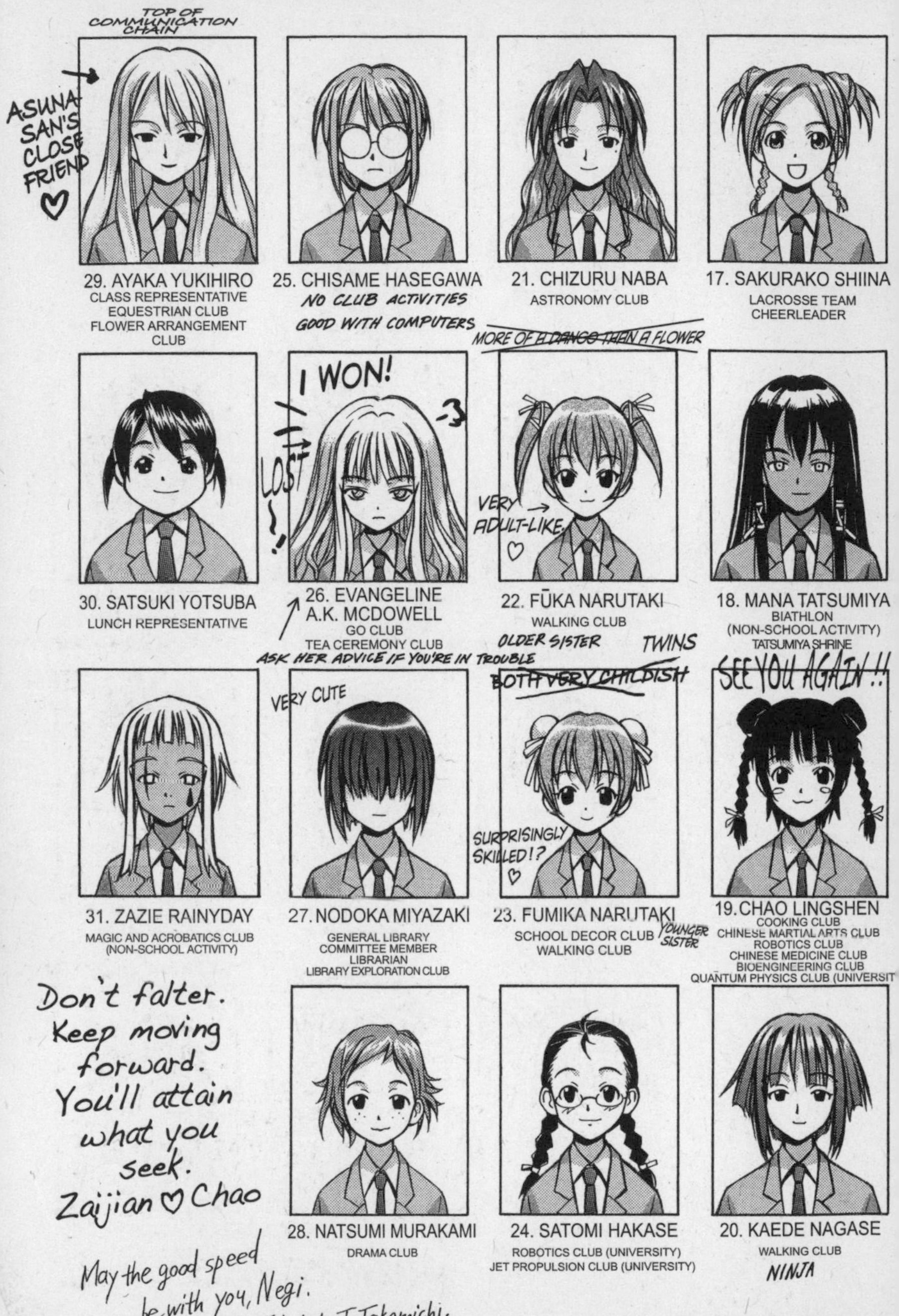
17. SAKURAKO SHIINA
LACROSSE TEAM
CHEERLEADER
21. CHIZURU NABA
ASTRONOMY CLUB
MORE OF A DANGO THAN A FLOWER
25. CHISAME HASEGAWA
NO CLUB ACTIVITIES
GOOD WITH COMPUTERS
TOP OF COMMUNICATION CHAIN
ASUNA-SAN'S CLOSE FRIEND ♡
29. AYAKA YUKIHIRO
CLASS REPRESENTATIVE
EQUESTRIAN CLUB
FLOWER ARRANGEMENT CLUB
18. MANA TATSUMIYA
BIATHLON
(NON-SCHOOL ACTIVITY)
TATSUMIYA SHRINE
VERY ADULT-LIKE ♡
22. FŪKA NARUTAKI
WALKING CLUB
OLDER SISTER
I WON!
LOST
26. EVANGELINE A.K. MCDOWELL
GO CLUB
TEA CEREMONY CLUB
ASK HER ADVICE IF YOU'RE IN TROUBLE
30. SATSUKI YOTSUBA
LUNCH REPRESENTATIVE
SEE YOU AGAIN!!
19. CHAO LINGSHEN
COOKING CLUB
CHINESE MARTIAL ARTS CLUB
ROBOTICS CLUB
CHINESE MEDICINE CLUB
BIOENGINEERING CLUB
QUANTUM PHYSICS CLUB (UNIVERSIT
TWINS
BOTH VERY CHILDISH
SURPRISINGLY SKILLED!? ♡
23. FUMIKA NARUTAKI
SCHOOL DECOR CLUB
WALKING CLUB
YOUNGER SISTER
VERY CUTE
27. NODOKA MIYAZAKI
GENERAL LIBRARY
COMMITTEE MEMBER
LIBRARIAN
LIBRARY EXPLORATION CLUB
31. ZAZIE RAINYDAY
MAGIC AND ACROBATICS CLUB
(NON-SCHOOL ACTIVITY)
20. KAEDE NAGASE
WALKING CLUB
NINJA
24. SATOMI HAKASE
ROBOTICS CLUB (UNIVERSITY)
JET PROPULSION CLUB (UNIVERSITY)
28. NATSUMI MURAKAMI
DRAMA CLUB
Don't falter. Keep moving forward. You'll attain what you seek. Zaijian ♡ Chao
May the good speed be with you, Negi.
Takahata T. Takamichi.

魔法先生 ネギま!
MAGISTER NEGI MAGI

赤松 健 SHONEN MAGAZINE COMICS
KEN AKAMATSU

27

なぜなにネギま
THE WHAT AND WHY OF *NEGIMA!*

Q. ラカンとナギは、やっぱりチュ〜♡したんですか?
Q. DID RAKAN AND NAGI REALLY SMOOCH♡?

A. パクティオーには様々なやり方があって、例えばエヴァと茶々丸は「ドール契約」だったりします。
A. THERE ARE ALL KINDS OF WAYS TO FORM A PACTIO. FOR EXAMPLE, EVA AND CHACHAMARU HAVE A "DOLL PACTIO."

タマシイがなくてもできる
YOU DON'T NEED A SOUL FOR THAT.

だから、ラカンとナギがチュ〜♡したと決めつけるのは早計です。
SO IT WOULD BE HASTY TO CONCLUDE THAT RAKAN AND NAGI HAVE SMOOCH♡ED.

しかし、しなかった証拠もまたありません。(笑)
HOWEVER, THERE'S ALSO NO PROOF THAT THEY DIDN'T. (LAUGH)

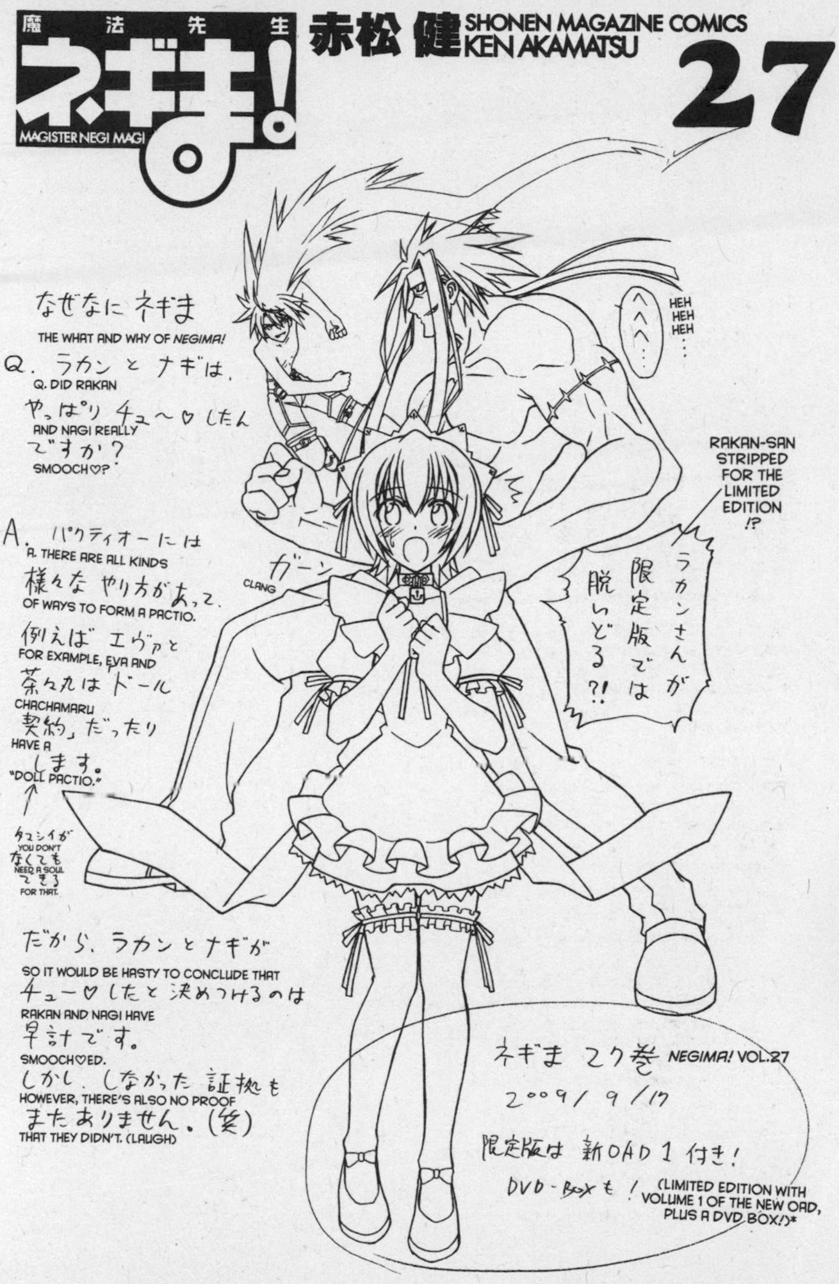

へへへ…
HEH HEH HEH...
ラカンさんが限定版では脱いどる?!
RAKAN-SAN STRIPPED FOR THE LIMITED EDITION !?
ガーン
CLANG

ネギま 27巻 NEGIMA! VOL.27
2009/9/17
限定版は新OAD 1付き!
DVD-BOXも!
(LIMITED EDITION WITH VOLUME 1 OF THE NEW OAD, PLUS A DVD BOX!)*

*OFFER AVAILABLE ONLY IN JAPAN

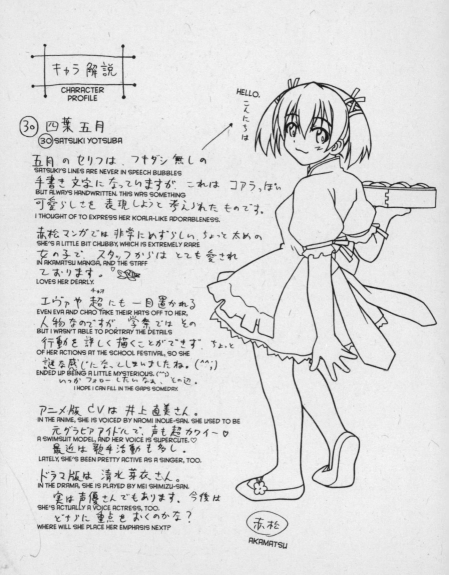

キャラ解説
CHARACTER PROFILE

㉚ 四葉五月
㉚ SATSUKI YOTSUBA

五月の セリフは、フキダシ無しの
SATSUKI'S LINES ARE NEVER IN SPEECH BUBBLES
手書き文字に なっていますが、これは コアラっぽい
BUT ALWAYS HANDWRITTEN. THIS WAS SOMETHING
可愛らしさを 表現しようと 考えられた ものです。
I THOUGHT OF TO EXPRESS HER KOALA-LIKE ADORABLENESS.

赤松マンガでは 非常にめずらしい、ちょっと 太めの
SHE'S A LITTLE BIT CHUBBY, WHICH IS EXTREMELY RARE
女の子で、 スタッフがぶは とても 愛され
IN AKAMATSU MANGA, AND THE STAFF
ております。♡
LOVES HER DEARLY.

エヴァや 超にも 一目置かれる
EVEN EVA AND CHAO TAKE THEIR HATS OFF TO HER,
人物なのですが、 学祭では その
BUT I WASN'T ABLE TO PORTRAY THE DETAILS
行動を 詳しく 描くことができず、ちょっと
OF HER ACTIONS AT THE SCHOOL FESTIVAL, SO SHE
謎な 感じに なってしまいましたね。(^^;)
ENDED UP BEING A LITTLE MYSTERIOUS. (^^)
いつか フォロー したいなぁ、その辺。
I HOPE I CAN FILL IN THE GAPS SOMEDAY.

アニメ版 CVは 井上直美さん。
IN THE ANIME, SHE IS VOICED BY NAOMI INOUE-SAN. SHE USED TO BE
元 グラビアアイドルで、 声も 超カワイー♡
A SWIMSUIT MODEL, AND HER VOICE IS SUPERCUTE.♡
最近は 歌手活動も 多し。
LATELY, SHE'S BEEN PRETTY ACTIVE AS A SINGER, TOO.

ドラマ版は 清水芽衣さん。
IN THE DRAMA, SHE IS PLAYED BY MEI SHIMIZU-SAN.
実は 声優さんでも あります。 今後は
SHE'S ACTUALLY A VOICE ACTRESS, TOO.
どチらに 重点を おくのかな?
WHERE WILL SHE PLACE HER EMPHASIS NEXT?

HELLO.
こんにちは

赤松
AKAMATSU

Translation Notes

Japanese is a tricky language for most Westerners, and translation is often more art than science. For your edification and reading pleasure, here are notes on some of the places where we could have gone in a different direction with our translation of the work, or where a Japanese cultural reference is used.

Ossan, page 16

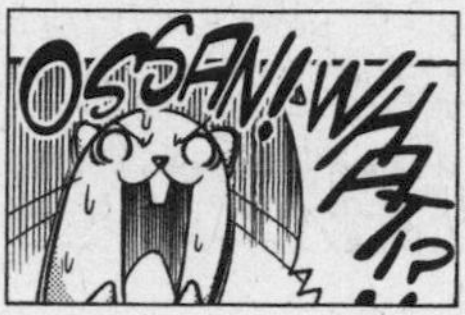
OSSAN!
WHAT!?

Ossan is an abbreviation of *Oji-san,* a way of addressing middle-aged men. Obviously Chamo isn't polite enough to use *Oji-san,* so *Ossan* is how he chooses to address Rakan.

Rakan-han, page 16

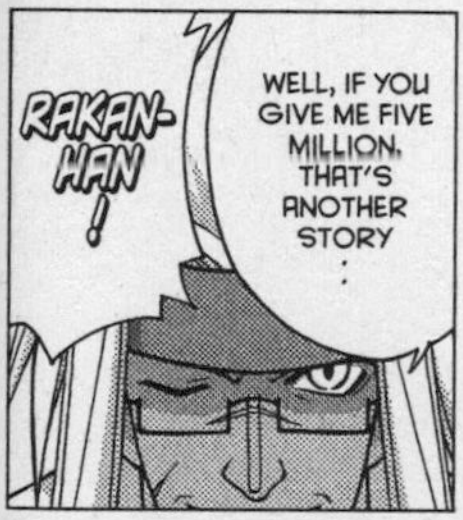
WELL, IF YOU GIVE ME FIVE MILLION, THAT'S ANOTHER STORY
RAKAN-HAN!

Konoka is close enough friends with everyone that she hasn't used *-han* much until now. Being from the Kansai region, Konoka speaks with a Kansai dialect, including saying *-han* instead of *-san.*

No-panties hygiene, page 19

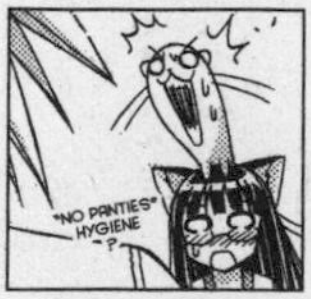
"NO PANTIES" HYGIENE—?

As the name suggests, "no-panties hygiene" is a method of staying healthy by removing underwear before sleeping. The theory was that the elastic band restricts the body, making it harder to relax, and that removing the panties improves ventilation, thus preventing the breeding of germs. If Tamaki does in fact believe in this method of hygiene, she has taken it so far as to use it even while awake.

Shirabe vs. Brigitte, page 24

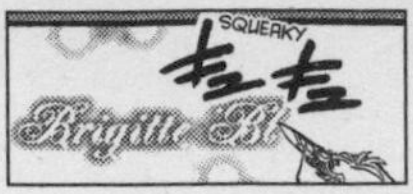
SQUEAKY
キュキュ
Brigitte B.

Apparently everyone in Fate's party has a code name, to protect them from having their real names used against them. Each of the girls' code names has something to do with her artifact. *Shirabe* is Japanese for "tune," *koyomi* means "calendar," and *tamaki* means "circle."

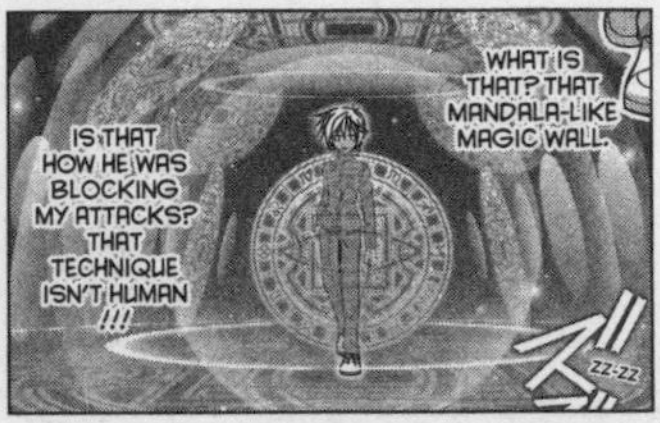
WHAT IS THAT? THAT MANDALA-LIKE MAGIC WALL.
IS THAT HOW HE WAS BLOCKING MY ATTACKS? THAT TECHNIQUE ISN'T HUMAN !!!
ZZ-ZZ

Mandala, page 89

A mandala is a set of geometric designs that represent the universe, looking much like the magic wall Fate is using. Mandalas are usually circular, and are generally used in Hinduism and Buddhism to help with meditation.

Super Kapa-kun, page 105

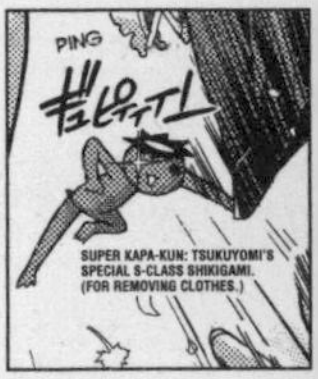
PING
SUPER KAPA-KUN: TSUKUYOMI'S SPECIAL S-CLASS SHIKIGAMI. (FOR REMOVING CLOTHES.)

As we learned when we first met Tsukuyomi, she uses various demon *shikigami,* including *kappa shikigami.* A *kappa* is a water sprite known for a whole range of evil deeds, from acts as heinous as dragging people underwater and sucking their blood to acts as mild as looking under women's skirts. Super Kapa-kun falls somewhere in the middle.

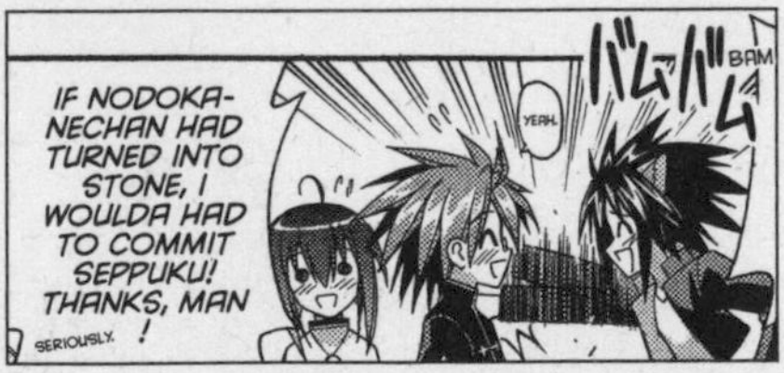
BAM
YEAH.
IF NODOKA-NECHAN HAD TURNED INTO STONE, I WOULDA HAD TO COMMIT SEPPUKU! THANKS, MAN !
SERIOUSLY.

Seppuku, page 110

Also known as *harakiri, seppuku* is ritual suicide committed in order to restore honor that is lost. Kotarō is saying that if he hadn't been able to prevent Nodoka's death, the only way to make up for such a serious mistake would be to kill himself.

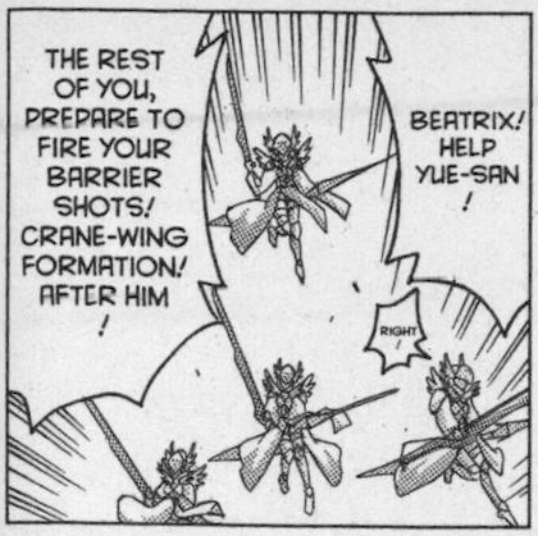
BEATRIX! HELP YUE-SAN!
THE REST OF YOU, PREPARE TO FIRE YOUR BARRIER SHOTS! CRANE-WING FORMATION! AFTER HIM!
RIGHT!

Crane-wing formation, page 116

Crane-wing is one of eight Japanese tactical formations. The soldiers line up in a V, taking the shape of a crane's spread wings. As to why the Ariadne Magic Knights would be using Japanese tactical formations—that remains a mystery.

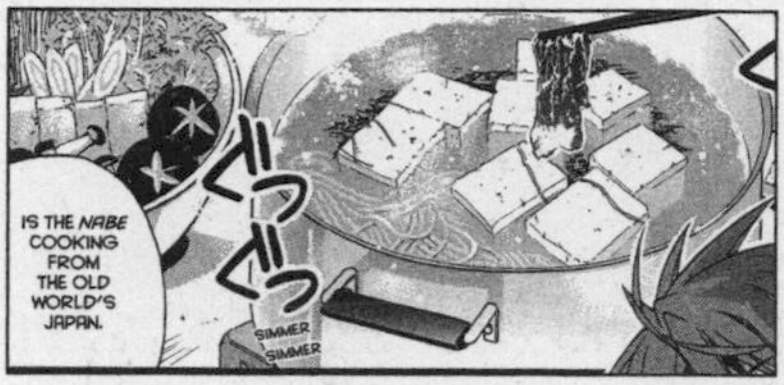
IS THE *NABE* COOKING FROM THE OLD WORLD'S JAPAN.
SIMMER SIMMER

Nabe, page 133

Nabe is Japanese for "pot," so, as expected, nabe cooking refers to cooking that is done in a pot. Meat, vegetables, etc. are all cooked together in a big pot, and those sitting around the pot take out what they want to eat.

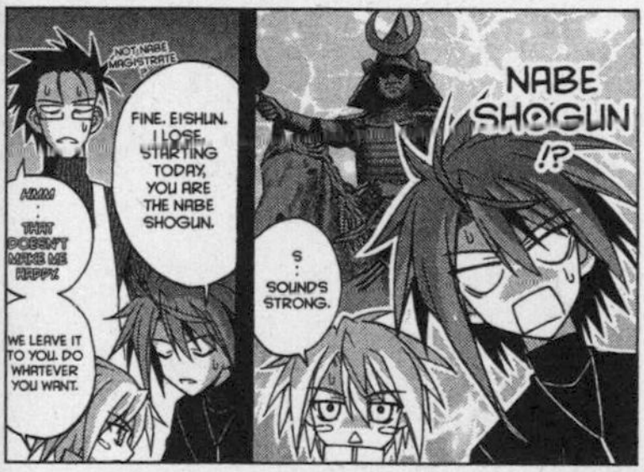
NABE SHOGUN!?
S... SOUND'S STRONG.
NOT NABE MAGISTRATE...?
FINE. EISHUN. I LOSE. STARTING TODAY, YOU ARE THE NABE SHOGUN.
HMM... THAT DOESN'T MAKE ME HAPPY.
WE LEAVE IT TO YOU. DO WHATEVER YOU WANT.

Nabe Shogun, Nabe Magistrate, page 134

Nabe Bugyō, or Nabe Magistrate, is what they call someone who is very picky about how to cook the *nabe*—what ingredients to add, when to add them, etc. A Nabe Shogun is someone who is even stricter than a Nabe Magistrate.

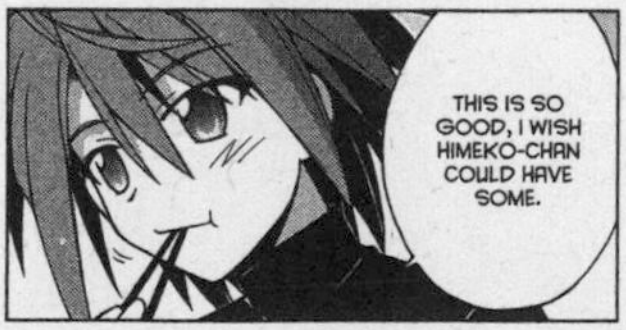
THIS IS SO GOOD, I WISH HIMEKO-CHAN COULD HAVE SOME.

Himeko, page 134

Himeko is the nickname Nagi has given to the Imperial Princess of Ostia. *Hime* is Japanese for "princess," and adding *ko* turns it into a cute girl's name.

Tara-chan and “Hello *desu*,” page 505

Tara-chan is a character from the popular anime and manga series, *Sazae-san*. He always ends his sentences with *desu,* a polite way to end sentences, even when it is grammatically incorrect. “Hello *desu*” is an example; most Japanese people do not add *desu* to *konnichi wa* (hello).

Volume 26

Bakabon’s papa, page 166

Bakabon is the main character of the anime *Tensai Bakabon* (*Genius Bakabon*). The main character is really his papa, who is forty-one years old.

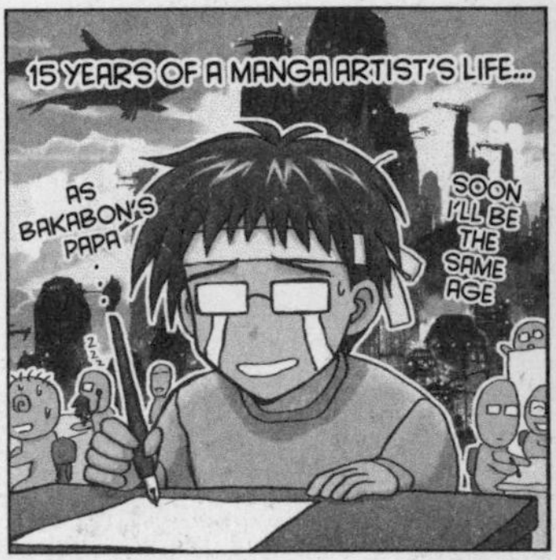
15 YEARS OF A MANGA ARTIST'S LIFE...
SOON I'LL BE THE SAME AGE
AS BAKABON'S PAPA

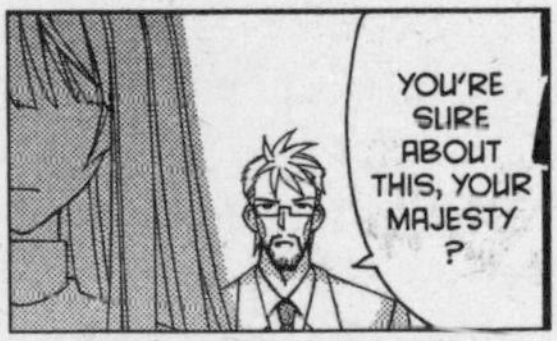
YOU'RE SURE ABOUT THIS, YOUR MAJESTY?

Your Majesty, page 196

Until this point, everyone (except Nagi) called Arika “Your Highness,” which is the proper form of address for a prince or princess. Now, Gateau addresses her as “Your Majesty,” indicating that she is no longer a princess, but a queen.

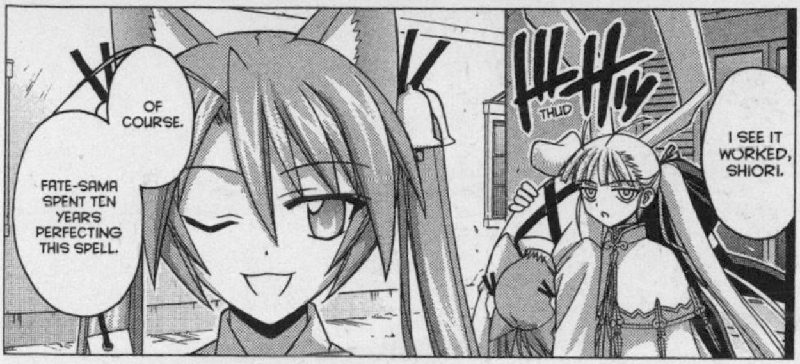
I SEE IT WORKED, SHIORI.
THUD
OF COURSE.
FATE-SAMA SPENT TEN YEARS PERFECTING THIS SPELL.

Homura and Shiori, page 207

As mentioned before, the name of each member of Fate's party has something to do with her artifact and/or magic power. *Homura* means "flame," and *shiori* means "bookmark."

I may be inexperienced, page 218

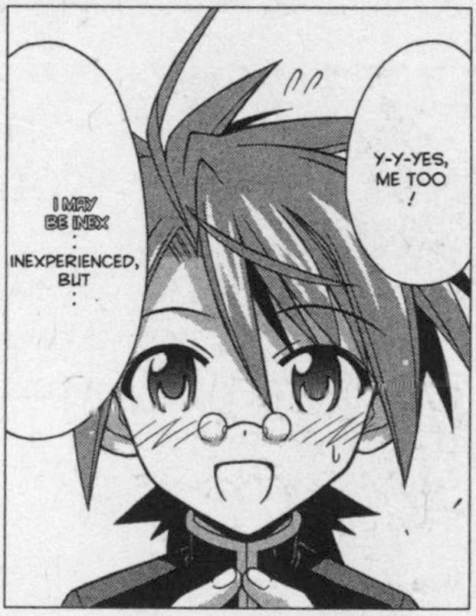
Y-Y-YES, ME TOO!
I MAY BE INEX... INEXPERIENCED, BUT...

What Negi says here is commonly said by newlyweds to their new spouse or their new in-laws as a sort of apology for not being perfect yet. Here, Negi is saying that he's not used to being a ninja's master, but there is a similarity.

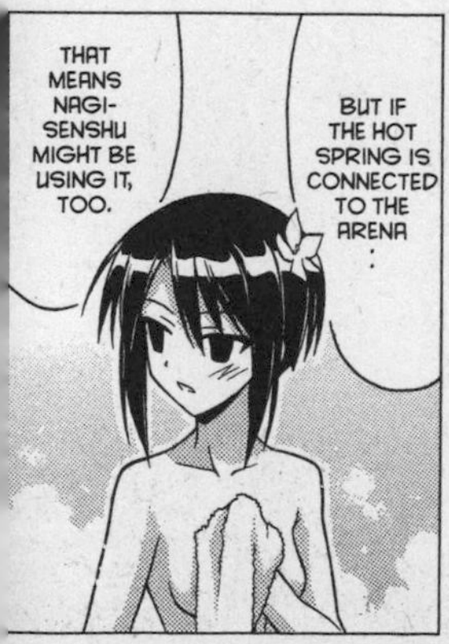
BUT IF THE HOT SPRING IS CONNECTED TO THE ARENA...
THAT MEANS NAGI-SENSHU MIGHT BE USING IT, TOO.

Senshu, page 232

Senshu is another title attached to people's names in order to show respect, like *sensei*. It is given to athletes, such as the fighters in this martial arts tournament. In the Magical World, they don't actually speak Japanese, so they are probably using their language's equivalent. Either way, it's a handy device for distinguishing "legendary hero Nagi" from "fighter in the tournament Nagi."

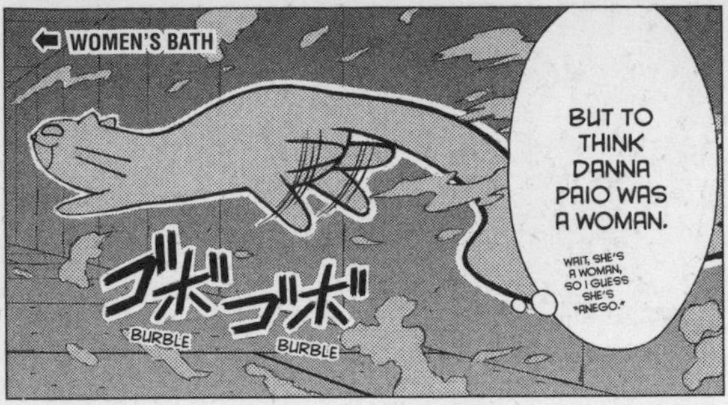
WOMEN'S BATH
BUT TO THINK DANNA PAIO WAS A WOMAN.
WAIT, SHE'S A WOMAN, SO I GUESS SHE'S "ANEGO."
ゴボゴボ
BURBLE
BURBLE

Danna and *anego*, page 237

Danna is a Japanese term of respect, roughly meaning "master." Chamo respects Paio Zi greatly as a kindred spirit, but since *danna* is used specifically for men, Chamo has to correct himself and use a female equivalent: *anego*.

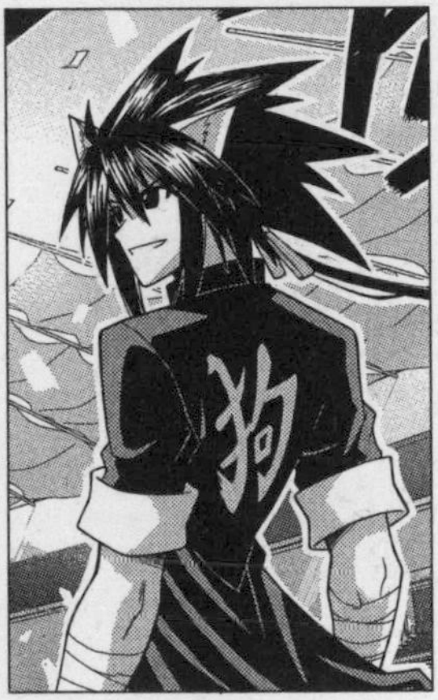

Kotarō's shirt, page 324

The Chinese character on the back of Kotarō's fancy new battle shirt means "dog," a fitting symbol for a dog boy like Kotarō.

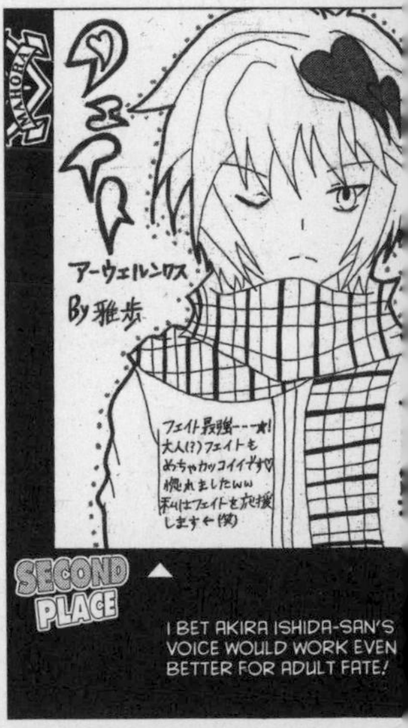
MAHORA
アーウェルンクス
By 雅歩
フェイト最強ーーー★!
大人(?)フェイトも
めちゃカッコイイです♡
惚れましたww
私はフェイトを応援
します←(笑)
SECOND PLACE
I BET AKIRA ISHIDA-SAN'S VOICE WOULD WORK EVEN BETTER FOR ADULT FATE!

Akira Ishida, page 333

As you may have figured out from the context, Akira Ishida is the voice actor who portrayed Fate in the *Negima!* anime, and he has come back to reprise the role in the new OADs coming out in Japan. He also happens to be the translators' very favorite Japanese voice actor.♡

Volume 27

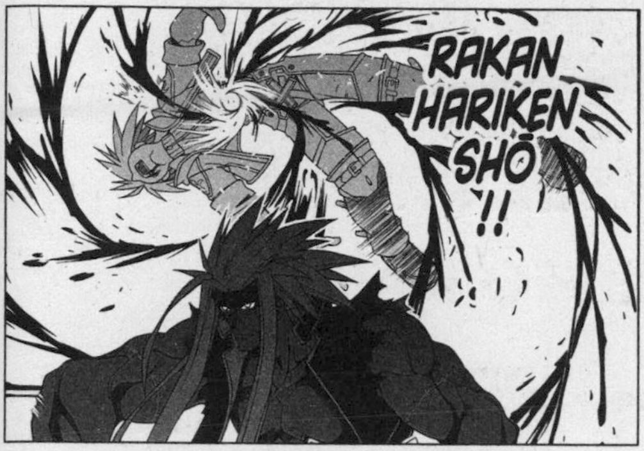
RAKAN HARIKEN SHŌ !!

Rakan Hariken Shō, page 386

The name of this attack is packed with meaning. Of course, Rakan also refers to Jack Rakan himself, but when he puts his name in an attack, he gives it *kanji* meaning "achiever of Nirvana." In English, it could be translated as "enlightened destructive reverse sword palm." And "*hariken*" can also be the English word "hurricane," which, based on the shower of blood from Negi, is also very appropriate, and the attack could also be "Rakan Hurricane Palm."

Complete training match, page 467

More literally, Negi says, "This was a complete chest-borrowing match." The phrase comes from sumo, when a lower-level wrestler will "borrow the chest" of a higher-level, stronger wrestler to practice his fighting skills and techniques.

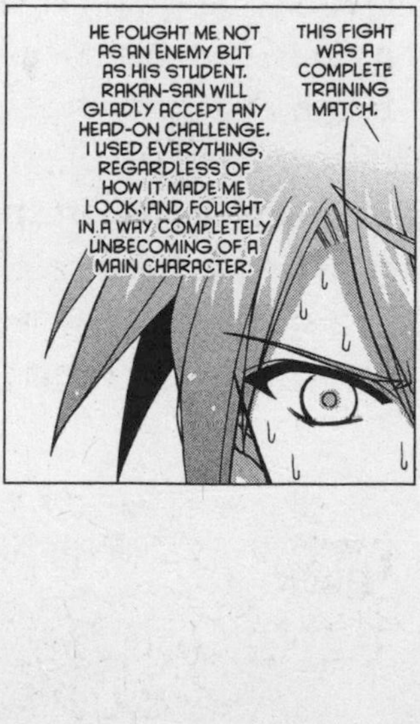
THIS FIGHT WAS A COMPLETE TRAINING MATCH.
HE FOUGHT ME NOT AS AN ENEMY BUT AS HIS STUDENT. RAKAN-SAN WILL GLADLY ACCEPT ANY HEAD-ON CHALLENGE. I USED EVERYTHING, REGARDLESS OF HOW IT MADE ME LOOK, AND FOUGHT IN A WAY COMPLETELY UNBECOMING OF A MAIN CHARACTER.

ANIMAL LAND

BY MAKOTO RAIKU

In a world of animals, where the strong eat the weak, Monoko the tanuki stumbles across a strange creature the likes of which has never been seen before—a human baby! While the newborn has no claws or teeth to protect itself, it does have the special ability to speak to and understand all different animals. Can the gift of speech between species change the balance of power in a land where the weak must always fear the strong?

ANIMAL LAND 1

MAKOTO RAIKU

Ages 13+

VISIT KODANSHACOMICS.COM TO:

- View release date calendars for upcoming volumes
- Find out the latest about upcoming Kodansha Comics series

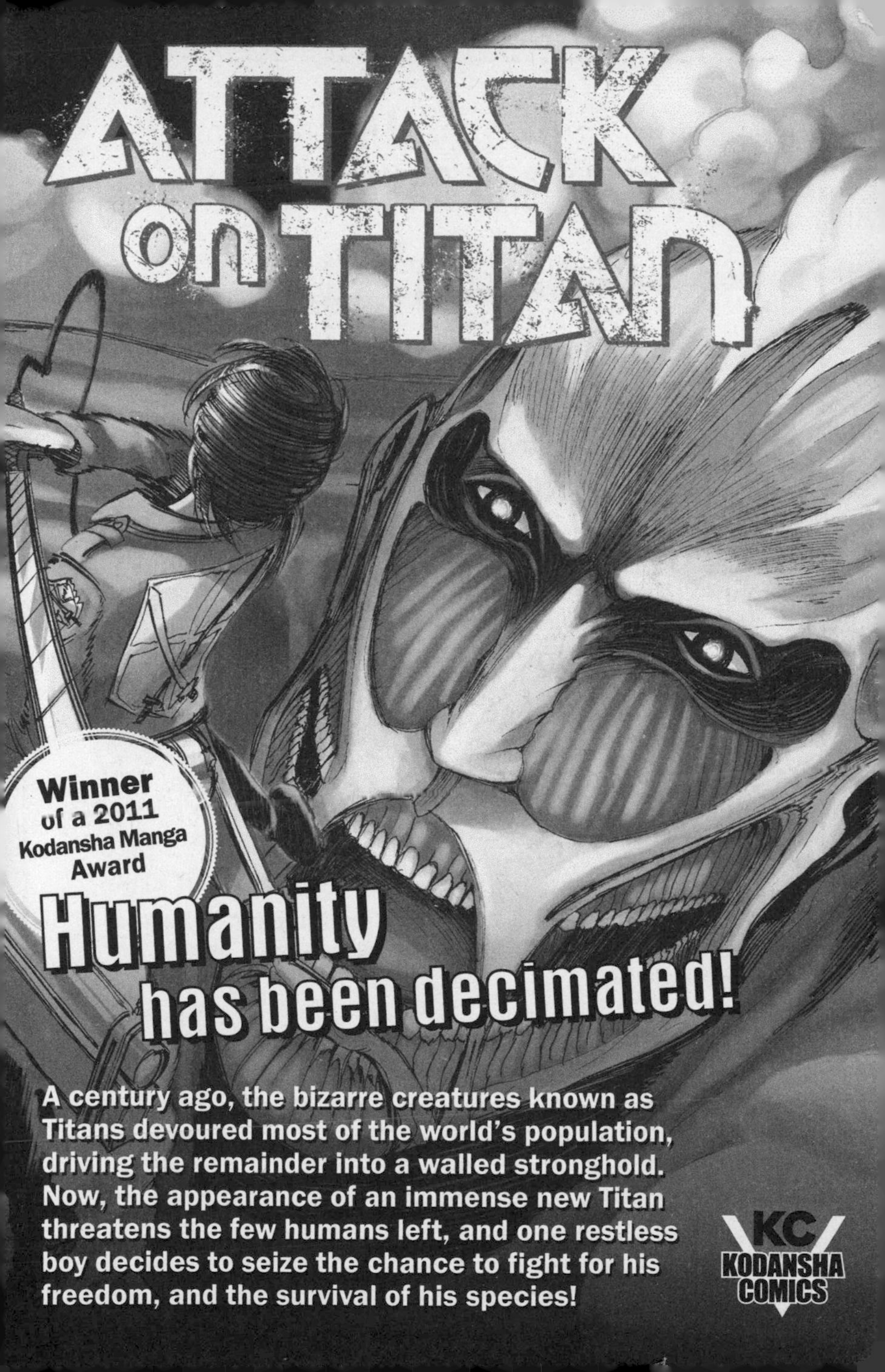
ATTACK on TITAN
Winner of a 2011 Kodansha Manga Award
Humanity has been decimated!
A century ago, the bizarre creatures known as Titans devoured most of the world's population, driving the remainder into a walled stronghold. Now, the appearance of an immense new Titan threatens the few humans left, and one restless boy decides to seize the chance to fight for his freedom, and the survival of his species!
KC KODANSHA COMICS

FROM HIRO MASHIMA, CREATOR OF **RAVE MASTER**

FAIRY TAIL

FAIRY TAIL
1
Hiro Mashima Creator of Rave Master

FAIRY TAIL
2
FAIRY
Hiro Mashima Creator of Rave Master

Lucy has always dreamed of joining the Fairy Tail, a club for the most powerful sorcerers in the land. But once she becomes a member, the fun really starts!

Special extras in each volume! Read them all!

RATING T AGES 13+

VISIT WWW.KODANSHACOMICS.COM TO:

- View release date calendars for upcoming volumes
- Find out the latest about new Kodansha Comics series

KC KODANSHA COMICS

TOMARE!

[STOP!]

You're going the wrong way!

Manga is a completely different type of reading experience.

To start at the *beginning*, go to the *end*!

That's right! Authentic manga is read the traditional Japanese way—from right to left, exactly the *opposite* of how American books are read. It's easy to follow: Just go to the other end of the book, and read each page—and each panel—from right side to left side, starting at the top right. Now you're experiencing manga as it was meant to be.